lonely planet

Central
Europe

Poland
p355

Germany
p159

Czech Republic
p95

Slovakia
p435

Austria
p40

Hungary
p295

Switzerland
p521

Slovenia
p481

Contents

OLD TOWN, PRAGUE,
CZECH REPUBLIC P99

RESIDENZPLATZ,
SALZBURG, AUSTRIA P65

MATTERHORN, ZERMATT,
SWITZERLAND P537

Contents

Contents

ON THE ROAD

SCHLOSS SCHÖNBRUNN, VIENNA, AUSTRIA P45

HOFBURG, VIENNA, AUSTRIA P44

Contents

GELLÉRT BATHS,
BUDAPEST, HUNGARY P302

ČESKÝ KRUMLOV, CZECH
REPUBLIC P134

welcome to Central Europe

Old-World Appeal

Teutonic half-timbered villages, graffiti-decorated Renaissance squares, medieval walled towns...if you're looking for old-world appeal, you've come to the right place. Wander the darkly Gothic alleyways of Prague, admire the baroque excess of Salzburg or take in the colourful old-Venetian influence on the Slovenian port of Piran. Poland and the Czech Republic seem to have more than their fair share of medieval masterpieces, but you can find narrow lanes and quaint townscapes throughout the region, from Bern, Switzerland to Bardejov, Slovakia. Smaller gems such as Bamberg, Germany are often far from the tourist radar. On mornings when the mists lie heavy and crowds are few, you might imagine yourself in an earlier century.

Atmospheric Eating & Drinking

Nourishing yourself is more fun in a great atmosphere, and Central Europe's abundance of outdoor cafes, beer halls and coffee houses offer just that. When the temperatures rise in spring, outdoor tables proliferate, along with the daffodils and tulips. Enjoy a plate of pasta while admiring the Slovenian coast, nosh *pierogi* (dumplings) on a Polish cobblestone street or dip into fondue while lakeside in Switzerland. Beer gardens across the region

At once natural and refined, folksy and cultured: the combination of mountain rusticity with old-world style captivates in Central Europe.

BEAUTIFUL PHOTOS FROM ALL OVER THE WORLD/GETTY IMAGES ©

(left) Prague (p98), Czech Republic
(below) Hikers on Mt Triglav (p501), Slovenia

ENRIQUE UGARTE/GETTY IMAGES ©

offer an opportunity to enjoy hearty food, a convivial atmosphere and a good brew alfresco. Once the weather cools, move inside to a boisterous beer hall. Or, for something a little sweeter, try a cake at a coffee house or pastry cafe. The most famous are in Vienna and Budapest, but you'll find many options – and other interesting places to eat and drink – all across the region.

Outdoor Adventures

With mountains covering so many Central European states, it's no wonder that the outdoors holds such an attraction in the region. The Alps rise to their highest in Switzerland, with jagged, Toblerone-like peaks such as the Matterhorn, and march on through southern Germany, across Austria and south into Slovenia. You can hike, bike, ski or just ride the gondolas and funiculars to enjoy the Alpine views. Other mountains, like the Swiss Jura and the Polish–Slovak Tatras, offer no less adventure. There are also sculptural sandstone 'rock towns' in the Czech Republic to climb, waterfall-filled gorges in Slovakia and Slovenia to hike and the bucolic Black Forest in Germany to walk. There's a new part of nature to explore almost around every corner.

›Central Europe

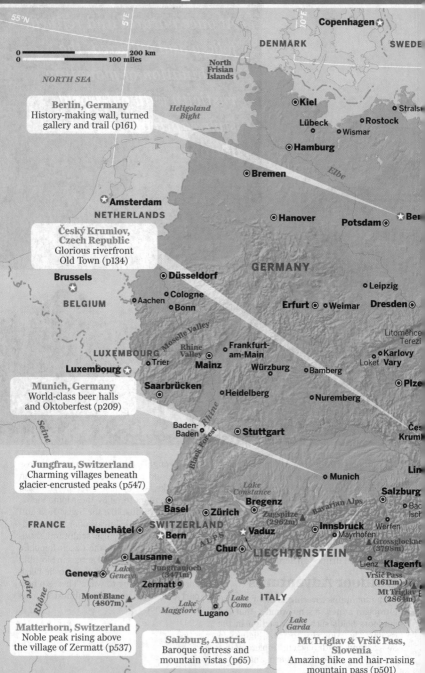

Berlin, Germany
History-making wall, turned gallery and trail (p161)

Český Krumlov, Czech Republic
Glorious riverfront Old Town (p134)

Munich, Germany
World-class beer halls and Oktoberfest (p209)

Jungfrau, Switzerland
Charming villages beneath glacier-encrusted peaks (p547)

Matterhorn, Switzerland
Noble peak rising above the village of Zermatt (p537)

Salzburg, Austria
Baroque fortress and mountain vistas (p65)

Mt Triglav & Vršič Pass, Slovenia
Amazing hike and hair-raising mountain pass (p501)

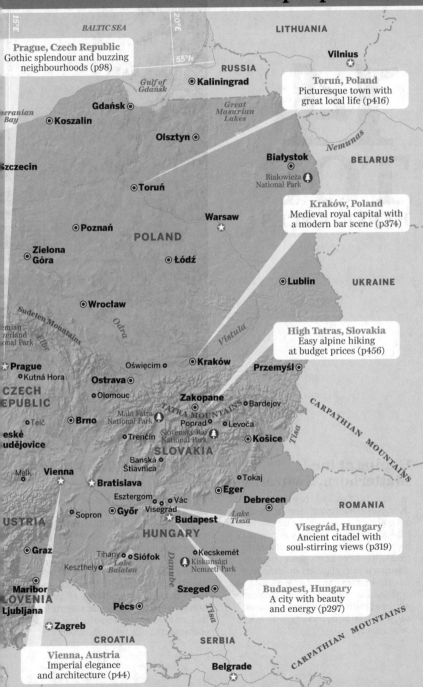

Prague, Czech Republic
Gothic splendour and buzzing neighbourhoods (p98)

Toruń, Poland
Picturesque town with great local life (p416)

Kraków, Poland
Medieval royal capital with a modern bar scene (p374)

High Tatras, Slovakia
Easy alpine hiking at budget prices (p456)

Visegrád, Hungary
Ancient citadel with soul-stirring views (p319)

Budapest, Hungary
A city with beauty and energy (p297)

Vienna, Austria
Imperial elegance and architecture (p44)

BALTIC SEA

LITHUANIA

Vilnius

RUSSIA

Kaliningrad

Gulf of
Gdańsk

Great
Masurian
Lakes

Nemunas

BELARUS

Gdańsk

Koszalin

Olsztyn

Białystok

Białowieża
National Park

eranian
Bay

Szczecin

Toruń

Warsaw

Poznań

POLAND

Łódź

Zielona
Góra

Lublin

UKRAINE

Wrocław

Sudeten Mountains

Odra

Vistula

emian
zerland
onal Park

Elbe

Prague

Kutná Hora

CZECH
REPUBLIC

Ostrava

Olomouc

Oświęcim

Kraków

Przemyśl

Telč

Brno

Malá Fatra
National Park

TATRA MOUNTAINS

Zakopane

Bardejov

CARPATHIAN MOUNTAINS

eské
udějovice

Trenčín

Poprad

Levoča

Slovenský Raj
National Park

Košice

Tisa

Banská
Štiavnica

SLOVAKIA

Melk

Vienna

Bratislava

Tokaj

Eger

Debrecen

Esztergom

Vác

Győr

Visegrád

Budapest

Lake
Tisza

ROMANIA

Sopron

USTRIA

Graz

HUNGARY

Tihany

Siófok

Kecskemét

Keszthely

Lake
Balaton

Kiskunsági
Nemzeti Park

Maribor

LOVENIA

Ljubljana

Pécs

Danube

Szeged

Tisa

Zagreb

CROATIA

SERBIA

CARPATHIAN MOUNTAINS

Belgrade

14
TOP
EXPERIENCES

Gaping at the Matterhorn, Switzerland

1 Sure, it graces Toblerone packages and evokes stereotypical 'Heidi' scenes, but nothing prepares you for the allure of the Matterhorn. As soon as you step into the timber-chalet-filled village of Zermatt (p537), this loner looms above you, mesmerising with its chiselled, majestic peak. Gaze at it from a tranquil sidewalk cafe, hike in its shadow along tangles of Alpine paths with cowbells clinking in the distance, or pause on a ski slope and admire its magnetic stance.

Singing in Salzburg, Austria

2 A fortress on a hill, 17th-century cobbled streets, Mozart, the ultimate singalong: if Salzburg (p65) didn't exist, someone would have to invent it just to keep all the acolytes who visit each year happy. It's hard to say what's more popular, but you just have to see all the kitsch for sale to know that this is *Sound of Music* country. Faster than you can say 'Do-Re-Mi' you can be whisked into the gorgeous steep hills that are alive with the sound of tour groups year-round. Concert at Salzburg Dom

MARTIN MOOS/GETTY IMAGES ©

PRITZ PRITZ/GETTY IMAGES ©

TRAVEL INK/GETTY IMAGES ©

Visiting Jungfrau Villages, Switzerland

3 Three of Europe's most impressive, glacier-encrusted peaks form the backdrop to the quaint towns and ski villages throughout Switzerland's Jungfrau region (p547). By day, take advantage of 200km of ski and snowboard pistes (and hundreds more kilometres of hiking trails). By night, return to an atmospheric chalet in resort towns like bustling Grindelwald or car-free Mürren. Here every home and hostel has a postcard-worthy view, and cowbells echo in the valleys. This is story-book Switzerland at its best. Mürren village

Touring Toruń, Poland

4 This beautiful Gothic city (p416) has just the right balance between sightseeing and relaxing. Grab a *zapiekanka* (toasted roll with cheese, mushrooms and tomato sauce) from the window of the milk bar just off the main square, then saunter past the locals to check out the curious statuary around the square's edge, including a monument to local hero Copernicus. Finish the day at one of the fancy beer-garden decks perched on the cobblestones. Statue of Copernicus, Toruń

Climbing Mt Triglav & Vršič Pass, Slovenia

5 They say you're not really a Slovene until you've climbed Mt Triglav (p501). There's no rule about which particular route to take – there are around 20 ways up – but if you're a novice, ascend with a guide from the Pokljuka plateau north of Lake Bohinj. If time is an issue and you're driving, head for the Vršič Pass, which stands (literally) head and shoulders above the rest. It leads from Alpine Gorenjska, past Mt Triglav itself and down to sunny Primorska and the bluer-than-blue Soča River in one hair-raising, spine-tingling hour.

JAN GREUNE/GETTY IMAGES ©

Appreciating Budapest, Hungary

6 Hungary's capital (p297) has cleaned up its act in recent years. Gone are the Soviet-era cars that used to spew their choking blue haze over the flat landscape of Pest. Now, the hills on the Buda side of the city are gleaming, and Pest itself is teeming with energy and life. It's no stretch to say that these days Budapest combines the beauty of Prague and buzz of Berlin into something that's uniquely Hungarian. Matthias Church, with Parliament in background

DAVID L RYAN/GETTY IMAGES ©

Exploring Prague, Czech Republic

7 Prague Castle and the Old Town Square are highlights of the Czech capital (p98), but for a more insightful look at life two decades after the Velvet Revolution, head to local neighbourhoods around the centre. Working-class Žižkov and energetic Smíchov are crammed with pubs, while elegant, tree-lined Vinohrady features a diverse menu of cosmopolitan restaurants. Gritty Holešovice showcases many forms of art, from iconic works from the last century to more recent but equally challenging pieces. Church of Our Lady Before Týn

Admiring Imperial Vienna, Austria

8 Imagine having unlimited riches and top architects at your hands for 640 years – that's the Vienna (p44) of the Habsburgs. The monumentally graceful Hofburg (p44) whisks you back to the age of empires as you marvel at the treasury's imperial crowns, the equine ballet of the Spanish Riding School and the chandelier-lit apartments of Empress Elisabeth. The palace is rivalled in grandeur only by the 1441-room Schloss Schönbrunn (p45), a Unesco World Heritage site, and the baroque Schloss Belvedere (p49), set in exquisite landscaped gardens. Napoleon's Room, Schloss Schönbrunn

KRZYSZTOF DYDYNSKI/GETTY IMAGES ©

Remembering the Berlin Wall, Germany

9 It's hard to believe, 25 years on, that the Berlin Wall really divided this ever-surprising city. The best way to examine its role in Berlin is to make your way – on foot or by bike – along the Berlin Wall Trail. Passing the Brandenburg Gate (p165), analysing graffiti at the East Side Gallery (p172) or learning about its history at the Gedenkstätte Berliner Mauer (p170): the path brings it all into context. It's heartbreaking, hopeful and sombre, and integral to understanding Germany's capital.

Viewing Visegrád, Hungary

10 A lonely, abandoned fortress (p319) high atop the Danube River marks what was once the northern border of the Roman Empire. Long after the Romans decamped, the ancient Hungarian kings, the Ottoman Turks and the Austrian Habsburgs in turn all marked this turf as their own. Climb to the top for some soul-stirring vistas over the surrounding countryside and ponder for a moment the kingdoms and peoples who have come and gone over sixteen centuries of history.

Checking out Český Krumlov, Czech Republic

11 Showcasing quite possibly Europe's most glorious Old Town, Český Krumlov (p134) is, for many travellers, a popular day trip from Prague. But a rushed few hours navigating the town's meandering lanes and clifftop castle sells the experience short. Stay at least one night to lose yourself in the Old Town's after-dark shadows, and get cosy in riverside restaurants, cafes and pubs. The following morning go rafting or canoeing on the Vltava River before exploring the nearby Newcastle Mountains by horse or mountain bike.

Hiking the High Tatras, Slovakia

12 The rocky, alpine peaks of the High Tatras (p456) in Slovakia are the highest in the Carpathians, with 25 peaks soaring over 2500m. But hiking this impressive little range needn't require an Olympian effort. In the morning, ride a cable car up to 1800m and you can hike along mid-elevation trails, stopping at a log cabin hikers' hut with a restaurant for lunch. A few hours more and you're at the Hrebienok funicular terminus, which will take you down to turn-of-the-20th-century Starý Smokovec below, well in time for dinner.

13

14

Beer-Drinking in Munich, Germany

13 It's not just the fact that you can drink beer in Munich (p209) – everybody knows you can. It's the variety of places where you can drink it that astounds and makes this a must-stop. There's Oktoberfest, of course, and then there are the famous beer halls, from the huge and infamous (Hofbräuhaus) to the huge and merely wonderful (Augustiner Bräustuben). And why stay inside for your frothy litre of lager? You can drink it in a park (Chinesischer Turm) or in the city centre (Viktualienmarkt) – or really just about anywhere. Beer tent at Oktoberfest

Discovering Kraków, Poland

14 As popular as it is, Poland's former royal capital (p374) never disappoints. It's hard to pinpoint exactly why it's so special, but there's a satisfying aura of history radiating from the sloping stone buttresses of the medieval buildings in the Old Town that makes its streets seem, well, just right. Add to that the extremes of a spectacular castle and the low-key, oh-so-cool bar scene situated within the tiny worn buildings of the Kazimierz backstreets, and it's a city you want to seriously get to know. Rynek Główny (Main Market Square)

need to know

Buses
» For travel in the mountains or between villages.

Trains
» Go almost everywhere; the fastest connections are in the west.

When to Go

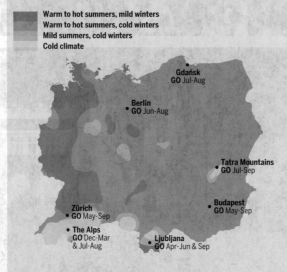

Warm to hot summers, mild winters
Warm to hot summers, cold winters
Mild summers, cold winters
Cold climate

Gdańsk
GO Jul-Aug

Berlin
GO Jun-Aug

Tatra Mountains
GO Jul-Sep

Budapest
GO May-Sep

Zürich
GO May-Sep

The Alps
GO Dec-Mar & Jul-Aug

Ljubljana
GO Apr-Jun & Sep

Your Daily Budget

Budget less than
€60
» Dorm bed: €10–35
» Fresh-food markets and cheap eats
» Camping, hiking and free museum days keep costs down

Midrange
€60– €180
» Double room in a pension or small hotel: €40–160
» Dinners average from €10 in the east to €30 in the west
» Great-value daily lunch menus at top restaurants

Top End over
€180
» International or boutique hotel: €180 and up
» High prices in Switzerland, Berlin and Prague
» Pocket the duty-free refunds from shopping sprees

High Season
(Jul–Aug)
» Expect crowds at major attractions; book hotels ahead
» Temperatures soar, especially in Hungary and Slovenia
» Higher-elevation hiking trails become accessible

Shoulder
(Apr–Jun & Sep–Oct)
» Prices remain high, but crowds ease off
» Moderate weather
» Village museums and castles remain open
» Bad timing for Alpine hiking or skiing

Low Season
(Nov–Mar)
» Outside the holidays prices drop 30% to 50%
» Christmas markets light up cities in late November and December
» Ski season kicks in
» Some attractions close

Driving

» Car hire readily available at airports throughout Central Europe; roads are good.

Ferries

» Travel by sea between Poland or Germany and Scandinavia, or from Slovenia to Italy.

Bicycles

» Beware of mountainous terrain and bring bike locks for the cities; the west has more dedicated cycle paths than the east.

Planes

» Budget airlines connect with many destinations in Western Europe and the UK.

Websites

» **Deutsche Bahn** (www.bahn.com) Best online train timetable for the region

» **Like a Local** (www.likealocalguide. com) Online guides to eastern capitals

» **In Your Pocket** (www.inyourpocket. com) Events listings for major cities

» **Lonely Planet** (www.lonelyplanet. com) Destination coverage, hotel booking and travellers' forum

» **Michelin** (www.viamichelin.com) Calculates the best route from A to B by car

Money

See individual country chapters for more information on specific currencies and exchange rates.

» **Crown** (Koruna česká; Kč) Czech Republic

» **Euro** (€) Germany, Austria, Slovenia and Slovakia

» **Forint** (HUF; Ft) Hungary

» **Swiss Franc** (Sfr) Switzerland, Liechtenstein

» **Złoty** (PLN; zł) Poland

Visas

» Visitors from Australia, New Zealand, Canada, Japan and the US can travel visa-free in Central Europe for 90 days.

» All countries in Central Europe are part of the Schengen Agreement and are considered one 'country' in terms of your 90-day stay.

» As part of the Schengen Agreement, EU citizens generally do not need visas and may be able to work across the region.

Arriving in Central Europe

» **Berlin Tegel Airport** Bus – 30 minutes to centre; frequent service

» **Frankfurt Airport** Train – 15 minutes to centre; frequent service

» **Vienna Airport** Train – 15 to 20 minutes to centre; every 30 minutes

» **Zürich Airport** Train – 10 to 15 minutes to main train station; frequent service

What to Take

» **Earplugs** Helpful for sleeping at hostels and in busy cities, plus you can tune out chatterboxes on planes, trains and buses.

» **Ecofriendly shopping bag** To use at all the fruit and vegetable markets.

» **Extra ziplock bags** Keep products from leaking and wet clothes separate from dry.

» **Hiking boots** For conquering the Alps or the Tatras.

» **Lonely Planet's Central Europe Phrasebook** For chatting with the locals.

» **Pocket knife with bottle-opener** For picnics on trains (but check it with your luggage on planes).

» **Sandals or thongs (flip-flops)** Useful at Baltic beaches and Hungarian spas.

» **Plug adaptors** If you're coming from the UK, North America or down under.

» **Unlocked mobile phone** Get a local SIM card and make cheap local calls.

if you like...

World Heritage Sites

Unesco's World Heritage list contains more than 80 of Central Europe's cultural and natural gems. Following their trail would take you to all of the region's states but one (alas, little Liechtenstein has yet to garner recognition). Here's a sampling.

Škocjan Caves, Slovenia Cross an unimaginably deep chasm by footbridge to explore these caves (p506)

Wartburg, Germany A timber-and-stone edifice near where Bach was born is the only German castle to make the list (p197)

Kutná Hora, Czech Republic A 14th-century townscape built outside Prague by silver-mining interests (p123)

Białowieża National Park, Poland In the furthest eastern reaches of Poland, the drawcard here is the magnificent European bison (p372)

Bardejov, Slovakia Slovakia's best Gothic-Renaissance town square, surrounded by 15th-century walls (p474)

Pannonhalma Abbey, Hungary Buildings in northeastern Hungary's most ancient abbey date to the 13th century, but the library boasts even older treasures (p323)

Hiking

Icy blue glacial lakes, crashing waterfalls, technical ascents...with so much striking mountain scenery, hiking in Central Europe is almost always a superlative – and challenging – experience.

Slovenský Raj National Park, Slovakia Ladders and chain-assists line the trails of the waterfall-filled gorge hikes in this national park (p468)

Zakopane, Poland Southern Poland's Tatra Mountain trails lead to emerald-green lakes like Morskie Oko (p393)

Julian Alps, Slovenia Centered on iconic Mt Triglav, trails lace this beautiful mountain region on the Italian border (p495)

Jungfrau region, Switzerland Spend a day or a month on the myriad trails – easy to hard – through this spectacular playground of Alpine peaks and valleys. The views will astound (p547)

Black Forest, Germany Seemingly endless paths lead from bucolic villages to misty peaks and crags (p239)

Kitzbühel Alps, Austria Peak-to-peak hiking here is well-served by cable cars, with plenty of alpine accommodation to boot (p83)

Castles

Defence was long a priority here at the crossroads of Europe. In some countries it seems that at the top of every craggy cliff you'll find a castle ruin. Stony fortresses typically date from between 12th and the 17th centuries. Then, as peace reigned, ruling families expanded and constructed chateaux and ornate palaces.

Karlštejn Castle, Czech Republic A finely restored, high Gothic castle built by Emperor Charles IV in the 14th century (p122)

Spiš Castle, Slovakia Impressive fortress ruins sprawl over more than four hilltop hectares (p465)

Schloss Neuschwanstein, Germany Mad King Ludwig's over-the-top castle inspired Walt Disney to create Fantasyland (p224)

Wawel Castle, Poland Kraków's town castle contains a large cathedral and is an enduring symbol of the country (p374)

Vienna's palaces, Austria The Hofburg palace served as the imperial Habsburg home for six centuries, while Schönbrunn was their ornate summer residence (p44)

AMOS CHAPPLE/GETTY IMAGES ©

» Memento Park – Statue Park Museum,
Hungary, Budapest, www.mementopark.hu
(p302)

Nightlife

Just about every one of the larger capitals in Central Europe, such as Prague and Budapest, will have a club scene, plus some live music. Smaller towns like Ljubljana and Bratislava rely on a calmer cafe culture for their evening entertainment. Your choice: dancing until dawn or a quiet, alfresco conversation with friends.

Berlin, Germany With more cutting-edge clubs than seems possible, Berlin is where DJs experiment with the sounds of tomorrow (p161)

Zürich, Switzerland Blows the staid Swiss cliché out of the (lakeside) water with trendy bar 'hoods and cutting-edge clubs (p550)

Warsaw, Poland Clubbers flock to Poland's main city for fabulous dance clubs, but don't miss the live jazz venues either (p368)

Budapest, Hungary Venues change by the week, giving Budapest a pumping, blade-sharp club scene (p297)

Sacred Spaces

Christianity, Judaism and Islam have all influenced Central Europe. Impressive cathedrals inhabit many of the town castles and squares, and other sacred sites are scattered around the region.

Old Jewish Cemetery, Czech Republic The approximately 12,000 ancient graves here date from 1439; it's an evocative setting that's just one of the many sacred Jewish sights in Prague (p102)

Mosque Church, Hungary Originally constructed during the 16th-century Turkish occupation of Hungary, this mosque-turned-church retains several Islamic elements (p329)

Wooden churches, Slovakia The onion domes on the nail-less village churches reflect the eastern-facing faith of the Slovakian hinterland (p475)

Wieskirche, Germany A jaw-dropping example of 18th-century rococo excess, covered with gilt decorations and hand-painted stucco, sits in a peaceful German valley (p222)

Kölner Dom, Germany Dominating the skyline of Cologne from any distance, this is one of Europe's most perfect large cathedrals (p256)

History

We can learn a lot from history in a region that was ripped apart by several world wars – both hot and cold.

Berlin Wall, Germany Reverberations were felt across Europe when the wall dividing East and West Germany came down in 1989; what remains is part outdoor art gallery, part walking trail (p170)

Memento Park, Hungary An amazing collection of Hungary's socialist and Soviet-inspired statues that were removed from public spaces after the fall of communism (p302)

Auschwitz-Birkenau, Poland Two of the most infamous Nazi concentration camps remain partially standing as a heart-wrenching memorial and museum (p385)

Vienna, Austria In this rococo capital of a vanished empire, history looms grandly around every corner (p44)

Terezín, Czech Republic A fortress 'community' that was actually a waypoint for Nazi death camps; exhibits include poignant pictures and poems by children once held there (p126)

STUART BLACK/GETTY IMAGES ©

» Hundertwasser-House (p49), Vienna.
A Hundertwasser Architecture Project,
architect Josef Krawina

Artistic Haunts

With so many cultural
capitals, it's easy to follow in
the footsteps of a favourite
author or musician. Read
or listen to their works as
you experience their home
cities.

Salzburg, Austria Native
son Wolfgang Mozart's music
resonates in all corners of this
Austrian Alpine town – as does
The Sound of Music (p65)

Weimar, Germany Bach, Liszt,
Goethe and Nietzsche were just
some of the luminaries who
lived and worked here (p195)

Prague, Czech Republic Postmodern authors Milan Kundera
and Franz Kafka both left their
mark on the Old Town streets of
Prague (p98)

Warsaw, Poland Nobel Laureate
and poet Czeslaw Milosz spent
WWII attending underground
lectures in Poland's capital city
(p358)

Vienna, Austria As the cultural
capital of the Austro-Hungarian
empire, Vienna attracted the
likes of Ludwig van Beethoven,
Joseph Haydn and Béla Bartók;
their classical music can still be
heard at venues today (p44)

Old Towns

Central Europe's Old Towns
are legendary. You'll hardly
turn a corner without
bumping into a Gothic arch
or a medieval buttress. The
ancient aura is perhaps best
experienced in the more
compact pedestrian centres.

**Český Krumlov, Czech
Republic** A stunning castle,
baroque buildings and the winding Vltava River make this one
of the Czech Republic's most
charming Old Towns (p134)

Bratislava, Slovakia The
rabbit-warren-like streets in the
Slovakian capital are studded
with more outdoor cafes than
you can shake a drink at (p438)

Ljubljana, Slovenia This
lovely town has a hilltop castle
perched above narrow streets
and riverfront plazas (p483)

Kraków, Poland The stunning
medieval centre escaped the
ravages of WWII and, as such,
is one of the region's best
preserved Old Towns (p374)

Salzburg, Austria 'If it's
baroque, don't fix it' seems to be
the motto of this incredible Old
Town in the Austrian Alps (p65)

Drinks

Definitely don't miss the
dark, light, sweet and wheat
beers crafted in Germany.
But don't limit yourself to
hops as there's plenty more
regional imbibing to do.

Bison vodka, Poland Locals
claim vodka was invented in
Poland; try it here, flavoured
with cherries or berries – or
with grass from the bison fields
(p428)

New wine, Austria In autumn
when an evergreen branch
appears over the *Heurigen*
(wine tavern) door, you know
effervescent new wine is
available (p89)

Budvar, Czech Republic
The original 'Budweiser' beer
is still made today in České
Budějovice; tour the factory or
taste it at a beer hall (p132)

Wine, Switzerland Unesco-
recognised vineyards climb from
the shores of beautiful Lake
Geneva and across the neighbouring region of Valais (p571)

Fruit brandy, everywhere Look
for fruit-flavoured firewater (OK,
they usually call it 'brandy') all
across the region. *Slivovica* is
flavoured with plums, *pálinka*
with apricots...

If you like... Extreme Sports

The Jungfrau region around Switzerland's Interlaken is an adventure-sports mecca (p547)

Go canyoning, parasailing or hydro-speed rafting in Bovec, Slovenia (p503)

Try rock climbing, rafting or paragliding in the Zillertal in Austria (p82)

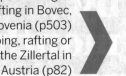

Modern Architecture

Sure, Central Europe is known for age-old architecture. But there's also a more modern side to the region.

Elbphilharmonie, Germany
Pritzker Prize–winning Swiss architects Jacques Herzog and Pierre de Meuron designed this modern glass facade in an old district of Hamburg (p269)

Hundertwasserhaus, Austria A mish-mash of uneven floors, misshapen windows and industrial materials make this apartment house in Vienna (p49)

Bauhaus school, Germany Examples of the less-is-more, early-1900s aesthetic can be found in Weimar, Dessau and Berlin (p172)

Museum of Czech Cubism, Czech Republic A monument of the indigenous cubist style (p103)

Paul Klee Centre, Switzerland Renzo Piano's sensitive building in Bern is the perfect homage to Klee's brilliant work within (p539)

Secessionist style, Austria and Hungary Austro-Hungarian Secessionist style emerged at the turn of the 20th century; examples include Vienna's Secession building (p49) and Kecskemét's Ornamental Palace (p333)

Off the Beaten Track

Everyone's heard of Berlin and Budapest. But if you feel you've been there, done that, then why not explore smaller, off-the-beaten-track towns? You're likely to have a more local experience as you discover these gems.

Toruń, Poland A beautiful Gothic city with curious statuary and plenty of beer gardens to enjoy (p416)

Kecskemét, Hungary Full of art nouveau architecture and small museums; the town itself is worth visiting before you set off to see the famous horses in the adjacent national park (p333)

Bern, Switzerland Often underrated, this capital city is a melange of medieval charm, folkloric and cartoonish fountains and a pulsating cafe scene (p538)

Piran, Slovenia There are Venetian alleyways to explore and fresh seafood to eat at this port town on the tip of a peninsula (p508)

Bamberg, Germany Cute little bridges span the canal that bisects one of Germany's best small towns; they also have smoked beer (p230)

Bathing

Opportunities abound in Central Europe if you enjoy a good soak. Thermal mineral waters bubble under parts of Germany and the Czech Republic, and beneath all of Hungary and Slovakia. We list the main sites, but many smaller spas exist across these countries.

Budapest, Hungary The queen of the spa towns, Budapest has thermal bathhouses dating back to Turkish times; the most popular are the ginormous Széchenyi Baths and the more intimate Gellért Baths (p297)

Piešťany, Slovakia A neoclassical thermal spa where you can be wrapped naked in hot mud or soak in a 'mirror pool' (p448)

Baden-Baden, Germany A 16-step Roman bathing experience is on offer in Germany's ritzy spa town (p238)

Karlovy Vary, Czech Republic Book a steam inhalation or just soak among the international set at the Czech answer to Baden-Baden (p126)

month by month

Top Events

1 **Oktoberfest**, September

2 **Christmas markets**, December

3 **Carnival**, February

4 **Summer music festivals**, July

5 **Zürich Street Parade**, August

January

Sure it's cold, but what better time to go skiing? While the rest of the region is quiet, the mountains buzz with crowded runs, full cable cars and aprés-ski activities.

☆ Ball Season, Austria

More than 300 balls take place in Vienna during January and February, including the season's highlight, the Opera Ball (p50). Expect men in full tails and women in dazzling dresses gliding elegantly around the polished dance floor.

February

Frigid temperatures and prime ski conditions continue, but an abundance of pre-Lenten festivals start to warm things up in towns big and small across the region.

 Kurentovanje, Slovenia

Parades of horned and feathered Carnival characters wearing painted masks and sheepskins highlight the 10-day festival (p514) leading up to Shrove Tuesday in Ptuj. This ethnographic tradition, which includes bonfires and performances, has taken place for more than 50 years.

✨🌙 Karneval/ Fasching, Germany

Towns in the traditional Catholic regions of Germany – Bavaria, along the Rhine and deep in the Black Forest – celebrate Carnival with costumed parties and parades in the week leading up to Lent. Don't miss Cologne (p255).

✨🌙 Fasnacht, Switzerland

At least six days of celebrating precede Fat Tuesday in Switzerland. The towns of Basel and Lucerne (p544), in particular, live it up: masked revellers party to bands in the streets and bars stay open all night long.

March

As the first green shoots emerge in the lowlands, snow still lies heavy in the mountains above. Concert seasons start and continue until autumn.

☆ Budapest Spring Festival, Hungary

Classical music (p307) is king late in March when Hungary's capital hosts two weeks of world-class opera, symphonic music and ballet performances. Venues include gilt concert halls and open-air stages set up on pedestrian squares.

April

The proliferation of outdoor cafe tables proves that spring has well and truly sprung. Thankfully, high season hasn't arrived yet; prices remain low and crowds relatively few.

☆ Music Festivals, Poland

A number of towns in Poland have small spring and summer music festivals. In Kraków (p374) the focus is organ concerts, while in Wrocław (p398) jazz takes centre stage for three days when performances are held on the Odra River.

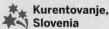 Sechseläuten, Switzerland

On the third Monday in April (p551), Zürich

celebrates spring with a costumed parade and ceremonial burning of the snowman (*Böögg*). At 6pm a fire is lit under the 4m-high effigy; when the fireworks in his head explode, winter is finished.

★ Festival of Sacred Music, Czech Republic

During the weeks leading up to Easter, six ancient churches in Brno serve as a blessed backdrop for Lenten concerts. Events include the likes of the Prague Philharmonic performing Beethoven's celebrated mass, *Missa Solemnis*.

May

Asparagus season is in full swing; look for seasonal menus that include the much-prized white variety. Castles and outdoor village museums are now fully open, but it's too soon for high-altitude hiking.

★ Prague Spring, Czech Republic

Czech composer Bedřich Smetana inspired Prague's most famous classical-music festival (p107), which runs from mid-May into June. It kicks off with a parade from Smetana's grave to the performance hall where his opera *Má Vlast* is staged.

Czech Beer Festival, Czech Republic

In Prague, for two weeks from mid- to late May, the Czech Beer Festival pours more than 70 brews from around the country. It may be mild compared to

Germany's Oktoberfest, but the three big exhibition-ground tents do give off a similar vibe.

★ Druga Godba, Slovenia

In mid-May, Ljubljana hosts a week-long festival (p489) of alternative and world music with bands from around the globe. The venue, a sprawling 18th-century monastic complex, is a rich contrast to the modern sounds.

June

Frequent rains help the alpine wildflowers bloom, and more and more hikers head to the hills – the lower ranges especially. It's strawberry season, so watch for little red morsels of joy.

★ Christopher Street Day, Germany

First held in 1978, this Berlin event in late June is one of the oldest gay and lesbian festivals in the world. Pride-related activities go on all week, culminating with floats and walking GLBT groups parading through the streets and the Tiergarten.

★ Jodler Fest Luzern, Switzerland

Lucerne is at its Alpine best for three days in June, when 12,000 yodellers and alp-horn players come to town. With a variety of colourful national costumes, the performances are wonderful to see as well as hear.

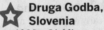 Olomouc Beer Festival, Czech Republic

More than 20 breweries participate in this three-day outdoor festival in the eastern Czech Republic. In addition to beers to sample, there are beer souvenirs to buy and more than 40 folk and rock bands to listen to.

★ Wrocław Non Stop, Poland

For 10 days in late June, quirky art installations, alternative movies and music, and experimental theatre and dance take centre stage in Wrocław. Public squares become art galleries and concert halls as the whole town gets in on the act.

July

Summer crowds arrive in earnest, so be sure to book lodging and hikers' huts ahead of time. It seems like every town and village is celebrating something with outdoor food stands and frivolities.

★ Jewish Culture Festival, Poland

Concerts, films, theatre performances and scholarly lectures are all part of this week-long celebration of Jewish culture in Kraków in early July. Join local tours and excursions to towns in the area for art and memorial sightseeing.

★ Karlovy Vary International Film Festival, Czech Republic

International celebrities often appear at this Czech festival (www.kviff.com), which screens more than 200 films each year. Tickets are easy to get and concurrent outdoor events add to the energetic atmosphere.

☆ Montreux Jazz Festival, Switzerland

For two weeks in early to mid-July, a distinct air of glamour surrounds this fabulous Swiss festival (p534) in Montreux. The world's biggest names in jazz play to rapt audiences who have paid well for the tickets. There are also free outdoor performances to enjoy.

☆ More Music, Music Everywhere

Musical festivals abound across the region in July; Geneva, Vienna, Warsaw, Ljubljana, Bratislava and Kraków are just a few of the other towns that have concerts and cultural events.

☆ Salzburg Festival, Austria

In late July some 250,000 people crowd into this quaint Austrian city for a month-long, world-renowned festival of music, theatre and opera (p69). Book tickets ahead: as one of Europe's largest classical events, first held in 1920, it's not unknown.

August

The year's hottest month is also the busiest. Despite the throngs, this is a good time to visit if you want plenty to do. City-planned events continue and thermal waterparks open for extended hours.

★☆ Street Parade, Switzerland

In early August 'love mobiles' (giant floats filled with revellers) cruise along the streets of Zürich blasting techno music. Hundreds of thousands of ravers dance in the streets in celebration of life, love and a good beat.

☆ Sziget Music Festival, Hungary

The week-long outdoor international-music bash (p307) in late July/early August is quite the party. Camp on Hungary's Óbuda Island in central Budapest and listen to world music, including rock, ska, hip hop and Romani – a little of everything, with an indie edge.

☆ Motor Sports, Czech Republic & Hungary

Hotels fill up early during the Moto Grand Prix, a famous motorcycle race in Brno, Czech Republic. But that's nothing compared to the popularity of the Formula One Grand Prix auto race (p307) held 24km north of Budapest, Hungary in late July/early August.

★☆ Folk Festivals

Keep an eye out for placards advertising small summer folk festivals at weekends. These festivals usually include all kinds of revelry, such as folk dances, music, food and drink. Towns and villages in Slovakia, Czech Republic, Poland and Hungary, especially, have them.

September

While some warmth may linger, autumn has already arrived in the mountains. Weather is unpredictable, but often a week or so of 'Indian summer' in late September provides excellent hiking potential.

★☆ Bohinj Cows' Ball, Slovenia

On a mid-September weekend, the residents of Bohinj mark the return of their cows from high pastures to the valleys by parading wreath-laden bovines through town. Food and folk music are part of the fun that culminates in a town dance.

★☆ Oktoberfest, Germany

Six million people guzzle 5 million litres of beer and 400,000 sausages each year at what may be one of the biggest festivals in the world (p214). But don't show up in October, the carousing actually takes place on the last 15 days in September.

🏃 Mushroom Picking

Locals know that September is prime time for picking mushrooms in the hilly forests of Central Europe. Go with a local or a reliable field guide – the prettiest specimens are often the most poisonous.

October

You're likely to have the museums and castles to yourself if you travel in mild October, but don't forget a raincoat. Avoid

the higher altitudes, which are usually wet and sloshy rather than beautifully snow-covered.

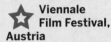

Viennale Film Festival, Austria

Austria's largest film festival (p50) takes place for two weeks in mid- to late October. The screenings have a decidedly independent, fringe-like feel, which attracts a youthful audience. Parties and related events are suitably cool and urban.

New Wine

From September into October, the new wines (unaged, usually light and effervescent) become available. Buy them at the local markets and vintners cellars, or attend town wine festivals in places like Budapest and Kecskemét in Hungary, and Neuchâtel and Lugano in Switzerland.

November

The best we can say is that prices fall and tourists are scarce in this way off-season. Outdoor attractions close, a chill

hangs about and places lack the holiday and ski season charm to come.

Low Season, Alps

Sure many resorts and hotels close for the month in cities across the Alps, but this just means that you'll have some of the world's most beautiful places to yourself. Book early at the few choices available to enjoy good rates.

December

Twinkly lights and mulled wine spice up long, cold winter nights in December. Christmas markets and city-wide decorations create a festive atmosphere across the region. Avoid the holiday itself and prices remain remarkably low.

Christkindlmärkte, Austria

Atmospheric Christmas joy abounds at Vienna's Christmas markets (p51), which run from mid-November to Christmas Eve.

Christkindlesmarkt, Germany

More than two million people attend Germany's most popular Christmas market, which fills most of Nuremberg's centre. Look for the Christmas angel and handmade ornaments, and don't miss the chance to eat *Lebkuchen* (large, soft gingerbread cookies).

Yet More Christmas Markets

Austria and Germany may have the largest fairs, but many towns across the region put up craft booths and decorations, sell hot food and wine and hold outdoor concerts. Check what's going on in your city.

New Years Eve

Central squares from Vienna to Prague pulse with fireworks, flying champagne corks and spontaneous kisses. Look for rousing special concerts and festive cheer everywhere.

itineraries

Two Weeks
Top Capital Tour

> Spending two to three days per capital will give you a great overview of the region. Start your trip in the dynamic, delightfully idiosyncratic **Berlin**; the history-filled capital of reunited Germany is also something of a party place. Then ride the rails to sprawling **Warsaw**, with a reconstructed Old Town that became the capital of the Commonwealth of Poland and Lithuania back in the mid-16th century. After a few days, continue south to mystical **Prague**. The Czech seat of power is famous for its fantasyland of Gothic architecture – and for great beer. Next? Slovakia's **Bratislava** is a fascinating mix of Old Town charm and new development, while the imperial opulence of the long-reigning Habsburg empire is still evident in Austria's capital, **Vienna**. Just don't satiate yourself on coffee-house culture there; you have more cafes to visit in one-time cocapital **Budapest**. Today Hungary's main city is abuzz with a mix of the modern and the historic. If you have time, detour to **Ljubljana** in Slovenia and tiny **Vaduz** in Liechtenstein; otherwise World Heritage–listed **Bern**, the Swiss capital fought over by the Holy Roman and Habsburg Empires alike, is your final stop. It's so beautiful, it's no wonder everyone wanted a piece of it.

Central Europe In-Depth

With two months, you can cover the entire region, but it will still be a bit of a 'Best of' trip. Skyscraper-filled **Frankfurt-am-Main** is most useful as an air hub, but you may want to spend a night. From there, shake off jet lag at the chi-chi spa centre **Baden-Baden** before exploring the bucolic towns of the **Black Forest**. Just across the Swiss border, the cobblestone streets and cafes of **Basel** await. Move on to the modern art and ancient architecture of the capital, **Bern**.

Soon the Alps beckon: **Interlaken** and the Jungfrau region have some of the most extreme mountain scenery around. Check out the cafe scene of **Zürich** before crossing the spine of the Alps and getting ready to imbibe in the beer halls of **Munich**. Spend a few days, so you can bus it along the Romantic Road and see the fantasyland-like Schloss Neuschwanstein in **Füssen.** Next stop is the baroque, music-filled city of **Salzburg**. Then it's south into the Julian Alps and picture-postcard, lakeside **Bled,** in Slovenia.

The lovely Slovenian capital of **Ljubljana** is also worth a stop before you ride the rails on to impressively imperial **Vienna** for a couple of nights. A riverboat ride along the vineyard-laden **Danube Valley** is a worthy detour before travelling downstream to the bathhouses and bars of **Budapest**. To the south, the architecture in **Pécs** retains some remarkable Turkish relics.

Heading north again, myriad Old Town cafes in **Bratislava** make a good pit stop en route to the **Tatra Mountains**. On the Slovak side, the most atmospheric midmountain village is Ždiar; in Poland, it's Zakopane. Hike rugged area trails before you continue to **Kraków**, one of Europe's prettiest Old Towns, near the notorious Auschwitz concentration camp. A local favourite and another lively Old Town, **Wrocław** is next, then **Dresden**, a restored German city that exhibits some impressive art.

The whole of Czech captial **Prague** is like a museum, so you'll want to take several days wandering its neighbourhoods, or side trip to spend a night in even more medieval **Český Krumlov**. From Prague exciting and edgy **Berlin** is only three hours north by fast train, or you can return west to catch a flight in Frankfurt-am-Main (7½ hours by train).

Three Weeks
Northern Route

Mild weather makes summer the best time for seeing the northernmost reaches of Germany and Poland. Start by spending a few nights in multicultural **Cologne**. Pass two days touring the country's largest cathedral and several small museums. By evening heft a glass of locally brewed Kölsch beer in one of the town's lively beer halls and bars. From there day-trip over to character-filled **Aachen**, where you can float in bubbling thermal baths before wandering the quirky cobblestone streets. Moving on to charming **Bremen** for a night or two, you'll explore art nouveau alleyways and an ornate market hall before winding up at a cafe on the waterfront promenade.

Next, Germany's most energetic port town, **Hamburg**, will keep you entertained for at least three days. You'll enjoy the maritime history, the old brick warehouse district and the new glass-encased philharmonic hall. Take the ferry out to the windswept beaches and seafood restaurants of Germany's northernmost point, the **North Frisian Islands**.

Back on the mainland, **Lübeck** is a 12th-century, Unesco-recognised townscape of medieval merchants' houses and towers that is well worth a stopover. Save at least three days – and nights – for the rich history, museums, bars and clubs of **Berlin**. The Brandenburg Gate, Holocaust Memorial and East Side Gallery at the Berlin Wall are must-sees. In the evening you have your choice of subdued-but-happening nightlife in Prenzlauer Berg, the hipster havens in Friedrichshain or alternative clubs in slightly grungy Kreuzberg.

Entering Poland, make the Old Town of **Poznań**, where the lively university population keeps the ancient centre buzzing, your first overnight stop. Two days in the impressively Gothic, church-filled **Toruń** has a much slower pace. To the north, **Gdańsk** is Poland's largest Baltic Sea port town. You can easily spend a few days wandering the waterfront, taking boat excursions and exploring resorts like Sopot.

Five hours or so south, **Warsaw** may not be the prettiest city, but it has loads of history hidden among the big-city sprawl. Take two days exploring the Old Town and war monuments. End your tour with an outing to **Białowieża National Park**, a biosphere reserve where the once nearly extinct European bison roams. The small village has plenty of places to stay overnight before your journey onward.

Three Weeks
Alpine Adventure

> Getting up close and personal with the Alps takes time; connections are almost never direct. Allow at least three to four days per region.

Starting out in **Geneva**, take a day and night to enjoy the city's cosmopolitan lakefront, cafes and fountains. If you want to gain altitude immediately, transfer on to quainter, also-lakeside **Lausanne** – part former fishing village with a summer beach-resort feel, part upscale, elegant shopping and dining town.

Next, explore Valais and Switzerland's 10 tallest peaks. Don your stylish togs and base yourself beneath the Matterhorn in the ritzy 19th-century resort town of **Zermatt**. Nearby, cogwheel trains and cable cars provide access to amazing hiking, skiing and mountain views.

From Zermatt take the 7½-hour Glacier Express train ride over high mountain passes to **St Moritz**. This region has 11,000km of hiking trails and incredible black diamond ski runs – and the town has fab nightlife to boot.

To the north, the **Swiss National Park** area is a quieter, more peaceful stop with rugged dolomite peaks, sprawling larch woodlands and untouched, topaz lakes. Stay in the village of Zernez or in the park itself.

Continuing on to the Liechtenstein Alps, you'll have to connect through **Vaduz** to get to the famous alpine hike, the thrilling Fürstensteig Trail. Don't forget to snap a shot of the town's famous hilltop castle.

Neighbouring Austria's wild and beautiful Arlberg region is home to **St Anton am Arlberg**, a huge draw for skiers and boarders, with an active party scene.

The Tyrolean Zillertal Valley is as much a summer playground as a winter one. Set off from the town of **Mayrhofen** to go cycling, hiking, rock climbing or rafting.

One of the best drives in the Alps awaits you in **Hohe Tauern National Park**, a nearly 1800-sq-km wilderness with 3000m peaks. You'll undoubtedly pass over Grossglockner Road, a 1930s engineering marvel with 36 switchbacks.

South in Slovenia, Triglav National Park encompasses almost all of the Julian Alps. A postcard-perfect mountain setting and cute village make **Bled** the most popular base. But you should also check out the larger, less-crowded lake at **Bohinj** or adventure-sports-oriented **Bovec** before connecting on from the capital, **Ljubljana**.

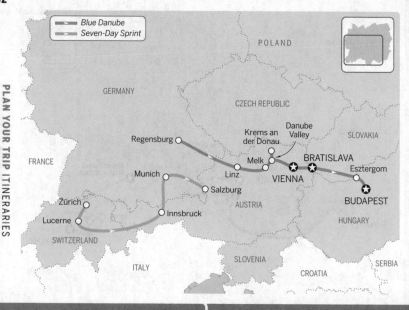

Blue Danube
Seven-Day Sprint

POLAND

GERMANY

CZECH REPUBLIC

FRANCE

Regensburg

Danube
Valley

Krems an
der Donau

SLOVAKIA

Melk

BRATISLAVA

Munich

Linz

VIENNA

Esztergom

Salzburg

Zürich

AUSTRIA

BUDAPEST

Lucerne

Innsbruck

HUNGARY

SWITZERLAND

ITALY

SLOVENIA

SERBIA

CROATIA

One Week
Seven-Day Sprint

> Only have a week to spend in Central Europe? You don't actually have to run far. The picture-perfect towns close to the borders of Switzerland, Austria and Germany are tailor-placed for a quick highlights tour. Fly into **Zürich**, and spend a night in the lively urban centre that retains an Old World heart; don't miss hip Züri-West. From there, head to the mountains and the ever-idyllic lakeside city of **Lucerne**, where iconic half-timbered bridges cross glacier-cold waters.

Leave Switzerland for its immediate neighbour to the east, Austria. **Innsbruck** has hosted the Winter Olympics twice and is a great mountain base; from there you can ski or hike, taking sustenance in mountain huts. The beer halls of **Munich** are now only a short hop away. This atmospheric Bavarian town with good museums is worth a couple of days; when it's clear, you can see the Alps. A short final jaunt brings you to the perfect combination of hills and music: **Salzburg**. Mozart's one-time home has an abundance of old architecture, including an impressive castle, surrounded by mountains and Alpine lakes.

10 Days
Blue Danube

> Build on Johann Strauss' classical attempt to capture the mood of Central Europe by exploring the region around the 'Blue Danube' river. Start with a water-view meal in Germany's **Regensburg**, a city replete with historical constructions. Then visit **Linz** and its stunning riverside art gallery before boarding a tour boat. Cruises stop in pretty **Melk**, dominated by an intimidating Benedictine monastery. After that, head to the **Danube Valley**, crowded with castles and vineyards, and best seen by water. On the northern bank of the Danube, **Krems an der Donau** has a pretty cobblestone centre.

Meander on by train to **Vienna**. Take a couple of days to tour the city before going by boat, train or bus to spend a night in the Slovakian capital, **Bratislava**, with its interesting mix of ancient Old Town and communist concrete. From there you can cruise along, following the Danube east into Hungary. Look up at **Esztergom** to see the awesome walled basilica high above. Finish with a few days in **Budapest**, where renting a bike and tootling around midriver Margaret Island caps off your Danube adventure.

» (above) Stift Melk (p60), Austria
» (left) Kapellbrücke (p543), Lucerne

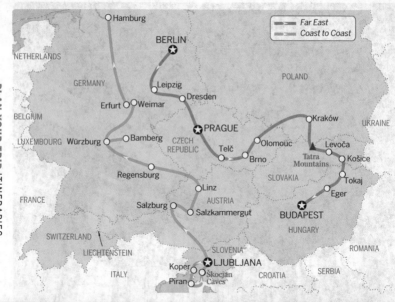

Two Weeks
Coast to Coast

From the Adriatic to the Baltic, going coast to coast takes you right up the centre of Central Europe. Connect to Slovenia through capital **Ljubljana**, and make your way to the water. Divide several days between the modern-day port of **Koper** and the old Venetian gem **Piran**. Backtracking north, a side trip to the colossal **Škocjan Caves** is in order before you head into Austria.

From Ljubljana, you go through **Salzburg** (and may want to stop) en route to boating, bobbing and nature-walking in the Lake District, **Salzkammergut**. Next, it's avant-garde and arty **Linz**. North in Germany, medieval **Regensburg** lies on the Danube riverfront. From there head north to **Würzburg** to taste the wines of the valley (or to oh-so-cute **Bamberg** for smoked beer). Spend a couple of days of cultural pursuit in **Weimar** – like Goethe, Liszt and Nietzsche before you. You might detour to see **Erfurt** and the nearby castle, or Buchenwald concentration camp. Transferring on to happening **Hamburg**, you've reached the coast and a lively last port of call.

One Month
Far East

Taking an eastern tack you'll be travelling through former communist countries, but you'd hardly know it today. Start in **Berlin**, where, instead of a wall dividing the city, you'll find an art gallery and walking path. Then travel to the dynamic East German city of **Leipzig**, where Bach and Wagner once lived. Make a stop in reconstructed baroque **Dresden** before staying a few days in tourist-filled **Prague**. You'll have a more authentic Czech experience in a smaller, Unesco-recognised town like **Telč**. Then, see modern Moravian life in upbeat **Brno**, and head east for another astronomical clock in laid-back **Olomouc**. If you like medieval construction, you'll love **Kraków**, in Poland. To get to Slovakia, you pass through the **Tatra Mountains**, so you may as well stop. Below the mountains, the walled city of **Levoča** is close to the impressive Spiš Castle ruins. A musical fountain and Gothic cathedral highlight **Košice**. Thirsty? Because little **Tokaj**, in Hungary, has been producing great dessert wines for ages. Vineyards also cover the hills surrounding the old town of **Eger** and its walkable wine-tasting valley. From there **Budapest** – and your onward journey – are not far west.

countries at a glance

Central Europe's charm lies in the common characteristics shared by some of its nations, juxtaposed with each country's individual attractions. Tuck into veal schnitzel and raise a stein to toast *Prost!* in Germany, Austria and Switzerland. Study communist history and Slavic cultures in Poland, Slovakia, Slovenia and the Czech Republic. Hike scenic trails and wander ancient Old Town streets all across the region. For more country-specific pursuits, soak up the warm coastal sun at Slovenian ports or ski the continent's most extreme slopes in Switzerland. For high art and opera, visit Austria. Into WWII history? Poland has numerous well-preserved sites. For great brews, choose between German stouts and Czech Pilsners. Hungary boasts countless thermal spas; Slovakia has castles galore. Exploring the contrasts and commonalities of this intriguing region could well consume a lifetime.

Austria

Culture ✓✓✓
Mountains ✓✓✓
Architecture ✓✓

Music, Opera & Art
Vienna is home to a cultural scene that includes world-class opera and art. But you'll also find Mozart's music resounding in Salzburg, modern art in Linz, and plays and festivals wherever you go.

Mountains
The Austrian Alps have hiking and skiing galore, and upland lakes serve as a summer playground. Whether swimming in Salzkammergut, climbing in Kitzbühel or driving over Grossglockner Road, the mountains offer quite a high.

Architecture
Ornate palaces, baroque castles and wacky modern constructions – Austria has it all. Look for impressive architecture in the cities and picture-perfect villages in the hills.

p40

Czech Republic

Old Towns ✓✓✓
Outdoors ✓✓✓
Beer ✓✓

Old Towns
The Czech Republic has more than its fair share of Central Europe's beautiful Old Towns. Prague tops the list, but don't miss Telč, Český Krumlov or Olomouc, either.

Great Outdoors
The interesting landscapes around the country can inspire and amuse. Pinnacles, spires and other sandstone shapes punctuate Bohemian Switzerland National Park and 'rock towns' like Adršpach and Teplice.

Beer
Czech brews are enjoyed the world over; why not go straight to the source? Throw back a Pilsner in Plzeň and a Budvar in České Budějovice before you indulge in the emerging microbrewery scene.

p95

Germany

History ✓✓✓
Entertainment ✓✓
Culture ✓✓✓

History

Events in Germany have often dominated the Central European stage, especially during the two world wars. Travelling through the country, you'll feel the weight of history in places like Berlin, Weimar, Dachau and beyond.

Party On

Oktoberfest in Munich is perhaps the world's biggest party, and it's just one of the country's many festivals. At other times of year check out the pulsing club scene in cities like Berlin.

Culture

The Bavarian culture, from oompah bands to beer halls, is enough reason to visit. You can also shop for cuckoo clocks in the Black Forest, or just admire the Teutonic half-timbered buildings as you go.

p159

Hungary

Spas ✓✓✓
Architecture ✓✓
Gastronomy ✓✓

Soaking in Spas

Sure, the thermal baths scattered across Hungary are recuperative, but they're also just plain fun. Try the big ones in Budapest then move on to the bubbles and squirts of smaller spas countrywide.

Architecture

Art nouveau in Budapest and Kecskemét, Moorish elements in Pécs and Eger...Hungary has a different style to much of Central Europe.

Gastronomy

From the country that made paprika famous comes a variety of delicious stews and sauces flavoured with this 'red gold'. Savour it with a glass of noteworthy Bull's Blood red or Tokaj white wine.

p295

Poland

History ✓✓✓
Old Towns ✓✓
Mountains ✓✓

History

WWII history is ever present, whether you're at the Warsaw Rising Museum or the infamous Auschwitz concentration camp in Oświęcim. It can be both enlightening and emotionally challenging.

Old Towns

Well-preserved towns like Kraków, Toruń and Wrocław will wow you. But even big cities like Warsaw and Gdańsk have compact Old Town centres worth exploring.

Tatra Mountains

In the south of the country, the surprisingly tall peaks of the compact Tatra Mountains provide hiking, lodging and lower prices than the Central European Alps to the west.

p355

Slovakia

Hiking ✓✓✓
Castles ✓✓
Old Towns ✓

Hiking

More than 20% of this country is reserved parkland, but the whole thing is covered with trails. Hike the alpine peaks of the High Tatras, climb up waterfall-filled gorges in Slovenský Raj and traverse forests in the Malá Fatra.

Castles

Of the hundreds of fortress ruins in Slovakia, the 4-hectare Spiš Castle is the most impressive. More complete, fairytale-worthy castles include those in Trenčín, Devín and Bojnice.

Old Towns

The rabbit-warren Old Town of capital Bratislava is worth a wander before you explore the medieval walled town of Levoča, the perfect Renaissance square in Bardejov and a Middle Ages mining town, Banská Štiavnica.

p435

Slovenia

Mountains ✓✓
Coast ✓✓✓
Wine ✓

Julian Alps

Whether hiking up Mt Triglav, crossing Vršič Pass or rowing on Lake Bled, the Slovenian mountain scenery is truly impressive. Towns like Bovec and Bohinj serve as both summer and winter sports centres.

Coast

The Adriatic coast of Slovenia is reminiscent of neighbouring Italy. The narrow old Venetian alleyways of Piran attract hordes of summer visitors. Avoid the crowds by seeking out other port towns like Koper and Izola.

Wine

Distinct Slovenian wines include peppery reds and dry rosés. Because exports are limited, the best local vintages can often be had nowhere but here.

p481

Switzerland

Mountains ✓✓✓
Skiing ✓✓✓
Nightlife ✓✓

Mountain Scenery

More than 65% of Switzerland is mountainous. The different regions of Valais, Jungfrau and the Jura each have their own character, but all offer spectacular vistas. Admire the views from cable cars, trains and the towns below.

Skiing

Some of the top skiing in the world is to be had on the Swiss slopes. Klein Matterhorn has Europe's highest runs and extensive summer skiing. Beginners can try one of more than 200 ski schools.

Nightlife

Zürich and Bern are well known for lively club scenes. Outside the cities, après-ski provides vibrant nightlife in mountain towns like chi-chi Zermatt and St Moritz.

p521

Every listing is recommended by our authors, and their favourite places are listed first

Look out for these icons:

 Our author's top recommendation

 A green or sustainable option

 No payment required

On the Road

See the Index for a full list of destinations covered in this book.

Austria

Why Go?

For such a small country, Austria has made it big. This is, after all, the land where Mozart was born, Strauss taught the world to waltz and Julie Andrews grabbed the spotlight with her twirling entrance in *The Sound of Music*. This is where the Habsburgs built their 600-year empire, and where past glories still shine in the resplendent baroque palaces and chandelier-lit coffee houses of Vienna, Innsbruck and Salzburg. This is a perfectionist of a country and whatever it does – mountains, classical music, new media, castles, cake, you name it – it does exceedingly well.

Beyond its grandiose cities, Austria's allure lies outdoors. And whether you're schussing down the legendary slopes of Kitzbühel, climbing high in the Alps of Tirol or pedalling along the banks of the sprightly Danube (Donau), you'll find the kind of inspiring landscapes that no well-orchestrated symphony, camera lens or singing nun could ever quite do justice.

Best Places to Eat

» Mill (p52)
» Magazin (p70)
» Chez Nico (p80)
» Der Steirer (p63)
» Restaurant Maria Loretto (p64)

Best Places to Stay

» Hotel Rathaus Wein & Design (p51)
» Haus Ballwein (p69)
» Hotel Weisses Kreuz (p79)
» Hotel Schloss Dürnstein (p60)
» Himmlhof (p84)

When to Go
Vienna

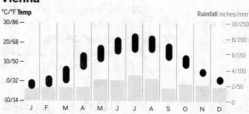

Jul–Aug Alpine hiking in Tirol, lake swimming in Salzkammergut and lots of summer festivals.

Sep–Oct New wine in vineyards near Vienna, golden forest strolls and few crowds.

Dec–Jan Christmas markets, skiing in the Alps and Vienna waltzing into the New Year.

Connections

Bang in the heart of Europe, Austria has speedy connections to its eight neighbouring countries. Trains from Vienna run to many Eastern European destinations, including Bratislava, Budapest, Prague and Warsaw; there are also connections south to Italy via Klagenfurt and north to Berlin. Salzburg is within sight of the Bavarian border, and there are many trains Munich-bound and beyond from the baroque city. Innsbruck is on the main rail line from Vienna to Switzerland, and two routes also lead to Munich. Look out for the fast, comfortable RailJet services to Germany and Switzerland.

ITINERARIES

Two Days

Spend this entire time in Vienna, making sure to visit the Habsburg palaces and Stephansdom before cosying up in a *Kaffeehäus* (coffee house). At night, check out the pumping bar scene.

One Week

Spend two days in Vienna, plus another day exploring the Wachau wine region, a day each in Salzburg and Innsbruck, one day exploring the Salzkammergut lakes, and finally one day in St Anton am Arlberg or Kitzbühel hiking or skiing (depending on the season).

Essential Food & Drink

» **Make it meaty** Go for a classic Wiener schnitzel, *Tafelspitz* (boiled beef with horseradish sauce) or *Schweinebraten* (pork roast). The humble wurst (sausage) comes in various guises.

» **On the side** Lashings of potatoes, either fried (*Pommes*), roasted (*Bratkartoffeln*), in a salad (*Erdapfelsalat*) or boiled in their skins (*Quellmänner*); *Knödel* (dumplings) and *Nudeln* (flat egg noodles).

» **Kaffee und Kuchen** Coffee and cake is Austria's sweetest tradition. Must-tries: flaky apple strudel, rich, chocolatey *Sacher Torte* and *Kaiserschmarrn* (sweet pancakes with raisins).

» **Wine at the source** Jovial locals gather in rustic *Heurigen* (wine taverns) in the wine-producing east, identified by an evergreen branch above the door. Sip crisp grüner veltliner whites and spicy blaufränkisch wines.

» **Cheese fest** Dig into gooey *Käsnudeln* (cheese noodles) in Carinthia, *Kaspressknodel* (fried cheese dumplings) in Tirol and *Käsekrainer* (cheesy sausages) in Vienna. The hilly Bregenzerwald is studded with dairies.

AT A GLANCE

» **Currency** euro (€)
» **Language** German
» **Money** ATMs widely available; banks open Mon-Fri
» **Visas** Schengen rules apply

AUSTRIA

Fast Facts

» **Area** 83,871 sq km
» **Capital** Vienna
» **Country code** 43
» **Emergency** 112

Exchange Rates

Australia	A$1	€0.82
Canada	C$1	€0.77
Japan	¥100	€0.83
New Zealand	NZ$1	€0.65
UK	UK£1	€1.18
USA	US$1	€0.78

Set Your Budget

» **Budget hotel room** €50
» **Two-course meal** €15
» **Museum entrance** €8
» **Beer** €3
» **City transport ticket** €2

Resources

» **ÖAV** (www.alpenverein.at) Austrian Alpine Club
» **ÖBB** (05 17 17; www.oebb.at) Austrian Federal Railways
» **Österreich Werbung** (www.austria.info) National tourism authority

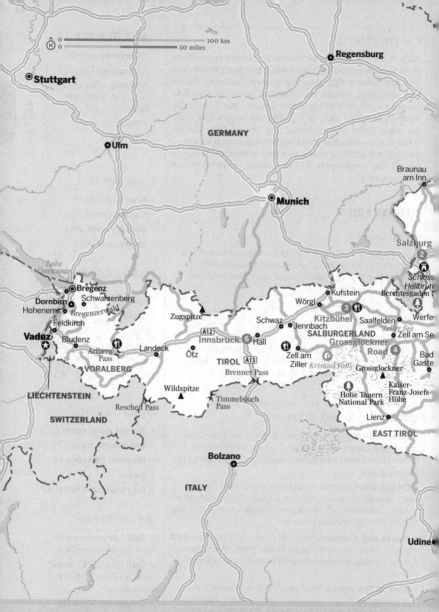

Austria Highlights

1 Discover the opulent Habsburg palaces, coffee houses and cutting-edge galleries of **Vienna** (p44)

2 Survey the baroque cityscape of **Salzburg** (p65) from the giddy height of 900-year-old Festung Hohensalzburg

3 Send your spirits soaring from peak to peak hiking and skiing in **Kitzbühel** (p82)

4 Buckle up for a roller-coaster ride of Alps and glaciers on the **Grossglockner Road** (p85), one of Austria's greatest drives

5 Dive into the crystal-clear lakes of **Salzkammergut** (p73), Austria's summer playground

6 Whiz up to the Tyrolean Alps in Zaha Hadid's space-age funicular from picture-perfect **Innsbruck** (p76)

7 Explore the romantic Wachau and technology trailblazer Linz in the **Danube Valley** (p59)

VIENNA

🎵01 / POP 1.72 MILLION

Few cities in the world waltz so effortlessly between the present and the past like Vienna. Its splendid historical face is easily recognised: grand imperial palaces and bombastic baroque interiors, revered opera houses and magnificent squares.

But Vienna is also one of Europe's most dynamic urban spaces. A stone's throw from Hofburg (the Imperial Palace), the MuseumsQuartier houses some of the world's most provocative contemporary art behind a striking basalt facade. In the Innere Stadt (inner city), up-to-the-minute design stores sidle up to old-world confectioners, and Austro-Asian fusion restaurants stand alongside traditional *Beisl* (small taverns). In this Vienna, it's OK to mention poetry slam and Stephansdom in one breath.

Throw in the mass of green space within the confines of the city limits and the 'blue' Danube cutting a path east of the historical centre, and this is a capital that is distinctly Austrian.

History

Vienna was probably an important trading post for the Celts when the Romans arrived around 15 BC. They set up camp and named it Vindobona, after the Celtic tribe Vinid, and by the 3rd century it had developed into a town and vineyards were introduced to the area. It was first officially recorded as 'Wenia' in 881 and became a Babenberg stronghold in the 11th century. The Babenbergs ruled for 200 years, until the Habsburgs took control of the city's reins and held them firm until the end of WWI.

Over the centuries Vienna suffered Ottoman sieges in 1529 and 1683, and occupation in 1805 and 1809 by Napoleon and his armies. In the years in between, it received a major baroque makeover, the remnants of which can be seen in many buildings throughout the city. The mid-19th century saw Vienna blossom again, and the royal coffers were emptied to build the celebrated Ringstrasse and accompanying buildings.

Between the two world wars Vienna's political pendulum swung from one extreme to the other – the 1920s saw the influx of socialism and the 1930s the rise of fascism. Vienna suffered heavily under Allied bombing, and on 11 April 1945 advancing Russian troops liberated the city. The Allies joined them until Austria became independent in 1955, and since then it has gone from the razor's edge of Cold War to the focal point between new and old EU member nations.

◉ Sights

Vienna's stately buildings and beautifully tended parks are made for the aimless ambler. Humming with street entertainers, pedestrian-only shopping lanes in the Innere Stadt such as Kärntner Strasse and Graben are great for a shop 'n' stroll.

Some former homes of the great composers, including those of Mozart and Beethoven, are open to the public; ask at the tourist office.

Many sights and attractions open slightly later in July and August, and close earlier from November to March.

Hofburg   PALACE

(Imperial Palace; www.hofburg-wien.at; Michaelerkuppel; 🚊1A, 2A Michaelerplatz, Ⓜ Herrengasse, 🚋1, 2, D, 71, 46, 49 Burgring) Nothing symbolises the culture and heritage of Austria more than its Hofburg, home base of the Habsburgs for six centuries, from the first emperor (Rudolf I in 1273) to the last (Karl I in 1918). The Hofburg owes its size and architectural diversity to plain old one-upmanship; the oldest section is the 13th-century Schweizerhof (Swiss Courtyard).

The Kaiserappartements (Imperial Apartments; www.hofburg-wien.at; adult/child with audio guide €10.50/6.50, with guided tour €13/7.50; ⊙9am-5.30pm; Ⓜ Herrengasse), once occupied by Franz Josef I and Empress Elisabeth, are extraordinary for their chandelier-lit opulence. Included in the entry price, the Sisi Museum is devoted to the life of Austria's beauty-obsessed Empress Elisabeth, nicknamed 'Sisi'. Highlights include a reconstruction of her luxurious coach and the dress she wore on the eve of her wedding. A ticket to the Kaiserappartements also includes entry to the Silberkammer (Silver Chamber), showcasing fine silverware and porcelain.

Among several other points of interest within the Hofburg you'll find the Burgkapelle (Royal Chapel), where the Vienna Boys' Choir performs (p56); the Spanische Hofreitschule (p56); and the Schatzkammer (Imperial Treasury; www.kaiserliche-schatz kammer.at; 01, Schweizerhof; adult/under 19yr €12/free; ⊙9am-5.30pm Wed-Mon), which holds all manner of wonders including the 10th-century Imperial Crown, a 2860-carat Columbian emerald and even a thorn from Christ's crown.

Stephansdom
CHURCH

(www.stephanskirche.at; 01, Stephansplatz; side aisle free, main nave adult/child €3.50/free; cathedral, catacombs & towers with audioguide adult plus child €16; ⊙6am-10pm Mon-Sat, 7am-10pm Sun, main nave & Domschatz audio tours 9-11.30am & 1-5.30pm Mon-Sat, 1-5.30pm Sun ; MStephansplatz) Rising high and mighty above Vienna with its dazzling mosaic tiled roof is Stephansdom, or Steffl (little Stephen) as the Viennese call it. The cathedral was built on the site of a 12th-century church but its most distinctive features are Gothic. Only limited areas can be visited without a ticket. Entry is free for worshippers.

Taking centre stage inside is the magnificent Gothic stone pulpit, fashioned in 1515 by Anton Pilgram. The baroque high altar in the main chancel depicts the stoning of St Stephen; the left chancel contains a winged altarpiece from Wiener Neustadt, dating from 1447; the right chancel houses the Renaissance-style red marble tomb of Friedrich III.

Dominating the cathedral is the skeletal, 136.7m-high Südturm (adult/child €3.50/1; ⊙9am-5.30pm). Negotiating 343 steps brings you to a cramped viewing platform for a stunning panorama of Vienna. You can also explore the cathedral's Katakomben (tours adult/child €5/2.50; ⊙10-11.30am & 1.30-4.30pm Mon-Sat, 1.30-4.30pm Sun), housing the remains of plague victims in a bone house, plus urns containing some of the organs of Habsburg rulers – gripping stuff.

TOP CHOICE Albertina
GALLERY

(www.albertina.at; 01, Albertinaplatz 3; adult/child €11/free; ⊙10am-6pm Thu-Tue, 10am-9pm Wed; MKarlsplatz, Stephansplatz, ⛒D, 1, 2, 71 Kärntner Ring/Oper) Simply reading the highlights should have any art fan lining up for entry into this gallery. Among its enormous collection (1.5 million prints and 50,000 drawings) are 70 Rembrandts, 145 Dürers (including the famous Hare) and 43 Raphaels, as well as works by da Vinci, Michelangelo, Rubens, Cézanne, Picasso, Klimt and Kokoschka.

In addition to the mostly temporary exhibitions, a series of Habsburg staterooms are always open.

Schloss Schönbrunn
PALACE, MUSEUM

(www.schoenbrunn.at; 13, Schönbrunner Schlossstrasse 47; Imperial Tour with audioguide adult/child €10.50/7.50, gardens admission free, maze adult/child €3.50/2.20; ⊙8.30am-5.30pm, gardens 6am-dusk, maze 9am-6pm) The Habsburgs' opulent summer palace is now a Unesco World Heritage site. Of the palace's 1441 rooms, 40 are open to the public; the Imperial Tour takes you into 26 of these. Because of the popularity of the palace, tickets are stamped with a departure time and there may be a time lag before you can enter, so buy your ticket straight away and then explore the gardens.

Fountains dance in the French-style formal gardens. The gardens harbour the world's oldest zoo, the Tiergarten (www.zoovienna.at; adult/child €15/7; ⊙9am-6.30pm), founded in 1752; a 630m-long hedge maze; and the Gloriette (adult/child €3/2.20; ⊙9am-btwn 4pm & 7pm, closed early Nov-late Mar), whose roof offers a wonderful view over the palace grounds and beyond.

TOP CHOICE Kaisergruft
CHURCH

(Imperial Burial Vault; www.kaisergruft.at; 01, Neuer Markt; adult/child €5/2; ⊙10am-6pm; MStephansplatz, Karlsplatz, ⛒D, 1, 2, 71 Kärntner Ring/Oper) Beneath the Kapuzinerkirche (Church of the Capuchin Friars), the high-peaked Kaisergruft is the final resting place of most of the Habsburg elite. The tombs range from simple to elaborate, such as the 18th-century baroque double casket of Maria Theresia and Franz Stephan. Empress Elisabeth's ('Sisi') coffin receives the most attention, however: lying alongside that of her husband, Franz Josef, it is often strewn with fresh flowers.

Kunsthistorisches Museum
GALLERY

(Museum of Fine Arts; www.khm.at; Maria-Theresien-Plaz, 01; adult/under 19yr €14/free; ⊙10am-6pm Tue-Sun, to 9pm Thu; MMuseumsQuartier, ⛒1, 2, D) When it comes to classical works of art, nothing comes close to the Kunsthistorisches Museum. It houses a huge range of art amassed by the Habsburgs and includes works by Rubens, Van Dyck, Holbein and Caravaggio. Paintings by Pieter Bruegel the Elder, including Hunters in the Snow, also feature. There is an entire wing of ornaments, clocks and glassware, and Greek, Roman and Egyptian antiquities.

MuseumsQuartier
MUSEUM COMPLEX

(Museum Quarter; www.mqw.at; combi ticket €25; ⊙information & ticket centre 10am-7pm) Small books have been written on this popular site, so only a taste can be given here. This remarkable ensemble of museums, cafes, restaurants and bars occupies the former imperial stables designed by Fischer von Erlach. Spanning 60,000 sq metres, it's one of the world's most ambitious cultural spaces.

Central Vienna

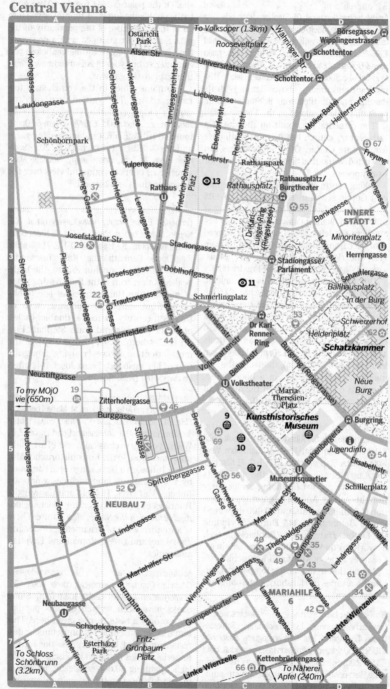

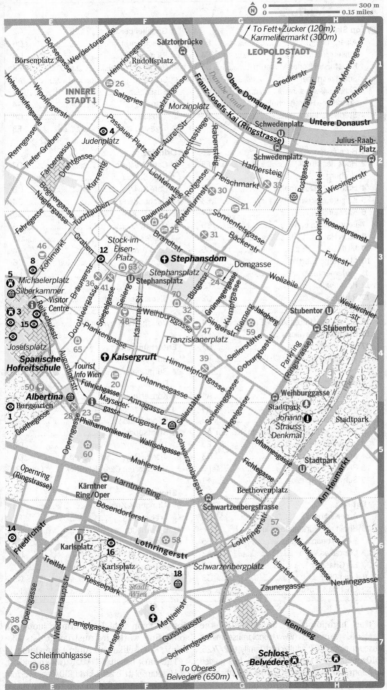

0   300 m
0   0.15 miles

To Fett+Zucker (120m);
Karmelitermarkt (300m)

LEOPOLDSTADT
2

Börsenplatz

Werdertorgasse

Salztorbrücke

Rudolfsplatz

Heinrichsgasse

Hohenstaufengasse

Wipplingerstr

INNERE
STADT 1

Salzgries

Börsengasse

26

Salzgries

Sartorigasse

Franz-Josefs-Kai (Ringstrasse)

Obere Donaustr

Gredlerstr

Grosse Mohrengasse

Taborstr

Praterstr

Passauer Platz

Morzinplatz

Schwedenplatz

Untere Donaustr

Renngasse

4

Judenplatz

Marc-Aurel-Str

Rabensteig

Schwedenplatz

Julius-Raab-
Platz

Tiefer Graben

Farbergasse

Drahtgasse

Kurrentg

Tuchlauben

Lichtensteg

Ruprechtsstiege

Rotgasse

Hafnersteig

Postgasse

Wiesingerstr

Bognergasse

Naglergasse

Fahrgasse

Fleischmarkt

33

Rosenburgstr

Bauernmarkt

Rotenturmstr

21

Sonnenfelsgasse

Bäckerstr

Dominikanerbastei

Falkestr

46

Kohlmarkt

Graben

Stock-im-
Eisen-
Platz

12

64

25

Brandstätte

Brandstr

30

31

Stephansdom

Domgasse

Wollzeile

Weiskirchner-
str

8

5

Michaelerplatz

Silberkammer

Visitor
Centre

36

Braunerstr

63

Stephansplatz

Stephansplatz

24

Bluttgasse

Schulerstr

Spiegelgasse

Seilergasse

70

Grünangergasse

Kumpfgasse

Riemergasse

Jakobeng

Stubentor

Stubentor

3

15

Dorotheergasse

Plankengasse

48

Kärntner Str

Weihburggasse

32

Singerstr

59

Seilerstätte

Parking
(Ringstrasse)

Josefsplatz

65

Augustinerstr

Franziskanerplatz

47

Spanische
Hofreitschule

Kaisergruft

Himmelpfortgasse

39

Coburgbastei

Weihburggasse

50

Albertina

Tourist
Info Wien

20

Führichgasse

Johannesgasse

Schellinggasse

Heegelgasse

Stadtpark

Johann
Strauss
Denkmal

Stadtpark

1

Burggarten

28

23

Mayseder-
gasse

Annagasse

2

Seilerstätte

Johannesgasse

Goethegasse

Opernring

Philharmonikerstr

Krugerstr

Walfischgasse

Schwarzenbergstr

Fichtegasse

Stadtpark

60

Mahlerstr

Am Heumarkt

Opernring
(Ringstrasse)

Kärntner
Ring/Oper

Kärntner Ring

Beethovenplatz

Bösendorferstr

Schwartzenbergstrasse

57

14

Friedrichstr

58

Lothringerstr

Lothringerstr

Treitlstr

Karlsplatz

16

Karlsplatz

18

Schwarzenbergplatz

Lisztstr

Marokkanergasse

Neulinggasse

38

Opernring

Wiedner Hauptstr

Resselpark

Stadt
Wien

Zaunergasse

6

Mattiellistr

Karlsgasse

Paniglgasse

Gusshausstr

Rennweg

Schleifmühlgasse

68

Schwindgasse

To Oberes
Belvedere (650m)

Schloss
Belvedere

17

Central Vienna

The highpoint is undoubtedly the **Leopold Museum** (www.leopoldmuseum.org; Museumsplatz 1, 07; adult/child/family €12/7/25; ⊙10am-6pm Wed-Mon, to 9pm Thu, free guided tour 3pm Sun; Ⓜ MuseumsQuartier, Volkstheater), which showcases the world's largest collec-

tion of Egon Schiele paintings, alongside some fine works by Austrian artists like Klimt, Kokoschka and Albin Egger-Lienz.

The dark basalt **MUMOK** (www.mumok.at; 07, Museumsplatz 1; adult/child €10/free; ⊙2-7pm Mon, 10am-7pm Tue-Sun, to 9pm Thu, free guided tour 2pm Sat & Sun, 7pm Thu; ⓂMuseumsQuartier, Volkstheater, ⓖ49 Volkstheater) is alive with Vienna's premier collection of 20th-century art, centred on fluxus, nouveau realism, pop art and photo-realism.

Schloss Belvedere
PALACE, GALLERY

(www.belvedere.at; combined ticket adult/child €16/free; ⓖD) Belvedere is a masterpiece of total art and one of the world's finest baroque palaces, designed by Johann Lukas von Hildebrandt (1668–1745).

The first of the palace's two main buildings is the **Oberes Belvedere** (Upper Belvedere; 03, Prinz-Eugen-Strasse 27; adult/child €11/free; ⊘10am-6pm; ⓖD). Pride and joy of the gallery is Gustav Klimt's rich gold *The Kiss* (1908), which perfectly embodies Viennese art nouveau, accompanied by other late-19th- to early-20th-century Austrian works. The second is the grandiose **Unteres Belvedere** (Lower Belvedere; 03, Rennweg 6; adult/child €11/free; ⊘10am-6pm Thu-Tue, to 9pm Wed; ⓖD), which contains a baroque museum. The buildings sit at opposite ends of a manicured garden.

KunstHausWien
MUSEUM

(www.kunsthauswien.com; 03, Untere Weissgerberstrasse 13; adult/child €10/5, audioguide €3; ⊘10am-7pm; Ⓜ1, O Radetzkyplatz) Like something out of a toy shop, this gallery was designed by eccentric Viennese artist and architect Friedensreich Hundertwasser (1928–2000), whose love of uneven floors, colourful mosaic ceramics, irregular corners and rooftop greenery shines through. The permanent collection is a tribute to Hundertwasser, showcasing his paintings, graphics and philosophy on ecology and architecture.

Down the road there's a block of residential flats by Hundertwasser, the **Hundertwassershaus** (cnr Löwengasse & Kegelgasse; ⓖ1). It's not possible to see inside, but you can visit the **Kalke Village** (www.kalke-village.at; Kegelgasse 37-39; ⊘9am-6pm), also the handiwork of Hundertwasser, created from an old Michelin factory, in typical fashion with a distinct absence of straight lines.

Trams trams 1 and O to Radetzkyplatz stop close by.

Prater
AMUSEMENT PARK

(www.wiener-prater.at; ⓈU1 Praterstern, ⓖ5, O) This large park encompasses grassy meadows, woodlands, an amusement park known as the **Würstelprater** and one of the city's icons, the **Riesenrad** (www.wienerriesenrad.com; 02, Prater 90; adult/child €9/4; ⊘9am-11.45pm, shorter hrs in winter). Built in 1897, this 65m-high

Ferris wheel takes about 20 minutes to rotate its 430-tonne weight, offering far-reaching views of Vienna. It achieved celluloid fame in *The Third Man*. Take U1 to Praterstern.

Secession
LANDMARK, MUSEUM

(www.secession.at; 01, Friedrichstrasse 12; adult/child €8.50/5, audioguide €3; ⊘10am-6pm Tue-Sun; ⓈU1, U2, U4 Karlsplatz) This popular art nouveau 'temple of art' building was built in 1898 and bears an intricately woven gilt dome that the Viennese nickname the 'golden cabbage'. The highlight inside is the 34m-long *Beethoven Frieze* by Klimt.

Haus der Musik
MUSIC MUSEUM

(☑513 4850; www.hdm.at; 01, Seilerstätte 30; adult/child €12/5.50, with Mozarthaus €17/7; ⊘10am-10pm; ⓂKarlsplatz, ⓖD, 1, 2 Kärntner Ring/Oper) Delving into the physics of sounds and paying tribute to Austria's great composers, this interactive museum is a fascinating journey through music. Most fun of all is the room where you can virtually conduct the Vienna Philharmonic.

Pestsäule
MEMORIAL

Graben is dominated by the knobbly outline of this memorial, designed by Fischer von Erlach in 1693 to commemorate the 75,000 victims of the Black Death.

Holocaust-Denkmal
MEMORIAL

(01, Judenplatz; ⓂStephansplatz) This is Austria's first Holocaust memorial, the 'Nameless Library'. The squat, boxlike structure pays homage to the 65,000 Austrian Jews who were killed during the Holocaust.

FREE Zentralfriedhof
CEMETERY

(www.friedhoefewien.at; 11, Simmeringer Hauptstrasse 232-244; ⊘7am-8pm, shorter hours in winter; ⓖ6, 71) Situated about 4km south of the centre, this is one of Europe's largest cemeteries. With two and a half million graves, it

WANT MORE?

For in-depth information, reviews and recommendations at your fingertips, head to the Apple App Store to purchase Lonely Planet's *Vienna City Guide* iPhone app.

Alternatively, head to **Lonely Planet** (www.lonelyplanet.com/austria/vienna) for planning advice, author recommendations, traveller reviews and insider tips.

AUSTRIA VIENNA

VIENNA IN...

One Day

Jump on tram 1 or 2 and circle the **Ringstrasse** (Ring road) for a brief but rewarding tour of the boulevard's monumental buildings. Get out at Kärntner Strasse and wander towards the Gothic **Stephansdom** before heading to the **Hofburg** and the breathtaking art collection of the **Kunsthistorisches Museum**. Dine at an **Innere Stadt restaurant** before a night at the **Staatsoper**.

Two Days

On day two, visit imperial palace **Schönbrunn** before a feast of Austrian art at the **Leopold Museum**. Eat at Vienna's celebrated **Naschmarkt**, then cross the city for a twilight ride on the **Riesenrad**. Finish the day with local wine and food at a **Heuriger**.

has more 'residents' than Vienna. Beethoven, Schubert and Brahms have memorials here. Take tram 6 or 71 to Zentralfriedhof.

Sigmund Freud Museum   MUSEUM
(www.freud-museum.at; 09, Berggasse 19; adult/child €8/3.50; ⊙9am-6pm; ⑤U2 Schottentor, U4 Schottenring, ⊠1, D) Former house of the famous psychologist, now housing a small museum featuring some of his personal belongings. The museum is 600m north of Schottentor.

Wien Museum   MUSEUM
(www.wienmuseum.at; 04, Karlsplatz 8; adult/under 19yr €8/free, free first Sun of month; ⊙10am-6pm Tue-Sun; ⑤U1, U2, U4 Karlsplatz) Provides a snapshot of the city's history, and contains a handsome art collection with paintings by Klimt and Schiele.

Loos Haus   ARCHITECTURE
(01, Michaelerplatz; ⊙9am-5pm Mon-Fri, to 5.30pm Thu; ⊠2A, ⓜHerrengasse) A perfect example of the clean lines of Loos' work. Franz Josef hated it and described the windows, which lack lintels, as 'windows without eyebrows'.

Stadtbahn Pavillons   LANDMARK
(www.wienmuseum.at; 04, Karlsplatz; adult/under 19yr €4/free; ⊙10am-6pm Tue-Sun Apr-Oct; ⑤U1, U2, U4 Karlsplatz) Jugendstil pavilions designed by Otto Wagner for Vienna's first public transport system.

⚡ Activities

Dividing the Danube from the Neue Donau is the svelte Donauinsel (Danube Island), which stretches some 21.5km from opposite Klosterneuburg in the north to the Nationalpark Donau-Auen in the south. The island features long sections of swimming areas, concrete paths for walking and cycling, and restaurants and snack bars. The Alte Donau is a landlocked arm of the Danube, a favourite of sailing and boating enthusiasts, swimmers, walkers, fisherfolk and, in winter (when it's cold enough), ice skaters.

⟳ Tours

The tourist office publishes a monthly list of guided walks, *Wiener Spaziergänge,* and can advise on bus tours and river cruises.

Vienna Tour Guides   WALKING TOUR
(☑774 89 01; www.wienguide.at; adult/child €14/7) Conducts 60 different guided walking tours, some of which are in English, from art nouveau architecture to Jewish traditions and the ever-popular *Third Man* tour.

✦ Festivals & Events

Pick up a copy of the monthly booklet of events from the tourist office. Tickets for many events are available at Wien-Ticket Pavillon in the hut by the Staatsoper.

Opernball   BALL
(01, Staatsoper) Of the 300 or so balls held in January and February, the Opernball (Opera Ball) is the ultimate. It's a supremely lavish affair, with the men in tails and women in shining white gowns.

Wiener Festwochen   ARTS FESTIVAL
(www.festwochen.at) Wide-ranging program of arts from around the world, from May to mid-June.

Donauinselfest   MUSIC FESTIVAL
(https://donauinselfest.at) Free three-day festival of rock, pop, hardcore, folk and country music on the Donauinsel in June.

Musikfilm Festival   FILM FESTIVAL
(01, Rathausplatz) Screenings of operas, operettas and concerts outside the Rathaus in July and August.

Viennale Film Festival   FILM FESTIVAL
(☑01 526 59 47; www.viennale.at) The country's biggest and best film festival, featuring fringe and independent films from around the world in October.

Christkindlmärkte   CHRISTMAS MARKET
(www.christkindlmarkt.at) Vienna's much-loved Christmas market season runs from mid-November to Christmas Eve.

🛏 Sleeping

Hotel Rathaus

Wein & Design   BOUTIQUE HOTEL €€€
(☑400 11 22; www.hotel-rathaus-wien.at; 08, Lange Gasse 13; s/d/tr €150/210/240; ✳@☎; Ⓢ U2 Rathaus, U3 Volkstheater, 🚋46) Each stylish room in this boutique hotel is dedicated to an Austrian winemaker and the chandelier-lit wine bar zooms in on a different winery every month. The open-plan, minimalist-chic rooms reveal a razor-sharp eye for design, especially the opalescent ones with hybrid beds and bathtubs.

Pension Sacher   PENSION €€
(☑533 32 38; www.pension-sacher.at; 01, Rothenturmstrasse 1; apt €90-136; ✳☎) Filled with chintzy knick-knacks, florals and solid wood furnishings, these super-central, spacious apartments are lovingly kept by the Sacher family of chocolate cake fame. There's everything you need to feel right at home and the views of Stephansdom are phenomenal.

Boutiquehotel Stadthalle   HOTEL €€
(☑982 42 72; www.hotelstadthalle.at; Hackengasse 20, 15; s €78-138, d €118-198; ☎; Ⓢ U3 Schweglerstrasse, 🚋9, 49) Welcome to Vienna's most sustainable hotel, which makes the most of solar power, rainwater collection and LED lighting, and has a roof planted with fragrant lavender. Rooms are a blend of modern with polished antiques. An organic breakfast is served in the leafy garden in summer. Arrive by bike or train for a 10%

ℹ **MORE FOR YOUR MONEY**

If you're planning on doing a lot of sightseeing, consider purchasing the Wien-Karte (Vienna Card; €19.90) for 72 hours of unlimited travel plus discounts at selected museums, attractions, cafes and shops. It's available from hotels and ticket offices.

The City of Vienna runs some 20 municipal museums (www.museum.vienna.at), which are included in a free booklet available at the Rathaus. Permanent exhibitions in all are free on the first Sunday of the month.

---

discount. The hotel is located 650m northwest of Westbahnhof.

TOP CHOICE Altstadt   PENSION €€
(☑522 66 66; www.altstadt.at; 07, Kirchengasse 41; s €125-175, d €145-215, ste €195-350; @☎; Ⓢ U2, U3 Volkstheater, 🚋46) One of Vienna's finest pensions, Altstadt has charming, individually decorated rooms, with high ceilings, plenty of space and a cosy lounge with free afternoon tea and cakes. Staff are genuinely affable and artworks are from the owner's personal collection.

my MOjO vie   HOSTEL €
(☑0676-551 11 55; http://mymojovie.at; 07, Kaiserstrasse 77; dm/d/tr/q €26/58/84/108; @☎; Ⓢ U6 Burggasse, 🚋5) An old-fashioned cage lift rattles up to these incredible backpacker digs. Everything you could wish for is here: design-focused dorms complete with dressing tables and snug-as-a-bug rugs, a kitchen with free

---

SPIN OF THE RING

The Ringstrasse, often just called the Ring, is a wide, tree-lined boulevard encircling much of the Innere Stadt. The best way to see its monumental buildings is by jumping on tram 1 or 2 for a brief but rewarding self-guided tour. For the price of a single ticket you'll take in the neo-Gothic Rathaus (City Hall; ☑525 50; www.wien.gv.at; 01, Rathausplatz 1; ☺guided tours 1pm Mon, Wed & Fri; ℳRathaus), the Greek Revival–style Parlament (www.parlament.gv.at; 01, Dr-Karl-Renner-Ring 3; tours adult/child €5/2.50, visitor centre admission free; ☺guided tours hourly 11am-4pm Mon-Sat, visitor centre 8.30am-6.30pm Mon-Fri, 9.30am-4.30pm Sat), the 19th-century Burgtheater (National Theatre; ☑514 44 4440; www.burgtheater.at; 01, Universitätsring 2; ☺box office 9am-5pm Mon-Fri; ℳRathaus) and the baroque Karlskirche (St Charles' Church; www.karlskirche.at; Karlsplatz; adult/child €8/4, audioguide €2; ☺9am-5.30pm Mon-Sat, 11.30am-5.30pm Sun; Ⓢ U1, U2, U4 Karlsplatz), among others.

Or hop off to relax in one of the Ring's three parks: flower-strewn Burggarten (www.bundesgaerten.at; 01, Burgring; ☺6am-10pm Apr-Oct, 6.30am-7pm Nov-Mar; ℳMuseumsquartier), Volksgarten or Stadtpark, with its gold statue of Johann Strauss.

supplies, netbooks for surfing, books for browsing and even musical instruments for your own jam session. Tram 5 stops close by.

Aviano
PENSION €€

(☎512 83 30; www.secrethomes.at; 01, Marco-d'Aviano-Gasse 1; s €87-112, d €127-187; ☜; ⓂStephansplatz) Aviano is a supremely central, good-value choice. The small high-ceilinged rooms feature whitewashed antique furnishings and decorative moulding. In summer, the sunny breakfast room opens onto a small balcony.

Believe It Or Not
HOSTEL €

(☎0676-550 00 55; www.believe-it-or-not-vienna.at; 07, Myrthengasse 10; dm €25-30; ☺☜; ⒮48A, ⓈU2, U3 Volkstheater) It may seem nondescript on the face of things, but you really won't believe what a cosy, homely hostel this is. We love the dorms with mezzanine-style beds, laid-back lounge, kitchen with free basics, and laptops for guest use. Lily, your South African host, puts on a great spread at breakfast.

König von Ungarn
HOTEL €€€

(☎51 584; www.kvu.at; 01, Schulerstrasse 10; s/d €155/220, ste €350; ☜; ⓂStephansplatz) Vienna's oldest hotel (1746) balances class and informality. Rooms are individually furnished with antiques (the best face Domgasse) and the inner courtyard is wonderful.

Hotel Sacher
LUXURY HOTEL €€€

(☎514 560; www.sacher.com; 01, Philharmonikerstrasse 4; r €480-1350, ste €1600-2900; ☒☺☜; ⓂKarlsplatz, ⒭D, 1, 2, 71 Kärntner Ring/Oper) Walking into the Sacher is like turning back the clock a hundred years. All of the lavishly decorated rooms boast baroque furnishings and 19th-century oil paintings, and the top-floor spa pampers with chocolate treatments.

Pension Kraml
PENSION €

(☎587 85 88; 06, www.pensionkraml.at; Brauergasse 5; s €35, d €56-76, tr €78-87, q €120; ☺☜; ⓈU3 Zieglergasse) A quiet and cosy family-run pension, where old-school politeness and comfort are paramount. Rooms are large (if a little dated).

Hotel Kärtnerhof
HOTEL €€

(☎512 19 23; www.karntnerhof.com; 01, Grashofgasse 4; s €99-129, d €135-195, tr €199-235, ste €279-299; ☺☜; ⓂStephansplatz) Tucked away from the bustle, this treasure oozes old Vienna charm, from the period paintings to the wood- and frosted-glass-panelled lift to the roof terrace. Rooms mix a few plain pieces with antiques, chandeliers and elegant curtains.

Schweizer Pension
PENSION €

(☎533 81 56; www.schweizerpension.com; 01, Heinrichsgasse 2; s €56-75, d €75-98; ⓂSchottentor, ⒭1 Salztorbrücke) This small, family-run pension is a superb deal, with homely touches and eco credentials. Book in advance, though, as it has only 11 rooms and is popular among those on squeezed budgets.

Altwienerhof
HOTEL €€

(☎892 60 00; www.altwienerhof.at; 15, Herklotzgasse 6; s €50-65, d €89-99, q €125; @; ⓈU6 Gumpendorfer Strasse) This pseudo-plush family-run hotel, just outside the Gürtel ring, offers ridiculously romantic abodes – think miniature chandeliers, antique pieces, floral bedding and lace tablecloths. Breakfast is taken in the conservatory or large inner courtyard. The hotel is a minute's walk west of U6 station Gumpendorfer Strasse.

✗ Eating

Vienna has thousands of restaurants covering all budgets and styles of cuisine, but dining doesn't stop there. *Kaffeehäuser* (coffee houses), *Beisl* (small taverns) and *Heurigen* (wine taverns) are just as fine for a good meal. *Würstel Stande* (sausage stands) are conveniently located on street corners and squares.

Mill
AUSTRIAN €€

(☎966 40 73; www.mill32.at; 06, Millergasse 32; mains €8-17.50; ☯11.30am-3pm & 5pm-midnight Mon-Fri, 11am-4pm Sun; ⓈU3, U6 Westbahnhof, ⒭9, 18, 52, 58) This art-slung bistro, with a hidden courtyard for summer days, still feels like a local secret. Scarlet brick walls and wood floors create a warm backdrop for spot-on seasonal food like chanterelle cannelloni and Styrian chicken salad drizzled with pumpkin-seed oil. The two-course lunch is a snip at €6.90. Mill is 400m south of the U3 Westbahnhof station on Mariahilfer Strasse.

TOP CHOICE Tian
VEGETARIAN €€

(☎890 4665; www.tian-vienna.com; 01, Himmelpfortgasse 23; 3-course lunch €12.50-16, 3–6-course evening menu €39-69, mains €18; ☯noon-4pm, 6pm-midnight Mon-Fri, from 9am Sat; ☝; ⓂStephansplatz, ⒭2 Weihburggasse) Vaulted charm meets urban attitude at this sleek lounge-style restaurant which takes vegetarian cuisine to delicious heights. Lunch menus offer the best value; you can also enjoy a drink at the cocktail bar.

Schnattl
INTERNATIONAL €€€

(☎405 34 00; www.schnattl.com; 08, Lange Gasse 40; mains €21-26, 3-course menus €33-38; ☯6pm-midnight Mon-Fri; 🚲; 🚌13A, 🚋2) Wilhelm Schnattl gives flight to culinary fantasy at this wood-panelled bistro, centred on an inner courtyard and attracting a food-loving crowd of artists and actors. The menu puts a creative spin on whatever is seasonal, be it mushrooms, shellfish, asparagus or game.

Gasthaus Pöschl   AUSTRIAN €€
(📞513 52 88; 01, Weihburggasse 17; mains €9-18; ⏰lunch & dinner) Close to pretty Franziskanerplatz, this small, wood-panelled *Beisl* brims with Viennese warmth and bonhomie. Austrian classics like *Tafelspitz* (boiled beef) and schnitzel are cooked to a T.

✎Tongues   DELI, CAFE €
(www.tongues.at; 06, Theobaldgasse 16; lunch mains €3.60; ⏰11am-9pm Mon-Fri, 11am-6pm Sat; 🚲) DJs can sometimes be found on the decks at this record shop and rustic deli, where you can pop in for a healthy lunch, electro on vinyl or some locally sourced cheese, salami, honey and wood-oven bread.

Reinthaler's Beisl   AUSTRIAN €
(📞513 12 49; 01, Dorotheergasse 2-4; mains €9-13) This warm, woody *Beisl* has got everything going for it: a cracking location just off Graben, a buzzy pavement terrace and a menu championing Viennese home cooking from brothy goulash with dumplings to perfectly crisp schnitzel.

Ra'mien   ASIAN €€
(📞585 47 98; www.ramien.at; 06, Gumpendorfer Strasse 9; mains €7-16; ⏰Tue-Sun; 🚲) Bright young things gravitate towards this minimalist-chic noodle bar, with a choice of Thai, Japanese, Chinese and Vietnamese noodle soups and rice dishes. The lounge bar downstairs has regular DJs and stays open until at least 2am.

Bitzinger Würstelstand
am Albertinaplatz   SAUSAGE STAND €
(01, Albertinaplatz; sausages €3.70-4.10; ⏰9.30-5am, drinks from 8am) Located behind the Staatsoper, this is one of Vienna's best sausage stands. Watch ladies and gents dressed to the nines while enjoying your wurst and a beer.

Amerlingbeisl   AUSTRIAN €
(📞526 16 60; www.amerlingbeisl.at; Stiftgasse 8, 07; mains €7-14; ⏰9am-2am; 🚲; Ⓜ️Volkstheater, 🚋49 Stiftgasse) The cobbled inner courtyard of this Spittelberg *Beisl*, with tables set up under the trees, is a summer evening magnet. The chef cooks Austro-Italian, hitting

SWEETNESS & LIGHT

Indulge your sweet tooth at these three Viennese favourites.

Cupcakes Wien (www.cupcakes-wien.at; 08, Josefstädter Strasse 17 ; cupcakes €3.90; ⏰10am-7.30pm Mon-Fri, 10am-6pm Sat; 🚲; ⒮U2 Rathaus, 🚋2) A pretty pink wonderland of cupcakes, with mascarpone toppings in flavours like lime, peanut and mint.

Süssi (📞943 13 24; www.suessi.at; 04, Operngasse 30; desserts €3.50-6, afternoon tea €17; ⏰11am-9pm Tue-Sat, 1-9pm Sun; ⒮U1, U2, U4 Karlsplatz) This tiny and fabulously OTT French tea room serves Mariage Frères brews with delectable nut tarts, cream cakes and macarons.

Fett+Zucker (www.fettundzucker.at; 02, Hollandstrasse 16; cakes & snacks €2.50-6; ⏰1-9pm Wed-Fri, 11am-9pm Sat & Sun; 🚲; ⒮U2 Taborstrasse, 🚋2) As the name suggests, the cheesecakes, strudels and brownies at this retro cafe don't skimp on the fat and sugar.

the mark with homemade pasta and dishes like pike perch with saffron noodles.

Figlmüller   BISTRO, PUB €€
(📞512 61 77; www.figlmueller.at; 01, Wollzeile 5; mains €12.90-22.90; ⏰11am-10.30pm; 🚲; Ⓜ️Stephansplatz) This famous *Beisl* has been sizzling up some of the biggest (and best) schnitzels in town since 1905. Sure, the rural decor is contrived, but it doesn't get more Viennese than this.

Trzesniewski   SANDWICHES €
(01, Dorotheergasse 1; sandwiches from €1.10; ⏰8.30am-7.30pm Mon-Fri, 9am-5pm Sat; Ⓜ️Stephansplatz) Possibly Austria's finest open-sandwich shop, with delectably thick spreads, from tuna with egg to Swedish herring. Two bites and they're gone. Wash them down with a tiny *Pfiff* beer.

Eis Griessler   ICE CREAM €
(01, Rotenturmstrasse 14; scoop €1.30; ⏰10.30am-11pm) Organic milk and fresh fruit go into dreamily smooth ice creams like Alpine caramel and Wachau apricot at this hole-in-the-wall parlour.

DON'T MISS

FOOD MARKET FINDS

Foodies gravitate towards the sprawling **Naschmarkt** (06, Linke & Rechte Wienzeile; ⊙6am-7.30pm Mon-Fri, to 6pm Sat; ⑤U1, U2, U4 Karlsplatz, U4 Kettenbrückengasse), the place to *nasch* (snack) in Vienna. Assemble your own picnic from stalls piled high with meats, fruits, vegetables, cheeses, olives, spices and wine. There are also plenty of people-watching cafes dishing up good-value lunches, and delis and takeaway stands where you can grab a falafel or kebab.

Freyung Market (www.biobauern-markt-freyung.at; 01, Freyung; ⊙9am-6pm Fri & Sat ; ☐1A, ⑤U2 Schottentor) sells farm-fresh produce, as does the bustling **Karmelitermarkt** (02, Karmelitermarkt; ⊙6am-7.30pm Mon-Fri, 6am-5pm Sat; ☐5A, ⑤U2 Taborstrasse, ☐2). Head to the Saturday farmers market at the latter for brunch at one of the excellent deli-cafes, followed by a mooch around stalls selling top-quality local goodies.

TOP CHOICE Griechenbeisl BISTRO, PUB €€
(☑533 19 77; 01, Fleischmarkt 11; mains €11.60-24.90; ⊙11am-1am; ☒Schwedenplatz, ☐1, 2) This is Vienna's oldest *Beisl* (dating from 1447), once frequented by the likes of Beethoven, Schubert and Brahms. The vaulted, wood-panelled rooms are a cosy setting for classic Viennese dishes.

🍷 Drinking

Pulsating bars cluster north and south of the Naschmarkt, around Spittelberg and along the Gürtel (mainly around the U6 stops of Josefstädter Strasse and Nussdorfer Strasse). The Bermuda Dreieck (Bermuda Triangle), near the Danube Canal in the Innere Stadt, also has many bars, but they are more touristy.

Vienna's *Heurigen* cluster in the wine-growing suburbs to the north, southwest, west and northwest of the city. They are identified by a *Busch'n* (a green wreath or branch) hanging over the door. Opening times are approximately from 4pm to 11pm, and wine costs around €3 per *Viertel* (250mL).

Palmenhaus BAR, CAFE
(www.palmenhaus.at; 01, Burggarten; ⊙10am-2am) Housed in a beautifully restored Jugendstil palm house, the Palmenhaus has a relaxed vibe. In summer, tables spill out onto the terrace overlooking the Burggarten, and DJs spin here on Friday nights.

Phil BAR, CAFE
(www.phil.info; 06, Gumpendorfer Strasse 10-12; ⊙5pm-1am Mon, 9am-1am Tue-Sun) A retro bar, book and record store, Phil attracts a bohemian crowd happy to squat on kitsch furniture your grandma used to own. Staff are super-friendly and the vibe is as relaxed as can be.

Volksgarten Pavillon BAR
(www.volksgarten-pavillon.at; 01, Burgring 1; ⊙11am-2am Apr–mid-Sep; ☎; ☒Volkstheater, ☐1, 2, D, 71 Dr-Karl-Renner-Ring) A lovely 1950s-style pavilion with views of Heldenplatz and an ever-popular garden.

Das Möbel BAR, CAFE
(http://dasmoebel.at; 07, Burggasse 10; ⊙10am-midnight; ☎; ☒Volkstheater) The interior is never dull at this bar near the Museums-Quartier. It's remarkable for its funky decor and furniture – cube stools, assorted moulded lamps – and everything is up for sale.

Mon Ami BAR
(www.monami.at; 06, Theobaldgasse 9; ⊙6pm-1am Wed-Sat; ⑤U2 MuseumsQuartier) This former pet-grooming salon morphed into a lovely '60s-style bar mixes excellent cocktails, has DJ and jam session nights, and attracts a laid-back, unpretentious crowd.

TOP CHOICE Dachboden BAR
(25hours Hotel, 07, Lerchenfelder Strasse 1-3; ⊙2pm-1am Tue-Sat, 2-10pm Sun; ☎☒; ☒Volkstheater, ☐2) The terrace with knockout views of Vienna is the big deal, but even in winter this arty attic bar is wonderfully relaxed, with low cushion seating and the occasional DJ night.

Vis-à-vis WINE BAR
(☑512 93 50; www.weibel.at; 01, Wollzeile 5; ⊙4.30-10.30pm Tue-Sat; ☒Stephansplatz) Hidden down a narrow, atmospheric passage is this wee wine bar. It may only seat close to 10 but it makes up for it with over 350 wines on offer (with a strong emphasis on Austrian faves) and great antipasti.

TOP CHOICE Strandbar Herrmann BAR
(www.strandbarherrmann.at; 03, Herrmannpark; ⊙10am-2am Apr–early Oct; ☎; ☐1, 0) You'd swear you're by the sea at this hopping canalside beach bar, with beach chairs, and sand

and hordes of Viennese livin' it up on hot summer evenings.

Loos American Bar
TOP CHOICE · COCKTAIL BAR

(www.loosbar.at; 01, Kärntner Durchgang 10; ⊙noon-5am Thu-Sat, to 4am Sun-Wed; ⓂStephansplatz) Designed by Adolf Loos in 1908, this tiny box decked head-to-toe in onyx is *the* spot for a classic cocktail in the Innere Stadt, expertly whipped up by talented mixologists.

10er Marie
WINE BAR

(16, Ottakringerstrasse 222-224; ⊙3pm-midnight Mon-Sat; ⓂU3) Vienna's oldest *Heuriger* has been going strong since 1740 – Schubert, Strauss and Crown Prince Rudolf all kicked back a glass or three here. The usual buffet is available. The *Heuriger* is 400m northwest of U3 Ottakring station.

Siebensternbräu
FREE · MICROBREWERY

(www.7stern.at; 07, Siebensterngasse 19; ⊙11am-midnight; ⓂNeubaugasse, 🚋49) Large brewery with all the main varieties, plus hemp beer, chilli beer and smoky beer. The hidden back garden is sublime in summer.

☆ Entertainment

Vienna is, and probably will be till the end of time, the European capital of opera and classical music. The line-up of music events is never-ending and even the city's buskers are often classically trained musicians.

Box offices are generally open from Monday to Saturday.

Staatsoper
TOP CHOICE · OPERA

(📞514 44 7880; www.wiener-staatsoper.at; 01, Opernring 2) Performances at Vienna's premier opera and classical music venue are lavish, formal affairs, where people dress up. Standing-room tickets (€3 to €4) are sold 80 minutes before performances begin.

Musikverein
CONCERT VENUE

(📞505 81 90; www.musikverein.at; 01, Bösendorferstrasse 12) The opulent Musikverein, home to the Vienna Philharmonic Orchestra, is celebrated for its acoustics. Standing-room tickets in the main hall cost €5 to €6.

Pratersauna
CLUB

(www.pratersauna.tv; Waldsteingartenstrasse 135; ⊙club 9pm-6am Wed-Sun, pool 1-9pm Fri & Sat Jun-Sep; ⓈU2 Messe-Prater) Pool, cafe, bistro and club converge in a former sauna. These days, you'll sweat it up on the dance floor any given night, with DJs playing mostly techno and electro. Take U2 to Messe-Prater and walk south 600m.

Porgy & Bess
JAZZ

(📞512 88 11; www.porgy.at; 01, Riemergasse 11; €18 most nights; ⊙concerts from 7pm or 8pm; ⓂStubentor, 🚋2) Quality is the cornerstone of Porgy & Bess' popularity. The sophisticated

AUSTRIA VIENNA

COFFEE HOUSE CULTURE

Vienna's legendary *Kaffeehäuser* (coffee houses) are wonderful places for people-watching, daydreaming and catching up on gossip or world news. Most serve light meals alongside mouth-watering cakes and tortes. Expect to pay around €8 for a coffee with a slice of cake. These are just five of our favourites.

Café Sperl (www.cafesperl.at; 06, Gumpendorfer Strasse 11; ⊙7am-11pm Mon-Sat, 11am-8pm Sun; 🛜; 🚋57A, ⓈU2 Museumsquartier) Gorgeous Jugendstil fittings, grand dimensions, cosy booths and an unhurried air. The must-try is *Sperl Torte* – an almond and chocolate cream dream.

Kleines Café (01, Franziskanerplatz 3; ⊙10am-2am) Tiny bohemian cafe with wonderful summer seating on Franziskanerplatz.

Café Sacher (01, Philharmonikerstrasse 4; ⊙8am-midnight) This opulent coffee house is celebrated for its *Sacher Torte* (€4.90), a rich chocolate cake with apricot jam once favoured by Emperor Franz Josef.

Demel (01, Kohlmarkt 14; ⊙9am-7pm; 🚋1A, 2A Michaelerplatz, ⓂHerrengasse, Stephansplatz) An elegant, regal cafe near the Hofburg. Demel's speciality is the *Anna Torte*, a chocolate and nougat calorie-bomb.

Café Drechsler (www.cafedrechsler.at; 06, Linke Wienzeile 22; ⊙open 23hr, closed 2-3am; 🛜; ⓈKettenbrückengasse) Sir Terence Conran revamped this stylish yet distinctly Viennese cafe. Its goulash is legendary, as are the DJ tunes that keep the vibe hip and upbeat.

club presents a top-drawer line-up of modern jazz acts, and DJs fill spots on weekends.

Volksoper
CONCERT VENUE

(People's Opera; ☑514 44 36 70; www.volksoper.at; 09, Währinger Strasse 78) Vienna's second opera house features operettas, dance and musicals. Standing tickets go for as little as €2 to €6.

Donau
CLUB

(www.donautechno.com; 07, Karl-Schweighofer-Gasse 10; ⊙8pm-btwn 2am & 6am) DJs spin techno to a friendly, cocktail-sipping crowd at this columned, strikingly illuminated club. It's easily missed – look for the grey metal door.

Konzerthaus
CONCERT VENUE

(☑242 002; www.konzerthaus.at; 03, Lothringerstrasse 20; ⊙box office 9am-7.45pm Mon-Fri, 9am-1pm Sat, plus 45 mins before performance; MStadtpark, ☐71, D) This is a major venue in classical music circles, but throughout the year ethnic music, rock, pop or jazz can also be heard in its hallowed halls.

Volksgarten ClubDiskothek
CLUB

(www.volksgarten.at; 01, Burgring 1; admission from €6; ⊙10pm-4am Tue & Thu-Sat ; MMuseumsQuartier, Volkstheater, ☐1, 2, D, 71 Dr-Karl-Renner-Ring) This club attracts a well-dressed crowd keen to strut their stuff and scan for talent from the long bar. The quality sound system pumps out an array of music styles.

Theater an der Wien
THEATRE

(☑588 85; www.theater-wien.at; 06, Linke Wienzeile 6; ☐59A, SU1, U2, U4 Karlsplatz) Once the host of monumental premieres such as Mozart's *Die Zauberflöte (The Magic Flute)*, this theatre now showcases opera, dance and concerts.

Burg Kino
CINEMA

(☑587 84 06; www.burgkino.at; 01, Opernring 19; SU2 MuseumsQuartier, ☐1, 2, D) English films; has regular screenings of *The Third Man*.

🔒 Shopping

In the alley-woven Innere Stadt, go to Kohlmarkt for designer chic, Herrengasse for antiques and Kärntnerstrasse for high-street brands. Naglergasse's old-world speciality stores are pure nostalgia. Tune into Vienna's creative pulse in the idiosyncratic boutiques and concept stores in Neubau, especially along Kirchengasse and Lindengasse.

Dorotheum
ANTIQUES

(www.dorotheum.com; 01, Dorotheergasse 17; ⊙10am-6pm Mon-Fri, 9am-5pm Sat; MStephansplatz) One of Europe's largest auction houses, where surprisingly not every item is priced out of this world. Stop by and simply browse – it's as entertaining as visiting many of Vienna's museums.

TOP CHOICE Blühendes Konfekt
FOOD

(www.bluehendes-konfekt.com; 06, Schmalzhofgasse 19; ⊙10am-6.30pm Wed-Fri; SU3 Zieglergasse, Westbahnhof, ☐5) Violets, forest strawberries and cherry blossom, wild mint and oregano – Michael Diewald makes the most of the seasons and what grows in his garden to create one-of-a-kind candied bouquets and confectionery. The shop is 350m southwest of U3 Zieglergasse station on Mariahilfer Strasse.

Näherei Apfel
FOOD, FASHION

(www.naeherei-apfel.at; Kettenbrückengasse 8; ⊙11am-7pm Tue-Fri, 10am-4pm Sat; SU4 Kettenbrückengasse) At this little workshop-store

---

IMPERIAL ENTERTAINMENT

Founded over five centuries ago by Maximilian I, the world-famous **Vienna Boys' Choir** (www.wsk.at) is the original boy band. These cherubic angels in sailor suits still hold a fond place in Austrian hearts. **Tickets** (☑533 99 27; www.hofburgkapelle.at; 01, Hofburg, Schweizerhof; Sunday in Burgkapelle €5-29) for their Sunday performances at 9.15am (September to June) in the Burgkapelle (Royal Chapel) in the Hofburg should be booked around six weeks in advance. The group also performs regularly in the Musikverein.

Another throwback to the Habsburg glory days is the **Spanische Hofreitschule** (Spanish Riding School; ☑533 90 31; www.srs.at; 01, Michaelerplatz 1; ⊙performances 11am Sat & Sun mid-Feb–Jun & late Aug-Dec). White Lipizzaner stallions gracefully perform equine ballet to classical music, while chandeliers shimmer from above and the audience cranes to see from pillared balconies. Tickets, costing between €23 and €158, are ordered through the website, but be warned that performances usually sell out months in advance. Unclaimed tickets are sold about two hours before performances. **Morning Training** (adult/child/family €14/7/28; ⊙10am-noon Tue-Fri Feb-Jun & mid-Aug–Dec) same-day tickets are available at the **visitor centre** (⊙9am-4pm Tue-Sun) on Michaelerplatz.

you can learn to sew (a two-hour intro course costs €23), browse Ursula's hand-crafted clothing and bags, and buy Burgenland apples dried, preserved, juiced and by the kilo.

✐ Gabarage Upcycling Design DESIGN
(www.gabarage.at; 06, Schleifmühlgasse 6; ☺10am-6pm Mon-Thu, 10am-7pm Fri, 11am-5pm Sat; ⓢU1 Taubstummengasse, 🚋1, 62) Upcycling is the word at this innovative design store, turning waste into wonders, from rubbish bin couches to bowling pin vases.

TOP CHOICE Art Up FASHION, ACCESSORIES
(www.artup.at; 01, Bauernmarkt 8; ☺11am-6.30pm Mon-Fri, 11am-5pm Sat; ⓜStephansplatz) Take the temperature of Vienna's contemporary design scene at Art Up, showcasing the latest designs of around 80 Austrian creatives.

Woka HOMEWARES
(www.woka.at; 01, Singerstrasse 16; ☺10am-6pm Mon-Fri, 10am-5pm Sat; 🚋Stephansplatz) Accurate re-creations of Wiener Werkstätte lamps are the hallmark of Woka.

Altmann & Kühne FOOD
(www.altmann-kuehne.at; Graben 30; ☺9am-6.30pm Mon-Fri, 10am-5pm Sat) Altmann & Kühne has been producing, and beautifully packaging, handmade bonbons for over 100 years. Stop by for a box of its famous *Liliputkonfekt* (miniature pralines).

Lomoshop PHOTOGRAPHY
(07, Museumsplatz 1; ☺11am-7pm; ⓢU2 Museums-Quartier) Cult Lomo cameras, gadgets and accessories in the MuseumsQuartier.

ⓘ Information

Many cafes and bars offer free wi-fi for their customers. Free public hotspots include Rathausplatz, Naschmarkt and Prater.

Airport Information Office (☺6am-11pm) Located in the arrivals hall.

Allgemeines Krankenhaus (🗹404 000; www.akhwien.at; 09, Währinger Gürtel 18-20) Hospital with a 24-hour casualty ward.

Jugendinfo (Vienna Youth Information; 🗹4000-84 100; www.jugendinfowien.at; 01, Babenbergerstrasse 1; ☺2-7pm Mon-Wed, 1-6pm Thu-Sat) Offers various reduced-price tickets for people aged 13 to 26.

Main Post Office (01, Fleischmarkt 19; ☺7am-10pm Mon-Fri, 9am-10pm Sat & Sun)

Police Station (🗹31 310; 01, Schottenring 7-9)

Tourist Info Wien (🗹245 55; www.wien.info; 01, Albertinaplatz; ☺9am-7pm; ☎;

TO MARKET

Vienna's atmospheric **Flohmarkt** (Flea Market; 05, Kettenbrückengasse; ☺dawn-4pm Sat; ⓢU4 Kettenbrückengasse) shouldn't be missed, with goods piled up in apparent chaos on the walkway. Books, clothes, records, ancient electrical goods, old postcards, ornaments, carpets...you name it, it's all here. Come prepared to haggle.

From mid-November, *Christkindlmärkte* (Christmas markets) bring festive sparkle to Vienna, their stalls laden with gifts, *glühwein* (mulled wine) and *Maroni* (roasted chestnuts). Some of the best include the pretty but touristy **Rathausplatz market** (🚋1, 2), the traditional **Spittelberg market** (🚋48A, ⓢU2, U3 Volkstheater, 🚋49) in Spittelberg's cobbled streets, where you can pick up quality crafts, and the authentic, oft-forgotten **Heiligenkreuzerhof market** (ⓜSchwedenplatz, 🚋2 Stubentor).

ⓜStephansplatz, 🚋1, 2, D, 71 Kärntner Ring/Oper) Vienna's main tourist office, with a ticket agency, hotel booking service, free maps and every brochure you could ever wish for.

ⓘ Getting There & Away

Air

For details on flying to Vienna, see p92.

Boat

Fast hydrofoils travel eastwards to Bratislava (one way €19 to €33, return €38 to €66, 1¼ hours) daily from April to October. From May to September, they also travel twice weekly to Budapest (one way/return €109/125, 5½ hours). Bookings can be made through **DDSG Blue Danube** (🗹58 880; www.ddsg-blue-danube.at; Handelskai 265).

Heading west, a series of boats ply the Danube between Krems and Melk, with a handful of services originating in Vienna. Two respectable operators include DDSG Blue Danube and **Brandner** (🗹07433-25 90 21; www.brandner.at; Ufer 50, Wallsee), the latter located in Wallsee. Both run trips from April through October that start at around €15 one way. For trips into Germany, contact **Donauschiffahrt Wurm + Köck** (🗹0732-783 607; www.donauschiffahrt.de; Untere Donaulände 1, Linz).

Bus

Vienna currently has no central bus station. National Bundesbuses arrive and depart from several different locations, depending on the

MEDIA

Tune into Vienna's cultural scene on the following websites:

About Vienna (www.aboutvienna.org) General website with cultural and sight-seeing information.

City of Vienna (www.wien.gv.at) Comprehensive government-run website.

Falter (www.falter.at, in German) Online version of the ever-popular *Falter* magazine.

Vienna Online (www.vienna.at, in German) Site with info on parties, festivals and news.

destination. Bus lines serving Vienna include **Eurolines** (798 29 00; www.eurolines.com; Erdbergstrasse 200; 6.30am-9pm).

Car & Motorcycle

The Gürtel is an outer ring road that joins up with the A22 on the north bank of the Danube and the A23 southeast of town. All the main road routes intersect with this system, including the A1 from Linz and Salzburg, and the A2 from Graz.

Train

Vienna is one of central Europe's main rail hubs. **Österreichische Bundesbahn** (ÖBB; www.oebb. at; Austrian Federal Railway) is the main operator. There are direct services and connections to many European cities. Sample destinations include Budapest (2½ to three hours, €37.40), Munich (four to five hours, €88), Paris (11½ to 15 hours, €88), Prague (4½ hours, €64.40) and Venice (seven to 11 hours, €63 to €99).

Vienna has multiple train stations. At press time, a massive construction project was in progress at Vienna's former Südbahnhof: an eastern section had been set up as a temporary station to serve some trains to/from the east, including Bratislava. The complex is due to reopen as Hauptbahnhof Wien (Vienna Central Station) in 2013, and as the main station it will receive international trains. As a result, all long-distance trains are being rerouted among the rest of Vienna's train stations, including the recently revamped Westbahnhof. Further train stations include Franz-Josefs-Bahnhof (which handles trains to/from the Danube Valley), Wien Mitte, Wien Nord and Meidling.

Vienna's shiny new **Hauptbahnhof** (Vienna Central Station; www.hauptbahnhof-wien. at; 13A, 69A, U1, D, O, 18) partially reopened in December 2012, with an eastern section set up to serve some trains to/from the east, including Bratislava. The rail project is a

massive €987 million undertaking and operations are expected to fully resume in 2015, with the main station receiving international trains. Currently, most long-distance trains are being rerouted among the rest of Vienna's train stations, including the recently revamped Westbahnhof. Further train stations include Franz-Josefs-Bahnhof (which handles trains to/from the Danube Valley), Wien Mitte, Wien Nord and Meidling.

Getting Around

To/From the Airport

It is 19km from the city centre to **Vienna International Airport** (VIE; www.viennaairport. com) in Schwechat. The **City Airport Train** (CAT; www.cityairporttrain.com; return adult/child under 15 yrs €19/free; 5.36am-11.06pm from airport) runs every 30 minutes and takes 16 minutes between the airport and Wien Mitte; book online for a €2 discount. The S-Bahn (S7) does the same journey (single €4), but in 25 minutes.

Buses run every 20 or 30 minutes, between 5am and 11pm, from the airport (one way/return €8/13). Services run to Meidling, Westbahnhof and Schwedenplatz.

Taxis cost about €35. **C&K Airport Service** (444 44; www.cundk.at) charges €32 one way for shared vans.

Bicycle

Cycling is an excellent way to get around and explore the city – over 800km of cycle tracks criss-cross the capital. Popular cycling areas include the 7km path around the Ringstrasse, the Donauinsel, the Prater and along the Danube Canal (Donaukanal).

Vienna's city bike scheme is called **Vienna City Bike** (www.citybikewien.at; 1st hr free, 2nd/3rd hr €1/2, per hr thereafter €4), with more than 60 bicycle stands across the city. A credit card is required to rent bikes – just swipe your card in the machine and follow the instructions (in a number of languages).

Car & Motorcycle

Due to a system of one-way streets and expensive parking, you're better off using the excellent public transport system. If you do plan to drive in the city, take special care of the trams: they always have priority and vehicles must wait behind trams when they stop to pick up or set down passengers.

Fiakers

More of a tourist novelty than anything else, a *Fiaker* is a traditional-style horse-drawn carriage. Bowler-hatted drivers generally speak English and point out places of interest en route. Expect to pay a cool €80/105 for a

40-/60-minute ride from Stephansplatz, Albertinaplatz or Heldenplatz.

Public Transport

Vienna's unified public transport network encompasses trains, trams, buses, and underground (U-Bahn) and suburban (S-Bahn) trains. Free maps and information pamphlets are available from **Wiener Linien** (☑7909-100; www.wienerlinien.at).

Before use, all tickets must be validated at the entrance to U-Bahn stations and on buses and trams (except for weekly and monthly tickets). Tickets are cheaper to buy from ticket machines in U-Bahn stations and in *Tabak* (tobacconist) shops, where singles cost €2. On board, they cost €2.20. Singles are valid for an hour, and you may change lines on the same trip.

A 24-hour ticket costs €6.70, a 48-hour ticket €11.70 and a 72-hour ticket €14.50. Weekly tickets (valid Monday to Sunday) cost €15; the Vienna Card (€19.90) includes travel on public transport for up to three days. The Strip Ticket (*Streifenkarte*) costs €8 and gives you four single tickets.

Taxi

Taxis are metered for city journeys and cost €2.60 flag fall during the day and €2.70 at night, plus a small per kilometre fee. It's safe to hail taxis from the street.

THE DANUBE VALLEY

The stretch of Danube between Krems and Melk, known locally as the Wachau, is arguably the loveliest along the entire length of the mighty river. Both banks are dotted with ruined castles and medieval towns, and lined with terraced vineyards. Further upstream is the industrial city of Linz, Austria's avant-garde art and new technology trailblazer.

Krems an der Donau

☑02732 / POP 24,100

Sitting on the northern bank of the Danube against a backdrop of terraced vineyards, Krems marks the beginning of the Wachau. It has an attractive cobbled centre, a small university, some good restaurants and the gallery-dotted Kunstmeile (Art Mile).

◉ Sights & Activities

It's a pleasure to wander the cobblestone streets of Krems, especially at night. Don't miss the baroque treasures of Schürerplatz.

Kunsthalle   GALLERY
(www.kunsthalle.at; Franz-Zeller-Platz 3; adult/concessions €10/9; ◷10am-6pm) The flagship of Krems' **Kunstmeile** (www.kunstmeile-krems. at), an eclectic collection of galleries and museums, the Kunsthalle has a program of small but excellent changing exhibitions.

⊫ Sleeping & Eating

Arte Hotel Krems   HOTEL €€
(☑71 123; www.arte-hotel.at; Dr-Karl-Dorrek-Strasse 23; s €85-105, d €128-162; P🅿🛜) This comfortable new art hotel close to the university has large, well-styled rooms in bright colours and with open-plan bathrooms.

Hotel Unter den Linden   HOTEL €€
(☑82 115; www.udl.at; Schillerstrasse 5; s €50, d €74-98) This big, yellow, family-run hotel has knowledgeable and helpful owners, bright comfortable rooms and a convenient location in Krems itself.

Mörwald Kloster Und   AUSTRIAN €€€
(☑70 493; www.moerwald.at; Undstrasse 6; mains €35-39, 5-course menu €75, 3-course lunch €29; ◷lunch & dinner Tue-Sat) Run by celebrity chef and winemaker Toni Mörwald, this is one of the Wachau's best restaurants. Delicacies from roast pigeon breast to fish dishes with French touches are married with top wines. There's a lovely garden.

❶ Information

Krems Tourismus (☑82 676; www.krems.info; Utzstrasse 1; ◷9am-6pm Mon-Fri) Has excellent city walk and vineyard maps, and stocks a *Heurigen* calendar.

❶ Getting There & Away

Frequent daily trains connect Krems with Vienna's Franz-Josefs-Bahnhof (€15.20, one hour) and Melk (€11.90, 1¼ hours). It is slightly quicker to take a bus to Melk (€10.20, one hour) rather than a train. The boat station is near Donaustrasse, about 2km west of the train station.

ON YOUR BIKE

Many towns in the Danube Valley are part of a bike-hire network called **Nextbike** (☑02742-229 901; www.nextbike.at; per hour/24 hours €1/8). After registering using a credit card (either by calling the hotline or on the website), a refunded €1 is deducted and you can begin renting bicycles.

Dürnstein

02711 / POP 870

The pretty town of Dürnstein, on a supple curve in the Danube, is known for its hilltop castle, **Kuenringerburg castle**, where Richard I (the Lionheart) of England was imprisoned in 1192. His unscheduled stopover on the way home from the Crusades came courtesy of Austrian archduke Leopold V, whom he had insulted.

There's not much left of the castle today. It's basically just a pile of rubble. Still, it's worth snapping a picture and the views from the top are breathtaking.

Sleeping & Eating

The tourist office has a list of private rooms and *Gasthöfe* (guesthouses) in Dürnstein.

Hotel Schloss Dürnstein   HOTEL €€
(212; www.schloss.at; Dürnstein 2; s €139-169, d €185-225; P@🕸🏊) This castle is the last word in luxury in town, with antique-furnished rooms, a spa, two pools and a high-end restaurant (mains €16 to €30) with staggering views over the river.

Hotel Sänger Blondel   HOTEL €€
(253; www.saengerblondel.at; Klosterplatz/Dürnstein 64; s €72, d €98-118; P@🕸) Expect a warm welcome from the Schendl family at this hotel, with good-sized rooms facing the Danube, castle or tree-shaded garden. Breakfast is jazzed up with regional produce like Wachau apricot jam.

Restaurant Loibnerhof   AUSTRIAN €€
(82 890; www.loibnerhof.at; Unterloiben 7; mains €15-26; Wed-Sun) Situated 1.5km east of Dürnstein in Unterloiben, this family-run restaurant inside a 400-year-old building has a leafy garden for enjoying local specialities and homegrown wines.

Information

For more about Dürnstein, contact the **tourist office** (200; www.duernstein.at; 9am-noon daily, plus 4-6pm Fri & Sat, closed mid–Oct–Mar), a two-minute walk south of the centre.

Getting There & Away

Dürnstein can be reached from Krems by train (€2.50, 18 minutes, hourly).

Melk

02752 / POP 5260

With its sparkling and majestic abbey-fortress, Melk is a highlight of any visit to the Danube Valley. Many visitors cycle here for the day – wearily pushing their bikes through the cobblestone streets.

Sights

TOP CHOICE **Stift Melk**   ABBEY
(Benedictine Abbey of Melk; 5550; www.stift-melk.at; Abt Berthold Dietmayr Strasse 1; adult/child €9.50/5, with guided tour €11.50/7; 9am-5.30pm) Rising like a vision on a hill overlooking the town, Stift Melk is Austria's most famous abbey. It has been home to Benedictine monks since the 11th century, though it owes its current good looks to 18th-century mastermind Jakob Prandtauer.

The interior of the twin-spired monastery church is baroque gone barmy, with endless prancing angels and gold twirls. Other highlights include the **Bibliothek** (Library) and the **Marmorsaal** (Marble Hall); the trompe l'oeil on the ceiling (by Paul Troger) gives the illusion of greater height. Eleven of the imperial rooms, where dignitaries (including Napoleon) stayed, now house a **museum**.

From around November to March, the monastery can only be visited by guided tour (11am and 2pm daily). Always phone ahead to ensure you get an English-language tour.

Sleeping & Eating

Restaurants and cafes with alfresco seating line the Rathausplatz.

Hotel Restaurant zur Post   HOTEL €€
(523 45; www.post-melk.at; Linzer Strasse 1; s €62-74, d €102-117, tr €125-145, q €150; P@🕸) This bright hotel in the heart of town has large, comfortable rooms. There's a sauna, free bike use for guests and a decent restaurant serving Austrian classics.

Hotel Wachau   HOTEL €€
(525 31; www.hotel-wachau.at; Am Wachberg 3; s €58-88, d €96-126; P♿@🕸) For comfortable, modern rooms, try this hotel 2km southeast of the train station. The restaurant (mains €12 to €20, gourmet menu €45) is open for dinner Monday to Saturday and specialises in well-prepared regional cuisine.

ℹ️ Information

The centrally located **tourist office** (📞51 160; www.niederoesterreich.at/melk; Kremser Strasse 5; ⊙9.30am-6pm Mon-Sat, 9.30am-4pm Sun) has maps and plenty of useful information.

ℹ️ Getting There & Away

Boats leave from the canal by Pionierstrasse, 400m north of the abbey. There are hourly trains to Vienna (€17.10, 1¼ hours).

Linz

📞0732 / POP 191,100

In Linz beginnt's (It begins in Linz) goes the Austrian saying, and it's spot on. The technology trailblazer and European Capital of Culture 2009 is blessed with a leading-edge cyber centre and world-class contemporary art gallery.

🔴 Sights & Activities

Linz' baroque Hauptplatz and sculpture-strewn Danube Park are made for aimless ambling.

Ars Electronica Center MUSEUM
(www.aec.at; Ars Electronica Strasse 1; adult/child €8/5; ⊙9am-5pm Wed-Fri, to 9pm Thu, 10am-6pm Sat & Sun) Ars Electronica Center zooms in on tomorrow's technology, science and digital media. In themed labs you can interact with robots, animate digital objects and (virtually) travel to outer space. The shipshape centre kaleidoscopically changes colour after dark.

Lentos GALLERY
(www.lentos.at; Ernst-Koref-Promenade 1; adult/child €6.50/4.50; ⊙10am-6pm Wed-Mon, to 9pm Thu) Ars Electronica's rival icon across the Danube is the rectangular glass-and-steel Lentos, also strikingly illuminated by night. The gallery guards one of Austria's finest modern art collections, including works by Warhol, Schiele and Klimt, which sometimes feature in the large-scale exhibitions.

Neuer Dom CHURCH
(New Cathedral; Herrenstrasse 26; ⊙7.30am-7pm Mon-Sat, 8am-7pm Sun) This neo-Gothic giant of a cathedral was designed in the mid-19th century by Vinzenz Statz of Cologne Dom fame. The tower's height was restricted to 134m, so as not to outshine Stephansdom in Vienna.

Schlossmuseum MUSEUM
(Castle Museum; www.schlossmuseum.at; Schlossberg 1; adult/child €6.50/4.50; ⊙9am-6pm Tue-Fri, to

9pm Thu, 10am-5pm Sat & Sun) Linz' hilltop castle is a treasure trove of art and history. The Gothic ecclesiastical paintings are a highlight.

Pöstlingbergbahn VIEWPOINT
(adult/child €5.60/2.80; ⊙6am-10.30pm Mon-Sat, 7.30am-10.30pm Sun) This gondola features in the *Guinness Book of Records* as the world's steepest mountain railway – quite some feat for such a low-lying city! Far-reaching city and Danube views await at the summit.

🍴 Sleeping & Eating

Spitz Hotel HOTEL €€
(📞73 37 33; www.spitzhotel.at; Fiedlerstrasse 6; r €99-250; ℗🅿️@🛜) Much-lauded Austrian architect Isa Stein has left her avant-garde imprint on the Spitz. Each of the hotel's rooms has unique artworks. Minimalism rules here, with clean lines, open-plan bathrooms and hardwood floors.

Hotel am Domplatz HOTEL €€
(📞77 30 00; www.hotelamdomplatz.at; Stifterstrasse 4; s €125-145, d €154-184; ℗🅿️@🛜) Sidling up to the Neuer Dom, this glass-and-concrete design hotel reveals light, streamlined interiors. Wind down with a view at the rooftop spa.

k.u.k. Hofbäckerei CAFE €
(Pfarrgasse 17; coffee & cake €3-6; ⊙6.30am-6pm Mon-Fri, 7am-12.30pm Sat) The empire lives on at this gloriously stuck-in-time cafe. Here Fritz Rath bakes *the* best *Linzer Torte* in town – rich, spicy and with lattice pastry that crumbles just so.

Cubus FUSION €€
(Ars-Electronica-Strasse 1; mains €10.50-23.50; ⊙9am-1am Mon-Sat, 9am-6pm Sun; 🛜) On the 3rd floor of the Ars Electronica Center, this glass cube has stellar Danube views. The menu is strictly fusion and the two-course lunch a snip at €7.20.

ℹ️ Information

Hotspot Linz (www.hotspotlinz.at) Free wi-fi at 120 hotspots in the city, including the Ars Electronica Center and Lentos.

Post Office (Domgasse 1; ⊙8am-6pm Mon-Fri, 9am-noon Sat) Handy to the centre.

Tourist Information Linz (☑7070 2009; www.linz.at; Hauptplatz 1; ⊙9am-7pm Mon-Sat, 10am-7pm Sun, shorter hours winter) Free city maps and room reservation service.

❶ Getting There & Around

AIR Austrian Airlines, Lufthansa, Ryanair and Air Berlin fly to the **Blue Danube Airport** (www.linz-airport.at), 13km southwest of Linz. An hourly shuttle bus (€2.70, 20 minutes) links the airport to the main train station.

PUBLIC TRANSPORT Bus and tram tickets are bought before you board from pavement dispensers or *Tabak* (tobacconist) shops. Single tickets cost €2 and day passes €4.

TRAIN Linz is halfway between Salzburg and Vienna on the main road and rail routes. Trains to Salzburg (€23.70, 1¼ hours) and Vienna (€34.30, 1½ hours) leave approximately twice hourly.

THE SOUTH

Austria's two main southern states, Styria (Steiermark) and Carinthia (Kärnten), often feel worlds apart from the rest of the country, both in climate and attitude. Styria is a blissful amalgamation of genteel architecture, rolling green hills, vine-covered slopes and soaring mountains. Its capital, Graz, is one of Austria's most attractive cities.

A fashion-conscious crowd heads to sun-drenched Carinthia in summer. Sidling up to Italy, the region exudes an atmosphere that's as close to Mediterranean as this staunch country gets.

Graz

☑0316 / POP 265,300

Austria's second-largest city is probably its most relaxed and, after Vienna, its liveliest for after-hours pursuits. It's an attractive place with bristling green parkland, red rooftops and a small, fast-flowing river gushing through its centre. Architecturally, it has Renaissance courtyards and provincial baroque palaces complemented by innovative modern designs.

The surrounding countryside, a mixture of vineyards, mountains, forested hills and thermal springs, is within easy striking distance.

⊙ Sights & Activities

Graz is a city easily enjoyed by simply wandering aimlessly. Admission to all of the major museums with a 24-hour ticket costs €11/4 for adults/children.

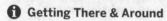

TOP CHOICE **Universalmuseum Joanneum** MUSEUM COMPLEX
(www.museum-joanneum.at; Raubergasse 10) The crowning glory of this Styria-wide ensemble of museums and palaces is the new **Joanneumsviertel** (www.joanneumsviertel.at; Kalchberggasse ; ⊙visitor centre 10am-5pm) quarter, gathered around squares and courtyards and seamlessly bringing together baroque and contemporary architecture. Besides the state library and multimedia collections, the complex is home to the **Neue Galerie Graz** (Joanneumsviertel, Kalchberggasse; adult/child €8/3; ⊙10am-5pm Tue-Sun), with an outstanding collection of 19th- and 20th-century art, placing the emphasis on Austrian masters from Klimt to Otto Wagner.

Kunsthaus Graz GALLERY
(www.kunsthausgraz.at; Lendkai 1; adult/child €8/3; ⊙10am-5pm Tue-Sun) Designed by British architects Peter Cook and Colin Fournier, this world-class contemporary art space looks something like a space-age sea slug. Exhibitions change every three to four months.

Schloss Eggenberg PALACE
(Eggenberger Allee 90; adult/child €8/3; ⊙palace tours 10am-4pm Tue-Sun Apr-Oct) A blend of gothic, Renaissance and baroque styles, this beautiful Unesco World Heritage palace can be reached by tram 1 from Hauptplatz. Admission includes a guided tour (on the hour except at 1pm), taking in 24 *Prunkräume* (staterooms), which are based around astronomy, the zodiac and classical or religious mythology.

FREE **Murinsel** BRIDGE
This artificial island-cum-bridge in the Mur River is an open seashell of glass, concrete and steel by New York artist Vito Acconci. It houses a trendy cafe-bar in aqua blue and a small stage.

Schlossberg VIEWPOINT
The wooded slopes of Schlossberg (473m) can be reached on foot, with the funicular **Schlossbergbahn** (Castle Hill Railway; 1hr ticket adult/child €2/1) from Kaiser-Franz-Josef-Kai, or by **Glass Lift** (Glass Lift 1hr ticket €1.90) from Schlossbergplatz. Napoleon was hard-pressed to raze this fortress, but raze it he did. Today the medieval **Uhrturm** (Clock Tower) is the legacy. The townsfolk paid Napoleon a ransom of 2987 florins and 11 farthings to spare the tower during the 1809 invasion.

Landeszeughaus MUSEUM
(www.zeughaus.at; Herrengasse 16; adult/child €8/3; ⊙10am-5pm Mon & Wed-Sun) A must-see for fans of armour and weapons, housing an astounding array of 30,000 gleaming exhibits.

FREE **Burg** CASTLE, PARK
(Hofgasse) At the far end of Graz' 15th-century castle is an ingenious double staircase (1499). Adjoining it is the Stadtpark, the city's largest green space.

🛏 Sleeping

Hotel zum Dom HOTEL €€
(☎82 48 00; www.domhotel.co.at; Bürgergasse 14; s €84-99, d €124-219, ste €194-239; P❄📶) Hotel zum Dom's individually furnished rooms come with power showers or whirlpools, and one suite even has a terrace whirlpool.

Hotel Daniel HOTEL €
(☎711 080; www.hoteldaniel.com; Europaplatz 1; r €59-79, breakfast per person €9; P❄@) Perched at the top of Annenstrasse, the Daniel is an exclusive design hotel. All rooms are tastefully furnished in minimalist designs. You can rent a Vespa (€15 per day) and there's a 24-hour espresso bar.

Augarten Hotel HOTEL €€
(☎20 800; www.augartenhotel.at; Schönaugasse 53; s €89-169, d €114-194; P❄📶🏊) The arty Augarten is decorated with the owner's private collection. All rooms are bright and modern, and the pool and sauna round off an excellent option.

Gasthof-Pension zur Steirer-Stub'n GUESTHOUSE €€
(☎71 68 55; www.pension-graz.at; Lendplatz 8; s/d €43/86, apt €120-180; P📶) A bright and breezy guesthouse where many of the good-sized rooms have patios overlooking Lendplatz.

🍴 Eating

With leafy salads dressed in pumpkin-seed oil, fish specialities and *Pfand'l* (pan-grilled) dishes, Styrian cuisine is Austrian cooking at its light and healthy best.

Stock up for a picnic at the farmers markets (⊙4.30am-1pm, closed Sun) on Kaiser-Josef-Platz and Lendplatz. For fast-food stands, head for Hauptplatz and Jakominiplatz.

TOP CHOICE **Der Steirer** TAVERNA €€
(www.dersteirer.at; Belgiergasse 1; mains €10-19.50, tapas €2, lunch menu from €7.90; ⊙11am-midnight) This Styrian neo-*Beisl* and wine bar

HUNDERTWASSER SPA

East Styria is famed for its thermal springs. Fans of Friedensreich Hundertwasser's playful architectural style won't want to miss the surreal **Rogner-Bad Blumau** (☎03383-51 00; www.blumau.com; adult/child €40/22; ⊙9am-11pm), 50km east of Graz. The spa has all the characteristics of his art, including uneven floors, grass on the roof, colourful ceramics and golden spires. Overnight accommodation includes entry to the spa. Call ahead to book treatments from sound meditation to invigorating Styrian elderberry wraps.

has a small but excellent selection of local dishes and a large choice of wines. The goulash with fried polenta is easily one of the best in the country. Or go for Styrian tapas like chanterelle tartar with speck.

Magnolia AUSTRIAN €€
(☎823 835; Schöngaugasse 53; 3-course menu €55-59, mains €15-20; ⊙lunch & dinner Mon-Fri) Alongside Augarten Hotel, with outdoor seating, this stylish restaurant with a seasonal menu and Austro-international cuisine is highly rated.

Landhauskeller AUSTRIAN €€
(☎83 02 76; Schmiedgasse 9; mains €11.50-26.50; ⊙11.30am-midnight Mon-Sat) What started as a spit-and-sawdust pub in the 16th century evolved into an atmospheric, medieval-style restaurant serving specialities like its four different sorts of *Tafelspitz* (prime boiled beef).

🍷 Drinking & Entertainment

The bar scene in Graz is split between three main areas: around the university; adjacent to the Kunsthaus; and on Mehlplatz and Prokopigasse (dubbed the 'Bermuda Triangle').

Orange BAR, CLUB
(www.cbo.at; Elisabethstrasse 30; ⊙8am-3am) A student crowd flocks to this modern cafe, bar and club, with a patio for summer evenings. DJs spin regularly here.

Kulturhauskeller BAR,
(Elisabethstrasse 30; ⊙9pm-5am Wed-Sat) Next to Orange, the Kulturhauskeller is a cavernous cellar bar that heaves with raunchy students on weekends.

❶ Information

Graz Tourismus (☑80 75; www.graztouris
mus.at; Herrengasse 16; ⊙10am-6pm) Graz'
main tourist office, with loads of free information on the city. Inside the train station is an
information stand and terminal, and a free
hotline to the tourist office.

Main Post Office (Neutorgasse 46; ⊙8am-
7pm Mon-Fri, 9am-noon Sat).

❶ Getting There & Away

AIR Ryanair (www.ryanair.com) has regular
flights from London Stansted to **Graz Airport**,
10km south of the centre, while **Air Berlin** (www.
airberlin.com) connects the city with Berlin.

BICYCLE Bicycle rental is available from **Bicycle** (☑688 645; Körösistrasse 5; per 24hr €15;
⊙7am-1pm & 2-6pm Mon-Fri).

PUBLIC TRANSPORT Single tickets (€2) for
buses, trams and the Schlossbergbahn are valid
for one hour, but you're usually better off buying
a 24-hour pass (€4.50).

TRAIN Trains to Vienna (€37, 2½ hours) depart
hourly, and six daily go to Salzburg (€48.60,
four hours). International train connections from
Graz include Ljubljana (€37.60, 3½ hours) and
Budapest (€64, 5½ hours).

Klagenfurt

☑0463 / POP 94,800

With its dreamy location on Wörthersee
and more Renaissance than baroque beauty,
Carinthia's capital Klagenfurt has a distinct
Mediterranean feel. While there isn't a huge
amount here to see, it makes a handy base
for exploring Wörthersee's lakeside villages
and elegant medieval towns to the north.

◉ Sights & Activities

Boating and swimming are usually possible
from May to September. Free guided tours
depart from the tourist office at 10am every
Friday and Saturday during July and August.

TOP CHOICE Wörthersee   LAKE

Owing to its thermal springs, the Wörthersee
is one of the region's warmer lakes (an average 21°C in summer) and is great for swimming, lakeshore frolicking and water sports.
The 40km **cycle path** circumnavigating the
lake is one of Austria's best. In summer the
tourist office cooperates with a hire company
for bicycles (per 24 hours €10).

Europapark   PARK

Europapark's green expanse and *Strandbad*
(beach) on the shores of the Wörthersee are

especially good for kids. The park's biggest
draw is **Minimundus** (www.minimundus.at;
Villacher Strasse 241; adult/child €13/8; ⊙9am-btwn
6pm & 8pm Mar-Oct), a 'miniature world' with
150 replicas of the world's architectural icons,
downsized to a scale of 1:25. To get there, take
bus 10 or 20 from Heiligengeistplatz.

🛏 Sleeping & Eating

When you check into accommodation in
Klagenfurt, ask for a *Gästekarte* (guest
card), which entitles you to discounts.

Hotel Geyer   HOTEL €€

(☑578 86; www.hotelgeyer.com; Priesterhausgasse
5; s €70-88, d €102-135, q €155-170; ℗@🛜) Colourful fabrics, paintings and objets d'art lend
a personal feel to this central pick. Rooms
are bright and contemporary, there is a little
spa area for relaxing moments, and breakfast
is served on a pretty patio in summer.

Arcotel Moser Verdino   HOTEL €€

(☑578 78; www.arcotel.at/moserverdino; Domgasse 2; s €80-144, d €104-256, ste €128-180, apt
€148-1920; @🛜) This excellent pick has high-
quality modern rooms with flair, very helpful staff and often discounted rates.

Restaurant Maria Loretto   AUSTRIAN €€

(☑24 465; Lorettoweg 54; mains €15-25; ⊙lunch
& dinner) A wonderful restaurant situated
on a headland above Wörthersee near the
Strandbad, serving fresh lake fish and
dishes prepared with home-grown herbs.
Reserve for an outside table.

Dolce Vita   ITALIAN €€€

(☑554 99; Heuplatz 2; lunch menu €29-49, dinner
mains €28, 4-6 course menu €59-79; ⊙Mon-Fri)
In a region strongly influenced by northern
Italian cuisine, this restaurant is something
of a local flagship, building a seasonal menu
mostly around fresh local produce and game.

❶ Information

Tourist Office (☑53 722 23; www.info.klagen-
furt.at; Neuer Platz 1, Rathaus; ⊙8am-6pm
Mon-Fri, 10am-5pm Sat, 10am-3pm Sun) Books
accommodation and sells Kärnten cards (www.
kaerntencard.at, adult/child €36/15.50) which
give free entry to 100 sights in the region over a
one-week period.

❶ Getting There & Around

AIR Klagenfurt's **airport** (www.klagenfurt
-airport.com; Flughafenstrasse 60-66) is served
by Ryanair from London Stansted and **TUIfly**
(www.tuifly.com) from major German cities.

BUS Bus drivers sell single tickets (€2) and 24-hour passes (€4.40). Bus 42 shuttles between the Hauptbahnhof and the airport.

TRAIN Two hourly direct trains run from Klagenfurt to Vienna (€50, 3¾ hours) and Salzburg (€38.70, three hours). Trains to Graz depart every two to three hours (€38.70, 2¾ hours). Trains to western Austria, Italy, Slovenia and Germany go via Villach (€7.80, 30 to 40 minutes, two to four per hour).

SALZBURG

⏷ 0662 / POP 149,500

The joke 'If it's baroque, don't fix it' is a perfect maxim for Salzburg; the tranquil Old Town burrowed below steep hills looks much as it did when Mozart lived here 250 years ago. Second only to Vienna in numbers of visitors, this compact city is centred on a tight grouping of narrow, cobbled streets overshadowed by ornate 17th-century buildings, which are in turn dominated by the medieval Hohensalzburg fortress from high above. Across the fast-flowing Salzach River rests the baroque Schloss Mirabell, surrounded by gorgeous manicured gardens.

If this doesn't whet your appetite, then bypass the grandeur and head straight for kitsch-country by joining a tour of *The Sound of Music* film locations.

◉ Sights

Old Town HISTORIC AREA
A Unesco World Heritage site, Salzburg's Old Town centre is equally entrancing whether viewed from ground level or the hills above.

The grand **Residenzplatz**, with its horse-drawn carriages and mythical fountain, is a good starting point for a wander. The overwhelmingly baroque **Dom** (Cathedral; Domplatz; ⊗8am-7pm Mon-Sat, from 1pm Sun), slightly south, is entered via bronze doors symbolising faith, hope and charity. The adjacent **Dommuseum** (adult/concession €5/1.50;

SALZBURG CARD

The money-saving **Salzburg Card** (1-/2-/3-day card €26/35/41) gets you entry to all of the major sights and attractions, a free river cruise, unlimited use of public transport (including cable cars) plus numerous discounts on tours and events. The card is half-price for children and €3 cheaper in the low season.

WANT MORE?

Head to **Lonely Planet** (www.lonely planet.com/austria/salzburg) for planning advice, author recommendations, traveller reviews and insider tips.

⊗10am-5pm Mon-Sat, 11am-6pm Sun May-Oct) is a treasure-trove of ecclesiastical art.

From here, head west along Franziskanergasse and turn left into a courtyard for **Stiftskirche St Peter** (St Peter's Abbey Church; St Peter Bezirk 1-2; ⊗church 8.30am-noon & 2.30-6.30pm, cemetery 6.30am-7pm), an abbey church founded around 700. Among the lovingly tended graves in the grounds you'll find the **Katakomben** (adult/student €1.50/1; ⊗10.30am-5pm Tue-Sun), or catacombs, cavelike chapels and crypts hewn out of the Mönchsberg cliff face.

The western end of Franziskanergasse opens out into Max Reinhardt Platz, where you'll see the back of Fisher von Erlach's **Kollegienkirche** (Universitätsplatz; ⊗8am-6pm), another outstanding example of baroque architecture. The **Stift Nonnberg** (Nonnberg Convent; Nonnberggasse 2; ⊗7am-dusk), where Maria first appears in *The Sound of Music*, is back in the other direction, a short climb up the hill to the east of the Festung Hohensalzburg.

Festung Hohensalzburg FORT
(www.salzburg-burgen.at; Mönchsberg 34; adult/child/family €7.80/4.40/17.70, with Festungsbahn funicular €11/6.30/25.50; ⊗9am-7pm) Salzburg's most visible icon is this mighty clifftop fortress, one of the best preserved in Europe. Built in 1077, it was home to many prince-archbishops who ruled Salzburg from 798. Inside are the impressively ornate staterooms, torture chambers and two museums.

It takes 15 minutes to walk up the hill to the fortress, or you can catch the **Festungsbahn funicular** (Festungsgasse 4).

Salzburg Museum MUSEUM
(www.salzburgmuseum.at; Mozartplatz 1; adult/child/family €7/3/14; ⊗9am-5pm Tue-Sun, to 8pm Thu) Housed in the baroque Neue Residenz palace, this flagship museum takes you on a romp through Salzburg past and present. Ornate rooms showcase medieval sacred art, prince-archbishop portraits and highlights such as Carl Spitzweg's renowned *Sonntagsspaziergang* (Sunday Stroll; 1841) painting.

Salzburg's famous 35-bell glockenspiel, which chimes daily at 7am, 11am and 6pm, is on the palace's western flank.

Salzburg

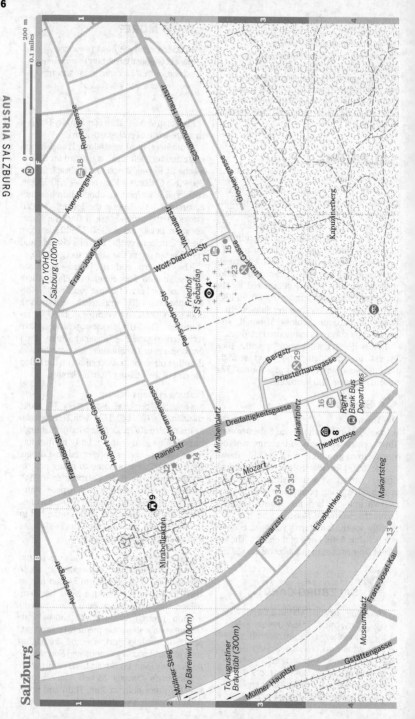

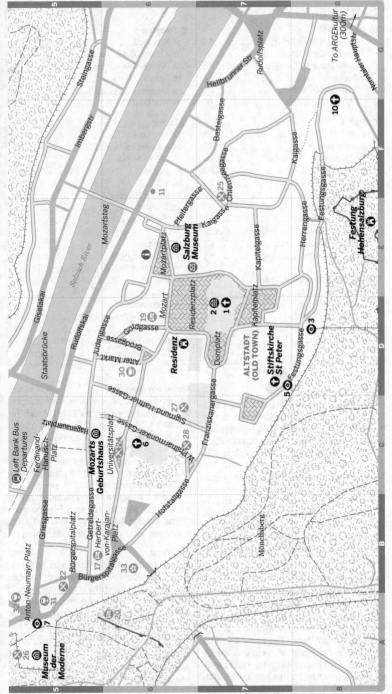

Salzburg

FREE **Schloss Mirabell** PALACE

(Mirabellplatz 4; ☺palace 8am-4pm Mon, Wed & Thu, 1-4pm Tue & Fri, gardens dawn-dusk) Prince-Archbishop Wolf Dietrich built this splendid palace in 1606 for his beloved mistress Salome Alt. Its lavish baroque interior, replete with stucco, marble and frescos, is free to visit. The **Marmorsaal** (Marble Hall) provides a sublime backdrop for evening chamber concerts.

For stellar fortess views, take a stroll in the manicured, fountain-dotted **gardens**. *The Sound of Music* fans will of course recognise the Pegasus statue, the gnomes and the steps where the mini von Trapps practised 'Do-Re-Mi'.

Mozarts Geburtshaus MUSEUM

(Mozart's Birthplace; www.mozarteum.at; Getreidegasse 9; adult/child/family €10/3.50/21; ☺9am-5.30pm) Mozart was born in this bright-yellow town house in 1756 and spent the first 17 years of his life here. The museum today harbours a collection of memorabilia, including the miniature violin the child prodigy played, plus a lock of his hair and buttons from his jacket.

Mozart-Wohnhaus MUSEUM

(Mozart's Residence; www.mozarteum.at; Makartplatz 8; adult/child/family €10/3.50/21, incl Mozarts Geburtshaus €17/5/36; ☺9am-5.30pm) The Mozart family moved to this more spacious abode in 1773, where a prolific Mozart composed works such as the *Shepherd King* and *Idomeneo*. Alongside family portraits and documents, you'll find Mozart's original fortepiano.

Under the same roof and included in your ticket is the **Mozart Ton-und Filmmuseum** (☺9am-1pm Mon, Tue & Fri, 1-5pm Wed & Thu), a film and music archive for the ultra-enthusiast.

Residenz PALACE

(www.residenzgalerie.at; Residenzplatz 1; adult/child €9/3; ☺10am-5pm) This resplendent baroque palace is where the prince-archbishops held court until the 19th century. You can visit their opulently frescoed staterooms, while the gallery spotlights Dutch and Flemish masters of the Rubens and Rembrandt ilk.

Museum der Moderne GALLERY

(www.museumdermoderne.at; Mönchsberg 32; adult/child €8/6; ☺10am-6pm Tue-Sun, to 8pm

Wed) Straddling Mönchsberg's cliffs, this contemporary gallery shows first-rate exhibitions of 20th- and 21st-century art. The works of Alberto Giacometti, Emil Nolde and John Cage have previously featured. There's a free guided tour of the gallery at 6.30pm every Wednesday.

The **Mönchsberg Lift** (Gstättengasse 13; one-way/return €2.10/3.40, incl gallery ticket €9.70/6.80; ⊙8am-7pm Thu-Tue, to 9pm Wed) whizzes up to the gallery year-round.

Friedhof St Sebastian   CEMETERY
(Linzer Gasse 41; ⊙9am-7pm) Tucked away behind the baroque St Sebastian's Church, this peaceful cemetery is the final resting place of Mozart family members and 16th-century physician Paracelsus. Outpomping them all, though, is Prince-Archbishop Wolf Dietrich von Raitenau's mosaic-tiled **mausoleum**, an elaborate memorial to himself.

⟳ Tours

If you would rather go it alone, the tourist office has four-hour iTour audioguides (€9), which take in big-hitters like the Residenz, Mirabellgarten and Mozartplatz.

Fräulein Maria's Bicycle Tours   BICYCLE TOUR
(www.mariasbicycletours.com; Mirabellplatz 4; adult/child €26/18; ⊙9.30am & 4.30pm May-Sep) Belt out *The Sound of Music* faves as you pedal on one of these 3½-hour bike tours of the film locations. No booking is required; just turn up at the Mirabellplatz meeting point.

Segway Tours   SEGWAY TOUR
(www.segway-salzburg.at; Wolf-Dietrich-Strasse 3; city/Sound of Music tour €33/65 ; ⊙tours 9am, noon, 3pm & 5pm Mar-Oct) These guided Segway tours take in the big sights by zippy battery-powered scooter.

Bob's Special Tours   BUS TOUR
(☎84 95 11; www.bobstours.com; Rudolfskai 38; ⊙office 10am-3pm Mon-Fri, noon-2pm Sat & Sun) Minibus tours to *The Sound of Music* locations (€45), the Bavarian Alps (€45) and Grossglockner (€90). Reservations essential.

Salzburg Sightseeing Tours   BUS TOUR
(www.salzburg-sightseeingtours.at; Mirabellplatz 2; adult/child €16/8; ⊙office 8am-6pm) Sells a 24-hour ticket for a multilingual hop-on, hop-off bus tour of the city and *The Sound of Music* locations.

Salzburg Schiffsfahrt   BOAT TOUR
(www.salzburghighlights.at; Makartsteg ; adult/child €14/7; ⊙Apr-Oct) Hour-long cruises depart from Makartsteg bridge, with some chugging on to Schloss Hellbrunn (the ticket price does not cover entry to the palace).

✪ Festivals & Events

Austria's most renowned classical music festival, the **Salzburg Festival** (www.salzburger festspiele.at) attracts international stars from late July to late August. Book on its website before January, or ask the **ticket office** (☎80 45-500; info@salzburgfestival.at; Herbert-von-Karajan-Platz 11; ⊙9.30am-1pm & 2-5pm Mon-Sat) about cancellations during the festival.

🛏 Sleeping

Ask for the tourist office's hotel brochure, which gives prices for hotels, pensions, hostels and camping grounds. Accommodation is at a premium during festivals.

TOP CHOICE **Haus Ballwein**   GUESTHOUSE €
(☎82 40 29; www.haus-ballwein.at; Moosstrasse 69a; s €35-45, d €58-68, apt €100-115; P🅿🛜) Country or city? Why not both at this farmhouse guesthouse, a 10-minute trundle from the Altstadt on bus 21. With its bright, pine-filled rooms, mountain views, free bike hire and garden patrolled by duck duo, Rosalee and Clementine, this place is big on charm. Breakfast is a wholesome spread of fresh rolls, eggs, fruit, muesli and cold cuts.

TOP CHOICE **Arte Vida**   GUESTHOUSE €€
(☎87 31 85; www.artevida.at; Dreifaltigkeitsgasse 9; s €55-140, d €80-152; 🛜) Arte Vida has the boho-chic feel of a Marrakesh *riad*, with its lantern-lit salon, communal kitchen and individually designed rooms done out in rich colours and fabrics. Your affable host Reinhold arranges yoga sessions in the quiet garden, and outdoor activities.

Hotel Am Dom   BOUTIQUE HOTEL €€
(☎84 27 65; www.hotelamdom.at; Goldgasse 17; s €90-160, d €130-280; ❄🛜) Antique meets boutique at this Altstadt hotel, where the original vaults and beams of the 800-year-old building contrast with razor-sharp design features. Artworks inspired by the Salzburg Festival grace the strikingly lit rooms.

Hotel & Villa Auersperg   BOUTIQUE HOTEL €€
(☎88 94 40; www.auersperg.at; Auerspergstrasse 61; s €129-155, d €165-205, ste 235-310; P🅿@🛜) This charismatic villa-hotel hybrid fuses late-19th-century flair with contemporary design. Relax by the lily pond in the garden

or in the rooftop wellness area with mountain views. Free bike hire is a bonus.

Haus Steiner
GUESTHOUSE €

(☑83 00 31; www.haussteiner.com; Moosstrasse 156; s/d/tr €34/56/78; P🐾) Kind-natured Rosemarie runs a tight ship at this chalet-style guesthouse. The pick of the petite rooms, furnished in natural wood, come with fridges and balconies with mood-lifting mountain views. The Altstadt is a 15-minute ride away on bus 21.

Haus Wartenberg
GUESTHOUSE €€

(☑84 84 00; www.hauswartenberg.com; Riedenburgerstrasse 2; d €128; P@🐾) Set in vine-strewn gardens, this 17th-century chalet guesthouse is a 10-minute stroll west of the Altstadt. Country-style rooms done out in chunky pinewood and florals are in keeping with the character of the place.

Wolf Dietrich
HISTORIC HOTEL €€

(☑87 12 75; www.salzburg-hotel.at; Wolf-Dietrich-Strasse 7; s €90-130, d €152-222, ste €197-277; P🐾🏊) For old-fashioned elegance you can't beat this central hotel, where rooms are dressed in polished wood furnishings and floral fabrics. In contrast, the spa and pool are ultramodern. Organic produce is served at breakfast.

Arthotel Blaue Gans
BOUTIQUE HOTEL €€€

(☑84 24 91; www.hotel-blaue-gans-salzburg.at; Getreidegasse 41-43; s €125-175, d €159-320; ✻🐾) Contemporary design blends harmoniously with the original vaulting and beams of this 660-year-old hotel, with sleek yet comfortable rooms.

YOHO Salzburg
HOSTEL €

(☑879 649; www.yoho.at; Paracelsusstrasse 9; dm €19-23, d €65-75; @🐾) Comfy bunks, free wi-fi, plenty of cheap beer – what more could a backpacker ask for? Except, perhaps, a merry sing-along: *The Sound of Music* is screened daily (yes, *every* day). The friendly crew can arrange tours, adventure sports and bike hire.

Stadtalm
HOSTEL €

(☑84 17 29; www.diestadtalm.com; Mönchsberg 19C; dm €19) This turreted hostel plopped on top of Mönchsberg takes in the entire Salzburg panorama, from the city's spires and fortress to Kapuzinerberg.

✗ Eating

Self-caterers can find picnic fixings at the **Grüner Markt** (Green Market; Universitätsplatz; ⊙Mon-Sat).

TOP CHOICE Magazin
MODERN EUROPEAN €€€

(☑84 15 84; www.magazin.co.at; Augustinergasse 13a; mains €25-31, tasting menus €57-79, cookery classes €130-150; ⊙Mon-Sat) Gathered around a courtyard below Mönchsberg's sheer rock wall, Magazin shelters a deli, wine store, cookery school and restaurant. Chef Richard Brunnauer's menus, fizzing with seasonal flavours like scallops with vine-ripened peaches and venison medallions in porcini sauce, are matched with wines from the 850-bottle cellar. Buses 4 and 21 stop at Augustinergasse.

TOP CHOICE Bärenwirt
AUSTRIAN €€

(☑42 24 04; www.baerenwirt-salzburg.at; Müllner Hauptstrasse 8; mains €9-18; ⊙11am-11pm) Sizzling and stirring since 1663, Bärenwirt combines a woody, hunting-lodge-style interior with a river-facing terrace. Go for hearty *Bierbraten* (beer roast) with dumplings, locally caught trout or organic wild boar bratwurst.

Alter Fuchs
AUSTRIAN €€

(☑88 20 22; Linzer Gasse 47-49; mains €10-17; ⊙noon-midnight Mon-Sat; ✐🐕) This old fox prides itself on serving up old-fashioned Austrian fare, such as schnitzels fried to golden perfection. Foxes clad in bandanas guard the bar in the vaulted interior and there's a courtyard for good-weather dining.

Zum Fidelen Affen
AUSTRIAN €€

(☑87 73 61; www.fideleraffe.at; Priesterhausgasse 8; mains €10.50-16.50; ⊙5pm-midnight Mon-Sat) At the jovial monkey you'll dine heartily on Austrian classics like goulash and sweet curd dumplings in the vaulted interior or on the pavement terrace. Reservations are recommended.

Afro Café
AFRICAN €

(☑84 48 88; www.afrocoffee.com; Bürgerspitalplatz 5; lunch €6.70, mains €10-15; ⊙9am-midnight Mon-Sat) Hot-pink walls, beach-junk art and *big* hair...this afro-chic cafe keeps the good vibes coming. Fruity cocktails wash down dishes like springbok in a sesame-coriander crust and lemongrass-zucchini cake.

Riedenburg
MODERN EUROPEAN €€€

(☑83 08 15; www.riedenburg.at; Neutorstrasse 31; lunch €18, mains €26-35; ⊙Tue-Sat) At this romantic Michelin-starred pick, creative Austrian signatures such as venison and guinea fowl crêpes with wild herbs are expertly matched with top wines. Take bus 1, 4 or 5 to Moosstrasse.

NO TOURIST TRAPP

Did you know that there were 10 (not seven) von Trapp children? Or that Rupert was the eldest (so long Liesl) and the captain a gentle-natured man? For the truth behind the Hollywood legend, stay at Villa Trapp (☑630 860; www. villa-trapp.com; Traunstrasse 34; d €109-500) in Aigen district, 3km southeast of the Altstadt. Marianne and Christopher have transformed the von Trapp's elegant 19th-century villa into a beautiful guesthouse, brimming with family heirlooms and snapshots. The villa sits in Salzburg's biggest private park.

M32
FUSION €€

(☑84 10 00; www.m32.at; Mönchsberg 32; 3-course lunch €27, 5-course dinner €68-70, mains €14-23; ☺9am-1am Tue-Sun; ☑⌖) Bold colours and a forest of stag antlers reveal architect Matteo Thun's imprint at Museum der Moderne's glass-walled restaurant. The seasonal food and views are fantastic.

Triangel
AUSTRIAN €€

(☑84 22 29; Wiener-Philharmoniker-Gasse 7; lunch from €4.90, mains €9-29; ☺noon-midnight Mon-Sat) Arty bistro near the Festspielhaus, with a market-fresh menu.

Mensa Toskana
CAFE €

(Sigmund-Haffner-Gasse 11; lunch €4.50-5.40; ☺lunch Mon-Fri) Atmospheric university cafe in the Altstadt, with a sunny terrace and decent lunches.

IceZeit
ICE CREAM €

(Chiemseegasse 1; scoop €1.20; ☺11am-8pm) Grab a cone at Salzburg's best ice-cream parlour.

🍷 Drinking

You'll find the biggest concentration of bars along both banks of the Salzach and the hippest around Gstättengasse and Anton-Neumayr-Platz.

TOP CHOICE Augustiner Bräustübl
BREWERY

(www.augustinerbier.at; Augustinergasse 4-6; ☺3-11pm Mon-Fri, 2.30-11pm Sat & Sun) Who says monks can't enjoy themselves? Since 1621, this cheery monastery-run brewery has been serving potent home brews in the vaulted hall and beneath the chestnut trees in the 1000-seat beer garden.

Republic
BAR

(www.republic-cafe.at; Anton-Neumayr-Platz 2; ☺8am-1am Sun-Thu, to 4am Fri & Sat) One of Salzburg's most happening haunts, with regular DJs and free events from jazz breakfasts to Tuesday salsa nights.

Unikum Sky
CAFE

(Unipark Nonntal; ☺10am-7pm Mon-Fri, 9.30am-6pm Sat) For knockout fortress views, drinks and inexpensive snacks, head up to this sun-kissed terrace atop the new Unipark Nonntal campus.

Humboldt Stub'n
BAR

(Gstättengasse 4-6; ☺10am-2am, to 4am Fri & Sat) A nail-studded Mozart punk guards this upbeat bar opposite Republic. Try a sickly Mozart cocktail (liqueur, cherry juice, cream and chocolate). Beers are €2.50 at Wednesday's student night.

Café Tomaselli
CAFE

(www.tomaselli.at; Alter Markt 9; ☺7am-9pm Mon-Sat, 8am-9pm Sun) If you like your service with a dollop of Viennese grumpiness and strudel with a dollop of cream, this grand, wood-panelled coffee house in the city centre is just the ticket.

☆ Entertainment

Some of the high-brow venues include the Schlosskonzerte (☑84 85 86; www.salzburger-schlosskonzerte.at; Theatergasse 2; ☺8pm), in Schloss Mirabell's sublime baroque Marble Hall, and the Mozarteum (☑889 40; www. mozarteum.at; Schwarzstrasse 26-28). Marionettes bring *The Sound of Music* and Mozart's operas magically to life at Salzburger Marionettentheater (☑87 24 06; www. marionetten.at; Schwarzstrasse 24; ☺May-Sep, Christmas, Easter; ⌖).

Most bands with a modern bent will invariably play at either the Rockhouse (www. rockhouse.at; Schallmooser Hauptstrasse 46) or ARGEkultur (www.argekultur.at; Ulrike-Gschwandtner-Strasse 5); both double as popular bars.

ℹ Information

Many hotels and bars offer free wi-fi, and there are several cheap internet cafes near the train station. *Bankomaten* (ATMs) are all over the place.

City Net Café (Gstättengasse 11; per hr €2; ☺10am-10pm) Central internet cafe also offering discount calls.

Hospital (☑44 82; Müllner Hauptstrasse 48) Just north of Mönchsberg.

Main Post Office (Residenzplatz 9; ⊙8am-6pm Mon-Fri, 9am-noon Sat)

Police Headquarters (⌀63 83; Alpenstrasse 90)

STA Travel (www.statravel.at; Rainerstrasse 2) Student and budget travel agency.

Tourist Office (⌀889 87-330; www.salzburg.info; Mozartplatz 5; ⊙9am-6pm, closed Sun Sep-Mar) Has plenty of information about the city and its immediate surrounds; there's a ticket booking agency in the same building. For information on the rest of the province, visit the **Salzburgerland Tourismus** (www.salzburgerland.com) website.

 ## Getting There & Away

Air

Salzburg airport (www.salzburg-airport.com) has regular scheduled flights to destinations all over Austria and Europe. Low-cost flights from the UK are provided by **Ryanair** (www.ryanair.com) and **easyJet** (www.easyjet.com). Other airlines include **British Airways** (www.britishairways.com) and **Jet2** (www.jet2.com).

Bus

Buses depart from just outside the Hauptbahnhof on Südtiroler Platz. For more information on buses in and around Salzburg and an online timetable, see www.svv-info.at and www.postbus.at.

Car & Motorcycle

Three motorways converge on Salzburg to form a loop around the city: the A1/E60 from Linz, Vienna and the east; the A8/E52 from Munich and the west; and the A10/E55 from Villach and the south. The quickest way to Tirol is to take the road to Bad Reichenhall in Germany and continue to Lofer (B178) and St Johann in Tirol.

Train

Salzburg has excellent rail connections with the rest of Austria, though its Hauptbahnhof is undergoing extensive renovation until 2014.

Fast trains leave hourly for Vienna (€49.90, three hours) via Linz (€23.70, 1¼ hours). There is a two-hourly express service to Klagenfurt (€38.70, three hours). The quickest way to Innsbruck (€41.30, two hours) is by the 'corridor' train through Germany via Kufstein; trains depart at least every two hours. There are trains every hour or so to Munich (€34, 1¾ hours).

 ## Getting Around

TO/FROM THE AIRPORT Salzburg airport (www.salzburg-airport.com) is located 5.5km west of the city centre. Bus 2 goes there from the Hauptbahnhof (€2.30, 19 minutes). A taxi costs about €20.

BICYCLE Top Bike (www.topbike.at; Staatsbrücke; ⊙10am-5pm) rents bikes for around €15 per day (half-price for kids). The Salzburg Card yields a 20% discount.

BUS Bus drivers sell single (€2.30) and 24-hour (€5.20) tickets. Weekly tickets (€13.60) can be purchased from machines and *Tabak* shops.

Bus 1 starts from the Hauptbahnhof and skirts the pedestrian-only Altstadt. Another central stop is Hanuschplatz.

CAR & MOTORCYCLE Parking places are limited and much of the Altstadt is pedestrian-only, so it's easier to leave your car at one of three park-and-ride points to the west, north and south of the city. The largest car park in the centre is the Altstadt Garage under Mönchsberg (€14 per day).

FIAKER A *Fiaker* (horse-drawn carriage) for up to four people costs €40 for 25 minutes. The drivers line up on Residenzplatz.

AROUND SALZBURG

Schloss Hellbrunn

A prince-archbishop with a wicked sense of humour, Markus Sittikus built Italianate Schloss Hellbrunn (www.hellbrunn.at; Fürstenweg 37; adult/concession/family €9.50/6.50/24; ⊙9am-5.30pm, to 9pm Jul & Aug; ⚐) as a 17th-century summer palace and an escape from his Residenz functions.

The ingenious trick fountains and water-powered figures are the big draw. When the tour guides set them off, expect to get wet! Admission includes entry to the baroque palace. The rest of the sculpture-dotted gardens are free to visit. Look out for *The Sound of Music* pavilion of 'Sixteen Going on Seventeen' fame.

Bus 25 runs to Hellbrunn, 4.5km south of Salzburg, every 20 minutes from Rudolfskai in the Altstadt.

Werfen

 06468 / POP 3000

Framed by the limestone turrets of the Tennengebirge, Werfen's Alpine beauty hasn't escaped Hollywood producers – it stars in WWII action film *Where Eagles Dare* (1968) and makes a cameo appearance in the picnic scene of *The Sound of Music*.

Both its ice caves and fortress can be visited as a day trip from Salzburg if you start early (tour the caves first and be at the fortress for the last falconry show), otherwise consult the tourist office (⌀53 88; www.werfen.at; Markt 24;

⊙9am-12.30pm & 1-6pm Mon-Fri year-round, 2-4pm Sat May-Sep) for accommodation options.

⊙ Sights & Activities

TOP CHOICE **Eisriesenwelt** ICE CAVE
(www.eisriesenwelt.at; adult/concession €9/8, with cable car €20/18; ⊙9am-3.30pm May-Oct; 🚸) Billed as the world's largest accessible ice caves, more than 1000m above Werfen in the Tennengebirge mountains, this glittering ice empire is a once seen, never forgotten experience. The 1¼-hour tour takes you through twinkling passageways and chambers, the carbide lamps picking out otherworldly ice sculptures. Dress for subzero temperatures.

Burg Hohenwerfen CASTLE
(adult/concession/family €14/12/33; ⊙9am-5pm Apr-Oct; 🚸) High on a wooded clifftop, Burg Hohenwerfen has kept watch over the Salzach Valley since 1077, although its current appearance dates from the 16th century. Highlights include far-reaching views over Werfen from the belfry, dungeons containing some pretty nasty torture instruments, and a dramatic **falcony show** (11.15am and 2.15pm or 3.15pm). The walk up from the village takes 20 minutes.

⊙ Getting There & Around

Werfen is 45km south of Salzburg on the A10/E55 motorway. Trains run frequently to Salzburg (€10, 40 minutes). In summer, minibuses (single/return €3.10/6.10) run every 25 minutes between Eisriesenstrasse in Werfen and the car park, a 20-minute walk from the cable car to Eisriesenwelt.

SALZKAMMERGUT

A wonderland of glassy blue lakes and tall craggy peaks, Austria's Lake District is a long-time favourite holiday destination. The peaceful lakes attract visitors in droves from Salzburg and beyond, with limitless opportunities for boating, fishing, swimming or just lazing on the shore.

Bad Ischl

☏06132 / POP 13,900
During the last century of the Habsburg reign, Bad Ischl became the favourite summertime retreat for the imperial family and its entourage. Today the town and many of its dignified buildings still have a stately aura,

and a perhaps surprisingly high proportion of the local women still go about their daily business in *Dirndl* (Austria's traditional full pleated skirt). It makes a good base for exploring the entire Salzkammergut region.

⊙ Sights & Activities

Kaiservilla PALACE
(www.kaiservilla.com; Jainzen 38; adult/child €13/7.50, grounds only €4.50/3.50; ⊙9.30am-4.45pm, closed Thu-Tue Jan-Mar, closed Nov) This Italianate building was Franz Josef's summer residence and shows that he loved huntin', shootin' and fishin' – it's decorated with an obscene number of animal trophies. It can be visited only by guided tour, during which you'll pick up little gems, like the fact that it was here that the Kaiser signed the letter declaring war on Serbia, which led to WWI.

What was once the teahouse of Franz Josef's wife, Elisabeth, now contains a small **Photomuseum** (adult/child €2/1.50; ⊙9.30am-5pm, closed Nov-Mar).

Cable Car CABLE CAR
(www.katrinseilbahn.com; return adult/child €18.50/12; ⊙9am-5pm May-early Nov) The local mountain (1542m) with walking trails and limited skiing in winter is served by a cable car.

Salzkammergut Therme SPA
(www.eurothermen.at; Voglhuberstrasse 10; adult/child €14.50/10.50; ⊙9am-midnight) If you'd like to follow in Princess Sophie's (mother of Franz Josef) footprints, take the thermal waters at this effervescent spa.

✯ Festivals & Events

Bad Ischl stages the works of operetta composer Franz Lehár at the **Lehár Festival** (www.leharfestival.at) in July and August.

🛏 Sleeping & Eating

Staff at both the tourist offices can help find rooms.

Hotel Garni Sonnhof HOTEL €€
(☏230 78; www.sonnhof.at; Bahnhofstrasse 4; s €65-95, d €90-150; 🅿🛜) Nestled in a leafy glade of maple trees next to the station, this hotel has cosy, traditional decor, a beautiful garden, chickens that deliver breakfast eggs, and a sunny conservatory. There's a sauna and a steam bath on site.

Goldenes Schiff HOTEL €€
(☏242 41; www.goldenes-schiff.at; Adalbert-Stifter-Kai 3; s €95-112, d €134-180, apt €180-196; 🅿@🛜)

The best rooms at this comfortable pick have large windows overlooking the river. There's also a spa area and an excellent restaurant (mains €14 to €21) serving regional cuisine from game to Wolfgangsee fish.

Weinhaus Attwenger
AUSTRIAN €€

(☑248 10; www.weinhaus-attwenger.com; Lehárkai 12; mains €14-22; ☺closed Mon, also closed Tue Sep-early May) This quaint chalet with a riverside garden serves prime-quality Austrian cuisine from a seasonal menu, with wines to match.

Grand Café & Restaurant Zauner Esplanade
AUSTRIAN €€

(Hasner Allee 2; mains €10-18.50; ☺10am-10pm) This offshoot of Café Zauner, the famous pastry shop at Pfarrgasse 7, serves Austrian staples, some using organic local meats, in a pleasant location beside the river.

ℹ Information

Post Office (Auböckplatz 4; ☺8am-6pm Mon-Fri, 9am-noon Sat)

Salzkammergut Touristik (☑0613 224 000; www.salzkammergut.co.at; Götzstrasse 12; ☺9am-7pm, closed Sun Oct-Mar) Has bike rental (per 24 hours €13) and internet (per 10 minutes €1.10).

Tourist Office (☑277 57; www.badischl.at; Auböckplatz 5; ☺9am-6pm Mon-Sat, 10am-6pm Sun) Has a telephone service (8am to 10pm) for rooms and information.

ℹ Getting There & Around

BUS Buses depart from outside the train station, with hourly buses to St Gilgen (€5.10, 40 minutes). Buses to St Wolfgang (€3.80, 32 minutes) go via Strobl.

CAR & MOTORCYCLE Most major roads in the Salzkammergut go to or near Bad Ischl; Hwy 158 from Salzburg and the north–south Hwy 145 intersect just north of the town centre.

TRAIN Hourly trains to Hallstatt (€3.80, 25 minutes) go via Steeg/Hallstätter See, at the northern end of the lake, and continue on the eastern side via Hallstatt station to Obertraun (€5.70, 30 minutes). A boat from Hallstatt station (€2.40) takes you to the township. There are also frequent trains to Gmunden (€7.80, 40 minutes) and Salzburg (€22.70, two hours) via Attnang-Puchheim.

Hallstatt

☑06134 / POP 790

With pastel-hued homes, swans and towering mountains on either side of a glassy green lake, Hallstatt looks like some kind of greeting card for tranquillity. Boats chug lazily across the water from the train station to the village itself, which clings precariously to a tiny bit of land between mountain and shore. So small is the patch of land occupied by the village that its annual Corpus Christi procession takes place largely in small boats on the lake.

◉ Sights & Activities

Hallstatt has been classified a Unesco World Heritage site for its natural beauty and for evidence of human settlement dating back 4500 years. Over 2000 graves have been discovered in and around the village, most dating from 1000 to 500 BC.

Salzbergwerk
SALT MINE

(funicular return plus tour adult/child €24/12, tour only €12/6; ☺9.30am-4.30pm, closed early Nov–late Apr) The region's major cultural attraction is situated high above Hallstatt on Salzberg (Salt Mountain). In 1734 the fully preserved body of a prehistoric miner was found and today he is known as the 'Man in Salt'. The standard tour revolves around his fate, with visitors travelling down an underground railway and miners' slides (a photo is taken of you while sliding) to an illuminated subterranean salt lake.

The mine can be reached on foot or with the funicular.

Beinhaus
CHURCH

(Bone House; Kirchenweg 40; admission €1.50; ☺10am-6pm, closed Nov-Apr) Don't miss the macabre yet beautiful Beinhaus behind Hallstatt's parish church. It contains rows of stacked skulls painted with flowery designs and the names of the deceased. The old Celtic pagan custom of mass burial has been practised here since 1600 (mainly due to the lack of graveyard space), and the last skull in the collection was added in 1995.

Hallstätter See
LAKE

(boat hire per hr from €11) If you don't fancy a chilly dip in the crystal-clear waters, hire a rowboat, kayak or pedalo for a scenic spin of the lake.

🍴 Sleeping & Eating

Rooms fill quickly in summer, so book ahead, arrive early, or go straight for the tourist office and the staff will help you find something.

Pension Sarstein
GUESTHOUSE €

(☑82 17; Gosaumühlstrasse 83; d €55-70, apt €65-100; ☎) The affable Fischer family take

OBERTRAUN

At nearby Obertraun you'll find the intriguing Dachstein Rieseneishöhle (www.dachstein-salzkammergut.com; cable car return plus one cave adult/child €27/15, all-inclusive ticket adult/child €39/23). The caves are millions of years old and extend into the mountain for almost 80km in places. The ice itself is around 500 years old, and is increasing in thickness each year – the 'ice mountain' is 8m high, twice as high now as it was when the caves were first explored in 1910.

From Obertraun it's also possible to catch a cable car to Krippenstein (return adult/child €23/14; ⊙closed mid-Oct–Nov & Easter–mid-May), where you'll find the freaky 5 Fingers viewing platform, which protrudes over a sheer cliff face. Not for sufferers of vertigo.

pride in their little guesthouse, a few minutes' walk along the lakefront from central Hallstatt. The old-fashioned rooms are nothing flash, but they are neat, cosy and have balconies with dreamy lake and mountain views. Family-sized apartments come with kitchenettes.

Pension Hallberg　　GUESTHOUSE **€€**
(☑87 09; www.pension-hallberg.at.tf; Seestrasse 113; s €60-80, d €70-130) Interesting artefacts rescued from the lake line the staircase leading up to the rooms, the best of which are light and airy, furnished with pale wood and have superb views over the lake.

Gasthof Simony　　AUSTRIAN **€€**
(☑206 46; www.gasthof-simony.at; Wolfengasse 105; mains €9-17; ⊙lunch Thu-Sun, dinner Thu-Tue) What a view! With a garden right on the lakeshore, this is a prime setting for a panoramic lunch or dinner. Tuck into good old-fashioned home cooking: smoked trout with horseradish, goulash, strudel and the like.

ℹ Information

Tourist Office (☑82 08; www.dachstein-salzkammergut.at; Seestrasse 169; ⊙9am-6pm Mon-Fri, 9am-4pm Sat & Sun, closed Sat & Sun Sep-Jun) Turn left from the ferry to reach the office. It stocks the free leisure map of lakeside towns, and hiking and cycling trail maps.

ℹ Getting There & Away

BOAT The last ferry connection leaves Hallstatt train station at 6.50pm (€2.40, 10 minutes). Ferry excursions do the circuit Hallstatt Lahn via Hallstatt Markt, Obersee, Untersee and Steeg return (€10, 90 minutes) three times daily from July to early September.

BUS Eight to 10 buses connect Hallstatt (Lahn) town with Obertraun (€2.20, eight minutes) daily.

TRAIN Hallstatt train station is across the lake. The boat service from there to the village coincides with train arrivals. About a dozen trains daily connect Hallstatt and Bad Ischl (€3.80, 22 minutes) and Hallstatt with Bad Aussee (€3.80, 15 minutes).

Wolfgangsee

Wolfgangsee is a hugely popular place to spend the summer swimming, boating, walking or simply lazing by its soothing waters. Its two main resorts are St Wolfgang and St Gilgen, the first of which takes first prize in the beauty stakes.

Coming from Salzburg, the first town you come across is St Gilgen. It's a fine point from which to explore the surrounding region, and its tourist office (☑06227-23 48; www.wolfgangsee.at; Mondsee Bundesstrasse 1a; ⊙9am-7pm) can help with accommodation and activities.

St Wolfgang, towards the southern end of Wolfgangsee, is squeezed between the northern shoreline of the lake and the towering peak of Schafberg (1783m). Its tourist office (☑06138-80 03; www.wolfgangsee.at; Au 140; ⊙9am-7pm Mon-Fri, 9am-6pm Sat, 10am-5pm Sun) has plenty of information for travellers.

In the heart of the village you'll find the 14th-century Pilgrimage Church (donation €1; ⊙9am-6pm), a highly ornate example that still attracts pilgrims. Reaching the top of Schafberg is an easy exercise – from May to October, a cogwheel railway climbs to its summit in 40 minutes (one way/return €20.40/29.80). Otherwise it's a three- to four-hour walk.

Both St Wolfgang and St Gilgen have numerous pensions, starting from about €25 per person; the local tourist offices have details.

On the lakefront, 1km east of St Wolfgang, Camping Appesbach (☑06138 22 06; www.appesbach.at; Au 99; campsite per adult/child/tent €7/4.20/10; ℗) is a favourite with Austrian holidaymakers. A plusher option with lake views, a wellness area and two pools is **Im Weissen Rössl** (⌨06138-23 06; www.weissesroessl.at; Markt 74; s €128-184, d €156-318; **P@☎☜**), the setting for Ralph Benatzky's operetta *The White Horse*.

A ferry operates May to October between Strobl and St Gilgen (one way €9, 75 minutes), stopping at points en route. Services are most frequent from June to early September. Boats run from St Wolfgang to St Gilgen almost hourly during the day (one way €6.80, 50 minutes); the free *Eintauchen & Aufsteigen* timetable from local tourist offices gives exact times.

A Postbus service from St Wolfgang via Strobl to St Gilgen (€4.20, 30 minutes) is frequent out of season, but tails off somewhat in summer when the ships run. For Salzburg you need to connect in Strobl (€2.20, 12 minutes).

Northern Salzkammergut

Mondsee is popular for two reasons – its close proximity to Salzburg (only 30km) and its warm water. The main village on the lake, also called Mondsee, is home to an attractive 15th-century church that was used in the wedding scene of *The Sound of Music* and a small and helpful **tourist office** (⌨06232-22 70; www.mondsee.at; Dr Franz Müller Strasse 3; ☺8am-6pm Mon-Fri, 9am-6pm Sat & Sun, closed Sat & Sun Oct-May).

Lying to the east of Mondsee is **Attersee**, Salzkammergut's largest lake and a favourite with sailors. East again from Attersee you'll find **Traunsee** and its three main resorts: Gmunden, Traunkirchen and Ebensee. **Gmunden** is famous for its twin castles, linked by a causeway on the lake, and its green and white ceramics. Contact the local **tourist office** (⌨07612-64 305; www.traunsee.at; Toscanapark 1; ☺8am-8pm Mon-Fri, 10am-7pm Sat & Sun) for information on accommodation and activities on and around the lake.

Buses run every hour to Mondsee from Salzburg (€9.10, 55 minutes). Gmunden is connected to Salzburg by train (€17, 1¼ hours), via Attnang-Puchheim.

TIROL

With converging mountain ranges behind lofty pastures and tranquil meadows, Tirol (also Tyrol) captures a quintessential Alpine panoramic view. Occupying a central position is Innsbruck, the region's jewel, while in the northeast and southwest are superb ski resorts. In the southeast, separated somewhat from the main state since part of South Tirol was ceded to Italy at the end of WWI, lies the protected natural landscape of the Hohe Tauern National Park, an Alpine wonderland of 3000m peaks, including the country's highest, the Grossglockner (3798m).

Innsbruck

📞0512 / POP 121.300

Tirol's capital is a sight to behold. The mountains are so close that within 25 minutes it's possible to travel from the heart of the city to over 2000m above sea level. Summer and winter outdoor activities abound, and it's understandable why some visitors only take a peek at Innsbruck proper before heading for the hills. But to do so is a shame, for Innsbruck has its own share of gems, including an authentic medieval Altstadt (Old Town), inventive architecture and vibrant student-driven nightlife.

◉ Sights

Innsbruck's atmospheric, Altstadt is ideal for a lazy stroll. Many of the following sights listed close an hour or two earlier in winter.

TOP
CHOICE **Goldenes Dachl & Museum** MUSEUM
(Golden Roof; Herzog-Friedrich-Strasse 15; adult/child €4/2; ☺10am-5pm, closed Mon Oct-Apr) Innsbruck's golden wonder is this Gothic oriel, built for Emperor Maximilian I in 1500 and glittering with 2657 fire-gilt copper tiles. An audioguide whizzes you through the history in the museum; look for the grotesque tournament helmets designed to resemble the Turks of the rival Ottoman Empire.

Hofkirche CHURCH
(www.tiroler-landesmuseum.at; Universitätstrasse; adult/child €5/4, combined Volkskunstmuseum ticket adult/child €10/6; ☺9am-5pm Mon-Sat, 12.30-5pm Sun) The 16th-century Hofkirche is one of Europe's finest royal court churches. Top billing goes to the empty **sarcophagus** of Emperor Maximilian I (1459–1519), a masterpiece of German Renaissance sculpture, guarded by 28 giant bronze figures including Dürer's legendary King Arthur. You're now forbidden to touch the statues, but

numerous inquisitive hands have already polished parts of the dull bronze, including Kaiser Rudolf's codpiece!

Volkskunstmuseum   MUSEUM
(Folk Art Museum; www.tiroler-landesmuseum. at; Universitätstrasse; combined Hofkirche ticket adult/child €10/6; ⊙9am-5pm) Next door to the Hofkirche, the Volkskunstmuseum houses Tyrolean folk art from handcarved sleighs and Christmas cribs to carnival masks and cow bells.

Hofburg   PALACE
(Imperial Palace; www.hofburg-innsbruck.at; Rennweg 1; adult/child €8/free, Hofgarten admission free; ⊙palace 9am-5pm, garden 6am-dusk) Empress Maria Theresia gave this Habsburg palace a total baroque makeover in the 16th century. The highlight of the state apartments is the Riesensaal (Giant's Hall), lavishly adorned with frescos and paintings of Maria Theresia and her 16 children, including Marie Antoinette.

Tucked behind the palace is the Hofgarten, an attractive garden for a botanical stroll.

Bergisel   SKI JUMP
(www.bergisel.info; adult/child €9/4; ⊙9am-6pm) Rising above Innsbruck like a celestial staircase, this glass-and-steel ski jump was designed by much-lauded Iraqi architect Zaha Hadid. From May to July, fans pile in to see athletes train, while preparations step up a gear in January for the World Cup Four Hills Tournament.

It's 455 steps or a two-minute funicular ride to the 50m-high **viewing platform**. Here, the panorama of the Nordkette range,

Inn Valley and Innsbruck is breathtaking, though the cemetery at the bottom has undoubtedly made a few ski jumping pros quiver in their boots.

Tram 1 trundles from central Innsbruck to Bergisel.

Tiroler Landesmuseum
Ferdinandeum   GALLERY
(www.tiroler-landesmuseum.at; Art Museum; adult/child €10/6; ⊙9am-5pm Tue-Sun) This treasure-trove of Tyrolean history and art contains the original reliefs used to design the Goldenes Dachl. In the gallery you'll find old master paintings, Gothic altarpieces, a handful of Kokoschka and Klimt originals, and Viennese actionism works with shock factor.

Schloss Ambras   CASTLE
(www.khm.at/ambras; Schlossstrasse 20; adult/child €10/free; ⊙10am-5pm) Archduke Ferdinand II transformed Schloss Ambras from a fortress into a Renaissance palace in 1564. A visit takes in the ever-so-grand banquet hall, shining armour (look out for the 2.6m suit created for giant Bartlmä Bon) and room upon room of Habsburg portraits, with Titian, Velázquez and van Dyck originals. It's free to stroll or picnic in the expansive **gardens**.

Schloss Ambras is 4.5km southeast of the centre. Take bus 4134 from the Hauptbahnhof for discounted entry and a free return journey. The Sightseer bus also stops here.

FREE Dom St Jakob   CHURCH
(St James' Cathedral; Domplatz; ⊙10.15am-7.30pm Mon-Sat, 12.30-7.30pm Sun) Innsbruck's 18th-century cathedral is a feast of over-the-top baroque. The Madonna above the high altar is by the German Renaissance painter Lucas Cranach the Elder.

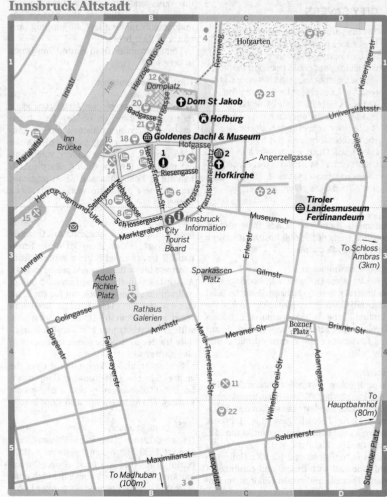

Alpenzoo
ZOO

(www.alpenzoo.at; Weiherburggasse 37; adult/child €8/4; ⊙9am-6pm) Home to Alpine wildlife like golden eagles, chamois and ibexes. To get there, walk up the hill from Rennweg or take bus W from Marktplatz.

Stadtturm
TOWER

(Herzog-Friedrich-Strasse 21, City Tower; adult/child €3/1.50; ⊙10am-8pm) Climb this tower's 148 steps for 360-degree views of the city's rooftops, spires and surrounding mountains.

⚡ Activities

Anyone who loves playing in the great outdoors will be itching to head up into the Alps in Innsbruck.

Nordkettenbahnen
FUNICULAR

(www.nordkette.com; one way/return to Hungerburg €4/6.80, Seegrube €14.60/23.40, Hafelekar €16.20/27; ⊙Hungerburgbahn 7am-7.15pm Mon-Fri, 8am-7.15pm Sat, Seegrubenbahn 8.30am-5.30pm, Hafelekarbahn 9am-5pm) Zaha Hadid's space-age funicular runs every 15 minutes, whizzing you from the Congress Centre to the slopes in no time. Walking trails head

Innsbruck Altstadt

off in all directions from **Hungerburg** and **Seegrube**. For more of a challenge, there is a downhill track for mountain bikers and two fixed-rope routes (*Klettersteige*) for climbers.

Patrolled by inquisitive Alpine sheep, the 2334m summit of **Hafelekar** affords tremendous views over Innsbruck to the snow-capped giants of the Austrian Alps, including 3798m Grossglockner.

Inntour   ADVENTURE SPORTS
(☑214 466; www.inntour.com; Leopoldstrasse 4; ☺9am-6.30pm Mon-Fri, to 5pm Sat) A one-stop adrenalin shop taking you canyoning (€75), tandem paragliding (€95), white-water rafting (€45) and bungee jumping (€140) from the 192m Europabrücke.

Olympia SkiWorld Innsbruck   SKIING
Innsbruck is the gateway to this massive ski arena, covering nine surrounding resorts and 300km of slopes to test all abilities. The most central place to pound powder is the **Nordkette/Seegrube**, accessed by the Nordkettenbahnen. A three-day/seven-day OlympiaWorld Ski Pass covering all areas costs €117/218; ski buses are free to anyone with a Club Innsbruck Card.

⌂ Sleeping

The tourist office has lists of private rooms costing between €20 and €40 per person.

Hotel Weisses Kreuz   HISTORIC HOTEL €€
(☑594 79; www.weisseskreuz.at; Herzog-Friedrich-Strasse 31; s €38-78, d €78-142; ☐@☎) Beneath the Altstadt's arcades, this atmospheric 500-year-old pile has played host to famous guests including a 13-year-old Mozart. With its wood-panelled parlours and twisting staircase, the hotel oozes history with every creaking beam. Rooms are supremely comfortable, staff charming and breakfast is a lavish spread.

TOP CHOICE Nepomuks   HOSTEL €
(☑584 118; www.nepomuks.at; Kiebachgasse 16; dm €23-25, d €56; ☎) Could this be backpacker heaven? Nepomuks sure comes close, with its Altstadt location, well-stocked kitchen and high-ceilinged dorms with homely touches like CD players. The delicious breakfast in attached Café Munding, with homemade pastries, jam and fresh-roasted coffee, gets your day off to a grand start.

Goldener Adler   HISTORIC HOTEL €€
(☑571 111; www.goldeneradler.com; Herzog-Friedrich-Strasse 6; s €85-125, d €126-240; ☐✳☎)

Since opening in 1390, the grand Goldener Adler has welcomed kings, queens and Salzburg's two biggest exports: Mozart and Mrs von Trapp. Rooms are elegant with gold drapes and squeaky-clean marble bathrooms.

Weisses Rössl
GUESTHOUSE €€

(☎583 057; www.roessl.at; Kiebachgasse 8; s €70-110, d €100-160; P@🖘) An antique rocking horse greets you at this late-16th-century guesthouse, with vaulted interiors and bright, spacious rooms. Host Mr Plank is a keen hunter and the restaurant (mains €10 to €26) has a meaty menu.

Mondschein
HOTEL €€

(☎227 84; www.mondschein.at; Mariahilfstrasse 6; s €87-105, d €105-180; P✳@🖘) As the name suggests, the moon lights the way to this riverside hotel. Done up in midnight blue and cream tones, rooms are light, spacious and classically elegant. Most have Altstadt views and the best sport Swarovski–crystal studded bathrooms.

Weinhaus Happ
GUESTHOUSE €€

(☎582 980; www.weinhaus-happ.at; Herzog-Friedrich-Strasse 14; s/d €75/110) Happ exudes old-world atmosphere. The '70s-style rooms could do with a lick of paint, but its plus points are many: prime views of the Goldenes Dachl, a cavernous wine cellar and a rustic restaurant (mains €7 to €21).

Pension Paula
GUESTHOUSE €

(☎292 262; www.pensionpaula.at; Weiherburggasse 15; s/d €41/65; P) Nestled in the hills above Innsbruck and with great city views, this family-run pension has super-clean,

homely rooms (most with balcony). It's 1km north of the Altstadt, near the Alpenzoo.

✕ Eating

TOP CHOICE Chez Nico
VEGETARIAN €€

(☎0650-451 06 24; www.chez-nico.at; Maria-Theresien-Strasse 49; lunch from €12.50, 6-course menu €51; ☺lunch & dinner Tue-Fri, dinner Sat; 🖉) Take a creative Parisian chef with an artistic eye and a passion for herbs, et voilà, you get Chez Nico. Nicolas Curtil (Nico) cooks seasonal vegetarian delights like porcini-sage ravioli and baked figs with rose sorbet at this intimate bistro.

Lichtblick
FUSION €€€

(☎566 550; www.restaurant-lichtblick.at; Rathaus Galerien; lunch €9.50-13, set menus €40-50; ☺10am-1am Mon-Sat) On the 7th floor of the Rathaus Galerien, this glass-walled restaurant has knockout views over Innsbruck to the mountains beyond. Season-driven specialities like homemade leek-truffle ravioli and schnitzel with chanterelles are all beautifully cooked and presented.

Cafe Munding
CAFE €

(www.munding.at; Kiebachgasse 16; cake €2-4; ☺8am-8pm) Scrumptious fruit tortes, cheesecakes, chocolate cake and home-roasted coffee.

Fischerhäusl
AUSTRIAN €€

(☎583 535; www.fischerhaeusl.com; Herrengasse 8; mains €9-21; ☺10.30am-1am Mon-Sat) The lemon-fronted Fischerhäusl has stood in this hidden spot between Domplatz and the Hofburg since 1758. On the menu is Tyrolean grub such as Kaspressknödelsuppe, cheesy dumplings swimming in broth, and Gröstl, a

---

DON'T MISS

AROUND INNSBRUCK

Just 9km east of Innsbruck is the town of Hall in Tirol. The labyrinth of pretty cobbled streets at its medieval heart pays testament to the massive wealth it accumulated from silver mines over the centuries. You can learn more about this legacy at **Burg Hasegg** (Burg Hasegg 6; adult/child €8/6; ☺10am-5pm Tue-Sun), a 14th-century castle that had a 300-year career as a mint for silver Thalers (coins, the root of the modern word 'dollar').

Another 9km east along the valley in Wattens is **Swarovski Kristallwelten** (Swarovski Crystal Worlds; http://kristallwelten.swarovski.com; Kristallweltenstrasse 1; adult/child €11/free; ☺9am-6.30pm), one of Austria's most-visited attractions. A crystal winterscape by Alexander McQueen, a kaleidoscopic crystal dome and a striking Terence Conran–designed shop are part of the fabulously glittering experience.

From Innsbruck, trains run frequently to Hall in Tirol (€2, eight minutes) and Fritzens-Wattens (€3.60, 16 minutes), 3km north of Swarovski Kristallwelten.

PICNIC GOODIES

s'Speckladele (Stiftgasse 4; ⊙9am-1pm & 2-6pm Mon-Fri, 9am-3pm Sat) This hole-in-the-wall shop has been doing a brisk trade in regional sausages, hams and speck made from 'happy pigs' for the past 60 years. Mini *Teufel* sausages with a chilli kick are the must-try.

s'Culinarium (Pfarrgasse 1; ⊙10am-6pm Mon-Sat) Herby Signor will help you pick an excellent bottle of Austrian wine at his shop-cum-bar.

Markthalle (www.markthalle-innsbruck.at; Innrain; ⊙7am-6.30pm Mon-Fri, to 1pm Sat) Freshly baked bread, Tyrolean cheese, organic fruit, smoked ham and salami – it's all under one roof at this riverside covered market.

potato, bacon and onion fry-up. The terrace fills quickly on warm days.

Ottoburg　　　　　　　　AUSTRIAN €€
(☑584 338; www.ottoburg.at; Herzog-Friedrich-Strasse 1; mains €16.50-28; ⊙lunch & dinner Tue-Sun; 🖩) This medieval castle hides a warren of wood-panelled *Stuben* (parlours). Dig into tournedos of venison, *Topfenknödel* (cottage-cheese dumplings) and other hearty fare.

Madhuban　　　　　　　　INDIAN €
(☑589 157; www.madhuban.at; Templstrasse 2; mains €7-12; ⊙lunch & dinner Mon-Fri, dinner Sat & Sun) If you've had your fill of schnitzel and strudel and fancy a little spice, Madhuban does a spot-on curry. The two-course lunch is a snip at €7.50.

Mamma Mia　　　　　　　　PIZZERIA €
(☑562 902; Kiebachgasse 2; mains €7-9; ⊙lunch & dinner) No-frills Italian bistro with a great buzz, huge pizzas and a shady terrace.

🍷 Drinking

Moustache　　　　　　　　BAR
(www.cafe-moustache.at; Herzog-Otto-Strasse 8; ⊙11am-2am Tue-Sun) You too can try your hand at playing Spot-the-Moustache (Einstein, Charlie Chaplin and others), the preferred pastime at this retro newcomer. It has a terrace overlooking pretty Domplatz, as well as Club Aftershave in the basement.

Hofgarten Café　　　　　　　　BAR
(Rennweg 6a; ⊙11am-2am Tue-Thu, to 4am Fri-Sun) DJs spin at this tree-shaded beer garden and star-studded pavilion. The happening events line-up skips from summer festivals to weekend house parties.

360°　　　　　　　　BAR
(Rathaus Galerien; ⊙10am-1am Mon-Sat) There's no better place to see Innsbruck start to twinkle. Grab a cushion and drink in 360-degree views of the city and Alps from the balcony skirting the circular bar.

Theresienbräu　　　　　　　　PUB
(Maria-Theresien-Strasse 53; ⊙11am-1am Mon-Wed, to 2am Thu-Sat, noon-9pm Sun) A lively microbrewery with a big beer garden for quaffing a cold one.

Elferhaus　　　　　　　　PUB
(Herzog-Friedrich-Strasse 11; ⊙10am-2am) Nurse a beer beside gothic gargoyles at the bar or take a church-like pew to hear live rock bands play.

☆ Entertainment

For up-to-date entertainment listings, visit www.innsider.at (in German).

Tiroler Landestheater　　　　　　　　COMEDY
(☑0512-520 744; www.landestheater.at; Rennweg 2; tickets €3-38; ⊙ticket office 8.30am-8.30pm Mon-Sat, 5.30-8.30pm Sun) This neoclassical theatre is the city's main stage for opera, dance and drama.

Treibhaus　　　　　　　　CULTURAL CENTRE
(www.treibhaus.at; Angerzellgasse 8; ⊙10am-1am) Young Innsbruckers flock to this cultural complex to enjoy the big garden terrace, the chilled atmosphere and regular DJs. There's free live music on Friday evenings.

❶ Information

Bubble Point (Innstrasse 11; ⊙7.30am-10.30pm Mon-Fri, 7.30am-10pm Sat & Sun) A laundry with high-speed internet for €2 per hour.

Innsbruck Information (☑535 60; www.innsbruck.info; Burggraben 3; ⊙9am-6pm) Main tourist office with truckloads of info on the city and surrounds, including skiing and walking. Sells ski passes, public-transport tickets and city maps (€1); will book accommodation (€3 commission) and has an attached ticketing service.

❶ Getting There & Away

AIR Innsbruck Airport, 4km to the west of the city centre, caters to national and international flights, handled mostly by Austrian Airlines, BA, easyJet and Welcome Air.

CAR & MOTORCYCLE The A12 and the parallel Hwy 171 are the main roads heading west and east. The B177, to the west of Innsbruck, continues north to Munich (Germany). The A13 is a toll road (€8) running south through the Brenner Pass to Italy and crossing the 192m Europabrücke, spanning the Sill River. Toll-free Hwy 182 follows the same route, passing under the bridge.

TRAIN Fast trains depart at least every two hours for Bregenz (€34.40, 2½ hours), Salzburg (€41.30, two hours), Kitzbühel (€19.20, 1½ hours) and Munich (€39.60, two hours). There are several daily services to Lienz (€19.20 to €35.20, 3¼ to 4½ hours).

❶ Getting Around

To/From the Airport The airport is 4km west of the centre and served by bus F. Buses depart every 15 or 20 minutes from Maria-Theresien-Strasse (€1.90); taxis charge about €10 for the same trip.

Car & Bicycle Street parking is very limited in the city centre. Parking garages (eg under the Altstadt) cost around €17 per day. At the same address as Inntour (p79) Die Börse rents

SUMMER IN THE ZILLERTAL

The Zillertal is one of Austria's greatest outdoor playgrounds. Come summer the valley buzzes with cyclists, with 1000km of well-marked trails reaching from easygoing valley jaunts to gruelling mountain passes. Bicycles are available for hire at train stations throughout the Zillertal for €8/12 per half/full day; www.zillertal.at has interactive maps and route descriptions.

Hikers head for the pristine Alpine landscapes of **Naturpark Zillertaler Alpen** (www.naturpark-zillertal.at). From May to October, the nature reserve runs 250 guided walks, from llama trekking to sunrise photo excursions, most costing around €5. For adrenalin-fuelled pursuits like rock climbing, rafting and paragliding, try **Action Club Zillertal** (☑62 977; www.actionclub-zillertal.com; Hauptstrasse 458 ; ☺9am-noon & 3-6pm) in Mayrhofen.

city, mountain, electric and children's bikes for €18/25/25/13 per day respectively.

Public Transport Single tickets on buses and trams cost €1.90 (from the driver; valid upon issue). A 24-hour ticket is €4.30.

Mayrhofen

☑05285 / POP 3820

Tirol is ribbed by beautiful valleys, but the Zillertal is among the best, its soaring peaks begging outdoor escapades. A central place to base yourself is Mayrhofen, a mecca for skiers and après-skiers in winter, and mountain bikers, hikers and lederhosen-clad *Volksmusik* (folk music) fans in summer.

Snow-sure Mayrhofen has varied skiing on 159km of slopes, one of Europe's best terrain parks for snowboarders and the infamous Harakiri, Austria's steepest piste with a 78% gradient. A one-day ski pass, valid for all cable cars and lifts, costs €45.

The **tourist office** (☑67 600; www.mayrhofen.at; Durfterstrasse 225; ☺9am-6pm Mon-Fri, 2-6pm Sat, 10am-2pm Sun) should be your first port of call for a handy accommodation booklet and the lowdown on activities.

Right in the centre, 500-year-old **Hotel Kramerwirt** (☑67 00; www.kramerwirt.at; Am Marienbrunnen 346; s incl half-board €91-117, d €158-210, mains €8-21; ☑🐾) has spacious rooms, a whirlpool for relaxing moments and a traditional restaurant.

To gorge on *Schlutzkropf'n* (fresh pasta filled with cheese) and the like in the cosiest of surrounds, head to woodsy chalet **Wirtshaus zum Griena** (☑62 778; www.wirtshaus-griena.at; Dorfhaus 768; mains €8-16; ☺Tue-Sun). Or assemble your own meaty snack at **Metzgerei Kröll** (Scheulingstrasse 382; snacks €3-8; ☺7.30am-12.30pm & 2.30-6pm Mon-Fri, 7am-noon Sat), famous for its aromatic *Schlegeis-Speck* ham cured at 1800m. Pizza and pasta dominate the menu at **Mamma Mia** (☑67 68; Einfahrt Mitte 432; mains €7-9; ☺11am-midnight).

Trains run regularly to Jenbach (€6.90, 55 minutes), where they connect with services to Innsbruck (€7.80, 20 minutes).

Kitzbühel

☑05356 / POP 8450

Kitzbühel began life in the 16th century as a silver- and copper-mining town, and today preserves a charming medieval centre despite its other persona – as a fashionable

KRIMML FALLS

The thunderous, three-tier Krimml Falls (www.wasserfaelle-krimml.at; adult/child €2.50/0.50, free Dec-Apr; ticket office 8am-6pm mid-Apr–late Oct) is Europe's highest waterfall at 380m, and one of Austria's most unforgettable sights. The pretty Alpine village of Krimml has a handful of places to sleep and eat; contact the tourist office (72 39; www.krimml.at; Oberkrimml 37; 8am-noon & 2-6pm Mon-Fri, 8.30-10.30am & 4.30-6pm Sat) for more information.

Krimml is on Hwy 168 (which becomes Hwy 165). Buses run year-round from Krimml to Zell am See (€9.90, 1¼ hours, hourly), with frequent onward train connections to Salzburg (€21.50, 1½ hours) .

and prosperous winter resort. It's renowned for the white-knuckled Hahnenkamm downhill ski race in January and the excellence of its slopes.

🏃 Activities

There's an Alpine flower garden (free) on Kitzbüheler Horn (note there's a toll road for drivers). The forest-fringed Schwarzsee, 3km to the northwest, is a fine location for summer swimming.

Skiing
SKIING
In winter there's first-rate intermediate skiing and freeriding on 170km of well-groomed slopes. A one-day AllStarCard ski pass covering Kitzbühel and the surrounding region costs €46.50.

Hiking
HIKING
Dozens of summer hiking trails thread through the Kitzbühel Alps; the tourist office gives walking maps and runs free guided hikes for guests staying in town. The Flex-Ticket covering all cable cars costs €43.50/36 with/without bus for three out of seven days.

🍴 Sleeping & Eating

The tourist office can help with accommodation, but it's best to book well ahead. Rates leap up by 50% in the high winter season.

For self-caterers, there's a Spar supermarket (Bichlstrasse 22) and Metzgerei

Huber (Bichlstrasse 14; snacks €3.50-7; 8am-6pm Mon-Fri, 8am-12.30pm Sat) for carnivorous snacks.

Villa Licht
HOTEL €€
(62 293; www.villa-licht.at; Franz-Reich-Strasse 8; d €150-230;) Pretty gardens, warm-hued rooms with pine trappings, mountain views – this charming Tyrolean chalet has the lot. Kids love the tree house and outdoor pool.

Snowbunny's Hostel
HOSTEL €
(067-6794 0233; www.snowbunnys.co.uk; Bichlstrasse 30; dm €25-40, d €74-100;) Friendly, laid-back hostel, a bunny-hop from the slopes. Breakfast is DIY-style in the kitchen, and there's a TV lounge, ski storage and shop for backpacker staples (Vegemite, Jägermeister etc).

Pension Kometer
PENSION €€
(622 89; www.pension-kometer.com; Gerbergasse 7; s €65-90, d €110-160;) Make yourself at home in the bright, sparkling clean rooms at this family run guesthouse. There's a relaxed lounge with games and DVDs. Breakfast is a treat with fresh breads, fruit and eggs.

Huberbräu Stüberl
AUSTRIAN €
(656 77; Vorderstadt 18; mains €7-13) This vaulted tavern serves hearty portions of Austrian classics, such as schnitzel and liver dumplings, cooked to perfection.

Hosteria
ITALIAN €
(733 02; Alf Petzoldweg 2; mains €8-16; lunch Thu-Mon, dinner Wed-Mon) Authentic antipasti and wood-fired pizzas are matched with fine wines and genuine smiles at this stylish little Italian.

ℹ Information

The tourist office (66 660; www.kitzbuehel.com; Hinterstadt 18; 8.30am-6pm Mon-Fri, 9am-6pm Sat, 10am-noon & 4-6pm Sun) has loads of info in English and a 24-hour accommodation board.

ℹ Getting There & Away

BUS It's quicker and cheaper to get from Kitzbühel to Lienz by bus (€14.70, two hours, twice daily) than by train.

CAR & MOTORCYCLE Kitzbühel is on the B170, 30km east of Wörgl and the A12/E45 motorway. Heading south to Lienz, you pass through some marvellous scenery. Hwy 108 (Felber Tauern Tunnel) and Hwy 107 (Grossglockner Rd; closed in winter) both have toll sections.

TRAIN Trains run frequently from Kitzbühel to Innsbruck (€19.20, 1¾ hours) and Salzburg (€28, 2½ hours). For Kufstein (€10, one hour), change at Wörgl.

St Anton am Arlberg

☏ 05446 / POP 2564

At the heart of the wild and austerely beautiful Arlberg region lies St Anton am Arlberg. In 1901 the first ski club in the Alps was founded here, downhill skiing was born and the village never looked back. Today the resort has legendary slopes and is Austria's unrivalled king of après ski.

☆ Activities

Skiing
SKIING

St Anton attracts both intermediate and advanced skiers and boarders, with challenging slopes, fantastic backcountry opportunities and a freestyle park on Rendl. A ski pass covering the whole Arlberg region and valid for all 85 ski lifts costs €47/257 for one/seven days in the high season.

Hiking
HIKING

(Wanderpass €31/36 for three/seven days) Naturally, hiking is the number-one summer pastime: the Wanderpass gives you a head start with access to all lifts.

H2O Adventure
ADVENTURE SPORTS

(☏ 05472-66 99; www.h2o-adventure.at; Bahnhofstrasse 1, Arlrock; ⊙May–mid-Oct) H2O Adventures gets adrenalin pumping, with activities from rafting to canyoning and mountain biking.

🛏 Sleeping & Eating

Rates can be almost double in the high winter season, when you'll need to book well ahead. Hit Dorfstrasse for snack bars and restaurants serving everything from tapas to Tex-Mex with a side order of après-ski. Most restaurants and bars close in summer.

Himmlhof
GUESTHOUSE €€

(☏ 232 20; www.himmlhof.com; Im Gries 9; d €164-304; P@🗑) This *himmlisch* (heavenly) Tyrolean chalet has wood-clad rooms brimming with original features (tiled ovens, four-poster beds and the like). An open fire and spa beckon after a day's skiing.

Altes Thönihaus
GUESTHOUSE €€

(☏ 28 10; www.altes-thoenihaus.at; Im Gries 1; s €60-64, d €116-124; P🗑) Dating to 1465, this listed wooden chalet oozes Alpine charm from every last beam. Fleecy rugs and pine keep the mood cosy in rooms with mountain-facing balconies. Downstairs there's a superb little spa and restored *Stube* (parlour).

Museum Restaurant
AUSTRIAN €€

(☏ 24 75; Rudi-Matt-Weg 10; mains €17.50-32.50; ⊙dinner) Arlberger hay soup, succulent Tyrolean beef and fresh-from-the-pond trout land on your plate at this wood-panelled restaurant, picturesquely housed in the village museum.

❶ Information

The **tourist office** (☏ 22 690; www.stanton-amarlberg.com; Dorfstrasse 8; ⊙8am-6pm Mon-Fri, 9am-6pm Sat, 9am-noon & 3-6pm Sun) has maps and information on accommodation and activities, and an accommodation board with free telephone outside.

❶ Getting There & Away

St Anton is on the main railway route between Bregenz (€19.20, 1½ hours) and Innsbruck (€21.50, 1¼ hours). The town is close to the eastern entrance of the Arlberg Tunnel, the toll road connecting Vorarlberg and Tirol. The tunnel toll is €8.50 one way. You can avoid the toll by taking the B197, but no vehicles with trailers are allowed on this winding road.

Lienz

☏ 04852 / POP 11.800

The Dolomites rise like an amphitheatre around Lienz, straddling the Isel and Drau rivers, and just 40km north of Italy. Those same arresting river and mountain views welcomed the Romans, who settled here some 2000 years ago. Lienz is also a stopover for skiers and hikers passing through or on the way to the Hohe Tauern National Park.

◉ Sights & Activities

Schloss Bruck
CASTLE

(Schlossberg 1; adult/child €7.50/2.50; ⊙10am-6pm mid-May–late Oct) Lienz' biggest crowd-puller is its medieval fortress. The museum displays everything from Tyrolean costumes to emotive paintings by famous local son Albin Egger-Lienz.

Stadtpfarrkirche St Andrä　CHURCH
(Pfarrgasse 4; ☺daylight hours) More of Albin
Egger-Lienz' sombre works can be seen at
the Gothic St Andrew's Church.

Aguntum　ARCHAEOLOGICAL SITE
(www.aguntum.info; Stribach 97; adult/child €6/4;
☺9.30am-5pm, closed Nov-Apr) For an insight
into Lienz' Roman past, visit the Aguntum
archaeological site.

Skiing　SKIING
A €36 day pass covers skiing on the nearby
Zettersfeld and **Hochstein** peaks. However, the area is more renowned for its 100km
of cross-country trails; the town fills up for
the annual **Dolomitenlauf** cross-country
skiing race in mid-January.

Dolomiten Lamatrekking　HIKING
(☑68 087; www.dolomitenlama.at) The Dolomites make for highly scenic hiking, with
cable cars rising to Hochstein (return €13)
and Zettersfeld (€10). From this outfitter
you can enlist a gentle-natured llama to accompany you.

🍴 Sleeping & Eating

The tourist office can point you in the direction of good-value guesthouses and camping
grounds.

Hotel Haidenhof　HOTEL €€
(☑624 40; www.haidenhof.at; Grafendorferstrasse
12; s €89-101, d €140-186; P🐾🛜) High above
Lienz, this country retreat has a dress-circle
view of the Dolomites. The spacious rooms
and roof terrace maximise those views.
Home-grown produce features in the restaurant (mains €16.50 to €26).

Romantik Hotel Traube　HOTEL €€
(☑644 44; www.hoteltraube.at; Hauptplatz 14;
s €65-99, d €134-190; P@🏊) Right on the
main square, Traube races you back to the
Biedermeier era with its high ceilings and
antique-meets-boutique rooms. The 6th-
floor pool affords views over Lienz to the
Dolomites.

Kirchenwirt　AUSTRIAN €€
(☑625 00; www.kirchenwirt-lienz.at; Pfarrgasse
7; mains €9-18; ☺9am-midnight) Up on a hill
opposite Stadtpfarrkirche St Andrä, this is
Lienz' most atmospheric restaurant. Dine
under the vaults or on the streamside terrace on local dishes like East Tyrolean
milk-fed lamb.

❶ Information

The **tourist office** (☑050-212 400; www.lien-
zerdolomiten.info; Europaplatz 1; ☺8am-6pm
Mon-Fri, 9am-noon & 4-6pm Sat) will find rooms
free of charge, or you can use the hotel board
(free telephone) outside. Free internet access
is available at the local **library** (Muchargasse 4;
☺9am-noon & 3-6pm Tue-Fri, 9am-noon Sat).

❶ Getting There & Away

There are several daily services to Innsbruck
(€19.20 to €35.20, 3¼ to 4½ hours). Trains run
every two hours to Salzburg (€37, 3½ hours). To
head south by car, you must first divert west or
east along Hwy 100.

Hohe Tauern National Park

If you thought Mother Nature pulled out all
the stops in the Austrian Alps, Hohe Tauern National Park was her magnum opus.
Straddling Tirol, Salzburg and Carinthia,
this national park is the largest in the Alps;
a 1786-sq-km wilderness of 3000m peaks,
Alpine meadows and waterfalls. At its heart
lies **Grossglockner** (3798m), Austria's highest mountain, which towers over the 8km-
long **Pasterze Glacier**, best seen from the
outlook at **Kaiser-Franz-Josefs-Höhe**
(2369m).

The 48km **Grossglockner Road** (www.
grossglockner.at; Hwy 107; car/motorcycle €32/22;
☺May-early Nov) from Bruck in Salzburgerland to Heiligenblut in Carinthia is one of
Europe's greatest Alpine drives. A feat of
1930s engineering, the road swings giddily
around 36 switchbacks, passing jewel-col-
oured lakes, forested slopes and wondrous
glaciers.

If you have wheels, you'll have more flexibility, although the road is open only between May and early November, and you
must pay tolls.

The major village on the Grossglockner Road is **Heiligenblut**, dominated by
mountain peaks and the needle-thin spire
of its 15th-century pilgrimage church.
Here you'll find a **tourist office** (☑04824-
27 00; www.heiligenblut.at; Hof 4; ☺9am-6pm),
which can advise on guided ranger hikes,
mountain hiking and skiing. The village
also has a campsite, a few restaurants
and a spick-and-span **Jugendherberge**
(hostel; ☑22 59; www.oejhv.or.at; Hof 36; dm/s/d
€20.50/28.50/49; P@).

Bus 5002 runs frequently between Lienz
and Heiligenblut on weekdays (€15.80, one

BREGENZERWALD

Only a few kilometres southeast of Bregenz, the forest-cloaked slopes, velvet-green pastures and limestone peaks of the Bregenzerwald unfold. In summer it's a glorious place to spend a few days hiking the hills and filling up on home-made cheeses in Alpine dairies. Winter brings plenty of snow, and the area is noted for its downhill and cross-country skiing. The Bregenzerwald tourist office (☑05512-23 65; www.bregenzerwald.at; Impulszentrum 1135, Egg; ☉9am-5pm Mon-Fri, 8am-1pm Sat) has information on the region.

hour), less frequently at weekends. From late June to mid-September, three buses run from Monday to Friday and Sunday, plus one on Saturday between Heiligenblut and Kaiser-Franz-Josefs-Höhe (€7.90, 30 minutes). Check the timetables with the tourist office in Lienz before setting off.

VORARLBERG

Vorarlberg has always been a little different. Cut off from the rest of Austria by the snow-capped Arlberg massif, this westerly region has often associated itself more with Switzerland than Vienna far to the east, and its citizens have developed a strong dialect even Tyroleans find hard to decipher.

Trickling down from the Alps to the shores of Bodensee (Lake Constance), Vorarlberg is an alluringly beautiful destination in its own right, attracting everyone from classical-music buffs to skiers. It's also a gateway, by rail or water, to Germany, Liechtenstein and Switzerland.

Bregenz

☑05574 / POP 28,000

Clichéd though it sounds, Vorarlberg's pocket-sized capital really does seem to have it all, with its mountains-meets-lake location, avant-garde art and monster of an opera festival. Every sunray is used to the max in summer for boating, cycling, swimming and lounging on the shores of Bodensee.

◉ Sights

Kunsthaus   GALLERY

(www.kunsthaus-bregenz.at; Karl-Tizian-Platz; adult/child €9/free; ☉10am-6pm Tue-Sun, to 9pm Thu) The architecturally eye-catching Kunsthaus, by award-winning Swiss architect Peter Zumthor, hosts first-rate contemporary art exhibitions.

Oberstadt   HISTORIC AREA

Set high above the modern centre is the Oberstadt, the storybook old town; look for the enormous onion dome of the Martinsturm (St Martin's Tower; www.martinsturm.at; Martinsgasse; adult/child €3.50/1; ☉10am-5pm Tue-Sun Apr-Oct), reputedly the largest in central Europe.

Pfänder Cable Car   CABLE CAR

(www.pfaenderbahn.at; Steinbruchgasse 4; one-way adult/child €6.50/3.20, return €11.20/5.60; ☉8am-7pm) For spectacular views of the lake, town and not-so-distant Alps, catch the cable car, which rises to 1064m.

🏃 Activities

Bregenz' shimmering centrepiece is the Bodensee, Europe's third-largest lake, straddling Austria, Switzerland and Germany. Lakeside activities include sailing and diving at Lochau, 5km north of town, and swimming.

Bodensee Radweg   CYCLING

(www.bodensee-radweg.com) In summer, the well-marked Bodensee Radweg that circumnavigates the Bodensee becomes an autobahn for lycra-clad *Radfahrer* (cyclists). Hire your own set of wheels at Fahrradverleih Bregenz (Seepromenade; per day city bike €15-18, e-bike €25; ☉9am-7pm Apr-Oct).

🎪 Festivals & Events

The Bregenzer Festspiele (Bregenz Festival; ☑407-6; www.bregenzerfestspiele.com), running from mid-July to mid-August, is the city's premier cultural festival. World-class operas and orchestral works are staged on the Seebühne, a floating stage on the lake, in the Festspielhaus and at the Vorarlberger Landestheater. Tickets are up for grabs about nine months before the festival.

🛏 Sleeping & Eating

Prices soar and beds are at a premium during the Bregenzer Festspiele – book ahead.

TOP CHOICE Deuring-Schlössle   HISTORIC HOTEL €€€
(☑478 00; www.deuring-schloessle.at; Ehre-
Guta-Platz 4; d €212-240, ste €314-420; P@⑤)
Bregenz' best rooms are found in this fabulously renovated old castle. Each one is
decorated differently, but all have loads of
medieval charm and grace. Its restaurant
(mains around €30) is also Bregenz' best,
with a sophisticated look and a market-
fresh menu.

JUFA Gästehaus Bregenz   HOSTEL €
(☑05708-35 40; www.jufa.at/bregenz; Mehrerauer-
strasse 5; dm €28.20; P@) Housed in a former
needle factory near the lake, this HI hostel
now reels backpackers in with its super-
clean dorms and excellent facilities including a common room and restaurant.

Hotel Weisses Kreuz   HOTEL €€
(☑498 80; www.hotelweisseskreuz.at; Römerstrasse 5; s €109-119, d €126-186, mains €14-29;
P❋@⑤) Service is attentive at this central
pick, with a restaurant rolling out seasonal
Austrian fare. The smart rooms sport cherry
wood furnishings, flat-screen TVs and organic bedding.

Wirtshaus am See   AUSTRIAN €€
(☑422 10; www.wirtshausamsee.at; Seepromenade
2; mains €11-18; ⊙9am-midnight) Snag a table
on the lakefront terrace at this mock half-
timbered villa, dishing up local specialities
like buttery Bodensee whitefish and venison
ragout. It's also a relaxed spot for quaffing
a cold one.

Cafesito   CAFE €
(Maurachgasse 6; bagels €3-4; ⊙7.45am-6.30pm
Mon-Fri, 9am-2.30pm Sat) Tiny Cafesito does
the best create-your-own bagels, smoothies
and fair-trade coffee in town.

❶ Information

Bregenz' **tourist office** (☑49 59; www.bregenz.
travel; Rathausstrasse 35a; ⊙9am-6pm Mon-
Fri, to noon Sat) has information on the city and
the surrounding area, and can help with
accommodation.

❶ Getting There & Away

BOAT From April to mid-October, there's a
frequent boat service between Bregenz and a
number of towns and cities on the Bodensee,
including Konstanz (one way €16.40, 4¼
hours), Lindau (€5.30, 22 minutes) and Friedrichshafen (€13.50, two hours) in Germany.

For information, consult www.bodenseeschiff-
fahrt.at.

TRAIN Trains to Munich (€45.40, three hours)
often go via Lindau (€2.20, nine minutes), and
Zürich (€34, 2¼ hours) via St Gallen (€14, 50
minutes). Twelve trains depart daily for Innsbruck (€34.40, 2½ hours). Trains to Konstanz
(€32.40, 1¾ to 2½ hours) may be frequent, but
require between one and four changes.

UNDERSTAND AUSTRIA

History

Austria has been a galvanic force in shaping
Europe's history. This landlocked little country was once the epicentre of the mighty
Habsburg empire and, in the 20th century, a
pivotal player in the outbreak of WWI.

Civilisation & Empire

Like so many European countries, Austria
has experienced invasions and struggles
since time immemorial. There are traces of
human occupation since the ice age, but it
was the Celts who made the first substantial
mark on Austria around 450 BC. The Romans followed 400 years later, and in turn
were followed by Bavarians and, in 1278, the
House of Habsburg, which took control of
the country by defeating the head of the Bavarian royalty.

The Habsburg Monarchy

For six centuries the Habsburgs used strategic marriages to maintain their hold over a
territory that encompassed much of central
and Eastern Europe and, for a period, even
Germany. But defeat in WWI brought that
to an end, when the Republic of Austria was
formed in 1918.

The 16th and 17th centuries saw the Ottoman threat reach the gates of Vienna, and in
1805 Napoleon defeated Austria at Austerlitz. Austrian Chancellor Metternich cleverly
reconsolidated Austria's power in 1815 after
Waterloo, but the loss of the 1866 Austro-
Prussian War, and creation of the Austro-
Hungarian empire in 1867, diminished the
Habsburg's influence in Europe.

However, these setbacks pale beside
Archduke Franz Ferdinand's assassination
by Slavic separatists in Sarajevo on 28 June
1914. When his uncle, the Austro-Hungarian
emperor Franz Josef, declared war on Serbia

in response, the ensuing 'Great War' (WWI) would prove the Habsburgs' downfall.

WWII & Postwar Austria

During the 1930s the Nazis began to influence Austrian politics, and by 1938 the recession-hit country was ripe for picking. Invading German troops met little resistance and Hitler was greeted on Heldenplatz as a hero by 200,000 Viennese.

Austria was heavily bombed during WWII, but the country recovered well, largely through the Marshall Plan and sound political and economic decisions (excluding its foray with the far-right Freedom Party and its controversial leader, Jörg Haider, in the 1990s). Austria has maintained a neutral stance since 1955, been home to a number of international organisations, including the UN, since 1979, and joined the EU in 1995.

Austria today enjoys the kind of economic, social and political stability that many other nations would dream of. Cities forging ahead include Linz, which seized the reins as European Capital of Culture in 2009, and Innsbruck, which hosted the first Winter Youth Olympics in 2012. Vienna, too, has plenty to look pleased about, topping the Mercer Quality of Living List in 2011 and with a shiny new Hauptbahnhof in the making.

Arts & Architecture

Classical Music

What other country can match the musical heritage of Austria? Great composers were drawn to Vienna by the Habsburgs' generous patronage during the 18th and 19th centuries. The era most strongly associated with Austrian music is *Wiener Klassik* (Vienna Classic), which dates back to the mid- and late 18th century and has defined the way we perceive classical music today. It began life as a step down from the celestial baroque music of the royal court and church, and shifted the focus of performance onto the salons and theatres of upper middle-class society.

Joseph Haydn (1732–1809) is considered to be the first of the great composers of the *Wiener Klassik* era, followed by Salzburg wunderkind Wolfgang Amadeus Mozart (1756–91). Beethoven's musical genius reached its zenith in Vienna. *Lieder* (song) master Franz Schubert (1797–1828) was the last of the heavyweight *Wiener Klassik* composers.

Vienna Secession & Expressionism

In 1897, 19 progressive artists broke away from the conservative artistic establishment and formed the Vienna Secession (*Sezession*) movement, synonymous with art nouveau. Vienna turned out such talents as the painter Gustav Klimt (1862–1918); Schloss Belvedere showcases one of his finest works, *The Kiss*. Vienna-born architect Otto Wagner (1841–1918) ushered in a new, functional direction around the turn of the 20th century and gave the capital a metro system replete with attractive art nouveau stations.

Gustav Klimt strongly influenced the work of well-known Austrian expressionists like Egon Schiele (1890–1918), who was obsessed with capturing the erotic on canvas, and Oskar Kokoschka (1886–1980). The paintings of these three Austrian greats hang out in the Leopold Museum in Vienna's MuseumsQuartier.

Baroque Heyday

Thanks to the Habsburg monarchy and its obsession with pomp and splendour, Austria is packed with high-calibre architecture, which reached giddy heights of opulence during the baroque era of the late 17th and early 18th century. It took the graceful column and symmetry of the Renaissance and added elements of the grotesque, burlesque and the saccharin.

Johann Bernhard Fischer von Erlach (1656–1723), the mastermind behind Schloss Schönbrunn, was the country's greatest baroque architect. Like Fischer von Erlach, Austria's second architect of the era, Johann Lukas von Hildebrandt (1668–1745), was famous for his interior decorative work of palaces for the aristocracy, such as Schloss Belvedere. Paul Troger (1698–1762) is Austria's master of the baroque fresco and his work is best appreciated at Stift Melk. Other baroque highlights include Karlskirche in Vienna, Salzburg's Dom and the Hofburg in Innsbruck.

Food & Drink

Staples & Specialities

Austria is famous for its Wiener schnitzel, goulash and desserts like *Sacher Torte*

(Sacher cake) and *Kaiserschmarrn* (sweet pancakes with raisins). Certainly, these classics are not to be missed, but the Austrian table offers a host of other regional and seasonal delights. Throw in excellent red wines from Burgenland and quality whites and reds from Lower Austria, Styria and elsewhere, and you have the makings of an exciting and unexpected culinary experience.

In Lower Austria try Waldviertel game, beef and poppy dishes, tangy cider from the Mostviertel, and pike and carp from Burgenland. The Wachau goes mad for *Marillen* (apricots) around mid-July. Styria is renowned for its *Almochsen* (meadow beef) and healthy, nutty pumpkin oil. Upper Austria is *Knödel* (dumpling) country, while the must-eat in neighbouring Salzburgerland is *Salzburger Nockerln,* a sweet soufflé. Freshwater fish in Carinthia, *Heumilchkäse* (hay milk cheese) from Vorarlberg and Tirol's hearty *Gröstl* (a fry-up from leftover potatoes, pork and onions) are other regional specialities.

Where to Eat & Drink

Solid Austrian fare is on the menu in Vienna's homely, good-value inns called *Beisl* (small taverns; from the Yiddish word for 'little houses'). Besides cake, most coffee houses serve light or classic dishes like goulash. In the winegrowing regions, rustic *Heurigen* (wine taverns) sell their wine directly from their own premises and food is available buffet-style. They open on a roster so pick up the local *Heurigenkalendar* (*Heurigen* calendar) from the tourist offices.

For cheap food, try *Mensen* (university canteens). Another money-saving trick is to make lunch the main meal of the day, as many Austrians do; most restaurants provide a good-value *Tagesteller* or *Tagesmenü* (fixed-price menu). You can assemble your own picnic at local farmers markets.

SURVIVAL GUIDE

Directory A–Z
Accommodation

From simple mountain huts to five-star hotels fit for kings – you'll find the lot in Austria. Tourist offices invariably keep lists and details, and some arrange bookings for free or for a nominal fee. Some useful points:

» It's wise to book ahead at all times, particularly during the high seasons: July and August and December to April (in ski resorts).
» Be aware that confirmed reservations in writing are considered binding, and cancellations within several days of arrival often involve a fee or full payment.
» Some hostels and some rock-bottom digs have an *Etagendusche* (communal shower).
» Very often a hotel won't have lifts; if this is important, always check ahead.
» In mountain resorts, high-season prices can be up to double the prices charged in the low season (May to June and October to November).
» In some resorts (not often in cities), a *Gästekarte* (guest card) is issued if you stay overnight, which offers discounts on things such as cable cars and admission.
» Locally, always check the city or region website, as many (such as in Vienna, Salzburg and Graz) have an excellent booking function.

Some useful websites:
Austrian Hotelreservation (www.austrian-hotelreservation.at)
Austrian National Tourist Office (www.austria.info)
Booking.com (www.booking.com)
Hostelling International (HI; www.hihostels.com)
Hostelworld (www.hostelworld.com)

THROUGH THE GRAPEVINE

The 830km **Weinstrasse Niederösterreich** (www.weinstrassen.at; Lower Austria Wine Rd) wends through eight wine-producing regions in Lower Austria, including the Kremstal, Kamptal and Weinviertel, passing beautiful terraced vineyards, bucolic villages, castles and abbeys. Visit the website for the low-down on local wineries (some with accommodation), wine shops and rustic *Heurigen* (wine taverns), where you can taste the region's pinot blanc (Weissburgunder), grüner veltliner, Riesling and red wines. Autumn is the time for semifermented *Sturm* (new wine).

PRACTICALITIES

» **Opening Hours** Most sights and tourist offices operate on reduced hours from November to March. Opening hours we provide are for the high season, so outside those months it can be useful to check ahead.

» **Seasonal Closures** In the Alps, many hotels, restaurants and sometimes tourist offices close between seasons, from around May to mid-June and mid-September to early December.

» **Concessions** Museums and sights have concessions for families, children (generally under 16 year olds), students and senior citizens; you may need to show proof of age. Children under 12 years usually receive a substantial discount on rooms they share with parents.

» **Smoking** Unless a separate room has been set aside, smoking is not allowed in restaurants. It's legal to smoke anywhere on outdoor terraces.

PRICE RANGES

Our reviews refer to double rooms with private bathrooms, except in hostels or where otherwise specified. Quoted rates are for the high season: December to April in the Alps, June and August everywhere else.

€€€ more than €200

€€ €80 to €200

€ less than €80

Activities

Austria is a wonderland for outdoorsy types, with much of the west given over to towering Alpine peaks. Opportunities for hiking and mountaineering are boundless in Tirol, Salzburgerland and the Hohe Tauern National Park, all of which have extensive Alpine hut networks (see www.alpenverein.at). Names like St Anton, Kitzbühel and Mayrhofen fire the imagination of serious skiers, but you may find cheaper accommodation and lift passes in little-known resorts; visit www.austria.info for the lowdown.

Business Hours

Banks 8am-3pm Mon-Fri, to 5.30pm Thu

Clubs 10pm to late

Post offices 8am-noon & 2-6pm Mon-Fri, 8am-noon Sat

Pubs 6pm-1am

Cafes 7.30am-8pm; hours vary widely

Restaurants noon-3pm, 7-11pm

Shops 9am-6.30pm Mon-Fri, 9am-5pm Sat

Supermarkets 9am-8pm Mon-Sat

Discount Cards

Regional Various discount cards are available, many of them covering a whole region or province. Some are free with an overnight stay.

Student & Youth Cards International Student Identity Cards (ISIC) and the European Youth Card (Euro<26; check www.euro26.org for discounts) will get you discounts at most museums, galleries and theatres. Admission is generally a little higher than the price for children.

Discount Rail Cards See p94.

Embassies & Consulates

All of the embassies and consulates listed following are located in Vienna (telephone prefix ☑01).

Australian Embassy (☑506 740; www.australian-embassy.at; Mattiellistrasse 2-4, Vienna)

Canadian Embassy (☑5313 83 000; www.canadainternational.gc.ca; Laurenzerberg 2, Vienna)

New Zealand Embassy (☑505 30 21; www.nzembassy.com/austria; Mattiellistrasse 2-4, Vienna)

UK Embassy (☑716 130; http://ukinaustria.fco.gov.uk; Jaurèsgasse 12, Vienna)

US Embassy (☑313 390; http://austria.usembassy.gov; Boltzmanngasse 16, Vienna)

Food

Price ranges in this chapter are for a two-course meal excluding drinks:

€€€ more than €30

€€ €15 to €30

€ less than €15

Money

ATMs Some *Bankomaten* (ATMs) are 24 hours. Most accept at the very least Maestro debit cards and Visa and MasterCard credit cards.

Credit Cards Visa and MasterCard (Eurocard) are accepted a little more widely than American Express (Amex) and Diners Club.

Taxes *Mehrwertsteuer* (MWST; value-added tax) is set at 20% for most goods.

Tipping It's customary to tip about 10% in restaurants, bars and cafes, and in taxis.

Transfers For emergency transfers, Western Union (www.westernunion.com) offices are available in larger towns.

Public Holidays

New Year's Day (Neujahr) 1 January

Epiphany (Heilige Drei Könige) 6 January

Easter Monday (Ostermontag) March/April

Labour Day (Tag der Arbeit) 1 May

Whit Monday (Pfingstmontag) Sixth Monday after Easter

Ascension Day (Christi Himmelfahrt) Sixth Thursday after Easter

Corpus Christi (Fronleichnam) Second Thursday after Whitsunday

Assumption (Maria Himmelfahrt) 15 August

National Day (Nationalfeiertag) 26 October

All Saints' Day (Allerheiligen) 1 November

Immaculate Conception (Mariä Empfängnis) 8 December

Christmas Day (Christfest) 25 December

St Stephen's Day (Stephanitag) 26 December

Telephone

Austrian telephone numbers consist of an area code followed by the local number.

Country code ☑43

International access code ☑00

Mobile Phones The network works on GSM 1800 and is compatible with GSM 900 phones. Phone shops sell prepaid SIM cards for about €10.

Public Telephones Phonecards in different denominations are sold at post offices and *Tabak* (tobacconist) shops. Call centres are widespread in cities, and many internet cafes are geared for Skype calls.

WHERE TO STAY

Hotels & Pensions Hotels and pensions (B&Bs) are rated by the same criteria from one to five stars.

Hostels In Austria over 100 hostels (*Jugendherberge*) are affiliated with Hostelling International (HI). Facilities are often excellent. Four- to six-bed dorms with shower/toilet are the norm, though some places also have doubles and family rooms. See www.oejhv. or.at or www.oejhw.at for details.

Private Rooms *Privatzimmer* (private rooms) are cheap (often about €50 per double). On top of this, you will find *Bauernhof* (farmhouses) in rural areas, and some *Öko-Bauernhöfe* (organic farms).

Alpine Huts There are over 530 of these huts in the Austrian Alps; most are maintained by the Österreichischer Alpenverein (ÖAV; Austrian Alpine Club; www.alpenverein.at, in German). Meals are often available. Bed prices for nonmembers are around €26 to €44 in a dorm; ÖAV members pay half-price.

Rental Accommodation *Ferienwohnungen* (self-catering apartments) are ubiquitous in Austrian mountain resorts; advance booking is recommended. Contact a local tourist office for lists and prices.

Camping Austria has over 490 camping grounds, many well equipped and scenically located. Prices can be as low as €4 per person or small tent and as high as €10. Many close in winter, so phone ahead to check. Search for camping grounds by region at www. camping-club.at (in German).

Eco-Hotels To search *Bio-* or *Öko-* ('eco') hotels by region, see www.biohotels.info.

Tourist Information

Tourist offices, which are dispersed far and wide in Austria, tend to adjust their hours from one year to the next, so business hours may have changed slightly by the time you arrive.

The Austrian National Tourist Office (www.austria.info) has a number of overseas offices. There is a comprehensive listing on the ANTO website.

Visas

Schengen visa rules apply. See p585 for further details. The Austrian Foreign Ministry website, www.bmeia.gv.at, lists embassies.

Getting There & Away

Air

Vienna is the main transport hub for Austria, but Graz, Linz, Klagenfurt, Salzburg and Innsbruck all receive international flights. Flights to these cities are often a cheaper option than those to the capital, as are flights to Airport Letisko (Bratislava Airport), 85km east of Vienna in Slovakia.

Among the low-cost airlines, Ryanair and Air Berlin fly to Graz, Innsbruck, Klagenfurt, Linz, Salzburg and Vienna (Ryanair to Bratislava for Vienna).

Following are the key international airports in Austria:

Graz Airport (✆29 020; www.flughafen-graz.at)

Innsbruck Airport (INN; ✆0512-22 525; www.innsbruck-airport.com)

Klagenfurt Airport (KLU; ✆0463-41 500; www.klagenfurt-airport.com)

Blue Danube Airport (LNZ; ✆0722-16 00; www.flughafen-linz.at)

Salzburg Airport (SZG; ✆0662-85 800; www.salzburg-airport.com)

Vienna Airport (VIE; ✆01-7007 22 233; www.viennaairport.com)

Airport Bratislava (BTS; ✆421 2 3303 33 53; www.airportbratislava.sk) Serves Bratislava and has good transport connections to Vienna. Used by Ryanair.

Land

BUS

Buses depart from Austria for as far afield as England, the Baltic countries, the Netherlands, Germany and Switzerland. But most significantly, they provide access to Eastern European cities small and large – from the likes of Sofia and Warsaw, to Banja Luka, Mostar and Sarajevo.

Services operated by Eurolines (www.eurolines.at) leave from Vienna and from several regional cities.

CAR & MOTORCYCLE

There are numerous entry points into Austria by road from Germany, the Czech Republic, Slovakia, Hungary, Slovenia, Italy and Switzerland. All border-crossing points are open 24 hours.

Standard European insurance and paperwork rules apply.

TRAIN

Austria has excellent rail connections. The main services in and out of the country from the west normally pass through Bregenz, Innsbruck or Salzburg en route to Vienna. Trains to Eastern Europe leave from Vienna. Express services to Italy go via Innsbruck or Villach; trains to Slovenia are routed through Graz.

Express & High-Speed Trains Express trains are identified by the symbols EC (EuroCity; serving international routes) or IC (InterCity; serving national routes).

Online Timetables ÖBB (✆05 17 17; www.oebb.at) Austrian National Railways, with national and international connections. Only national connections have prices online.

Reservations Extra charges can apply on fast trains and international trains, and it is a good idea (sometimes obligatory) to make seat reservations for peak times.

SparSchiene (discounted ÖBB tickets) These are often available when you book online in advance and can cost as little as a third of the standard train fare.

River & Lake

Hydrofoils run to Bratislava and Budapest from Vienna; slower boats cruise the Danube between the capital and Passau. The Danube Tourist Commission (www.danube-river.org) has a country-by-country list of operators and agents who can book tours. Germany and Switzerland can be reached from Bregenz.

Getting Around

Air

Flying within a country the size of Austria is not usually necessary. The main airline serving longer routes is **Austrian Airlines** (www.austrian.com) The national carrier and its joint flight operator Tyrolean offer several flights daily between Vienna and Graz, Innsbruck, Klagenfurt, Linz and Salzburg.

Bicycle

Bike Hire All cities have at least one bike shop that doubles as a rental centre; expect to pay around €10 to €15 per day.

Bike Touring Most tourist boards have brochures on cycling facilities and plenty of designated cycling routes within their region. Separate bike tracks are common in cities, and long-distance tracks and routes also run along major rivers such as the Danube and lakes such as Wörthersee in Carinthia and Bodensee (Lake Constance) in Vorarlberg.

Bike Transport You can take bicycles on any train with a bicycle symbol at the top of its timetable. A day ticket costs €5 for regional, €10 for national (InterCity) and €12 for international trains. You can't take bicycles on buses.

Boat

The Danube serves as a thoroughfare between Vienna and Lower and Upper Austria. Services are generally slow, scenic excursions rather than functional means of transport.

Bus

Postbus services usually depart from outside train stations. In remote regions, there are fewer services on Saturday and often none on Sunday. Generally, you can only buy tickets from the drivers. For information inside Austria, call ☑0810 222 333 (6am to 8pm); from outside Austria, call ☑+43 1 71101, or visit the website, www.postbus.at.

Car & Motorcycle

Autobahns ('A') and *Bundesstrassen* ('B') are major roads, while *Landstrassen* ('L') let you enjoy the ride and are usually good for cyclists. A daily motorail service links Vienna to Innsbruck, Salzburg and Villach.

AUTOMOBILE ASSOCIATIONS

Annual membership for Austria's two automobile associations costs €75.60 and includes a free 24-hour breakdown service. The two associations:

ARBÖ (☑24hr emergency assistance 123, office 123 123; www.arboe.at; Mariahilfer Strasse 180, Vienna; ⊙office telephone 6am-7pm daily, office premises 8am-5.30pm Mon-Fri)

ÖAMTC (☑24hr emergency assistance 120, office 01-711 99-0; www.oeamtc.at; Schubertring 1-3, Vienna; ⊙8am-6pm Mon-Fri, 9am-1pm Sat)

HIRE

Multinational car-hire firms Avis (www.avis.at), Budget (www.budget.at), Europcar (www.europcar.co.at) and Hertz (www.hertz.at) all have offices in major cities; ask at tourist offices for details. The minimum age for hiring small cars is 19 years, or 25 years for larger, 'prestige' cars. Customers must have held a driving licence for at least a year. Many contracts forbid customers to take cars outside Austria, particularly into Eastern Europe.

MOTORWAY & TUNNEL TOLLS

A *Vignette* (toll sticker) is imposed on all motorways; charges for cars/motorbikes are €8.30/4.80 for 10 days and €24.20/12.10 for two months. *Vignette* can be purchased at border crossings, petrol stations and *Tabak* shops. There are additional tolls (usually €2.50 to €10) for some mountain tunnels.

ROAD RULES

» The minimum driving age is 18.

» Drive on the right, overtake on the left.

» Give way to the right at all times except when a priority road sign indicates otherwise. Trams always have priority.

» An international driving licence should always be carried.

» Seat belts are compulsory.

» The speed limit is 50km/h in built-up areas, 130km/h on motorways and 100km/h on other roads. Except for the A1 (Vienna–Salzburg) and the A2 (Vienna–Villach), the speed limit is 110km/h on the autobahn from 10pm to 5am.

» The penalty for drink-driving – over 0.05% – is a hefty on-the-spot fine and confiscation of your driving licence.

» Crash helmets are compulsory for motorcyclists and their passengers, not for cyclists.

» Children under the age of 14 who are shorter than 1.5m must have a special seat or restraint.

» Carrying a warning triangle, safety vest and first-aid kit in your vehicle is compulsory.

» Winter tyres and/or snow chains are compulsory from November to mid-April.

» It's illegal to hitchhike on Austrian motorways.

Train

Austria has a clean, efficient rail system, and if you use a discount card it's very inexpensive.

Disabled Passengers Use the 24-hour ⏰05-17 17 customer number for special travel assistance; do this at least 24 hours ahead of travel (48 hours ahead for international services). Staff at stations will help with boarding and alighting.

Fares Fares quoted here are for 2nd-class tickets.

Information ÖBB (www.oebb.at) is the main operator, supplemented with a handful of private lines. Tickets and timetables are available online.

RailJet It's worth seeking out RailJet train services connecting Vienna, Graz, Villach, Salzburg, Innsbruck, Linz and Klagenfurt, as they travel up to 200km/h.

Reservations In 2nd class within Austria this costs €3.50 for most express services; recommended for travel on weekends.

RAIL PASSES

Depending on the amount of travelling you intend to do in Austria, rail passes can be a good deal.

Eurail Austria Pass This handy pass is available to non-EU residents; prices start at €123 for three days' unlimited 2nd-class travel within one month, and youths under 26 receive substantial discounts. See the website at www.eurail.com for all options.

InterRail Passes are for European citizens and include One Country Pass Austria (three/four/six/eight days €181/205/267/311). Youths under 26 receive substantial discounts. See www.interrail net.com for all options.

Vorteilscard Reduces fares by at least 45% and is valid for a year, but not on buses. Bring a photo and your passport or ID. It costs adult/under 26 years/senior €100/20/27.

Czech Republic

Why Go?

Since the fall of communism in 1989 and the opening of Central and Eastern Europe, Prague has evolved into one of Europe's most popular travel destinations. The city offers an intact medieval core that transports you back 500 years in time. The 14th-century Charles Bridge, traversing two historic riverside neighbourhoods, is one of the continent's most beautiful sights. The city is not just about history. It's a vital urban centre with a rich array of cultural offerings. Outside the capital, castles and palaces abound – including the audacious hilltop chateau at Český Krumlov – which illuminate the stories of powerful families and individuals whose influence was felt throughout Europe. Beautifully preserved Renaissance towns that withstood the ravages of the communist era link the centuries, and idiosyncratic landscapes provide a stage for active adventures.

Best Places to Eat

» Sansho (p114)

» Aberdeen Angus Steakhouse (p131)

» Moritz (p145)

» Koishi (p140)

» Cukrkávalimonáda (p114)

Best Places to Stay

» Golden Well Hotel (p108)

» Fusion Hotel (p109)

» Hotel Templ (p149)

» Hostel Mitte (p139)

» Savic Hotel (p109)

When to Go

Prague

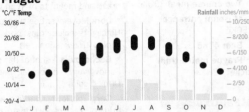

°C/°F Temp — Rainfall inches/mm

30/86 — — 10/250
20/68 — — 8/200
10/50 — — 6/150
0/32 — — 4/100
-10/14 — — 2/50
-20/-4 — — 0

J F M A M J J A S O N D

May Prague comes alive with festivals from classical music and beer to fringe arts.

Jul Karlovy Vary shows off its arty side at the sleepy spa town's annual film festival.

Dec Prague's Christmas Market draws visitors from around the world.

AT A GLANCE

» **Currency** Crown (Kč)

» **Language** Czech

» **Money** ATMs all over; banks open Monday to Friday

» **Visas** Schengen rules apply; visas not required for most nationalities

Fast Facts

» **Area** 78,864 sq km
» **Capital** Prague
» **Country code** ☑420
» **Emergency** ☑112

Exchange Rates

Australia	A$1	21.06Kč
Canada	C$1	19.84Kč
Euro Zone	€1	25.77Kč
Japan	¥100	21.37Kč
New Zealand	NZ$1	16.88Kč
UK	UK£1	30.51Kč
USA	US$1	20.17Kč

Set Your Budget

» **Budget hotel room** 1500Kč

» **Two-course meal** 300Kč

» **Museum entrance** 150Kč

» **Beer** 40Kč

» **Prague metro-tram ticket** 32Kč

Resources

» **Czech Tourism** (www.czechtourism.com)

Connections

The Czech Republic lies along major European road and rail lines and is a convenient hub for exploring neighbouring countries. Prague has excellent rail connections to Dresden and Berlin as well as Krakow, Bratislava, Budapest and Vienna. Major four-lane highways link Prague to German cities, Bratislava and Budapest.

ITINERARIES

One Week

Experience Prague's exciting combination of its tumultuous past and energetic present. Top experiences include the grandeur of Prague Castle, Josefov's Jewish Museum, and getting pleasantly lost amid the bewildering labyrinth of the Old Town. Take an essential day trip to Terezín, and then head south to Český Krumlov for a few days of riverside R&R.

Two Weeks

Begin in Prague before heading west for the spa scenes at Mariánské Lázně or Karlovy Vary. Balance the virtue and vice ledger with a few Bohemian brews in Plzeň before heading south for relaxation and rigour around Český Krumlov. Head east to the Renaissance grandeur of Telč and Brno's cosmopolitan galleries and museums. Use the Moravian capital as a base for exploring the Moravian Karst caves and Mikulov's wine country, before continuing to underrated Olomouc to admire the Holy Trinity Column.

Essential Food & Drink

» **Beer** Czechs claim to have the best *pivo* (beer) in the world and who are we to argue?

» **Dumplings** Every culture has its starchy side dish; for Czechs it's *knedliky* – big bread or potato balls sliced like bread and meant to mop up gravy.

» **Pork** Move over beef, *vepřové maso* (pork) is king here. Highlights include roast pork, pork *guláš* (goulash) or pork *vepřový řízek* (schnitzel).

» **Becherovka** A shot of this sweetish herbal liqueur from Karlovy Vary is a popular way to start (or end) a big meal. Drink it cold.

» **Carp** This lowly river fish, known locally as *kapr*, is given pride of place every Christmas at the centre of the family meal.

Czech Republic Highlights

1 Stroll across the **Charles Bridge** (p105) in the early morning or late evening when the crowds thin out.

2 Enjoy a beer in the open air on a warm summer evening at Prague's **Letná Beer Garden** (p115).

3 Join the appreciative throngs at Prague's **Astronomical Clock** (p99) at the top of the hour.

4 Repair to **Český Krumlov** (p134) to see the prettiest town in Central Europe.

5 Tour the **Pilsner Urquell Brewery** (p130) in Plzeň to see where it all started.

6 Amble through the stately town of **Olomouc** (p142), the most amazing place you've never heard of.

PRAGUE

POP 1.22 MILLION

It's the perfect irony of Prague: you are lured here by the past, but compelled to linger by the present and the future. Fill your days with its illustrious artistic and architectural heritage – from Gothic and Renaissance to art nouveau and cubist – but after dark move your focus to the lively restaurants, bars and clubs in emerging neighbourhoods like Vinohrady and Žižkov. If Prague's seasonal legions of tourists wear you down, that's okay. Just drink a glass of the country's legendary lager, relax and rest reassured that quiet moments still exist: a private dawn on Charles Bridge, a chilled beer in the Letná Beer Garden as you gaze upon the glorious cityscape of Staré Město or getting lost in the intimate lanes of Malá Strana.

⊙ Sights

Prague nestles on the Vltava River, separating Hradčany (the Castle district) and Malá Strana (Lesser Quarter) on the west bank, from Staré Město (Old Town) and Nové Město (New Town) on the east. Prague Castle overlooks Malá Strana, while the twin Gothic spires of Týn Church dominate Old Town Sq (Staroměstské nám). The broad avenue of Wenceslas Sq (Václavské nám) stretches southeast from Staré Město towards the National Museum and the main train station.

HRADČANY

Hradčany (which translates as Castle District) is an attractive and peaceful residential area stretching west from Prague Castle to Strahov Monastery. It became a town in its own right in 1320, and twice suffered heavy damage – once in the Hussite Wars and again in the Great Fire of 1541 – before becoming a borough of Prague in 1598.

TOP
CHOICE ⟩ **Prague Castle**   CASTLE

(Pražský hrad; Map p104; ☎224 372 423; www.hrad. cz; Hradčanské náměstí; grounds free, sights adult/ concession full 350/175Kc, reduced 250/125Kc; ⊙grounds 5am-midnight Apr-Oct, 6am-11pm Nov-Mar; gardens 10am-6pm Apr & Oct, to 7pm May & Sep, to 9pm Jul & Aug, closed Nov-Mar; historic buildings 9am-6pm Apr-Oct, to 4pm Nov-Mar; Ⓜ Malostranská, ☐22) Immense Prague Castle is the city's most popular sight. Its has always been the seat of Czech rulers as well as the official residence of the head of state. The main attractions of the castle complex include the Old Royal Palace, Basilica of St George, Golden Lane (Zlatá ulička; Map p104), and St Vitus Cathedral, among many others.

Entry to the castle grounds is free, but to visit the sights, including St Vitus Cathedral, requires a combined-entry ticket. Several options are available, depending on how much time you have. Two main options are available: full-price and reduced-price tickets. The latter includes admission to most major sights and will satisfy the demands of most visitors.

St Vitus Cathedral

(Katedrála Sv Víta; Map p104; ☎257 531 622; www. katedralasvatehovita.cz; III nádvoří, Pražský hrad) Prague's principal cathedral anchors the castle grounds and is visible from around the city. Though it looks ancient, it was only completed in 1929. Its many treasures include art nouveau stained glass by Alfons Mucha.

The spectacular, baroque silver tomb of St John of Nepomuk, towards the back, contains two tonnes of silver in all. The biggest and most beautiful of the cathedral's numerous side chapels is the Chapel of St Wenceslas. Its walls are adorned with gilded panels containing polished slabs of semi-precious stones.

PRAGUE IN TWO DAYS

Beat the tourist hordes with an early-morning stroll across **Charles Bridge**, and continue uphill on Nerudova to Hradčany and the glories of **Prague Castle**. Don't miss also seeing the superb 'Princely Collections' at the **Lobkowicz Palace**. Cross the river again to the **Charles Bridge Museum**.

On day two, explore **Josefov**, Prague's original Jewish quarter, and then pack a hilltop picnic for the view-friendly fortress at **Vyšehrad**. Make time for a few Czech brews, either at the relaxed **Letná Beer Garden** or the excellent **Pivovarský Klub**, before kicking on for robust Czech food at **U Modré Kachničky** or some high-quality Asian-influenced fusion at **Sansho**. For a nightcap head to a cool late-night spot like **Čili Bar**.

Old Royal Palace

(Starý královský Palác; Map p104) The Old Royal Palace is one of the oldest parts of the castle, dating from 1135. At its heart is the grand **Vladislav Hall** (Map p104) and the **Bohemian Chancellery** (Map p104), scene of the famous Defenestration of Prague.

Basilica of St George

(Bazilika Sv Jiří; Map p104; Jiřské náměstí) The striking, brick-red, early-baroque facade that dominates St George Sq (Jiřské náměstí) conceals the Czech Republic's best-preserved Romanesque church, the Basilica of St George, established in the 10th century by Vratislav I. Next to the basilica is the **Convent of St George** (Klášter Sv Jiří; Map p104; ☎257 531 644; www.ngprague.cz; Jiřské náměstí 33; adult/concession 150/80Kč; ☺10am-6pm Tue-Sun), the current home of the National Gallery's Museum of 19th-Century Czech Art.

Lobkowicz Palace

(Lobkovický Palác; Map p104; ☎233 312 925; www.lobkowicz.cz; Jiřská 3; adult/concession/family 275/200/690Kč; ☺10.30am-6pm) This 16th-century palace houses a private museum known as the 'Princely Collections', which includes priceless paintings, furniture and musical memorabilia. You tour with an audio guide dictated by owner William Lobkowicz and his family – this personal connection really brings the displays to life, and makes the palace one of Prague Castle's most interesting attractions.

Šternberg Palace   GALLERY

(Šternberský palác; Map p104; ☎233 090 570; www.ngprague.cz; Hradčanské náměstí 15; adult/child 150/80Kč; ☺10am-6pm Tue-Sun; ☐22) The baroque Šternberg Palace is home to the National Gallery's collection of 14th- to 18th-century European art, including works by Goya and Rembrandt. Fans of medieval altarpieces will be in heaven; there are also several Rubens, some Rembrandts and Breughels, and a large collection of Bohemian miniatures.

Sanctuary of Our Lady of Loreta   CHURCH

(Map p100; www.loreta.cz; Loretánské náměstí 7; adult/child 110/90Kč; ☺9am-4.30pm Tue-Sun; ☐22, 23 to Pohořelec) The baroque Sanctuary of Our Lady of Loreta showcases precious religious artefacts, and the cloister houses a 17th-century replica of the Santa Casa from the Italian town of Loreta, reputedly the Virgin Mary's house in Nazareth, transported to Italy by angels in the 13th century.

MIND YOUR MANNERS

It's customary to say *dobrý den* (good day) when entering a shop, cafe or bar, and *na shledanou* (goodbye) when leaving.

Strahov Library   HISTORIC BUILDING

(Strahovská knihovna; Map p100; ☎233 107 718; www.strahovskyklaster.cz; Strahovské nádvoří 1; adult/concession 80/50Kč; ☺9am-noon & 1-5pm; ☐22, 25) Strahov Library is the largest monastic library in the country, with two magnificent baroque halls dating from the 17th and 18th centuries. The main attractions are the two-storey-high **Philosophy Hall** (Filozofický sál; 1780–97) and the older but even more beautiful **Theology Hall** (Teologiský sál; 1679).

STARÉ MĚSTO

One of Europe's most beautiful urban spaces, the **Old Town Square** (Staroměstské náměstí; Map p110; MStaroměstská), usually shortened in Czech to Staromák, has been Prague's principal public square since the 10th century, and was its main marketplace until the beginning of the 20th century. There are busking jazz bands and alfresco concerts, plus Christmas and Easter markets in season, all watched over by Ladislav Šaloun's brooding art nouveau **statue of Jan Hus** (Map p110; MStaroměstská). It was unveiled on 6 July 1915, which was the 500th anniversary of Hus' death at the stake.

Old Town Hall   HISTORIC BUILDING

(Staroměstská radnice; Map p110; ☎12444; www.prazskeveze.cz; Staroměstské náměstí 1; guided tour adult/child 105/85Kč; ☺11am-6pm Mon, 9am-6pm Tue-Sun; MStaroměstská) Prague's Old Town Hall, founded in 1338, is a hotchpotch of medieval buildings acquired over centuries, presided over by a tall Gothic tower with its splendid Astronomical Clock. As well as housing the main tourist information office (p120), the town hall has several historic attractions, and hosts art exhibitions on the ground floor. The tower view is the best in town.

Astronomical Clock   HISTORIC SITE

(Map p110; MStaroměstská) Ironically, if you wish to tell the time in Old Town Sq, it's easier to look at the clock above this, because the 1490 mechanical marvel is tricky to decipher. The clock's creator, Master Hanuš, was

Greater Prague

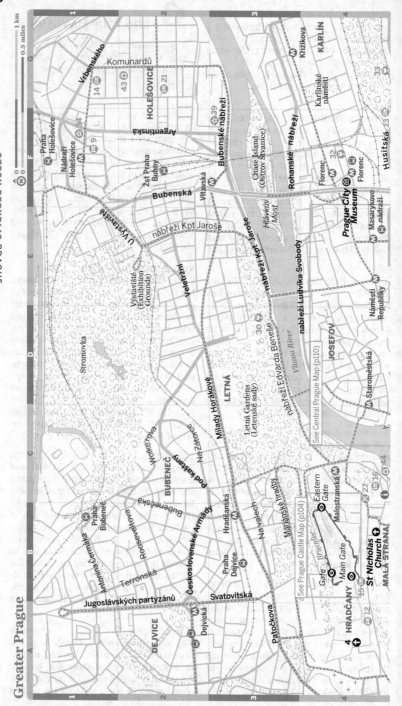

0 —— 1 km
0 —— 0.5 miles

KARLÍN

Karlínské náměstí

Husitská

Komunardů

Vrbenského

14
43
21

HOLEŠOVICE

39

Argentinská

Bubenské nábřeží

Rohanské nábřeží

34
9

Praha
Holešovice

Nádraží
Holešovice

Žst Praha
Bubny

Bubenská

Vltavská

Chase Island
(Ostrov Štvanice)

Florenc

Florenc

Prague City
Museum

Masarykovo
nádraží

nábřeží Kpt Jaroše

Hlávkův
Most

Bubenská

U Výstaviště

Výstaviště
(Exhibition
Grounds)

Veletržní

nábřeží Kpt Jaroše

nábřeží Ludvíka Svobody

Náměstí
Republiky

Stromovka

Vltava River

30

nábřeží Edvarda Beneše

JOSEFOV

LETNÁ

Milady Horákové

Letná Gardens
(Letenské sady)

Staroměstská

See Central Prague Map (p110)

Wolkerova

Na Zátorce

pod kaštany

BUBENEČ

Bubenečská

Hradčanská

Na Valech

Mariánské hradby

Eastern
Gate

Malostranská

M

16

22

44

Praha
Bubeneč

Roosveltova

Antonína Čermáka

Československé Armády

Praha
Dejvice

Hradčanská

Gate
Bruská

Gate

Main Gate

St Nicholas
Church

MALÁ
STRANA

Terronská

Jugoslávských partyzánů

DEJVICE

Dejvická

Svatovítská

Patočkova

See Prague Castle Map (p104)

12

4

HRADČANY

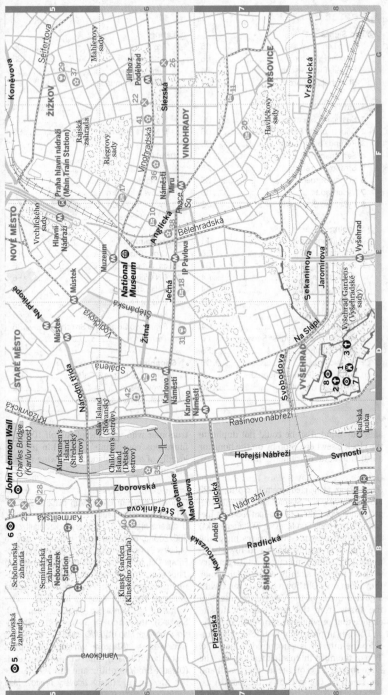

Greater Prague

allegedly blinded so he could not duplicate the clock elsewhere. Stop by on the hour for a little medieval marionette show.

Church of Our Lady Before Týn   CHURCH
(Kostel Panny Marie před Týnem; Map p110; ☑222 318 186; www.tyn.cz; Staroměstské náměstí; suggested donation 25Kč; ◎10am-1pm & 3-5pm Tue-Sat, 10.30am-noon Sun Mar-Oct; Ⓜ Staroměstská) Its distinctive twin Gothic spires make the Týn church an unmistakable Old Town landmark. Like something out of a 15th-century – and probably slightly cruel – fairy tale, they loom over Old Town Sq, decorated with a golden image of the Virgin Mary made in the 1620s from the melted-down Hussite chalice that previously adorned the church.

Though impressively Gothic on the outside, the interior is smothered in baroque. Two of the most interesting features are the huge rococo **altar** on the northern wall and the **tomb of Tycho Brahe**, the Danish as-

tronomer who was one of Rudolf II's most illustrious 'consultants' (he died in 1601, allegedly of a burst bladder following a royal piss-up).

Prague Jewish Museum   MUSEUM
(Židovské muzeum Praha; Map p110; ☑222 317 191; www.jewishmuseum.cz; Reservation Centre, U starého hřbitova 3a; ordinary ticket adult/child 300/200Kč, combined ticket including entry to Old-New Synagogue 480/320Kč; ◎9am-6pm Sun-Fri Apr-Oct, to 4.30pm Nov-Mar; Ⓜ Staroměstská) This museum consists of six Jewish monuments: the **Maisel Synagogue** (Maiselova synagóga; Map p110; Maiselova 10); the **Pinkas Synagogue** (Pinkasova synagóga; Map p110; Široká 3); the **Spanish Synagogue** (Spanélská synagóga; Map p110; Vězeňská 1); the **Klaus Synagogue** (Klauzová synagóga; Map p110; U starého hřbitova 1); the **Ceremonial Hall** (Obřadní síň; Map p110); and the **Old Jewish Cemetery** (Starý židovský hřbitov; Map

p110; Pinkas Synagogue, Široká 3); see p106 for a museum itinerary. The monuments are clustered together in Josefov, a small corner of the Old Town that was home to Prague's Jews for some 800 years before it was brought to an end by an urban renewal project at the start of the 20th century and the Nazi occupation during WWII.

The monuments cannot be visited separately but require a combined entry ticket which is good for all of the sights and available at ticket windows throughout Josefov. A fifth synagogue, the Old-New Synagogue (Staronová synagóga; Map p110; Červená 2; adult/child 200/140Kč), is still used for religious services, and requires a separate ticket or additional fee.

The Jewish Museum was first established in 1906 to preserve objects from synagogues that were demolished during the slum clearance at the turn of the 20th century. The collection grew richer as a result of one of the most grotesquely ironic acts of WWII. During the Nazi occupation, the Germans took over management of the museum in order to create a 'museum of an extinct race'. To that end, they brought in objects from destroyed Jewish communities throughout Bohemia and Moravia.

Municipal House   HISTORIC BUILDING
(Obecní dům; Map p110; ☎222 002 101; www.obec-nidum.cz; náměstí Republiky 5; guided tour adult/child 290/240Kč; ☷public areas 7.30am-11pm, information centre 10am-8pm; ⓂNáměstí Republiky) Restored in the 1990s, Prague's most exuberant and sensual building is a labour of love, every detail of its design and decoration carefully considered, every painting loaded with symbolism. The restaurant and cafe flanking the entrance are like walk-in museums of art nouveau design; upstairs are half a dozen sumptuously decorated halls that you can visit by guided tour.

The Municipal House stands on the site of the Royal Court, seat of Bohemia's kings from 1383 to 1483 (when Vladislav II moved to Prague Castle), which was demolished at the end of the 19th century. Between 1906 and 1912 this magnificent art nouveau palace was built in its place – a lavish joint effort by around 30 leading artists of the day.

Convent of St Agnes   GALLERY
(Klášter sv Anežky; Map p110; ☎224 810 628; www.ngprague.cz; U Milosrdných 17; adult/child 150/80Kč; ☷10am-6pm Tue-Sun; ☖5, 8, 14) In the northeastern corner of Staré Město is the former Convent of St Agnes, Prague's oldest surviving Gothic building. The 1st-floor rooms hold the National Gallery's permanent collection of medieval and early Renaissance art (1200–1550) from Bohemia and Central Europe, a treasure house of glowing Gothic altar paintings and polychrome religious sculptures.

Museum of Czech Cubism   GALLERY
(Muzeum Českého Kubismu; Map p110; ☎224 211 746; www.ngprague.cz; Ovocný trh 19; adult/child 100/50Kč; ☷10am-6pm Tue-Sun; ⓂNáměstí Republiky) Though dating from 1912, Josef Gočár's dům U černé Matky Boží (House of the Black Madonna) – Prague's first and finest example of cubist architecture – still looks modern and dynamic. It now houses three floors of remarkable cubist paintings and sculpture, as well as furniture, ceramics and glassware in cubist designs.

Estates Theatre   HISTORIC BUILDING
(Stavovské divadlo; Map p110; ☎224 902 231; www.narodni-divadlo.cz; Ovocný trh 1; ⓂMůstek)

CHEAP THRILLS

Prague has become more expensive in recent years, but there are still some things you can do for free or to reduce your costs:

» Stroll through the gardens and courtyards at Prague Castle (p98).

» Visit Charles Bridge (p105) at dawn.

» Explore the fortress at Vyšehrad (p108).

» Catch tram 22 from Peace Sq in Vinohrady all the way to Prague Castle for a DIY city tour. It might be the best 32Kč you ever spend.

» Make lunch your main meal of the day to save money on eating out, taking advantage of restaurants' denní menu (daily menus).

» Combine people-watching and great river views while grabbing a cheap-as-chips sunset beer at the Letná Beer Garden (p115).

Prague Castle

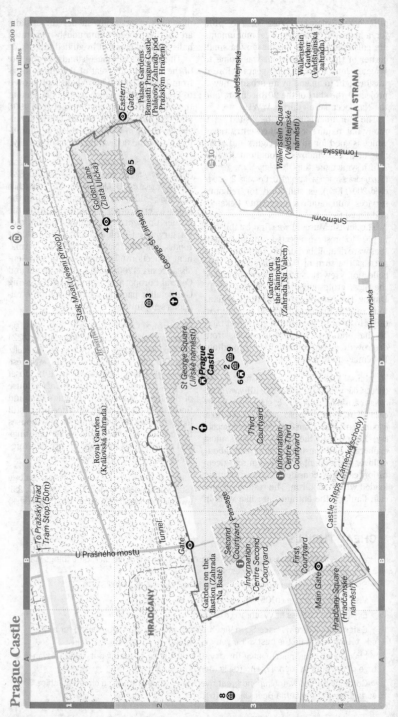

0 — 200 m
0 — 0.1 miles

HRADČANY

To Pražský Hrad
Tram Stop (50m)

Royal Garden
(Královská zahrada)

Stag Moat (Jelení příkop)

Tunnel

Palace Gardens
Beneath Prague Castle
(Palácový Zahrady pod
Pražským Hradem)

Eastern
Gate

Golden Lane
(Zlatá Ulička)

George St (Jiřská)

U Prašného mostu

Gate

Garden on the
Bastion (Zahrada
Na Baště)

Information
Centre Second
Courtyard

Second
Courtyard

Passage

Information
Centre Third
Courtyard

Third
Courtyard

St George Square
(Jiřské náměstí)

Prague
Castle

Garden on
the Ramparts
(Zahrada Na Valech)

First
Courtyard

Main Gate

Hradčany Square
(Hradčanské
náměstí)

Castle Steps (Zámecké schody)

MALÁ STRANA

Valdštejnská

Wallenstein
Garden
(Valdštejnská
zahrada)

Wallenstein Square
(Valdštejnské
náměstí)

Sněmovní

Tomášská

Thunovská

Prague Castle

◎ **Top Sights**
Prague Castle D2

◎ **Sights**
1 Basilica of St George............................E2
2 Bohemian Chancellery.......................D3
3 Convent of St George.........................E2
4 Golden Lane..E1
5 Lobkowicz Palace F2
6 Old Royal Palace D3
7 St Vitus Cathedral...............................C2
8 Šternberg Palace A3
9 Vladislav Hall D3

🛏 **Sleeping**
10 Golden Well Hotel F3

Prague's oldest theatre and finest neoclassical building, the Estates Theatre is where the premiere of Mozart's *Don Giovanni* was performed on 29 October 1787, with the maestro himself conducting. Opened in 1783 as the Nostitz Theatre (after its founder, Count Anton von Nostitz-Rieneck), it was patronised by upper-class German citizens and thus came to be called the Estates Theatre.

MALÁ STRANA
Across the river from the Old Town are the baroque backstreets of Malá Strana (Little Quarter), built in the 17th and 18th centuries by victorious Catholic clerics and nobles on the foundations of their Protestant predecessors' Renaissance palaces.

Charles Bridge BRIDGE
(Karlův most; Map p110; Malostranské náměstí; 🚋17, 18 to Karlovy lázně) Strolling across the 14th-century Charles Bridge is everybody's favourite Prague activity. In 1357 Charles IV commissioned Peter Parler (the architect of St Vitus Cathedral) to replace the 12th-century Judith Bridge, which had been washed away by floods in 1342. The new bridge was completed in 1390, and took Charles' name only in the 19th century.

Despite occasional flood damage, it withstood wheeled traffic for 500-odd years – thanks, legend says, to eggs mixed into the mortar (though recent investigations have disproved this myth) – until it was made pedestrian-only in the decades after WWII.

St Nicholas Church CHURCH
(Kostel sv Mikuláše; Map p100; 🕿257 534 215; Malostranské náměstí 38; adult/child 70/35Kč; ⊗9am-

5pm Mar-Oct, to 4pm Nov-Feb; 🚋12, 20, 22) Malá Strana is dominated by the huge green cupola of St Nicholas Church, one of Central Europe's finest baroque buildings. Don't confuse it with the other Church of St Nicholas, on Old Town Sq. It was begun by famed German baroque architect Kristof Dientzenhofer; his son Kilian continued the work and Anselmo Lurago finished the job in 1755.

On the ceiling, Johann Kracker's 1770 *Apotheosis of St Nicholas* is Europe's largest fresco (clever *trompe l'œil* technique has made the painting merge almost seamlessly with the architecture). In the first chapel on the left is a mural by Karel Škréta, which includes the church official who kept track of the artist as he worked; he is looking out through a window in the upper corner.

John Lennon Wall HISTORIC SITE
(Map p100; Velkopřevorské náměstí; 🚋12, 20, 22) After his murder in New York on 8 December 1980, John Lennon became a pacifist hero for young Czechs. An image of Lennon was painted on a wall in a secluded square opposite the French Embassy (there is a niche on the wall that looks like a tombstone), along with political graffiti and Beatles lyrics.

Despite repeated coats of whitewash, the secret police never managed to keep it clean for long, and the Lennon Wall became a political focus for Prague youth. These days, it's still fun to take a look and scrawl something on the wall yourself.

Vrtbov Garden GARDENS
(Vrtbovská zahrada; Map p100; 🕿257 531 480; www.vrtbovska.cz; Karmelitská 25; adult/concession 60/50Kč; ⊗10am-6pm Apr-Oct; 🚋12, 20, 22) This 'secret garden', hidden along an alley at the corner of Tržiště and Karmelitská, was built in 1720 for the Earl of Vrtba, the senior chancellor of Prague Castle. It's a formal baroque garden, climbing steeply up the hillside to a terrace graced with baroque statues of Roman mythological figures by Matthias Braun.

NOVÉ MĚSTO & VYŠEHRAD
Nové Město surrounds the Old Town on all sides and was originally laid out in the 14th century. Its main public area is Wenceslas Sq. This piece of Prague has witnessed a great deal of Czech history – a giant Mass was held here during the revolutionary upheavals of 1848; in 1918 the creation of the new Czechoslovak Republic was celebrated here; and in 1989 the fall of communism was announced here. At the southern end

A STROLL THROUGH PRAGUE'S JEWISH MUSEUM

The Prague Jewish Museum (p102), a collection of four synagogues, the former Ceremonial Hall and the Old Jewish Cemetery, is one of the city's treasures. Start your exploration at the Pinkas Synagogue, built in 1535 and used for worship until 1941. After WWII it was converted into a memorial, with walls inscribed with the names of the 77,297 Czech victims of the Nazis. It also has a collection of drawings by children held in the Terezín concentration camp during WWII.

The Pinkas Synagogue leads to the Old Jewish Cemetery, Europe's oldest surviving Jewish graveyard. Founded in the 15th century, it has a palpable atmosphere of mourning even after two centuries of disuse (it was closed in 1787). Around 12,000 crumbling stones are heaped together, but beneath them are tens of thousands of graves, piled in layers because of lack of space.

Exit through a gate between the Klaus Synagogue (Klausová Synagóga) and the Ceremonial Hall (Obřadní síň), both of which house exhibitions on Jewish forms of worship, family ceremonies and traditions.

A block southeast lies the neo-Gothic Maisel Synagogue, which replaced a Renaissance original built by Mordechai Maisel, the mayor of the Jewish community, in 1592. It houses an exhibit on the history of the Jews in Bohemia and Moravia from the 10th to 18th centuries.

East of the Maisel is the Spanish Synagogue. Named after its striking Moorish interior and dating from 1868, its exhibit continues the story of the Jews in the Czech lands from the 19th century to the present.

Separate from the Jewish Museum, the Old-New Synagogue dates from 1270 and is Europe's oldest working synagogue. Around the central chamber are an entry hall, a winter prayer hall and the room from which women watch the men-only services. The interior, with a pulpit surrounded by a 15th-century wrought-iron grill, looks much as it would have 500 years ago.

of the square is Josef Myslbek's muscular equestrian statue of St Wenceslas (sv Václav; Map p110; Václavské náměstí; MMuzeum), the 10th-century pacifist Duke of Bohemia and the 'Good King Wenceslas' of Christmas-carol fame. Near the statue, a small memorial to the victims of communism bears photographs and handwritten epitaphs to anticommunist heroes.

National Museum
MUSEUM

(Národní muzeum; Map p100; ☑224 497 111; www.nm.cz; Václavské náměstí 68; ☺closed until 2015; MMuzeum) Looming above Wenceslas Sq is the neo-Renaissance bulk of the National Museum, designed in the 1880s by Josef Schulz as an architectural symbol of the Czech National Revival. The museum mainly displays rocks, fossils and stuffed animals but was closed during our research for renovation and not expected to reopen until 2015. The museum's exterior is impressive and worth checking out.

Mucha Museum
GALLERY

(Muchovo muzeum; Map p110; ☑221 451 333; www.mucha.cz; Panská 7; adult/child 180/120Kč; ☺10am-6pm; MMůstek) This fascinating (and busy) museum features the sensuous art nouveau posters, paintings and decorative panels of Alfons Mucha (1860–1939), as well as many sketches, photographs and other memorabilia. The exhibits include countless artworks showing Mucha's trademark Slavic maidens with flowing hair and piercing blue eyes, bearing symbolic garlands and linden boughs.

Prague City Museum
MUSEUM

(Muzeum hlavního města Prahy; Map p100; ☑224 816 773; www.muzeumprahy.cz; Na Poříčí 52, Karlin; adult/child 120/50Kč; ☺9am-6pm Tue-Sun; MFlorenc) This excellent museum, opened in 1898, is devoted to the history of Prague from prehistoric times to the 20th century. Among the many intriguing exhibits are the Astronomical Clock's original 1866 calendar wheel with Josef Mánes' beautiful painted panels representing the months – that's January at the top, toasting his toes by the fire.

What everybody comes to see is Antonín Langweil's astonishing 1:480 scale model of Prague as it looked between 1826 and 1834. The display is most rewarding after you get to know Prague a bit, as you can spot the changes – look at St Vitus Cathedral, for example, still only half-finished. Labels are in English as well as Czech.

Museum of Communism
MUSEUM

(Muzeum Komunismu; Map p110; ☑224 212 966; www.muzeumkomunismu.cz; Na Příkopě 10; adult/concession/child under 10 190/150Kč/free; ☺9am-9pm; Ⓜ️Můstek) It's difficult to think of a more ironic site for a museum of communism – an 18th-century aristocrat's palace, between a casino and a McDonald's. Put together by an American expat and his Czech partner, the museum tells the story of Czechoslovakia's years behind the Iron Curtain in photos, words and a fascinating collection of... well, stuff.

Charles Bridge Museum
MUSEUM

(Muzeum Karlova Mostu; Map p110; ☑776 776 779; www.charlesbridgemuseum.com; Křížovnické náměstí 3; adult/concession 150/70Kč; ☺10am-8pm May-Sep, to 6pm Oct-Apr; ⬛17, 18) Founded in the 13th century, the Order of the Knights of the Cross with the Red Star were the guardians of Judith Bridge (and its successor Charles Bridge), with their 'mother house' at the Church of St Francis Seraphinus on Křížovnické náměstí. This museum, housed in the order's headquarters, covers the history of Prague's most famous landmark.

⚲ Tours

Amazing Walks of Prague
WALKING TOUR

(☑777 069 685; www.amazingwalks.com; per person 300-500Kč) Guide Roman Bílý is especially strong on WWII, the communist era and the Jewish Quarter.

Prague Walks
WALKING TOUR

(☑222 322 309; www.praguewalks.com; per person 220-990Kč) Runs interesting walking tours with themes such as Prague architecture, Žižkov pubs and the Velvet Revolution. Meet at the Astronomical Clock, or you can arrange to be met at your hotel.

Wittmann Tours
GUIDED TOUR

(Map p110; ☑222 252 472; www.wittmann-tours.com; Novotného lávka 5; per person 880Kč ; ☺Josefov tours 10.30am & 2pm Sun-Fri mid-Mar–Dec; ⬛17, 18) Offers a three-hour walking tour of Josefov, and seven-hour day trips to Terezín (1250Kč per person), daily May to October, four times a week April, November and December.

✹ Festivals & Events

Prague Spring
CLASSICAL MUSIC

(www.festival.cz; ☺May) The Czech Republic's biggest annual cultural event, and one of Europe's most important festivals of classical music.

Khamoro
MUSIC & CULTURE

(www.khamoro.cz; ☺late May) Annual celebration of Roma culture.

Prague Fringe Festival
ARTS

(www.praguefringe.com; ☺late May-early Jun) Eclectic action.

Christmas Market
SEASONAL

(☺1-24 Dec) In Old Town Sq.

🛏 Sleeping

At New Year, Christmas or Easter, and from May to September, book in advance. Prices quoted are for the high season: generally

---

THE STATUES OF CHARLES BRIDGE

The Charles Bridge is known best of all for its statues that line the bridge on both sides. The statues were not part of the original design but were added centuries later as part of the Austrian Habsburgs' efforts to convert sceptical Czechs to Catholicism.

The first monument erected on the bridge was the crucifix near the eastern end, in 1657. The first statue – the Jesuits' 1683 tribute to St John of Nepomuk – inspired other Catholic orders, and over the next 30 years a score more went up, like ecclesiastical billboards. New ones were added in the mid-19th century, and one (plus replacements for some lost to floods) was added in the 20th. As most of the statues were carved from soft sandstone, several weathered originals have been replaced with copies.

The most famous figure is the monument to **St John of Nepomuk**. According to the legend on the base of the statue, Wenceslas IV had him trussed up in armour and thrown off the bridge in 1393 for refusing to divulge the queen's confessions (he was her priest), though the real reason had to do with the bitter conflict between church and state; the stars in his halo allegedly followed his corpse down the river. Tradition says that if you rub the bronze plaque, you will one day return to Prague.

VYŠEHRAD: WHERE IT ALL BEGAN

Legend has it that **Vyšehrad** (Map p100; www.praha-vysehrad.cz; ⏰9.30am–6pm Apr–Oct, to 5pm Nov–Mar; MVyšehrad) hill, south of Nové Město, is the place where Prague was born. According to myth, a wise chieftain named Krok built a castle here in the 7th century, and Libuše, the cleverest of his three daughters, prophesied that a great city would arise here. Taking as her king a ploughman named Přemysl, she founded both the city of Prague and the Přemysl dynasty.

While this is probably not entirely true, the site may have been permanently settled as early as the 9th century, and early ruler Boleslav II (r 972–99) lived here for a time. By the mid-11th century there was a fortified settlement, and Vratislav II (r 1061–92) moved his court here from Hradčany, beefing up the walls and adding a castle, the **Basilica of St Lawrence** (Map p100; admission 10Kč; ⏰11am–5pm Mon–Fri, 11.30am–4pm Sat & Sun), the original **Church of SS Peter & Paul** (Kostel sv Petra a Pavla; Map p100; ☎249 113 353; www.praha-vysehrad.cz; K Rotundě 10, Vyšehrad; adult/child 30/10Kč; ⏰9am–noon & 1–5pm Wed–Mon; MVyšehrad) and the **Rotunda of St Martin** (Rotunda sv Martina; Map p100; ☎241 410 348; www.praha-vysehrad.cz; V Pevnosti, Vyšehrad; ⏰open only during mass; MVyšehrad). His successors stayed until 1140, when Vladislav II returned to Hradčany.

Charles IV was well aware of Vyšehrad's symbolic importance. In the 14th century, he repaired the walls and joined them to those of his new town, Nové Město. He built a small palace, no longer standing, and decreed that the coronations of Bohemian kings should begin with a procession from here to Hradčany.

Nearly everything was wiped out during the Hussite Wars of the 15th century. The fortress remained a ruin – except for a ramshackle township of artisans and traders – until after the Thirty Years' War, when Leopold I refortified it. Vyšehrad served as an Austrian fortress in the late 17th and18th centuries and was occupied for a time by both the French and the Prussians. These days it's peaceful park and a great spot to throw down a blanket and uncork a bottle of wine.

Don't miss **Vyšehrad Cemetery** (Vyšehradský hřbitov; Map p100; ☎249 198 815; www.praha-vysehrad.cz; K Rotundě 10, Vyšehrad ; ⏰8am–7pm May–Sep, shorter hr rest of yr; MVyšehrad), the city's most prestigious burial ground and the final resting place of dozens of Czech luminaries, including composers Antonín Dvořák and Bedřich Smetana and artist Alfons Mucha.

April to October. For better value stay outside of the Old Town (Staré Město) and take advantage of Prague's excellent public transport network.

HRADČANY & MALÁ STRANA

Golden Well Hotel   HOTEL €€€
(Map p104; ☎257 011 213; www.goldenwell.cz; U Zlaté Studně 4; d/ste from 6250/12,500Kč; P🅿❄🐕@🛜; MMalostranská) The Golden Well is one of Malá Strana's hidden secrets, tucked away at the end of a cobbled cul-de-sac – a Renaissance house that once belonged to Emperor Rudolf II, perched on the southern slope of the castle hill. The rooms are quiet and spacious, with polished wood floors, reproduction period furniture, and blue-and-white bathrooms with underfloor heating.

Domus Henrici   HOTEL €€
(Map p100; ☎220 511 369; www.domus-henrici. cz; Loretánská 11; d/ste from 3250/4000Kč; @🛜;

🚌22, 25) This historic building in a quiet corner of Hradčany is intentionally nondescript out front, hinting that peace and privacy are top priorities here. There are eight spacious and stylish rooms, half with private fax, scanner/copier and internet access (via an ethernet port), and all with polished wood floors, large bathrooms, comfy beds and fluffy bathrobes.

Lokál Inn   INN €€
(Map p100; ☎257 014 800; www.lokalinn.cz; Míšeňská 12; d/ste from 3475/4475Kč; 🍴🛜; 🚌12, 20, 22) Polished parquet floors and painted wooden ceilings abound in this 18th-century house designed by Prague's premier baroque architect, Kilian Dientzenhofer. The eight rooms and four suites are elegant and uncluttered, and the rustic, stone-vaulted cellars house a deservedly popular pub and restaurant run by the same folk as Lokál (p114).

Hotel Neruda
BOUTIQUE HOTEL €€

(Map p100; ☑257 535 557; www.hotelneruda.cz; Nerudova 44; r from 2225Kč; ✹✳✿; 🖸12, 20, 22) Set in a tastefully renovated Gothic house dating from 1348, the Neruda has decor that is chic and minimalist in neutral tones enlivened by the odd splash of colour, with a lovely glass-roofed atrium and a sunny roof terrace. The bedrooms share the modern, minimalist decor and are mostly reasonably sized.

STARÉ MĚSTO

Residence Karolina
APARTMENT €€

(Map p110; ☑224 990 900; www.residence-karolina.com; Karoliny Světlé 4; 2-/4-person apt 3175/5475Kč; ✹@✿; 🖸6, 9, 19, 21, 22) We're going to have to invent a new category of accommodation – boutique apartments – to cover this array of 20 beautifully furnished flats. Offering one- or two-bedroom options, all apartments have spacious seating areas with comfy sofas and flat-screen TVs, sleek modern kitchens and dining areas.

Savic Hotel
HOTEL €€€

(Map p110; ☑224 248 555; www.savic.eu; Jilská 7; r from 4125Kč; ✳@✿; 🇲Můstek) From the complimentary glass of wine when you arrive to the comfy king-size beds, the Savic certainly knows how to make you feel welcome. Housed in the former monastery of St Giles, the hotel is bursting with character and full of delightful period details including old stone fireplaces, beautiful painted timber ceilings and fragments of frescoes.

Perla Hotel
BOUTIQUE HOTEL €€

(Map p110; ☑221 667 707; www.perlahotel.cz; Perlová 1; s/d from 1975/2225Kč; ✹✿; 🇲Můstek) The 'Pearl' on Pearl St is typical of the slinky, appealing designer hotels that have sprung up all over central Prague. Here the designer has picked a – surprise, surprise – pearl motif that extends from the giant pearls that form the reception desk to the silky, lustrous bedspreads and huge screen prints on the bedroom walls.

Old Prague Hostel
HOSTEL €

(Map p110; ☑224 829 058; www.oldpraguehostel.com; Benediktská 2; dm/s/d from 375/1000/1200Kč; ✹@✿; 🇲Náměstí Republiky) Cheerful and welcoming, with colourful homemade murals brightening the walls, this is one of Prague's most sociable hostels, with a good mix of people from backpackers to families. Facilities are good, with lockers in the dorms, luggage storage and 24-hour reception, though

the mattresses on the bunks are a bit on the thin side.

NOVÉ MĚSTO

Mosaic House
HOTEL, HOSTEL €€

(Map p100; ☑221 595 350; www.mosaichouse.com; Odboru 4; dm/s/d from 300/1840/2520Kč; ✹✿; 🇲Karlovo Náměstí) A blend of four-star hotel and boutique hostel, Mosaic House is a cornucopia of designer detail, from the original 1930s' mosaic in the entrance hall to the silver spray-painted tree branches used as clothes-hanging racks. The backpackers dorms are kept separate from the private rooms, but have the same high-quality decor and design.

Fusion Hotel
BOUTIQUE HOTEL, HOSTEL €

(Map p110; ☑226 222 800; www.fusionhotels.com; Panská 9; dm/d/tr 400/2000/2600Kč; @✿; 🖸3, 9, 14, 24) Billing itself as an 'affordable design hotel', Fusion certainly has style in abundance. From the revolving bar and the funky sofas that litter the public areas, to the individually decorated bedrooms that resemble miniature modern-art galleries – all white walls and black trim with tiny splashes of colour – the place exudes 'cool'.

Icon Hotel
BOUTIQUE HOTEL €€€

(Map p110; ☑221 634 100; www.iconhotel.eu; V ámě 6; r from 3000Kč; ✳@✿; 🖸3, 9, 14, 24) Staff clothes by Diesel, computers by Apple, beds by Hästens – pretty much everything in this gorgeous boutique hotel has a designer stamp on it. Appearing on Europe's trendiest hotels lists, the Icon's sleekly minimalist rooms are enlivened with a splash of purple from the silky bedspreads, while the curvy,

---

ACCOMMODATION AGENCIES

Useful accommodation agencies include the following:

Hostel.cz (☑415 658 580; www.hostel.cz) Website database of hostels and budget hotels, with a secure online booking system.

Mary's Travel & Tourist Service (Map p100; ☑222 254 007; www.marys.cz; Italská 31, Vinohrady; ☺9am-7pm Mon-Fri, 10am-5pm Sat & Sun) Friendly, efficient agency offering private rooms, hostels, pensions, apartments and hotels in all price ranges in Prague and surrounding areas.

Central Prague

Vltava River

JOSEFOV

U Milosrdných

JOSEFOV

Dvořákovo nábřeží

Elišky Krásnohorské

Dušní

Bílkova

Kozí

U obecního dvora

Vězeňská

17

Franz
Kafka
Monument

Kozí

Dušní

Masná

Alšovo nábřeží

17.listopadu

2

8

15

Maiselova

Pařížská

Prague
Jewish Museum

16

13

Široká

9

Mánes Bridge
(Mánesův
most)

49

Jan Palach Square
(Náměstí
Jana Palacha)

28

M Staroměstská

29

Valentinská

Kaprova

Zatecká

U radnice

Dlouhá

Czech
Tourism

Týn Courtyard
(Týnský dvůr)

7

14

4

Veleslavínova

Platnéřská

Mariánské
náměstí

Linhartská

Prague
Welcome

1

Charles
Bridge

3

Křižovnická

Křižovnické
náměstí

Karlova

Little Square
(Malé náměstí)

Old Town
Hall

STARÉ MĚSTO

54

19

Anenská

Liliová

Husova

42

53

33

Prague
Welcome

6

Anenské
náměstí

40

25

37

Jilská

Michalská

Melantrichova

Open-Air
Market

Rytířská

Náprstkova

Zlatá

43

Havelská

V Kotcích

Provaznická

36

Bethlehem Square
(Betlémské
náměstí)

Skořepka

Uhelný
trh

23

Můstek M

Betlémská

Konviktská

Na Perštýně

Martinská

Perlová

28. října

Bartolomějská

39

Jungmannovo
náměstí

24

M Můstek

26

Národní třída

Franciscan Garden
(Františkánská
zahrada)

Legion
Bridge
(Legií most)

P

46

Mikulandská

Purkyňova

Jungmannova

Palackého

Voršilská

Ostrovní

Vladislavova

Spálená

Vodičkova

Slav Island
(Slovanský
ostrov)

V Jirchářích

Smetanovo nábřeží

Divadelní

Karoliny Světlé

Masarykovo nábřeží

Nastruze

Pštrossova

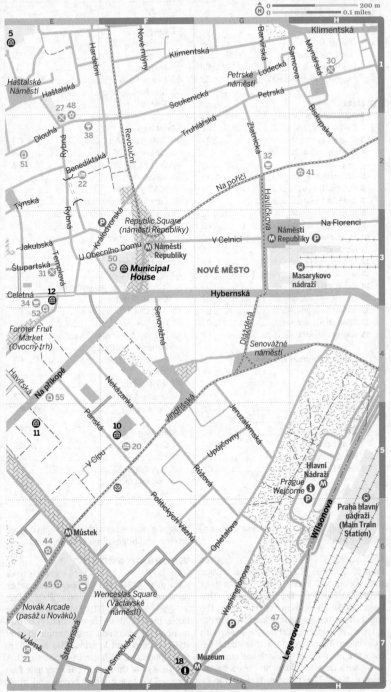

Central Prague

reproduction art-deco armchairs are supplied by Modernista (p119).

Miss Sophie's   HOSTEL €
(Map p100; ☏296 303 530; www.miss-sophies.com; Melounova 3; dm from 410Kč, s/d/apt 1760/2000/2360Kč; ❄@🛜; Ⓜ IP Pavlova) This hostel makes a pleasant change from the usual characterless backpacker hive. There's a touch of contemporary style here, with oak-veneer floors and stark, minimalist decor – the main motif is 'distressed' concrete, along with neutral colours and black metal-framed beds. The place is famous for its

'designer' showers, with autographed glass screens and huge rainfall shower heads.

VINOHRADY & ŽIŽKOV

Arkada   BOUTIQUE HOTEL €€
(Map p100; ☏242 429 111; www.arkadahotel.cz; Balbínová 8, Vinohrady; s/d from 1750/2250Kč; Ⓟ❄@🛜; ⓂMuzeum, 🚊11) This relatively new hotel in Vinohrady comes highly recommended for offering a great combination of style, comfort and location. The rooms are well appointed, with a retro-1930s feel that fits the style of the building. Rooms have flat-screen TVs, free internet access and mini-

bars. Ask to see a couple before choosing, since the decor differs from room to room.

Czech Inn
HOSTEL, HOTEL €

(Map p100; ☑267 267 600; www.czech-inn.com; Francouzská 76, Vinohrady; dm 285-385Kč; s/d 1320/1540Kč, apt from 1650Kč; P☺@☎; 🚊4, 22) The Czech Inn calls itself a hostel, but the boutique label wouldn't be out of place. Everything seems sculpted by an industrial designer, from the iron beds to the brushed-steel flooring and minimalist square sinks. The Czech Inn offers a variety of accommodation, from standard hostel dorm rooms to good-value private doubles (with or without attached bathroom) and apartments.

Pension Královský Vinohrad
PENSION €

(Map p100; ☑222 515 093; www.kralovskyvinohrad. cz; Šmilovského 10, Vinohrady; d from 1500Kč, ste from 2100Kč; P☺@; 🚊4, 22) This pension occupies a lovely 1910 apartment building in a leafy backstreet. The cheaper rooms are plain but functional, while the larger rooms and 'suites' (two-room apartments) are more stylishly decorated and furnished with antiques and stripped pine furniture. The suites also have minibars and tables and chairs. Offers steep discounts on the website.

Hostel Elf
HOSTEL €

(Map p100; ☑222 540 963; www.hostelelf. com; Husitská 11, Žižkov; dm from 340Kč; s/d 1230/1960Kč; @☎; Ⓜ Florenc) Young, hip and sociable, Hostel Elf welcomes a steady stream of party-hearty backpackers from across the globe to its well-maintained dorms. The dorms are immaculately clean and brightly decorated with graffiti art and murals. There's a little beer-garden terrace and cosy lounge, with free tea and coffee and cheap beer, and Žižkov with its pubs is right on the doorstep.

HOLEŠOVICE

Absolutum Hotel
BOUTIQUE HOTEL €€

(Map p100; ☑222 541 406; www.absolutumhotel.cz; Jablonského 639/4; s/d 2500/3200Kč; P☺✱@☎; Ⓜ Nádraží Holešovice, 🚋 Praha-Holešovice) A highly recommended, eye-catching boutique hotel, the Absolutum is located across from Nádraží Holešovice metro station. While the neighbourhood wouldn't win a beauty contest, the hotel compensates with a nice list of amenities, including beautifully designed rooms with exposed brickwork, well-appointed modern bathrooms (many rooms have a tub), air-conditioning, an excellent restaurant, a wellness centre and free parking.

Sir Toby's Hostel
HOSTEL €

(Map p100; ☑246 032 610; www.sirtobys.com; Dělnická 24; dm 200-400Kč, s/d 950/1200Kč; P☺@☎; 🚊1, 3, 5, 25) Set in a refurbished apartment building with a spacious kitchen and common room, Sir Toby's is only 10 minutes north of the city centre by tram. The dorms have between six and 10 bunks, including all-female rooms, and the bigger dorms are some of the cheapest in Prague. All rooms are light and clean, but don't expect anything fancy.

Hotel Leon
HOSTEL, HOTEL €

(Map p100; ☑220 941 351; www.antee.cz; Ortenovo náměstí 26; s/d from 940/1440Kč; P☺@; Ⓜ Nádraží Holešovice, 🚊5, 12, 15) The Hotel Leon advertises itself as something between a hostel and a small hotel. In truth, it's actually much nicer than a standard hostel and not much more expensive (especially if you share a three- or four-bed room). The rooms are basic, with no TV or much of anything else, but are quiet and clean, with adjoining bathrooms.

✗ Eating

Eating in Prague's tourist areas is pricey, but cheaper eats are available just a block or two away. Regular lunch specials (look for *denní menu* in Czech) will stretch your travel budget. Most restaurants open from 11am to 11pm.

HRADČANY & MALÁ STRANA

Café Lounge
CAFE €

(Map p100; ☑257 404 020; www.cafe-lounge.cz; Plaská 8; mains 100-300Kč; ⊗7.30am-10pm Mon-Fri, 9am-1pm Sat, 9am-5pm Sun; ☺☎; 🚊6, 9, 12, 20, 22) Cosy and welcoming, Café Lounge sports an art-deco atmosphere, superb coffee, exquisite pastries and an extensive wine list. The all-day cafe menu offers freshly made salads and cornbread sandwiches, while lunch and dinner extends to dishes such as venison goulash or roast pike-perch with caraway seeds.

Lichfield
INTERNATIONAL €€

(Map p100; ☑266 112 284; www.theaugustine. com; Letenská 12; mains 270-460Kč; ⊗11am-11pm; ☎; 🚊12, 20, 22) Named after society photographer Lord Lichfield, whose images of celebrities adorn the walls, this stylish yet relaxed restaurant is worth seeking out (it's hidden away in the Augustine Hotel). The menu ranges from down-to-earth but delicious dishes such as ox cheeks braised

WANT MORE?

For in-depth information, reviews and recommendations at your fingertips, head to the Apple App Store to purchase Lonely Planet's *Prague City Guide* and *Czech Phrasebook* iPhone apps.

Alternatively, head to www.lonelyplanet.com/czech-republic/prague for planning advice, author recommendations, traveller reviews and insider tips.

in the restaurant's own St Thomas beer, to top-end favourites such as grilled lobster and caviar.

Cukrkávalimonáda
INTERNATIONAL €

(CKL; Map p100; ☑257 225 396; www.cukrkavalimonada.com; Lázeňská 7; mains 100-180Kč; ☺9am-7pm; ⛴12, 20, 22) A cute little cafe-cum-restaurant that combines minimalist modern styling with Renaissance-era painted timber roof-beams, CKL offers fresh pastas, frittatas, ciabattas, salads and pancakes (sweet and savoury) by day and a slightly more sophisticated bistro menu in the early evening. There's also a good breakfast menu offering ham and eggs, croissants, and yoghurt, and the hot chocolate is to die for.

U Modré Kachničky
CZECH €€€

(Map p100; ☑257 320 308; www.umodrekachnicky. cz; Nebovidská 6; mains 450-600Kč; ☺noon-4pm & 6.30pm-midnight; ⛴12, 20, 22) A plush 1930s-style hunting lodge hidden away on a quiet side street, 'At the Blue Duckling' is a pleasantly old-fashioned place with quiet, candlelit nooks perfect for a romantic dinner. The menu is heavy on traditional Bohemian duck and game dishes, such as roast duck with *slivovice* (plum brandy), plum sauce and potato pancakes.

Café de Paris
FRENCH €€

(Map p100; ☑603 160 718; www.cafedeparis.cz; Maltézské náměstí 4; mains 230-290Kč; ☺noon-midnight; ⛴12, 20, 22) A little corner of France tucked away on a quiet square, the Café de Paris is straightforward and unpretentious. So is the menu – just a couple of choices, onion soup or foie gras terrine to start, followed by entrecôte steak with chips, salad and a choice of sauces (they're very proud of the Café de Paris sauce, made to a 75-year-old recipe with 35 ingredients).

STARÉ MĚSTO

Mistral Café
BISTRO €

(Map p110; ☑222 317 737; www.mistralcafe.cz; Valentinská 11; mains 130-250Kč; ☺9am-11pm Mon-Fri, 10am-11pm Sat & Sun; ☎; Ⓜ Staroměstská) Is this the coolest bistro in the Old Town? Pale stone, bleached birchwood and potted shrubs make for a clean, crisp, modern look, and the clientele of local students and office workers clearly appreciate the competitively priced, well-prepared food. Fish and chips in crumpled brown paper with lemon and black-pepper mayo – yum!

Maitrea
VEGETARIAN €

(Map p110; ☑221 711 631; www.restaurace-maitrea. cz; Týnská ulička 6; mains 130-160Kč; ☺11.30am-11.30pm Mon-Fri, noon-11.30pm Sat & Sun; ☑; Ⓜ Staroměstská) Maitrea (a Buddhist term meaning 'the future Buddha') is a beautifully designed space full of flowing curves and organic shapes, from the sensuous polished-oak furniture and fittings to the blossom-like lampshades. The menu is inventive and wholly vegetarian, with dishes such as red bean chilli tortillas, beetroot cakes with sauerkraut and polenta, and pasta with smoked tofu, spinach and parmesan.

Vino di Vino
ITALIAN €€

(Map p110; ☑222 311 791; www.vinodivinopraha. cz; Štupartská 18; mains 250-300Kč; ☺noon-10pm; Ⓜ Náměstí Republiky) This Italian wine shop and delicatessen doubles as a restaurant, with a menu that makes the most of all those imported goodies – bresaola with smoked mozzarella, *spaghetti alla chitarra* (with squid and pecorino), and *saltimbocca alla Romana* (beef fillet with prosciutto and sage). Good list of Italian wines, too, including excellent Montepulciano d'Abbruzzo at 590Kč a bottle.

Lokál
CZECH €

(Map p110; ☑222 316 265; lokal-dlouha.ambi.cz; Dlouhá 33; mains 100-200Kč; ☺11am-1am Mon-Fri, noon-1am Sat, noon-10pm Sun; ☻; ⛴5, 8, 14) Who'd have thought it possible? A classic Czech beer hall (albeit with slick modern decor); excellent *tankové pivo* (tanked Pilsner Urquell); a daily changing menu of traditional Bohemian dishes; smiling, efficient, friendly service; and a no-smoking area!

NOVÉ MĚSTO & VINOHRADY

Sansho
ASIAN, FUSION €€

(Map p110; ☑222 317 425; www.sansho.cz; Petrská 25; mains 120-300Kč, 6-course dinner 750Kč;

⊘11.30am-10.30pm Tue-Thu, to 11.30pm Fri, 6-11.30pm Sat; ⊜; 🚃3, 8, 24) Friendly and informal best describes the atmosphere at this ground-breaking restaurant where British chef Paul Day champions Czech farmers by sourcing all his meat and vegetables locally. There's no menu – the waiter will explain what dishes are available, depending on market produce – typical dishes include salmon sashimi, pork belly with Asian spices, and 12-hour beef rendang.

Kofein
SPANISH €€
(Map p100; ☑273 132 145; www.ikofein.cz; Nitranská 9, Vinohrady; tapas plates 55-75Kč; ⊘11am-midnight Mon-Fri, 5pm-midnight Sat & Sun; 🐾🛋; Ⓜ Jiřího z Poděbrad, 🚃11) One of the hottest restaurants in town is this Spanish-style tapas place not far from the Jiřího z Poděbrad metro station. Descend into a lively space to see a red-faced chef minding the busy grill. Our faves include marinated trout with horseradish and pork belly confit with celeriac. Book ahead.

Mozaika
INTERNATIONAL €€
(Map p100; ☑224 253 011; www.restaurantmozaika.cz; Nitranská 13, Vinohrady; mains 180-450Kč; ⊜🛋; Ⓜ Jiřího z Poděbrad) One of the most dependably good restaurants in the neighbourhood. The theme is an updated French bistro, with beef tournedos and *boeuf bourguignon* sharing the spotlight with international entrees such as stir-fries and BBQ pork ribs. Advance booking essential.

Le Patio
INTERNATIONAL €€
(Map p110; ☑224 934 375; www.lepatio.cz; Národní třída 22; mains 200-420Kč; ⊘8am-11pm Mon-Fri, 9am-11pm Sat & Sun; Ⓜ Můstek) It's easy to walk past this place on bustling Národní třída without noticing it, but it's well worth dropping in to sample its accomplished menu of local and international dishes in a relaxed atmosphere that hints of oriental travel – a ship's prow, lots of Asian-style lamps, paintings and textiles.

Aromi
ITALIAN €€€
(Map p100; ☑222 713 222; www.aromi.cz; Mánesova 78, Vinohrady; mains 400-600Kč; ⊘noon-11pm Mon-Sat, to 10pm Sun; 🛋; Ⓜ Jiřího z Poděbrad, 🚃11) Red brick, polished wood and country-style furniture create a rustic atmosphere in this gourmet Italian restaurant. Brisk and businesslike at lunchtime, romantic in the evening, Aromi has a reputation for authentic, excellent Italian cuisine. Advance booking essential.

Drinking
Czech beers are among the world's best. The most famous brands are Budvar, Plzeňský Prazdroj (Pilsner Urquell) and Prague's own Staropramen. Independent microbreweries and regional Czech beers are also becoming more popular in Prague.

Bars & Pubs

Prague Beer Museum
PUB
(Map p110; ☑732 330 912; www.praguebeermuseum.com; Dlouhá 46; ⊘noon-3am; 🚃5, 8, 14) Although the name seems aimed at the tourist market, this lively and always heaving pub is very popular with Praguers. There are no fewer than 31 beers on tap (plus an extensive beer menu with tasting notes to guide you).

TOP CHOICE Pivovarský Klub
BEER HALL
(Map p100; ☑222 315 777; www.gastroinfo.cz/pivoklub; Křižíkova 17, Karlín; ⊘11am-11.30pm; Ⓜ Florenc) This bar is to beer what the Bodleian Library is to books – wall-to-wall shelves lined with myriad varieties of bottled beer from all over the world, and six guest beers on tap. Perch on a bar stool or head downstairs to the snug cellar and order some of the pub's excellent grub (such as authentic *guláš* with bacon dumplings for 235Kč) to soak up the beer.

TOP CHOICE Letná Beer Garden
BEER GARDEN
(Letenský zámeček; Map p100; ☑233 378 208; www.letenskyzamecek.cz; Letenské sady 341, Bubeneč; ⊘11am-11pm summer only; 🚃1, 8, 15, 25, 26 to Letenské náměstí) No accounting of watering holes would be complete without a nod toward the city's best beer garden, situated at the eastern end of Letna park. Buy a takeaway beer from a small kiosk and grab a picnic table, or sit on a small terrace where you can order beer-by-the-glass and decent pizza.

Pivovarský Dům
BREWERY
(Map p100; ☑296 216 666; www.gastroinfo.cz/pivodum; cnr Ječná & Lipová; ⊘11am-11pm; 🚃4, 6, 10, 16, 22) While the tourists flock to U Fleků, locals gather here to sample the classic Czech lager (40Kč per 0.5L) that is produced on the premises, as well as wheat beer and a range of flavoured beers (including coffee, banana and cherry, 40Kč per 0.3L).

Bukowski's
COCKTAIL BAR
(Map p100; ☑222 212 676; Bořivojova 86, Žižkov; ⊘6pm-2am; 🚃5, 9, 26) Like many of the drinking dens that are popular among expats,

Bukowski's is more a cocktail dive than a cocktail bar. Named after hard-drinking American writer Charles Bukowski, it cultivates a dark and slightly debauched atmosphere – the decor is self-consciously 'interesting' (when you can see it through the smoke-befogged candlelight).

TOP CHOICE U Vystřeleného oka PUB

(Map p100; ☎222 540 465; www.uvoka.cz; U Božích Bojovníků 3, Žižkov; ☺4.30pm-1am Mon-Sat; ☐133, 207) You've got to love a pub that has vinyl pads on the wall above the gents' urinals to rest your forehead on. 'The Shot-Out Eye' – the name pays homage to the one-eyed Hussite hero atop the hill behind the pub – is a bohemian (with a small 'b') hostelry with a raucous Friday-night atmosphere where the cheap Pilsner Urquell pulls in a typically heterogeneous Žižkov crowd.

Čili Bar COCKTAIL BAR

(Map p110; ☎777 945 848; www.cilibar.cz; Kožná 8; ☺5pm-2am; Ⓜ Můstek) This tiny cocktail bar could not be further removed in atmosphere from your typical Old Town drinking place. Cramped and smoky – there are Cuban cigars for sale – with battered leather armchairs competing for space with a handful of tables, it's friendly, relaxed and lively.

U Medvídků BEER HALL

(At the Little Bear; Map p110; ☎224 211 916; www.umedvidku.cz; Na Perštýně 7; ☺beer hall 11.30am-11pm, museum noon-10pm; ☎; Ⓜ Můstek) The most micro of Prague's microbreweries, with a capacity of only 250L, U Medvídků started producing its own beer only in 2005, though its beer hall has been around for years. What it lacks in size, it makes up for in strength – the dark lager produced here is the strongest in the country, with an alcohol content of 11.8%.

U Zlatého Tygra PUB

(Map p110; ☎222 221 111; www.uzlatehotygra.cz; Husova 17; ☺3-11pm; Ⓜ Staroměstská) The 'Golden Tiger' is one of the few Old Town drinking holes that has hung onto its soul, considering its location. It was novelist Bohumil Hrabal's favourite hostelry – there are photos of him on the walls – and the place that Václav Havel took Bill Clinton in 1994 to show him a real Czech pub.

Cafes

Krásný ztráty CAFE

(Map p110; ☎775 755 143; www.krasnyztraty.cz; Náprstkova 10; ☺9am-1am Mon-Fri, noon-1am Sat & Sun; ☎; ☐17, 18) This cool cafe doubles as an art gallery and occasional music venue, and is hugely popular with students from nearby Charles University. There are Czech newspapers and books to leaf through, chilled tunes on the sound system, and a menu of gourmet teas and coffees to choose from.

Kávovarna CAFE

(Map p110; ☎296 236 233; Štěpánská 61, Pasáž Lucerna; ☺8am-midnight; Ⓜ Můstek) This retro-styled place has bentwood chairs and curved wooden benches in the smoky, dimly lit front room (there's a nonsmoking room beyond the bar), with exhibitions of arty black-and-white photography on the walls. The coffee is good and reasonably priced, and there's delicious Kout na Šumavě beer on tap at a very reasonable 37Kč per half litre.

Café Imperial CAFE

(Map p110; ☎246 011 440; www.cafeimperial.cz; Na Poříčí 15; ☺7am-11pm; Ⓜ Náměstí Republiky) First opened in 1914, and given a complete facelift in 2007, the Imperial is a tour de force of art nouveau tiling – the walls and ceiling are covered in original ceramic tiles, mosaics, sculptured panels and bas-reliefs. The coffee is good, there are cocktails in the evening, and the Czech lunch and dinner offerings are first rate.

Literární Kavárna Řetězová CAFE

(Map p110; ☎222 220 681; Řetězová 10; ☺noon-11pm Mon-Fri, 5-11pm Sat & Sun; ☐17, 21) This is the kind of place where you can imagine yourself tapping out the Great Prague Novel on your laptop with a half-finished coffee on the table beside you. It's a plain, vaulted room with battered wooden furniture, a scatter of rugs on the floor and old black-and-white photos on the wall.

Grand Cafe Orient CAFE

(Map p110; Ovocný trh 19, Nové Město; Ⓜ Náměstí Republiky) Prague's only cubist café, the Orient was designed by Josef Gočár and is cubist down to the smallest detail, including the lampshades and coat-hooks. It was restored and reopened in 2005, having been closed since 1920. Decent coffee and inexpensive cocktails.

☆ Entertainment

From clubbing to classical music, puppetry to performance art, Prague offers plenty of entertainment. It's an established centre of classical music and jazz. For current listings see www.prague.tv. Try the following ticket agencies to see what might be on during your visit and to snag tickets online: **Bohemia Ticket International** (BTI; Map p110; 📞224 227 832; www.ticketsbti.cz; Malé náměstí 13; ⊘9am-5pm Mon-Fri), **Ticketpro** (Map p110; www.ticketpro.cz; Vodičkova 36, Pasáž Lucerna, Nové Město; ⊘noon-4pm & 4.30-8.30pm Mon-Fri) and **Ticketstream** (www.ticketstream.cz).

Performing Arts

Prague offers a nightly array of classic music, dance, opera and theatre in season (September to May). Buy tickets in advance at venue box offices or at the theatre an hour before the performance starts.

National Theatre   OPERA, BALLET
(Národní divadlo; Map p110; 📞224 901 377; www.narodni-divadlo.cz; Národní třída 2; tickets 30-1000Kč; ⊘box offices 10am-6pm; 🚋6, 9, 18, 21, 22) The much-loved National Theatre provides a stage for traditional opera, drama and ballet by the likes of Smetana, Shakespeare and Tchaikovsky, sharing the program alongside more modern works by composers and playwrights such as Philip Glass and John Osborne. The box offices are in the Nový síň building next door, and in the Kolowrat Palace (opposite the Estates Theatre).

Prague State Opera   OPERA, BALLET
(Státní opera Praha; Map p110; 📞224 901 886; www.opera.cz; Wilsonova 4; opera tickets 100-1150Kč; ballet tickets 100-800Kč; ⊘box office 10am-5.30pm Mon-Fri, 10am-noon & 1-5.30pm Sat & Sun; Ⓜ Muzeum) The impressive neo-rococo home of the Prague State Opera provides a glorious setting for performances of classical, mostly Italian, opera and ballet.

Smetana Hall   CLASSICAL MUSIC
(Smetanova síň; Map p110; 📞222 002 101; www.obecnidum.cz; náměstí Republiky 5; tickets 250-600Kč; ⊘box office 10am-6pm; Ⓜ Náměstí Republiky) Smetana Hall is the home venue of the Prague Symphony Orchestra (Symfonický orchestr hlavního města Prahy), and also stages performances of folk dance and music.

Rudolfinum   LIVE MUSIC
(Map p110; 📞227 059 227; www.ceskafilharmonie.cz; náměstí Jana Palacha, Staré Město; ⊘box office 10am-6pm Mon-Fri; Ⓜ Staroměstská) One of Prague's main venues for classical music concerts is the Dvořák Hall in the neo-Renaissance Ruldolfinum, home to the Czech Philharmonic Orchestra.

Estates Theatre   OPERA, BALLET
(Stavovské divadlo; Map p110; 📞224 902 322; www.narodni-divadlo.cz; Ovocný trh 1; tickets 30-1260Kč; ⊘box office 10am-6pm; Ⓜ Můstek) The Estates Theatre (p103) is the oldest theatre in Prague, famed as the place where Mozart conducted the premiere of *Don Giovanni* on 29 October 1787. The repertoire includes various opera, ballet and drama productions.

Archa Theatre   THEATRE
(Divadlo Archa; Map p110; 📞221 716 111; www.archatheatre.cz; Na poříčí 26; tickets 150-880Kč; ⊘box office 10am-6pm Mon-Fri; 🚋5, 8, 14) The Archa has been described as Prague's alternative National Theatre, a multifunctional venue for the avant garde and the experimental. As well as contemporary drama (occasionally in English), dance and performance art, the theatre also stages live music, from Indian classical to indie rock.

Švandovo Divadlo Na Smíchově   THEATRE
(Šandovo Theatre in Smíchov; Map p100; 📞257 318 666; www.svandovodivadlo.cz; Štefaníkova 57, Smíchov; tickets 150-300Kč; ⊘box office 11am-2pm & 2.30-7pm Mon-Fri, 5-7pm Sat & Sun; 🚋6, 9, 12, 20) This experimental theatre space, performing Czech and international dramatic works, is admired for its commitment to staging 'English-friendly' performances. It also hosts occasional live music and dance, as well as regular 'Stage Talks' – unscripted discussions with noted personalities.

Nightclubs

Cross Club   CLUB
(Map p100; 📞736 535 053; www.crossclub.cz; Plynární 23, Holešovice; admission free-150Kč; ⊘cafe noon-2am, club 6pm-4am; 📶; Ⓜ Nádraží Holešovice) An industrial club in every sense of the word: the setting in an industrial zone; the thumping music (both DJs and live acts); and the interior, an absolute must-see jumble of gadgets, shafts, cranks and pipes, many of which move and pulsate with light to the music. The program includes occasional live music, theatre performances and art happenings.

Roxy   CLUB, PERFORMING ARTS
(Map p110; 📞224 826 296; www.roxy.cz; Dlouhá 33; admission Fri & Sat free-300Kč; ⊘7pm-midnight Mon-Thu, to 6am Fri & Sat; 🚋5, 8, 14) Set in the ramshackle shell of an art-deco cinema, the legendary Roxy is the place to see the country's top DJs and frequent live acts. On the 1st floor is NoD, an 'experimental space' that stages drama, dance, performance art, cinema and live music.

TOP CHOICE Sasazu
CLUB

(Map p100; ☑284 097 455; www.sasazu.com; block 25, Holešovice market, Bubenské nábřeží 306, Holešovice; admission 200-1000Kč; ☻9pm-5am; ☎; Ⓜ Vltavská, 🚊1, 3, 5, 25) One of the most popular dance clubs in the city, Sasazu attracts the fashionable elite and hangers-on in equal measure. If you're into big dance floors and long lines (hint: go early), this is your place.

Radost FX
CLUB

(Map p100; ☑224 254 776; www.radostfx.cz; Bělehradská 120, Vinohrady; admission 100-250Kč; ☻10pm-6am; ☎; Ⓜ IP Pavlova) Though not quite as trendy as it once was, slick and shiny Radost is still capable of pulling in the crowds, especially for its Thursday hip-hop and R&B night, **FXbounce** (www.fxbounce.com). The place has a chilled-out, bohemian atmosphere, with an excellent lounge and vegetarian restaurant that keeps serving into the small hours.

Live Music

Palác Akropolis
LIVE MUSIC, CLUB

(Map p100; ☑296 330 911; www.palacakropolis.cz; Kubelíkova 27, Žižkov; admission free-50Kč; ☻club 7pm-5am; 🚊5, 9, 26 to Lipanska) The Akropolis is a Prague institution, a labyrinthine, sticky-floored shrine to alternative music and drama. Its various performance spaces host a smorgasbord of musical and cultural events, from DJs to string quartets to Macedonian Roma bands to local rock gods to visiting talent – Marianne Faithfull, the Flaming Lips and the Strokes have all played here.

Lucerna Music Bar
LIVE MUSIC

(Map p110; ☑224 217 108; www.musicbar.cz; Palác Lucerna, Vodičkova 36; admission 100-500Kč; ☻8pm-4am; Ⓜ Můstek, 🚊3, 9, 14, 24) Nostalgia reigns supreme at this atmospheric old theatre, now looking a little dog-eared, with anything from Beatles tribute bands to mainly Czech artists playing jazz, blues, pop, rock and more on midweek nights. But the most popular events are the regular 1980s and '90s video parties held every Friday and Saturday night.

JazzDock
JAZZ

(Map p100; ☑774 058 838; www.jazzdock.cz; Janáčkovo nábřeží 2, Smíchov; admission 90-150Kč; ☻4pm-3am; Ⓜ Anděl, 🚊7, 9, 12, 14) Most of Prague's jazz clubs are smoky cellar affairs. This riverside club is a definite step up, with a clean, modern decor and a decidedly romantic view out over the Vltava. This place draws some of the best local talent and oc-

casional international acts. Go early or book to get a good table.

Jazz Club U Staré Paní
JAZZ

(Map p100; ☑602 148 377; www.jazzstarapani.cz; Michalská 9; admission 250Kč; ☻7pm-1am Wed-Sun, music from 9pm; Ⓜ Můstek) Located in the basement of the Hotel U Staré Paní, this long-established but recently revamped jazz club caters to all levels of musical appreciation. There's a varied program of modern jazz, soul, blues and Latin rhythms, and a dinner menu if you want to make a full evening of it.

Gay & Lesbian Venues

The neighbourhood of Vinohrady is developing as a gay quarter, and the city enjoys a relaxed scene.

FREE Termix
CLUB

(Map p100; ☑222 710 462; www.club-termix.cz; Třebízského 4a, Vinohrady; ☻8pm-5am Wed-Sun; Ⓜ Jiřího z Poděbrad) Termix is one of Prague's most popular gay dance clubs, with an industrial high-tech vibe (lots of shiny steel and glass and plush sofas) and a young crowd that contains as many tourists as locals. The smallish dance floor fills up fast and you may have to queue to get in.

ON Club
CLUB, LIVE MUSIC

(Map p100; www.onclub.cz; Vinohradská 40, Vinohrady; ☻10pm-5am; Ⓜ Muzeum, 🚊11) The ON Club is the latest incarnation in a series of gay and gay-friendly clubs to occupy the cavernous Radio Palác building. The crowd is mostly men, but there are some women, and everyone is welcome. Most nights there's a disco, but weekends usually bring big-name DJs and occasional live music.

Cinemas

Most films are screened in their original language with Czech subtitles (*české titulky*), but some Hollywood blockbusters, especially those aimed at kids, are dubbed into Czech (*dabing*).

Kino Světozor
CINEMA

(Map p110; ☑608 330 088; www.kinosvetozor.cz; Vodičkova 41; tickets 90-120Kč; ☎; Ⓜ Můstek) The Světozor is under the same management as Kino Aero but is more central, and has the same emphasis on classic cinema and art-house films screened in their original language – everything from *Battleship Potemkin* and *Casablanca* to *Annie Hall* and *The Motorcycle Diaries*.

Kino Aero
CINEMA

(📞271 771 349; www.kinoaero.cz; Biskupcova 31, Žižkov; tickets 60-100Kč; 🚊5, 9, 10, 16, 19) The Aero is Prague's best-loved art-house cinema, with themed programs, retrospectives and unusual films, often in English or with English subtitles. This is the place to catch reruns of classics from *Smrt v Benátkách (Death in Venice)* to *Život Briana (The Life of Brian)*.

🛍 Shopping

Near Old Town Sq, explore the antique shops of Týnská and Týnská ulička.

Granát Turnov
JEWELLERY

(Map p110; 📞222 315 612; www.granat.eu; Dlouhá 28-30; ⊙10am-6pm Mon-Fri, to 1pm Sat; Ⓜ Náměstí Republiky) Part of the country's biggest jewellery chain, Granát Turnov specialises in Bohemian garnet, and has a huge range of gold and silver rings, brooches, cufflinks and necklaces featuring the small, dark, blood-red stones.

Kubista
HOMEWARES

(Map p110; 📞224 236 378; www.kubista.cz; Ovocný trh 19; ⊙10am-6pm Tue-Sun; Ⓜ Náměstí Republiky) Appropriately located in the Museum of Czech Cubism in Prague's finest cubist building, this shop specialises in limited-edition reproductions of distinctive cubist furniture and ceramics, and designs by masters of the form such as Josef Gočár and Pavel Janák.

Manufaktura
ARTS & CRAFTS

(Map p110; 📞257 533 678; www.manufaktura.cz; Melantrichova 17; ⊙10am-8pm; Ⓜ Můstek) There are several Manufaktura outlets across town, but this small branch near Old Town Sq seems to keep its inventory especially enticing.

Modernista
HOMEWARES

(Map p110; 📞224 241 300; www.modernista.cz; Celetná 12; ⊙11am-7pm; Ⓜ Náměstí Republiky) Modernista is an elegant gallery specialising in reproduction 20th-century furniture in classic styles ranging from art deco and cubist to functionalist and Bauhaus. The shop is inside the arcade at Celetná 12 (not visible from the street).

Moser
GLASS

(Map p110; 📞224 211 293; www.moser-glass.com; Na Příkopě 12; ⊙10am-8pm; Ⓜ Můstek) One of the most exclusive and respected of Bohemian glassmakers, Moser was founded in Karlovy Vary in 1857 and is famous for its rich and flamboyant designs. The shop on Na Příkopě is worth a browse as much for the decor as for the goods.

Pivní Galerie
FOOD & DRINK

(Map p100; 📞220 870 613; www.pivnigalerie.cz; U Průhonu 9, Holešovice; ⊙noon-7pm Tue-Fri; 🚊1, 3, 5, 25) If you think Czech beer begins and ends with Pilsner Urquell, a visit to the tasting room at Pivní Galerie (the Beer Gallery) will lift the scales from your eyes. Here you can sample and purchase a huge range of Bohemian and Moravian beers – nearly 150 varieties from 30 different breweries.

Shakespeare & Sons
BOOKS

(Map p100; 📞257 531 894; www.shakes.cz; U Lužického Semináře 10; ⊙11am-7pm; 🚊12, 20, 22) Excellent English-language bookshop with heaps of books in several rooms on several levels.

Globe Bookstore & Café
BOOKS

(Map p100; 📞224 934 203; www.globebookstore. cz; Pštrossova 6; ⊙9.30am-midnight Sun-Wed, 9.30am-1am Thu-Sat; 🛜; Ⓜ Karlovo Náměstí) A popular hangout for book-loving expats, the Globe is a cosy English-language bookshop with an excellent cafe.

ℹ Information

Dangers & Annoyances

Pickpockets work the crowds at the Astronomical Clock, Prague Castle and Charles Bridge, and on the central metro and tramlines, especially crowded trams 9 and 22.

Most taxi drivers are honest, but some operating from tourist areas overcharge their customers. Phone a reputable taxi company or look for the red and yellow signs for the 'Taxi Fair Place' scheme, indicating authorised taxi stands.

The park outside the main train station is a hangout for dodgy types and worth avoiding late at night.

Emergency

If your passport or valuables are stolen, obtain a police report and crime number. You'll need this for an insurance claim. There's usually an English-speaker on hand. The emergency phone number for the police is 📞158.

Internet Access

Many hotels, bars and fast-food restaurants provide wi-fi hotspots.

Globe Bookstore & Café (📞224 934 203; www.globebookstore.cz; Pštrossova 6; per min 1Kč; ⊙9.30am-midnight; 🛜; Ⓜ Karlovo Náměstí) No minimum. Also has ethernet ports so you can connect your own laptop, and free wi-fi.

Relax Café-Bar (☎224 211 521; www.relaxcafe-bar.cz; Dlážděná 4; per 15min 20Kč; ☺8am-10pm Mon-Fri, 2-10pm Sat; 🛜; Ⓜ Náměstí Republiky) A conveniently located internet cafe. Wi-fi is free.

Medical Services

Canadian Medical Care (☎235 360 133, 724 300 301; www.cmcpraha.cz; Veleslavínská 1, Veleslavín; ☺8am-6pm Mon-Fri, to 8pm Tue & Thu; 🚌20, 26) A pricey but professional private clinic with English-speaking doctors; an initial consultation will cost from 1500Kč to 2500Kč.

Na Homolce Hospital (☎257 271 111; www.homolka.cz; 5th fl, Foreign Pavilion, Roentgenova 2, Motol; 🚌167, Ⓜ Anděl) The best hospital in Prague, equipped and staffed to Western standards, with staff who speak English, French, German and Spanish.

Polyclinic at Národní (Poliklinika na Národní; ☎222 075 120, 24hr emergencies 777 942 270; www.poliklinika.narodni.cz; Národní třída 9, Nové Město; ☺8.30am-5pm Mon-Fri; Ⓜ Můstek) A central clinic with staff who speak English, German, French and Russian. Expect to pay around 800Kč to 1500Kč for an initial consultation.

Money

The major banks are best for changing cash, but using a debit card in an ATM gives a better rate of exchange. Avoid *směnárna* (private exchange booths), which advertise misleading rates and have exorbitant charges.

Post

Main post office (☎221 131 111; www.cpost.cz; Jindřišská 14, Nové Město; ☺2am-midnight; Ⓜ Můstek) Collect a ticket from the automated machines outside the main hall (press 1 for stamps and parcels, 4 for Express Mail Service – EMS).

Tourist Information

Prague Welcome (Map p110; ☎221 714 444; www.praguewelcome.cz; Old Town Hall, Staroměstské náměstí 5; ☺9am-7pm; Ⓜ Staroměstská) is the city's tourist information office, with branches at **Staré Město** (Map p110; Rytířská 31, Staré Město; ☺10am-7pm Mon-Sat; Ⓜ Můstek) and the **Malá Strana Bridge Tower** (Map p100; Mostecká; ☺10am-6pm Apr-Oct; 🚌12, 20, 22) as well as at Prague airport and the **main train station** (Map p110; Wilsonova 8, Nové Město; ☺10am-6pm Mon-Sat; Ⓜ Hlavní Nádraží). The offices stock maps and brochures, all free.

❶ Getting There & Away

Bus

The main terminal for international and domestic buses is **Florenc bus station** (ÚAN Praha Florenc; Map p100; ☎900 144 444; www.florenc.cz; Křižíkova 4; ☺4am-midnight, information counter 6am-9.30pm; Ⓜ Florenc), 600m northeast of the main train station. Short-haul tickets are sold on the bus, and long-distance domestic tickets are sold in the newly renovated central hall.

For convenience, some regional buses arrive at and depart from outlying metro stations, including Dejvická, Černý Most, Nádraží Holešovice, Smíchovské nádraží, Roztyly and Haje. Check timetables and departure points at www.idos.cz. Recommended bus lines include the following:

Eurolines (☎245 005 245; www.elines.cz) Big international coach service that runs buses to all over Europe.

Student Agency (☎800 100 300; www.studentagency.cz) Links major Czech cities; also services throughout Europe.

Train

Prague is well integrated into European rail networks and if you're arriving from somewhere in Europe, chances are you're coming by train. The Czech rail network is operated by **České dráhy** (ČD; Czech Railways; ☎840 112 113; www.cd.cz). Timetable information is available online at www.vlak-bus.cz.

Most trains arrive at **Praha hlavní nádraží** (Main Train Station; ☎840 112 113; www.cd.cz; Wilsonova 8, Nové Město). Some trains, particularly from Berlin, Vienna and Budapest, also stop at **Praha-Holešovice** (☎840 112 113; www.cd.cz; Vrbenského, Holešovice), north of the city centre. Both stations have their own stops on the metro line C (red).

❶ Getting Around

To/From the Airport

To get into town from the airport, buy a full-price public transport ticket (32Kč) from the Prague Public Transport Authority (p122) desk in the arrivals hall and take bus 119 (20 minutes, every 10 minutes, 4am to midnight) to the end of metro line A (Dejvická), then continue by metro into the city centre (another 10 to 15 minutes; no new ticket needed).

Note you'll need a half-fare (16Kč) ticket for your bag or suitcase (per piece) if it's larger than 25cm x 45cm x 70cm.

If you're heading to the southwestern part of the city, take bus 100, which goes to the Zličín metro station (line B).

There's also an **Airport Express** (tickets 50Kč; ☺5am-10pm) bus which takes 35 minutes and runs every 30 minutes. It goes to Praha hlavní nádraží (main train station), where you can connect to metro line C (buy a ticket from the driver; luggage goes free).

Alternatively, take a **Cedaz** (☎220 116 758; www.cedaz.cz; ticket 130Kč; ☺7.30am-7pm)

TRANSPORT FROM PRAGUE

Domestic Bus

DESTINATION	PRICE (KČ)	DURATION (HR)	FREQUENCY
Brno	165	2½	hourly
České Budějovice	150	2¾	several daily
Český Krumlov	180	3	7 daily
Karlovy Vary	150	2¼	8 daily
Kutná Hora	80	1¼	6 daily
Plzeň	100	1½	hourly

International Bus

DESTINATION	PRICE (KČ)	DURATION (HR)	FREQUENCY
Berlin (Germany)	1310	4½	daily
Budapest (Hungary)	1000	6	daily
Dresden (Germany)	840	2¼	daily
Munich (Germany)	1420	5¼	2 daily
Vienna (Vienna)	990	4½	several daily
Warsaw (Poland)	1590	12	3 weekly

Domestic Train

DESTINATION	PRICE (KČ)	DURATION (HR)	FREQUENCY
Brno	210	3	frequent
České Budějovice	220	2¾	several daily
Kutná Hora	100	1	4 daily
Olomouc	220	2¾	several daily
Plzeň	100	1½	hourly

International Train

DESTINATION	PRICE (KČ)	DURATION (HR)	FREQUENCY
Berlin (Germany)	737	5	daily
Bratislava (Slovakia)	381	4¼	several daily
Dresden (Germany)	483	2¼	several daily
Frankfurt (Germany)	1245	8	2 daily
Munich (Germany)	737	5	4 daily
Vienna (Austria)	483	4-5	several daily
Warsaw (Poland)	483	8½	2 daily

minibus from outside either arrival terminal to the Czech Airlines office near náměstí Republiky (20 minutes, every 30 minutes); buy a ticket from the driver. The minibus service also runs in the opposite direction for returning to the airport.

AAA Radio Taxi (p122) operates a 24-hour taxi service, charging around 500Kč to 700Kč to get to the centre of Prague. You'll find taxi stands outside both arrivals terminals. Drivers usually speak some English and accept credit cards.

Bicycle

Biking is gaining in popularity and several parts of the city now have marked bike lanes (look for yellow bike-path signage). Still, with its cobblestones, tram tracks and multitudes of pedestrians, Prague has a long way to go to catch up with far more bike-friendly cities like Vienna or Amsterdam.

The black market for stolen bikes is thriving, so don't leave bikes unattended for longer than a few minutes and always use the sturdiest lock money can buy.

City Bike (☑776 180 284; www.citybike-prague.com; Královdorská 5, Staré Město; rental per day 500Kč, tours per person 550-800Kč; ☺9am-7pm Apr-Oct; Ⓜ Náměstí Republiky) Rental includes helmet, padlock and map; good-quality Trek mountain bikes are available for 750Kč per 24 hours.

Praha Bike (☑732 388 880; www.prahabike.cz; Dlouhá 24; rental per day 500Kč, tours per person 490Kč; ☺9am-8pm; Ⓜ Náměstí Republiky) Hires out good, new bikes with lock, helmet and map, plus offers free luggage storage. It also offers student discounts and group bike tours.

Car & Motorcycle

Challenges to driving in Prague include cobblestones, trams and one-way streets. Try not to arrive or leave on a Friday or Sunday afternoon or evening, when Prague folk are travelling to and from their weekend houses.

Central Prague has many pedestrian-only streets, marked with *pěší zóna* (pedestrian zone) signs, where only service vehicles and taxis are allowed; parking can be a nightmare. Meter time limits range from two to six hours at around 50Kč per hour. Parking in one-way streets is normally only allowed on the right-hand side.

Public Transport

Prague's excellent public-transport system combines tram, metro and bus services. It's operated by the **Prague Public Transport Authority** (DPP; ☑800 191 817; www.dpp.cz) which has information desks at Prague airport (7am to 10pm) and in several metro stations, including Muzeum, Můstek, Anděl and Nádraží Holešovice. The metro operates daily from 5am to midnight.

The metro has three lines: line A (shown on transport maps in green) runs from the north-western side of the city at Dejvická to the east at Depo Hostivař; line B (yellow) runs from the southwest at Zličín to the northeast at Černý Most; and line C (red) runs from the north at Letňany to the southeast at Háje. Convenient stops for visitors include Staroměstská (closest to Old Town Sq), Malostranská (Malá Strana), Můstek (Wenceslas Sq), Muzeum (National Museum) and Hlavní nádraží (main train station).

After the metro closes, night trams (51 to 58) rumble across the city about every 40 minutes through the night (only full-price 32Kč tickets are valid on these services). If you're planning a late evening, find out if one of these lines passes near where you are staying.

TICKETS

Tickets are sold from machines at metro stations and some tram stops (coins only), as well as at DPP information offices and many newsstands and kiosks. Tickets are valid on all metros, trams and buses.

Tickets can be purchased individually or as discounted day passes valid for one or three days. A full-price individual ticket costs 32/16Kč per adult/child aged six to 15 years and senior aged 65 to 70 (kids under six ride free) and is valid for 90 minutes of unlimited travel, including transfers. For shorter journeys, buy short-term tickets that are valid for 30 minutes of unlimited travel. These cost 24/12Kč per adult/child and senior. Bikes and prams travel free.

If you're planning on staying more than a few hours, it makes sense to buy either a one- or three-day pass. One-day passes cost 110/55Kč per adult/child and senior; three-day passes cost 310Kč (no discounts available for children or seniors).

Taxi

Taxis are frequent and relatively expensive. The official rate for licensed cabs is 40Kč flagfall plus 28Kč per kilometre and 6Kč per minute while waiting. On this basis, any trip within the city centre – say, from Wenceslas Sq to Malá Strana – should cost around 170Kč. A trip to the suburbs, depending on the distance, should run from around 200Kč to 400Kč, and to the airport between 500Kč and 700Kč.

While the number of dishonest drivers has fallen in recent years, taxi rip-offs are still an occasional problem, especially among drivers who congregate in popular tourist areas like Old Town Sq and Wenceslas Sq.

Instead of hailing cabs off the street, call a radio taxi, as they're better regulated and more responsible. From our experience the following companies have honest drivers and offer 24-hour service and English-speaking operators:

AAA Radio Taxi (☑222 333 222, 14014; www.aaataxi.cz)

City Taxi (☑257 257 257; www.citytaxi.cz)

ProfiTaxi (☑14015; www.profitaxi.cz)

AROUND PRAGUE

Karlštejn

Rising above the village of Karlštejn, 30km southwest of Prague, this medieval castle is in such good shape it wouldn't look out of place on Disneyworld's Main St. The crowds come in theme-park proportions as well, but the peaceful surrounding countryside offers views of Karlštejn's stunning exterior that rival anything you'll see on the inside.

Karlštejn Castle (Hrad Karlštejn; ☑311 681 617; www.hradkarlstejn.cz; adult/child Tour 1 270/180Kč, Tour 2 300/200Kč, Tour 3 120/60Kč; ☺9am-6.30pm Jul & Aug, to 5.30pm Tue-Sun May, Jun & Sep, to 4.30pm Tue-Sun Apr & Oct, reduced hr Nov-Mar) was born of a grand pedigree, starting life in 1348 as a hideaway for the crown jewels and treasury of the Holy Roman Emperor, Charles IV. Run by an appointed burgrave, the castle was surrounded by a network of landowning knight-vassals, who came to the castle's aid whenever enemies moved against it.

Karlštejn again sheltered the Bohemian and the Holy Roman Empire crown jewels during the Hussite Wars of the 15th century, but fell into disrepair as its defences became outmoded. Considerable restoration work in the late-19th century returned the castle to its former glory.

There are three guided tours available. Tour 1 (50 minutes) passes through the Knight's Hall, still daubed with the coats-of-arms and names of the knight-vassals, Charles IV's bedchamber, the Audience Hall and the Jewel House, which includes treasures from the Chapel of the Holy Cross and a replica of the St Wenceslas Crown.

Tour 2 (70 minutes, May to October only) must be booked in advance and takes in the the Marian Tower, with the Church of the Virgin Mary and the Chapel of St Catherine, then moves on the Great Tower for the castle's star attraction, the exquisite Chapel of the Holy Cross.

Tour 3 (40 minutes, May to October only) visits the upper levels of the Great Tower, the highest point of the castle, which provides stunning views over the surrounding countryside.

❶ Getting There & Away

From Prague, there are frequent train departures daily from Prague's *hlavní nádraží* (main station). The journey takes about 40 minutes and costs around 50Kč.

Konopiště

Archduke Franz Ferdinand d'Este, heir to the Austro-Hungarian throne, is famous for being dead – after all, it was his assassination in 1914 in Sarajevo that sparked WWI. But the archduke was an enigmatic figure who avoided the intrigues of the Vienna court and for the last 20 years of his life hid away in what became his ideal country retreat.

Konopiště Chateau (Zámek Konopiště; ☑317 721 366; www.zamek-konopiste.cz; adult/child Tour 1 or 2 210/130Kč, Tour 3 310/210Kč; ☺10am-noon & 1-5pm Tue-Sun Jun-Aug, to 4pm Apr, May & Sep, 10am-noon & 1-3pm Sat & Sun Oct & Nov, closed Dec-Mar), lying amid extensive grounds 3km west of the town of Benešov, is a testament to the archduke's twin obsessions – hunting and St George. Having renovated the massive Gothic and Renaissance building in the 1890s and installed all the latest technology – including electricity, central heating, flush toilets, showers and a luxurious lift – Franz Ferdinand decorated his home with his hunting trophies.

His game books record that he shot about 300,000 creatures in his lifetime, from foxes and deer to elephants and tigers. About 100,000 animal trophies adorn the walls, each marked with the date and place it met its end – the crowded Trophy Corridor (Tours 1 and 3), with a forest of mounted animal heads, and the antler-clad Chamois Room (Tour 3), with its 'chandelier' fashioned from a stuffed condor, are truly bizarre sights.

❶ Getting There & Away

To reach Konopiště from Prague, take any one of the frequent trains to Benešov (70Kč, 50 minutes) and hike along a marked trail for 30 minutes. Infrequent buses (60Kč, one hour) leave from a small bus station at the top of the Roztyly metro stop on Prague's line C (red).

Kutná Hora

In the 14th century, the silver-rich ore under Kutná Hora, 60km southeast of Prague, gave the now-sleepy town an importance in Bohemia second only to Prague. The local mines and mint turned out silver *groschen* for use as the hard currency of Central Europe. The silver ore ran out in 1726, leaving the medieval townscape largely unaltered. Now, with several fascinating and unusual historical attractions, the Unesco World Heritage–listed town is a popular day trip from Prague.

◉ Sights

Sedlec Ossuary   CHURCH
(Kostnice; ☑327 561 143; www.ossuary.eu; Zámecká 127; adult/concession 60/40Kč; ☺8am-6pm Mon-Sat Apr-Sep, 9am-5pm Mar & Oct, 9am-4pm Nov-Feb) When the Schwarzenberg family

Kutná Hora

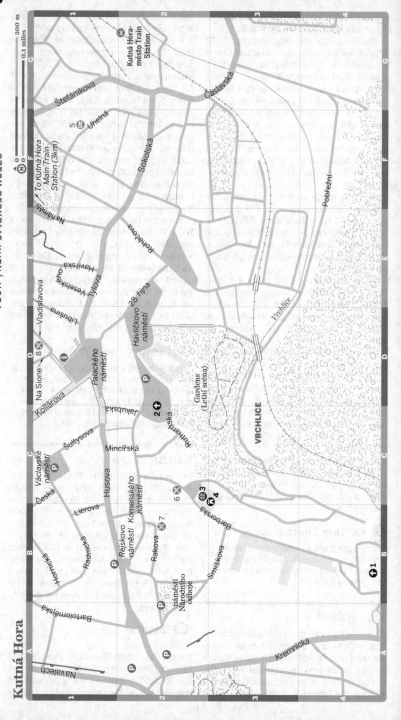

Kutná Hora-město Train Station

To Kutná Hora Main Train Station (3km)

VRCHLICE

Gardens (Letní scéna)

Vrchlice

náměstí Národního odboje

Rejskovo náměstí

Komenského náměstí

Václavské náměstí

Palackého náměstí

Havlíčkovo náměstí

Na náměti

Štefáníkova

Sokolská

Rohákova

Čáslavská

Pobřežní

Kremnická

Na valech

Bartolomějská

Horniká

Radnická

Lierova

Česká

Šultysova

Mincířská

Husova

Rakova

Smíškova

Barborská

Ruthardská

Jakubská

28. října

Tylova

Veselská

Havířská

Libušina

Vladislavova

Na Sione

Kollárova

Uhelna

200 m
0.1 miles

Kutná Hora

◎ **Sights**

purchased Sedlec monastery in 1870 they allowed a local woodcarver to get creative with the bones that had been piled in the crypt for centuries. But this was no piddling little heap of bones: it was the remains of no fewer than 40,000 people. The result was the remarkable 'bone church' of Sedlec Ossuary.

Garlands of skulls and femurs are strung from the vaulted ceiling like Addams Family Christmas decorations, while in the centre dangles a vast chandelier containing at least one of each bone in the human body. Four giant pyramids of stacked bones squat in each of the corner chapels, and crosses, chalices and monstrances of bone adorn the altar. There's even a Schwarzenberg coat of arms made from bones – note the crow pecking the eyes from the Turk's head, a grisly motif of the Schwarzenberg family.

Cathedral of St Barbara　　　CHURCH
(Chrám sv Barbora; ☑327 512 115; Barborská; adult/concession 60/40Kč; ☺10am-4pm Mon, 9am-5.30pm Tue-Sun May-Sep, 10am-4pm daily Oct-Apr) Kutná Hora's greatest monument is the Gothic Cathedral of St Barbara. Rivalling Prague's St Vitus in size and magnificence, its soaring nave culminates in elegant, six-petalled ribbed vaulting, and the ambulatory chapels preserve original 15th-century frescoes, some of them showing miners at work.

Construction began in 1380, interrupted during the Hussite Wars and abandoned in 1558 when the silver began to run out. It was finally completed in neogothic style at the end of the 19th century. Take a walk around the outside of the church, too; the terrace at the east end enjoys the finest view in town.

Czech Silver Museum　　　MUSEUM
(České muzeum stříbra; ☑327 512 159; www.cms-kh.cz; Barborská 28; adult/concession Tour 1 70/40Kč, Tour 2 120/80Kč, combined 140/90Kč; ☺10am-6pm Jul & Aug, 9am-6pm May, Jun & Sep, 9am-5pm Apr & Oct) From the southern side of St James Church, a narrow cobbled lane (Ruthardská) leads down and then up to the Hrádek (Little Castle). Originally part of the town's fortifications, it was rebuilt in the 15th century as the residence of Jan Smíšek, administrator of the royal mines, who grew rich from silver he illegally mined right under the building. It now houses the Czech Silver Museum.

Visiting is by guided tour. Tour I (one hour) leads through the main part of the museum where the exhibits celebrate the mines that made Kutná Hora wealthy, including a huge wooden device once used to lift loads weighing as much as 1000kg from the 200m-deep shafts.

Tour II (90 minutes) allows you to don a miner's helmet and explore 500m of medieval mine shafts beneath the town. Kids need to be aged at least seven for this tour.

🛏 Sleeping

Penzión U Kata　　　PENSION €
(☑327 515 096; www.ukata.cz; Uhelná 596; s/d/tr 500/760/1140Kč; ᴘ◉☺) You won't lose your head over the rates at this good-value family hotel called the 'Executioner'. Bikes can be hired for 200Kč per hour and it's a short stroll from the bus station. Downstairs is a welcoming Czech beer hall and restaurant.

🍴 Eating & Drinking

Pivnice Dačický　　　BEER HALL €
(☑327 512 248; www.dacicky.com; Rakova 8; mains 120-330Kč; ☺11am-11pm) Get some froth on your moustache at this old-fashioned, wood-panelled Bohemian beer hall, where you can dine on dumplings and choose from five different draught beers, including Pilsner Urquell, Budvar and Primátor Dark.

U Sňeka Pohodáře　　　ITALIAN €
(☑327 515 987; www.usneka.cz; Vladislavova 11; mains 100-235Kč; ☺) Kutná Hora's best Italian flavours are found at this cosy local favourite that's very popular for takeaway or dine-in pizza and pasta. And no, we don't know why it's called 'The Contented Snail'.

Kavárna Mokate　　　CAFE
(Barborská 37; ☺8am-10pm Mon-Fri, 10am-10pm Sat, 10am-8pm Sun) This cosy little cafe, with

ancient earthenware floor tiles, timber beams, mismatched furniture and oriental rugs dishes up a wide range of freshly ground coffees and exotic teas, as well as iced tea and coffee in summer.

ℹ️ Information

The **Kutná Hora tourist office** (Informační centrum; ☎327 512 378; www.guide.kh.cz; Palackého náměstí 377; ☺9am-6pm Apr-Sep, 9am-5pm Mon-Fri, 10am-4pm Sat & Sun Oct-Mar) books accommodation, provides internet access (1Kč per minute) and rents out bicycles (220Kč per day).

ℹ️ Getting There & Away

Kutná Hora can be reached from Prague by either bus or train. The town's bus station is located on the Old Town's northeastern edge, which is convenient to the Old Town sites, but 3km from the Sedlec Ossuary. There's regular bus service throughout the day from Prague (68Kč, 1¼ hours). Some buses depart from the main Florenc bus station, while others leave from a small stop at the Haje metro station on line C (red).

Kutná Hora's main train station, by contrast, is just 800m from the ossuary, but about 3km from the Old Town. Sporadic trains throughtout the day leave from Prague's main station (101Kč, one hour).

Terezín

The military fortress at Terezín (*Theriesenstadt* in German), 60km north of Prague, was built by the Habsburgs in the 18th century to guard the empire's northern frontier against possible incursion by the Prussian army, but the place is better known as a notorious WWII prison and concentration camp.

Around 150,000 men, women and children, mostly Jews, were detained here en route to the Auschwitz-Birkenau extermination camps: 35,000 of them died here of hunger, disease or suicide, and only 4000 ultimately survived. From 1945 to 1948 the fortress served as an internment camp for the Sudeten Germans, who were expelled from Czechoslovakia after the war.

Terezín also played a tragic role in deceiving the world about the ultimate goals of the Nazi's 'Final Solution'. Official visitors were immersed in a charade, with Terezín being presented as a Jewish 'refuge', complete with shops, schools and cultural organisations – even an autonomous Jewish 'government'.

As late as April 1945, Red Cross visitors delivered positive reports.

The **Terezín Memorial** (www.pamatnik-terezin.cz) consists of the **Ghetto Museum** (muzeum ghetta; ☎416 782 225; adult/child 170/140Kč, combined with Lesser Fortress 210/160Kč; ☺9am-6pm Apr-Oct, to 5.30pm Nov-Mar) in the Main Fortress, the **Magdeburg Barracks** (cnr Tyršova & Vodárenská; ☺9am-6pm Apr-Oct, to 5.30pm Nov-Mar) and the **Lesser Fortress** (Malá pevnost; ☎416 782 576; Pražská; adult/child 170/140Kč, combined with Ghetto Museum 210/170Kč; ☺8am-6pm Apr-Oct, to 4.30pm Nov-Mar), a 10-minute walk east across the Ohře River.

The Ghetto Museum records daily life in the camp during WWII, through moving displays of paintings, letters and personal possessions. Displays at the Magdeburg Barracks highlight the rich cultural life – including music, theatre, fine arts and literature – that flourished against this backdrop of fear.

The Lesser Fortress was used to hold political prisoners, including anti-Nazi Czech partisans. Take the grimly fascinating self-guided tour through the prison barracks, workshops, morgues and mass graves, before arriving at the bleak execution grounds, where more than 250 prisoners were shot.

ℹ️ Getting There & Away

Direct buses from Prague to Litoměřice (165Kc return, one hour) normally stop at Terezín. Buses leave from outside the Praha-Holešovice train station.

BOHEMIA

The Czech Republic's western province boasts surprising variety. Český Krumlov, with its riverside setting and dramatic Renaissance castle, is in a class by itself, but lesser-known towns like Loket exude unexpected charm. Big cities like České Budějovice and Plzeň offer urban attractions like great museums and restaurants. The spa towns of western Bohemia were world famous in the 19th century and retain old-world lustre.

Karlovy Vary

POP 60,000

Karlovy Vary (KV) is the closest the Czech Republic has to a glam resort, but it is still only glam with a small 'g'. While the resort was famous across Europe in the 19th century as a *kurort* (health spa), these days the town attracts mostly day trippers, content to stroll the main colonnade area and sip on allegedly health-restoring sulphuric compounds from ceramic, spouted drinking cups. Despite the spa rep, Karlovy Vary is not entirely welcoming to walk-ins looking for high-end treatments like exotic massages and peelings; these services are available, but require advance bookings. Good bus services from Prague makes this an easy return day trip.

◉ Sights

FREE **Hot Spring Colonnade** SPRING
(Vřídelní Kolonáda; www.karlovyvary.cz; Vřídelní Kolonáda; ⊘Pramen Vřídlo 6am-7pm) The Hot Spring Colonnade houses the most impressive of the town's geysers, **Pramen Vřídlo**. The building itself is an incongruous, mid-'70s structure once dedicated to Soviet cosmonaut Yuri Gagarin. The geyser belches some 15m into the air; people lounge about inhaling the vapours or sampling the waters from a line of taps in the next room.

Church of Mary Magdalene CHURCH
(kostel sv Maří Magdaléná; www.karlovyvary.cz; náměstí Svobody 2; ⊘open during Mass) Whatever your thoughts on the excesses of baroque architecture, it's hard not to fall for this confection by Kilian Ignatz Dientzenhofer, dating from the 1730s. You can arrange a tour through a branch of the Infocentrum to see the baroque **crypt** and the unique **funeral chapel**.

Church of SS Peter & Paul CHURCH
(kostel Sv Petra a Pavla; Krále Jiřího; ⊘9am-6pm) The impressive Orthodox Church of SS Peter & Paul, with five polished onion domes and art nouveau exterior murals, was apparently modelled after a similar church near Moscow. One of the church's most prominent decorations is a relief depicting Tsar Peter the Great.

Karlovy Vary Museum MUSEUM
(Krajské muzeum Karlovy Vary; ☎353 226 252; www.kvmuz.cz; Nová Louka 23; adult/concession 60/30Kč; ⊘9am-noon & 1-5pm Wed-Sun) The Karlovy Vary Museum has extensive exhibits on the town's history as a spa resort, Czech glasswork and the area's natural history.

Moser Glass Museum MUSEUM
(Sklářské muzeum Moser; ☎353 416 132; www.moser-glass.com; Kpt Jaroše 19; adult/child 80/50Kč, glassworks 120/70Kč, combined ticket 180/100Kč;

⊘9am-5pm, glassworks to 2.30pm; ☐1) The Moser Glass Museum has more than 2000 items on display. Tours of the adjacent **glassworks** and combined tickets are also available. There is a shop here, too, but the prices are not anything special, and there's another shop in town. To get here catch bus 1 from the Tržnice bus station.

FREE **Diana Lookout Tower** TOWER
(☎353 222 872; www.karlovy-vary.cz/en/diana-tower; ⊘9am-7pm Jun-Sep, to 6pm Apr, May & Oct, to 5pm Feb, Mar, Nov & Dec) This lookout tower, atop a wooded hill to the west of the historic spa area, is the perfect destination for a short afternoon hike.

🏃 Activities

Castle Spa SPA
(Zámecké Lázně; ☎353 225 502; www.castle-spa.com; Zámecký vrch 1; ⊘7.30am-7.30pm Mon-Fri, from 8.30am Sat & Sun) Most KV accommodation offers some kind of spa treatment for a fee, but if you're just a casual visitor or day tripper, consider Castle Spa, a modernised spa centre complete with a subterranean thermal pool. Consult the website for a full menu of treatments and prices.

Swimming Pool SWIMMING
(☎359 001 111; www.thermal.cz; IP Pavlova 11; adult/child 100/80Kč; ⊘8.30am-8pm) The Hotel Thermal's 50m pool is open to the public year-round. The waters are heated by thermal springs. To find it, follow the 'Bazén' signs up the hill behind the hotel to the pool.

🎬 Festivals & Events

Karlovy Vary International Film Festival FILM
(www.kviff.com; ⊘Jul) The Karlovy Vary Film Festival always features the year's top films as well as attracting plenty of (B-list) stars. It's rather behind the likes of Cannes, Venice and Berlin but is well worth the trip.

🛏 Sleeping

Accommodation prices in Karlovy Vary have risen steeply in recent years to be similar to those in Prague, especially in July during the film festival. Indeed, if you're planning a July arrival, make sure to book well in advance. Expect to pay an additional 'spa tax' (15Kč per bed per night). The city's Infocentrum offices can help out with hostel, pension and hotel bookings. Alternatively, consider staying in Loket and visiting Karlovy Vary as a day trip.

TOP CHOICE **Hotel Maltézský Kříž**　　　HOTEL €€
(☑353 169 011; www.maltezskykriz.cz; Stará Louka 50; s/d 1650/2800Kč; @☎) Welcome to Karlovy Vary's best-value midrange hotel. Oriental rugs and wooden floors combine at this spiffy property, with cosy rooms and a more spacious double-storeyed apartment. The bathrooms are decked out in warm, earthy tones.

Carlsbad Plaza　　　HOTEL €€€
(☑353 225 501; www.carlsbadplaza.cz; Mariánsko-lázeňská 23; s/d 4000/6000Kč; P☺✳@☎☲) Seriously stylish, this relatively new hotel has raised the bar in spa town, with soothingly modern treatment facilities, classy rooms and a vegetarian-friendly Asian restaurant.

Embassy Hotel　　　HOTEL €€
(☑353 221 161; www.embassy.cz; Nová Luka 21; s/d from 2260/3130Kč; @☎) KV's not short of top-end hotels, but most lack the personal touch of the family-owned Embassy, with its riverside location and perfectly pitched heritage rooms. The hotel's pub and restaurant have seen visits from plenty of film-fest luminaries.

Grandhotel Pupp　　　HOTEL €€€
(☑353 109 631; www.pupp.cz; Mírové náměstí 2; r 4000-7000Kč; P☺✳@☎☲) No accounting of KV's hotels would be complete without mentioning the granddaddy, the Pupp, whose history dates back to the 18th century. Take a look at a few rooms, as layouts and furnishings differ from wing to wing.

OPLÁTKY

To quote Monty Python, 'Do you get wafers with it?' The answer is a resounding 'yes' according to Karlovry Vary locals, who prescribe the following method of taking your spring water: have a sip from your *lázeňský pohárek* (spa cup), then dull the sulphurous taste with a big, round, sweet wafer called *oplatky*. *Oplatky* are sold for around 10Kč each at a few spa hotels and speciality shops, or you can pick them up at **Kolonada Oplatky** (cnr Nehrova & Masarykova). Steer clear of the fancy chocolate or hazelnut flavours, though; they're never as crunchily fresh and warm as the standard vanilla flavour.

Even if you're not staying here, take a peek inside; the restaurants are very good, and the period-piece atmosphere is perfect.

Hotel Romania　　　HOTEL €€
(☑353 222 822; www.romania.cz; Zahradni 49; s/d 1200/1950Kč; ☎) Don't be put off by the ugly monolith of the Hotel Thermal dominating the views from this good-value, reader-recommended hotel (just squint a little). The spacious rooms are very tidy and the English-speaking staff very helpful.

Hotel Boston　　　HOTEL €
(☑353 362 711; www.boston.cz; Luční vrch 9; s/d 1390/1570Kč; ☺☎) Tucked away down a quiet lane, this family-owned hotel has relatively spacious rooms decorated in bright colours with updated bathrooms. The flash cafes of Stará Louka are just around the corner.

🍴 Eating & Drinking

Hospoda U Švejka　　　CZECH €€
(☑353 232 276; www.svejk-kv.cz; Stará Louka 10; mains 160-370Kč; ☺11am-11pm; ☺) A great choice for lunch or dinner, right in the heart of the spa centre. Though the presentation borders on extreme kitsch, the food is actually very good and the atmosphere not unlike a classic Czech pub.

Embassy Restaurant　　　CZECH €€€
(☑353 221 161; www.embassy.cz; Nová Louka 21; mains 200-500Kč) The in-house restaurant of the Embassy Hotel (p128) is a destination in its own right. The dining room is richly atmospheric and the food, mostly Czech standards like roast pork or duck, is top notch. There's an excellent wine list, and in nice weather they sometimes offer outdoor seating.

Tandoor　　　INDIAN €€
(☑608 701 341; www.tandoor-kv.cz; IP Pavlova 25; mains 150-250Kč; ☺noon-10pm Mon-Sat, to 6pm Sun; ☺) Located under a block of flats, Tandoor turns out a winning combo of authentic Indian flavours, Gambrinus beer and smooth, creamy lassis. Vegetarian options abound, or if you're after a serious chilli hit, order the Chicken Phall.

Promenáda　　　INTERNATIONAL €€€
(☑353 225 648; www.hotel-promenada.cz; Tržiště 31; mains 250-650Kč) The house restaurant of the Hotel Promenáda has appeared in some 'best of' lists for the Czech Republic and is a perennial favourite on online forums. The elegant

dining area is conducive to a memorable evening, and the food is very good (though perhaps not always worth the steep prices).

Sklípek CZECH €
(☑353 220 222; www.restaurantsklipek.com; Moskevská 2; meals 120-180Kč) Red-checked tablecloths and an emphasis on good steaks, fish and pasta give this place an honest, rustic ambience missing from the more expensive chi-chi spots down the hill in the spa district.

Café Elefant CAFE
(☑353 223 406; Stará Louka 30; coffee 50Kč) Classy old-school spot for coffee and cake. A tad touristy, but still elegant and refined.

Retro Cafe Bar BAR
(☑353 100 710; www.retrocafebar.cz; TG Masaryka 18; ⊙10am-midnight Sun-Thu, to 3am Fri & Sat) A retro-themed bar, cafe and restaurant that defies easy categorisation. A nice place to chill for coffee or a cocktail, and the food is not bad either. Retro Cafe Bar also has music in the evenings and retro-themed nights.

ℹ Information

Karlovy Vary has several tourist information offices scattered around town – the main office is at **Dolní nádrazi** (☑353 232 838; www.karlovyvary.cz; Západní 2a, lower bus station; ⊙9am-6pm Mon-Fri, 10am-5pm Sat & Sun) and there are others at **Hotel Thermal** (☑355 321 171; www.karlovyvary.cz; IP Pavlova 11; ⊙9am-5pm Mon-Fri, 10am-5pm Sat & Sun) and **Hot Spring Colonnade** (☑773 291 243; www.karlovyvary.cz; Vřídelní kolonáda; ⊙9am-5pm Mon-Fri, 10am-5pm Sat & Sun). In addition to providing maps and helpful advice, the offices can help find accommodation in private rooms and apartments that are much cheaper than hotels.

ℹ Getting There & Away

Buses are the only practical way of reaching Karlovy Vary. **Student Agency** (www.studentagency.cz) runs frequent buses to/from Prague Florenc (from 155Kč, 2¼ hours, several daily) departing from the main bus station beside Dolní nádraží train station. Buses to nearby Loket (30Kč, 30 minutes) run throughout the day.

Loket
POP 3200

Surrounded by a wickedly serpentine loop in the Ohře River, the picturesque village of Loket may as well be on an island. According to the local tourist office, it was Goethe's favourite town and, after a lazily subdued stroll around the gorgeous main square and castle, it may be yours as well. Most people visit Loket as a day trip from Karlovy Vary, but it's also a sleepy place to ease off the travel accelerator for a few days, especially when the day trippers have departed. Loket also makes a good base for visiting Karlovy Vary.

◉ Sights

Hrad Loket CASTLE
(Loket Castle; ☑352 684 648; www.hradloket.cz; Hrad; adult/concession with English guide 110/90Kč, with English text 95/75Kč; ⊙9am-4.30pm Apr-Oct, 9am-3.30pm Nov-Mar) Built on the site of a Romanesque fort, of which the only surviving bits are the tall, square tower and fragments of a rotunda. Its present late-Gothic look dates from the late 14th century. From 1788 to 1947 it was used as a prison. Highlights include two rooms filled with the town's lustrous porcelain and views from the castle tower.

🏃 Activities

Ask at the Infocentrum about **hiking** possibilities in the surrounding forests, including a semi-ambitious day hike to Karlovy Vary (around four hours) along a 17km blue-marked trail. Karlovy Vary is also the destination for **rafting** trips.

🛏 Sleeping & Eating

There are plenty of cafes and pizzerias that come and go with the season scattered around the main square.

Hotel Císař Ferdinand HOTEL €€
(☑352 327 130; www.hotel-loket.cz; TG Masaryka 136; s/d 1060/1850Kč; P❋@🖙🏊) Located in the centre of town, this former malt house of a local brewery has recently renovated rooms and the best little microbrewery and restaurant in town.

ℹ Information

Infocentrum Loket (Loket Information Centre; ☑352 684 123; www.loket.cz; TG Masaryka 12; ⊙10.30am-12.30pm & 1-5pm) Decent source of local info, though most brochures and maps are in German. Has internet access (10Kč per 15 minutes).

ℹ Getting There & Away

Frequent bus departures link Karlovy Vary to Loket (30Kč, 20 minutes). The bus arriving from Karlovy Vary stops across the bridge from the Old Town. Walk across the bridge to reach the castle, accommodation and tourist information.

Plzeň

POP 173,000

Plzeň, the regional capital of western Bohemia and the second-biggest city in Bohemia after Prague, is best known as the home of the Pilsner Urquell Brewery, but it has a handful of other interesting sights and enough good restaurants and night-time pursuits to justify an overnight stay. Most of the sights are located near the central square, but the brewery itself is about a 15-minute walk outside the centre. Try to arrive in the morning to tour the non-drinking attractions first, and save the brewery tour and inevitable post-tour beers for the late afternoon (which makes for a more natural progression to dinner, continuing the pub crawl after dark).

◎ Sights

Pilsner Urquell Brewery   BREWERY
(Prazdroj; ☏377 062 888; www.prazdroj.cz; U Prazdroje 7; guided tour adult/child 150/80Kč; ◷8.30am-6pm Apr-Sep, to 5pm Oct-Mar; tours in English 12.45pm, 2.15pm & 4.15pm) Plzeň's most popular attraction is the Pilsner Urquell Brewery, in operation since 1842 and arguably home to the world's best beer. Entry is by guided tour only, with three tours in English available daily. Tour highlights include a trip to the old cellars (dress warmly) and a glass of unpasteurised nectar at the end.

Brewery Museum   MUSEUM
(☏377 235 574; www.prazdroj.cz; Veleslavínova 6; adult/child guided tour 120/90Kč, English text 90/60Kč; ◷10am-6pm Apr-Dec, to 5pm Jan-Mar) The Brewery Museum offers an insight into how beer was made (and drunk) in the days before Prazdroj was founded. Highlights include a mock-up of a 19th-century pub, a huge wooden beer tankard from Siberia and a collection of beer mats. All have English captions and there's a good English written guide available.

Underground Plzeň   UNDERGROUND
(Plzeňské historické podzemí; ☏377 235 574; www. plzenskepodzemi.cz; Veleslavínova 6; adult/child

---

WORTH A TRIP

MARIÁNSKÉ LÁZNĚ & CHODOVÁ PLANÁ

Mariánské Lázně (known abroad as Marienbad) is smaller, less urban and arguably prettier than Karlovy Vary. In the resort's heyday, Mariánské Lázně drew such luminaries as Goethe, Thomas Edison, Britain's King Edward VII and even author Mark Twain.

These days most visitors seem to be day trippers from Germany, hauled in by coach to stroll the gardens and colonnades before repairing to a cafe for the inevitable *apfelstrudel* (apple strudel) then the ride back home.

The restored cast-iron **Colonnade** (Lázeňská kolonáda; Lázeňská kolonáda; ◷6am-6pm) is the spa's striking centrepiece, with a whitewashed pavilion that houses taps for the various springs. Do as others do and purchase a porcelain drinking mug for walking and sipping. Notices on the walls (in English too) describe the various properties of the spa waters.

The colonnade is the site of numerous classical and brass-band concerts throughout the day in high season. In the evening, there's a **singing fountain**, where lights and water sashay to the sounds of Bach and Chopin.

The centrally located **Infocentrum** (☏354 622 474; www.marianskelazne.cz; Hlavní třída 47; ◷9am-6pm) is a good place to turn for information on spa treatments and hiking possibilities in the ample forests surrounding the town.

Mariánské Lázně is easy to reach from both Prague and Plzeň. Half a dozen trains a day run from Prague (250Kč, three hours), passing through Plzeň en route. Regular (slow) trains link Mariánské Lázně and Karlovy Vary (63Kč, 1¾ hours).

If you prefer your spas with suds, so to speak, not far from Mariánské Lázně, in the village of **Planá**, you'll find a unique beer spa, **Beer Wellness Land**, at the **Chodovar Brewery** (☏374 617 100; www.chodovar.cz; Pivovarská 107; treatments from 660Kc). As the name implies, it's similar to a water bath, but here the liquid is heated beer, complete with confetti-sized fragments of hops. This may very well be the perfect spot to simultaneously sample both of Bohemia's claims to fame: world-class spas and beer.

90/70Kč; ⊙10am-6pm Apr-Dec, to 5pm Feb-Mar, closed Jan; English tour 1pm daily) This extraordinary tour explores the passageways below the old city. The earliest were probably dug in the 14th century, perhaps for beer production or defence; the latest date from the 19th century. Of an estimated 11km that have been excavated, some 500m of tunnels are open to the public. Bring extra clothing (it's a chilly 10°C underground).

St Bartholomew Church
CHURCH

(kostel Sv Bartoloměje; ☑377 226 098; www.katedralaplzen.org; náměstí Republiky; adult/concession church 20/10Kč, tower 35/25Kč; ⊙10am-6pm Wed-Sat Apr-Sep, Wed-Fri Oct-Dec) Gigantic Gothic St Bartholomew Church looms over the surrounding facades from the centre of náměstí Republiky. Ask at the City Information Centre (p132) about guided tours. Look inside at the delicate marble 'Pilsen Madonna' (dating from c 1390) on the main altar, or climb the 301 steps to the top of the tower (weather permitting) for serious views.

Puppet Museum
MUSEUM

(muzeum Loutek; ☑378 370 801; www.muzeumloutek.cz; náměstí Republiky 23; adult/concession 60/30Kč; ⊙10am-6pm Tue-Sun; 🚼) Since opening in 2011, this museum has been a hit with the younger set. The exhibitions are well done, and many are interactive, allowing visitors to indulge their inner puppeteers.

Great Synagogue
SYNAGOGUE

(Velká Synagoga; ☑377 223 346; www.zoplzen.cz; sady Pětatřicátníků 11; adult/child 60/40Kč; ⊙10am-6pm Sun-Fri Apr-Oct) The Great Synagogue, west of the Old Town, is the third-largest in the world – only those in Jerusalem and Budapest are bigger. It was built in the Moorish style in 1892 by the 2000 Jews who lived in Plzeň at the time. English guides cost 500Kč. The building is often used for concerts and art exhibitions.

Patton Memorial Pilsen
MUSEUM

(☑378 037 954; www.patton-memorial.cz; Podřežni 10; adult/concession 60/40Kč; ⊙9am-1pm & 2-5pm Tue-Sun) The Patton Memorial Pilsen details the liberation of Plzeň in May 1945 by the American army, under General George S Patton. Especially poignant are the handwritten memories of former American soldiers who have returned to Plzeň over the years, and the museum's response to the communist-era revisionist fabrications that claimed Soviet troops, not Americans, were responsible for the city's liberation.

🛏 Sleeping

Pension Stará Plzeň
PENSION €

(☑377 259 901; www.pension-sp.cz; Na Roudné 12; s 600-1000Kč, d 800-1200Kč; 🅿😊@🛜) The pension 'Old Pilsen' offers light-and-sunny rooms with skylights, wooden floors and comfy beds. The more expensive rooms offer antique-style beds, Persian rugs and exposed, wood-beam ceilings. To get here, walk north on Rooseveltova across the river, then turn right onto Na Roudné and continue for 300m.

Courtyard by Marriott
HOTEL €€

(☑373 370 100; www.marriott.com; sady 5 května 57; r 2000-2600Kč; 🅿😊✳@🛜) This handsome branch of the Marriott has a good location, near the Brewery Museum and central sights. The rooms are relatively spacious, clean and bright, with all of the conveniences you'd expect. The reception desk is particularly helpful and can arrange brewery tours and sightseeing options. Expect sizeable discounts on weekends.

U Salzmannů
PENSION €

(☑377 235 476; www.usalzmannu.cz; Pražská 8; s & d 950-1350Kč, ste 1500Kč; 😊🛜) This pleasant pension, right in the heart of town, sits above a historic pub. The standard rooms are comfortable but basic; the more luxurious double 'suites' have antique beds and small sitting rooms, as well as kitchenettes. The pub location is convenient if you overdo it; to reach your bed, just climb the stairs.

Pension City
PENSION €

(☑377 326 069; www.pensioncityplzen.cz; sady 5 kvetna 52; s/d 1050/1450Kč; 😊🛜) On a quiet street near the river, Pension City has comfortable rooms and friendly, English-speaking staff armed with lots of local information.

Hotel Central
HOTEL €€

(☑378 011 855; www.central-hotel.cz; náměstí Republiky 33; s/d 1800/2700Kč; 😊@🛜) This rather modern building across from St Bartholomew Church has an excellent location, right on the main square. The renovated rooms are clean and inviting, with the best rooms being those that face the square.

🍴 Eating & Drinking

Aberdeen Angus Steakhouse
STEAKHOUSE €€

(☑725 555 631; www.angusfarm.cz; Pražská 23; mains 180-400Kč) For our money, this may be the best steakhouse in all of the Czech Republic. The meats hail from the nearby

Angus Farm, where the livestock is raised organically. There are several cuts and sizes on offer; lunch options include a tantalising cheeseburger. The downstairs dining room is cosy; there's also a creekside terrace. Book in advance.

Na Parkánu
CZECH €

(☑377 324 485; www.naparkanu.com; Veleslavínova 4; mains 80-180Kč; 🛜) Don't overlook this pleasant pub-restaurant, attached to the Brewery Museum. It may look a bit touristy, but the traditional Czech food is top rate, and the beer, naturally, could hardly be better. Try to snag a spot on the summer garden. Don't leave without trying the *nefiltrované pivo* (unfiltered beer).

U Mansfelda
CZECH, PUB €€

(☑377 333 844; www.umansfelda.cz; Dřevěná 9; mains 155-229Kč; 🍽🛜) Sure, it's a pub – remember you're in Plzeň now – but it's also more refined and has more interesting food than many other places. Try Czech cuisine like wild boar *guláš* (spicy meat and potato soup). Downstairs from the beer-fuelled terrace is a more relaxed *vinárna* (wine bar).

Groll Pivovar
CZECH €€

(☑602 596 161; www.pivovargroll.cz; Truhlářska 10; mains 129-259Kč) If you've come to Plzeň on a beer pilgrimage, then another essential visit is for a beer-garden lunch at this spiffy microbrewery. Meals include well-priced steaks and salads. The highlight is the drinks menu: homemade light and dark beers, complemented by an excellent (and still relatively rare) yeast beer.

Na Spilce
CZECH €

(☑377 062 755; www.naspilce.com; U Prazdroje 7; mains 80-230Kč; ⊘11am-10pm Sun-Thu, to 11pm Fri & Sat) This excellent pub and restaurant within the confines of the Pilsner Urquell Brewery feels like a factory canteen. The traditional Czech cooking is above average, and the beer is fresh from tanks next door.

Slunečnice
VEGETARIAN €

(☑377 236 093; www.slunecniceplzen.cz; Jungmanova 4; baguettes 60Kč; ⊘7.30am-6pm; 🌱) For fresh sandwiches, self-service salads and vegetarian dishes. Around 100Kč will buy a plateful.

❶ Information

City Information Centre (Informační centrum města Plzně; ☑378 035 330; www.icpilsen.cz; náměstí Republiky 41; ⊘9am-7pm Apr-Sep, to 6pm Oct-Mar) Reserves accommodation, organises guides, sells maps and changes money.

American Center Plzeň (☑377 237 722; www.americancenter.cz; Dominikánská 9; ⊘9am-10pm) Mainly a business resource centre, with a restaurant-bar, internet access and CNN news.

❶ Getting There & Away

BUS From Prague, the bus service to Plzeň (100Kč, one hour) is frequent (hourly), relatively fast and inexpensive. The main bus station is west of the centre on Husova.

TRAIN From Prague, eight trains (150Kč, 1½ hours) leave daily from the main station, *hlavní nádraží*. It's on the eastern side of town, 10 minutes' walk from Old Town Sq (náměstí Republiky).

České Budějovice
POP 96,000

České Budějovice (chesky bood-yo-vit-zah) is the provincial capital of southern Bohemia and a natural base for exploring the region. Transport connections to nearby Český Krumlov are good, meaning you could easily spend the day there and evenings here. While České Budějovice lacks top sights, it does have one of Europe's largest main squares (the biggest in the Czech Republic) and a charming labyrinth of narrow lanes and winding alleyways. It's also the home of 'Budvar' beer (aka Czech 'Budweiser'), and a brewery tour usually tops the 'must-do' list.

❷ Sights

Budweiser Budvar Brewery
BREWERY

(www.budvar.cz; cnr Pražská & K Světlé; adult/child 100/50Kč; ⊘9am-5pm Mar-Dec, closed Sun & Mon Jan-Feb) The Budweiser Budvar Brewery is 3km north of the main square. Group tours run every day and the 2pm tour (Monday to Friday only) is open to individual travellers. The highlight is a glass of real-deal Budvar deep in the brewery's chilly cellars. Catch bus 2 to the Budvar stop.

Náměstí Přemysla Otakara II
SQUARE

(náměstí Přemysla Otakara II) This mix of arcaded buildings centred on **Samson's Fountain** (Samsonova kašna; 1727) is the broadest plaza in the country, spanning 133m. Among the architectural treats is the 1555 Renaissance **Town Hall** *(radnice)*, which received a baroque facelift in 1731. The figures on the balustrade – Justice, Wisdom, Courage and Prudence – are matched by an exotic quartet of bronze gargoyles.

BOHEMIAN ROOTS – TÁBOR

The Old Town of Tábor was a formidable natural defence against invasion. Six centuries ago, the Hussite religious sect founded Tábor as a military bastion in defiance of Catholic Europe.

Based on the biblical concept that 'nothing is mine and nothing is yours, because everyone owns the community equally', all Hussites participated in communal work, and possessions were allocated equally in the town's main square.

This exceptional nonconformism may have given the word 'bohemian' the connotations we associate it with today. Religious structures dating from the 15th century line the town square, and it's possible to visit a 650m stretch of **underground tunnels** the Hussites used for refuge in times of war.

There are also excellent hotels and a handful of clean, reasonably priced pensions. The **Hotel Nautilus** (☑380 900 900; www.hotelnautilus.cz; Žižkovo náměstí 20; s/d from 2250/2700Kč; P⊛❋⤵) on the central square is the cream of the crop. **Pension Jana** (☑381 254 667; www.bedandbreakfast.euweb.cz; Kostinická 161; s/d/tr from 700/1100/1350Kč; P⤵) is a step down in price, but is friendly and also centrally located.

Tábor has excellent bus connections to Prague and neighbouring towns. Buses for Prague's Florenc station (93Kč) leave approximately every two hours. Train travel to Prague (140Kč, 1½ hours) is about as frequent but more expensive.

Black Tower
TOWER

(Černá věž; ☑386 801 413; U Černé věže 70/2; adult/concession 30/20Kč; ☺10am-6pm Tue-Sun Apr-Oct) The dominating, 72m Gothic-Renaissance Black Tower was built in 1553. Climb its 225 steps (yes, we counted them) for fine views. The tower's two **bells** – the Marta (1723) and Budvar (1995), are a gift from the brewery and are rung daily at noon.

Museum of South Bohemia
MUSEUM

(Jihočeské muzeum; ☑387 929 311; www.muzeumcb.cz; Dukelská 1) The Museum of South Bohemia holds an enormous collection of historic books, coins and weapons. It was closed in 2012 for reconstruction and, during research for this book, it wasn't clear when it would reopen: check the website for the latest information.

South Bohemian Motorcycle Museum
MUSEUM

(Jihočeské Motocyklové muzeum; ☑723 247 104; www.motomuseum.cz; Piaristické náměstí; adult/concession 50/20Kč; ☺10am-6pm) There are nearly 100 historic motorcycles on display here at this unlikely, ecclesiastical setting for a motorcycle museum. In addition to motorbikes, there are old-time bicycles and model airplanes on display.

🛏 Sleeping

Hotel Budweis
HOTEL €€

(☑389 822 111; www.hotelbudweis.cz; Mlýnská 6; s/d 2200-2800Kč; P⊛❋@⤵) The Hotel Budweis opened its doors in 2010, hived out of an old grain mill with a picturesque canalside setting. The owners have opted for a smart contemporary look. All of the rooms have air-conditioning and are wheelchair accessible. There are two good restaurants in-house, and the central location puts other eating and drinking options a short walk away.

Grandhotel Zvon
HOTEL €€

(☑381 601 611; www.hotel-zvon.cz; náměstí Přemysla Otakara II 28; r 2600-4400Kč; ⊛❋⤵) 'Since 1533' says the sign, but we're pretty sure Zvon – one of the city's leading hotels – has been renovated since then. The ritzy facade across three main-square buildings is let down by standard rooms, but the executive rooms (add a whopping 80% to listed prices) would be classy in any town.

Hotel Bohemia
HOTEL €€

(☑386 360 691; www.bohemiacb.cz; Hradební 20; s/d 1490/1790Kč; ⤵) Carved wooden doors open to a restful interior inside these two old burghers' houses in a quiet street. The restaurant comes recommended by the tourist information office.

Penzión Centrum
PENSION €€

(☑387 311 801; www.penzioncentrum.cz; Biskupská 130/3; s/d/tr 1000/1400/1800Kč; ⊛@⤵) Huge rooms with satellite TV, queen-sized beds with crisp white linen, and thoroughly professional staff all make this a top reader-recommended spot near the main square.

Hotel Malý Pivovar
HOTEL €€

(☏386 360 471; www.malypivovar.cz; Karla IV 8-10; s/d 2000/2800Kč; P🕸😾@) With a cabinet of sports trophies and sculpted leather sofas, the lobby resembles a gentlemen's club. However the elegant and traditionally furnished rooms will please both the men and the ladies, and it's just a short stroll to the cosy Budvarka beer hall downstairs.

Ubytovna U Nádraží
HOSTEL €

(☏972 544 648; www.ubytovna.vors.cz; Dvořákova 161/14; s 450-490Kč, d 660-730Kč; 😾@🕸) Recently renovated, this tower block a few hundred metres from the bus and train stations has good-value accommodation with shared bathrooms (usually with just one other room). Shared kitchens are available; a good option for longer-stay students.

✗ Eating

Masné Krámy
CZECH €

(☏387 201 301; www.masne-kramy.cz; Krajinská 13; mains 129-239Kč) No visit to České Budějovice would be complete without stopping at this renovated 16th-century meat market (now a popular pub) for excellent Czech food and a cold Budvar. You'll find all the Czech staples, including the house 'brewer's goulash', on the food menu. The drinks menu is equally important: try the superb unfiltered yeast beer. Advance booking essential.

U Tří Sedláku
CZECH €

(☏387 222 303; www.utrisedlaku.cz; Hroznová 488; mains 100-170Kč) Locals celebrate that nothing much has changed at U Tří Sedláku since its opening in 1897. Tasty meaty dishes go with the Pilsner Urquell that's constantly being shuffled to busy tables.

Indická
INDIAN €€

(Gateway of India; ☏777 326 200; www.indick-arestaurace.cz; Piaristická 22; mains 120-220Kč; 🕙11am-11pm Mon-Sat; 🕸🍴) From Chennai to the Czech Republic comes respite for travellers wanting something different. Request spicy because they're used to dealing with more timid local palates. Daily lunch specials (85Kč to 100Kč) are good value.

Fresh Salad & Pizza
PIZZERIA €

(☏387 200 991; Hroznová 21; salads 70-100Kč, pizza 100-130Kč; 😾🕸🍴) This lunch spot with outdoor tables does exactly what it says on the tin: healthy salads and (slightly) less healthy pizza dished up by a fresh and funky, youthful crew.

🍷 Drinking

Café Hostel
CAFE

(☏387 204 203; www.cafehostel.cz; Panská 13; 🕙noon-10pm Mon-Fri, from 5pm Sat & Sun; 🕸) This cosy cafe and bar features occasional DJ sets and live music. The scruffy rear garden could charitably be described as a work in progress. Upstairs are a couple of simple, but spotless, dorm rooms.

Singer Pub
PUB

(☏386 360 186; www.singerpub.cz; Česká 55) With Czech and Irish beers, and good cocktails, don't be surprised if you get the urge to rustle up something on the Singer sewing machines scattered around here. If not, challenge the regulars to a game of *foosball* with a soundtrack of noisy rock.

ℹ Information

Česká Spořitelna (☏956 744 630; www.csas.cz; FA Gerstnera 2151/6; 🕙8.30am-4pm Mon-Fri) Change money at this bank.

Municipal Information Centre (Městské Informační Centrum; ☏386 801 413; www.c-budejovice.cz; náměstí Přemysla Otakara II 2; 🕙8.30am-6pm Mon-Fri, to 5pm Sat, 10am-4pm Sun May-Sep, 9am-5pm Mon-Fri, to 1pm Sat, closed Sun Oct-Apr) Books tickets, tours and accommodation, and has free internet.

ℹ Getting There & Away

BUS From Prague, Student Agency (p120) yellow buses leave from Na Knížecí bus station (150Kč, 2½ hours) at the Anděl metro station (Line B). There are decent bus services from České Budějovice to Český Krumlov (35Kč, 45 minutes) and Tábor (70Kč, one hour). České Budějovice's bus station is 300m southeast of the train station above the Mercury Central shopping centre on Dvořákova.

TRAIN From Prague, there's a frequent train service (222Kč, 2½ hours, hourly). Regular (slow) trains trundle to Český Krumlov (32Kč, 45 minutes). From the train station it's a 10-minute walk west down Lannova třída, then Kanovnická, to nám Přemysla Otakara II, the main square.

Český Krumlov
POP 14,100

Outside of Prague, Český Krumlov is arguably the Czech Republic's only other world-class sight and must-see. From a distance, the town looks like any other in the Czech countryside, but once you get closer and see the Renaissance castle towering over the undisturbed 17th-century townscape, you'll feel the appeal; this really is that fairy-tale

HLUBOKÁ NAD VLTAVOU

The delightful confection known as **Hluboká Chateau** (☏387 843 911; www.zamek-hluboka.eu; Zámek; adult/concession Tour 1 250/160Kč, Tour 2 230/160Kč, Tour 3 170/80Kč; ⊙9am-5pm Tue-Sun May & Jun, to 6pm Jul & Aug, shorter hr Sep-Feb, closed Mar) is one of the most popular day trips from České Budějovice. Built by the Přemysl rulers in the latter half of the 13th century, Hluboká was taken from the Protestant Malovec family in 1662 as punishment for supporting an anti-Habsburg rebellion, and then sold to the Bavarian Schwarzenbergs. Two centuries later, they gave the chateau the English Tudor/Gothic face it wears today, modelling its exterior on Britain's Windsor Castle.

Crowned with crenellations and surrounded by a dainty garden, Hluboká is too prissy for some, but this remains the second-most-visited chateau in Bohemia after Karlštejn, and for good reason.

There are three English-language tours available: Tour 1 (called the 'representation room' on the website) focuses on the castle's public areas; Tour 2 goes behind the scenes in the castle apartments; Tour 3 explores the kitchens. Tour 1 is all most visitors will need to get the flavour of the place.

The surrounding park is open throughout the year (admission free). Buses make the journey to the main square in Hluboká nad Vltavou every 30 to 60 minutes (20 minutes, 20Kč).

town the tourist brochures promised. Český Krumlov is best approached as an overnight destination; it's too far for a comfortable day trip from Prague. Consider staying two nights, and spend one of the days hiking or biking in the surrounding woods and fields.

◉ Sights

TOP CHOICE **Český Krumlov Castle**   CASTLE
(☏380 704 711; www.castle.ckrumlov.cz; Zámek; adult/concession Tour 1 250/160Kč, Tour 2 240/140Kč, Theatre Tour 380/220Kč, tower 50/30Kč; ⊙9am-6pm Tue-Sun Jun-Aug, 9am-5pm Apr, May, Sep & Oct) Český Krumlov's striking Renaissance castle, occuping a promontory high above the town, began life in the 13th century. It acquired its present appearance in the 16th to 18th centuries under the stewardship of the noble Rožmberk and Schwarzenberg families. The interiors are accessible by guided tour only, though you can stroll the grounds and climb the tower on your own.

Three main tours are offered: Tour 1 takes in the opulent Renaissance rooms, including the chapel, baroque suite, picture gallery and masquerade hall, while Tour 2 visits the Schwarzenberg portrait galleries and their apartments used in the 19th century; and the Theatre Tour explores the chateau's remarkable rococo theatre, complete with original stage machinery.

Egon Schiele Art Centrum   MUSEUM
(☏380 704 011; www.schieleartcentrum.cz; Široká 71; adult/concession 120/70Kč; ⊙10am-6pm Tue-Sun) This excellent private gallery houses a small retrospective of the controversial Viennese painter Egon Schiele (1890–1918), who lived in Krumlov in 1911 and raised the ire of townsfolk by hiring young girls as nude models. For this and other sins he was eventually driven out. The centre also houses interesting temporary exhibitions.

🏃 Activities

Maleček   CANOEING
(☏380 712 508; http://en.malecek.cz; Rooseveltova 28; 2-person canoe per 30min 390Kč; ⊙9am-5pm) In summer, messing about on the river is a great way to keep cool. You can rent boats – a half-hour splash in a two-person canoe costs 390Kč, or you can rent a canoe for a full-day trip down the river from the town of Rožmberk (850Kč, six to eight hours).

Expedicion   ADVENTURE TOUR
(☏607 963 868; www.expedicion.cz; Soukenická 33; ⊙9am-7pm) Expedicion rents out bikes (290Kč per day), arranges horse riding (250Kč per hour), and operates action-packed day trips (1680Kč including lunch) incorporating horse riding, fishing, mountain biking and rafting in the nearby Newcastle Mountains region.

Český Krumlov

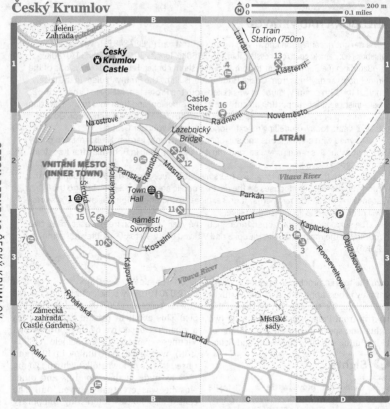

👉 Tours

Sebastian Tours
GUIDED TOUR

(☎607 100 234; www.sebastianck-tours.com; 5 Května Ul, Plešivec; day trip to Hluboká nad Vltavou per person 599Kč) Sebastian Tours can get you discovering South Bohemia on guided tours including stops at Hluboká nad Vltavou and České Budějovice. Also offers shuttle bus service to destinations further afield like Linz, Vienna and Salzburg in Austria.

🛏 Sleeping

Castle Apartments
APARTMENT €€

(☎380 725 110; www.zameckaapartma.cz; Latrán 45-47; apt 1800-3800Kč; 🞀🞂) Three adjoining houses near the castle district have been transformed into comfortable private apartments that offer wooden floors, and modern kitchenettes and bathrooms (no additional charge for the romantic views). Castle Apartments just may be Český Krumlov's best-value accommodation option.

🏆 Dilettante's Hangout
GUESTHOUSE €

(☎728 280 033; www.dilettanteshangout.com; Plesivecke náměstí 93; r 790-990Kč; 🞀) Don't be fooled by the bland exterior. Inside this intimate homestay are three romantic, arty rooms decorated with mementoes of the owner's global wanderings. Each room is unique, but they're all cosy and eclectic. There are kitchenettes for self-catering.

U Malého Vítka
HOTEL €€

(☎380 711 925; www.vitekhotel.cz; Radniční 27; d 1500Kč; 🄿🞀🞂) We really like this small hotel in the heart of the Old Town. The room furnishings are of high-quality, hand-crafted wood, and each room is named after a traditional Czech fairy-tale character. The downstairs restaurant and cafe are very good too.

Pension Kapr
PENSION €

(☎602 409 360; www.penzionkapr.cz; Rybářská 28; s 1000Kč; d 1200-1800Kč; @🞂) OK, it may be named after a fish (carp), but this river-

Český Krumlov

side pension, with exposed bricks and 500 years of history, has a quiet location and wonderful views of the Old Town. The lovely rooms, with whitewashed walls and wooden floors, are all named after the owners' children.

Krumlov House   HOSTEL €
(☎380 711 935; www.krumlovhostel.com; Rooseveltova 68; dm/d/tr 300/750/1350Kč; ✳🛜) Perched above the river, Krumlov House is friendly and comfortable, and has plenty of books, DVDs, and local information to feed your inner wanderer. Lots of day trips are on offer. The owners are English-speaking and traveller-friendly.

Pension Myší Díra   PENSION €
(☎380 712 853; www.ceskykrumlov-info.cz; Rooseveltova 28; s/d from 1290/1590Kč; 🅿😊@) This welcoming pension has a great location overlooking the river, and bright, beautiful rooms with lots of pale wood and quirky handmade furniture. Deluxe rooms and weekend accommodation (June to August) are 300Kč extra, but rates fall by 40% in winter. Breakfast is served in your room.

✗ Eating

Laibon   VEGETARIAN €€
(☎728 676 654; www.laibon.cz; Parkán 105; mains 90-180Kč; 😊🛜🍴) Candles and vaulted ceilings create a great boho ambience in the best little vegetarian teahouse in Bohemia. Just paging through the menu with seldom-seen words like guacamole and hummus can start the mouth watering. The riverside setting's pretty fine as well. Order the blueberry dumplings for dessert.

Nonna Gina   ITALIAN €
(☎380 717 187; Klášteriní 52; pizza 90-155Kč; 😊) Authentic Italian flavours from the authentic Italian Massaro family feature in this *pizzerie* down a quiet lane. Grab an outdoor table and pretend you're in Naples.

Krčma v Šatlavské   CZECH €€
(☎380 713 344; www.satlava.cz; Horní 157; mains 150-260Kč) Nirvana for meat-lovers, this medieval barbecue cellar serves sizzling platters in a funky labyrinth illuminated by candles and the flickering flames of open grills. Booking ahead is essential. Be forewarned: summer months bring tour-bus crowds.

Hospoda Na Louži   CZECH €
(☎380 711 280; www.nalouzi.cz; Kájovská 66; mains 90-170Kč; 😊) Nothing's changed in this wood-panelled *pivo* (beer) parlour for almost a century. Locals and tourists pack Na Louži for huge meals and tasty dark (and light) beer from the Eggenberg brewery.

U Dwau Maryí   CZECH €
(☎380 717 228; www.2marie.cz; Parkán 104; mains 100-200Kč) This medieval tavern recreates old recipes and is your best chance to try dishes made with buckwheat and millet: all tastier than they sound. Wash the food down with a goblet of mead or choose a 21st-century Pilsner. In summer it's a tad touristy, but the stunning riverside castle views easily compensate.

◧ Drinking

Café Schiele   CAFE
(☎380 704 011; www.schieleartcentrum.cz; Široká 71; ⊙10am-7pm; 🛜) A lovely cafe housed in the art gallery, with ancient oak floorboards, mismatched furniture and a grand piano with sawn-off legs serving as a coffee table. Excellent fair-trade coffee.

Zapa Cocktail Bar   COCKTAIL BAR
(☎380 712 559; www.zapabar.cz; Latrán 15; ⊙6pm-1am) Český Krumlov empties out after dinner,

CZECH REPUBLIC ČESKÝ KRUMLOV

but Zapa keeps going most nights until after midnight. Expect great cocktails and a relaxed vibe.

ℹ Information

Infocentrum (☑380 704 622; www.ckrumlov. info; náměstí Svornosti 1; ☺9am-7pm Jun-Aug, to 6pm Apr, May, Sep & Oct, to 5pm Nov-Mar) Transport and accommodation info, maps, internet access (5Kč per five minutes) and audio guides (100Kč per hour). A guide for disabled visitors is available.

ℹ Getting There & Away

BUS From Prague, Student Agency (p120) coaches (195Kč, three hours) leave regularly from the Na Knížecí bus station at Anděl metro station (Line B). Book in advance for weekends or in July and August.

TRAIN From Prague, the train journey (260Kč, 3½ hours) requires a change in České Budějovice. Buses are usually quicker and cheaper. There's a regular train service between České Budějovice and Český Krumlov (32Kč, 45 minutes).

MORAVIA

The Czech Republic's eastern province, Moravia, is yin to Bohemia's yang. If Bohemians love beer, Moravians love wine. If Bohemia is towns and cities, Moravia is rolling hills and pretty landscapes. Once you've seen the best of Bohemia, head east for a different side of the Czech Republic. The capital, Brno, has the museums, but the northern city of Olomouc has captivating architecture. The south is dominated by vineyards and, naturally, wine-drinking day-tipplers.

Brno

POP 387,200

Among Czechs, Moravia's capital has a dull rep: a likeable place where not much actually happens. There was even a hit movie a few years back called *Nuda v Brně (Boredom in Brno)*. The reality, though, is different. Tens of thousands of students ensure lively cafe and club scenes that easily rival Prague's. The museums are great too. Brno was one of the leading centres of experimental architecture in the early 20th century, and the Unesco-protected Vila Tugendhat is considered a masterwork of functionalist design.

◉ Sights

ŠPILBERK CASTLE & AROUND

Špilberk Castle CASTLE
(☑542 123 611; www.spilberk.cz; combined entry adult/concession 200/120Kč; ☺9am-5pm Tue-Sun Oct-Apr, to 5pm daily May & Jun, 10am-6pm daily Jul-Sep) Brno's dramatic hilltop castle is considered the city's most important landmark, and is home to the **Brno City Museum** (muzeum města Brna; ☑542 123 611; www. spilberk.cz; Špilberk Castle; combined entry including admission to Špilberk Castle adult/concession 200/120Kč; ☺9am-5pm Tue-Sun Oct-Apr, to 5pm daily May & Jun, 10am-6pm daily Jul-Sep). You can also visit the **casemates** (small rooms within the castle walls) and climb the lookout **tower**. Buy a combined entry ticket for all sights or purchase separate tickets; see the website for a full menu.

The two most popular exhibitions at the museum are **From Castle to Fortress**, on the castle's history, and **Prison of Nations**, on the role Špilberk played in the 18th and 19th centuries. Other exhibitions focus on the history, art and architecture of Brno. A combined ticket (adult/child 120/60Kč) gives access to all displays.

Cathedral of SS Peter & Paul CHURCH, TOWER
(katedrála sv Petra a Pavla; www.katedrala-petrov.cz; Petrov Hill; adult/concession tower 40/30Kč, crypts 20/10Kč; ☺11am-6pm Mon-Sat, from 11.45am Sun) This 14th-century cathedral atop Petrov Hill was originally built on the site of a pagan temple to Venus, and has been reconstructed many times since. The highly decorated 11m-high main altar with figures of SS Peter and Paul was carved by Viennese sculptor Josef Leimer in 1891. You can also climb the **tower** for dramatic views, or visit the **crypts**.

The Renaissance **Bishop's palace** (closed to the public) adjoins the cathedral. To the left is the pleasant **Denisovy sady**, a verdant park sweeping around Petrov Hill.

HISTORIC CENTRE

Spacious **náměstí Svobody** is the city's bustling central hub. It dates from the early 13th century, when it was called Dolní trh (lower market). The **plague column** here dates from 1680, and the **House of the Lords of Lipá** (Dům Pánů z Lipé; nám Svobody 17) is a Renaissance palace (1589–96) with a 19th-century sgraffito facade and arcaded courtyard. On the eastern side of the square is the **House of the Four Mamlases** (Dům U čtyř mamlasů; nám Svobody 10). The facade here is supported by a quartet of well-muscled but clearly moronic 'Atlas' figures, each struggling to hold up the building and their loincloths at the same time.

FREE Old Town Hall HISTORIC BUILDING
(Stará radnice; Radnická 8; adult/concession tower 30/15Kč; ⊙9am-5pm) Brno's atmospheric Old Town Hall dates from the early 13th century. The tourist office (p142) is here, plus oddities including a crocodile hanging from the ceiling (known affectionately as the Brno 'dragon') and a wooden wagon wheel with a unique story. You can also climb the tower.

Capuchin Monastery CEMETERY
(Kapucínský klášter; www.kapucini.cz; adult/concession 60/30Kč; ⊙9am-noon & 1pm-4.30pm May-Sep, closed Mon mid-Feb–Apr & Oct–mid-Dec, closed mid-Dec–mid-Feb) One of the city's leading attractions is this ghoulish cellar crypt that holds the mummified remains of several city noblemen from the 18th century. Apparently the dry, well-ventilated crypt has the natural ability to turn dead bodies into mummies. Up to 150 cadavers were deposited here prior to 1784, the desiccated corpses including monks, abbots and local notables.

Brno Underground UNDERGROUND
(Brněnské podzemí; www.ticbrno.cz; Zelný trh 21; adult/concession 150/75Kč; ⊙9am-6pm Tue-Sun) In 2011 the city opened the first of what will be several opportunities to explore the underground passages of the medieval city. This tour takes around 40 minutes to explore several of the cellars situated 6m to 8m below the Cabbage Market. The cellars were built for two purposes: to store goods and to hide in during wars.

Church of St James CHURCH
(kostel sv Jakuba; ☑542 212 039; www.svatyjakub-brno.wz.cz; Jakubská 11; ⊙8am-6pm) This austere 15th-century church contains a baroque pulpit with reliefs of Christ dating from 1525. But the biggest drawcard is a small stone figure known as the 'Nehaňba' (The Shameless): above the 1st-floor window on the south side of the clock tower at the church's west end is the figure of a man baring his buttocks towards the cathedral. Local legend claims this was a disgruntled mason's parting shot to his rivals working on Petrov Hill.

OUTSIDE THE CENTRE

TOP CHOICE Vila Tugendhat ARCHITECTURE
(Villa Tugendhat; ☑515 511 015; www.tugendhat.eu; Černopolni 45; adult/concession 300/180Kč; ⊙10am-6pm Tue-Sun; 🚋3, 5, 11) Brno had a reputation in the 1920s as a centre for modern architecture in the functionalist and Bauhaus styles. Arguably the finest example is this family villa, designed by modern master Mies van der Rohe in 1930. Entry is by guided tour, booked in advance by phone or via the website.

Mendel Museum MUSEUM
(Mendelianum; ☑543 424 043; www.mendel-museum.com; Mendlovo náměstí 1; adult/concession 60/30Kč; ⊙10am-6pm Tue-Sun Apr-Oct, to 5pm Nov-Mar) Gregor Mendel (1822–84), the Augustinian monk whose studies of peas and bees at Brno's Abbey of St Thomas established modern genetics, is commemorated here. In the garden are the foundations of Mendel's original greenhouse.

Museum of Romany Culture MUSEUM
(Muzeum romské kultury; ☑545 571 798; www.rommuz.cz; Bratislavská 67; adult/concession 40/20Kč; ⊙10am-6pm Mon-Fri, to 5pm Sun) This excellent museum provides an overdue positive showcase of Romany culture. Highlights include a couple of music-packed videos, period photographs from across Europe, and regular special exhibitions.

🛏 Sleeping

In February, April, August, September and October, Brno hosts major international trade fairs, and hotel rates increase by 40% to 100%. Book ahead if possible. For budget options, see the tourist information office for private rooms from around 400Kč. It can also help with accommodation in student dorms during July and August.

TOP CHOICE Hostel Mitte HOSTEL €
(☑734 622 340; www.hostelmitte.com; Panská 22; dm incl breakfast 490Kč; s/d 1000/1100Kč; ➋@🛜) Set in the heart of the Old Town, this clean and stylish hostel opened in 2011 and still smells and looks brand new. The rooms are named after famous Moravians (like Milan Kundera) or famous events (Austerlitz) and decorated accordingly. There's a cute cafe on the ground floor with free wi-fi.

Hotel Europa HOTEL €€
(☑545 421 400; www.hotel-europa-brno.cz; třída kpt Jaroše 27; s/d 1375/1625Kč; 🅿➋🛜) Set in a quiet neighbourhood a 10-minute walk from the centre, this self-proclaimed 'art' hotel (presumably for the wacky futuristic

lobby furniture) offers clean and tastefully furnished modern rooms in a historic 19th-century building. The lobby has free wi-fi, while the rooms have cable (ethernet) connections. There is free street parking out the front.

Hotel Pod Špilberkem HOTEL €€

(☎543 235 003; www.hotelpodspilberkem.cz; Pekařská 10; s/d/tr 1400/1600/2500Kč; P🖘@🛜) Tucked away near the castle are these quiet rooms, all clustered around a central courtyard. The secure car park is a good option for self-drive travellers.

Hotel & Pivnice Pegas HOTEL €€

(☎542 210 104; www.hotelpegas.cz; Jakubská 4; s/d 2000/2500Kč; 🖘🛜) Centrally located, the Pegas has been refurbished to include huge beds, flat-screen TVs and updated bathrooms. Expect a friendly welcome at reception and the lure of the Pegas microbrewery and pub downstairs. The rooms are on the 4th floor, so there is no problem with noise from the bar.

Grandhotel HOTEL €€

(☎542 518 111; www.grandhotelbrno.cz; Benešova 18-20; r from 2500Kč; P🖭@🛜) Under Austrian ownership, Brno's oldest hotel has been refurbished to emerge as one of the city's most comfortable and characterful sleeping options. The building's heritage style now includes all modcons, including a gym and sauna. Rooms are spacious and quiet, despite the location opposite the train station. Check online for good discounts.

Hostel Fléda HOSTEL €

(☎533 433 638; www.hostelfleda.com; Štefánikova 24; dm/d from 300/800Kč; 🖘🛜) A quick tram ride from the centre, one of Brno's best music clubs offers funky and colourful rooms. A nonsmoking cafe and good bar reinforce the social vibe. Catch tram 1 or 6 to the Hrnčírská stop.

Eating

Koishi ASIAN €€€

(☎777 564 744; www.koishi.cz; Údolní 11; mains 395-490Kč; ⊙11am-11pm Mon-Fri, 9am-11pm Sat

---

WORTH A TRIP

EXPLORING MORAVIA'S CAVES

The area to the immediate north of Brno has some of the Czech Republic's best caving in a region known as the Moravian Karst (Moravský kras). Carved with canyons and some 400 caves, the landscape is very pretty, with lots of woods and hills. See the excellent website www.cavemk.cz for information on the various caves in the area.

The karst formations here result from the seepage of faintly acidic rainwater through limestone, which over millions of years slowly dissolves it, creating hollows and fissures. In the caves themselves, the slow dripping of this water has produced extraordinary stalagmites and stalactites.

The organisational centre for any caving expedition is the town of **Blansko**, which has a good **tourist information office** (Blanenská Informační Kancelář; ☎516 410 470; www.blansko.cz; Rožmitálova 6, Blansko; ⊙9am-6pm Mon-Fri, to noon Sat) that sells maps and advance tickets to two of the main caves: the Punkva and Kateřinská Caves. The office can field transport questions and can help with accommodation. On weekends, particularly in July and August, cave-tour tickets sell out in advance, so try to book ahead with the tourist information office.

The most popular tour is through the **Punkva Cave** (Punkevní jeskyně; ☎516 418 602; www.smk.cz; adult/child 170/80Kč; ⊙8.40am-2pm Tue-Sun Jan-Mar, 8.20am-4pm Tue-Sun Apr-Sep, 8.40am-2pm Tue-Sun Oct-Dec). It involves a 1km walk through limestone caverns to the bottom of the Macocha Abyss, a 140m-deep sinkhole. Small, electric-powered boats then cruise along the underground river back to the entrance.

Another popular tour is to the **Kateřinská Cave** (Kateřinská jeskyně; ☎516 413 161; www. moravskykras.net; adult/child 80/60Kč; ⊙8.20am-4pm daily May-Aug, 9am-4pm Tue-Sun Apr & Sep, 9am-2pm Tue-Sun Oct, 10am-2pm Tue-Fri Mar & Nov, closed Dec-Feb). It's usually a little less crowded than the Punkva option. The 30-minute tour here explores two massive chambers.

Though it's easiest to explore the cave region with your own wheels, it is possible to see the caves on a day trip from Brno with public transport. Trains make the 30-minute run to Blansko hourly most days (37Kč): ask at Brno's tourist information office (p142).

& Sun; ☺☎) Sushi master Tadayoshi Ebina and top seafood chef Petr Fučík have combined to bring award-winning cooking to Brno. Koishi has earned a reputation for excellent sushi, but it has since expanded its range to include more traditional European and Czech cooking, with an Asian touch. It has an excellent wine list as well. Reserve in advance.

Spolek   CZECH €
(☏774 814 230; www.spolek.net; Orli 22; mains 60-140Kč; ☺9am-10pm Mon-Fri, 10am-10pm Sun; ☎) You'll get friendly, unpretentious service at this coolly 'bohemian' (yes, we're in Moravia) haven with interesting salads and soups, and a concise but diverse wine list. Photojournalism on the walls is complemented by a funky mezzanine bookshop. It has excellent coffee too.

Sabaidy   ASIAN €
(☏545 428 310; www.sabaidy.cz; třída kpt Jaroše 29; mains 150-230Kč; ☺5-11pm Mon-Fri; ☺☑) With decor incorporating Buddhist statues and a talented Laotian chef delivering authentic flavours, Sabaidy delivers both 'om' and 'mmmm'. After lots of same-ish Czech food, this really is different. The easiest access is via Hotel Amphone at třída kpt Jaroše 29.

Špaliček   CZECH €€
(☏542 215 526; Zelný trh 12; mains 160-310Kč; ☺) Brno's oldest restaurant sits on the edge of the Cabbage Market. Ignore the irony and dig into huge Moravian meals, partnered with a local Starobrno beer or something from the decent local wine list.

Rebio   VEGETARIAN €
(☏542 211 110; www.rebio.cz; Orli 26; mains 80-100Kč; ☺8am-7pm Mon-Fri, 10am-3pm Sat; ☑) Healthy risottos and vegie pies stand out in this self-service spot that changes its tasty menu every day. Organic beer and wine is available. There's another all-vegie branch at the **Velký Špaliček shopping centre** (Mečova 2, 1st fl; ☺9am-9pm Mon-Fri, 11am-8pm Sat & Sun).

🍷 Drinking

U Richarda   PUB
(☏775 027 918; www.uricharda2.cz; Údolní 7) This microbrewery is highly popular with students, who come for the great house-brewed, unpasteurised yeast beers, including a rare cherry-flavoured lager, and good

traditional Czech cooking (mains 109Kč to 149Kč). Book in advance.

Pivnice Pegas   PUB
(☏542 210 104; www.hotelpegas.cz; Jakubská 4) *Pivo* melts that old Moravian reserve as the locals become pleasantly noisy. Don't miss the wheat beer with a slice of lemon. Try to book a table in advance, or grab a spot at one of Brno's longest bars. The food's pretty good too, but the interior can get smoky.

Avia   CAFE
(☏739 822 215; www.aviacafe.cz; Botanická 1; ☺11am-10pm; ☎) Popular student cafe-restaurant situated on the ground floor of the Jan Hus Congregational Church, a landmark functionalist building from 1929. The architecture and location, close to the university, lend an intellectual atmosphere. When you've tired of talking Proust, you can shoot pool in the adjoining billiard room.

Kavárna Vladimíra Menšíka   CAFE
(☏777 001 411; Veselá 3; coffee 30-50Kč; ☺9am-11pm Mon-Sat, 11.30am-10pm Sun; ☎) One of our favourite places to hide away in Brno is this corner cafe dedicated to late Czech film star Vladimír Menšík, a leading actor of the Czech New Wave. You'll find a relaxed space and good coffee, with pictures and film stills of Menšík all over the walls.

☆ Entertainment

Stará Pekárna   CLUB, LIVE MUSIC
(☏541 210 040; www.starapekarna.cz; Štefánikova 8; ☺5pm-late Mon-Sat) Old and new music with blues, world beats, DJs and rock. Catch a 1, 6 or 7 tram to Pionýrská. Gigs usually kick off at 8pm.

Fléda   LIVE MUSIC
(☏533 433 559; www.fleda.cz; Štefánikova 24; ☺to 2am) DJs, Brno's best up-and-coming bands and occasional touring performers all rock the stage at Brno's top music club. Catch tram 1 or 6 to the Hrnčířská stop.

Brno State Philharmonic
Orchestra   CLASSICAL MUSIC
(☏539 092 811; www.filharmonie-brno.cz; Komenského náměstí 8) City's main venue for classical music. Buy tickets at the **Philharmonic Orchestra Box Office** (Besední ul; ☺9am-2pm Mon & Wed, 1-6pm Tue, Thu & Fri).

Janáček Theatre
OPERA, BALLET

(Janáčkovo divadlo; Rooseveltova 1-7, sady Osvobození) Hosts high-quality opera and ballet. Buy tickets at the National Theatre Box Office (Národní Divadlo v Brně Prodej Vstupnek; ☑542 158 120; www.ndbrno.cz; Dvořákova 11; ⊙8am-5.30pm Mon-Fri, to noon Sat).

Reduta Theatre
CLASSICAL MUSIC, OPERA

(Reduta divadlo; www.ndbrno.cz; Zelný trh 4) Opera and classical music with an emphasis on Mozart (he played here in 1767). Buy tickets at the National Theatre Box Office.

Kino Art
CINEMA

(☑541 213 542; www.kinoartbrno.cz; Cihlářská 19) Screens art-house films.

ℹ Information

Cyber Café (www.facebook.com/cybercafebrno; Mečova 2, Velký Spaliček shopping centre; per hr 60Kč; ⊙10am-10pm Mon-Sat; 🛜) Has computers for surfing the web. There's also a free wi-fi hot spot in the Velký Spaliček shopping centre.

Tourist information office (☑542 211 090; www.ticbrno.cz; Radnická 8, Old Town Hall; ⊙8am-6pm Mon-Fri, 9am-6pm Sat & Sun) Sells maps and books accommodation. Free internet up to 15 minutes.

ℹ Getting There & Away

BUS Brno is well connected by bus; service to and from Prague (165Kč, 2½ hours) via the local coach service **Student Agency** (☑841 101 101; www.studentagency.cz) is especially good. The main bus station is behind the train station, though buses to Prague often leave from a small stop in front of the Grandhotel (p140). From Prague, buses depart from Florenc bus station hourly through the day.

TRAIN Express trains run between Brno's **train station** (☑541 171 111) and Prague's hlavní nádraží every couple of hours during the day (210Kč, 2½ hours). Brno is also a handy junction for onward train travel to Vienna (220Kč, two hours) and Bratislava (218Kč, 1½ hours).

ℹ Getting Around

Brno has a reliable system of trams and buses that hits most of the major spots (though you'll have to hike up to Špilberk (p138) on your own two legs). Buy public transport tickets from vending machines and newsstands. Tickets valid for 60 minutes cost 25Kč and allow unlimited transfers; 24-hour tickets are 70Kč. For taxis, try **City Taxis** (☑542 321 321).

Olomouc
POP 105,000

Olomouc is a sleeper. Practically unknown outside the Czech Republic and underappreciated at home, the city is surprisingly majestic. The main square is among the country's nicest, surrounded by historic buildings and blessed with a Unesco-protected trinity column. The evocative central streets are dotted with beautiful churches, testifying to the city's long history as a bastion of the Catholic Church. Explore the foundations of ancient Olomouc Castle at the must-see Archdiocesan Museum, then head for one of the city's many pubs or microbreweries. Don't forget to try the cheese, Olomoucký sýr, reputedly the smelliest in the country.

◉ Sights & Activities
HORNÍ NÁMĚSTÍ & AROUND

Olomouc's main square, Horní (or 'upper') náměstí, will be your first port of call. This is where the tourist office is, as well the city's most important sight: a gargantuan trinity column. The square also contains two of the city's six baroque fountains. The Hercules Fountain (Herkulova kašna) dates from 1688 and features the muscular Greek hero standing astride a pit of writhing serpents, while the Caesar Fountain (Caeserova kašna), east of the town hall, was built in 1724 and is Olomouc's biggest.

Holy Trinity Column
MONUMENT

(Sousoší Nejsvětější trojice; Horní náměstí) The town's pride and joy is this 35m-high (115ft) baroque sculpture that dominates the square and is a popular meeting spot for local residents. The trinity column was built between 1716 and 1754 and is allegedly the biggest single baroque sculpture in Central Europe. In 2000, the column was awarded an inscription on Unesco's World Heritage list.

The individual statues depict a bewildering array of Catholic religious motifs, including the Holy Trinity, the 12 apostles, the assumption of Mary, and some of the best-known saints. There's a small chapel at the base of the column that's sometimes open during the day for you to poke your nose in.

FREE Town Hall
TOWER

(Radnice; Horní náměstí; tower 15Kč) Olomouc's Town Hall dates from the 14th century and is home to one of the quirkier sights in town:

an astronomical clock from the 1950s, with a face in Socialist Realist style. The original was damaged in WWII. At noon the figures put on a little performance. The tower is open twice daily to climb, at 11pm and 3pm.

St Moritz Cathedral
CHURCH

(Chrám sv Mořice; www.moric-olomouc.cz; Opletalova 10; ☉tower 9am-5pm Mon-Sat, noon-5pm Sun) This vast Gothic cathedral is Olomouc's original parish church, built between 1412 and 1540. The western tower is a remnant of its 13th-century predecessor. The cathedral's amazing sense of peace is shattered every September with an International Organ Festival; the cathedral's organ is Moravia's mightiest. The tower provides the best view in town.

DOLNÍ NÁMĚSTÍ & AROUND

Dolní náměstí (lower square), runs south of Horní náměstí and sports its own Marian Plague Column (Mariánský morový sloup) and baroque fountains dedicated to Neptune and Jupiter. The 1661 Church of Annunciation of St Mary stands out with its beautifully sober interior.

St Michael Church
CHURCH

(kostel sv Michala; www.svatymichal.cz; Žerotínovo náměstí 1; ☉8am-6pm) This church on Žerotínovo náměstí has a green dome and a robust baroque interior with a rare painting of a pregnant Virgin Mary. Wrapped around the entire block is an active Dominican seminary (Dominikánský klášter).

NÁMĚSTÍ REPUBLIKY & AROUND

Olomouc Museum of Art
MUSEUM

(Olomoucký muzeum umění; ☑585 514 111; www.olmuart.cz; Denisova 47; adult/child 50/25Kč, Wed & Sun free; ☉10am-6pm Tue-Sun) This popular museum houses an excellent collection of 20th-century Czech painting and sculpture. Admission includes entry to the Archdiocesan Museum (p143).

Archbishop's Palace
MUSEUM

(Arcibiskupský palác; ☑587 405 421; www.arcibiskupskypalac.ado.cz; Wurmova 9; adult/concession 60/30Kč; ☉10am-5pm Tue-Sun May-Sep, 10am-5pm Sat & Sun Apr & Oct) This expansive former residence of the archbishop was built in 1685. Entry to see the lavish interiors is by guided tour only (free audioguide provided in English). It was here that Franz-Josef I was crowned Emperor of Austria in 1848 at the tender age of 18.

VÁCLAVSKÉ NÁMĚSTÍ & AROUND

It's hard to believe now, but this tiny square, northeast of the centre, was where Olomouc began. A thousand years ago this was the site of Olomouc Castle. You can still see the castle foundations in the lower levels of the Archdiocesan Museum. The area holds Olomouc's most venerable buildings and darkest secrets. Czech King Wenceslas III (Václav III) was murdered here in 1306 under circumstances that are still unclear to this day.

Archdiocesan Museum
MUSEUM

(Arcidiecézni muzeum; ☑585 514 111; www.olmuart.cz; Václavské náměstí 3; adult/concession 50/25Kč, Sun & Wed free; ☉10am-6pm Tue-Sun) The impressive holdings of the Archdiocesan Museum trace the history of Olomouc back 1000 years. The thoughtful layout, with helpful English signage, takes you through the original Romanesque foundations of Olomouc Castle, and highlights the cultural and artistic development of the city during the Gothic and baroque periods.

St Wenceslas Cathedral
CHURCH

(dóm sv Václava; Václavské náměstí; ☉8am-6pm) Adjacent to the museum, this cathedral, the seat of the Olomouc Archbishop, was originally a Romanesque basilica first consecrated back in 1131. It was rebuilt several times before having a neo-Gothic makeover in the 1880s. There's a crypt inside that you can enter.

🛏 Sleeping

Penzión Na Hradě
PENSION €€

(☑585 203 231; www.penzionnahrade.cz; Michalská 4; s/d 1390/1890Kč; ❀🗑) Tucked away in the robust shadow of St Michael Church, this designer pension has sleek, cool rooms and professional service, creating a contemporary ambience in the heart of the Old Town.

Poet's Corner
HOSTEL €

(☑777 570 730; www.hostelolomouc.com; Sokolská 1, 3rd fl; dm/tw/tr/q 350/900/1200/1600Kč; ❀🗑) The Australian-Czech couple who mind this friendly and exceptionally well-run hostel are a wealth of local information. Bicycles can be hired from 100Kč to 200Kč per day. In summer there's a two-night minimum stay, but Olomouc is definitely worth it, and there's plenty of day-trip information on offer.

Pension Angelus
PENSION €€

(☑776 206 936; www.pensionangelus.cz; Wurmova 1; s/d 1250/1850Kč; P❀🗑) With antique

Olomouc

400 m
0.2 miles

Morava

Na Letné
Komenského
Dobrovského
třída 1 máje
Masarykova
17. listopadu
To Train Station (1km);
Bus Station (2km)
Kosinova
Smetanova
17. listopadu
Morava

Nábřeží Přemyslovc

9

2
Václavské
náměstí
Mlčochova
Dómská
11
Wurmova
1
Biskupské
náměstí
Mariánská
Palacký
University

Michalské stromořadí
Stadium

Bezručovy
sady

Mlýnský potok

Hanáckého pluku
Kozelužská
Denisova
náměstí
Republiky
6
20
Křížkovského
19

Boleslavova
Franklinova
Dobrovského
Na střelnici
Zámečnická
Kačeni
Pekařská
Ostružnická
Zlatnická
Universitní
21
12
3 7
Žerotínovo
náměstí
Panská
Školní
Purkrabská
Hrnčířská
Church of the
Annunciation
of St Mary
U Výpadu
Kateřinská

Studentská
Slovenská
Sokolská
Opletalova
28. října
Riegrova
Horní
náměstí
8
Úzká
Pavelčákova
10
4
i
5
Dolní
náměstí
16
Lafayettova
14
Mlýnská

U stadiónu
Legionářská
Hynaisova
Palackého
8. května
Mlýnská
třída Svobody
Svornova
Tylova
Spojenců
15
18
Palachovo
náměstí
Nešporova
Havlíčkova
Videňská
17
Sněžtanovy
sady
Čechovy
sady
Krapkova

Olomouc

furniture, crisp white duvets and oriental rugs on wooden floors, the Angelus is a spacious and splurge-worthy romantic getaway. To get here catch bus 2 or 6 from the train station or bus 4 from the bus station, jumping off at the U Domú stop.

Ubytovna Marie GUESTHOUSE €
(☎585 220 220; www.ubytovnamarie.cz; třída Svobody 41; per person 500Kč; ⊜⊛) Spick and span (if spartan) double and triple rooms with shared bathrooms and kitchens make this spot popular with long-stay overseas students. Significant discounts kick in after two nights.

✗ Eating & Drinking

Moritz CZECH €€
(☎585 205 560; www.hostinec-moritz.cz; Nešverova 2; mains 120-260Kč; ⊜⊛) This microbrewery and restaurant is a firm local favourite. We reckon it's a combination of the terrific beers, good-value food and a praise-worthy 'no smoking' policy. In summer, the beer garden's the only place to be. Advance booking a must.

Nepal NEPALESE €
(☎585 208 428; www.nepalska.cz; Mlýnská 4; mains 110-150Kč; ⊛⊿) Located in a popular Irish pub, this Nepalese-Indian eatery is the place to go for something a little different. The 100Kč buffet lunch is the best deal, but loyal patrons say the quality of the food is better in the evening.

Drápal CZECH €
(☎585 225 818; www.restauracedrapal.cz; Havlíčkova 1; mains 110-150Kč; ⊛) It's hard to go wrong with this big, historic pub on a busy corner near the centre. The unpasteurised Pilsner Urquell is arguably the best beer in Olomouc. The smallish menu is loaded with Czech classics, like the ever-popular *Španělský ptáček* (literally 'Spanish bird'), a beef roulade stuffed with smoked sausage, parsley and a hard-boiled egg.

Svatováclavský Pivovar CZECH €€
(☎585 207 517; www.svatovaclavsky-pivovar.cz; Mariánská 4; mains 170-290Kč; ⊛) Another microbrewery (what's in the water in Olomouc?), this is a bit bigger than Moritz and it's easier to find a walk-in table here. The microbrewery produces several excellent versions of unpasteurised yeast beer. The menu features mostly Czech standards done well, plus a few dishes that experiment with Olomouc's signature stinky cheese.

Hanácacká Hospoda CZECH €
(Dolní náměstí 38; mains 100-180Kč; ⊌) The menu lists everything in the local Haná dialect at this popular pub-restaurant. It's worth persevering though because the huge Moravian meals are tasty and supreme value. Don't worry – they've got an English menu if you're still getting up to speed with Haná.

TOP CHOICE Cafe 87 CAFE
(☎585 202 593; Denisova 47; chocolate pie 35Kč; coffee 40Kč; ⊗7.30am-9pm Mon-Fri, 8am-9pm Sat & Sun; ⊛) Locals come in droves to this funky cafe beside the Olomouc Museum of Art for coffee and its famous chocolate pie. Some people still apparently prefer the dark chocolate to the white chocolate. When will they learn? It's a top spot for breakfast and toasted sandwiches too.

Vertigo BAR
(www.klubvertigo.cz; Univerzitní 6; ⊗1pm-midnight Mon-Thu, 4pm-2am Fri-Sun) A dark, dank student bar that reeks of spilled beer and stale

CZECH BEER

There is an increasing number of excellent Czech regional beers worth investigating. Buy the *Good Beer Guide to Prague & the Czech Republic* by long-time Prague resident Evan Rail. In Prague it's available at Shakespeare & Sons (p119) or the Globe Bookstore & Cafe (p119). Here are our picks to get you started on your hoppy way:

» Pivovarský Klub (p115)
» Prague Beer Museum (p115)
» Na Parkánu (p132)
» U Richarda (p141)
» Svatováclavský Pivovar (p145)

smoke. In other words, a very popular drinking spot in a college town like Olomouc.

 Information

Slam (www.slam.cz; Slovenská 12; per min 1Kč; ◷9am-9pm Mon-Fri, from 10am Sat & Sun; 🛜) Internet.

Tourist information office (Olomoucká Informační Služba; 📞585 513 385; www.tourism.olomouc.eu; Horní náměstí ; ◷9am-7pm) Sells maps and makes accommodation bookings.

 Getting There & Away

BUS There are around 15 buses daily to/from Brno (92Kč, 1¼ hours), as well as dozens of other lines that service regional towns and cities; see www.jizdnirady.idnes.cz. The bus station is 1km east of the train station.

TRAIN Olomouc is on a main rail line, with regular services from both Prague (240Kč, three hours) and Brno (100Kč, 1½ hours). The train station (*hlavní nádraží*) is 2km east of the centre, over the Morava River and its tributary the Bystřice.

Telč

POP 6000

The Unesco-protected town of Telč, perched on the border between Bohemia and Moravia, possesses one of the country's prettiest and best-preserved historic town squares. Actually, we can't think of another that comes close. The main attraction is the beauty of the square itself, lined with Renaissance and baroque burgers' houses, with their brightly coloured yellow, pink and green facades.

Spend part of your visit simply ambling about, taking in the classic Renaissance chateau on the square's northwestern end and the parklands and ponds that surround the square on all sides. Telč empties out pretty quickly after the last tour bus leaves, so plan an overnight stay only if you're looking for some peace and quiet. In late July/early August the town holds the Prázdniny v Telči (www.prazdninyvtelci.cz) folk festival.

 Sights

Telč's sumptuous Renaissance chateau (Zámek; www.zamek-telc.cz; náměstí Zachariáše z Hradce; adult/concession Route A 110/70Kč, Route B 90/60Kč; ◷9-11.45am & 1-6pm Tue-Sun Apr-Oct), part of which is known as the Water Chateau, guards the north end of the Telč peninsula. Entry is by guided tour only: Route A takes one hour, passing through the Renaissance halls; Route B takes 45 minutes, exploring the castle's apartment rooms.

The chateau was rebuilt from the original Gothic structure by Antonio Vlach (between 1553 and 1556) and Baldassare Maggi (from 1566 to 1568). The surviving structure remains in remarkably fine fettle, with immaculately tended lawns and beautifully kept interiors. In the ornate Chapel of St George (kaple sv Jiří), opposite the ticket office, are the remains of the castle's founder Zachariáš z Hradce.

Telč's stunning town square, Náměstí Zachariáše z Hradce, is a tourist attraction in its own right. Most houses here were built in Renaissance style in the 16th century after a fire levelled the town in 1530. Some facades were given baroque facelifts in the 17th and 18th centuries, but the overall effect is harmoniously Renaissance.

Some famous houses on the square include No 15, which shows the characteristic Renaissance sgraffito. The house at No 48 was given a baroque facade in the 18th century. No 61 has a lively Renaissance facade rich in sgraffito. The Marian column in the middle of the square dates from 1717, and is a relatively late baroque addition.

Dominating the town centre are the Gothic towers of the Church of St James the Elderly (kostel sv Jakuba Staršího; adult/concession 20/15Kč; ◷10-11.30am & 1-6pm Tue-Sun Jun-Aug, 1-5pm Sat & Sun May & Sep). Also watching over the square is the baroque Holy Name of Jesus Church (kostel Jména Ježíšova; náměstí Zachariáše z Hradce 3; ◷8am-6pm), completed in 1667 as part of a Jesuit college.

North of the square is a narrow lane leading to the old town's Small Gate (Malá brána), through which is a large English-style park surrounding the duck ponds (once the town's defensive moat). South along Palackého, toward the Great Gate (Velká brána), is the imposing Romanesque Church of the Holy Spirit (kostel sv Ducha; Palackého; ⊙7am-6pm) from the early 13th century. Outside the Great Gate you can walk along parts of Telč's remaining bastions.

🛏 Sleeping

Accommodation can be hard to get and expensive during the annual Prázdniny v Telči folk music festival in late July/early August, so book ahead. The tourist information office can book private rooms from 300Kč per night.

Pension Steidler   PENSION €
(☑721 316 390; www.telc-accommodation.eu; náměstí Zachariáše z Hradce 52; s/d without breakfast 500/800Kč) Rooms reconstructed with skylights and wooden floors combine with an absolute town square location to deliver one of Telč's best-value places to stay. Some rooms have views of the lake. Breakfast costs 50Kč per person. Note there's a surcharge of 100Kč per room in summer (June to August) for stays of less than two nights.

Hotel Celerin   HOTEL €€
(☑567 243 477; www.hotelcelerin.cz; náměstí Zachariáše z Hradce 43; s/d 980/1530Kč; ❀❂⊛) Variety is king in the Celerin's 12 comfortable rooms, with decor ranging from cosy wood to white-wedding chintz (take a look first). Rooms 4, 5, 9 and 10 have views out onto the square. The hotel sometimes closes in winter.

Penzin Kamenné Slunce   PENSION €
(☑732 193 510; www.kamenne-slunce.cz; Palackého 2; s/d 450/900Kč; ℗⊖⊛) Lots of brick, exposed beams and warm wooden floors make this a very welcoming spot just off the main square. Hip bathrooms with colourful tiles are further proof that this is arguably Telč's coolest place to stay. Breakfast costs 70Kč.

Hotel Černý Orel   HOTEL €€
(☑567 243 222; www.cernyorel.cz; náměstí Zachariáše z Hradce 7; s/d 1200/1800Kč; ℗⊖⊛) Right on the main square, the 'Black Eagle' is just the ticket if you're into slightly faded, old-world ambience. While the rooms are comfortable, they don't rise to the level of the exquisite exterior. The ground-floor restaurant is one of the town's more popular lunch venues.

🍴 Eating & Drinking

U Marušky   CZECH €
(☑602 432 904; Palackého 28; mains 90-170Kč) This simple pub caters more to locals than visitors, but offers decent home-cooked Czech meals with the added bonus of very good Ježek beer on tap. There's also a small beer garden open during summer. The daily lunch menu is a steal at 75Kč.

Švejk   CZECH €
(www.svejk-telc.cz; náměstí Zachariáše z Hradce 1; mains 105-165Kč; ⊛) Classic Czech cooking in a publike setting next to the castle. The names of menu items, unsurprisingly, are taken from classic WWI comic novel *The Good Soldier Švejk*. 'Cadet Biegler' chicken, for example, turns out to be a schnitzel that's stuffed with ham and cheese. The outdoor terrace is popular in nice weather.

Pizzerie   ITALIAN €
(☑567 223 246; náměstí Zachariáše z Hradce 32; pizza 80-130Kč) Right on the main square and right on the money for better-than-average pizza.

Kavarná Antoniana   CAFE
(☑603 519 903; náměstí Zachariáše z Hradce 23; coffee 24-30Kč, cake 35Kč; ⊙8am-2am) The best coffee on the square, plus beer and alcoholic drinks, and inspirational black-and-white photos of Telč plastered on the wall. There are only limited food options, but the late opening hours mean it's one of the few places in the centre where you can get a drink in the evening.

❶ Getting There & Around

BUS Around half a dozen buses make the run daily from Prague's Florenc bus station (170Kč, 2½ hours), with many connections requiring a change in Jihlava. Regional service is decent, with around five daily buses to and from Brno (100Kč, two hours). Check www.bus-vlak.cz for times and prices.

TRAIN Passenger train services have been greatly scaled back and are not recommended.

Mikulov

POP 7600

The 20th-century Czech poet Jan Skácel (1922–89) bequeathed Mikulov a tourist slogan for the ages when he penned that the town was a 'piece of Italy moved to Moravia by God's hand'. Mikulov is arguably the most attractive of the southern Moravian wine towns, surrounded by white, chalky hills and adorned with an amazing hill-top Renaissance chateau, visible for miles around. Mikulov was also once a thriving cultural centre for Moravia's Jewish community, and the former Jewish Quarter is slowly being rebuilt. Once you've tired of history, explore the surrounding countryside (on foot or bike) or relax with a glass of local wine.

◉ Sights & Activities

Mikulov Chateau CASTLE
(Zámek; ☑519 309 019; www.rmm.cz; Zámek 1; adult/concession 100/50Kč; ☺9am-5pm Tue-Sun May-Sep, to 4pm Apr & Oct) This chateau was the seat of the Dietrichstein family from 1575 to 1945, and played an important role in the 19th century, hosting on separate occasions French Emperor Napoleon, Russia's Tsar Alexander and Prussian King Frederick. Much of the castle was destroyed by German forces in February 1945: the lavish interiors are the result of a painstaking reconstruction.

The castle is accessible by guided tour only. The full history tour takes two hours and visits significant castle rooms as well as exhibitions on viticulture and archaeology. There are three more specialised, shorter tours also available.

Jewish Quarter NEIGHBOURHOOD
(Husova) Mikulov was a leading centre of Moravian Jewish culture for several centuries until WWII. The former synagogue (Synagóga; ☑519 510 255; Husova 11; ☺1-5pm Tue-Sun 15 May-30 Sep) has a small exhibition on the Jews of Mikulov. It was under reconstruction during our research and it wasn't clear when it would reopen.

The evocative Jewish Cemetery (Židovský hřbitov; Vinohrady; adult/concession 20/10Kč; ☺9am-5pm Mon-Fri Jul & Aug) is a 10-minute walk from the tourist office. To find it, walk out Brněnská and look for a sign leading off to the right. Additionally, an 'instructive trail' runs through the Jewish Quarter, with information plaques in English. You can pick it up at the end of Husova near Alfonse Muchy.

WORTH A TRIP

LEDNICE & VALTICE

A few kilometres east of Mikulov, the Unesco-protected historic landscape of Lednice and Valtice is a popular weekend destination for Czechs, who tour the historic architecture, hike and bike, and sample the region's wines. The two towns are about 10km apart, connected by regular buses. Neither offers much in terms of nightlife, so they're best visited as a day trip from either Mikulov or Brno.

If you've got more time, either town makes a perfect base for exploring the rolling hills of the southern Moravian wine country: hundreds of miles of walking and cycling trails criss-cross a mostly unspoiled landscape.

Owned by the Liechtenstein family from 1582 to 1945, Lednice Chateau (Zámek; ☑519 340 128; www.zamek-lednice.com; Zámek, Lednice; adult/child standard tour 1 150/100Kč, tour 2 150/100Kč; ☺9am-6pm Tue-Sun May-Aug, to 5pm Tue-Sun Sep, to 4pm Sat & Sun only Apr & Oct) is one of the country's most popular weekend destinations. The crowds come for the splendid interiors and extensive gardens, complete with an exotic-plant greenhouse, lakes with pleasure boats, and a mock Turkish minaret – architectural excess for the 19th-century nobility.

Valtice Chateau (Zámek; ☑519 352 423; www.zamek-valtice.cz; Zámek 1, Valtice; standard tour adult/concession 100/80Kč; ☺9am-noon & 1-6pm Tue-Sun May-Aug, to 5pm Sep, to 4pm Apr & Oct), dating originally from the 12th century before getting a baroque facelift, is one of the Czech Republic's finest baroque structures, the work of JB Fischer von Erlach and Italian architect Domenico Martinelli. Entry is by guided-tour only, with two different tours on offer (in Czech, with English text available). The grounds and gardens are free for you to explore during opening times.

Valtice has regular train service throughout the day to/from Mikulov (23Kč, 12 minutes) and Břeclav (25Kč, 15 minutes), which has excellent onward connections to Brno, Bratislava and Vienna.

Both Lednice and Valtice are easily reachable by bus from Brno or Mikulov. Regular buses shuttle the short distance between Lednice and Valtice (20Kč, 15 minutes).

Goat Hill
HILL, LOOKOUT

(Kozí hrádek; tower 20Kč; ⊙tower 9am-6pm May-Sep) Goat Hill is topped with an abandoned 15th-century lookout tower offering stunning views over the Old Town. To find it, walk uphill from the Jewish Cemetery, following a red-marked trail. Note that the tower keeps irregular hours: it's only open when the flag is flying. But even if the tower is closed, the views from the hilltop are spectacular.

Holy Hill
HILL, CHURCH

(Svatý kopeček; Gernerála Svobody) Another uphill venture is to scale the 1km path up this 363m peak, through a nature reserve and past grottos depicting the Stations of the Cross, to the compact Church of St Sebastian. The blue-marked trail begins at the bottom of the main square on Svobody. The whitewashed church and the limestone on the hill give it a Mediterranean ambience.

Dietrichstein Burial Vault
MAUSOLEUM

(Dietrichštejnská hrobka; náměstí 5; adult/concession 50/25Kč; ⊙10am-6pm daily Jun-Aug, 9am-5pm Tue-Sun Apr, May, Sep & Oct) The Dietrichstein family mausoleum occupies the former St Anne's Church. The front of the building features a remarkable baroque facade – the work of Austrian master Johann Bernhard Fischer von Erlach – dating from the early 18th century. The tombs, dating from 1617 to 1852, hold the remains of 45 family members.

Mikulov Wine Trail
HIKING, CYCLING

A pleasant way to visit smaller, local vineyards across the rolling countryside is by bicycle on the Mikulov Wine Trail. The tourist office can recommend a one-day ride that also takes in the nearby chateaux at Valtice and Lednice. Bicycles and additional cycle touring information are available from RentBike (⏲737 750 105; www.rentbike.cz; Kostelní náměstí 1; rental per hr/day 110/330Kč).

🛏 Sleeping

TOP CHOICE / Hotel Templ
HOTEL €€

(⏲519 323 095; www.templ.cz; Husova 50; s/d from 1390/1650Kč; P😊🛜) This beautifully reconstructed, family-run hotel comprises a main building and an annex, two doors down. The updated rooms are done out in cheerful tiles and stained glass. The baths are as stylish as the rooms. Some rooms, such as ours (No 11 in the annex), open onto a secluded patio with tables for relaxing in the evening.

Pension Baltazar
PENSION €€

(⏲519 324 327; www.pensionbaltazar.cz; Husova 44; d 1200-1800Kč; P😊🛜) You'll find this place a few doors up from the Hotel Templ. Beautifully resurrected rooms effortlessly combine modern furniture with exposed-brick walls and wooden floors.

Penzión Husa
PENSION €€

(⏲731 103 283; www.penzionhusa.cz; Husova 30; d 1590Kč; P😊🛜) Yet another beautiful pension on Husova, the 'Goose' boasts furnishings with period flare, like canopy beds and big oriental rugs on top of hardwood floors. This place is popular, so try to book well in advance.

🍴 Eating & Drinking

Restaurace Templ
CZECH €€

(⏲519 323 095; www.templ.cz; Husova 50; mains 165-280Kč; 😊🛜) The best restaurant in town is matched by a fine wine list specialising in local varietals. The menu features an appetising mix of duck, pork and chicken dishes. Choose from either the formal restaurant or relaxed wine garden. There's also a small terrace out the back for dining alfresco on warm evenings.

Hospůdka Pod Zámkem
CZECH €

(⏲519 512 731; www.hospudkapodzamkem.cz; Husova 49; daily special 69Kč; 🛜) This funky combination of old-school pub and coffee bar serves simple but very good Czech meals, usually limited to a few daily specials like soup plus roast pork or chicken drumsticks. It's also the unlikely home of Mikulov's best coffee and serves very good Gambrinus beer to boot. Find it across the street from the Hotel Templ.

Restaurace Alfa
CZECH €

(⏲519 510 877; náměstí 27; mains 130-200Kč) The Alfa's beautiful sgraffito building, just across the square from the tourist information office, hides what's basically an ordinary Czech pub on the inside. That said, the kitchen turns out well-done Czech cooking, and there are even a few game dishes on the menu.

Petit Café
CAFE

(⏲733 378 264; náměstí 27; crepes 40-70Kč; 🛜) Tasty crepes and coffee are dished up in a hidden courtyard/herb-garden setting. Later at night, have a beer or a glass of wine.

Vinařské Centrum WINE BAR
(☎519 510 368; www.vinarskecentrum.com; náměstí 11; ⊘9am-9pm Mon-Sat, 10am-9pm Sun) This drinking room has an excellent range of local wines available in small tasting glasses (15Kč to 50Kč), or whole bottles when you've finally made up your mind.

ⓘ Information

Tourist information office (☎519 510 855; www.mikulov.cz; náměstí 1; ⊘8am-6pm Mon-Fri, 9am-6pm Sat & Sun Jun-Sep, 8am-noon & 12.30-5pm Mon-Fri, 9am-4pm Sat & Sun Apr, May & Oct) Organises tours (including specialist outings for wine buffs) and accommodation, and has internet access (1Kč per minute).

ⓘ Getting There & Away

BUS Mikulov is easily reached by bus from Brno (65Kč, 1½ hours), with coaches leaving hourly. From Prague, there are few direct buses; the best approach is to catch a bus for Brno and change. Regional bus services are good, with frequent buses to/from Valtice and Lednice.

TRAIN There are several daily trains to and from Břeclav (39Kč, 30 minutes), an important junction for onward services to Brno, Bratislava and Vienna. See the online timetable at www.vlak-bus.cz.

UNDERSTAND CZECH REPUBLIC

History

Over the centuries, the Czechs have been invaded by the Habsburgs, the Nazis and the Soviets, and the country's location has meant domestic upheavals have not stayed local for long. Their rejection of Catholicism in 1418 resulted in the Hussite Wars. The 1618 revolt against Habsburg rule ignited the Thirty Years' War, and the German annexation of the Sudetenland in 1938 helped fuel WWII. The liberal reforms of 1968's Prague Spring led to tanks rolling in from across the Eastern Bloc, and the peaceful ousting of the government during 1989's Velvet Revolution was a model for freedom-seekers everywhere.

Bohemian Beginnings

Ringed by hills, the ancient Czech lands of Bohemia and Moravia have formed natural territories since the earliest times. Slavic tribes from the east settled and were united from 830 to 907 in the Great Moravian Empire. Christianity was adopted after the arrival in 863 of the Thessalonian missionaries Cyril and Methodius, who created the first Slavic (Cyrillic) alphabet.

In the 9th century, the first home-grown dynasty, the Přemysls, erected some huts in what was to become Prague. This dysfunctional clan gave the Czechs their first martyred saints – Ludmila, killed by her daughter-in-law in 874, and her grandson, the pious Prince Václav (or Good 'King' Wenceslas; r 921-29), murdered by his brother Boleslav the Cruel.

The Přemysls' rule ended in 1306, and in 1310 John of Luxembourg came to the Bohemian throne through marriage, and annexed the kingdom to the German empire. The reign of his son, Charles IV (1346-78), who became Holy Roman Emperor, saw the first of Bohemia's two 'Golden Ages'. Charles founded Prague's St Vitus Cathedral, built Charles Bridge and established Charles University. The second was the reign of Rudolf II (1576-1612), who made Prague the capital of the Habsburg Empire and attracted artists, scholars and scientists to his court. Bohemia and Moravia remained under Habsburg dominion for almost four centuries.

Under the Habsburg Thumb

In 1415 Protestant religious reformer Jan Hus, rector of Charles University, was burnt at the stake for heresy. He inspired the nationalist Hussite movement that plunged Bohemia into civil war (1419-34).

When the Austrian and Catholic Habsburg dynasty ascended the Bohemian throne in 1526, the fury of the Counter-Reformation was unleashed after Protestants threw two Habsburg councillors from a Prague Castle window. This escalated into the Catholic-Protestant Thirty Years' War (1618-48), which devastated much of Central Europe.

The defeat of the Protestants at the Battle of White Mountain in 1620 marked the start of a long period of rule from Vienna, including forced re-Catholicisation, Germanisation and oppression of Czech language and culture.

National Reawakening

The Czechs started to rediscover their linguistic and cultural roots at the start of the

19th century, during the so-called Národní obrození (National Revival). Overt political activity was banned, so the revival was culturally based. Important figures included historian Josef Palacký and composer Bedřich Smetana.

An independent Czech and Slovak state was realised after WWI, when the Habsburg empire's demise saw the creation of the Czechoslovak Republic in October 1918. Three-quarters of the Austro-Hungarian empire's industrial power was inherited by Czechoslovakia, as were three million Germans, mostly in the border areas of Bohemia (the *pohraniči*, known in German as the Sudetenland).

The Czechs' elation was to be short-lived. Under the Munich Pact of September 1938, Britain and France accepted the annexation of the Sudetenland by Nazi Germany, and in March 1939 the Germans occupied the rest of the country (calling it the Protectorate of Bohemia and Moravia).

Most of the Czech intelligentsia and 80,000 Jews died at the hands of the Nazis. When Czech paratroopers assassinated Nazi governor Reinhardt Heydrich in 1942, the entire town of Lidice was wiped out in revenge.

Communist Coup

After the war, the Czechoslovak government expelled 2.5 million Sudeten Germans – including antifascists who had fought the Nazis – from the Czech borderlands and confiscated their property. During the forced marches from Czechoslovakia many were interned in concentration camps and tens of thousands died.

In 1947 a power struggle began between the communist and democratic forces, and in early 1948 the Social Democrats withdrew from the postwar coalition. The result was the Soviet-backed coup d'état of 25 February 1948, known as Vítězný únor (Victorious February). The new communist-led government established a dictatorship, which resulted in years of oppression. In the 1950s thousands of noncommunists fled the country. Others were captured and imprisoned, and hundreds were executed or died in labour camps.

Prague Spring & Velvet Revolution

In April 1968 the new first secretary of the Communist Party, Alexander Dubček, introduced liberalising reforms to create 'socialism with a human face' – known as the 'Prague Spring'. Censorship ended, political prisoners were released and economic decentralisation began. Moscow was not happy, but Dubček refused to buckle and Soviet tanks entered Prague on 20 August 1968, closely followed by 200,000 Soviet and Warsaw Pact soldiers.

Many pro-reform Communist Party functionaries were expelled and 500,000 party members lost their jobs after the dictatorship was re-established. Dissidents were summarily imprisoned and educated professionals were made manual labourers.

The 1977 trial of the underground rock group the Plastic People of the Universe (for disturbing the peace at an unauthorised music festival) inspired the formation of the human-rights group Charter 77. The communists saw the musicians as threatening the status quo, but others viewed the trial as an assault on human rights. Charter 77's group of Prague intellectuals, including late playwright–philosopher Václav Havel, continued their underground opposition throughout the 1980s.

By 1989 Gorbachev's reforms, called *perestroika*, and the fall of the Berlin Wall on 9 November raised expectations of change. On 17 November an official student march in Prague was smashed by police. Daily demonstrations followed, culminating in a general strike on 27 November. Dissidents led by Havel formed the Anti-Communist Civic Forum and negotiated the resignation of the Communist government on 3 December, less than a month after the fall of the Berlin Wall.

A 'Government of National Understanding' was formed, with Havel elected president on 29 December. With no casualties, the days after 17 November became known as Sametová revoluce (the Velvet Revolution).

Velvet Divorce

Following the end of communist central authority, antagonisms between Slovakia and Prague re-emerged. The federal parliament granted both the Czech and Slovak Republics full federal status within a Czech and Slovak Federated Republic (ČSFR), but this failed to satisfy Slovak nationalists.

Elections in June 1992 sealed Czechoslovakia's fate. Václav Klaus' Civic Democratic Party (ODS) took 48 seats in the 150-seat federal parliament, while 24 went to the Movement for a Democratic Slovakia (HZDS), a left-leaning Slovak nationalist party led by Vladimír Mečiar.

In July the Slovak parliament declared sovereignty, and on 1 January 1993 Czechoslovakia ceased to exist for the second time. Prague became capital of the new Czech Republic, and Havel was elected its first president.

A New Country

Thanks to booming tourism and a solid industrial base, the Czech Republic enjoyed negligible unemployment and by 2003 Prague enjoyed Eastern Europe's highest standard of living. However, capitalism also meant a lack of affordable housing, rising crime and a deteriorating health system.

The Czech Republic became a member of NATO in 1999, and joined the EU on 1 May 2004. With EU membership, greater numbers of younger Czechs are now working and studying abroad, seizing opportunities their parents didn't have.

The celebrated dissident and first president after the Velvet Revolution, Václav Havel, died in 2011 after a long battle with cancer. His death rallied Czechs of all political stripes and marked what many saw as a formal end to the post-communist transition period.

People

The population of the Czech Republic is 10.5 million (2012 estimate); 95% of the population are Czech and 3% are Slovak. Only 150,000 of the three million Sudeten Germans evicted after WWII remain. A significant Roma population (0.3%) is subject to hostility and racism, suffering from poverty and unemployment.

Most Czechs profess to be atheist (39.8%) or nominally Roman Catholic (39.2%), but church attendance is low. There are small Protestant (4.6%) and Orthodox (3%) congregations. The Jewish community (1% in 1918) today numbers only a few thousand.

Arts

Literature

The communist period produced two Czech writers of world standing, both of whom hail originally from Brno: Milan Kundera (b 1929) and Bohumil Hrabal (1914–97).

For many visitors, Kundera remains the undisputed champ. His wryly told stories weave elements of humour and sex along with liberal doses of music theory, poetry and philosophy to appeal to both our low- and high-brow literary selves. His best known book, *The Unbearable Lightness of Being* (also made into a successful film in 1988), is set in Prague in the uncertain days ahead of the 1968 Warsaw Pact invasion. Look out too for Kundera's *The Joke* and *The Book of Laughter and Forgetting*.

Ask any Czech who their favourite author is and chances are they'll say Hrabal, and it's not hard to see why. Hrabal's writing captures what Czechs like best about themselves, including a keen wit, a sense of the absurd and a fondness for beer. Hrabal is also a great storyteller, and novels such as *I Served the King of England* and *The Little Town Where Time Stood Still* are both entertaining and insightful. Hrabal died in 1997 in classic Czech fashion: falling from a window.

No discussion of Czech literature would be complete without mentioning Franz Kafka (1883–1924), easily the best-known writer to have ever lived in Prague and the author of modern classics *The Trial* and *The Castle*, among many others. Though Kafka was German-speaking and Jewish, he's as thoroughly connected to the city as any Czech writer could be.

Kafka's Czech contemporary, and polar opposite, was the pub scribe Jaroslav Hašek (1883–1923), author of *The Good Soldier Švejk*, a book that is loved and reviled in equal doses. For those who get the jokes, it is a comic masterpiece of a bumbling, likeable Czech named Švejk and his (intentional or not) efforts to avoid military service for Austria-Hungary during WWI. Czechs tend to bridle at the assertion that an idiot like Švejk could somehow embody any national characteristic.

Art & Music

Czechs have always been active contributors to the arts, and no trip to Prague would be complete without a stroll through the city's major museums and galleries to admire the work of local painters, photographers and sculptors. For evenings, you'll be spoiled for choice among offerings of classical music, jazz and rock.

Two Czechs, Antonín Dvořák (1841–1904) and Bedřich Smetana (1824–84), are household names in classical music. Dvořák was heavily influenced by the Czech National Revival, which inspired his two *Slavonic Dances* (1878 and 1881), the operas *Rusalka*

THE CHALLENGING MR ČERNÝ

Czech installation artist David Černý (b 1967) has cultivated a reputation as the enfant terrible of the Prague and European art scenes. He first made international headlines in 1991 when he painted a WWII memorial with a Soviet tank bright pink, and his installations (several around Prague) manage to amuse and provoke in equal measure.

In Prague's Lucerna pasáž, he's hung St Wenceslas and his horse upside down, and across the river outside the Kafka Museum, Černý's *Piss* sculpture invites contributions by SMS. Rising above the city, like a faded relic from *Star Wars*, is the Žižkov TV Tower with Černý's giant babies crawling up the exterior.

Černý's other recent project is **MeetFactory** (www.meetfactory.cz), a multipurpose gallery, artists' collective and performance space in a former factory in Smíchov.

and *Čert a Káča (The Devil and Kate)*, and his religious masterpiece, *Stabat Mater*. He spent four years in the USA, where he composed his famous *Symphony No 9, From the New World*. Smetana wrote several operas and symphonies, and his signature work remains his *Moldau (Vltava)* symphony.

Alfons Mucha (1860–1939) is probably the most famous visual artist to come out of the Czech lands, though because he attained his fame mostly in Paris, and not in Prague, his reputation remains more exalted abroad than at home.

Film

The 1960s was a decade of relative artistic freedom, and talented young directors such as Miloš Forman and Jiří Menzel crafted bittersweet films that charmed moviegoers with their grit and wit, while at the same time poking critical fun at their communist overlords.

During that period, dubbed the 'Czech New Wave', Czechoslovak films twice won the Oscar for 'Best Foreign Film', for the *Little Shop on Main Street* in 1965 and *Closely Watched Trains* in 1967. Forman eventually left the country and went on to win 'Best Picture' Oscars for *One Flew Over the Cuckoo's Nest* and *Amadeus*, which was partly filmed in Prague.

Since the Velvet Revolution, directors have struggled to make meaningful films, given the tiny budgets and a constant flood of Hollywood blockbusters. At the same time, they've had to endure nonstop critical scrutiny that their output meet the high standards set during the New Wave.

In recent years historical films have made a comeback, particularly films that explore WWII and the Nazi occupation. The best include director Adam Dvořák's *Lidice* (2011), Jan Hřebejk's *Kawasaki Rose* (2009) and Tomáš Lunák's *Alois Nebel* (2010). The latter is an inventive interpretation of a graphic novel on the final days of WWII and the subsequent expulsion of Czech Germans.

Environment

The landlocked Czech Republic is bordered by Germany, Austria, Slovakia and Poland. The land is made up of two river basins: Bohemia in the west, drained by the Labe (Elbe) River flowing north into Germany; and Moravia in the east, drained by the Morava River flowing southeast into the Danube. Each basin is ringed by low, forest-clad hills, notably the Šumava range along the Bavarian–Austrian border in the southwest, the Krušné hory (Ore Mountains) along the northwestern border with Germany, and the Krkonoše mountains along the Polish border east of Liberec. The country's highest peak, Sněžka (1602m), is in the Krkonoše.

Food & Drink

The classic Bohemian dish is *vepřo-knedlo-zelo*, slang for a plate of roast pork, bread dumplings and sauerkraut. Also look out for *svíčková na smetaně* (braised beef in a cream sauce) and *kapr na kmíní* (fried or baked carp with caraway seed).

A *bufet* or *samoobsluha* is a self-service cafeteria with *chlebíčky* (open sandwiches), salads, *klobásy* (spicy sausages), *špekačky* (mild pork sausages), *párky* (frankfurters), *guláš* (goulash) and of course *knedlíky* (those ubiquitous dumplings).

A *pivnice* is a pub without food, while a *hospoda* or *hostinec* is a pub or beer hall serving basic meals. A *vinárna* (wine bar) has anything from snacks to a full-blown menu. The occasional *kavárna* (cafe) has a full menu, but most only serve snacks and desserts. A *restaurace* is any restaurant.

In Prague and other main cities you'll find an increasing number of excellent vegetarian restaurants, but smaller towns' choices remain limited. There are a few standard *bezmasá jídla* (meatless dishes) served by most restaurants. The most common are *smažený sýr* (fried cheese) and vegetables cooked with cheese sauce.

For nonsmoking premises, look out for signs saying *Kouření zakázano*.

Beer & Wine

One of the first words of Czech you'll learn is *pivo* (beer). Most famous are Budvar and Pilsner Urquell, but there are many other local brews to be discovered.

Most beer halls have a system of marking everything you eat or drink on a small piece of paper that is left on your table, then totted up when you pay (say *zaplatím, prosím* – I'd like to pay, please).

The South Moravian vineyards around the town of Mikulov produce improving *bílé víno* (white wines).

SURVIVAL GUIDE

Directory A–Z

Accommodation

Outside the peak summer season, hotel rates can fall by up to 40%. Booking ahead – especially in Prague – is recommended for summer and around Christmas and Easter. Many hotels are now completely or mostly nonsmoking.

Prices quoted here are for rooms with a private bathroom and a simple breakfast, unless otherwise stated. The following price indicators apply (for a high-season double room):

€ less than 1600Kč

€€ 1600Kč to 3700Kč

€€€ more than 3700Kč

CAMPING

Most campsites are open from May to September only and charge around 80Kč to 100Kč per person. Camping on public land is prohibited. See Czech Camping (www.czech-camping.com) and Do Kempu (www.czech-camping.com) for information and online booking.

HOSTELS

Prague and Český Krumlov are the only places with a choice of backpacker-oriented hostels. Dorm beds costs around 450Kč in Prague and 350Kč to 450Kč elsewhere. Booking ahead is recommended. Czech Youth Hostel Association (www.czechhostels.com) offers information and booking for Hostelling International (HI) hostels.

HOTELS

Hotels in central Prague, Český Krumlov and Brno can be expensive, but smaller towns are usually significantly cheaper. Two-star hotels offer reasonable comfort for 1000Kč to 1200Kč for a double, or 1200Kč to 1500Kč with private bathroom (around 50% higher in Prague). It's always worth asking for a weekend discount in provincial Czech cities and towns. See Czech Hotels (www.czechhotels.net) and Discover Czech (www.discoverczech.com).

PRIVATE ROOMS & PENSIONS

Look for signs advertising *privát* or *Zimmer frei* (private rooms). Most tourist information offices can book for you. Expect to pay from 450Kč to 550Kč per person outside Prague. Bathrooms are usually shared.

Penzióny (pensions) are small, often family-run, accommodation offering rooms with private bathroom and breakfast. Rates range from 1000Kč to 1500Kč for a double room (1900Kč to 2500Kč in Prague). See Czech Pension (www.czechpension.cz).

Business Hours

Banks 8.30am to 4.30pm Monday to Friday

Bars 11am to midnight

Museums & Castles Usually closed Monday year-round

Restaurants 11am to 11pm

Shops 8.30am to 6pm Monday to Friday, 8.30am to noon Saturday

Embassies & Consulates

Most embassies and consulates are open at least 9am to noon Monday to Friday. All of the following are in Prague.

Australian Consulate (☎221 729 260; www.dfat.gov.au/missions/countries/cz.html; 6th fl, Klimentská 10, Nové Město; ⓜ5, 8, 14, 26) Honorary consulate for emergency assistance only (eg a stolen passport); the nearest Australian embassy is in Vienna.

Canadian Embassy (☎272 101 800; www.canadainternational.gc.ca; Muchova 6, Bubeneč; ⓜHradčanská)

French Embassy (☎251 171 711; www.france.
cz; Velkopřevorské náměstí 2, Malá Strana; 🚊12,
20, 22)

German Embassy (☎257 113 111; www.
deutschland.cz; Vlašská 19, Malá Strana; 🚊12,
20, 22)

Irish Embassy (☎257 530 061; www.embas-
syofireland.cz; Tržiště 13, Malá Strana; 🚊12,
20, 22)

Netherlands Embassy (☎233 015 200;
www.netherlandsembassy.cz; Gotthardská 6/27,
Bubeneč; 🚊1, 8, 15, 25, 26 then walk)

New Zealand Consulate (☎222 514 672;
egermayer@nzconsul.cz; Dykova 19, Vinohrady;
Ⓜ Jiřího z Poděbrad)

Russian Embassy (☎233 375 650; www.
czech.mid.ru; Korunovační 34, Bubeneč; 🚊1, 8,
15, 25, 26)

UK Embassy (☎257 402 111; http://ukinc-
zechrepublic.fco.gov.uk; Thunovská 14, Malá
Strana; 🚊12, 20, 22)

US Embassy (☎257 022 000; http://czech.
prague.usembassy.gov; Tržiště 15, Malá Strana;
🚊12, 20, 22)

Food

Restaurants open as early as 11am and carry
on till midnight; some take a break between
lunch and dinner. The following price indicators apply to a main meal.

€ less than 200Kč

€€ 200Kč to 500Kč

€€€ more than 500Kč

Gay & Lesbian Travellers

Homosexuality is legal in the Czech Republic, but Czechs are not yet used to seeing public displays of affection; it's best
to be discreet. For online information including links to accommodation and bars,
see the Prague Gay Guide (www.prague.gay
guide.net).

Internet Access

Most Czech accommodation now offers wi-
fi access, and internet cafes remain common throughout the country. An increasing
number of Infocentrum (tourist information) offices also offer internet access. In this
guide, we've used the 🛜 symbol to denote
places that offer wi-fi and the @ symbol for
places that allow access to a computer.

Money

ATMS

ATMS linked to the most common global
banking networks can be easily located in all
major cities, and smaller towns and villages.

CASH & CREDIT CARDS

Keep small change handy for use in public toilets, telephones and tram-ticket
machines, and try to keep some small-
denomination notes for shops, cafes and restaurants. Changing larger notes from ATMs
can be a problem.

Credit cards are widely accepted in petrol
stations, midrange and top-end hotels, restaurants and shops.

EXCHANGING MONEY

Change cash or get a cash advance on
credit cards at the main banks. Beware of
směnárna (private exchange offices), especially in Prague – they advertise misleading
rates, and often charge exorbitant commissions or 'handling fees'. There is no black
market for currency exchange, and anyone
who offers to change money in the street is
dodgy.

TIPPING

» In bars, leave small change as a tip.

» Tipping is optional in restaurants, but
increasingly expected in Prague; round the
bill up the next 20Kč or 30Kč (5% to 10%).

» Tip taxi drivers the same as you would in
restaurants.

Public Holidays

New Year's Day 1 January

Easter Monday March/April

Labour Day 1 May

Liberation Day 8 May

SS Cyril and Methodius Day 5 July

Jan Hus Day 6 July

Czech Statehood Day 28 September

Republic Day 28 October

Freedom and Democracy Day 17
November

Christmas 24 to 26 December

Post

The Czech Republic has a reliable postal
service. Mail can be held at Prague Poste Restante, Jindřišská 14, 11000 Praha 1, Czech
Republic.

Telephone

All Czech phone numbers have nine digits; dial all nine for any call, local or long distance. Buy phonecards for public telephones from post offices and newsstands from 100Kč.

Mobile-phone coverage (GSM 900/1800) is excellent. If you're from Europe, Australia or New Zealand, your own mobile phone should be compatible. Purchase a Czech SIM card from any mobile-phone shop for around 500Kč (including 300Kč of calling credit). Local mobile phone numbers start with the following: ☑601–608 and ☑720–779. The Czech Republic's country code is ☑420.

Tourist Information

Czech Tourism (Map p110; www.czechtourism. com) Official tourist information.

IDOS (www.idos.cz) Train and bus timetables.

Mapy (www.mapy.cz) Online maps.

Travellers with Disabilities

Ramps for wheelchair users are becoming more common, but cobbled streets, steep hills and stairways often make getting around difficult. Public transport is still problematic, but a growing number of trains and trams have wheelchair access. Major tourist attractions such as Prague Castle also offer wheelchair access. Anything described as *bezbarierová* is 'barrier free'. Resouces including the following:

Prague Integrated Public Transport (www.dpp.cz) See the 'Barrier Free' information online.

Prague Wheelchair Users Organisation (Pražská organizace vozíčkářů; ☑224 827 210; www.pov.cz; Benediktská 6, Staré Město) This is a watchdog organisation for the disabled. While it's mostly geared toward local residents, it can help to organise a guide and transportation at about half the cost of a taxi, and has information on the barrier-free Prague in Czech, English and German.

Visas

The Czech Republic is part of the Schengen Agreement, and citizens of most countries can spend up to 90 days in the country in a six-month period without a visa. For travellers from some other countries, a Schengen Visa is required; you can only get this from your country of residence.

Getting There & Away

Located in the middle of Europe, the Czech Republic is easily reached by air from key European hubs or overland by road or train from neighbouring countries. Flights, tours and rail tickets can be booked online at www.lonelyplanet.com/travel_services.

Entering the Country

Entering the country is straightforward and you are not likely to encounter serious problems or delays. If arriving by air from outside the EU's common border and customs area, the Schengen zone (this includes arrivals from Ireland and the UK), you must go through passport control. If arriving from a European hub within the Schengen zone, such as Amsterdam or Frankfurt, you will not pass through passport control in Prague.

If arriving overland by train, bus or car, the Czech Republic is surrounded on all sides by EU Schengen countries and there are no passport or customs checks on the border.

Air

Nearly all international flights arrive at **Václav Havel Airport Prague** (Letiště Praha; ☑220 111 888; www.prg.aero). Flights to and from destinations outside the EU's Schengen zone use the airport's Terminal 1, which has standard passport and customs checks. Flights within the Schengen zone use Terminal 2 and are treated as domestic flights.

The national carrier **Czech Airlines** (www. czechairlines.com) has a good safety record and is a member of the Skyteam airline alliance.

Land

The Czech Republic has border crossings with Germany, Poland, Slovakia and Austria. These are all EU member states within the Schengen zone, meaning there are no longer any passport or customs checks.

BUS

The main international bus terminal is **Florenc** (ÚAN Praha Florenc; ☑900 144 444; www. florenc.cz; Křižíkova 4; ☺4am-midnight, information counter 6am-9.30pm; Ⓜ Florenc) bus station in Prague. The station is equipped with an information booth, a large announcements board, ticket windows, shops and a Burger King restaurant.

Several bus lines run long-haul coach services to and from destinations around Europe. The leaders on the local market are Student Agency (☏800 100 300; www.studentagency. cz) and Eurolines (www.elines.cz). Both have offices at the Prague bus station.

CAR & MOTORCYCLE

The Czech Republic lies along major European highways. On entering the country, motorists are required to display on their windscreen a special prepaid sticker (*dálniční známka*), purchased at petrol stations and kiosks near the border. A sticker valid for 10 days costs 310Kč, for 30 days 440Kč, and for a year 1500Kč.

TRAIN

Prague's Praha hlavní nádraží (main train station; ☏840 112 113; www.cd.cz; Wilsonova 8, Nové Město) is the country's international train gateway, with frequent service to and from Germany, Poland, Slovakia and Austria. Trains to/from the south and east, including from Bratislava, Vienna and Budapest, normally stop at Brno's main train station as well.

In Prague, buy international train tickets in advance from ČD Travel (☏972 241 861; www.cdtravel.cz; Wilsonova 8) agency, which has a large ticketing office on the lower level of Praha hlavní nádraží and a city centre office (☏972 233 930; V Celnici 6) not far from náměstí Republiky. Sales counters are divided into those selling domestic tickets (*vnitrostátní jízdenky*) and international tickets (*mezinárodní jizdenky*), so make sure you're in the right line. The windows also sell seat reservations. Credit cards are accepted.

Both InterRail and Eurail passes are valid on the Czech rail network.

Getting Around

Bus

Within the Czech Republic, buses are often faster, cheaper and more convenient than trains. Many bus routes have reduced frequency (or none) at weekends. Buses occasionally leave early so get to the station at least 15 minutes before the official departure time. Check bus timetables and prices at www.idos.cz. Main bus companies:

CSAD (☏information line 900 144 444) The national bus company links cities and smaller towns.

Student Agency (☏800 100 300; www.studentagency.cz) Popular, private bus company with several destinations, including Prague, Brno, České Budějovice, Český Krumlov, Karlovy Vary and Plzeň.

Car & Motorcycle

DRIVING LICENCE

Foreign driving licences are valid for up to 90 days. Strictly speaking, licences that do not include photo identification need an International Driving Permit as well, although this rule is rarely enforced.

FUEL

Unleaded petrol is available as *natural* (95 octane) or *natural plus* (98 octane). The Czech for diesel is *nafta* or just *diesel*. *Autoplyn* (LPG gas) is available in every major town but at very few outlets.

CZECH REPUBLIC GETTING AROUND

TYPES OF TRAINS

Several different categories of train run on Czech rails, differing mainly in speed and comfort.

EC (EuroCity) Fast, comfortable international trains, stopping at main stations only, with 1st- and 2nd-class coaches; supplementary charge of 60Kč; reservations recommended. Includes 1st-class only SC Pendolino trains that run from Prague to Olomouc, Brno and Ostrava, with links to Vienna and Bratislava.

IC (InterCity) Long-distance and international trains with 1st- and 2nd-class coaches; supplement of 40Kč; reservations recommended.

Ex (express) Similar to IC trains, but no supplementary charge.

R (*rychlík*) The main domestic network of fast trains with 1st- and 2nd-class coaches and sleeper services; no supplement except for sleepers; express and *rychlík* trains are usually marked in red on timetables.

Os (*osobní*) Slow trains using older rolling stock that stop in every one-horse town; 2nd class only.

CAR HIRE

Small local companies offer better prices, but are less likely to have fluent, English-speaking staff. It's often easier to book by email than by phone. Typical rates for a Škoda Fabia are around 800Kč a day, including unlimited kilometres, collision-damage waiver and value-added tax (VAT). Bring your credit card as a deposit. A motorway tax coupon is included with most rental cars. One reliable rental outfit is Secco Car (☏220 802 361; www.seccocar.cz; Přístavní 39, Holešovice).

ROAD RULES

The minimum driving age is 18. Traffic moves on the right. The use of seat belts is compulsory for front- and rear-seat passengers.

» Children under 12 or shorter than 1.5m (4ft 9in) are prohibited from sitting in the front seat and must use a child-safety seat.

» Headlights must always be on, even in bright daylight.

» The legal blood-alcohol limit is zero; if the police pull you over for any reason, they are required to administer a breathalyser.

Local Transport

Local transport is affordable, well organised and runs from around 4.30am to midnight daily. Purchase tickets in advance from newsstands and vending machines. Validate tickets in time-stamping machines on buses and trams and at the entrance to metro stations.

Tours

AVE Bicycle Tours (☏251 551 011; www.bicycle-tours.cz; guided tour 1190Kč, self-guided tour 600Kč; ☉Apr-Oct) Cycle touring specialists.

E-Tours (www.etours.cz) Nature, wildlife and photography tours.

Top Bicycle (www.topbicycle.com) Biking and multisport tours.

Train

Czech Railways provides efficient train services to almost every part of the country. See www.idos.cz and www.cd.cz for fares and timetables.

Germany

Best Places to Eat

» Cafe Jacques (p178)
» Café Schäfer (p242)
» Bratwursthäusle (p229)
» Auerbachs Keller (p193)

Best Places to Stay

» Circus Hotel (p175)
» Romantik Hotel
Theophano (p203)
» Steigenberger Grandhotel
Handelshof (p193)
» Grüne Zitadelle (p199)
» Hotel Elch (p229)

Why Go?

Beer or wine? That sums up the German conundrum. One is at the heart of a pilsner-swilling culture, is the very reason for one of the world's great parties (Oktoberfest) and is consumed with pleasure across the land. The other is responsible for gorgeous vine-covered valleys, comes in myriad forms and is enjoyed everywhere, often from cute little green-stemmed glasses.

And the questions about Germany continue. Berlin or Munich? Castle or club? Ski or hike? East or west? BMW or Mercedes? In fact, the answers are simple: both. Why decide? The beauty of Germany is that rather than choosing, you can revel in the contrasts.

Berlin, edgy and vibrant, is a grand capital in a constant state of reinvention. Munich rules Bavaria, the centre of national traditions. Half-timbered villages bring smiles as you wander the cobblestoned and castle-shadowed lanes. Exploring this country and all its facets keeps visitors happy for weeks.

When to Go
Berlin

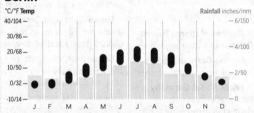

Jun–Aug Warm summers cause Germans to shed their clothes; night never seems to come.

Sep The real month of Oktober fest; autumn celebrations are found throughout Bavaria.

Dec It's icy, it's cold and you can drink hot wine at Christmas markets country-wide.

Fast Facts

» **Area** 356,866 sq km

» **Capital** Berlin

» **Country code** ✆49

» **Emergency** ✆112

Exchange Rates

Australia	A$1	€0.82
Canada	C$1	€0.77
Japan	¥100	€0.83
New Zealand	NZ$1	€0.65
UK	UK£1	€1.18
USA	US$1	€0.78

Set Your Budget

» **Budget hotel room** €80

» **Two-course meal** €15-25

» **1L of beer** €6-8

» **Bottle of wine in shop** from €4

» **U-Bahn ticket** around €2

Resources

» **German National Tourist Office** (www.germany.travel)

» **Online German Course** (www.deutsch-lernen.com)

» **Facts About Germany** (www.tatsachen-ueber-deutschland.de) Info on all aspects of German society.

» **Deutschland Online** (www.magazine-deutsch land.de) Insightful features on culture, business and politics.

Connections

At the heart of Europe, Germany has a superb railway network that's well linked to surrounding countries. Freiburg and Stuttgart have services south to Switzerland and Italy, Munich is close to the Czech Republic and Austria (including Salzburg and Innsbruck), Berlin is close to Poland, Hamburg has frequent services to Denmark, Cologne is good for fast trains to the Netherlands and Belgium (including Brussels for Eurostar to London), and Frankfurt is the base for high-speed trains to Paris, Strasbourg and other parts of France.

ITINERARIES

One Week

Spend three days in and around Berlin (eg Potsdam), then marvel at Dresden's rebirth and Nuremberg's historical pedigree before wrapping up your journey with a couple of days in Munich.

Two Weeks

Start in Munich for some Bavarian joy followed by an Alpine side trip to the top of Germany – the Zugspitze – aboard a spectacular train–cable-car combo. Admire the sugary confection of Schloss Neuschwanstein before dipping into medieval times along the Romantic Road and being enchanted by Heidelberg. The Romantic Rhine delivers fine wine and ancient castles galore. Climb the grand cathedral in charismatic Cologne and finish it all in Berlin.

Essential Food & Drink

» **Sausage** (*Wurst*) More than 1500 types are made countrywide. From sweet, smoky and tiny Nürnbergers, to crunchy Thüringers, to that fast-food remedy for the munchies, the sliced and tomato-sauce-drowned *currywurst*.

» **Mustard** (*Senf*) The perfect accompaniment to sausages, schnitzels and more, German mustards can be hot, laced with horseradish or rich with seeds – or all three.

» **Bread** (*Brot*) Get Germans talking about bread and often their eyes will water as they describe their favourite type – usually hearty and wholegrained in infinite variations.

» **Cakes** (*Kuchen*) From the confectionery fantasy of the Black Forest cake to all manner of apple-laden, crumb-covered delights, sweet tooths never feel ignored.

» **Beer** (*Bier*) For most Germans, intensely hoppy pilsner is the poison of choice, although wheat beer is popular in summer and regional varieties abound, such as Kölsch in Cologne and Rauchbier in Bamberg.

» **Wine** (*Wein*) Winning competitions and critics' praises, German wine in the 21st century is leagues removed from that cloyingly sweet stuff of yore. The country's crisp rieslings are the world's best.

BERLIN

♫ 030 / POP 3.5 MILLION

There's just no escaping history in Berlin. You might be distracted by the trendy, edgy, gentrified streets, by the bars bleeding a laid-back cool factor, by the galleries sprouting talent and pushing the envelope, but make no mistake – reminders of the German capital's past assault you while modernity sits around the corner. Norman Foster's Reichstag dome, Peter Eisenman's Holocaust Memorial and the iconic Brandenburg Gate are all contained within a few neighbouring blocks. Potsdamer Platz and its shiny Sony Center hosts Berlin's star-studded film festival each year, on the very site where only 25 years ago you could climb up a viewing platform in the West and peer over the Berlin Wall for a glimpse behind the Iron Curtain.

Renowned for its diversity and its tolerance, its alternative culture and its night-owl stamina, the best thing about Berlin is the way it reinvents itself and isn't shackled by its mind-numbing history. And the world knows this – a steady stream of Germans from other parts of the country and a league of global expatriates are flocking here to see what all the fuss is about.

History

By German standards, Berlin entered onto the stage rather late and puttered along in relative obscurity for centuries. Founded in the 13th century as a trading post, it achieved a modicum of prominence after coming under the rule of the powerful Hohenzollern from southern Germany in 1411. The clan managed to cling to power until the abolition of the monarchy in 1918.

In 1701, Elector Friedrich III was elevated to King Friedrich I, making Berlin a royal residence. The promotion significantly shaped the city, which blossomed under Friedrich I's grandson, Frederick the Great, who sought greatness as much on the battlefield as through building and embracing the ideals of the Enlightenment. The best bits of Unter den Linden date back to his reign, when Berlin blossomed into a cultural centre nicknamed 'Athens on the Spree'.

As throughout northern Europe, the Industrial Revolution began its march on Berlin in the 19th century, vastly expanding the city's population and spawning a new working class. Berlin boomed politically, economically and culturally, especially after becoming capital of the German Reich in 1871. By 1900 the population had reached two million.

World War I stifled Berlin's momentum, while the 1920s were marred by instability, corruption and inflation. Berliners responded like there was no tomorrow and made their city as much a den of decadence as a cauldron of creativity. Artists of all stripes flocked to this city of cabaret, Dada and jazz.

Hitler's rise to power put an instant dampener on the fun as the dark ages of the Third Reich descended upon the world. Berlin suffered heavy bombing in WWII and a crushing invasion of 1.5 million Soviet soldiers during the final Battle of Berlin in April 1945. Few original Nazi-era sights remain, but memorials and museums keep the horror in focus.

After WWII, Germany fell into the cross hairs of the Cold War; a country divided ideologically and literally by a fortified border and the infamous Berlin Wall, whose construction began in 1961. Just how differently

BERLIN IN ...

One Day

Book ahead for an early time slot on the lift to the **Reichstag** dome, then snap a picture of the **Brandenburger Tor** before stumbling around the **Holocaust Memorial** and admiring the contemporary architecture of **Potsdamer Platz**. Ponder Cold War madness at **Checkpoint Charlie**, then head to **Museumsinsel** to admire Queen Nefertiti and the Pergamonaltar. Finish up with a night of mirth and gaiety around **Hackescher Markt**.

Two Days

Kick off day two coming to grips with what life was like in divided Berlin at the **Gedenkstätte Berliner Mauer**. Intensify the experience at the **DDR Museum** and on a walk along the **East Side Gallery**. Spend the afternoon soaking up the urban spirit of Kreuzberg with its sassy shops and street art, grab dinner along the canal, drinks around Kottbusser Tor and finish up with a night of clubbing at **Watergate** or **Berghain**.

Germany Highlights

1 Party day and night in **Berlin** (p161): save sleep for somewhere else as there's no time here with the clubs, museums, bars and ever-changing Zeitgeist

2 Time your journey for **Oktoberfest** (p214), Munich's orgy of suds, or just hang out in a beer garden

3 Go slow in Germany's alluring small towns like **Bamberg** (p230), with winding lanes, smoked beer (!) and a lack of cliché

4 Compare the soaring peaks of the Dom in **Cologne** (p255) with the slinky glasses of the city's famous beer

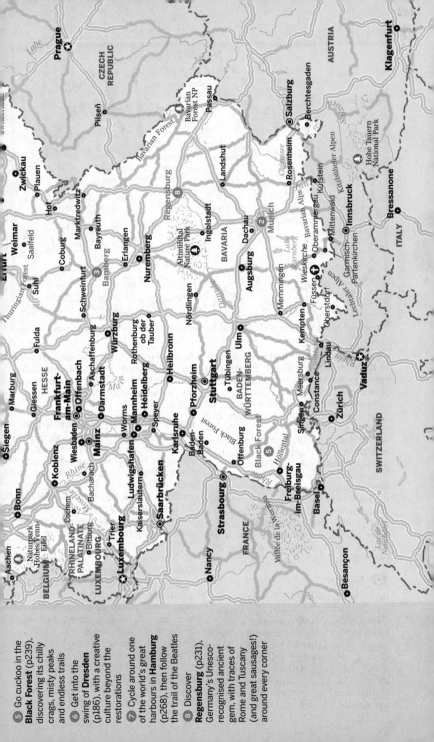

5 Go cuckoo in the **Black Forest** (p239), discovering its chilly crags, misty peaks and endless trails

6 Get into the swing of **Dresden** (p186), with a creative culture beyond the restorations

7 Cycle around one of the world's great harbours in **Hamburg** (p268), then follow the trail of the Beatles

8 Discover **Regensburg** (p231), Germany's Unesco-recognised ancient gem, with traces of Rome and Tuscany (and great sausages!) around every corner

Berlin

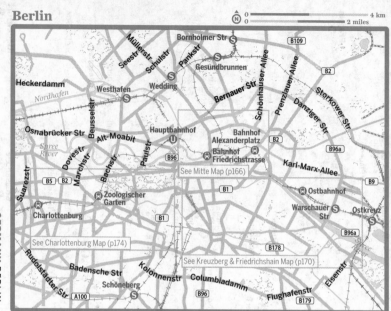

the two Germanys developed is still palpable in Berlin, expressed not only through Wall remnants but through vastly different urban planning and architectural styles.

Since reunification, Berlin has again become a hotbed of creativity, with unbridled nightlife, an explosive art scene and booming fashion and design industries. Sure, problems persist – empty city coffers, high unemployment, the delayed Berlin Brandenburg Airport, to name a few – but Berlin's allure to tourists and newcomers from around the world remains unabated. It's a city that dances to its own tune, where individualism triumphs over conformity and brilliant ideas are celebrated and welcome. Few people who live here don't love it. Few people who visit will ever forget it.

⊙ Sights

Key sights like the Reichstag, Brandenburger Tor, Checkpoint Charlie and Museumsinsel cluster in the historic city centre – Mitte – which is also home to a maze-like hipster quarter around Hackescher Markt. North of here, residential Prenzlauer Berg has a lively cafe and restaurant scene, while to the south loom the contemporary high-rises of Potsdamer Platz. Further south, gritty but cool Kreuzberg is party central, as is student-

flavoured Friedrichshain east across the Spree River and home to the East Side Gallery stretch of the Berlin Wall. Western Berlin's hub is Charlottenburg, with great shopping and a famous royal palace.

REICHSTAG & UNTER DEN LINDEN

The Reichstag is the historic anchor of the federal government quarter, which also includes the postmodern chancellery and office buildings for the parliamentarians. Just south of here, chic Unter den Linden boulevard stretches 1.5km from the Brandenburger Tor to the giant treasure chest of the Museumsinsel, past a phalanx of grand old structures reflecting one-time Prussian grandeur.

TOP CHOICE Reichstag   HISTORIC BUILDING

(Map p166; www.bundestag.de; Platz der Republik 1; ☺lift ride 8am-midnight, last entry 11pm; ☐100, Ⓢ Bundestag, Ⓡ Hauptbahnhof) One of Berlin's most iconic buildings, the Reichstag has been burned, bombed, rebuilt, buttressed by the Berlin Wall, wrapped in fabric and eventually turned into the modern home of Germany's parliament, the Bundestag.

The grand old structure was designed by Paul Wallot in 1894 and given a total post-reunification makeover by Norman Foster. The famous architect preserved only its historical shell while adding the glistening glass dome, which can be reached by lift (reservations mandatory). At the top, pick up a free auto-activated audioguide and learn about the building, city landmarks and the workings of the parliament while following the ramp spiralling up and around the dome's mirror-clad central funnel.

Brandenburger Tor & Pariser Platz
HISTORIC SITE

(Map p166; ⑤Brandenburger Tor, ⑨Brandenburger Tor) A symbol of division during the Cold War, the landmark Brandenburg Gate now epitomises German reunification. Its architect Carl Gotthard Langhans found inspiration in Athen's Acropolis for this elegant triumphal arch, completed in 1791 as the royal city gate. It is crowned by the Quadriga sculpture of the winged goddess of victory piloting a chariot drawn by four horses. The Brandenburg Gate stands sentinel over Pariser Platz, a harmoniously proportioned square once again framed by banks as well as the US, British and French embassies, just as it was during its 19th-century heyday.

FREE Holocaust Memorial
MEMORIAL

(Map p166; ☑2639 4336; www.stiftung-denk-mal.de; Cora-Berliner-Strasse 1; audioguide €3; ⊙field 24hr, information centre 10am-8pm Tue-Sun, last entry 7.15pm Apr-Sep, 6.15pm Oct-Mar; ⑤Brandenburger Tor, ⑨Brandenburger Tor) The football-field-sized Memorial to the Murdered European Jews is Germany's central memorial to the Nazi-planned genocide and is colloquially known as the Holocaust Memorial. American architect Peter Eisenman created a maze of 2711 sarcophagi-like concrete columns rising in sombre silence from undulating ground. For context, visit the subterranean Ort der Information (information centre).

Hitler's Bunker
HISTORIC SITE

(Map p170; cnr In den Ministergärten & Gertrud-Kolmar-Strasse; ⑤Brandenburger Tor, ⑨Brandenburger Tor) Berlin was burning and Soviet tanks advancing relentlessly when Adolf Hitler committed suicide on 30 April 1945 alongside Eva Braun, his long-time female companion, hours after their marriage. Today, a parking lot covers the site, revealing its dark history only via an information panel with a diagram of the vast bunker network, and information on its construction and post-WWII history.

WANT MORE?

For in-depth information, reviews and recommendations at your fingertips, head to the Apple App Store to purchase Lonely Planet's *Berlin City Guide* iPhone app.

Alternatively, head to Lonely Planet (www.lonelyplanet.com/germany/berlin) for planning advice, author recommendations, traveller reviews and insider tips.

Unter den Linden
STREET

(Map p166; ☑100, 200, ⑤Brandenburger Tor, ⑨Brandenburger Tor) This chic boulevard stretches 1.5km from the Brandenburger Tor to the giant treasure chest of the Museumsinsel, past a phalanx of grand old structures built under various Prussian kings and reflecting the one-time grandeur of the royal family.

Bebelplatz
MEMORIAL

(Map p166; Bebel Sq; ☑100, 200, ⑤Französische Strasse, Hausvogteiplatz) Unter den Linden runs past this treeless square, where books by Brecht, Mann, Marx and other 'subversives' went up in flames during the first full-blown public book burning staged by Nazi students in 1933. Michael Ullmann's underground installation, *Empty Library*, beneath a glass pane at the square's centre, poignantly commemorates the event.

Bebelplatz was first laid out in the mid-18th century as part of the Forum Fridericianum, a cluster of cultural buildings envisioned by Frederick the Great. The Staatsoper Unter den Linden, the Alte Königliche Bibliothek, a palace for Fritz' brother Heinrich (now the Humboldt Universität), and the copper-domed Sankt-Hedwigs-Kathedrale all date from this time.

Deutsches Historisches Museum
MUSEUM

(Map p166; ☑203 040; www.dhm.de; Unter den Linden 2; adult/concession €8/4; ⊙10am-6pm; ☑100, 200, ⑨Alexanderplatz, Hackescher Markt) This engaging museum zeroes in on two millennia of German history in all its gore and glory; not in a nutshell but on two floors of a Prussian-era armoury. Check out the Nazi globe, the pain-wrecked faces of dying warrior sculptures in the courtyard, and the temporary exhibits in the boldly modern annex designed by IM Pei.

Mitte

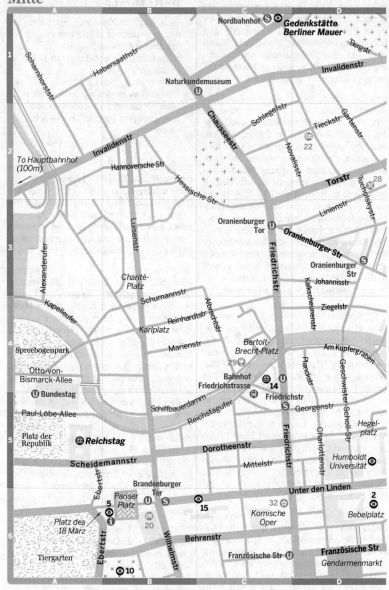

Checkpoint Charlie   HISTORIC SITE
(Map p170; cnr Zimmerstrasse & Friedrichstrasse; ⊙24hr; ⑤Kochstrasse, Stadtmitte)
Checkpoint Charlie was the principal gateway for foreigners and diplomats between the two Berlins from 1961 to 1990. Unfortunately, this potent symbol of the Cold War has become a tacky tourist trap, although a free **open-air exhibit** that illustrates milestones in Cold War history is one redeeming aspect. New since September 2012 is Yadegar Asisi's **Berlin Wall Panorama** (Map

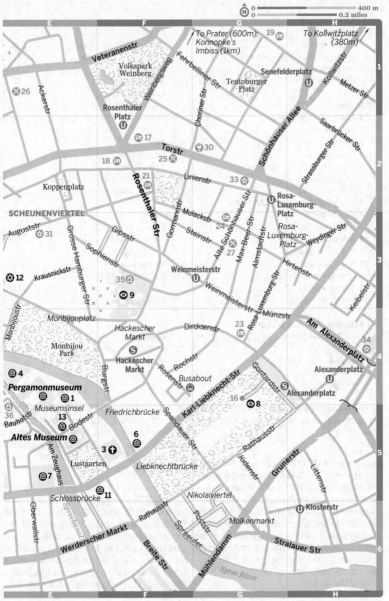

p170; www.asisi.de; cnr Friedrichstrasse & Zimmerstrasse; adult/concession €10/8.50; ⏰10am-6pm; Ⓢ Kochstrasse). An official Cold War Museum is in the planning stages and may open by 2015. Until then, a 'Blackbox' offers a preview.

Nearby, the privately run **Haus am Checkpoint Charlie** (Map p170; ☎253 7250; www.mauermuseum.de; Friedrichstrasse 43-45; adult/concession €12.50/9.50; ⏰9am-10pm; ♿; Ⓢ Kochstrasse, Stadtmitte) is especially strong when it comes to documenting spectacular escape attempts (through tunnels, in hot-air balloons and even using a one-man submarine).

Tränenpalast MUSEUM
(Map p166; ☑4677 7790; www.hdg.de; Reichstagsufer 17; ☺9am-7pm Tue-Fri, 10am-6pm Sat & Sun; ⑤Friedrichstrasse, ☐100) East Berliners had to bid adieu to family visiting from West Germany in this glass-and-steel border crossing pavilion – hence its moniker 'Palace of Tears'. Photographs, historical footage and the original claustrophobic passport control booths help illustrate the social impact the division had on the daily lives of Germans on both sides of the border.

MUSEUMSINSEL & SCHEUNENVIERTEL
Museumsinsel (Museum Island) is Berlin's most important treasure trove, spanning 6000 years worth of art, artefacts, sculpture and architecture from Europe and beyond. It segues into the Scheunenviertel (Barn Quarter), a compact and charismatic quar-

ter filled with idyllic courtyards, bleeding-edge art galleries, local-designer boutiques, shabby-chic bars and even a belle époque ballroom. Since reunification, the Scheunenviertel has also reprised its historic role as Berlin's main Jewish quarter.

Museumsinsel MUSEUM
(☑2090 5577; www.smb.museum; day pass for all museums €14/7; ☐100, 200, ⑤Hackescher Markt, Friedrichstrasse) Spread across five grand museums built between 1830 and 1930, the complex takes up the entire northern half of the little Spree Island where Berlin's settlement began in the 13th century and has been a Unesco World Heritage Site since 1999.

The Pergamonmuseum (Map p166; ☑266 424 242; www.smb.museum; Am Kupfergraben 5; adult/concession €8/4; ☺10am-6pm Fri-Wed, to 9pm Thu; ☐Hackescher Markt, Friedrichstrasse, bus 100) is the island's top draw with monumental architecture from ancient worlds, including the namesake Pergamon Altar and the stunning Babylonian Ishtar Gate.

The Altes Museum (Old Museum; Map p166; ☑266 424 242; www.smb.museum; Am Lustgarten; adult/concession €8/4; ⊘10am-6pm Fri-Wed, to 8pm Thu; 🚇100, 200, 🚊Friedrichstrasse) was the first repository to open on the island, in 1830, and presents Greek, Etruscan and Roman antiquities. Note the *Praying Boy* bronze sculpture, Roman silver vessels and portraits of Caesar and Cleopatra.

The show-stopper of the Egyptian collection at the Neues Museum (New Museum; Map p166; ☑266 424 242; www.smb.museum; adult/concession €10/5; ⊘10am-6pm Sun-Wed, to 8pm Thu-Sat; 🚇100, 200, 🚊Hackescher Markt) is the 3300-year-old bust of Queen Nefertiti; the equally enthralling Museum of Pre- and Early History has treasure from Troy.

Famous for its European sculpture from the Middle Ages to the 18th century (Riemenschneider, Donatello, Pisano, etc), the Bodemuseum (Map p166; ☑266 424 242; www.smb.museum; Monbijoubrücke; adult/concession €8/4; ⊘10am-6pm Tue, Wed & Fri-Sun, to 10pm Thu; 🚊Hackescher Markt) has a huge coin collection and Byzantine art.

The Alte Nationalgalerie (Old National Gallery; Map p166; ☑266 424 242; www.smb.museum; Bodestrasse 1-3; adult/concession €8/4; ⊘10am-6pm Fri-Wed, to 10pm Thu; 🚇100, 200, 🚊Hackescher Markt) trains its focus on 19th-century European art.

Berliner Dom   CHURCH
(Berlin Cathedral; Map p166; ☑2026 9110; www.berlinerdom.de; Am Lustgarten; adult/concession €7/4; ⊘9am-8pm Mon-Sat, noon-8pm Sun Apr-Sep, to 7pm Oct-Mar; 🚇100, 200, 🚊Hackescher Markt) Pompous yet majestic, the Italian Renaissance–style former royal court church (1905) does triple duty as house of worship, museum and concert hall. Inside it's gilt to the hilt and outfitted with a lavish marble-and-onyx altar, a 7269-pipe Sauer organ and elaborate royal sarcophagi. Climb up the 267 steps to the gallery for glorious city views.

DDR Museum   MUSEUM
(GDR Museum; Map p166; ☑847 123 731; www.ddr-museum.de; Karl-Liebknecht-Strasse 1; adult/concession €6/4; ⊘10am-8pm Sun-Fri, to 10pm Sat; 🚇; 🚇100, 200, 🚊Hackescher Markt) The touchy-feely GDR Museum does a delightful job at pulling back the Iron Curtain on an extinct society. You'll learn that in East Germany, kids were put through collective potty training, engineers earned little more than farmers and everyone, it seems, went on nudist holidays. The more sinister sides of GDR life are also addressed, including the chronic supply shortages and Stasi surveillance.

Humboldt-Box   MUSEUM
(Map p166; ☑0180-503 0707; www.humboldt-box.com; Schlossplatz; adult/concession €4/2.50; ⊘10am-8pm Apr-Oct, to 6pm Nov-Mar; 🚇100, 200, 🚊Alexanderplatz, Hackescher Markt) This oddly shaped structure offers a sneak preview of the planned reconstruction of the Berlin City Palace, to be known as Humboldtforum, on Schlossplatz, opposite the Museumsinsel museums. On display are teasers from each future resident – the Ethnological Museum, the Museum of Asian Art and a library – along with a fantastically detailed model of the historic city centre. Great views from the upstairs cafe terrace.

Fernsehturm   LANDMARK
(Map p166; www.tv-turm.de; Panoramastrasse 1a; adult/child €12/7.50, VIP tickets €19.50/11.50; ⊘9am-midnight Mar-Oct, from 10am Nov-Feb; 🚇Alexanderplatz, 🚊Alexanderplatz) Germany's tallest structure, the needle-like TV Tower is as iconic to Berlin as the Eiffel Tower is to Paris and has been soaring 368m high (including the antenna) since 1969. Come early to beat the queue for the lift to the panorama platform at 203m. There's also lovably stuffy cafe, which makes one revolution in 30 minutes.

FREE Hackesche Höfe   HISTORIC SITE
(Map p166; ☑2809 8010; www.hackesche-hoefe.com; Rosenthaler Strasse 40/41, Sophienstrasse 6; 🚇M1, 🚊Hackescher Markt) The Hackesche Höfe is the largest and most famous of the interlinked courtyard complexes peppered throughout the Scheunenviertel. Take your sweet time pottering around this tangle of cafes, galleries, boutiques and entertainment venues. Court I, festooned with art nouveau tiles, is the prettiest.

Neue Synagoge   SYNAGOGUE
(Map p166; ☑8802 8300; www.cjudaicum.de; Oranienburger Strasse 28-30; adult/concession €3/2; ⊘10am-8pm Sun & Mon, to 6pm Tue-Thu, to 5pm Fri, reduced hours Nov-Apr; 🚇Oranienburger Tor, 🚊Oranienburger Strasse) The sparkling gilded dome of the New Synagogue is the most visible symbol of Berlin's revitalised Jewish community. The 1866 original was Germany's largest synagogue but its modern incarnation is more a place of remembrance called Centrum Judaicum.

GERMANY BERLIN

Kreuzberg & Friedrichshain

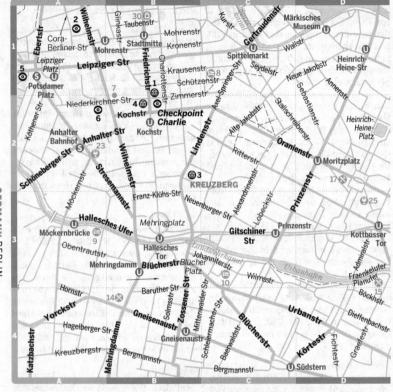

TOP CHOICE Gedenkstätte

Berliner Mauer   MEMORIAL

(☎467 986 666; www.berliner-mauer-gedenkstaette
.de; Bernauer Strasse btwn Gartenstrasse & Brun-
nenstrasse; ⏰9.30am-7pm Apr-Oct, to 6pm Nov-
Mar, open-air exhibit 24hr; ☒Nordbahnhof) The
central memorial site of German division
incorporates a stretch of original Berlin
Wall along with vestiges of the border installations, escape tunnels, a chapel and a
monument. Multimedia stations, 'archaeological windows' and markers sprinkled
throughout the memorial provide detailed
background.

POTSDAMER PLATZ & TIERGARTEN

Berlin newest quarter, Potsdamer Platz, was
forged in the 1990s from ground once bisected by the Berlin Wall. It's a showcase of
contemporary architecture by such illustrious architects as Renzo Piano and Helmut
Jahn whose flashy Sony Center – anchored
by a plaza canopied by a tentlike glass roof –
is the most eye-catching complex.

Just west of Potsdamer Platz, is the Kulturforum, a cluster of art museums of which the
Gemäldegalerie and the Neue Nationalgalerie
are standouts. Also here is the world-class
Berliner Philharmonie. The leafy Tiergarten,
meanwhile, with its rambling paths and hidden beer gardens, makes for a perfect sightseeing break.

Museum für Film und Fernsehen   MUSEUM

(☎300 9030; www.deutsche-kinemathek.de;
Potsdamer Strasse 2; adult/concession €6/4.50;
⏰10am-6pm Tue, Wed & Fri-Sun, to 8pm Thu;
☒200, ⓈPotsdamer Platz, ☒Potsdamer Platz)
Every February, celluloid celebs sashay down
the red carpet at Potsdamer Platz venues
during the Berlin International Film Festival. Germany's film history, meanwhile, gets
the star treatment year-round in this engaging museum. Skip through galleries dedicated
to pioneers like Fritz Lang, groundbreaking

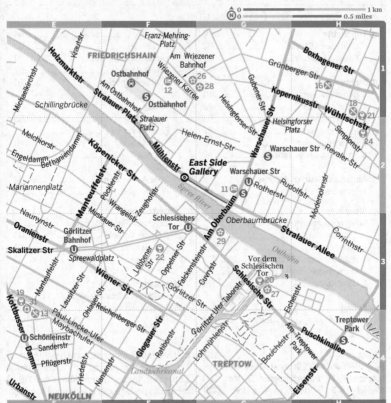

movies like Leni Riefenstahl's *Olympia* and legendary divas like Marlene Dietrich. The TV exhibit has more niche appeal but is still fun if you want to know what *Star Trek* sounds like in German.

Panoramapunkt
VIEWPOINT

(Map p170; ☑2593 7080; www.panoramapunkt. de; Potsdamer Platz 1; adult/concession €5.50/4; ☉10am-8pm, last ride 7.30pm, reduced hours in winter; ☐M41, 200, ⑤Potsdamer Platz, ⓇPotsdamer Platz) A super-speedy lift yo-yos up and down the red-brick Kollhoff Building on Potsdamer Platz for fabulous 360-degree views from a lofty 100m. Information panels trace the square's history and there's a cafe to boot.

Neue Nationalgalerie
GALLERY

(Map p174; ☑266 2951; www.neue-nationalgalerie. de; Potsdamer Strasse 50; adult/concession €10/5; ☉10am-6pm Tue, Wed & Fri, to 10pm Thu, 11am-6pm Sat & Sun; ⑤Potzdamer Platz, ⓇPotsdamer Platz) The New National Gallery is a glass

and steel temple designed in 1968 by Ludwig Mies van der Rohe. It presents changing exhibits of paintings and sculpture created by 20th-century European artists before 1960. Look for works by Picasso, Miró and Klee, along with German expressionists like Otto Dix, George Grosz and Ernst Ludwig Kirchner.

Gemäldegalerie
GALLERY

(Map p174; ☑266 424 242; www.smb.museum/ gg; Matthäikirchplatz 8; adult/concession €8/4; ☉10am-6pm Tue, Wed & Fri-Sun, to 10pm Thu; ☐M29, M41, 200, ⑤Potsdamer Platz, ⓇPotsdamer Platz) The principal Kulturforum museum boasts one of the world's finest and most comprehensive collections of European art from the 13th to the 18th centuries. Wear comfy shoes when exploring the 72 galleries: a walk past masterpieces by Rembrandt, Dürer, Vermeer, Gainsborough and many more Old Masters covers almost 2km.

Kreuzberg & Friedrichshain

Bauhaus Archiv　　　　　　MUSEUM
(Map p174; ☎254 0020; www.bauhaus.de; Klingel-höferstrasse 14; adult/concession Sat-Mon €7/4, Wed-Fri €6/3; ⊙10am-5pm Wed-Mon; ⑤Nollendorfplatz) Changing exhibits using study notes, workshop pieces, photographs, blueprints, models and other objects and documents, illustrate the theories of this influential 20th-century design movement. Bauhaus founder Walter Gropius himself drafted the blueprints for the distinctive white shed-roofed building.

FREE **Topographie des Terrors**　　MEMORIAL
(Topography of Terror; Map p170; ☎2548 6703; www.topographie.de; Niederkirchner Strasse 8; ⊙10am-8pm May-Sep, to dusk Oct-Apr; 🚻; ⑤Potsdamer Platz, ⓇPotsdamer Platz) In the same spot where once stood the most feared institutions of Nazi Germany (including the Gestapo headquarters and the SS central command), this compelling exhibit dissects the anatomy of the Nazi state. A short stretch of the Berlin Wall runs along Niederkirchner Strasse.

KREUZBERG & FRIEDRICHSHAIN

Kreuzberg gets its street cred from being delightfully edgy and wacky. While the western half around Bergmannstrasse has an upmarket, genteel air, eastern Kreuzberg (around Kottbusser Tor and still nicknamed SO36 after its old postal code) is a multicultural mosaic of tousled students, aspiring creatives, shisha-smoking immigrants and international life artists. Spend a day searching for great street art, soaking up the multi-culti vibe, scarfing a shawarma, browsing vintage stores and hanging by the river or canal, then find out why Kreuzberg is also known as a night-crawler's paradise. Same goes for equally free-spirited Friedrichshain, across the Spree River in the former East Berlin.

FREE **East Side Gallery**　　HISTORIC SITE
(Map p170; www.eastsidegallery-berlin.de; Mühlenstrasse btwn Oberbaumbrücke & Ostbahnhof; ⊙24hr; ⑤Warschauer Strasse, ⓇOstbahnhof, Warschauer Strasse) At 1.3km, the East Side Gallery is not only the longest surviving stretch of Berlin Wall, it is also the world's largest open-air mural collection. In 1989, dozens of international artists translated the era's global euphoria and optimism into more than 100 paintings that are a mix of political statements, drug-induced musings and truly artistic visions. It was restored in 2009.

Jüdisches Museum
MUSEUM

(Jewish Museum; Map p170; 2599 3300; www.jmberlin.de; Lindenstrasse 9-14; adult/concession €5/2.50; 10am-10pm Mon, to 8pm Tue-Sun, last admission 1hr before closing; SHallesches Tor, Kochstrasse) This engaging museum offers a chronicle of the trials and triumphs in 2000 years of Jewish history in Germany but it's Daniel Libeskind's landmark building that steals the show. A 3D metaphor for the tortured history of the Jewish people, its zigzag outline symbolises a broken Star of David, and its silvery titanium-zinc facade is sharply angled and pierced with small gashes.

Stasimuseum
MUSEUM

(553 6854; www.stasimuseum.de; Haus 1, Ruschestrasse 103; adult/concession €5/4; 11am-6pm Mon-Fri, noon-6pm Sat & Sun; SMagdalenenstrasse) The former headquarters of East Germany's much-feared Ministry of State Security is now the Stasi Museum. Marvel at cunningly low-tech surveillance devices (hidden in watering cans, neckties, even rocks), a claustrophobic prisoner transport van and the obsessively neat offices of Stasi chief Erich Mielke. Other rooms introduce the ideology, rituals and institutions of GDR society. Panelling is partly in English.

Stasi Prison
MEMORIAL SITE

(Gedenkstätte Hohenschönhausen; 9860 8230; www.stiftung-hsh.de; Genslerstrasse 66; tour adult/concession €5/2.50; tours hourly 11am-3pm Mon-Fri, 10am-4pm Sat & Sun, English tour 2.30pm daily; M5 to Freienwalder Strasse) Victims of Stasi persecution often ended up in this grim prison. Tours reveal the full extent of the terror and cruelty perpetrated upon thousands of suspected regime opponents, many utterly innocent. The prison is in the district of Lichtenberg, deep in the former East Berlin. Take tram M5 from Alexanderplatz to Freienwalder Strasse, then walk 10 minutes along Freienwalder Strasse.

CHARLOTTENBURG

The glittering heart of West Berlin during the Cold War, Charlottenburg has been eclipsed by historic Mitte and other eastern districts since reunification, but is now trying hard to stage a comeback with major construction and redevelopment around Zoo station. Its main artery is the 3.5km-long Kurfürstendamm (Ku'damm for short), Berlin's busiest shopping strip. Its main tourist attraction is the nicely restored Charlottenburg palace.

TOP CHOICE Schloss Charlottenburg
PALACE

(320 911; www.spsg.de; Spandauer Damm 20-24; day pass adult/concession €15/11; 145, 309, SRichard-Wagner-Platz, Sophie-Charlotte-Platz) The grandest Prussian palace to survive in Berlin consists of the main building and three smaller structures scattered about the sprawling park. Each building charges separate admission; the day pass (*Tageskarte*) is good for one-day admission to every open building.

Charlottenburg palace started out as the summer residence of Sophie Charlotte, wife of King Friedrich I. The couple's baroque living quarters in the palace's oldest section, the **Altes Schloss** (320 911; www.spsg.de; Spandauer Damm; adult/concession €12/8; 10am-6pm Tue-

(side text) GERMANY BERLIN

TICKETS TO SAVINGS

If you're on a budget, various ticket deals and passes can help you stretch your euros further.

Bereichskarten The museum clusters on Museumsinsel and the Kulturforum offer area tickets good for same-day admission to all permanent collections in that particular area.

Berlin Museum Pass (www.visitberlin.de; adult/concession €19/9.50) Buys admission to the permanent exhibits of about 60 museums for three consecutive days, including top draws like the Pergamonmuseum. Sold at tourist offices and participating museums.

Berlin Welcome Card (www.visitberlin.de; 48-/72hr €17.90/23.90, 48hr incl Potsdam & up to 3 children under 15yr €19.90, 72hr incl Museumsinsel €34) Unlimited public transport and up to 50% discount to 200 sights, attractions and tours for periods of two, three or five days. It's also sold at tourist offices, U-Bahn and S-Bahn ticket vending machines and many hotels.

CityTourCard (www.citytourcard.com; 48hr/72hr/5 days €16.90/22.90/29.90) Similar to the Berlin Welcome Card, but a bit cheaper and with fewer discounts.

GERMANY BERLIN

Charlottenburg

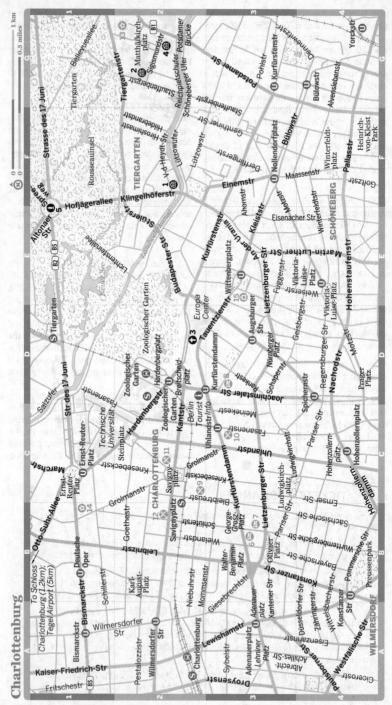

Charlottenburg

Sun Apr-Oct, to 5pm Tue-Sun Nov-Mar; 🚌145, 309, Ⓢ Richard-Wagner-Platz, Sophie-Charlotte-Platz), are an extravaganza in stucco, brocade and overall opulence, although the private chambers of Frederick the Great in the **Neuer Flügel** (New Wing; 🕿 320 911; www.spsg. de; Spandauer Damm 20-24; adult/concession incl audioguide €6/5; ⊙10am-6pm Wed-Mon Apr-Oct, to 5pm Wed-Mon Nov-Mar; 🚌M45, 309, Ⓢ Richard-Wagner-Platz, Sophie-Charlotte-Platz) – designed in flamboyant rococo style – are even more impressive.

Other buildings dotted around the park house 19th-century paintings (**Neuer Pavillon**), fancy porcelain (**Belvedere**) and dead royals (**Mausoleum**).

Kaiser-Wilhelm-Gedächtniskirche CHURCH (Kaiser Wilhelm Memorial Church; Map p174; 🕿 218 5023; www.gedaechtniskirche.com; Breitscheidplatz; ⊙9am-7pm; Ⓢ Zoologischer Garten, Kurfürstendamm, Ⓡ Zoologischer Garten) The bombed-out tower of this landmark church in Charlottenburg serves as an antiwar memorial, standing quiet and dignified amid the roaring traffic. The 1895 original was a real beauty, as you can tell from the before and after pictures on the ground floor. The adjacent octagonal hall of worship, added in 1961, has amazing midnight-blue glass walls and a giant 'floating' Jesus.

⬅ Tours

Most of these English-language walking tours don't require reservations – just show up at one of the meeting points. Since these can change quite suddenly, we have not listed them here. Keep an eye out for flyers in hotel or hostel lobbies, or at tourist offices, or contact the companies directly.

Berlin Walks WALKING TOUR (🕿 301 9194; www.berlinwalks.de; adult €12-15, concession €9-12) Get under the skin of Berlin's history and what makes the city tick today with the local expert guides of Berlin's longest-running English-language walking tour company.

New Berlin Tours WALKING TOUR (www.newberlintours.com; adult €12-15, concession €10-15) Energetic and entertaining English-language walking tours by the pioneers of the donation-based 'free tour' and the pub crawl.

Fat Tire Bike Tours BICYCLE TOUR (Map p166; 🕿 2404 7991; www.fattirebiketours. com/berlin; Panoramastrasse 1a; adult €24, concession €22; Ⓢ Alexanderplatz, Ⓡ Alexanderplatz) Offers a huge range of tours, from standard city tours to themed tours along the former course of the Berlin Wall and/or a Cold War tour, historical tours and more.

Trabi Safari DRIVING TOUR (Map p170; 🕿 2759 2273; www.trabi-safari.de; Zimmerstrasse 97; per person €30-90, Wall Ride €79-89, prices depending on group size; Ⓢ Kochstrasse) Catch the *Good Bye, Lenin!* vibe on tours of Berlin's classic sights or the 'Wild East' with you driving or riding in convoy of a 'Trabi', East Germany's (now) cult car with live commentary (in English by prior arrangement) piped into your vehicle. Bring your drivers' license.

🛏 Sleeping

MITTE & PRENZLAUER BERG

TOP CHOICE **Circus Hotel** HOTEL €€ (Map p166; 🕿 2000 3939; www.circus-berlin.de; Rosenthaler Strasse 1; d €80-110; @🛜; Ⓢ Rosenthaler Platz) At our favourite budget boutique

DON'T MISS

BERLIN'S TIERGARTEN, A SWATH OF GREEN

Lolling about in the grass on a sunny afternoon is the quintessential Berlin pastime. Germans adore the outdoors and flock to urban green spaces whenever the weather is fine. They also dislike tan lines, so don't be surprised if you stumble upon locals sunbathing in the nude.

The Tiergarten is criss-crossed by a series of major roads and anchored by the Brandenburg Gate and the Reichstag on its northwestern edge. It's a tangle of curved walking and cycling paths, tiny ponds, open fields and thick woods. You'll probably get lost, but there are dozens of maps scattered about to help you find your way.

From the Reichstag, the Tiergarten's **carillon** (John-Foster-Dulles-Allee; ▣100 or 200) and the **Haus der Kulturen der Welt** (House of World Cultures; ☏397 870; www.hkw.de; John-Foster-Dulles-Allee 10; admission varies; ◷exhibits 11am-7pm Wed-Mon; ▣100, ⓢBundestag) are clearly visible. The latter was the US contribution to the 1957 International Building Exposition and it's easy to see why locals call it the 'pregnant oyster.'

Further west, the wings of the **Siegessäule** (Victory Column; Map p174; Grosser Stern; ▣100, 200) were the *Wings of Desire* in that famous Wim Wenders film. This golden angel was built to commemorate Prussian military victories in the 19th century. However, there are better views than those at the column's peak.

hotel, none of the mod rooms are alike but all feature upbeat colours, thoughtful design details, sleek oak floors and quality beds. Unexpected perks include a well-stocked library and free iPod, netbook and DVD player rentals. Fabulous breakfast buffet to boot.

TOP CHOICE **EastSeven Berlin Hostel** HOSTEL €
(Map p166; ☏9362 2240; www.eastseven.de; Schwedter Strasse 7; dm €17-19, d €50; @⏆; ⓢSenefelderplatz) Friendly and fun, this small hostel is within strolling distance of hip hangouts and public transport. Cultural and language barriers melt quickly over a BBQ in the idyllic back garden, dinners in the modern kitchen (with dishwasher!) or chilling in the retro lounge. Come bedtime, retreat to comfy pine beds in brightly painted dorms or private rooms (baby beds are available).

Hotel Honigmond HOTEL €€
(Map p166; ☏284 4550; www.honigmond-berlin. de; Tieckstrasse 12; d €145-235; P@⏆; ⓢOranienburger Tor) This delightful hotel scores a perfect 10 on our 'charmometer', not for being particularly lavish but for its homey yet elegant ambience. The nicest rooms flaunt such historic features as ornate stucco ceilings, frescoes and parquet floors.

Hotel Amano HOTEL €€
(Map p166; ☏809 4150; www.amanogroup.de; Auguststrasse 43; d €80-160; P✳@⏆; ⓢRosenthaler Platz) This hit with designer-hotel devotees has inviting public areas dressed in brushed-copper walls and cocoa-hued banquettes. In

the rather twee rooms, white furniture, oak floors and natural-toned fabrics create crisp cosiness. Great bar and fabulous summer rooftop terrace.

Motel One Berlin-Alexanderplatz HOTEL €
(Map p166; ☏2005 4080; www.motel-one.de; Dircksenstrasse 36; d from €69; P✳@⏆; ⓢAlexanderplatz, ⒭Alexanderplatz) If you value location over luxury, this fast-growing budget designer chain makes for an excellent crash pad. Though small, rooms come with up-to-the-minute touches (flat-screen TVs, granite counters, massage showerheads, air-con) normally the staples of posher players. Check the website for other Motel One properties around town. Optional breakfast is €7.50.

Adina Apartment Hotel Berlin Checkpoint Charlie APARTMENT €€
(Map p170; ☏200 7670; www.adina.eu; Krausenstrasse 35-36; d €110-160, 1-bedroom apt from €140; P✳@⏆; ⓢStadtmitte, Spittelmarkt) Adina's contemporary and roomy one- and two-bedroom apartments with full kitchens are tailor-made for cost-conscious families, anyone in need of elbow room, and self-caterers (a supermarket is a minute away). Kitchenless rooms also available. See the website about other Berlin Adina properties. Optional breakfast is €15.

Hotel Adlon Kempinski LUXURY HOTEL €€€
(Map p166; ☏226 10; www.kempinski.com; Pariser Platz, Unter den Linden 77; r from €250; ✳@⏆; ⓢBrandenburger Tor, ⒭Brandenburger Tor)

Opposite Brandenburger Tor, the Adlon has been Berlin's most high-profile defender of the grand tradition since 1907. The striking lobby is a mere overture to the full symphony of luxury awaiting in spacious, amenity-laden rooms and suites where the decor is old-fashioned in a regal sort of way. A ritzy day spa, gourmet restaurants and the swank Felix nightclub add 21st-century spice.

Wombats City Hostel Berlin HOSTEL €

(Map p166; ☎8471 0820; www.wombats-hostels.com; Alte Schönhauser Strasse 2; dm/d €25/70; @☎; ⓈRosa-Luxemburg-Platz) Wombat's has a long track record at getting hostelling right. From backpack-sized in-room lockers to individual reading lamps and a guest kitchen with dishwasher, the attention to detail here is impressive. Spacious rooms with bathrooms are as de rigueur as freebie linen and a welcome drink, best enjoyed with fellow party pilgrims in the 7th-floor Wombar.

Circus Hostel HOSTEL €

(Map p166; ☎2000 3939; www.circus-hostel.de; Weinbergsweg 1a; dm €23-29, d from €80, with shared bathroom from €64, 2-/4-person apt €95/150; @☎; ⓈRosenthaler Platz) Clean, cheerfully painted rooms, abundant showers and competent, helpful staff are among factors that keep Circus at the top of the hostel heap. Welcome tech touches include laptop and Skype phone rentals and laptop-sized in-room lockers with integrated electrical plug. To download its free self-guided MP3 city tour, go to www.circus-berlin.de/bustour.

KREUZBERG & FRIEDRICHSHAIN

Grand Hostel HOSTEL €

(Map p170; ☎209 5450; www.grandhostel-berlin.de; Tempelhofer Ufer 14; dm €12-15, d €58; @☎; ⓈMöckernbrücke) Afternoon tea in the library? Check. Rooms with stucco-ornamented ceilings? Got 'em. Canal views? Yup. OK, the Grand Hostel may be no five-star hotel, but it is one of Berlin's most comfortable and atmospheric hostels in an 1870s building. Dorms and private rooms have quality single beds (linen costs €3) and large lockers.

Ostel Hostel HOSTEL €

(Map p170; ☎2576 8660; www.ostel.eu; Wriezener Karree 5; dm/d/apt from €15/64/80; ℗@☎; ⓈOstbahnhof) Fancy a stay with a *Good Bye, Lenin!* vibe? Book a bed in this unusual hostel, which resuscitates socialist GDR charm with original furnishings sourced from flea markets, grannies' attics and eBay. Rates include linen, towels and wi-fi. It's within

stumbling distance to Berghain/Panorama Bar (p181).

ᴛᴏᴘ/ᴄʜᴏɪᴄᴇ Michelberger Hotel HOTEL €€

(Map p170; ☎2977 8590; www.michelbergerhotel.com; Warschauer Strasse 39; d €80-180; ☎; ⓈWarschauer Strasse, ⓇWarschauer Strasse) The pinnacle of creative crash pads, Michelberger perfectly encapsulates Berlin's offbeat DIY spirit. Rooms don't hide their factory pedigree but are comfortable and come in sizes suitable for lovebirds, families or rock bands. The bar-reception-lobby often doubles as a party venue. Great for the young and forever young.

Hotel Johann HOTEL €€

(Map p170; ☎225 0740; www.hotel-johann-berlin.de; Johanniterstrasse 8; d €95-120; ℗@☎; ⓈPrinzenstrasse, Hallesches Tor) This 33-room hotel consistently tops the popularity charts, thanks to its eager-to-please service and rooms pairing minimalist designer style with historic flourishes. Nice garden and within strolling distance of the Jüdisches Museum.

CHARLOTTENBURG

ᴛᴏᴘ/ᴄʜᴏɪᴄᴇ Hotel Askanischer Hof HOTEL €€

(Map p174; ☎881 8033; www.askanischer-hof.de; Kurfürstendamm 53; d €120-180; ☎; ⓈAdenauerplatz) If you're after character and vintage flair, you'll find heaps of both at this 17-room jewel with a Roaring Twenties pedigree. No two rooms are alike but all are filled with antiques, lace curtains, frilly chandeliers and time-worn oriental rugs; often used for fashion shoots.

Hotel Bogota HOTEL €€

(Map p174; ☎881 5001; www.bogota.de; Schlüterstrasse 45; d €90-150, with shared bathroom €64-77; ☎; ⓈUhlandstrasse) Bogota has charmed travellers with charisma and vintage flair since 1964. Helmut Newton studied with

---

ℹ BUS TOUR ON THE CHEAP

Get a crash course in 'Berlinology' by hopping on the upper deck of bus 100 or 200 at Zoologischer Garten or Alexanderplatz and letting the landmarks whoosh by for the price of a standard bus ticket (€2.40, day pass €6.50). Bus 100 goes via the Tiergarten, 200 via Potsdamer Platz. Without traffic, trips take about 30 minutes. Watch out for pickpockets.

fashion photographer Yva here in the 1930s and to this day the retro landmark hosts glam-mag photo shoots. Room sizes and amenities vary greatly, so ask to see a few before settling in.

Hotel Concorde Berlin
HOTEL €€€

(Map p174; ☑800 9990; www.concorde-hotels.com/concordeberlin; Augsburger Strasse 41; d €150-300; P❋@🛜; SKurfürstendamm) Designed by German architect Jan Kleihues, from the curved limestone facade to the door knobs, the Concorde channels New York efficiency, French lightness of being and Berlin-style unpretentiousness. Rooms and suites are supersized and accented with contemporary German art. Free wi-fi. Optional breakfast is €28.

✖ Eating

If you crave traditional German comfort food, you'll certainly find plenty of places in Berlin to indulge in pork knuckles, smoked pork chops and calves liver. These days, though, 'typical' local fare is lighter, healthier, creative and more likely to come from organic eateries, a UN worth of ethnic restaurants and gourmet kitchens, including 13 that flaunt Michelin stars.

Berlin is a snacker's paradise, with Turkish (your best bet), *Wurst* (sausage), Greek, Italian and Chinese snack stalls throughout the city. Meat eaters should not leave the city without trying Berlin's famous *Currywurst*.

Excellent farmers markets include those at **Kollwitzplatz** (Kollwitzstrasse; ⊗noon-7pm Thu, 9am-4pm Sat; SSenefelderplatz) in Prenzlauer Berg and the **Türkenmarkt** (Turkish Market; Map p170; www.tuerkenmarkt.de; Maybachufer; ⊗11am-6.30pm Tue & Fri; SSchönleinstrasse, Kottbusser Tor) in Kreuzberg.

MITTE & PRENZLAUER BERG

TOP CHOICE Katz Orange
INTERNATIONAL €€€

(Map p166; ☑983 208 430; www.katzorange.com; Bergstrasse 22; mains €13-22; ⊗dinner Tue-Sat year-round, lunch May-Sep; SRosenthaler Platz) Wits its gourmet organic farm-to-table menu, feel-good country styling and swift and smiling servers, the 'Orange Cat' hits a gastro grand slam. The setting in a castle-like former brewery is stunning, especially in summer when the patio opens.

Oderquelle
GERMAN €€

(☑4400 8080; Oderberger Strasse 27; mains €8-16; ⊗dinner; SEberswalder Strasse) It's always fun to pop by this woodsy resto and see what's inspired the chef today. Most likely, it'll be a delicious well-crafted German meal, perhaps with a slight Mediterranean nuance. The generously topped and crispy *Flammekuche* (Alsatian pizza) are a reliable standby.

Hartweizen
ITALIAN €€

(Map p166; ☑2849 3877; www.hartweizen.com; Torstrasse 96; mains €11-24; ⊗dinner Mon-Sat; SRosenthaler Platz) This hipster favourite is eons away from Chianti-bottle kitsch. Instead, it is quite simply a top Italian restaurant focused on the feisty flavours of the Puglia region. The most creativity goes into the appetisers, but fish and meat are also first-rate, the pastas are homemade and the wines are fairly priced.

Konnopke's Imbiss
GERMAN €

(Schönhauser Allee 44a; sausages €1.30-1.70; ⊗10am-8pm Mon-Fri, noon-8pm Sat; SEberswalder Strasse) Brave the inevitable queue for great *Currywurst* from one of the city's cult sausage kitchens, now in shiny new glass digs but in the same historic spot since 1930.

Monsieur Vuong
ASIAN €€

(Map p166; ☑9929 6924; www.monsieurvuong.de; Alte Schönhauser Strasse 46; mains around €8; ⊗noon-midnight; SWeinmeisterstrasse, Rosa-Luxemburg-Platz) At Berlin's 'godfather' of upbeat Indochina nosh-stops, the mini-menu features flavour-packed soups and two or three oft-changing mains. Come in the afternoon to avoid the feeding frenzy.

Schwarzwaldstuben
GERMAN €€

(Map p166; ☑2809 8084; Tucholskystrasse 48; mains €7-14; 🚆Oranienburger Strasse) In the mood for a Hansel and Gretel moment? Then join the other 'lost kids' in this send-up of the Black Forest complete with plastic pines and baseball-capped Bambi heads. We can't get enough of the '*geschmelzte Maultaschen*' (sautéed ravioli-like pasta), the giant schnitzel and the Rothaus Tannenzäpfle beer.

Lucky Leek
VEGAN €€

(☑6640 8710; www.lucky-leek.de; Kollwitzstrasse 46; mains around €12; ⊗dinner Tue & Thu-Sun; ☑; SSenefelderplatz) At this popular vegan restaurant, quality ingredients, fearless flavour combinations, creative and colourful presentation and enthusiastic staff should make believers of even the most dedicated carnivores.

KREUZBERG & FRIEDRICHSHAIN

TOP CHOICE Cafe Jacques
INTERNATIONAL €€€

(Map p170; ☑694 1048; Maybachufer 8; mains €12-20; ⊗dinner; SSchönleinstrasse) A favourite with off-duty chefs and local foodies, Jacques infallibly charms with flattering candlelight, warm decor and fantastic wine. It's the perfect date spot but, quite frankly, you only have to be in love with good food to appreciate the French- and north African–inspired blackboard menu. Reservations essential.

TOP CHOICE **Max und Moritz**　　　GERMAN €€
(Map p170; ☑6951 5911; www.maxundmoritzberlin.de; Oranienstrasse 162; mains €9-15; ☺dinner; ⓢMoritzplatz) This ode-to-old-school brewpub has lured hungry diners and drinkers with sudsy home brews and granny-style Berlin fare since 1902. A menu favourite is the *Kutschergulasch* (goulash cooked with beer).

Defne　　　TURKISH €€
(Map p170; ☑8179 7111; www.defne-restaurant.de; Planufer 92c; mains €7.50-16; ☺dinner; ⓢKottbusser Tor, Schönleinstrasse) If you thought Turkish cuisine stopped at the doner kebab, canal-side Defne will teach you otherwise. The appetizer platter alone elicits intense food cravings (fabulous walnut-chilli paste!), but inventive mains such as *ali nacik* (sliced lamb with pureed eggplant and yoghurt) also warrant repeat visits.

Curry 36　　　GERMAN €
(Map p170; www.curry36.de; Mehringdamm 36; snacks €2-6; ☺9am-4pm Mon-Sat, to 3pm Sun; ⓢMehringdamm) Top-ranked *Currywurst* purveyor that's been frying 'em up since the days when Madonna was singing about virgins.

Lemon Leaf　　　ASIAN €
(Map p170; ☑2900 9471; Grünberger Strasse 69; mains €5-9; ☺noon-midnight; ☑; ⓢFrankfurter Tor) Cheap and cheerful, this place is always swarmed by local loyalists thanks to its light, inventive and fresh Indochina menu supplemented by daily specials. Raveworthy homemade mango lassi.

Spätzle & Knödel　　　GERMAN €€
(Map p170; ☑2757 1151; Wühlischstrasse 20; mains €8-15; ☺dinner; ⓢSamariterstrasse) This elbows-on-the-table gastropub is a great place to get your southern German comfort food fix, with waist-expanding portions of roast pork, goulash and of course the eponymous *Spätzle* (German mac 'n' cheese) and *Knödel* (dumplings).

Schalander　　　GERMAN €€
(☑8961 7073; www.schalander-berlin.de; Bänschstrasse 91; snacks €3.50-10, mains €8-14;

☺4pm-1am Mon-Fri, noon-1am Sat & Sun; ☎; ⓢSamariterstrasse, ⓡFrankfurter Allee) See the pub action reflected in the very shiny steel vats that churn out the full-bodied pilsner, *dunkel* and *weizen* at this old-school gastropub far off the tourist track. The menu is big on southern German comfort food, along with *Flammkuche*.

CHARLOTTENBURG

Ali Baba　　　ITALIAN €
(Map p174; ☑881 1350; www.alibaba-berlin.de; Bleibtreustrasse 45; dishes €3-9; ☺11am-2am Sun-Thu, to 3am Fri & Sat; ⓡSavignyplatz) Everybody feels like family at this been-here-forever port of call where the thin-crust pizza is delicious, the pasta piping hot and nothing costs more than €9.

Dicke Wirtin　　　GERMAN €€
(Map p174; ☑312 4952; www.dicke-wirtin.de; Carmerstrasse 9; mains €6-15; ☺noon-1am or later; ⓡSavignyplatz) Old Berlin charm oozes from every nook and cranny of this been-here-forever pub, which pours eight draught beers (including the superb Kloster Andechs) and nearly three dozen homemade schnapps varieties. Hearty local fare like roast pork, fried liver or breaded schnitzel keeps brains balanced.

Café-Restaurant Wintergarten im Literaturhaus　　　INTERNATIONAL €€
(Map p174; ☑882 5414; www.literaturhaus-berlin.de; Fasanenstrasse 23; mains €8-16; ☺9.30am-1am; ⓢUhlandstrasse) Tuck into dependably good seasonal bistro cuisine amid elegant Old Berlin flair in this graceful art nouveau villa or, if weather permits, in the idyllic garden. Breakfast is served until 2pm.

Good Friends　　　CHINESE €€
(Map p174; ☑313 2659; www.goodfriends-berlin.de; Kantstrasse 30; mains €10-20; ☺noon-2am; ⓡSavignyplatz) Sinophiles tired of the Kung Pao school of Chinese cooking will appreciate the real thing at this authentic Cantonese restaurant. The ducks dangling in the window are the overture to a menu long enough to confuse Confucius.

🍺 Drinking

Snug pubs, riverside beach bars, clubs, beer gardens, underground dives, DJ bars, snazzy hotel lounges, cocktail caverns – with such variety, finding a party pen to match your mood is not exactly a tall order. Kreuzberg and Friedrichshain are currently the edgiest bar-hopping grounds, with swanky Mitte and Charlottenburg being more suited for date nights than late nights. The line between cafe and bar is often blurred, with many places changing stripes as the hands move around the clock.

Madame Claude
PUB

(Map p170; Lübbener Strasse 19; ⊖from 7pm; Ⓢ Schlesisches Tor) Gravity is literally upended at Kreuzberg's David Lynch-ian booze burrow, where the furniture dangles from the ceiling and the moulding's on the floor. Don't worry, there are still comfy sofas for entertaining your posse, plus Wednesday's music quiz night, live music or DJs, and open-mike Sundays. Doesn't fill up until around 11pm.

Hops & Barley
PUB

(Map p170; ☏2936 7534; Wühlischstrasse 40; Ⓢ Warschauer Strasse, Ⓡ Warschauer Strasse) Conversation flows as freely as the unfiltered pilsner, malty *dunkel* (dark), fruity *weizen* (wheat) and potent cider produced right at this congenial Friedrichshain microbrewery inside a former butchers shop.

Würgeengel
BAR

(Map p170; www.wuergeengel.de; Dresdener Strasse 122; ⊖from 7pm; Ⓢ Kottbusser Tor) For a swish night out, point the compass to this '50s-style Kreuzberg cocktail cave, complete with glass ceiling, chandeliers and shiny black tables. The name, by the way, pays homage to the surreal 1962 Buñuel movie *Exterminating Angel*. Smoking allowed.

⭐ Prater
BEER GARDEN

(☏448 5688; www.pratergarten.de; Kastanienallee 7-9; ⊖from noon Apr-Sep in good weather; Ⓢ Eberswalder Strasse) In Prenzlauer Berg, Berlin's oldest beer garden (since 1837) has kept much of its traditional charm and is a fantastic place to hang and guzzle a cold one beneath the ancient chestnut trees (self-service). In foul weather or winter, the adjacent woodsy restaurant is a fine place to sample classic local fare (mains €8 to €19).

Neue Odessa Bar
BAR

(Map p166; Torstrasse 89; Ⓢ Rosenthaler Platz) Rub shoulders with a global mix of grown-ups with a hot fashion sense at this comfy-chic and always busy Mitte staple. The patterned wallpaper, velvet sofas and smart lamps create cosy ambience, no matter if your taste runs towards Krusovice or cocktails. Smoking allowed.

Ankerklause
PUB

(Map p170; ☏693 5649; www.ankerklause.de; Kottbusser Damm 104; ⊖from 4pm Mon, from 10am Tue-Sun; Ⓢ Kottbusser Tor) Ahoy there! This nautical kitsch tavern with an ass-kicking jukebox sets sail in an old harbour-master's shack, and is great for quaffing and waving to the boats puttering along the canal.

Süss War Gestern
BAR

(Map p170; Wühlischstrasse 43; Ⓢ Warschauer Strasse, Samariterstrasse, Ⓡ Warschauer Strasse, Ostkreuz) Chilled electro and well-mixed cocktails fuel the party spirit, and the low light makes everyone look good. Try the eponymous house cocktail made with real root ginger, ginger ale and whisky. Smoking ok. In Friedrichshain.

Berliner Republik
PUB

(Map p166; www.die-berliner-republik.de; Schiffbauerdamm 8; ⊖10am-6am; Ⓢ Friedrichstrasse, Ⓡ Friedrichstrasse) Just as in a mini–stock exchange, the cost of drinks fluctuates with demand at this raucous riverside pub near Friedrichstrasse. Everyone goes Pavlovian when a heavy brass bell rings, signalling rock-bottom prices. Not too many locals but fun nonetheless.

Solar
BAR

(Map p170; ☏0163-765-2700; www.solar-berlin.de; Stresemannstrasse 76; ⊖6pm-2am Sun-Thu, to 4am Fri & Sat; Ⓡ Anhalter Bahnhof) Views of Potsdamer Platz and surrounds are truly impressive from this chic 17th-floor sky lounge above a posh restaurant (mains €18 to €29). Great for sunset drinks. Getting there aboard an exterior glass lift is half the fun. It's in a chunky high-rise behind the Pit Stop auto shop.

Freischwimmer
BEER GARDEN

(Map p170; ☏6107 4309; www.freischwimmer-berlin.de; Vor dem Schlesischen Tor 2a; mains €7-15; ⊖from 4pm Tue-Fri, from 10am Sat & Sun; Ⓢ Schlesisches Tor) In summertime, few places are more idyllic than this rustic ex-boathouse turned all-day, canal-side chill zone. Snacks and light meals are served, but they're more of an afterthought. It's sometimes open in winter – call ahead for hours.

⭐ Entertainment

Sometimes it seems as though Berliners are the lotus eaters of Germany, people who love nothing better than a good time. Pack some stamina if you want to join them. With no curfew, this is a notoriously late city, where bars stay packed from dusk to dawn and beyond and some clubs don't hit their stride until 6am.

Zitty and *Tip* are the most widely read of the biweekly German-language listings magazines, available at news kiosks.

Nightclubs

Few clubs open before 11pm (and if you arrive before midnight you may be dancing solo) but they stay open well into the early hours – usually sunrise at least. With so many top electro DJs living in Berlin – and others happy to visit – the city is a virtual musical testing lab. Line-ups are often amazing and may include such DJ royalty as André Galluzzi, Ellen Allien, Ricardo Villalobos, Paul Kalkbrenner, Booka Shade and Richie Hawtin. To determine which clubs best match your style, go to www.clubmatcher.de.

Berghain/Panorama Bar   CLUB
(Map p170; www.berghain.de; Wriezener Bahnhof; ☺midnight Fri-Mon morning; ☒Ostbahnhof) Still the holy grail of techno-electro clubs. Only world-class spinmasters heat up this hedonistic bass junkie hellhole inside a labyrinthine ex-power plant. The big factory floor (Berghain) is gay-leaning and pounds with minimal techno beats. One floor up, Panorama Bar is smaller, more mixed and pulsating with house and electro. Provocative art more than hints at the club's sexually libertine nature with its busy darkrooms, alcoves and toilets. Best time: after 4am. Strict door, no cameras.

Kaffee Burger   CLUB
(Map p166; ☎2804 6495; www.kaffeeburger.de; Torstrasse 60; ⓢRosa-Luxemburg-Platz) Noth-

ing to do with either coffee or meat patties, this sweaty cult club with lovingly faded commie-era decor is the famous home of the twice-monthly Russendisko, fun-for-all concerts and parties with a sound policy that swings from indie and electro to klezmer punk without missing a beat.

Watergate   CLUB
(Map p170; ☎6128 0394; www.water-gate.de; Falckensteinstrasse 49a; ☺from 11pm Fri & Sat; ⓢSchlesisches Tor) Top DJs keep electro-hungry hipsters hot and sweaty till way past sunrise at this high-octane riverside club with two floors, panoramic windows and a floating terrace overlooking the Oberbaumbrücke. Long queues, tight door on weekends.

Cookies   CLUB
(Map p166; www.cookies.ch; cnr Friedrichstrasse & Unter den Linden; ☺from midnight Tue, Thu & Sat; ⓢFranzösische Strasse) This indoor playground complete with wicked little theme rooms (a mirror cabinet, a 'wedding' chapel) is still an essential after-dark player in Berlin. Top local and international electro DJs heat up the sexy crowd on the mosaic dance floor.

Clärchens Ballhaus   CLUB
(Map p166; ☎282 9295; www.ballhaus.de; Auguststrasse 24; ☺restaurant 12.30-11.30pm, dancing nightly; ☒M1, ☒Oranienburger Strasse) Yesteryear is now at this late, great 19th-century dance hall where groovers and grannies hoof it across the parquet without even a touch of irony. There are different sounds nightly – salsa to swing, tango to disco – and a live band on Saturday.

GERMANY BERLIN

GAY & LESBIAN BERLIN

Berlin's legendary liberalism has spawned one of the world's biggest and most diverse GLBT playgrounds. The closest that Berlin comes to a 'gay village' is Schöneberg (Motzstrasse and Fuggerstrasse especially, get off at U-Bahn station Nollendorfplatz), where the rainbow flag has proudly flown since the 1920s. There's still plenty of (old-school) partying going on here.

Current hipster central is Kreuzberg, which teems with party pens along Mehringdamm and Oranienstrasse. Across the river, Friedrichshain has such key clubs as Berghain and the hardcore **Lab.oratory** (Map p170; www.lab-oratory.de; Am Wriezener Bahnhof; ☺Thu-Mon; ⓢOstbahnhof).

Mann-O-Meter (☎216 8008; www.mann-o-meter.de; Bülowstrasse 106; ☺5-10pm Tue-Fri, 4-8pm Sat & Sun; ⓢNollendorfplatz) is a one-stop information centre that also operates a hotline to report attacks on gays. **Siegessäule** (www.siegesaeule.de) is a weekly freebie mag that's the bible to all things gay and lesbian in town.

Weekend CLUB

(Map p166; www.week-end-berlin.de; Am Alexanderplatz 5; ⊙Thu-Sat; ⑤Alexanderplatz, ⑧Alexanderplatz) This house and electro den has an unbeatable location in a tower overlooking Alexanderplatz (in summer from the rooftop terrace) and is popular with suburban weekend warriors. Prices are hefty, door is middling.

Club der Visionäre CLUB

(Map p170; ☑6951 8942; www.clubdervisionaere.com; Am Flutgraben 1; ⊙from 2pm Mon-Fri, from noon Sat & Sun; ⑤Schlesisches Tor, ⑧Treptower Park) It's drinks, pizza and fine electro at this summertime chill and party playground in an old canalside boatshed. Hang out beneath the weeping willows or stake out some turf on the upstairs deck. On weekends party people invade 24/7.

Music & Opera

Berliner Philharmonie CLASSICAL MUSIC

(Map p174; ☑2548 8999; www.berliner-philharmoniker.de; Herbert-von-Karajan-Strasse 1; ☑200, ⑤Potsdamer Platz, ⑧Potsdamer Platz) This landmark concert hall has supreme acoustics and, thanks to Hans Scharoun's clever terraced vineyard design, not a bad seat in the house. It's the home base of the world-famous Berliner Philharmoniker, currently led by Sir Simon Rattle.

Staatsoper unter den Linden @ Schillertheater OPERA

(Map p174; ☑information 203 540, tickets 2035 4555; www.staatsoper-berlin.de; Bismarckstrasse 110; ⑤Ernst-Reuter-Platz) Point your highbrow compass towards the Daniel Barenboim–led Staatsoper, Berlin's top opera company. While its historic digs on Unter den Linden are getting a facelift (probably until 2014), the high-calibre productions are staged at the Schiller Theater in Charlottenburg. All operas are sung in their original language.

🔒 Shopping

For high street shopping, head to Berlin's main shopping boulevard Kurfürstendamm and its extension Tauentzienstrasse, which are chock-a-bloc with the usual-suspect high-street chains. You'll find more of the same in malls such as Alexa near Alexanderplatz and Potsdamer Platz Arkaden at Potsdamer Platz. Indeed, getting the most out of shopping in Berlin means venturing off the high street and into the *Kieze* (neighbourhoods) for local flavour. Each comes with its

SHOPPING BY NEIGHBOURHOOD

Unter den Linden Tacky souvenir shops meet big-label glamour haunts and top-flight galleries along Friedrichstrasse.

Scheunenviertel Boutique haven with Berlin-made fashions and accessories; also a high-end international designer and gallery quarter.

Charlottenburg Mainstream and couture on Kurfürstendamm, indie boutiques in the side streets, homewares on Kantstrasse.

Kreuzberg & Friedrichshain Vintage fashion, streetwear and music in indie boutiques, especially along Oranienstrasse and around Boxhagener Platz.

Prenzlauer Berg Berlin labels, niche boutiques around Kollwitzplatz, Helmholtzplatz and along Kastanienallee.

own flair, identity and mix of stores calibrated to the needs, tastes and bank accounts of local residents.

Big shops in the centre are open from 10am to 8pm or 9pm. Local boutiques keep flexible hours, usually opening around 11am or noon and closing at 7pm.

Flea-market-hopping is a popular local pastime on the weekend, particularly Sundays. The Berlin Art & Nostalgia Market (Map p166; Georgenstrasse, Mitte; ⊙8am-5pm Sat & Sun; ⑤ Friedrichstrasse) is heavy on collectables, books, ethnic crafts and GDR memorabilia; the Flohmarkt am Mauerpark (p183) is known for its vintage wear and young-designer retro fashions; and the Flohmarkt am Arkonaplatz (www.mauerparkmarkt.de; Arkonaplatz; ⊙10am-4pm Sun; ⑤Bernauer Strasse) is the best spot to hit if you're looking for retro 1960s and 1970s furniture and accessories.

TOP CHOICE KaDeWe DEPARTMENT STORE

(Map p174; www.kadewe.de; Tauentzienstrasse 21-24; ⊙10am-8pm Mon-Thu, to 9pm Fri, 9.30am-8pm Sat; ⑤Wittenbergplatz) This venerable department store has an assortment so vast that a pirate-style campaign is the best way to plunder its bounty. Don't miss the legendary 6th-floor gourmet food hall.

Flohmarkt am Mauerpark   MARKET
(www.mauerparkmarkt.de; Bernauer Strasse 63-64;
☺10am-5pm Sun; ⑤Eberwalder Strasse) On Sunday afternoons, join the throngs of thrifty
trinket hunters, bleared-eyed clubbers and
excited tourists sifting for treasure at this always busy flea market right where the Berlin
Wall once ran.

Friedrichstadtpassagen   SHOPPING CENTRE
(Map p170; Friedrichstrasse btwn Französische
Strasse & Mohrenstrasse; ☺10am-8pm Mon-Sat;
⑤Französische Strasse, Stadtmitte) Even if you're
not part of the Gucci and Prada brigade, the
wow factor of this trio of indoor shopping arcades (called *Quartiere*) is undeniable.

Ampelmann Galerie   SOUVENIRS
(Map p166; ☏4472 6438; www.ampelmann.de;
Court V, Hackesche Höfe, Rosenthaler Strasse 40-
41; ☺9.30am-10pm Mon-Sat, 10am-7pm Sun; ⓜM1,
ⓡHackescher Markt) It took a vociferous grassroots campaign to save the little Ampelmann, the endearing fellow on East German
pedestrian traffic lights. Now the beloved
cult figure and global brand graces an entire
store worth of T-shirts, fridge magnets and
other knick-knacks.

ⓘ Information

Berlin Tourismus (☏2500 2333; http://visit
berlin.de; ☺call centre 9am-7pm Mon-Fri, 10am-
5pm Sat, 10am-2pm Sun) Berlin's tourist board
operates three walk-in offices and a call centre
with multilingual staff who field general questions and can make hotel and ticket bookings.
Hauptbahnhof (Europaplatz, ground fl, north entrance; ☺8am-10pm; ⑤Hauptbahnhof, ⓡHaupt-
bahnhof) Extended hours April to October.
Brandenburger Tor (Brandenburger Tor, Pariser
Platz; ☺9.30am-7pm daily; ⑤Brandenburger
Tor, ⓡBrandenburger Tor)
Kurfürstendamm (Neues Kranzler Eck, Kurfürstendamm 22; ☺9.30am-8pm Mon-Sat, to
6pm Sun; ⑤Kurfürstendamm) Extended hours
April to October.

ⓘ Getting There & Away
Air

Berlin's brand-new airport, Berlin Brandenburg Airport has been taking shape next to
Schönefeld Airport, about 24km southeast of
the city centre, since 2006. At the time of writing, construction problems and safety concerns
have repeatedly delayed the original 2011 opening date; at press time, no new opening date had
been announced. In the meantime, most major
international airlines, as well as many discount
carriers, including Ryanair, easyJet, Air Berlin

and germanwings, continue to fly into Berlin's
two other airports.
Tegel Airport (TXL; ☏01805 000 186; www.
berlin-airport.de) About 8km northwest of the
city centre.
Schönefeld Airport (SXF; ☏0180 5000 186;
www.berlin-airport.de) About 22km southeast.

Bus

ZOB Berlin's 'central' bus station is in deepest
western Berlin, next to the trade-fair grounds,
about 4km west of Zoo Station.
BerlinLinienBus (☏861 9331; www.berlin
linienbus.de) The main operator; buy tickets
online or at the ZOB Reisebüro ticket office at
the bus station.
Deutsche Touring/Eurolines (☏069 790
3501; www.touring.de) Also has many domestic
and international departures.
Busabout (www.busabout.com) Backpacker-
oriented hop-on, hop-off service stops at the
Citystay Hostel in Mitte.

Train

Berlin is well connected by train to other German cities, as well as to popular European
destinations, including Prague, Warsaw and
Amsterdam. All long-distance trains converge at
the **Hauptbahnhof** (www.berlin-hauptbahnhof.
de; Europaplatz, Washingtonplatz; ⑤Hauptbahnhof, ⓡHauptbahnhof).

The left-luggage office (€5 per piece per 24
hours) is behind the ReiseBank currency exchange
on the first upper level, opposite the Reisezentrum. Self-service lockers are hidden on the lower
level of the parking garage, accessible near the
Kaiser's supermarket on the first lower floor.

ⓘ Getting Around
To/From the Airport

TEGEL

The TXL bus connects Tegel with Alexanderplatz
(40 minutes) every 10 minutes. For Kurfürsten-
amm and Zoo Station, take bus X9 (20 minutes).
Tegel is not directly served by the U-Bahn, but
both bus 109 and X9 stop at Jakob-Kaiser-Platz
(U7), the station closest to the airport. Each of
these trips costs €2.40. Taxi rides cost about €20
to Zoologischer Garten and €23 to Alexanderplatz
and should take between 30 and 45 minutes.

SCHÖNEFELD

Airport-Express trains make the 30-minute trip
to central Berlin twice hourly. Note: these are
regular regional trains, identified as RE7 and RB14
in timetables. The S-Bahn S9 runs every 20 minutes and is slower but useful if you're headed to
Friedrichshain or Prenzlauer Berg. For the Messe
(trade-fair grounds), take the S45 to Südkreuz and
change to the S41. Trains stop about 400m from

PUBLIC TRANSPORT TICKETS

Three tariff zones exist – A, B and C. Unless venturing to Potsdam or Schönefeld Airport, you'll only need an AB ticket.

TICKET	AB (€)	BC (€)	ABC (€)
Single	2.40	2.80	3.10
Day pass	6.50	6.80	7
Group day pass (up to 5 people)	15.50	15.80	16
7-day pass	28	28.90	34.60

the airport terminals. Free shuttle buses run every 10 minutes; walking takes about five minutes. You'll need a transport ticket covering zones ABC (€3.10). Taxi rides average €40 and take 35 minutes to an hour.

Bicycle

Many hostels and hotels have bikes for guest use, often for free or a nominal fee. Rental stations are everywhere – from convenience stores to clothing boutiques to petrol stations to bike shops. Keep an eye out for 'Rent-A-Bike' signs.

Bicycles may be taken aboard designated U-Bahn and S-Bahn carriages (usually the last car) as well as on trams and regional trains (RE, RB) and on night buses (Sunday to Thursday only). You need to get a separate ticket called a *Fahrradkarte* (bicycle ticket, €1.50).

Car & Motorcycle

Garage parking is expensive (about €2 per hour) and vehicles entering the environmental zone (within the S-Bahn rail ring) must display a special sticker (*Umweltplakette;* €5 to €15). Order it online at www.berlin.de/sen/umwelt/luftqualitaet/de/luftreinhalteplan/doku_umweltzone.shtml. The fine for getting caught without the sticker is €40. Rental cars automatically have this sticker.

Public Transport

One type of ticket is valid on all public transport, including the U-Bahn, buses, trams and ferries run by **BVG** (☎194 49; www.bvg.de), as well as the S-Bahn and regional RE, SE and RB trains operated by **Deutsche Bahn** (www.bahn.com).

Buy tickets from vending machines (English instructions available) in U-Bahn or S-Bahn stations and aboard trams, from bus drivers and at station offices and news kiosks sporting the yellow BVG logo.

Stamp all tickets, except those bought from bus drivers, before boarding or risk a €40 on-the-spot fine if caught without a validated ticket.

Services operate from 4am until just after midnight on weekdays, with half-hourly *Nachtbus* (night bus) services in between. At weekends, the U-Bahn and S-Bahn run all night long (except the U4 and U55).

Taxi

You can order a **taxi** (☎44 33 11, 20 20 20) by phone, flag one down or pick one up at a rank. Flagfall is €3.20, then it's €1.65 per km up to 7km and €1.28 for each km after that. Up to four passengers travel for the price of one. Tip about 10%. There is no surcharge for night trips.

AROUND BERLIN

Sachsenhausen Concentration Camp

In 1936 the Nazis opened a *Konzentrationslager* (concentration camp) for men in a disused brewery in Sachsenhausen, 35km north of Berlin. By 1945 about 200,000 prisoners had passed through the gates – cynically labelled, as at Auschwitz in Poland, *Arbeit Macht Frei* (Work Sets You Free). Tens of thousands died from hunger, exhaustion, illness, medical experiments and executions.

After the war the Soviets imprisoned some 60,000 German POWs in what was now Speziallager No 7 (Special Camp No 7); about 12,000 died of malnutrition and disease before it was dissolved in 1950.

Once you get to the **Sachsenhausen Memorial and Museum** (☎03301-200 200; www.stiftung-bg.de; admission free; ☺8.30am-6pm mid-Mar–mid-Oct, to 4pm mid-Oct–mid-Mar), pick up a leaflet or, better yet, an audioguide at the visitor centre to get a better grasp of this huge site. Proceed to Tower A, the entrance gate, beyond which is the roll-call area and two restored barracks with exhibits illustrating the abysmal living conditions prisoners endured. Opposite, two original infirmary barracks have exhibits about the camp's poor medical care and on the horrid medical experiments performed on prisoners.

Further on, the Prisoners' Kitchen zeroes in on key moments in the camp's history during its various phases. Exhibits include instruments of torture, the original gallows and, in the cellar, heart-wrenching artwork scratched into the wall by prisoners. The most sickening displays, though, deal with the **Station Z extermination site**, a pit for shooting prisoners in the neck with a wooden 'catch' where bullets could be retrieved and recycled.

From Berlin take the frequent S1 train to Oranienburg station (€3.10, 45 minutes) from where it's a 2km signposted walk to the camp.

Potsdam

☑0331 / POP 150,000

Featuring ornate palaces and manicured parks, the Prussian royal seat of Potsdam is the most popular day trip from Berlin. Headlining the roll call of palaces is Schloss Sanssouci, the private retreat of King Friedrich II (Frederick the Great), who was also the visionary behind many of Potsdam's other fabulous pads and parks, which miraculously survived WWII with nary a shrapnel wound. When the shooting stopped, the Allies chose Schloss Cecilienhof for the Potsdam Conference of August 1945 to lay the groundwork for Germany's postwar fate.

◉ Sights

Park Sanssouci   GARDEN
(⊙dawn-dusk) Park Sanssouci is the heart of Potsdam and what everyone comes to see. Its most celebrated palace is **Schloss Sanssouci** (www.spsg.de; adult/concession incl audioguide Apr-Oct €12/8, Nov-Mar €8/5; ⊙10am-6pm Tue-Sun Apr-Oct, to 5pm Nov-Mar; ☑695, 606), a rococo extravaganza built by Frederick the Great in the 18th century. Admission is by timed ticket only; come early or, for guaranteed entry, join the city tour offered by the Potsdam tourist office. Standouts on the audio guided tours include the whimsically decorated Concert Hall, the intimate Library and the elegant Marble Room.

At the far western end of the park, the vast, domed **Neues Palais** (New Palace; ☑969 4200; Am Neuen Palais; adult/concession €6/5; ⊙10am-6pm Wed-Mon Apr-Oct, to 5pm Nov-Mar; ☑695 or 605 to Neues Palais, ☒to Potsdam, Park Sanssouci Bahnhof) was built for representational purposes and only used as a residence by the last German kaiser, Wilhelm II, until

1918. The interior is an opulent symphony of ceiling frescoes, gilded ornamentation and fanciful wall coverings.

Among the park's many other pearls, the **Chinesisches Haus** (Am Grünen Gitter; admission €2; ⊙10am-6pm Tue-Sun May-Oct; ☑605 to Schloss Charlottenhof, 606 or 695 to Schloss Sanssouci, ☒91 to Schloss Charlottenhof) is a standout. It's a circular pavilion of gilded columns, palm trees and figures of Chinese musicians and animals that houses a porcelain collection.

Schloss Cecilienhof   PALACE
(☑969 4244; www.spsg.de; Im Neuen Garten 11; tours adult/concession €6/5; ⊙10am-6pm Tue-Sun Apr-Oct, to 5pm Nov-Mar; ☑603) This rustic English-style country palace was completed in 1917 for crown prince Wilhelm and his wife Cecilie but is most famous for hosting the 1945 Potsdam Conference where Stalin, Truman and Churchill (later Atlee) hammered out Germany's postwar fate. The conference room, with its giant round table, looks as though the delegates just left.

Altstadt   HISTORIC AREA
Potsdam's historic town centre is east of Park Sanssouci. The baroque **Brandenburger Tor** (Brandenburg Gate) triumphal arch opens up to the Brandenburger Strasse shopping strip. Follow it to the pretty **Holländisches Viertel** (Dutch Quarter), a cluster of gabled red-brick houses filled with galleries, boutiques and restaurants.

⌖ Tours

Potsdam Sanssouci Tour   GUIDED TOUR
(tours with/without Sanssouci Palace €27/16; ⊙Tue-Sun Apr-Oct) The local tourist office runs the 3½-hour Potsdam Sanssouci Tour, which checks off the highlights and guarantees admission to Schloss Sanssouci. Tours are in English and German and leave at 11.10am from the tourist office at the Hauptbahnhof.

Schiffahrt in Potsdam   BOAT TOUR
(☑275 9210; www.schiffahrt-in-potsdam.de; Lange Brücke 6; ⊙9.45am-7pm Apr-Oct) Boats cruise the Havel and the lakes around Potsdam. The most popular tour is the palace cruise (*Schlösserrundfahrt*; €13).

ⓘ Information

Potsdam Tourist Office – Hauptbahnhof
(☑2755 8899; www.potsdamtourismus.com; inside the main train station; ⊙9.30am-8pm

Mon-Sat, 10am-6pm Sun) There's another office at Brandenburger Tor.

Sanssouci Visitors Centre (☑969 4200; www.spsg.de; An der Orangerie 1, at the Historic Windmill; ☺8.30am-6pm Apr-Oct, to 5pm Nov-Mar)

❶ Getting There & Away

Regional trains leaving from Berlin-Hauptbahnhof and Zoologischer Garten take about half an hour to reach Potsdam Hauptbahnhof; some continue on to Potsdam-Charlottenhof and Potsdam-Sanssouci, which are actually closer to Park Sanssouci. The S7 from central Berlin makes the trip in about 40 minutes. You need a ticket covering zones A, B and C (€3) for either service.

DRESDEN & SAXONY

Saxony has everything you could want in a holiday: storybook castles peering down from craggy mountaintops, cobbled marketplaces serenaded by mighty churches, exuberant palaces, nostalgic steam trains and indigenous Sorb folk traditions. And through it all courses the broad-shouldered Elbe in its steady eternal flow out to the North Sea, past neatly arrayed vineyards, sculpted sandstone cliffs and villa-studded hillsides.

Many heavyweights have shaped Saxony's cultural landscape; Bach, Canaletto, Goethe and Wagner among them. Dresden and Leipzig grab top historical billing. The former became synonymous with the devastation of WWII, but has since resurrected its baroque heritage. And it was Leipzig that sparked the 'peaceful revolution' of 1989 that brought down the Berlin Wall and led to the momentous reunification of Germany.

Dresden

☑0351 / POP 512,000

Proof that there is life after death, Dresden has become one of Germany's most popular attractions, and for good reason. Restorations have returned the city to the glory days when it was famous throughout Europe as 'Florence on the Elbe', owing to the efforts of Italian artists, musicians, actors and master craftsmen who flocked to the court of Augustus the Strong, bestowing countless masterpieces upon the city.

The devastating bombing raids in 1945 levelled most of these treasures. But Dresden is a survivor and many of the most important landmarks have since been rebuilt, including the elegant Frauenkirche. Today, there's a constantly evolving arts and cultural scene and zinging pub and nightlife quarters, especially in the Outer Neustadt.

◉ Sights

TOP CHOICE **Frauenkirche**　　　　　CHURCH
(www.frauenkirche-dresden.de; Neumarkt; admission free, audioguide €2.50; ☺usually 10am-noon & 1-6pm) The domed Frauenkirche – one of Dresden's most beloved symbols – has literally risen from the city's ashes. The original graced its skyline for two centuries before collapsing two days after the devastating February 1945 bombing. The East Germans left the rubble as a war memorial, but after reunification a grassroots movement helped raise the funds to rebuild the landmark. It was consecrated in November 2005.

A spitting image of the original, it may not bear the gravitas of age but that only slightly detracts from its festive beauty inside and out. The altar, reassembled from nearly 2000 fragments, is especially striking. You can also climb the **dome** (Neumarkt; adult/concession €8/5; ☺10am-6pm Mon-Sat, 12.30-6pm Sun Mar-Oct, to 4pm Nov-Feb) for sweeping city views. The galleried interior is also a wonderful place for concerts, meditations and services. Check the website for the current schedule or stop by the **Frauenkirche Visitors Centre** (☑6560 6701; Weisse Gasse 8; movie €2; ☺10am-7pm Mon-Fri, 10am-6pm Sat), which also screens a movie about the church's history and legacy.

Residenzschloss　　　　　PALACE
(☑4914 2000; www.skd.museum; Schlossplatz; adult/concession €10/7.50; ☺10am-6pm Wed-Mon) Dresden's fortresslike Renaissance city palace was home to the Saxon rulers from 1485 to 1918 and now shelters four precious collections, including the unmissable **Grünes Gewölbe** (Green Vault), a real-life Aladdin's Cave spilling over with precious objects wrought from gold, ivory, silver, diamonds and jewels. There's so much of it, two separate 'treasure chambers' – the Historisches Grünes Gewölbe and the Neues Grünes Gewölbe – are needed to display everything.

Another important collection in the palace is the **Kupferstich-Kabinett**, which counts around half a million prints and drawings by 20,000 artists (including Dürer, Rembrandt and Michelangelo) in its possession. Numismatists might want to drop by the Münzkabinett (Coin Cabinet) in the palace tower for a small array of historic coins and medals.

In 2013, the historic weapons and armour of the Rüstkammer (armoury), normally displayed in the Zwinger, also move into the Residenzschloss. Here, they join the exotic Türckische Cammer (Turkish Chamber), one of the richest collections of Ottoman art outside Turkey. A huge three-mast tent made of gold and silk is just one standout among many.

Tickets to the Residenzschloss are good for all these collections except for the Historisches Grünes Gewölbe (☑4914 2000; www.skd.museum; Residenzschloss, enter via Sophienstrasse or Kleiner Schlosshof; adult/under 16 incl audioguide €10/free; ☺10am-7pm Wed-Mon). Admission here is by timed ticket only and you're strongly advised to order advance tickets online or by phone since only 40% are sold at the palace box office for same-day admission.

Zwinger
MUSEUM

(☑4914 2000; www.skd.museum; Theaterplatz 1; adult/concession €10/7.50; ☺10am-6pm Tue-Sun) A ravishing baroque complex, the sprawling Zwinger was primarily a royal party palace and now houses numerous precious collections. The most important is the Gemäldegalerie Alte Meister, which features a roll call of Old Masters including Botticelli, Titian, Rubens, Vermeer and Dürer. A key work is the 500-year-old *Sistine Madonna* by Raphael.

Admission also gives you access to the dazzling Porzellansammlung (Porcelain Collection) and the ancient scientific instruments, globes and timepieces of the Mathematisch-Physikalischer Salon.

Fürstenzug
HISTORIC SITE

(Procession of Princes; Augustusstrasse) You'd need a really wide-angle lens to get a shot of Wulhelm Walther's amazing 102m-long tiled mural on the wall of the former Stendehaus (Royal Stables). The scene, a long row of royalty on horses, was painted in 1876 and then transferred to some 24,000 Meissen porcelain tiles in 1906.

Semperoper
HISTORIC BUILDING

(☑320 7360; www.semperoper-erleben.de; Theaterplatz 2; tour adult/concession €8/4; ☺varies) One of Germany's most famous opera houses, the original Semperoper burned down a mere three decades after its 1841 inauguration. Guided 45-minute tours operate almost daily (the 3pm tour is in English); exact times depend on the rehearsal and perform-

NAVIGATING DRESDEN

The Elbe River splits Dresden in a rough V-shape, with the Neustadt (new city) to the north and the Altstadt (old city) to the south.

From the Hauptbahnhof, pedestrian-only Prager Strasse leads north into the Altstadt. Here there's a mix of communist-era triumphalism and modern-day commercialism. The lovely Brühlsche Terrasse runs along the Elbe between the Albertinum and the Zwinger, with boat docks below.

In the Neustadt, home to much of the city's nightlife, the main attractions for visitors are the Albertplatz and Louisenstrasse quarters. Here you'll find all manner of shops, galleries, funky boutiques and dozens of cafes, bars and clubs.

ance schedule. Buy advance tickets online to skip the queue.

Albertinum
GALLERY

(www.skd.museum; enter from Brühlsche Terrasse or Georg-Treu-Platz 2; adult/concession €8/6; ☺10am-6pm; ℗) After massive renovations following severe 2002 flood damage, the Renaissance-era former arsenal is now the stunning home of the Galerie Neue Meister (New Masters Gallery), an ark of paintings by leading artistic lights since the Romantic period – Caspar David Friedrich to Claude Monet and Gerhard Richter – in gorgeous rooms orbiting a light-filled central courtyard.

Militärhistorisches Museum Dresden
MUSEUM

(☑823 2803; www.mhmbw.de; Olbrichtplatz 2; adult/concession €5/3; ☺10am-6pm Tue-Sun, to 9pm Mon; ☒7 or 8 to Stauffenbergallee) Even devout pacifists will be awed by this engaging museum which reopened in 2011 in a 19th-century arsenal bisected by a bold glass-and-steel wedge designed by Daniel Libeskind. Standouts among the countless intriguing objects are a 1975 Soyuz landing capsule, a V2 rocket and personal items of concentration-camp victims.

☞ Tours

Sächsische Dampfschiffahrt
RIVER TOUR

(www.saechsische-dampfschiffahrt.de; adult/child from €16/8) Ninety-minute Elbe paddle-wheel steamer tours leave from the Terrassenufer

Dresden

N 0 ____ 400 m
0 ____ 0.2 miles

Alaunplatz

Bischofsweg

Gothaer Str

Grossenhainer Str

Leipziger Str

Lössnitzstr

Dresden-Neustadt

Schlesischer Platz

Dr-Friedrich-Wolf-Str

Erna-Berger-Str

Dämmweg

15

Försterstr

18

Jordanstr

Louisenstr

16

Katharinenstr

21

23

22

8

19

NEUSTADT

Böhmische Str

Antonstr

Antonstr

Hainstr

Theresienstr   Albertplatz

Bautzner Str

17

9

Königstr

Albertstr

Hauptstr

Glacisstr

Hospitalstr

Hoyerswerdaer Str

Marienbrücke

Grosse Meissner Str

Bellevuegarten

Köpckestr   Wigardstr

Albertbrücke

Devrientstr

Augustusbrücke

Am Zwingerteich

Elbe River

Carolabrücke

Käthe-Kollwitz-Ufer

24

5

13

Schlossplatz

Theaterplatz

6

Brühlsche Terrasse

Terrassenufer

Ziegelstr

Residenzschloss

Sophienstr

4

Schlossstr

14

1

Steinstr

10   20

3

Frauenkirche

Neumarkt

Postplatz

11

ALTSTADT

Wilsdruffer Str

Landhausstr

Schless-gasse

St-Petersburger Str

Pillnitzer Str

Am See

Marienstr

Wallstr

Pfarrgasse

2

Altmarkt

Kreuzstr

12

Ringstr

Zirkusstr

Grunaerstr

Güntzstr

Dr-Külz-Ring

Waisenhausstr

Georgplatz

Blüherstr

Lennéstr

Reitbahnstr

Prager Str

St-Petersburger Str

Zinzendorfstr

Lingnerallee

Herkulesallee

To Dresden
Hauptbahnhof (200m)

Dresden

docks several times daily in summer along with services to Meissen and the villages of Saxon Switzerland.

Grosse Stadtrundfahrt　　　BUS TOUR
(☏899 5650; www.stadtrundfahrt.com; day pass adult/concession €20/18; ⊙9.30am-5pm) This narrated hop-on, hop-off tour stops at 22 sights and also includes short walking tours of the Zwinger, Fürstenzug and Frauenkirche.

🛏 Sleeping

Hotel Martha Dresden　　　HOTEL €€
(☏817 60; www.hotel-martha-hospiz.de; Nieritzstrasse 11; d €113-120; 🖥) Fifty rooms with big windows, wooden floors and Biedermeier-inspired furnishings combine with an attractive winter garden and friendly staff into a pleasant place to hang your hat. The rustic restaurant serves local food and wine.

Radisson Blu Gewandhaus Hotel　HOTEL €€
(☏494 90; www.radissonblu.com/gewandhaus hotel-dresden; Ringstrasse 1; d from €133; P🅿🌐 🖥🖧) Public areas in this restored and converted 18th-century trading house are stunning and the Biedermeier-style rooms have marble-fitted bathrooms with whirlpool tubs. Tops for class and personal service.

Hostel Mondpalast　　　HOSTEL €
(☏563 4050; www.mondpalast.de; Louisenstrasse 77; dm €14-19.50, d €48-56, linen €2, breakfast €6.50; 🌐) Check in at the out-of-this-world

bar-cafe (with cheap drinks) before being 'beamed up' to your room in the Moon Palace – each one dedicated to a sign of the zodiac or some other spacey theme. Bike rentals and large kitchen.

**Hotel Taschenbergpalais
Kempinski**　　　HOTEL €€€
(☏491 20; www.kempinski-dresden.de; Taschenberg 3; r €170-230; 🖥🌐🖧) Luxury is taken very seriously indeed at Dresden's grandest hotel. Checking in here buys views over the Zwinger from rakishly handsome rooms that beautifully bridge the traditional and the contemporary. In winter, the courtyard turns into an ice rink.

Pension am Zwinger　　　PENSION €€
(☏8990 0100; www.pension-zwinger.de; Ostra-Allee 27; d €80-90; P🅿🌐🖧) Self-caterers, families and space-cravers will appreciate these bright, functional but stylish apartment-style rooms with basic kitchens. It's supercentral and fairly quiet, despite being on a busy street. Note that the reception is at Maxstrasse 3 about 50m away.

Ibis Budget　　　HOTEL €
(☏8339 3820; www.etaphotel.com; Wilsdruffer Strasse 25; r from €39; 🖥🌐🖧) The ship cabin-sized rooms have few frills but the key sights are just a hop, skip and jump away. With its upbeat ambience and friendly service, this is definitely a great budget base. It's part of the Altmarkt-Galerie shopping mall.

✖ Eating

The Neustadt has oodles of cafes and restaurants, many found along Königstrasse and the streets north of Albertplatz. This is the most interesting part of town at night. Restaurants in the Altstadt are mostly tourist-geared.

La Casina Rosa

ITALIAN €€

(☏801 4848; www.la-casina-rosa.de; Alaunstrasse 93; pizza & pasta €6.50-9.50; ☺lunch Tue-Sat, dinner Mon-Sat) Everybody feels like family at this neighbourhood-adored trattoria with its warren of cosy rooms (plus idyllic summer garden) and feisty pasta and pizza, plus seasonally inspired specials. Menu stars include the 'piccola Capri' pizza topped with shrimp, zucchini and rucula. Reservations are key.

Raskolnikoff
CAFE, BAR €€

(☏804 5706; www.raskolnikoff.de; Böhmische Strasse 34; mains €5-13; ☺9am-2am) An artist squat in GDR times, Raskolnikoff still brims with artsy-bohemian flair. The menu is sorted by compass direction (borscht to fish soup and steak) and, in summer, the sweet little beer garden beckons. The beer itself comes from the Neustadt-based Schwingheuer brewery and is a steal at €2.40 per half litre. Upstairs are eight basic but handsomely done-up rooms (doubles €52 to €70).

Cafe Alte Meister
INTERNATIONAL €€

(☏481 0426; www.altemeister.net; Theaterplatz 1a; mains €7-15; ☺10am-1am) If you've worked up an appetite from museum-hopping, retreat to this elegant filling station between the Zwinger and the Semperoper for a smoked-trout sandwich, light salad, luscious cake or energy-restoring steak. A sculpture of composer Carl Maria von Weber guards the entrance.

PlanWirtschaft
INTERNATIONAL €€

(☏801 3187; Louisenstrasse 20; mains €7-14; ☺9am-1am) The winning formula at this long-time favourite: fresh ingredients sourced from local suppliers, a menu that dazzles with inventiveness and smiley staff that make even first-timers feel at home. Sit inside the cafe, the romantic garden or the cosy brick cellar.

Grand Café
CAKES, SAXON €€

(☏496 2444; www.coselpalais-dresden.de; An der Frauenkirche 12; mains €10-15; ☺10am-midnight) The cakes and imaginative mains are good, but, frankly, they almost play second fiddle to the gold-trimmed baroque setting of the Coselpalais. A stylish refuelling stop after climbing the Frauenkirche dome.

🍷 Drinking

If you're up for a night on the razzle, head out to the buzzing bars and cafes of the Neustadt, especially along Alaunstrasse, Louisenstrasse and Görlitzer Strasse.

Café 100
PUB

(☏273 5010; www.cafe100.de; Alaunstrasse 100; ☺8pm-late) One of the first pubs in the Neustadt to open after reunification, Café 100 does double duty as a studenty pub on the ground floor and a candle-lit wine bar in the cavernous cellar.

Combo
CAFE

(Louisenstrasse 66; ☺9am-2am) Laid-back to the point of toppling, this '70s-retro cafe has enormous windows that fold back when the heat is on, 1960s airport furniture, and great coffee served with a side of water and two gummi bears.

Queens & Kings
GAY BAR

(www.queens-dresden.de; Görlitzer Strasse 2b) The 'Queens' is dead, long live the 'Queens & Kings', across the street from the original gay fave party palace. The new version is more modern, a tad chicer and dressed in flamboyant colours.

Karl May Bar
BAR

(☏491 20; www.kempinski.com; Taschenberg 3; ☺6pm-2am) Cocktail connoisseurs gravitate to this sophisticated saloon inside the Taschenbergpalais hotel. Sink into a heavy burgundy-coloured leather chair to sip tried-and-true classics. Live music Friday and Saturday, happy hour 6pm to 8pm.

☆ Entertainment

Semperoper Dresden
OPERA

(☏491 1705; www.semperoper.de; Theaterplatz 2; ☺ticket office 10am-6pm Mon-Fri, 10am-5pm Sat & Sun) Dresden's famous opera house is the home of the Sächsische Staatsoper Dresden, which puts on brilliant performances that usually sell out. Tickets are sold by phone, in person and online.

Blue Note
JAZZ

(☏8014275; www.jazzdepartment.com; Görlitzer Strasse 2b; ☺8pm-5am) Small, smoky and smooth, this converted smithy has concerts featuring regional talent almost nightly (usually jazz, but also rock and Latin), then turns into a night-owl magnet until the wee hours. Many concerts are free. Global beers and awesome single malt whisky selection.

Katy's Garage LIVE MUSIC
(www.katysgarage.de; Alaunstrasse 48) As the name suggests, this cavernous party pit is set in a former tyre shop with matching decor and drinks named after car parts. You know the crowd skews young if one of their theme nights is the 'Älternabend' for people over 25.

ℹ Information

Tourist office - Hauptbahnhof (Hauptbahnhof; ◷9am-7pm)
Tourist office Frauenkirche (Schlossstrasse 23; ◷10am-7pm Mon-Fri, 10am-6pm Sat, 10am-3pm Sun, reduced hours Jan-Mar)

ℹ Getting There & Around

Dresden airport is about 9km north of the city centre. The S2 train links the airport with the city centre several times hourly (€2). Taxis are about €20.

By train, Dresden is linked to such major cities as Leipzig (€30, 70 minutes) and Berlin-Hauptbahnhof (€38, two hours) as well as to Meissen (€5.60, 40 minutes) by the local S1. Most trains stop at Hauptbahnhof (central train station) and at Dresden-Neustadt north of the river.

Buses and trams are run by **Dresdner Verkehrsbetriebe** (DVB; ☑857 1011). Fares within town cost €2, a day pass €5. Buy tickets from vending machines at stops or aboard trams. Trams 3, 7, 8 and 9 provide good links between the Hauptbahnhof, Altstadt and Neustadt.

Around Dresden

MEISSEN
☑03521 / POP 29,000

Straddling the Elbe around 25km upstream from Dresden, Meissen is the cradle of European porcelain manufacturing and still hitches its tourism appeal to the world-famous china first cooked up in its imposing 1710 castle. Adjacent to the soaring Gothic cathedral, it crowns a ridge above the Altstadt whose meandering cobbled lanes offer an escape from the porcelain pilgrims rolling in by tour bus.

◉ Sights

TOP CHOICE **Erlebniswelt**
Haus Meissen MUSEUM
(☑468 208; www.meissen.com; Talstrasse 9; adult/child €9/4.50; ◷9am-6pm May-Oct, 9am-

DRESDEN-CARD

The Dresden-Card, sold at the tourist offices, provides free public transportation as well as sweeping sightseeing discounts. Various schemes are available, including a one-day version (single/family €10/12.50), a two-day version (€25/46) and a three-day regional version (€48/68).

5pm Nov-Apr) There's no 'quiet time' to arrive at the popular and unmissable porcelain museum, where you can witness the astonishing artistry and craftsmanship that makes Meissen porcelain unique. It's next to the porcelain factory, about 1km south of the Altstadt. Visits start with a 30-minute tour (with English audioguide) of the **Schauwerkstätten**, where you can observe live demonstrations of vase throwing, plate painting, figure moulding and the glazing process. This helps you appreciate the fragile masterpieces displayed in the ensuing rooms.

Albrechtsburg CASTLE, MUSEUM
(☑352 147 070; www.albrechtsburg-meissen.de; Domplatz 1; adult/concession incl audioguide €8/4; ◷10am-6pm Mar-Oct, 10am-5pm Nov-Feb) Lording it over Meissen, the 15th-century Albrechtsburg is famous as the birthplace of European porcelain. Production began in the castle in 1710 and only moved to a custom-built factory in 1863. An exhibit on the second floor chronicles how it all began.

The adjacent **cathedral** (☑452 490; adult/child €4/2; ◷10am-6pm Mar-Oct, to 4pm Nov-Feb) contains an altarpiece by Lucas Cranach the Elder.

ℹ Information
Tourist office (www.touristinfo-meissen.de; Markt 3; ◷10am-6pm Mon-Fri, to 4pm Sat & Sun Apr-Oct, 10am-5pm Mon-Fri, to 3pm Sat Nov-Mar)

ℹ Getting There & Away
Half-hourly S1 trains run from Dresden's Hauptbahnhof and Neustadt train stations (€5.80, 40 minutes). For the Erlebniswelt, get off at Meissen-Triebischtal.

Steam boats operated by **Sächsische Dampfschiffahrt** (☑0331-452 139; www.saechsische-dampfschiffahrt.de; one-way/return €14/19.50; ◷May-Sep) depart from the Terrassenufer in Dresden. Consider going one way by boat and the other by train.

SAXON SWITZERLAND

About 40km south of Dresden, the Sächsische Schweiz embraces a unique and evocative landscape. This is wonderfully rugged country where nature has chiselled porous rock into bizarre columns, battered cliffs, tabletop mountains and deep valleys. The Elbe courses through thick forest, past villages and mighty hilltop castles.

Much of it is protected as a national park and popular with hikers and rock climbers. Even a short visit is rewarding, if you make your way to the **Bastei**, a stunning cluster of rock formations some 200m above the Elbe and the village of **Rathen**. It's a wonderland of fluted pinnacles and offers panoramic views of the surrounding forests, cliffs and mountains.

From April to October, steamers operated by Sächsische Dampfschiffahrt (p187) plough up the Elbe several times daily between Dresden and Bad Schandau, stopping in Rathen and other villages (5½ hours, adult/concession €23.90/19.10).

The region is also served frequently by the S1 train from Dresden. For the Bastei, get off at Rathen, catch the ferry across the Elbe, then follow a sweat-raising 30-minute trail to the top. Drivers can leave their car in the big car park near Rathen station.

Leipzig

☑0341 / POP 532,000

In Goethe's *Faust,* a character named Frosch calls Leipzig 'a little Paris'. He was wrong – Leipzig is more fun and infinitely less self-important than the Gallic capital. It's an important business and transport centre, a trade-fair mecca and – aside from Berlin – the most dynamic city in eastern Germany.

Culture has been big in Leipzig for centuries. After all, Bach's one-time backyard was also where Wagner was born and Mendelssohn-Bartholdy ran a music academy. Leipzig became known as the *Stadt der Helden* (City of Heroes) for its leading role in the 1989 'Peaceful Revolution' that led to the downfall of communist East Germany.

◉ Sights

Leipzig's compact centre lies within a ring road along the town's medieval fortifications. Don't rush from sight to sight – wandering around Leipzig is a pleasure in itself, with many of the blocks around the central Markt criss-crossed by historic shopping arcades. Four good ones: **Steibs Hof** (100-year-old blue tiles and classic cafes), **Specks Hof** (soaring atrium, bookshops, cafes), **Jägerhofpassage** (galleries, theatre, antiques) and the classic **Mädlerpassage** (grand design, Auerbachs Keller restaurant).

TOP CHOICE **Nikolaikirche**   CHURCH
(Church of St Nicholas; www.nikolaikirche-leipzig.de; Nikolaikirchhof 3; ☉10am-6pm Mon-Sat & during services 9.30am, 11.15am & 5pm Sun) The Church of St Nicholas has Romanesque and Gothic roots but since 1797 has sported a striking neoclassical interior with palmlike pillars and cream-coloured pews. It played a key role in the nonviolent movement that led to the collapse of East Germany by hosting 'peace prayers' every Monday at 5pm starting in 1982 (still held today).

FREE **Zeitgeschichtliches Forum**   MUSEUM
(Forum of Contemporary History; ☑222 00; www.hdg.de/leipzig; Grimmaische Strasse 6; ☉9am-6pm Tue-Fri, 10am-6pm Sat & Sun) This fascinating exhibit tells the political history of the GDR from division and dictatorship to fall-of-the-Wall ecstasy and post-*Wende* blues. It's essential viewing for anyone seeking to understand the late country's inner workings.

FREE **Stasi Museum**   MUSEUM
(☑961 2443; www.runde-ecke-leipzig.de; Dittrichring 24; ☉10am-6pm) In the GDR the walls had ears, as is chillingly documented in this exhibit in the former Leipzig headquarters of the East German secret police (the Stasi), a building known as the Runde Ecke (Round Corner). English-language audioguides aid in understanding the displays on propaganda, preposterous disguises, cunning surveillance devices, recruitment (even among children), scent storage and other chilling machinations that reveal the GDR's all-out zeal when it came to controlling, manipulating and repressing its own people.

Bach-Museum Leipzig   MUSEUM
(☑913 7202; www.bach-leipzig.de; Thomaskirchhof 16; adult/concession €6/4, under 16yrs free; ☉10am-6pm Tue-Sun) Completely updated, this interactive museum does more than tell you about the life and accomplishments of heavyweight musician Johann Sebastian Bach. Learn how to date a Bach manuscript,

listen to baroque instruments or treat your ears to recordings of any of his compositions.

Thomaskirche CHURCH

(☑222 240; www.thomaskirche.org; Thomaskirchhof 18; tower €2; ⊙church 9am-6pm, tower 1pm, 2pm & 4.30pm Sat, 2pm & 3pm Sun) The composer Johann Sebastian Bach worked in the Thomaskirche as a cantor from 1723 until his death in 1750, and his remains lie buried beneath a bronze plate in front of the altar. The Thomanerchor (p194), once led by Bach, has been going strong since 1212. The tower can be climbed for sweeping city views.

Museum der Bildenden Künste MUSEUM

(☑216 990; www.mdbk.de; Katharinenstrasse 10; adult/concession €5/4; ⊙10am-6pm Tue & Thu-Sun, noon-8pm Wed) An edgy glass cube shelters Leipzig's well-respected collection of paintings from the 15th century to today, including works by native sons Max Beckmann and Neo Rauch, a chief representative of the post-reunification New Leipzig School.

🛏 Sleeping

TOP
CHOICE Steigenberger

Grandhotel Handelshof HOTEL €€€

(☑350 5810; www.steigenberger.com/Leipzig; Salzgässchen 6; r from €160; ❄@🛜) Behind the imposing historic facade of a 1909 municipal trading hall, this luxe lodge outclasses most of Leipzig's hotels with its super-central location, charmingly efficient team and modern rooms dressed in crisp white-silver-purple colours. The stylish bi-level spa is the perfect bliss-out station.

Motel One HOTEL €

(☑337 4370; www.motel-one.de; Nikolaistrasse 23; d from €69, breakfast €7.50; P❄🛜) The Leipzig outpost of this increasingly ubiquitous budget designer chain has a five-star location opposite the Nikolaikirche and also gets most other things right, from the Zeitgeist-capturing lobby-lounge to the snug but smartly designed rooms. No surprise it's often booked out.

arcona Living Bach 14 HOTEL, STUDIOS €€

(☑496 140; http://bach14.arcona.de; Thomaskirchhof 13/14; d from €90) In this musically themed marvel, within earshot of the Thomaskirche, you'll sleep sweetly in sleek rooms decorated with sound-sculpture lamps, Bach manuscript wallpaper and colours ranging from subdued olive to perky raspberry. The

quietest ones are in the new garden wing but those in the historic front section have views of the church. Larger ones come with kitchenettes.

Quartier M APARTMENT €€

(☑2133 8800; www.apartment-leipzig.de; Markgrafenstrasse 10; apt €75-140; P) The building oozes old-world flair but the roomy apartments with full kitchens above an organic supermarket are state-of-the art and pack plenty of modern design cachet. Some units come with balcony or *terrasse*.

Hostel Sleepy Lion HOSTEL €

(☑993 9480; www.hostel-leipzig.de; Jacobstrasse 1; dm/d/apt from €12.50/42/55, linen €2.50, breakfast €3.50; @🛜) Thumbs up for this clean and cheerfully painted hostel with a super-central location and clued-in staff. Every budget and privacy need can be accommodated in dorms sleeping four to 10, as well as in private rooms and apartments.

✖ Eating

TOP
CHOICE **Auerbachs Keller** GERMAN €€€

(☑216 100; www.auerbachs-keller-leipzig.de; Mädlerpassage; mains €14-22) Founded in 1525, cosy Auerbachs Keller is touristy, but the food's actually quite good and the setting memorable. In Goethe's *Faust - Part I,* Mephistopheles and Faust carouse here with students before riding off on a barrel. The scene is depicted on a carved tree trunk in what is now the Goethezimmer (Goethe Room), where the great writer allegedly came for 'inspiration'.

Zum Arabischen Coffe Baum CAFE €€

(☑961 0060; www.coffe-baum.de; Kleine Fleischergasse 4; mains €8-16; ⊙11am-midnight) One of Europe's oldest coffeehouses, this rambling outpost has hosted poets, politicians, professors and everyone else since 1720. The warren of rooms spread over several floors is an atmospheric spot to try a *Leipziger Lerche* (lark), a locally famous marzipan-filled shortcrust pastry. Other cakes, light meals and alcoholic drinks are also served.

Telegraph CAFE €€

(☑149 4990; www.cafe-telegraph.de; Dittrichring 18-20; mains €5-11; ⊙8am-midnight; 🛜) Leipzig goes cosmopolitan at this high-ceilinged cafe with curved booths and wooden tables, a bilingual menu and a stack of international mags and dailies. It's a popular breakfast spot, available until a hangover-friendly 3pm. The menu is heavy on Austrian classics.

Gosenschenke
'Ohne Bedenken' BREWPUB €€
(☑566 2360; www.gosenschenke.de; Menckestrasse 5; mains €11-15; ⊙from noon daily Apr-Sep, from 4pm Mon-Fri & noon Sat & Sun Oct-Mar) This historic Leipzig institution, backed by the city's prettiest beer garden, is *the* place to sample *Gose*, a local top-fermented beer often served with a shot of liqueur. The menu requires that you surrender helplessly to your inner carnivore.

Drinking & Entertainment

Party activity centres on three main areas: the boisterous Drallewatsch pub strip, the more upmarket theatre district around Gottschedstrasse, and the mix of trendy and alt-vibe joints along Karl-Liebknecht-Strasse (aka 'Südmeile').

Moritzbastei CAFE, BAR
(☑702 590; www.moritzbastei.de; Universitätsstrasse 9; dishes €2-5; ⊙cafe & Schwalbennest from 10am Mon-Fri, noon Sat, 9am Sun, Fuchsbau from 8pm; ☎) This time-honoured warren of historic cellars below the old city fortifications keeps an all-ages crowd happy with three locations in one: the sprawling **Cafe Barbarkane** for coffee, drinks or light meals; the intimate **Schwalbennest** for wine; and the cool **Fuchsbau** bar for cocktails. Bands or DJs often take over the space after dark. Summer terrace, too.

Noels Ballroom PUB
(☑303 2007; noels-ballroom.com; Kurt-Eisner-Strasse 43; ⊙5pm-late; ☐10, 11 to Karl Liebknecht/ Kurt-Eisner-Strasse) McCormacks has renamed itself but the high-octane vibe, foamy pints of Guinness and lovely flower-filled beer garden still make Noels one of the best Irish pubs in town.

naTo PUB
(☑391 5539; www.nato-leipzig.de; Karl-Liebknecht-Strasse 46) The mother of Leipzig's alternative-music pub-clubs, with jazz, experimental and indie sounds alongside films and theatre. Great outdoor seating in summer.

Thomanerchor CLASSICAL MUSIC
(☑984 4211; www.thomaskirche.org; Thomaskirch-hof 18; tickets €2) This famous boys' choir performs Bach motets and cantatas at 6pm on Friday and 3pm on Saturday and also sings during Sunday services at 9.30am and 6pm at the Thomaskirche. To get a space, show

up when doors open 45 minutes before concerts begin.

Gewandhausorchester CLASSICAL MUSIC
(☑127 0280; www.gewandhaus.de; Augustusplatz 8; tours €4.50; ⊙tours usually 12.30pm Thu) Once led by Felix Mendelssohn-Bartholdy, the Gewandhaus is one of Europe's finest and oldest civic orchestras (since 1743). Tickets are available by email, by phone and in person.

Information

The Hauptbahnhof contains a large mall with shops open until 10pm Monday to Saturday and a few also on Sunday afternoon.

Tourist office (☑710 4260, room referral 710 4255; www.ltm-leipzig.de; Katharinenstrasse 8; ⊙9.30am-6pm Mon-Fri, to 4pm Sat, to 3pm Sun)

ⓘ Getting There & Away

Leipzig-Halle airport (LEJ; www.leipzig-halle -airport.de) is about 21km west of Leipzig and has domestic and international flights, including daily Ryanair service from London-Stansted, Rome, Milan and Malaga. It is linked to town by hourly RE train.

There are frequent trains to Frankfurt (€75, 3¾ hours), Dresden (€26, 1¼ hours) and Berlin (€45, 1¼ hours), among others. Private Interconnex trains also go to Berlin twice daily (€19, 1¼ hours).

ⓘ Getting Around

Buses and trams are run by **LVB** (☑194 49; www.lvb.de), which operates an information kiosk outside the Hauptbahnhof. The central tram station is here as well. Single tickets cost €1.50 for up to four stops and €2.10 for longer trips; day passes are €5.

WEIMAR & THURINGIA

Thuringia offers outstanding culture in its cities backed by the sprawling expanse of the Thuringian Forest. Top of the pops is Weimar, home to such seminal 18th-century poets and thinkers as Goethe and Schiller and the birthplace of the Bauhaus movement. Eisenach, where Bach was born, is dominated by the famous Wartburg castle, which is closely associated with the reformer Martin Luther, as is Erfurt, the state capital and a lively student town. It was the Nazis who put a dark stain on Thuringia's illustrious legacy when building Buchenwald concentration camp just outside Weimar.

Weimar

☎03643 / POP 65,500

Neither a monumental town nor a medieval one, Weimar appeals to those whose tastes run to cultural and intellectual pleasures. Over the centuries, it has been home to an entire pantheon of intellectual and creative giants, including Goethe, Schiller, Cranach, Bach, Herder, Liszt and Nietzsche. There are plenty of statues, plaques and museums to remind you of their legacy along with parks and gardens in which to take a break from the intellectual onslaught.

In the 20th century, Weimar won international name recognition as the place where the constitution of the Weimar Republic was drafted after WWI, though there are few reminders of this historical moment. Around the same time, Walter Gropius and other progressive architects founded the seminal Bauhaus design movement in town. The ghostly ruins of the nearby Buchenwald concentration camp, on the other hand, provide haunting evidence of the Nazi terror.

◉ Sights

TOP CHOICE **Goethe Haus & Nationalmuseum** MUSEUM

(Frauenplan 1; combined ticket Goethe Haus & museum adult/concession €10.50/8.50, permanent museum exhibition only adult/concession €6.50/5.50; ⊙9am-6pm Tue-Fri & Sun, to 7pm Sat) No other individual is as closely associated with Weimar as Johann Wolfgang von Goethe, who lived in this town from 1775 until his death in 1832, the last 50 years in what is now the

Goethe Haus. This is where he worked, studied, researched and penned and other immortal works. His study and the bedroom where he died are both preserved in their original state. To get the most from your visit, use the audioguide (free). Visitors numbers are limited and tickets timed.

The adjacent museum, which zeroes in on Goethe's life and times, was being revamped at the time of research.

Schiller Haus MUSEUM

(Schillerstrasse 12; adult/concession €5/4; ⊙9am-6pm Tue-Fri & Sun, to 7pm Sat) Dramatist (and Goethe's friend) Friedrich von Schiller lived in Weimar from 1799 until his early death in 1805. Study up on the man, his family and life before plunging on to the private quarters, including the study with his deathbed and the desk where he wrote *Wilhelm Tell* and other famous works.

Herzogin Anna Amalia Bibliothek LIBRARY

(www.klassik-stiftung.de; Platz der Demokratie 1; adult/concession incl audioguide €6.50/5.50; ⊙9.30am-2.30pm Tue-Sun) Anna Amalia was an art-loving 18th-century duchess who had a penchant for collecting precious books that are now exhibited in a magnificent library which was beautifully restored after a disastrous 2004 fire. The magnificent Rokokosaal (Rococo Hall) is crammed with 40,000 tomes once used for research purposes by Goethe, Schiller and other Weimar hot shots. Entry is limited and by timed ticket, so book in advance or start queuing before the ticket office opens at 9.30am.

GERMANY WEIMAR

BUCHENWALD

The Buchenwald concentration camp **museum and memorial** (☎03643-4300; www.buchenwald.de; Ettersberg; ⊙buildings & exhibits 10am-6pm Tue-Sun Apr-Oct, to 4pm Tue-Sun Nov-Mar, grounds open until sunset) is 10km northwest of Weimar. Between 1937 and 1945, more than one-fifth of the 250,000 people incarcerated here died, among them such prominent German communists and social democrats as Ernst Thälmann and Rudolf Breitscheid. After 1943, prisoners were exploited in the production of weapons. Shortly before the end of the war, some 28,000 prisoners were sent on death marches.

After the war, the Soviet victors established Special Camp No 2, in which 7000 so-called anticommunists and ex-Nazis were literally worked to death.

Pamphlets and books in English are sold at the bookshop, where you can also rent an excellent multilanguage audioguide (€3 or €5 with images). Last admission is 30 minutes before closing but you really need at least an hour to do the site justice.

From Weimar, take bus 6 (direction Buchenwald) from Goetheplatz. By car, head north on Ettersburger Strasse from Weimar train station and turn left onto Blutstrasse.

Park an der Ilm PARK

This sprawling park, just east of the Altstadt, is as inspiring and romantic now as it was in Goethe's time. **Goethes Gartenhaus** (Goethe's Garden House; Park an der Ilm; adult/concession €4.50/3.50; ⏲10am-6pm Wed-Mon), where the writer lived from 1776 to 1782, is a highlight. A few decades later, the composer Franz Liszt resided – and wrote the *Faust Symphony* – in what is now the **Liszt-Haus** (Liszt House; Marienstrasse 17; adult/concession €4/3; ⏲10am-6pm Tue-Sun Apr-Sep, to 4pm Sat & Sun Oct-Mar).

Bauhaus Museum MUSEUM

(www.das-bauhaus-kommt.de; Theaterplatz; adult/concession €4.50/3.50; ⏲10am-6pm) Considering that Weimar is the birthplace of the influential Bauhaus school, this museum is a rather modest affair. Plans are to move to newer, larger premises, so check the situation again from 2013.

Sleeping

TOP CHOICE **Casa dei Colori** PENSION €€

(☎489 640; www.casa-colori.de; Eisfeld 1a; r €84-114; P 📶) This charming pension convincingly imports cheerfully exuberant Mediterranean flair to provincial Thuringia. The mostly good-sized rooms are dressed in bold colours and come with a small desk, a couple of comfy armchairs and a stylish bathroom.

Labyrinth Hostel HOSTEL €

(☎811 822; www.weimar-hostel.com; Goetheplatz 6; dm €14-21, s/d €35/46, linen €2.50, breakfast €3; @ 📶) Loads of imagination has gone into this professionally run hostel with artist-designed rooms where you sleep in a bed perched on stacks of books. Bathrooms are shared and so are the kitchen and the lovely rooftop terrace.

Hotel Amalienhof HOTEL €€

(☎5490; www.amalienhof-weimar.de; Amalienstrasse 2; s €67-75, d €97-105, ste €115-130; P 📶) The charms of this hotel are manifold: classy antique furnishings, richly styled rooms that point to history without burying you in it, and a late breakfast buffet for those who take their holidays seriously.

Hotel Elephant Weimar LUXURY HOTEL €€€

(☎8020; www.luxurycollection.com/elephant; Markt 19; r €109-221, ste €291; P @ 📶) The moment you enter this charmer's elegant art deco lobby, you sense that it's luxury all the way to the top. For over 300 years, this classic has wooed statesmen, artists, scholars and the merely rich with first-class service and amenities.

Eating

TOP CHOICE **Jo Hanns** GERMAN €€

(☎493 617; Scherfgasse 1; mains €11.50-17.50; ⏲11am-midnight) The food is satisfying but it's the 130 local wines that give Jo Hanns a leg up on the competition. No matter whether you order the classic steak, roast lamb or scallops and shrimp with mint-lime spaghetti, there's a bottle to suit.

Versilia ITALIAN €€

(☎770 359; www.versilia-weimar.de; Frauentorstrasse 17; mains €17.50-23.50, pasta €6-8.50; ⏲11am-midnight) This delightful wine bar and restaurant serves delicious antipasti, homemade pasta dishes and pan-Italian mains in a spacious setting.

ACC GERMAN €

(www.acc-cafe.de; Burgplatz 1; dishes €5-10; ⏲11-1am; 📶) Goethe's first pad upon arriving in Weimar is now an alt-vibe, artsy hang-out, where the food and wine are organic whenever possible and the upstairs gallery delivers a primer on the local art scene. The owners also rent out a room and a holiday flat (www.goethezimmer.de), both handsomely furnished.

Estragon HEALTH FOOD €

(Herderplatz 3; soups €3-5.50; ⏲10am-7pm Mon-Sat, noon-6pm Sun) There are days when a bowl of steamy soup feels as warm and embracing as a hug from a good friend. This little soup kitchen turns mostly organic ingredients into delicious flavour combos served in three sizes. It shares digs with a small organic supermarket.

Residenz-Café INTERNATIONAL €€

(Grüner Markt 4; mains €5-18; ⏲8am-1am; ✎) Everyone should find something to their taste at the 'Resi', one of Weimar's enduring favourites, no matter if it's time for breakfast, lunch, cake or dinner.

Information

Tourist office (☎7450; www.weimar.de; Markt 10; ⏲9.30am-7pm Mon-Sat, to 3pm Sun)

Getting There & Away

Weimar's Hauptbahnhof is a 20-minute walk from the centre. Frequent connections include

Erfurt (€8, 15 minutes), Eisenach (€14.40, one hour), Leipzig (€22, 1¼ hours), Dresden (€43, 2½ hours) and Berlin-Hauptbahnhof (€54, 2¼ hours).

Erfurt

☏ 0361 / POP 205,000

Thuringia's state capital is a scene-stealing combo of sweeping squares, time-worn alleyways, perky church towers, idyllic river scenery, and vintage inns and taverns. On the little Gera River, Erfurt was founded as a bishopric in 742 by the indefatigable missionary St Boniface. Rich merchants laid the foundation of the university in 1392, allowing students to study common law, rather than religious law. Its most famous graduate was the later Reformer Martin Luther, who studied philosophy here before becoming a monk at the local Augustinian monastery in 1505.

◉ Sights

Mariendom CHURCH
(St Mary's Cathedral; Domplatz; ⊙9am-6pm Mon-Sat, 1-6pm Sun) Erfurt's cathedral began life as a simple chapel founded by St Boniface, but the Gothic pile you see today has the hallmarks of the 14th century. Look for the superb stained-glass windows; the 12th-century Wolfram candelabrum in the shape of a man; the Gloriosa bell (1497); a Romanesque stucco Madonna; and the 14th-century choir stalls. The **Domstufen-Festspiele** (www.domstufen.de) classical music festival is held on the cathedral steps in July or August.

Severikirche CHURCH
(Domplatz; ⊙9am-6pm Mon-Sat, 1-6pm Sun) This five-aisled hall church (1280) teems with such prized treasures as a stone Madonna (1345), a 15m-high baptismal font (1467), and the sarcophagus of St Severus.

GERMANY ERFURT

WORTH A TRIP

EISENACH

On the edge of the Thuringian forest, Eisenach is the birthplace of Johann Sebastian Bach, but even the great composer plays second fiddle to the awe-inspiring hilltop **Wartburg castle** (www.wartburg-eisenach.de; tour adult/concession €9/5, museum & Luther study only €5/4; ⊙tours 8.30am-5pm, in English 1.30pm). Budget at least two hours: one for the guided tour, the rest for the museum and the grounds (views!).

When it comes to medieval castles and their importance in German history, the Wartburg is the mother lode. According to legend, the first buildings were put up in 1067 by the hilariously named local ruler Ludwig the Springer in an effort to protect his territory. In 1206, Europe's best minstrels met for the medieval version of *Pop Idol*, a song contest later immortalised in Richard Wagner's opera *Tannhäuser*. Shortly thereafter, Elisabeth, the most famous Wartburg woman, arrived. A Hungarian princess, she was married off to the local landgrave at age four and later chose to abandon court life for charitable work, earning canonisation quickly after her death in 1235.

The Wartburg's most famous resident, however, was Martin Luther, who went into hiding here in 1521 under the assumed name of Junker Jörg after being excommunicated and placed under papal ban. During this 10-month stay, he translated the New Testament from Greek into German, contributing enormously to the development of the written German language.

Bach fans, meanwhile, should head down into town where the **Bachhaus** (www.bachhaus.de; Frauenplan 21; adult/concession €7.50/4; ⊙10am-6pm) has a modern exhibit about the great composer's life and work.

From April to October, bus 10 runs hourly from 9am to 5pm from the Hauptbahnhof (with stops at Karlsplatz and Mariental) to the Eselstation stop, from where it's a steep 10-minute walk up to the castle. In winter, buses are available on demand; call ☏228 822 for a pick-up.

Regional trains run frequently to Erfurt (€11.10, 45 minutes) and Weimar (€14.40, one hour). The **tourist office** (☏792 30; www.eisenach.de; Markt 24; ⊙10am-6pm Mon-Fri, to 5pm Sat & Sun) can help you find accommodation if your day trip gets extended.

Krämerbrücke
BRIDGE

Even if it were not the only bridge north of the Alps flanked by buildings, the medieval Merchant Bridge would still be a most charming spot. You can watch chocolate makers, potters, jewellers and other artisans at work in their teensy studios or pop into a cafe for refreshments. Of the two churches that once bookended the stone bridge only the Ägidienkirche remains. Its tower can sometimes be climbed.

Augustinerkloster
CHURCH

(Augustinian Monastery; Augustinerstrasse 10, enter on Comthurgasse; tour adult/concession €6/4; ⊙tours hourly 10am-noon & 2-5pm Mon-Sat, 11am & noon Sun) Reformer Martin Luther lived at this monastery from 1505 to 1511 and was ordained a priest here in 1507. You're free to roam the grounds and visit the church, with its ethereal Gothic stained-glass windows but to get inside the monastery itself to see the cloister, a recreated Luther cell and an exhibit on the history of the Bible and Luther's life in Erfurt, you need to join a guided tour. Lodging is also available here.

Zitadelle Petersberg
FORTRESS

(tour adult/concession €8/4; ⊙7pm Fri & Sat May-Oct) On the Petersberg hill northwest of Domplatz, this citadel ranks among Europe's largest and best-preserved baroque fortresses. It sits above a honeycomb of tunnels, which can be explored on two-hour guided tours run by the tourist office.

Alte Synagoge
SYNAGOGUE

(Old Synagogue; http://alte-synagoge.erfurt.de; Waagegasse 8; adult/concession €5/3; ⊙10am-5pm Tue-Thu, 11am-5pm Fri-Sun) The Alte Synagoge in Erfurt is one of the oldest Jewish houses of worship in Europe, with roots in the 12th century. After the pogrom of 1349, it was converted into a storehouse and is now an exhibit space and museum.

🛏 Sleeping

TOP CHOICE Re_4 Hostel
HOSTEL €

(☎600 0110; www.re4hostel.de; Puschkinstrasse 21; dm €13-16, s/d €26/52, without bathroom €20/40, linen €2; P@) This cool hostel in a former police station is run by an energetic, clued-in crew, happy to help you make the most out of your stay in Erfurt. Breakfast costs an extra €4.50. Room 13 has a 'chilling' surprise. The hostel's about 1.5km

southwest from the Hauptbahnhof (tram 5 to Pushkinstrasse).

Opera Hostel
HOSTEL €

(☎6013 1360; www.opera-hostel.de; Walkmühlstrasse 13; dm €13-18, s/d/tr €45/54/75, without bathroom €37/48/66, linen €2.50; @🖥) Run with smiles and aplomb, this upmarket hostel in a historic building scores big with wallet-watching global nomads. Rooms are bright and spacious, many with an extra sofa for chilling. Make friends in the communal kitchen and on-site lounge-bar. Take bus 51 from Hauptbahnhof to Alte Oper.

Hotel am Kaisersaal
HOTEL €€

(☎658 560; www.bachmann-hotels.de; Futterstrasse 8; s/d €89/104; P🖥) Tip-top rooms are appointed with all expected mod cons in this highly rated hotel. Request a yard-facing one if you're bothered by street noise. Take tram 1 or 5 to Futterstrasse.

🍴 Eating

TOP CHOICE Zwiesel
GERMAN €

(Michaelisstrasse 31; mains €6-9; ⊙6pm-late Mon-Thu, 3pm-late Fri-Sun) Been cut out of the family will? No problem at this reliable cheapie choice, which has 25 mains costing just €5.95 and drink prices to match. Even the rump steak is only €8.95. Any of the 350 cocktails cost €4.90.

Zum Goldenen Schwan
GERMAN €€

(Michaelisstrasse 9; snacks €3-7, mains €8-17; ⊙11am-1am) This authentic inn serves Thuringian classics, including *Puffbohnenpfanne* (fried broad beans with roast bacon), an Erfurt speciality. Excellent house brews wash everything down well.

Steinhaus
GERMAN €

(Allerheiligenstrasse 20-21; mains €4-8; ⊙11am-late, food till midnight) The ceiling beams may be ancient, but the crowd is intergenerational at this rambling gastro pub-cum-beer garden in the historic Engelsburg student centre.

ℹ Information

Tourist office (☎664 00; www.erfurt-tourismus.de; Benediktsplatz 1; ⊙10am-7pm Mon-Fri, to 6pm Sat, to 4pm Sun)

ℹ Getting There & Around

Fast trains leave frequently for Berlin (€60, 2½ hours, change in Leipzig), Dresden (€51, 2½ hours) and Frankfurt-am-Main (€54, 2¼ hours). Regional trains to Weimar (€5, 15 minutes) and Eisenach (€11.10, 45 minutes) run at least once hourly.

Trams 3, 4 and 6 run from Hauptbahnhof via Anger and Fischmarkt to Domplatz. Tickets cost €1.80, or €4.20 for a day pass.

SAXONY-ANHALT

Once the smog-filled heart of East Germany's chemical industry and open-pit coal mining, Saxony-Anhalt (Sachsen-Anhalt) has gone from humdrum to, well, not quite hip, but certainly more happening than its reputation would suggest. Open your eyes and you'll find deep wellsprings of beauty, ingenuity and historical magnitude. After all, Otto I, the first Holy Roman Emperor, is buried in Magdeburg; Martin Luther kick started the Reformation in Wittenberg; and, centuries later, the Bauhaus School revolutionised modern design and architecture from its base in Dessau.

Magdeburg

📞0391 / POP 231,500

Something old, something new: Magdeburg is constantly characterised by the juxtaposition of those two. Home to Germany's most ancient cathedral, the city also boasts the last of Austrian architect Friedensreich Hundertwasser's bonkers structures and teems with wide Cold War–era boulevards and enormous *Plattenbauten* (concrete tower blocks). Meanwhile, the historic cobbled streets around Hasselbachplatz are filled with cafes and bars.

⦿ Sights

Dom   CHURCH
(www.magdeburgerdom.de; Am Dom 1; tour adult/concession €3/1.50; ⊘10am-6pm Mon-Sat, 11.30am-6pm Sun, tours 2pm Mon-Sat, 11.30am Sun) Magdeburg's main historical landmark traces its roots to 937 when Otto I (912–73) founded a Benedictine monastery and had it built up into a full-fledged cathedral within two decades. He and his English wife Editha are buried here amid stunning artistic treasures ranging from the delicate 13th-century **Magdeburg Virgins** sculptures to a haunting **antiwar memorial** by Ernst Barlach.

Grüne Zitadelle   ARCHITECTURE
(Green Citadel; 📞620 8655; www.gruene-zitadelle. de; Breiter Weg 9; tour adult/concession €6/5; ⊘information office 10am-6pm, tours 11am, 3pm & 5pm Mon-Fri, hourly 10am-5pm Sat & Sun) Completed in 2005, Hunderwasser's piglet-pink final building sprouts trees from its roof and nicely reflects the architect's philosophy of creating highly unique spaces in harmony with nature. Inside are offices, flats and shops, as well as a small hotel and a cafe. Tours are in German only.

🛏 Sleeping & Eating

TOP CHOICE Grüne Zitadelle   BOUTIQUE HOTEL €€
(📞620 780; www.hotel-zitadelle.de; Breiter Weg 9; s €105-135, d €125-145, breakfast €11; P❋⊛🛜) Fans of Hundertwasser can ponder the architect's penchant for uneven, organic forms in these elegant rooms. The attached cafe (dishes €4 to €5, open 7am to 7pm) is open to the public, serving breakfast and light meals.

DJH Hostel   HOSTEL €
(📞532 1010; www.jugendherberge.de/jh/magde burg; Leiterstrasse 10; dm/s/tw €21/33/45, over 27yr extra €3; P@⊛🛜) The smart, modern premises, generous space, good facilities and quiet but central location make this a winner.

Petriförder   INTERNATIONAL €€
(📞597 9600; www.restaurant-petrifoerder-magde burg.eu; Petriförder 1; mains €8-24; ⊘from 11.30am Mon-Fri, from 10am Sat & Sun) Right on the Elbe River, this resto-bar has a toe in all doors, with pasta, pizza, schnitzel and a good range of well-prepared poultry, fish and red-meat dishes. A beach bar sets up nearby in summer.

ⓘ Information

Tourist office (📞194 33; www.magdeburg -tourist.de; Ernst-Reuter-Allee 12; ⊘10am-6.30pm Mon-Fri, to 4pm Sat)

ⓘ Getting There & Away

Magdeburg is directly connected to Berlin Hauptbahnhof (€27, two hours), Leipzig (€27, 1¼ hours) and Dessau-Rosslau (€11.10, 50 minutes). For Lutherstadt Wittenberg (€16.40, 70 minutes), change in Rosslau. Magdeburg is just south of the A2 to Berlin or Hanover and also served by the A14 to Leipzig.

Dessau-Rosslau

✆ 0340 / POP 87,000

'Less is more' and 'form follows function' – both these dictums were taught in Dessau, home of the influential Bauhaus School. Between 1925 and 1932, some of the century's greatest artists and architects breathed life into the groundbreaking principles of modernism here, among them Walter Gropius, Paul Klee, Wassily Kandinsky and Ludwig Mies Van der Rohe. Their legacy still stands proud, in the immaculate Bauhaus School building, the lecturers' purpose-built homes and other pioneering constructions.

◉ Sights

FREE **Bauhausgebäude** ARCHITECTURE
(Bauhaus Building; www.bauhaus-dessau.de; Gropiusallee 38; exhibition adult/concession €6/4, tour €4/3; ⊙10am-6pm, tours 11am & 2pm daily, also noon & 4pm Sat & Sun) Bauhaus founder Walter Gropius considered architecture the ultimate of all artistic endeavours, and this building was the first real-life example of his vision. It was revolutionary, bringing industrial construction techniques such as curtain walling and wide spans into the public domain and presaging untold buildings worldwide.

Today urban studies students use part of the building but much of it is open to the public. The gift shop sells cool trinkets, books, posters and postcards. Staff also rent English-language audioguides (adult/concession €4/3); note only the guided tours will get you inside the most interesting rooms.

Meisterhäuser ARCHITECTURE
(Masters' Houses; www.meisterhaeuser.de; Ebertallee 63, 65-67 & 69-71; admission to all 3 houses adult/concession €7.50/5.50, tours €11.50/8.50; ⊙11am-6pm Tue-Sun, tours 12.30pm & 3.30pm daily, also 1.30pm Sat & Sun) The leading lights of the Bauhaus movement – Gropius, Lyonel Feininger, Georg Muche, Wassily Kandisky and Paul Klee among them – lived together as neighbours in the so-called Meisterhäuser, white cubist structures that exemplify the Bauhaus aim of 'design for living' in a modern industrial world. They're on leafy Ebertallee, a 15-minute walk west of the Hauptbahnhof.

⌂ Sleeping & Eating

In Dessau-Rosslau, you really can eat, drink and sleep Bauhaus. For a different diet, investigate the main thoroughfare of Zerbster Strasse.

TOP CHOICE **Hotel-Pension An den 7 Säulen** HOTEL €
(✆ 619 620; www.pension7saeulen.de; Ebertallee 66; s €47-56, d €62-74; ℗) Rooms at this small pension are clean and nicely renovated; the owners are friendly, the garden is pleasant and the breakfast room overlooks the Meisterhäuser across the leafy street. Take bus 11 to Kornerhaus from Hauptbahnhof and walk back to Ebertallee.

NH Dessau HOTEL €€
(✆ 251 40; www.nh-hotels.com; Zerbsterstrasse 29; r €65-99, breakfast €16; ℗ ✳ @ ☎) This modern hotel in white-grey tones is set in the pedestrianised strip leading to the Rathaus and tourist office. Nice touch: the rooftop sauna with attached terrace. Take bus 12 from the train station to Zerbsterstrasse.

Bauhaus Klub CAFE €
(Gropiusallee 38; light dishes €3.50-8.90; ⊙8am-midnight Mon-Fri, 9am-midnight Sat, 8am-6pm Sun; ☎) Breakfasts, salads, snacks and *Flammkuchen* are served downstairs in the congenial cafe and snack bar in the Bauhaus Building.

TOP CHOICE **Pächterhaus** GERMAN €€
(✆ 650 1447; www.paechterhaus-dessau.de; Kirchstrasse 1; mains €18-25; ⊙lunch & dinner Tue-Sun) Foodies on a mission won't mind making the small detour to this gorgeously restored half-timbered farm house where seasonal and locally sourced ingredients get the gourmet treatment. Take bus 11 to Kirchstrasse.

❶ Information

Bauhaus Foundation (✆ 650 8251; www.bauhaus-dessau.de; Gropiusallee 38; ⊙10am-6pm) Offers educational info on, and tours of, Bauhaus buildings, sometimes in English.

Tourist office (✆ 204 1442, accommodation 220 3003; www.dessau-rosslau-tourismus.de; Zerbsterstrasse 2c; ⊙10am-6pm Mon-Fri, to 1pm Sat)

❶ Getting There & Away

For Berlin (€36, 1½ hours), change in Lutherstadt Wittenberg (€7.50, 30 minutes). Direct regional services go to Leipzig (€11.10, 45 minutes), Halle (€11.10, 55 minutes) and Magdeburg (€11.10, 50 minutes).

Lutherstadt Wittenberg

📞 03491 / POP 49,500

As its full name suggests, Wittenberg is first and foremost about Martin Luther (1483–1546), the monk who triggered the German Reformation by publishing his 95 theses against church corruption in 1517. Wittenberg back then was a hotbed of progressive thinking which also saw priests get married and educators like Luther's buddy Philipp Melanchthon argue for schools to accept female pupils. Today Wittenberg retains its significance for the world's 340 million Protestants, including 66 million Lutherans, as well as for those who simply admire Luther for his principled stand against authority. Sometimes called the 'Rome of the Protestants', its many Reformation-related sites garnered it the World Heritage Site nod from Unesco in 1996.

◎ Sights

Lutherhaus
MUSEUM

(www.martinluther.de; Collegienstrasse 54; adult/concession €5/3; ⊙9am-6pm) Even those with no previous interest in the Reformation will likely be fascinated by the state-of-the-art exhibits in the Lutherhaus, the former monastery turned Luther family home. Through an engaging mix of accessible narrative (in German and English), spotlit artefacts (eg his lectern from the Stadtkirche, indulgences chests, bibles, cloaks), famous oil paintings and interactive multimedia stations, you'll learn about the man, his times and his impact on world history. Highlights include Cranach's *Ten Commandments* in the refectory, and an original room furnished by Luther in 1535.

Schlosskirche
CHURCH

(Castle Church; Schlossplatz; ⊙10am-6pm Mon-Sat, 11.30am-6pm Sun) Did or didn't he nail those 95 theses to the door of the Schlosskirche? We'll never know for sure, for the original portal was destroyed by fire in 1760 and replaced in 1858 with this massive bronze version inscribed with the theses in Latin. Luther himself is buried below the pulpit, opposite his friend and fellow reformer Philipp Melanchthon.

Stadtkirche St Marien
CHURCH

(Jüdenstrasse 35; ⊙10am-6pm Mon-Sat, 11.30am-6pm Sun) This church was where Martin Luther's ecumenical revolution began, with

the world's first Protestant worship services in 1521. It was also here that Luther preached his famous Lectern sermons in 1522, and where he married ex-nun Katharina von Bora three years later. The centrepiece is the large altar, designed jointly by Lucas Cranach the Elder and his son. The side facing the nave depicts Luther, Melanchthon and other Reformation figures, as well as Cranach himself, in biblical contexts.

🛏 Sleeping & Eating

TOP CHOICE Alte Canzley
HOTEL €€

(📞429 190; www.alte-canzley.de; Schlossplatz 3-5; s €70-125, d €85-139; 🅿@🛜) The nicest place in town for your money is in a 14th-century building opposite the Schlosskirche. Each of the eight spacious units are furnished in dark woods and natural hues, named for a major historical figure and equipped with a kitchenette. The vaulted downstairs harbours Saxony-Anhalt's first certified organic restaurant (dishes €7.20 to €23.90).

DJH Hostel
HOSTEL €

(📞505 205; www.jugendherberge-wittenberg.de; Schlossstrasse 14/15; dm under/over 27yr €19/22, s/d €28.50/34, linen €3.50; 🅿@🛜) Wittenberg's excellent youth hostel has 40 bright rooms sleeping up to six people and come with bathrooms, bedside reading lamps and private lockers.

Brauhaus Wittenberg
GERMAN €€

(Markt 6, Im Beyerhof; mains €6.90-15.90; ⊙11am-11pm) This place – with a cobbled courtyard, indoor brewery and shiny copper vats – thrums with the noise of people having a good time. The menu is hearty but also features smaller dishes for waist-watchers. Upstairs are a few simple rooms with air-con (singles/doubles €57/79).

❶ Information

Tourist office (📞498 610; www.wittenberg.de; Schlossplatz 2; ⊙9am-6pm Mon-Fri, 10am-4pm Sat & Sun)

❶ Getting There & Away

Wittenberg is on the main train line to Halle and Leipzig (both €12.20, one hour). ICE (€30, 45 minutes) and RE trains (€21.50, 1¼ hours) travel to Berlin. Coming from Berlin, be sure to board for 'Lutherstadt Wittenberg', as there's also a Wittenberge west of the capital.

Harz Mountains

The Harz Mountains constitute a mini-Alpine region straddling Saxony-Anhalt and Lower Saxony. Here, medieval castles overlook fairy-tale historic towns, while there are caves, mines and numerous hiking trails to explore.

The region's highest – and most famous – mountain is the Brocken, where one-time visitor Johann Wolfgang von Goethe set the 'Walpurgisnacht' chapter of his play *Faust*. His inspiration came from folk tales depicting *Walpurgisnacht,* or *Hexennacht* (witches' night), as an annual witches' coven. Every 30 April to 1 May it's celebrated enthusiastically across the Harz region.

GOSLAR
📞 05321 / POP 41,000

Goslar has a charming medieval Altstadt, which, together with its historic Rammelsberg mine, is a Unesco World Heritage Site. Founded by Heinrich I in 922, the town's early importance centred on silver and the Kaiserpfalz, the seat of the Saxon kings from 1005 to 1219. It fell into decline after a second period of prosperity in the 14th and 15th centuries, reflecting the fortunes of the Harz as a whole, and relinquished its mine to Braunschweig in 1552 and then its soul to Prussia in 1802.

⊙ Sights

Altstadt
NEIGHBOURHOOD

One of the nicest things to do in Goslar is to wander through the historic streets around the Markt where the 1494 **Hotel Kaiserworth** is decorated with almost life-size figures. The **market fountain**, crowned by an ungainly eagle symbolising Goslar's status as a free imperial city, dates from the 13th century. Opposite the **Rathaus** (town hall), the **Glockenspiel** (carillon) depicts local mining scenes and plays at 9am, noon, 3pm and 6pm.

Kaiserpfalz
CASTLE

(Kaiserbleek 6; adult/concession €4.50/2.50; ⊙10am-5pm) Goslar's pride and joy is the reconstructed 11th-century Romanesque palace, Kaiserpfalz. The **St Ulrich Chapel** on the south side houses the heart of Heinrich III. Just below the palace, the **Domvorhalle** displays the 11th-century 'Kaiserstuhl' throne, used by German emperors.

Rammelsberg Museum & Besucherbergwerk
MUSEUM

(Rammelsberg Museum & Visitors' Mine; www.rammelsberg.de; Bergtal 19; admission €12; ⊙9am-6pm, last admission 4.30pm) About 1km south of town, the shafts and buildings of this 1000-year-old mine are now a museum and Unesco World Heritage Site. Admission includes a German-language tour and a pamphlet with English explanations of the 18th- and 19th-century Roeder Shafts, the mine railway and the ore processing section. Bus 803 stops here.

🛏 Sleeping & Eating

⬆TOP CHOICE Hotel Kaiserworth
HOTEL €€

(📞7090; www.kaiserworth.de; Markt 3; s €71-101, d €122-182, tr €172-207; P🐾😊📶) This magnificent 500-year-old former merchant guild building has tasteful rooms, a good restaurant and a cafe that's open until 2am or the last customer.

Gästehaus Schmitz
GUESTHOUSE €

(📞234 45; www.schmitz-goslar.de; Kornstrasse 1; s/d/tr €45/60/75; P) This slightly eccentric guesthouse is an excellent choice in the heart of town, especially for those on low budgets or looking for an apartment.

Die Butterhanne
GERMAN €€

(www.butterhanne.de; Marktkirchhof 3; mains €8.50-14; ⊙from 8.30am) The fare is traditional and regular here and the outdoor seating is nice. The name refers to a famous local frieze showing a milkmaid churning butter while clutching her buttock to insult her employer.

ⓘ Information

Tourist office (📞780 60; www.goslar.de; Markt 7; ⊙9.15am-6pm Mon-Fri, 9.30am-4pm Sat, 9.30am-2pm Sun)

ⓘ Getting There & Away

Bad Harzburg–Hanover trains stop here often, as do trains on the Braunschweig–Göttingen line. There are direct trains to Wernigerode (€9.10, 45 minutes, every two hours) and other services requiring a change at Vienenburg.

The B6 runs north to Hildesheim and east to Bad Harzburg, Wernigerode and Quedlinburg. The north–south A7 is reached via the B82.

QUEDLINBURG
📞 03946 / POP 28,400

With over 1400 half-timbered houses dating from six centuries ago, Quedlinburg is a

NARROW-GAUGE RAILWAYS

Fans of old-time trains or unusual journeys will be in their element on any of the three narrow-gauge railways crossing the Harz. This 140km integrated network – the largest in Europe – is served by 25 steam and 10 diesel locomotives, which tackle gradients of up to 1:25 (40%) and curves as tight as 60m in radius. There are three lines:

Harzquerbahn Runs 60km on a north–south route between Wernigerode and Nordhausen; the 14km between Wernigerode and Drei Annen Hohne includes 72 bends.

Brockenbahn From the junction at Drei Annen Hohne, this classic trains begins the steep climb up the Brocken, northern Germany's highest mountain. Direct trains also leave from Wernigerode and Nordhausen.

Selketalbahn Begins in Quedlinburg, crosses the plain to Gernrode and follows a creek through deciduous forest before joining the Selke Valley and climbing past Alexisbad to high plains around Friedrichshöhe and beyond.

For timetables and information, see **Harzer Schmalspurbahnen** (☎03943-5580; www.hsb-wr.de).

highlight of any trip to the Harz. In 1994 the city became a Unesco World Heritage Site; since then, work to save the crumbling treasures lining its romantic cobblestone streets has gradually progressed. You can also pick up a narrow-gauge railway from here.

◎ Sights

With so many historic buildings, Quedlinburg is perfect for just strolling around and soaking up the atmosphere.

Stiftskirche St Servatius CHURCH
(Schlossberg 1; adult/concession €4.50/3, combined ticket Dom, treasury, crypt & Schlossmuseum adult/concession €8.50/5.50; ◎10am-6pm Tue-Sat) This 12th-century church is one of Germany's most significant from the Romanesque period. Its treasury contains reliquaries and early bibles, while the crypt features early frescoes and royal graves.

Schlossmuseum MUSEUM
(Schlossberg 1; adult/concession €4/2.50, combined ticket Dom, treasury, crypt & Schlossmuseum adult/concession €8.50/5.50; ◎10am-6pm Tue-Sun) The present-day Renaissance palace, on a 25m-high plateau above Quedlinburg, contains the Schlossmuseum, with some fascinating Ottonian-period items dating from 919 to 1056.

Fachwerkmuseum Ständebau MUSEUM
(Wordgasse 3; adult/concession €3/2; ◎10am-5pm Fri-Wed) Germany's earliest half-timbered houses were built using high perpendicular struts, a technique perfectly illustrated by this 1310 building, which also contains exhibits on the style and construction technique.

🛏 Sleeping

TOP CHOICE **Romantik Hotel Theophano** HOTEL €€
(☎963 00; www.hoteltheophano.de; Markt 13-14; s €69, d €99-140; P@🛜) Each room is decorated in an individual style at this rambling, rustic hotel. Most are spacious and very comfortable, but the many staircases (no lift) and low thresholds might be a problem for some.

DJH Hostel HOSTEL €
(☎03946-811 703; www.jugendherberge.de; Neuendorf 28; dm €16.50-19.50, bedding €3) This excellent hostel offers four- and 10-bed dorms in a quiet and very central location. It's relatively small and fills quickly in summer.

❶ Information

Tourist office (☎905 625; www.quedlinburg.de; Markt 2; ◎9.30am-6pm Mon-Fri, to 3pm Sat, to 2pm Sun)

❶ Getting There & Away

Frequent services to Thale (€2.20, 12 minutes). For trains to Wernigerode (€9.10, 45 minutes), change at Halberstadt. The narrow-gauge Selketalbahn runs to Gernrode (€3, 15 minutes) and beyond.

MECKLENBURG-WESTERN POMERANIA

Mecklenburg-Vorpommern combines historic Hanseatic-era towns like Schwerin, Wismar and Stralsund with holiday areas such as Warnemünde and Rügen Island. Often skipped by international travellers, in summer it seems like half of Germany is lolling on the sands and relaxing in a *Strandkorb* (basket-like beach wicker chairs). At other times of the year, intrepid visitors will be rewarded with discoveries far from the maddening crowds.

Schwerin

 0385 / POP 95,200

State capital Schwerin has a modest dignity befitting its status. Picturesquely sited around seven lakes, the centrepiece of this engaging city is its Schloss (castle), built in the 14th century when the city was the seat of the Grand Duchy of Mecklenburg. It's small enough to explore on foot and, if you're on the move, as part of a half-day break on a train journey. But Schwerin's beauty and charm are invariably infectious, and few people regret spending extra time here.

👁 Sights

Schloss Schwerin
CASTLE

(☑525 2920; www.schloss-schwerin.de; adult/child €4/2.50; ☉10am-6pm mid-Apr–mid-Oct, 10am-5pm Tue-Sun mid-Oct–mid-Apr) Gothic and Renaissance turrets, Slavic onion domes, Ottoman features and terracotta Hanseatic step gables are among the mishmash of architectural styles that make up Schwerin's inimitable Schloss, which is crowned by a gleaming golden dome. Nowadays the Schloss earns its keep as the state parliament building.

Inside the palace's opulently furnished rooms, highlights include a huge collection of Meissen porcelain and richly coloured stained glass windows in the **Schlosskirche**. Surrounding the palace, the **Burggarten** has a lovely orangerie with a restaurant and summer terrace cafe overlooking the water. Across the causeway south of here is the canal-laced, baroque **Schlossgarten** (Palace Garden).

Staatliches Museum
MUSEUM

(☑595 80; www.museum-schwerin.de; Alter Garten 3; adult/concession €8/6; ☉10am-6pm Tue-Sun & noon-8pm Thu Apr-Oct, 10am-5pm Tue-Sun & 1pm-8pm Thu Nov-Mar) An enormous neoclassical building, the state museum displays such old masters as Rembrandt, Rubens and Brueghel, as well as oils by Lucas Cranach the Elder and collections of more modern works by Marcel Duchamp and Ernst Barlach.

Dom
CHURCH

(☑565 014; Am Dom 4; adult/child €2/1; ☉11am-3pm Mon-Fri, 11am-4pm Sat, noon-3pm Sun) You don't get better examples of north German red-brick architecture than the 14th-century Gothic Dom, towering above the Markt. The tower was added in the 19th century and can be climbed (adult/child €1.50/0.50). Inside, check out the elaborately carved pews.

🛏 Sleeping

Zur guten Quelle
HOTEL €

(☑565 985; www.zur-guten-quelle.m-vp.de; Schusterstrasse 12; s from €54, d from €78; ℗🐾) In a pretty half-timbered house, bang in the Altstadt, this hotel has half a dozen simple but comfortable rooms and is also known for its cosy traditional restaurant and beer garden.

Hotel Niederländischer Hof
HOTEL €€

(☑591 100; www.niederlaendischer-hof.de; Karl-Marx-Strasse 12-13; s €84-124, d €125-170; ℗🐾) Overlooking the Pfaffenteich pond, this regal 1901-established hotel has 33 elegant rooms with black marble bathrooms, a library warmed by an open fire, and a lauded restaurant. Room decor ranges from trad luxe to whimsical seaside.

DJH Hostel
HOSTEL €

(☑326 0006; www.jugendherberge.de; Waldschulweg 3; dm from €20) Though popular with school groups, this 91-bed/20-room hostel is in a peaceful, leafy location south of the city centre. Take bus 14.

🍴 Eating & Drinking

Zum Stadtkrug
BREWERY €€

(☑593 6693; www.altstadtbrauhaus.de; Wismarsche Strasse 126; mains €10-20) The dark beer at this 1936-established microbrewery/pub consistently rates among the best in Germany. It's full of antique brewing equipment, and opens to a convivial beer garden. The menu features the usual assortment of schnitzels and porky mains but everything is well prepared. Sandwiches are excellent.

Weinhaus Wöhler
GERMAN €€

(☑555 830; www.weinhaus-woehler.de; Puschkinstrasse 26; mains €9-22; 🐾) In addition to wood-lined dining rooms, a large covered courtyard and a tapas/cocktail bar, this half-timbered inn also offers six rooms (€80 to €130). The seasonal regional menu is best enjoyed amidst the grape vines on the terrace.

Zum Freischütz PUB
(www.zum-freischuetz.de; Ziegenmarkt 11; ⊙11am-late Mon-Fri, 6pm-late Sat & Sun) A life-size bronze goat stands on the square near this characterful cafe overlooking Schwerin's old goat market. The storied pub has an old interior that features wooden chairs dating back decades. Sandwiches, soups and various cheap specials are served long into the night.

ℹ Information

Schwerin-Information (☑592 5212; www.schwerin.de; Markt 14; ⊙9am-7pm Mon-Fri, 10am-6pm Sat & Sun Apr-Oct, 9am-6pm Mon-Fri, 10am-4pm Sat & Sun Nov-Mar)

ℹ Getting There & Away

Train links include Hamburg (from €27, one hour), Rostock (from €20, one hour), Stralsund (from €33, two hours) and Wismar (€8, 30 minutes), with less frequent direct connections to/from Berlin (€35, 2¼ hours).

Wismar

☑03841 / POP 44,400

Wismar, a Hanseatic gem that's fast being discovered, joined the powerful trading league in the 13th century. For centuries it was in and out of Swedish control – hence the 'Swedish heads' dotted across town. The entire Altstadt was Unesco-listed in 2002. Quieter than Rostock or Stralsund, Wismar can fill up with visitors quickly in high season.

◉ Sights & Activities

The old harbour, Alter Hafen, with old boats swaying in the breeze, evokes the trading days of yore. **Adler-Schiffe** (☑01805-123 344; www.adler-schiffe.de; adult/child €9.50/5.50; ⊙daily Apr-Oct, weekends Nov-Mar) operates hour-long harbour cruises.

Markt SQUARE
Dominating the central Markt is the landmark **Wasserkunst** (waterworks, 1602), an ornate, 12-sided well that supplied Wismar's drinking water until 1897. Behind it, the red-brick **Alter Schwede** (1380), with its striking step-gabled facade, houses a restaurant and guesthouse.

The 19th-century Rathaus (town hall) at the square's northern end houses the excellent **Rathaus Historical Exhibition** (adult/child €2/1; ⊙10am-6pm). Note the 15th-century murals, a glass-covered medieval well, and the elaborate coffin of a Swedish general named Wrangel.

St-Nikolai-Kirche CHURCH
(St-Nikolai-Kirchhof; www.kirchen-in-wismar.de; admission €2; ⊙8am-8pm May-Sep, 10am-6pm Apr & Oct, 11am-4pm Nov-Mar) Of the three great red-brick churches that once rose above Wismar before WWII, only the sober red-brick St-Nikolai-Kirche, the largest of its kind in Europe, was left intact. Today it contains a font from its older sister church, the St-Marien-Kirche.

Fürstenhof HISTORIC BUILDING
The restored Italian Renaissance Fürstenhof is now the city courthouse. The facades are slathered in terracotta reliefs depicting episodes from folklore and the town's history.

🛏 Sleeping & Eating

Boats along Alter Hafen sell fresh fish and seafood from 9am to 6pm daily.

TOP CHOICE **Hotel Reingard** HOTEL €€
(☑284 972; www.hotel-reingard.de; Weberstrasse 18; s €68-72, d €98-102; P) This charismatic boutique hotel has a dozen artistic rooms, a leafy little garden and wonderfully idiosyncratic touches such as a nightly classical music lightshow playing across the facade.

Pension Chez Fasan HOTEL €
(☑213 425; www.unterkunft-pension-wismar.de; Bademutterstrasse 20a; s/d €25/47, s without bathroom €22) The 25 simple but perfectly comfortable rooms in these three linked houses, just one block north of the Markt, are fantastic value. Call ahead if you're not arriving during reception hours (normally 2pm to 8pm).

Alter Schwede SEAFOOD €
(☑283 552; mains €10-21; ⊙11.30am-late; ☑) Baltic eel with herbed potatoes, and catfish with mustard are among the specialities of this landmark spot. The facade alone is a tourist attraction, but the reproduction Swedish head over the door puts it over the top. Get a table out front and enjoy Markt action.

To'n Zägenkrog SEAFOOD €€
(☑282 716; www.ziegenkrug-wismar.de; Ziegenmarkt 10; mains €10-15; ⊙5-9pm) Excellent fish dishes are the mainstay of this cosy 1897-established pub. It's crammed with maritime mementoes and great harbour views.

SWEDISH HEADS

A 'Swedish head' isn't something you need to successfully assemble an IKEA bookcase. In Wismar, Swedish Heads refers to two baroque busts of Hercules that once graced mooring posts at the harbour entrance.

Semicomical, with great curling moustaches and wearing lions as hats, the statues are believed to have marked either the beginning of the harbour or the navigable channels within it. The originals were damaged when a Finnish barge rammed them in 1902, at which time replicas were made. One original is now in the Schabbellhaus (www.schabbellhaus.de; Schweinsbrücke 8), the town's historical museum (under renovation until at least 2014).

ℹ Information

Tourist office (☑251 3025; www.wismar.de; Am Markt 11; ⊙9am-6pm daily Apr-Oct, 9am-6pm Mon-Sat, 10am-4pm Sun Nov-Mar)

ℹ Getting There & Away

Trains travel every hour to/from Rostock (€12, 70 minutes) and Schwerin (€8, 40 minutes).

Rostock & Warnemünde

☑0381 / POP 202,700

Rostock is a major Baltic port and shipbuilding centre and was once an important Hanseatic trading city. Parts of the city centre, especially along Kröpeliner Strasse, retain the flavour of this period.

Its chief suburb – and chief attraction – is Warnemünde, 12km north of the centre. Among eastern Germany's most popular beach resorts, its broad, sandy beach is chocka-block with bathers on hot summer days.

◉ Sights

It takes just a couple of hours to see the city sights which cluster in the pedestrianised zone between Neuer Markt and Universitätsplatz.

TOP CHOICE Marienkirche   CHURCH
(☑453 325; www.marienkirche-rostock.de; Am Ziegenmarkt; €1.50 donation requested; ⊙10am-6pm Mon-Sat, 11.15am-5pm Sun May-Sep, 10am-4pm Mon-Sat, 11.15am-noon Sun Oct-Apr) Rostock's pride and joy, the Marienkirche, built in 1290, was the only one of its four main churches to survive WWII unscathed. Notable features include the 12m-high astrological clock (1470–72) and the Gothic bronze baptismal font (1290).

Kröpeliner Strasse & Universitätsplatz   SQUARE
Kröpeliner Strasse, a broad, shop-filled, cobblestone pedestrian mall lined with 15th- and 16th-century burghers' houses, runs from Neuer Markt west to the 55m-high Kröpeliner Tor (city gate).

At its centre is Universitätsplatz, a square lined with university buildings. At the southwestern end is the 13th-century convent Kloster Zum Heiligen Kreuz, which today houses the Kulturhistorisches Museum Rostock (☑203 590; www.kulturhistorisches-museum-rostock.de; Klosterhof 7; admission free; ⊙10am-6pm Tue-Sun), whose collection includes Victorian furniture and sculptures by Ernst Barlach.

🛏 Sleeping

Hanse Hostel   HOSTEL €
(☑128 6006; www.hanse-hostel.de; Doberaner Strasse 136; dm €14-18, s/d without bathroom €24/44, breakfast €4; ❁@🖧) On the edge of Rostock's trendy bar district, the KTV, is this family-run operation with great facilities spread over two buildings. Recently added rooms have private bathrooms (single/double €35/56). From the Hauptbahnhof, take tram 4 or 5 to the Volkstheater stop.

Hotel Kleine Sonne   HOTEL €€
(☑497 3153; www.die-kleine-sonne.de; Steinstrasse 7; per person €52-102; @🖧) This lovely place lives up to its name, the Little Sun, with sunny yellow and red detailing against otherwise starkly minimalist decor. Guests may use the wellness centre at the nearby Steigenberger Hotel Sonne.

Hotel-Pension Zum Kater   GUESTHOUSE €€
(☑548 210; www.pension-zum-kater.de; Alexandrinenstrasse 115; s/d from €72/100; 🅿) Less than 10 minutes' stroll from the beach in Warnemünde, and even closer to the harbour, this guesthouse is sweet and cosy. Get a room with a roof terrace. Short stays may incur slightly higher rates.

🍴 Eating

Excellent fish and *Wurst* stalls set up shop on Rostock's Neuer Markt and Warnemünde's harbour most mornings.

Café Central
CAFE €€

(☎490 4648; Leonhardstrasse 20; mains €6-15; ⊙from 10am) Café Central has cult status among Rostock's students, artists, hipsters and suits who loll around sipping long drinks on the banquettes or gabbing with friends at sidewalk tables. There are a lot of cheap ethnic restaurants nearby. It's 500m northwest of the Kröpeliner Tor.

Weineckeck Krahnstöver
PUB €€

(Grosse Wasser Strasse 30; mains €10-18; ⊙closed Sun) One side is a wine bar with a pub feel, the other side a proper restaurant: both sides have a loyal local following and offer a lengthy list of wines that you sip in the warm, old-fashioned atmosphere between dark wood walls.

Zur Kogge
GERMAN €

(☎493 4493; www.zur-kogge.de; Wokrenter-strasse 27; mains €9-17; ⊙11am-9pm Mon-Sat; ⊕) At this Rostock institution, cosy wooden booths are cradled by nautical decor and local fish dominate the menu. You can also stop by for coffee and cake between meal times, and there's an above-average kids' menu to boot.

Fischerklause
SEAFOOD €€

(☎525 16; www.fischer-klause.de; Am Strom 123; mains €9-15; ☎) One of Warnemünde's atmospheric old fishermen's cottages along Alter Strom crawls with tourists thanks to its fun ship's cabin decor and succulent fishy fare.

❶ Information

Tourist office (☎381 2222; www.rostock.de; Neuer Markt 3; ⊙10am-6pm Mon-Fri, to 4pm Sat & Sun, shorter hours May-Sep)

Warnemünde-Information (☎548 000; www.warnemuende.de; Am Strom 59; ⊙9am-6pm Mon-Fri, 10am-4pm Sat & Sun, shorter hours Nov-Feb)

❶ Getting There & Around

Ferries serving Denmark, Sweden, Latvia and Finland depart from Warnemünde's **Überseehafen** (Overseas Seaport; www.rostock-port.de).

There are frequent direct trains to Berlin (from €38, 2½ hours) and Hamburg (from €33, 2¼ hours), and hourly services to Stralsund (€15, one hour) and Schwerin (€20, one hour).

Rostock and Warnemünde are linked by frequent S-Bahn trains (single/day pass €2.70/5.40, 22 minutes).

Stralsund

☎03831 / POP 57,700

You instantly know you're next to the sea here. Possessing an unmistakable medieval profile, Stralsund was the second-most powerful member of the medieval Hanseatic League, after Lübeck. An attractive town of imposing churches and elegant town houses, it brims with classic red-brick Gothic gabled architecture and is great for getting a feel for Baltic culture.

◉ Sights

Alter Markt
SQUARE

Seven copper turrets and six triangular gables grace the red-brick Gothic facade of Stralsund's splendid **Rathaus** (1370). The upper portion of the northern facade, or *Schauwand* (show wall), has openings to prevent strong winds from knocking it over. Inside, the sky-lit colonnade boasts shiny black pillars on carved and painted bases; on the western side of the building is an ornate portal.

Through the Rathaus' eastern walkway you'll come to the main portal of the 1270 **Nikolaikirche** (☎299 799; www.nikolai-stralsund.de; adult/child €2/free; ⊙9am-7pm Mon-Sat, 1-5pm Sun May-Sep, 10am-6pm Mon-Sat, 1-5pm Sun Oct-Apr), which was modelled on Lübeck's Marienkirche and is filled with art treasures. The **main altar** (1708), designed by the baroque master Andreas Schlüter, shows the eye of God flanked by cherubs and capped by a depiction of the Last Supper. Also worth a closer look are the huge **high altar** (1470), showing scenes from Jesus' life, and, behind the altar, a 1394-built (but no longer operational) **astronomical clock**.

Opposite the Rathaus you'll find the **Wulflamhaus** (Alter Markt 5), a beautiful 15th-century town house named after an old mayor. Its turreted step gable imitates the Rathaus facade.

Marienkirche
CHURCH

(☎298 965; www.st-mariengemeinde-stralsund.de; ⊙9am-6pm Apr-Oct) The Neuer Markt is dominated by the massive 14th-century Marienkirche, another superb example of north German red-brick construction. You can climb the steep wooden steps up the tower for a sweeping view of the town, with its lovely red-tiled roofs, and over to Rügen Island. The ornate 17-century **organ** is a stunner.

WORTH A TRIP

RÜGEN ISLAND

Germany's largest island, Rügen is at times hectic, relaxed, windblown and naked – fitting, perhaps, since the resort tradition here reflects all aspects of Germany's recent past. In the 19th century, luminaries such as Einstein, Bismarck and Thomas Mann came to unwind in its fashionable coastal resorts. Later both Nazi and GDR regimes made Rügen the holiday choice for dedicated comrades.

The largest and most celebrated seaside resort is **Binz**, an alluring confection of ornate, white 19th-century villas, white sand and blue water. North of here, **Prora** was built by the Nazis as the 'world's largest holiday camp', a set of outside buildings hugging one of the island's most beautiful beaches.

The ruggedly beautiful area further north is protected as the **Jasmund National Park**. Its highlight is the **Stubbenkammer**, where jagged white-chalk cliffs plunge into the jade-coloured sea. Also here is Rügen's highest point – the 117m **Königsstuhl** – which offers views that inspired such artists as Caspar David Friedrich. The best view of the peak itself is from the **Viktoria-Sicht** some hundred metres to the east.

Other popular tourist destinations are **Jagdschloss Granitz** (1834), a castle surrounded by lush forest, and the twin lighthouses at **Kap Arkona** on the island's northern edge.

Tourismuszentrale Rügen (www.ruegen.de) and the **tourist office** (www.ostseebad-binz.de; Kurverwaltung, Heinrich-Heine-Strasse 7; ⊙9am-6pm Mon-Fri, 10am-6pm Sat & Sun Feb-Oct, 9am-4pm Mon-Fri, 10am-4pm Sat & Sun Nov-Jan) in Binz are your best bets for information.

Direct IC trains connect Binz with Hamburg (€58, four hours) and beyond and there is hourly service to Stralsund (€12, 50 minutes) as well. To get around the island and really appreciate it, a car is vital.

TOP CHOICE Ozeaneum
AQUARIUM

(☎265 0610; www.ozeaneum.de; Hafeninsel Stralsund; adult/child €14/8, combination ticket with Meeresmuseum €18/11; ⊙9.30am-9pm Jun–mid-Sep, 9.30am-7pm mid-Sep–May) In an arctic-white wavelike building that leaps out from the surrounding red-brick warehouses, the state-of-the-art Ozeaneum takes you into an underwater world of creatures from the Baltic and North Seas and the Atlantic Ocean up to the polar latitudes.

Meeresmuseum
AQUARIUM

(Maritime Museum; ☎265 010; www.meeres museum.de; Katharinenberg 14-20; adult/child €7.50/5, combination ticket with Ozeaneum €18/11; ⊙10am-6pm Jun-Sep, 10am-5pm Oct-May) Affiliated with the Ozeaneum, the Meeresmuseum aquarium is in a 13th-century ex-convent. Exhibits include a popular huge sea-turtle tank and polychromatic tropical fish.

🛏 Sleeping & Eating

TOP CHOICE Altstadt Hotel Peiss
HOTEL €€

(☎303 580; www.altstadt-pension-peiss.de; Tribseer Strasse 15; s €50-85, d €55-115; P🐾🛜) Thirteen spacious rooms with Paul Gauguin prints and sparkling bathrooms combine with cheery service at this bright and appealing guesthouse. With a terrace, small garden and bike rack, it's especially popular with cyclists.

Younior Hotel
HOSTEL

(☎0800-233 388 234; www.younior-hotel.de; Tribseer Damm 78; dm €21-26; P🐾@) In an expanse of parkland near the train station, a grand old 1897 building that once housed Stralsund's railway offices now has a much more active life as a 300-bed hostel. Dorms have comfy, capsule-like triple-decker bunks, and fun facilities include a guest-only bar, a BBQ area and beach volleyball.

TOP CHOICE Restaurant

Esszimmer
MODERN EUROPEAN €€€

(www.esszimmer-stralsund.de; Am Querkanal 5; lunch mains from €12, set dinner menus from €40; ⊙noon-2.30pm, 5.30-10.30pm Thu-Tue) Esszimmer has a fresh and ever-changing menu that has a creative take on local seasonal foods and dishes. Service is excellent. Tables outside catch the clang of harbour bells in summer.

Hansekeller
GERMAN €€

(www.hansekeller-stralsund.de; Mönchstrasse 48; mains €8-16) Entering an inconspicuous archway and descending a flight of steps brings you to this 16th-century cross-vaulted brick cellar illuminated by glowing lamps and flickering candles. Taking a seat near the open kitchen lets you watch its chefs prepare regional specialities.

Nur Fisch SEAFOOD €€
(☏306 609; www.nurfisch.de; Heilgeiststrasse 92; mains €6-15; ⊙10am-6pm Mon-Fri, 11am-2pm Sat) Simple canteen-style bistro dedicated to marine delights – from fish sandwiches to sumptuous platters of seafood and even a fine seafood paella.

ℹ Information

Tourist office (☏246 90; www.stralsundtouris mus.de; Alter Markt 9; ⊙10am-6pm Mon-Fri, to 4pm Sat & Sun May-Oct, 10am-5pm Mon-Fri, to 2pm Sat Nov-Apr)

ℹ Getting There & Away

Regional trains travel to/from Rostock (€15, one hour), Berlin Hauptbahnhof (from €40, 3½ hours) and other towns in the region at least every two hours.

BAVARIA

From the cloud-shredding Alps to the fertile Danube plain, Bavaria is a place that keeps its clichéd promises. Story-book castles bequeathed by an oddball king poke through dark forest, cowbells tinkle in flower-filled meadows, the thwack of palm on lederhosen accompanies the clump of frothy stein on timber benches, and medieval walled towns go about their time-warped business.

But diverse Bavaria offers much more than the chocolate-box idyll. Learn about Bavaria's state-of-the-art motor industry in Munich, discover its Nazi past in Nuremberg and Berchtesgaden, sip world-class wines in Würzburg, get on the Wagner trail in Bayreuth or seek out countless kiddy attractions across the state. Destinations are often described as possessing 'something for everyone', but in Bavaria's case this is no exaggeration.

Munich

☏089 / POP 1.38 MILLION
Munich is a flourishing success story that revels in its own contradictions. It's the natural habitat of well-heeled power dressers and lederhosen-clad thigh-slappers, Mediterranean-style street cafes and olde-worlde beer halls, high-brow art and high-tech industry. If you're looking for Alpine clichés, they're all here, but the Bavarian capital also has plenty of unexpected cards down its Dirndl.

Statistics show Munich is enticing more visitors than ever, especially in summer and during Oktoberfest. Munich's walkable centre retains a small-town air but holds some world-class sights, especially its art galleries and museums, along with a king's ransom of royal Bavarian heritage.

History

Munich derives its name from monks who first settled here in the 8th century, but the town itself was only first mentioned in an official document in 1158. In 1240 the city passed to the Wittelsbach dynasty who would rule over Munich (as well as Bavaria) until the 1918.

In the Middle Ages, Munich prospered as a salt trade hub but was hit hard by the outbreak of the plague in 1349. When the epidemic finally subsided 150 years later, the *Schäffler* (coopers) invented a ritualistic dance to remind residents of their good fortune. The *Schäfflertanz* is re-enacted daily by the little figures of the Glockenspiel (carillon) on Marienplatz.

By the early 19th century, furious monument-building gave Munich its spectacular architecture and wide Italianate avenues. Culture and the arts flourished, especially under King Ludwig I. His grandson, Ludwig II, took royal expenditure a bit too far; his grandiose projects, including numerous lavish palaces, bankrupted the royal house and threatened the government. Ironically, today they are the biggest money-spinners in Bavaria's booming tourism industry.

By 1901 Munich had a population of half a million souls but last century was a hard time for most of them. WWI practically starved the city; the Nazis first rose to prominence here and the next world war nearly wiped the city off the map. The 1972 Olympic Games ended in tragedy when 17 people were killed in a terrorist hostage-taking incident.

Today Munich is recognised for its high living standards, the most millionaires per capita in Germany after Hamburg, and for an appreciation of the good life.

◉ Sights

ALTSTADT

Marienplatz SQUARE
(Ⓢ Marienplatz) The heart and soul of the Altstadt, Marienplatz is a popular gathering

Central Munich

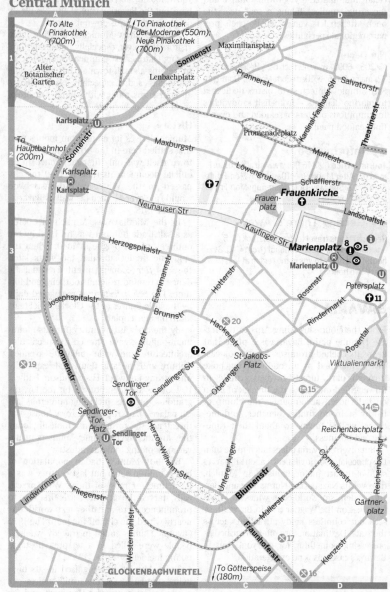

The square is dominated by the heavily ornamented neo-Gothic **Neues Rathaus** (New Town Hall) whose highlight is the en-

GERMANY MUNICH

Lothringen, while the bottom half portrays the *Schäfflertanz*). For pinpointing Munich's landmarks without losing your breath, catch the lift up the 85m-tall **tower** (adult/child €2/€1; ⊙9am-7pm Mon-Fri, 10am-7pm Sat & Sun).

Altes Rathaus   HISTORICAL BUILDING
(Old Town Hall; Marienplatz; Ⓢ Marienplatz, Ⓡ Marienplatz) The eastern side of Marienplatz is dominated by the Altes Rathaus (Old Town Hall). On 9 November 1938 Joseph Goebbels gave a hate-filled speech here that launched the nationwide *Kristallnacht* pogroms. Today it houses the adorable **Spielzeugmuseum** (Toy Museum;

dearing **Glockenspiel** whose 43 bells and 32 figures perform two actual historic events. The top half tells the story of a knight's tournament held in 1568 to celebrate the marriage of Duke Wilhelm V to Renata of

DON'T MISS

RESIDENZ

The Residenz is a suitably grand palace that reflects the splendour and power of the Bavarian rulers who lived here from 1385 to 1918. Taking up half the compound is the treasure-packed **Residenzmuseum** (📞290 671; www.residenz-muenchen.de; adult/child €7/free, combination ticket for the museum, Schatzkammer & Cuvilliés-Theater €13/free; ⊕9am-6pm Apr–mid-Oct, 10am-5pm mid-Oct–Mar). Start at the **Grottenhof** (Grotto Court), home of the wonderful **Perseusbrunnen** (Perseus Fountain), with its namesake holding the dripping head of Medusa. Next door is the famous **Antiquarium**, a barrel-vaulted hall smothered in frescoes and built to house the Wittelsbach's enormous antique collection. It's widely regarded as the finest Renaissance interior north of the Alps.

Upstairs are the **Kurfürstenzimmer** (Electors Rooms), with some stunning Italian portraits and a passage lined with two dozen views of Italy. Also up here are François Cuvilliés' **Reiche Zimmer** (Rich Rooms), a six-room extravaganza of exuberant rococo. More rococo magic awaits in the **Ahnengallery** (Ancestors Gallery), a chronological roll call of 121 portraits of Bavarian rulers. The superb rococo **Steinzimmer** (Stone Rooms) are awash in intricately patterned and coloured marble.

The Residenzmuseum entrance also leads to the **Schatzkammer der Residenz** (Residence Treasury; adult/concession/under 18yr with parents €7/6/free; ⊕9am-6pm Apr–mid-Oct, 10am-5pm mid-Oct–Mar), a veritable banker's bonus worth of jewel-encrusted bling of yesteryear, from golden toothpicks to finely crafted swords, miniatures in ivory to gold entombed cosmetics trunks.

Another highlight is the **Cuvilliés-Theater** (adult/child €3.50/free; ⊕2-6pm Mon-Sat, from 9am Sun Apr-Jul & mid-Sep–mid-Oct, 9am-6pm daily Aug–mid-Sep, shorter hours mid-Oct–Mar), named for its architect and one of Europe's finest rococo theatres. Famous for hosting the premiere of Mozart's opera *Idomeneo*, restoration work in the mid-2000s revived the theatre's former glory, and its stage once again hosts high-brow musical and operatic performances.

www.toymuseum.de; Marienplatz 15; adult/child €4/1; ⊕10am-5.30pm) with its huge collection of rare and precious toys from Europe and the US.

St Peterskirche CHURCH
(Church of St Peter; Rindermarkt 1; church admission free, tower adult/child €1.50/1; ⊕tower 9am-5.30pm Mon-Fri, from 10am Sat & Sun; ⑤Marienplatz, ⒭Marienplatz) Some 306 steps divide you at ground level and the best view of central Munich from the 92m tower of St Peterskirche, Munich's oldest church (1150). Also known as Alter Peter (Old Peter), it's a virtual textbook of art through the centuries, with highlights including the Gothic St-Martin-Altar, Johann Baptist Zimmermann's baroque ceiling fresco, and Ignaz Günther's rococo sculptures.

Viktualienmarkt MARKET
(⊕Mon-Fri & Sat morning; ⑤Marienplatz, ⒭Marienplatz) Viktualienmarkt is a feast of flavours and one of Germany's finest gourmet markets where many of the stalls have been run by generations of the same family. Prices are predictably high, but so is the

quality and many items sold here are hard to find elsewhere.

FREE **Hofbräuhaus** BEER HALL
(www.hofbraeuhaus.de; Am Platzl 9; ⑤Marienplatz, ⒭Marienplatz) Even teetotalling cliché-haters will at some point gravitate, out of simple curiosity, to the Hofbräuhaus, the world's most celebrated beer hall. The writhing hordes of tourists tend to overshadow the sterling interior, where dainty twirled flowers and Bavarian flags adorn the medieval vaults.

Frauenkirche CHURCH
(Church of Our Lady; Frauenplatz 1; tower €2; ⊕7am-7pm Sat-Wed, to 8.30pm Thu, to 6pm Fri) This 15th-century church is Munich's spiritual heart. No other building in the central city may stand taller than the 99m of its onion-domed twin towers. From April to October, you can enjoy panoramic city views from the **south tower**.

Michaelskirche CHURCH
(Church of St Michael; Kaufingerstrasse 52; crypt admission €2; ⊕crypt 9.30am-4.30pm Mon-Fri,

9.30am-2.30pm Sat & Sun; ⑤Karlsplatz, ⓇKarl-splatz, ⓇKarlsplatz). Completed in 1597 as the then-largest Renaissance church north of the Alps, St Michaels boasts an impressive unsupported barrel-vaulted ceiling but is really most famous as the final resting place of King Ludwig II, whose humble tomb in the crypt is usually drowned in flowers. The building has been, and is set to be, under heavy renovation for years.

Bier & Oktoberfestmuseum   MUSEUM
(Beer&OktoberfestMuseum;www.bier-und-oktober festmuseum.de; Sterneckerstrasse 2; adult/concession €4/2.50; ⊘1-5pm Tue-Sat; ⓇIsartor, ⓇIsartor) If you can't be in town for the real thing, head to this popular museum to learn all about Bavarian suds and the world's most famous booze-up. The four floors heave with old brewing vats, historic photos and some of the earliest Oktoberfest regalia.

Asamkirche   CHURCH
(Sendlinger Strasse 34; ⑤Sendlinger Tor, ⓇSendlinger Tor) Though pocket-sized, late baroque Asamkirche (1746) is as rich and epic as a giant's treasure chest. Its creators, the brothers Cosmas Damian and Egid Quirin, dipped deeply into their considerable talent box to swathe every inch of wall space with paintings, *Putti* (cherubs), gold leaf and stucco flourishes.

MAXVORSTADT, SCHWABING & ENGLISCHER GARTEN
North of the Altstadt, Maxvorstadt is home to Munich's *Kunstareal* (art district), a cluster of top-drawer art museums. It segues into cafe-filled Schwabing which rubs up against the vast Englischer Garten.

Alte Pinakothek   ART MUSEUM
(www.pinakothek.de; Barer Strasse 27; adult/child €7/5, Sun €1, audioguide €4.50; ⊘10am-8pm Tue, to 6pm Wed-Sun; ⓇPinakotheken, ⓇPinakotheken) Munich's main repository of Old European Masters is crammed with all the major players that decorated canvases between the 14th and 18th centuries.

The collection is world famous for its exceptional quality and depth, especially when it comes to German masters such as Lucas Cranach the Elder and Albrecht Dürer. Rubens fans also have reason to rejoice thanks, in part, to the 6m-high *Last Judgment* in its custom-designed hall. The Italians are represented by Botticelli, Raphael, Titian and many others, while the Spaniards field such heavy hitters as El Greco, Murillo and Velázquez.

Neue Pinakothek   ART MUSEUM
(www.pinakothek.de; Barer Strasse 29; adult/child €7/5, Sun €1; ⊘10am-6pm Thu-Mon, to 8pm Wed; ⓇPinakotheken, ⓇPinakotheken) Picking up where the Alte Pinakothek leaves off, the Neue Pinakothek harbours a well-respected collection of 19th- and early 20-century paintings and sculpture, from rococo to *Jugendstil* (art nouveau).

All the main household names get wall space here, including crowd-pleasing Impressionists such as Monet, Cézanne, Degas and Van Gogh. Memorable canvases also include the brooding landscapes of German Romantic painter Caspar David Friedrich and those of local artists Carl Spitzweg and Franz Lenbach.

Pinakothek der Moderne   ART MUSEUM
(www.pinakothek.de; Barer Strasse 40; adult/child €10/7, Sun €1; ⊘10am-6pm Tue, Wed & Fri-Sun, 10am-8pm Thu; ⓇPinakotheken, ⓇPinakotheken) This vast modern art museum has a spectacular four-storey interior centred on an eye-like dome which spreads soft natural light throughout white galleries.

The museum unites four significant collections under a single roof, most notably the **State Gallery of Modern Art**, which showcases exemplary modern classics by Picasso, Klee, Dalí, Kandinsky and more recent big shots like Andy Warhol, Cy Twombly and Joseph Beuys.

Retro fans gravitate to the **New Collection** which focuses on applied design from the industrial revolution via art nouveau

---

LOCAL KNOWLEDGE

NO WAVE GOODBYE

Munich is famous for beer, sausages and surfing. Yep, you read that right. Just go to the southern tip of the English Garden at Prinzregentenstrasse and you'll see scores of people leaning over a bridge to cheer on wetsuit-clad daredevils as they 'hang 10' on an artificially created wave in the Eisbach creek. It's only a single wave, but it's a damn fine one. In fact, the surfers are such an attraction, the tourist office even includes them in its brochures.

and Bauhaus to today. VW Beetles, Eames chairs and early Apple Macs stand alongside more obscure interwar items that wouldn't be out of place in a Kraftwerk video.

Also here is the State Graphics Collection, which boasts drawings, prints and engravings by such masters as Leonardo da Vinci and Paul Cézanne, and the Architecture Museum, which illustrates how such famous practiciners as baroque architect Balthasar Neumann and Bauhaus maven Le Corbusier have influenced the genre.

TOP CHOICE Englischer Garten PARK

(S Universität) The sprawling English Garden is among Europe's biggest city parks – bigger than even London's Hyde Park and New York's Central Park – and a favourite playground for locals and visitors alike.

Several historic follies lend the park a playful charm. The wholly unexpected Chinesischer Turm (Chinese Tower), now at the heart of Munich's oldest beer garden, was built in the 18th century during a pan-European craze for all things oriental. Further south, at the top of a gentle hill, stands the heavily photographed Monopteros (1838), a small Greek temple whose ledges are often knee-to-knee with dangling legs belonging to people admiring the view of the Munich skyline.

Further Afield

Schloss Nymphenburg PALACE

(www.schloss-nymphenburg.de; adult/child €6/5; 9am-6pm Apr–mid-Oct, 10am-4pm mid-Oct–Mar; Schloss Nymphenburg) This command-ing palace and its lavish gardens sprawl around 5km northwest of the Altstadt. Begun in 1664 as a villa for Electress Adelaide of Savoy, the stately pile was extended over the next century to create the royal family's summer residence.

The main palace building consists of a large villa and two wings of creaking parquet floors and sumptuous period rooms. Right at the beginning of the self-guided tour comes the highpoint of the entire Schloss, the Schönheitsgalerie (Gallery of Beauties), housed in the former apartments of Queen Caroline. Some 38 portraits of attractive females chosen by an admiring King Ludwig I peer prettily from the walls.

Further along the tour route comes the Queen's Bedroom, which still contains the sleigh bed on which Ludwig II was born, and the King's Chamber resplendent with 3D ceiling frescoes.

Also in the main building is the Marstall-Museum (adult/concession €4.50/3.50; 9am-6pm Apr–mid-Oct, 10am-4pm mid-Oct–Mar), displaying royal coaches and riding gear. This includes Ludwig II's fairy-tale-like rococo sleigh, ingeniously fitted with oil lamps for his crazed nocturnal outings.

BMW Museum MUSEUM

(www.bmw-welt.de; adult/child €12/6; 10am-6pm Tue-Sun) The BMW Museum is like no other car museum on the planet. The seven themed 'houses' examine the development of BMW's product line and include sections on motorcycles and motor racing. However, the interior design of this truly unique building, with its curvy retro feel, futuristic bridg-

---

DON'T MISS

OKTOBERFEST

Hordes come to Munich for Oktoberfest (www.oktoberfest.de), running the 15 days before the first Sunday in October. Reserve accommodation well ahead and go early in the day so you can grab a seat in one of the hangar-sized beer 'tents'. The action takes place at the Theresienwiese grounds, about a 10-minute walk southwest of the Hauptbahnhof. While there is no entrance fee, those €9 1L steins of beer (called Mass) add up fast. Although its origins are in the marriage celebrations of Crown Prince Ludwig in 1810, there's nothing regal about this beery bacchanalia now: expect mobs, expect to meet new and drunken friends, expect decorum to vanish as night sets in and you'll have a blast.

A few tips:

» Locals call it Wiesn (meadow)

» The Hofbräu tent is big with tourists

» The Augustiner tent draws traditionalists

» Traditional Oktoberfest beer should be a rich copper colour; order it instead of the tourist-satisfying pale lager

es, squares and huge backlit wall screens, almost upstages the exhibits.

Deutsches Museum
MUSEUM

(📞21 791; www.deutsches-museum.de; Museuminsel 1; adult/child €8.50/3; ⊙9am-5pm; 🚇Deutsches Museum) Spending a few hours in this temple to technology is an eye-opening journey of discovery and a likely hit with young, sponge-like minds. There are tons of interactive displays (including glass blowing and papermaking), live demonstrations and experiments, model coal and salt mines, and engaging sections on cave paintings, geodesy, microelectronics and astronomy. In the fabulous KinderReich (Childrens Kingdom; ⊙9am-4.30pm), 1000 activities, from a kid-size mouse wheel to a fully explorable fire engine and heaps of colourful blocks, await.

🖙 Tours

Radius Tours
GUIDED TOUR

(📞543 487 7720; www.radiustours.com; opp track 32, Hauptbahnhof; ⊙8.30am-6pm Apr-Oct, to 2pm Nov-Mar) Entertaining and informative English-language tours include the two-hour pay-what-you-like Priceless Munich Walk (⊙10am daily), the fascinating 2½-hour Hitler & The Third Reich Tour (adult/student €12/10; ⊙3pm Apr–mid-Oct, 11.30am Fri-Tue mid-Oct–Mar), and the three-hour Prost! Beer & Food tour (adult/student €29/27; ⊙6pm selected days). The company also runs popular excursions to Neuschwanstein, Salzburg and Dachau as well as a range of other themed tours.

Munich Walk Tours
WALKING TOUR

(📞2423 1767; www.munichwalktours.de; Arnulfstrasse 2; tours from €12) In addition to running an almost identical roster of tours to Munich's other tour companies and acting as an agent for them (see website for times and prices), these guys also rent out bicycles (€15 per 24 hours) and offer internet access at Thomas-Wimmer-Ring 1 (€1 per 45 minutes).

Mike's Bike Tours
BIKE TOURS

(📞2554 3987; www.mikesbiketours.com; departs Altes Rathaus, Marienplatz; tours from €24) This outfit runs guided bike tours of the city from the Altes Rathaus on Marienplatz. The standard tour is around four hours long (with a one-hour beer garden break; lunch not included); the extended tour goes for seven hours and covers 15km.

City Bus 100
BUS

Ordinary city bus that runs from the Hauptbahnhof to the Ostbahnhof via 21 of the city's museums and galleries.

🛌 Sleeping

Munich has no shortage of places to stay – except during Oktoberfest or some busy summer periods, when the wise (meaning those with a room) will have booked. Many budget and midrange places can be found in the cheerless streets around the train station. If you can, avoid this area as you'll find hotels with more charm and atmosphere elsewhere.

Hotel Blauer Bock
HOTEL €€

(📞231 780; www.hotelblauerbock.de; Sebastiansplatz 9; s €55-99, d €90-153; 🛜; 🚇Marienplatz, 🚇Marienplatz) A stuffed olive's throw away from the Viktualienmarkt, this simple hotel has successfully slipped through the net of gentrification to become the Altstadt's best deal. The cheapest, unmodernised rooms have shared facilities, the updated ensuite chambers are of a 21st-century vintage and all are quiet, despite the location. Great restaurant to boot.

Hotel Cocoon
DESIGN HOTEL €€

(📞5999 3907; www.hotel-cocoon.de; Lindwurmstrasse 35; s/d €79/99; 🚇Sendlinger Tor, 🚇Sendlinger Tor) If retro-design is your thing, you just struck gold. Things kick off in the reception with its faux '70s veneer and suspended '60s ball chairs, and continue in the rooms, all identical and decorated in cool retro oranges and greens.

The glass showers actually stand in the sleeping area, with only a kitschy Alpine meadow scene veiling life's vitals. Another branch, Cocoon Stachus (Adolf-Kolping-Strasse 11), opened in 2012.

Schiller 5
HOTEL €€

(📞515 040; www.schiller5.com; Schillerstrasse 5; s/d from €102/144; 🅿🗶@; 🚇Hauptbahnhof, 🚇Hauptbahnhof, 🚇Hauptbahnhof) Not only are the pads at this semi-apartment hotel smartly trimmed, you also get a lot for your euro here in the shape of a well-equipped kitchenette, sound system, coffee machine and extra large bed. Street noise may be an issue.

Sofitel Munich Bayerpost
HOTEL €€€

(📞599 480; www.sofitel.com; Bayerstrasse 12; s/d from €140/160; 🅿🗶@🗶; 🚇Hauptbahnhof, 🚇Hauptbahnhof Süd, 🚇Hauptbahnhof) This high-concept jewel wraps all that's great about Munich – history, innovation, elegance, the art of living – into one neat and appealing package. Be sure to make time for the luxurious spa whose grotto-like pool juts into the atrium lobby.

Hotel am Viktualienmarkt
HOTEL €€

(☑231 1090; www.hotel-am-viktualienmarkt.de; Utzschneiderstrasse 14; d €50-120; ☎; Ⓢ Marienplatz, Ⓡ Marienplatz) Owners Elke and her daughter Stephanie run this good-value property with panache and a sunny attitude. The best of the up-to-date 26 rooms have wooden floors and framed poster art. All this, plus the city-centre location, makes it a superb deal.

Meininger's
HOSTEL, HOTEL €

(☑5499 8023; www.meininger-hostels.de; Landsbergerstrasse 20; dm/s/d without breakfast from €15/45/80; @☎☒; Ⓡ Holzapfelstrasse.) About 800m west of the Hauptbahnhof, this hostel-hotel combo has basic, clean, bright rooms with big dorms divided into two for a bit of privacy. Room rates vary wildly depending on the date, special events and occupancy. Breakfast is an extra €4, bike hire €12 per day.

Hotelissimo Haberstock
HOTEL €€

(☑557 855; www.hotelissimo.com; Schillerstrasse 4; s/d from €74/104; ☎; Ⓢ Hauptbahnhof, Ⓡ Hauptbahnhof, Ⓡ Hauptbahnhof) The cheery decor at this value-for-money pick reflects the vision of the owners, a husband-and-wife team with a knack for colour, fabrics and design.

Wombats City Hostel Munich
HOSTEL €

(☑5998 9180; www.wombats-hostels.com; Senefelderstrasse 1; dm €12-24, d from €70; @☎; Ⓢ Hauptbahnhof, Ⓡ Hauptbahnhof) This professionally run affair near the train station has a whopping 300 dorm beds plus private rooms. Dorms come with ensuite facilities, sturdy lockers and comfy pine bunks. A free welcome drink awaits in the bar, but breakfast is €3.80 extra.

La Maison
DESIGN HOTEL €€

(☑3303 5550; www.hotel-la-maison.com; Occamstrasse 24; s/d from €109/119; Ⓟ❋❄@; Ⓢ Münchner Freiheit) Discerningly retro, this sassy number flaunts heated oak floors, jet-black basins and starkly contrasting design throughout. Cool bar on ground level.

Gästehaus Englischer Garten
GUESTHOUSE €€

(☑383 9410; www.hotelenglischergarten.de; Liebergesellstrasse 8; s €68-177, d €79-177; Ⓟ@☎; Ⓢ Münchner Freiheit) Cosily inserted into a 200-year-old ivy-clad mill, this small guesthouse on the edge of the English Garden of-

fers a Bavarian version of the British B&B experience. Not all rooms are ensuite, but the breakfast is generous and there's cycle hire (€12 per day).

Hotel Mariandl
HOTEL €€

(☑552 9100; www.mariandl.com; Goethestrasse 51; s €65-115, d €70-165; Ⓢ Sendlinger Tor, Ⓡ Sendlinger Tor) If you like your history laced with quirkiness, you'll find both aplenty in this rambling neo-Gothic mansion where rooms ooze art noveau flair with hand-selected antiques and ornamented ceilings. Breakfast is served until 4pm in the Vienna-style downstairs cafe, which also has live jazz or classical music nightly.

Hotel Uhland
HOTEL €€

(☑543 350; www.hotel-uhland.de; Uhlandstrasse 1; s/d from €69/87; Ⓟ☎; Ⓢ Theresienwiese) The Uhland is an enduring favourite with regulars who expect their hotel to feel like a home away from home. Three generations of family are constantly finding ways to improve their guests' experience, be it with wi-fi, bathroom phones, ice cubes, bike rentals or mix-your-own organic breakfast muesli.

Tent
CAMPGROUND €

(☑141 4300; www.the-tent.com; In den Kirschen 30; tent bunk/floor space €10.50/7.50, tent pitch from €11; ☺Jun-Nov; Ⓡ Botanischer Garten) A kilometre north of Schloss Nymphenburg, this youth-oriented camping ground has classic tent pitches, as well as a 160-bunk main tent with floor space and foam mats for shoe-string nomads.

✖ Eating

TOP CHOICE Fraunhofer
BAVARIAN €€

(Fraunhoferstrasse 9; mains €7-17.50; ☺4pm-1am; ✎; Ⓡ Müllerstrasse) With its screechy parquet floors, stuccoed ceilings, wood panelling and virtually no trace that the last century even happened, this characterful brewpub is one of the city centre's best places to explore the region with a fork. The menu also features at least a dozen vegetarian dishes as well as local fish.

Prinz Myshkin
VEGETARIAN €€

(☑265 596; www.prinzmyshkin.com; Hackenstrasse 2; mains €10-17; ☺11am-12.30am; ✎; Ⓢ Marienplatz, Ⓡ Marienplatz) Munich's premier meat-free dining spot fills out an open-plan, but strangely intimate vaulted dining space in a former brewery with health-conscious eaters. Join them in savouring such imaginative dishes as tofu stroganoff, 'Save the Tuna' pizza and succulent curries.

Wirtshaus in der Au BAVARIAN €€
(☑448 1400; Lilienstrasse 51; mains €8-19; ☺5pm-midnight Mon-Fri, from 10am Sat & Sun; ☐Deutsches Museum) Though this traditional Bavarian restaurant has a solid 21st-century vibe, it's that time-honoured staple, the dumpling, that's been declared top speciality here. Once a brewery, the space-rich indoor dining area has chunky tiled floors, a lofty ceiling and a crackling fireplace in winter. When spring springs, the beer garden fills.

Königsquelle ALPINE €€
(☑220 071; Baaderplatz 2; mains €9-18; ☺dinner; ☐Isartor, ☐Isartor) This Munich institution is well loved for its attentive service, expertly prepared food, and dark, well-stocked hardwood bar (with a great selection of malt whiskys). The handwritten, Alpine-inflected menu hopscotches from schnitzel to linguine and goat's cheese to cannelloni.

Tantris FINE DINING €€€
(☑361 9590; www.tantris.de; Johann-Fichte-Strasse 7; menu from €75; ☺lunch & dinner Tue-Sat; ☐Dietlindenstrasse) Tantris means 'the search for perfection' and here, at one of Germany's most famous restaurants, they're not far off it. The interior design is full-bodied '70s – all postbox reds, truffle blacks and illuminated yellows – the food gourmet sublimity and the service sometimes as unintrusive as it is efficient. Great wine cellar to boot.

Weisses Brauhaus BAVARIAN €€
(Tal 7; mains €8-15; ☐Marienplatz, ☐Marienplatz) This brewpub's *Weisswurst* (veal sausage) sets the standard for the rest to aspire to; sluice down a pair with the unsurpassed Schneider Weissbier. At night, the dining halls are charged with red-faced, ale-infused hilarity where Alpine whoops accompany the rabble-rousing oompah band.

La Vecchia Masseria ITALIAN €€
(Mathildenstrasse 3; mains €6-15; ☺11.30am-12.30am; ☐Sendlinger Tor, ☐Sendlinger Tor) One of Munich's more typically Italian *osterie*, this loud but still romantic place has earthy wood tables, antique tin buckets, baskets and clothing irons conjuring up the ambience of an Apennine farmhouse.

Bergwolf FAST FOOD €
(Fraunhoferstrasse 17; ☺noon-2am Mon-Thu, noon-4am Fri & Sat, noon-10pm Sun, closed 3-6pm Sun-Fri; ☐Fraunhoferstrasse) At this favourite pit

---

BEER HALLS & BEER GARDENS

Beer drinking is not just an integral part of Munich's entertainment scene, it's a reason to visit. Beer halls can be vast, boozy affairs seating thousands, or much more modest neighbourhood hang outs. The same goes for beer gardens. What's common is a certain camaraderie among strangers, huge 1L glasses of beer and lots of pretzels and sausages. In beer gardens you are usually allowed to bring your own picnic as long as you sit at tables without tablecloths and order something to drink.

Here are our top choices:

Augustiner Bräustuben (Landsberger Strasse 19; ☺10am-midnight; ☐Holzapfelstrasse) At this authentic beer hall inside the actual Augustiner brewery, the Bavarian grub here is superb, especially the *Schweinshaxe* (pork knuckles). Giant black draught horses are stabled behind glass on your way to the restroom. It's about 700m west of the Hauptbahnhof.

Hofbräuhaus (Am Platzl 9; ☺9am-11.30pm; ☐Marienplatz, ☐Kammerspiele, ☐Marienplatz) The ultimate cliché of Munich beer halls where tourists arrive by the busload but no one seems to mind. Wander upstairs for echoes of the past, a small museum and possibly a seat.

Hirschgarten (Hirschgartenallee 1; ☺11am-11pm; ☐Kriemhildenstrasse, ☐Laim) The Everest of Munich beer gardens can accommodate up to 8000 Augustiner lovers, but still manages to feel airy and uncluttered. It's in a lovely spot in a former royal hunting preserve a short walk south of Schloss Nymphenburg.

Chinesischer Turm (Chinese Tower; ☑383 8730; Englischer Garten 3; ☺10am-11pm; ☐Chinesischer Turm, ☐Tivolistrasse) This one's hard to ignore because of its English Garden location and pedigree as Munich's oldest beer garden (open since 1791). Join a motley crowd of fellow beer lovers around the wooden pagoda, showered by the strained sounds of possibly the world's drunkest oompah band.

stop for night owls, the poison of choice is *Currywurst*, a sliced spicy sausage provocatively dressed in a curried ketchup and best paired with a pile of crisp fries. Hangover prevention at its tastiest.

Götterspeise
CAFE €

(Jahnstrasse 30; snacks from €3; ⊙8am-7pm Mon-Fri, 9am-6pm Sat; 🚋Müllerstrasse) The name of this place translates as 'food of the gods' and the edible in question is that most sinful of treats, chocolate. This comes in many forms, both liquid and solid, but there are also teas, coffees and cakes, and we love the little smokers' perches outside for puffing chocoholics.

Cafe an der Uni
CAFE €

(Ludwigstrasse 24; snacks & mains €5-9; ⊙8am-1am Mon-Fri, from 9am Sat & Sun; 🚇💵; Ⓢ Universität) Anytime is a good time to be at charismatic CADU. Enjoy breakfast (served until a hangover-friendly 11.30pm!), a cuppa Java or a Helles in the lovely garden hidden by a wall from busy Ludwigstrasse.

Drinking

Apart from the beer halls and garden, Munich has no shortage of lively pubs. Schwabing and the Glockenbachviertel are good places to follow your ears. Many places serve food; most are open until 1am or later on weekends.

Alter Simpl
PUB

(Türkenstrasse 57; ⊙11am-3am Mon-Fri, 11am-4am Sat & Sun; 🚋Schellingstrasse) Thomas Mann and Hermann Hesse used to knock 'em back at this well-scuffed and wood-panelled thirst parlour. A bookishly intellectual ambience still pervades and this is an apt spot to curl up with a weighty tome over a few Irish ales.

GAY & LESBIAN MUNICH

In Munich, the rainbow flag flies especially proudly along Müllerstrasse and the adjoining Glockenbachviertel. Keep an eye out for the freebie mags *Our Munich* and *Sergej*, which contain up-to-date listings and news about the community and gay-friendly establishments around town. Another source is www.gaymunich.de, which has a small section in English. For help with lodging, check out www.gaytouristoffice.com.

Baader Café
CAFE

(Baaderstrasse 47; ⊙9.30am-1am; 🚋Fraunhoferstrasse) This literary think-and-drink institution lures all sorts, from short skirts to tweed jackets who linger over daytime coffees and night-hour cocktails. Popular Sunday brunch.

Trachtenvogl
CAFE, LOUNGE

(Reichenbachstrasse 47; ⊙10am-1am Sun-Thu, to 2am Fri & Sat; 🚋Fraunhoferstrasse) At night you'll have to shoehorn your way into this buzzy lair favoured by a chatty, boozy crowd of scenesters, artists and students. Daytimes are mellower, all the better to slurp its hot-chocolate menu and check out the cuckoo clocks and antlers, left over from the days when this was a folkoric garment shop.

⭐ Entertainment

Kultfabrik
CLUB COMPLEX

(www.kultfabrik.de; Grafingerstrasse 6; 🚋Ostbahnhof) This former dumpling factory is party central with more than a dozen venues along with numerous fast-food eateries. Go to **11er** for electro and house, **Titty Twister** for hard rock and **Refugium** for metal. Nostalgic types can become dancing queens at **Noa**, **Rafael** and **Q Club** while rock-a-billies jive till the wee hours at **Eddy's**.

Münchner Philharmoniker
CLASSICAL MUSIC

(☎480 980; www.mphil.de; Rosenheimer Strasse 5; 🚋Am Gasteig) Munich's premier orchestra regularly performs at the Gasteig Cultural Centre. Book tickets early as performances usually sell out.

Jazzclub Unterfahrt im Einstein
BLUES, JAZZ

(☎448 2794; www.unterfahrt.de; Einsteinstrasse 42; Ⓢ Max-Weber-Platz) Join a diverse crowd at this long-established, intimate club for a mixed bag of acts ranging from old bebop to edgy experimental. The Sunday open jam session is legendary.

Atomic Café
CLUB

(www.atomic.de; Neuturmstrasse 5; ⊙from 10pm Tue-Sat; 🚋Kammerspiele) This bastion of indie sounds with funky '60s decor is known for bookers with a knack for catching upwardly hopeful bands before their big break. Otherwise it's party time; long-running Britwoch is the hottest Wednesday club night in town.

FC Bayern München
SOCCER

(www.fcbayern.de; Ⓢ Fröttmaning) Germany's most successful team plays at the impressive Allianz Arena, built for the 2006 World Cup. Tickets can be ordered online.

🛍 Shopping

Munich is a fun and sophisticated place to shop that goes far beyond chains and department stores. If you want those, head to Neuhauser Strasse and Kaufingerstrasse. Southeast of there, Sendlinger Strasse has smaller and somewhat more individualistic stores, including a few resale and vintage emporia.

To truly unchain yourself, though, you need to hit the Gärtnerplatzviertel and Glockenbachviertel, the bastion of well-edited indie stores and local designer boutiques. Hans-Sachs-Strasse and Reichenbachstrasse are especially promising.

Maxvorstadt, especially Türkenstrasse, also has an interesting line-up of stores with stuff you won't find on the high street back home.

ℹ Information

Tourist office (☏2339 6500; www.muenchen. de) There are two branches: Hauptbahnhof (Bahnhofplatz 2; ⊗9am-8pm Mon-Sat, 10am-6pm Sun) and Marienplatz (Marienplatz 8, Neues Rathaus; ⊗10am-7pm Mon-Fri, to 5pm Sat, to 2pm Sun).

City Tour Card (www.citytourcard-muenchen. com; 1/3 days €9.90/19.90) Includes public transport in the *Innenraum* (zones 1 to 4, marked white on transport maps) and discounts of between 10% and 50% for more than 50 attractions, tours, eateries and theatres. Available at some hotels, tourist offices, and U-Bahn, S-Bahn and DB vending machines.

ℹ Getting There & Away

Air

Munich Airport (MUC; www.munich-airport.de), aka Flughafen Franz-Josef Strauss, is second in importance only to Frankfurt's. It's linked to the Hauptbahnhof every 20 minutes by S-Bahn (S1 and S8, €10, 40 minutes) and by the Lufthansa Airport Bus (€10.50, 45 minutes, between 5am and 8pm). Budget between €50 and €70 for a taxi ride.

Note that Ryanair flies into Memmingen's **Allgäu Airport** (www.allgaeu-airport.de), 125km to the west. Seven buses daily shuttle between here and the Hauptbahnhof (€13, 1¾ hours).

Bus

Europabus links Munich to the Romantic Road. For times and fares for this service and all other national and international coaches contact **Sindbad** (☏5454 8989; Arnulfstrasse 20) near the Hauptbahnhof. Buses leave from **Zentraler Omnibusbahnhof** (Central Bus Station, ZOB; Arnulfstrasse 21) at S-Bahn station Hackerbrücke.

Car & Motorcycle

Munich has autobahns radiating in all directions. Take the A9 to Nuremberg, the A8 to Salzburg, the A95 to Garmisch-Partenkirchen and the A8 to Ulm or Stuttgart.

Train

Train connections from Munich to destinations within Bavaria, as well as to other German and European cities, are numerous. All services leave from the Hauptbahnhof, where **Euraide** (www.euraide.de; Desk 1, Reisezentrum, Hauptbahnhof; ⊗ 9.30am-8pm Mon-Fri May-Jul, 10am-7pm Mon-Fri Aug-Apr) is a friendly English-speaking agency that sells train tickets, makes reservations and can create personalised rail tours of Germany and beyond.

Useful connections from Munich include:
Baden-Baden (€81, five hours, hourly) Change in Mannheim.
Berlin (€121, six hours, every two hours)
Cologne (€134, 4½ hours, hourly)
Frankfurt (€95, 3¼ hours, hourly)
Nuremberg (€52, 1¼ hours, twice hourly)
Prague (€66, five hours 50 minutes, two daily)
Vienna (€85.80, 4½ hours, every two hours)
Würzburg (€67, two hours, twice hourly)

ℹ Getting Around

Car & Motorcycle

It's not worth driving in the city centre – many streets are pedestrian-only. The tourist office has a map that shows city-wide parking places (from €2 per hour).

Public Transport

Munich's efficient public transport system is run by **MVV** (www.mvv-muenchen.de) and is composed of buses, trams, the U-Bahn and the S-Bahn. The U-Bahn and S-Bahn run almost 24 hours a day, with a short gap between 2am and 4am.

The city is divided into four zones with most places of visitor interest (except Dachau and the airport) falling within the *Innenraum* (inner zone), which is marked white on public transport maps.

Short rides (*Kurzstrecke*; four bus or tram stops or two U-Bahn or S-Bahn stops) cost €1.20, longer trips cost €2.50. Children aged six to 14 pay a flat €1.20. Day passes are €5.60 for individuals and €10.20 for up to five people travelling together.

Bus drivers sell single tickets and day passes, but tickets for the U-/S-Bahn and other passes must be purchased from station vending machines. Tram tickets are available from vending machines aboard. Tickets must be stamped

WORTH A TRIP

DACHAU

Construction of the first Nazi concentration camp in **Dachau** (Dachau Memorial Site; www.kz-gedenkstaette-dachau.de; Alte Römerstrasse 75; admission free, tours €3; ⊗9am-5pm, tours 11am & 1pm Tue-Sun), some 16km northwest of central Munich, began in March 1933. More than 200,000 Jews, political prisoners, homosexuals and others deemed 'undesirable' were imprisoned here; more than 30,000 died. Pick up an audioguide (€3.50) at the visitors centre or join a 2½-hour tour (€3) offered at 11am and 1pm Tuesday to Sunday. A visit includes camp relics, memorials and a sobering museum that shows a 22-minute English-language documentary (10am, 11.30am, 12.30pm, 2pm and 3pm) that uses mostly post-liberation footage to outline what took place here.

The S2 makes the trip from Munich Hauptbahnhof (two-zone ticket, €5) to Dachau station in 21 minutes from where bus 726 (direction Saubachsiedlung) runs straight to the camp. Show your stamped ticket to the driver. By car, follow Dachauer Strasse straight out to Dachau and follow the 'KZ-Gedenkstätte' signs.

(validated) before use. The fine for getting caught without a valid ticket is €40.

Taxi

Taxis (☎216 10) are expensive and not much more convenient than public transport.

Bavarian Alps

Stretching west from Germany's remote southeastern corner to the Allgäu region near Lake Constance, the Bavarian Alps (Bayerische Alpen) form a stunningly beautiful natural divide along the Austrian border. Ranges further south may be higher, but these mountains shoot up from the foothills so abruptly that the impact is all the more dramatic.

The region is packed with cute villages, sprightly spas and plenty of possibilities for skiing, snowboarding, hiking, canoeing and paragliding. The ski season lasts from about late December until April.

GARMISCH-PARTENKIRCHEN
☑08821 / POP 26,000

An incredibly popular hangout for outdoorsy types and moneyed socialites, the double-barrelled resort of Garmisch-Partenkirchen is blessed with a fabled setting a snowball's throw from Germany's highest peak, the 2964m-high Zugspitze. Garmisch has a cosmopolitan feel, while Partenkirchen retains its old-world Alpine village vibe.

⊙ Sights & Activities

Zugspitze 　　　　　　　　　　MOUNTAIN
(www.zugspitze.de) Views from Germany's rooftop are quite literally breathtaking and,

on good days, extend into four countries. Skiing and hiking are the main activities here. The trip to the Zugspitze summit is as memorable as it is popular; beat the crowds by starting early in the day and, if possible, skip weekends altogether.

In Garmisch, board the **Zahnradbahn** (cogwheel train) at its own station behind the Hauptbahnhof. Trains first chug along the mountain base to the **Eibsee**, a forest lake, then wind their way through a mountain tunnel up to the **Schneeferner Glacier** (2600m). Here, you'll switch to the **Gletscherbahn** cable car for the final ascent to the summit. When you're done soaking in the panorama, board the **Eibsee-Seilbahn**, a steep cable car, that sways and swings its way back down to the Eibsee in about 10 minutes.

Most people come up on the train and take the cable car back down, but it works just as well the other way around. Either way, the entire trip costs €39/21.50 per adult/child in winter and €49.50/28 in summer. Winter rates include a day ski pass.

Partnachklamm 　　　　　　　GORGE
(www.partnachklamm.eu; adult/child €3/1.50; ⊗9am-5pm Oct-Easter, 8am-6pm Easter-Sep) One of the area's main attractions is the dramatically beautiful Partnachklamm, a narrow 700m-long gorge with walls rising up to 80m. A circular walk hewn from the rock takes you through the gorge, which is spectacular in winter when you can walk beneath curtains of icicles and frozen waterfalls.

🛏 Sleeping & Eating

Hotel Garmischer Hof HOTEL €€
(📞9110; www.garmischer-hof.de; Chamonixstrasse 10; s €59-94, d €94-136; 📶🅿) Property of the Seiwald family since 1928, many a climber, skier and Alpine adventurer has creased the sheets at this welcoming inn. Rooms are simply furnished but cosy, breakfast is served in the vaulted cafe-restaurant and there's a sauna providing *après-piste* relief.

Hostel 2962 HOSTEL €
(📞957 50; www.hostel2962.com; Partnachauenstrasse 3; dm/d from €20/60; 📶) A bed in one of the four-bed dorms in this converted hotel is the cheapest sleep in town. For dorm dwellers breakfast costs €6.

Bräustüberl GERMAN €€
(📞2312; Fürstenstrasse 23; mains €6-17) A short walk from the centre, this quintessentially Bavarian tavern is the place to cosy up with some local nosh, served by *Dirndl*-trussed waitresses, while the enormous enamel coal-burning stove revives chilled extremities.

ℹ Information

Tourist office (📞180 700; www.gapa.de; Richard-Strauss-Platz 2; ⏰8am-6pm Mon-Sat, 10am-noon Sun)

ℹ Getting There & Away

From Garmisch there is train service to Munich (€19, 80 minutes, hourly) and to Innsbruck, Austria (€15, 80 minutes, every two hours) via Mittenwald. **RVO bus 9606** (www.rvo-bus.de) runs to Füssen (€3, 2¼ hours, five to six daily), via Oberammergau and Wieskirche, from the train station.

The A95 from Munich is the direct road route. The most central parking is at the Kongresshaus (next to the tourist office) for €1 per hour.

Bus tickets cost €1.50 for journeys in town. For bike hire, try **Fahrrad Ostler** (📞3362; Kreuzstrasse 1; per day/week from €10/50).

OBERAMMERGAU
📞08822 / POP 5230

Quietly quaint Oberammergau occupies a wide valley surrounded by the dark forests and snow-dusted peaks of the Ammergauer Alps. The centre is packed with traditional painted houses, woodcarving shops and awe-struck tourists who come here to learn about the town's world-famous **Passion Play**, a blend of opera, ritual and Hollywood epic that's been performed since the late 17th century as a collective thank you from the villagers for being spared the plague. Half the village takes part, sewing amazing costumes

ℹ ALP-HOPPING

While the public transport network is good, the mountain geography means there are few direct routes between the top Alpine draws; sometimes a shortcut via Austria is quicker (such as by road between Füssen and Garmisch-Partenkirchen). Bus rather than rail routes are often more practical. For those driving, the German Alpine Road (Deutsche Alpenstrasse) is a scenic way to go.

and growing hair and beards for their roles (no wigs or false hair allowed). The next performances are in 2020 but, meanwhile, tours of the **Passionstheater** (📞945 8833; Passionswiese 1; combined tour & Oberammergau Museum entry adult/child/concession €8/3/6; ⏰tours 9.30am-5pm Apr-Oct) let you take a peek at the costumes and sets any time.

Oberammergau's other claim to fame is **Lüftmalerei**, the eye-popping house facades painted in an illusionist style. The pick of the crop is the amazing **Pilatushaus** (Ludwig-Thoma-Strasse 10; ⏰3-5pm Tue-Sat May-Oct), whose painted columns snap into 3D as you approach. It contains a gallery and several craft workshops.

The town is also celebrated for its intricate **woodcarvings**. At workshops throughout town skilled craftspeople produce anything from an entire nativity scene in single walnut shell to a life-size Virgin Mary. Speciality shops and the **Oberammergau Museum** (📞941 36; www.oberammergaumuseum.de; Dorfstrasse 8; combined museum entry & Passiontheater tour adult/child/concession €8/3/6; ⏰10am-5pm Tue-Sun Apr-Oct) display fine examples of the carvings.

Oberammergau has a **DJH hostel** (📞4114; www.oberammergau.jugendherberge.de; Malensteinweg 10; dm from €16.80) as well as several guesthouses, including the exceptionally good-value **Gästehaus Richter** (📞935 765; www.gaestehaus-richter.de; Welfengasse 2; s €28-35, d €56-70; 📶) with immaculate ensuite rooms, a guest kitchen, free wi-fi and a filling Alpine breakfast. Recently updated **Hotel Turmwirt** (📞926 00; www.turmwirt.de; Ettalerstrasse 2; s/d from €75/99; 🅿) next to the church has pristine business-standard rooms, some with Alpine views from the balconies and bits of woodcarving art throughout.

GERMANY BAVARIAN ALPS

DON'T MISS

WIESKIRCHE

Known as 'Wies' for short, the **Wieskirche** (☑08862-932 930; www.wieskirche.de; ☺8am-5pm) is one of Bavaria's best-known baroque churches and a Unesco-listed heritage site. About a million visitors a year flock to see this stuccoed wonder by the artist brothers Dominikus and Johann Baptist Zimmermann.

In 1730, a farmer in Steingaden, about 30km northeast of Füssen, witnessed the miracle of his Christ statue shedding tears. Pilgrims poured into the town in such numbers over the next decade that the local abbot commissioned a new church to house the weepy work. Inside the almost circular structure, eight snow-white pillars are topped by gold capital stones and swirling decorations. The unsupported dome must have seemed like God's work in the mid-17th century, its surface adorned with a pastel ceiling fresco celebrating Christ's resurrection.

From Füssen, regional RVO bus 73 (www.rvo-bus.de) makes the journey up to six times daily. The Europabus also stops here long enough in both directions to have a brief look round then get back on. By car, take the B17 northeast and turn right (east) at Steingaden.

The **tourist office** (☑922 740; www.ammergauer-alpen.de; Eugen-Papst-Strasse 9a; ☺9am-6pm Mon-Fri, 9am-1pm Sat) can help find accommodation.

Hourly trains connect Munich with Oberammergau (change at Murnau; €18.10, 1¾ hours). **RVO bus 9606** (www.rvo-bus.de) travels hourly direct to Garmisch-Partenkirchen via Ettal; change at Echelsbacher Brücke for Füssen.

BERCHTESGADEN
☑08652 / POP 7600

Steeped in myth and legend, the Berchtesgadener Land is almost preternaturally beautiful. Framed by six formidable mountain ranges and home to Germany's second-highest mountain, the Watzmann (2713m), its dreamy, fir-lined valleys are filled with gurgling streams and peaceful Alpine villages.

Much of the terrain is protected as the Nationalpark Berchtesgaden, which embraces the pristine Königssee, one of Germany's most photogenic lakes. Yet, Berchtesgaden's history is also indelibly entwined with the Nazi period, as chronicled at the disturbing Dokumentation Obersalzberg. The Eagle's Nest, a mountaintop lodge built for Hitler, is now a major tourist attraction.

☉ Sights & Activities

Königssee   LAKE
Crossing the serenely picturesque, emerald-green Königssee makes for some unforgettable memories. Contained by steep mountain walls some 5km south of Berchtesgaden, it's Germany's highest lake (603m), with drinkable waters shimmering into fjordlike depths. Bus 841 makes the trip out here from the Berchtesgaden Hauptbahnhof roughly every hour.

Escape the hubbub of the bustling lakeside tourist village by taking an electric **boat tour** (www.seenschifffahrt.de; return adult/child €13.30/6.70) to **St Bartholomä**, a quaint onion-domed chapel on the western shore. At some point, the boat will stop while the captain plays a horn towards the Echo Wall – the sound will bounce seven times. Pure magic! The effect only fails during heavy fog. From the dock at St Bartholomä, an easy trail leads to the wondrous **Eiskapelle** in about one hour.

TOP CHOICE **Dokumentation Obersalzberg**   MUSEUM
(www.obersalzberg.de; Salzbergstrasse 41, Obersalzberg; adult/child €3/free; ☺9am-5pm daily Apr-Oct, 10am-3pm Tue-Sun Nov-Mar) In 1933 the quiet mountain retreat of **Obersalzberg** (3km from the town of Berchtesgaden) became the southern headquarters of Hitler's government, a dark period that's given the full historical treatment at the Dokumentation Obersalzberg. All facets of Nazi terror are dealt with, including Hitler's near-mythical appeal, his racial politics, the resistance movement, foreign policy and the death camps. Half-hourly bus 838 runs here from Berchtesgaden Hauptbahnhof.

Eagle's Nest   HISTORIC SITE
(☑2969; www.kehlsteinhaus.de; ☺mid-May–Oct) Berchtesgaden's most sinister draw is Mt Kehlstein (as the Eagle's Nest is known in

German), a sheer-sided peak at Obersalzberg where Martin Bormann, a key henchman of Hitler's, engaged 3000 workers to build a diplomatic meetinghouse for the Führer's 50th birthday. The Allies never regarded the site worth bombing, and so it survived WWII untouched and today houses a restaurant that donates profits to charity.

To get there, drive or take half-hourly bus 838 from the Hauptbahnhof to the Hotel InterContinental. From here the road is closed to private traffic and you must take a special **bus** (adult/child €15.50/9) up the mountain (35 minutes). The final 124m stretch to the summit is aboard a snazzy brass-clad lift (elevator).

You can also experience the sinister legacy of the Obersalzberg area, including the Eagle's Nest and the underground bunker system, on a four-hour guided English-language tour run by **Eagle's Nest Tours** (☑649 71; www.eagles-nest-tours.com; Königsseer Strasse 2; adult/child €50/35; ☐1.15pm mid-May–Oct). Reservations are advised.

Salzbergwerk HISTORIC SITE
(www.salzzeitreise.de; Bergwerkstrasse 83; adult/child €15.50/9.50; ☐9am-5pm May-Oct, 11am-3pm Nov-Apr) Once a major producer of 'white gold', Berchtesgaden has thrown open its salt mines for fun-filled 90-minute tours. Kids especially love donning miners' garb and whooshing down a wooden slide into the depth of the mine. Down below, highlights include mysteriously glowing salt grottoes and the crossing of a 100m-long subterranean salt lake on a wooden raft.

🛏 Sleeping & Eating

Hotel Bavaria HOTEL €€
(☑660 11; www.hotelbavaria.net; Sunklergässchen 11; r €50-130; 🅿) In the same family for over a century, this well-run hotel offers a romantic vision of Alpine life with rooms bedecked in frilly curtains, canopied beds, heart-shaped mirrors and knotty wood galore. Five of the pricier rooms have their own whirlpools. Gourmet breakfasts include sparkling wine.

Holzkäfer CAFE, BAR €
(☑600 90; Buchenhöhe 40; dishes €4-9; ☐11am-1am Wed-Mon) This funky log cabin in the Obersalzberg hills is a great spot for a night out with fun-loving locals. Cluttered with antlers, carvings and backwoods oddities,

HITLER'S MOUNTAIN RETREAT

Of all the German towns tainted by the Third Reich, Berchtesgaden has a burden heavier than most. Hitler fell in love with nearby Obersalzberg in the 1920s and bought a small country home, later enlarged into the imposing Berghof.

After seizing power in 1933, Hitler established a part-time headquarters here and brought much of the party brass with him. They bought, or often confiscated, large tracts of land and tore down farmhouses to erect a 7ft-high barbed-wire fence. Obersalzberg was sealed off as the fortified southern headquarters of the NSDAP (National Socialist German Workers' Party).

In the final days of WWII, the Royal Air Force levelled much of Obersalzberg, though the Eagle's Nest, Hitler's mountaintop eyrie, was left unscathed.

it's known for its tender pork roasts, dark beer and Franconian wines.

ℹ Information

The **tourist office** (www.berchtesgaden.de; Königsseer Strasse 2; ☐8.30am-6pm Mon-Fri, to 5pm Sat, 9am-3pm Sun Apr–mid-Oct, reduced hours mid-Oct–Mar) is just across the river from the train station.

ℹ Getting There & Away

Travelling from Munich by train involves a change at Freilassing (€30.90, three hours, five daily). The best option between Berchtesgaden and Salzburg is **RVO bus** (www.rvo-bus.de) 840 (45 minutes) which links both towns' train stations twice hourly. Berchtesgaden is south of the Munich–Salzburg A8 autobahn.

Romantic Road

From the vineyards of Würzburg to the foot of the Alps, the almost 400km-long Romantic Road (Romantische Strasse) draws two million visitors every year, making it by far the most popular of Germany's holiday routes. It passes through more than two dozen cities and towns, including Rothenburg ob der Tauber, Dinkelsbühl and Augsburg. Expect tourist coaches and kitsch galore, but also a fair wedge of *Gemütlichkeit* (cosiness) and genuine hospitality.

❶ Getting There & Around

Though Frankfurt is the most popular gateway for the Romantic Road, Munich is a good launchpad as well, especially if you decide to take the bus.

It is possible to do this route using train connections and local buses, but the going is complicated, tedious and slow, especially at weekends. The ideal way to travel is by car, though Deutsche Touring's **Europabus** (✆0171-653 2340719 126 268; www.touring-travel.eu) is an alternative. Note that it gets incredibly crowded in summer. From April to October the special coach runs daily in each direction between Frankfurt and Füssen (for Neuschwanstein); the entire journey takes around 12 hours. There's no charge for breaking the journey and continuing the next day.

Tickets are available for short segments of the trip, and reservations are only necessary during peak-season weekends. Reservations can be made through travel agents, **Deutsche Touring** (www.touring.de), EurAide (p219) in Munich, and Deutsche Bahn's Reisezentrum offices in the train stations. Students, children, pensioners and rail-pass holders qualify for discounts of between 10% and 50%.

Füssen

✆08362 / POP 14,200

In the foothills of the Alps, the town of Füssen itself is often overlooked by the mobs swarming to Schloss Neuschwanstein and Hohenschwangau, the two fantasy castles associated with King Ludwig II. It has some baroque architecture and you can actually sense a certain Alpine serenity after dark while locals count the change from the day's day-tripper invasion.

---

❶ VISITING THE CASTLES

Both Neuschwanstein and Hohenschwangau must be seen on guided tours (in German or English), which last about 35 minutes each. Timed tickets are only available from the **Ticket Centre** (✆930 40; www.hohenschwangau.de; Alpenseestrasse 12; ⊙tickets 8am-5pm Apr-Sep, 9am-3pm Oct-Mar) at the foot of the castles. In summer, come as early as 8am to ensure you get in that day.

All Munich's tour companies run day excursions out to the castles.

◉ Sights

TOP CHOICE **Schloss Neuschwanstein** CASTLE
(✆930 830; www.hohenschwangau.de; adult/concession €12/11, with Hohenschwangau €23/21; ⊙8am-5pm Apr-Sep, 9am-3pm Oct-Mar) Appearing through the mountaintops like a misty mirage is the world's most famous castle, and the model for Disney's citadel, fairy-tale Schloss Neuschwanstein.

King Ludwig II planned this castle himself, with the help of a stage designer rather than an architect, and it provides a fascinating glimpse into the king's state of mind. Ludwig foresaw his showpiece palace as a giant stage on which to recreate the world of Germanic mythology in the operatic works of Richard Wagner. At its centre is the lavish **Sängersaal** (Minstrels' Hall), created to feed the king's obsession with Wagner and medieval knights. Wall frescos in the hall depict scenes from the opera *Tannhäuser*.

Other completed sections include Ludwig's *Tristan and Isolde*–themed **bedroom**, dominated by a huge Gothic-style bed crowned with intricately carved cathedral-like spires; a gaudy artificial grotto (another allusion to *Tannhäuser*); and the Byzantine **Thronsaal** (Throne Room) with an incredible mosaic floor containing over two million stones.

At the end of the tour visitors are treated to a 20-minute **film** on the castle and its creator, and there's a reasonably priced cafe and the inevitable gift shops.

For the postcard view of Neuschwanstein and the plains beyond, walk 10 minutes up to **Marienbrücke** (Mary's Bridge), which spans the spectacular Pöllat Gorge over a waterfall just above the castle. It's said Ludwig liked to come here after dark to watch the candlelight radiating from the Sängersaal.

Schloss Hohenschwangau CASTLE
(✆930 830; www.hohenschwangau.de; adult/concession €12/11, with Neuschwanstein €23/21; ⊙8am-5.30pm Apr-Sep, 9am-3.30pm Oct-Mar) Ludwig spent his formative years at the sun-yellow Schloss Hohenschwangau. Far less showy than Neuschwanstein, Hohenschwangau has a distinctly lived-in feel and every piece of furniture is original. After his father died, Ludwig's main alteration was having stars, illuminated with hidden oil lamps, painted on the ceiling of his bed-

room. Some rooms have frescos from German history and legend (including the story of the Swan Knight, *Lohengrin*). The swan theme runs throughout.

Museum der Bayerischen Könige   MUSEUM
(Museum of the Bavarian Kings; www.museumder bayerischenkoenige.de; Alpseestrasse 27; adult/ concession €8.50/7; ☺8am-7pm Apr-Sep, 10am-6pm Oct-Mar) This architecturally stunning museum is packed with historical background on Bavaria's first family. The big-window lake views to the Alps are almost as stunning as the royal bling on show, which includes Ludwig II's famous blue and gold robe.

🛏 Sleeping & Eating

Altstadt Hotel zum Hechten   HOTEL €€
(☑916 00; www.hotel-hechten.com; Ritterstrasse 6; s €59-65 d €90-99; 🎧) This is one of Füssen's oldest hotels and a barrel of fun. Public areas are traditional in style but the bedrooms are mostly airy, light and brightly renovated. One of Füssen's better eateries awaits downstairs.

Franziskaner Stüberl   BAVARIAN €€
(☑371 24; Kemptener Strasse 1; mains €5.50-15; ☺lunch & dinner) This quaint restaurant specialises in *Schweinshaxe* (pork knuckle) and schnitzel, prepared in more varieties than you can shake a haunch at. Non-carnivores go for the scrumptious *Käsespätzle* (rolled cheese noodles) and the huge salads.

ℹ Information

Tourist Office (☑938 50; www.fuessen.de; Kaiser-Maximillian-Platz 1; ☺9am-5pm Mon-Fri, 10am-2pm Sat, 10am-noon Sun)

ℹ Getting There & Away

Trains from/to Munich (€24, two hours) run every two hours. RVO buses 78 and 73 serve the castles from Füssen Bahnhof (€4 return).

The Europabus (p224) leaves from stop 3 outside Füssen train station at 8am. It arrives in Füssen after 8pm.

Augsburg

☑0821 / POP 264,700
The largest city on the Romantic Road, Augsburg is also one of Germany's oldest, founded over 2000 years ago by the stepchildren of Roman emperor Augustus. Today it's a lively provincial city, criss-crossed by little streams and imbued with an appealing ambience and vitality. It makes a good day trip from Munich or a stop on a Romantic Road foray.

⊙ Sights

Look for the very impressive onion-shaped towers on the 17th-century **Rathaus** and the adjacent **Perlachturm**, a former guard tower. North of here is the 10th-century **Dom Maria Heimsuchung** (Hoher Weg; ☺7am-6pm), which has more 'modern' additions, such as the 14th-century doors showing scenes from the Old Testament.

The Fuggers – a 16th-century banking family – left their mark everywhere. They have lavish tombs inside **St Anna Kirche** (Im Annahof 2, off Annastrasse; ☺10am-12.30pm & 3-6pm Tue-Sat, 10am-12.30pm & 3-4pm Sun), a place also known for being a Martin Luther bolt-hole. The 16th-century **Fuggerei** (www.fugger.de; Jakober Strasse; adult/concession €4/3; ☺8am-8pm Apr-Sep, 9am-6pm Oct-Mar) was built with banking riches to house the poor, which, remarkably, it still does. The excellent **museum** (Mittlere Gasse 14; free with Fuggerei admission) shows how the family lived.

🛏 Sleeping & Eating

Hotel am Rathaus   HOTEL €€
(☑346 490; www.hotel-am-rathaus-augsburg.de; Am Hinteren Perlachberg 1; s €79-98 d €98-125; 🎧) Just steps from Rathausplatz and Maximilianstrasse, this super-central boutique hotel hires out 31 rooms with freshly neutral decor and a sunny little breakfast room.

Bauerntanz   GERMAN €€
(Bauerntanzgässchen 1; mains €7-16; ☺11am-11.30pm) Belly-satisfying helpings of creative Swabian and Bavarian food (*Spätzle*, veal medallions and more *Spätzle*) are plated up by friendly staff at this prim Alpine tavern with lace curtains, hefty timber interior and chequered fabrics.

ℹ Information

Tourist Office (☑502 0724; www.augsburg-tourismus.de; Maximilian Strasse 57; ☺9am-6pm Mon-Fri, 10am-5pm Sat, 10am-2pm Sun Apr-Oct, 9am-5pm Mon-Fri, 10am-2pm Sat Nov-Mar)

ℹ Getting There & Away

Trains between Munich and Augsburg are frequent (€12 to €20, 40 minutes); it's on the main line to Frankfurt. The Romantic Road bus stops at the train station and the Rathaus.

Rothenburg ob der Tauber

📞 09861 / POP 11,000

In the Middle Ages, Rothenburg's town fathers built strong walls to protect the town from siege; today they are the reason the town is under siege from tourists. The most stereotypical of all German walled towns, Rothenburg can't help being so cute. Granted 'free imperial city' status in 1274, it's a confection of twisting cobbled lanes and pretty architecture enclosed by towered stone walls. Swarmed during the day, the underlying charm oozes out after the last bus leaves.

◉ Sights

Jakobskirche   CHURCH
(Klingengasse 1; adult/child €2/0.50; ⊙9am-5pm) Rothenburg's most famous church sports wonderful stained-glass windows, but its real pièce de résistance is the Heilig Blut Altar (Sacred Blood Altar) carved with dizzying intricacy by medieval master Tilmann Riemenschneider.

Rathaus   HISTORIC BUILDING
(Marktplatz; Rathausturm adult/concession €2/0.50; ⊙tower 9.30am-12.30pm & 1-5pm daily Apr-Oct, noon-3pm daily Dec, shorter hours Sat & Sun Nov & Jan-Mar) The highlight of Rothenburg's Renaissance town hall is the widescreen views of the city and surrounds from the tower's viewing platform (220 steps).

Mittelalterliches Kriminalmuseum   MUSEUM
(📞5359; www.kriminalmuseum.rothenburg.de; Burggasse 3-5; adult/child €4.20/2.60; ⊙10am-6pm May-Oct, shorter hours Nov-Apr) Chastity belts, a cage for cheating bakers and a beer-barrel pen for drunks are among the medieval implements of torture and punishment at this gruesomely fascinating museum.

DRINK AND YE SHALL BE FREE

According to legend, Rothenburg was spared destruction during the Thirty Years' War when the mayor won a challenge by Catholic General Tilly and downed more than 3L of wine at a gulp. This 'Meistertrunk' scene is re-enacted several times daily by the clock figures on the tourist office building and at a festival during Whitsuntide.

🛏 Sleeping & Eating

Burg-Hotel   HOTEL €€
(📞948 90; www.burghotel.eu; Klostergasse 1-3; s €100-135, d €100-170; 🅿🌐🛜) Each of the 15 elegantly furnished guest rooms at this boutique hotel built into the town walls has its own private sitting area. The lower floors shelter a decadent spa while phenomenal valley views unfurl from the breakfast room and stone terrace.

Altfränkische Weinstube   HOTEL €
(📞6404; www.altfraenkische-weinstube-rothenburg.de; Klosterhof 7; r €59-89; 🛜) In a quiet side street, this characterful inn has six atmosphere-laden rooms, most with four-poster or canopied beds. The restaurant (dinner only) serves up sound regional fare.

Zur Höll   GERMAN €€
(📞4229; Burggasse 8; mains €6.50-18; ⊙dinner) This medieval wine tavern, with an appreciation for slow food, is in the town's oldest original building, dating back to the year 900. There's a small regional menu and some excellent wines from nearby Würzburg.

ℹ Getting There & Away

There are hourly trains to/from Steinach, a transfer point for service to Würzburg (€12.20, 1¼ hours). The Europabus pauses here for 35 minutes.

Würzburg

📞 0931 / POP 133,500

Tucked in among river valleys lined with vineyards, Würzburg beguiles even before you reach the city centre, and is renowned for its art, architecture and delicate wines. For centuries the resident prince-bishops wielded enormous power and wealth, and the city grew in opulence under their rule. Its crowning glory is the Residenz, one of the finest baroque structures in Germany and a Unesco World Heritage site.

◉ Sights

Residenz   PALACE
(www.residenz-wuerzburg.de; Balthasar-Neumann-Promenade; adult/child €7.50/6.50; ⊙9am-6pm Apr-Oct, 10am-4.30pm Nov-Mar) The Unesco-listed Residenz is one of Germany's most important and beautiful baroque palaces. Its undisputed highlight is the Grand Staircase designed by Balthasar Neumann, a single set of steps that splits and

zigzags up to the 1st floor and is lidded by a humonguous Tiepolo fresco (667 sq metres). It allegorically depicts the four then-known continents (Europe, Africa, America and Asia).

Visits are by guided tour only and also take in the **Weisser Saal** (White Hall) with its ice-white stucco, the **Kaisersaal** (Imperial Hall) canopied by yet another impressive fresco by Tiepolo, and the gilded stucco **Spiegelkabinett** (Mirror Hall). German-language groups leave half-hourly; English tours leave at 11pm and 3pm year-round and, additionally, at 4.30pm April to October. The **Hofgarten** at the back is a beautiful relaxation spot.

Festung Marienberg   FORTRESS
Panoramic views over the city's red rooftops and vine-covered hills extend from Marienberg Fortress. It has presided over Würzburg since the city's prince-bishops commenced its construction in 1201; they governed from here until 1719. Their pompous lifestyle is on show at the **Fürstenbau-museum** (adult/child €4.50/3.50; ☺9am-6pm Tue-Sun mid-Mar–Oct), while city history is laid out upstairs.

Also here is the **Mainfränkisches Museum** (www.mainfraenkisches-museum.de; adult/child €4/2; ☺10am-5pm Tue-Sun) with a striking collection of Tilman Riemenschneider sculptures.

The fortress is a 30-minute walk up the hill from the Alte Mainbrücke via the **Tellsteige trail**, which is part of the 4km-long **Weinwanderweg** (wine hiking trail) through the vineyards around Marienberg.

🛏 Sleeping & Eating

Würzburg's many *Weinstuben* (wine taverns) are great for sampling the local vintages.

Babelfish   HOSTEL €
(☎304 0430; www.babelfish-hostel.de; Haugerring 2; dm €17-23, s/d €45/70) This uncluttered and spotlessly clean hostel has 74 beds spread over two floors, a rooftop terrace, 24-hour reception and a well-equipped guest kitchen.

Hotel Rebstock   HOTEL €€
(☎309 30; www.rebstock.com; Neubaustrasse 7; s/d from €101/120; 🅿️@🛜) Don't be misled by the Best Western sign out front: Würzburg's top digs, in a squarely renovated rococo townhouse, has 70 unique, stylishly finished rooms, impeccable service and an Altstadt location.

Bürgerspital Weinstube   WINE RESTAURANT €€
(☎352 880; Theaterstrasse 19; mains €7-23; ☺lunch & dinner) The cosy nooks of this labyrinthine medieval place are among Würzburg's most popular eating and drinking spots. Choose from a broad selection of Franconian wines and wonderful regional dishes, including *Mostsuppe,* a tasty wine soup.

Alte Mainmühle   FRANCONIAN €€
(☎167 77; Mainkai 1; mains €7-21; ☺10am-midnight) Accessed straight from the old bridge, tourists and locals alike cram onto the double-decker terrace suspended above the Main River to savour modern twists on old Franconian favourites.

ℹ Information

Tourist Office (☎372 398; www.wuerzburg.de; Marktplatz; ☺10am-6pm Mon-Fri, 10am-2pm Sat Apr-Dec, plus 10am-2pm Sun May-Oct, reduced hours Jan-Mar)

ℹ Getting There & Away

The Europabus stops next to the Hauptbahnhof and at the Residenzplatz.

Train connections from Würzburg:

Bamberg (€19, one hour, twice hourly)

Frankfurt (€33, one hour, hourly)

Nuremberg (€19.20 to €27, one hour, twice hourly)

Rothenburg ob der Tauber (€12.20, one hour, hourly) Change in Steinach.

Nuremberg

☎0911 / POP 503,000

Nuremberg (Nürnberg) woos visitors with its wonderfully restored medieval Altstadt, its grand castle and, in December, its magical *Christkindlmarkt* (Christmas market). Thriving culinary traditions include sizzling *Nürnberger Bratwürste* (finger-sized sausages) and *Lebkuchen* – large, soft gingerbread cookies, traditionally eaten at Christmas time but available here year-round. Both within and beyond the high stone wall encircling the Altstadt is a wealth of major museums that shed light on Nuremberg's significant history.

Nuremberg played a major role during the Nazi years. It was here that the fanatical party rallies were held, the boycott of Jewish businesses began and the infamous Nuremberg Laws outlawing Jewish citizenship were enacted. After WWII the city was chosen as the site of the War Crimes Tribunal, now known as the Nuremberg Trials.

CHRISTMAS MARKETS

Beginning in late November every year, central squares across Germany are transformed into Christmas markets or *Christkindlmärkte* (also known as *Weihnachtsmärkte*). Folks stamp about between the wooden stalls, perusing seasonal trinkets (from hand-carved ornaments to plastic angels) while warming themselves with *Glühwein* (mulled, spiced red wine) and grilled sausages. Locals love 'em and, not surprisingly, the markets are popular with tourists, so bundle up and carouse for hours. Markets in Nuremberg, Dresden, Cologne and Munich are especially famous.

◉ Sights

Hauptmarkt   SQUARE
This bustling square in the heart of the Altstadt is the site of daily markets as well as the famous *Christkindlesmarkt*. At the eastern end is the ornate Gothic **Pfarrkirche Unsere Liebe Frau** (Hauptmarkt 14), also known as the Frauenkirche. Daily at noon crowds crane their necks to witness the clock's figure enact a spectacle called *Männleinlaufen*. Rising from the square like a Gothic spire is the gargoyle-adorned, 19m-tall **Schöner Brunnen** (Beautiful Fountain). Touch the seamless golden ring in the ornate wrought-iron gate for good luck.

Kaiserburg   CASTLE
(www.schloesser.bayern.de; adult/child incl museum €7/6; ⊙9am-6pm Apr-Sep, 10am-4pm Oct-Mar) Construction of Nuremberg's landmark, the immensely proportioned Kaiserburg, began in the 12th century and dragged on for about 400 years. The complex, for centuries the receptacle of the Holy Roman Empire's treasures, consists of three parts: the Kaiserburg and Stadtburg (the Emperor's Palace and City Fortress) and the Burggrafenburg (Count's Residence), which was largely destroyed in 1420.

The **Kaiserburg Museum** chronicles the history of the castle and provides a survey of medieval defence techniques. You can also visit the **royal living quarters**, the **Imperial and Knights' Halls**, and the **Romanesque Doppelkapelle** (Twin Chapel).

Enjoy panoramic city views from atop the **Sinwellturm** (Sinwell Tower; 113 steps) or peer into the amazing 48m-deep **Tiefer Brunnen** (Deep Well).

The grassy knoll at the southeast corner of the castle gardens (open seasonally) is called **Am Ölberg** and is a good spot to sit and gaze out over the city's rooftops.

Memorium
Nuremberg Trials   HISTORIC BUILDING
(☑3217 9372; www.memorium-nuremberg.de; Bärenschanzstrasse 72; adult/concession €5/3; ⊙10am-6pm Wed-Mon) Nazis were tried in 1945 and 1946 for crimes against peace and humanity in Schwurgerichtssaal 600 (Court Room 600) of what is still Nuremberg's regional courthouse. The proceedings became known as the Nuremberg Trials, and were held by the Allies in the city for obvious symbolic reasons. The initial and most famous trial, conducted by international prosecutors, saw 24 people accused, of whom 19 were convicted and sentenced, many to death by hanging. Hermann Göring, the Reich's field marshall, cheated the hangman by taking a cyanide capsule in his cell hours before his scheduled execution.

In addition to viewing the courtroom (if not in use), a new exhibition provides comprehensive background on the trials. The courthouse is about 2km from the Altstadt centre. To get here, take the U1 towards Bärenschanze and get off at 'Sielstrasse'.

Reichsparteitagsgelände   HISTORIC SITE
(Luitpoldhain) If you've ever wondered where the infamous black-and-white images of ecstatic Nazi supporters hailing their Führer were filmed, it was here in Nuremberg. This orchestrated propaganda began as early as 1927 but, after 1933, Hitler opted for a purpose-built venue, the Reichsparteitagsgelände, about 4km southeast of the centre. Much of the outsize grounds were destroyed during Allied bombing raids, but 4 sq km remain, enough to get a sense of the megalomania behind it.

Exhibits at the **Dokumentationszentrum** (☑231 7538; Bayernstrasse 110; adult/concession €5/3; ⊙9am-6pm Mon-Fri, 10am-6pm Sat & Sun; 🚊) in the north wing of the Kongresshalle put the grounds into historical context by examining the rise of the NSDAP, the Hitler cult, the party rallies and the Nuremberg Trials. East of here, across an artificial pond, is the **Zeppelinfeld**, fronted by a 350m-long grandstand, where most of the big Nazi parades, rallies and events took place.

Take tram 9 from the Hauptbahnhof to 'Doku-Zentrum'.

Germanisches Nationalmuseum
MUSEUM

(www.gnm.de; Kartäusergasse 1; adult/child €6/4; ⊙10am-6pm Tue & Thu-Sun, to 9pm Wed) Spanning prehistory to the early 20th century, the German National Museum is the country's most important museum of German culture. It features paintings and sculptures, an archaeological collection, arms and armour, musical and scientific instruments and toys. Among its many highlights is Dürer's anatomically detailed *Hercules Slaying the Stymphalian Birds*.

At the museum's entrance is the inspired Way of Human Rights, a symbolic row of 29 white concrete pillars (and one oak tree) bearing the 30 articles of the Universal Declaration of Human Rights.

Museums
MUSEUMS

Nuremberg has a lot of toy companies and the Spielzeugmuseum (Toy Museum; Karlstrasse 13-15; adult/child €5/3; ⊙10am-5pm Tue-Fri, to 6pm Sat & Sun) presents their products in their infinite variety.

The Deutsche Bahn Museum (☎0180-444 22 33; www.db-museum.de; Lessingstrasse 6; adult/child €5/2.50, free with InterRail pass; ⊙9am-5pm Tue-Fri, 10am-6pm Sat & Sun) has a trainload of exhibits on the German railways.

Albrecht-Dürer-Haus (Albrecht-Dürer-Strasse 39; adult/child €5/2.50; ⊙10am-5pm Fri-Wed, to 8pm Thu) is where Dürer, Germany's renowned Renaissance draughtsman, lived from 1509 to 1528. A digital version of his wife Agnes 'leads' tours.

🛏 Sleeping

Nuremberg hosts many a trade show through the year (including a huge toy fair in February). During these times – and Christmas market weekends – rates soar like a model rocket.

TOP CHOICE Hotel Elch
HOTEL €€

(☎249 2980; www.hotel-elch.com; Irrerstrasse 9; s/d from €75/95; 🛜) This 14th-century, half-timbered house is a snug and romantic 12-room gem. Rooms 2 and 7 have half-timbered walls and ceilings, but modern touches include contemporary art, glazed terracotta bathrooms and rainbow-glass chandeliers. Note the multicoloured elk heads throughout (the hotel's name means 'Elk').

Lette'm Sleep
HOSTEL €

(☎992 8128; www.backpackers.de; Frauentormauer 42; dm €16-20, r from €50; @🛜) A backpacker favourite, this indie hostel near the Hauptbahnhof has colourfully painted dorms and some groovy self-catering apartments. The retro-styled kitchen and common room are great chill areas; internet, tea and coffee are free, and staff are wired into what's happening around town.

Art & Business Hotel
HOTEL €€

(☎232 10; www.art-business-hotel.com; Gleissbühlstrasse 15; s/d €89/115; 🛜) You don't have to be an artist or a business person to stay at this up-to-the-minute place near the Hauptbahnhof. From the trendy bar to slate bathrooms, design here is bold, but not overpoweringly so. Small sculpture garden out back. Rates tumble at weekends.

Hotel Deutscher Kaiser
HOTEL €€

(☎242 660; www.deutscher-kaiser-hotel.de; Königstrasse 55; s/d from €89/108; @🛜) Super-central and with posh design and service, this treat of a historic hotel has been in the same family for over a century. Climb the castle-like granite stairs to find rooms of understated simplicity, flaunting oversize beds, Italian porcelain, silk lampshades and period furniture. Renovation work is ongoing.

Hotel Drei Raben
HOTEL €€€

(☎274 380; www.hotel3raben.de; Königstrasse 63; s/d €130/150; 🛜🛜) The design of this hotel builds upon the legend of the three ravens perched on the building's chimney stack, who tell stories from Nuremberg lore. Each of the 'mythology' rooms uses decor and art – including sandstone-sculpted bedheads and etched-glass bathroom doors – to reflect a particular tale.

🍴 Eating

Don't leave Nuremberg without trying its famous *Nürnberger Bratwürste*. Order 'em by the half dozen with *Meerrettich* (horseradish) on the side. Restaurants line the hilly lanes above the Burgstrasse.

TOP CHOICE Bratwursthäusle
GERMAN €€

(http://die-nuernberger-bratwurst.de; Rathausplatz 2; meals €6-14; ⊙closed Sun) Seared over a flaming beech-wood grill, the little links sold at this rustic inn arguably set the standards for grilled sausages across the land. You can dine in the timbered restaurant or on the

GERMANY NUREMBERG

terrace with views of the Hauptmarkt. Service can be flustered at busy times.

TOP CHOICE **Goldenes Posthorn** FRANCONIAN €€
(☎225 153; Glöckleinsgasse 2, cnr Sebalder Platz; mains €6-19; ⏰11am-11pm; ☑) Push open the heavy copper door to find a real culinary treat that has been serving the folk of Nuremberg since 1498. The miniature local sausages are big here, but there's plenty else on the menu including many an obscure country dish and some vegie options. The choice of dining spaces ranges from formal to folksy, chunky wood to wood panelled.

Hütt'n GERMAN €€
(Bergstrasse 20; mains €5.50-15; ⏰4pm-midnight Mon-Fri, 11am-12.30am Sat, 11am-10.30pm Sun) This local haunt perpetually overflows with admirers of *Krustenschäufele* (roast pork with crackling, dumplings and sauerkraut salad) and the finest *Bratwurst* put to work in various dishes, though menus change daily (Friday is fish day). Also try a tankard of the Franconian *Landbier*.

Café am Trödelmarkt CAFE €
(Trödelmarkt 42; dishes €4-8.50; ⏰9am-6pm Mon-Sat, 11am-6pm Sun) A gorgeous place on a sunny day, this multilevel waterfront cafe overlooks the covered Henkersteg bridge. It's especially popular for its continental breakfasts, and has fantastic cakes as well as good blackboard lunchtime specials.

❶ Information

Tourist Office (www.tourismus.nuernberg.de) Two branches: Künstlerhaus (☎233 60; Königstrasse 93; ⏰9am-7pm Mon-Sat, 10am-4pm Sun) and Hauptmarkt (Hauptmarkt 18; ⏰9am-6pm Mon-Sat, 10am-4pm Sun May-Oct).

❶ Getting There & Around

Nuremberg **airport** (NUE; www.airport-nuernberg.de), 5km north of the centre, is served by regional and international carriers, including Lufthansa, Air Berlin and Air France. U-Bahn 2 runs every few minutes from the Hauptbahnhof to the airport (€2.40, 12 minutes). A taxi costs about €16.

Rail connections from Nuremberg include:
Berlin (€93, five hours, at least hourly)
Frankfurt (€51, two hours, at least hourly)
Munich (€52, one hour, twice hourly)
Vienna (€94.20, five hours, every two hours)

The best transport around the Altstadt is on foot. Public-transport day passes cost €4.80. Passes bought on Saturday are valid all weekend.

Bamberg

☑0951 / POP 70,000

Off the major tourist routes, Bamberg is revered by those in the know. It boasts a beautifully preserved collection of 17th- and 18th-century merchants' houses, palaces and churches. A canal and fast-flowing river spanned by cute little bridges run through the town, which even has its own local style of beer. No wonder it has been recognised by Unesco as a World Heritage site. Could it be the best small town in Germany?

◉ Sights

Bamberger Dom CATHEDRAL
(www.erzbistum-bamberg.de; Domplatz; ⏰8am-6pm Apr-Oct, to 5pm Nov-Mar) The quartet of spires of Bamberg's Dom soars above the cityscape. Its star attraction is the statue of the chivalric knight-king, the **Bamberger Reiter**. Also note the **Lächelnde Engel** (Smiling Angel), who smirkingly hands the martyr's crown to the headless St Denis in the north aisle, and the **marble tomb** of Pope Clemens II, the only papal burial place north of the Alps, in the west choir.

Altes Rathaus HISTORIC BUILDING
(Obere Brücke) The best views of the Gothic 1462 Altes Rathaus (Old Town Hall), which perches on a tiny artificial island between two bridges like a ship in dry dock, are from the small Geyerswörthsteg footbridge across the Regnitz. See if you can spot the cherub's leg sticking out from the fresco on the east side.

Neue Residenz PALACE
(☎519 390; www.schloesser.bayern.de; Domplatz 8; adult/child €4.50/3.50; ⏰9am-6pm Apr-Sep, 10am-4pm Oct-Mar) The 45-minute guided tours of the former residence of Bamberg's prince-bishops take in some 40 stuccoed rooms crammed with furniture and tapestries from the 17th and 18th centuries. The palace also hosts a small branch of the **Bayerische Staatsgalerie** (Bavarian State Gallery) which has mostly medieval, Renaissance and baroque paintings

🛏 Sleeping

Hotel Sankt Nepomuk HOTEL €€
(☎984 20; www.hotel-nepomuk.de; Obere Mühlbrücke; r €95-145; 🛜) Named aptly after the patron saint of bridges, this is a classy establishment in a half-timbered former mill right on the Regnitz. It has a superb

restaurant (mains €15 to €30) with a terrace, along with 24 comfy rustic rooms.

Backpackers Bamberg HOSTEL €
(☎222 1718; www.backpackersbamberg.de; Heiliggrabstrasse 4; dm €15-18, s/d €27/40; 🖃) This indie hostel is a well-kept old-school affair with clean dorms, a guest kitchen and a quiet, family-friendly atmosphere. It's left unstaffed for most of the day so let them know your arrival time. Located around 400m north along Luitpoldstrasse from the Luitpoldbrücke.

Hotel Europa HOTEL €€
(☎309 3020; www.hotel-europa-bamberg.de; Untere Königstrasse 6-8; r €89-119) The Europa is a spick-and-span but unfussy affair above a well-respected Italian restaurant just outside the Altstadt. Ask for a room with views of the Dom and the red-tiled roofs of the Altstadt.

✗ Eating & Drinking

Bamberg's unique style of beer is called *Rauchbier,* which literally means smoked beer. With a bacon flavour at first, it is a smooth brew that goes down easily.

TOP CHOICE Schlenkerla GERMAN €€
(Dominikanerstrasse 6; mains €8-15; ⊘Wed-Mon) A warren of rooms decked out with antler lamps, this 16th-century restaurant is famous for tasty Franconian specialities and *Rauchbier,* served directly from oak barrels. This should be your one stop if you only have time for one (stop, not beers...).

Messerschmidt FRANCONIAN €€
(☎297 800; Lange Strasse 41; mains €12-25; ⊘lunch & dinner) This stylish gourmet eatery in the birth house of aviation engineer Willy Messerschmidt oozes old-world charm, with dark woods, white linens and formal service. Tuck into hearty local fare out on the park-facing terrace or in the attached wine tavern.

Klosterbräu BREWERY €
(☎522 65; Obere Mühlbrücke 1-3; mains €6-12; ⊘10.30am-11pm Mon-Fri, 10am-11pm Sat, 10am-10pm Sun) This beautiful half-timbered brewery is Bamberg's oldest. It draws *Stammgäste* (regulars) and tourists alike who wash down filling slabs of meat and dumplings with its excellent range of ales. English-language brewery tours on request.

❶ Information

Tourist office (☎297 6200; www.bamberg.info; Geyerswörthstrasse 5; ⊘9.30am-6pm Mon-Fri, to 4pm Sat, to 2.30pm Sun)

❶ Getting There & Away

Rail connections include:
Berlin (€76, 4¼ hours, every two hours)
Munich (€59, two to 2½ hours, every two hours)
Nuremberg (€12 to €21, 40 to 60 minutes, four hourly)
Würzburg (€19, one hour, twice hourly)

Regensburg
☎0941 / POP 135,500

On the wide Danube River, Regensburg has relics of historic periods reaching back to the Romans, yet doesn't have the tourist mobs you'll find in other equally attractive German cities. Oh well, their loss. At least Unesco noticed – it recognised that Regensburg has the only intact medieval centre in Germany. Amid the half-timbers, Renaissance towers that could be in Tuscany mix with Roman ruins. Meanwhile, some 25,000 students keep things lively.

◉ Sights

Steinerne Brücke BRIDGE
A veritable miracle of engineering for its day, the Stone Bridge was cobbled together between 1135 and 1146 and for centuries remained the only solid crossing along the entire Danube.

Dom St Peter CHURCH
(Domplatz; ⊘6.30am-6pm Apr-Oct, to 5pm Nov-Mar) One of Bavaria's grandest Gothic cathedrals, St Peter's impressive features include kaleidoscopic stained-glass windows and the intricately gilded altar. The **Domschatzmuseum** (adult/child €2/1; ⊘10am-5pm Tue-Sat, noon-5pm Sun) brims with monstrances, tapestries and other church treasures.

Altes Rathaus HISTORIC BUILDING
(Rathausplatz; adult/concession €7.50/4; ⊘English tours 3pm Apr-Oct, 2pm Nov-Mar) The seat of the Reichstag for almost 150 years, the Altes Rathaus is now home to Regensburg's mayors and the **Reichstagsmuseum.** Tours take in not only the lavishly decorated **Reichssaal** (Imperial Hall), but also the original **torture chambers** in the basement.

🛏 Sleeping

Petit Hotel Orphée HOTEL €€

(📞596 020; www.hotel-orphee.de; Wahlenstrasse 1; s €35-125, d €70-135) Behind a humble door in the heart of the city lies a world of genuine charm, unexpected extras and real attention to detail. The wrought-iron beds, original sinks and cosy common rooms create the feel of a lovingly attended home. Another somewhat grander branch of the hotel is located above the Café Orphée (📞529 77; Untere Bachgasse 8; mains €7-18; ⏰9am-1am).

Brook Lane Hostel HOSTEL €

(📞696 5521; www.hostel-regensburg.de; Obere Bachgasse 21; dm/s/d from €16/40/50, apt per person €55; ➕🛜) Check-in at this small hostel is in the integrated convenience store; late landers should let staff know in advance. Dorms do the minimum required but the apartments and doubles here are applaudable deals. Access to kitchens and washing machines throughout.

Altstadthotel am Pach HOTEL €€

(📞298 610; www.regensburghotel.de; Untere Bachgasse 9; s €98-124, d €118-144; @🛜) Those who have shaped Regensburg history, from Marcus Aurelius to Emperor Karl V, are commemorated in the 21 rooms of this sleek hotel. All are warmly furnished with thick carpets, comfy mattresses and a minifridge with complimentary beer and water.

🍴 Eating & Drinking

Historische Wurstkuchl GERMAN €

(Thundorfer Strasse 3; 6 sausages €7.80; ⏰8am-7pm) This titchy riverside eatery has been serving the city's traditional finger-size sausages, grilled over beech wood and dished up with sauerkraut and sweet grainy mustard, since 1135, giving cred to its claim of being the world's oldest sausage kitchen.

Dicker Mann BAVARIAN €€

(www.dicker-mann.de; Krebsgasse 6; mains €6.50-20; ⏰9am-11pm) Stylish, traditional and serving all the staples of Bavarian sustenance, the 'Chubby Chappy' is one of the oldest restaurants in town, allegedly dating back to the 14th century. On a balmy eve, be sure to bag a table in the lovely beer garden out back.

Spitalgarten BEER GARDEN

(St Katharinenplatz 1) A thicket of folding chairs and slatted tables by the Danube, this is one of the best places in town for some alfresco quaffing. It claims to have brewed beer (today's Spital) here since 1350, so it probably knows what it's doing by now.

ℹ Information

Tourist Office (www.regensburg.de; Altes Rathaus; ⏰9am-6pm Mon-Fri, to 4pm Sat & Sun)

ℹ Getting There & Away

Train connections include:

Munich (€25.20, 1½ hours, hourly)

Nuremberg (€19, one to two hours, hourly)

Passau (from €22 to €27, one to 1½ hours, hourly) Additional services via Plattling.

STUTTGART & THE BLACK FOREST

Germany's southwest is taken up by Baden-Württemberg, a prosperous, modern state created in 1951 out of three smaller regions: Baden, Württemberg and Hohenzollern (thank goodness the names stopped at two!). With the exception of cuckoo clocks in the Black Forest, it runs a distant second in the cliché race to Bavaria. But that's really all the better, as it leaves more for you to discover on your own.

This pretty land of misty hills, shadowy conifers and cute villages rewards exploration. If you want a big and quaint historical town, there's Heidelberg. Baden-Baden is the sybaritic playground for spa-goers, and Freiburg has youthful vibrancy in an intriguing historical package. Finally, Lake Constance is a lovely redoubt bordering Switzerland and has all the pleasures a large body of water can offer.

Stuttgart

📞0711 / POP 581,000

Hemmed in by vine-covered hills, comfortable Stuttgart enjoys a quality of life founded on its fabled car companies: Porsche and Mercedes. It's also Baden-Württemberg's state capital and the hub of its industries. At the forefront of Germany's economic recovery from the ravages of WWII, Stuttgart started life less auspiciously in 950 as a horse stud farm. About 80% of the city centre was destroyed in WWII, but there are a few historical buildings left and – no surprise – excellent car museums.

Stuttgart

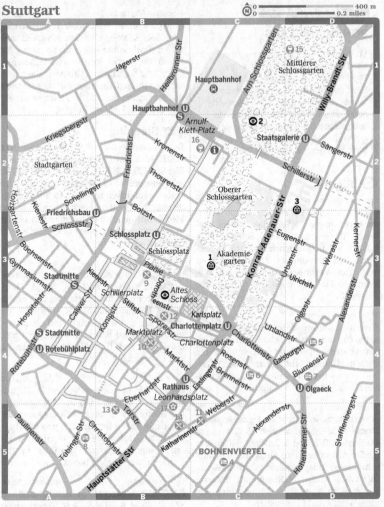

N 0 ———— 400 m
0 ———— 0.2 miles

Stuttgart

◎ Sights
1 Neues Schloss	C3
2 Schlossgarten	C2
3 Staatsgalerie	D2

🛏 Sleeping
4 Abalon Hotel	C5
5 City Hotel	D4
6 Der Zauberlehrling	C4
7 Hostel Alex 30	D4
8 Interhostel	A5

✕ Eating
9 Alte Kanzlei	B3
10 Food Market	B4
11 Irma la Douce	C5
12 Markthalle	B4
13 Reiskorn	B5
14 Weinstube Fröhlich	B5

🍷 Drinking
15 Biergarten im Schlossgarten	D1
16 Sky Beach	C2

☆ Entertainment
17 Kiste	B5

LOCAL KNOWLEDGE

BOHEMIAN BEANS

Stuttgart's most interesting neighbourhood is a short stroll from the centre. The **Bohnenviertel** (Bean District) takes its name from the diet of the poor tanners, dyers and craftsmen who lived here. Today the district's cobbled lanes and gabled houses harbour idiosyncratic galleries, workshops, bookstores, wine taverns, cafes and a red-light district.

Sights

Neues Schloss HISTORIC BUILDING
(Schlossplatz) Duke Karl Eugen von Württemberg's answer to Versailles was the exuberant three-winged Neues Schloss (New Palace), a baroque-neoclassical royal residence that now houses state government ministries. A bronze statue of Emperor Wilhelm I, looking dashing on his steed, graces nearby **Karlsplatz**.

Schlossgarten GARDEN
Stretching southwest from the Neckar River to the city centre is the Schlossgarten, an extensive strip of parkland divided into three sections (Unterer, Mittlerer and Oberer Garten), complete with ponds, swans, street entertainers and modern sculptures.

Staatsgalerie GALLERY
(www.staatsgalerie-stuttgart.de; Konrad-Adenauer-Strasse 30-32; adult/concession €5.50/4, special exhibitions €10/8, Wed & Sat free; ⏲10am-6pm Tue-Sun, to 8pm Tue & Thu) Alongside big-name exhibitions, this prestigious art museum showcases works by Rembrandt, Picasso, Monet, Dalí as well as 20th-century pop idols Warhol and Lichtenstein.

Mercedes-Benz Museum MUSEUM
(www.museum-mercedes-benz.com; Mercedesstrasse 100; adult/concession €8/4; ⏲9am-6pm Tue-Sun; 🚉Neckarpark) A futuristic swirl on the cityscape, the Mercedes-Benz Museum takes a chronological spin through the Mercedes empire. Look out for legends like the 1885 Daimler Riding Car, the world's first gasoline-powered vehicle, and the record-breaking Lightning Benz that hit 228km/h on Daytona Beach in 1909. Free English tour at 11am.

Porsche Museum MUSEUM
(www.porsche.com; Porscheplatz 1; adult/concession €8/4; ⏲9am-6pm Tue-Sun; 🚉Neuwirtshaus) Like a pearly white spaceship preparing for lift-off, the barrier-free Porsche Museum is every little boy's dream. Groovy audioguides race you through the history of Porsche from its 1948 beginnings. Break to glimpse the 911 GT1 that won Le Mans in 1998.

Sleeping

Der Zauberlehrling BOUTIQUE HOTEL €€€
(☎237 7770; www.zauberlehrling.de; Rosenstrasse 38; s €135-180, d €180-290, ste €195-320; P 📶) The self-consciously cool 'sorcerer's apprentice' reveals design-driven rooms, from Titanic with its waterbed to the hi-tech wizardry of the Media Suite. Yet it's hard to conjure up a smile at reception and the place lacks a little soul. Nice, but not quite magic.

Interhostel HOSTEL €
(☎6648 2797; www.inter-hostel.com; Paulinenstrasse 16; dm/s/d €25/42/64; 📶) A short toddle from Stadtmitte station, this hostel makes backpackers' hearts sing with its free coffee and wi-fi, bright and characterful digs, relaxed lounge and chipper team, plus handy stuff like luggage storage and a guest kitchen.

City Hotel HOTEL €€
(☎210 810; www.cityhotel-stuttgart.de; Uhlandstrasse 18; s €79-89, d €99-115; P 📶) Eschew the anonymity of Stuttgart's cookie-cutter chains for this intimate hotel just off Charlottenplatz. Rooms are light, clean and modern, if slightly lacklustre. Breakfast on the terrace in summer is a bonus.

Ochsen Hotel HISTORIC HOTEL €€
(☎407 0500; www.ochsen-online.de; Ulmer Strasse 323; s €89-99, d €119-129; P 📶; 🚉Inselstrasse) It's worth going the extra mile to this charismatic 18th-century hotel where some of the spacious, warm-hued rooms have whirlpool tubs perfect for a post-sightseeing bubble. The wood-panelled restaurant dishes up delicious local fare.

Abalon Hotel HOTEL €€
(☎217 10; www.abalon.de; Zimmermannstrasse 7-9; s €74-89, d €89-112; P 📶) Affable staff, a top location and wallet-friendly rates make Abalon a great pick. The bright parquet-floored rooms are large and spotless.

Hostel Alex 30 HOSTEL €

(☑838 8950; www.alex30-hostel.de; Alexander-strasse 30; dm/s/d/q €24/36/58/100, breakfast €8; P☏) Backpackers find a relaxed base in these mellow digs with a bar, sun deck and communal kitchen. The spotless, citrus-bright rooms are light and contemporary.

✗ Eating

Stuttgart is a great place to sample Swabian specialities such as *Spätzle* (noodles) and *Maultaschen* (a hearty ravioli in broth). Local wines edge out beer in popularity.

The **food market** (Marktplatz; ☉7.30am-1pm Tue, Thu & Sat) and the **Markthalle** (Market Hall; Dorotheenstrasse 4; ☉7am-6.30pm Mon-Fri, 7am-4pm Sat), with their bounty of local produce and gourmet items, are the best features of the otherwise humdrum Marktplatz.

TOP CHOICE **Irma la Douce** MEDITERRANEAN €€€

(☑470 4320; www.irmaladouce.de; Katharin-enstrasse 21b; lunch €11-14, dinner €25-39.50; ☉closed lunch Sat & Sun) An ornate fireplace and chandeliers cast flattering light across the polished wood, bookshelves and paintings at this 19th-century bistro where the food is inspired by the seasons and Mediterranean flavours.

Weinstube Fröhlich SWABIAN €€

(☑242 471; www.weinstube-froehlich.de; Leonhardstrasse 5; mains €12-23; ☉5.30pm-12.30am) True, it's bang in the heart of the red-light district, but don't be put off. This softly lit, dark wood-panelled restaurant is an atmospheric choice for well-executed Swabian fare (cheese-rich *Käsespätzle*, *Maultaschen* with potato salad) and regional wines.

Alte Kanzlei GERMAN €€

(☑294 457; Schillerplatz 5a; mains €10.50-20.50) Empty tables are gold-dust rare at this convivial, high-ceilinged restaurant. Feast on Swabian favourites like *Spanferkel* (roast suckling pig) and *Flädlesuppe* (pancake soup), washed down with regional tipples.

Reiskorn INTERNATIONAL €

(☑664 7633; Torstrasse 27; mains €5.50-12.90; ☉closed Sun lunch; ☑) With an easygoing vibe and bamboo-green retro interior, this culinary globetrotter serves everything from tangy Caribbean prawn salad to dim sum.

☕ Drinking & Entertainment

Hans-im-Glück Platz is a hub of bars, while club- and lounge-lined Theodor-Heuss-Strasse is thronged with sashaying hipsters.

Biergarten im Schlossgarten BEER GARDEN

(www.biergarten-schlossgarten.de; ☉10.30am-1am May-Oct; ☏) Toast summer with beer and pretzels at Stuttgart's best-loved, 2000-seat beer garden in the green heart of the Schlossgarten. Regular live music gets steins a-swinging.

Sky Beach BAR

(www.skybeach.de; Königstrasse 6, top floor Galeria Kaufhof; ☉noon-12.30am Mon-Sat, 11am-midnight Sun Easter-Sep) When the sun comes out, Stuttgarters live it up at this urban beach, complete with sand, cabana beds, DJs spinning mellow lounge beats and grandstand city views.

Kiste LIVE MUSIC

(www.kiste-stuttgart.de; Hauptstätter Strasse 35; ☉6pm-1am Mon-Thu, to 2am Fri & Sat) Jam-packed at weekends, this hole-in-the-wall bar is Stuttgart's leading jazz venue, with nightly concerts starting at 9pm or 10pm.

ℹ Information

StuttCard (72hr with/without VVS ticket €18/9.70) Free entry to most museums, plus discounts on events, activities and guided tours. Sold at the tourist office and some hotels.

Tourist Office (www.stuttgart-tourist.de; Königstrasse 1a; ☉9am-8pm Mon-Fri, 9am-6pm Sat, 11am-6pm Sun)

ℹ Getting There & Around

Stuttgart International Airport (www.stuttgart-airport.com), a major hub for germanwings, is 13km south of the city. S2 and S3 trains take about 30 minutes to get from the airport to the Hauptbahnhof (€3.50).

Trains head to all major German cities and many international ones, such as Zürich and Paris. Services include:

Frankfurt (€59, 1¼ hour)

Munich (€54, 2¼ hour)

Nuremberg (€39, 2¼ hour)

For travel within the city, single tickets are €2.10. A day pass, good for two zones (including the car museums), is better value at €6.10.

Tübingen

☎07071 / POP 84,000

Forty kilometres south of Stuttgart, Tübingen mixes all the charms of a late-medieval city – a hilltop fortress, cobbled alleys and half-timbered houses – with the erudition and mischief of a university town. Wander the winding alleys of old stone walls, then take a boat ride down the Neckar River.

The central **Marktplatz** is dominated by the 1435 **Rathaus**, which sports a baroque facade and astronomical clock. The nearby late-Gothic **Stiftkirche** (Am Holz-markt; ⊙9am-5pm) houses the tombs of the Württemberg dukes and has excellent medieval stained-glass windows. Above town, the Renaissance **Schloss Hohentübingen** (Burgsteige 11; museum adult/concession €5/3; ⊙castle 7am-8pm daily, museum 10am-5pm Wed-Sun, to 7pm Thu) was where Friedrich Miescher discovered DNA in 1869. It has fine views over the town's steep, red-tiled rooftops and an archaeology museum whose starring attraction is the collection of 35,000-year-old Vogelherd figurines, the world's oldest figurative artworks.

🛏 Sleeping & Eating

TOP CHOICE **Hotel am Schloss**   HISTORIC HOTEL €€
(☎929 40; www.hotelamschloss.de; Burgsteige 18; s €75, d €108-135; P🅿🛜) So close to the castle you can almost reach out and touch it, this flower-bedecked hotel has dapper rooms ensconced in a 16th-century building. Rumour has it Kepler was partial to the wine here.

Wurstküche   GERMAN €€
(☎927 50; Am Lustnauer Tor 8; mains €9-17.50; ⊙11am-midnight) The rustic, wood-panelled Wurstküche brims with locals quaffing wine and contentedly munching *Schupfnudeln* (potato noodles) and *Spanferkel* (roast suckling pig).

Weinhaus Beck   BAR
(Am Markt 1; ⊙9am-11pm) There's rarely an empty table at this wine tavern beside the Rathaus, a convivial place to enjoy a local tipple or coffee and cake.

❶ Getting There & Away

The definition of a day trip: trains between Tübingen and Stuttgart run every 30 minutes (€12.20, one hour).

Heidelberg

☎06221 / POP 147,000

Germany's oldest and most famous university town is renowned for its baroque old town, lively university atmosphere, excellent pubs and evocative half-ruined castle, which draw 3.5 million visitors a year. They are following in the footsteps of the late 18th- and early 19th-century romantics, most notably Johann Wolfgang von Goethe. Mark Twain kicked off his European travels in 1878 with a three-month stay in Heidelberg, later recounting his bemused observations in *A Tramp Abroad*.

◉ Sights

The tourist office runs English-language **walking tours** (adult/concession €7/5; ⊙10.30am Fri & Sat Apr-Oct) of the Altstadt.

TOP CHOICE **Schloss**   CASTLE
(www.schloss-heidelberg.de; adult/child incl Bergbahn €5/3, audioguide €4; ⊙24hr, ticket required 8am-5.30pm) Sticking up above the Altstadt like a picture-book pop-up, Heidelberg's ruined Schloss is one of the most romantic spots in Germany. Palatinate princes, stampeding Swedes, rampaging French, Protestant Reformers and lightning strikes – this Renaissance castle has seen the lot. Its tumultuous history, lonely beauty and changing moods helped inspire the German Romantic movement two centuries ago. One of its biggest attractions is the **Grosses Fass**, a massive wine barrel capable of holding about 228,000L.

To reach the red-sandstone castle, perched above the Altstadt, either hoof it up the steep, cobbled Burgweg in about 10 minutes, or take the historic funicular called **Bergbahn** (Funicular Railway; www.bergbahn-heidelberg.de; ⊙every 10min 9am-about 5pm) from Kornmarkt. Schloss tickets include travel on the Bergbahn.

Studentenkarzer   HISTORIC SITE
(Augustinergasse 2; adult/student incl Universitäts-museum €3/2.50; ⊙10am-6pm Tue-Sun Apr-Sep, 10am-4pm Tue-Sat Oct-Mar) Dominating Universitätsplatz are the 18th-century Alte Universität and the Neue Universität. On the back side, find the Studentenkarzer, the student jail from 1823 to 1914. Crimes that could get you locked up included public drunkenness, nocturnal singing and duelling.

Heiliggeistkirche
CHURCH

(Marktplatz; spire adult/student €2/1; ⏰11am–5pm Mon-Sat, 12.30-5pm Sun & holidays mid-Mar–Oct, 11am-3pm Fri & Sat, 12.30-3pm Sun Nov–mid-Mar) Heidelberg's most famous church, the Gothic Church of the Holy Spirit, was built from 1398 to 1441. For a bird's-eye view of Heidelberg, you can climb 208 stairs to the top of the spire. Stop by at 12.30pm from Monday to Saturday (except in winter) for 10 minutes of exquisite organ music.

Philosophenweg
TRAIL

Passing through steep fields and orchards on the slopes across the river from the Altstadt, the Philosophers' Way commands panoramic views of the Schloss as it wends its way through the forest to various monuments, towers, ruins, a beer garden and the Thingstätte, a Nazi-era amphitheatre.

🛏 Sleeping

Finding any accommodation during Heidelberg's high season can be difficult. Arrive early in the day or book ahead.

TOP CHOICE Arthotel
BOUTIQUE HOTEL €€

(📱650 060; www.arthotel.de; Grabengasse 7; d without breakfast €115-198; P✳🛜) For 21st-century German style, head to this charmer. The red and black lobby, lit by a wall of windows, sets the tone, while the 24 rooms, equipped with huge bathrooms, are spacious and cleanly minimalist – except for three, which come with painted ceilings that date from 1790.

Hotel Goldener Hecht
HOTEL €€

(📱166 025; www.hotel-goldener-hecht.de; Steingasse 2; d without breakfast €73-94; 🛜) This atmospheric hotel, near the Alte Brücke, has just 13 rooms, six with bridge views; the three corner rooms are bright and gorgeous. It's very central but potentially noisy.

Hotel am Kornmarkt
HOTEL €€

(📱905 830; www.hotelamkornmarkt.de; Kornmarkt 7; s/d from €65/85, without bathroom €40/70, breakfast €9; 🛜) A block from the Marktplatz, this hotel is a beacon to euro-conscious travellers. The 20 rooms are no-frills but still comfortable and spotless, the priciest have Kornmarkt views.

Steffis Hostel
HOSTEL €

(📱778 2772; www.hostelheidelberg.de; Alte Eppelheimer Strasse 50; dm from €18, d without bathroom €52; ⏰reception 8am-10pm; P@🛜) Tucked

ⓘ HEIDELBERG FAST TRACK

Heidelberg's captivating **old town** starts to reveal itself only after a charm-free 15-minute walk east from the main train station. Cut to the chase and go direct to the heart of town with bus 32 to Universitätsplatz or bus 33 to Bergbahn.

into a 19th-century tobacco factory, Steffis offers bright, well-lit rooms (all with shared bathrooms), a colourful lounge, a spacious kitchen and an ineffable old-time hostel vibe. Perks include free wi-fi, tea, coffee and bicycles (deposit €20). It's just north of the Hauptbahnhof, above a Lidl supermarket, and reached by an industrial-size lift.

🍴 Eating

TOP CHOICE Zur Herrenmühle
GERMAN €€€

(📱602 909; www.herrenmuehle-heidelberg.de; Hauptstrasse 237-239; mains €14.50-28.50; ⏰6-10pm Mon-Sat) A flour mill from 1690 has been turned into an elegant and highly cultured place to enjoy traditional 'country house' cuisine, including fish, under 300-year-old wood beams, a candle flickering romantically at each table. A five-course menu costs €36.50.

Schiller's Café
CAFE €

(Heiliggeiststrasse 5; cakes €2.50; ⏰10am-8pm Sun-Wed, 10am-midnight Thu-Sat) Housed in one of Heidelberg's oldest residential buildings (the cellar and first floor date from the 1500s) this homey, wholesome cafe serves over 60 kinds of hot chocolate, homemade cakes, quiche and wines. Most dishes are organic and some are gluten-free.

KulturBrauerei
CAFE €€

(📱502 980; Leyergasse 6; mains €10.50-26.50; ⏰7am-11pm or later) With its wood-plank floor, black iron chandeliers and time-faded ceiling frescoes, this microbrewery – in a hall that dates from 1903 – is an atmospheric spot to tuck into salad, soup or regional dishes such as Schäufele (pork shoulder) with sauerkraut (€10.50), or to quaff homebrews in the beer garden.

Café Burkardt
CAFE €

(Untere Strasse 27; cake & snacks €3-8; ⏰9am-11pm Tue-Sat, 9am-6pm Sun) Full of doily-draped tables and dark-wood crannies, this friendly cafe serves salads, German dishes, pasta and some of Heidelberg's scrummiest tarts and cheesecakes. Also on offer are great breakfasts and local wines.

🍺 Drinking & Entertainment

Lots of the action centres on Untere Strasse. Two ancient pubs, **Zum Roten Ochsen** (209 77; Hauptstrasse 213) and **Zum Sepp'l** (230 85; Hauptstrasse 217), are now filled with tourists.

Kulturhaus Karlstorbahnhof   LIVE MUSIC
(978 711; www.karlstorbahnhof.de; Am Karlstor 1; ⊙closed Aug) This edgy cultural centre shelters a concert venue, an art-house cinema and the popular **Klub K** (⊙10 or 11pm-5 or 6am Thu-Sat), whose DJs play everything from techno and dubstep to indie rock for a mixed crowd. It's train-track-adjacent, 100m east of the Karlstor.

Nachtschicht   CLUB
(www.nachtschicht.com; Bergheimerstrasse 147; admission €3-6; ⊙10pm-4am Thu, 8pm-1am Fri, 11pm-5am Sat) Two blocks north of the Hauptbahnhof, this old tobacco factory has morphed into one of Heidelberg's most popular student clubs.

❶ Information

Heidelberg Card (1/2/4 days €11/13/16, 2-day family pass €28) Includes public transport, admission to the Schloss (including the Bergbahn) and discounts at most museums, for bike and boat rental, and for tours. Available at the tourist offices.

Tourist Office (194 33, 584 4444; www.heidelberg-marketing.de) Branches include Hauptbahnhof (Willy-Brandt-Platz 1; ⊙9am-7pm Mon-Sat, 10am-6pm Sun & holidays Apr-Oct, 9am-6pm Mon-Sat Nov-Mar) and Marktplatz (Marktplatz 10; 8am-5pm Mon-Fri, 10am-5pm Sat).

❶ Getting There & Away

There are hourly IC trains to/from Frankfurt (from €16.40, one hour) and Stuttgart (from €21.20, 40 minutes) along with frequent service to the railway hub of Mannheim (€4.90, 19 minutes), with connections throughout Germany.

The fastest way to get to Frankfurt airport (€23, one hour, every hour or two) is to take the eight-seat **Lufthansa Airport Shuttle** (06152-976 9099; www.transcontinental-group.com).

Baden-Baden
07221 / POP 54,500

'So nice that you have to name it twice', enthused Bill Clinton about Baden-Baden, whose air of old-world luxury and curative waters have attracted royals, the rich and celebrities over the years – Bismarck, Queen Victoria and Victoria Beckham included. 'Nice', however, does not really convey the amazing grace of this Black Forest town, with its grand colonnaded buildings and whimsically turreted art nouveau villas spread across the hillsides and framed by forested mountains. Add to that temple-like thermal baths – which put the *baden* (bathe) in Baden – and a palatial casino and you'll understand that the allure of this grand dame of German spa towns is as timeless as it is enduring.

⊙ Sights & Activities

Kurhaus & Casino   LANDMARK
(www.kurhaus-baden-baden.de; Kaiserallee 1; guided tour €5; ⊙guided tour 9.30am-11.30am daily) The belle époque facade of the Kurhaus towers above well-groomed gardens and an alley of chestnut trees, flanked by boutiques, linking it with Kaiserallee. Inside is the sublime **casino** (www.casino-baden-baden.de; admission €5; ⊙2pm-2am Sun-Thu, 2pm-3am Fri & Sat), which seeks to emulate the gilded splendour of Versailles. Gents must wear a jacket and tie, rentable for €8 and €3 respectively. No need to dress up for the 25-minute guided tour.

Friedrichsbad   TOP CHOICE   SPA
(275 920; www.roemisch-irisches-bad.de; Römerplatz 1; 3hr ticket €23, incl soap-and-brush massage €33; ⊙9am-10pm, last admission 7pm) Abandon modesty (and clothing) to wallow in thermal waters at this sumptuous 19th-century spa as you slip into the regime of steaming, scrubbing, hot-cold bathing and dunking in the Roman-Irish bath. With its cupola, mosaics and Carrera marble pool, the bathhouse is the vision of a neo-Renaissance palace.

Caracalla Therme   SPA
(www.caracalla.de; Römerplatz 11; 2/3/4hr €14/17/20; ⊙8am-10pm, last admission 8pm) Keep your bathing suit on at this glass-fronted spa as you make the most of the mineral-rich spring water in indoor and

outdoor pools, grottoes and surge channels. For those who dare to bare, saunas range from the rustic 'forest' to the roasting 95°C 'fire' variety.

🛏 Sleeping & Eating

Most restaurants huddle in the pedestrianised stretch around Leopoldsplatz. Nightlife is suited for people who've had the life boiled out of them.

Hotel Beek B&B €€

(☑367 60; www.hotel-beek.de; Gernsbacherstrasse 44-46; s €85-95, d €109-119; @) On a tree-fringed street in the heart of town, this pretty-in-pink hotel doubles as an excellent patisserie, going strong since 1885. Facing either a courtyard or the Neues Schloss, the bright rooms sport comfy beds; the best ones come with balconies.

Hotel am Markt HISTORIC HOTEL €

(☑270 40; www.hotel-am-markt-baden.de; Marktplatz 18; s €37-53, d €70-92; P@🛜) Sitting pretty in front of the Stiftskirche, this 250-year-old hotel has 23 homely, well-kept rooms. It's quiet up here apart from your wake-up call of church bells, but you wouldn't want to miss out on the great breakfast.

Weinstube im Baldreit GERMAN €€€

(☑231 36; Küferstrasse 3; mains €12.50-19; ⊙5-10pm Mon-Sat) Tucked down cobbled lanes, this wine-cellar restaurant is tricky to find, but persevere. Baden-Alsatian fare such as *Flammkuchen* topped with Black Forest ham, Roquefort and pears is expertly matched with local wines. Eat in the ivy-swathed courtyard in summer, the vaulted interior in winter.

Café König CAFE €

(Lichtentaler Strasse 12; cake €3.50-5; ⊙9.30am-6.30am Mon-Sat, 10.30am-6.30pm Sun) Liszt and Tolstoy once sipped coffee at this venerable cafe, which has been doing a brisk trade in top cakes, tortes, pralines and truffles for 250 years.

Rathausglöckel GERMAN €€

(☑906 10; Steinstrasse 7; mains €10-16; ⊙6-11pm Mon-Sat, 11.30am-2pm & 6-11pm Sun, closed Wed; 🗷🍴) Strong on old-school charm, this low-beamed tavern is cosily clad in dark wood and oil paintings and serves historic regional and German dishes.

❶ Information

The **tourist office** (www.baden-baden.com; Kaiserallee 3; ⊙10am-5pm Mon-Sat, 2-5pm Sun) is in the Trinkhalle.

❶ Getting There & Around

Karlsruhe-Baden-Baden airport (Baden Airpark; www.badenairpark.de), 15km west of town, is linked to London and other European cities by Ryanair.

Buses to Black Forest destinations depart from the bus station, next to the Bahnhof.

Baden-Baden is close to the A5 (Frankfurt–Basel autobahn) and is the northern starting point of the zigzagging Schwarzwald-Hochstrasse, which follows the B500.

Baden-Baden is on a major north–south rail corridor. Twice-hourly destinations include Freiburg (€19.20 to €28, 45 to 90 minutes) and Karlsruhe (€10 to €15, 15 to 30 minutes).

Black Forest

The Black Forest (Schwarzwald) gets its name from its dark canopy of evergreens, which evoke mystery and allure. Although some parts heave with visitors, a 20-minute walk from even the most crowded spots will put you in quiet countryside interspersed with hulking traditional farmhouses and patrolled by amiable dairy cows. It's not nature wild and remote, but bucolic and picturesque. And, yes, there are many, many

❶ **BLACK FOREST SAVINGS**

Check into almost any hotel in Baden-Württemberg, pay the nominal *Kurtaxe* (holiday tax) and you automatically receive the money-saving **Gästekarte** (Guest Card), entitling you to free or discounted entry to many attractions and activities plus hefty discounts on everything from bike hire and spas to ski lifts and boat trips. Versions with the Konus symbol mean free use of public transport.

Most tourist offices in the Black Forest sell the three-day **Schwarzwald-Card** for admission to around 150 attractions in the Black Forest. Details on both cards are available at www.blackforest-tourism.com.

Black Forest

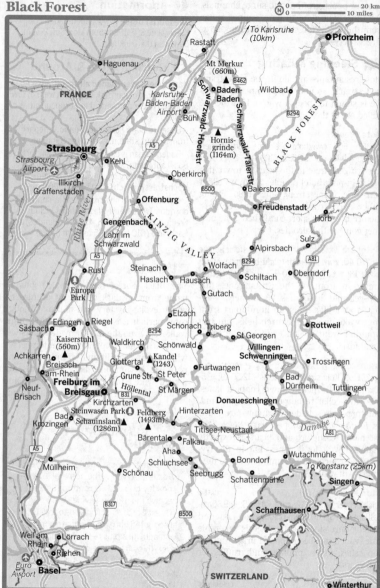

places to buy cuckoo clocks (you pay at least €150 for a good one).

❶ Getting Around

With a car you'll find a visit especially rewarding, as you can explore the rolling hills and deep valleys at will. One of the main tourist roads is the scenic **Schwarzwald-Hochstrasse** (B500), which runs from Baden-Baden to Freudenstadt and from Triberg to Waldshut.

An hourly train line links Freudenstadt with Offenburg via Alpirsbach, Schiltach and other villages. From Hausach, trains run roughly hourly southeast to Triberg and Constance.

FREUDENSTADT
📞 07441 / POP 23,550

Freudenstadt is a good base for exploring the northern Black Forest and hikes into the surrounding countryside. It's most notable feature is a vast cafe- and shop-lined **market square** that is the largest in the country. Stop by the **tourist office** (www.freudenstadt. de; Marktplatz 64; ⊙9am-6pm Mon-Fri, 10am-2pm Sat & Sun May-Oct, shorter hours other times) for hiking suggestions.

The Gaiser family extend a warm welcome at **Hotel Adler** (📞915 20; www.adler-fds. de; Forststrasse 15-17; s €45-53, d €74-90, mains €12 to €17; P🐕), a guesthouse with comfy, fusty rooms and a terrace. The bistro serves Swabian faves like *Spätzle*.

ALPIRSBACH

A small town, Alpirsbach, is worth a trip for its 12th-century Benedictine abbey, **Kloster Alpirsbach** (adult/concession €4/3.30; ⊙10am-5.30pm Mon-Sat, 11am-5.30pm Sun), which conveys the simple, spiritual life in its flat-roofed church, spartan cells and Gothic cloister. The museum has a stash of 16th-century clothing, caricatures (of artistic scholars) and lines (of misbehaving ones).

Just across the old complex you'll find what's kept the monks busy all these years: the **Alpirsbacher Klosterbräu** (📞670; www.alpirsbacher.com; Marktplatz 1; tours €6.90; ⊙2.30pm daily) brewery. Tours include a couple of glasses of the brew.

For more information, stop by the **tourist office** (📞951 6281; www.stadt-alpirsbach.de; Krähenbadstrasse 2; ⊙10am-noon & 2-5pm Mon-Fri, closed Wed afternoon).

Alpirsbach is a stop for the hourly trains linking Schiltach and Freudenstadt.

SCHILTACH
📞 07836 / POP 3875

A contender for the prettiest town in the Black Forest is Schiltach, where there is the always-underlying roar of the intersecting Kinzig and Schiltach Rivers. Half-timbered buildings lean at varying angles along the criss-crossing hillside lanes. Centred on a trickling fountain, the sloping, triangular **Marktplatz** is Schiltach at its picture-book best.

Don't miss the **Schüttesäge Museum** (Gerbegasse; ⊙11am-5pm daily Apr-Oct, Sat & Sun

---

FOREST FOODIE FAVES

Black Forest specialities include *Schwarzwälder Schinken* (ham), which is smoked and served in a variety of ways. Rivalling those ubiquitous clocks in fame (but not price), *Schwarzwälder Kirschtorte* (Black Forest cake) is a chocolate and cherry concoction. A popular local beer is the crisp pilsener called Rothaus.

---

only Nov-Mar), which illustrates Schiltach's rafting tradition with a reconstructed workshop, a functioning watermill and touchy-feely exhibits for kids.

Nineteen generations of the same family have run the 16th-century inn **Weysses Rössle** (📞387; www.weysses-roessle.de; Schenkenzeller Strasse 42; s/d €52/75; P🐕), where countrified rooms feature snazzy bathrooms. The woodsy tavern uses locally sourced, organic fare.

The **tourist office** (www.schiltach.de; Hauptstrasse 5; ⊙10am-5pm Mon-Fri, to 2pm Sat Apr-Oct) can help with accommodation and has a lot of English-language information.

TRIBERG
📞 07722 / POP 5000

Heir to the Black Forest cake recipe, nesting ground of the world's biggest cuckoos and spring of Germany's highest waterfall – Triberg is a torrent of Schwarzwald superlatives and attracts gushes of guests.

Niagara they ain't, but Germany's highest **waterfalls** (adult/concession €3.50/3; ⊙Mar-early Nov, 25-30 Dec) do exude their own wild romanticism. The Gutach River feeds the seven-tiered falls, which drop a total of 163m. The trail starts near the tourist office, which also has a small museum.

Triberg is Germany's undisputed cuckoo-clock capital. Two timepieces claim the title of world's largest cuckoo clock, giving rise to the battle of the birds. To the casual observer, the biggest is undeniably the commercially savvy **Eble Uhren−Park** (www.uhren-park.de; Schonachbach 27; admission €2; ⊙9am-6pm Mon-Sat, 10am-6pm Sun), listed in the Guinness World Records, on the B33 between Triberg and Hornberg. At the other end of town, in Schonach, is its underdog rival, the **1. Weltgrösste Kuckuckuhr** (📞07722-4689; Untertalstrasse

28; adult/concession €1.20/0.60; ⊙9am-6pm May-Oct, 10am-5pm Nov-Apr), nestled inside a snug chalet and complete with gear-driven innards. This giant timepiece – unable to compete in size alone – has taken to calling itself the world's oldest, largest cuckoo clock. It was built in the 1980s.

Above the shop of master woodcarver Gerald Burger is **Kukucksnest** (☑869 487; Wallfahrtstrasse 15; d €58), a beautiful nest he has carved for guests.

The kirsch-scented Black Forest cake at **Café Schäfer** (www.cafe-schaefer-triberg.de; Hauptstrasse 33; cake €3-4; ⊙9am-6pm Mon-Fri, 8am-6pm Sat, 11am-6pm Sun, closed Wed) is the real deal; it has the original recipe to prove it.

The hourly Schwarzwaldbahn train line loops southeast to Constance (€23.30, 1½ hours), and northwest to Offenburg (€11.10, 45 minutes). Bus 7150 travels north via Gutach to Offenburg; bus 7265 heads south to Villingen via St Georgen.

Triberg's train station is 1.7km from the centre; take any bus to the Markt.

Freiburg im Breisgau

☑0761 / POP 224,200

Sitting plump at the foot of the Black Forest's wooded slopes and vineyards, Freiburg is a sunny, cheerful university town; its medieval Altstadt a story-book tableau of gabled town houses, cobblestone lanes and cafe-rimmed plazas lorded over by a monumental 13th-century cathedral. Party-loving students spice up the local nightlife. Blessed with 2000 hours of annual sunshine, this is Germany's warmest city.

◉ Sights & Activities

^{TOP} **Münster**   CATHEDRAL

(Münsterplatz; tower adult/concession €1.50/1; ⊙10am-5pm Mon-Sat, 1-7.30pm Sun, tower 9.30am-5pm Mon-Sat, 1-5pm Sun) Freiburg's 13th-century minster is a red-sandstone pile whose punctured spires and gargoyles flush scarlet in the dusk light. Ascend the tower for an excellent view of the church's intricate construction; on clear days you can spy the Vosges Mountains in France.

Inside, the kaleidoscopic stained-glass windows dazzle. The **high altar** features a masterful triptych of the coronation of the Virgin Mary by Hans Baldung.

Rathausplatz   SQUARE

(Town Hall Square) Freiburg locals hang out by the fountain in chestnut-shaded Rathausplatz. On its western side, note the red-sandstone, step-gabled **Neues Rathaus** (New City Hall; Rathausplatz).

Across the way is the mid-16th-century **Altes Rathaus** (Old City Hall; Universtitat-strasse), a flamboyant, ox-blood red edifice, embellished with gilt swirls and crowned by a clock and a fresco of the twin-headed Habsburg eagle.

On the square's northern side, the medieval **Martinskirche** demands attention with its covered cloister. Once part of a Franciscan monastery, the church was severely damaged in WWII, it was rebuilt in the ascetic style typical of this mendicant order.

Augustinermuseum   MUSEUM

(☑201 2531; Salzstrasse 32; adult/child €6/4; ⊙10am-5pm Tue-Sun) This beautiful Augustinian monastery showcases prized medieval,

WORTH A TRIP

SOARING ABOVE THE FOREST

Freiburg seems tiny as you drift up above the city and a tapestry of meadows and forest on the **Schauinslandbahn** (adult/concession return €12/11, one-way €8.50/8; ⊙9am-5pm, to 6pm Jul-Sep) to the 1284m **Schauinsland peak** (www.bergwelt-schauinsland.de). The lift provides a speedy link between Freiburg and the Black Forest highlands.

Up top, enjoy commanding views to the Rhine Valley and Alps from the lookout tower, then hit a trail to capture the scenery from many different angles. You can also bounce downhill on the 8km off-road **scooter track** (www.rollerstrecke.de; €20; ⊙2pm & 5pm Sun May-Jun, Sat & Sun Jul & Sep-Oct, Wed-Sun Aug), one of Europe's longest; it takes around an hour from top to bottom station.

The Schauinslandbahn valley station is about 9km southeast of central Freiburg. Take tram 2 to Günterstal and then bus 21 to Talstation.

baroque and 19th-century art by such hot shots as Hans Baldung, Matthias Grünewald and Lucas Cranach. There's also lavish medieval stained glass.

🛏 Sleeping

TOP CHOICE **Hotel Oberkirch**　　HISTORIC HOTEL €€€
(📞202 6868; www.hotel-oberkirch.de; Münsterplatz 22; s €102-123, d €155-169, mains €13-23; 🅿) Wake up to Münster views at this 250-year-old green-shuttered hotel, whose country-style rooms feature floral wallpaper and half-canopied beds. The dark-wood **tavern** downstairs does a roaring trade in hearty local fare like venison ragout with *Knödel* (dumplings).

Hotel Schwarzwälder Hof　　HOTEL €€
(📞380 30; www.schwarzwaelder-hof.eu; Herrenstrasse 43; s/d/tr €65/99/120; 📶) This bijou hotel has an unrivalled style-for-euro ratio. A wrought-iron staircase sweeps up to snazzy rooms that are temples to chalk whites and chocolate browns. Some have Altstadt views.

Black Forest Hostel　　HOSTEL €
(📞881 7870; www.blackforest-hostel.de; Kartäuserstrasse 33; dm €14-23, s/d €30/50; 📶) Funky budget digs with chilled common areas, a shared kitchen, bike rental and spacey stainless-steel showers. It's a five-minute walk from the centre of town.

🍴 Eating & Drinking

Wolfshöhle　　MEDITERRANEAN €€€
(📞303 03; Konviktstrasse 8; mains €16-27; ⏱closed Mon lunch, Sun) With tables set up on a pretty square, Wolfshöhle is a summer-evening magnet. The menu whisks you off on a gastro tour of the Mediterranean, with well-executed dishes like Iberian pork with wild garlic puree and scampi with saffron-infused risotto.

Hausbrauerei Feierling　　BREWERY €€
(Gerberau 46; mains €6-12; 📞) Starring one of Freiburg's best beer gardens, this brewpub serves great vegetarian options and humungous schnitzels with *Brägele* (chipped potatoes).

Englers Weinkrügle　　GERMAN €€
(📞383 115; Konviktstrasse 12; mains €9-16; ⏱Tue-Sun) A warm, woody Baden-style *Weinstube* (wine tavern) with wisteria growing out front and regional flavours on the menu. The trout in various guises (for instance

with riesling or almond-butter sauce) is delicious.

Schlappen　　PUB
(Löwenstrasse 2; ⏱11am-btwn 1am & 3am Mon-Sat, 3pm-1am Sun) With its jazz-themed back room and poster-plastered walls, this pub is a perennial favourite. Try one of 10 absinthe varieties and you'll be away with the green fairies. Punters spill onto the terrace in summer.

ℹ Information

Tourist office (📞388 1880; www.freiburg.de; Rathausplatz 2-4; ⏱8am-8pm Mon-Fri, 9.30am-5pm Sat, 11am-4pm Sun)

ℹ Getting There & Around

Freiburg shares **EuroAirport** (www.euroairport. com) with Basel (Switzerland) and Mulhouse (France). It buzzes with low-cost carriers. From Freiburg it is served hourly by the **Airport Bus** (📞500 500; www.freiburger-reisedienst.de; one-way/return €23/39; ⏱55 minutes).

The Frankfurt–Basel A5 passes just west of Freiburg. The scenic B31 leads east through the Höllental to Lake Constance. The B294 goes north into the Black Forest.

Fast trains connect Freiburg to Basel (from €16.40, 45 minutes) and Baden-Baden (from €19.20, 45 minutes). Freiburg is also the western terminus of the Höllentalbahn to Donaueschingen via Titisee-Neustadt (€5.10, 38 minutes, twice an hour).

LAKE CONSTANCE

Straddling Germany, Austria and Switzerland, Lake Constance (known locally as Bodensee) is Central Europe's third largest lake. Formed by the Rhine Glacier during the last ice age and fed and drained by that same sprightly river today, this whopper of a lake measures 63km long, 14km wide and up to 250m deep. Even if you never make contact with the water, this giant bulge in the sinewy course of the Rhine offers a delightful splash of refreshment. Historic towns line its vineyard-dappled periphery, which can be explored by boat or bicycle or on foot.

ℹ Getting There & Around

Trains link Lindau and Constance, and buses fill in the gaps to places like Meersburg. By car, the B31 hugs the northern shore of Lake Constance, but it can get rather busy.

TICKETS TO SAVINGS

EuregioBodensee Tageskarte
(www.euregiokarte.com) All-day access to land transport around Lake Constance, including areas in Austria and Switzerland. It's sold at train stations and ferry docks and costs €16.50/22/29 for one/two/all zones.

Bodensee Erlebniskarte (adult/child €72/36, not incl ferries €40/21) This three-day card, available at local tourist and ferry offices from early April to mid-October, is good for unlimited travel on almost all boats and mountain cableways on and around Lake Constance (including its Austrian and Swiss shores) as well as free entry to around 180 tourist attractions and museums.

The most enjoyable, albeit slowest, way to get around is by ferry. Constance is the main hub, but Meersburg and Friedrichshafen also have plentiful ferry options. The most useful lines, run by **German BSB** (www.bsb-online.com) and **Austrian ÖBB** (www.bodenseeschifffahrt.at), link Constance with Meersburg (€5.30, 30 minutes), Friedrichshafen (€11.70, 1¾ hours), Lindau (€15.40, three hours) and Bregenz (€16.40, 3½ hours); children aged six to 15 years pay half-price. The websites list timetables.

Euregio Bodensee (www.euregiokarte.com), which groups all Lake Constance–area public transport, publishes a free *Fahrplan* with schedules for all train, bus and ferry services.

Constance

📞 07531 / POP 84,700

Hugging the Swiss border, Constance (Konstanz) is a feelgood university town with a lively buzz and upbeat bar scene, particularly in the cobbled Altstadt and along the lively waterfront.

It achieved historical significance in 1414, when the Council of Constance convened to try to heal huge rifts in the Catholic Church. The consequent burning at the stake of the religious reformer Jan Hus as a heretic, and the scattering of his ashes over the lake, did nothing to block the Reformation.

◎ Sights & Activities

TOP CHOICE **Münster** CATHEDRAL

(tower adult/child €2/1; ⊙10am-6pm Mon-Sat, 10am-6pm Sun, tower 10am-5pm Mon-Sat, 12.30pm-

5.30pm Sun) Crowned by a filigree spire and looking proudly back on 1000 years of history, the sandstone Münster is an architectural potpourri of Romanesque, Gothic, Renaissance and baroque styles. Standouts include the 15th-century Schnegg, an ornate spiral staircase, the 1000-year-old crypt and the sublime Gothic cloister. On cloudless days, it's worth ascending the tower for broad views over the city and lake.

Mainau GARDEN

(www.mainau.de; adult/concession €16.90/9.50; ⊙sunrise-sunset) Jutting out over the Lake Constance and bursting with flowers, the lusciously green islet of Mainau is a 45-hectare Mediterranean garden dreamed up by the Bernadotte family, relatives of the royal house of Sweden. Take bus 4 from Constance's train station or hop aboard a passenger ferry.

🛏 Sleeping & Eating

Münsterplatz and Markstätte are peppered with pizzerias and snack bars. Watch out for rip-offs around Stadtgarten.

Hotel Barbarossa HISTORIC HOTEL €€

(📞128 990; www.barbarossa-hotel.com; Obermarkt 8-12; s €55-75, d €95-130; 🐾) This 600-year-old patrician house harbours parquet-floored, individually decorated rooms, which are bright and appealing, if a tad on the small side. The terrace has views over Constance's rooftops and spires.

Riva BOUTIQUE HOTEL €€€

(📞363 090; www.hotel-riva.de; Seestrasse 25; s €110-150, d €200-240; 🅿🐾🏊) This ultrachic contender has crisp white spaces, glass walls and a snail-like stairwell. Zen-like rooms with hardwood floors feature perks including free minibars. The rooftop pool and Mediterranean-style restaurant (mains €18 to €25) overlook the lake.

Münsterhof GERMAN €€

(📞3638 427; Münsterplatz 3; mains €8.50-17; 🐾) Tables set up in front of the Münster, a slick bistro interior and a lunchtime buzz have earned Münsterhof a loyal local following. The two-course €6.90 lunch is a bargain.

Voglhaus CAFE €

(Wessenbergstrasse 8; light meals €2.50-6; ⊙9am-6.30pm Mon-Sat, 11am-6pm Sun; 🐾) Locals flock to the 'bird house' for its chilled vibe and contemporary wood-and-stone interior, warmed by an open fire in winter. Wood-oven bread with spreads, wholegrain bagels and cupcakes pair nicely with smoothies and speciality coffees like Hansel and Gretel (with gingerbread syrup).

Brauhaus Johann Albrecht   BREWPUB
(Konradigasse 2; ☉11.30am-1pm) This step-gabled microbrewery is a relaxed haunt for quaffing wheat beer or hoppy lager by the glass or metre, with a terrace for summer imbibing.

ℹ Information

The **tourist office** (☏133 030; www.konstanz
-tourismus.de; Bahnhofplatz 43; ☉9am-6.30pm Mon-Fri, 9am-4pm Sat, 10am-1pm Sun Apr-Oct, 9.30am-6pm Mon-Fri Nov-Mar) is in the train station.

ℹ Getting There & Away

Constance is Lake Constance's main ferry hub. By car, it's served by the B33, which links up with the A81 to and from Stuttgart near Singen. Or you can take the B31 to Meersburg and then catch a car ferry.

The town is also the southern terminus of the scenic Schwarzwaldbahn, which trundles hourly through the Black Forest. For northern shore towns, change in Radolfzell.

Meersburg
☏07532 / POP 5630
Tumbling down vine-streaked slopes to Lake Constance and crowned by a perkily turreted medieval castle, Meersburg lives up to all those clichéd knights-in-armour, damsel-in-distress fantasies. Its highlight is the **Altes Schloss** (adult/concession €8.50/6.50; ☉9am-6.30pm Mar-Oct, 10am-6pm Nov-Feb), an archetypal medieval stronghold, complete with keep, drawbridge, knights' hall and dungeons.

The **tourist office** (☏440 400; www.meers burg.de; Kirchstrasse 4; ☉9am-12.30pm & 2-6pm Mon-Fri, 10am-3pm Sat, 10am-1pm Sun, shorter hours in winter) is housed in a one time Dominican monastery.

Meersburg has no train station but is linked eight times daily by express bus 7394 to Constance (€3.25, 40 minutes) and Friedrichshafen (€3.10, 26 minutes).

Lindau
☏08382 / POP 24,800
Cradled in the southern crook of Lake Constance and almost dipping its toes into Austria, Lindau is a good-looking, car-free little town, with a candy-coloured postcard of an Altstadt, clear-day Alpine views and lakefront cafes. The town's biggest architectural stunner is the 15th-century, step-gabled **Altes Rathaus** (Old Town Hall; Bismarckplatz), a frescoed frenzy of cherubs, merry minstrels and galleons.

Spend at the night at the 18th-century **Hotel Garni-Brugger** (☏934 10; www.hotel -garni-brugger.de; Bei der Heidenmauer 11; s €56-78, d €92-106; @), where bright rooms are done up in floral fabrics and pine, and the owner-family bends over backwards to please. A good bet for regional fare is **Weinstube Frey** (☏947 9676; Maximilianstrasse 15; mains €13-22; ☉closed Mon), a 500-year-old wine tavern oozing Bavarian charm. For a drink with a cool view, head to Seepromenade.

The **tourist office** (☏260 030; www.lindau. de; Ludwigstrasse 68; ☉9am-6pm Mon-Fri, 2-6pm Sat & Sun May-Sep, 9am-5pm Mon-Fri Oct-Apr) is opposite the train station.

Lindau is on the B31 and is connected to Munich by the A96. The Deutsche Alpenstrasse (German Alpine Route), which winds eastward to Berchtesgaden, begins here. It is also at the eastern terminus of the rail line that goes along the northern lake shore as far as Radolfzell.

RHINELAND-PALATINATE

Rhineland-Palatinate (Rheinland-Pfalz) is deeply riven by rivers, and the two best known – the Rhine and the Moselle – are synonymous with the wines made from the grapes growing on their hillsides. Created after WWII from parts of the former Rhineland and Rhenish Palatinate regions, the area's turbulent history goes all the way back to the Romans, best demonstrated in Trier. In recent centuries it was hotly contested by the French and a variety of German states, which produced many of its charismatically crumbling medieval castles.

ROMANCING THE RHINE

Nearly every Rhine village has its own charms and is worth at least a quick spin on foot. Just pick one at random and make your own discoveries. Here are a few enticing teasers:

Boppard Roman walls and ruins and cable to Vierseenblick viewpoint. On the left bank.

Oberwesel Famous for its 3km-long partly walkable medieval town wall, punctuated by 16 guard towers. On the left bank.

Assmannhausen Relatively untouristed village known for its red wines, sweeping views and good hikes. On the right bank.

Rüdesheim Escape the day-tripper deluged *Drosselgasse* (alley) to soar above the vineyards to the mighty *Niederwalddenkmal* (memorial). On the right bank.

Romantic Rhine

A trip along the mighty Rhine is a highlight for most travellers to Germany. The section between Koblenz and Mainz is Unesco-protected and is called Romantic Rhine for good reason. This is Germany's landscape at its most dramatic – forested hillsides alternate with craggy cliffs and nearly-vertical terraced vineyards. Idyllic villages appear around each bend, their neat half-timbered houses and Gothic church steeples seemingly plucked from the world of fairy tales.

High above the river, which is busy with barge traffic, and the rail lines that run along each bank, are the famous medieval castles, some ruined, some restored, all shrouded in mystery.

Spring and autumn are the best times to visit; the area is overrun in summer and goes into hibernation in winter. Every river town brims with cute places to stay, eat and drink.

Although Koblenz and Mainz are the best starting points, the Rhine Valley is also easily accessible from Frankfurt on a (very long) day trip. Note that there are only car ferries (no bridges) along this stretch of river.

Getting There & Around

Each mode of transport on the Rhine has its own advantages and all are equally enjoyable. Try combining several. The **Köln-Düsseldorfer Line** (KD; ☏0221-2088 318; www.k-d.com) runs numerous boat services daily between Koblenz and Mainz (as well as the less-interesting stretch between Cologne and Koblenz) which stop at riverside towns along the way.

Villages on the Rhine's left bank (eg Bingen, Bacharach, Oberwesel and Boppard) are served hourly by local trains on the Koblenz–Mainz run. Right-bank villages such as Rüdesheim, Assmannshausen, Kaub, St Goarshausen and Braubach are linked hourly to Koblenz' Hauptbahnhof and Wiesbaden by the RheingauLinie, operated by Vias.

ST GOAR & ST GOARSHAUSEN
☏06741 / POP 3100

These twin towns face each other across the Rhine. On the left bank, St Goar is lorded over by **Burg Rheinfels** (www.st-goar.de; adult/child €4/2; ⏰9am-6pm mid-Mar–early Nov, 11am-5pm Sat & Sun in good weather early Nov–mid-Mar), one of the most impressive castles on the river. Its labyrinthine ruins reflect the greed and ambition of the local count who built the behemoth in 1245 to levy tolls on passing ships.

Across the river, just south of St Goarshausen, is the most fabled spot along the Romantic Rhine, the **Loreley Rock**. This vertical slab of slate owes its fame to a mythical maiden whose siren songs are said to have lured sailors to their death in the river's treacherous currents. Learn more at the multimedia visitor's centre **Loreley Besucherzentrum** (☏599 093; www.loreley-besucherzentrum.de; adult/student €2.50/1.50; ⏰10am-6pm Apr-Oct, 10am-5pm Mar, 11am-4pm Sat & Sun Nov-Feb). The outcrop can be reached by car, by shuttle bus from Goarshausen's Marktplatz (€2.65, hourly 10am to 5pm) and via the 400-step Treppenweg stairway, which begins about 2km upriver from St Goarshausen at the base of the breakwater.

St Goar's **Jugendherberge** (youth hostel; ☏388; www.djh.de; Bismarckweg 17; dm/s/d €18/30/50) is right below the castle, which also houses the upmarket **Romantik Hotel Schloss Rheinfels** (☏06741-8020; www.schloss-rheinfels.de; d €115-265, cheaper in winter; @🛜🏊) and its three restaurants.

BACHARACH
☏06743 / POP 2250

One of the prettiest of the Rhine villages, Bacharach conceals its considerable charms behind a 14th-century wall (you can stroll on top along most of it). Beyond the thick arched gateways awaits a beautiful medieval old town graced with half-timbered mansions such as the **Altes Haus**, the **Posthof** and the off-kilter **Alte Münze** along Oberstrasse. All house places to eat, drink and be merry.

The local youth hostel, **DJH Burg Stahleck** (🖉1266; www.jugendherberge.de; Burg Stahleck; dm/d €20.50/52), has a dream location in a hillside medieval castle. Right on the medieval ramparts, the **Rhein Hotel** (🖉1243; www.rhein-hotel-bacharach.de; Langstrasse 50; s €39-65, d €78-130; ❄🗐) has 14 well-lit, soundproofed rooms with original artwork. The restaurant serves regional dishes.

MAINZ
🖉06131 / POP 199,000

An easy day trip from Frankfurt, Mainz has an attractive old town anchored by its massive **Dom** (Marktplatz; ⏰9am-6.30pm Mon-Fri, 9am-4pm Sat, 12.45-6.30pm Sun & holidays, shorter hrs Nov-Feb), which has a blend of Romanesque, Gothic and baroque architecture.

Sampling local wines in a half-timbered Altstadt tavern is as much a part of any Mainz visit as viewing the ethereal Marc Chagall–designed windows in **St-Stephan-Kirche** (Kleine Weissgasse 12; ⏰10am-4.30pm) or the first printed Bible in the **Gutenberg Museum** (www.gutenberg-museum.de; Liebfrauenplatz 5; adult/child €5/3; ⏰9am-5pm Tue-Sat, 11am-5pm Sun), which honours local boy and moveable-type inventor Johannes Gutenberg.

For more information, visit the **tourist office** (🖉286 210; www.touristik-mainz.de; Brückenturm am Rathaus; ⏰9am-6pm Mon-Fri, 10am-4pm Sat, 11am-3pm Sun).

In a 15th-century Carmelite nunnery near the cathedral, **Hotel Hof Ehrenfels** (🖉971 2340; www.hof-ehrenfels.de; Grebenstrasse 5-7; s/d/tr €80/100/120, €10 less Fri-Sun) has Dom views that are hard to beat. For wine and sustenance, sit beneath the soaring Gothic vaults of a medieval hospital at **Heiliggeist** (www.heiliggeist-mainz.de; Mailandsgasse 11; mains €9.80-19.80; ⏰4pm-1am Mon-Fri, 9am-1am or 2am Sat, Sun & holidays).

Moselle Valley

Like a vine right before harvest, the Moselle hangs heavy with visitor fruit. Castles and half-timbered towns are built along the sinuous river below steep, rocky cliffs planted with vineyards. It's one of the country's most scenic regions, with a constant succession of views rewarding the intrepid hikers who brave the hilly trails. Unlike the Romantic Rhine, it's spanned by plenty of bridges. The region is busiest in May, on summer weekends and during the local wine harvest (mid-September to mid-October).

❶ Getting There & Around

The most scenic part of the Moselle Valley runs 195km from Trier to Koblenz; it's most practical to begin your Moselle Valley trip from either town. Driving is the easiest way to explore this area. If you're coming from Koblenz, the B49 and then, after Bullay, the B53 follow the river all the way to Trier, crossing it several times.

Trains linking Koblenz with Trier (€19.20, 1½ to two hours, at least hourly) stop at river villages only as far as Bullay. From there, hourly shuttle trains head upriver to Traben-Trarbach. The villages between Traben-Trarbach and Trier, including Bernkastel-Kues, are served by bus 333, run by Moselbahn buses.

Frankfurt-Hahn Airport (www.hahn-airport.de), served by Ryanair, is 22km east of Traben-Trarbach and 17km east of Bernkastel-Kues. A shuttle bus links the airport with the railhead of Bullay (€6.80, 51 minutes).

KOBLENZ
🖉0261 / POP 106,000

Founded by the Romans, Koblenz sits at the confluence of the Rhine and Moselle Rivers, a point known as **Deutsches Eck** (German 'Corner'), and is dominated by a bombastic 19th-century statue of Kaiser Wilhelm I on horseback. On the right Rhine bank high above the Deutsches Eck, the **Festung Ehrenbreitstein** (www.diefestungehrenbreitstein.de;

WORTH A TRIP

BURG ELTZ

South of Koblenz, at the head of the beautiful Eltz Valley, Burg Eltz is not to be missed. Towering over the surrounding hills, this superb medieval castle has frescoes, paintings, furniture and ornately decorated rooms.

By car, you can reach Burg Eltz via the village of Münstermaifeld; the castle is 800m from the car park (shuttle bus €1.50). Trains link Koblenz and Moselkern (also reachable by boat), where a 35-minute trail to the castle begins at the Ringelsteiner Mühle car park.

adult/child €6/3; ☉10am-6pm Apr-Oct, to 5pm Nov-Mar)is one one of Europe's mightiest fortresses. Views are great and there's a regional museum inside. The castle is reached by an 850m-long Seilbahn (aerial cable car; www.seilbahn-koblenz.de; adult/6-14yr return €8/4, incl fortress €11.20/5.60, bicycle one-way €3; ☉10am-6pm or 7pm Apr-Oct, to 5pm Nov-Mar).

The tourist office (☑313 04; Bahnhofplatz 17; ☉9am-6pm Mon-Fri) is outside the Hauptbahnhof. Restaurants and pubs cluster around Münzplatz and Burgstrasse in the Altstadt and along the Rhine.

Several boat companies dock on the Rhine, south of the Deutsches Eck. Koblenz has two train stations, the main Hauptbahnhof on the Rhine's left bank about 1km south of the city centre, and Koblenz-Ehrenbreitstein on the right bank (right below the fortress).

BEILSTEIN

On the right bank of the Moselle, about 50km upriver from Koblenz, Beilstein is a pint-sized village right out of the world of fairy tales. Little more than a cluster of houses surrounded by steep vineyards, its historic highlights include the Marktplatz and Burg Metternich, a hilltop castle reached via a staircase.

The Zehnthauskeller (Marktplatz; ☉11am-evening Tue-Sun) houses a romantically dark, vaulted wine tavern owned by the same family that also runs two local hotels (☑1850; www.hotel-lipmann.de).

TRABEN-TRARBACH

Full of fanciful art nouveau villas, the double town of Traben-Trarbach provides respite from the 'romantic half-timbered town' circuit. Pick up a map of the town at the tourist office (☑839 80; www.traben-trarbach. de; Am Bahnhof 5, Traben; ☉10am-5pm Mon-Fri May-Aug, to 6pm Sep & Oct, to 4pm Nov-Apr, 11am-3pm Sat May-Oct; ☏). The ruined medieval Grevenburg castle sits high in the craggy hills above Trarbach and is reached via a steep footpath, the Sponheimer Weg, that begins a block north of the bridge.

Weingut Caspari (☑5778; www.weingut -caspari.de; Weiherstrasse 18, Trarbach; mains €6.50-16.90) is a rustic, old-time wine restaurant serving hearty local specialities; it's six short blocks inland from the bridge.

BERNKASTEL-KUES

The twin town of Bernkastel-Kues is at the heart of the middle Moselle region. On the right bank, Bernkastel has a charming Markt, a romantic ensemble of half-timbered houses with beautifully decorated gables. On Karlstrasse, the alley to the right as you face the Rathaus, the tiny Spitzhäuschen resembles a giant bird's house, its narrow base topped by a much larger, precariously leaning, upper floor.

Get your heart pumping by hoofing it from the Spitzhäuschen up to Burg Landshut, a ruined 13th-century castle – framed by vineyards and forests – on a bluff above town; allow 30 minutes. You'll be rewarded with glorious valley views and a cold drink at the beer garden (☉10am-6pm mid-Feb–Nov).

Trier

☑0651 / POP 105,250

Founded by the Romans around 16 BC as Augusta Treverorum, Trier became the capital of Roman Gaul in the 3rd century and the residence of Constantine the Great in the 4th century. To this day, you'll find more – and better preserved – Roman ruins here than anywhere else north of the Alps. Trier's proximity to France can be tasted in its cuisine, while its large student population injects life among the ruins.

◉ Sights

Porta Nigra ROMAN GATE
(adult/student €3/2.10, incl Stadtmuseum Simeonstift €7.20/5.80; ☉9am-6pm Apr-Sep, to 5pm Mar & Oct, to 4pm Nov-Feb) Trier's chief landmark, the brooding 2nd-century city gate is held together by nothing but gravity and iron rods.

Amphitheater ROMAN SITE
(Olewiger Strasse; adult/child €3/2.10; ☉9am-6pm Apr-Sep, to 5pm Mar & Oct, to 4pm Nov-Feb) This classic outdoor space once held 20,000 spectators during gladiator tournaments and animal fights – or when Constantine the Great crowned his battlefield victories by feeding his enemies to voracious animals.

Kaiserthermen ROMAN SITE
(Imperial Baths; Palastgarten; adult/student €3/2.10) This vast thermal bathing complex was created by Constantine.

Dom CHURCH
(www.dominformation.de; Liebfrauenstrasse 12; ☉10am-5pm Mon-Sat, 12.30-5pm Sun, shorter hours Nov-Mar) Built above the palace of Constantine the Great's mother, Helena, this fortress-like cathedral is mostly Romanesque, with some

soaring Gothic and eye-popping baroque embellishments.

Konstantin Basilika
CHURCH

(www.konstantin-basilika.de; Konstantinplatz; ◎10am-6pm Apr-Oct, 10am or 11am-noon and 2 or 3pm-4pm Tue-Sat, noon-1pm Sun Nov-Mar) Constructed around AD 310 as Constantine's throne hall, the brick-built Konstantin Basilika (Aula Palatina) is now a typically austere Protestant church with mind-blowing dimensions.

Karl Marx Haus
HISTORIC SITE

(www.fes.de/karl-marx-haus; Brückenstrasse 10; adult/child €3/2; ◎10am-6pm daily Apr-Oct, 2-5pm Tue-Sun Nov-Mar) The suitably modest birthplace of the author of *Das Kapital* is fast becoming a major pilgrimage stop for the growing numbers of mainland Chinese tourists to Europe.

🛏 Sleeping

Hotel Römischer Kaiser
HOTEL €€

(☑977 00; www.friedrich-hotels.de; Porta-Nigra-Platz 6; s/d from €73.50/111; 🖥) Built in 1894, this hotel – convenient to the train station and the old centre – offers 43 bright, comfortable rooms with solid wood furnishings, parquet floors and spacious bathrooms.

Hille's Hostel
HOSTEL €

(☑710 2785, outside office hrs 0171-329 1247; www.hilles-hostel-trier.de; Gartenfeldstrasse 7; dm from €14, s/d €40/50, breakfast €8; ◎reception 9am-noon & 4-6pm or later; @🖥) This laid-back indie hostel has a piano in the common kitchen and 12 attractive, spacious rooms, most with private bathrooms. Call ahead if arriving outside reception hours so they'll leave the door code and the key.

⬛TOP CHOICE Becker's Hotel
BOUTIQUE HOTEL €€

(☑938 080; www.beckers-trier.de; Olewiger Strasse 206; d €110-220; P🌼@🖥) This classy establishment pairs 31 supremely tasteful rooms – some ultramodern, others rustically traditional – with stellar dining. It's 3km southeast of the centre in the quiet wine district of Olewig, across the creek from the old monastery church. Served by buses 6, 16 and 81.

🍴 Eating

In the warm months, cafes fill Trier's public squares, including the Kornmarkt. The Olewig district, 3km southeast of the centre, is home to traditional wine taverns.

Zum Domstein
ROMAN €€

(www.domstein.de; Hauptmarkt 5; mains €8.90-18.50, Roman dinner €17-35) A German-style bistro where you can either dine like an ancient Roman or feast on more conventional German and international fare.

Kartoffel Kiste
POTATOES €€

(www.kiste-trier.de; Fahrstrasse 13-14; mains €7.20-17; ◎11am-midnight; 🍴) A local favourite, this place specialises in baked, breaded, gratineed, soupified and sauce-engulfed potatoes, as well as delicious schnitzel and steaks.

ℹ️ Information

Tourist Office (☑978 080; www.trier-info.de; just inside Porta Nigra; ◎9 or 10am-5 or 6pm Mon-Sat, 9 or 10am-1pm or later Sun).

ℹ️ Getting There & Away

Trier has at least hourly train connections to Koblenz (€20.80, 1½ to two hours) and frequent service to Luxembourg (same-day return €10.80, 50 minutes, at least hourly), with onward connections to Paris.

HESSE

About two-thirds of Hesse's population lives in the Rhine-Main region, a sprawling urban conglomeration – with excellent public transport – that stretches from Frankfurt-am-Main in the north to Darmstadt in the south and Wiesbaden in the west. The attractive spa-city of Wiesbaden is the state capital, but it is Frankfurt, home of the European Central Bank, that wields the financial – and especially stock market – clout.

Frankfurt-am-Main

☑069 / POP 680,000

Unashamedly high-rise, Frankfurt-on-the-Main (pronounced 'mine') is unlike any other German city. Bristling with jagged skyscrapers, 'Mainhattan' is a true capital of finance and business, home base for one of the world's largest stock exchanges and the European Central Bank. It also hosts some of Europe's key trade fairs, including famous book and auto fairs.

Despite its business demeanour, Frankfurt consistently ranks high among Germany's most liveable cities thanks to its rich collection

Frankfurt-am-Main

Westend

Bockenheimer Landstrasse

Liebigstr

Reuterweg

Bockenheimer Anlage

Eschenheimer Tor

Hochstr

Taubenstr

INNENSTADT

Schillerstr

Alte Oper

Börsenplatz

Hauptwache

16

Biebergasse

Goethestr

Börsenstr

Taunusanlage

Neue Mainzer Str

Westendplatz

Niedenau

3

Rossmarkt

Töngesgasse

Grosser Hirschgraben

Kaisermarkt

12

Berliner Str

1

Niedenau

Weserstr

Taunusanlage

Gallusanlage

Bethmannstr

Tourist Office

8

BAHNHOFSVIERTEL

Elbestr

Willy-Brandt-Platz

Karlstr

Taunusstr

6

Untermainbrücke

Kaiserstr

Hauptbahnhof

Münchener Str

5

Tourist Office

Windmühlstr

Mainkai

Baseler Str

7

Eurolines

Holbeinsteg

Museumsufer

MUSEUMSUFER

Wilhelm-Leuschner-Str

Baselerplatz

Städel Museum

Dürerstr

Städelstr

Untermainkai

Main River

Holbeinstr

Gartenstr

Schweizerplatz

Friedensbrücke

Schaumainkai

2

SACHSENHAUSEN

Steinlestr

Holbeinstr

Gartenstr

Schwanthaler Str

Textorstr

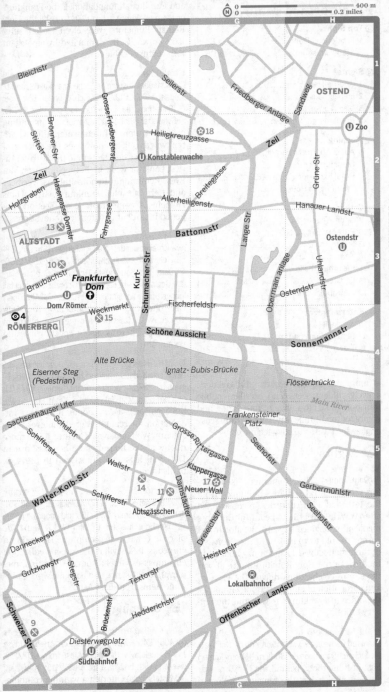

0   400 m
0   0.2 miles

Bleichstr

Grosse Friedbergstr

Sellerstr

Friedberger Anlage

Sandweg

OSTEND

Zoo

Brönner Str

Stiftstr

Heiligkreuzgasse

18

Zeil

Grüne Str

Konstablerwache

Zeil

Holzgraben

Hasengasse Domstr

Fahrgasse

Allerheiligenstr

Breitegasse

Hanauer Landstr

13

ALTSTADT

Battonnstr

Lange Str

Ostendstr

10

Kurt-Schumacher-Str

Obermain anlage

Uhlandstr

Frankfurter Dom

Braubachstr

Dom/Römer

Weckmarkt

Fischerfeldstr

Ostendstr

4

RÖMERBERG

15

Schöne Aussicht

Sonnemannstr

Alte Brücke

Ignatz- Bubis-Brücke

Eiserner Steg
(Pedestrian)

Flösserbrücke

Main River

Sachsenhäuser Ufer

Schulstr

Frankensteiner
Platz

Seehofstr

Schifferstr

Grosse Rittergasse

Wallstr

Klappergasse

Walter-Kolb-Str

14

11

Neuer Wall

17

Gerbermühlstr

Schifferstr

Damstädter

Abtsgässchen

Dreieichstr

Seehofstr

Danneckerstr

Heisterstr

6

Gutzkowstr

Stegstr

Textorstr

Lokalbahnhof

Offenbacher   Landstr

Schweizer Str

9

Brückenstr

Hedderichstr

Diesterwegplatz

Südbahnhof

Frankfurt-am-Main

of museums, expansive parks and greenery, a lively student scene and excellent public transport. Take advantage of fine dining and plenty of night-time diversions, from cosy apple-wine taverns to edgy techno clubs.

◎ Sights

Römerberg　　　　　　　　　　　PLAZA

(🚇Dom/Römer) The Römerberg is Frankfurt's old central square. Buildings from the 14th and 15th centuries, reconstructed after WWII, hint at how beautiful the city's medieval core once was. In the northwest corner, the old town hall, or **Römer**, consists of three step-gabled 15th-century houses. In the time of the Holy Roman Empire, it was the site of celebrations during the election and coronation of emperors; today it houses the office of Frankfurt's mayor and the registry office.

Frankfurter Dom　　　　　　　CATHEDRAL

(Frankfurt Cathedral; www.domkonzerte.de; Domplatz 14; ⊙church 9am-noon & 2.30-8pm; 🚇Dom/Römer) East of Römerberg, behind the **Historischer Garten** (which has the remains of Roman

and Carolingian foundations), the Frankfurter Dom as where, from 1356 to 1792, the Holy Roman Emperors were elected (and, after 1562, crowned). It's dominated by an elegant 15th-century Gothic **tower**.

Städel Museum　　　　　　　　MUSEUM

(www.staedelmuseum.de; Schaumainkai 63; adult/student/family €12/10/20, child under 12yr free; ⊙10am-5pm Tue & Fri-Sun, to 9pm Wed & Thu; 🚇Schweizer Platz) The most outstanding collection along Museumsufer, this world-renowned gallery showcases the talents of key painters from the 14th to the 20th centuries. Look for work by Botticelli, Dürer, Van Eyck, Rembrandt, Renoir, Rubens, Vermeer and Cézanne, plus Frankfurt native Hans Holbein. A contemporary art section reopened in 2012 after extensive renovations.

Main Tower　　　　　　　　　VIEWPOINT

(www.maintower.de; Neue Mainzer Strasse 52-58; elevator adult/child/family €5/3.50/13.50; ⊙10am-9pm Sun-Thu, to 11pm Fri & Sat late Mar-late Oct, closes 2hr earlier late Oct-late Mar, cocktail lounge 9pm-midnight or 1am Tue-Sat; 🚇Alte Oper) Get your head in the clouds atop the Main Tower, with its open-air viewing platform 200m up. There is also a cocktail bar and restaurant.

Goethe-Haus　　　　　　HISTORIC BUILDING

(www.goethehaus-frankfurt.de; Grosser Hirschgraben 23-25; adult/student/family €7/3/11; ⊙10am-6pm Mon-Sat, 10am-5.30pm Sun; 🚇Willy-Brandt-Platz) 'Few people have the imagination for reality' uttered the ever-pithy Johann Wolfgang von Goethe. Read more quotes at the house where he was born in 1749, which is again furnished in the style of his time.

Liebieghaus　　　　　　　　　MUSEUM

(www.liebieghaus.de; Schaumainkai 71; adult/student & senior/family €7/5/16, child under 12yr free; ⊙10am-6pm Tue-Sun, to 9pm Wed & Thu) *The* place to come to see sculpture. Housed in a gorgeous 1890s villa, the superb collection encompasses Greek, Roman, Egyptian, medieval, Renaissance and baroque works, plus some items from East Asia.

🛏 Sleeping

TOP CHOICE Villa Orange　　　　　HOTEL €€

(🚇405 840; www.villa-orange.de; Hebelstrasse 1; s/d weekday without breakfast from €118/138, weekend with breakfast from €90/115; 🅿✳@🛜; 🚇Musterschule) Offering a winning combina-

NAVIGATING FRANKFURT

The airport is 11 minutes by train southwest of the city centre. The Hauptbahnhof is on the western side of the city, within walking distance of the centre, best reached via Kaiserstrasse. This leads to Kaiserplatz and another square called An der Hauptwache. This is the retail hub, with stores stretching along in all directions, principally along the Zeil. The area between Hauptwache and the Römerberg contains vestiges of Frankfurt's Altstadt (Old Town).

The Main River flows just south of the Altstadt, with several bridges leading to charming Sachsenhausen whose northeastern corner, known as Alt-Sachsenhausen, has quaint old houses and wine taverns.

Numerous museums line the south bank of the Main River along the so-called Museumsufer. To sample them all, buy a 48-hour Museumsufer ticket (www.kultur -frankfurt.de; adult/concession/family €15/8/23).

Just northeast of the centre, Frankfurt's village roots are most strongly felt in Bornheim, whose spine – Berger Strasse – is lined with funky small shops, cafes and pubs.

GERMANY FRANKFURT-AM-MAIN

tion of tranquillity, modern German design and small-hotel comforts (eg a quiet corner library), this century-old villa has 38 spacious rooms.

Twenty-Five Hours BOUTIQUE HOTEL €€
(25h; ☎256 6770; www.25hours-hotels.com; Niddastrasse 58; d without breakfast weekday/ weekend from €107/77, during fairs up to €390; ✳@☎; ᴙFrankfurt Hauptbahnhof) Inspired by Levi's jeans, the 76 themed rooms are styled by decade from the 1940s (calm colours) through the 1980s (tiger-print walls). Guests can jam on the drums and guitars in the Gibson-designed basement music room or admire skyline views from the roof terrace.

TOP CHOICE **Frankfurt Hostel** HOSTEL €
(☎247 5130; www.frankfurt-hostel.com; Kaiserstrasse 74, 3rd fl; dm €19-25, s/d from €35/45, during fairs up to €80/100; @☎; ᴙFrankfurt Hauptbahnhof) This 200-bed hostel is reached via a marble-and-tile lobby and a mirrored lift. Kudos for the chill-out area, guest kitchen and the free spaghetti dinners. Dorms have three to 10 metal bunks and free lockers.

Adina Apartment Hotel HOTEL €€
(☎247 4740; www.adina.eu; Wilhelm-Leuschner-Strasse 6; d without breakfast from €84-135, during fairs up to €377; ☎✳; ᴙWilly-Brandt-Platz) Self-caterers and families will appreciate these spacious studios and one- and two-bedroom apartments, all with kitchenettes.

Hotel Excelsior HOTEL €
(☎256 080; www.hotelexcelsior-frankfurt.de; Mannheimer Strasse 7-9; s/d from €61/75, during fairs €199/239; P@☎; ᴙFrankfurt Hauptbahnhof)

Behind a light-green facade, this 197-room place offers excellent value and plenty of freebies: a business centre, landline phone calls within Germany, and coffee, tea, fruit and cakes in the lobby.

 Eating & Drinking

The pedestrian strip linking the Alte Oper and the western end of the Zeil is also known as *Fressgass* thanks to its many eateries. Another cluster of places to drink and eat is in Alt-Sachsenhausen.

LOCAL KNOWLEDGE

APPLE-WINE TAVERNS

Apple-wine taverns are Frankfurt's great local tradition. They serve *Ebbelwei* (Frankfurt dialect for *Apfelwein*), an alcoholic apple cider, along with local specialities like *Handkäse mit Musik* (literally, 'hand-cheese with music'). This is a round cheese soaked in oil and vinegar and topped with onions; your bowel supplies the music. Anything with the sensational local sauce made from herbs, *Grüne Sosse*, is a winner. Some good *Ebbelwei* taverns are in Alt-Sachsenhausen, where Fichtekränzi (☎612 778; www.fichtekraenzi.de; Wallstrasse 5; mains €7.20-15.50; ⏰5-11pm; ☑; ᴙLokalbahnhof) and Adolf Wagner (☎612 565; www.apfelwein-wagner.com; Schweizer Strasse 71; mains €4.50-13.90; ⏰11am-midnight; ☑; ᴙSüdbahnhof) are recommended.

ALL ABOARD THE EBBELWEI-EXPRESS

The Ebbelwei-Express (Apple Wine Express; www.ebbelwei-express.com; adult/child under 14yr €7/3; ⊙half-hourly 1.30-5.30pm Sat, Sun & holidays Apr-Oct & Sat Nov-Mar, approx hourly 1.30-5pm Sun & holidays Nov-Mar) is a historic tram whose 70-minute circuit takes in both banks of the Main between the Zoo and the Messe. Jump on at any stop marked with the letters EE – including the Hauptbahnhof and Börneplatz. As you'd expect, the price includes *Ebbelwei* (apple wine) or juice, and pretzels.

Eckhaus
GERMAN €€

(☑491 197; Bornheimer Landstrasse 45; mains €8-17.90; ⊙5pm-midnight or 1am; ☒Merianplatz) We love this place with its smoke-stained walls and ancient floorboards. The hallmark *Kartoffelrösti* (shredded potato pancake) has been served here for over 100 years.

[TOP CHOICE] Kleinmarkthalle
MARKET €

(Hasengasse 5; ⊙7.30am-6pm Mon-Fri, to 3pm Sat; ☑; ☒Dom/Römer) This traditional covered food market has loads of fruit, vegetables and meats, as well as hot food.

Karin
CAFE €€

(☑295 217; Grosser Hirschgraben 28; mains €8-14; ⊙9am-midnight Mon-Sat, 10am-7pm Sun, 10am-midnight holidays; ☒Willy-Brandt-Platz) This Frankfurt-style cafe serves German and international dishes and nine different breakfasts (until 6pm). Changing exhibits by local artists grace the walls. Cash only.

Bitter & Zart
CAFE €

(www.bitterundzart.de; Braubachstrasse 14; ⊙10am-8pm Mon-Sat, 10am-6pm Sun; ☒Dom/Römer) Walk past the chocolate chair then turn left and you're in a delightful shop whose shelves are piled high with the finest chocolates; turn right and order espresso, light meals and breakfast (until noon) or yummy cakes.

Lobster
BISTRO €€€

(☑612 920; www.lobster-weinbistrot.de; Wallstrasse 21; mains €15-20; ⊙6pm-1am Mon-Sat, hot dishes until 10.30pm; ☒Südbahnhof) In a 1950s grocery and milk shop, this cosy, friendly 'wine bistro' is renowned for mouth-watering meat

and fish dishes that are 'a little bit French'. Serves three dozen wines by the glass. It's teensy, so book ahead.

Metropol
BISTRO €€

(☑288 287; Weckmarkt 13-15; mains €9.50-14.50; ⊙9am-1am or 2am Tue-Sat, 9am-midnight Sun; ☒Dom/Römer) Serves dishes from a changing menu that ranges from bistro staples to the inspired. Has a lovely courtyard out the back where children can chill out. Cash only.

Wein-Dünker
WINE CELLAR

(www.weinkellerei-duenker.de; Berger Strasse 265; ⊙2pm-1am Mon-Thu, 2pm-3am Fri & Sat, 6pm-midnight Sun; ☒Bornheim Mitte) Descend to this little wine cellar to try some of Germany's finest wines. It serves only snacks, but you can BYO and picnic atop an upturned barrel.

☆ Entertainment

[FREE] Summa Summarum
LIVE MUSIC

(Klappergasse 3; ⊙8pm-1am Tue-Sat) This vaulted stone cellar with just a half-dozen tables reverberates with traditional New Orleans jazz on Wednesday and Friday, and singer-songwriters (blues, rock etc) on Thursday and Saturday. Tuesday is open-mic night.

King Kamehameha
CLUB

(☑4800 9610; www.king-kamehameha.de; Hanauer Landstrasse 192; admission Thu €8, Fri & Sat €10; ⊙9pm-4am or later Thu, 10pm-4am or later Fri & Sat) 'KingKa' is legendary, with DJs on weekends and a house band on Thursdays. It's about 2km southeast of the zoo (tram 11).

Tigerpalast
CABARET

(☑restaurant 9200 2225, tickets 920 0220; www.tigerpalast.com; Heiligkreuzgasse 16-20; adult €58.75-64.25, child halfprice; ⊙shows 7pm & 10pm Tue-Thu, 7.30pm & 10.30pm Fri & Sat, 4.30pm & 8pm Sun, closed mid-Jun–mid-Aug; ☒Konstablerwache) Shows at this top-rated variety theatre often include acrobats and circus and magic performances. Hugely enjoyable even if you don't speak German. Book ahead.

Jazzkeller
JAZZ

(www.jazzkeller.com; Kleine Bockenheimer Strasse 18a; admission €5-25; ⊙8pm-2am Tue-Thu, 10pm-3am Fri, 9pm-2am Sat, 8pm-1am Sun; ☒Alte Oper) A great jazz venue since 1952. Check out the walls for photos of jazz greats who've played here over the years. Concerts begin an hour after opening except on Friday, when there's dancing to Latin and funk. In a cellar across from Goethestrasse 27.

255

Information

Tourist Office (☎2123 8800; www.frankfurt
-tourismus.de) Two branches: Hauptbahnhof
(Hauptbahnhof; ⊗8am-9pm Mon-Fri, 9am-6pm
Sat, Sun & holidays; ℝFrankfurt Hauptbahnhof) and Römer (Römerberg 27; ⊗9.30am-
5.30pm Mon-Fri, 9.30am-4pm Sat, Sun &
holidays; ℝDom/Römer).

Getting There & Away

Air

Frankfurt Airport (FRA; www.frankfurt-airport.
com), 12km southwest of the city centre, is
Germany's busiest. Terminals 1 and 2 are linked
by a driverless railway, the SkyLine.

The airport has two train stations accessible
from Terminal 1. The *Regionalbahnhof* handles
regional train and S-Bahn connections, while
long-distance IC, EC and ICE trains stop at the
Fernbahnhof. Coming from Terminal 2, use the
yellow shuttle buses (rather than the SkyLine).

To get into town, take S-Bahn lines S8 and S9
from the Regionalbahnhof (€4.10, 15 minutes). A
taxi costs about €27.

Note that **Frankfurt-Hahn airport** (HHN;
www.hahn-airport.de) is 125km west of Frankfurt near the Moselle Valley.

Bus

Long-distance buses leave from the south side
of the Hauptbahnhof, where you'll find **Eurolines** (☎790 3253; www.eurolines.eu; Mannheimer Strasse 15; ⊗7.30am-7.30pm Mon-Fri,
7.30am-2pm Sat, 7.30am-1pm Sun; ℝFrankfurt
Hauptbahnhof), with services to most European
destinations. The Europabus (p224) headed to
the Romantic Road also leaves from here.

Train

The Hauptbahnhof has train services to pretty
much everywhere, including Berlin (€118, four
hours).

Getting Around

Public Transport

Both single and day tickets for Frankfurt's excellent transport network called **traffiQ** (☎01801-
069 960; www.traffiq.de) can be purchased from
vending machines at most stops and stations.
Single tickets cost €2.50 and a *Tageskarte* (24-
hour ticket) costs €6.20 (€14.50 including the
airport).

Taxi

Flagfall is €2.75 (€3.25 at night) and each kilometre is charged at €1.65 (€1.75 at night). There
are taxi ranks throughout the city, or call a cab
through **Taxi Frankfurt** (☎250 001, 230 001;
www.taxi-frankfurt.de).

NORTH RHINE-WESTPHALIA

North Rhine-Westphalia harbours within
its boundaries flat, windswept expanses and
forested hills high enough to hold onto snow
during winter. Villages sweetly lost in time
contrast with frenzied metropolises habitu-
ally on fast-forward. Through it all carves
the muscular Rhine, fed by tributaries such
as the Ruhr that gives its name to an entire
region.

Must-sees include Cologne with its lofty
Dom (cathedral), Bonn with its Beethoven
legacy and fabulous museums, and Charlemagne's imperial capital of Aachen. There
are historical cities like Münster, where the
Thirty Years' War peace treaty was signed,
and elegant ones like Düsseldorf, the state
capital and art-world hub.

Cologne

☎0221 / POP 1 MILLION

Cologne (Köln) offers lots of attractions, led
by its famous cathedral whose filigree twin
spires dominate the skyline. The city's museum landscape is especially strong when it
comes to art but it also has something in
store for fans of chocolate, sports and Roman history. Its people are well known for
their joie de vivre and it's easy to have a
good time right along with them year-round
in the beer halls of the Altstadt (Old Town).

Sights

**Römisch-Germanisches
Museum**   MUSEUM
(Roman Germanic Museum; ☎2212 2304; www.
museenkoeln.de; Roncalliplatz 4; adult/child €8/4;
⊗10am-5pm Tue-Sun) Sculptures and ruins
displayed outside are merely the overture

COLOGNE CARNIVAL

Ushering in Lent in late February or
early March, Cologne's **Carnival**
(Karneval) rivals Munich's Oktoberfest
for exuberance, as people dress in creative costumes and party in the streets.
Things kick off the Thursday before the
seventh Sunday before Easter, culmi-
nate on Monday (*Rosenmontag*), when
there are televised street parades, and
end on Ash Wednesday.

GERMANY COLOGNE

DON'T MISS

KÖLNER DOM

As easy as it is to get church fatigue in Germany, the huge **Kölner Dom** (Cologne Cathedral; ☎1794 0200; www.koelner-dom.de; ⊙6am-10pm May-Oct, to 7.30pm Nov-Apr, south tower 9am-6pm May-Sep, to 5pm Mar-Apr & Oct, to 4pm Nov-Feb) is one you shouldn't miss. Blackened with age, this gargoyle-festooned Gothic cathedral has a footprint of 12,470 sq metres, with twin spires soaring to 157m. Although its ground stone was laid in 1248, stop-start construction meant it wasn't finished until 1880, as a symbol of Prussia's drive for unification. Just over 60 years later it escaped WWII's heavy bombing largely intact.

Sunshine filtering softly through stained-glass windows and the weak glow of candles are the only illumination in the moody, high-ceilinged interior. Behind the altar lies the cathedral's most precious reliquary, the **Shrine of the Three Magi** (c 1150–1210), which reputedly contains the bones of the Three Wise Men. Brought to Cologne from Milan in the 12th century, it can just be glimpsed through the gates to the inner choir.

To see the shrine properly, you need to take a guided tour. For fine views, embark on the seriously strenuous climb of 509 steps of the Dom's south tower, passing the 24-tonne **Peter Bell**, the world's largest working clanger.

to a full symphony of Roman artefacts found along the Rhine. Highlights include the giant **Poblicius tomb** (AD 30–40), the magnificent 3rd-century **Dionysus mosaic** and astonishingly well-preserved glass items.

Museum Ludwig   MUSEUM
(☎2212 6165; www.museenkoeln.de; Bischofs-gartenstrasse 1; adult/child €10/7; ⊙10am-6pm Tue-Sun) This grand art museum gets extra big kudos for its collections of 1960s pop art (Warhol's *Brillo Boxes* are a highlight), German expressionism and Russian avant garde painting, as well as photography.

Kolumba   MUSEUM
(☎933 1930; www.kolumba.de; Kolumbastrasse 4; adult/child €5/free; ⊙noon-5pm Wed-Mon, to 7pm Thu) Art, history, architecture and spirituality form a harmonious tapestry in this spectacular collection of religious treasures. Coptic textiles, Gothic reliquary and medieval painting are juxtaposed with works by Bauhaus legend Andor Weiniger and edgy room installations. Don't miss the 12th-century carved ivory crucifix.

NS Dokumentationszentrum   MUSEUM
(☎2212 6332; www.museenkoeln.de; Appellhof-platz 23-25; adult/child €5/2; ⊙10am-6pm Tue-Fri, 11am-6pm Sat & Sun) An exhibit in the basement of the Gestapo (Nazi-era secret police) prison, where scores of people were interrogated, tortured and murdered, documents the history of Cologne during the Third Reich. Inscriptions on the cell walls offer a gut-wrenching record of the emotional and physical pain endured by prisoners.

Wallraf-Richartz-Museum & Fondation Corboud   MUSEUM
(☎2212 1119; www.museenkoeln.de; Obenmars-pforten; adult/child €9/6; ⊙10am-6pm Tue-Sun, to 9pm Thu) A famous collection of paintings from the 13th to the 19th centuries, this museum occupies a postmodern cube designed by the late OM Ungers. Standouts include brilliant examples from the Cologne School, known for its distinctive use of colour. Upstairs are Dutch and Flemish artists, including Rembrandt and Rubens, Italians such as Canaletto and Spaniards such as Murillo.

Chocolate Museum   MUSEUM
(Schokoladen Museum; ☎931 8880; www.schoko ladenmuseum.de; Am Schokoladenmuseum 1a; adult/concession €8.50/6; ⊙10am-6pm Tue-Fri, 11am-7pm Sat & Sun) At this hi-tech temple to the art of chocolate-making, exhibits on the origin of the 'elixir of the gods', as the Aztecs called it, and the cocoa-growing process are followed by a live-production factory tour and a stop at a chocolate fountain for a sample.

 Tours

KD River Cruises   BOAT TOUR
(☎258 3011; www.k-d.com; Frankenwerft 35; tour €10; ⊙10.30am-5pm) One of several companies offering one-hour spins taking in the splendid Altstadt panorama; other options include sunset cruises.

🛏 Sleeping

TOP CHOICE **Hotel Hopper et cetera** HOTEL €€
(☏924 400; www.hopper.de; Brüsseler Strasse 26; s €95-120, d €135-180; 🅿@🛜) A waxen monk welcomes you to this former monastery, whose 49 rooms sport eucalyptus floors, cherry furniture and marble baths, along with such Zeitgeist-compatible touches as iPod docks. The sauna and bar, both in the vaulted cellars, are great for reliving the day's exploits.

Cerano Hotel HOTEL €€
(☏925 7300; www.cerano-hotels.de; Elisenstrasse 16; r €60-120; 🛜) This unassuming five-storey hotel near the train station is peppered with extra touches: mineral water, juices and more apples than you'd find in an orchard. Staff are helpful and the breakfast is a delight.

Hotel Cristall HOTEL €€
(☏163 00; www.hotelcristall.de; Ursulaplatz 9-11; s €70-180, d €90-250; ✳@🛜) This stylish boutique hotel makes excellent use of colour, customised furniture and light accents. Some rooms are rather compact; light sleepers should not get a street-facing one.

Lint Hotel HOTEL €€
(☏920 550; www.lint-hotel.de; Lintgasse 7; s €60-90, d €90-130; 🛜) The 18 rooms of this cute, contemporary and ecoconscious (solar-panelled roof) hotel in the heart of the Altstadt are comfortable and sport hardwood floors. Partly organic breakfast buffet.

Station Hostel for Backpackers HOSTEL €
(☏912 5301; www.hostel-cologne.de; Marzellenstrasse 44-56; dm €17-20, s/d from €32/48; @🛜) This is a hostel as hostels should be: central, convivial and economical. A lounge gives way to clean, colourful rooms sleeping one to six people. There's lots of free stuff, including linen, internet access, lockers, city maps and a guest kitchen.

Meininger City Hostel & Hotel HOSTEL €
(☏355 332 014; www.meininger-hostels.com; Engelbertstrasse 33-35; dm €18-24, s/d from €48/70; @🛜) This charming hostel in the Zülpicher Viertel student quarter is loaded with retro appeal coupled with modern rooms featuring lockers, bunkside reading lamps, a small TV and private bathrooms. Freebies include linen, towels, and pasta that you can whip up in the small basement kitchen.

🍴 Eating

The largest variety and most happening restaurants are in the Zülpicher Viertel and Belgisches Viertel (Belgian Quarter) areas, both in the city centre.

Alcazar PUB €
(Bismarckstrasse 39; snacks €4-9, mains €10-16; 🛜) This is the kind of place that never goes out of fashion, thanks to its winning combination of freshly prepared international dishes, unpretentious ambience and chirpy service. No food service in the afternoon.

TOP CHOICE **Salon Schmitz** MODERN EUROPEAN €
(Aachener Strasse 28; snacks €4-8) No matter whether you prefer sidling up to the long bar or grabbing an ultracomfy sofa in the retro lounge, Schmitz is a perfect pit stop for relaxed chats over coffee, cocktails or its house-brand Kölsch beer. If hunger strikes, pop next door to the affiliated deli in a former butcher's shop.

Bei Oma Kleinmann GERMAN €€
(www.beiomakleinmann.de; Zülpicher Strasse 9; mains €12; ⏱5pm-1am Tue-Sun, kitchen to 11pm) Named for its long-time owner, who was still cooking almost to her last day at age 95 in 2009, this cosy trad restaurant has timeless dishes, including 14 kinds of schnitzel. Pull up a seat at the small wooden tables for a classic Cologne night out.

Feynsinn INTERNATIONAL €€
(☏240 9210; www.cafe-feynsinn.de; Rathenauplatz 7; mains €7-18) At this well-respected restaurant organic ingredients are woven into sharp-flavoured dishes. The owners raise their own meat. Get a table overlooking the park for a meal or just a drink.

Engelbät EUROPEAN €
(☏246 914; www.engelbaet.de; Engelbertstrasse 7; crepes €3-9; ⏱11am-1am) This cosy restaurant-pub is famous for its habit-forming crepes, which come as sweet, meat or vegetarian. The sidewalk tables are popular for drinks and there are many other choices nearby.

🍷 Drinking & Entertainment

As in Munich, beer in Cologne reigns supreme. Local breweries turn out a variety called *Kölsch*, which is relatively light and served in skinny 200mL glasses.

GERMANY COLOGNE

BONN

South of Cologne on the Rhine River, Bonn (population 312,000) became West Germany's capital in 1949. Now that Berlin has resumed this role, Bonn is doing just fine, sporting a healthy economy and lively urban vibe. For visitors, the birthplace of Ludwig van Beethoven has plenty in store, not least the great composer's birth house, a string of top-rated museums and a lovely riverside setting.

The **tourist office** (☑775 000; www.bonn.de; Windeckstrasse 1; ☺10am-6pm Mon-Fri, to 4pm Sat, to 2pm Sun) is a three-minute walk along Poststrasse from the Hauptbahnhof, and can fill in the details.

Beethoven fans will head straight to the **Beethoven-Haus** (☑981 7525; www.beethoven-haus-bonn.de; Bonngasse 24-26; adult/child €5/4; ☺10am-6pm Mon-Sat, 11am-6pm Sun Apr-Oct, to 5pm Nov-Mar), where the composer was born in 1770. The house contains memorabilia concerning his life and music, including his last piano, with an amplified sounding board to accommodate his deafness.

The **Haus der Geschichte der Bundesrepublik Deutschland** (FRG History Museum; ☑916 50; www.hdg.de; Willy-Brandt-Allee 14; ☺9am-7pm Tue-Fri, 10am-6pm Sat & Sun) presents Germany's postwar history. It is part of the Museumsmeile, a row of museums in the old government quarter south of the city centre along the B9. It also includes the **Kunstmuseum Bonn** (☑776 260; www.kunstmuseum-bonn.de; Friedrich-Ebert-Allee 2; adult/concession €7/3.50; ☺11am-6pm Tue & Thu-Sun, to 9pm Wed), which presents 20th-century art, especially by August Macke and other Rhenish expressionists.

The unfiltered ale is a must at **Brauhaus Bönnsch** (☑650 610; www.boennsch.de; Sterntorbrücke 4; mains €7-15; ☺11am-1am), a congenial brew-pub adorned with photographs of famous politicians: Willy Brandt to, yes, Arnold Schwarzenegger. Schnitzel, spare ribs and sausages dominate the menu, but the *Flammkuchen* (Alsatian pizza) is also a winner.

Bonn is linked to Cologne many times hourly by U-Bahn lines U16 and U18 as well as by regional trains.

Früh am Dom   BEER HALL
(☑258 0394; www.frueh.de; Am Hof 12-14; mains €5-12) This warren of a beer hall near the Dom epitomises Cologne earthiness. Sit inside amid loads of knick-knacks or on the flower-filled terrace next to a fountain. It's also known for great breakfasts.

TOP CHOICE Päffgen   BEER HALL
(www.paeffgen-koelsch.de; Friesenstrasse 64-66) Busy, loud and boisterous, Päffgen has been pouring *Kölsch* since 1883 and hasn't lost a step since. In summer you can enjoy the refreshing brew and local specialities beneath starry skies in the beer garden.

Malzmühle   BEER HALL
(☑210 117; www.muehlenkoelsch.de; Heumarkt 6; mains €6-15; ☺10am-midnight) Expect plenty of local colour at this convivial beer hall off the beaten tourist track. It brews *Kölsch* with organic ingredients and is also known for its lighter *Malzbier* (malt beer, 2% alcohol).

Stadtgarten   CLUB
(☑952 9940; www.stadtgarten.de; Venloer Strasse 40) In a small park, this Belgian Quarter favourite hosts vibrant dance parties and live jazz, soul and world music concerts in its cellar hall, but is also a great spot just for a drink (summer beer garden).

Papa Joe's Klimperkasten   PIANO BAR
(☑258 2132; www.papajoes.de; Alter Markt 50) A piano player tickles the ivories nightly in this museumlike place where the smoky brown walls are strewn with yesteryear's photographs. There are Markt-facing outdoor tables in fine weather.

Alter Wartesaal   CLUB
(☑912 8850; www.wartesaal.de; Johannisstrasse 11; ☺Thu-Sat) In a former train station waiting hall, this is a stylish bar-disco-restaurant combo. Themed nights range from the erotic KitKatClub to SoulChannel. There are cafe tables out front in the shadow of the Dom where you can take a pause.

ℹ️ Information

Tourist Office (☎2213 0400; www.koelntouris mus.de; Unter Fettenhennen 19; ⊙9am-8pm Mon-Sat, 10am-5pm Sun)

ℹ️ Getting There & Away

Air

About 18km southeast of the city centre, **Köln Bonn Airport** (CGN; ☎02203-404 001; www. airport-cgn.de) has direct flights to 130 cities and is served by numerous airlines,with destina-tions across Europe.The S13 train connects the airport and the Hauptbahnhof every 20 minutes (€2.80, 15 minutes). Taxis charge about €30.

Train

Cologne's Hauptbahnhof sits just a Frisbee toss away from the Dom. Services are fast and frequent in all directions. A sampling: Berlin (€113, 4¼ hours), Frankfurt (€67, 1¼ hours) and Munich (€134, 4½ hours). In addition there are fast trains to Brussels (for connecting to the Eurostar for London or Paris).

ℹ️ Getting Around

Cologne's comprehensive mix of buses, trams, and U-Bahn and S-Bahn trains is operated by **VRS** (☎01803-504 030; www.vrsinfo.de) in cooperation with Bonn's system. Short trips (up to four stops) cost €1.80, longer ones €2.60. Day passes are €7.50 for one person and €11.10 for up to five people travelling together. Buy your tickets from the orange ticket machines at sta-tions and aboard trams; be sure to validate them.

Düsseldorf

☎0211 / POP 589,000

Düsseldorf dazzles with boundary-pushing architecture, zinging nightlife and an art scene to rival any other. It's a posh and mod-ern city that seems all buttoned-up business at first: banking, advertising, fashion and tel-ecommunications are among the fields that fuel the wealth of the state capital of North Rhine-Westphalia. Yet all it takes is a few hours of bar-hopping around the Altstadt, the historical quarter along the Rhine, to re-alise that locals have no problem letting their hair down once they slip out of those Boss jackets. The Altstadt may claim to be the 'longest bar in the world' but some attention has strayed a bit further south to Medienhaf-en, a redeveloped harbour area and a feast of international avant garde architecture.

◉ Sights

Marktplatz   SQUARE

Düsseldorf's historic Marktplatz is framed by the Renaissance **Rathaus** (town hall) and accented by an equestrian **statue of Jan Wellem**, an art-loving late 17th-century lo-cal ruler who's buried nearby in the early-ba-roque **Andreaskirche** (www.dominikaner-dues-seldorf.de; Andreasstrasse 27; ⊙8am-6.30pm).

TOP CHOICE **Kunstsammlung Nordrhein-Westfalen**   MUSEUM

(Art Collection of North Rhine Westphalia; www. kunstsammlung.de; combined ticket adult/child €20/5; ⊙10am-6pm Tue-Fri, 11am-6pm Sat & Sun) It's this modern art collection that gives Düsseldorf an edge in the art world. **K20 Grabbeplatz** (☎838 1130; Grabbeplatz 5; adult/child €12/9.50) has fabulous canvas-es by Paul Klee alongside other big-shots, including Pablo Picasso, Henri Matisse, and Düsseldorf's own Joseph Beuys. It is linked by shuttle to the **K21 Stände-haus** (☎838 1630; Ständehausstrasse 1; adult/ child €10/2.50), a showcase of cutting-edge paintings, photographs, installations and video art created after 1980 by the likes of Nam June Paik and Bill Viola. A third gal-lery, the **Schmela Haus** (Mutter-Ey-Strasse 3), was being redeveloped at the time of research.

Rheinuferpromenade   PROMENADE

(Rhine River Walk) **Burgplatz**, on the northern end of the Altstadt, marks the beginning of the Rhine promenade, whose cafes and benches fill with people in fine weather, cre-ating an almost Mediterranean flair. Mark-ing the south end of the Rhine promenade, the **Rheinturm** (Stromstrasse 20; adult/child €4/2.50; ⊙10am-11.30pm) has an observation deck at 168m with – yes indeed! – sweeping views on a clear day.

Medienhafen   ARCHITECTURE

(Am Handelshafen) South of the Rheinturm, the old harbour area has been reborn as the Media Harbour, which is mostly an of-fice quarter but noteworthy for its cutting-edge architecture by celebrated interna-tional architects. Frank Gehry's warped **Neuer Zollhof** is especially photogenic. A few cafes and restaurants let you give your feet a rest.

Sleeping

Stage 47 BOUTIQUE HOTEL €€
(☎388 030; www.stage47.de; Graf-Adolf-Strasse 47; s/d from €130/145; P❄@🛜) Behind the drab exterior, movie glamour meets design chic at this urban boutique hotel. Rooms are named for famous people, who appear in enormous black-and-white prints framed on the wall, so let's hope you like who you sleep with...

Max Hotel Garni HOTEL €€
(☎386 800; www.max-hotelgarni.de; Adersstrasse 65; s/d from €70/85; @🛜) Upbeat, contemporary and run with personal flair, this charmer is a Düsseldorf favourite. The 11 rooms are good-sized and decked out in bright hues and warm woods. Rates include coffee, tea, soft drinks and a regional public transport pass. Call ahead to arrange an arrival time.

Sir & Lady Astor HOTEL €€
(☎173 370; www.sir-astor.de; Kurfürstenstrasse 18 & 23; s €85-170, d €95-250; @🛜) Never mind the ho-hum setting on a residential street near the Hauptbahnhof, this unique twin boutique hotel brims with class, originality and charm. Check-in is at Sir Astor, furnished in 'Scotland-meets-Africa' style, while Lady Astor across the street goes more for French floral sumptuousness. Book early.

Backpackers-Düsseldorf HOSTEL €
(☎302 0848; www.backpackers-duesseldorf.de; Fürstenwall 180; dm €15-23; @🛜) Düsseldorf's adorable indie hostel sleeps 60 in clean four- to 10-bed dorms outfitted with individual backpack-sized lockers. It's a low-key place with a kitchen and a relaxed lounge where cultural and language barriers melt quickly. The reception is generally staffed from 8am to 9pm. Breakfast is included.

Eating & Drinking

On balmy nights, restaurants set up tables outside and the atmosphere – especially in the Altstadt – is electric and often raucous. The beverage of choice is *Altbier*, a dark and semisweet beer typical of Düsseldorf.

Brauerei im Füchschen GERMAN €€
(☎137 470; www.fuechschen.de; Ratinger Strasse 28; mains €5-15; ⊙9am-1am) Boisterous, packed and drenched with local colour – the 'Little Fox' in the Altstadt is all you expect a Rhenish beer hall to be. Mean *Schweinshaxe* (roast pork leg) and some of the best *Altbier* in town.

Weinhaus Tante Anna MODERN EUROPEAN €€€
(www.tanteanna.de; Andreasstrasse 2; mains/menus from €25/45) This is like your aunt's place (if she was a baroness); silver serving plates, subdued carved wood interior, wines decanted and poured properly – the details do go on. The constantly changing menu shows the range of the kitchen.

Libanon Express MIDDLE EASTERN €
(Berger Strasse 19-21; mains €3-20) Great kebabs, falafel and other Middle Eastern specialities.

TOP CHOICE **Zum Uerige** BEER HALL
(☎866 990; www.uerige.de; Berger Strasse 1) This cavernous beer hall is a superb place to soak up local colour along with your beer. The suds flow so quickly from giant copper vats that the waiters – called *Köbes* – simply carry huge trays of brew and plonk down a glass whenever they spy an empty.

Information

Altstadt Tourist Office (Marktstrasse/Ecke Rheinstrasse; ⊙10am-6pm)
Hauptbahnhof Tourist Office (Immermannstrasse 65b; ⊙9.30am-7pm Mon-Fri, to 5pm Sat)

Getting There & Away

Düsseldorf International Airport (DUS; www.dus-int.de) has three terminals and is served by a wide range of airlines. S-Bahns, regional RE and long-distance trains link it with Düsseldorf Hauptbahnhof, and cities beyond, every few minutes. A taxi into town costs about €16.

Düsseldorf is part of a dense S-Bahn and regional train network in the Rhine-Ruhr region, including Cologne (€12, 30 minutes). ICE/IC train links include Berlin (€107, 4¼ hours), Hamburg (€78, 3¾ hours) and Frankfurt (€78, 1¾ hours).

Getting Around

Rheinbahn (www.rheinbahn.de) operates an extensive network of U-Bahn trains, trams and buses throughout Düsseldorf. Most trips within the city cost €2.40. Day passes are €5.70.

Aachen

☎0241 / POP 258,700

A spa town founded by the Romans, with a hopping student population and tremendous amounts of character, Aachen has narrow cobbled streets, quirky fountains, shops full of delectable *Printen* (local biscuit, a bit

AACHENER DOM

It's impossible to overstate the significance of Aachen's magnificent cathedral (☑477 090; www.aachendom.de; Münsterplatz; ☉7am-7pm Apr-Dec, 7am-7pm Jan-Mar). The burial place of Charlemagne, it's where more than 30 German kings were crowned and where pilgrims have flocked since the 12th century.

Start your church visit at the new Dom Visitors Centre (☑4770 9127; Klosterplatz 2; ☉10am-1pm Mon, to 5pm Tue-Sun Jan-Mar, 10am-1pm Mon, to 6pm Tue-Sun Apr-Dec) for info and tickets for tours, and the Domschatzkammer (Cathedral Treasury; ☑4770 9127; adult/child €6.50/5.50; ☉10am-1pm Mon, to 5pm Tue-Sun Jan-Mar, 10am-1pm Mon, to 6pm Tue, Wed & Fri-Sun, to 9pm Thu Apr-Dec), an Aladdin's Cave of religious treasures.

The cathedral's oldest and most impressive section is the emperor's private palace chapel, the Pfalzkapelle, an outstanding example of Carolingian architecture. Completed in 800, the year of the Charlemagne's coronation, the octagonal structure boasts a colossal brass chandelier that was a gift from Emperor Friedrich Barbarossa during whose reign Charlemagne was canonised in 1165.

Pilgrims have poured into town ever since, drawn in as much by the cult surrounding Charlemagne as by several prized relics, including the loincloth said to have been worn by Jesus at his crucifixion. These days, they're only displayed once every seven years (next in 2014).

To accommodate the growing numbers of pilgrims, a Gothic choir was docked to the chapel in 1414 and fancifully decorated with a pala d'oro, a gold-plated altar-front depicting Christ's Passion, and the jewel-encrusted gilded copper pulpit, both fashioned in the 11th century. At the far end is the gilded shrine of Charlemagne that has held the emperor's remains since 1215. In front, the equally frilly shrine of St Mary shelters the cathedral's famous relics.

Unless you join a guided tour (adult/child €5/4; ☉11am-4.30pm Mon-Fri, 1-4pm Sat & Sun, tours in English 2pm), you'll barely catch a glimpse of Charlemagne's white marble imperial throne in the upstairs gallery. Reached via six steps – just like King Solomon's throne – it served as the coronation throne of 30 German kings between 936 and 1531.

GERMANY AACHEN

like gingerbread), and – most famously – an ancient cathedral. It makes for an excellent day trip from Cologne or Düsseldorf or a worthy overnight stop.

◉ Sights

Rathaus HISTORIC BUILDING
(Markt; adult/concession €5/3; ☉10am-6pm) Aachen's mighty Gothic town hall is festooned with 50 life-size statues of German rulers, including 30 German kings that were crowned in town. Inside, highlights are the Kaisersaal with its epic 19th-century frescoes by Alfred Rethel and the replicas of the imperial insignia: a crown, orb and sword (the originals are in Vienna).

**Ludwig Forum für
Internationale Kunst** MUSEUM
(Ludwig Forum for International Art; ☑180 7104; www.ludwigforum.de; Jülicherstrasse 97-109; adult/child €5/3; ☉noon-6pm Tue, Wed & Fri, noon-8pm Thu, 11am-6pm Sat & Sun) In a former umbrella factory, this art museum trains the spotlight on modern art (Warhol, Immendorf, Holzer, Penck, Haring etc) and also stages progressive changing exhibits.

Suermondt Ludwig Museum MUSEUM
(☑479 800; www.suermondt-ludwig-museum.de; Wilhelmstrasse 18; adult/child €5/3; ☉noon-6pm Tue, Thu & Fri, noon-8pm Wed, 10am-6pm Sat & Sun) The Suermondt Ludwig is especially proud of its medieval sculpture but also has fine works by Cranach, Dürer, Macke, Dix and other masters.

⌂ Sleeping

Hotel Drei Könige HOTEL €€
(☑483 93; www.h3k-aachen.de; Büchel 5; s €90-130, d €120-180, apt €140-240; ☎) The radiant Mediterranean decor is an instant mood enhancer at this family-run favourite with its doesn't-get-more-central location. Some

rooms are a tad twee but the two-room apartment sleeps up to four. Breakfast on the 4th floor comes with dreamy views over the rooftops and the cathedral.

DJH Hostel HOSTEL €

(☑0241 711 010; www.aachen.jugendherberge.de; Maria-Theresia-Allee 260; dm/s/d from €26/45/68) Aachen's modernised 180-bed hostel is nicely located in a park overlooking the city. About a third of the 55 rooms have private bathrooms. Take bus 2 (direction Preuswald) to the Ronheide stop.

✗ Eating & Drinking

Aachen's students have their own 'Latin Quarter' along Pontstrasse, with dozens of bars and cheap eats. It runs for about 1km northeast of the Markt.

TOP **CHOICE** **Leo van den Daele** CAFE €

(www.van-den-daele.de; Büchel 18; treats from €3) Leather-covered walls, tiled stoves and antiques forge the yesteryear flair of this rambling cafe institution. Come for all-day breakfast, a light lunch or divine cakes.

Am Knipp GERMAN €€

(☑331 68; www.amknipp.de; Bergdriesch 3; mains €8-18; ◷dinner Wed-Mon) Hungry grazers have stopped by this traditional inn since 1698, and you too will have a fine time enjoying hearty German cuisine served amid a flea market's worth of twee knick-knacks. A vast, lovely beer garden as well.

Apollo Kino & Bar BAR/CLUB

(☑900 8484; www.apollo-aachen.de; Pontstrasse 141-149) This cavernous basement joint does double duty as an art-house cinema and a sweaty dance club for the student brigade with a sound spectrum that covers all the bases.

❶ Information

Tourist Office (☑0241 180 2961, 0241 180 2960; www.aachen-tourist.de; Friedrich-Wilhelm-Platz; ◷9am-6pm Mon-Fri, to 2pm Sat, also 10am-2pm Sun Easter-Dec)

❶ Getting There & Around

Regional trains to Cologne (€16, one hour) run twice hourly, with some proceeding beyond. Aachen is a stop for high-speed trains to/from Brussels and Paris.

Local bus tickets are €1.60; drivers sell tickets.

LOWER SAXONY

Lower Saxony (Niedersachsen) likes to make much of its half-timbered towns. Hamelin is certainly a true fairy-tale beauty, and lovely Lüneburg is quite unlike any other town you'll see. The state is also home to the global headquarters of Volkswagen and the business-minded capital, Hanover, as well as the western stretches of the pretty Harz mountains.

Hanover

☑0511 / POP 518,000

German comedians like to dismiss Hanover (Hannover in German) as 'the autobahn exit between Göttingen and Walsrode'. However, the capital of Lower Saxony is far livelier than its reputation assumes, and its residents are remarkably friendly and proud of their small city. While it's famous for hosting trade fairs, particularly the huge CEBIT computer show in March, it also boasts acres of greenery in the Versailles-like gardens, Herrenhäuser Gärten.

Less well-known but buried deep within its identity is a British connection – for over 100 years from the early 18th century, monarchs from the house of Hanover also ruled Great Britain and everything that belonged to the British Empire.

◉ Sights & Activities

Neues Rathaus HISTORIC BUILDING

(Trammplatz 2; elevator adult/concession €3/2; ◷9.30am-6.30pm Mon-Fri, 10am-6.30pm Sat & Sun, elevator closed mid-Nov–Mar) An excellent way to get your bearings in Hanover is to visit the Neues Rathaus (built in 1901–13) and travel 98m to the top in the **curved lift** inside its green dome. There are four viewing platforms here.

Die Nanas SCULPTURE

(Leibnizufer) Hanover's city fathers and mothers were inundated with nearly 20,000 letters of complaint when these three earth-mama sculptures were first installed beside the Leine River in 1974. Now, the voluptuous and fluorescent-coloured 'Sophie', 'Charlotte' and 'Caroline', by the late French artist Niki de Saint Phalle, are among the city's most recognisable, and most loved, landmarks.

TOP CHOICE Sprengel Museum · MUSEUM

(www.sprengel-museum.de; Kurt-Schwitters-Platz; adult/concession €7/4, Fri free; ⊗10am-6pm Wed-Sun, to 8pm Tue) The Sprengel Museum is held in extremely high esteem, both for the design of the building as well as for the art it houses. Its cavernous interior is perfectly suited to showcase modern figurative, abstract and conceptual art, including a sprinkling of works by Nolde, Chagall and Picasso. A selection of scuptures by Niki de Saint Phalle is usually on show as well. Take bus 100 from Kröpcke to the Maschsee/Sprengel Museum stop.

TOP CHOICE Herrenhäuser Gärten · GARDEN

(☑1684 7576; www.herrenhaeuser-gaerten.de; ⊗9am-sunset) Situated about 5km northwest of the centre, Herrenhäuser Gärten (Herrenhausen Gardens) is a remarkable ensemble of parks and gardens largely modelled on those at Versailles. The jewel in the crown, **Grosser Garten** (adult/concession incl Berggarten €5/4 Nov–mid-May, €8/5 mid-May-Oct) is grand both in format and history and peppered with statues, fountains and the colourfully tiled **Niki de Saint Phalle Grotto** (creator of the city's much-loved *Die Nanas* sculptures). The **Grosse Fontäne** (Great Fountain; the tallest in Europe) at the park's south end jets water up to 80m high. Popular summer attractions are the **Wasserspiele** (Fountain Display; ⊗11am-noon & 3-5pm Mon-Fri, 11am-noon & 2-5pm Sat & Sun Apr-Oct), water fountains that are synchronised to do some spectacular spurting, and the **Illuminations**, when the Grosser Garten is lit up for between one and two hours. Also part of the ensemble are two other gardens, the **Berggarten** (www.herrenhaeuser-gaerten.de; adult/concession late Mar-Oct €3.50/1.50, combination ticket with Grosser Garten adult/concession €5/4 Nov–mid-May, €8/5 mid-May–Oct), with its great assortment of flora from around the world, and the lake-dotted **Georgengarten** (admission free). Take tram/U-Bahn 4 or 5 from Kröpke to Herrenhäuser Gärten.

🛏 Sleeping

City Hotel am Thielenplatz · HOTEL €

(☑327 691; www.smartcityhotel.com; Thielenplatz 2; s/d from €59/69, breakfast €9.50; P🕐) This very central 'budget boutique' beauty has a reception and bar (open until 5am) styled with leather seating, black-and-white leaf-patterned wallpaper and lots of wood

laminate. Rooms have been renovated, mostly in a minimalist style.

City Hotel Flamme · HOTEL €€

(☑388 8004; www.city-hotel-flamme.de; Lammstrasse 3; s/d €70/125; P@🕐) Most of the 24 rooms of this attractively mural-painted hotel-pension open onto balconies facing a large atrium courtyard, which has a quirky eating area and glassed-in front wall.

DJH Hostel · HOSTEL €

(☑131 7674; www.jugendherberge.de/jh/hannover; Ferdinand-Wilhelm-Fricke-Weg 1; 4-bed dm under/over 27yr from €21.80/25.80, s/d €38.50/57; P@🕐; ⑤3 or 7 to Bahnhof Linden/Fischerhof) This huge, space-lab-like structure houses a modern hostel with breakfast room and terrace bar overlooking the river. It's only a short walk from here to the Maschsee (lake).

GästeResidenz PelikanViertel · APARTMENT €€

(☑399 90; www.gaesteresidenz-pelikanviertel.de; Pelikanstrasse 11; s €49-83, d €69-105, tr €100-125; P🕐; ⑤3, 7 or 9 to Pelikanstrasse) Upmarket student residence meets budget hotel, this well-managed complex has a wide range of pleasant Ikea-ish rooms and apartments, some split over two levels. Use of kitchen utensils costs an additional €8 (plus €50 deposit) per apartment.

✕ Eating & Drinking

TOP CHOICE Markthalle · MARKET €

(www.hannover-markthalle.de; Kamarschstrasse 49; dishes €3.50-10; ⊗7am-8pm Mon-Wed, to 10pm Thu & Fri, to 4pm Sat; 🖉) This huge covered market of food stalls and gourmet delicatessens is fantastic for a quick bite, both carnivorous and vegetarian.

Brauhaus Ernst August · PUB

(www.brauhaus.de; Schmiedestrasse 13; ⊗8am-3am Mon-Thu, to 5am Fri & Sat, 9am-3pm Sun) A Hanover institution, this sprawling brewpub makes a refreshing unfiltered pilsner called Hannöversch. A party atmosphere reigns nightly, helped along by a varied roster of live bands and DJs.

Café Mezzo · CAFE, BAR

(www.cafe-mezzo.de; Lister Meile 4; ⊗9am-2am Tue-Thu, to 3am Fri & Sat, to midnight Sun & Mon; 🕐) This classic bar and cafe used to be a student hang-out, but today gets a balance of ages. It's popular any time of day (including for breakfast), but doubles well as a place to warm up in the evening before moving on to a club or performance.

Hiller
VEGETARIAN €€

(www.hannover-vegetarisch.de; Blumenstrasse 3; mains €7.70-10.50, lunch menu €7.90-10.70; ⊗lunch & dinner Mon-Sat; ⊘) Germany's oldest vegetarian restaurant is a tad hushed and old-fashioned but the interior, with colourful draped cloth on the walls, is cheery. Food is well prepared and excellent value.

Georxx
INTERNATIONAL €€

(www.georxx-hannover.de; Georgsplatz 3; pasta €8.50-13.50, mains €9.50-28.80; ⊗from 9am) Popular with businesspeople, office workers, shoppers, tired travellers and arty types, Georxx has pleasant outdoor seating in summer, a menu offering a taste for everyone (a bit of Asia, a bit of the Balkans etc) and good lunch specials (€6.50 to €9.50). Breakfast is served until 5pm.

❶ Information

Hannover Tourismus (⊘information 1234 5111, room reservations 1234 555; www.hannover.de; Ernst-August-Platz 8; ⊗9am-6pm Mon-Fri, to 2pm Sat, also 9am-2pm Sun Apr-Sep)

❶ Getting There & Around

Hanover's **airport** (HAJ; www.hannover-airport.de) has many connections, including on Air Berlin.

Hanover is a major rail hub for European and national services, with frequent ICE trains to/from Hamburg Hauptbahnhof (€43, 1¼ hours), Bremen (€31, one hour), Munich (€125, 4¼ hours), Cologne (€68, 2¾ hours) and Berlin (€65, 1¾ hours), among others.

U-Bahn lines from the Hauptbahnhof are boarded in the station's north (follow signs towards Raschplatz), including the U8 to the Messe (fairgrounds). The U10 and U17 are overground trams leaving from south of the station near the tourist office.

Most visitors only ever travel in the central 'Hanover' zone. Single tickets are €2.30 and day passes €4.50.

Around Hanover

WOLFSBURG

Volkswagen *is* the Lower Saxon town of Wolfsburg – and the huge VW emblem adorning the company's global headquarters (and a factory the size of a small country) won't let you forget it.

Arriving in Wolfsburg, the first thing you see is the enormous Volkswagen emblem adorning the company's global headquar-ters. The top reason people come here is to experience the theme park called Auto-stadt (Car City; www.autostadt.de; Stadtbrücke; adult/concession €15/12, car tower discovery adult/concession €8/6; ⊗9am-6pm), where exhibitions run the gamut of automotive design and engineering, the history of the Beetle and the marketing of individual marques, including VW itself, Audi, Bentley and Lamborghini.

Nearby, Phaeno (www.phaeno.de; Willy Brandt-Platz 1; adult/child/concession/family €12/7.50/9/26.50; ⊗9am-5pm Tue-Fri, 10am-6pm Sat & Sun, last entry 1hr before closing) is a science centre housed in a sleek piece of futuristic architecture by celebrity architect Zaha Hadid. Serious car-ficionados might also want to check out the great collection of rare and unsual vehicles in the AutoMuseum (http://automuseum.volkswagen.de; Dieselstrasse 35; adult/concession/family €6/3/15; ⊗10am-6pm Tue-Sun).

Wolfsburg is about 90km east of Hanover via the A2 autobahn and is frequently served by direct train (from €17.50, 30 minutes).

CELLE
⊘05141 / POP 70,250

With row upon row of ornate half-timbered houses, all decorated with scrolls and allegorical figures, Celle is graced with a picture-book town centre that is among the most attractive in the region. It's a pleasant place for a leisurely day trip from Hanover.

The tourist office (in the Altes Rathaus) has a good *Walk Through Celle* map in English that takes you from sight to sight.

◉ Sights

Schloss
PALACE

(Ducal Palace; Schlossplatz; Residenzmuseum €5, combined Residenzmuseum, Bomann Museum & Kunstmuseum €8, Fri free, guided tours adult €6; ⊗10am-5pm Tue-Sun) Celle's wedding-cake Schloss was built in 1292 as a town fortification and in 1378 was expanded and turned into a residence. Today it houses administrative offices and the Palace Museum. One-hour guided tours take you the Renaissance Schlosskapelle (chapel), the 19th-century Schlossküche (kitchen) and – rehearsals permitting – the baroque Schlosstheater (⊘tickets 127 14; www.schlosstheater-celle.de; Schlossplatz; ⊗closed Jul & Aug).

The frilly palace contrasts with the ultra-modern Kunstmuseum (Art Museum; ⊘123 55; www.kunst.celle.de; Schlossplatz 7; adult/concession incl Bomann Museum €5/3, free Fri; ⊗10am-

BERGEN-BELSEN

The Nazi-built concentration camp at **Bergen-Belsen** (www.bergenbelsen.de; Lohheide; ⊙10am-6pm) began its existence in 1940 as a POW camp, but was partly taken over by the SS from April 1943 to hold Jews as hostages in exchange for German POWs held abroad. In all, 70,000 Jews, Soviet soldiers, political hostages and other prisoners died here, most famously Anne Frank, whose posthumously published diary became a modern classic. The Documentation Centre today is one of the best of its kind and deals sensitively but very poignantly with the lives of the people who were imprisoned here – before, during and after incarceration.

Bergen-Belsen is about 25km northwest of Celle and 60km northeast of Hannover. It is difficult to reach by public transport. If you're driving, take the B3 to the town of Bergen and follow the signs to Belsen. A taxi from Celle costs about €35.

5pm Tue-Fri, to 6pm Sat & Sun) opposite, which presents contemporary German art and is illuminated at night into a '24-hour' museum.

Altes Rathaus HISTORIC BUILDING
Cellle's 16th-century town hall boasts a wonderful Weser Renaissance stepped gable, topped with the ducal coat of arms and a golden weather vane. At the tourist office door, on the building's south side, there are two **whipping posts**, used from 1786 to 1850 to punish minor offenders. Prisoners weren't in fact whipped but merely left here for 12 hours, to allow their neighbours to spit at them or throw insults and eggs.

Stadtkirche CHURCH
(www.stadtkirche-celle.de; An der Stadtkirche 8; tower adult/concession €1/0.50; ⊙church 10am-6pm Tue-Sat year-round, tower 10-11.45am & 2-4.45pm Tue-Sat Apr-Oct) The highlight of the 13th-century Stadtkirche is the 235 steps you can climb to the top of the church steeple for a view of the city. The city trumpeter climbs 220 steps to the white tower below the steeple for a trumpet fanfare in all four directions at 9.30am and 5.30pm daily.

✖ Eating

Restaurant Bier Akademie GERMAN €€
(www.bier-akademie-celle.de; Weisser Wall 6; mains €11.10-22.50; ⊙lunch Mon-Thu, dinner Mon-Sat) This family-run restaurant serves an excellent range of beef, poultry and lamb as well as pork, but its speciality is a local roulade, which you can order as a starter or main course. It's just northeast of Schlossplatz.

❶ Information

Tourist office (☎1212; www.region-celle.com; Markt 14-16; ⊙9am-6pm Mon-Fri, 10am-4pm Sat, 11am-2pm Sun)

❶ Getting There & Away
Various train services run to Celle from Hanover (from €9.10, 45 minutes) and Lüneburg (€16.40, 1¼ hours). The Altstadt is about a 15-minute walk east of the Hauptbahnhof.

HAMELIN
📱05151 / POP 57,800
If you were to believe the 'Pied Piper of Hamelin' fairy tale, this quaint, ornate town on the Weser River ought to be devoid of both rats and children. According to legend, the Pied Piper *(Der Rattenfänger)* was employed by Hamelin's townsfolk to lure their pesky rodents into the river in the 13th century. When they refused to pay him, however, he picked up his flute again and led their kids away.

However, it is a bedtime story, after all. International tourism means the reality is very different. Everywhere you look along Hamelin's cobbled streets are – you guessed it – fake rats and happy young children.

⊙ Sights

Rattenfängerhaus HISTORIC BUILDING
(Rat Catcher's House; Osterstrasse 28) This is among the finest of the houses built in the ornamental Weser Renaissance style so prevalent throughout the Altstadt. Note the typically steep and richly decorated gable.

Hochzeitshaus HISTORIC BUILDING
(Wedding House; Osterstrasse 2) The Hochzeitshaus (1610–17) does double duty as city council offices and a police station. The **Rattenfänger Glockenspiel** at the far end of the building chimes daily at 9.35am and 11.35am, while a carousel of Pied Piper figures twirls at 1.05pm, 3.35pm and 5.35pm.

WORTH A TRIP

LÜNEBURG, THE WOBBLY TOWN

With an off-kilter church steeple, buildings leaning on each other and houses with swollen 'beer-belly' facades, it's as if charming Lüneburg has drunk too much of the pilsner lager it used to brew.

Of course, the city's wobbly angles and uneven pavements have a more prosaic cause. For centuries until 1980, Lüneburg was a salt-mining town, and as this 'white gold' was extracted from the earth, ground shifts and subsidence knocked many buildings sideways. Inadequate drying of the plaster in the now-swollen facades merely added to this asymmetry. But knowing the scientific explanation never detracts from the pleasure of being on Lüneburg's comic-book crooked streets.

Between Hanover (€26, one hour by train) and Hamburg (€12, 30 minutes), the city's an easy day trip from either. From the train station, head west into town towards the highly visible, 14th-century **St Johanniskirche** (435 94; Am Sande; admission €2; ⊙10am-5pm Sun-Wed, to 6pm Thu-Sat Apr-Oct, 9am-6pm Thu-Sat, to 4pm Sun Nov-Mar), the 106m-high spire of which leans 2.2m off true. Local legend has it that the architect tried to kill himself by jumping off it. (He fell into a hay cart and was saved, but celebrating his escape later in the pub he drank himself into a stupor, fell over, hit his head and died after all.)

The church stands at the eastern end of the city's oldest square, **Am Sande**, full of typically Hanseatic stepped gables. At the western end stands the beautiful black-and-white **Industrie und Handelskammer** (Chamber of Industry & Trade).

Continue one block past the Handelskammer and turn right into restaurant-lined Schröderstrasse, which leads to the Markt, where the ornate **Rathaus** (town hall) contains the **tourist office** (04131 207 6620; www.lueneburg.de; ⊙9am-6pm Mon-Fri, to 4pm Sat, 10am-4pm Sun May-Sep, 9am-5pm Mon-Fri, to 2pm Sat Oct-Apr).

Admire the square before continuing west along Waagestrasse and down our favourite Lüneburg street, **Auf dem Meere**, en route to the **St Michaeliskirche** (314 00; Johann-Sebastian-Bach-Platz; ⊙10am-5pm Mon-Sat, 2-5pm Sun May-Sep, to 4pm Oct-Apr). Here the wonky facades and wavy pavements are like something from a Tim Burton film.

It's too late now to regain your equilibrium, so head back along Am Flock for the pubs on **Am Stintmarkt** on the bank of the Ilmenau River.

Museum Hamelin   MUSEUM
(Osterstrasse 8-9; adult/concession €5/4; ⊙11am-6pm Tue-Sun) Two gorgeous Weser Renaissance–style houses are home to the revamped regional history museum. The **Leisthaus** at No 9 was built for a patrician grain trader in 1585–89, whereas the **Stiftsherrenhaus** dates from 1558 and is the only surviving building in Hamelin decorated with figures, some of them planetary gods, others biblical figures.

🛏 Sleeping & Eating

TOP CHOICE **Hotel La Principessa**   HOTEL €€
(956 920; www.laprincipessa.de; Kupferschmiedestrasse 2; s/d €78/99; P🐾) Cast-iron balustrades, tiled floors throughout and gentle Tuscan pastels and ochre shades make this Italian-themed hotel an unusual and distinguished option in Hamelin.

TOP CHOICE **Rattenfängerhaus**   GERMAN €€
(Osterstrasse 28; mains €10-23; ⊙11am-10pm) Hamelin's traditional restaurants are unashamedly aimed at tourists, such as this cute half-timbered tavern with a speciality of 'rats' tails' flambéed at your table (fortunately, like most of the theme dishes here, it's based on pork). Schnitzels, herrings, vegie dishes and 'rat killer' herb liquor are also offered.

ℹ Information

Tourist office (957 823; www.hameln.de; Diesterallee 1; ⊙9am-6pm Mon-Fri, 9.30am-3pm Sat, 9.30am-1pm Sun)

ℹ Getting There & Away

By car, take the B217 to/from Hanover.

Frequent S-Bahn trains (S5) head to Hamelin from Hanover's Hauptbahnhof (€11.10, 45 minutes). The train station is about 800m east of the centre.

Bremen

📞0421 / POP 548,000

Bremen, the smallest of the German states, brings together culture and nightlife. It's a shame the donkey, dog, cat and rooster in Grimm's Town Musicians of Bremen never actually made it here – they would have fallen in love with the place. This little city is big on charm, from the fairy-tale character statue to a jaw-dropping art nouveau laneway and impressive town hall. On top of that, the Weser riverside promenade is a relaxing, cafe-lined refuge and the student district along Ostertorsteinweg knows it's got a good thing going.

◉ Sights & Activities

Markt   SQUARE

Bremen's Markt is striking, particularly because of its ornate, gabled **Rathaus**. In front stands a 13m-tall medieval statue of the knight **Roland**, Bremen's protector. On the building's western side, you'll find a sculpture of the **Town Musicians of Bremen** (1951). Local artist Gerhard Marcks has cast them in their most famous pose, scaring the robbers who invaded their house, with the rooster atop the cat, perched on the dog, on the shoulders of the donkey.

Dom St Petri   CHURCH

(St Petri Cathedral; tower €1; ⊙10am-4.45pm Mon-Fri, to 1.30pm Sat, 2-4.45pm Sun, tower closed Nov-Easter) The 13th-century twin-towered Dom has great ribbed vaults and chapels, but its most intriguing – and certainly macabre – feature is the **Bleikeller** (Lead Cellar; adult/child €1.40/1; ⊙10am-5pm Mon-Fri, to 1.45pm Sat, noon-4.45pm Sun Apr-Oct) accessed via a separate entrance south of the main door. Eight bodies mummified in the incredibly dry air are displayed in open coffins, including a soldier with his mouth opened in a silent scream, and a student who died in a duel in 1705.

Böttcherstrasse   STREET

This charming lane is a superb example of expressionist architecture and was largely designed by Bernhard Hoetger (1874–1959). Enter via the golden relief called the *Lichtbringer* (Bringer of Light), which shows a scene from the Apocalypse with the archangel Michael fighting a dragon. Hoetger's **Haus Atlantis** (now the Hilton Hotel) features a show-stopping, multicoloured, glass-walled spiral staircase. He also fused the 16th-century Roselius Haus with the adjoining Paula-Modersohn-Becker-Haus with its rounded edges and wall reliefs. Today these two are museums comprising the **Kunstsammlungen Böttcherstrasse** (Art Collection Böttcherstrasse; www.pmbm.de; Böttcherstrasse 6-10; combined ticket adult/concession €5/3; ⊙11am-6pm Tue-Sun).

Schnoor   NEIGHBOURHOOD

The maze of narrow, winding alleys known as the Schnoorviertel was once the fishermen's quarter and then the red-light district. Now its doll's-house–sized cottages house souvenir shops and restaurants.

Beck's Brewery   BREWERY

(📞01805-101 030; www.becks.de/besucherzentrum; Am Deich; tours €10.50; ⊙10am, 11.30am, 1pm, 3pm, 4.30pm & 6pm Thu-Sat May-Oct, less frequently Jan-Apr) You can see where the wares come from during a two-hour tour of the Beck's brewery, run in conjunction with the tourist office. Book online or by telephone and meet at the brewery by taking tram 1 or 8 to Am Brill. *Prost!*

🛏 Sleeping

Bremer Backpacker Hostel   HOSTEL €

(📞223 8057; www.bremer-backpacker-hostel.de; Emil-Waldmann-Strasse 5-6; dm/s/d €18/29/48; 🅿@🛜) This private hostel is simply furnished but spotless, with a kitchen, communal room and a small courtyard out front for soaking up the sun.

TOP CHOICE **Hotel Bölts am Park**   HOTEL €€

(📞346 110; www.hotel-boelts.de; Slevogtstrasse 23; s/d €65/85; 🅿🛜) This cosy family-run hotel in a leafy neighbourhood has real character, from the wonderfully old-fashioned breakfast hall to its well-proportioned doubles.

TOP CHOICE **Hotel Überfluss**   BOUTIQUE HOTEL €€€

(📞322 860; www.hotel-ueberfluss.com; Langenstrasse 72/Schlachte 36; s €120-160, d €131-195, ste from €339; ❄🛜) Quite literally 7m above river level, this designer hotel has black bathrooms and stunning views from its more expensive rooms.

Hotel Lichtsinn   HOTEL €€

(📞368 070; www.hotel-lichtsinn.com; Rembertistrasse 11; s/d €85/110; 🅿@🛜) Wooden floorboards, Persian carpets and vaguely Biedermeier-style furniture characterise most of this hotel's rooms, a favourite with the theatre world.

✖ Eating & Drinking

The student quarter around Ostertorstein-weg brims with inexpensive restaurants and cafes. The waterfront promenade, Schlachte, is pricier and more mainstream. The Markt-platz is home to oodles of cheap snack stands.

TOP CHOICE Casa
MEDITERRANEAN €€

(http://casa-bremen.com; Ostertorsteinweg 59; mains €8.40-19.60; ⊙from 10am; ✍) Formerly known as Casa Blanca, Bremen's long-standing favourite now has a slightly more upmarket splash. It serves lava-grill fish and meat dishes alongside salads and pizza – often with a Mediterranean edge.

Piano
INTERNATIONAL €

(www.cafepiano-bremen.de; Fehrfeld 64; mains €6.50-11.40; ⊙9am-1am; ✍) Enduringly popular, this bustling cafe place serves pizza, pasta, a few heartier dishes and vegie casseroles to all comers – from media types to young mums. On weekends, breakfast is served until the afternoon.

TOP CHOICE Engel Weincafe
BAR, CAFE

(www.engelweincafe-bremen.de; Ostertorsteinweg 31; breakfast €4.90-8.60, Flammkuchen €6.70-9.50, cheeses & meats €4-13.30; ⊙8am-1am Mon-Fri, 10am-1am Sat & Sun; 🐾) Housed in a former pharmacy, this popular hang-out recently morphed into a double act of cafe and wine bar that does good breakfasts and serves cheeses, cold cuts of meat and platters to accompany the fine wines.

Katzen Café
INTERNATIONAL €€

(✆326 621; www.katzen-cafe.de; mains €15.50-24; ⊙lunch & dinner) This popular Moulin Rouge–style restaurant opens out into a rear sunken terrace bedecked with flowers. The menu runs the gamut from Alsatian to Norwegian, with seafood a strong theme.

TOP CHOICE Wohnzimmer
BAR

(www.wohnzimmer-bremen.de; Ostertorsteinweg 99; ⊙from 4pm May-Aug, from 10am Sep-Apr) This bar and lounge mostly gets a relaxed 20s and early 30s crowd, who hang out on the sofas – which explains the name 'Living Room' – or lounge around on the mezzanine levels.

ℹ Information

Tourist Office (✆01805-101030; www.bremen-tourism.de) Two branches:

Hauptbahnhof (www.bremen-tourism.de; main train station; ⊙9am-7pm Mon-Fri, 9.30am-5pm Sat & Sun) and the branch office (Marktplatz, cnr Obernstrasse/Liebfraukirchhof; ⊙10am-6.30pm Mon-Sat, to 4pm Sun).

ℹ Getting There & Around

Bremen's **airport** (BRE; www.airport-bremen.de) is about 3.5km south of the city centre and has flights to German and European destinations. Ryanair flies to Edinburgh and London-Stansted. Tram 6 travels between the Hauptbahnhof and the airport (€2.35, 15 minutes). A taxi from the airport costs about €15.

Frequent IC trains go to Hamburg (€26, one hour), Hanover (€31, one hour) and Cologne (€63, three hours).

HAMBURG

✆040 / POP 1.8 MILLION

'The gateway to the world' might be a bold claim, but Germany's second-largest city and biggest port has never been shy. Hamburg has engaged in business with the world ever since it joined the Hanseatic League trading bloc back in the Middle Ages, and this 'harbourpolis' is now the nation's premier media hub and among its wealthiest cities. It's also the site of Europe's largest urban-renewal project, the HafenCity, that is efficiently transforming the old docklands into a bold new city quarter.

Hamburg's maritime spirit infuses the entire city; from architecture to menus to the cry of gulls, you always know you're near the water. The city has given rise to vibrant neighbourhoods awash with multicultural eateries, as well as the gloriously seedy Reeperbahn red-light district.

◎ Sights & Activities

Old Town
HISTORIC AREA

Hamburg's medieval Rathaus (✆4283 120 10; tours adult/child €3/0.50; ⊙English-language tours hourly 10.15am-3.15pm Mon-Thu, to 1.15pm Fri, to 5.15pm Sat, to 4.15pm Sun; ⑤Rathausmarkt or Jungfernstieg) is one of Europe's most opulent. North of here, you can wander through the Alsterarkaden, the Renaissance-style arcades sheltering shops and cafes alongside a canal or 'fleet'.

For many visitors, however, the city's most memorable building is south in the Merchants' District. The 1920s, brown-brick Chile Haus (cnr Burchardstrasse &

Johanniswall; ⓢMönckebergstrasse/Messberg) is shaped like an ocean liner, with remarkable curved walls meeting in the shape of a ship's bow and staggered balconies that look like decks.

Speicherstadt & Harbour HISTORIC AREA

The seven-storey red-brick warehouses lining the Speicherstadt archipelago are a well-recognised Hamburg symbol, stretching to Baumwall in the world's largest continuous warehouse complex. It's best appreciated by simply wandering through its streets or taking a boat up its canals.

The Speicherstadt merges into Europe's biggest inner-city urban development, the HafenCity. Here, a long-derelict port area of 155 hectares is being redeveloped with restaurants, shops, apartments and offices, all built to very strict sustainability standards. In the next 20 years, it's anticipated that some 40,000 people will work and 12,000 will live here. The main architectural highlight is the stunning concert hall called Elbphilharmonie (Elbe Philharmonic Hall; www.elbphilharmonie.de; ⓢMessberg). For a project overview, head to the HafenCity InfoCenter (☑3690 1799; www.hafencity.com; Am Sandtorkai 30; ⊙10am-6pm Tue-Sun; ⓢMessberg).

Reeperbahn NEIGHBOURHOOD

(ⓢReeperbahn) No discussion of Hamburg is complete without mentioning St Pauli, home of the Reeperbahn, Europe's biggest red-light district. Sex shops, peep shows, dim bars and strip clubs line the streets, which generally start getting crowded with the masses after 8pm or 9pm. This is also where you find the notorious Herbertstrasse (a block-long street lined with brothels that's off-limits to men under 18 and to female visitors of all ages).

Fischmarkt MARKET

(⊙5-10am Sun; ⓡReeperbahn) Here's the perfect excuse to stay up all Saturday night. Every Sunday between 5am and 10am, curious tourists join locals of every age and walk of life at the famous Fischmarkt in St Pauli. The market has been running since 1703, and its undisputed stars are the boisterous *Marktschreier* (market criers) who hawk their wares at full volume. Live bands also entertainingly crank out cover versions of ancient German pop songs in the adjoining Fischauktionshalle (Fish Auction Hall).

Internationales Maritimes Museum MUSEUM

(☑3009 3300; www.internationales-maritimes-museum.de; Koreastrasse 1; adult/concession €12/8.50; ⊙10am-6pm Tue, Wed & Fri-Sun, 10am-8pm Thu; ⓢMessberg) Hamburg's maritime past – and future – is fully explored in this excellent private museum sprawls which over 10 floors of a rehabbed brick shipping warehouse. The vast collection includes 26,000 model ships.

Museum für Völkerkunde MUSEUM

(☑01805-308 888; www.voelkerkundemuseum.com; Rothenbaumchaussee 64; adult/child €7/free; ⊙10am-6pm Tue, Wed & Fri-Sun, to 9pm Thu; ⓢHallerstrasse or Dammtor) The famous ethnology museum is packed with traditional and modern artefacts from Africa, Asia and the South Pacific, including masks, jewellery, costumes, musical instruments, carved wooden canoes and even a complete, intricately carved, Maori meeting hall.

Hamburger Kunsthalle MUSEUM

(☑428 131 200; www.hamburger-kunsthalle.de; Glockengiesserwall; adult/concession €8.50/5; ⊙10am-6pm Tue, Wed & Fri-Sun, to 9pm Thu; ⓡHauptbahnhof) Consists of two buildings, the old one housing old masters and 19th-century art, and a white concrete cube – the Galerie der Gegenwart – showcasing contemporary German artists, including Georg Baselitz and Gerhard Richter, alongside international stars such as David Hockney and Jeff Koons.

St Michaeliskirche CHURCH

(www.st-michaelis.de; tower adult/child €4/3, crypt €3/2, combo ticket €6/4; ⊙10am-7.30pm May-Oct, to 5.30pm Nov-Apr; ⓡStadthausbrücke) Northeast of the landing piers, the St Michaeliskirche, or 'Der Michel' as it's commonly called, is one of Hamburg's most recognisable landmarks and northern Germany's largest Protestant baroque church. Ascending the tower (by steps or lift) rewards with great panoramas across the canals.

Mahnmal St-Nikolai MEMORIAL

(Memorial St Nicholas; www.mahnmal-st-nikolai.de; Willy-Brandt-Strasse 60; adult/child €4/2; ⊙10am-5pm; ⓢRödingsmarkt) Destroyed in WWII, this memorial now houses an unflinching

Hamburg

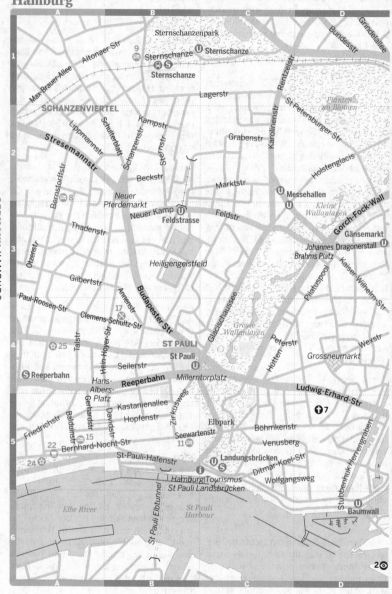

exhibit on the horrors of war focusing on three events in World War II: the German bombing of Coventry in 1940, the German destruction of Warsaw, and Operation Gomorrha, the combined British and American bombing of Hamburg over three days and nights in 1943 that killed 35,000 and incinerated much of the centre. Great views from the 76.3m-high viewing platform inside the surviving spire.

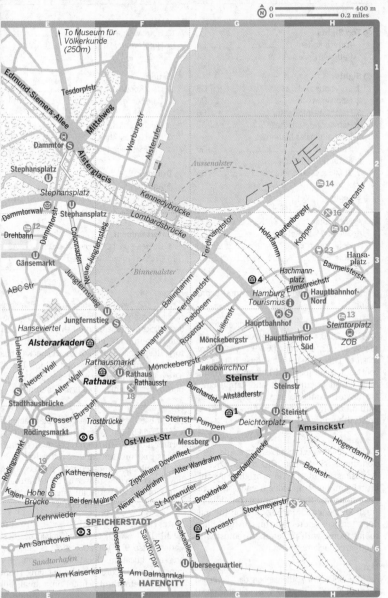

💤 Sleeping

TOP CHOICE **Hotel Wedina** HOTEL €€

(☏280 8900; www.wedina.de; Gurlittstrasse 23; s €70-195, d €120-225; @🛜; ⓢHauptbahnhof) You might find a novel instead of a chocolate on your pillow at this literary hotel, which has bedded Margaret Atwood, Jonathan Franzen, and JK Rowling among others. The 59 rooms spread over four colourful buildings

Hamburg

offer a choice of traditional or mod-urban decor.

Fritz Hotel　　　　　　BOUTIQUE HOTEL €€
(☎8222 2830; www.fritzhotel.com; Schanzen-strasse 101-103; s/d from €65/95; 🖥; ⑤Stern-schanze) This stylish town-house hotel is as cool as a cucumber and has only 17 rooms total. Fresh organic fruit and cappuccinos are always available. If you want a room with a balcony, be prepared for some street noise, otherwise get one in back.

Backpackers St Pauli　　　　HOSTEL €
(☎2351 7043; www.backpackers-stpauli.de; Bern-storffstrasse 98; dm from €20, d from €60; 🖥; ⑤Feldstrasse) Entered via a bright cafe, this hostel-cum-hotel includes a cool, subterra-nean maritime-themed lounge containing a small kitchenette. Make friends on the out-door terrace before returing to light-filled rooms (some with private bathrooms) with good-sized lockers.

Hotel SIDE　　　　　　HOTEL €€€
(☎309 990; www.side-hamburg.de; Drehbahn 49; r €120-300; P🖥✳@🖥✳; ⑤Gänsemarkt) This Matteo Thun–designed stunner is built around a prism-shaped central atrium and has suites featuring vividly coloured free-standing bath-tubs. The 8th-floor chill-out lounge, strewn with 1950s-style saucers-from-outer-space sofas, opens to a panoramic sun deck.

Kogge　　　　　　　　HOTEL €
(☎312 872; www.kogge-hamburg.de; Bernhard-Nocht-Strasse 59; s €30-35, d €50-60; @🖥; ⑤Land-ungsbrücken or Reeperbahn) At this rock-and-roll pub deep in noisy, grungy Reeperbahn terri-tory, sleepyhead party-goers can check out as late as 2pm from 'Bollywood', 'Punk Royal', 'Disco Dream' or other artist-designed rooms outfitted with sinks. Toilets are shared.

Hotel Village　　　　　HOTEL €
(☎480 6490; www.hotel-village.de; Steindamm 4; s €50-75, d €65-100; @🖥; ⑤Hauptbahnhof) This former bordello turned edgy gem has 20 rooms that mix and match red velvet, gold flock wallpaper and leopard prints; some have huge mirrors above the bed. It attracts a mix of gay and straight guests. Economy rooms have shared bathrooms.

Hotel Hafen　　　　　HOTEL €€
(☎311 1370; www.hotel-hafen-hamburg.de; See-wartenstrasse 9; r €70-200; @🖥; ⑤Landungs-brücken) Location, location, location. For superb views, score a harbour-facing gem at this behemoth of a hotel on a small hill overlooking the port action. In addition to the refurbished, historic main building, a former seamen's home, there are newer modern wings.

Galerie-Hotel Petersen　　PENSION €€
(☎0173-200 0746, 249 826; www.ghsp.eu; Lange Reihe 50; s €60-100, d €70-170; ✳@🖥; ⑤Haupt-

bahnhof) This delightful B&B inside a historic 1790 town house is an extension of its welcoming artist-owner's personality. Furnishings include a mix of contemporary, antique and artdeco styles. Our pick of its five rooms is the top-floor studio, with a romantic terrace, kitchenette and separate living area.

✗ Eating

The Schanzenviertel swarms with cheap eateries; try Schulterblatt for Portuguese outlets or Susanenstrasse for Asian and Turkish. Many fish restaurants around the Landungsbrücken are overrated and touristy. St Georg's Lange Reihe offers many characterful eating spots to suit every budget, and there is a seemingly endless selection of simple but quality, high-value sushi joints all over town.

TOP CHOICE Oberhafenkantine   GERMAN €€
(www.oberhafenkantine-hamburg.de; Stockmeyerstrasse 39; mains €7-16; ℝSteinstrasse) Serving traditional local fare since 1925, this is where you can order a 'Hamburger' and get the real thing: a patty made with various seasonings and onions. Fresh pollack, haddock and more conjure the days when the surrounding piers echoed to the shouts of seamen and the crash of cargo-laden nets.

Fleetschlösschen   INTERNATIONAL €€
(Brooktorkai 17; snacks €7-10; ⊘8am-8pm Mon-Fri, 11am-6pm Sat & Sun; ⓈMessberg) One of the cutest cafes you ever saw, this former customs post overlooks a Speicherstadt canal and has brilliant outdoor seating areas. The owner's knick-knack collection includes centuries-old Dutch pottery unearthed during the construction of HafenCity.

TOP CHOICE Café Paris   FRENCH €€
(www.cafeparis.net; Rathausstrasse 4; mains €10-20; ⊘9am-11.30pm Mon-Fri, from 10am Sat & Sun; ⓈRathaus) Within a spectacularly tiled 1882 butchers' hall and adjoining art-deco salon, this elegant yet relaxed brasserie serves classical French cafe fare and a killer breakfast for two.

Deichgraf   GERMAN €€€
(☑364 208; www.deichgraf-hamburg.de; Deichstrasse 23; mains €18-29; ⊘lunch Mon-Sat, dinner Sat; ⓈRödingsmarkt) In a prime setting, with the water on one side and long street-side tables on the other, Deichgraf excels in Hamburg specialties cooked to a high standard. Much of the food is sourced regionally.

Café Koppel   VEGETARIAN €
(www.cafe-koppel.de; Lange Reihe 66; mains €5-10; ✐; ⓈHauptbahnhof) Set back from busy Lange Reihe, with a garden in summer, this vegie cafe is a refined oasis, where the menu could be an ad for the fertile fields of northern Germany. Salads, soups and much more are all made with fresh, seasonal ingredients.

Café Mimosa   CAFE €
(www.cafemimosa.de; Clemens-Schultz-Strasse 87; mains €5-12; ⓈSt Pauli) Skip the greasy fast-food joints on the nearby Reeperbahn for this gem of a neighbourhood cafe and indulge in delicious pastas, salads and home-made cakes in a theatrical space or outside at a pavement table.

⬤ Drinking & Entertainment

Listings in Szene (www.szene-hamburg.de) are helpful for navigating the enormous bar scene. Clubkombinat (www.neu.clubkombinat.de) is the go-to source for club listings.

THE HISTORY OF THE HAMBURGER

A classic *Calvin and Hobbes* comic strip once asked if hamburgers were made out of people from Hamburg. And while Hamburg's citizens are, of course, known as Hamburgers, it was the city's role as an international port that gave rise to its most famous namesake.

The origins of the ubiquitous fast food date back to the 12th century. The Tartars (Mongolian and Turkish warriors) wedged pieces of beef between their saddles and the horses' backs, softening the meat as they rode until it was tender enough to be eaten raw. By the 17th century, Hamburg ships brought 'steak tartare' back to Germany, which visiting seafarers then referred to as 'steak in the Hamburg style'. These patties of salted minced beef – usually slightly smoked and mixed with breadcrumbs and onions – were highly durable, making them ideal for long sea voyages.

Hamburg emigrants to America continued making the patties, which they served in bread. As for who in America officially launched the burger remains a fanatical culinary debate.

Bar M & V
BAR

(www.mvbar.de; Lange Reihe 22; 🚉Hauptbahnhof) The drinks menu is like a designer catalogue at this grand old St Georg bar that's had a beautiful restoration. Settle into one of the wooden booths, smell the freesias and enjoy.

Amphore
CAFE

(www.cafe-amphore.de; Hafenstrasse 140; 🚉Reeperbahn) Beguiling in its trad beauty, non-fussy Amphore has terrace views out to the Elbe and pavement tables for neighbourhood gawking. An excellent St Pauli spot for a drink.

Strandperle
BAR

(www.strandperle-hamburg.de; Schulberg 2; ⊙almost year-round; 🚌112) The mother of Hamburg's beach bars, Strandperle should not be missed. All ages and classes gather and mingle, especially at dusk as the sun sets while huge freighters glide past. From Altona station, take bus 112 west to Neumühlen/Övelgönne.

Tower Bar
LOUNGE

(www.hotel-hafen-hamburg.de; Seewartenstrasse 9; ⊙6pm-1am Mon-Thu, 6pm-2.30am Fri-Sun; 🚇Landungsbrücken) For a more elegant, mature evening, repair to this 14th-floor eyrie at the Hotel Hafen for unbeatable harbour views.

TOP CHOICE Hafenklang
CLUB

(www.hafenklang.org; Grosse Elbstrasse 84; 🚉Königstrasse) A collective of Hamburg industry insiders presents established and emerging DJs and bands, as well as clubbing events and parties. Look for the spray-painted name on the dark-brick harbour store above a blank metal door.

TOP CHOICE Golden Pudel Club Live Music
LIVE MUSIC

(☎3197 9930; www.pudel.com; St-Pauli-Fischmarkt 27; ⊙from 10pm; 🚉St Pauli) In a ramshackle wooden fisherman's hut, this bar-club was established by members of legendary Hamburg band Die Goldenen Zitronen and gets packed to the rafters for its quality electro, hip-hop, R&B and reggae gigs.

Grosse Freiheit 36/Kaiserkeller
LIVE MUSIC

(☎3177 7811; Grosse Freiheit 36; 🚉Reeperbahn) The Beatles once played in the basement Kaiserkeller at this now-mainstream venue mounting pop and rock concerts. It's the best reason today to detour up the Grosse Freiheit.

🛈 Information

Tourist Information

Hamburg Tourismus (☎3005 1200; www.hamburg-tourismus.de)

Hauptbahnhof (Kirchenallee exit; ⊙8am-9pm Mon-Sat, 10am-6pm Sun)

Landungsbrücken (btwn piers 4 & 5; ⊙8am-6pm Apr-Oct, 10am-6pm Nov-Mar; 🚇Landungsbrücken)

Airport (Airport Plaza btwn Terminals 1 & 2; ⊙6am-11pm)

🛈 Getting There & Away

Air

Hamburg's **airport** (HAM; www.flughafen-hamburg.de) has frequent flights to domestic and European cities. The S1 S-Bahn travels to the city centre in 24 minutes (€2.85).

Bus

The **Zentral Omnibus Busbahnhof** (Busbahnhof, Central Bus Station; ☎247 576; www.zob-hamburg.de; Adenauerallee 78; ⊙ticket counters 5am-10pm Mon-Tue, Thu, Sat & Sun, to midnight Wed & Fri) is southeast of the Hauptbahnhof. **Eurolines** (www.eurolines.com) has buses to such eastern European destinations as Prague (€59) and Warsaw (€50).

Car & Motorcycle

The major A1 and A7 autobahns cross south of the Elbe River.

Train

Reading timetables, remember that Hamburg has four mainline train stations: the Hauptbahnhof, Dammtor, Altona and Harburg. Frequent trains serve Lübeck (€18.50, 40 minutes), Hanover (€40, 1¼ hours) and Bremen (from €20.80, 55 minutes). A direct service to Westerland on Sylt Island leaves every two hours (€44, 3¼ hours). Direct ICE trains depart frequently for Berlin-Hauptbahnhof (€68, 2¼ hours), Cologne (€79, four hours), Munich (€127, six hours), Frankfurt (€106, three hours) and Copenhagen (€78.80, five hours).

🛈 Getting Around

HVV (☎194 49; www.hvv.de) operates buses, ferries, and U-Bahn and S-Bahn trains. The city is divided into zones. **Ring A** covers the city centre, inner suburbs and airport. Single tickets are €2.85, day passes €6.95. Services run around the clock on weekends; between 12.30am and 4am Sunday to Thursday the night bus network takes over, converging on Rathausmarkt.

SCHLESWIG-HOLSTEIN

Sandwiched between the North and Baltic Seas, Schleswig-Holstein is Germany's answer to the Côte d'Azur. Of course, the weather here often makes it a pretty funny sort of answer, as dark clouds and strong winds whip in across the flat peninsula. Still, people flock to the beaches on the coasts, and the countryside in between has a stark beauty.

Lübeck

📞 0451 / POP 210,300

Two pointed cylindrical towers of Lübeck's Holstentor (city gate) greet you upon arrival – if you think they're a tad crooked, you're not seeing things: they lean towards each other across the stepped gable that joins them. Right behind them, the streets are lined with medieval merchants' homes and spired churches forming the city's so-called 'crown'. It's hardly surprising that this 12th-century gem is on Unesco's World Heritage list.

◉ Sights & Activities

TOP CHOICE Holstentor   LANDMARK

Built in 1464, the impossibly cute city gate serves as Lübeck's museum as well as its symbol. The six gabled brick buildings east of the Holstentor are the Salzspeicher, once used to store the salt from Lüneburg that was pivotal to Lübeck's Hanseatic trade.

Marienkirche   CHURCH

(Schüsselbuden 13; admission €1; ☺10am-6pm Apr-Sep, to 5pm Oct, to 4pm Tue-Sun Nov-Mar) This 13th-century church is most famous for its shattered bells, left where they fell after a WWII bombing raid. Outside there's a little devil sculpture with an amusing folk tale (in German and English).

Petrikirche   CHURCH

(📞397 730; www.st-petri-luebeck.de; Schüsselbuden 13; adult/child €3/2; ☺9am-9pm Apr-Sep, 10am-7pm Oct-Mar) Panoramic city views unfold from the 50m-high viewing platform reached by lift.

Rathaus   HISTORIC BUILDING

(📞122 1005; Breite Strasse 64; adult/concession €3/1.50; ☺tours 11am, noon & 3pm Mon-Fri) Some described as a 'fairy tale in stone', Lübeck's medieval town hall is widely regarded as one of the most beautiful in Germany.

BEHIND THE SCENES

In the Middle Ages, Lübeck was home to numerous craftspeople and artisans. In response to a housing shortage, tiny single-storey homes were built in courtyards – accessible via little walkways – behind existing rows of houses. Almost 90 such *Gänge* (walkways) and *Höfe* (courtyards) still exist, including the **Füchtingshof** (Glockengiesserstrasse 25) with its beautiful carvings and the 1612 **Glandorps Gang** (Glockengiesserstrasse 41-51), which you can peer into.

Quandt-Linie   BOAT TOUR

(📞777 99; www.quandt-linie.de; Holstentorterrassen; adult/child from €12/6) The Trave River forms a moat around the Altstadt, and cruising it aboard a boat is a fine way to get a feel for Lübeck. One-hour tours leave every half-hour between 10am and 6pm (May to October) from just south of the Holstenbrücke bridge.

🛏 Sleeping

TOP CHOICE Klassik

Altstadt Hotel   BOUTIQUE HOTEL €€

(📞702 980; www.klassik-altstadt-hotel.de; Fischergrube 52; s €60-100, d €130-160; 🛜) Rooms at this elegantly furnished boutique hotel are dedicated to a famous artist or writer such as Thomas Mann and Johann Sebastian Bach. Single rooms (some share baths) feature travelogues by famous authors.

Hotel an der Marienkirche   HOTEL €

(📞799 410; www.hotel-an-der-marienkirche.de; Schüsselbuden 4; s €58-78, d €75-95; 🛜) This small and bright budget hotel could not be better located; in fact, one of the 18 rooms has a view of the namesake church. The staff is as cheery as the Ikea-like furnishings. The breakfast buffet is especially healthy.

Hotel Lindenhof   HOTEL €€

(📞872 100; www.lindenhof-luebeck.de; Lindenstrasse 1a; s €65-95, d €85-135; @🛜) The 66 rooms at this family-run hotel in a quiet side street are small, but the breakfast buffet, friendly service and thoughtful touches such as free biscuits and newspapers give the Lindenhof an edge.

Rucksackhotel
HOSTEL €

(706 892; www.rucksackhotel-luebeck.com; Kanalstrasse 70; dm €15-16, s €28, d €40; ⓟ@🛜) This 30-bed hostel has a relaxed atmosphere, good facilities including a well-equipped kitchen, and colourful decor with the odd tropical touch.

✗ Eating

TOP CHOICE Schiffergesellschaft
GERMAN €€€

(767 76; www.schiffergesellschaft.com; Breite Strasse 2; mains €12-25) Opened in 1535, Lübeck's cutest – if not best – restaurant is stuffed with ships' lanterns, old model ships and orange Chinese-style lamps. As you sit on long benches resembling church pews, staff in long white aprons bring you Frisian specialities. On balmy nights, head up a flight of steps to the hidden garden out back. Book.

Brauberger
GERMAN €€

(702 0606; Alfstrasse 36; mains €9-14; ⊙5pm-midnight Mon-Thu, 5pm-late Fri & Sat) The brewing kettles are right in the dining room and the humid air is redolent with hops at this traditional German brewer, which has been serving its own golden amber since 1225. Get a stein of the cloudy house brew and enjoy one of many excellent schnitzels or other trad fare.

Krützfeld
DELI €

(728 32; Hüxstrasse 23; snacks from €2; ⊙8am-6pm Tue-Fri, 8am-2pm Sat) This classic deli has been serving all manner of fresh and smoked seafood for decades. There's no better place in town to assemble a picnic.

🔒 Shopping

TOP CHOICE Niederegger
FOOD

(530 1126; www.niederegger.de; Breite Strasse 89; ⊙9am-7pm Mon-Fri, 9am-6pm Sat, 10am-6pm Sun) Niederegger is Lübeck's mecca for marzipan, which has been made locally for centuries. Even if you're not buying, the shop's elaborate seasonal displays are a feast for the eyes. At the back of the shop there's an elegant cafe.

ℹ Information

Lübeck Travemünde Tourismus (01805 882 233; www.luebeck-tourismus.de; Holstentorplatz 1; ⊙9.30am-7pm Mon-Fri, 10am-3pm Sat & 10am-2pm Sun Jun-Sep, 9.30am-6pm Mon-Fri &10am-3pm Sat Oct-May)

ℹ Getting There & Away

Ryanair and Wizzair serve **Lübeck airport** (LBC; www.flughafen-luebeck.de). Buses take passengers straight to Hamburg (€10, 55 minutes), while local bus 6 serves Lübeck's Hauptbahnhof and central bus station (€2.70).

Lübeck has hourly trains to Hamburg (€19, 40 minutes) and Rostock (€24, 2¼ hours, change in Bad Kleinen).

NORTH FRISIAN ISLANDS

With their grass-covered dunes, shifting sands, birds, seal colonies, lighthouses and rugged cliffs, you'd imagine Germany's North Frisian Islands to be the domain of intrepid nature lovers. Instead, these North Sea islands are a favourite of the German elite. On glamorous Sylt in particular, you'll find designer boutiques housed in quintessential reed-thatched cottages, gleaming Porches and Mercedes jamming the car parks, luxurious accommodation and some of the country's most extravagant restaurants. Those with less cash to splash can still enjoy the pure sea air, especially in Sylt's more remote corners. The islands of Amrum and Föhr are more peaceful still.

Sylt

04651 / POP 21,100

Sylt can't be labelled without scratching your head. Westerland, the largest town, is largely filled with high-rises that obscure views of the beach, although some of the world's best windsurfing can be found off its shore.

Further north, pretty Kampen teems with ritzy restaurants and celebrity guests who come to see and be seen along the main promenade, Stroenwai, aka Whiskey Alley. Its main natural attraction is the 52.5m-tall, Uwe Dune. Climb the wooden steps for stunning 360-degree views.

Historic reed-thatched houses strangled with ivy, lush gardens of colourful blooms, stone walls and the occasional garden gate made from two curving whalebones combine to create the island's prettiest village in Keitum.

⊨ Sleeping

Tourist offices have details about all accommodation options, including private rooms.

Village BOUTIQUE HOTEL €€€
(☑469 70; www.village-kampen.de; Alte Dorfstrasse 7, Kampen; r from €300; ℙ⌂✆☒) This flawless 10-room boutique hotel has service standards worthy of a palace. Discretion is the rule, whether at the indoor pool or out in the lovely gardens. Superb breakfasts.

Single Pension PENSION €
(☑920 70; www.singlepension.de; Trift 26, Westerland; s €38-70, d €55-80; ℙ) Not only for singles, but certainly a social spot for solo travellers young and old, who can strike up a rapport over tea or lounging in the garden. The rooms are humble, but the location central and breakfast is served to 1pm.

DJH Hostel Dikjen Deel HOSTEL €
(☑835 7825; www.jugendherberge.de; Fischerweg 36-40, Westerland; dm under/over 26yr €23/28; ⊙closed mid-late Dec) Set amid the dunes, Westerland's hostel is a 45-minute walk from the Bahnhof. Alternatively, take bus 2 in the direction of Rantum/Hörnum to the Dikjen Deel stop. There are also DJH hostels in remote List-Mövenberg and Hörnum.

✕ Eating

Kupferkanne CAFE €€
(☑410 10; www.kupferkanne-sylt.de; Stapelhooger Wai, Kampen; mains €6-15; ⊙8am-5pm) Enjoy coffee and yummy cake – or a full meal – surrounded by a maze of low bramble hedges in the enchanting gardens or in the knick-knack-filled thatched Frisian house.

TOP CHOICE **Gosch** SEAFOOD €€
(www.gosch.de; Hafenstrasse 16, List; mains €4-15) Coming to Sylt without visiting Gosch would be like coming to Germany without ordering a beer. A Sylt institution, it offers exceptionally fresh fish sandwiches, seafood pasta and smoked fish at its original kiosk in List harbour and at branches across the island.

Sansibar SEAFOOD, STEAK €€€
(☑964 646; www.sansibar.de; Hörnumer Strasse 80, Rantum; mains €14-35; ⊙11am-11pm, shorter hours in winter) Dining among the dunes in this large grass-roof beach pavilion is an unforgettable experience (book *well* ahead). Alternatively, stop by for a drink on its terrace at sunset.

❶ Information

Tourist Information Desk (www.westerland. de; Bahnhofplatz, Westerland; ⊙9am-6pm) Inside the train station. A good first stop.

❶ Getting There & Around

Sylt is connected to the mainland by a causeway used exclusively by trains. IC trains serve Hamburg Hauptbahnhof (€47, 3¼ hours), while regional trains have hourly direct services to Hamburg Altona (€34, 3½ hours).

Vehicles use the **car train** (www.syltshuttle. de; one-way/return €47/86 Fri-Mon, return €73 Tue-Thu) from Niebüll. There's at least one connection per hour in both directions; it doesn't take reservations. With loading and unloading, expect the journey to take about an hour.

GERMANY SYLT

WORTH A TRIP

AMRUM & FÖHR

Amrum is the smallest North Frisian Island; you can walk around it in a day. It's also the prettiest, with reed-thatched Frisian houses, a patchwork of dunes, woods, heath and marsh, and glorious Kniepsand – 12km of fine, white sand, sometimes up to 1km wide – that takes up half the island. Crowning the central village of **Wittdün** is northern Germany's tallest lighthouse, which stands 63m tall. The island's largest village is **Nebel**. The **tourist office** (☑04682 940 30; www.amrum.de; ferry landing, Wittdün; ⊙hours vary) can help find accommodation.

The 'green isle' of Föhr is interesting for its Frisian culture. Its main village, **Wyk**, boasts plenty of windmills; there are 16 northern hamlets tucked behind dikes up to 7m tall; and there's the large 12th-century church of **St Johannis** in Nieblum. The **tourist office** (☑04681-300; www.foehr.de; Poststraat 2, Nieblum; ⊙9am-5pm Mon-Fri, 9am-noon Sat, 10am-noon Sun) can help with more details. There is no camping here.

Ferries to Amrum and Föhr are operated by **WDR** (☑800; www.wdr-wyk.de) from Dagebüll Hafen.

UNDERSTAND GERMANY

History

Events on German soil have often dominated the European stage, but the country itself is a relatively recent invention: for most of its history Germany has been a patchwork of semi-independent principalities and city-states, occupied first by the Roman Empire, then the Holy Roman Empire and finally the Austrian Habsburgs. Perhaps because of this, many Germans retain a strong regional identity, despite the momentous events that have occurred since.

The most significant medieval events in Germany were pan-European in nature – Martin Luther brought on the Protestant Reformation with his criticism of the Catholic Church in Wittenberg in 1517, a movement that ultimately sparked the Thirty Years' War (1618–48). Germany became the battlefield of Europe, only regaining stability after the Napoleonic Wars with increasing industrialisation and the rise of the Kingdom of Prussia. In 1866 legendary Prussian 'Iron Chancellor' Otto von Bismarck brought the German states together, largely by force, and a united Germany emerged for the first time in 1871, under Kaiser Wilhelm I.

WWI & the Rise of Hitler

With the advent of the 20th century, Germany's rapid growth soon overtaxed the political talents of Kaiser Wilhelm II and led to mounting tensions with England, Russia and France. When war broke out in 1914, Germany's only ally was a weakened Austria-Hungary. Gruelling trench warfare on two fronts sapped the nation's resources, and by late 1918 Germany sued for peace. The Kaiser abdicated and escaped to the Netherlands. Amid widespread public anger and unrest, a new government – the Weimar Republic – was proclaimed.

The Treaty of Versailles in 1919 chopped huge areas off Germany and imposed heavy reparation payments. These were impossible to meet, and when France and Belgium occupied the Rhineland to ensure continued payments, the subsequent hyperinflation and miserable economic conditions provided fertile ground for political extremists. One party waiting in the wings was the Nationalsozialistische Deutsche Arbeiterpartei (National Socialist German Workers' Party, NSDAP, or Nazi Party), led by a failed Austrian artist and WWI German army veteran corporal named Adolf Hitler.

After the 1929 US stock market crash plunged the world in to economic depression, the Nazis increased their strength in general elections, and in 1933 replaced the Social Democrats as the largest party in the *Reichstag* (parliament). Hitler was appointed chancellor. Within one year, he consolidated absolute power with him as *Führer* and turned Germany into a one-party dictatorship.

WWII & Jewish Persecution

From 1935 Germany began to re-arm and build its way out of the economic depression with strategic public works such as the autobahns (freeways). Hitler reoccupied the Rhineland in 1936, and in 1938 annexed Austria and, following a compromise agreement with Britain and France, parts of Czechoslovakia.

All of this took place against a backdrop of growing racism at home. The Nuremberg Laws of 1935 deprived non-Aryans – mostly Jews and Roma (sometimes called Gypsies) – of their German citizenship and many other rights. On 9 November 1938 the horror escalated into *Kristallnacht* (Night of Broken Glass), in which synagogues and other Jewish institutions and businesses across Germany were desecrated, burned or demolished.

In September 1939, after signing a pact that allowed both Stalin and himself a free hand in the east of Europe, Hitler attacked Poland, which led to war with Britain and France. Germany quickly occupied large parts of Europe, but after 1942 began to suffer increasingly heavy losses. Massive bombing reduced Germany's cities to rubble, and the country lost 10% of its population. Germany surrendered unconditionally in May 1945, soon after Hitler's suicide.

After the war, the full scale of Nazi terror was exposed. 'Concentration camps' had exterminated some six million Jews and one million more Roma, communists, homosexuals and others in what has come to be known as the Holocaust.

The Two Germanies

At conferences in Yalta and Potsdam, the Allies (the Soviet Union, the USA, the UK and France) redrew the borders of Germany and divided it into four occupation zones.

In the Soviet zone of the country, the communist Socialist Unity Party (SED) won the 1946 elections and began a rapid nationalisation of industry. In September 1949 the Federal Republic of Germany (FRG) was created out of the three western zones; in response the German Democratic Republic (GDR) was founded in the Soviet zone the following month, with (East) Berlin as its capital.

As the West's bulwark against communism, the FRG received massive injections of US capital and experienced rapid economic growth (the *Wirtschaftswunder* or 'economic miracle') under the leadership of Konrad Adenauer. The GDR, on the other hand, had to pay massive war reparations to the Soviet Union and rebuild itself from scratch.

The widening economic gulf between the two Germanys prompted 3.6 million mostly young and well-educated East Germans to seek a future in the West, thus putting the GDR on the brink of economic and political collapse. To stop the exodus, the GDR government – with Soviet consent – built a wall around West Berlin in 1961 and fenced off the intra-German border.

The appointment of the more politically flexible Erich Honecker as government leader in 1971, combined with the *Ostpolitik* (East-friendly policy) of FRG chancellor Willy Brandt, eased the political relationship between the two Germanys. In the same year, all four Allies formally accepted the division of Berlin, and signed an accord that guaranteed West Berliners the right to visit East Berlin, whilst the GDR also granted GDR citizens the right to travel to West Germany in cases of family emergency.

Honecker's policies produced higher living standards in the GDR, yet East Germany barely managed to achieve a level of prosperity half that of the FRG. After Mikhail Gorbachev came to power in the Soviet Union in March 1985, the East German communists gradually lost Soviet backing.

Reunification

German reunification caught even the most insightful political observers by surprise. The fall of communism was a gradual development that ended in a big bang – the collapse of the Berlin Wall on 9 November 1989.

Once again, East Germans were leaving their country in droves, this time via Hungary, which had opened its borders with Austria. Some people sought refuge in the West German embassy in Prague. Meanwhile, mass demonstrations in Leipzig spread to other cities, including East Berlin.

As the situation escalated, Erich Honecker relinquished leadership to his security chief, Egon Krenz. Then suddenly on 9 November 1989, a decision to allow direct travel to the West was mistakenly interpreted as the immediate opening of all GDR borders with West Germany. That same night thousands of people streamed into the West past stunned border guards. Millions more followed in the next few days, and the dismantling of the Berlin Wall began soon thereafter.

Plans to reform the GDR were dismissed after East German citizens clearly voted in favour of the pro-reunification Christian Democratic Union (CDU) in the early 1990 elections. Unification was enacted on 3 October 1990. In the midst of national euphoria, the CDU-led coalition, led by Helmut Kohl, soundly defeated the Social Democrat opposition in elections on 2 December that year.

Since Reunification

Under Kohl's leadership East German assets were privatised; state industries were trimmed back, sold or closed; and infrastructure was modernised, all resulting in economic growth of about 10% each year until 1995. The trend slowed dramatically thereafter, however, creating an eastern Germany that consisted of unification winners and losers.

Amid allegations of widespread financial corruption, the Kohl government was replaced with a coalition government of SPD and Alliance 90/The Greens in 1998. This marked the first time an environmentalist party had governed nationally worldwide. The rise of the Greens and, more recently, the left, has changed the political landscape of Germany dramatically, making absolute majorities by the 'big two' all the more difficult to achieve. In 2005 the CDU/CSU and SPD formed a grand coalition and Angela Merkel became the first woman to hold the job of German chancellor. She won a second term in the 2009 election that also confirmed the trend towards a five-party political system in Germany.

Germany Today

Europe's Economic Engine

Germany seems to have weathered the recent financial crisis better than most industrial nations, in large part because it now bears the fruits of decade-old key reforms, especially the liberalisation of its labour laws. The German government launched a slew of proactive measures, such as allowing companies to put workers on shorter shifts without loss of pay and stimulating the economy by providing incentives for Germans to scrap older cars and buy new ones. The beginning of the millennium's second decade has seen the importance of Germany's stable economy grow, as the debt-driven crisis in the Eurozone has spread from Greece to threaten all of southern Europe. Germany is seen to have a key position in propping up the euro, the collapse of which could plunge economies across the globe back into recession. So far, so good.

Environmental Leadership

With a Green Party active in politics since the 1980s, Germany has long played a leading role in environmental and climate protection and is considered a pioneer in the development of renewable energies. In 2011, about 20% of total energy production came from alternative sources. The country has also reduced its greenhouse gas emissions by 24% since 1990, thus exceeding the 21% reduction called for by the 2005 Kyoto Protocol.

In 2011, following the nuclear disaster in Fukushima, Japan, Germany became the first industrial nation to completely opt out of nuclear power, immediately shutting down the eight oldest of its 17 reactors, with rest going off the grid by 2022.

Land of Immigration

Some 15 million people living in Germany have an immigrant background (foreign born or have at least one immigrant parent), accounting for about 18% of the total population. According to the United Nations, only the USA and Russia absorb a greater number of international migrants. The largest group are people of Turkish descent, a legacy of the post-WWII economic boom when 'guest workers' were recruited to shore up the war-depleted workforce.

Many stayed. After reunification, the foreign population soared again as repatriates from the former USSR and refugees from war-ravaged Yugoslavia arrived by the millions.

Whether immigration enriches or endangers German culture has been the subject of much recent debate, but the fact is that – thanks to an ageing population and a low birth rate – the country needs newcomers to keep it, and its economy, running.

Arts

Germany's creative population has made major contributions to international culture, particularly during the 18th century when the courts at Weimar and Dresden attracted some of the greatest minds of Europe. With such rich traditions to fall back on, inspiration has seldom been in short supply for the new generations of German artists, despite the upheavals of the country's recent history.

Fine Arts

German art hit its first heyday in the Renaissance, which came late to Germany but flourished quickly. The heavyweight of the period is Albrecht Dürer, (1471–1528), who was the first to seriously compete with the Italian masters. Dürer influenced court painter Lucas Cranach the Elder (1472–1553) who worked in Wittenberg for more than 45 years.

Two centuries later, the baroque period brought great sculpture, including works by Andreas Schlüter in Berlin. Neoclassicism in the 19th century, meanwhile, ushered back interest in the human figure and an emphasis on Roman and Greek mythology. This segued into Romanticism, which drew heavily on dreamy idealism nicely captured in the paintings of Caspar David Friedrich and Otto Runge.

In 1905 Ernst Ludwig Kirchner, along with Erich Heckel and Karl Schmidt-Rottluff, founded the artist group *Die Brücke* (The Bridge) in Dresden that turned the art world on its head with ground-breaking visions that paved the way for German expressionism. By the 1920s art had become more radical and political, with artists such as George Grosz, Otto Dix and Max Ernst exploring the new concepts of Dada and surrealism. Käthe Kollwitz is one of the era's few major female artists, known for her social-realist drawings.

After 1945 abstract art became a mainstay of the West German scene, with key figures such as Joseph Beuys, Monica Bonvicini and Anselm Kiefer enjoying worldwide reputations. After reunification, the New Leipzig School achieved success at home and abroad with figurative painters such as Neo Rauch generating much acclaim.

Architecture

The scope of German architecture is such that it could easily be the focus of an entire visit. The first great wave of buildings in Germany came with the Romanesque period (800–1200), outstanding examples of which include the cathedrals at Worms, Speyer and Mainz. Gothic architecture brought such traits as ribbed vaults, pointed arches and flying buttresses nicely exemplified by Cologne's cathedral, Freiburg's Münster and Lübeck's Marienkirche.

For classic baroque, Balthasar Neumann's Residenz in Würzburg and the many classic buildings in Dresden are must-sees. The neoclassical period of the 19th century was dominated by Karl Friedrich Schinkel, who was especially prolific in Berlin and northern Germany.

No modern movement has had greater influence on design than Bauhaus, founded in 1919 by Walter Gropius. You can still visit the seminal school and private homes of Gropius and his fellow professors in Dresden-Rosslau. For an overview, drop by the Bauhaus Archive in Berlin. The Nazis shut down the Bauhaus in 1932 and reverted to the pompous and monumental. Berlin's Olympic Stadium and the Reichsparteitagsgelände (party rally grounds) in Nuremberg are among the few surviving buildings from that dark period.

Frankfurt shows Germany's take on the modern high-rise. For the boldest new architecture head to Berlin where such international starchitects as Daniel Libeskind, David Chipperfield and Lord Norman Foster have put their stamp on the city's post-reunification look.

Music

Forget brass bands and oompah music – few countries can claim the impressive musical heritage of Germany, which generated the greatness of Johann Sebastian Bach, Georg Friedrich Händel, Ludwig van Beethoven, Richard Strauss, Robert Schumann, Johannes Brahms and Richard Wagner, to name a few.

Germany has also made significant contributions to the contemporary-music scene. Internationally renowned artists include punk icon Nina Hagen, '80s balloon girl Nena, and rock bands from the Scorpions to Die Toten Hosen to Rammstein. Kraftwerk pioneered the original electronic sounds, which morphed into techno and became the seminal club music since the 1990s, especially in Berlin and Frankfurt. Today, Germany has the largest electronic-music scene in the world, and DJs such as Ellen Allien, Paul Kalkbrenner, Paul van Dyk and Sven Väth have become household names on the global party circuit.

Food & Drink

German Cuisine

Germany might not have the culinary kudos of its neighbours, but its robust, fresh flavours have made it a rising star in Europe's kitchen. Of course, if you crave traditional comfort food, you'll certainly find plenty of places to indulge in pork, potatoes and cabbage. These days, though, 'typical German' fare is lighter, healthier, creative and more likely to come from organic eateries, a UN worth of ethnic restaurants and gourmet kitchens. In fact, in 2012 Germany's Michelin skies twinkled brighter than ever before, with 208 one-star, 32 two-star and nine three-star restaurants.

When it comes to bread, Germany is a world-beater with over 300 tasty and textured varieties, often mixing wheat and

GERMANY FOOD & DRINK

VEGETARIANS

Germany was slow in embracing vegetarianism – let alone veganism – but of late health-conscious cafes and restaurants serving meatless fare have been sprouting faster than alfalfa, at least in the cities. Even rural restaurants will have at least a couple of vegetarian dishes on the menu. Otherwise, Asian and Indian eateries are the usual good bet for vegie-based dishes. For a comprehensive list of vegan and vegetarian restaurants in Germany, see www.happycow.net/europe/germany.

DINING TIPS

Restaurants are often formal places with full menus, crisp white linen and high prices. Many are open all day as are cafes, which serve coffee and alcohol alongside light inexpensive meals. In cities, some eateries serve good-value 'business lunches' including a starter, main course and drink for under €10.

Handy speed-feed shops, called *Imbiss*, serve all sorts of savoury fodder, from sausage-in-a-bun to doner and pizza. Many bakeries serve sandwiches alongside pastries.

Rather than leaving money on the table, tip when you pay by stating a rounded-up figure or saying '*es stimmt so*' (that's the right amount). A tip of 10% is generally about right.

rye flour. *Brezeln* are traditional pretzels covered in rock salt. Seasonal specialities include *Bärlauch* (wild garlic), which starts showing up in salads and as pesto in early spring; white asparagus in May and June; fresh berries and cherries in summer and handpicked mushrooms such as *Steinpilze* (porcini) and loamy *Pfifferlinge* (chanterelles) in autumn.

Pastries and cakes such as the famous *Schwarzwälder Kirschtorte* (Black Forest cake) are often enjoyed during the traditional afternoon *Kaffee und Kuchen* (coffee and cake) break.

Beer

Beer, Germany's national beverage, is both excellent and inexpensive. Its 'secret' dates back to the *Reinheitsgebot* (purity law) – passed in 1516 – demanding breweries to use only malt, yeast, hops and water. Although no longer a legal requirement, most German brewers still conform to it. Here's a rundown of the most common beer types:

Pils (Pilsner) Full beer with pronounced hop flavour and a creamy head.

Weizenbier/Weissbier Fruity and a bit spicy, lovely on a hot day. *Hefeweizen* has a stronger shot of yeast, whereas *Kristallweizen* is clearer with more fizz.

Bockbier Strong, dark beer brewed seasonally (eg *Maibock* in May and *Weihnachtsbock* at Christmas).

Helles Bier Has strong malt aromas and is slightly sweet.

Dunkles Bier Dark and full-bodied.

Wine

The reputation of German wine was long sullied by the cloyingly sweet taste of Liebfraumilch and the naff image of Blue Nun. Now, thanks to rebranding campaigns, a new generation of wine growers and an overall rise in quality, German wine is winning critics' praise and international awards left and right.

There are 13 wine-growing regions, the Rhine and the Moselle being the internationally best known. Typical white wine varieties include riesling, Müller-Thurgau (aka Rivaner), Silvaner, Grauburgunder (Pinot gris) and Weissburgunder (Pinot blanc). Among the reds, Spätburgunder (Pinot noir), is the best of the bunch.

For a comprehensive rundown, visit www.winesofgermany.co.uk, www.germanwines.de or www.germanwineusa.org.

SURVIVAL GUIDE

Directory A–Z

Accommodation

Germany has all types of places to unpack your suitcase, from hostels, camping grounds and family hotels to chains, business hotels and luxury resorts.

» Reservations are a good idea, especially if you're travelling in the busy summer season (June to September). Local tourist offices will often go out of their way to find something in your price range.

» Camping grounds abound. Fees consist of charges per person (between €3 and €10), tent (€6 to €16, depending on size) and car (€3 to €8), plus additional fees for hot showers, resort tax, electricity and sewage disposal.

» **Deutsches Jugendherbergswerk** (DJH; www.jugendherberge.de) coordinates the official Hostelling International (HI) hostels in Germany. Rates in gender-segregated dorms, or in family rooms, range from €13 to €30 per person, including linen and breakfast. People over 27 are charged an extra €3 or €4. Indie hostels are more relaxed and can be found in most large cities.

Unless noted in reviews, price ranges in this chapter refer to a double room with private bathroom and breakfast in high season.

€€€ more than €150

€€ €80 to €150

€ less than €80

Business Hours

We've listed business hours where they differ from the following standards. Where hours vary across the year, we've provided those applicable in high season.

Banks 9am to 4pm Monday to Friday, extended hours usually on Tuesday or Thursday

Bars 6pm to 1am

Cafes 8am to 8pm

Clubs 10pm to 4am

Post offices 9am to 6pm Monday to Friday, some Saturday mornings

Restaurants 11am to 10pm (varies widely, food service often stops at 9pm in rural areas)

Major stores & supermarkets 9.30am to 8pm Monday to Saturday (shorter hours in suburbs and rural areas, possible lunchtime break)

Customs Regulations

Duty-free shopping is only available if you're leaving the EU. Duty-free allowances (for anyone over 17) arriving from non-EU countries:

» 200 cigarettes or 100 cigarillos or 50 cigars or 250g of loose tobacco

» 1L of strong liquor or 2L of less than 22% alcohol by volume plus 4L of wine plus 16L of beer

» other goods up to the value of €300 if arriving by land or €430 if arriving by sea or air (€175 for under 15yr)

Discount Cards

Tourist offices in many cities sell 'Welcome Cards' entitling visitors to free or reduced admission on museums, sights and tours, plus unlimited local public transportation for the period of their validity (usually 24 or 48 hours). They can be good value if you want to fit a lot in.

Embassies & Consulates

All foreign embassies are in Berlin, but many countries have consular offices in such cities as Frankfurt, Munich, Hamburg and Düsseldorf.

Australia (☎030-880 0880; www.australian-embassy.de; Wallstrasse 76-79; ⑤Märkisches Museum)

Canada (☎030-203 120; www.kanada-info.de; Leipziger Platz 17; ⑤Potsdamer Platz, ⓡPotsdamer Platz)

New Zealand (☎030-206 210; www.nz embassy.com; Friedrichstrasse 60; ⑤Stadtmitte)

UK (☎030-204 570; www.britischebotschaft. de; Wilhelmstrasse 70; ⑤Brandenburger Tor, ⓡBrandenburger Tor)

USA (☎030-830 50; www.germany.usembassy. gov; Clayallee 170; ⑤Oskar-Helene-Heim)

Food

Price categories used in reviews in this chapter refer to the the cost of a main course.

€€€ more than €15

€€ €8 to €15

€ less than €8

Gay & Lesbian Travellers

» Germany is a magnet for *schwule* (gay) and *lesbische* (lesbian) travellers, with the rainbow flag flying especially proudly in Berlin and Cologne, with sizeable communities in Hamburg, Frankfurt and Munich.

» Generally speaking, attitudes towards homosexuality tend to be more conservative in the countryside, among older people and in the eastern states.

Legal Matters

» By law you must carry some form of photographic identification, such as your passport, national identity card or driving licence.

» The permissible blood alcohol limit is 0.05%; drivers caught exceeding this amount are subject to stiff fines, a confiscated licence and even jail time. Drinking in public is legal, but be discreet about it.

» There is no universal nationwide smoking law, with regulations left to each of the 16 German states. It's best to ask first before lighting up.

TIPPING

Restaurant bills always include a service charge (*Bedienung*) but most people add 5% or 10% unless the service was truly abhorrent.

Bartenders 5%

Hotel porters €1 to €1.50 per bag

Room cleaners €1 per night per person

Taxi drivers around 10%

Money

» Cash is king in Germany, so always carry some with you and plan to pay in cash almost everywhere.

» The easiest and quickest way to obtain cash is by using your debit (bank) card at an ATM (*Geldautomat*) linked to international networks such as Cirrus, Plus, Star and Maestro.

» Credit cards are becoming more widely accepted, but it's best not to assume that you'll be able to use one – enquire first.

» Change currency in foreign-exchange offices (*Wechselstuben*) at airports and train stations, particularly those of the Reisebank.

Public Holidays

Germany observes eight religious and three secular holidays nationwide. Shops, banks, government offices and post offices are closed on these days. States with predominantly Catholic populations, such as Bavaria and Baden-Württemberg, also celebrate Epiphany (6 January), Corpus Christi (10 days after Pentecost), Assumption Day (15 August) and All Saints' Day (1 November). Reformation Day (31 October) is only observed in eastern Germany.

The following are *gesetzliche Feiertage* (public holidays):

Neujahrstag (New Year's Day) 1 January

Ostern (Easter) Good Friday, Easter Sunday and Easter Monday

Christi Himmelfahrt (Ascension Day) Forty days after Easter

Maifeiertag/Tag der Arbeit (Labour Day) 1 May

Pfingsten (Whit/Pentecost Sunday & Monday) Fifty days after Easter.

Tag der Deutschen Einheit (Day of German Unity) 3 October

Weihnachtstag (Christmas Day) 25 December

Zweiter Weihnachtstag (Boxing Day) 26 December

Telephone

German phone numbers consist of an area code followed by the local number, which can be between three and nine digits long.

Country code ☑49

International access code ☑00

Directory inquiries ☑11837 for an English-speaking operator (charged at €1.99 per minute)

Travellers with Disabilities

Germany is fair at best (but better than much of Europe) for the needs of travellers with disabilities, with access ramps for wheelchairs and/or lifts in some public buildings. Resources include:

Deutsche Bahn Mobility Service Centre (☑ext 9 for English 0180-599 6633512; www. bahn.com; ◔24hr) Train access information and route-planning assistance. The website has useful information in English (search for 'barrier-free travel').

German National Tourism Office (www. germany.travel) Your first port of call, with inspirational information in English.

Natko (www.natko.de) Central clearing house for inquiries about barrier-free travel in Germany.

Visas

» EU nationals only need their passport or national identity card to enter, stay and work in Germany, even for stays over six months.

» Citizens of Australia, Canada, Israel, Japan, New Zealand, Poland, Switzerland and the US need only a valid passport but no visa if entering Germany as tourists for up to three months within a six-month period. Passports must be valid for another three months beyond the intended departure date.

» Nationals from other countries need a Schengen Visa.

Getting There & Away

Most travellers arrive in Germany by air, or by rail and road connections from neighbouring countries. Flights, tours and rail tickets can be booked online at lonelyplanet.com/bookings.

Entering Germany

If you're arriving from any of the 24 other Schengen countries, such as the Netherlands, Poland, Austria or the Czech Republic, you no longer have to show your passport or go through customs in Germany, no matter which nationality you are.

Air

Budget carriers, **Lufthansa** (www.lufthansa.com) and international airlines serve numerous German airports from across Europe and the rest of the world. Frankfurt and Munich are the hubs, but there are also sizeable airports in Berlin, Hamburg, Cologne/Bonn and Stuttgart, and smaller ones in Bremen, Dresden, Hanover, Leipzig, Münster-Osnabrück and Nuremberg.

Lufthansa, Germany's national flagship carrier and Star Alliance member, operates a vast network of domestic and international flights and has one of the world's best safety records. Practically every other national carrier from around the world serves Germany, along with budget carriers **Air Berlin** (www.airberlin.com), **easyJet** (☑0900-1100 161; www.easyjet.com), **Flybe** (www.flybe.com), **airBaltic** (www.airbaltic.com), **Ryanair** (☑0900-116 0500; www.ryanair.com) and **germanwings** (www.germanwings.com).

Note that Ryanair usually flies to remote airports, which are often little more than recycled military airstrips. Frankfurt-Hahn, for instance, is actually near the Moselle River, about 125km west of Frankfurt proper.

Land

BUS

Travelling by bus between Germany and the rest of Europe is cheaper than by train or plane, but journeys will take a lot longer.

Eurolines (www.eurolines.com) is a consortium of national bus companies operating routes throughout the continent. The German affiliate is **Deutsche Touring** (www.touring.de). Sample one-way fares and travel times:

ROUTE	PRICE	DURATION (HR)
Budapest–Frankfurt	€96	14½–18
Florence–Munich	€78	8½
London–Cologne	€69	12
Paris–Munich	€64	13
Krakow–Berlin	€41	10

Children between the ages of four and 12 pay half price, while teens, students and seniors get 10% off regular fares. Tickets can be purchased online and at most train stations throughout Germany.

Backpacker-geared hop-on, hop-off **Busabout** (www.busabout.com) runs coaches along three interlocking European loops between May and October. Passes are sold online and through travel agents. Germany is part of the North Loop with buses stopping in Berlin, Dresden, Munich and Stuttgart.

CAR & MOTORCYCLE

When bringing your own vehicle to Germany, you need a valid driving licence, your car registration certificate and proof of insurance. Foreign cars must display a nationality sticker unless they have official European plates. You also need to carry a warning (hazard) triangle and a first-aid kit.

To decrease air pollution caused by fine particles, many German cities have introduced low-emissions Green Zones that may only be entered by cars displaying an *Umweltplakette* (emissions sticker). Check with your local automobile association or order a sticker online www.tuev-sued.de or www.tuev-nord.de (English instructions provided). The cost is €6.

TRAIN

A favourite way to get to Germany from elsewhere in Europe is by train. In Germany ticketing is handled by **Deutsche Bahn** (www.bahn.com). Long-distance trains connecting major German cities with those in other countries are called EuroCity (EC) trains. Seat reservations are essential during the peak summer season and around major holidays.

Germany is also linked by overnight train to many European cities; routes include Amsterdam to Munich, Zurich to Berlin and Paris to Hamburg.

SEA

Germany's main ferry ports are Kiel, Lübeck and Travemünde in Schleswig-Holstein, and Rostock and Sassnitz (on Rügen Island) in

Mecklenburg-Western Pomerania. All have services to Scandinavia and the Baltic states.

There are no longer any direct ferry services between Germany and the UK, but you can go via the Netherlands, Belgium or France and drive or train it from there. For fare details and to book tickets, check the ferry websites or go to www.ferrybooker.com or www.ferrysavers.com.

Getting Around

Germans are whizzes at moving people around, and the public-transport network is among the best in Europe. The best ways of getting around the country are by car and by train. Regional bus services fill the gaps in areas not well served by the rail network.

Air

There are lots of domestic flights, many with budget carriers such as Air Berlin (www.air berlin.com) and germanwings (www.german wings.com), as well as Lufthansa (www.lufthansa.com). Unless you're flying from one end of the country to the other, say Berlin to Munich or Hamburg to Munich, planes are only marginally quicker than trains once you factor in the check-in and transit times.

Bicycle

» Cycling is allowed on all roads and highways but not on the autobahns (motorways). Cyclists must follow the same rules of the road as cars and motorcycles. Helmets are not compulsory (not even for children), but wearing one is common sense.

» Bicycles may be taken on most trains but require a separate ticket (Fahrradkarte). These cost €9 per trip on long-distance trains (IC and EC and City Night Line), or €10 per trip for international travel. You need to reserve a space at least one day ahead and leave your bike in the bike compartment usually at the beginning or end of the train. Bicycles are not allowed on high-speed ICE trains. The fee on local and regional trains (IRE, RB, RE, S-Bahn) is €5 per day.

» There is no charge at all on some local trains, which are listed in Deutsche Bahn's Bahn & Bike brochure (in German). The brochures also notes the almost 250 stations where you can rent bikes. It's available for download at www.bahn.de/bahnundbike.

» Otherwise, most towns and cities have private bicycle-hire stations, often at or near the train station. Hire costs range from €7 to €20 per day and from €35 to €85 per week, depending on the model of bicycle. A minimum deposit of €30 (more for fancier bikes) and/or ID are required.

» Hotels, especially in resort areas, sometimes keep a stable of bicycles for their guests, often at no charge.

Boat

With two seas and a lake- and river-filled interior, don't be surprised to find yourself in a boat at some point.

» Regular ferries serve the East Frisian Islands in Lower Saxony; the North Frisian Islands in Schleswig-Holstein; and the islands of Poel, Rügen and Hiddensee in Mecklenburg-Western Pomerania.

» Scheduled boat services also operate along sections of the Rhine, the Elbe and the Danube, and on major lakes such as the Chiemsee and Lake Starnberg in Bavaria and Lake Constance in Baden-Württemberg.

Bus

» In some rural areas buses may be your only option for getting around without your own vehicle. This is especially true of the Harz Mountains, sections of the Bavarian Forest and the Alpine foothills.

» The frequency of services varies from 'rarely' to 'constantly'. Commuter-geared routes offer limited or no service in the evenings and at weekends, so keep this in mind or risk finding yourself stuck in a remote place on a Saturday night.

» In cities, buses generally converge at the Busbahnhof or Zentraler Omnibus Bahnhof (ZOB; central bus station), which is often near the Hauptbahnhof (central train station).

» For long-distance travel between German cities, the main operators are Deutsche Touring (www.touring.de) and Berlin Linien Bus (www.berlinlinienbus.de). Discounts are available for children, students, seniors and groups.

Car & Motorcycle

» Germany's pride and joy is its 11,000km network of autobahns (motorways, freeways). Every 40km to 60km, you'll find elaborate service areas with petrol stations, toilet facilities and restaurants; many are open 24 hours. In between are rest stops (Rastplatz), which usually have picnic tables and toilet facilities. Orange emergency call boxes are spaced about 2km apart.

» Autobahns are supplemented by an extensive network of Bundesstrassen (secondary 'B' roads, highways) and smaller Landstrassen (country roads, 'L'). No tolls are charged on any public roads.

» If your car is not equipped with a navigational system, having a good map or road atlas is essential, especially in rural areas. Navigating is not done by the points of the compass. That is to say that you'll find no signs saying 'north' or 'west'. Rather, you'll see signs pointing you in the direction of a city, so you'd best have that map right in your lap to stay oriented. Maps are sold at every petrol station.

» Cars are impractical in urban areas. Leaving your car in a central *Parkhaus* (car park) can cost €20 per day or more.

AUTOMOBILE ASSOCIATIONS

ADAC (Allgemeiner Deutscher Automobil-Club; ☎0180-222 2222; www.adac.de) offers roadside assistance to members of its affiliates, including British AA, American AAA and Canadian CAA.

DRIVING LICENCES

Visitors do not need an international driving licence to drive in Germany; bring your licence from home.

HIRE

» To hire your own wheels, you'll need to be at least 25 years old and possess a valid driving licence and a major credit card. Some companies lease to drivers between the ages of 21 and 24 for an additional charge (about €12 to €20 per day). Younger people or those without a credit card are usually out of luck.

» For insurance reasons, driving into an eastern European country, such as the Czech Republic or Poland, is usually a no-no.

» All the main international companies maintain branches at airports, major train stations and towns.

» Rental cars with automatic transmission are rare in Germany and will usually need to be ordered well in advance.

INSURANCE

You must have third-party insurance to enter Germany with a vehicle.

ROAD RULES

Road rules are easy to understand, and standard international signs are in use. You drive on the right, and cars are left-hand drive. Right of way is usually signed, with major roads given priority, but at unmarked intersections traffic coming from the right always has right of way.

The blood-alcohol limit for drivers is 0.05%. Obey the road rules carefully: the German police are very efficient and issue heavy on-the-spot fines. Germany also has one of the highest concentrations of speed cameras in Europe.

Speed limits:

Towns & cities On bigger roads 50km/h, on residential streets 30km/h (or as posted).

Open road/country 100km/h

Autobahn Unlimited but many exceptions as posted.

Public Transport

» Public transport is excellent within big cities and small towns and may include buses, trams (Strassenbahn), S-Bahn (light rail) and U-Bahn (underground/subway trains).

» Tickets cover all forms of transit, and fares are determined by zones or time travelled, sometimes both. Multiticket strips and day passes are generally available, offering better value than single-ride tickets.

» Tickets must usually be bought from vending machines at the stations or stops. Only buses and some trams let you buy tickets from the driver.

» Normally, tickets must be stamped upon boarding in order to be valid. Inspections are random but fines (usually €40) are levied if you're caught without a valid ticket.

Train

» Operated almost entirely by **Deutsche Bahn** (www.bahn.com), the German train system is the finest in Europe and is generally the best way to get around the country.

» Several private operators provide train services on regional routes, such as the Ostdeutsche Eisenbahn in Saxony and the Bayerische Oberlandbahn in Bavaria.

» It's rarely worth buying a 1st-class ticket on German trains; 2nd class is usually quite comfortable. There's more difference between the train classifications – basically the faster a train travels, the plusher (and pricier) it is.

» Most train stations have coin-operated lockers costing from €1 to €4 per 24-hour period. Larger stations have staffed left-luggage offices (*Gepäckaufbewahrung*).

A PRIMER ON TRAIN TYPES

Here's the low-down on the alphabet soup of trains operated by Deutsche Bahn (DB):

InterCity Express (ICE) Long-distance, high-speed trains that stop at major cities only and run at one- or two-hour intervals.

InterCity (IC), EuroCity (EC) Long-distance trains that are fast but slower than the ICE; also run at one- and two-hour intervals and stop in major cities. EC trains run to major cities in neighbouring countries.

InterRegio-Express (IRE) Regional train connecting cities with few intermediary stops.

City Night Line (CNL) Night trains with sleeper cars and couchettes.

Regional Bahn (RB) Local trains, mostly in rural areas, with frequent stops; the slowest in the system.

Regional Express (RE) Local trains with limited stops that link rural areas with metropolitan centres and the S-Bahn.

S-Bahn Local trains operating within a city and its suburban area.

» Seat reservations (€4) for long-distance travel are highly recommended, especially on Friday or Sunday afternoons, during holiday periods or in summer. Reservations can be made online and at ticket counters up to 10 minutes before departure.

TICKETS

» Tickets may be bought online at www. bahn.de, using a credit card, at no surcharge. However, you will need to present a printout of your ticket, as well as the credit card used to buy it, to the conductor.

» Many train stations have a *Reisezentrum* (travel centre), where staff sell tickets (for a small fee) and can help you plan an itinerary (ask for an English-speaking agent).

» Smaller stations may only have a few ticket windows and the smallest ones aren't staffed at all. In this case, you must buy tickets from multilingual vending machines. These are also plentiful at staffed stations and convenient if you don't want to queue at a ticket counter. Both agents and machines accept major credit cards.

» Only conductors on long-distance trains sell tickets on board, at a surcharge; major credit cards are usually accepted. Not having a ticket carries a stiff penalty.

SPECIAL DEALS

Deutsche Bahn offers several permanent rail deals:

» **Schönes-Wochenende-Ticket** (Nice Weekend Ticket; €40 for up to five people travelling together) Valid for one day of unlimited 2nd-class travel on regional trains (IRE, RE, RB, S-Bahn), plus on local public transport. Available from midnight Saturday or Sunday until 3am the next day.

» **Quer-durchs-Land-Ticket** (Around Germany Ticket; €42 for the first person and €6 each for up to four additional persons) A weekday variation of the Schönes-Wochenende-Ticket.

» **Länder-Tickets** (Regional Tickets) One day of unlimited travel on regional trains and public transport within one of the German states (or, in some cases, also in bordering states). Tickets are generally valid for travel Monday to Friday from 9am to 3am the following day and on weekends from midnight until 3am the following day. Some passes are priced at a flat rate for up to five people travelling together (eg the Brandenburg-Berlin-Ticket costs €28); others have staggered pricing: the first person buys the main ticket and up to four people may join for a just few euros more per ticket (eg in Bavaria, the first person pays €22, additional tickets cost €4).

» On any of these schemes, children under 15 travel for free if accompanied by their parents or grandparents. See the website for details or check with a *Reisezentrum* if already in Germany.

» Tickets can be purchased online, from vending machines or, for a €2 surcharge, from station ticket offices.

GERMAN RAIL PASS

If your permanent residence is outside Europe, including Turkey and Russia, you qualify for the German Rail Pass. Tickets are sold through www.bahn.com, www.raileurope. com, or through agents in your home country.

Central Europe Revealed

Natural Attractions »
Regal Residences »
Pivo & Vino »

Lake Bled (p496), Slovenia

RACHEL LEWIS/GETTY IMAGES ©

Natural Attractions

With the mountain rooftop of Europe, the Alps, stretching across four Central European countries, it should come as no surprise that nature is a strong drawcard here. Wide river valleys, age-old forests and interesting rock formations add to the attraction.

Soča Valley, Slovenia

1 More turquoise than seems natural, the Soča River cleaves through its namesake valley for over 90km. It's a magnet for anyone who wants to hike, ski, raft and more in stunning natural beauty.

Valais, Switzerland

2 The Swiss Alps have the tallest peaks of Europe's tallest mountains. So whether you don your boots and go hiking, ride the world's highest train or enjoy the view from a glacial lakeside cafe, it's superlative.

Danube Valley, Austria

3 The Danube Valley is arguably the most picturesque section of Central Europe's central river. Terraced vineyards line river banks, castle ruins sit high above and medieval cities dot the landscape.

Black Forest, Germany

4 Large stands of evergreens interspersed with farmhouses and wandering cows make for a bucolic scene in the Black Forest. Though the villages can get quite busy, venture down the path and you'll find solitude among the trees.

Clockwise from top left
1 Soča River (p503), Slovenia 2 The Swiss Alps, Switzerland
3 Dürnstein (p60), Austria 4 Black Forest (239), Germany

Regal Residences

Kings, queens and the nobles of old sure knew how to live. They've left behind an impressive legacy of ornate palaces, romantic castles and stony fortresses for modern-day travellers to wonder at all across Central Europe.

Spiš Castle, Slovakia

1 The sprawling hilltop remains of this Slovakian fortress are impressive enough – just imagine the daunting sight the castle once posed. A Romanesque palace and small chapel are intact, but walking among the ruined rooms is almost more evocative.

Schloss Mirabell, Austria

2 At this palace it's not just the Marble Hall, open for concerts, that attracts. People are also drawn to the meticulous, fountain-filled garden surrounds. You may recognise them as where the von Trapp children sang 'Do-Re-Mi' in the *Sound of Music*.

Neuschwanstein Castle, Germany

3 A sugary pastiche of architectural styles, Neuschwanstein is the crenulated castle of fairy tale and legend. 'Mad' King Ludwig II's obsession with swans, Wagnerian opera and theatrical design are evident in the flights of fancy throughout.

Bellinzona, Switzerland

4 A trio of medieval castles sits lakefront where three Swiss valleys converge. With such a setting, it's surprising the crowds aren't larger. All the better for you to enjoy Castelgrande, Castello di Montebello and Castello di Sasso Corbaro.

Clockwise from top left
1 Spiš Castle (p465), Slovakia 2 Schloss Mirabell (p68), Salzburg, Austria 3 Schloss Neuschwanstein (224), Füssen, Germany

Pivo & Vino

Whether you call it _Bier_ or _pivo_, _Wein_ or _vino_, the region's beer and wine are worth talking about. Germany and the Czech Republic are known worldwide for their hoppy brews and beer halls, and the wine cellars of Austria and Hungary provide an excellent alternative for imbibing.

Beer, Czech Republic

1 Beer gardens and halls are the establishments of choice for enjoying a good Czech brew. And you can always go straight to the factory – for Pilsner Urquell in Plzeň and Budvar in České Budějovice.

Wine, Hungary

2 Hungary's Tokaj dessert wines have been famous for centuries; sample them from a 600-year-old cellar. Even more fun are the outdoor tasting tables in Eger's wine valley, which produces a full-bodied red called Bikavér (Bull's Blood).

1. Beer billboard in Staré Město, Prague, Czech Republic
2. Wine varieties on display, Budapest, Hungary

Hungary

Includes »

Best Places to Eat

» Ikon (p344)

» Padlizsán (p321)

» Imola Udvarház Borétterem (p341)

» Kisbuda Gyöngye (p309)

» La Maréda (p322)

Best Places to Stay

» Four Seasons Gresham Palace Hotel (p308)

» Fábián Panzió (p334)

» Tisza Hotel (p337)

» Hotel Senator Ház (p341)

Why Go?

Hungary is just the place to kick off an Eastern European trip. A short hop from Vienna, this land of Franz Liszt and Béla Bartók, paprika-lashed dishes and the romantic Danube River continues to enchant visitors. The allure of Budapest, once an imperial city, is obvious at first sight, and it also boasts the hottest nightlife in the region. Other cities, too, like Pécs, the warm heart of the south, and Eger, the wine capital of the north, have much to offer travellers, as does the sprawling countryside, particularly the Great Plain, where cowboys ride and cattle roam. And where else can you laze about in an open-air thermal spa while snow patches glisten around you? In Hungary you'll find all the glamour, excitement and fun of Western Europe – at half the cost.

When to Go
Budapest

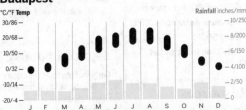

May Spring is in full swing, which means reliable weather, cool temperatures and flowers.

Jul & Aug Sunny but very hot, so decamp to the hills or Lake Balaton (and book ahead).

Sep & Oct Sunshine, mild temperatures and harvest festivals; perhaps the best time to visit.

HUNGARY

AT A GLANCE

» **Currency** Forint (Ft)

» **Language** Hungarian

» **Money** ATMs abound

» **Visas** None for EU, USA, Canada, Australia & New Zealand

Fast Facts

» **Area** 93,030 sq km

» **Capital** Budapest

» **Country code** 36

» **Emergency** Ambulance ☏104, emergency assistance ☏112, fire ☏105, police ☏107

Exchange Rates

Australia	A$1	248Ft
Canada	C$1	234Ft
Euro Zone	€1	303Ft
Japan	¥100	252Ft
New Zealand	NZ$1	199Ft
UK	UK£1	359Ft
USA	US$1	238Ft

Set Your Budget

» **Budget hotel room** 9000Ft (15,000Ft Budapest)

» **Two-course meal** 3500Ft (4500Ft Budapest)

» **Museum entrance** 900Ft

» **Beer** 500Ft

» **City transport ticket** 320Ft

Resources

» **Budapest Sun** (www.budapestsun.com)

» **Hungarian National Tourist Office** (www.gotohungary.com)

» **Hungary Museums** (www.museum.hu)

Connections

Hungary lies at the heart of Central Europe and is easy to reach by rail, road or even boat. Rail connections are particularly good to and from Vienna; high-speed express trains cover the 260km between the Austrian capital and Budapest in just under three hours. Rail connections are also good to Bratislava and Prague, with continuing services to popular travel destinations like Berlin and Kraków. Rail connections to Croatia, Serbia and Romania are less frequent, though they're also reliable with some advance planning. Buses fan out in all directions from Budapest, and nearly all corners of Europe can be reached within 24 hours. Regular hydrofoil services link Budapest with Bratislava and Vienna. Budapest is the country's only practical destination by air but is well served by commercial and budget carriers.

ITINERARIES

One Week

Spend at least three days in Budapest, checking out the sights, museums, cafes and *romkertek* (outdoor clubs) On your fourth day take a day trip to a Danube Bend town: see the open-air museum in Szentendre or the cathedral at Esztergom. Day five can be spent on a day trip to Pécs to see the lovely Turkish remains and check out the many museums and galleries in town. If you've still got the travel bug, on day six try some local wine in Eger, a baroque town set in red-wine country. On your last day recuperate in one of Budapest's wonderful thermal baths.

Two Weeks

In summer spend some time exploring the towns and grassy beaches around Lake Balaton. Tihany is a rambling hillside village filled with craftsmen's houses set on a protected peninsula. Keszthely is an old town with a great palace in addition to a beach and Hévíz has a thermal lake. Try to see something of the Great Plain as well. Szeged is a splendid university town on the Tisza River, and Kecskemét is a centre of art nouveau. Finish your trip in Tokaj, home of Hungary's most famous sweet wine.

Essential Food & Drink

» **Gulyás** (goulash) Hungary's signature dish, though here it's more like a soup than a stew and made with beef, onions and tomatoes.

» **Pörkölt** Paprika-infused stew; closer to what we would call goulash.

» **Halászlé** Recommended fish soup made from poached freshwater fish, tomatoes, green peppers and paprika.

» **Savanyúság** Literally 'sourness'; anything from mildly sour-sweet cucumbers to almost acidic sauerkraut, eaten with a main course.

BUDAPEST

♪1 / POP 1.75 MILLION

There's no other Hungarian city like Budapest in terms of size and importance. Home to almost 20% of the national population, Hungary's *főváros* (main city) is the nation's administrative, business and cultural centre; everything of importance starts, finishes or is taking place here.

But it's the beauty of Budapest – both natural and manmade – that makes it stand apart. Straddling a gentle curve in the Danube, the city is flanked by the Buda Hills on the west bank and the beginnings of the Great Plain to the east. Architecturally it is

Hungary Highlights

① Get lost in Hungary's best nightlife, especially the bars and pubs of **Budapest** (p311).

② Learn about the bravery of **Eger** (p339) while under Turkish attack, and how the city's Bull's Blood wine got its name.

③ Watch the cowboys ride at Bugac in **Kiskunság**

National Park (p333), in the heart of the Great Plain.

④ Absorb the Mediterranean-like climate and historic architecture of **Pécs** (p329), including its iconic Mosque Church.

⑤ Take a pleasure cruise across **Lake Balaton** (p325), Central Europe's largest body of fresh water.

⑥ Ease your aching muscles in the warm waters at the thermal lake in **Hévíz** (p328) and try one of the special treatments on offer.

⑦ Mill about with artists, free thinkers and day-trippers at the too-cute-for-words artists' colony of **Szentendre** (p316).

a gem, with enough baroque, neoclassical, eclectic and art nouveau elements to satisfy anyone.

In recent years, Budapest has taken on the role of the region's party town. In the warmer months outdoor beer gardens called *romkertek* heave with partygoers, and the world-class Sziget music festival in August is a major magnet. Fun can always be found on your doorstep; indeed, the city's scores of new hostels offer some of the best facilities and most convivial company in Europe.

History

Strictly speaking, the story of Budapest begins only in 1873 with the administrative union of three cities: Buda, west of the Danube; the even older Óbuda to the north; and Pest on the eastern side of the river. But the area had already been occupied for thousands of years.

The Romans had a colony at Aquincum in Óbuda till the 5th century AD. In the 1500s the Turks arrived uninvited and stayed for almost 150 years. The Habsburg Austrians helped kick the occupiers out, but then made themselves at home for more than two centuries.

In the late 19th century, under the dual Austro-Hungarian monarchy, the population of Budapest soared; many notable buildings date from that boom period. The 20th century was less kind. Brutal fighting towards the end of WWII, with Hungary on the losing side, brought widespread destruction and new overlords, this time the Soviets. The futile 1956 revolution left thousands dead and buildings that to this day remain pockmarked with bullet holes.

Thankfully, those times are long gone. With Hungary a member of the European Union, Budapest is once again a sophisticated capital of a proud nation with a distinctive heritage.

WANT MORE?

For in-depth information, reviews and recommendations at your fingertips, head to the Apple App Store to purchase Lonely Planet's *Budapest City Guide* iPhone app.

Alternatively, head to www.lonelyplanet.com/hungary/budapest for planning advice, author recommendations, traveller reviews and insider tips.

◎ Sights & Activities

Budapest is an excellent city for sightseeing, especially on foot. The Castle District in Buda contains a number of museums, both major and minor, but the lion's share is in Pest. Think of Margaret Island as a green buffer between the two – short on things to see, but a great place for a breather.

BUDA

Castle Hill (Várhegy) is arguably Budapest's biggest tourist attraction and a first port of call for any visit to the city. Here, you'll find most of Budapest's remaining medieval buildings, the Royal Palace, some sweeping views over Pest across the river and a festive mood year-round.

You can walk to Castle Hill up the Király lépcső, the 'Royal Steps' that lead northwest off Clark Ádám tér, or else take the Sikló (Map p300; I Szent György tér; one way/return adult 900/1800Ft, child 550/1000Ft; ⊙7.30am-10pm, closed 1st & 3rd Mon of month; 🚊16, 🚋19, 41), a funicular railway built in 1870 that ascends from Clark Ádám tér to Szent György tér near the Royal Palace.

The 'other peak' overlooking the Danube, south of Castle Hill, is Gellért Hill.

Royal Palace   PALACE
(Királyi Palota; Map p300; I Szent György tér) The massive former Royal Palace, razed and rebuilt at least a half-dozen times over the past seven centuries, occupies the southern end of Castle Hill. Here you'll find atmospheric medieval streets as well as the Hungarian National Gallery (Nemzeti Galéria; Map p300; www.mng.hu; I Szent György tér 6; adult/concession 1200/600Ft; ⊙10am-6pm Tue-Sun; 🚊16, 16/a, 116, 🚋19, 41) and the Budapest History Museum (Budapesti Történeti Múzeum; Map p300; www.btm.hu; I Szent György tér 2; adult/concession 1500/750Ft; ⊙10am-6pm Tue-Sun Mar-Oct, reduced hours Nov-Feb; 🚊16, 16/a, 116, 🚋19, 41).

Matthias Church   CHURCH
(Mátyás Templom; Map p300; www.matyastemplom.hu; I Szentháromság tér 2; adult/concession 1000/700Ft; ⊙9am-5pm Mon-Fri, 9am-1pm Sat, 1-5pm Sun) The pointed spire and the colourful tiled roof make neo-Gothic Matthias Church (so named because King Matthias Corvinus held both his weddings here) a Castle Hill landmark. Parts date back some 500 years, notably the carvings above the southern entrance, but the rest of it was designed by architect Frigyes Schulek in 1896.

Budapest

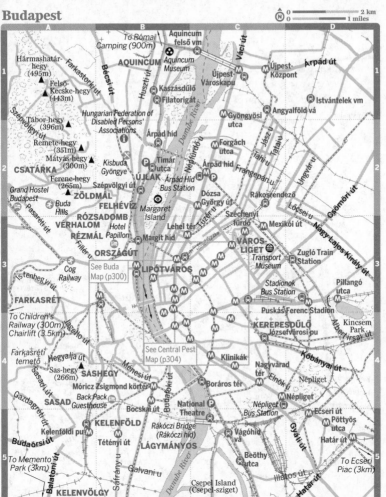

Fishermen's Bastion

MONUMENT

(Halászbástya; Map p300; I Szentháromság tér; adult/concession 540/220Ft; ⊙9am-11pm mid-Mar–mid-Oct) Just east of Matthias Church, Fishermen's Bastion is another neo-Gothic folly built as a viewing platform in 1905. In front of it is the ornate equestrian St Stephen statue (Szent István szobor) by sculptor Alajos Stróbl.

Royal Wine House & Wine Cellar Museum

MUSEUM

(Borház és Pincemúzeum; Map p300; ☑267 1100; www.kiralyiborok.com; I Szent György tér Nyugati sétány; adult/student & senior 990/750Ft; ⊙noon-8pm daily May-Sep, noon-8pm Tue-Sun Oct-Apr) Housed in what once were the royal cellars dating back to the 13th century, below Szent György tér, this place offers a crash course in Hungarian viticulture in the heart of the Castle District. Tastings cost 1990/2490/3790Ft for three/four/six wines.

FREE Citadella

FORTRESS

(Map p300; www.citadella.hu; ⊙24hr) Built by the Habsburgs after the 1848–49 War of Independence to defend the city from further insurrection, the Citadella was obsolete by the time it was ready (1851) and the political

Buda

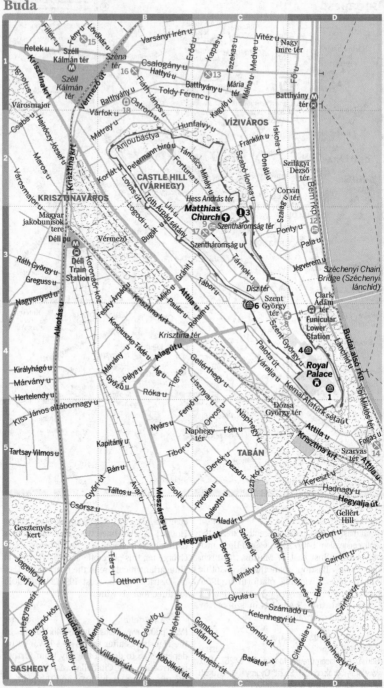

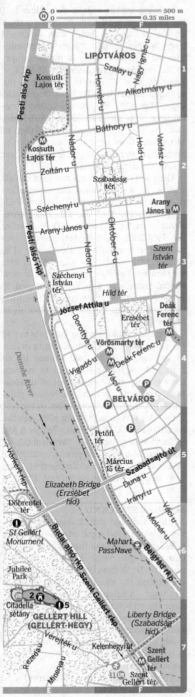

climate had changed. Today the Citadella contains some big guns and dusty displays in the central courtyard, the rather hokey **1944 Bunker Waxworks** (1944 Bunkér Panoptikum; Map p300; www.citadella.hu; admission 1200Ft; ⊙9am-8pm May-Sep, to 5pm Oct-Apr; ⬚27) inside a bunker used during WWII, and a hotel-cum-hostel (p308).

To reach here from Pest, cross Elizabeth Bridge and take the stairs leading up behind the statue of St Gellért, or cross Liberty Bridge and follow Verejték utca through the park starting opposite the entrance to the Gellért Baths.

Liberty Monument   MONUMENT
(Szabadság szobor; Map p300) The Liberty Monument – a lovely lady with a palm frond proclaiming freedom throughout the city – stands atop Gellért Hill. Some 14m high, she was raised in 1947 in tribute to the Soviet soldiers who died liberating Budapest in 1945,

but the victims' names in Cyrillic letters on the plinth and the statues of the Soviet soldiers were removed in 1992 and sent to Memento Park (p302).

TOP CHOICE **Memento Park**   HISTORIC SITE

(off Map p299; www.mementopark.hu; XXII Balatoni út 16; adult/student 1500/1000Ft; ⊙10am-dusk) Home to almost four dozen statues, busts and plaques of Lenin, Marx and 'heroic' workers that once 'graced' the streets of Budapest and elsewhere, this socialist Disneyland 10km southwest of the city centre is a mind-blowing place to visit.

To get here, take tram 19 from Batthyány tér in Buda or tram 47 or 49 from Deák Ferenc tér in Pest to Kosztolány Dezsö tér in southern Buda and board city bus 150 (25 minutes, every 20 to 30 minutes) for the park. There's also a more expensive direct bus (with park admission adult/child return 4900/3500Ft), which departs from in front of the Le Meridien Budapest Hotel on Deák Ferenc tér at 11am year-round, with an extra departure at 3pm in July and August.

Aquincum Museum   ARCHAEOLOGICAL SITE

(Aquincumi Múzeum; Map p299; www.aquincum. hu; III Szentendre út 139; adult/student & senior 1500/600Ft, archaeological park only 1000/300Ft; ⊙park 9am-6pm Tue-Sun May-Sep, reduced hours Apr & Oct; museum 10am-6pm Tue-Sun May-Sep, reduced hours Apr & Oct) Some 7km north of the centre is the Aquincum Museum, with the most complete ruins of a 2nd-century Roman civilian town in Hungary. Inside is a vast collection of coins and wall paintings. It can be reached by taking the HÉV from Batthyány tér in Buda to the Aquincum stop.

TOP CHOICE **Gellért Baths**   BATHHOUSE

(Gellért Fürdő; Map p300; ☎466 6166; www. spasbudapest.com; XI Kelenhegyi út, Danubius Hotel Gellért; without/with private changing room 3200/4300Ft ; ⊙6am-8pm) Soaking in the art nouveau Gellért Baths, open to both men and women in separate sections but mixed on Sunday, has been likened to taking a bath in a cathedral. The eight thermal pools range in temperature from 26°C to 38°C.

Buda Hills   HILL

(Map p299) With 'peaks' up to 500m, a comprehensive system of trails and no lack of unusual conveyances to get you around, the Buda Hills are the city's playground and a welcome respite from hot, dusty Pest in summer.

Heading for the hills is more than half the fun. From Széll Kálmán metro station on the M2 line in Buda, walk westward along Szilágyi Erzsébet fasor for 10 minutes (or take tram 18 or 56 for two stops) to the circular Hotel Budapest at Szilágyi Erzsébet fasor 47. Directly opposite is the terminus of the Cog Railway (Fogaskerekű vasút; Map p299; www.bkv.hu; Szilágyi Erzsébet fasor 14-16; admission 320Ft; ⊙5am-11pm). Built in 1874, the railway climbs 3.6km in 14 minutes three or four times an hour to Széchenyi-hegy (427m), one of the prettiest residential areas in Buda.

Here you can stop for a picnic in the attractive park south of the old-time station or board the narrow-gauge Children's Railway (Gyermekvasút; off Map p299; www.gyermekvasut.hu; adult/child 1 section 500/300Ft, entire line 700/350Ft; ⊙closed Mon Sep-Apr), two minutes to the south on Hegyhát út. The railway with eight stops was built in 1951 by Pioneers (socialist Scouts) and is now staffed entirely by schoolchildren aged 10 to 14 (the engineer excepted). The little train chugs along for 12km, terminating at Hűvösvölgy.

There are walks fanning out from any of the stops along the Children's Railway line, or you can return to Széll Kálmán station on tram 61 from Hűvösvölgy. A more interesting way down, however, is to get off at Jánoshegy, the fourth stop and the highest point (527m) in the hills. About 700m to the east is the chairlift (Libegő; off Map p299; www.bkv. hu; adult/child 800/500Ft; ⊙9am-7pm Jul & Aug, 9.30am-5pm May, Jun & Sep, 10am-4pm Oct-Apr, closed 2nd & 4th Mon of every month), which will take you down 1040m to Zugligeti út. From here bus 291 returns to Szilágyi Erzsébet fasor.

MARGARET ISLAND

Neither Buda nor Pest, 2.5km-long Margaret Island (Margit-sziget; admission free; Map p299), in the middle of the Danube, was the domain of one religious order or another until the Turks came and turned what was then called the Island of Rabbits into – of all things – a harem. It's been a public park since the mid-19th century.

While not huge on unmissable sights, the island's gardens and shaded walkways are lovely places to stroll around. As the island is mostly off-limits to cars, cyclists also feel welcome here.

The easiest way to get to Margaret Island from Buda or Pest is via tram 4 or 6. Bus 26 covers the length of the island as it makes the run from Nyugati train station to Árpád Bridge. You can hire a bicycle from one of several stands on the island.

PEST

TOP CHOICE **Great Synagogue** JEWISH
(Nagy zsinagóga; Map p304; ☑343 6756; www.dohanystreetsynagogue.hu; VII Dohány utca 2-8; adult/student & child 2750/2050Ft; ☉10am-5.30pm Sun-Thu, to 4pm Fri Apr-Oct, reduced hours Nov-Mar) Northeast of the Astoria metro stop is what remains of the Jewish quarter. The twin-towered, 1859 Great Synagogue, the largest Jewish house of worship in the world outside New York City and seating 3000, also contains the **Hungarian Jewish Museum** (Magyar Zsidó Múzeum; Map p304; ☑343 6756; www.zsidomuzeum.hu; VII Dohány utca 2; synagogue & museum adult/student & child 2750/2050Ft, call ahead for guided tours; ☉10am-6pm Sun-Thu, to 4pm Fri Mar-Oct, 10am-4pm Sun-Thu, to 2pm Fri Nov-Apr; ⊠M2 Astoria) with a harrowing exhibit on the Holocaust.

On the synagogue's north side, the **Holocaust Memorial** (Map p304; opp VII Wesselényi utca 6; ⊠M2 Astoria, ☒47, 49) stands over the mass graves of those murdered by the Nazis from 1944 to 1945. On the leaves of the metal 'tree of life' are the family names of some of the hundreds of thousands of victims.

Parliament HISTORIC BUILDING
(Országház; Map p304; ☑441 4904; www.parlament.hu; V Kossuth Lajos tér 1-3; adult/concession/EU citizen 3500/1750Ft/free; ☉8am-4pm Mon-Sat, 8am-2pm Sun) The huge riverfront Parliament, dating back to 1902, dominates Kossuth Lajos tér. English-language tours are given at 10am, noon and 2pm (Hungarian tours depart continually). To avoid disappointment, book ahead (in person).

Hősök tere SQUARE
(Heroes' Sq; Map p304) This public space holds a sprawling monument constructed to honour the millennium in 1896 of the Magyar conquest of the Carpathian Basin.

Museum of Fine Arts MUSEUM
(Szépművészeti Múzeum; www.mfab.hu; XIV Dózsa György út 41; adult/concession 1800/900Ft, temporary exhibitions 3800/2000Ft; ☉10am-6pm Tue-Sun) On the northern side of the square, this gallery houses the city's outstanding collection of foreign artworks in a building dating from 1906. The Old Masters'

collection is the most complete, with thousands of works from the Dutch and Flemish, Spanish, Italian, German, French and British schools between the 13th and 18th centuries, including seven paintings by El Greco.

City Park PARK
(Városliget; Map p304) City Park is Pest's green lung – an open space covering almost a square kilometre. It has boating on a small lake in summer, ice-skating in winter and duck-feeding year-round. The park's **Vajdahunyad Castle** (Map p304) was built in 1896 in various architectural styles from all over historic Hungary, including Gothic, Romanesque and baroque. It now contains the **Hungarian Agricultural Museum** (Magyar Mezőgazdasági Múzeum; Map p304; www.mmgm.hu; XIV Vajdahunyad sétány, Vajdahunyad Castle; adult/child 1100/550Ft; ☉10am-5pm Tue-Sun Apr-Oct, 10am-4pm Tue-Fri, to 5pm Sat & Sun Nov-Mar; ⊠M1 Hősök tere, ☒75, 79).

Further east the varied exhibits of the **Transport Museum** (Közlekedési Múzeum; Map p299; www.km.iif.hu; XIV Városligeti körút 11; adult/child 1400/700Ft; ☉10am-5pm Tue-Fri, to 6pm Sat & Sun May-Sep, reduced hours Oct-Apr; ⊛) make it one of the most enjoyable spots in the city for children.

In the park's northern corner is the art nouveau **Széchenyi Baths** (Széchenyi Fürdő; off Map p304; ☑363 3210; www.spasbudapest.com; XIV Állatkerti út 1; ticket with locker/cabin weekdays 3400/3800Ft, weekends 3550/3950F; ☉6am-10pm; ⊠M1 Széchenyi fürdő), its cupola visible from anywhere in the park. Built in 1908 this place has a dozen thermal baths and five swimming pools.

Terror House MUSEUM
(Terror Háza; Map p304; www.terrorhaza.hu; VI Andrássy út 60; adult/concession 2000/1000Ft; ☉10am-6pm Tue-Sun) The headquarters of the dreaded secret police has been turned into so-called Terror House, a museum focusing on the crimes and atrocities committed by both Hungary's fascist and Stalinist regimes. The years leading up to the 1956 uprising get the lion's share of the exhibition space. The excellent audio guide costs 1500Ft.

Hungarian State Opera House CULTURAL BUILDING
(Magyar Állami Operaház; Map p304; ☑332 8197; www.operavisit.hu; VI Andrássy út 22; tours adult/concession 3000/2000Ft; ☉tours 3pm & 4pm) Designed by Miklós Ybl in 1884, the neo-

Central Pest

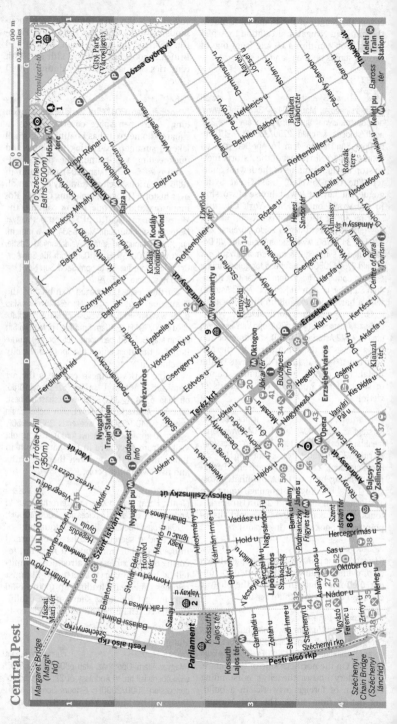

500 m
0.25 miles

City Park
(Városliget)

Dózsa György út

Keleti Train Station

To Széchenyi
Baths (500m)

Hősök
tere

Andrássy út

Munkácsy Mihály u

Kodály
körönd

Benczúr u

Rippl-Rónai u

Lendvay u

Délibáb u

Bajza u

Munkácsy Mihály u

Aradi u

Szondi u

Szinyei Merse u

Bajnok u

Szív u

Izabella u

Vörösmarty u

Csengery u

Eötvös u

Teréz krt

Terézváros

Kmetty György u

Bajza u

Munkácsy Mihály u

Lövölde
tér

Rottenbiller u

Szófia u

Vörösmarty u

Hunyadi
tér

Oktogon

Király u

Rózsa u

Rottenbiller u

Rózsa u

Izabella u

Csengery u

Hevesi
Sándor tér

Almássy u

Hársfa u

Budapest

Erzsébet krt

Kürt u

Erzsébetváros

Hegedűs u

Dob u

Kertész u

Akácfa u

Klauzál
tér

Csányi u

Kis Diófa u

Vasvári
Pál u

Opera

Andrássy út

Révay u

Bajcsy-
Zsilinszky út

Keleti pu

Baross
tér

Tököry út

Munkás u

Rózsák
tere

Aláerdősor u

Izabella u

Bethlen
Gábor tér

Bethlen Gábor u

Damjanich u

Peter u

Nefelejcs u

József u

István u

Marek u

Dembinszky u

Garay u

Péterfy Sándor u

Bácskai u

Centre of Rural
Tourism

Almássy u

Wesselényi u

Ferdinánd híd

Podmaniczky u

Nyugati
Train Station

Budapest
Info

Nyugati pu

Jókai u

Jókai
tér

Teréz krt

Szondi u

Weiner Leó u

Dessewffy u

Zichy Jenő u

Mozsár u

Nagymező u

Ó u

Lovag u

Hajós u

Dalszínház u

To Trófea Grill
(350m)

Váci út

ÚJLIPÓTVÁROS

Viseg rádi u

Kresz Géza u

Kádár u

Hollán Ernő u

Katona József u

Pannónia u

Hegedűs
Gyula u

Szent István krt

Bihari János u

Vadász u

Alkotmány u

Kálmán Imre u

Hold u

Nagy
Ignác u

Markó u

Honvéd u

Stollár Béla u

Falk Miksa u

Szalay u

Balassi Bálint u

Jászai
Mari tér

Margaret Bridge
(Margit
híd)

Balaton u

Balaton u

Honvéd u

Kossuth
Lajos tér

Parliament

Kossuth
Lajos tér

Pesti alsó rkp

Széchenyi rkp

Garibaldi u

Zoltán u

Steindl Imre u

Vécsey u

Báthory u

Perczel M u

Nagysándor J u

Szabadság
tér

Lipótváros

Bank u

Frigyes tér

Arany János u

Padmaniczky János u

Szent
István tér

Hercegprímás u

Sas u

Október 6 u

Arany János u

Nádor u

Zrínyi u

Mérleg u

Vigyázó
Ferenc u

Széchenyi u

Széchenyi rkp

Pesti alsó rkp

Széchenyi
Chain Bridge
(Széchenyi
lánchíd)

Vörösmarty u

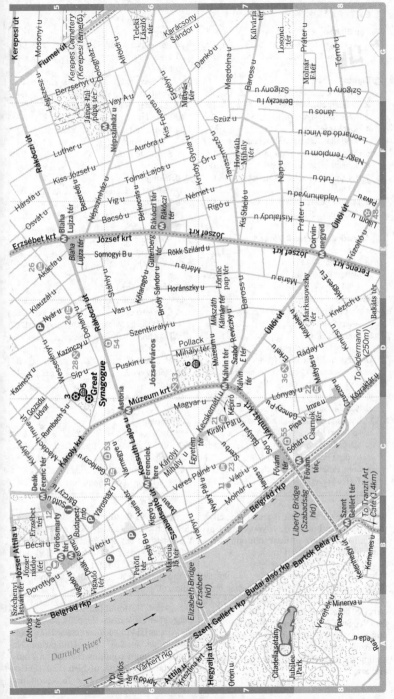

Central Pest

Renaissance opera house is among the city's most beautiful buildings. If you cannot attend a performance at least join one of the English-language guided tours.

Ethnography Museum MUSEUM
(Néprajzi Múzeum; Map p304; www.neprajz.hu; V Kossuth Lajos tér 12; adult/concession 1000/500Ft; combined ticket for all exhibitions 1400Ft; ☺10am-6pm Tue-Sun) The Ethnography Museum, opposite the Parliament building, has an extensive collection of national costumes among its permanent displays on folk life and art.

St Stephen's Basilica CHURCH
(Szent István Bazilika; Map p304; www.basilica.hu; V Szent István tér; adult/concession 500/300Ft; ☺9am-5pm Apr-Sep, 10am-4pm Oct-Mar) Look for the mummified right hand of St Stephen in the chapel of the colossal St Stephen's Basilica, off Bajcsy-Zsilinszky út.

Hungarian National Museum MUSEUM
(Magyar Nemzeti Múzeum; Map p304; www.mnm.hu; VIII Múzeum Q 14-16; adult/concession 1100/550Ft; ☺10am-6pm Tue-Sun) The Hungarian National Museum contains the nation's most important collection of historical relics – from archaeological finds to coronation

regalia – in a large neoclassical building purpose-built in 1847.

Tours

Free Budapest Tours
WALKING TOUR

(Map p304; ☑06 20 534 5819; www.freebudapest-tours.eu; Deák Ferenc tér; ☺10.30am & 2.30pm) Entertaining, knowledgeable guides offer two unique and highly professional tours of the city: 'Essential Pest', which takes in the highlights of Inner Town (1½ hours); and 'From Pest to Buda', which covers Inner Town's highlights, plus the banks of the Danube and the Castle District (2½ hours). The tours are free of charge; the guides work for tips only (be generous!) and departures are at 10.30am for 'From Pest to Buda' and 2.30pm for 'Essential Pest'. Meeting point is on Deák Ferenc tér (near the Deák tér metro) at the Budapest Sightseeing Bus stop. Evening thematic tours – 'Literary Walk' and 'Behind The Night' pub crawls – cost 3000Ft per person.

Mahart PassNave
BOAT TOUR

(Map p304; ☑484 4013; www.mahartpassnave.hu; V Belgrád Rakpart, Landing Stage pier 3; adult/concession 2990/1490Ft; ☺10am-10pm May-Sep, 11am-8pm Oct-Dec & Apr) Hour-long cruises between Margaret and Rákóczi bridges depart hourly in high season and at 1pm and 5pm in low season.

Festivals & Events

Many festivals and events are held in and around Budapest. Look out for the tourist board's annual *Events Calendar* for a complete listing.

Budapest Spring Festival
PERFORMING ARTS

(www.festivalcity.hu) The capital's largest and most important cultural event, with 200 events taking place over two weeks in late March/early April at dozens of venues.

Sziget Music Festival
MUSIC

(www.sziget.hu) Now one of the biggest and most popular music festivals in Europe, this 10-day event is held in mid-August on Budapest's Óbuda Island.

Hungarian Formula One Grand Prix
SPORT

(www.hungaroring.hu) Hungary's premier sporting event is held at Mogyoród, 24km northeast of Budapest, in early August.

Budapest International Wine Festival
WINE

(www.winefestival.hu) Hungary's foremost wine-makers introduce their wines at this popular event held in mid-September in the Castle District.

Budapest International Marathon
RUNNING

(www.budapestmarathon.com) Eastern Europe's most celebrated race goes along the Danube and across its bridges in early October.

Sleeping

Accommodation prices and standards are still quite reasonable in Budapest. Many year-round hostels occupy middle floors of old apartment buildings (with or without lift) in central Pest. Come summer (July to late August), student dormitories at colleges and universities open to travellers.

Private rooms in Budapest homes generally cost 6000Ft to 7500Ft for a single, 7000Ft to 8500Ft for a double and 10,000Ft to 13,000Ft for a small apartment. One centrally located broker is the **To-Ma Travel Agency** (Map p304; ☑353 0819; www.tomatour.hu; V Október 6 utca 22; ☺9am-noon & 1-8pm Mon-Fri, 9am-5pm Sat & Sun).

BUDA

TOP CHOICE Hotel Papillon
HOTEL €€

(☑212 4750; www.hotelpapillon.hu; II Rózsahegy utca 3/b; s/d/tr €60/75/95, apt €100-120; P❄@🖥🛎) This small 20-room hotel in Rózsadomb has a delightful back garden with a small swimming pool, and several rooms have balconies. There are also four apartments available in the same building, one of which boasts a lovely roof terrace.

Back Pack Guesthouse
HOSTEL €

(Map p299; ☑385 8946; www.backpackbudapest.hu; XI Takács Menyhért utca 33; beds in yurt 3000Ft, dm large/small 3800/4500Ft, d 11,000Ft; P❄🛎) A friendly and very laid-back place, though relatively small with just 50 beds. There's a lush garden in the back with a hammock stretched invitingly between trees. Take bus 7 to Tétényi út (from Keleti train station) or tram 18 to Móricz Zsigmond körtér to catch bus 7.

Hotel Victoria
HOTEL €€

(Map p300; ☑457 8080; www.victoria.hu; I Bem rakpart 11; s/d from €109/115; P❄@🛎) This rather elegant hotel has 27 comfortable and spacious rooms with larger-than-life views of Parliament and the Danube. Despite its small size it gets special mention for its friendly service and facilities, including the renovated 19th-century Jenő Hubay Music Hall, which now serves as a small theatre and function rooms.

Danubius Hotel Gellért
LUXURY HOTEL €€€

(Map p300; ✆889 5500; www.danubiusgroup.com/gellert; XI Szent Gellért tér 1; d/ste from €170/268; P✳@☎⊠) Peek through the doors of this turn-of-the-20th-century *grand dame*, even if you don't choose to stay here. The 234-room, four-star hotel has loads of character and its famous thermal baths (p302) are free for guests. Prices depend on your room's view and the quality of its bathroom.

Burg Hotel
HOTEL €€

(Map p300; ✆212 0269; www.burghotelbudapest.com; I Szentháromság tér 7-8; s/d/ste from €105/115/134; P✳☎) This small hotel with all the mod cons is in the Castle District, just opposite Matthias Church. The 26 partly refurbished rooms look fresher than they once did but are not much more than just ordinary. But, as they say, location is everything and midrange options are as scarce as hen's teeth on Castle Hill.

Grand Hostel Budapest
HOSTEL €

(Map p299; www.grandhostel.hu; XII Hüvösvölgyi utca 69; dm 3600-4500Ft, s/d from 8400/13,500Ft; P@☎) 'Grand' might be tooting its own horn a bit, but this colourful hostel does come pretty close, with its cavernlike cocktail bar, tiled rooms, communal barbecues and DJ nights. To get here, take tram 61 from Széll Kálmán tér to the Kelemen László utca stop.

Citadella Hotel
HOSTEL €

(Map p300; ✆466 5794; www.citadella.hu; XI Citadella sétány; dm 3200Ft, s & d with shared shower/shower/bath tub 10,500/11,500/12,500Ft; @) This hostel in the fortress atop Gellért Hill is pretty threadbare, though the dozen guest rooms are extra large, retain some of their original features and have their own shower (toilets are on the circular corridor). The single dorm room has 14 beds and shared facilities.

Római Camping
CAMPGROUND €

(off Map p299; ✆388 7167; www.romaicamping.hu; III Szentendrei út 189; campsite for 1/2/van/caravan 4720/6000/5665/7220Ft, bungalow for 2/4 6000/12,000Ft; ☉year-round; P@☎) Located in a leafy park north of the city, opposite the popular **Rómaifürdő swimming pool** complex, this is the city's largest camping ground. To get here, take the HÉV suburban railway from the Batthyány tér metro station in Buda to the Rómaifürdő station about 900m out of the city, which is almost opposite the site.

PEST

TOP CHOICE Four Seasons

Gresham Palace Hotel
LUXURY HOTEL €€€

(Map p304; ✆268 6000; www.fourseasons.com/budapest; V Széchenyi István tér 5-6; r/ste from €325/1125; P✳@☎⊠) Restored to its bygone elegance, with mushroom-shaped windows, whimsical ironwork and glittering gold decorative tiles on the exterior, the 179-room Four Seasons inhabits the art nouveau Gresham Palace (1907) and provides superb views of the Danube.

TOP CHOICE Gerlóczy Rooms

Delux
BOUTIQUE HOTEL €€

(Map p304; ✆501 4000; www.gerloczy.hu; V Gerlóczy utca 1; r €90; ✳@☎) Just 15 individually decorated rooms await you here, inside this revamped 1890s building. The rooms themselves are decked out in sombre shades (try to nab one of the two rooms with balconies) but it's details such as the stained glass, art-nouveau touches and original wrought-iron staircase that give the place character. Great cafe and restaurant downstairs, too.

Home-Made Hostel
HOSTEL €€

(Map p304; ✆302 2103; www.homemadehostel.com; VI Teréz körút 22; dm/d from 5500/15,000Ft; @☎) This cosy, extremely welcoming hostel with 20 beds in four rooms has unique decor, with recycled tables hanging upside down from the ceiling and old valises serving as lockers. The old-style kitchen is also a blast from the past.

Hotel Art
HOTEL €€€

(Map p304; ✆266 2166; www.hotelart.hu; V Király Pál utca 12; s €79-151, d €99-159; P✳☎) This Best Western property has art deco touches (including a pink facade) in the public areas, fitness centre and sauna, but the 32 guest rooms are, on the whole, quite ordinary except for the few that have separate sitting and sleeping areas. Rooms on the 5th floor have mansard roofs.

oKM Saga Guest
Residence
GUESTHOUSE €

(Map p304; ✆215 6883, 217 1934; www.km-saga.hu; IX Lónyay utca 17, 3rd fl; s €25-63, d €28-80; ✳@) This unique place has five themed rooms, an eclectic mix of 19th-century furnishings and a hospitable, multilingual Hungarian-American owner, Shandor. It's essentially a gay B&B but everyone is welcome. Two rooms share a bathroom.

Corinthia Grand
Hotel Royal
LUXURY HOTEL €€€

(Map p304; ☎479 4000; www.corinthia.hu; VII Erzsébet körút 43-49; r/ste from €140/347; P❋@🛜🏊) Decades in the remaking, this five-star beauty with 440 rooms has been carefully reconstructed in the Austro-Hungarian style of heavy drapes, sparkling chandeliers and large, luxurious ballrooms. Its restored Royal Spa, dating from 1886 but now as modern as tomorrow, is a legend reborn.

TOP CHOICE Connection
Guest House
GUESTHOUSE €€

(Map p304; ☎267 7104; www.connectionguesthouse.com; VII Király utca 41; s/d from €45/60; @🛜) This very central gay pension above a leafy courtyard attracts a young crowd due to its proximity to nightlife venues. Two of the nine rooms share facilities on the corridor and face partially pedestrianised Király utca.

Soho Hotel
BOUTIQUE HOTEL €€€

(Map p304; ☎872 8216; www.sohohotel.hu; VII Dohány utca 64; s/d/ste €189/199/249; P❋@🛜) This delightfully stylish boutique 74-room hotel sports a foyer bar in eye-popping reds, blues and lime greens. The non-allergenic rooms have bamboo matting on the walls, parquet floors and a music/film theme throughout.

Aventura Hostel
HOSTEL €€

(Map p304; ☎239 0789; www.aventurahostel.com; XIII Visegrádi utca 12, 1st fl; dm/d/apt 4300/15,000/18,800Ft; @🛜) This has got to be the most chilled hostel in Budapest, with four themed rooms (India, Japan, Africa and – our favourite – Space), run by two affable ladies. It's slightly out of the action, in Újlipótváros, but easily accessible by public transport.

Marco Polo Hostel
HOSTEL €

(Map p304; ☎1 413 2555; www.marcopolohostel.com; VII Nyár utca 6; dm/s/d/tr/q from 3500/12,000/15,000/19,000/24,000Ft; ❋@🛜) The Mellow Mood Group's very central flagship hostel is a swish, powder-blue, 47-room place, with telephones and TVs in all the rooms, except the dorms, and a lovely courtyard.

Medosz Hotel
HOTEL €€

(Map p304; ☎374 3000; www.medoszhotel.hu; VI Jókai tér 9; s €49-59, d €59-69; P🛜) Well priced for its central location, the Medosz is opposite the restaurants and bars of Liszt Ferenc tér. The 68 rooms are spare but comfortable and many have been renovated.

Loft Hostel
HOSTEL €

(Map p304; ☎328 0916; www.lofthostel.hu; V Veres Pálné utca 19; dm 4200-5000Ft, d 13,000Ft; @🛜) This hostel may well succeed in its loft-y aspirations to be the hottest backpacker magnet in town. There are excellent Hungarian dishes on offer and there's a friendly atmosphere. The showers are among the best in town and it feels like staying at a friend's house. Bike rental and tours available.

✖ Eating

Very roughly, a cheap two-course sit-down meal for one person with a glass of wine or beer in Budapest costs 3500Ft, while the same meal in a midrange eatery would be 7000Ft. An expensive meal will cost up to 10,000Ft. Restaurants are generally open from 10am or 11am to 11pm or midnight. It's always best to arrive by 9pm or 10pm, though, to ensure being served. It is advisable to book tables at medium-priced to expensive restaurants, especially at the weekend.

Ráday utca and Liszt Ferenc tér are the two most popular traffic-free streets. The moment the weather warms up, tables, and umbrellas spring up on the pavements and the people of Budapest crowd the streets.

BUDA

For self-catering in Buda, visit the **Fény utca Market** (Map p300; II Fény utca; ⊙6am-6pm Mon-Fri, to 2pm Sat), just next to the Mammut shopping mall.

Csalogány 26
HUNGARIAN €€€

(Map p300; ☎201 7892; www.csalogany26.hu; I Csalogány utca 26; 4-/8-course menus 8000/12,000Ft; ⊙noon-3pm & 7-10pm Tue-Sat) One of the best restaurants in Budapest turns out superb Hungarian and international dishes at prices that, while no bargain, are considered good value for the quality of what's on offer. Reserve for the evenings.

Kisbuda Gyöngye
HUNGARIAN €€

(Map p299; ☎368 6402; www.remiz.hu; III Kenyeres utca 34; mains 2680-5220Ft; ⊙closed Sun) This is a traditional and very elegant Hungarian restaurant in Óbuda; the antique-cluttered dining room and attentive service manage to create a *fin-de-siècle* atmosphere.

Éden
VEGETARIAN €

(Map p300; www.edenetterem.hu; I Iskola utca 31; mains 900-1200Ft; ⊙8am-9pm Mon-Thu, to 6pm Fri, 11am-7pm Sun; ☑) Located in a town house just below Castle Hill, this self-service place offers solid but healthy vegan and vegetarian fare.

Nagyi Palacsintázója
HUNGARIAN €

(Granny's Palacsinta Place; Map p300; www.nagyipali.hu; I Hattyú utca 16; pancakes 160-680Ft; ⏱24hr; 🖫) This place serves Hungarian pancakes – both the savoury and sweet varieties – round the clock and is always packed. There are other 24-hour branches in Buda (I Batthyány tér 5), Óbuda (III Szentendrei út 131) and Pest (V Petőfi Sándor tér 17–19).

Ruszwurm Cukrászda
CAFE €

(Map p300; www.ruszwurm.hu; I Szentháromság utca 7; cakes 380-580Ft; ⏱10am-7pm) This is the perfect place for coffee and cakes in the Castle District, though it can get pretty crowded – especially in high season when it's almost always impossible to get a seat.

PEST

The Nagycsarnok (Great Market; Map p304; IX Vámház körút 1-3; ⏱9am-6pm Mon-Sat) is a vast historic market built of steel and glass. Head here for fruit, vegetables, deli items, fish and meat.

TOP CHOICE Mák Bistro
INTERNATIONAL €€

(Map p304; ☎06 30 723 9383; www.makbistro.hu; V Vigyázó Ferenc utca 4; mains 3200-5600Ft; ⏱noon-3pm & 6pm-midnight Tue-Sat) With a new chef at the helm, Mák has gone from strength to strength. Try such ambitious pairings as scallops with grapefruit and sardine with mango, though you may be tempted by more traditional mains such as *mangalica* (a type of pork unique to Hungary) spare ribs and sirloin with polenta. The chocolate *millefeuille* really is to die for. Great wine selection too.

TOP CHOICE Klassz
INTERNATIONAL €€

(Map p304; www.klasszetterem.hu; VI Andrássy út 41; mains 1890-4390Ft; ⏱11.30am-11pm Mon-Sat, to 6pm Sun) Klassz is focused on wine, but the food is also of a very high standard. Varieties of foie gras and native *mangalica* are permanent stars on the menu, with dishes such as Burgundy-style leg of rabbit and lamb trotters with vegetable ragout playing cameo roles. Reservations not accepted; just show up and wait over a glass of wine.

Ring Cafe
BURGERS €

(Map p304; ☎331 5790; www.ringcafe.hu; VI Andrássy út 38; burgers 1490-3290Ft; ⏱9am-late Mon-Fri, 10am-1am Sat, 10am-10pm Sun; 🖫) When

we tell you that these guys do the best burgers in town – bar none – we're not messing about. And with imaginative sandwiches, salads and egg-and-bacon power breakfasts to boot, it's little wonder that this place is always packed.

Első Pesti Rétesház
SWEETS €€

(Map p304; ☎428 0135; www.reteshaz.com; V Október 6 utca 22; mains 2990-5990Ft; ⏱9am-11pm) It may be a bit overdone (think Magyar Disneyland, with old-world counters, painted plates on the walls and curios embedded in Plexiglas washbasins), but the 'First Strudel House of Pest' is just the place to taste Hungarian stretched pastry (360Ft) filled with apple, cheese, poppy seeds or sour cherry.

Momotaro Ramen
ASIAN €€

(Map p304; ☎269 3802; www.momotaroramen.com; V Széchenyi utca 16; dumplings 600-1400Ft, noodles 1150-1800Ft, mains 1800-4750Ft; ⏱11am-10.30pm Tue-Sun; 🖫) This is a favourite pit stop for noodles – especially the soup variety – and dumplings when *pálinka* (fruit-flavoured brandy) and other lubricants have been a-flowing the night before. But it's also good for more substantial dishes.

LaciPecsenye
HUNGARIAN €€

(Map p304; ☎333 1717; www.lacipecsenye.eu; V Sas utca 11; mains 2800-4700Ft; ⏱noon-midnight) Inside this minimalist chic bistro, the changing daily mains on black slate are largely for the carnivorous, though some are especially inspired, such as calamari stuffed with meat and anything with duck liver. Don't miss out on the pumpkin cake.

Soul Café
INTERNATIONAL €

(Map p304; ☎217 6986; www.soulcafe.hu; IX Ráday utca 11-13; mains 1800-3700Ft) One of the more reliable choices along a street heaving with so-so restaurants and iffy cafes, the Soul has inventive continental dishes and decor and a great terrace on both sides of this pedestrian street.

Múzeum
HUNGARIAN €€

(Map p304; ☎267 0375; www.muzeumkavehaz.hu; VIII Múzeum körút 12; mains 2800-6700Ft; ⏱6pm-midnight Mon-Sat) If you like to dine in old-world style, with a piano softly tinkling in the background, try this cafe-restaurant, still going strong after 125 years at the same location near the Hungarian National Museum. The goose liver dishes are above average and there's a good selection of Hungarian wines.

Trófea Grill BUFFET €€
(off Map p304; ☎270 0366; www.trofeagrill.hu; XIII
Visegrádi utca 50/a; lunch weekdays/weekends
3899/5499Ft, dinner 5499Ft; ☺noon-midnight
Mon-Fri, 11.30am-midnight Sat, 11.30am-9pm Sun)
This is the place to head when you *really*
could eat a horse (which might be found
sliced on one of the tables). It has an enormous buffet of more than 100 cold and hot
dishes over which diners swarm like bees
while being observed by the cooks from
their kitchen. There's a half-dozen branches
including one in **Buda** (II Margit körút 2).

Salaam Bombay INDIAN €€
(Map p304; ☎411 1252; www.salaambombay.hu;
V Mérleg utca 6; mains 1490-3900Ft; ☺noon-3pm &
6-11pm; ☝) If you hanker after a fix of authentic curry or tandoori in a bright, upbeat environment, look no further than this attractive
eatery just east of Széchenyi István tér. As
would be expected, there's a wide choice of
vegetarian dishes too.

Bors Gasztro Bár SANDWICHES €
(Map p304; www.facebook.com/BorsGasztroBar; VII
Kazinczy utca 10; mains from 790Ft; ☺11.30am-9pm;
☝) We love this thimble-sized place, not just
for its hearty imaginative soups but grilled
baguettes too. Not really a sit-down kind of
place; most people loiter by the doorway.

🍷 Drinking

Budapest is loaded with pubs and bars, and
there's enough variation to satisfy all tastes.
In summer, the preferred drinking venues
are the *romkertek* – outdoor spaces, for the
most part, in Pest that double as beer gardens and music clubs.

In the 19th century Budapest rivalled Vienna for cafe culture. The majority of the
surviving traditional cafes are in Pest, but
Buda can still lay claim to a handful of great
ones.

BUDA
Tranzit Art Café CAFE
(off Map p304; www.tranzitcafe.com; XI Kosztolányi
Dezső tér 7; lunch 1200Ft; ☺9am-11pm Mon-Fri,
10am-10pm Sat & Sun) An abandoned bus station now houses a friendly cafe with artwork
on walls, hammocks in the green courtyard
for sipping your shake in, and good breakfasts and two-course lunches. Occasional
events too.

PEST
For coffee in exquisite art nouveau surroundings, two places are particularly note-

worthy. **Gerbeaud** (Map p304; ☎429 9000;
www.gerbeaud.hu; V Vörösmarty tér 7; cakes from
750Ft; ☺9am-9pm; Ⓜ M1 Vörösmarty tér), Budapest's cake-and-coffee-culture king, has been
at the same location since 1870. Or station
yourself at the **Művész Kávéház** (Artist Cof-
feehouse; Map p304; ☎343 3544; www.muvesz-
kavehaz.hu; VI Andrássy út 29; cakes 590-790Ft;
☺9am-10pm Mon-Sat, 10am-10pm Sun; Ⓜ M1 Opera) for some of the best pastries and people-
watching in town.

DiVino Borbár WINE BAR
(Map p304; ☎06 70 935 3980; www.divinoborbar.
hu; V Szent István tér 3; ☺4pm-midnight Sun-Wed, to
2am Thu-Sat) Central, free-flowing and always
heaving, DiVino is Budapest's most popular
wine bar, and the crowds spilling out into the
square in front of the basilica will immediately tell you that. The choice of wines (sup-
posedly only from vintners aged under 35) at
this self-service place is enormous.

400 Bar BAR
(Map p304; www.400bar.hu; VII Kazinczy utca 52;
☺11am-3am Mon-Wed & Sun, to 5am Thu-Sat) This
large cafe-bar with an attractive terrace in
a pedestrian zone in the heart of the city is
great for coffee, cocktails, shooters and generally for meeting new people.

Kiadó Kocsma PUB
(Map p304; VI Jókai tér 3; ☺10am-1am Mon-Fri,
11am-1am Sat & Sun) The 'Pub for Rent' on two
levels is a great place for a swift pint and
a quick bite. It's a stone's throw physically
(but light years in attitude and presentation)
from the places on Liszt Ferenc tér.

Lukács Cukrászda CAFE
(Map p304; www.lukacscukraszda.com; VI Andrássy
út 70; ☺9am-7.30pm) This cafe is dressed up
in the finest of decadence – all mirrors and
gold – with soft piano music in the background. The selection of cakes is pricey but
superb.

☆ Entertainment

For a city of its size, Budapest has a huge
choice of things to do and places to go after
dark – from opera and (participatory) folk
dancing to live jazz and pulsating clubs with
some of the best DJs in the region.

Your best source of information in English
for what's on in the city is the freebie **Budapest Funzine** (www.budapestfunzine.hu), available at hotels, bars, cinemas and wherever
tourists congregate. The monthly freebie

Koncert Kalendárium has more serious offerings: classical concerts, opera, dance and the like.

Authentic *táncház*, literally 'dance house' but really folk-music workshops, are held at various locations throughout the week, but less frequently in summer. Very useful listings can be found on the **Dance House Guild** (www.tanchaz.hu) and **Folkrádió** (www.folkradio.hu) websites. The former also lists bands playing other types of traditional music, such as klezmer (Jewish folk music).

Performing Arts

You can book almost anything online at www.jegymester.hu and www.kulturinfo.hu. Another useful booking agency is **Ticket Express** (Map p304; ☎303 030 999; www.tex.hu; VI Andrássy út 18; ⊙10am-6.30pm Mon-Fri, to 3pm Sat), the largest ticket office network in the city.

Classical concerts are held regularly in the city's churches, including Matthias Church on Castle Hill in Buda.

Hungarian State Opera House OPERA
(Magyar Állami Operaház; Map p304; ☎bookings 814 7225; www.opera.hu; VI Andrássy út 22) Take in a performance while admiring the incredibly rich interior decoration of this sublime building. The ballet company performs here as well.

Ferenc Liszt Music Academy CLASSICAL MUSIC
(Liszt Ferenc Zeneakadémia; Map p304; ☎342 0179; www.zeneakademia.hu; VI Liszt Ferenc tér 8) Budapest's premier venue for classical concerts is not just a place to hear music but to ogle at the wonderful, decorative Hungarian Zsolnay porcelain and frescos as well.

Live Music

Aranytíz Cultural Centre TRADITIONAL MUSIC
(Aranytíz Művelődési Központ; Map p304; ☎354 3400; www.aranytiz.hu; V Arany János utca 10; ⊙bookings 2-9pm Mon & Wed, 9am-3pm Sat) At this cultural centre in the northern inner town in Pest, the wonderful Kalamajka Táncház, one of the best music and dance shows in town, has programs from 8.30pm on Saturday that run till about midnight.

Jedermann LIVE MUSIC
(www.jedermannkavezo.blogspot.com; XI Ráday utca 58; ⊙8am-1am) This very mellow spot attached to the Goethe Institute and decorated with jazz posters fills up with students and intellectuals. Jazz gigs most nights and, in summer, the courtyard terrace is a pleasant refuge.

Most! LIVE MUSIC
(Map p304; www.mostjelen.blogspot.com; VI Zichy Jenő utca 17; ⊙11am-2am Mon & Tue, to 4am Wed-Fri, 4pm-4am Sat, 4pm-2am Sun) This eclectic bar-cafe-performance space whose name means 'Now!' wears many hats. It's at its best when local pop and rock acts take to the stage, or when decent local DJs are spinning a set.

Nightclubs

Not all clubs and music bars in Budapest levy a cover charge, but those that do will ask for between 1500Ft and 3000Ft on the door. The trendier (and trashier) places usually let women in for free. Nightclubs usually open from 4pm to 2am Sunday to Thursday and until 4am on Friday and Saturday; some open only at weekends.

Mappa Club CLUB
(Map p304; http://mappaclub.com; IX Lilliom utca 41) An arty crowd and some of the best DJs in town makes the scene beneath the Trafó House of Contemporary Arts a must for locals and visitors alike.

Morrison's 2 CLUB
(Map p304; ☎374 3329; www.morrisons.hu; V Szent István körút 11; ⊙5pm-4am Mon-Sat) Far and away Budapest's biggest party venue, this cellar club attracts a younger crowd with its four dance floors, half-dozen bars (including one in a covered courtyard) and enormous games room upstairs. Live bands from 9pm to 11pm in the week.

Instant CLUB
(Map p304; ☎06 30 830 8747; www.instant.co.hu; VI Nagymező utca 38; ⊙1pm-3am) This cavernous space on Pest's most vibrant nightlife strip counts five bars on three levels with underground DJs and dance parties.

Gay & Lesbian Venues

Club AlterEgo GAY
(Map p304; www.alteregoclub.hu; VI Dessewffy utca 33; ⊙10pm-6am Fri & Sat) Budapest's premier gay club, with the chicest (think attitude) crowd and the best dance music.

Eklektika Restolounge LESBIAN
(Map p304; www.eklektika.hu; VI Nagymező utca 30; ⊙noon-midnight) There are no specifically lesbian bars in town, but this chilled-out eatery-bakery and lounge with a completely new look but the same ol' friendly vibe and gay-friendly crowd is probably the closest you'll find.

🛍 Shopping

As well as the usual folk arts, wines, spirits, food and music, Budapest has more distinctive items such as hand-blown glassware and antique books. But there are those who consider the city's flea markets their shopping highlight – and they certainly are a distinctive Budapest experience.

Shops are generally open from 9am or 10am to 6pm during the week, and till 1pm on Saturday.

TOP CHOICE Ecseri Piac MARKET

(off Map p299; XIX Nagykőrösi út 156; ⊙6am-4pm Mon-Fri, to 3pm Sat, 8am-1pm Sun) The biggest flea market in Central Europe. Saturday is said to be the best day; dealers get here early for the diamonds amid the rust. Take bus 54 from Boráros tér in Pest or, for a quicker journey, the red-numbered express bus 84E, 89E or 94E from the Határ út stop on the M3 metro line and get off at the Fiume utca stop. Then follow the crowds over the pedestrian bridge.

Bestsellers BOOKS

(Map p304; www.bestsellers.hu; V Október 6 utca 11; ⊙9am-6.30pm Mon-Fri, 10am-5pm Sat, 10am-4pm Sun) The best English-language bookshop in town, with lots of Hungarica too.

Holló Atelier HANDICRAFTS

(Map p304; ☑317 8103; V Vitkovics Mihály utca 12; ⊙10am-6pm Mon-Fri, to 2pm Sat) Attractive folk art with a modern look. Everything handmade on site at the workshop.

Treehugger Dan's Bookstore BOOKS

(Map p304; www.treehuggerdans.com; VI Lázár utca 16; ⊙10am-6pm Mon-Fri, to 4pm Sat) Tiny shop selling mostly secondhand English-language books; also does trade-ins and serves organic fairtrade coffee.

Bortársaság WINE

(Map p300; ☑212 2569; www.bortarsasag.hu; I Batthyány utca 59; ⊙10am-7pm Mon-Fri, to 6pm Sat) Original shop of what's now a chain of 10 stores, this place has an exceptional selection of Hungarian wines.

Magyar Pálinka Háza DRINK

(Hungarian Pálinka House; Map p304; ☑06 30 421 5463; www.magyarpalinkahaza.hu; VIII Rákóczi út 17; ⊙9am-7pm Mon-Sat) If *pálinka* (fruit-flavoured brandy) is your poison, this is the place for you.

ℹ Information

Dangers & Annoyances

No parts of Budapest are off limits to visitors, although some locals avoid Margaret Island after dark off-season, and both residents and visitors give the dodgier parts of the 8th and 9th districts (areas of prostitution) a wide berth.

Pickpocketing is most common in markets, the Castle District, Váci utca and Hősök tere, near major hotels and on certain popular buses (eg 7) and trams (2, 2A, 4, 6, 47 and 49).

Scams involving attractive young women, gullible guys, expensive drinks in nightclubs and a frog-marching to the nearest ATM by gorillas-in-residence have been all the rage in Budapest for nigh on two decades now. Guys, please: if it seems too good to be true, it certainly is. These scams have cost some would-be Lotharios hundreds, even thousands, of dollars and your embassy won't be able to help you. Trust us.

Discount Cards

Budapest Card (www.budapestinfo.hu; 24/48/72hr card 3900/7900/9900Ft) Offers access to many museums, unlimited public transport and discounts on tours and other services. You can buy it at hotels, travel agencies, large metro station kiosks and tourist offices, but it's cheaper online.

Medical Services

FirstMed Centers (☑24hr emergency hotline 224 9090; www.firstmedcenters.com; I Hattyú utca 14, 5th fl; ⊙8am-8pm Mon-Fri, to 2pm Sat) On call 24/7 for emergencies. Expensive.

SOS Dent (☑269 6010; www.smilistic.com; VI Király utca 14; ⊙24hr) Round-the-clock dental surgery.

Teréz Gyógyszertár (☑311 4439; VI Teréz körút 4; ⊙8am-8pm Mon-Fri, to 2pm Sat) Extended-hours pharmacy.

Money

There are ATMs everywhere, including in the train and bus stations and at the airport. ATMs at branches of OTP bank deliver difficult-to-break 20,000Ft notes. Moneychangers (particularly those along Váci utca) don't tend to give good rates, so go to a bank instead if possible.

Post

Main post office (Map p304; V Bajcsy-Zsilinsky út 16; ⊙8am-8pm Mon-Fri, to 2pm Sat) A few minutes' walk from central Deák Ferenc tér.

Tourist Information

Budapest Info (Map p304; ☑438 8080; V Sütő utca 2; ⊙8am-8pm) Also has an Oktogon **branch** (Map p304; VI Liszt Ferenc tér 11; ⊙10am-6pm Mon-Fri; Ⓜ M1 Oktogon, ☐4, 6) and desks in the arrivals sections of Ferenc Liszt International Airport's Terminals 1, 2A and 2B.

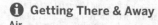 Getting There & Away

Air

Ferenc Liszt International Airport (☎296 7000; www.bud.hu) has two modern terminals next to one another, 24km southeast of the city. Terminal 2A is served by flights from countries within the Schengen border, while other international flights and budget carriers use 2B.

Boat

Mahart PassNave (Map p300; ☎484 4000; www.mahartpassnave.hu; V Belgrád rakpart; ⊙8am-6pm Mon-Fri) runs hydrofoils to Bratislava and Vienna from May to late September, which arrive at and depart from the **International Ferry Pier** (Nemzetközi hajóállomás; ☎318 1223; V Belgrád rakpart). Hydrofoils depart Budapest on Mondays and Wednesdays at 9am, returning from Vienna at the same time on Tuesdays and Thursdays. Adult one-way/return fares to Vienna are €99/125. Transporting a bicycle costs €25.

For information on ferry services to the towns of the Danube Bend, see p316.

Bus

Volánbusz (☎382 0888; www.volanbusz.hu), the national bus line, has an extensive list of destinations from Budapest. All international buses and some buses to/from western Hungary use **Népliget Bus Station** (Map p299; ☎219 8030; IX Üllői út 131). **Stadionok Bus Station** (Map p299; ☎220 6227; XIV Hungária körút 48-52) generally serves places to the east of Budapest. Most buses to the Danube Bend arrive at and leave from the **Árpád Híd Bus Station** (Map p299; ☎412 2597; XIII Árbóc utca 1, off XIII Róbert Károly körút), though some leave from the small suburban bus terminal next to **Újpest-Városkapu train station** (XIII Arva utca, off Váci út), which is on the M3 blue metro line. In fact, all stations are on metro lines, and all are in Pest. If the ticket office is closed, you can buy your ticket on the bus.

Car & Motorcycle

Driving around Budapest is not for the fainthearted. Dangerous manoeuvres, extensive roadworks and serious accidents abound and finding a place to park is next to impossible in some neighbourhoods. Use the public transport system instead.

If you want to venture into the countryside, travelling by car is an option. All major international rental firms, including **Avis** (☎318 4240; www.avis.hu; V Arany János utca 26-28; ⊙7am-6pm Mon-Sat, 8am-6pm Sun), **Budget** (☎214 0420; www.budget.hu; VII Krisztina körút 41-43, Hotel Mercure Buda; ⊙8am-8pm Mon-Fri, to 6pm Sat & Sun) and **Europcar** (☎505 4400; www.europcar.hu; V Erzsébet tér 7-8; ⊙8am-6pm Mon & Fri, to 4.30pm Tue-Thu, to noon Sat), have offices in Budapest and at the airport. The best independent rental company with highly competitive rates is **Fox Autorent** (☎382 9000; www.foxautorent. com; VII Hársfa utca 53-55, Bldg I, ground fl; ⊙8am-6pm), which also has an office at the airport. Compact cars per day/week rent from €35/170.

Train

Hungarian State Railways (MÁV) runs the country's extensive rail network. Contact **MÁV-Start passenger service centre** (☎512 7921; www. mav-start.hu; V József Attila utca 16; ⊙9am-6pm Mon-Fri) for 24-hour information on domestic train departures and arrivals. Its website has a useful timetable in English for planning routes. Fares are usually noted for destinations within Hungary.

Buy tickets at one of Budapest's three main train stations. **Keleti train station** (Eastern Train Station; VIII Kerepesi út 2-4) handles most international trains as well as domestic ones from the north and northeast. For some international destinations (eg Romania), as well as domestic ones to/from the Danube Bend and Great Plain, head for **Nyugati train station** (Western Train Station; VI Nyugati tér). For trains bound for Lake Balaton and the south, go to **Déli train station** (Southern Train Station; I Krisztina körút 37). All three stations are on metro lines.

Always confirm your departure station when you buy your tickets, since stations can vary depending on the train.

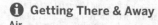 Getting Around

To/From the Airport

The cheapest (and slowest) way to get into the city centre from Ferenc Liszt International Airport is to take city bus 200E (320Ft) which terminates at the Kőbánya-Kispest metro station. From there, take the M3 metro into the city centre. Total cost: 640Ft to 720Ft.

The **Airport Shuttle Minibusz** (☎296 8555; www.airportshuttle.hu; one way/return 3200/5500Ft) ferries passengers in nine-seat vans from all three of the airport's terminals directly to the place you're staying. Tickets are available at a clearly marked desk in the arrivals hall, though you may have to wait while the van fills up.

Fő Taxi (☎222 2222; www.fotaxi.hu) has the monopoly on picking up taxi passengers at the airport. Fares to most locations in Pest are 5300Ft and in Buda 5500Ft to 6000Ft.

TRANSPORT FROM BUDAPEST

Bus

DESTINATION	PRICE (FT)	DURATION (HR)	FREQUENCY
Bratislava (Slovakia)	3400	3	1 daily
Prague (Czech Republic)	7900	7¼	1 daily
Rijeka (Croatia)	9900	8	1 weekly
Sofia (Bulgaria)	12,500	13½	1 daily
Subotica (Serbia)	3900	4½	2 daily
Vienna (Austria)	5900	3	5 daily

Train

DESTINATION	PRICE (€)	DURATION (HR)
Berlin (Germany)	95	12
Bratislava (Slovakia)	22	2½
Bucharest (Romania)	75	13-15
Frankfurt (Germany)	110	11
Lviv (Ukraine)	55	12
Ljubljana (Slovenia)	39	9
Munich (Germany)	95	10
Prague (Czech Republic)	45	7
Sofia (Bulgaria)	89	18
Zagreb (Croatia)	42	6½
Venice (Italy)	70	14
Vienna (Austria)	32	3
Warsaw (Poland)	72	12
Zürich (Switzerland)	94	12

Of course, you can take any taxi to the airport and several companies have a flat, discounted fare. **Rádió Taxi** (☑377 7777; www.radiotaxi. hu) charges from 4300Ft between Pest and the airport, and 4800Ft from Buda.

Public Transport

Public transport is run by **BKV** (Budapest Transport Company; ☑258 4636; www.bkv.hu). The three underground metro lines (M1 yellow, M2 red, M3 blue) meet at Deák tér in Pest; the long-awaited green M4 will open in 2014. The HÉV suburban railway runs north from Batthyány tér in Buda. Travel cards are only good on the HÉV within the city limits (south of the Békásmegyer stop).

There's also an extensive network of buses, trams and trolleybuses. Public transport operates from 4.30am until 11.30pm and some 40 night buses run along main roads. Tram 6 on the Big Ring Road now runs round the clock.

A single ticket for all forms of transport is 320Ft (60 minutes of uninterrupted travel on the same metro, bus, trolleybus or tram line *without* transferring/changing); a book of 10 tickets is 2800Ft. A transfer ticket (490Ft) is valid for one trip with one validated transfer within 90 minutes.

The three-day travel card (3850Ft) or the seven-day pass (4600Ft) make things easier, allowing unlimited travel inside the city limits. Keep your ticket or pass handy; the fine for 'riding black' is 8000Ft on the spot, or 16,000Ft if you pay later at the **BKV office** (☑461 6800; VII Akácfa utca 22; ☺6am-8pm Mon-Fri, 8am-1.45pm Sat).

Taxi

Taxi drivers overcharging foreigners in Budapest has been a problem since time immemorial. Never get into a taxi that lacks an official yellow licence plate, the logo of the taxi firm and a visible table of fares.

If you need a taxi, call one; this costs less than if you flag one down on the street. Make sure you know the number of the landline phone you're calling from, as that's how the dispatcher establishes your address (though you can call from a mobile as well). Dispatchers usually speak English.

Reliable companies include **City Taxi** (☑211 1111; www.citytaxi.hu), **Főtaxi** (☑222 2222; www.fotaxi.hu) and **Rádió Taxi** (☑377 7777; www.radiotaxi.hu). Note that rates are higher at night and in the early morning.

THE DANUBE BEND

North of Budapest, the Danube breaks through the Pilis and Börzsöny Hills in a sharp bend before continuing along the Slovak border. The Roman Empire had its northern border here and medieval kings ruled Hungary from majestic palaces overlooking the river at Esztergom and Visegrád. East of Visegrád the river divides, with Szentendre and Vác on different branches, separated by Szentendre Island. Today the easy access to historic monuments, rolling green scenery – and vast numbers of souvenir craft shops – lure many day trippers from Budapest.

❶ Getting There & Away

BUS Regular buses serve towns on the west bank of the Danube, but trains only go as far as Szentendre, with a separate line running to Esztergom; the east bank, including Vác, has excellent transport links.

BOAT The river itself is a perfect highway and regular boats ferry tourists to and from Budapest over the summer months. From May to September, a **Mahart PassNave** (www.mahartpassnave.hu) ferry departs Budapest's Vigadó tér at 10am Tuesday to Sunday bound for Szentendre (one way/return 1590/2390Ft, 1½ hours), returning at 5pm; the service runs on Saturday only in April.

Between May and late August there's a ferry from Vigadó tér at 9am, calling at Vác (one-way/return 1490/2240Ft, 11am) and Visegrád (1790/2690Ft, noon) before carrying on to Esztergom (1990/2990Ft, 1.45pm). It returns from Esztergom/Visegrád/Vác at 4.45/5.50/6.30pm, reaching Budapest at 8pm. The service is reduced to Saturday only in April and September.

Hydrofoils travel from Budapest to Visegrád (one way/return 2690/3990Ft, one hour) and Esztergom (one way/return 3990/5990Ft, 1½ hours) on Friday, Saturday and Sunday from early May to September; boats leave at 9.30am and return at 5pm from Esztergom and 5.30pm from Visegrád.

Szentendre

☑26 / POP 26,000

Once an artists' colony, now a popular day trip 19km north of Budapest, pretty little Szentendre (*sen*-ten-dreh) has narrow, winding streets and is a favourite with souvenir-shoppers. The charming old centre has plentiful cafes and galleries and there is a handful of noteworthy Serbian Orthodox churches, dating from the time when Christian worshippers fled here to escape the Turkish invaders. Expect things to get crowded in summer and at weekends. Outside town is Hungary's largest open-air village museum.

◎ Sights

Fő tér   SQUARE
(Main Sq) Colourful Fő tér, the town's main square, is the best place to begin sightseeing in Szentendre. Here you'll find many buildings and monuments from the 18th and 19th centuries, including the Memorial Cross (1763) and the 1752 Serbian Orthodox Blagoveštenska Church (Blagoveštenska templom; ☑310 554; Fő tér; admission 300Ft; ◉10am-5pm Tue-Sun), with a stunning iconostasis. The pedestrian lanes surrounding the square are filled with shops sellings gift items and folkcraft.

Margit Kovács Ceramic Collection   MUSEUM
(Kovács Margit Kerámiagyüjtemény; ☑310 244; www.pmmi.hu/hu/museum/6/intro; Vastagh György utca 1; adult/concession 1000/500Ft ; ◉10am-6pm) If you descend Görög utca from Fő tér and turn right onto Vastagh György utca you'll reach this museum in an 18th-century salt house, dedicated to the work of Szentendre's most famous artist. Kovács (1902–77) was a ceramicist who combined Hungarian folk, religious and modern themes to create Gothic-like figures.

Castle Hill   VIEWPOINT
(Vár-domb) Castle Hill, reached via Váralja lépcső, the narrow steps between Fő tér 8 and 9, was the site of a fortress in the Middle Ages. All that's left of it today is the walled early Gothic Church of St John the Baptist (Keresztelő Szent János Templom; Templom tér, Vár-domb; admission free), from where you get splendid views of the town and river.

Hungarian Open-Air
Ethnographical Museum   MUSEUM
(Magyar Szabadtéri Néprajzi Múzeum; ☑502 500; www.skanzen.hu; Sztaravodai út; adult/student

1500/750Ft, on festival days 1600/800Ft; ☺9am-5pm Tue-Sun Apr-Oct, 10am-4pm Sat & Sun Nov-early Dec, Feb & Mar) Just 5km northwest of Szentendre is Hungary's most ambitious *skanzen* (open-air folk museum), with farmhouses, churches, bell towers, mills and so on set up in eight regional divisions. Craftspeople and artisans do their thing on random days (generally at the weekend) from Easter to early December and the museum hosts festivals throughout the season. Reach it on bus 230 from bay/stop 7 at the bus station.

🛌 Sleeping & Eating

Seeing Szentendre on a day trip from Budapest is probably your best bet. For private rooms, visit the Tourinform (p317) office.

Mathias Rex GUESTHOUSE €€
(Mathias Rex Panzió; ☎505 570; www.mathiasrexhotel.hu; Kossuth Lajos utca 16; s/d 10,000/15,000Ft, studio from 30,000Ft; ❄@) This very central *panzió* (pension or guesthouse) has a dozen rooms so clean they border on sterile, but they're of a good size. The decor is modern and minimalist, and there's a pretty courtyard and an inexpensive cellar-restaurant.

Pap-sziget Camping CAMPGROUND €
(Pap-sziget Kemping; ☎310 697; www.pap-sziget.hu; small/large campsite for 2 4000/4400Ft, bungalows from 8600Ft; ☺May–mid-Oct; @☀) This big leafy camping ground takes up most of Pap Island, some 2km north of Szentendre. Motel (6400Ft per double) and hostel (4800Ft per double) rooms are very basic, though the 'comfort bungalows' are slightly more, well, comfortable. Take bus 11 from the station.

TOP CHOICE **Promenade** INTERNATIONAL €€
(☎312 626; www.promenade-szentendre.hu; Futó utca 4; mains 1850-4450Ft; ☺11am-11pm Tue-Sun) Vaulted ceilings, whitewashed walls, a huge cellar for tasting wine and a wonderful terrace overlooking the Danube are all highlights at the Promenade, one of Szentendre's best restaurants serving 'enlightened' Hungarian and international dishes.

Erm's HUNGARIAN €€
(☎303 388; www.erms.hu; Kossuth Lajos utca 22; mains 1590-3700Ft) Subtitled 'Csülök & Jazz', retro-style Erm's, with its walls festooned with early-20th-century memorabilia and simple wooden tables, is where to go for Hungarian-style pork knuckle in all its guises and live music at the weekend.

❶ Information

Main post office (Kossuth Lajos utca 23-25)
OTP Bank (Dumtsa Jenő utca 6)
Tourinform (☎317 966; www.iranyszentendre.hu; Dumtsa Jenő utca 22; ☺9.30am-4.30pm Mon-Fri, 10am-2pm Sat & Sun) Lots of information on Szentendre and the Bend.

DANUBE: THE DUSTLESS HIGHWAY

No other river in Europe is as evocative, or important, as the Danube. It has been immortalised in legends, tales, songs, paintings and films through the ages and has played an essential role in the cultural and economic life of millions of people since the earliest human populations settled along its banks.

Originating in Germany's Black Forest, the river cuts an unstoppable swathe through – or along the border of – 10 countries and, after more than 2800km, empties into the Black Sea in Romania. In Europe it is second only in length to the Volga (although, at 6400km, the Amazon dwarfs both) and, contrary to popular belief, is green-brown rather than blue (or 'blond', as the Hungarians say). About 2400km of its length is navigable, making it a major transport route across the continent.

Even though only 12% of the river's length is located in Hungary, the country is vastly affected by the Danube. The entire country lies within the Danube river basin and is highly prone to flooding. As early as the 16th century, large dyke systems were built for flood protection, but it's hard to stop water running where it wants to. The capital was devastated by flooding in 1775 and 1838; in 2006 the river burst its banks, threatening to fill Budapest's metro system and putting the homes of tens of thousands of people in danger. It came close to doing so again in 2009.

Despite the potential danger, the river is so loved that it actually has its own day. On 29 June every year cities along the river host festivals, family events and conferences on **Danube Day** (www.danubeday.org) in honour of the mighty river.

❶ Getting There & Away

The most convenient way to get to Szentendre is to take the HÉV suburban train from Buda's Batthyány tér metro station in central Budapest (630Ft, 40 minutes, every 10 to 20 minutes).

Vác

✈27 / POP 34,500

Lying on the eastern bank of the river, Vác *(vahts)* is a pretty town with interesting historic relics, from its collection of baroque town houses to its vault of 18th-century mummies. It's also the place to view glorious sunsets over the Börzsöny Hills reflected in the Danube.

Vác is an old town. Uvcenum – the town's Latin name – is mentioned in Ptolemy's 2nd-century *Geographia* as a river crossing on an important road. The town's medieval centre and Gothic cathedral were destroyed during the Turkish occupation; reconstruction under several bishops in the 18th century gave Vác its present baroque appearance.

◉ Sights

Március 15 tér SQUARE

Vác's renovated main square has the town's most colourful buildings, including the **Town Hall** (Március 15 tér 11) from 1764, considered a baroque masterpiece. Note the statue of Justice and the seals held by the two figures on the gable – they represent Hungary and Bishop Kristóf Migazzi, the driving force behind Vác's reconstruction more than two centuries ago. In the square's centre, you'll see the entrance to a **crypt** (Március 15 tér; adult/concession 600/350Ft; ⊙2-6pm Wed-Fri, 10am-6pm Sat & Sun May-Oct), the only remnant of the medieval Church of St Michael. Tourinform (p318) holds the key.

Memento Mori MUSEUM

(✆500 750; Március 15 tér 19; adult/concession 1000/500Ft; ⊙10am-6pm Tue-Sun) This bizarre exhibit contains three mummies and assorted artefacts recovered from the crypt of the Dominican Church on Március 15 tér. The crypt functioned as a place of burial in the 18th century, but was later bricked up and forgotten. A cool temperature and minimal ventilation kept the bodies and clothes of the deceased in good condition for centuries. When it was rediscovered in 1994 and a total of 262 bodies were exhumed, it proved a gold mine for historians and helped to shed light on the burial practices and way of life in the 18th century.

Vác Cathedral CHURCH

(Váci székesegyház; admission free; ⊙10am-noon & 1.30-5pm Mon-Sat, 7.30am-7pm Sun) Tree-lined Konstantin tér to the southeast of Március 15 tér is dominated by the town's colossal cathedral, which dates from 1775 and was one of the first examples of neoclassical architecture in Hungary. The frescos on the vaulted dome and the altarpiece are by celebrated artist Franz Anton Maulbertsch.

Triumphal Arch MONUMENT

(Diadalív-kapu; Dózsa György út) North of the main square is the only such structure in Hungary. It was built by Bishop Migazzi in honour of a state visit by Empress Maria Theresa in 1764.

🛏 Sleeping & Eating

TOP CHOICE Tabán Panzió GUESTHOUSE €€

(Alt Vendégház; ✆06 30 910 3428, 316 860; altvendeghaz@invitel.hu; Tabán utca 25; s/d 5000/12,000Ft; ✳🖨) Staying at this small guesthouse above the Danube is like staying with nice relatives. The four rooms (No 3 has a balcony) are kitschy but cosy and there's a fully equipped kitchen and small garden for guests' use.

Fónagy & Walter GUESTHOUSE €€

(✆310 682; www.fonagy.hu; Budapesti főút 36; r 12,500Ft; @🖨) Fónagy & Walter is a homely little guesthouse 850m southeast of the main square. Its five suitelike rooms accommodating up to four people are overly decorated but comfortable and there's a well-stocked wine cellar.

Váci Remete Pince HUNGARIAN €€

(✆06 30 944 3538, 302 199; Fürdő lépcső 3; mains 1850-3290Ft) This wonderful eatery, with its covered terrace and views of the Danube, impresses with its top-notch wine selection, fine spread of Hungarian specialities and excellent service.

Duna Presszó CAFE €

(✆305 839; Március 15 tér 13; cakes 450Ft; ⊙9am-9pm Sun-Thu, to 10pm Fri & Sat) Duna is the quintessential cafe, with dark-wood furniture, chandeliers and excellent cake and ice cream. It's very central.

❶ Information

Main post office (Posta Park 2) Some 300m east of Március 15 tér.

OTP Bank (Széchenyi utca) In the Dunakanyar shopping centre.

Tourinform (☏316 160; www.tourinformvac. hu; Március 15 tér 17; ⊗8am-5pm Mon-Fri, to 2pm Sat mid-Jun–Aug, 9am-5pm Mon-Fri, 10am-noon Sat Sep–mid-Jun) Overlooking the main square, Március 15 tér.

ℹ Getting There & Away

Car ferries (1500/430/430Ft per car/bicycle/ person, hourly 6am to 8pm) cross over to Szentendre Island; a bridge connects the island's west bank with the mainland at Tahitótfalu. From there hourly buses run to Szentendre (310Ft, 25 minutes). You can also catch half-hourly buses (560Ft, 50 minutes) and trains (650Ft, 45 minutes) from Vác to Budapest.

Visegrád

☏26 / POP 1860

The spectacular vista from what remains of the 13th-century hilltop citadel in Visegrád (*vish*-eh-grahd) is what pulls visitors to this sleepy town. The first fortress here was built by the Romans as a border defence in the 4th century. Hungarian kings constructed a mighty citadel on the hilltop, and a lower castle near the river, after the 13th-century Mongol invasions.

In the 14th century a royal palace was built on the flood plain at the foot of the hills and in 1323 King Charles Robert of Anjou, whose claim to the local throne was being fiercely contested in Buda, moved the royal household here. For nearly two centuries Hungarian royalty alternated between Visegrád and Buda.

Both the Turks and the Habsburgs played a role in the destruction of the citadel. All trace of the 350-room royal palace, situated close to the town centre, was lost until 1934 when archaeologists, by following descriptions in literary sources, uncovered the ruins that you can visit today.

The small town has two distinct areas: to the north around the Mahart PassNave ferry pier and another, the main town, about 1km to the south, near the Nagymaros ferry.

◉ Sights & Activities

Royal Palace   PALACE
(Királyi Palota; ☏597 010; www.visegradmuzeum.hu; Fő utca 29; adult/concession 1100/550Ft; ⊗9am-5pm Tue-Sun) The partial reconstruction of the royal palace, near the main town, only hints at the structure's former magnificence. The dozen or so rooms that can be visited are mostly the royal suites; the history of the palace and its reconstruction, along with ar-

chitectural finds such as richly carved stones dating from the 14th century, is told in an archaeological exhibition and lapidarium. To find the palace from the Mahart PassNave ferry, walk south for about 400m in the direction of the Nagymaros ferry and then turn left towards town to find Fő utca.

Solomon's Tower   TOWER
(Salamon Torony; ☏398 026; adult/concession 700/350Ft; ⊗9am-5pm Tue-Sun May-Sep) North of the main town and just a short walk up Görgey lépcső from the Mahart PassNave ferry port, 13th-century Solomon's Tower was once part of a lower castle used to control river traffic. These days, what's left of the stocky, hexagonal keep, with walls up to 8m thick, houses one of the palace's original Gothic fountains, along with exhibits related to town history.

Visegrád Citadel   FORTRESS
(Visegrádi Fellegvár; ☏598 080; adult/child & student 1400/700Ft; ⊗9am-5pm mid-Mar–Apr & Oct, to 6pm May-Sep, to 4pm Nov-Mar) Just north of Solomon's Tower, a trail marked 'Fellegvár' (Fortress) leads to Visegrád Citadel (1259) sitting atop a 350m hill and surrounded by moats hewn from solid rock. While the citadel ruins themselves are not as spectacular as their history, the **view** of the Danube Bend and the Börzsöny Hills from the walls is well worth the climb.

An alternative, less steep path leads to the citadel from the town centre area. Find the **trail** (Kálvária sétány) starting behind the Catholic church on Fő tér. You can also reach it by **City-Bus** (☏397 372; www.city-bus. hu; up to 6 people 2500Ft; ⊗9am-6pm Apr-Sep) minibus in season.

🛏 Sleeping & Eating

Hotel Honti   HOTEL €€
(☏398 120; www.hotelhonti.hu; Fő utca 66; hotel s/d €45/65, guesthouse s/d €40/55, campsites per person 1100Ft plus per tent/caravan 600/1200Ft; ✳@☎) This friendly establishment has seven homely rooms in its guesthouse on quiet Fő utca and 23 in the hotel facing Rte 11. The hotel's large garden and table-tennis table are for guest use, and bicycles are also available for rent (per day 2000Ft). There's now a camping ground next to the guesthouse as well.

Kovács-kert   HUNGARIAN €€
(☏398 123; www.kovacs-kertetterem.hu; Rév utca 4; mains 1590-2490Ft) This adorable restaurant just up from the Nagymaros ferry pier has

a large photo menu covering a fine array of Hungarian standards and a lovely, leafy terrace.

Don Vito Pizzeria PIZZERIA €
(☎397 230; www.donvitovisegrad.hu; Fő utca 83; pizza 990-1950Ft, pasta 1590-1890Ft; ☑) Don Vito is quite a joint for such a small town. Its collection of gangster memorabilia is impressive, as is its selection of pizzas, including vegetarian options.

Getting There & Away

No train line reaches Visegrád but buses are very frequent (745Ft, 1¼ hours, hourly) to/from Budapest's Újpest-Városkapu train station, Szentendre (465Ft, 45 minutes, every 45 minutes) and Esztergom (560Ft, 45 minutes, hourly).

Esztergom

☎33 / POP 30,850

It's easy to see the attraction of Esztergom – especially from a distance. The city's massive basilica, sitting high above the town and Danube River, is an incredible sight rising magnificently from its rural setting.

But the significance of this town is even greater than its architectural appeal. The 2nd-century Roman emperor-to-be Marcus Aurelius wrote his famous *Meditations* while he camped here. In the 10th century, Stephen I, founder of the Hungarian state, was born here and crowned at the cathedral. From the late 10th to the mid-13th centuries Esztergom served as the Hungarian royal seat. In 1543 the Turks ravaged the town and much of it was destroyed, only to be rebuilt in the 18th and 19th centuries.

Sights & Activities

Esztergom Basilica CHURCH
(Esztergomi Bazilika; ☎402 354; www.bazilika-esztergom.hu; Szent István tér 1; admission free; ⊙8am-6pm Apr-Sep, to 4pm Oct-Mar) The basilica, the largest church in Hungary, is on Castle Hill, and its 72m-high central dome can be seen for many kilometres around. The building of the present neoclassical church was begun in 1822 on the site of its 12th-century counterpart, which was destroyed by the Turks. The oldest part is the red-marble 1510 **Bakócz Chapel**, with splendid Italian Renaissance stone-carving and sculpture.

The **treasury** (kincstár; adult/child 800/400Ft; ⊙9am-5pm Mar-Oct, 11am-4pm Tue-Sun Nov & Dec) is an Aladdin's cave of vestments and church plate in gold and silver studded with jewels. The door to the right as you enter the basilica leads to the **crypt** (altemplom; admission 200Ft; ⊙9am-5pm Mar-Oct, 11am-2.45pm Nov-Feb), a series of eerie vaults down 50 steps. Among those at rest here is Cardinal József Mindszenty, who was imprisoned by the communists for refusing to allow Hungary's Catholic schools to be secularised. It's worth making the tortuous climb 400 steps up to the **cupola** (admission 600Ft; ⊙9.30am-5.30pm Apr-Oct) for the outstanding views over the city.

Castle Museum MUSEUM
(Vármúzeum; ☎415 986; www.mnmvarmuzeuma.hu; Szent István tér 1; adult/concession 1800/900Ft, courtyard only 500/250Ft; ⊙10am-6pm Tue-Sun Apr-Sep, to 4pm Tue-Sun Oct-Mar) At the southern end of Castle Hill, the Castle Museum is housed in the former **Royal Palace**, which was built mostly by French architects in the 12th century during Esztergom's golden age. The museum concentrates on archaeological finds from the town and its surrounding area, the majority of which is pottery dating from the 11th century onwards.

Christian Museum MUSEUM
(Keresztény Múzeum; ☎413 880; www.christianmuseum.hu; Berényi Zsigmond utca 2 ; adult/concession 900/450Ft; ⊙10am-5pm Wed-Sun Mar-Nov)

Below Castle Hill in the picturesque riverbank Watertown (Víziváros) district is the former **Bishop's Palace**, today housing the Christian Museum with the finest collection of medieval religious art in Hungary. Don't miss the sublime Hungarian Gothic triptychs and altarpieces. From Castle Hill walk down steep Macskaút, which can be accessed from just behind the basilica.

Aquasziget SPA
(☎511 100; www.aquasziget.hu; Táncsics Mihály utca 5; adult/child day pass 2950/1600Ft; ⊙10am-8pm Mon-Fri, from 9am Sat & Sun) At the northern end of Primate Island south of Castle Hill is this enormous spa and water park with a plethora of indoor and outdoor pools, curly water slides and a full wellness centre.

Sleeping & Eating

Alabárdos Panzió GUESTHOUSE €€
(☎312 640; www.alabardospanzio.hu; Bajcsy-Zsilinszky utca 49; s/d 8500/11,500Ft, apt from 20,100Ft; ❄📶) This mustard-yellow landmark up a

small hill isn't flashy but does provide neat, tidy and sizeable accommodation in 23 rooms and apartments.

Ria Panzió GUESTHOUSE €€
(☑06 20 938 3091, 313 115; www.riapanzio.com; Batthyány Lajos utca 11; s/d 9000/12,000Ft; ✿@☎) This 11-room guesthouse in a converted town house just down from the basilica has quiet, cosy rooms, a tiny fitness centre in the wine cellar and bicycles for rent (1000Ft per day).

Gran Camping CAMPGROUND €
(☑06 30 948 9563, 402 513; www.grancamping-fortanex.hu; Nagy-Duna sétány 3; campsites per adult/child/tent/tent & car 1400/800/1100/1400Ft, bungalows from 16,000Ft, dm/d/tr 3000/12,000/14,000Ft; ☺May-Sep; @☎) Small but centrally located on Primate Island, Gran Camping has space for 500 souls in various forms of accommodation (including a hostel with dormitory) as well as a good-sized swimming pool.

TOP CHOICE Padlizsán HUNGARIAN €€
(☑311 212; Pázmány Péter utca 21; mains 1550-3000Ft) With a sheer rock face topped by a castle bastion as its courtyard backdrop, Padlizsán has a dramatic setting. And its menu doesn't let the show down either, featuring modern Hungarian dishes and imaginative salads. Soft live music most nights.

Csülök Csárda HUNGARIAN €€€
(☑412 420; Batthyány Lajos utca 9; mains 1980-3890Ft) The 'Pork Knuckle Inn' – guess the speciality here – is a charming eatery that is popular with visitors and locals alike. It serves up good home cooking (try the bean soup, 1790Ft) and the portions are huge.

ℹ Information

Cathedralis Tours (☑520 260; Bajcsy-Zsilinszky utca 26; ☺9am-6pm Mon-Fri, 9am-noon Sat (in summer)) Private travel agency can provide information.

Post office (Arany János utca 2) Enter from Széchenyi tér.

OTP Bank (Rákóczi tér 2-4)

ℹ Getting There & Away

BUS Buses run to/from Budapest (930Ft, 1½ hours), Visegrád (560Ft, 45 minutes) and Szentendre (930Ft, 1½ hours) at least hourly.

TRAIN Trains depart from Budapest's Nyugati train station (1120Ft, 1½ hours) at least hourly. Cross the Mária Valéria Bridge into Štúrovo,

Slovakia, and you can catch a train to Bratislava, which is just 1½ hours away.

NORTHWESTERN HUNGARY

A visit to this region is a boon for anyone wishing to see remnants of Hungary's Roman legacy, medieval heritage and baroque splendour. Because it largely managed to avoid the Ottoman destruction of the 16th and 17th centuries, northwestern Hungary's main towns – Sopron and Győr – managed to retain their medieval cores; exploring their cobbled streets and hidden courtyards is a magical experience. Equally rewarding is the region's natural beauty.

Győr

☑96 / POP 131,300

Lying midway between Budapest and Vienna at the confluence of three rivers, Győr (*jyeur*) is a delightful city, with a medieval heart hidden behind a commercial facade. This was the site of a Roman town, Arrabona. In the 11th century, Stephen I established a bishopric here and in the 16th century a fortress was erected to hold back the Turks. The Ottomans captured Győr in 1594 but were able to hold on to it for only four years. For that reason Győr is known as the 'dear guard', watching over the nation through the centuries.

◉ Sights & Activities

Bécsí kapu tér PUBLIC SQUARE
(Vienna Gate Square) The enchanting 1725 **Carmelite Church** (Karmelita Templom; Bécsí kapu tér) and many fine baroque palaces line riverfront Bécsí kapu tér. On the northwestern side of the square are the fortifications built in the 16th century to stop the Turks. A short distance to the east is **Napoleon House** (Király utca 4; adult/senior & student 800/400Ft; ☺10am-6pm Mon-Fri, 9am-1pm Sat), named after the French military leader.

FREE Basilica CHURCH
(Bazilika; ☺8am-noon & 2-6pm) North up Káptalan-domb (Chapter Hill), in the oldest section of Győr, is the baroque Basilica. Situated on the hill, it was originally Romanesque, but most of what you see inside dates from the 17th and 18th centuries. Don't miss the Gothic **Héderváry Chapel** at the back of

the cathedral, which contains the glittering 15th-century **Herm of László**, a gold bust of the eponymous king and saint.

Diocesan Treasury and Library   MUSEUM
(Egyházmegyei kincstár és könyvtár; Káptalandomb 26; adult/senior & student 800/400Ft; ☉10am-4pm Tue-Sun Mar-Oct) East of the Basilica is one of the richest collections of sacred objects in Hungary, containing Gothic chalices and Renaissance mitres embroidered with pearls. But the showstopper is the precious **library**, containing almost 70,000 volumes printed before 1850, including an 11th-century codex.

Raba Quelle   SPA
(✆514 900; www.gyortermal.hu; Fürdő tér 1; adult/child 2450/1900Ft; ☉thermal baths 9am-8.30pm Sun-Thu, to 9pm Fri & Sat year-round, pool 6am-8pm Mon-Sat year-round, open-air pool 8am-8pm May-Aug) The water temperature in the pools at this thermal spa ranges from 29°C to 38°C. You can also take advantage of its fitness and wellness centres, offering every treatment imaginable.

🛏 Sleeping & Eating

Hotel Klastrom   BOUTIQUE HOTEL €€€
(✆516 910; www.klastrom.hu; Zechmeister utca 1; s/d/tr 12,500/17,500/20,000Ft; @) This delightful three-star hotel occupies a 300-year-old Carmelite convent south of Bécsi kapu tér. Rooms are charming and bright, and extras include a sauna, solarium, pub with a vaulted ceiling, and a restaurant with seating in a leafy courtyard garden.

Kertész Pension   GUESTHOUSE €€
(✆317 461; www.kerteszpanzio.com; Iskola utca 11; s/d 8000/12,000Ft; @) The 'Gardener' has very simple rooms, but it's well located in central Győr, staff couldn't be more friendly and there's an attractive, wood-panelled bar.

Soho Café & Pension   PENSION €
(✆550 465; www.sohocafe.hu; Kenyér köz 7; s/d/tr 7000/10,000/13,000Ft; @) Győr's cheapest in-town pension has simple no-frills rooms and two big pluses: it's just a block from Széchenyi tér and has a ground-floor cafe with free wi-fi, friendly staff, and good coffee and beer.

⌖TOP CHOICE La Maréda   INTERNATIONAL €€€
(✆510 982; www.lamareda.hu; Apáca utca 4; mains 2680-4850Ft) The most creative restaurant in town, La Maréda specialises in true fusion cuisine. Everything on the seasonal menu – from venison saddle with goat's cheese and spicy pumpkin cream to roast duck (pink and juicy in the middle!) with quince jelly – is expertly seasoned and presented beautifully enough to deserve the accolade 'food as art'. Yet the service is wonderfully unpretentious and attentive.

Matróz   SEAFOOD €€
(http://matroz-vendeglo.internettudakozo.hu; Dunakapu tér 3; mains 1200-2180Ft) Matróz makes the best fish dishes around, from warming carp soup to delicate pike-perch fillets. The handsome vaulted brick cellar, complete with dark-blue tiled oven and nautical memorabilia, completes this wonderful little eatery.

☆ Entertainment

A good source of information for what's on in Győr is the free magazine **Győri Est** (www.gyoriest.hu/).

Győr National Theatre   THEATRE
(Győri Nemzeti Színház; ✆box office 520 611; www.gyoriszinhaz.hu; Czuczor Gergely utca 7; ☉10am-1pm Mon-Fri, 2-6pm Tue-Fri) This modern venue is home to the celebrated **Győr Ballet** (www.gyoribalett.hu) as well as the city's opera company and philharmonic orchestra.

NAPOLEONIC PAUSE

Known only to pedants and Lonely Planet guidebook writers (until now) is the 'footnote fact' that France's Napoleon Bonaparte actually spent a night in Hungary – in Győr to be precise. The minuscule military commander slept over at Király utca 4, due east of Bécsi kapu tér, on 31 August 1809, in what is now called Napoleon-ház (Napoleon House). And why did NB choose Győr to make his grand entrée into Hungary? The city was near the site of the Battle of Raab (that's Győr in German), which had taken place just 11 weeks earlier between the Franco-Italian and Austrian-Hungarian armies. Bonaparte's side won and an inscription on the Arc de Triomphe in Paris still recalls 'la bataille de Raab'.

PANNONHALMA ABBEY

Take half a day and make the short, 20km trip from Győr to impressive **Pannonhalma Abbey** (Pannonhalmi főapátság; ☑570 191; www.bences.hu; Vár utca 1; foreign-language tours adult/student/family 2500/1500/6300Ft; ⊗9am-4pm Tue-Sun Apr & Oct–mid-Nov, 9am-5pm daily Jun-Sep, 10am-3pm Tue-Sun mid-Nov–Mar), a Unesco World Heritage Site since 1996. Most buildings in the complex date from the 13th to 19th centuries; highlights include the **Romanesque basilica and crypt** (1225), the **Gothic cloister** (1486) and the impressive collection of **ancient texts** in the library. Because it's an active monastery, the abbey must be visited with a guide. English and German tours leave at 11.20am and 1.20pm daily from May to September, with an extra tour at 3.20pm from June to September.

There are daily buses to the abbey from Győr (465Ft, 30 minutes) at 8am, 10.15am, 10.45am and noon.

ⓘ Information

Tourinform (☑311 771; www.gyortourism.hu; Baross Gábor utca 21-23; ⊗9am-6pm Mon-Fri, to 7pm Sat & Sun Jun-Aug, to 5pm Mon-Fri, to 1pm Sat Sep-May) Large new office with helpful staff and plenty of informative brochures.

OTP Bank (Baross Gábor utca 16)

Main post office (Bajcsy-Zsilinszky út 46; ⊗8am-6pm Mon-Fri) Opposite the Győr National Theatre.

ⓘ Getting There & Away

BUS Buses travel to Budapest (2520Ft, two hours, one to four daily), Pannonhalma (465Ft, 30 minutes, hourly), Esztergom (2200Ft, 2¼ hours, one daily) and Balatonfüred (2200Ft, 2½ hours, five daily).

TRAIN Győr is well connected by express train to Budapest's Keleti and Déli train stations (2520Ft, 1½ hours, half-hourly) and a dozen daily trains connect Győr with Vienna's Westbahnhof (3950Ft, 1½ hours).

Sopron

☑99 / POP 60,800

Sopron (*showp*-ron) is an attractive border town with a history that stretches back to Roman times. It boasts some well-preserved ancient ruins and a fetching medieval square, bounded by the original town walls, that invite an hour or two of aimless meandering.

The Mongols and Turks never got this far west so, unlike many Hungarian cities, numerous medieval buildings survived and are in use. The town's close history with nearby Austria goes back centuries and Sopron could easily have landed on the other side of the border if it weren't for a referendum

in 1921 in which town residents voted to remain part of Hungary. The rest of Bürgenland (the region to which Sopron used to belong) went to Austria. Once you've strolled through the quiet backstreets, have a glass or two of Kékfrancos, the local red wine.

◎ Sights & Activities

Fő tér   SQUARE

Fő tér is the main square in Sopron; there are several museums, monuments and churches scattered around it, including the massive **Firewatch Tower** (Tűztorony; Fő tér), a 60m-high tower rising above the Old Town's **Fidelity Gate** (Fő tér, below Firewatch Tower) and under renovation at the time of research.

The building is a true architectural hybrid: the 2m-thick square base, built on a Roman gate, dates from the 12th century; the middle cylindrical and arcaded balcony was built in the 16th century; and the baroque spire was added in 1680. In the centre of the square is the **Trinity Column** (Szentháromság oszlop; Fő tér) from 1701, among the finest examples of a 'plague pillar' in Hungary.

Just off the square, along the town wall, are the small **open-air ruins** (Szabadtéri rom), with reconstructed Roman walls and 2nd-century houses dating from the time when Sopron was the tiny Roman outpost Scarbantia.

Storno House   MUSEUM

(Storno Ház és Gyűjtemény; www.soprontourist.info/en/sopron//museums; adult/senior & student 1300/750Ft; ⊗10am-6pm Tue-Sun Apr-Sep, 2-6pm Oct-Mar) Storno House, built in 1417, was the residence of the Swiss–Italian family of Ferenc Storno, a chimney sweep turned art restorer, whose recarving of Romanesque and

Gothic monuments throughout Transdanubia divide opinions to this day. The wonderful **Storno Collection** of antiques and bric-a-brac on the 2nd floor includes much of their work. See what you think.

Fabricius House MUSEUM
(www.soprontourist.info/en/sopron//museums; Fő tér 6; adult/senior & student 1000/500Ft; ☺10am-6pm Tue-Sun Apr-Sep, to 2pm Oct-Mar) Baroque Fabricius House was built on Roman foundations and contains an **archaeological exhibition** of Celtic, Roman and early Hungarian finds on its lower floors and a **lapidarium** of sarcophagi and reconstructed Scarbantia-era statues. Upstairs are the so-called **urban apartments**, where you can see how Sopron's burghers lived in the 17th and 18th centuries.

Goat Church CHURCH
(Kecsketemplom; Templom utca 1; ☺7am-9pm May-Sep, 8am-6pm Mon-Sat Oct-Apr) Near the centre of Fő tér is this 13th-century Gothic church, whose name comes from the heraldic animal of its chief benefactor. Just off the main nave is the **Medieval Chapter Hall** (Középkori Káptalan Terem; ☑info 338 843; Templom utca 1; admission free; ☺10am-noon & 2-5pm mid-May–Sep), part of a 14th-century Franciscan monastery, with frescos and stone carvings.

Synagogues JEWISH
The **Old Synagogue** (Ó Zsinagóga; Új utca 22; adult/student 700/350Ft; ☺10am-6pm Tue-Sun May-Oct) and the **New Synagogue** (Új Zsinagóga; Új utca 11), both built in the 14th century, are reminders of the town's once substantial Jewish population. The former contains a reconstructed *mikvah* (ritual bath) in the courtyard.

🛏 Sleeping & Eating

Wieden Panzió GUESTHOUSE €€
(☑523 222; www.wieden.hu; Sas tér 13; s/d from 7000/9900Ft; 🖘) Sopron's cosiest pension is located in an attractive old town house within easy walking distance of the inner town. Rooms are spacious and bright, and the friendly staff will go out of its way to make you feel welcome.

Jégverem Fogadó GUESTHOUSE €
(☑510 113; www.jegverem.hu; Jégverem utca 1; s/d 6900/8900Ft; 🖘) An excellent and central bet, with five suitelike rooms in an 18th-century ice cellar. Even if you're not staying here, try the terrace restaurant for enormous portions of pork, chicken and fish.

Graben INTERNATIONAL €€
(☑340 256; www.grabenetterem.hu; Várkerület 8; mains 1690-3200Ft; ☺8am-10pm) Located in a cosy cellar near the old city walls, Graben attracts a largely Austrian clientele with its steaks, schnitzel and game dishes. Great flavours and friendly service. In summer its terrace spreads out over an inner courtyard.

Stubi HUNGARIAN €
(Balfi utca 16; meals 600-1000Ft; ☺noon-9pm) This is very much a local place for local people. Stick with the Hungarian-style daily specials – *gulyás* (goulash), hearty cabbage and potato stew, noodles with crushed poppy seeds and so on. Portions are very large.

Liszt Salon CAFE €
(Szent György utca 12; coffee 600Ft; ☺10am-10pm) This very stylish cafe attracts locals and tourists alike with a huge array of teas and coffees and two distinct areas – one with low, comfy couches and the other featuring upright chairs and tables. Occasional classical-music concerts.

☆ Entertainment

**Ferenc Liszt Conference
& Cultural Centre** PERFORMING ARTS
(☑517 517; www.prokultura.hu; Liszt Ferenc utca 1; ☺9am-5pm Mon-Fri, to noon Sat) A theatre, concert hall, casino and restaurant all rolled into one. The information desk has the latest on classical music and other cultural events in Sopron.

Petőfi Theatre THEATRE
(☑517 517; www.prokultura.hu; Petőfi tér 1) This beautiful theatre with national Romantic-style mosaics on the front facade is Sopron's leading theatre.

❶ Information

Main post office (Széchenyi tér 7-8)
OTP Bank (Várkerület 96/a)
Tourinform (☑517 560; sopron@tourinform. hu; Liszt Ferenc utca 1, Ferenc Liszt Conference & Cultural Centre; ☺9am-6pm Mon-Fri, to 7pm Sat-Sun mid-Jun–Aug, shorter hours rest of year) Free internet access and a plethora of information on Sopron and the surrounding area, including local vintners.

❶ Getting There & Away

BUS Bus travel to/from Budapest involves lengthy transfers/changes in cities like Veszprém and Székesfehérvár and is not recommended. There are hourly buses to Győr

(1680Ft, 2½ hours) and two a day to Balaton-füred (3130Ft, four hours).

TRAIN Trains run to Budapest's Keleti train station (4200Ft, three hours, eight daily) via Győr. Local trains run to Wiener Neustadt (2800Ft, 40 minutes, hourly) in Austria, where you change for Vienna.

Lake Balaton

Central Europe's largest expanse of fresh water is Lake Balaton, covering 600 sq km. The main activities here include swimming, sailing and sunbathing, but the lake is also popular with cyclists lured here by more than 200km of marked bike paths that encircle the lake.

The southern shore is mostly a forgettable jumble of tacky resorts, with its centre at Siófok. The northern shore, however, is yin to the southern coast's yang. Here the pace of life is more refined and the forested hills of Balaton Uplands National Park create a wonderful backdrop. Historical towns such as Keszthely and Balatonfüred dot the landscape, while Tihany, a peninsula cutting the lake almost in half, is home to an important historical church.

BALATONFÜRED
☑87 / POP 13,600

Balatonfüred (*bal*-ah-ton fuhr-ed) is the oldest and most fashionable resort on the lake. In its glory days in the 19th century the wealthy and famous built large villas along its tree-lined streets, hoping to take advantage of the health benefits of the town's thermal waters. More recently, the lake frontage received a massive makeover and now sports the most stylish marina on Balaton. The hotels here are a bit cheaper than those on the neighbouring Tihany peninsula, making this a good base for exploring.

◎ Sights & Activities

Gyógy tér   SQUARE
(Cure Sq; Gyógy tér) This leafy square is the heart of the Balatonfüred spa. In the centre is **Kossuth Pump House** (1853), which dispenses slightly sulphuric, but drinkable, thermal water. This is as close as you'll get to the hot spring; the mineral baths are reserved for patients of the **State Hospital of Cardiology** on the eastern side of the square.

On the northern side is the **Balaton Pantheon** (Gyógy tér), with memorial plaques from those who took the cure at the hospital, while on the western side is the late baroque **Horváth House** (Gyógy tér 3), the site of the first **Anna Ball** (www.annabal.hu; Anna Grand Hotel; tickets from Ft 25,000) – the town's red-letter annual event – in 1825. It's now held at the **Anna Grand Hotel** (☑342 044; www.annagrandhotel.eu; Gyógy tér 1; s/d from 25,000/35,000Ft; ❊@✿❊) every year on 26 July.

Public Beaches   BEACH
Balatonfüred's most accessible grassy beaches, measuring about a kilometre in length, are **Eszterházy Strand** (www.balatonfuredistrandok.hu; Tagore sétány; adult/child 900/540Ft; ◷8.30am-7pm mid-Jun–mid-Aug, 8.30am-7pm mid-May–mid-Jun & mid-Aug–mid-Sep), with a water park right in town, and the more attractive **Kisfaludy Strand** (www.balatonfuredistrandok.hu; Aranyhíd sétány; adult/child 640/400Ft; ◷8.30am-7pm mid-Jun–mid-Aug, 8.30am-7pm mid-May–mid-Jun & mid-Aug–mid-Sep) along the footpath about 800m northeast of the pier. Many beaches along the lake are 'managed' – that is, keep opening hours and charge admission. Facilities almost always include changing rooms and showers.

Cruises   CRUISE
The park along the central shore, near the ferry pier, is worth a promenade. You can take a one-hour **pleasure cruise** (☑342 230; www.balatonihajozas.hu; ferry pier; adult/concession 1500/6500Ft) four or five times a day, from late April to mid-September. The **retro disco boat** (Disco Hajo; ☑342 230; www.balatonihajozas.hu; ferry pier; cruise 1900Ft), a two-hour cruise with music and drinks, leaves at 9pm Monday and Wednesday to Saturday.

🛏 Sleeping

Prices fluctuate throughout the year and usually peak between early July and late August. There are lots of houses with rooms for rent on the streets north of Kisfaludy Strand. Tourinform (p326) can help find private rooms from roughly 4000Ft per person per night.

Hotel Blaha Lujza   HOTEL €€
(☑581 219; www.hotelblaha.hu; Blaha Lujza utca 4; s 11,000Ft, d 16,000-18,000Ft; ❊✿) This small hotel's 20 rooms are a little compact but very comfy. This was the summer home of the much-loved 19th-century actress-singer Lujza Blaha from 1893 to 1916.

Balaton Villa   HOTEL €€
(☑788 290; www.balatonvilla.hu; Deák Ferenc utca 38; s/d 6400/13,000Ft; ❊✿) The nine rooms at

this pastel-yellow villa uphill from the lake are large and bright. Each has its own balcony overlooking a sunny garden and grape vines, and guests can make use of a well-equipped kitchen and grill area.

Füred Camping
CAMPGROUND €

(✆580 241; fured@balatontourist.hu; Széchenyi utca 24; campsite per adult/child/tent 1600/1200/5500Ft; bungalows/caravans from 17,000/23,000Ft; ⊙mid-Apr–early Oct; @) This is one of the the largest camping grounds on the lake and has direct access to the water. Bungalows sleep up to four people.

✗ Eating & Drinking

La Riva
ITALIAN €€€

(✆06 20 391 4039; http://larivaristorante.hu; Zákonyi Ferenc sétány 4; mains 2000-4500Ft) Taking pride of place on the modern marina's waterfront is this imaginative restaurant. Pasta and pizza are the mainstays, but don't overlook the daily specials.

Balaton
HUNGARIAN €€

(Kisfaludy utca 5; mains 1800-3000Ft) This cool, leafy oasis amid all the hubbub is set back from the lake in the shaded park area. It serves generous portions and has an extensive fish selection.

Kedves
CAFE

(Blaha Lujza utca 7; cakes 400-650Ft) Join some of Lujza Blaha and take coffee and cake at the cafe where the famous 19th-century actress-singer used to while away the hours. It's also appealing for its location, away from the madd(en)ing crowds.

❶ Information

Post office (Zsigmond utca 14)

OTP Bank (Petőfi Sándor utca 8)

Tourinform (✆580 480; balatonfured@ tourinform.hu; Blaha Lujza utca 5; ⊙9am-7pm Mon-Fri, to 6pm Sat, to 1pm Sun Jul & Aug, 9am-5pm Mon-Fri, to 1pm Sat Jun & Sep, 9am-4pm Mon-Fri Oct-May) Well-stocked and well-run tourist office.

❶ Getting There & Around

The adjacent bus and train stations are on Dobó István utca, about 1km uphill from the lake. Buses to Tihany (310Ft, 30 minutes) leave every 30 minutes or so throughout the day. Several buses daily head to the northwestern lakeshore towns including Keszthely (1300Ft, 1½ hours, seven daily).

Buses and trains to Budapest (2520Ft, 2½ hours) are much of a muchness but the former are more frequent.

From April to October half a dozen daily ferries ply the water from Balatonfüred to Tihany (1100Ft, 30 minutes).

TIHANY
✔87 / POP 1350

The place with the greatest historical significance on Lake Balaton is Tihany (tee-haw-nee), a hilly peninsula jutting 5km into the lake. Activity here is centred on the tiny town of the same name, which is home to the celebrated Abbey Church. Contrasting with this are the hills and marshy meadows of the peninsula's nature reserve, which has an isolated, almost wild feel to it. It's ideal for hiking and birdwatching.

◉ Sights & Activities

Abbey Church
TOP CHOICE
CHURCH

(Bencés Apátság templom; http://tihany.osb. hu; András tér 1; adult/concession incl museum 1000/500Ft; ⊙9am-6pm May-Sep, 10am-5pm Apr & Oct, 10am-3pm Nov-Mar) You can spot the twin-towered ochre-coloured Benedictine Abbey Church (1754) from a long way off. The nave is filled with fantastic altars, pulpits and screens carved in the mid-18th century by an Austrian lay brother and all are baroque-rococo masterpieces in their own right. Entombed in the **Romanesque crypt** is the abbey's founder, King Andrew I. Admission includes entry to the attached **Benedictine Abbey Museum** (Bencés Apátsági Múzeum; admission incl with Abbey Church entry fee; ⊙9am-6pm May-Sep, 10am-5pm Apr & Oct, 10am-3pm Nov-Mar). Behind the church a path leads to a lookout with outstanding views.

Hiking
HIKING

Hiking is one of Tihany's main attractions; there's a good map outlining the colour-coded trails in the centre of the village at Kossuth Lajos utca and András tér. Following the Green Trail northeast of the village centre for an hour will bring you to the **Russian Well** (Oroszkút) and the ruins of the **Old Castle** (Óvár) at 219m, where Russian Orthodox monks, brought to Tihany by Andrew I, hollowed out cells in the soft basalt walls.

⌖ Sleeping & Eating

Kántás Panzió
GUESTHOUSE €€

(✆448 072; www.kantas-panzio-tihany.hu; Csokonai út 49; r 13,000Ft; ❄🛜) Kántás is a fine example of Tihany's cheaper accommodation. It's small and personal, with pleasant attic rooms (some with balcony) above a restaurant. Views are across the inner lake.

Adler
BOUTIQUE HOTEL €€€
(☑538 000; www.adler-tihany.hu; Felsőkopaszhegyi utca 1/a; r 14,700-16,900Ft, apt 29,700-32,400Ft; ❄🛜🏊) Adler counts 13 large, whitewashed rooms with balconies; good for families and also has a jacuzzi, sauna and restaurant.

TOP CHOICE Ferenc Pince
HUNGARIAN €€
(☑448 575; Cserhegy 9; mains from 2500Ft; ☺noon-11pm, closed Tue) About 2km south of the Abbey Church, Ferenc is a wine- and food-lover's dream. During the day, its terrace offers expansive views of the lake, while at night the lights of the southern shore are visible.

Rege Café
CAFE €
(Kossuth Lajos utca 22; cakes from 350Ft; ☺10am-6pm) From its high vantage point near the Benedictine Abbey Museum, this modern cafe has an unsurpassed panoramic view of the Balaton.

ⓘ Information
Tihany Tourist (☑448 481; www.tihanytourist. hu; Kossuth Lajos utca 11; ☺9am-5pm May-Sep, 10am-4pm Apr & Oct) Organises accommodation and local tours.

Tourinform (☑448 804; tihany@tourinform. hu; Kossuth Lajos utca 20; ☺9am-7pm Mon-Fri, 10am-5pm Sat & Sun mid-Jun–mid-Sep, shorter hours rest of year) Central.

ⓘ Getting There & Away
Buses travel along the 14km of mostly lakeside road between Tihany village and Balatonfüred's train and bus stations (310Ft, 30 minutes) throughout the day.

From April to October, half a dozen daily ferries ply the water from Balatonfüred to Tihany (1100Ft, 30 minutes). You can follow a steep path up to the village from the pier to reach the Abbey Church.

KESZTHELY
☑83 / POP 21,000
At the very western end of the lake sits Keszthely (*kest*-hey), a place of grand town houses and a gentle ambience far removed from the lake's tourist hot spots. Its small, shallow beaches are well suited to families, and the lavish Festetics Palace is a must-see.

The beaches and the ferry pier lie to the southeast through a small park. The main commercial centre, where everything happens, is about 500m north of the bus and train stations uphill, along the main street, Kossuth Lajos utca.

◉ Sights & Activities

TOP CHOICE Festetics Palace
PALACE
(Festetics Kastély; ☑312 190; www.helikonkastely. hu; Kastély utca 1; Palace & Coach Museum adult/ concession 2300/1150Ft; ☺9am-9pm Jul & Aug, 10am-4pm May, Jun & Sep, reduced hours & closed Mon Oct-Apr) The glimmering white, 100-room Festetics Palace was first built in 1745; the wings were extended out from the original building 150 years later. About a dozen rooms in the baroque south wing have been turned into the **Helikon Palace Museum** (Helikon Kastélymúzeum). Many of the decorative arts in the gilt salons were imported from England in the mid-1800s.

Also here is the palace's greatest treasure, the renowned **Helikon Library** (Helikon Könyvtár), with its 100,000 volumes and splendid carved furniture. Behind the palace in a separate building is the **Coach Museum** (Hintómúzeum; adult/concession 1000/500Ft; ☺9am-9pm Jul & Aug, 10am-4pm May, Jun & Sep, reduced hours & closed Mon Oct-Apr), which is filled with coaches and sleighs fit for royalty.

Lakeside Area
BEACH
Keszthely's best beaches for swimming or sunbathing are **City Beach** (Városi Strand; adult/child 890/630Ft, 3 days 1800/1300Ft; ☺8am-6pm mid-May–mid-Sept), which is close to the ferry pier and good for kids, and reedy **Helikon Beach** (Helikon Strand; adult/ child 500/350Ft, 3 days 1050/840Ft; ☺8am-6pm mid-May–mid-Sept) further south. There's windsurfing and kitesurfing rental at City Beach in summer. Many beaches keep opening hours and charge admission. Facilities almost always include changing rooms and showers.

You can take a one-hour **pleasure cruise** (☑312 093; www.balatonihajozas.hu; ferry pier; ☺adult/concession 1500/650Ft) several times daily from late March to late October. In high season there are up to seven sailings a day.

🛏 Sleeping
Tourinform (p328) can help find private rooms (from 3500Ft per person). Otherwise, strike out on your own (particularly along Móra Ferenc utca) and keep an eye out for '*szoba kiadó*' or '*zimmer frei*' signs (Hungarian and German, respectively, for 'room for rent').

HUNGARY LAKE BALATON

TOP CHOICE Bacchus HOTEL €€€

(☎510 450; www.bacchushotel.hu; Erzsébet királyné utca 18; s 13,500Fr, d 16,900-25,000Ft, apt 27,000Ft; ❋@✿) Bacchus' central position and immaculate rooms make it a popular choice with travellers. Equally pleasing is its atmospheric cellar, which includes a lovely restaurant with wine tastings.

Tokajer GUESTHOUSE €€

(Tokaji Panzió Keszthely; ☎319 875; www.pensiontokajer.hu; Apát utca 21; s/d/apt from 9200/15,000/18,000Ft; ❋@✿✉) Spread over four buildings in a quiet part of town, the Tokajer – its German name – has slightly dated rooms, but they're spacious and some have a balcony. Extras include two pools, a wellness centre and fitness room, and free use of bicycles.

Ambient Hostel HOSTEL €

(☎06 30 460 3536; http://keszthely-szallas.fw.hu; Sopron utca 10; dm/d from 3600/7900Ft; @) Only a short walk north of Festetics Palace is this hostel with basic, cheap dorm rooms, each of which comes with its own bathroom. Ambient also has a colourful, modern roadside cafe.

✗ Eating & Drinking

TOP CHOICE Margareta HUNGARIAN €

(www.margaretaetterem.hu; Bercsényi utca 60; mains 1400-3200Ft; ◷11am-10pm) Margareta is no beauty, but the wraparound porch and hidden backyard terrace is heaving in the warmer months and the small interior packs them in the rest of the year. Food sticks to the basic but hearty Hungarian staples, but be warned: portions are huge.

Pelso Café CAFE

(Fő tér; coffee & cake from 300Ft; ◷10am-10pm; ☎) This modern two-level cafe at the southern end of the main square does decent coffee and cake as well as cocktails. Wonderful terrace.

☆ Entertainment

Festetics Palace CLASSICAL MUSIC

(Festetics Kastély; ☎312 190; www.helikonkastely.hu; Kastély utca 1; ◷8pm Thu) Classical-music concerts are held every Thursday throughout the year in the music hall of the palace.

❶ Information

OTP Bank (Kossuth Lajos utca 38)

Tourinform (☎314 144; keszthely@tourinform.hu; Kossuth Lajos utca 28; ◷9am-8pm Mon-Fri, to 6pm Sat mid-Jun–mid-Sep, 9am-5pm Mon-Fri, to 12.30pm Sat mid-Sep–mid-Jun) Excellent source of information on Keszthely and the lake.

❶ Getting There & Away

BUS Buses from Keszthely run to destinations including Balatonfüred (1300Ft, 1½ hours, seven daily) and Budapest (3410Ft, three hours, seven daily).

TRAIN Keszthely is on a railway branch line linking the lake's southeastern shore with Budapest (3410Ft, four hours, six daily). To reach towns along Lake Balaton's northern shore by train, you have to change at Tapolca (465Ft, 30 minutes, hourly).

SOUTH CENTRAL HUNGARY

Southern Hungary is a region of calm; a place to savour life at a slower pace. It's only marginally touched by tourism, and touring

---

WORTH A TRIP

HÉVÍZ

Hévíz (population 4335), just 8km northwest of Keszthely, is the most famous of Hungary's spa towns because of the Gyógy-tó (Hévíz Thermal Lake; ☎501 700; www.spaheviz.hu; 3hr/5hr/whole day 2500/2800/3800Ft; ◷8am-7pm Jun-Aug, 9am-6pm May & Sep, 9am-5pm Apr & Oct, 9am-4pm Mar & Nov-Feb) – Europe's largest 'thermal lake'. A dip into this water lily-filled lake is essential for anyone visiting the Lake Balaton region.

It's an astonishing sight: a surface of almost 4.5 hectares in the Park Wood, covered for most of the year in pink and white lotuses. The source is a spring spouting from a crater some 40m below ground that disgorges up to 80 million L of warm water a day, renewing itself every 48 hours or so. The surface temperature averages 33°C and never drops below 22°C in winter, allowing bathing throughout the year, even when there's ice on the fir trees. Do as the locals do and rent a rubber ring (600Ft) and just float.

A covered bridge leads to the thermal lake's fin-de-siècle central pavilion, which contains a small buffet, sun chairs, showers, changing rooms and steps down into the lake.

Buses link Hévíz with Keszthely (250Ft, 15 to 20 minutes) almost every half-hour.

through the countryside is like travelling back in time. Passing through the region, you'll spot whitewashed farmhouses whose thatched roofs and long colonnaded porticoes decorated with floral patterns seem unchanged over the centuries.

Historically, the area bordering Croatia and Serbia has often been 'shared' between Hungary and these countries, and it's here that the remnants of the 150-year Turkish occupation can be most strongly felt.

The region is bounded by the Danube River to the east, the Dráva River to the south and west, and Lake Balaton to the north. It's generally flat, with the Mecsek and Villány Hills rising in isolation from the plain. The weather always seems to be a few degrees warmer here than in other parts of the country; the sunny clime is great for grape-growing and oak-aged Villány reds are well regarded.

Pécs

📞72 / POP 157,700

Blessed with a mild climate, an illustrious past and a number of fine museums and monuments, Pécs *(paich)* is one of the most pleasant and interesting cities to visit in Hungary. For those reasons and more – a handful of universities, the nearby Mecsek Hills, a lively nightlife and excellent wines – many travellers put it second only to Budapest on their Hungary must-see list.

The Roman settlement of Sopianae in what is now Pécs was the capital of the province of Lower Pannonia for 400 years. Christianity flourished here as early as the 4th century and in 1009 Stephen I made Pécs a bishopric. The Mongols swept through here in 1241, prompting the authorities to build massive city walls, parts of which are still standing. The Turkish occupation began in 1543 and lasted nearly a century and a half, lending Pécs an Ottoman patina that's immediately visible at the Mosque Church that stands at the heart of the city's main square.

⊙ Sights & Activities

The city's main sights are clustered in three areas: Széchenyi tér, with the Mosque Church; Dóm tér (dominated by the Basilica of St Peter); and Káptalan utca, Pécs' 'museum street'.

TOP CHOICE Mosque Church   MOSQUE

(Mecset templom; Széchenyi tér; adult/concession 750/500Ft; ⊙10am-4pm mid-Apr–mid-Oct, to noon mid-Oct–mid-Apr, shorter hours Sun) The erstwhile Pasha Gazi Kassim Mosque is now the Inner Town Parish Church (Belvárosi plébánia templom), but it's more commonly referred to as the Mosque Church. It is the largest building still standing in Hungary from the time of the Turkish occupation and the very symbol of the city.

Synagogue   SYNAGOGUE

(Zsinagóga; Kossuth tér; adult/concession 600/400Ft; ⊙10am-noon & 12.45-5pm Sun-Fri May-Oct) Pécs' beautifully preserved 1869 synagogue is south of Széchenyi tér.

Zsolnay Porcelain Museum   MUSEUM

(Zsolnay Porcélan Múzeum; Káptalan utca 2; adult/concession 1200/600Ft; ⊙10am-5pm Tue-Sun) From the northern end of Széchenyi tér, climb Szepessy Ignéc utca and turn left (west) onto Káptalan utca, a street lined with museums and galleries. The Zsolnay Porcelain Museum is on the eastern end of this strip. English translations provide a good history of the artistic and functional ceramics produced from this local factory's illustrious early days in the mid-19th century to the present time. The museum was once the home of the Zsolnay family and contains many original furnishings and personal effects.

Basilica of St Peter   CHURCH

(Szent Péter bazilika; Dóm tér; adult/concession 900/600Ft; ⊙9am-5pm Mon-Sat, 1-5pm Sun) The foundations of the four-towered basilica dedicated to St Peter date from the 11th century and the side chapels are from the 1300s. But most of what you see today of the neo-Romanesque structure is the result of renovations carried out in 1881. The 1770 Bishop's Palace (Püspöki palota; 📞513 030; Szent István tér 23; adult/child 1900/1000Ft; ⊙tours 2pm, 3pm & 4pm Thu late Jun–mid-Sep) is southwest of the cathedral. Also near the square is a 15th-century barbican (Barbakán; Esze Tamás utca 2; ⊙garden 7am-8pm May-Sep, 9am-5pm Oct-Apr), the only stone bastion to survive from the old city walls.

Cella Septichora
Visitors Centre   RUINS

(Cella Septichora látogatóközpont; www.pecsorokseg.hu; Janus Pannonius utca; adult/concession 1200/600Ft; ⊙10am-6pm Tue-Sun) On the

HUNGARY PÉCS

Pécs

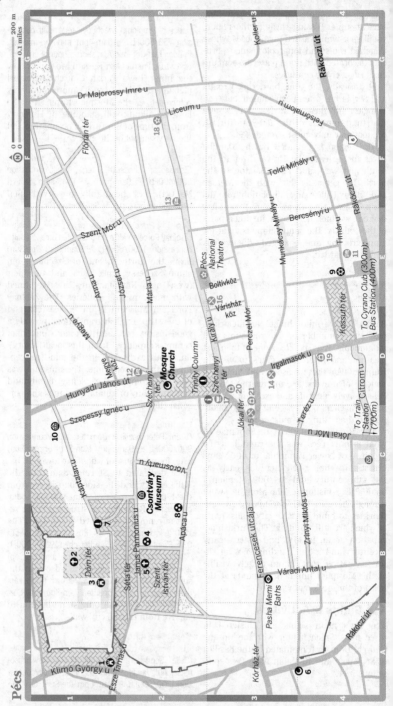

200 m
0.1 miles

Dr Majorossy Imre u

Liceum u

Rákóczi út

Koller u

Felsőmalom u

Florián tér

18

Szent Mór u

13

Toldi Mihály u

Bercsényi u

Munkácsy Mihály u

Pécs
National
Theatre

Boltívköz

Várisház
köz

Tímár u

Rákóczi út

11

9

Kossuth tér

To Cyrano Club (300m);
Bus Station (400m)

Megye u

Anna u

József u

Mária u

Meszye
köz

12

Mosque
Church

Trinity Column

Széchenyi
tér

Király u

Perczel Mór u

Irgalmasok u

14

19

20

To Train
Station
(700m)

Citrom u

Teréz u

Hunyadi János út

Szepessy Ignác u

1

17

21

15

Jókai tér

Jókai Mór u

10

Káptalan u

Vörösmarty u

Csontváry
Museum

8

Apáca u

Ferencesek utcája

Zrínyi Miklós u

To Train Station

Janus Pannonius u

Séta tér

4

5

Szent
István tér

2

Dóm tér

3

7

Pasha Memi
Baths

Váradi Antal u

Klimó György u

Esze Tamás u

Kórház tér

6

Rákóczi út

Pécs

southern side of Dom tér is the Cella Septichora Visitors Centre, which illuminates a series of early Christian burial sites that have been on Unesco's World Heritage list since 2000. The highlight is the so-called **Jug Mausoleum** (Korsós sírkamra; adult/child 300/150Ft; ⊙10am-6pm Tue-Sun), a 4th-century Roman tomb whose name comes from a painting of a large drinking vessel with vines.

Early Christian Tomb Chapel   CHURCH
(Ókeresztény sírkápolna; Szent István tér 12; adult/concession 500/300Ft; ⊙10am-6pm Tue-Sun) This early Christian tomb chapel dates from about AD 350 and has frescos of Adam and Eve and Daniel in the lion's den. Two **Roman tomb sites** (Apáca utca 8 & 14; adult/child/family 450/250/850Ft; ⊙10am-5pm Tue-Sun) containing 110 graves from the same era are a little further south.

⌷TOP⌷ **Csontváry Museum**   MUSEUM
(☑310 544; Janus Pannonius utca 11; adult/child 1500/750Ft; ⊙10am-6pm, closed Mon) The Csontváry Museum shows the major works of the 19th-century painter Tivadar Kosztka Csontváry (1853–1919), a unique symbolist artist whose tragic life is often compared with that of his great contemporary, Vincent Van Gogh.

Hassan Jakovali Mosque   MOSQUE
(Hassan Jakovali mecset; Rákóczi utca; adult/concession 600/300Ft; ⊙9.30am-6pm Wed-Sun late Mar-Oct) Though wedged between two mod-

ern buildings, this 16th-century mosque is more intact than its larger cousin, the Mosque Church, and comes complete with a **minaret**. There's a small **exhibition** on the Ottomans in Hungary inside.

⌷🛏⌷ Sleeping

In July and August more than a dozen of the city's colleges open up their doors to travellers, and prices average 4000Ft to 6000Ft for a dorm bed; Tourinform (p332) has the complete list.

Hotel Főnix   HOTEL €€
(☑311 682; www.fonixhotel.hu; Hunyadi János út 2; s/d from 8200/14,000Ft; ❄@🕾) Főnix appears to be a hotel too large for the land it's built on and some of the 16 rooms and suites are not even big enough to swing a, well, phoenix in. Try to bag a room with a balcony; the Mosque Church is just within reach.

Hotel Diána   GUESTHOUSE €€
(☑328 594; www.hoteldiana.hu; Tímár utca 4/a; s/d/tr from 11,350/16,350/20,350Ft; ❄@) This very central hotel-cum-guesthouse offers 20 spotless rooms, comfortable kick-off-your-shoes decor and a warm welcome.

Nap Hostel   HOSTEL €
(☑950 684; www.naphostel.com; Király utca 23-25; dm/d from 2800/12,350Ft; @🕾) Clean, friendly hostel with dorms and a double room on the 1st floor of a former bank. There's also a large kitchen. Enter from Szent Mór utca.

HUNGARY PÉCS

✕ Eating & Drinking

Pubs, cafes and fast-food eateries line pedestrian-only Király utca. Another good bet is tiny and more intimate Jókai tér.

TOP CHOICE **Enoteca & Bistro Corso** INTERNATIONAL €€€
(☎525 198; www.enotecapecs.hu; Király utca 14; mains 3200-5500Ft) One of Hungary's top restaurants, Corso offers dining on two levels: the top features refined Hungarian cooking with Italian and French influences, while the ground floor is slightly less expensive but equally good. The alfresco terrace is also a popular spot for snacks and drinks in the warmer months.

Áfium BALKAN €
(☎511 434; Irgalmasok utca 2; mains 1500-2200Ft; ⊙11am-1am) With Croatia and Serbia so close, it's a wonder that more restaurants don't offer cuisine from south of the border. Don't miss the bean soup with trotters. Weekday set lunch is just 520Ft.

Az Elefánthoz ITALIAN €€
(☎216 055; www.elefantos.hu; Jókai tér 6; mains 2600-4500Ft, pizza 1400-2600Ft) With its welcoming terrace overlooking Jókai tér and quality Italian dishes, this place is a sure bet for first-rate food in the centre. It has a wood-fired stove for pizzas, though the pasta dishes are also worth a try.

Coffein Café CAFE
(Széchenyi tér 9; ⊙8am-midnight Mon-Thu, to 2am Fri & Sat, 10am-10pm Sun; ☎) For the best views across Széchenyi tér to the Mosque Church and Király utca, find a perch at this cool cafe, which is done up in the warmest of colours.

☆ Entertainment

Pécs has well-established opera and ballet companies as well as a symphony orchestra. Tourinform has schedule information. The free biweekly PécsiEst (www.pecsiest.hu) also lists what's on around town.

Cyrano Club CLUB
(Czindery utca 6; men 800-1200Ft, women free; ⊙8pm-5am Fri & Sat) A big club, popular with a big-haired, big-nailed crowd that's been around for ages.

Varázskert CLUB
(Király utca 65; ⊙6pm-3am summer) Big open-air beer garden and late-hours music club at the far end of Király utca.

🔒 Shopping

Pécs has been known for its leatherwork since Turkish times and you can pick up a few bargains in several shops around the city, including **Blázek** (☎332 460; Teréz utca 1), which deals mainly in handbags and wallets. **Corvina Art Bookshop** (☎310 427; Széchenyi tér 7-8) stocks English-language books and guides and **Zsolnay** (☎310 220; Jókai tér 2) has a porcelain outlet south of Széchenyi tér. About 3km southwest of town, a Sunday **flea market** (Vásártér; Megyeri út; ⊙8am-3pm Sun) attracts people from around the region.

ℹ Information

Tourinform (☎213 315; baranya-m@tourinform.hu; Széchenyi tér 9; ⊙9am-5pm Mon-Fri & 10am-3pm Sat & Sun Jun-Aug, closed Sun May, Sep & Oct, closed Sat & Sun Nov-Apr) Knowledgeable staff, copious information on Pécs and region.

Main post office (Jókai Mór utca 10) In a beautiful art nouveau building (1904) south of Széchenyi tér.

ℹ Getting There & Away

BUS Some five buses a day connect Pécs with Budapest (3010Ft, 4½ hours), eight with Szeged (3010Ft, 4½ hours) and two with Kecskemét (3010Ft, 4½ hours).

TRAIN Pécs is on a main rail line with Budapest's Déli train station (3950Ft, three hours, nine daily). One daily train runs from Pécs to Eszék in Croatia (the town is called Osijek in Croatia; two hours), with continuing service to the Bosnian capital, Sarajevo (nine hours).

SOUTHEASTERN HUNGARY

Like the outback for Australians or the Wild West for Americans, the Nagy Alföld (Great Plain) holds a romantic appeal for Hungarians. Many of these notions come as much from the collective imagination, paintings and poetry as they do from history, but there's no arguing the spellbinding potential of big-sky country – especially around Hortobágy and Kiskunság National Parks. The Great Plain is home to cities of graceful architecture and history. Szeged is a centre of art and culture, Kecskemét is full of art nouveau gems and Debrecen is 'the Calvinist Rome'.

Kecskemét

📞76 / POP 107,000

Located about halfway between Budapest and Szeged, Kecskemét (*kech*-kah-mate) is a green, pedestrian-friendly city with delightful art nouveau architecture, many fine museums and the region's excellent *barackpálinka* (apricot brandy). And Kiskunság National Park is right at the back door. Day-trip opportunities include hiking in the sandy, juniper-covered hills, a horse show at Bugac or a visit to one of the area's many horse farms.

◎ Sights

Kossuth tér SQUARE

(P) Kossuth tér is dominated by the massive 1897 art nouveau **City Hall** (📞513 513, ext 2263; Kossuth tér 1; admission free; ⊙by arrangement), which is flanked by the baroque **Great Church** (Nagytemplom; 📞487 501; Kossuth tér 2; ⊙9am-noon year-round plus 3-6pm May-Sep, closed Mon) and the earlier **Franciscan Church of St Nicholas** (Szent Miklós Ferences Templom; 📞497 025; Lestár tér), parts of which date from the 13th century. Nearby is the magnificent 1896 **József Katona Theatre** (Katona József Színház; Katona József tér 5), a neobaroque venue with a statue of the **Holy Trinity** (1742) in front of it.

Ornamental Palace ARCHITECTURE

(Cifrapalota; Rákóczi út 1) The masterful art-nouveau-style Ornamental Palace, which dates from 1902, has multicoloured majolica tiles decorating its 'waving' walls. The palace contains the **Kecskemét Gallery** (Kecskeméti Képtár; 📞480 776; www.museum.hu/kecskemet/keptar; adult/concession 500/270Ft; ⊙10am-5pm Tue-Sun). Its collection of 20th-century Hungarian art is important, but visit mainly to see the aptly named **Decorative Hall** (Díszterem) and its amazing stuccowork and colourful tiles.

Hungarian Folk Craft Museum MUSEUM

(Népi Iparművészeti Múzeum; 📞327 203; www.nepiiparmuveszet.hu; Serfőző utca 19/a; adult/concession 500/250Ft; ⊙10am-5pm Tue-Sat Mar-Oct,

HUNGARY KECSKEMÉT

WORTH A TRIP

KISKUNSÁG NATIONAL PARK

Totalling more than 76,000 hectares, **Kiskunság National Park** (Kiskunsági Nemzeti Park; www.knp.hu) consists of nine 'islands' of protected land. Much of the park's alkaline ponds and sand dunes are off limits. Bugac (*boo*-gats) village (population 2850), 30km southwest of Kecskemét, is the most accessible part of the park.

The highlight of a trip here is a chance to see a popular **cowboy show** (csikósbemutató; www.bugacpuszta.hu; admission 1400Ft; ⊙12.15pm May-Oct), where the horse herders race one another bareback and ride 'five-in-hand', a breathtaking performance in which one *csikós* (cowboy) gallops five horses at full speed while standing on the backs of the back two.

There are also several nature and educational **hiking trails** in the vicinity, with explanatory sign-posting in English, where you can get out and see this amazing ecosystem of dunes, bluffs and swamps.

Getting to the show without your own vehicle is difficult. There's a morning bus from Kecskemét to Bugac (745Ft, one hour, 37km) but it won't get you there in time for the 12.15pm show. (Buses before that leave at an ungodly 5.25am weekdays and 6.30am at the weekend). An alternative but complicated way to go is to take the hourly train to Kiskunfélegyháza (465Ft, 16 minutes, 25km) at 9.11am and then the hourly bus to Bugac (370Ft, 30 minutes, 18km).

If you've got your own transportation, follow route 54 out of Kecskemét in the direction of Soltvadkert. Turn off the road at the 21km marker and follow a dirt track a couple of kilometres toward Bugacpuszta and then follow signs to the **Karikás Csárda** (📞575 112; www.bugacpuszta.hu/en/?pid=310; Nagybugac 135; mains 1600-3800Ft; ⊙10am-10pm May-Sep, to 8pm Apr & Oct), a kitschy but decent restaurant next to the park entrance that also doubles as a ticket and information booth to the show and small **Herder Museum** (Pásztormúzeum; 📞575 112; www.museum.hu/bugac/pasztormuzeum; admission free; ⊙10am-5pm May-Oct).

From there you can get to the show on foot or by **horse-driven carriage** (adult/child incl cowboy show 3500/2500Ft; ⊙11.30am May-Oct). Tourinform (p335) in Kecskemét can help plan an outing to the national park; the owners of the Fábián Panzió (p334) guesthouse in Kecskemét are another good source of information.

Kecskemét

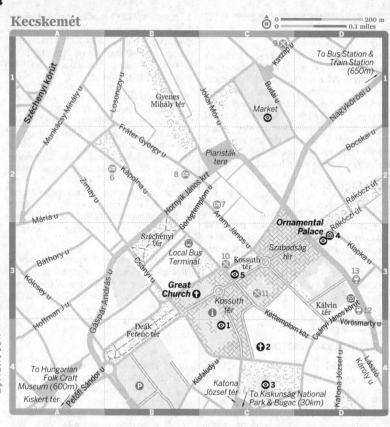

to 4pm Nov-Feb) A dozen rooms of a 200-year-old farm complex are crammed with embroidery, weaving, woodcarving, furniture, agricultural tools and textiles at the Hungarian Folk Craft Museum, the granddaddy of all Kecskemét museums.

Sleeping

Tourinform (p335) can help you locate the numerous colleges that offer dormitory accommodation in July and August.

Fábián Panzió GUESTHOUSE €€
TOP CHOICE
(☎477 677; www.panziofabian.hu; Kápolna utca 14; s 9800-10,800Ft; d 11,000-12,800Ft; ❇@☎) The world-travelling family that owns this 10-room guesthouse seems to know exactly what their guests want: fridges and tea- and coffee-making facilities are room standards; there are local restaurant menus and tourist brochures to peruse; bikes are available for rent. Quiet street, garden coutyard.

Pálma HOTEL €€
(☎321 045; www.hotelpalma.hu; Arany János utca 3; s 6100-8500Ft; d 8900-10,900Ft; ❇☎) The central Pálma counts 40 simple guest rooms in two modern buildings. The more expensive ones are on the 1st floor and have TV, fridge and air-conditioning. Free self-service laundry facilities.

Teachers' College HOSTEL €
(Tanítóképzö Főiskola; ☎486 977; www.kefo.hu; Piaristák tere 4; s/d 3500/7000Ft; ◷mid-Jun–Aug; @▥) The most central and friendly of Kecskemét's summer college accommodation, this dormitory has basic rooms with twin beds and (mostly) en suite bathrooms.

Eating

Cézár ITALIAN €€
TOP CHOICE
(☎328 849; www.clubcaruso.hu; Kaszap utca 4; mains 2200-4200Ft) As authentic a *ristorante italiano* as you'll find in the Hungarian

Kecskemét

provinces, Cézár serves dishes made with ingredients almost entirely sourced in Italy. The choice of pizza (980Ft to 1400Ft) and pasta dishes (1800Ft to 2700Ft) is huge and they do mains in half-portions.

Rozmaring HUNGARIAN €€€
(☎509 175; www.rozmaringbisztro.hu; Szabadság tér 2; mains 1800-4300Ft; ☑) Artistic presentations come standard at this silver-service restaurant on the city's pedestrian square. This is modern Hungarian done right.

Lordok CAFE €
(☎06 70 866 0223; Kossuth tér 6-7; mains 500-900Ft; ☯7am-midnight) This popular self-service canteen and adjoining trendier cafe-bar does triple duty as a cheap and tasty lunch option, a place for a midafternoon caffeine break and a spot for a sundowner.

🍷 Drinking & Entertainment

For drinks, the Western-themed pub **Wanted Söröző** (☎415 923; Csányi János körút 4; ☯8am-midnight Mon-Thu, 10am-2am Fri & Sat, 10am-midnight Sun) sits handily just up the road from the more alternative **Black Cat Pub** (☎06 70 299 4040; Csányi János körút 6; ☯11am-midnight Sun-Thu, to 2am Fri & Sat).

Tourinform has a list of what concerts and performances are on, or check out the free weekly magazine *Kecskeméti Est*.

ℹ Information

Main post office (Kálvin tér 10)
OTP Bank (Korona utca 2, Malom Centre) In central shopping centre.
Tourinform (☎481 065; www.kecskemet.hu; Kossuth tér 1; ☯8am-5pm Mon-Fri & 9am-1pm Sat & Sun Jun-Aug, 8am-6pm Mon-Fri Sep-May) In City Hall; rent out bikes and advises on excursions to Kiskunság National Park.

ℹ Getting There & Away

The main bus and train stations are opposite each other, near József Katona Park. Frequent buses depart for Budapest (1680Ft, 1¼ hours, hourly) and for Szeged (1860Ft, two hours, hourly).

A direct rail line links Kecskemét to Budapest's Nyugati train station (1900Ft, 1½ hours, hourly), Pécs (3690Ft, 4½ hours, two daily) and Szeged (1650Ft, one hour, hourly).

Szeged

☑62 / POP 170,300

Busting border town Szeged (*seh*-ged) has a handful of historic sights that line the embankment along the Tisza River and a clutch of sumptuous art nouveau town palaces that are in varying states of repair. Importantly, it's also a big university town, which means lots of culture, lots of partying and an active festival scene that lasts throughout the year.

For centuries, the city's position at the confluence of the Maros and Tisza Rivers brought prosperity and growth. That happy relationship turned sour in 1879, when the Tisza overflowed its banks, wiping out much of the central city. Most of the historic buildings you see today date from the late 19th and early 20th centuries.

The **Szeged Open-Air Festival** (☎541 205; www.szegediszabadteri.hu), held in Dom tér in July and August, is the largest festival outside Budapest in Hungary. Main events include an opera, an operetta, a play, folk dancing, classical music, ballet and a rock opera.

◎ Sights & Activities

Dóm tér SQUARE
'Cathedral Square' contains Szeged's most important buildings and monuments and is the centre of events during the annual

Szeged

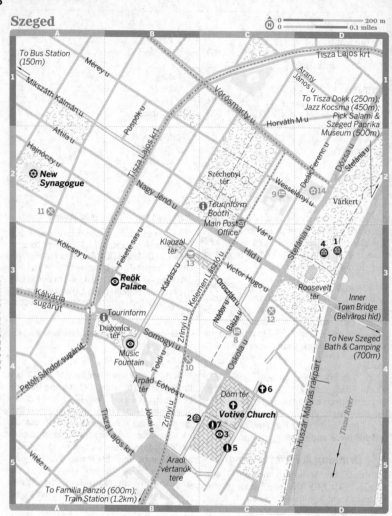

summer festival. Lording (as it were) above all else is the twin-towered **Votive Church** (Fogadalmi templom; ☎420 157; www.dom.szeged.hu; Dóm tér; admission free; ☺6.30am-7pm Mon-Sat, from 7.30am Sun), a disproportionate brick monstrosity that was pledged after the 1879 flood but built from 1913 to 1930. About the only things worth seeing inside are the organ, with more than 11,500 pipes, and dome covered with frescos.

Just in front is the Romanesque **St Demetrius Tower** (Dömötö-torony; Dóm tér), all that remains of a church erected here in the 12th century. At the northeastern end

of the square stands the **Serbian Orthodox church** (Görögkeleti Szerb ortodox templom; ☎424 246; Dóm tér; adult/child 400/300Ft; ☺8am-5pm), built in 1778. Take a peek inside at the fantastic iconostasis: a central gold 'tree', with 70 icons hanging from its 'branches'.

Back on Dóm tér, duck into the **Diocesan Museum & Treasury** (Egyházmegyei Múzeum és Kincstár; ☎420 932; www.museum.hu/szeged/egyhazmegyei; Dom tér 5; adult/concession 100/50Ft; ☺10am-6pm Apr-Oct, closed Mon) and wade through the collection of monstrances, chalices and other liturgical objects. Running along three sides of the square is the

Szeged

National Pantheon (Nemzeti Emlékcsarnok; admission free; ⊘24hr), with statues and reliefs of 70 Hungarian notables.

New Synagogue   SYNAGOGUE
(Új Zsinagóga; ☑423 849; www.zsinagoga.szeged.hu; Jósika utca 10; adult/concession 400/200Ft; ⊘10am-noon & 1-5pm Apr-Sep, 10am-2pm Oct-Mar, closed Sat) The art nouveau New Synagogue, which was designed by Lipót Baumhorn in 1903, is the most beautiful Jewish house of worship in Hungary and still in use, though the comunity has dwindled from 8000 before WWII to about 50 people. Dominating the enormous blue-and-gold interior is the cupola, decorated with stars and flowers and appearing to float skyward.

Reök Palace   ARCHITECTURE
(Reök Palota; ☑541 205; www.reok.hu; Tisza Lajos körút 56) The Reök Palace (1907) is a mind-blowing green and lilac art nouveau structure that looks like an aquarium decoration. It's been polished up to its original lustre and now hosts regular photography and visual-arts exhibitions.

Ferenc Móra Museum   MUSEUM
(☑549 040; www.mfm.u-szeged.hu; Roosevelt tér 1-3; adult/concession 900/600Ft; ⊘10am-6pm Tue, Wed & Fri-Sun, to 8pm Thu) The Palace of Education (1896) now houses this excellent museum containing a colourful collection of folk art from Csongrád County as well as traditional trades. After the 1879 flood claimed many of the walls of Szeged's riverfront castle, built around 1240, the city demolished the rest. For a closer look at the ancient subterranean walls, visit the nearby **Castle Museum & Lapidarium** (Varmuzéum

és kötár; ☑549 040; Stefánia sétány 15; adult/child 300/200Ft; ⊘10am-5pm, closed Mon).

Pick Salami & Szeged Paprika Museum   MUSEUM
(Pick szalámi és Szegedi paprika múzeum; ☑06 20 989 8000; www.pickmuzeum.hu; Felső Tisza-part 10; adult/child incl salami tasting & paprika sample 980/740Ft; ⊘3-6pm, closed Mon) Between the two bridges spanning the Tisza is this museum, with two floors of exhibits showing the methods of salami production and the cultivating, processing and packaging of Szeged's 'red gold'. It's a lot more interesting than you might think and you even get samples.

⊨ Sleeping

TOP CHOICE **Tisza Hotel**   HISTORIC HOTEL €€€
(☑478 278; www.tiszahotel.hu; Széchenyi tér 3; s/d classic 15,700/17,900Ft; superior 17,800/20,800Ft; ❋⊛) Szeged's fine old-world hotel drips with crystal chandeliers and gilt mirrors, but many of its 49 rooms don't match up to the public elegance. All in all, it's a lovely (if somewhat frayed) place with large, bright and airy rooms.

Dóm Hotel   BOUTIQUE HOTEL €€€
(☑423 750; www.domhotel.hu; Bajza utca 6; s/d/apt 26,500/30,500/47,000Ft; ❋@) A welcome addition to Szeged's top-end accommodation scene, this smart and extremely central 16-room hotel boasts a small wellness centre, popular in-house restaurant and multilingual staff for whom no request is too much.

Familia Panzió   GUESTHOUSE €€
(☑441 122; www.familiapanzio.hu; Szentháromság utca 71; s/d/tr from 7000/9500/14,000Ft; ❋⊛) Budget travellers book up this family-run

guesthouse, which has two-dozen contemporary (if nondescript) rooms in a great old building close to the train station.

New Szeged Bath & Camping
CAMPGROUND €

(Újszegedi partfürdő és kemping; ☑430 843; www.szegedcamping.hu; Középkikötő sor 1-3; campsites per person 990Ft plus per tent 390Ft; bungalows 8000-11,500Ft; ☉May-Sep; ☎⌨) The large grassy camping ground with sites for 700 on the Tisza River looks a bit like a public park. Bungalows on stilts are also available. Adjoining spa open May to September.

✗ Eating & Drinking

Vendéglő A Régi Hídhoz
HUNGARIAN €€

(☑420 910; www.regihid.hu; Oskola utca 4; mains 1400-2400Ft) For an authentic meal that won't break the bank head for 'At the Old Bridge', a traditional Hungarian restaurant with all the favourites and a lovely terrace just a block back from the river. Great place to try *Szögedi halászlé* (2000Ft), Szeged's famous fish soup.

Taj Mahal
INDIAN €€

(☑452 131; www.tajmahalszeged.hu; Gutenberg utca 12; mains 1540-2290Ft; ☑) If you get a hankering for a curry or a spot of tandoor, this pleasantly authentic subcontinental restaurant just metres from the New Synagogue is the place to come. Lots of vegetarian options too.

Boci Tejivó
FAST FOOD €

(☑423 154; www.bocitejivo.hu; Zrínyi utca 2; mains 260-500Ft; ☉24hr; ☑) This is a very modern take on an old-fashioned idea – the 'milk bar' so popular during socialist times. Order from among the dozens of meatless dishes – cheese and mushrooom omelettes, noodles with walnuts or poppyseed and anything with the ever-popular *túró* (curds), especially *túrógombóc* (curd dumplings; 590Ft).

A Cappella
CAFE

(☑559 966; Kárász utca 6; cakes 385-625Ft; ☉7am-9pm) This giant sidewalk cafe overlooking Klauzál tér has a generous choice of cakes and ice creams.

☆ Entertainment

As a university town Szeged boasts a vast array of bars, clubs and other nightspots. Nightclub programs are listed in the free *Szegedi Est* (www.szegediest.hu) magazine.

Szeged National Theatre
THEATRE

(Szegedi Nemzeti Színház; ☑479 279; www.szinhaz. szeged.hu; Deák Ferenc utca 12-14) This theatre,

where operas, ballet and classical concerts are staged, has been the centre of cultural life in Szeged since 1886.

Jazz Kocsma
LIVE MUSIC

(☑06 70 250 9279; jazzkocsma.blog.hu; Kálmány Lajos 14; ☉5pm-midnight Mon-Thu, to 2am Fri & Sat) Small, ever-popular music club that gets pretty crowded during the academic year for live music on Friday and Saturday nights.

Tisza Dokk
CLUB

(www.tiszadokk.hu; Arany János utca 1; ☉10am-1am Sun-Thu, to 5am Fri & Sat) This sophisticated bar-cum-dance-club on a dock on the Tisza attracts Szeged's beautiful people.

❶ Information

Main post office (Széchenyi tér 1)
OTP Bank (Klauzál tér 4)
Tourinform (☑488 690; http://tip.szeged-varos.hu; Dugonics tér 2; ☉9am-5pm Mon-Fri, to 1pm Sat) Exceptionally helpful office tucked away in a quiet courtyard near the university. There's a seasonal Tourinform booth (Széchenyi tér; ☉8am-8pm Mon-Fri, 9am-6pm Sat & Sun mid-Jun–mid-Sep) open in summer.

❶ Getting There & Around

The train station is south of the city centre on Indóház tér; from here, tram 1 or 2 will take you to the centre. The bus station is west of the centre in Mars tér and within easy walking distance via pedestrian Mikszáth Kálmán utca.

Buses run to Pécs (3410Ft, four hours, eight daily) and Debrecen (3950Ft, 4½ hours, up to three daily). Buses run to the Serbian city of Subotica (1200Ft, 1½ hours) up to four times daily.

Szeged is on the main rail line to Budapest's Nyugati train station (2420Ft, 2½ hours, hourly); trains also stop halfway along in Kecskemét (2100Ft, one hour). You have to change in Békéscsaba (1860Ft, two hours, half-hourly) to get to Arad in Romania.

NORTHEASTERN HUNGARY

If ever a Hungarian wine were worldfamous, it would be tokaj (or tokay). And this is where it comes from, a region of Hungary containing microclimates conducive to wine production. The chain of wooded hills in the northeast constitutes the foothills of the Carpathian Mountains, which stretch along the Hungarian border with Slovakia. Though you'll definitely notice the rise in elevation, Hungary's highest peak of Kékes is, at 1014m, still just a bump in the road. The highlights here are the wine towns of Eger and Tokaj.

Eger

📌 36 / POP 56,500

Filled with wonderfully preserved baroque buildings, Eger (*egg*-air) is a jewelbox of a town. Learn about the Turkish conquest and defeat at its hilltop castle, climb an original minaret, hear an organ performance at the massive basilica and, best of all, go from cellar to cellar in the Valley of Beautiful Women, tasting the celebrated Bull's Blood wine from the region where it's made.

It was at Eger in 1552 that the Hungarians fended off the Turks for the first time during the 170 years of occupation. The Turks came back in 1596 and this time captured the city, turning it into a provincial capital and erecting several mosques and other buildings, until they were driven out at the end of the 17th century. Eger played a central role in Ferenc Rákóczi II's attempt to overthrow the Habsburgs early in the 18th century and it was then that a large part of the castle was razed by the Austrians. Eger flourished in the 18th and 19th centuries, when the city acquired most of its wonderful baroque architecture.

👁 Sights & Activities

Eger Castle FORTRESS
(Egri Vár; www.egrivar.hu; Vár köz 1; castle grounds adult/child 800/400Ft, incl museum 1400/700Ft; ⏲exhibits 9am-5pm Tue-Sun Mar-Oct, 10am-4pm Tue-Sun Nov-Feb, castle grounds 8am-8pm May-Aug, to 7pm Apr & Sep, to 6pm Mar & Oct, to 5pm Nov-Feb) The best view of the city can be had by climbing up cobblestone Vár köz from Dózsa György tér to Eger Castle, erected in the 13th century. Models and drawings in the **István Dobó Museum**, housed in the former Bishop's Palace (1470), painlessly explain the history of the castle.

The 19th-century building on the northwestern side of the courtyard houses the **Eger Art Gallery**, with works by Canaletto and Ceruti. The terrace of the renovated **Dobó Bastion** (Dobó Bástya; adult/concession 500/250Ft), which dates back to 1549 but collapsed in 1976, offers stunning views of the town; it now hosts changing exhibits.

Beneath the castle are **casemates** (Kazamata) hewn from solid rock, which you may tour with a Hungarian-speaking guide included in the price (English-language guide 800Ft extra). Other attractions, including the **Panoptikum** (Waxworks; waxworks adult/concession 500/350Ft) and a **3D film** (admission 400-600Ft), cost extra.

Minaret ISLAMIC
(📌06 70 202 4353; Knézich Károly utca; admission 200Ft; ⏲10am-6pm Apr-Oct) This 40m-tall minaret, topped incongruously with a cross, is the only reminder of the Ottoman occupation of Eger. Nonclaustrophobes can brave the 97 narrow spiral steps to the top for the awesome views.

**Minorite Church of
St Anthony of Padua** CHURCH
(Páduai Szent Antal Minorita Templom; Dobó István tér 6; ⏲9am-5pm Tue-Sun) On the southern side of Eger's main square stands the Minorite church (1771), one of the most glorious baroque buildings in Hungary. In front of the church are statues of national hero István Dobó and his comrades-in-arms routing the Turks in 1552.

AS STRONG AS A BULL

The story of the Turkish attempt to take Eger Castle is the stuff of legend. Under the command of István Dobó, a mixed bag of 2000 soldiers held out against more than 100,000 Turks for a month in 1552. As every Hungarian kid in short trousers can tell you, the women of Eger played a crucial role in the battle, pouring boiling oil and pitch on the invaders from the ramparts.

Eger's wine also played a significant role. Apparently Dobó sustained his troops with a ruby-red local wine. When they fought on with increased vigour – and stained beards – rumours began to circulate among the Turks that the defenders were drinking the blood of bulls. The invaders departed, for the time being, and the name Bikavér (Bull's Blood) was born.

View the mockup of the siege in miniature in the castle museum or read Géza Gárdonyi's *Eclipse of the Crescent Moon* (1901), which describes the siege in thrilling detail.

Eger

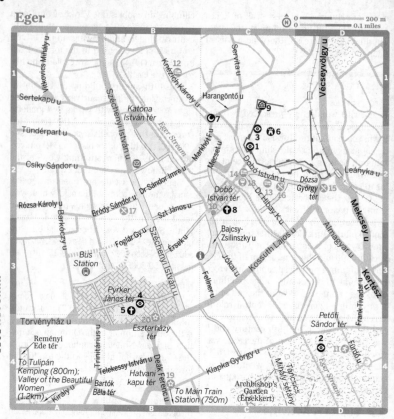

Eger Basilica
CHURCH

(Egri Bazilika; Pyrker János tér 1; ⏰7.30am-6pm Mon-Sat, from 1pm Sun) The first thing you see as you come into town from the bus or train station is the mustard-coloured neoclassical basilica, with its gigantic pillars built in 1836. Try to time your visit with one of the half-hour **organ concerts** (800Ft; ⏰11.30am Mon-Sat, 12.45pm Sun mid-May–mid-Oct). You can tour the caverns below the basilica to see the archbishop's enormous former wine cellar at the **City under the City** (Pyrker János tér, Város a Város Alat; adult/concession 950/500Ft; ⏰9am-7pm Apr-Sep, 10am-5pm Oct-Mar) exhibition.

Turkish Bath
SPA

(Török Fürdő; ☎510 552; www.egertermal.hu; Fürdő utca 3-4; 2½hr session adult/child 1900/1500Ft; ⏰4.30-9pm Mon & Tue, 3-9pm Wed-Fri, 9am-9pm Sat & Sun) A multimillion forint addition has added five pools, saunas, a steam room and a *hammam* (Turkish bath) to this historic spa dating back to 1617. Various kinds of massage and treatments are also available.

TOP CHOICE Valley of the Beautiful Women
WINE TASTING

(Szépasszony-völgy) Wine tasting is popular in the wine cellars of the evocatively named Valley of the Women. This is the place to sample Bull's Blood – one of very few reds produced in Eger – or any of the whites: Leányka, Olaszrizling and Hárslevelű, from nearby Debrő. The choice of wine cellars – there are two dozen – can be a bit daunting and their characters can change, so walk around and have a look yourself. But be careful: those 1dL (100Ft) glasses go down pretty fast. The valley is a little over 1km southwest across Rte 25 and off Király utca. Walk, or board the **City Eye Bus Tour** (☎06 20 457 7871; Dobó István tér; tour 700Ft; ⏰8am-6.30pm Apr-Oct) in season from the west side of Dobó István tér. A taxi costs about 1000Ft.

Eger

🛏 Sleeping

TOP CHOICE Hotel Senator Ház BOUTIQUE HOTEL €€

(Senator House; ☑411 711; www.senatorhaz.hu; Dobó István tér 11; s/d €50/70; ☀) Some 11 warm and cosy rooms with traditional white furnishings fill the upper floors of this delightful 18th-century inn on Eger's main square. The ground floor is shared between a quality restaurant and a reception area stuffed with antiques and curios.

Dobó Vendéghaz HOTEL €€

(☑421 407; www.vendeghaz.hu; Dobó István utca 19; s/d 9000/13,500Ft; ☎) Tucked away along one of the old town's pedestrian streets just below the castle, this lovely little hotel has seven spick-and-span rooms, some with little balconies.

Agria Retur Panzió GUESTHOUSE €

(☑416 650; http://agria.returvendeghaz.hu; Knézich Károly utca 18; s/d 3800/6400Ft; @☎) Walking up three flights of steps to this charming guesthouse near the Minaret, you enter a cheery communal kitchen/eating area central to four rooms. Out back is a huge garden with a barbecue at your disposal.

Tulipán Kemping CAMPGROUND €

(☑311 542; www.tulipancamping.com; Szépasszonyvölgy utca 71; campsites per person/tent/caravan 800/900/1600Ft, bungalows d/q 5000/6000Ft) Surrounded by vineyards, Tulipán Kemping is stumbling distance from the wine cellars of the Valley of the Beautiful Women. Bungalows are cabins, with no bath or kitchen.

🍴 Eating & Drinking

Lining the entry path to the Valley of the Beautiful Women are 10 food-stand eateries, with waiters that come to your covered picnic table with menus to point at (mains 850Ft to 1400Ft). There are also several *csárdák* (Hungarian-style inns) among the wine cellars to choose from.

TOP CHOICE Imola Udvarház Borétterem HUNGARIAN €€

(☑516 180; www.imolaudvarhaz.hu; Dósza György tér 4; mains 1930-3970Ft) With its inventive menu and excellent wine list, this very stylish eatery at the foot of the castle has been named among the top dozen restaurants in Hungary. We'll come back in particular for the ever-changing four-course tasting menu (4570Ft).

Palacsintavár CREPERIE €

(Pancake Castle; ☑413 986; www.palacsintavar.hu; Dobó István utca 9, enter from Fazola Henrik utca; mains 1490-1820Ft) Savoury *palacsinták* – pancakes, for want of a better word – are served at this eclectic eatery, with an abundance of fresh vegetables. Flavours range from Asian to Italian and there's a large choice of sweet ones too.

Szántófer Vendéglő HUNGARIAN €€

(Plough; ☑517 298; www.szantofer.hu; Bródy Sándor utca 3; mains 1700-2400Ft) Choose the 'Plough' for hearty, home-style Hungarian fare. A covered courtyard out back is perfect for escaping the summer heat.

HUNGARY EGER

Bikavér Borház

WINE BAR

(☎413 262; Dobó István tér 10; ⏱9am-10pm) Try one or two of the region's wines at this central wine bar. The waiters can guide you through their selection, and bring along a plate of cheese or grapes to help you cleanse your palate.

☆ Entertainment

The Tourinform office can tell you what concerts and musicals are on. The free Egri Est (www.est.hu) magazine has nightlife listings.

Géza Gárdonyi Theatre

THEATRE

(Gárdonyi Géza Színház; ☎510 700; www.gardony-iszinhaz.hu; Hatvani kapu tér 4) Dance, opera and drama are staged at the town's theatre, due south of the basilica.

Gödör Kult Klub

CLUB

(Pyrker János tér 3; ⏱10pm-6am Wed, Fri & Sat) This bizarre cavelike DJ dance club, beneath the cathedral steps, parties hard on weekends.

❶ Information

OTP Bank (Széchenyi István utca 2)

Post office (Széchenyi István utca 22)

Tourinform (☎517 715; http://mheger.hu; Bajcsy-Zsilinszky utca 9; ⏱9am-6pm Mon-Fri, to 1pm Sat & Sun mid-Jun–mid-Sep, 9am-5pm Mon-Fri, to 1pm Sat mid-Sep–mid-Jun) Covers Eger and surrounding areas.

❶ Getting There & Away

BUS The bus station is west of Széchenyi István utca, near Pyrker János tér. From Eger, buses serve Kecskemét (3130Ft, 4½ hours, three daily) and Szeged (3950Ft, 5¾ hours, two daily). To get to Tokaj by bus, you have to go to Nyíregy-háza (2520Ft, three hours, two daily) and catch another bus back.

TRAIN The main train station is on Vasút utca, south of the **Archbishop's Garden** (Érsek-kert; enter from Petőfi Sándor tér 2). To reach the city centre, walk north on Deák Ferenc utca and then head along pedestrian Széchenyi István utca.

Up to seven direct trains a day head to Budapest's Keleti train station (2830Ft, three hours). Otherwise, Eger is on a minor train line linking Putnok and Füzesabony, so you have to change at the latter for Debrecen (2230Ft, 2¾ hours).

Tokaj

☎47 / POP 4900

The world-renowned sweet wines of Tokaj (toke-eye) have been produced here since the 15th century. Today Tokaj is a pictur-esque little town of old buildings, nesting storks and wine cellars, offering plenty of opportunity to sample its famous tipple. And lying at the confluence of the Bodrog and Tisza Rivers there are ample options for recreation too.

◉ Sights & Activities

Wine Tasting

WINE TASTING

Pincék (private cellars) and restaurants for wine tastings are scattered throughout Tokaj. The correct order is to move from dry to sweet: very dry Furmint, dry Szamorodni, sweet Szamorodni and then the honey-sweet Aszú wines. A basic flight of six Tokaj wines costs 2600Ft to 3200Ft; an all-Aszú tasting can run between 4200Ft and 6000Ft.

The granddaddy of tasting places is the 600-year-old **Rákóczi Cellar** (Rákóczi Pince; ☎352 408; www.rakoczipince.hu; Kossuth tér 15; ⏱11am-6pm), where bottles of wine mature in long corridors. **Erzsébet Cellar** (☎06 20 802 0137; www.erzsebetpince.hu; Bem utca 16; ⏱10am-6pm, by appointment) is a smaller, family-run affair that usually needs to be booked ahead. The most friendly of all is **Hímesudvar** (☎352 416; www.himesudvar.hu; Bem utca 2; ⏱10am-6pm), with an atmospheric 16th-century cellar and shop northwest of the town centre.

Tokaj Museum

MUSEUM

(Tokaji Múzeum; ☎352 636; www.tokaj.hu/tokaj/culture/museum/index; Bethlen Gábor utca 7; adult/concession 600/300Ft; ⏱10am-4pm Tue-Sun) The Tokay Museum, in an 18th-century mansion built by Greek wine traders, leaves nothing unsaid about the history of Tokaj and the production of its wines. There's also a superb collection of Christian liturgical art and Judaica from the 19th-century **Great Synagogue** (Nagy Zsinagóga; ☎552 000; Serház utca 55) just around the corner, which was used as a German barracks during WWII but is once again gleaming after a total renovation.

🛏 Sleeping & Eating

Huli-Bodrog Panzió

GUESTHOUSE €

(☎06 20 465 5903; www.hulipanzio.hu; Rákóczi út 16; s 4000-5000Ft, d 8000Ft; ❄🔊) The 19 down-to-earth rooms spread across the 1st floor of a popular counter-service restaurant aren't huge and decor is basic, but there are small fridges and the possibility of air-con (1500Ft).

Vaskó Panzió GUESTHOUSE €

(☏352 107; http://vaskopanzio.hu; Rákóczi út 12; r 8000Ft; 🏵🌐) The very central Vaskó has 11 tidy rooms with window sills bedecked with flower pots. It's above a private wine cellar, and the proprietor can organise tastings.

Vízisport Turisztaház HOSTEL €

(☏06 20 971 6564, 552 187; www.tokaj-info.hu; Horgász utca 3; campsites/dm 1000/2000Ft; @) Three- to four-bed rooms share a bathroom at this bare-bones hostel (beds only, no kitchen or common room) across the river from the centre. It rents out bikes, canoes and kayaks and organise canoe trips too.

Toldi Fogadó HUNGARIAN €€

(☏353 403; www.toldifogado.hu; Hajdú köz 2; mains 1650-2590Ft; 🍴) Lovely restaurant offering quasi-fine dining down a small *köz* (lane) off the main drag, Toldi excels at fish dishes (try the catfish) but also has some excellent duck dishes (duck leg with *lecsó*, a kind of ratatouille) and a generous selection of vegetarian mains.

Fakapu HUNGARIAN €

(Wooden Gate; ☏06 20 972 6307; Rákóczi út 27; mains 1200-1850Ft) Enter the 'Wooden Gate' through its impressive, well, wooden gate and you'll find a cute wine restaurant that offers simple Hungarian soups, stews and plates of smoked meats.

ℹ Information

OTP Bank (Rákóczi Ferenc út 35)

Post office (Rákóczi Ferenc út 24)

Tourinform (☏950 603; www.tokaj-turizmus. hu; Serház utca 1; ⊙9am-5pm Mon-Sat, 10am-3pm Sun Jun-Aug, 9am-4pm Mon-Fri Sep-May) Just off Rákóczi út. Hands out a useful booklet of wine cellars in the area and rents out bikes (2000/2400Ft per half-/full day).

ℹ Getting There & Away

BUS Buses arrive and depart from stops outside Serház utca 38, east of Kossuth tér. No direct buses link Tokaj with Budapest or Eger, though you can reach Debrecen (1680Ft, two hours) on two buses a day.

TRAIN Trains arrive 1.2km south of the town centre; from there, walk north on Baross Gábor utca and turn left on Bajcsy-Zsilinszky út, which turns into Rákóczi út, the main thoroughfare. Up to 16 trains a day head west to Budapest Keleti station (3950Ft, 2¾ hours) and east to Debrecen (2250Ft, 1¾ hours).

Debrecen

☏52 / POP 208,000

Debrecen (*deb*-re-tsen) is Hungary's second-largest city and its name has been synonymous with wealth and conservatism since the 16th century. Flanked by the golden Great Church and the historic Aranybika Hotel, Debrecen's central square sets the rather subdued tone for this city.

During summer frequent street festivals fill the pedestrian core with revellers, but old-town bars and nightclubs create a lively scene for night crawlers on weekends year-round. Debrecen's array of museums and thermal baths will keep you busy for a couple of days. The **Flower Carnival** (www.iranydebrecen.hu/ info/flower-carnival) in mid-August is the event of the year.

The area around Debrecen has been settled for centuries. The city's wealth, based on salt, the fur trade and cattle-raising, grew steadily through the Middle Ages and increased during the Turkish occupation. Debrecen played a pivotal role in the 1848 nationalist revolt and it experienced a major building boom in the late 19th and early 20th centuries.

⊙ Sights & Activities

Great Church CHURCH

(Nagytemplom; ☏412 694; http://nagytemplom.hu; Paic tér 4-6; adult/concession 350/250Ft; ⊙9am-6pm Mon-Fri, to 2pm Sat, 10am-4pm Sun Apr-Oct, 10am-1pm daily Nov-Mar) Built in 1822, the iconic Great Church accommodates 3000 people and is Hungary's largest Protestant house of worship. The nave is rather austere apart from the magnificent organ; climb the 210 steps to the top of the west clock tower for grand views over the city.

Déri Museum MUSEUM

(☏322 207; www.derimuz.hu; Déri tér 1; adult/child 500/300Ft; ⊙10am-6pm Apr-Oct, to 4pm Nov-Mar, closed Mon) Folklore exhibits at the Déri Museum, a short walk northwest of the Great Church, offer excellent insights into life on the plain and the bourgeois citizens of Debrecen up to the 19th century. Mihály Munkácsy's mythical artistic interpretations of the Hortobágy and his *Christ's Passion* trilogy usually take pride of place in a separate art gallery.

Aquaticum Debrecen SPA

(☏514 174; www.aquaticum.hu; Nagyerdei Park; adult/concession 2350/1900Ft; ⊙11am-9pm Mon-Thu, 10am-9pm Fri-Sun) The main attraction in

Nagyerdei, a park 5km north of the centre, is Aquaticum, a complex of 'Mediterranean Enjoyment Baths' offering all manner of slides and waterfalls, spouts and grottoes within its pools. Rammed in summer.

🛏 Sleeping

TOP CHOICE Centrum Panzió
GUESTHOUSE €

(☑442 843; www.panziocentrum.hu; Péterfia utca 37/a; s/d 6500/8500Ft; ❈@🅿🛜) A bit north of centre but every bit worth the extra half-kilometre, the Centrum looks a little like your grandmother's house, with flowery odds and ends. Some of the two-dozen large rooms (eg room 15) are in the back, facing a long garden that seems to go on forever. All have a minifridge and microwave. Bike rental is available.

Aranybika
HOTEL €€

(☑508 600; www.hotelaranybika.com; Piac utca 11-15; s €46-88, d €56-106; ❈🛜🅿🏊) This landmark art nouveau hotel has been *the* place to stay in Debrecen since 1915 but, alas, standards have fallen. Many of the 205 rooms retain their drab carpets and plain, proletarian furnishings of a different era. Superior rooms have a bit more space than standard, though, as well as antique reproduction furniture.

Stop Panzió
GUESTHOUSE €

(☑420 302; www.stop.at.tf; Batthyányi utca 18; s/d/tr 6900/8900/11,900Ft; 🛜) The dozen renovated rooms here fill up because they're the right price for the right location – in a courtyard off a cafe-filled pedestrian street.

György Maróthi College
HOSTEL €

(Maróthi György Kollégium; ☑502 780; www.marothi kollegium.hu/; Blaháné utca 15; s/d 4130/6490Ft, without bathroom 2655/4550Ft; @) Just off the main pedestrian lanes, this central dormitory has fairly basic rooms, and bathroom facilities are shared. There's a kitchen on each floor.

🍴 Eating & Drinking

TOP CHOICE Ikon
INTERNATIONAL €€€

(☑06 30 555 7766; www.ikonrestaurant.hu; Piac utca 23; mains 2900-6900Ft) Ikon comands a prominent position on the main square, but despite the postmodern decor and classily clad wait staff, is discreet and very upscale. The inventive dishes are some of the best in town.

Trattoria Trinacria
ITALIAN €€

(☑416 988; http://dvklub.wix.com/trinacria; Batthyány utca 4; mains 1500-3500Ft) Charming Italian terrace eatery on a pedestrian side street. Serves well-prepared pasta dishes, including homemade ravioli, as well as very good wood-fired pizzas.

Csokonai Söröző
HUNGARIAN €€

(☑410 802; http://www.csokonaisorozo.hu/eng; Kossuth utca 21; mains 1850-3490Ft) Medieval decor, sharp service and excellent Hungarian specialities all help to create one of Debrecen's most-recommended eating experiences. This cellar pub-restaurant also serves pasta and (go figure) Mexican dishes like *fajitas*.

Eve's Cofe & Lounge
CAFE €

(☑322 222; http://hovamenjek.hu/debrecen/eve-s-cofe-lounge; Simonffy utca 1/b; sandwiches 800-1000Ft; ⊙8am-midnight Mon-Thu, 8am-1am Fri & Sat, 9am-10pm Sun) Pleasantly upscale cafe (that's what we think 'cofe' means) that serves breakfasts as well as very good sandwiches and salads throughout the day.

🍷 Drinking & Entertainment

Pick up a copy of the biweekly entertainment freebie Debreceni Est (www.debreceniest.hu) for music listings. For bars and late-night cafes, check out Simonffy utca. For clubs, most of the action is along Bajcy-Zsilinszky.

B4 Gösser
BAR

(☑06 70 943 7752; http://b4gosser.hu; Kálvin tér 4; ⊙10am-2am Sun-Thu, to 4am Fri & Sat) Tucked away in a courtyard just far enough east of the Great Church so as not to disturb the faithful, this pub/club/jazz bar is party central at the weekend.

Cool Music & Dance Club
CLUB

(Bajcsy-Zsilinszky utca 1-3; cover charge 500-800Ft; ⊙11pm-5am Mon, Fri & Sat) DJs spin house and techno tunes here most weekends; Fridays (and sometimes Mondays) see frequent theme parties.

Csokonai Theatre
THEATRE

(☑455 075; www.csokonaiszinhaz.hu; Kossuth utca 10) Three-tier gilt balconies, ornate ceiling frescos and elaborate chandeliers: the Csokonai is everything a 19th-century theatre should be. Musicals and operas are staged here.

ℹ Information

Main post office (Hatvan utca 5-9)

OTP Bank (Piac utca 45)

Tourinform (☑412 250; www.iranydebrecen. hu; Piac utca 20; ⊙9am-5pm year-round plus

9am-1pm Sat Jun-Sep) Helpful office in the central town hall. There's also a Tourinform **kiosk** (Kossuth tér; ☺10am-8pm Thu-Sun Jun-Sep) open in summer.

ℹ Getting There & Away

BUS The bus station is at the western end of Széchenyi utca. Buses are quickest if you're going directly to Eger (2520Ft, 2½ hours, six daily) or Szeged (3950Ft, 4½ hours, three daily).

TRAIN The train station is to the south on Petőfi tér; reach the centre by following Piac utca, which runs northward to Kálvin tér, site of the Great Church. Frequently departing trains will get you to Budapest (3950Ft, 3¼ hours) and Tokaj (2250Ft, 1¼ hours). The night train from Budapest to Moscow stops here at about 9.30pm.

UNDERSTAND HUNGARY

History

Hungary before the Magyars

The plains of the Carpathian Basin attracted waves of migration, from both east and west, long before the Magyar tribes settled here. The Celts occupied the area at the start of the 4th century BC, but the Romans conquered and expelled them just before the start of the Christian era. The lands west of the Danube (Transdanubia in today's Hungary) became part of the Roman province of Pannonia, where a Roman legion was stationed at the town of Aquincum (now Óbuda). The Romans brought writing, planted the first vineyards and built baths near some of the region's many thermal springs.

A new surge of nomadic tribespeople, the Huns, arrived on the scene in the 5th century AD led by a man who would become legendary in Hungarian history. By AD 441, Attila had conquered the Romans and his army acquired a reputation as great warriors. Many Hungarian boys and men bear the name Attila, even though the Huns have no connection with present-day Hungarians and the Huns' short-lived empire did not outlast Attila's death in AD 453.

Many tribes, including the Goths, the Longobards and the Avars – a powerful Turkic people who controlled parts of the area from the 5th to the 8th centuries – filled the vacuum left by the Huns and settled in the area. The Avars were subdued by Charlemagne in 796, leaving space for the Franks and Slavs to move in.

The Conquest

The Magyars, ancestors of modern-day Hungarians, are said to have moved into the Carpathian Basin at the very end of the 9th century. Legend has it that it was the *gyula* (supreme military commander) Árpád who led the alliance of seven tribes. The Magyars, a fierce warrior tribe, terrorised much of Europe with raids reaching as far as Spain and southern Italy. They were stopped at the Battle of Augsburg in 955 and subsequently converted to Christianity. Hungary's first king and its patron saint, Stephen (István), was crowned on Christmas Day in 1000, marking the foundation of the Hungarian state.

Medieval Hungary

Medieval Hungary was a powerful kingdom that included Transylvania (now in Romania), Transcarpathia (now in Ukraine), modern-day Slovakia and Croatia. Under King Matthias Corvinus (1458–90), Hungary experienced a brief flowering of Renaissance culture. However, in 1526 the Ottomans defeated the Hungarian army at Mohács in southern Hungary and by 1541 Buda Castle had been seized and Hungary sliced in three. The central part, including Buda, was controlled by the Ottomans, while Transdanubia, present-day Slovakia and parts of Transcarpathia were ruled by Hungarian nobility based in Pozsony (Bratislava) under the auspices of the Austrian House of Habsburg. The principality of Transylvania, east of the Tisza, prospered as a vassal state of the Ottoman Empire.

Habsburg Hegemony & War

After the Ottomans were evicted from Buda in 1686, the Habsburg domination of Hungary began. The 'enlightened absolutism' of the Habsburg monarchs Maria Theresa (r 1740–80) and her son Joseph II (r 1780–90) helped the country leap forward economically and culturally. Rumblings of Hungarian independence surfaced now and again, but it was the unsuccessful 1848 Hungarian revolution that really started to shake the Habsburg oligarchy. After Austria was defeated in war by France and then Prussia in 1859 and 1866, a weakened empire struck a compromise with Hungary in 1867, creating a dual monarchy. The two states would be self-governing in domestic affairs, but act jointly in matters of common interest, such as foreign relations. The Austro-Hungarian monarchy lasted until WWI.

After WWI and the collapse of the Habsburg Empire in November 1918, Hungary was proclaimed a republic. But Hungary had been on the losing side of the war; the 1920 Treaty of Trianon stripped the country of more than two-thirds of its territory – a hot topic of conversation to this very day.

In 1941 Hungary's attempts to recover lost territories saw the nation go to war on the side of Nazi Germany. When leftists tried to negotiate a separate peace in 1944, the Germans occupied Hungary and brought the fascist Arrow Cross Party to power. The Arrow Cross immediately began deporting hundreds of thousands of Jews to Auschwitz. By early April 1945 Hungary was defeated and occupied by the Soviet army.

Communism

By 1947 the communists assumed complete control of the government and began nationalising industry and dividing up large estates among the peasantry. On 23 October 1956, student demonstrators demanding the withdrawal of Soviet troops from Hungary were fired upon. The next day Imre Nagy, the reformist minister of agriculture, was named prime minister. On 28 October Nagy's government offered an amnesty to all those involved in the violence, promising to abolish the hated secret police, the ÁVH (known as ÁVO until 1949), and proclaim Hungary nonaligned. On 4 November Soviet tanks moved into Budapest, crushing the uprising. By the time the fighting ended on 11 November, thousands had been killed. Then the reprisals began: an estimated 20,000 people were arrested and 2000 executed, including Nagy. Another 250,000 fled to Austria.

After the revolt, the ruling party was reorganised as the Hungarian Socialist Workers' Party, which began a program to liberalise the social and economic structure, basing the

reforms on compromise. By the 1970s Hungary had abandoned strict central economic control altogether in favour of a limited market system, often referred to as 'Goulash Communism'. In June 1987 Károly Grósz took over as premier and Hungary began moving towards full democracy. The huge number of East Germans who were able to slip through the Iron Curtain by leaving via Hungary was a major catalyst for the fall of the Berlin Wall in 1989.

The Republic

At their party congress in February 1989 the communists agreed to surrender their monopoly on power. The Republic of Hungary was proclaimed in October and democratic elections were scheduled for March 1990. Hungary changed its political system with scarcely a murmur and the last Soviet troops left the country in June 1991.

The painful transition to a full market economy resulted in declining living standards for most people and a recession in the early 1990s, but the early years of the 21st century saw astonishing growth. Hungary became a member of NATO in 1999 and joined the European Union (EU) in 2004.

Late in 2008, reeling from the fallout of the global financial crisis, Hungary was forced to approach the International Monetary Fund for economic assistance. Economic woes have plagued the nation ever since, but an even bigger concern to many Hungarians is the rise of the far-right Jobbik party, which garnered over 16% of the vote in the national elections of 2010.

Hungary's most recent appearance on the world stage came in 2011 when it assumed presidency of the EU Council. A new constitution went into effect at the start of 2012.

People

Just over 10 million people live within the national borders, and another five million Hungarians and their descendants are abroad. The estimated 1.44 million Hungarians in Transylvania constitute the largest ethnic minority in Europe and there are another 293,000 in Serbia, 520,500 in Slovakia, 156,600 in Ukraine, 40,500 in Austria, 16,500 in Croatia and 6250 in Slovenia.

Ethnic Magyars make up approximately 92% of the population. Many minority groups estimate their numbers to be significantly higher than official counts. There

---

HABITS & CUSTOMS

The Magyar are an especially polite people and their language is filled with courtesies. To toast someone's health before drinking, say *egéségére* (*egg-eh-sheg-eh-ray*), and to wish them a 'bon appetit' before eating, *jo étvágyat* (*yo* ate-vad-yaht). If you're invited to someone's home, always bring a bunch of flowers or a bottle of good local wine.

are 13 recognised minorities in the country, including Germans (2.6%), Serbs and other South Slavs (2%), Slovaks (0.8%) and Romanians (0.7%). The number of Roma is officially put at 1.9% of the population – just under 200,000 people – some sources place the figure as high as 4% (800,000).

Of those Hungarians declaring religious affiliation, just under 52% are Roman Catholic, 16% Reformed (Calvinist) Protestant, 3% Evangelical (Lutheran) Protestant, and 2.7% Greek Catholic and Orthodox. Hungary's Jewish people number around 80,000, down from a pre-WWII population of nearly 10 times that.

Arts

The history of Hungarian highbrow culture includes world-renowned composers such as Béla Bartók and Franz Liszt, and the Nobel Prize-winning writer Imre Kértesz. Hungary's insatiable appetite for music and dance means that opera, symphony and ballet are high on the entertainment agenda and even provincial towns have decent companies.

For the more contemporary branches of artistic life Budapest is the focus, containing many art galleries, theatre and dance companies. The capital is also a centre for folk music and dance, which have got a new lease of life in recent years.

Literature

Hungary has some excellent writers, both of poetry and prose. Sándor Petőfi (1823–49) is Hungary's most celebrated poet. A line from his work *National Song* became the rallying cry for the 1848 War of Independence, in which he fought and died.

Contemporary Hungarian writers whose work has been translated into English and are worth a read include Péter Esterházy and Sándor Márai. The most celebrated Hungarian writer is the 2002 Nobel Prize winner Imre Kertész. Among his novels available in English are *Fateless* (1975) and *Kaddish for an Unborn Child* (1990). Hungary's most prominent contemporary female writer, who died in 2007 at age 90, was Magda Szabó (*Katalin Street*, 1969; *The Door*, 1975).

Making a big splash in literary circles both at home and abroad these days is László Krasznahorka (1954-), whose demanding postmodernist novels (*Satantango*, 1985; *The Melancholy of Resistance*, 1988) are called 'forbidding', even in Hungarian.

Classical & Traditional Music

Hungary's most influential musician was composer Franz (Ferenc) Liszt (1811–86). The eccentric Liszt described himself as 'part Gypsy' and in his *Hungarian Rhapsodies*, as well as in other works, he does indeed weave motifs of the Roma people into his compositions.

Ferenc Erkel (1810–93) is the father of Hungarian opera and his stirringly nationalist *Bánk Bán* is a standard at the Hungarian State Opera House in Budapest. Béla Bartók (1881–1945) and Zoltán Kodály (1882–1967) made the first systematic study of Hungarian folk music; both integrated some of their findings into their compositions.

Hungarian folk musicians play violins, zithers, hurdy-gurdies, bagpipes and lutes on a five-tone diatonic scale. Look out for Muzsikás, Marta Sebestyén, Ghymes (a Hungarian folk band from Slovakia) and the Hungarian group Vujicsics, which mixes in elements of southern Slav music. Another folk musician with eclectic tastes is the Paris-trained Bea Pálya, who combines such sounds as traditional Bulgarian and Indian music with Hungarian folk.

Romani music – as opposed to the schmaltzy Gypsy fare played at touristy restaurants – has become fashionable among the young, with Romani bands playing 'the real thing' in trendy bars till the wee hours: it's a dynamic, hopping mix of fiddles, bass and cymbalom (a stringed instrument played with sticks). A Romani band would never be seen without the tin milk bottle used as a drum, which gives Hungarian Romani music its characteristic sound. Some modern Romani music groups – Kalyi Jag (Black Fire) from northeastern Hungary, Romano Drom (Gypsy Road) and Romani Rota (Gypsy Wheels) – have added guitars, percussion and even electronics to create a whole new sound.

Klezmer (traditional Eastern European Jewish music) has also made a comeback in playlists recently.

Pop music is as popular here as anywhere. Indeed, Hungary has one of Europe's biggest pop spectacles – the annual Sziget Music Festival (p307). It has more than 1000 performances over a week and attracts an audience of up to 400,000 people.

Visual Arts

Favourite painters from the 19th century include realist Mihály Munkácsy (1844–1900), the so-called painter of the *puszta* (Great Plain) and the Symbolist Tivadar Kosztka

Csontváry (1853–1919). Győző Vásárhelyi (1908–97), who changed his name to Victor Vasarely when he emigrated to Paris, is considered the 'father of op art'. Probably the most successful Hunagarian painter in history was the beloved József Rippl-Rónai (1861–1927).

In the 19th and early 20th centuries, the Zsolnay family created world-renowned decorative art in porcelain. Ceramic artist Margit Kovács (1902–77) produced a large number of statues and ceramic objects during her career. The traditional embroidery, weavings and ceramics of the nation's *népművészet* (folk art) endure, and there is usually at least one handicraft store in every town.

Environment

The Landscape

Hungary occupies the Carpathian Basin to the southwest of the Carpathian Mountains. Water dominates much of the country's geography. The Danube (Duna) River divides the Great Plain (Nagyalföld) in the east from Transdanubia (Dunántúl) in the west. The Tisza (596km in Hungary) is the country's longest river and historically has been prone to flooding. Hungary has hundreds of small lakes and is riddled with thermal springs. Lake Balaton (596 sq km), in the west, is the largest freshwater lake in Europe outside Scandinavia. Hungary's 'mountains' to the north are really hills, with the country's highest peak being Kékes (1014m) in the Mátra range.

Wildlife

There are a lot of common European animals in Hungary (deer, hares, wild boar and foxes), as well as some rare species (wild cat, lake bat and Pannonian lizard), but most of the country's wildlife comes from the avian family. Around 75% of the country's 480 known vertebrates are birds, for the most part waterfowl attracted by the rivers, lakes and wetlands. Some rare species include the saker falcon, eastern imperial eagle, great bustard and black stork.

National Parks

There are 10 *nemzeti park* (national parks) in Hungary. Bükk, north of Eger, is a mountainous limestone area of forest and caves. Kiskunság National Park (p333), near Kecskemét, and Hortobágy, outside Debrecen, protect the unique grassland environment of the plains.

Food & Drink

Hungary enjoys perhaps the most varied and interesting cuisine in all of Eastern Europe.

Hungarian Cuisine

The omnipresent seasoning in Hungarian cooking is paprika, a mild red pepper that appears on restaurant tables as a condiment beside the salt and black pepper, as well as in many recipes. *Pörkölt*, a paprika-infused stew, can be made from different meats, especially *borjúhús* (veal), and usually has no vegetables. *Galuska* (small, gnocchilike dumplings) are a good accompaniment to soak up the sauce. The well-known *csirke paprikás* (chicken paprika) is stewed chicken in a tomato, cream and paprika sauce. *Töltött káposzta/paprika* (cabbage/peppers stuffed with meat and rice) is cooked in a roux made with paprika, and topped with sour cream. Another local favourite is *halászlé* (fisherman's soup), a rich mix of several kinds of poached freshwater fish, tomatoes, green peppers and (you guessed it) paprika.

Leves (soup) is the start to any main meal in a Hungarian home. *Gulyás* (goulash), although served as a stew outside Hungary, is a soup here, cooked with beef, onions and tomatoes. Traditional cooking methods are far from health-conscious, but they are tasty. Frying is a nationwide obsession and you'll often find breaded and fried turkey, pork and veal schnitzels on the menu.

For dessert you might try *palincsinta* (crêpes filled with jam, sweet cheese or chocolate sauce). A good food-stand snack is *lángos,* fried dough that can be topped with cheese and/or *tejföl* (sour cream).

Vegetarians & Vegans

Traditional Hungarian cuisine and vegetarianism are definitely not a match made in heaven. However, things are changing and there are places even in the provinces that serve good vegetarian dishes or even full meals. Where there are no vegetarian restaurants, you'll have to make do with what's on the regular menu or shop for ingredients in the markets.

Cold *gyümölcs leves* (fruit soup) made with sour cherries and other berries is a summertime mainstay. Some not very light but widely available dishes for vegetarians to look for are *rántott sajt* (fried cheese), *gombafejek rántva* (fried mushroom caps), *gomba leves* (mushroom soup) and *túrós csusza* (short, wide pasta with cheese). Note, *bableves* (bean soup) almost always contains meat.

Where to Eat & Drink

An *étterem* is a restaurant with a large selection and formal service. A *vendéglő* is smaller and more casual, and serves home-style regional dishes. The overused term *csárda*, which originally meant a rustic country inn with Roma music, can now mean anything – including 'tourist trap'. To keep prices down, look for *étkezde* (a tiny eating place that may have a counter or sit-down service), *önkiszolgáló* (a self-service canteen), *grill* (which generally serves gyros or kebabs and other grilled meats from the counter) or a *szendvics bár* (which has open-faced sandwiches to go).

Wine has been produced in Hungary for hundreds of years and you'll find it available by the glass or bottle everywhere. There are plenty of pseudo-British/Irish/Belgian pubs, smoky *sörözők* (Hungarian pubs, often in a cellar, where drinking is taken very seriously), *borozók* (wine bars, usually dives) and nightclubs, but the most pleasant place to enjoy a cocktail or coffee may be in a cafe. A *kávéház* may primarily be an old-world dessert shop, or it may be a bar with an extensive drinks menu; either way they sell alcoholic beverages in addition to coffee. In spring, tables sprout up along the pavement.

SURVIVAL GUIDE

Directory A–Z

Accommodation

Hungary has a wide variety of accommodation options, ranging from hostels and camping grounds at the budget level, private rooms and guesthouses or *panziók* (pensions) at midrange, and hotels and luxury boutiques at the top end. The high season for lodging typically runs from April to October and over the Christmas and New Year holidays, and prices are highest in Budapest. We define price ranges for a double with private bathroom as the following:

€ less than 9000Ft/€30 (15,000Ft/€50 in Budapest)

€€ 9000Ft/€30 to 16,5000Ft/€55 (15,000Ft/€50 to 33,500Ft/€110 in Budapest)

€€€ more than 16,500Ft/€55 (33,500Ft/€110 in Budapest)

Prices in shops and restaurants in Hungary are uniformly quoted in forint, but many hotels and guesthouses and even MÁV, the national rail company, give their rates in euros. In such cases, we have followed suit and you can usually pay in either euros or forint.

Hungary's camping grounds are listed in Tourinform's *Camping Hungary* map and brochure; also try the website of the **Hungarian Camping Association** (MKSZ; www.camping.hu). Facilities are generally open April or May to September or October and can sometimes be difficult to reach without a car.

The **Hungarian Youth Hostels Association** (MISZSZ; www.miszsz.hu) keeps a list of official year-round hostels throughout Hungary. In general, these hostels have a communal kitchen, laundry and internet service, and sometimes a lounge; a basic bread-and-jam breakfast may be included. Having an HI card is not required anywhere, but it may get you a 10% discount.

From July to August, students throughout Hungary vacate college and university dorms, and the administration opens them to travellers. Facilities are usually – but not always – pretty basic and shared. We list them under Sleeping; the local Tourinform office can help you find such places.

Renting a private room in a Hungarian home is a good budget option and can be a great opportunity to get up close and personal with the culture. Prices outside Budapest run from 4000Ft to 6500Ft per person per night. Tourinform offices can usually help with finding these too. Otherwise look for houses with signs reading *szoba kiadó* or *Zimmer frei* ('room available' in Hungarian and German) .

An engaging alternative is to stay in a rural village or farmhouse, but only if you have wheels: most of these places are truly remote. Contact **Tourinform** (from abroad 36 1 438 80 80, within Hungary 800 36 000 000; www.tourinform.hu), the **Association of Hungarian Rural & Agrotourism** (FATOSZ; Map p304; 1-352 9804; www.fatozs.eu; VII Király utca 93; 73, 76) or the **Centre of Rural Tourism** (1-321 2426; www.falutur.hu; VII Dohány utca 86) in Budapest.

Activities

CANOEING

For canoeists, Ecotours leads week-long Danube River canoe and camping trips (tent rental and food extra) for about €500, as well as shorter Danube Bend and Tisza River trips.

CYCLING

Hungary's flat terrain makes it ideal for cycling. Velo-Touring, a large cycling travel agency, has a great selection of seven-night trips in all regions, from a senior-friendly Southern Transdanubia wine tour (€835) to a bike ride between spas on the Great Plain (€750). Lake Balaton is circled by a 200km-long cycling track that takes four to five days to complete at a leisurely pace.

HIKING/BIRDWATCHING

Hiking enthusiasts may enjoy the trails around Tihany at Lake Balaton, the Bükk Hills north of Eger or the plains at Bugac Puszta south of Kecskemét. The birdwatching expert in Hungary is Gerard Gorman, who owns and operates Probirder, an information website and guide service.

HORSEBACK RIDING

See the Hungarian National Tourist Office (HNTO; www.gotohungary.com) website and its *Hungary on Horseback* brochure. Equus Tours leads seven-night horseback tours (from €750) in the Hortobágy, Mátra Hills and Northeast Hungary.

SPAS

Hungary has more than 100 thermal baths open to the public. The HNTO puts out a booklet called *Hungary: A Garden of Well-Being* and has listings online. Also try the Spas in Hungary (www.spasinhungary.com) website.

Business Hours

Banks 8am or 9am to 4pm or 5pm Monday to Friday

Museums 9am or 10am to 5pm or 6pm Tuesday to Sunday

Restaurants Roughly 11am to midnight

Discount Cards

The Hungary Card (www.hungarycard.hu; basic/standard/plus 2550/5800/9300Ft) offers free entry to many museums; 50% off on six return train fares and some bus and boat travel; up to 20% off selected accommodation; and 50% off the price of the Budapest Card (www.buda-pestinfo.hu; 24/48/72hr card 3900/7900/9900Ft). It's available at Tourinform offices.

Embassies & Consulates

Embassies in Budapest (phone code ☏1) include the following:

Australian Embassy (☏457 9777; www.hungary.embassy.gov.au; XII Királyhágó tér 8-9, 4th fl; ⊙visas 9-11am, general enquiries 8.30am-4.30pm Mon-Fri)

Austrian Embassy (☏479 7010; www.austrian-embassy.hu; VI Benczúr utca 16; ⊙8-11am Mon-Fri)

Canadian Embassy (☏392 3360; www.hungary.gc.ca; II Ganz utca 12-14; ⊙8.30-11am & 2-3.30pm Mon-Thu)

Croatian Embassy (☏354 1315; veleposlanstvo.budimpesta@mvpei.hr; VI Munkácsy Mihály utca 15; ⊙9am-5pm Mon-Fri)

French Embassy (☏374 1100; www.ambafrance-hu.org; VI Lendvay utca 27; ⊙9am-12.30pm Mon-Fri)

German Embassy (☏488 3567; www.budapest.diplo.de; I Úri utca 64-66; ⊙9am-noon Mon-Fri)

Irish Embassy (☏301 4960; www.embassyofireland.hu; V Szabadság tér 7, Bank Center, Granit Tower, 5th fl; ⊙9.30am-12.30pm & 2.30-4.30pm Mon-Fri)

Netherlands Embassy (☏336 6300; www.netherlandsembassy.hu; II Füge utca 5-7; ⊙10am-noon Mon-Fri)

Romanian Embassy (☏384 0271; http://budapesta.mae.ro; XIV Thököly út 72; ⊙8.30am-12.30pm Mon-Fri; ⊜5, 7, 173)

Serbian Embassy (☏322 9838; ambjubp@mail.datanet.hu; VI Dózsa György út 92/a; ⊙10am-1pm Mon-Fri)

Slovakian Embassy (☏273 3500; www.mzv.sk/Budapest; XIV Gervay út 44; ⊙9am-noon Mon-Fri)

Slovenian Embassy (☏438 5600; http://budimpesta.veleposlanistvo.si; II Csatárka köz 9; ⊙9am-noon Mon-Fri)

South African Embassy (☏392 0999; budapest.admin@foreign.gov.za; II Gárdonyi Géza út 17; ⊙9am-12.30pm Mon-Fri)

UK Embassy (☏266 2888; http://ukinhungary.fco.gov.uk/en; V Harmincad utca 6; ⊙9.30am-12.30pm & 2.30-4.30pm Mon-Fri)

Ukrainian Embassy (☏422 4122; www.mfa.gov.ua; XIV Stefánia út 77; ⊙9am-noon Mon-Wed)

US Embassy (☏475 4400; www.usembassy.hu; V Szabadság tér 12; ⊙8.30am-4.30pm Mon-Fri)

Food

Price ranges are as follows:

€ less than 2000Ft (3000Ft in Budapest)

€€ 2000Ft to 3500Ft (3000Ft to 6500Ft in Budapest)

€€€ more than 3500Ft (6500Ft in Budapest)

Gay & Lesbian Travellers

Budapest has a large and active gay scene, though there is virtually nothing 'out' in the rest of the country. The Háttér Gay & Lesbian Association (☏1-329 2670; www.hatter. hu; ◷6-11pm) in Budapest has an advice and help line operating daily. Company (www. companymedia.hu) is a monthly magazine featuring info on events, venues and parties (available at gay venues around Budapest). The Labrisz Lesbian Association (☏1-252 3566; www.labrisz.hu) has info on Hungary's cultural lesbian scene.

Internet Access

Most hostels and hotels offer internet access. Wi-fi is almost always free of charge. Use of a terminal will cost between 200Ft and 400Ft per hour.

Language Courses

Debreceni Nyári Egyetem (Debrecen Summer University; ☏52-532 595; www.nyariegyetem. hu; Egyetem tér 1, Debrecen) is the best-known school for studying Hungarian. It organises intensive two- and four-week courses during July and August and 80-hour, two-week advanced courses during the academic year. The branch (Map p304; ☏1-320 5751; www.nyariegyetem.hu/bp; V Váci utca 63, 2nd fl; ▓M2 Kossuth Lajos tér) in Budapest also offers similar courses.

Media

Budapest has two English-language newspapers: the weekly Budapest Times (www. budapesttimes.hu; 750Ft), with interesting reviews and opinion pieces, and the business-oriented biweekly Budapest Business Journal (www.bbjonline.hu; 1250Ft). Both are available on newsstands. An excellent online newspaper is the Budapest Sun (www.budapestsun.com).

Money

The unit of currency is the Hungarian forint (Ft). Coins come in denominations of five, 10, 20, 50, 100 and 200Ft, and notes are denominated in 500, 1000, 2000, 5000, 10,000 and 20,000Ft. ATMs are everywhere, even in small villages. Tip waiters, hairdressers and taxi drivers approximately 10% of the total.

Post

Postcards and small letters mailed within Europe cost 220Ft. To addresses outside Europe, expect to pay 240Ft.

Public Holidays

New Year's Day 1 January

1848 Revolution Day 15 March

Easter Monday March/April

International Labour Day 1 May

Whit Monday (Pentecost) May/June

St Stephen's/Constitution Day 20 August

1956 Remembrance/Republic Day 23 October

All Saints' Day 1 November

Christmas Holidays 25 & 26 December

Telephone

Hungary's country code is ☏36. To make an outgoing international call, dial ☏00 first. To dial city-to-city within the country, first dial ☏06, wait for the second dial tone and then dial the city code and phone number. All localities in Hungary have a two-digit city code, except for Budapest, where the code is ☏1.

In Hungary you must always dial 06 when ringing mobile telephones, which have specific area codes depending on the telecom company. Telecom companies include Telenor (☏06 20; www.telenor.hu), T-Mobile (☏06 30; www.t-mobile.hu) and Vodafone (☏06 70; www.vodafone.hu).

Consider buying a rechargeable SIM chip, which will reduce the cost of making local calls. Vodafone, for example, sells prepaid vouchers for 1680Ft, with 500Ft worth of credit. Top-up cards cost from 2000Ft to 12,000Ft and are valid for from one month to a year.

There's also a plethora of phonecards for public phones on offer, including Magyar Telekom's Barangoló (www.t-home.hu) and NeoPhone (www.neophone.hu), with cards valued at between 1000Ft and 5000Ft.

Tourist Information

The **Hungarian National Tourist Office** (www.gotohungary.com) has a chain of more than 140 **Tourinform** (www.tourinform.hu) information offices across the country. These are the best places to ask general questions and pick up brochures across the country. In the capital, you can also visit **Budapest Info** (✆1-438 8080; www.budapestinfo.hu).

Travellers with Disabilities

Wheelchair ramps and toilets fitted for people with disabilities do exist, though they are not as common as in Western Europe. Audible traffic signals are becoming more common in big cities. For more information, contact the Budapest-based **Hungarian Federation of Disabled Persons' Associations** (MEOSZ; ✆1-250 9013; www.meoszinfo.hu; III San Marco utca 76).

Visas

Citizens of virtually all European countries, as well as Australia, Canada, Israel, Japan, New Zealand and the USA, do not require visas to visit Hungary for stays of up to 90 days. Check current visa requirements on the Consular Services page of the **Ministry for Foreign Affairs** (http://konzuliszolgalat.kormany.hu/en) website.

Getting There & Away

Air

The vast majority of international flights land at **Ferenc Liszt International Airport** (✆296 7000; www.bud.hu) on the outskirts of Budapest. The national carrier, Malév Hungarian Airlines, went into liquidation at the start of 2012. Airlines now serving Hungary include the following:

Aeroflot (SU; ✆1-318 5955; www.aeroflot.com; hub Moscow)

Air Berlin (AB; ✆06 80 017 110; www.airberlin.com; hub Cologne)

Air France (AF; ✆1-483 8800; www.airfrance.com; hub Paris)

Alitalia (AZ; ✆1-483 2170; www.alitalia.it; hub Rome)

Austrian Airlines (OS; ✆1-296 0660; www.aua.com; hub Vienna)

British Airways (BA; ✆1-777 4747; www.ba.com; hub London)

CSA Czech Airlines (OK; ✆1-318 3045; www.csa.cz; hub Prague)

EasyJet (U2; www.easyjet.com; hub London)

EgyptAir (MS; www.egyptair.com; hub Cairo)

El Al (LY; ✆1-266 2970; www.elal.co.il; hub Tel Aviv)

Finnair (AY; ✆1-296 5486; www.finnair.com; hub Helsinki)

German Wings (4U; ✆1-526 7005; www.germanwings.com; hub Cologne)

LOT Polish Airlines (LO; ✆1-266 4771; www.lot.com; hub Warsaw)

Lufthansa (LH; ✆1-411 9900; www.lufthansa.com; hub Frankfurt)

Ryanair (FR; www.ryanair.com; hub London)

SAS (SK; www.flysas.com; hub Copenhagen)

Tarom Romanian Airlines (RO; www.tarom.ro; hub Bucharest)

Turkish Airlines (TK; ✆1-266 4291; www.thy.com; hub Istanbul)

Wizz Air (W6; ✆06 90 181 181; www.wizzair.com; hub Katowice (Poland))

Land

Hungary is well connected with all seven of its neighbours by road, rail and even ferry, though most transport begins or ends its journey in Budapest.

Border formalities with its EU neighbours – Austria, Romania, Slovenia and Slovakia – are virtually nonexistent. But Hungary must implement the strict Schengen border rules, so expect a somewhat closer inspection of your documents when travelling to/from Croatia, Ukraine and Serbia.

BUS

Most international buses arrive at the **Népliget bus station** (✆219 8030; IX Üllői út 131) in Budapest and most services are run by **Eurolines** (www.eurolines.com) in conjunction with its Hungarian affiliate, Volánbusz. Useful international routes include buses from Budapest to Vienna in Austria, Bratislava in Slovakia, Subotica in Serbia, Rijeka in Croatia, Prague in the Czech Republic and Sofia in Bulgaria.

CAR & MOTORCYCLE

Foreign driving licences are valid for one year after entering Hungary. Drivers of cars and riders of motorbikes will need the vehicle's registration papers. Third-party insurance is compulsory for driving in Hungary; if your car is registered in the EU, it's assumed you have it. Other motorists must show a Green Card or buy insurance at the border.

Travel on Hungarian motorways requires pre-purchase of a *matrica* (highway pass) available from petrol stations and post offices. Your licence-plate/registration number will be entered into a computer database where it can be screened by highway-mounted surveillance cameras. Prices are 2975Ft for a week and 4780Ft for a month.

TRAIN

Magyar Államvasutak (MÁV; ☏06 40 494 949, 1-371 9449; http://elvira.mav-start.hu), the Hungarian State Railways, links up with international rail networks in all directions, and its schedule is available online.

Eurail passes are valid, but not sold, in Hungary. EuroCity (EC) and Intercity (IC) trains require a seat reservation and payment of a supplement. Most larger train stations in Hungary have left-luggage rooms open from at least 9am to 5pm. There are three main train stations in Budapest, so always note the station when checking a schedule online.

Some direct train connections from Budapest include Austria, Slovakia, Romania, Ukraine (continuing to Russia), Croatia, Serbia, Germany, Slovenia, Czech Republic, Poland, Switzerland, Italy, Bulgaria and Greece.

River

A hydrofoil service on the Danube River between Budapest and Vienna operates twice a week from May to late September.

Getting Around

Note that Hungary does not have any scheduled domestic flights.

Boat

In summer there are regular passenger ferries on the Danube from Budapest to Szentendre, Vác, Visegrád and Esztergom as well as on Lake Balaton.

Bus

Domestic buses, run by the Volán (www.volan. eu) association of coach operators, cover an extensive nationwide network.

Timetables are posted at all stations. Some footnotes you could come across include *naponta* (daily), *hétköznap* (weekdays), *munkanapokon* (on work days), *munkaszüneti napok kivételével naponta* (daily except holidays) and *szabad és munkaszüneti napokon* (on Saturday and holidays). A few large bus stations have luggage rooms, but these generally close by 6pm.

Car & Motorcycle

Most cities and towns require that you pay for street parking (usually 9am to 6pm workdays) by buying temporary parking passes from machines. Most machines take only coins (so keep a lot handy); place the time-stamped parking permit on the dashboard. The cost averages about 200Ft an hour in the countryside and up to 450Ft on central Budapest streets.

AUTOMOBILE ASSOCIATIONS

The so-called 'Yellow Angels' of the Hungarian Automobile Club (Magyar Autóklub; ☏1-345 1800; www.autoklub.hu; IV Berda József utca 15, Budapest; Ⓜ M3 Újpest Városkapu) do basic breakdown repairs for free if you belong to an affiliated organisation such as AAA in the USA or AA in the UK. You can call 24 hours a day on ☏188 nationwide.

FUEL & SPARE PARTS

Ólommentes benzin (unleaded petrol 95/98 octane) is available everywhere. Most stations also have *gázolaj* (diesel).

HIRE

In general, you must be at least 21 years old and have had your licence for at least a year to rent a car. Drivers under 25 sometimes have to pay a surcharge. Rental agencies are common in large cities and at Budapest airport. The competition is fierce but local rental rates can be high; your best bet is to book online before you travel.

ROAD RULES

The most important rule to remember is that there's a 100% ban on alcohol when you are driving, and this rule is strictly enforced.

Using a mobile phone while driving is prohibited in Hungary. *All* vehicles must have their headlights switched on throughout the day outside built-up areas. Motorcyclists must have their headlights on at all times.

Hitching

Hitching is never entirely safe in any country and we don't recommend it. Travellers who decide to hitch are taking a small but potentially serious risk. Hitchhiking is legal everywhere in Hungary except on motorways. Though it isn't as popular as it once was, the road to Lake Balaton is always jammed with hitchhikers in the holiday season.

Local Transport

Public transport is efficient and extensive, with bus and, in many towns, trolleybus services. Budapest, Szeged and Debrecen also have trams, and there's an extensive metro and a suburban commuter railway in Budapest. Purchase tickets at newsstands before travelling and validate them once aboard. Inspectors do check tickets, especially on the metro lines in Budapest.

Train

MÁV ([✆]1-444 4499; www.mav-start.hu) operates reliable train services on its 7600km of tracks. Schedules are available online and computer information kiosks are popping up at rail stations around the country. Second-class domestic train fares range from 155Ft for a journey of less than 5km to about 4660Ft for a 300km trip.

First-class fares – where available – are usually 25% more. IC trains are express trains, the most comfortable and modern. *Gyorsvonat* (fast trains) take longer and use older cars; *személyvonat* (passenger trains) stop at every village along the way. *Helyjegy* (seat reservations) cost extra and are required on IC and some fast trains; these are indicated on the timetable by an 'R' in a box or a circle (a plain 'R' means seat reservations are available but not required).

In all stations a yellow board indicates *indul* (departures) and a white board is for *érkezik* (arrivals). Express and fast trains are indicated in red, local trains in black.

On certain trains (look for the bicycle symbol on the schedule), bicycles can be transported in special carriages for 235Ft per 50km travelled. You can freight a bicycle for 25% of a full 2nd-class fare.

If you plan to travel extensively in Hungary consider purchasing the Hungary pass from Eurail (www.eurail.com), available to non-European residents only, before entering the country. It costs US$92/132 for five/10 days of 1st-class travel in a 15-day period, and US$80/101 for those under 26 years of age in 2nd class. Children aged six to 14 pay half price.

Poland

Why Go?

If they were handing out prizes for 'most eventful history', Poland would be sure to get a medal. The nation has spent centuries at the pointy end, grappling with war and invasion. Nothing, however, has succeeded in suppressing the Poles' strong sense of nationhood and cultural identity. As a result, centres such as bustling Warsaw and cultured Kraków exude a sophisticated energy that's a heady mix of old and new.

Away from the cities, Poland is a diverse land, from its northern beaches to its magnificent southern mountains. In between are towns and cities dotted with ruined castles, picturesque squares and historic churches.

Although prices have steadily risen in the postcommunist era, Poland is still good value for travellers. As the Polish people work on combining their distinctive national identity with their place in the heart of Europe, it's a fascinating time to visit this beautiful country.

Best Places to Eat

» Glonojad (p382)

» Warung Bali (p407)

» Bernard (p402)

» Sketch (p366)

» Restauracja Pod Łososiem (p412)

Best Places to Stay

» Hostel Mleczarnia (p401)

» Castle Inn (p365)

» Wielopole (p381)

» Grand Hotel Lublinianka (p389)

When to Go
Warsaw

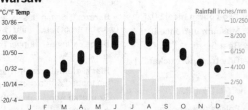

May–Jun Indulge in the asparagus season, when restaurant menus feature this vegetable.

Jul–Aug Hit the beaches on Poland's long, sandy Baltic coast.

Sep Walk in the Tatra Mountains, bedding down in a cosy hikers' refuge.

AT A GLANCE

» **Currency** Złoty (zł)

» **Language** Polish

» **Money** ATMs all over; banks open Monday to Friday

» **Visas** Not required for citizens of the EU, Canada, New Zealand and Australia

Fast Facts

» **Area** 312, 685 sq km

» **Capital** Warsaw

» **Country code** ☏48

» **Emergency** Ambulance ☏999, fire ☏998, police ☏997

Exchange rates

Australia	A$1	3.42zł
Canada	C$1	3.22zł
Euro Zone	€1	4.18zł
Japan	¥100	3.47zł
New Zealand	NZ$1	2.74zł
UK	UK£1	4.95zł
USA	US$1	3.27zł

Set Your Budget

» **Budget hotel room** 200zł

» **Two-course meal** 50zł

» **Museum entrance** 10zł

» **Beer** 6–9zł

» **City transport ticket** 3zł

Resources

» **Polska** (www.poland.travel)

» **Poland.pl** (www.poland.pl)

Connections

Poland offers plenty of possibilities for onward travel. The country is well connected by train: among its useful connections are direct services to Berlin from both Warsaw (via Poznań) and Kraków; to Prague from Warsaw and Kraków; and to Kyiv in Ukraine from Warsaw and Kraków (via Przemyśl and Lviv). Trains also link Warsaw to Minsk in Belarus and Moscow in Russia, and Gdańsk to Kaliningrad in Russia and Berlin in Germany. International buses head in all directions, including eastward to the Baltic States. From southern Zakopane, it's easy to hop to Slovakia via bus, or even minibus. And from the Baltic coast ports of Gdańsk, Gydnia and Świnoujscie, ferries head to various ports in Denmark and Sweden.

ITINERARIES

One Week

Spend a day exploring Warsaw with a stroll around the Old Town and a stop at the Warsaw Rising Museum for a glimpse of the city's wartime history. The next day, head to historic Kraków for three days, visiting the beautiful Old Town, striking Wawel Castle, the former Jewish district of Kazimierz and Wieliczka's impressive salt mine. Take a day trip to Auschwitz-Birkenau, the Nazi German concentration and extermination camp. Afterwards, head to Zakopane for two days for some mountain air.

Two Weeks

Follow the above itinerary, then travel to Wrocław for two days, visiting its unique Panorama. Progress north to Gothic Toruń for a day, then onward to Gdańsk for two days, exploring the attractive architecture and bars of the Old Town and visiting the monuments at Westerplatte. Wind down with a couple of days at the seaside in Sopot.

Essential Food & Drink

» **Żurek** This hearty sour soup includes sausage and hard-boiled egg.

» **Barszcz** This famous soup comes in two varieties: red (with beetroot) and white (with wheat flour and sausage).

» **Bigos** Extinguish hunger pangs with this thick sauerkraut and meat stew.

» **Placki ziemniaczane** These filling potato pancakes are often topped with a meaty sauce.

» **Szarlotka** Apple cake with cream is a Polish classic.

» **Sernik** Baked cheesecake – weighty but tasty.

» **Piwo** Poland's beer is good, cold and inexpensive, and often served in colourful beer gardens.

» **Wódka** Try it plain, or ask for *myśliwska* (flavoured with juniper berries).

» **Herbata z rumem** Tea with rum is the perfect pick-me-up after a heavy day of sightseeing.

Poland Highlights

① Experience the beauty and history of Kraków's **Wawel Castle** (p374).

② Encounter European bison and other magnificent fauna at **Białowieża National Park** (p372).

③ Hunt for **gnome statues** (p399) in the Old Town of Wrocław.

④ Remember the victims of Nazi German genocide at former extermination camp **Auschwitz-Birkenau** (p385).

⑤ Soak up the cosmopolitan vibe of **Gdańsk** (p408) and take a dip in the Baltic at nearby **Sopot** (p415).

⑥ Enjoy the skiing or hiking life of the **Tatra Mountains** (p395).

⑦ Discover Warsaw's tragic wartime history at the **Warsaw Rising Museum** (p364).

WARSAW

Warsaw (Warszawa in Polish, var-*shah*-va) may not be the prettiest of Poland's cities, but there's no mistaking its dynamism. As the bustling capital and business centre of the nation, Warsaw is home to an array of dining and nightlife that's the equal of any European city its size.

It's true, however, that Warsaw can be hard work. The city centre sprawls across a wide area, quite separate from the attractive but tourist-heavy Old Town, and its traffic-choked streets lined with massive concrete buildings can be less than enthralling.

However, look at Warsaw with a historic perspective and you'll see the capital in an entirely new light. As a city that's survived everything fate could throw at it – including the complete destruction of its historic heart in WWII – Warsaw is a place with an extraordinary backstory.

When you factor in its entertainment options; the beauty of its reconstructed Old Town, Royal Way and former Royal Parks; and the history represented by the Stalinist-era Palace of Culture and the Warsaw Rising Museum, what emerges is a complex city that well repays a visit.

History

The Mazovian dukes were the first rulers of Warsaw, establishing it as their stronghold in the 14th century. The city's strategic central location led to the capital being transferred from Kraków to Warsaw in 1596, following the earlier union of Poland and Lithuania.

Although the 18th century was a period of catastrophic decline for the Polish state, Warsaw underwent a period of prosperity during this period. Many magnificent churches, palaces and parks were built, and cultural and artistic life blossomed. The first (short-lived) constitution in Europe was instituted in Warsaw in 1791.

In the 19th century Warsaw declined in status to become a mere provincial city of the Russian Empire. Following WWI, the city was reinstated as the capital of a newly independent Poland and once more began to thrive. Following the Warsaw Rising of 1944, when the Poles revolted against German rule, the city centre was devastated and the entire surviving population forcibly evacuated. When the war ended, the people of Warsaw returned to the capital and set about rebuilding its historic heart.

Since the fall of communism, and particularly since Poland's entry into the EU, Warsaw has undergone a surge of economic development which has reshaped its commercial heart.

◉ Sights

The Vistula River divides the city. The western left-bank sector is home to the city centre, including the Old Town – the historic nucleus of Warsaw. Almost all tourist attractions, as well as most tourist facilities, are on this side of the river.

OLD TOWN

Plac Zamkowy   HISTORIC SQUARE
(Castle Square; Map p360) This square is the main gateway to the Old Town. All the buildings here were superbly rebuilt from their foundations after WWII, earning the Old Town a place on Unesco's World Heritage List. Within the square stands the **Monument to Sigismund III Vasa** (Map p360; Plac Zamkowy), who moved the capital from Kraków to Warsaw in 1596.

Royal Castle   CASTLE
(Map p360; Plac Zamkowy 4; adult/concession 22/15zł; ⊙10am-4pm Mon-Sat, 11am-4pm Sun, closed

---

WARSAW IN TWO DAYS

Wander through the **Old Town** and tour the **Royal Castle**. Head along the **Royal Way**, checking out the impressive **Chopin Museum** en route, then have lunch at ever-so-cool **Sketch**. Take the lift to the top of the **Palace of Culture & Science** for views of the city, before promenading through the nearby **Saxon Gardens**.

The next day, visit the **Warsaw Rising Museum** in the morning, followed by lunch at one of the many restaurants along ul Nowy Świat. Spend the afternoon exploring **Łazienki Park**, before sipping a local brew at chilled bar **Relax**. Finish off the day with a visit to the nightclub district around **ul Mazowiecka**, or take in a concert at **Filharmonia Narodowa**.

Warsaw

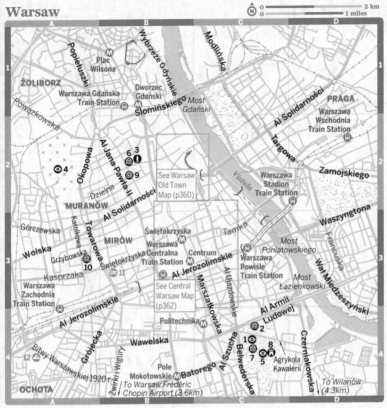

Warsaw

◎ Sights

1 Botanical Gardens C4
2 Centre for Contemporary Art C4
3 Ghetto Heroes Monument B2
4 Jewish Cemetery A2
5 Łazienki Park C4
6 Museum of the History of
   Polish Jews B2
7 Old Orangery C4
8 Palace on the Water C4
9 Pawiak Prison Museum B2
10 Warsaw Rising Museum A3

⌨ Sleeping

11 Hotel Premiere Classe B3
12 Majawa Motor Inn & Camping 123 .... A4

Mon Oct-Apr) The dominant feature of Castle Square is this massive 13th-century castle, also reconstructed after the war. The highlight of the sumptuously decorated rooms is the Senators' Antechamber, where landscapes of 18th-century Warsaw by Bernardo Bellotto (Canaletto's nephew) are on show.

Historical Museum of Warsaw   MUSEUM
(Map p360; www.mhw.pl; Rynek Starego Miasta 42; adult/concession 8/4zł; ⏲11am-6pm Tue & Thu,

10am-3.30pm Wed & Fri, 10.30am-4.30pm Sat & Sun) Off the magnificent **Rynek Starego Miasta** (Old Town Market Sq) is this institution devoted to Warsaw's tumultuous history. At noon it shows an English-language film depicting the wartime destruction of the city (admission 6zł).

Barbican   FORTIFICATION
(Map p360; ul Nowomiejska) Northwest of the Rynek Starego Miasta along ul Nowomiejska

Warsaw Old Town

Map labels:
Franciszkańska · Kościelna · Bonifraterska · Koźla · Freta · New Town Sq · Stara · Wybrzeże Gdańskie · Vistula · Świętojerska · Mostowa · Boleść · Brzozowa · Bugaj · **Historical Museum of Warsaw** · Nowomiejska · Rynek Starego Miasta · Kilińskiego · Jezuicka · Plac Krasińskich · **Monument to the Warsaw Rising** · Krasiński Gardens · Podwale · Tourist Office · Świętojańska · Piwna · Warsaw Tourist Information Centre · **Royal Castle** · Schillera · Miodowa · Długa · Ratusz-Arsenał · Senatorska · Koźla · Rynek Mariensztacki · Bednarska · Bielańska · Gen Andersa · Plac Teatralny · Krakowskie Przedmieście · Molibra · Trebacka · Wierzbowa · Plac Bankowy · Niecała · Saxon Gardens · Tourist Office

---

is this imposing fortified section of the medieval city walls. You can clamber onto the city walls via walkways here and get a feel for the height of the Old Town above the Vistula River.

Marie Skłodowska-Curie Museum
MUSEUM

(Map p360; ul Freta 16; adult/concession 11/6zł; ⊘10am-5pm) North of the Old Town along ul Freta, this museum features displays about Poland's great lady, Marie Curie, who, along with her husband Pierre, discovered radium and polonium, and laid the foundations for radiography, nuclear physics and cancer therapy.

St John's Cathedral
CHURCH

(Map p360; ul Świętojańska 8; crypt 2zł; ⊘10am-1pm & 3-5.30pm Mon-Sat) Near the castle is this 15th-century Gothic cathedral, Warsaw's oldest church. Its relatively simple but elegant interior is worth a look.

Monument to the Warsaw Rising
MONUMENT

(Map p360; cnr ul Długa & ul Miodowa) West of the Old Town, this striking set of statuary honours the heroic Polish revolt against German rule in 1944.

Warsaw Old Town

ROYAL WAY

This 4km route (called Szlak Królewski in Polish) links the Royal Castle with Łazienki Park via ul Krakowskie Przedmieście, ul Nowy Świat and Al Ujazdowskie. Bus 180 runs along or near this route and continues south to Wilanów Park.

TOP CHOICE Chopin Museum   MUSEUM
(Map p362; www.chopin.museum; ul Okólnik 1; adult/concession 22/13zł, Tue free; ☺11am-8pm Tue-Sun) To learn about Poland's most renowned composer, head to this institution. Renovated and expanded on the 200th anniversary of his birth in 2010, it presents an immersive audiovisual exhibition covering Chopin's work, possessions and his life in Paris. You're encouraged to take your time through four floors of displays, including stopping by the listening booths in the basement.

Saxon Gardens   GARDENS
(Map p362; ☺24hr) West of the Royal Way are these attractive gardens, at whose entrance stands the small but poignant **Tomb of the Unknown Soldier** (Map p362; Saxon Gardens). It's housed within the only surviving remnant of the Saxon Palace that once stood here and was destroyed by the Germans during WWII. The ceremonial **changing of the guard** takes place at noon here on Sunday.

Church of the
Holy Cross   CHURCH
(Map p362; ul Krakowskie Przedmieście 3) South of the Old Town is this prominent 17th-century church. **Chopin's heart** is preserved in the second pillar on the left-hand side of the main nave. It was brought from Paris, where he died of tuberculosis aged only 39.

National Museum   MUSEUM
(Map p362; www.mnw.art.pl; Al Jerozolimskie 3; adult/concession 15/10zł, incl temporary exhibitions 20/15zł, Tue free; ☺10am-6pm Tue-Sun) East of the junction of ul Nowy Świat and Al Jerozolimskie, the National Museum houses an impressive collection of Greek and Egyptian antiquities, Coptic frescos, medieval woodcarvings and Polish paintings. Look out for the surreal fantasies of Jacek Malczewski.

Łazienki Park   GARDENS
(Map p359; www.lazienki-krolewskie.pl; ul Agrykola; gardens free; ☺dawn-dusk) This large, shady and popular park is best known for the 18th-century **Palace on the Water** (Map p359; ul Agrykola 1; adult/concession 15/10zł, Thu free; ☺9am-4pm Tue-Sun) It was the summer residence of Stanisław August Poniatowski, the last king of Poland, who abdicated once the Third Partition of Poland dissolved his realm in 1795. The park was once a royal

POLAND WARSAW

Central Warsaw

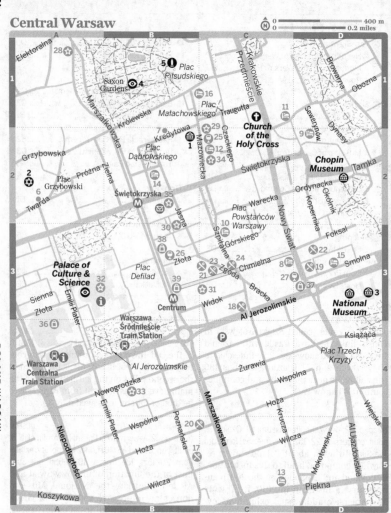

hunting ground attached to Ujazdów Castle.

Also within the park is the **Old Orangery** (Map p359; Łazienki Park; adult/student 10/5zł, Thu free; ⊙9am-4pm Tue-Fri), which contains a sculpture gallery and 18th-century theatre. **Piano recitals** are held among the nearby rose gardens between noon and 4pm every Saturday and Sunday from May to September.

St Anne's Church CHURCH
(Map p360; ul Krakowskie Przedmieście 68) Just south of the Royal Castle, this ornate 15th-century church has impressive views from

its **tower** (ul Krakowskie Przedmieście 68; adult/concession 5/4zł; ⊙11am-9pm May-Oct).

Museum of Caricature MUSEUM
(Map p360; www.muzeumkarykatury.pl; ul Kozia 11; adult/concession 5/3zł, Sat free; ⊙11am-6pm Tue-Sun) Along a side street off ul Krakowskie Przedmieście is this quirky museum, exhibiting numerous original works by Polish and foreign caricaturists, created from the 18th century onwards.

Radziwiłł Palace PALACE
(Map p360; ul Krakowskie Przedmieście 48/50) This palace, off ul Krakowskie Przedmieście,

Central Warsaw

POLAND WARSAW

is the imposing residence of the Polish president. It's not open to the public.

Ethnographic Museum   MUSEUM
(Map p362; www.ethnomuseum.website.pl; ul Kredytowa 1; adult/concession 12/6zł, Wed free; ⊙10am-4pm Tue-Sat, noon-5pm Sun) South of the Saxon Gardens is the Ethnographic Museum. It displays Polish folk costumes, as well as regional arts and crafts.

Polish Army Museum   MUSEUM
(Map p362; Al Jerozolimskie 3; adult/concession 10/5zł, Wed free; ⊙10am-4pm Wed-Sun) Next door to the National Museum is this museum recording the history of the Polish army, with military vehicles outside and miscellaneous militaria within.

**Centre for
Contemporary Art**   ART GALLERY
(Map p359; www.csw.art.pl; ul Jazdów 2; adult/concession 12/6zł, Thu free; ⊙noon-7pm Tue-Sun) This cutting-edge gallery is housed in the reconstructed **Ujazdów Castle**, originally built during the 1620s.

Botanical Gardens   GARDENS
(Map p359; adult/concession 6/3zł; ⊙10am-8pm Apr-Aug, 10am-5pm Sep-Oct) South of the Centre for Contemporary Art are these small but pleasant gardens, suitable for whiling away an idle hour on a sunny day.

WILANÓW

To reach Wilanów, take bus 116 or 180 from ul Nowy Świat or Al Ujazdowskie.

Wilanów Park   GARDENS
(www.wilanow-palac.pl; ul Wisłostrada; adult/concession 5/3zł, Thu free; ⊙9am-dusk) This magnificent park lies 6km southeast of Łazienki Park. Its centrepiece is the splendid **Wilanów Palace** (www.wilanow-palac.pl; adult/concession 20/15zł, Sun free; ⊙9.30am-4.30pm Mon-Sat, 10.30am-6.30pm Sun), the summer residence of King Jan III Sobieski, who ended the Turkish threat to Central Europe by defeating the

Turks at Vienna in 1683. In summer, be prepared to wait for entry. The last tickets are sold one hour before closing time.

In the well-kept park behind the palace is the Orangery (ul Wisłostrada; admission varies with temporary exhibitions; ☺10am-6pm), which houses an art gallery with changing exhibitions. The Poster Museum (www.postermuseum.pl; ul Kostki Potockiego 10/16; adult/student 10/7zł, Mon free; ☺noon-4pm Mon, 10am-4pm Tue-Fri, 10am-6pm Sat & Sun; 🚌116, 180) in the former royal stables is a repository of Poland's world-renowned poster art.

CITY CENTRE

Palace of Culture & Science LANDMARK
(Map p362; www.pkin.pl; Plac Defilad 1; ☺9am-6pm) Massive, brooding and inescapable, this towering structure has become an emblem of the city, as it's slowly rehabilitated from its Stalinist past. It has a particularly sinister aspect at dusk, though it's also a handy landmark. The palace was built in the early 1950s as a 'gift of friendship' from the Soviet Union (the kind of unwanted gift that's hard to hide away), and is still one of Europe's tallest buildings (over 230m). The clock faces were added to the building in the postcommunist period.

The observation terrace (adult/concession 20/15zł) on the 30th floor provides a panoramic view, though it can be very cold and windy up there.

WEST OF THE CITY CENTRE

Warsaw Rising Museum MUSEUM
(Map p359; www.1944.pl; ul Grzybowska 79; adult/concession 14/10zł, Sun free; ☺8am-6pm Mon, Wed & Fri, 8am-8pm Thu, 10am-6pm Sat & Sun) This impressive museum commemorates Warsaw's insurrection against its Nazi German occupiers in 1944, which ended in defeat and the destruction of much of the city and its population. The Rising was viciously suppressed by the Germans (while the Red Army stood by on the opposite bank of the Vistula River), with more than 200,000 Poles dying by its conclusion.

The moving story of the Rising is retold here via photographs, exhibits and audiovisual displays. The centrepiece is a massive memorial wall emitting a heartbeat and selected audio recordings. At the end of the journey there's a replica 1944 cafe, underlining the fact that life went on, even in the worst days of the struggle. Captions are in Polish and English. Catch trams 22 or 24 from Al Jerozolimskie, heading west.

FORMER JEWISH DISTRICT

The suburbs northwest of the Palace of Culture & Science were once predominantly inhabited by Jewish Poles. During WWII the Nazi German occupiers established a Jewish ghetto in the area, but razed it to the ground after crushing the Warsaw Ghetto Uprising in April 1943.

Jewish Cemetery CEMETERY
(Map p359; ul Okopowa 49/51; admission 4zł; ☺10am-5pm Mon-Thu, 9am-1pm Fri, 11am-4pm Sun) The most poignant remainder of the wartime tragedy is Europe's largest Jewish resting place. Founded in 1806, it has more than 100,000 gravestones. Visitors must wear a head covering to enter. It's accessible from the Old Town on bus 180, heading north from ul Nowy Świat.

Ghetto Heroes Monument MONUMENT
(Map p359; cnr ul Anielewicza & ul Zamenhofa) This monument was established to remember the victims of the Jewish ghetto, which was established here by the occupying Germans. It features pictorial plaques.

Museum of the History of Polish Jews MUSEUM
(Map p359; www.jewishmuseum.org.pl; cnr ul Anielewicza & ul Zamenhofa; ☺10am-6pm Wed-Mon) Opposite the Ghetto Heroes Monument is this new multimedia and education centre, which opened on the 70th anniversary of the Ghetto Uprising in April 2013. Check with the tourist office for entry fees.

Pawiak Prison Museum MUSEUM
(Map p359; ul Dzielna 24/26; adult/concession 6/4zł; ☺10am-4pm Wed-Sun) Once a Gestapo prison during the Nazi German occupation, this institution now contains moving exhibits, including letters and other personal items.

Nożyk Synagogue SYNAGOGUE
(Map p362; ul Twarda 6; admission 6zł; ☺9am-8pm Mon-Fri, 11am-8pm Sun) This neo-Romanesque place of worship is the only Warsaw synagogue to survive WWII.

☞ Tours

Our Roots TOUR
(Map p362; ☎22 620 0556; www.our-roots.jewish.org.pl; ul Twarda 6) Offers Jewish heritage tours.

Trakt TOUR
(Map p362; ☎22 827 8068; www.trakt.com.pl; ul Kredytowa 6) Guided tours of Warsaw and beyond.

⭐ Festivals & Events

Mozart Festival MUSIC
(www.operakameralna.pl; ⊙Jun/Jul)

Warsaw Summer Jazz Days MUSIC
(www.adamiakjazz.pl; ⊙Jul)

Street Art Festival THEATRE
(www.sztukaulicy.pl; ⊙Jul)

**Warsaw Autumn International
Festival of Contemporary Music** MUSIC
(www.warsaw-autumn.art.pl; ⊙Sep)

Warsaw Film Festival FILM
(www.wff.pl; ⊙Oct)

🛏 Sleeping

Not surprisingly, Warsaw is the most expensive Polish city for accommodation, though there's a number of reasonably priced hostels around town. The tourist offices can help you find a room.

TOP CHOICE **Castle Inn** HOTEL €€
(Map p360; ☑22 425 0100; www.castleinn.eu; ul Świętojańska 2; s/d from 290/330zł; 🛜) Proceed up the stairs to the striking purple decor and shiny tiles of this Old Town hotel, situated in a 17th-century tenement house. All rooms overlook either Castle Sq or St John's Cathedral and come in a range of playful styles.

Oki Doki Hostel HOSTEL €
(Map p362; ☑22 828 0122; www.okidoki.pl; Plac Dąbrowskiego 3; dm 39-93zł, s/d from 120/149zł; 🛜) There are no drab dorms here. Each is decorated thematically using the brightest paints available; try the communist (red with a big image of Lenin). Lower bunks have good head room and the shared bathrooms are clean and bright. The hostel also has a bar, free washing machine and a kitchen, as well as bikes for hire (28zł per day).

Nathan's Villa Hostel HOSTEL €
(Map p362; ☑22 622 2946; www.nathansvilla.com; ul Piękna 24/26; dm 47-60zł, r 175-205zł; 🛜) Nathan's sunlit courtyard leads to well-organised dorms and comfortable private rooms. The kitchen is well set up and there's a laundry, book exchange and games to while away rainy days.

Hotel Le Regina HOTEL €€€
(Map p360; ☑22 531 6000; www.mamaison.com/leregina; ul Kościelna 12; r/ste from €150/450; ❋🛜🏊) It's not cheap, but Le Regina is a jaw-dropping combination of traditional architecture and contemporary design. The enormous rooms feature king-size beds with headboards of dark, polished wood. Deluxe rooms also have timber floors and terraces with courtyard views. All rooms sport spectacular bathrooms with marble benchtops.

Apartments Apart APARTMENTS €€
(Map p362; ☑22 351 2250; www.apartmentsapart.com; ul Nowy Świat 29/3; apt from €45; 🛜) Company offering a range of apartments dotted throughout the Old Town and the city centre. Most include a washing machine in addition to a kitchen. Check online first, as last-minute web specials can be great value.

Hotel Bristol LUXURY HOTEL €€€
(Map p360; ☑22 551 1000; www.lemeridien.pl; ul Krakowskie Przedmieście 42/44; r from 750zł; ❋🛜🏊) Established in 1899 and restored to its former glory after a massive renovation, the Bristol is touted as Poland's most luxurious hotel. Its neoclassical exterior houses a feast of original art nouveau features and huge, traditionally decorated rooms. Attentive staff cater to your every whim.

Hotel Premiere Classe HOTEL €€
(Map p359; ☑22 624 0800; www.premiere-classe-warszawa.pl; ul Towarowa 2; r 199zł; 🛜) If you're not bothered too much by room size, this modern hotel makes a good base. Rooms are small but bright, and neatly set up with modern furnishings. Guests can use the restaurants, bars and fitness centre in its neighbouring sister hotels. Catch tram 22 or 24 west from Al Jerozolimskie.

Sofitel Victoria HOTEL €€€
(Map p362; ☑22 657 8011; www.sofitel.com; ul Królewska 11; r from 400zł; 🛜🏊) The very model of a modern business hotel, with a spacious marble foyer and a lounge area housing a small library of books on Polish culture and history. The rooms are conservatively decorated, with gleaming bathrooms.

Hostel Helvetia HOSTEL €
(Map p362; ☑22 826 7108; www.hostel-helvetia.pl; ul Kopernika 36/40; dm/r 59/220zł; 🛜) Bright hostel with an attractive combined lounge and kitchen. Dorms have lockers, and there's one small women-only dorm. Bike hire is 30zł per day. Enter from the street behind, ul Sewerynów.

Hostel Kanonia HOSTEL €
(Map p360; ☑22 635 0676; www.kanonia.pl; ul Jezuicka 2; dm/s/d 45/90/160zł; 🛜) Housed in a historic building in the heart of the Old

POLAND WARSAW

Town, accommodation is mostly in dorms, with only one double and one triple. Some rooms have picturesque views onto the cobblestone streets. There's a dining room with basic kitchen facilities, and a washing machine.

Dom Literatury HOTEL €€

(Map p360; ☑22 635 0404; www.fundacjadl.com; ul Krakowskie Przedmieście 87/89; s/d 220/370zł; ☎) Within a grand historic building, this accommodation features rambling halls and staircases bedecked with pot plants and sizeable paintings. There's a maze of comfortable rooms, many of which have excellent views of the Old Town and the Vistula. You're paying for the location, however, rather than the standard of accommodation.

Hotel Harenda HOTEL €€

(Map p362; ☑22 826 0071; www.hotelharenda. com.pl; ul Krakowskie Przedmieście 4/6; s/d from 310/340zł; ☎) Boasting a great location just off the Royal Way, the Harenda's rooms are neat and clean, with solid timber furniture and an old-fashioned vibe. Breakfast is an additional 25zł.

Hotel Gromada Centrum HOTEL €€

(Map p362; ☑22 582 9900; www.gromada.pl; Plac Powstańców Warszawy 2; s/d from 210/240zł; ❋☎) Centrally located, the Gromada is a big concrete box but also a great launching pad for exploring the central city. Upstairs from the spacious foyer with folkloric decor, the corridors stretch out into the distance like an optical illusion. The rooms are plain, but clean and spacious.

Smolna Youth Hostel HOSTEL €

(Map p362; ☑22 827 8952; www.hostelsmolna30. pl; ul Smolna 30; dm/s/d 50/85/150zł; ☎) Very central and very popular, though there's a midnight curfew (2am in July and August) and reception is closed between 10am and 4pm. It's simple but clean, and there's a lounge and kitchen area. Note that guests are separated into dorms according to gender, and reception is up four flights of stairs.

Dom Przy Rynku Hostel HOSTEL €

(Map p360; ☑22 831 5033; www.cityhostel.net; Rynek Nowego Miasta 4; dm 60zł; ☉Jul-Sep; ☎) Only open in summer and located in a quiet corner of the busy New Town, Przy Rynku is a neat, clean and friendly hostel occupying a 19th-century house. Its rooms accommodate two to five people, and there's a kitchen and laundry for guest use.

Majawa Motor Inn & Camping 123 CAMPING GROUND €

(Map p359; ☑22 823 3748; www.astur.waw.pl; ul Bitwy Warszawskiej 1920r 15/17; site per person/ tent 25/20zł, bungalows s/d from 50/80zł, hotel s/d from 70/120zł; ☎❋) Set in extensive grounds near the Dworzec Zachodnia bus station. The bungalows are available from mid-April to mid-October and there's a tennis court nearby. Catch tram 9 or 25 west from Al Jerozolimskie.

Hotel Mazowiecki HOTEL €€

(Map p362; ☑22 827 2365; www.hotelewam.pl; ul Mazowiecka 10; s/d from 160/200zł; ☎) One-star accommodation in a handy location on one of the city centre's nightlife strips. Most rooms have shared bathrooms, but a few have en suites.

✗ Eating

The most recent revolution in the Polish capital has been a gastronomic one. A good selection of restaurants can be found in the Old Town and New Town, and in the area between ul Nowy Świat and the Palace of Culture & Science.

Self-caterers can buy groceries at the **Carrefour Supermarket** (Map p362; ul Złota 59) in the Złote Tarasy shopping centre behind Warszawa Centralna train station; and at **ML Delikatesy** (Map p360; ul Piwna 47) in the Old Town.

TOP CHOICE Sketch INTERNATIONAL €€

(Map p362; ul Foksal 19; mains 12-41zł; ☉8am-1am) Shiny bright restaurant and bar with orange furniture and cool wait staff. There's lots of natural light and it's a great relaxed place for taking a break from sightseeing. Mains include baguettes, salads, pasta and grilled dishes. Sharing plates come in Polish, Spanish and Italian variants.

Bar Mleczny Pod Barbakanem CAFETERIA €

(Map p360; ul Mostowa 27/29; mains 5-9zł; ☉8am-5pm Mon-Fri, from 9am Sat & Sun; ☑) Near the Barbican, this popular former milk bar that survived the fall of the Iron Curtain continues to serve cheap, unpretentious food in an interior dominated by tiles. Fill up while peering out through the lace curtains at the passing tourist hordes.

Podwale Piwna Kompania GRILL €€

(Map p360; ul Podwale 25; mains 22-50zł; ☉11am-1am Mon-Sat, noon-1am Sun) The restaurant's name (The Company of Beer) gives you an idea of the lively atmosphere in this eatery just outside the Old Town's moat. The menu features lots of grilled items and dishes such as roast duck, schnitzel, pork ribs and steak. There's a courtyard for outdoor dining.

Fret Á Porter
POLISH €€

(Map p360; ul Freta 37; mains 25-56zł; ⊙noon-11pm; 🛜) Choose between the pavement terrace, with views of the New Town Sq, and the eccentric dining room with modern art on the walls. The menu indulges in similarly bold contrasts, ranging from traditional Polish dishes to exotic offerings such as kangaroo steaks.

Beirut
MIDDLE EASTERN €

(Map p362; ul Poznańska 12; mains 12-19zł; 🛜🍴) Very hip, the small Beirut 'Hummus and Music Bar' brings together two of the best things in life. The menu features hummus in several variations, as well as salads, falafel and pitta bread. There's a DJ turntable on hand for later in the evening, when the music part kicks in.

Cô tú
ASIAN €

(Map p362; Hadlowo-Usługowe 21; mains 12-18zł; ⊙10am-9pm Mon-Fri, 11am-7pm Sat & Sun) The wok at this simple Asian diner never rests, as hungry Poles can't get enough of the excellent dishes coming from the kitchen. The menu is enormous, covering seafood, vegetables, beef, chicken and pork. Duck through the archway at ul Nowy Świat 26 to find it.

Restauracja Pod Samsonem
JEWISH €€

(Map p360; ul Freta 3/5; mains 10-30zł) Situated in the New Town and frequented by locals looking for inexpensive and tasty meals with a Jewish flavour. Interesting appetisers include Russian pancakes with mushroom sauce, and 'Jewish caviar' (fried chopped liver). Spot the bas relief of Samson and the lion above the next door along from the entrance.

Tukan Salad Bar
VEGETARIAN €

(Map p360; Plac Bankowy 2; mains 5-19zł; ⊙8am-8pm Mon-Fri, 10am-6pm Sat; 🍴) Vegetarian-friendly outlet offering a wide choice of salads. As the name suggests, look for the toucan on the door. It's hidden from the street in the arcade running parallel.

Restauracja Przy Zamku
POLISH €€€

(Map p360; Plac Zamkowy 15; mains 38-120zł) An attractive, old-world kind of place with hunting trophies on the walls and attentive, apron-wearing waiters. The top-notch Polish menu includes fish and game and a bewildering array of entrees – try the excellent hare pâté served with cranberry sauce.

Dżonka
ASIAN €€

(Map p362; ul Hoża 54; mains 15-31zł; ⊙11am-7pm Mon-Fri, noon-6pm Sat & Sun) This hidden gem serves a range of Asian dishes, covering Chinese, Japanese, Korean and Thai cuisine. Though small (just six tables), it has loads of personality, with dark timber surfaces and bamboo place mats. There's some spicy food on the menu, including Sichuan cuisine, though it's been toned down a little for Polish palates.

British Bulldog
BRITISH PUB €

(Map p362; Al Jerozolimskie 42; mains 9-27zł; 🛜) If you must go to a faux-British pub, this is a good choice in the city centre. Serves steaks and fish and chips, along with an all-day breakfast. Happy hour runs from 4pm to 7pm.

Bazyliszek Restauracja
POLISH €€

(Map p360; Rynek Starego Miasta 1/3; mains 17-48zł) Step beneath the red-eyed basilisk into this restaurant in a prime spot on the Rynek Starego Miasta. It serves mainly Polish-style dishes, with forays into foreign cuisine such as Argentinian steak.

Taqueria Mexicana
MEXICAN €€

(Map p362; ul Zgoda 5; mains 24-50zł) Brightly hued place festooned with Mexican rugs and featuring a central bar. Varieties of tacos, enchiladas and fajitas adorn the menu; there's a 15zł set lunch from Monday to Friday.

Krokiecik
CAFETERIA €

(Map p362; ul Zgoda 1; mains 6-25zł) Attractive cafeteria serving a range of inexpensive and tasty dishes, including good soups. The house speciality is *krokiety* (filled savoury pancakes).

POLAND WARSAW

WANT MORE?

For in-depth information, reviews and recommendations at your fingertips, head to the Apple App Store to purchase Lonely Planet's *Warsaw City Guide* and *Polish Phrasebook* iPhone apps.

Alternatively, head to www.lonelyplanet.com/poland/warsaw for planning advice, author recommendations, traveller reviews and insider tips.

Zgoda Grill Bar POLISH **€€**

(Map p362; ul Zgoda 4; mains 24-69zł) A bright, informal place serving up a range of tasty Polish standards. There's also a decent salad selection.

🍷 Drinking

TOP CHOICE **Polyester** CAFE-BAR

(Map p360; ul Freta 49/51; 🕾) Polyester, with its fashionably retro furnishings and vibe, is arguably the hippest cocktail bar in the vicinity of the Old Town. Serves excellent cocktails, as well as a full range of coffee variants and light food.

Relax CAFE-BAR

(Map p362; ul Złota 8a; ◷8am-11pm Mon-Fri, 10.30am-11pm Sat & Sun; 🕾) Compact, friendly place with retro-grungy charm at the back of a derelict cinema building. Serves a range of Polish microbrewery beers.

Sense BAR

(Map p362; ul Nowy Świat 19; ◷noon-late; 🕾) A very modern venue with a mellow atmosphere. Comfortable banquettes sit beneath strings of cube-shaped lights and there's an extensive wine and cocktail list. Try the house speciality – ginger rose vodka. There's also an impressive food menu if you're hungry.

Paparazzi BAR

(Map p362; ul Mazowiecka 12; ◷6pm-late; 🕾) This is one of Warsaw's flashest venues, where you can sip a bewildering array of cocktails under blown-up photos of Hollywood stars. It's big and roomy, with comfortable seating around the central bar.

☆ Entertainment

Nightclubs

There's no shortage of good clubs in Warsaw. Explore ul Mazowiecka, ul Sienkiewicza and the area around ul Nowy Świat for nightclub action. Free jazz concerts also take place in the Rynek Starego Miasta on Saturdays at 7pm in July and August.

Enklawa CLUB

(Map p362; www.enklawa.com; ul Mazowiecka 12; ◷9pm-4am Tue-Sat) Funky space with comfy plush seating, two bars and plenty of room to dance. Check out the long drinks list, hit the dance floor or observe the action from a stool on the upper balcony. Wednesday night is 'old school' night, with music from the '70s and '80s.

Tygmont JAZZ CLUB

(Map p362; ☑22 828 3409; www.tygmont.com.pl; ul Mazowiecka 6/8; ◷7pm-late) Hosting both local and international acts, the live jazz here is both varied and plentiful. Concerts start around 8pm but the place fills up early, so either reserve a table or turn up at opening time. Dinner is also available.

Capitol CLUB

(Map p362; ul Marszałkowska 115; ◷10pm-late Sat) If scarcity excites you, squeeze through the doors of this oh-so-cool club on the one night of the week it's open – Saturday. Low lighting gleams off pillars, retro decor and the shining faces of Warsaw's beautiful people as they gyrate within the dance-floor throng.

Underground Music Cafe CLUB

(Map p362; www.under.pl; ul Marszałkowska 126/134; ◷1pm-late) A swarm of students and backpackers pour into this basement club for its cheap beer, dark lighting and selection of music that varies from '70s and '80s to house, R & B and hip hop.

Performing Arts

Teatr Roma MUSICAL THEATRE

(Map p362; ☑22 628 8998; www.teatrroma.pl; ul Nowogrodzka 49) Theatre staging big-budget musicals sung in Polish, such as the ever-popular *Deszczowa Piosenka* (aka *Singin' in the Rain*).

Teatr Wielki OPERA

(Map p360; ☑22 692 0200; www.teatrwielki.pl; Plac Teatralny 1) The Grand Theatre hosts opera and ballet in its aptly grand premises.

Filharmonia Narodowa CLASSICAL MUSIC

(Map p362; ☑22 551 7111; www.filharmonia.pl; ul Jasna 5) Classical-music concerts are held here.

Cinemas

To avoid watching Polish TV in your hotel room, catch a film at the central Kino Atlantic (Map p362; ul Chmielna 33) or enjoy a flick in socialist-era glory at Kinoteka (Map p362; Plac Defilad 1) within the Palace of Culture & Science. English-language movies are subtitled in Polish.

🛍 Shopping

There are also plentiful antique and arts and crafts shops around the Rynek Starego Miasta, so brandish your credit card and explore.

Wars & Sawa MALL

(Map p362; ul Marszałowska 104/122) A sprawling modern shopping mall in the city centre.

Lapidarium JEWELLERY
(Map p360; www.lapidarium.pl; ul Nowomiejska 15/7) One of the most interesting shops on the Rynek Starego Miasta; offers jewellery and communist-era collectables.

EMPiK BOOKS
Has several stores across Warsaw, including branches in the **Wars & Sawa shopping mall** (Map p362; ul Marszałkowska 116/122, Wars & Sawa shopping mall) and on **Royal Way** (Map p362; ul Nowy Świat 15/17). A good source of English-language books, newspapers and magazines.

ⓘ Information
Discount Cards
Warsaw Tourist Card (www.warsawcard.com; 1/3 days 35/65zł) Free or discounted access to museums, public transport and some theatres, sports centres and restaurants. Available from tourist offices and some accommodation.

Internet Access
Expect to pay about 5zł per hour for internet access in Warsaw. Several convenient but dingy internet cafes are also located within Warszawa Centralna train station.

Verso Internet (ul Freta 17; ☺8am-8pm Mon-Fri, 9am-5pm Sat, 10am-4pm Sun) Enter from the rear, off ul Świętojerska.

Warsaw Point Gallery (ul Złota 59, Złote Tarasy; ☺9am-10pm) Pay at the information desk of this shopping mall.

Medical Services
Apteka Grabowskiego (Warszawa Centralna; ☺24hr) At the train station.

Centrum Medyczne LIM (☎22 332 2888; www.cmlim.pl; Al Jerozolimskie 65/79, 3rd fl, Marriott Hotel) Offers specialist doctors, laboratory tests and house calls.

EuroDental (☎22 627 5888; www.eurodental.com.pl; ul Śniadeckich 12/16; ☺8am-8pm Mon-Sat, 10am-2pm Sun) Private dental clinic with multilingual staff.

Money
Banks, *kantors* (foreign-exchange offices) and ATMs are easy to find around the city centre. *Kantors* that open 24 hours can be found at Warszawa Centralna train station and the airport, but exchange rates at these places are about 10% lower than in the city centre. Avoid changing money in the Old Town, where the rates can be even lower.

Post
Main Post Office (Map p362; ul Świętokrzyska 31/33; ☺24hr)

Tourist Information
Each tourist office provides free city maps and free booklets, such as the handy *Warsaw in Short* and the *Visitor*, and sells maps of other Polish cities; offices can also help with booking hotel rooms.

Free monthly tourist magazines worth seeking out include the comprehensive *Warsaw Insider* (10zł) and *Warsaw in Your Pocket* (5zł).

Tourist Office (☎22 19431; www.warsawtour.pl) Old Town (Map p360; Rynek Starego Miasta 19; ☺9am-9pm May-Sep, 9am-7pm Oct-Apr); Royal Way (Map p360; ul Krakowskie Przedmieście 15; ☺11am-8pm Tue-Sun); Palace of Culture & Science (Map p362; Plac Defilad 1; ☺8am-6pm); Warszawa Centralna train station (Map p362; Al Jana Pawła II; ☺8am-8pm May-Sep, 8am-7pm Oct-Apr); Warsaw Frédéric Chopin Airport (ul Żwirki i Wigury 1; ☺8am-8pm May-Sep, 8am-7pm Oct-Apr)

Warsaw Tourist Information Centre (Map p360; ☎22 635 1881; www.wcit.waw.pl; Plac Zamkowy 1/13; ☺9am-6pm Mon-Fri, 10am-6pm Sat & Sun) Helpful privately run tourist office in the Old Town.

ⓘ Getting There & Away
Air
The **Warsaw Frédéric Chopin Airport** (www.lotnisko-chopina.pl; ul Żwirki i Wigury 1), 7km from the city centre, is more commonly called Okęcie Airport.

There is a useful tourist office on the arrivals level, along with ATMs and several *kantors*. There are also car-hire companies, a left-luggage room and a newsagent where you can buy public transport tickets.

Domestic and international flights run by Poland's national carrier, LOT, can be booked at the **LOT office** (☎0801 703 703; Al Jerozolimskie 65/79) in town, or at any travel agency.

In July 2012, a new low-cost airport, **Warsaw Modlin** (www.modlinairport.pl; ul Generała Wiktora Thommée 1a, Nowy Dwór Mazowiecki), opened 35km north of the city. If you're flying on a budget carrier such as Ryanair or Wizz Air, you're likely to arrive here. It offers the usual services such as ATMs and car hire.

Bus
Warsaw's major bus station is **Dworzec Zachodnia** (Western Bus Station; www.pksbilety.pl; Al Jerozolimskie 144). This complex is southwest of the city centre and adjoins the Warszawa Zachodnia train station. To reach it, take the commuter train that leaves from Warszawa Śródmieście station. From here you can catch PKS buses in every direction.

Services run by the private company **Polski Bus** (www.polskibus.com) depart from the small bus station next to the Wilanowska metro station. Check its website for its timetable and fluctuating fares, as tickets must be purchased online.

International buses also depart from and arrive at Dworzec Zachodnia or, occasionally, outside Warszawa Centralna train station. Tickets are available from the bus offices at Dworzec Zachodnia, from agencies at Warszawa Centralna or from any of the major travel agencies in the city. **Eurolines Polska** (22 621 3469; www.eurolinespolska.pl) operates a huge number of buses to destinations throughout Europe; check its website for fares and special offers.

Train

Warsaw has several train stations, but the one that most travellers will use is **Warszawa Centralna** (Warsaw Central; Al Jerozolimskie 54). Opened in 1975 as a shining example of socialism, it became grimy and sinister in later years. It was impressively refurbished for the Euro 2012 football championships, but the shop-lined corridors beneath the main hall are still a confusing maze.

Warszawa Centralna is not always where trains start or finish, so make sure you get on or off promptly. Guard your belongings against pick-pocketing and theft at all times.

The station's main hall houses ticket counters, ATMs and snack bars, as well as a post office, newsagents and a tourist office. Along the underground mezzanine level leading to the platforms are several *kantors* (one of which is open 24 hours), a **left-luggage office** (7am-midnight), lockers, eateries, outlets for local public transport tickets, internet cafes and bookshops.

Tickets for domestic and international trains are available from counters at the station (but allow at least an hour for possible queuing). Alternatively, automatic ticket machines are avail-

TRANSPORT FROM WARSAW

Bus

DESTINATION	COMPANY	PRICE (ZŁ)	DURATION (HR)	FREQUENCY
Berlin (Germany)	Polski Bus	Varies	10¼	2 daily
Gdańsk	PKS	56	6	Hourly
Gdańsk	Polski Bus	Varies	5¾	Hourly
Kraków	PKS	58	6	8 daily
Kraków	Polski Bus	Varies	5	4 daily
Lublin	Polski Bus	Varies	3	5 daily
Prague (Czech Republic)	Polski Bus	Varies	12	2 daily
Toruń	PKS	50	4	hourly
Vienna (Austria)	Polski Bus	Varies	12½	2 daily
Wrocław	PKS	63	7	6 daily
Wrocław	Polski Bus	Varies	7¼	2 daily
Zakopane	PKS	65	8	6 daily

Train

DESTINATION	DURATION (HR)	FREQUENCY
Berlin (Germany)	5	5 daily
Bratislava (Slovakia)	8	2 daily
Budapest (Hungary)	11½	1 daily
Kyiv (Ukraine)	15½	1 daily
Minsk (Belarus)	9½-12	2-3 daily
Moscow (Russia)	18-21	2-3 daily
Prague (Czech Republic)	8½-10½	2 daily
Vienna (Austria)	8	3 daily

able, displaying instructions in English. You can check prices and book international train tickets online via **PKP Intercity** (☏22 391 9757; www.intercity.pl). Tickets for immediate departures on domestic and international trains can also be bought at numerous, well-signed booths in the underpasses leading to Warszawa Centralna.

For train connections between Warsaw and other Polish locations, check the Getting There & Away section under each specific town or city in this chapter.

Some domestic trains also stop at Warszawa Śródmieście station, 300m east of Warszawa Centralna, and Warszawa Zachodnia, next to Dworzec Zachodnia bus station.

🛈 Getting Around

To/From the Airport

In 2012 a train service began running from the new Okęcie airport station, Warszawa Lotnisko Chopina, stopping at either Warszawa Centralna or Warszawa Śródmieście stations in the city centre. Some services also stop at useful intermediate stations such as Warszawa Zachodnia. Trains depart approximately every 15 minutes from 4.30am to 11.30pm daily; the 20-minute journey costs 3.60zł on a regular one-trip public transport ticket.

Another way of getting from Warsaw's main airport to the city centre is bus 175 (3.60zł), which leaves every 10 to 15 minutes and travels via Warszawa Centralna train station and ul Nowy Świat, terminating at Plac Piłsudskiego, about a 500m walk from Castle Sq in the Old Town. If you arrive in the wee small hours, night bus N32 links the airport with Warszawa Centralna every 30 minutes.

The taxi fare between Okęcie airport and the city centre is about 45zł to 50zł. Official taxis displaying a name, telephone number and fares can be arranged at the official taxi counters at the international arrivals level.

From the new Warsaw Modlin airport, the easiest way to get to the city centre is aboard the regular **Modlin Bus** (☏503 558 148; www.modlinbus.com; adult/child 33/23zł; ⊗4am–midnight). Alternatively, a taxi to the centre will cost between 100zł and 130zł, depending on the time of day.

Car

Warsaw traffic isn't fun, but there are good reasons to hire a car for jaunts into the countryside. Major car-rental companies are listed in the local English-language publications. They include **Avis** (☏22 650 4872; www.avis.pl), **Hertz** (☏22 500 1620; www.hertz.pl) and **Sixt** (☏22 511 1550; www.sixt.pl).

Public Transport

Warsaw's public transport operates from 5am to 11pm daily. The standard fare (3.60zł) is valid for one ride only on a bus, tram or metro train travelling anywhere in the city.

Time-based tickets are available for 20/40/60 minutes (2.60/3.80/5.20zł), one day (12zł) and three days (24zł); with these you can transfer between vehicles within the time limit. Buy tickets from kiosks (including those marked 'RUCH') before boarding, and validate them on board.

Warsaw is the only place in Poland where ISIC cards get a public-transport discount (of 48%).

A metro line operates from the suburb of Ursynów (Kabaty station) at the southern city limits to Młociny in the north, via the city centre (Centrum), but is of limited use to visitors. Local commuter trains head out to the suburbs from the Warszawa Śródmieście station.

Taxi

Taxis are a quick and easy way to get around – as long as you use official taxis and drivers use their meters. Beware of unauthorised 'Mafia' taxis parked in front of top-end hotels, at the airport, outside Warszawa Centralna train station and in the vicinity of most tourist sights – they'll take you the long way round and overcharge for it.

MAZOVIA & PODLASIE

After being ruled as an independent state by a succession of dukes, Mazovia shot to prominence during the 16th century, when Warsaw became the national capital. The region has long been a base for industry, the traditional mainstay of Poland's third-largest city, Łódź. To the east of Mazovia, toward the Belarus border, lies Podlasie, which means 'land close to the forest'. The main attraction of this region is the impressive Białowieża National Park.

Łódź

POP 729,000

Little damaged in WWII, Łódź (pronounced 'woodge') is a lively, likeable place with a wealth of attractive art nouveau architecture and the added bonus of being off the usual tourist track. It's also an easy day trip from Warsaw. Łódź became a major industrial centre in the 19th century, attracting immigrants from across Europe. In the 20th century, it became the hub of Poland's cinema industry – giving rise to the nickname 'Holly-Woodge'. Though its textile industry slumped in the postcommunist years, the centrally located city has had some success in attracting new investment in more diverse commercial fields.

POLAND ŁÓDŹ

BIAŁOWIEŻA NATIONAL PARK

Once a centre for hunting and timber-felling, Białowieża (Byah-wo-*vyeh*-zhah) on Poland's eastern border is the nation's oldest national park. Its significance is underlined by Unesco's unusual recognition of the park as both a Biosphere Reserve *and* a World Heritage Site. The forest contains more than 100 species of birds, along with elk, wild boars and wolves. Its major drawcard is the magnificent European bison, which was once extinct outside zoos, but has been successfully reintroduced to its ancient home.

The main attraction is the **Strict Nature Reserve** (www.bpn.com.pl; adult/concession 6/3zł; ☺9am-5pm), which can only be visited on a three-hour tour with a licensed guide along an 8km trail (195zł for an English-speaking guide). The creatures can be shy of visitors and you may not see them at all. Even without bison for company, however, being immersed in one of Europe's last remnants of primeval forest is a special experience.

For a guarantee of spotting *żubry* (bison), visit the **European Bison Reserve** (Rezerwat Żubrów; www.bpn.com.pl; adult/concession 6/3zł; ☺9am-5pm May-Sep, 8am-4pm Tue-Sun Oct-Apr) on the Hajnówka–Białowieża road. It's an open-plan zoo containing many mighty bison, as well as wolves, strange horselike tarpans and the mammoth *żubroń* (a hybrid of bison and cow).

The logical visitor base is the charming village of Białowieża, with a range of accommodation from budget to top end. To arrange guides, bike hire or transport via horse-drawn cart, visit the **PTTK office** (☎85 681 2295; www.pttk.bialowieza.pl; ul Kolejowa 17; ☺8am-4pm) at the southern end of **Palace Park**, the former location of the Russian tsar's hunting lodge.

Białowieża can be a tricky place to reach by public transport. From Warsaw, the only direct option is a single daily bus to the village departing at 2.20pm from Dworzec Zachodnia (45zł, five hours). Alternatively, head first from Warsaw by train or bus to Białystok, from where you can catch buses to Białowieża either directly or by changing at Hajnówka.

For more details, check out Lonely Planet's *Poland* country guide or visit www.pttk.bialowieza.pl.

Many of the attractions are along ul Piotrkowska, the main thoroughfare. You'll find banks and *kantors* (foreign-exchange offices) here and on ul Kopernika, one street west. You can't miss the bronze statues of local celebrities along ul Piotrkowska, including director Roman Polański and pianist Artur Rubinstein, seated at a baby grand. The helpful **tourist office** (www.turystyczna.lodz.pl; ul Piotrkowska 87; ☺9am-5pm) hands out free brochures and advice.

◉ Sights & Activities

Cinematography Museum   MUSEUM
(www.kinomuzeum.pl; Plac Zwycięstwa 1; adult/concession 10/7zł, Tue free; ☺10am-4pm Tue, Wed & Fri, 11am-6pm Thu, Sat & Sun) Three blocks east of ul Piotrkowska's southern pedestrian zone. Worth a look both for its collection of old cinema gear and its mansion setting.

City Museum of Łódź   MUSEUM
(www.muzeum-lodz.pl; ul Ogrodowa 15; adult/concession 9/5zł, Sun free; ☺10am-2pm Mon, 2-6pm Wed, 11am-4pm Tue, Thu, Sat & Sun) Northwest of Plac Wolności, at the north end of the main drag,

this splendid museum tells the lively story of the city from its 19th-century industrial heyday onwards.

Manufaktura   MALL
(www.manufaktura.com; ul Karskiego 5) Close by the City Museum is this fascinating shopping mall and entertainment centre, constructed within a massive complex of historic red-brick factory buildings.

Jewish Cemetery   CEMETERY
(www.jewishlodzcemetery.org; ul Bracka 40; admission 6zł, 1st Sun of month free; ☺9am-5pm Sun-Thu, 9am-3pm Fri Apr-Oct, 9am-3pm Sun-Fri Nov-Mar) One of the largest in Europe. It's 3km northeast of the city centre and accessible by tram 6 from a stop one block north of Plac Wolności to its terminus at Strykowska. Enter from ul Zmienna.

Dętka   TOUR
(Plac Wolności 2; adult/concession 5/3zł; ☺noon-7pm Thu-Sun May-Oct) Guided tours every half-hour through the old red-brick sewer system beneath the city's streets, demonstrating the city's industrial heritage via photographs

and documents exhibited along the route. Operated by the City Museum.

🛏 Sleeping & Eating

The tourist office can provide information about all kinds of accommodation.

Youth Hostel   HOSTEL €
(☑42 630 6680; www.yhlodz.pl; ul Legionów 27; dm 18-40zł, s/d from 65/80zł; 🛜) This place is excellent, so book ahead. It features nicely decorated rooms in a spacious old building, with free laundry and a kitchen. It's 250m west of Plac Wolności.

Hotel Savoy   HOTEL €€
(☑42 632 9360; www.centrumhotele.pl; ul Traugutta 6; s/d from 149/249zł; 🛜) Well positioned just off central ul Piotrkowska, with simple but spacious light-filled rooms with clean bathrooms.

Hotel Centrum   HOTEL €€
(☑42 632 8640; www.centrumhotele.pl; ul Kilińskiego 59; s/d from 207/308zł; ❉🛜) East of ul Piotrkowska, this communist-era behemoth offers neatly renovated rooms and will be handy for the Łódź Fabryczna train station once it reopens after reconstruction in 2014.

Chłopska Izba   POLISH €€
(☑42 630 8087; ul Piotrkowska 65; mains 11-28zł; ⊙noon-11pm) On ul Piotrkowska is this restaurant with folksy decor, serving up tasty versions of all the Polish standards.

Esplanada   EUROPEAN €€
(☑42 630 5989; ul Piotrkowska 100; mains 19-59zł) A vibrant eatery serving quality Polish and German cuisine in an attractive historic venue. Beware the enormous (if tasty) schnitzels.

❶ Getting There & Around

AIR From **Łódź airport** (www.airport.lodz.pl; ul Maczka 35), which can be reached by city buses 55 and 65 (3.20zł, 20 minutes), there are flights to a number of British destinations including London and Dublin via Ryanair and Wizz Air. Dublin has four Ryanair connections per week. There are no domestic flights.

TRAIN At time of research the most convenient train station to the city centre, Łódź Fabryczna, had closed for reconstruction and was expected to reopen in 2014. In the meantime, the best option for travellers is busy Łódź Kaliska station, 1.2km southwest of central Łódź and accessible by tram 12 from the city centre. Trains are generally a better option than bus services from Łódź.

TRANSPORT FROM ŁÓDŹ

Bus

DESTINATION	DURATION (HR)	FREQUENCY
Berlin (Germany)	7½	2 daily
Poznań	2¾	2 daily
Prague (Czech Republic)	9½	2 daily
Warsaw	2¾	5 daily
Wrocław	4½	3 daily

Train

DESTINATION	COST(ZŁ)	DURATION (HR)	FREQUENCY
Częstochowa	38	2	4 daily
Gdańsk	61	6½	6 daily
Kraków	52	4½	4 daily
Poznań	32	4½	5 daily
Toruń	34	3	10 Daily
Warsaw	36	2	at least hourly
Wrocław	48	4¼	5 daily

BUS **Polski Bus** (www.polskibus.com) has useful connections to some destinations from its stop at Łódź Kaliska station. Check fares and buy tickets online.

MAŁOPOLSKA

Małopolska (literally 'lesser Poland') is a stunning area within which the visitor can spot plentiful remnants of traditional life amid green farmland and historic cities. The region covers a large swathe of southeastern Poland, from the former royal capital Kraków, to the eastern Lublin Uplands.

Kraków

POP 758,000

While many Polish cities are centred on an attractive Old Town, none can compare with Kraków (*krak*-oof) for sheer, effortless beauty. With a charming origin involving the legendary defeat of a dragon by either Prince Krakus or a cobbler's apprentice (depending on which story you believe), and with a miraculous escape from destruction in WWII, the city seems to have led a lucky existence.

As a result, Kraków is blessed with magnificent buildings and streets dating back to medieval times, with a stunning historic centrepiece – Wawel Castle.

Just south of the castle lies Kazimierz, the former Jewish quarter, reflecting both new and old. Its silent synagogues are a reminder of the tragedy of WWII, while the district's tiny streets and low-rise architecture have become home in recent years to a lively nightlife scene.

Not that you'll have trouble finding nightlife anywhere in Kraków, or a place to sleep. As the nation's biggest tourist drawcard, the city has hundreds of restaurants, bars and other venues tucked away in its laneways and cellars. Though hotel prices are above the national average, and visitor numbers high in summer, this vibrant, cosmopolitan city is an essential part of any tour of Poland.

◎ Sights & Activities

WAWEL HILL

Kraków's main draw for tourists is Wawel Hill. South of the Old Town, this prominent mount is crowned with a castle containing a cathedral; both are enduring symbols of Poland.

Wawel Castle   CASTLE

(☑12 422 5155; www.wawel.krakow.pl; grounds free; ⊙6am–dusk) You can choose from several attractions within this magnificent structure, each requiring a separate ticket, valid for a specific time. There's a limited daily quota of tickets for some parts, so arrive early if you want to see everything.

Most popular are the splendid **State Rooms** (adult/concession 18/11zł, Sun Nov-Mar free; ⊙9.30am–5pm Tue-Fri, from 10am Sat & Sun Apr-Oct, 9.30am–4pm Tue-Sun Nov-Mar) and the **Royal Private Apartments** (adult/concession 25/19zł; ⊙9.30am–5pm Tue-Sun Apr-Oct, to 4pm Tue-Sat Nov-Mar). Entry to the latter is only allowed on a guided tour; you may have to accompany a Polish-language tour if it's the only one remaining for the day. If you want to hire a guide who speaks English or other languages, contact the on-site **guides office** (☑12 422 1697).

The 14th-century **Wawel Cathedral** (www.katedra-wawelska.pl; ⊙9am–5pm Mon-Sat, from 12.30pm Sun) was the coronation and burial place of Polish royalty for four centuries. Ecclesiastical artefacts are displayed in its small **Cathedral Museum** (adult/concession 12/7zł; ⊙9am–5pm Tue-Sun). Admission also gives access to the **Royal Tombs**, including that of King Kazimierz Wielki; and the **bell tower** of the golden-domed **Sigismund Chapel** (1539), which contains the country's largest bell (11 tonnes).

Other attractions within the castle grounds include the **Museum of Oriental Art** (adult/concession 8/5zł; ⊙9.30am–5pm Tue-Sun Apr-Oct, to 4pm Tue-Sat Nov-Mar), the **Crown Treasury & Armoury** (adult/concession 18/11zł, Mon free; ⊙9.30am–1pm Mon, to 5pm Tue-Sun Apr-Oct, 9.30am–4pm Tue-Sun Nov-Mar) and the **Lost Wawel** (adult/concession 8/5zł, Mon Apr-Oct & Sun Nov-Mar free; ⊙9.30am–1pm Mon, to 5pm Tue-Sun Apr-Oct, 9.30am–4pm Tue-Sun Nov-Mar), a well-displayed set of intriguing archaeological exhibits.

In the warmer months there's also the **Former Buildings & Fortifications** tour (adult/concession 18/10zł; ⊙1pm Sat-Mon May-Sep) of the grounds, and you can climb the 137-step **Sandomierska Tower** (admission 4zł; ⊙10am–5pm May-Sep).

Finish your visit by entering the atmospheric cave known as the **Dragon's Den** (admission 3zł; ⊙10am–5pm Apr-Oct), as its exit leads out onto the riverbank where you'll encounter a fire-spitting bronze dragon.

Hi-Flyer Balloon   BALLOON RIDE
(Rondo Grunwaldzkie; adult/concession 38/20zł; ☺9am-10pm) Located on the opposite bank of the Vistula River from Wawel Castle, this tethered balloon lifts its passengers 150m into the air, enabling great views of the city.

OLD TOWN
Kraków's Old Town is a harmonious collection of historic buildings dating back centuries, ringed by a linear park known as the Planty which replaced the old city walls in the 19th century. It's an eminently walkable area.

Rynek Główny   HISTORIC SQUARE
(Main Market Square) This vast square is the focus of the Old Town and is Europe's largest medieval town square at 200m by 200m. Its most prominent feature is the 15th-century **Town Hall tower** (Wieża Ratuszowa; Rynek Główny 1; adult/concession 7/5zł; ☺10.30am-6pm Apr-Oct), which you can climb.

Cloth Hall   HISTORIC BUILDING
(Sukiennice; Rynek Główny 1) At the centre of the square is this 16th-century Renaissance building, housing a large souvenir market (p384). Here you can enter **Rynek Underground** (www.podziemiarynku.com; Rynek Główny 1; adult/concession 17/14zł, Tue free; ☺10am-8pm Mon, to 4pm Tue, to 10pm Wed-Sun), a fascinating attraction beneath the market square, consisting of an underground route through medieval market stalls and other long-forgotten chambers. The experience is enhanced by holograms and other audiovisual wizardry.

Upstairs, the **Gallery of 19th-Century Polish Painting** (http://muzeum.krakow.pl; Rynek Główny 1; adult/concession 12/6zł; ☺10am-8pm Tue-Sat, to 6pm Sun) exhibits art from a range of genres, including Polish Impressionism.

On the west side of the Cloth Hall is the useful **Historical Museum Visitor Centre** (☎12 426 5060; Rynek Główny 1; ☺10am-7pm), where you can buy tickets for many of the city's museums.

St Mary's Church   CHURCH
(Rynek Główny 4; adult/concession 6/4zł; ☺11.30am-6pm Mon-Sat, 2-6pm Sun) This 14th-century place of worship fills the northeastern corner of the square. The huge main altarpiece by Wit Stwosz (Veit Stoss in German) of Nuremberg is the finest Gothic sculpture in Poland and is opened ceremoniously each day at 11.50am.

FREE THRILLS

If you're short of a złoty, take advantage of these *gratis* Kraków attractions:

» Visit the beautiful courtyard of the Collegium Maius.

» Soak up the heady historical atmosphere of the grounds of Wawel Castle.

» Examine the intriguing collection of the Jewish Museum (p379) in Kazimierz for free on Mondays.

» Catch the historic *hejnał* (bugle call) being played from the tower of St Mary's Church each hour.

» Observe the crowds watching the artists displaying their work on the wall next to the 14th-century Florian Gate.

Every hour a *hejnał* (bugle call) is played from the highest tower of the church. The melody, played in medieval times as a warning call, breaks off abruptly to symbolise the moment when, according to legend, the throat of a 13th-century trumpeter was pierced by a Tatar arrow. In summer you can climb the church's highest **tower** (St Mary's Church; adult/concession 5/3zł; ☺9-11.30am & 1-5.30pm May-Aug).

Collegium Maius   HISTORIC BUILDING
(www.maius.uj.edu.pl; ul Jagiellońska 15; adult/concession 12/6zł; ☺10am-2.20pm Mon-Fri, to 1.20pm Sat) West of the Rynek Główny is the oldest surviving university building in Poland. Guided tours of its fascinating academic collection run half-hourly and there's usually a couple in English, at 11am and 1pm. Even if you don't go on a tour, step into the magnificent arcaded courtyard for a glimpse of the beautiful architecture.

Florian Gate   FORTIFICATION
(ul Floriańska) From St Mary's Church, walk up ul Floriańska to this 14th-century gate. It's a tourist hot spot, with crowds, buskers and artists selling their work along the remnant section of the old city walls. Beyond it is the **Barbican** (Barbakan; ul Basztowa; adult/concession 7/5zł; ☺10.30am-6pm May-Oct), a defensive bastion built in 1498.

Czartoryski Museum   MUSEUM
(www.czartoryski.org; ul Św Jana 19) Near the Florian Gate, this museum features an impressive collection of European art, including Leonardo da Vinci's *Lady with an Ermine*.

Kraków – Old Town & Wawel

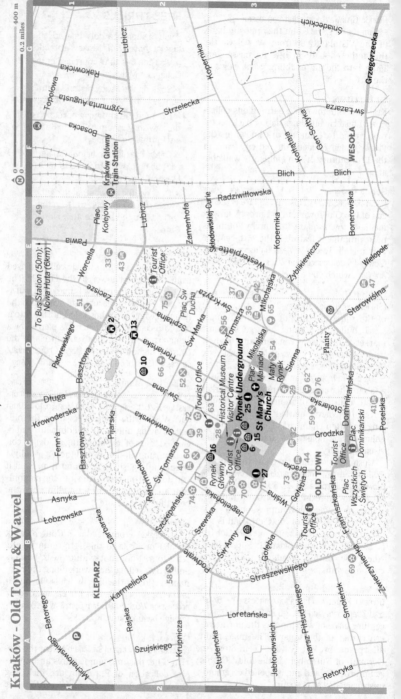

0 _____ 400 m
0 _____ 0.2 miles

KLEPARZ

WESOŁA

OLD TOWN

Rynek Underground

St Mary's Church

Historical Museum Visitor Centre

Kraków Główny Train Station

To Bus Station (50m);
Nowa Huta (6km)

Tourist Office

Tourist Office

Tourist Office

Tourist Office

Tourist Office

Tourist Office

Rynek Główny

Mały Rynek

Plac Mariacki

Plac Nowy

Plac Kolejowy

Plac Sw Ducha

Plac Wszystkich Świętych

Plac Dominikański

Plac Sw Krzyża

Planty

Streets:
Batorego, Michałowskiego, Szujskiego, Szlak, Krupnicza, Studencka, Garbarska, Asnyka, Łobzowska, Rajska, Karmelicka, Fenn'a, Długa, Krowoderska, Paderewskiego, Basztowa, Pijarska, Reformacka, Szczepańska, Szewska, Sw Anny, Jagiellońska, Sw Tomasza, Sławkowska, Sw Jana, Floriańska, Sw Marka, Szpitalna, Worcella, Zacisze, Pawia, Lubicz, Topolowa, Bosacka, Rakowicka, Zygmunta Augusta, Strzelecka, Kopernika, Zamenhofa, Radziwiłłowska, Skłodowskiej-Curie, Westerplatte, Sw Tomasza, Mikołajska, Zyblikiewicza, Starowiślna, Wielopole, Sw Krzyża, Mikołajska, Sienna, Stolarska, Grodzka, Bracka, Wiślna, Gołębia, Franciszkańska, Dominikańska, Poselska, Straszewskiego, Smoleńsk, marsz Piłsudskiego, Loretańska, Jabłonowskich, Retoryka, Zwierzyniecka, Bonerowska, Gen Sokółka, Kołłątaja, Blich, Sw Łazarza, Grzegórzecka, Śniadeckich

Podwale, Gołębia

Numbered locations: 2, 13, 10, 66, 51, 33, 43, 49, 15, 56, 37, 36, 65, 42, 47, 62, 76, 59, 41, 44, 73, 70, 74, 40, 60, 39, 72, 34, 28, 16, 7, 58, 69, 6, 25, 27, 15, 29, 32, 54, 52, 63

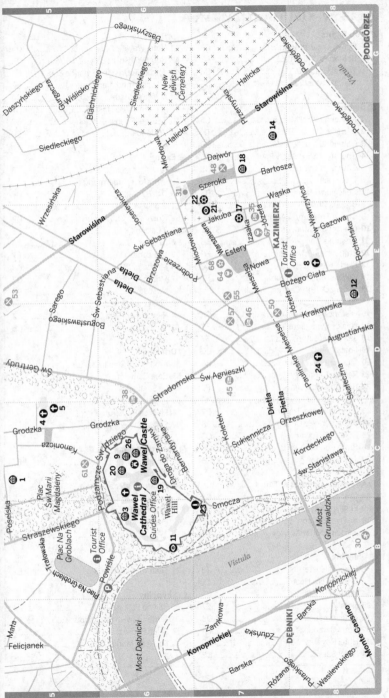

POLAND KRAKÓW

Kraków - Old Town & Wawel

◎ Top Sights

◎ Sights

◎ Activities, Courses & Tours

◎ Sleeping

◎ Eating

◎ Drinking

◎ Entertainment

◎ Shopping

Also on display are Turkish weapons and artefacts, including a campaign tent from the 1683 Battle of Vienna. At the time of research it was closed for a major renovation, expected to take until 2013; check with the tourist office for an update.

Historic Churches   CHURCH
South of the Rynek Główny along ul Grodzka is the early-17th-century Jesuit **Church of SS Peter & Paul** (ul Grodzka 64; ⊙dawn-dusk), Poland's first baroque church. The nearby Romanesque 11th-century **Church of St Andrew** (ul Grodzka 56; ⊙9am-6pm Mon-Fri) was the only building in Kraków to withstand the Tatars' attack of 1241.

Archaeological Museum   MUSEUM
(ul Poselska 3; adult/concession 7/5zł, Sun free; ⊙9am-3pm Mon-Wed, 2-6pm Thu, 10am-3pm Fri & Sun) Between the churches in the southern section of the Old Town you'll find this small but interesting museum, with displays on local prehistory and ancient Egyptian artefacts, including animal mummies.

Historical Museum of Kraków   MUSEUM
(www.mhk.pl; Rynek Główny 35; adult/concession 6/4zł, Sat free; ⊙10am-5.30pm Wed-Sun) On the northwest corner of the Rynek Główny, this institution contains paintings, documents and oddments relating to the city's history.

English Language Club   SOCIAL GROUP
(ul Sienna 5; admission 2zł; ⊙6-8pm Wed) Just south of St Mary's Church on the Rynek Główny, this social group has met weekly since the dying days of communism, when local students wanted to make contact with foreign visitors. Its weekly catch-ups are a fun way to meet a mixed bunch of Poles, expats and tourists in a relaxed setting.

KAZIMIERZ
Founded by King Kazimierz Wielki in 1335, Kazimierz was originally an independent town. In the 15th century, Jews were expelled from Kraków and forced to resettle in a small prescribed area in Kazimierz, separated from the rest of the town by a wall. The Jewish quarter later became home to Jews fleeing persecution throughout Europe.

By the outbreak of WWII there were 65,000 Jewish Poles in Kraków (around 30% of the city's population) and most lived in Kazimierz. Tragically, this thriving community was devastated in the Holocaust.

Nowadays the district's eastern quarter is dotted with synagogues and other reminders of Jewish culture and history, while the western half is home to a lively bar and dining scene. Kazimierz lies southeast of the Old Town.

Jewish Museum   MUSEUM
(www.mhk.pl; ul Szeroka 24; adult/concession 8/6zł, Mon free; ⊙10am-2pm Mon & 9am-5pm Tue-Sun) This museum is housed within the 15th-century Old Synagogue, the oldest in Poland. Within its walls are exhibitions on Jewish traditions.

Galicia Jewish Museum   MUSEUM
(www.galiciajewishmuseum.org; ul Dajwór 18; adult/concession 15/10zł; ⊙10am-6pm) South of the Old Synagogue, this fine museum features an impressive photographic exhibition, depicting modern-day traces of southeastern Poland's once thriving Jewish community.

Remuh Synagogue   SYNAGOGUE
(www.remuh.jewish.org.pl; ul Szeroka 40; adult/concession 5/2zł; ⊙9am-6pm Sun-Fri) A short walk north from the Old Synagogue is this small 16th-century place of worship, still used for religious services. Behind it, the **Remuh Cemetery** (ul Szeroka 40; admission free; ⊙9am-6pm Mon-Fri) boasts some extraordinary Renaissance gravestones.

Izaak's Synagogue   SYNAGOGUE
(ul Kupa 18; adult/concession 5/3zł; ⊙9am-7pm Sun-Thu, to 3pm Fri) Heading west from ul Szeroka, you'll find this restored synagogue, decorated with impressive frescos from the 17th century.

Ethnographic Museum   MUSEUM
(www.etnomuzeum.eu; Plac Wolnica 1; adult/concession 9/5zł, Sun free; ⊙11am-7pm Tue-Sat, to 3pm Sun May-Sep, 10am-6pm Mon, to 3pm Wed-Fri, to 2pm Sat & Sun Oct-Apr) Kazimierz's Old Town Hall contains this museum, displaying a collection of regional crafts and costumes.

Historic Churches   CHURCH
Kazimierz's western Catholic quarter includes the 14th-century Gothic **St Catherine's Church** (ul Augustiańska 7), with an imposing 17th-century gilded high altar, while the 14th-century **Corpus Christi Church** (ul Bożego Ciała 26) is crammed with baroque fittings.

PODGÓRZE
During the war the Germans relocated Jews to a walled ghetto in this district, just south of Kazimierz across the Vistula River. They were exterminated in the nearby Płaszów

NOWA HUTA

There's another side to Kraków that few tourists see. Catch tram 4 or 15 from Kraków Główny train station, or tram 22 from Kazimierz, east to Plac Centralny in Nowa Huta. This suburb was a 'workers' paradise' district built by the communist regime in the 1950s to counter the influence of the city's religious and intellectual traditions. Its immense, blocky concrete buildings stretch out along broad, straight streets; a fascinating contrast to the Old Town's delicate beauty.

Concentration Camp, as portrayed in Steven Spielberg's haunting film, *Schindler's List*.

TOP CHOICE Schindler's Factory   MUSEUM
(www.mhk.pl; ul Lipowa 4; adult/concession 17/14zł; ⏰10am-4pm Mon, 10am-8pm Tue-Sun) This impressive museum covering the German occupation of Kraków in WWII is housed in the former enamel factory of Oskar Schindler, which was immortalised in *Schindler's List*. Well-organised, innovative exhibits tell the moving story of the city from 1939 to 1945, recreating urban elements such as a tram carriage, a train station underpass and a crowded ghetto apartment within the factory's walls. It's an experience that shouldn't be missed.

From the main post office in the Old Town, catch any tram down ul Starowiślna and alight at the first stop over the river at Plac Bohaterów Getta. From here, follow the signs east along ul Kącik, under the railway line to the museum.

Museum of Contemporary Art in Kraków   GALLERY
(MOCAK; www.mocak.com.pl; ul Lipowa 4; adult/concession 10/5zł, Tue free; ⏰11am-7pm Tue-Sun) Opened in 2011, MOCAK is a major museum of modern art and the first such building in Poland to be constructed from scratch. As it's right next to Schindler's Factory, the two attractions could be combined for an absorbing day out.

WIELICZKA

Wieliczka Salt Mine   UNDERGROUND MUSEUM
(www.kopalnia.pl; ul Daniłowicza 10; adult/concession 68/54zł; ⏰7.30am-7.30pm Apr-Oct, 8am-5pm Nov-Mar) Wieliczka (vyeh-*leech*-kah), 15km

southeast of the city centre, is famous for this former salt mine. It's an eerie but richly decorated world of pits and chambers, and every single element from chandeliers to altarpieces was hewn by hand from solid salt. The mine is included on Unesco's World Heritage List.

The highlight of a visit is the richly ornamented Chapel of the Blessed Kinga, a church measuring 54m by 17m and 12m high. Construction of this underground temple took more than 30 years (1895–1927), resulting in the removal of 20,000 tonnes of rock salt.

The obligatory guided tour through the mine takes about two hours (a 2km walk). Tours in English operate approximately hourly between 10am and 5pm, increasing to half-hourly from 8.30am to 6pm in July and August. If you're visiting independently, you must wait for a tour to start. Last admission to the mine is shortly before closing time.

To avoid queues at Wieliczka, buy your ticket in advance from the Kopalnia Soli office (ul Wiślna 12; ⏰9am-5pm Mon-Fri) in Kraków before setting out.

An easy way to get to Wieliczka is by minibus (3zł; look for the 'Salt Mine' sign on the windscreen), departing frequently between 6am and 8pm from ul Pawia near the Galeria Krakowska shopping mall next to Kraków Główny train station. Alternatively, bus 304 travels from the same area to the salt mine and requires a suburban ticket (3.40zł), which you can obtain from ticket vending machines. Get off at the 'Wieliczka Kopalnia Soli' stop.

☞ Tours

These companies operate tours of Kraków and surrounding areas.

Jarden Tourist Agency   JEWISH HERITAGE
(☏12 429 1374; www.jarden.pl; ul Szeroka 2) The best agency for tours of Polish Jewish heritage, based in Kazimierz. Its showpiece, 'Retracing Schindler's List' (two hours by car), costs 80zł per person. All tours require a minimum of three and must be booked in advance. Tours are in English, but other languages can be arranged.

Cracow Tours   GUIDED TOURS
(☏12 430 0726; www.cracowtours.pl; ul Krupnicza 3) This company runs various tours, including a four-hour general bus tour of the city (adult/concession 130/65zł).

Crazy Guides COMMUNIST HERITAGE
(☎50 009 1200; www.crazyguides.com) Offers entertaining tours of the city's communist-era suburbs, in restored cars of the socialist era. Guides collect tour members from their accommodation.

⚜ Festivals & Events

Krakow International Film Festival FILM
(www.kff.com.pl; ☺May/Jun)

Lajkonik Pageant HISTORIC
(☺May/June) Held seven days after Corpus Christi, this centuries-old parade is led by a man in a pointed hat riding a hobbyhorse, symbolising an ancient victory over invaders.

Jewish Culture Festival JEWISH
(www.jewishfestival.pl; ☺Jun/Jul)

International Festival of Street Theatre THEATRE
(www.teatrkto.pl; ☺Jul)

Summer Jazz Festival MUSIC
(www.cracjazz.com; ☺Jul)

Organ Music Festival MUSIC
(☺Jul/Aug) A series of concerts held in churches each summer; check with the tourist office for the latest schedule.

Live Festival MUSIC
(www.livefestival.pl; ☺Aug) Big open-air music festival with a diverse range of performers.

Kraków Christmas Crib Competition CHRISTMAS
(☺Dec) Competitive display of elaborate nativity scenes, exhibited in the Rynek each winter.

🛏 Sleeping

Kraków is unquestionably Poland's major tourist destination, with prices to match. Booking ahead in the busy summer months is recommended.

An agency offering decent rooms around town is **Jordan Tourist Information & Accommodation Centre** (☎12 422 6091; www.jordan.pl; ul Pawia 8; s/d around 150/250zł; ☺8am-6pm Mon-Fri, 9am-2pm Sat).

TOP CHOICE Wielopole HOTEL €€
(☎12 422 1475; www.wielopole.pl; ul Wielopole 3; s/d 299/359zł; ❄☎) Smart and simple modern rooms in a renovated block on the eastern edge of the Old Town, with narrow beds but

spotless bathrooms. The tariff includes an impressive buffet breakfast.

Mama's Hostel HOSTEL €
(☎12 429 5940; www.mamashostel.com.pl; ul Bracka 4; dm 50-60zł, d 150zł; ☎) Centrally located, brightly hued lodgings with a beautiful sunlit lounge overlooking a courtyard and the aroma of freshly roasted coffee drifting up from a cafe below in the mornings. There's a washing machine on-site.

Nathan's Villa Hostel HOSTEL €
(☎12 422 3545; www.nathansvilla.com; ul Św Agnieszki 1; dm from 42zł, d 184zł; ☎) Comfy rooms, sparkling bathrooms, a laundry and a friendly atmosphere make this place a big hit with backpackers, and its cellar bar, minicinema, beer garden and pool table add to the appeal. Conveniently located between the Old Town and Kazimierz.

AAA Kraków Apartments APARTMENTS €€
(☎12 346 4670; www.krakow-apartments.biz; apt from 300zł; ☎) Company renting out renovated apartments in the vicinity of the Old Town, with a smaller selection in Kazimierz. Cheaper rates are available for longer stays.

Hotel Amadeus HOTEL €€€
(☎12 429 6070; www.hotel-amadeus.pl; ul Mikołajska 20; s/d 540/620zł; ☎) Everything about this hotel says 'class'. The rooms are tastefully furnished, though singles are rather small given the price. One room has wheelchair access, and there's a sauna, fitness centre and well-regarded restaurant. While hanging around the lobby, you can check out photos of famous guests.

Hotel Stary HOTEL €€€
(☎12 384 0808; www.stary.hotel.com.pl; ul Szczepańska 5; s/d 800/900zł; ❄☎☀) Setting a classy standard, the Stary is housed in an 18th-century aristocratic residence that exudes charm. The fabrics are all natural, the bathroom surfaces Italian marble, and there's a fitness centre, swimming pool and rooftop terrace to enjoy.

Hotel Abel HOTEL €€
(☎12 411 8736; www.hotelabel.pl; ul Józefa 30; s/d 160/220zł; ☎) Reflecting the character of Kazimierz, this hotel has a distinctive personality, evident in its polished wooden staircase, arched brickwork and age-worn tiles. The comfortable rooms make a good base for exploring the historic Jewish neighbourhood.

POLAND KRAKÓW

Greg & Tom Hostel
HOSTEL€

(☑12 422 4100; www.gregtomhostel.com; ul Pawia 12; dm 57zł, d from 150zł; 🛜) This well-run hostel is in a handy location near the train station. There's a free Polish dinner served each Tuesday, the staff are friendly and laundry facilities are included.

Cracow Hostel
HOSTEL€

(☑12 429 1106; www.cracowhostel.com; Rynek Główny 18; dm 40-72zł, d 188zł; 🛜) This hostel spread over three floors may not be the best in town, with somewhat cramped dorms, but it's perched high above the Rynek Główny and has an amazing view from its comfortable lounge.

Hostel Flamingo
HOSTEL€

(☑12 422 0000; www.flamingo-hostel.com; ul Szewska 4; dm 55-85zł, d 190zł; 🛜) Colourful hostel with pink and lilac decor, a friendly attitude and a great location not far west of the Rynek Główny. Dorms have four to 10 beds.

Hotel Royal
HOTEL €€

(☑12 421 3500; www.hotelewam.pl; ul Św Gertrudy 26-29; s/d from 249/360zł; 🛜) Impressive art nouveau edifice with loads of old-world charm, just below Wawel Castle. It's split into two sections: the higher-priced rooms are cosy and far preferable to the fairly basic rooms at the back.

Tournet Pokoje Gościnne
HOTEL €€

(☑12 292 0088; www.accommodation.krakow.pl; ul Miodowa 7; s/d from 150/200zł; 🛜) This is a neat pension in Kazimierz, offering simple but comfortable and quiet rooms with compact bathrooms. The in-house restaurant serves Polish dishes.

Hotel Wit Stwosz
HOTEL €€€

(☑12 429 6026; www.wit-stwosz.com.pl; ul Mikołajska 28; s/d 330/420zł; 🛜) In a historic town house belonging to St Mary's Church, decorated in a suitably religious theme. Rooms are compact and simply furnished, but tasteful and attractive.

Hotel Wawel
HOTEL €€€

(☑12 424 1300; www.hotelwawel.pl; ul Poselska 22; s/d 340/480zł; ❄🛜) Ideally located just off busy ul Grodzka, this is a pleasant place offering tastefully decorated rooms with timber highlights. It's far enough from the main drag to minimise noise.

Hotel Saski
HOTEL €€

(☑12 421 4222; www.hotelsaski.com.pl; ul Sławkowska 3; s/d 295/395zł; 🛜) The Saski occupies a historic mansion, complete with a uniformed doorman, rattling old lift and ornate furnishings. The rooms themselves are comparatively plain.

Hotel Campanile
HOTEL €€

(☑12 424 2600; www.campanile.com.pl; ul Św Tomasza 34; r 369zł; 🛜) Straightforward modern hotel in a quiet corner of the Old Town, just a few blocks from the Rynek. It has attractive, bright rooms done out in corporate decor. Breakfast is 35zł extra.

Camping Smok
CAMPING GROUND €

(☑12 429 8300; www.smok.krakow.pl; ul Kamedulska 18; site per person/tent 25/15zł, r 180zł) It's small, quiet and pleasantly located 4km west of the Old Town, with both tent space and rooms. To get here from outside the Kraków Główny train station building, take tram 1, 2 or 6 to the end of the line in Zwierzyniec (destination marked 'Salwator') and change for any westbound bus (except bus 100).

🍴 Eating

Kraków is a food paradise, tightly packed with restaurants serving a wide range of international cuisines.

One local speciality is *obwarzanki* (ring-shaped pretzels powdered with poppy seeds, sesame seeds or salt) available from street vendors who can often be found dozing next to their barrows throughout the city.

Self-caterers can stock up at the **Carrefour Supermarket** (ul Pawia 5, Galeria Krakowska; ⊙9am-10pm Mon-Sat, 10am-9pm Sun) within the Galeria Krakowska shopping mall, next to the Kraków Główny train station.

TOP CHOICE Glonojad
VEGETARIAN €

(Plac Matejki 2; mains 8-14zł; ⊙8am-10pm; 🛜🍴) Attractive modern vegetarian restaurant with a great view onto Plac Matejki, just north of the Barbican. The diverse menu has a variety of tasty dishes including samosas, curries, potato pancakes, burritos, gnocchi and soups. There's also an all-day breakfast menu, so there's no need to jump out of your hotel bed too early.

Deli Bar
HUNGARIAN €€

(ul Meiselsa 5; mains 10-53zł; ⊙1-10pm) A Hungarian guy called László told us this was the best Magyar restaurant in Kraków, and he was right on the money. Its Hungarian owners turn out tasty paprika-laced classics such as goulash, *palacsinta* (crepes in Hungarian) and 'Budapest pork'.

Milkbar
POLISH €
(ul Św Tomasza 24; mains 10-18zł; ☉9am-9pm)
Cleverly modernised version of the traditional *bar mleczny* (milk bar), serving affordable
dishes including breakfast in a pleasant dining area. The two-course set menu for 18zł is
great value.

Restauracja Pod Gruszką
POLISH €€
(ul Szczepańska 1; mains 12-29zł; ☉noon-midnight)
A favourite haunt of writers and artists, this
upstairs establishment is the eatery that
time forgot, with its elaborate old-fashioned
decor featuring chandeliers, lace tablecloths, age-worn carpets and sepia portraits.
The menu covers a range of Polish dishes,
the most distinctive being the soups served
within small bread loaves.

Momo
VEGETARIAN €
(ul Dietla 49; mains 10-16zł; ☉11am-8pm; ☑) Vegans
will cross the doorstep of this Kazimierz restaurant with relief – the majority of the menu
is completely animal-free. The space is decorated with Indian craft pieces and serves up
subcontinental soups, stuffed pancakes and
rice dishes, with a great range of cakes. The
Tibetan dumplings are a treat worth ordering.

Il Calzone
ITALIAN €€
(ul Starowiślna 15a; mains 16-44zł; ☉noon-11pm
Mon-Thu) This pleasant slice of Italy is a well-
kept secret, tucked away in a quiet nook set
back from the street. Considering its pleasant whitewashed decor and charming outdoor terrace, the food is excellent value.

Ariel
JEWISH €€
(ul Szeroka 18; mains 19-78zł) Atmospheric Jewish restaurant packed with old-fashioned
timber furniture and portraits, serving a
range of kosher dishes. Try the Berdytchov
soup (beef, honey and cinnamon) for a tasty
starter. There's often live music here at night.

Nostalgia
POLISH €€
(ul Karmelicka 10; mains 19-76zł; ☉noon-11pm) A
refined version of the traditional Polish eatery, Nostalgia features a fireplace, overhead
timber beams, uncrowded tables and courteous service. Wrap yourself around Russian
dumplings, a 'Hunter's Stew' of cabbage,
meat and mushrooms, or vegie options such
as potato pancakes. In warm weather diners
can enjoy the outdoor eating area.

Manzana
MEXICAN €€
(ul Miodowa 11; mains 19-32zł; ☉7.30am-1am) Long
opening hours, a breakfast menu and some
impressively authentic dishes make this a
compelling dining choice. The interior is done
out in soothing burnt orange tones, with only
a minimum of sombreros as decoration.

Pimiento
ARGENTINIAN €€€
(ul Stolarska 13; mains 44-159zł) This upmarket
grill serves a dizzying array of steaks to suit
both appetite and budget, and offers some
reasonable vegetarian alternatives for the
meat averse. Factor the South American
wine list into your calculations and you have
a classy night out.

Il Forno
ITALIAN €€
(Mały Rynek 2; mains 21-79zł; ☉noon-late) This
place has an attractive view of the Mały
Rynek (Small Market Sq). It serves pizzas
and pasta, along with more ambitious meat
and fish dishes. The downstairs bar section
is the Arabian-styled Shisha Club, serving
Middle Eastern food.

Gruzińskie Chaczapuri
GEORGIAN €€
(ul Floriańska 26; mains 16-29zł; ☉noon-11pm; ☑)
Cheap and cheerful place serving up tasty
Georgian dishes. Grills, salads and steaks fill
the menu and there's a separate vegetarian
selection with items such as the traditional
Georgian cheese pie with stewed vegetables.

Smak Ukraiński
UKRAINIAN €€
(ul Kanonicza 15; mains 18-30zł; ☉noon-10pm)
This Ukrainian restaurant presents authentic dishes in a cosy little cellar decorated
with provincial flair. Expect lots of dumplings, *borshch* (beetroot soup) and waiters
in waistcoats.

🍸 Drinking

There are hundreds of pubs and bars in
Kraków's Old Town, many housed in ancient
vaulted cellars. Kazimierz also has a lively
bar scene, centred on Plac Nowy and its surrounding streets.

Ambasada Śledzia
BAR
(ul Stolarska 6; ☉8am-6am) The 'Herring Embassy' sits neatly, if cheekily, on this street
lined with consulates. It serves cheap beer
and vodka along with snack-sized servings
of *śledź* (herring), *kiełbasa* (sausage) or
golonka (pork knuckle) for around 10zł. It's
a good place to chow down if you're out late
clubbing.

Paparazzi
BAR
(ul Mikołajska 9; ☉noon-1am Mon-Fri, 4pm-1am Sat
& Sun; ☎) Bright, modern place, with B&W
press photos of celebrities covering the walls.
The drinks menu includes cocktails such as

POLAND KRAKÓW

the Polish martini, built around bison grass vodka. There's also inexpensive bar food.

Singer
CAFE-BAR

(ul Estery 20; ⊙9am-4am) Laid-back hang-out of the Kazimierz cognoscenti, this relaxed cafe-bar's moody candlelit interior is full of character. Alternatively, sit outside and converse over a sewing machine affixed to the table.

Piwnica Pod Złotą Pipą
PUB

(ul Floriańska 30; ⊙noon-midnight) Less claustrophobic than other cellar bars, with lots of tables for eating or drinking. Decent bar food and international beers on tap.

Le Scandale
BAR

(Plac Nowy 9; ⊙8am-3am; 🛜) Smooth Kazimierz drinking hole with low black-leather couches, ambient lighting and a gleaming well-stocked bar. Full of mellow drinkers sampling the extensive cocktail list.

Cafe Camelot
CAFE

(ul Św Tomasza 17; ⊙9am-midnight) For coffee and cake, try this genteel haven hidden around an obscure street corner in the Old Town. Its cosy rooms are cluttered with lace-covered candlelit tables and a quirky collection of wooden figurines featuring spiritual or folkloric scenes.

☆ Entertainment

The comprehensive Polish-English booklet *Karnet* (4zł), published by the city authorities' tourist office, lists almost every event in the city. In addition, the tourist office located at ul Św Jana 2 specialises in cultural events and can book tickets to many of them.

Nightclubs

TOP CHOICE Baccarat
CLUB

(ul Stolarska 13; ⊙8pm-late Thu-Sat) Luxuriously appointed nightclub playing a mix of house,

dance and disco sounds, via DJs and occasional live performers. Move your body beneath the shiny chandeliers and mirror balls.

Alchemia
BAR/CLUB

(ul Estery 5; ⊙9am-3am) This Kazimierz venue exudes a shabby-is-the-new-cool look with rough-hewn wooden benches, candlelit tables and a companionable gloom. It hosts regular live-music gigs and theatrical events through the week.

Harris Piano Jazz Bar
JAZZ

(Rynek Główny 28; ⊙9am-2am May-Oct, 1pm-2am Nov-Apr) Subterranean jazz haunt with one of Kraków's most varied programs. There's jazz, blues, big band, fusion or soul music every night, interspersed with free jam sessions. Ticketed events range from 15zł to 35zł.

Rdza
CLUB

(ul Bracka 3/5) This basement club attracts some of Kraków's more sophisticated clubbers, with its Polish house music bouncing off exposed brick walls and comfy sofas. Guest DJs start spinning at 9pm.

Performing Arts

Stary Teatr
THEATRE

(☑12 422 9080; www.stary.pl; ul Jagiellońska 5) Accomplished theatre company offering quality productions. To overcome the language barrier, pick a Shakespeare play you know well from the repertoire and take in the distinctive Polish interpretation.

Teatr im Słowackiego
OPERA, THEATRE

(☑12 424 4528; www.slowacki.krakow.pl; Plac Św Ducha 1) This grand place, built in 1893, focuses on Polish classics, large theatrical productions and opera.

Filharmonia Krakowska
CLASSICAL MUSIC

(☑12 619 8722; www.filharmonia.krakow.pl; ul Zwierzyniecka 1) Hosts one of the best orchestras in the country; concerts are usually held on Friday and Saturday.

Cinemas

Two convenient cinemas are **Krakowskie Centrum Kinowe Ars** (ul Św Jana 6) and **Kino Pod Baranami** (Rynek Główny 27), the latter located within a courtyard off the Rynek Główny. Films are in their original languages, with Polish subtitles.

Shopping

The place to start (or perhaps end) your Kraków shopping is at the large **souvenir**

market (Rynek Główny 3; 10am-6pm) within the Cloth Hall (p375), selling everything from fine amber jewellery to tacky plush dragons.

Galeria Plakatu ART
(ul Stolarska 8; 11am-6pm Mon-Fri, 11am-2pm Sat) Fascinating examples of Polish poster art can be purchased here.

Sklep Podróżnika BOOKS
(ul Jagiellońska 6; 11am-7pm Mon-Fri, 10am-2pm Sat) For regional and city maps, as well as Lonely Planet titles.

Jarden Jewish Bookshop BOOKS
(ul Szeroka 2) Located in Kazimierz; well stocked with titles on Poland's Jewish heritage.

Information

Discount Cards
Kraków Tourist Card (www.krakowcard.com; 2/3 days 60/75zł) Available from tourist offices, the card includes travel on public transport and entry to many museums.

Internet Access
Centrum Internetowe (ul Stolarska 5; 9am-midnight) Within the Pasaż Bielaka arcade.
Klub Garinet (ul Floriańska 18; per hr 4zł; 9am-10pm)

Money
Kantors (foreign-exchange offices) and ATMs can be found all over the city centre. It's worth noting, however, that many *kantors* close on Sunday and some located near the Rynek Główny and Kraków Główny train station offer terrible exchange rates – check around before proffering your cash. There are also exchange facilities at the airport, with even less attractive rates.

Post
Main Post Office (ul Westerplatte 20; 7.30am-8.30pm Mon-Fri, 8am-2pm Sat)

Tourist Information
Two free magazines, *Welcome to Cracow & Małopolska* and *Visitor: Kraków & Zakopane*, are available at upmarket hotels. The *Kraków in Your Pocket* booklet (5zł) is also very useful, packed with entertaining reviews of local sights and eateries.

POLAND KRAKÓW

DON'T MISS

AUSCHWITZ-BIRKENAU

Few place names have more impact than Auschwitz, which is seared into public consciousness as the location of history's most extensive experiment in genocide.

Established within disused army barracks in 1940, Auschwitz was initially designed to hold Polish prisoners, but was expanded by the German military occupiers into their largest centre for the extermination of European Jews.

Two more camps were subsequently established: Birkenau (Brzezinka, also known as Auschwitz II), 3km west of Auschwitz; and Monowitz (Monowice), several kilometres west of Oświęcim, the Polish town which contains the former death camp. In the course of their operation, between one and 1.5 million people were murdered by the Nazi Germany regime in these death factories – 90% of them Jews.

Auschwitz was only partially destroyed by the fleeing Nazis, so many of the original buildings remain as a bleak document of the camp's history. A dozen of the 30 surviving prison blocks house sections of the **State Museum Auschwitz-Birkenau** (33 844 8100; www.auschwitz.org.pl; ul Więźniów Oświęcimia 20; admission free; 8am-7pm Jun-Aug, 8am-6pm May & Sep, 8am-5pm Apr & Oct, 8am-4pm Mar & Nov, 8am-3pm Dec-Feb).

Between May and October it's compulsory to join a tour if you arrive between 10am and 3pm. English-language tours of the Auschwitz-Birkenau complex (adult/concession 40/30zł, 3½ hours) leave at half-hourly intervals from 9.30am.

Auschwitz-Birkenau is an easy day trip from Kraków. Most convenient are the approximately hourly buses to Oświęcim (12zł, 1½ hours) departing from the bus station in Kraków, which either pass by or terminate at the museum. There are also numerous minibuses to Oświęcim (10zł, 1½ hours) from the minibus stands off ul Pawia, next to Galeria Krakowska.

Most travel agencies in Kraków offer organised tours of Auschwitz (including Birkenau), costing from 90zł to 130zł per person. Check with the operator for exactly how much time the tour allows you at each site, as some run to a very tight schedule.

For more about Oświęcim, including accommodation, check out Lonely Planet's *Poland* country guide or visit www.mpit-oswiecim.neostrada.pl.

TRANSPORT FROM KRAKÓW

Domestic Bus

DESTINATION	PRICE (ZŁ)	DURATION (HR)	FREQUENCY
Cieszyn (on the Czech border)	20	3	Hourly
Lublin	48	5½	6 daily
Oświęcim (Auschwitz)	12	1½	hourly
Zakopane	18	2	at least hourly
Zamość	52	8	9 daily

Domestic Train

DESTINATION	PRICE (ZŁ)	DURATION (HR)	FREQUENCY
Częstochowa	38	2¼	3 daily
Gdynia & Gdańsk	69	8-12	10 daily
Lublin	58	4½	2 daily
Poznań	61	8½	9 daily
Przemyśl	50	5	9 daily
Toruń	69	8½	3 daily
Warsaw	56	3	at least hourly
Wrocław	52	5½	hourly
Zakopane	24	3¾	8 daily

International Train

DESTINATION	DURATION (HR)	FREQUENCY
Berlin (Germany)	10	1 daily
Bratislava (Slovakia)	7½	1 daily
Budapest (Hungary)	10½	1 daily
Kyiv (Ukraine)	19½	1 daily
Lviv (Ukraine)	7½-9½	2 daily
Prague (Czech Republic)	10	1 daily
Vienna (Austria)	8	1 daily

Tourist Office ul Św Jana (☎12 421 7787; www.
karnet.krakow.pl; ul Św Jana 2; ☺9am-7pm);
Cloth Hall (☎12 433 7310; Rynek Główny 1;
☺9am-7pm May-Sep, 9am-5pm Oct-Apr); northeastern Old Town (☎12 432 0110; ul Szpitalna
25; ☺9am-7pm May-Sep, 9am-5pm Oct-Apr);
southern Old Town (☎12 616 1886; Plac Wszystkich Świętych 2; ☺9am-5pm); Wawel Hill (ul
Powiśle 11; ☺9am-7pm); Kazimierz (☎12 422
0471; ul Józefa 7; ☺9am-5pm); airport (☎12 285
5431; John Paul II International airport, Balice;
☺9am-7pm). Helpful city-run service; the office
at ul Św Jana 2 specialises in cultural events.

❶ Getting There & Away

Air

The **John Paul II International airport** (www.
lotnisko-balice.pl; ul Medweckiego 1) is more
often called Balice airport, after the suburb in
which it's located, about 15km west of the Old
Town. The airport terminal hosts car-hire desks,
along with currency exchanges offering un-
appealing rates. To get to the Old Town by public
transport, step aboard the free shuttle bus to
the nearby train station. Buy a ticket (12zł) on
board the train from a vending machine or the
conductor for the 20-minute train journey to
Kraków Główny station.

If you land instead at Katowice airport, catch the
Matuszek (☎32 236 1111; www.matuszek.com.
pl; one-way/return 44/88zł) shuttle bus to the
Kraków bus station; the journey takes two hours.

LOT flies between Kraków and Warsaw several times a day and offers direct connections
from Kraków to Frankfurt, Paris, Vienna and
Athens. Bookings for all flights can be made at

the **LOT office** (☑12 422 8989; ul Basztowa 15; ⊘9am-5pm Mon-Fri). There are also twice daily domestic flights via Eurolot to Gdańsk, Poznań and Szczecin.

A range of other airlines, including several budget operators, connect Kraków to cities in Europe, including an array of destinations across Britain and Ireland. There are direct flights daily to and from London via EasyJet and Ryanair. Dublin is serviced daily by Ryanair and Aer Lingus.

Bus

If you've been travelling by bus elsewhere in Poland, Kraków's modern main **bus station** (ul Bosacka 18) will seem like a palace compared with the usual facility. It's located on the other side of the main train station, northeast of the Old Town. Taking the train will generally be quicker, but several PKS buses head to places of interest; check fares and buy tickets online.

Two private bus companies, **Trans Frej** (www.trans-frej.com.pl) and **Szwagropol** (www.szwagropol.pl), also serve Zakopane frequently (19zł, two hours). **Polski Bus** (www.polskibus.com) departs from here to Warsaw (five hours, four daily) and Zakopane (2¼ hours, two daily).

Train

Kraków Główny train station (Plac Dworcowy), on the northeastern outskirts of the Old Town, handles all international trains and most domestic rail services. The railway platforms are about 150m north of the station building, and you can also reach them from the adjacent Galeria Krakowska shopping mall.

Lublin

POP 349,000

If the crowds are becoming too much in Kraków, you could do worse than jump on a train to Lublin. This attractive eastern city has many of the same attractions – a beautiful Old Town, a castle, and good bars and restaurants – but is less visited by international tourists.

Though today the city's beautifully preserved Old Town is a peaceful blend of Gothic, Renaissance and baroque architecture, Lublin has an eventful past. In 1569 the Lublin Union was signed here, uniting Poland and Lithuania; and at the end of WWII, the Soviet Union set up a communist government in Lublin, prior to the liberation of Warsaw.

⊙ Sights & Activities

OLD TOWN

Lublin Castle   CASTLE
(www.zamek-lublin.pl; ul Zamkowa; ⊘10am-5pm Tue-Sat, 10am-6pm Sun) This substantial fortification, standing on a hill at the northeastern edge of the Old Town, has a dark history. It was built in the 14th century, then rebuilt as a prison in the 1820s. During the occupation under Nazi Germany, more than 100,000 people passed through its doors before being deported to the death camps. The castle's major occupant is now the **Lublin Museum** (www.zamek-lublin.pl; ul Zamkowa 9; adult/concession 8.50/6.50zł; ⊘10am-5pm Wed-Sat, 9am-6pm Sun). On display are paintings, silverware, porcelain, woodcarvings and weaponry, mostly labelled in Polish. Check out the alleged 'devil's paw-print' on the 17th-century table in the foyer, linked to a local legend.

At the eastern end of the castle is the gorgeous 14th-century **Chapel of the Holy Trinity** (ul Zamkowa 9; adult/concession 8.50/6.50zł; ⊘10am-5pm Tue-Sat, 10am-6pm Sun), accessible via the museum. Its interior is covered with polychrome Russo-Byzantine frescos painted in 1418 – possibly the finest medieval wall paintings in Poland.

Historical Museum of Lublin   MUSEUM
(www.zamek-lublin.pl; Plac Łokietka 3; adult/concession 5.50/4.50zł; ⊘9am-4pm Wed-Sat, 9am-5pm Sun) Situated within the 14th-century **Kraków Gate**, a remnant of medieval fortifications, this institution displays documents and photos relating to the city's history. Daily at noon, a bugler plays a special tune atop the **New Town Hall** opposite the gate (if you like bugling, don't miss the annual National Bugle Contest here on 15 August).

Cathedral   CHURCH
(Plac Katedralny; ⊘dawn-dusk) A 16th-century place of worship that houses impressive baroque frescos. The painting of the Virgin Mary is said to have shed tears in 1949, so it's a source of pride and reverence for local believers.

Archdiocesan Museum   MUSEUM
(Plac Katedralny; adult/concession 7/5zł; ⊘10am-5pm) This museum of sacred art also offers expansive views of the Old Town, as it's housed within the lofty **Trinitarian Tower** (1819).

Underground Route   WALK
(Rynek 1; adult/concession 9/7zł; ⊘10am-4pm Tue-Fri, noon-5pm Sat & Sun) This guided tour winds its way through 280m of connected cellars beneath the Old Town, with historical exhibitions along the way. Entry is from the neoclassical **Old Town Hall** in the centre of the pleasant Rynek (Market Sq) at approximately

Lublin

0 0
0.1 miles
200 m

Bus Station

Minibus Station

Lublin Castle

2

4

Al Tysiąclecia

Plac Zamkowy

Zamkowa

Furmańska

Kowalska

Grodzka

Podwale

Plac po Farze

Archidiakońska

Dominikańska

18

Złota

15

10

Cathedral

1

Podwale

Plac Katedralny

Jezuicka

Rynek

12

Grodzka

14

Rybna

Bartowa

Olejna

Szambelańska

3

Historical Museum of Lublin

5

Plac Łokietka

Kozia

Ku Farze

Plac Ofiar Getta

Świętoduska

Lubartowska

Wodopojna

To Kozłówka (38km)

Przechodnia

To Train Station (1.8km); Majdanek (5km)

Narutowicza

11

13

Plac Wolności

19

Staszica

Kapucyńska

Niecała

8

Radziwiłłowska

Plac Litewski

Krakowskie Przedmieście

16

17

Kościuszki

7

Peowiaków

Kołłątaja

3 Maja

Chmielna

Unii Lubelskiej

Unii Lubelskiej

Lublin

two-hourly intervals; check with the tourist office for exact times.

MAJDANEK

FREE **Majdanek State Museum** MEMORIAL
(www.majdanek.pl; ⊙9am-4pm) About 4km southeast of the Old Town is one of the largest Nazi German death camps, where some 235,000 people, including more than 100,000 Jews, were massacred. Barracks, guard towers and barbed-wire fences remain in place; even more chilling are the crematorium and gas chambers.

A short explanatory film (3zł) can be seen in the visitors centre, from which a marked 'visiting route' (5km) passes the massive stone **Monument of Fight & Martyrdom** and finishes at the domed **mausoleum** holding the ashes of many victims.

Trolleybus 156 and bus 23 depart from a stop on ul Królewska near Plac Katedralny, and travel to the entrance of Majdanek.

🛏 Sleeping

TOP CHOICE **Grand Hotel Lublinianka** HOTEL €€
(☑81 446 6100; www.lublinianka.com; ul Krakowskie Przedmieście 56; s/d from 310/370zł; ✳🖥) The swankiest place in town includes free use of a sauna and spa. The cheaper (3rd-floor) rooms have skylights but are relatively small, while 'standard' rooms are spacious and have glitzy marble bathrooms. One room is designed for wheelchair access and there's a good restaurant on-site.

Vanilla Hotel HOTEL €€
(☑81 536 6720; www.vanilla-hotel.pl; ul Krakowskie Przedmieście 12; s/d 330/370zł; 🖥) This beautiful boutique hotel is anything but vanilla. The rooms are filled with inspired styling, featuring vibrant colours, big headboards behind the beds and cool retro furniture. The attention to detail continues into the restaurant and coffee bar, which serves the best ice-cream concoctions in town.

Hotel Waksman HOTEL €€
(☑81 532 5454; www.waksman.pl; ul Grodzka 19; s/d 210/230zł; 🖥) This small gem is excellent value for its quality and location. Just within the Grodzka Gate in the Old Town, it offers elegantly appointed rooms with different colour schemes and an attractive lounge with tapestries on the walls.

Hostel Lublin HOSTEL €
(☑79 288 8632; www.hostellublin.pl; ul Lubartowska 60; dm/r 50/120zł; 🖥) The city's first modern hostel is situated within a former apartment building and contains neat, tidy dorms, a basic kitchenette and a cosy lounge. Take trolleybus 156 or 160 north from the Old Town.

Hotel Europa HOTEL €€€
(☑81 535 0303; www.hoteleuropa.pl; ul Krakowskie Przedmieście 29; s/d from 410/450zł; ✳🖥) Central hotel offering smart, thoroughly modernised rooms with high ceilings and elegant furniture in a restored 19th-century building. Two rooms are designed for wheelchair access and there's a nightclub downstairs.

POLAND LUBLIN

TRANSPORT FROM LUBLIN

Bus

DESTINATION	PRICE (ZŁ)	DURATION (HR)	FREQUENCY
Kraków	48	5½	6 daily
Olsztyn	61	8¾	1 daily
Przemyśl	35		5 daily
Warsaw	30	3	at least hourly
Zakopane	70	8½	2 daily
Zamość	23	2	2 daily

Train

DESTINATION	PRICE (ZŁ)	DURATION (HR)	FREQUENCY
Gdańsk	69	9	2 daily
Kraków	58	4½	2 daily
Kyiv (Ukraine)		13-14	1 daily
Warsaw	40	2½	10 daily
Zamość	21	2¼	4 daily

Lubelskie Samorządowe Centrum Doskonalenia Nauczycieli　　HOSTEL €
(☑81 532 9241; ul Dominikańska 5; dm 66zł) This place is in an atmospheric Old Town building and has rooms with between two and five beds. It's good value and often busy, so book ahead.

🍴 Eating & Drinking

There's a handy **Lux Supermarket** (Plac Wolności 1) located in the city centre, on Plac Wolności.

TOP CHOICE Magia　　INTERNATIONAL €€
(ul Grodzka 2; mains 16-65zł; ⊘noon-midnight) Charming, relaxed restaurant with numerous vibes to choose from within its warren of dining rooms and large outdoor courtyard. Dishes range from tiger prawns and snails to beef and duck, with every sort of pizza, pasta and pancake in between.

Mandragora　　JEWISH €€€
(Rynek 9; mains 14-63zł) They're aiming for the *Fiddler on the Roof* effect here with lace tablecloths, knick-knacks and photos of old Lublin on the walls. The food is a hearty mix of Polish and Jewish.

Oregano　　MEDITERRANEAN €€
(ul Kościuszki 7; mains 18-54zł; ⊘noon-11pm) This pleasant, upmarket restaurant specialises in Mediterranean cuisine, featuring pasta, paella and seafood. There's a well-organised English-language menu and the chefs aren't scared of spice.

Biesy　　POLISH €
(Rynek 18; mains 12-24zł) Atmospheric cellar eatery with multiple nooks and crannies. Its tasty speciality is large pizzalike baked tarts with a variety of toppings.

Złoty Osioł　　PUB
(ul Grodzka 5a; ⊘noon-midnight; 🐕) A classic example of the hidden Polish pub, the Golden Donkey is tucked away well back from the street. Its dimly lit but atmospheric rooms are a good place for a quiet drink.

Caram'bola Pub　　PUB
(ul Kościuszki 8; ⊘10am-late Mon-Sat, noon-late Sun) This pub is a pleasant place for a beer or two. It also serves inexpensive bar food, including pizzas.

☆ Entertainment

Club Koyot　　CLUB
(ul Krakowskie Przedmieście 26; ⊘5pm-late Wed-Sun) This club is concealed in a courtyard set way back from ul Krakowskie Przedmieście. Features live music or DJs most nights.

Filharmonia Lubelska CLASSICAL MUSIC
(☑81 531 5112; www.filharmonialubelska.pl; ul Skłodowskiej-Curie 5) Institution with a large auditorium that hosts classical and contemporary music concerts. To get here from the Old Town, head west on ul Krakowskie Przedmieście and then go south one block along ul Grottgera.

ⓘ Information

Main Post Office (ul Krakowskie Przedmieście 50; ⊘24hr)

Net Box (ul Krakowskie Przedmieście 52; per hr 10zł; ⊘10am-8pm Mon-Sat, 2-6pm Sun) Internet access in a courtyard off the street.

Tourist Office (☑81 532 4412; www.loitik. eu; ul Jezuicka 1/3; ⊘9am-7pm Mon-Fri, from 10am Sat & Sun May-Oct, 9am-5pm Mon-Fri, from 10am Sat & Sun Nov-Apr) Lots of free brochures, including the city walking-route guide *Tourist Routes of Lublin*, which includes a chapter outlining the *Heritage Trail of the Lublin Jews*.

ⓘ Getting There & Away

AIR The brand-new **Lublin airport** (www. airport.lublin.pl) is 10km east of Lublin, with budget airline flights from London and Dublin.

BUS From the **bus station** (Al Tysiąclecia), opposite the castle, PKS buses head to various national destinations and **Polski Bus** (www. polskibus.com) heads to Warsaw (three hours, five daily; book tickets online).

Private minibuses also run to various destinations, including Zamość (15zł, 1½ hours, half-hourly), from the **minibus station** north of the bus terminal.

TRAIN The **train station** (Plac Dworcowy) is 1.8km south of the Old Town and accessible by bus 1 or 13. When leaving the station, look for the bus stop on ul Gazowa, to the left of the station entrance as you walk down the steps (not the trolleybus stop).

Kozłówka

The hamlet of Kozłówka (koz-*woof*-kah), 38km north of Lublin, is famous for its sumptuous late-baroque **palace**, which houses the **Museum of the Zamoyski Family** (☑81 852 8310; www.muzeumzamoyskich.pl; adult/concession incl all sections 25/13zł; ⊘10am-4pm Apr-Nov). The collection in the **main palace** (adult/concession 17/8zł) features original furnishings, ceramic stoves and a large collection of paintings. You must see this area on a Polish-language guided tour, the start-

ing time for which will be noted at the top of your ticket. An English-language tour (best organised in advance) costs an extra 50zł. The entrance fee to this section also includes entry to the 1907 **chapel**.

Even more interesting is the incongruous **Socialist-Realist Art Gallery** (adult/concession 6/3zł), decked out with numerous portraits and statues of communist-era leaders. It also features many idealised scenes of farmers and factory workers striving for socialism. These stirring works were originally tucked away here in embarrassment by the communist authorities, after Stalin's death led to the decline of this all-encompassing artistic style.

You can pay the overall museum fee to see everything on the grounds, which also includes temporary exhibitions (5/2zł) and transport exhibitions within a coach-house (5/2zł); or if you prefer, just pay for each section you wish to view.

From Lublin, catch one of the frequent buses to Lubartów (7zł, 40 minutes, at least half-hourly), then change for Kozłówka by taking a PKS bus or private minibus (5zł, 10 minutes).

Zamość

POP 66,000

While most Polish cities' attractions centre on their medieval heart, Zamość (*zah-moshch*) is pure Renaissance. The streets of its attractive, compact Old Town are perfect for exploring and its central market square is a symmetrical delight, reflecting the city's glorious 16th-century origins.

Zamość was founded in 1580 by Jan Zamoyski, the nation's chancellor and commander-in-chief. Designed by an Italian architect, the city was intended as a prosperous trading settlement between Western Europe and the region stretching east to the Black Sea.

In WWII, the Nazis earmarked the city for German resettlement, sending the Polish population into slave labour or concentration camps. Most of the Jewish population of the renamed 'Himmlerstadt' was exterminated.

The splendid architecture of Zamość's Old Town was added to Unesco's World Heritage list in 1992. Since 2004, EU funds have been gradually restoring Zamość to its former glory.

⊙ Sights

Rynek Wielki
HISTORIC SQUARE

(Great Market Square) The heart of Zamość's attractive Old Town, this impressive Italianate Renaissance square (exactly 100m by 100m) is dominated by the lofty, pink Town Hall and surrounded by colourful arcaded houses once owned by wealthy citizens.

The Museum of Zamość (ul Ormiańska 30; adult/concession 8/4zł; ⊙9am-5pm Tue-Sun) is based in two of the loveliest buildings on the square and houses interesting exhibits, including paintings, folk costumes, archaeological finds and a scale model of the 16th-century town.

Synagogue
SYNAGOGUE

(www.zamosc.fodz.pl; ul Pereca 14; admission 6zł; ⊙10am-6pm Tue-Sun) Before WWII, Jewish citizens accounted for 45% of the town's population and most lived in the area north and east of the palace. The most significant Jewish architectural relic is this Renaissance place of worship, built in the early 17th century. It was recently renovated and reopened to the public as a cultural centre, giving access to its beautiful interior decoration and an impressive digital presentation on the town's Jewish history.

Cathedral
CHURCH

(ul Kolegiacka; ⊙dawn-dusk) Southwest of the Rynek Wielki, this mighty 16th-century holy place hosts the tomb of Jan Zamoyski in the chapel to the right of the high altar. The bell tower (ul Kolegiacka; admission 2zł; ⊙10am-4pm Mon-Sat May-Sep) can be climbed for good views of the historic cathedral bells and the Old Town. In the grounds, the Sacral Museum (ul Kolegiacka 2; admission 2zł; ⊙10am-4pm Mon-Fri, 10am-1pm Sat & Sun May-Sep, 10am-1pm Sun Oct-Apr) features various robes, paintings and sculptures.

Bastion
FORTIFICATION

(ul Łukasińskiego) On the eastern edge of the Old Town is the best surviving bastion from the original city walls. You can take a tour (ul Łukasińskiego; adult/concession 7.50/4.50zł; ⊙8am-6pm) through the renovated fortifications, checking out displays of military gear and views over the city. Tickets can be bought from the souvenir shop next to the entrance and the tour only runs when a minimum of three people have gathered.

Zamoyski Palace
PALACE

This former palace directly west of the Old Town (closed to the public) lost much of its character when it was converted into a military hospital in the 1830s. To the north of the palace stretches a beautifully landscaped park. To its south is the Arsenal Museum (ul Zamkowa 2), though at the time of research this was closed for a major renovation. Check with the tourist office for an update.

🛏 Sleeping

TOP CHOICE Hotel Senator
HOTEL €€

(☑84 638 9990; www.senatorhotel.pl; ul Rynek Solny 4; s/d from 164/229zł; 🖳) Charming accommodation with tastefully furnished rooms, an on-site restaurant with its own fireplace and an unusual medieval vibe to its decor. The expansive breakfast buffet costs 25zł extra.

Hotel Zamojski
HOTEL €€

(☑84 639 2516; www.accorhotels.com; ul Kołłątaja 2/4/6; s/d from 191/253zł; ❄🖳) This comfortable joint is situated within three connected old houses, just off the square. The rooms are modern and tastefully furnished, and there's a good restaurant and cocktail bar, along with a fitness centre.

Hotel Arkadia
HOTEL €

(☑84 638 6507; www.arkadia-zamosc.pl; Rynek Wielki 9; s/d from 100/140zł; 🖳) With just nine rooms, this compact place offers a pool table and restaurant in addition to lodgings. It's charming but shabby, though its location right on the Rynek Wielki is hard to beat.

Hotel Renesans
HOTEL €€

(☑84 639 2001; www.hotelrenesans.pl; ul Grecka 6; s/d from 136/192zł; 🖳) It's ironic that a hotel named after the Renaissance is housed in the Old Town's ugliest building. However, it's central and the rooms are surprisingly modern and pleasant.

Camping Duet
CAMPING GROUND €

(☑84 639 2499; www.duet.virgo.com.pl; ul Królowej Jadwigi 14; s/d 80/95zł, per tent/person 12zł/10zł; ❄) Only 600m west of the Old Town, Camping Duet has neat bungalows, tennis courts, a restaurant, sauna and spa. There's also a pleasant camping ground in a partly wooded area. Larger bungalows sleep up to six.

✗ Eating & Drinking

For self-caterers, there's a handy Lux minisupermarket (ul Grodzka 16; ⊙6am-8pm Mon-Fri, 8am-6pm Sat & Sun) one block east of the Rynek Wielki.

Restauracja Muzealna   POLISH €€
(ul Ormiańska 30; mains 14-29zł; ⊙11am-10pm
Mon-Sat, 11am-9pm Sun) Subterranean restaurant in an atmospheric cellar below the
Rynek Wielki, bedecked with ornate timber
furniture and portraits of nobles. It serves
a good class of Polish cuisine at reasonable
prices and has a well-stocked bar.

Bar Asia   POLISH €
(ul Staszica 10; mains 10-19zł; ⊙8am-5pm Mon-Fri,
8am-4pm Sat) For hungry but broke travellers, this old-style *bar mleczny* (milk bar) is
ideal. It serves cheap and tasty Polish food,
including several variants of *pierogi* (dumplings), in a minimally decorated space.

Corner Pub   PUB
(ul Żeromskiego 6) This cosy Irish-style pub is
a good place to have a drink. It has comfy
booths and the walls are ornamented with
bric-a-brac such as antique clocks, swords
and model cars.

❶ Information

K@fejka Internetowa (Rynek Wielki 10; per
hr 3zł; ⊙9am-5pm Mon-Fri, 10am-2pm Sat)
Internet access.

Main Post Office (ul Kościuszki 9; ⊙7am-8pm
Mon-Fri, 8am-3pm Sat)

Tourist Office (☏84 639 2292; Rynek Wielki
13; ⊙8am-6pm Mon-Fri, 10am-5pm Sat & Sun
May-Sep, 8am-5pm Mon-Fri, 9am-2pm Sat &
Sun Oct-Apr) Sells the glossy *Zamość – The
Ideal City* (9.50zł).

❶ Getting There & Away

Bus

The **bus station** (ul Hrubieszowska) is 2km east
of the Old Town and linked by frequent city buses, primarily buses 0 and 3. From here, buses
head to the following destinations:

Kraków (52zł, eight hours, three daily)
Lublin (23zł, two hours, two daily)
Warsaw (42zł, 5½ hours, two daily)

Two buses a day also travel to Jarosław (24zł,
three hours), from where you can continue to
Przemyśl near the Ukrainian border.

A quicker way to and from Lublin is via the
minibuses that depart every 30 minutes (15zł,
1½ hours) from the minibus station opposite the
bus station. Check the changeable timetable
for departures to other destinations, including
Warsaw and Kraków.

Train

From the **train station** (ul Szczebrzeska 11), 1km
southwest of the Old Town, infrequent services

run to Lublin (21zł, 2¼ hours, four daily) and
Kraków (61zł, seven hours, one daily). The two
trains per day to transport junction Jarosław
(26zł, 3¾ hours) may be handy if you're heading
to Przemyśl for Ukraine.

CARPATHIAN MOUNTAINS

The Carpathians (Karpaty) stretch from the
southern border with Slovakia into Ukraine
and their wooded hills and snowy mountains are a beacon for hikers, skiers and
cyclists. The most popular destination here
is the resort town of Zakopane in the heart
of the Tatra Mountains (Tatry). Elsewhere,
historic regional towns such as Przemyśl
and Sanok offer a relaxed pace and unique
insights into the past.

Zakopane

POP 27,900

Nestled at the foot of the Tatra Mountains,
Zakopane is Poland's major winter sports
centre, though it's a popular destination
year-round. It may resemble a tourist trap,
with its overcommercialised, overpriced
exterior, but it also has a relaxed, laid-back
vibe that makes it a great place to chill for a
few days, even if you're not planning to ski
or hike.

Zakopane also played an important role
in sustaining Polish culture during the long
period of foreign rule in the 19th century,
thanks to the many artistic types who settled in the town during this period.

❍ Sights & Activities

Tatra Museum   MUSEUM
(www.muzeumtatrzanskie.pl; ul Krupówki 10; adult/
concession 7/5.50zł, Sun free; ⊙9am-5pm Tue-Sat,
9am-3pm Sun) Check out exhibits about regional history, ethnography and geology at
this centrally located museum, along with
displays on local flora and fauna.

Museum of Zakopane Style   MUSEUM
(www.muzeumtatrzanskie.pl; ul Kościeliska 18;
adult/concession 7/5.50zł; ⊙9am-5pm Wed-Sat,
9am-3pm Sun) Fittingly housed in the 1892
Villa Koliba, which was the first house to be
designed by artist and architect Stanisław
Witkiewicz in the Zakopane style. This distinctive architectural style became the trademark of the town in the late 19th century.

POLAND ZAKOPANE

Szymanowksi Museum · MUSEUM

(www.muzeum.krakow.pl; ul Kasprusie 19; adult/concession 6/3zł, Sun free; ⊙10am-4pm Tue-Sun) This institution within the Villa Atma is dedicated to the great composer Karol Szymanowski, who once lived here. It hosts piano recitals in summer.

Mt Gubałówka · MOUNTAIN

Behind the township, this mountain (1120m) offers excellent views over the Tatras and is a popular destination for tourists who don't feel overly energetic. The **funicular** (ul Nowotarska; adult/concession one way 10/8zł, return 17/14zł; ⊙8am-9.45pm Jul & Aug, 9am-8pm Mar-Jun, Sep & Oct, 8.30am-6pm Nov & Dec) covers the 1388m-long route in less than five minutes, climbing 300m from the funicular station just north of ul Krupówki. You can also hike up or down if you like.

🛏 Sleeping

Given the abundance of private rooms and decent hostels, few travellers actually stay in hotels.

Some travel agencies in Zakopane can arrange private rooms, but in the high season they may not want to offer anything for less than three nights. Expect a double room (singles are rarely offered) to cost about 80zł in the high season in the town centre and about 60zł for somewhere further out.

Locals offering private rooms may approach you at the bus or train stations; alternatively, just look out for signs posted in the front of private homes – *noclegi* and *pokoje* both mean 'rooms available'.

Like all seasonal resorts, accommodation prices fluctuate considerably between low season and high season (December to February and July to August). Always book accommodation in advance at peak times, especially on weekends.

┌TOP┐CHOICE Hotel Sabała · HOTEL €€€

(☑18 201 5092; www.sabala.zakopane.pl; ul Krupówki 11; s/d from 340/460zł; 🕿🏊) Built in 1894 but thoroughly up to date, this striking timber building has a superb location overlooking the picturesque pedestrian thoroughfare. It offers cosy attic-style rooms and there's a sauna and solarium on the premises. A candlelit restaurant has views of street life.

Carlton · HOTEL €€

(☑18 201 4415; www.carlton.pl; ul Grunwaldzka 11; s/d 80/160zł; 🕿) Affordable pension in a grand old house away from the main drag, featuring light-filled rooms with modern furniture. There's an impressive shared balcony overlooking the road and a big comfy lounge lined with potted plants.

Youth Hostel Szarotka · HOSTEL €

(☑18 201 3618; www.schroniskomlodziezowe.zakopane.org.pl; ul Nowotarska 45; dm/d 41/102zł) This friendly, homey place gets packed in the high season. There's a kitchen and washing machine on-site. It's on a noisy road about a 10-minute walk from the town centre.

🍴 Eating & Drinking

The main street, ul Krupówki, is lined with all sorts of eateries.

Czarny Staw · GRILL €€

(ul Krupówki 2; mains 12-46zł; ⊙10am-1am) Offers a tasty range of Polish dishes, including a variety of dumplings, and much of the menu is cooked before your very eyes on the central grill. There's a good salad bar and live music most nights.

Pstrąg Górski · SEAFOOD €€

(ul Krupówki 6; mains 15-33zł; ⊙9am-10pm) This self-service fish restaurant, done up in traditional style and overlooking a narrow stream, serves some of the freshest trout, salmon and sea fish in town. It's excellent value.

Stek Chałupa · POLISH €€

(ul Krupówki 33; mains 17-44zł; ⊙8am-midnight) Big friendly barn of a place, with homey decor and waitresses in traditional garb. The menu features meat dishes, particularly steaks, though there are vegetarian choices among the salads and *pierogi* (dumplings).

Appendix · CAFE-BAR

(ul Krupówki 6; ⊙3pm-midnight; 🛜) A mellow venue for an alcoholic or caffeine-laden drink, hidden away above the street with an ambient old-meets-new decor. It hosts live music most weekends.

ℹ Information

Centrum Przewodnictwa Tatrzańskiego (Tatra Guide Centre; ☑18 206 37 99; ul Chałubińskiego 42a; ⊙9am-3pm) Arranges English- and German-speaking mountain guides.

Księgarnia Górska (ul Zaruskiego 5) Bookshop in the reception area of the Dom Turysty PTTK hostel, sells regional hiking maps.

TRANSPORT FROM ZAKOPANE

Bus

DESTINATION	COST(ZŁ)	DURATION (HR)	FREQUENCY
Kraków	18	2	almost hourly
Lublin	70	8½	2 daily
Przemyśl	53	9	1 daily
Warsaw	65	8	6 daily

Train

DESTINATION	PRICE (ZŁ)	DURATION (HR)	FREQUENCY
Częstochowa	56	7	1 daily
Gdynia & Gdańsk	76	16	1 daily
Kraków	24	3¾	8 daily
Łódź	63	10½	1 daily
Poznań	65	11½	1 daily
Warsaw	63	9	3 daily

Main Post Office (ul Krupówki 20; ⊙7am-7.30pm Mon-Fri, 8am-2pm Sat)

PTTK Office (☎18 201 2429; www.pttkzakopane.pl; ul Krupówki 12) Provides handy info about hiking and mountain refuges.

Tourist Office (☎18 201 2211) Bus station (☎18 201 2211; ul Kościuszki 17; ⊙8am-8pm daily Jul-Aug, 9am-5pm Mon-Sat Sep-Jun); Town (ul Kościeliska 7; ⊙9am-5pm Mon-Sat) These offices offer advice, sell hiking and city maps, and provide information about rafting trips down the Dunajec River.

Widmo (ul Galicy 6; per hr 5zł; ⊙7.30am-11pm Mon-Fri, 9am-11pm Sat & Sun) Internet access.

❶ Getting There & Away

From the **bus station** (ul Chramcówki), PKS buses run to several destinations. Two private companies, **Trans Frej** (www.trans-frej.com.pl) and **Szwagropol** (www.szwagropol.pl) run comfortable Kraków-bound buses (19zł) every 45 minutes to an hour, and **Polski Bus** (www.polskibus.com) heads to Warsaw twice daily (seven hours) via Kraków (2¼ hours); book tickets online.

Locally, PKS buses – and minibuses from opposite the bus terminal – regularly travel to Lake Morskie Oko and on to Polana Palenica. To cross into Slovakia, get off this bus/minibus at Łysa Polana, cross the border on foot, and take another bus to Tatranská Lomnica and the other Slovak mountain towns.

Trains head to a number of destinations around Poland from Zakopane's **train station** (ul Chramcówki).

Tatra Mountains

The Tatras, 100km south of Kraków, are the highest range of the Carpathian Mountains, providing a dramatic range of rugged scenery that's a distinct contrast to the rest of Poland's flatness. Roughly 60km long and 15km wide, this mountain range stretches across the Polish–Slovak border. A quarter is in Poland and is mostly part of the Tatra National Park (about 212 sq km). The Polish Tatras contain more than 20 peaks over 2000m, the highest of which is Mt Rysy (2499m).

◎ Sights & Activities

Lake Morskie Oko   LAKE

The emerald-green Lake Morskie Oko (Eye of the Sea) is among the loveliest lakes in the Tatras, completely surrounded by mountains and reached via a small pass. There's a restaurant and bar in the hostel by the lake. PKS buses and minibuses regularly depart from Zakopane for Polana Palenica (30 minutes), from where a road (9km) continues uphill to the lake. Cars, bikes and buses are not allowed up this road, so you'll have to walk, but it's not steep (allow about two hours one way). Alternatively, take a horse-drawn carriage (50/30zł per person uphill/downhill, but negotiable) to within 2km of the lake. In winter, transport is by horse-drawn four-seater sledge, which is more expensive. The last minibus to Zakopane returns between 5pm and 6pm.

Mt Kasprowy Wierch Cable Car CABLE CAR

(www.pkl.pl; adult/concession return 49/39zł; ◔7.30am-4pm Jan-Mar, 7.30am-6pm Apr-Jun, Sep & Oct, 7am-9pm Jul & Aug, 9am-4pm Nov & Dec) The cable-car trip from Kuźnice (2km south of Zakopane) to the summit of Mt Kasprowy Wierch (1985m) is a classic tourist experience enjoyed by Poles and foreigners alike. At the end of the trip you can get off and stand with one foot in Poland and the other in Slovakia. The one-way journey takes 20 minutes and climbs 936m. The cable car normally shuts down for one week in May and won't operate if the snow or winds are dangerous.

The view from the top is spectacular (clouds permitting). Two chairlifts transport skiers to and from various slopes between December and April. A restaurant serves skiers and hikers alike. In summer, many people return to Zakopane on foot down the Gąsienicowa Valley, and the most intrepid walk the ridges all the way across to Lake Morskie Oko via Pięciu Stawów, a strenuous hike taking a full day in good weather.

If you buy a return ticket, your trip back is automatically reserved for two hours after your departure, so if you want to stay longer than that buy a one-way ticket to the top (39zł) and another one when you want to come down (25zł). Mt Kasprowy Wierch is popular; in summer, arrive early and expect to wait. PKS buses and minibuses to Kuźnice frequently leave from Zakopane.

Hiking HIKING

If you're doing any hiking in the Tatras get a copy of the *Tatrzański Park Narodowy* map (1:25,000), which shows all hiking trails in the area. Better still, buy one or more of the 14 sheets of *Tatry Polskie*, available at Księgarnia Górska (p394) in Zakopane. In July and August these trails can be overrun by tourists, so late spring and early autumn are the best times. Theoretically you can expect better weather in autumn, when rainfall is lower.

Like all alpine regions, the Tatras can be dangerous, particularly during the snow season (November to May). Remember the weather can be unpredictable. Bring proper hiking boots, warm clothing and waterproof rain gear – and be prepared to use occasional ropes and chains (provided along the trails) to get up and down some rocky slopes.

Guides are not necessary because many of the trails are marked, but they can be arranged in Zakopane for about 350zł per day.

There are several picturesque valleys south of Zakopane, including the Dolina Strążyska. You can continue from the Strążyska by the red trail up to Mt Giewont (1909m), 3½ hours from Zakopane, and then walk down the blue trail to Kuźnice in two hours.

Two long and beautiful forested valleys, the Dolina Chochołowska and the Dolina Kościeliska, are in the western part of the park, known as the Tatry Zachodnie (West Tatras). These valleys are ideal for cycling. Both are accessible by PKS buses and minibuses from Zakopane.

The Tatry Wysokie (High Tatras) to the east offer quite different scenery: bare granite peaks and glacial lakes. One way to get there is via cable car to Mt Kasprowy Wierch, then hike eastward along the red trail to Mt Świnica (2301m) and on to the Zawrat pass (2159m) – a tough three to four hours from Mt Kasprowy. From Zawrat, descend northwards to the Dolina Gąsienicowa along the blue trail and then back to Zakopane.

Alternatively, head south (also along the blue trail) to the wonderful Dolina Pięciu Stawów (Five Lakes Valley), where there is a mountain refuge 1¼ hours from Zawrat. The blue trail heading west from the refuge passes Lake Morskie Oko, 1½ hours from the refuge.

Skiing SKIING

Zakopane boasts four major ski areas (and several smaller ones) with more than 50 ski lifts. Mt Kasprowy Wierch offers the best conditions and the most challenging slopes in the area, with its ski season extending until early May. Lift tickets cost 10zł for one ride at Mt Kasprowy Wierch. Alternatively, you can buy a day card (90zł), which allows you to skip the queues.

Another alternative is the Harenda chairlift (www.harendazakopane.pl; ul Harenda 63; 5zł; ◔9am-6pm) just outside Zakopane, in the direction of Kraków.

Ski equipment rental is available at all ski areas except Mt Kasprowy Wierch. Outlets in Zakopane such as Sport Shop & Service (☎18 201 5871; ul Krupówki 52a) also rent ski gear.

🛏 Sleeping

Tourists are not allowed to take their own cars into the Tatra National Park; you must walk in, take the cable car or use an official vehicle owned by the park or a hotel or hostel.

Camping is also not allowed in the park, but several PTTK mountain refuges/hostels provide simple accommodation. Most refuges are small and fill up fast; in midsummer and midwinter they're invariably packed beyond capacity. No one is ever turned away, however, though you may have to crash on the floor if all the beds are taken. Don't arrive too late in the day and remember to bring along your own bed mat and sleeping bag. All refuges serve simple hot meals, but the kitchens and dining rooms close early (sometimes at 7pm).

Most refuges are open all year but some may be temporarily closed for renovations or because of inclement weather. Check the current situation at the PTTK office (p395) in Zakopane. Its staff will be able to give you the location of all refuges and may be able to make bookings.

Kalatówki Mountain Hotel HOTEL €€
(☑18 206 3644; www.kalatowki.pl; dm/s/d from 66/89/170zł) This large and decent accommodation is the easiest to reach from Zakopane. It's a 40-minute walk from the Kuźnice cable-car station.

Dolinie Pięciu Stawów Hostel HOSTEL €
(☑781 055 555; www.piecstawow.pl; dm/d 45/120zł) This is the highest (1700m) and most scenically located refuge in the Polish Tatras. Breakfast is 14zł extra.

Morskie Oko Hostel HOSTEL €
(☑18 207 7609; www.schroniskomorskieoko.pl; dm 39-54zł) An early start from Zakopane would allow you to visit Morskie Oko in the morning and stay here at night.

Dunajec Gorge

An entertaining way to explore the Pieniny Mountains is to go rafting on craft piloted by the Polish Association of Pieniny Oarsmen (☑18 262 9721; www.flisacy.com.pl) along the Dunajec River, which traces the Polish–Slovak border through a spectacular and deep gorge. The rafts are large flat timber vessels which can hold a dozen or so passengers.

The trip starts at the wharf (Przystan Flisacka) in Sromowce Wyżne-Kąty, 46km northeast of Zakopane, and you can finish either at the spa town of Szczawnica (adult/concession 46/23zł, 2¼ hours, 18km), or further

on at Krościenko (adult/concession 55/28zł, 2¾ hours, 23km). The raft trip operates between April and October, but only starts when there's a minimum of 10 passengers.

The gorge is an easy day trip from Zakopane. Catch a regular bus to Nowy Targ (7zł, 30 minutes, hourly) from Zakopane to connect with one of five daily buses (10zł, 45 minutes) to Sromowce-Kąty. From Szczawnica or Krościenko, take the bus back to Nowy Targ (10zł, one hour, hourly) and change for Zakopane. You can also return to the Sromowce-Kąty car park by bus with the raftsmen.

To avoid waiting around in Sromowce-Kąty for a raft to fill up, reserve a place via any travel agency in Zakopane for around 50zł per person. You'll still have to make your own way to the wharf by car or bus.

Przemyśl
POP 65,000 / TRANSPORT HUB

Przemyśl (*psheh*-mishl) is a significant transport hub and a logical jumping-off point for the Ukrainian border about 15km east of the city.

The city has a selection of inexpensive accommodation, including the central Dom Wycieczkowy PTTK Podzamcze (☑16 678 5374; www.przemysl.pttk.pl; ul Waygarta 3; dm from 26zł, s/d 49/72zł; ☑) hostel on the western edge of the Old Town. More comfort is available at the two-star Hotel Europejski (☑16 675 7100; www.hotel-europejski.pl; ul Sowińskiego 4; s/d 110/140zł; ☑) in a renovated old building facing the train station. Another option is Hotel Gromada (☑16 676 1111; www.gromada.pl; ul Wybrzeże Piłsudskiego 4; s/d from 130/180zł; ☑), a big chain hotel west of the Old Town.

For restaurants and bars, head to the the sloping Rynek (Market Sq). The tourist office (☑16 675 2163; www.przemysl.pl; ul Grodzka 1; ⊙10am-6pm Mon-Fri, 9am-5pm Sat & Sun) is situated above the southwest corner of the square.

From Przemyśl, buses run regularly to Lviv in Ukraine (25zł, two hours). Another option is to take a private minibus to the border (5zł, 15 minutes), then walk across to connect with Ukrainian transport on the other side. Buses also operate regularly to all towns in southeastern Poland, including Sanok (14zł, two hours, five daily).

Trains run to Kraków (50zł, five hours, nine daily) and Warsaw (61zł, eight hours,

LAKE SOLINA & SANOK

In the far southeastern corner of Poland, wedged between the Ukrainian and Slovakian borders, lies Lake Solina. This sizeable reservoir (27km long and 60m deep) was created in 1968 when the San River was dammed. Today it's a popular centre for water sports and other recreational pursuits.

The best place to base yourself is **Polańczyk**. This pleasant town on the lake's western shore offers a range of attractions, including sailing, windsurfing, fishing and beaches. There are also numerous hotels and sanatoriums offering spa treatments.

On the route to the lake, the town of **Sanok** is noted for its unique **Museum of Folk Architecture** (www.skansen.mblsanok.pl; ul Rybickiego 3; adult/concession 12/8zł; ☉8am-6pm May-Sep, 9am-2pm Oct-Apr), which features the buildings of regional ethnic groups.

Outside Sanok, the marked **Icon Trail** takes hikers or cyclists along a 70km loop, passing by 10 village churches as well as attractive mountain countryside.

There are regular buses from Przemyśl to Sanok (14zł, two hours, five daily), from where you can continue to Polańczyk (9zł, one hour, hourly). You can also reach Sanok directly by bus from Kraków (36zł, five hours, six daily). For more details about Sanok and its attractions, check out Lonely Planet's *Poland* country guide or step into the Sanok **tourist office** (☏13 464 4533; Rynek 14; ☉9am-5pm Mon-Fri, 9am-1pm Sat & Sun).

twice daily); and international sleeper trains operate to Lviv (2¾ hours, twice daily) and Kyiv (13 hours, once daily) in Ukraine.

The bus terminal and adjacent train station in Przemyśl are about 1km northeast of the Rynek.

SILESIA

Silesia (Śląsk, *shlonsk*, in Polish) is a fascinating mix of landscapes. Though the industrial zone around Katowice has limited attraction for visitors, beautiful Wrocław is a historic city with lively nightlife, and the Sudeten Mountains draw hikers and other nature lovers.

The history of the region is similarly diverse, having been governed by Polish, Bohemian, Austrian and German rulers. After two centuries as part of Prussia and Germany, the territory was largely included within Poland's new borders after WWII.

Wrocław

POP 630,000

When citizens of beautiful Kraków enthusiastically encourage you to visit Wrocław (*vrots*-wahf), you know you're onto something good. The city's delightful Old Town is a gracious mix of Gothic and baroque styles and its large student population ensures a healthy number of restaurants, bars and nightclubs.

Wrocław has been traded back and forth between various rulers over the centuries, but began life in the year 1000 under the Polish Piast dynasty and developed into a prosperous trading and cultural centre. In the 1740s it passed to Prussia, under the German name of Breslau. Under Prussian rule, the city became a major textile manufacturing centre, greatly increasing its population.

Upon its return to Poland in 1945, Wrocław was a shell of its former self, having sustained massive damage in WWII. Though 70% of the city was destroyed, sensitive restoration has returned the historic centre to its former beauty.

◉ Sights

OLD TOWN

Rynek   HISTORIC SQUARE

(Market Square) In the centre of the Old Town is Poland's second-largest old market square (after Kraków). It's an attractive, rambling space, lined by beautifully painted facades and with a complex of old buildings in the middle. The southwestern corner of the square opens into **Plac Solny** (Salt Place), once the site of the town's salt trade and now home to a 24-hour flower market.

City Museum of Art   MUSEUM

(www.muzeum.miejskie.wroclaw.pl; Stary Ratusz; adult/concession 10/7zł; ☉10am-5pm Wed-Sat, 10am-6pm Sun) The beautiful **Town Hall** (in Polish, Stary Ratusz), built 1327–1504, on the southern side of the square houses this museum with stately rooms on show, including exhibits on the art of gold and the stories of famous Wrocław inhabitants.

Jaś i Małgosia
HISTORIC BUILDINGS

(ul Św Mikołaja) In the northwestern corner of the Rynek are these two attractive small houses linked by a baroque gate. Whimsically, they've been named after a couple better known to English speakers as Hansel and Gretel.

Gnomes of Wrocław
STATUES

See if you can spot the diminutive statue of a gnome at ground level, just to the west of the Jaś i Małgosia houses on the edge of the Rynek; he's one of more than 200, which are scattered through the city. Whimsical as they are, they're attributed to the symbol of the Orange Alternative – a communist-era dissident group that used ridicule as a weapon and often painted gnomes where graffiti had been removed by the authorities. You can buy a gnome map (6zł) from the tourist office and go gnome-spotting.

Church of St Elizabeth
CHURCH

(www.kosciolgarnizon.wroclaw.pl; ul Św Elżbiety 1; admission 5zł; ⊙10am-7pm Mon-Sat, noon-7pm Sun) Behind decorative houses and miniature gnome statues is this monumental 14th-century church with its 83m-high tower, which you can climb for city views.

Church of St Mary Magdalene
CHURCH

(ul Łaciarska; bridge adult/concession 4/3zł; ⊙10am-6pm Mon-Sat) One block east of the Rynek is this Gothic church with a Romanesque portal from 1280 incorporated into its southern external wall. Climb the 72m high tower and its connected bridge (⊙10am-6pm Apr-Oct) for a lofty view.

EAST OF THE OLD TOWN

TOP CHOICE **Panorama of Racławice**
MONUMENTAL ARTWORK

(www.panoramaraclawicka.pl; ul Purkyniego 11; adult/concession 25/18zł; ⊙9am-5pm) Wrocław's pride and joy (and major tourist attraction) is this giant 360-degree painting housed in a circular building east of the Old Town. The painting depicts the 1794 Battle of Racławice, in which a Polish peasant army led by Tadeusz Kościuszko defeated Russian forces intent on partitioning Poland. Created by Jan Styka and Wojciech Kossak for the centenary of the battle in 1894, it is an immense 114m long and 15m high and was brought here

by Polish immigrants displaced from Lviv (Ukraine) after WWII. Due to the communist government's uneasiness about glorifying a famous Russian defeat, however, the panorama wasn't re-erected until 1985.

Obligatory tours (with audio in English and other languages) run every 30 minutes between 9am and 4.30pm from April to November, and 10am and 3pm from December to March. The ticket also allows same-day entry to the nearby National Museum.

National Museum
MUSEUM

(www.mnwr.art.pl; Plac Powstańców Warszawy 5; adult/concession 15/10zł, Sat free; ⊙10am-5pm) Treasure trove of fine art on three floors, with extensive permanent collections and a stunning skylit atrium.

ECCLESIASTICAL DISTRICT

Cathedral of St John the Baptist
CHURCH

(Plac Katedralny; tower adult/concession 5/4zł; ⊙10am-4pm Mon-Sat, 2-4pm Sun) This Gothic cathedral has a unique lift to whisk you to the top of its tower for superb views. Next door to the cathedral is the Archdiocesan Museum (Plac Katedralny 16; adult/concession 4/3zł; ⊙9am-3pm Tue-Sun) featuring sacred art.

Church of Our Lady on the Sand
CHURCH

(ul Św Jadwigi) North of the river is Piasek Island (Sand Island), where you'll find this 14th-century place of worship with lofty Gothic vaults and a year-round nativity scene.

Church of the Holy Cross & St Bartholomew
CHURCH

(Plac Kościelny) Across a small bridge from Piasek Island lies Ostrów Tumski (Cathedral Island), a picturesque area full of churches. Admire this two-storey Gothic structure, which was built between 1288 and 1350.

Botanical Gardens
GARDENS

(ul Sienkiewicza 23; adult/concession 10/5zł; ⊙8am-6pm Apr-Nov) North of the Cathedral of St John the Baptist are these charming gardens, where you can chill out among the chestnut trees and tulips.

SOUTH OF THE OLD TOWN

Historical Museum
MUSEUM

(www.mmw.pl; ul Kazimierza Wielkiego 35; adult/concession 15/10zł; ⊙10am-5pm Tue-Sun) Housed in a grand former palace, this museum highlights the main events in Wrocław's thousand-year history and includes an art collection covering the past two centuries.

Wrocław

0.25 miles
500 m

Księcia Witolda

Podwale

Pomorska

Plac Uniwersytecki

Plac Katedralny
Katedralny

Ostrów Tumski
(Cathedral Island)

Piasek Island
(Sand Island)

Św Jadwigi

Stąromłyńska

Grodzka

Św Ducha

Odra

Odra

Plac Nowy Targ

Piaskowa

Krańskiego

Janickiego

Purkyniego

Bernardyńska

Panorama of Racławice

Plac Powstańców Warszawy

Al Słowackiego

Plac
Dominikański

Nowa

Oławska

Piotra
Skargi

Panorama of Racławice

Szewska

Plac Biskupa Nankiera

Nożownicza

Kuźnicza

Wita Stwosza

Kurza

Krowia

Plac Nowy Targ

Szewska

Oławska

Świdnicka

Szewska

City Museum of Art

To Hostel

Babel (800m); Wrocław
Główny Train Station (1km);
Bus Terminal (1.3km)

Grodzka

Więzienna

Kotlarska

Bielna

Igielna

Rynek

Lower Silesia Tourist
Information Centre

Kiełbaśnicza

Kiełbaśnicza

Malarska

Św
Elżbiety

Odrzańska

Rzeźnicza

Św Mikołaja

Nowy Świat

Ruska

Ruska

Psie Budy

Kazimierza Wielkiego

Krupnicza

Cieszyńskiego

Św Mikołaja

Antoniego

Włodkowica

To Copernicus
Airport (12km)

To Passage
sculpture (700m)

Szajnochy

Tourist
Office

Wrodawie

1. Plac Katedralny
2. ◎2
3. ✝3
4. ✝4
5. ◎5
6. ✝6
7. ✝7
8. 🏛8
9. ◎9
10. 🏛10
11. 11
12. 12
13. 13
14. 14
15. 15
16. 16
20. 20
21. 21
22. 22
23. 23
24. 24
25. 25
26. 26
27. 27
28. 28
29. 29

Wrocław

Passage PUBLIC ART
(cnr ul Świdnicka & ul Piłsudskiego) This fascinating sculpture depicts a group of pedestrians being swallowed by the pavement, only to re-emerge on the other side of the street.

✹ Festivals & Events

Jazz on the Odra International Festival MUSIC
(www.jazznadodra.pl; ◷Apr)

Musica Polonica Nova Festival MUSIC
(www.musicapolonicanova.pl; ◷Apr) Celebrates new orchestral compositions, with a focus on Polish works.

Wratislavia Cantans MUSIC
(www.wratislaviacantans.pl; ◷Sep) Features music with a vocal component, including opera and choral works.

Wrocław Marathon SPORT
(www.wroclawmaraton.pl; ◷Sep)

🛏 Sleeping

TOP CHOICE **Hostel Mleczarnia** HOSTEL €
(☎71 787 7570; www.mleczarniahostel.pl; ul Włodkowica 5; dm from 40zł, d 220zł; ⊛) This hostel, on a quiet road not far from the Rynek, has bags of charm: it has been decorated in a deliberately old-fashioned style within a former residential building. There's a women-only dorm available, along with a kitchen and laundry facilities. Downstairs is a good cafe-bar.

Hotel Patio HOTEL €€
(☎71 375 0400; www.hotelpatio.pl; ul Kiełbaśnicza 24; s/d from 300/360zł; ⊛⊛) Pleasant lodgings a short hop from the Rynek, housed within two buildings linked by a covered sunlit courtyard. Rooms are clean and light, sometimes small but with reasonably high ceilings. There's a restaurant and bar on-site.

Art Hotel HOTEL €€
(☎71 787 7100; www.arthotel.pl; ul Kiełbaśnicza 20; s/d from 270/290zł; ⊛⊛) Elegant but affordable accommodation in a renovated apartment building. Rooms feature tastefully restrained decor, quality fittings and gleaming bathrooms. Within the hotel is a top-notch restaurant and there's a fitness room to work off the resultant kilojoules.

Hostel Babel HOSTEL €
(☎71 342 0250; www.babelhostel.pl; ul Kołłątaja 16; dm from 45zł, d 140zł; ⊛) A tatty old staircase leads up to pleasant budget accommodation. Dorms are set in renovated apartment rooms with ornate lamps and decorative ceilings. Guests have access to a kitchen and washing machine.

POLAND WROCŁAW

Hotel Tumski
HOTEL €€

(☑71 322 6099; www.hotel-tumski.com.pl; Wyspa Słodowa 10; s/d from 260/380zł; ☎) This is a neat hotel in a peaceful setting overlooking the river on Piasek Island, offering reasonable value for money. It's ideal for exploring the lovely ecclesiastical quarter and there's a good restaurant attached.

Hotel Zaułek
HOTEL €€

(☑71 341 0046; www.hotelzaulek.pl; ul Garbary 11; s/d from 270/380zł; ☎) Run by the university, this guesthouse accommodates just 18 visitors in a dozen homey rooms. The 1pm checkout is a plus for heavy sleepers, and weekend prices are a steal. Breakfast is an additional 11zł; half and full board are also available.

Hotel Europejski
HOTEL €€

(☑71 772 1000; www.silfor.pl; ul Piłsudskiego 88; s/d from 200/250zł; ☀☎) Pleasant hotel a stone's throw from the train station, with high ceilings, quality furniture and a cafe-bar and restaurant. Check its website for last-minute cheap deals.

AS Apartments
APARTMENTS €€

(☑71 341 8759; www.asapart.pl; Rynek 18; apt from €55; ☎) Company offering a choice of apartments in the Old Town, many of them with a view of the Rynek. The fixtures and fittings can be old-fashioned, but the locations are fabulous for the price.

Hotel Europeum
HOTEL €€

(☑71 371 4500; www.europeum.pl; ul Kazimierza Wielkiego 27a; s/d 320/350zł; ☀☎) Business-oriented hotel with stylish rooms in a great location near the Rynek. Rates drop dramatically at weekends.

✗ Eating & Drinking

TOP CHOICE **Bernard**
INTERNATIONAL €€

(Rynek 35; mains 27-77zł; ⊙10.30am-11pm) Bernard is one cool dude – this lively split-level bar-restaurant-brewery is a cut above its Rynek rivals. It serves a selection of upmarket comfort food including burgers, steak and fish dishes, along with a Polish choice or two; all washed down with the in-house lager. There's live music most nights and a breakfast menu from 10.30am to noon.

Restauracja Jadka
POLISH €€€

(ul Rzeźnicza 24/25; mains 58-83zł; ⊙1-11pm) One of the best restaurants in town, presenting impeccable modern versions of Polish classics amid elegant table settings in delightful Gothic surrounds. There's loads of character in the interior, with tables bearing lacy white tablecloths dotted beneath brick archways, illuminated by low-lit lamps.

Bazylia
CAFETERIA €

(Plac Uniwersytecki; mains per 100g 2.49zł; ⊙10am-6pm Mon-Fri, from 11am Sat & Sun) Inexpensive and bustling modern take on the classic *bar mleczny* (milk bar), set in a curved space with huge plate-glass windows overlooking the venerable university buildings. The menu has a lot of Polish standards such as *bigos* (thick sauerkraut and meat stew) and *gołąbki* (cabbage leaves stuffed with mince and rice), and a decent range of salads and other vegetable dishes. Everything is priced by weight at the same rate; order and pay at the till before receiving your food.

Darea
JAPANESE, KOREAN €€€

(ul Kuźnicza 43/45; mains 26-65zł; ⊙noon-11pm) Over time the menu at this place has become steadily more Japanese, but you'll still find authentic Korean dishes such as *bibimbab* and *bulgogi* on the list. It's all good Asian food in atmospheric surrounds.

La Scala
ITALIAN €€

(Rynek 38; mains 19-145zł) Offers authentic Italian food and particularly tasty desserts. Some dishes are pricey, but you're really paying for the location. The cheaper trattoria at ground level serves good pizza and pasta.

Mexico Bar
MEXICAN €€

(ul Rzeźnicza 34; mains 15-45zł; ⊙noon-11pm) Compact, warmly lit restaurant featuring sombreros, backlit masks and a chandelier made of beer bottles. There's a small bar to lean on while waiting for a table. All the Tex-Mex standards are on the menu.

Bar Wegetariański Vega
VEGETARIAN €

(Rynek 1/2; mains 4-11zł; ⊙8am-7pm Mon-Fri, 9am-5pm Sat & Sun; ☑) This cheap cafeteria in the centre of the Rynek offers vegie dishes in a light green space, with a good choice of soups and crepes. Upstairs there's a vegan section, open from noon.

Pub Guinness
PUB

(Plac Solny 5; ⊙noon-2am) No prizes for guessing what this pub serves. A lively, fairly authentic Irish pub, spread over three levels on a busy corner. The ground-floor bar buzzes with student and traveller groups getting together, and there's a restaurant and beer cellar as well. A good place to wind down after a hard day's sightseeing.

TRAINS FROM WROCŁAW

DESTINATION	PRICE (ZŁ)	DURATION (HR)	FREQUENCY
Berlin (Germany)	Varies	5	1 daily
Częstochowa	40	3	6 daily
Kraków	52	5½	hourly
Łódź	48zł	4¼	5 daily
Poznań	46	3½	at least hourly
Szczecin	61	5	6 daily
Toruń	56	5	5 daily
Warsaw	61	6½	hourly

Cafe Artzat CAFE
(ul Malarska 30; ☎) This low-key cafe just north of the landmark Church of St Elizabeth is one of the best places in town to recharge the batteries over coffee or tea and a good book.

☆ Entertainment

PRL CLUB
(Rynek Ratusz 10; ⊙noon-late) The dictatorship of the proletariat is alive and well in this tongue-in-cheek venue inspired by communist nostalgia. Disco lights play over a bust of Lenin, propaganda posters line the walls and red-menace memorabilia is scattered through the maze of rooms. Descend to the basement – beneath the portraits of Stalin and Mao – if you'd like to hit the dance floor.

Bezsenność CLUB
(ul Ruska 51; ⊙7pm-late) With its alternative/rock/dance line-up and distressed decor, 'Insomnia' attracts a high-end clientele and is one of the most popular clubs in town.

Filharmonia CLASSICAL MUSIC
(☑71 342 2459; www.filharmonia.wroclaw.pl; ul Piłsudskiego 19) Southwest of the Old Town, across the river, this place hosts classical music concerts.

❶ Information

Internet Netvigator (ul Igielna 14; per hr 4zł; ⊙9am-midnight)
Lower Silesia Tourist Information Centre (☑71 342 2291; www.wroclaw-info.pl; ul Sukiennice 12; ⊙10am-6pm)
Main Post Office (Rynek 28; ⊙6.30am-8.30pm Mon-Sat)
Tourist Office (☑71 344 3111; www.wroclaw-info.pl; Rynek 14; ⊙9am-9pm Apr-Oct, 9am-7pm Nov-Mar)

❶ Getting There & Away

AIR From **Copernicus Airport** (www.airport.wroclaw.pl), national carrier LOT flies frequently between Wrocław and Warsaw. Internationally, it heads three times daily to Frankfurt and four times daily to Munich. Tickets can be bought at the **LOT office** (☑71 342 5151; ul Piłsudskiego 36). Eurolot also links Wrocław to Gdańsk.

A range of budget carriers connect Wrocław with other European cities, including several British and Irish regional destinations. Ryanair and Wizz Air fly daily to London, while Ryanair heads five times a week to Dublin.

The airport is in Strachowice, about 12km west of the Old Town. The frequent bus 406 and infrequent night bus 249 link the airport with Wrocław Główny train station and the bus terminal.

BUS The **bus station** (ul Sucha 11) is south of the main train station, and offers five daily PKS buses to Warsaw (60zł, six hours). For most other destinations the train is a better choice, though handy **Polski Bus** (www.polskibus.com) services run from here to Łódź (4½ hours, twice daily) and Prague (five hours, twice daily), as well as Warsaw (7¼ hours, twice daily); check fares and book tickets online.

TRAIN Wrocław Główny train station (ul Piłsudskiego 105), formerly Breslau Hauptbahnhof, was opened in 1857 as a lavish architectural confection resembling a castle with turrets and Gothic arches. Extensively renovated and restored for the UEFA football championship in 2012, it's easily Poland's most attractive railway station and is worth visiting even if you're not travelling by train.

Sudeten Mountains

The Sudeten Mountains (Sudety) run for more than 250km along the Czech–Polish border. The Sudetes feature dense forests,

CZĘSTOCHOWA

This pilgrimage destination 114km northwest of Kraków and 150km east of Wrocław is dominated by the graceful **Paulite Monastery of Jasna Góra** (☏34 377 7408; www. bop.jasnagora.pl; admission free; ☉dawn-dusk), sited atop a hill in the centre of town. Founded in 1382, it's the home of the *Black Madonna*, a portrait claimed to be the source of miracles. In recognition of these feats, in 1717 the painting was crowned Queen of Poland. It's well worth a trip to the monastery to check out its three museums, and of course to meet the *Black Madonna*.

Częstochowa has regular train connections with Kraków, Łódź, Warsaw, Zakopane and Wrocław. For more details, browse Lonely Planet's *Poland* country guide, visit www. info.czestochowa.pl, or step into the Częstochowa **tourist office** (☏34 368 2250; Al Najświętszej Marii Panny 65; ☉9am-5pm Mon-Sat), which can assist with accommodation should you like to stay over.

amazing rock formations and deposits of semi-precious stones and can be explored along the extensive network of trails for hiking or mountain biking. The highest part of this old eroded chain is Mt Śnieżka (1602m).

Szklarska Poręba, at the northwestern end of the Sudetes, offers superior facilities for hiking and skiing. It's at the base of Mt Szrenica (1362m) and the town centre is at the upper end of ul Jedności Narodowej. The small tourist office (☏75 754 7740; www.szklarskaporeba.pl; ul Jedności Narodowej 1a; ☉8am-4pm Mon-Fri, 9am-5pm Sat & Sun) can book accommodation and has info and maps. Nearby, several trails begin at the intersection of ul Jedności Narodowej and ul Wielki Sikorskiego. The red trail goes to Mt Szrenica (two hours) and offers a peek at Wodospad Kamieńczyka, a spectacular waterfall.

Karpacz to the southeast has more nightlife on offer, although it attracts fewer serious mountaineers. It's loosely clustered along a 3km road winding through Łomnica Valley at the base of Mt Śnieżka. The tourist office (☏75 761 8605; www.karpacz.pl; ul Konstytucji 3 Maja 25; ☉9am-5pm Mon-Sat, 10am-2pm Sun) should be your first port of call. To reach the peak of Mt Śnieżka on foot, take one of the trails (three to four hours) from Hotel Biały Jar. Some of the trails pass by one of two splendid postglacial lakes: Mały Staw and Wielki Staw.

The bus is the fastest way of getting around the region. Every day from Szklarska Poręba, two buses head to Wrocław (31zł, three hours), as does one train (38zł, 3¾ hours). From Karpacz, get one of the frequent buses to Jelenia Góra (9zł, 30 minutes), from where buses and trains go in all directions, including to Wrocław. The two mountain towns are also linked to each other by two buses each day (9zł, 45 minutes).

For the Czech Republic, at least three trains cross the border each day from Szklarska Poręba to Harrachov (5zł, 30 minutes). You can also take a bus from Szklarska Poręba to Jakuszyce (5zł, 15 minutes), cross the border on foot to Harrachov and take a Czech bus from there.

WIELKOPOLSKA

Wielkopolska (Greater Poland) is the region where Poland came to life in the Middle Ages and is referred to as the Cradle of the Polish State. As a result of this ancient eminence, its cities and towns are full of historic and cultural attractions.

The royal capital moved from Poznań to Kraków in 1038, though Wielkopolska remained an important province. Its historic significance didn't save it from international conflict, however, and the region became part of Prussia in 1793. Wielkopolska rose against German rule at the end of WWI and became part of the reborn Poland. The battles of WWII later caused widespread destruction in the area.

Poznań

POP 555,000

No one could accuse Poznań of being too sleepy. Between its regular trade fairs, student population and visiting travellers, it's a vibrant city with a wide choice of attractions. There's a beautiful Old Town at its centre, with a number of interesting museums and a range of lively bars, clubs and restaurants. The surrounding countryside is also good for cycling and hiking.

Poznań grew from humble beginnings, when 9th-century Polanian tribes built a wooden fort on the island of Ostrów Tumski. From 968 to 1038 Poznań was the de facto capital of Poland. Its position between Berlin and Warsaw has always underlined its importance as a trading town and in 1925 a modern version of its famous medieval trade fairs was instituted. The fairs, filling up the city's hotels for several days at a time, are the lynchpin of the city's economy.

As it's at the heart of Wielkopolska, Poznań makes a good transport hub from which to explore the region.

◉ Sights

OLD TOWN

Poznań's Old Town is centred on its attractive and ever-busy **Stary Rynek** (Old Market Sq), lined with restaurants and bars. There are several small museums of varying degrees of interest dotted around the square, in its central buildings and nearby; ask at the tourist office (p408) for the full list.

Historical Museum of Poznań MUSEUM
(www.mnp.art.pl; Stary Rynek 1; adult/concession 7/5zł, Sat free; ⊙9am-3pm Tue-Thu, noon-9pm Fri, 11am-6pm Sat & Sun) Located within the Renaissance **Town Hall** (Stary Rynek), which was built 1550–60, this museum displays splendid period interiors. If you're outside the building at noon, look up. Every midday two mechanical metal goats above its clock butt their horns together 12 times, echoing an improbable centuries-old legend of two animals escaping a cook and fighting each other in the town hall tower.

Fish Sellers' Houses HISTORIC BUILDINGS
(Stary Rynek) Located on the southeast side of the Stary Rynek, this endearing row of small arcaded buildings with colourful facades was built in the 16th century on the former site of fish stalls. It was later reconstructed after major damage in WWII.

Wielkopolska Military Museum MUSEUM
(www.mnp.art.pl; Stary Rynek 9; adult/concession 7/5zł, Sat free; ⊙9am-3pm Tue-Thu, noon-9pm Fri, 11am-6pm Sat & Sun) Exhibits of arms from Poland's many conflicts over the centuries, dating from the 11th century to the present.

Museum of Musical Instruments MUSEUM
(www.mnp.art.pl; Stary Rynek 45; adult/concession 5.50/3.50zł, Sat free; ⊙9am-3pm Tue-Thu, noon-9pm Fri, 11am-6pm Sat & Sun) Large though unimaginative collection of music-making devices, displayed over multiple levels.

Franciscan Church CHURCH
(ul Franciszkańska 2) This 17th-century church, one block west of the square, has an ornate baroque interior, complete with wall paintings and rich stucco work.

Parish Church of St Stanislaus CHURCH
(ul Gołębia 1) Two blocks south of Stary Rynek is this large, pink baroque place of worship with monumental altars dating from the mid-17th century.

Museum of Applied Arts MUSEUM
(www.mnp.art.pl; Góra Przemysława 1) Collection of furniture, gold and silverware, glass, ceramics, weapons, clocks, watches and sundials from Europe and the Far East. At the time of research the museum was undergoing a major renovation as part of a restoration of the castle it's housed within, but should have reopened by the time you read this.

WEST OF THE OLD TOWN

**Monument to the Victims
of June 1956** MONUMENT
(Plac Mickiewicza) Emotive memorial to the dead and injured of the massive 1956 strike by the city's industrial workers, which was crushed by tanks. It's in a park west of the prominent Kaiserhaus building.

Palm House GREENHOUSE
(Palmiarnia; www.palmiarnia.poznan.pl; ul Matejki 18; adult/concession 7/5zł; ⊙9am-5pm Tue-Sat, 9am-6pm Sun) This huge greenhouse (built in 1910) contains 17,000 species of tropical and subtropical plants. It's located in Park Wilsona, 1km southwest of the train station.

NORTH OF THE OLD TOWN

Museum of Armaments MUSEUM
(Al Armii Poznań; adult/concession 4/2zł, Fri free; ⊙9am-4pm Tue-Sat, from 10am Sun) This museum of weaponry is located in Citadel Park about 1.5km north of the Old Town, within the remains of a 19th-century Prussian citadel. Some 20,000 German troops held out for a month here in February 1945, when the fortress was destroyed by artillery fire. Exhibits include Russian tanks and rocket launchers.

EAST OF THE OLD TOWN

Ostrów Tumski HISTORIC AREA
This river island is dominated by the monumental, double-towered **Poznań Cathedral** (ul Ostrów Tumski 17; ⊙dawn-dusk), originally built in 968. The Byzantine-style **Golden Chapel**

GNIEZNO

If you're staying in Poznań, it's worth checking out historic Gniezno, one of Poland's oldest settlements. It was probably here that Poland's Duke Mieszko I was baptised in 966, the starting point of Catholicism's major role in the nation's story. In 1025, Bolesław Chrobry was crowned in the city's cathedral as the first Polish king. Gniezno probably also functioned as Poland's first capital before Poznań achieved that honour, though history is murky on this point.

Whatever the case, Gniezno makes a good day trip from Poznań, or a short stopover. Setting out from its attractive broad market square you can investigate its historic cathedral, dating from the 14th century, and a museum dedicated to Poland's origins, situated on the nearby lakeside.

An hour north of Gniezno is the Iron Age village of Biskupin, unearthed in the 1930s and partly reconstructed. Passing by it is a tourist train that links the towns of Żnin and Gąsawa, both of which have regular bus transport to Gniezno. Gniezno itself is linked to Poznań by frequent trains (45-minute trip) and buses (one-hour trip) throughout the day.

For more details, check out Lonely Planet's *Poland* country guide or drop into Gniezno's tourist office (☑61 428 4100; www.szlakpiastowski.com.pl; Rynek 14).

(1841) and the mausoleums of Mieszko I and Boleslaus the Brave are behind the high altar.

A new attraction under construction opposite the island's eastern shore is the Cathedral Island Heritage Centre (www.trakt.poznan.pl; ul Gdańska). A cutting-edge multimedia history museum, it should be open by mid-2013.

The island is 1km east of the Old Town (take any eastbound tram from Plac Wielkopolski).

Lake Malta RECREATIONAL ZONE

Some 1.6km east of the Old Town is this body of water, a favourite weekend destination for Poles. It holds sailing regattas, outdoor concerts and other events in summer and in winter there's a ski slope in operation.

A fun way to visit the lake is to take tram 4, 8 or 17 from Plac Wielkopolski to the Rondo Środka stop on the other side of Ostrów Tumski. From the nearby terminus, you can catch a miniature train along the Malta Park Railway (http://mpk.poznan.pl/maltanka; ul Jana Pawła II; adult/concession 6/4zł; ⏱10am-6.30pm Apr-Oct), which follows the lake's shore to the New Zoo (www.zoo.poznan.pl; ul Krańcowa 81; adult/concession 20/10zł; ⏱9am-7pm Apr-Sep, to 4pm Oct-Mar). This sprawling institution houses diverse species, including Baltic grey seals.

✰✰ Festivals & Events

St John's Fair CULTURAL

(⏱Jun) Held on the Stary Rynek, featuring craft items, local foods and street artist performances. The fair runs for two weeks.

Malta International Theatre Festival THEATRE

(www.malta-festival.pl; ⏱Jul)

Ethno Port Poznań Festival WORLD MUSIC

(www.ethnoport.pl; ⏱Aug)

Transatlantyk Poznań International Film & Music Festival FILM, MUSIC

(www.transatlantyk.org; ⏱Aug)

🛏 Sleeping

The largest trade fairs take place in January, June, September and October; during these times (and at other times when trade fairs are on), the rates of Poznań's accommodation dramatically increase. A room may also be difficult to find, so it pays to book ahead. Prices given here are for outside trade fair periods. You can check the dates of the fairs online at www.mtp.pl.

Rooms can also be found via Biuro Zakwaterowania Przemysław (☑61 866 3560; www.przemyslaw.com.pl; ul Głogowska 16; ⏱10am-6pm Mon-Fri, to 2pm Sat), an accommodation agency with an office not far from the train station.

TOP CHOICE Hotel Stare Miasto HOTEL €€

(☑61 663 62 42; www.hotelstaremiasto.pl; ul Rybaki 36; s/d from 224/390zł; ✳🅿) Elegant, value-for-money hotel with a tasteful chandeliered foyer and a spacious breakfast room. Rooms can be small, but are clean and bright with lovely starched white sheets. Some upper rooms have skylights in place of windows.

Rezydencja Solei
HOTEL €€

(☎61 855 7351; www.hotel-solei.pl; ul Szewska 2; s/d 199/299zł; ☜) Temptingly close to Stary Rynek, this tiny hotel offers small but cosy rooms in an old-fashioned residential style, with wallpaper and timber furniture striking a homey note. The attic suite is amazingly large and can accommodate up to four people. Breakfast is 20zł extra.

Frolic Goats Hostel
HOSTEL €

(☎61 852 4411; www.frolicgoatshostel.com; ul Wrocławska 16/6; dm from 44zł, d 170zł; ☜) Named after the feisty goats who fight above the Town Hall clock, this hostel is aimed squarely at the international backpacker. There's a washing machine on the premises, bike hire is available for 30zł per day and room rates are unaffected by trade fairs. Enter from ul Jaskółcza.

Brovaria
HOTEL €€

(☎61 858 6868; www.brovaria.pl; Stary Rynek 73/74; s/d from 250/290zł; ☜) This multi-talented hotel also operates as a restaurant and bar, but most impressive is its in-house microbrewery. The elegant rooms have tasteful dark timber tones and some have views onto the Rynek.

Hostel Cameleon
HOSTEL €

(☎61 639 3041; www.hostel-cameleon.com; ul Świętosławska 12; dm 55zł, s/d from 120/165zł; ☜) Centrally located hostel with contemporary decor and a spacious kitchen and lounge. The cheaper private rooms have shared bathrooms. Also has a washing machine.

Hotel Lech
HOTEL €€

(☎61 853 0151; www.hotel-lech.poznan.pl; ul Św Marcin 74; s/d 200/295zł; ☜) Hotel Lech has standard two-star decor, but rooms are relatively spacious and the bathrooms are modern. Flash your ISIC card for a discount.

✖ Eating & Drinking

TOP CHOICE **Warung Bali**
INDONESIAN €€€

(ul Żydowska 1; mains 36-62zł; ☉noon-10pm) Excellent Indonesian restaurant not far from the main square, with a tastefully decorated interior. Indonesian music plays softly while you order *gado gado* (mixed vegetables with peanut sauce), satays, *nasi goreng* (fried rice) and other delicious classics.

Tapas Bar
SPANISH €€

(Stary Rynek 60; mains 19-88zł; ☉9am-midnight) Atmospheric place dishing up authentic tapas and Spanish wine in a room lined with intriguing bric-a-brac. Most tapas dishes

cost about 26zł, so forget the mains and share with friends. Also serves breakfast.

Gospoda Pod Koziołkami
POLISH €€

(Stary Rynek 95; mains 13-78zł; ☉11am-10pm) Homey bistro within Gothic arches on the ground floor and a grill in the cellar. The menu is crammed with tasty Polish standards, including some distinctively Wielkopolska specialities.

Bar Caritas
CAFETERIA €

(Plac Wolności 1; mains 6-12zł; ☉8am-7pm Mon-Fri, 9am-5pm Sat, from 11am Sun) You can point at what you want without resorting to your phrasebook at this cheap and convenient milk bar. There are many variants of *naleśniki* (crepes) on the menu. Lunchtimes get crowded, so be prepared to share a table.

Ptasie Radio
CAFE-BAR

(ul Kościuszki 74; ☉8am-midnight Mon-Fri, from 10am Sat & Sun; ☜) This funky drinking hole, named after a famous Polish poem 'Bird Radio', is a retro riot of chipped wooden tables, pot plants and bird images everywhere along its shelves and walls. It's a mellow place for a coffee or something stronger.

Proletaryat
BAR

(ul Wrocławska 9; ☉1pm-late Mon-Sat, 3pm-late Sun) Small, red communist nostalgia bar with an array of socialist-era gear on the walls, including the obligatory bust of Lenin in the window and various portraits of the great man and his comrades. Play 'spot the communist leader' while sipping a boutique beer.

☆ Entertainment

Czarna Owca
CLUB

(ul Jaskółcza 13; ☉6pm-late Wed-Sat) Literally 'Black Sheep', this is a popular club with nightly DJs playing a mix of genres including R & B, house, rock, Latin, soul and funk.

Teatr Wielki
THEATRE

(☎61 659 0280; www.opera.poznan.pl; ul Fredry 9) The main venue for opera and ballet.

Filharmonia
CLASSICAL MUSIC

(☎61 853 6935; www.filharmonia.poznan.pl; ul Św Marcin 81) Offers classical music concerts.

ℹ Information

Adax (ul Półwiejska 28; per hr 2.50zł; ☉8am-9pm Mon-Fri, from 10am Sat, from noon Sun) Internet access south of Stary Rynek.

City Information Centre (☎61 851 9645; ul Ratajczaka 44; ☉10am-7pm Mon-Fri, until 5pm Sat) Handles bookings for cultural events.

POLAND POZNAŃ

TRANSPORT FROM POZNAŃ

Domestic Train

DESTINATION	PRICE (ZŁ)	DURATION (HR)	FREQUENCY
Gdańsk & Gdynia	58	5	8 daily
Kraków	61	8½	9 daily
Szczecin	46	2¾	at least hourly
Toruń	24	2½	10 daily
Warsaw	56	3¼	at least hourly
Wrocław	46	3½	at least hourly
Zakopane	65	11½	1 daily

International Train

DESTINATION	DURATION (HR)	FREQUENCY
Berlin (Germany)	2½	6 daily
Kyiv (Ukraine)	19	1 daily
Moscow (Russia)	21	1 daily

Main Post Office (ul Kościuszki 77; ⊙7am-8pm Mon-Fri, 8am-3pm Sat)

Tourist Office (☑61 852 6156; www.poznan.pl; Stary Rynek 59; ⊙9am-8pm Mon-Sat, 10am-6pm Sun May-Sep, 10am-6pm Mon-Fri Oct-Apr)

ⓘ Getting There & Away

AIR From **Poznań Airport** (www.airport-poznan.com.pl; ul Bukowska 285), national carrier LOT flies up to three times a day to Warsaw, once daily to Frankfurt and twice daily to Munich. Tickets are available from the **LOT office** (☑61 849 2261; ul Bukowska 285) at the airport. There are also two domestic flights daily via Eurolot to Kraków.

A vast array of other European cities are serviced from Poznań, including London via Wizz Air and Ryanair (daily), and Dublin via Ryanair (four times a week). The airport is in the western suburb of Ławica, 7km from the Old Town and accessible by bus L from the main train station, or buses 48, 59 and night bus 242 from the Bałtyk stop near Rondo Kaponiera.

BUS The **bus station** (ul Towarowa 17) is a 10-minute walk east of the train station, though will eventually be integrated with the new Poznan Główny train station. In any case, most of its destinations can be reached more comfortably and frequently by train.

From the smaller Dworzec Górczyn bus station 5km southwest of the main train station along ul Głogowska, **Polski Bus** (www.polskibus.com) runs useful services to Warsaw (5¾ hours, three daily) and Berlin (4½ hours, twice daily) as well as other destinations around Poland; check fares and book online.

TRAIN The busy Poznań Główny train station was in two pieces at the time of research, with the partly opened new station building operating in conjuction with the old terminal next to it. The station is about 1.5km southwest of the Old Town.

POMERANIA

Pomerania (Pomorze in Polish) is an attractive region with diverse drawcards, from beautiful beaches to architecturally pleasing cities. It covers a large swathe of territory along the Baltic coast, from the German border in the west to the lower Vistula Valley in the east. A sandy coastline stretches from Gdańsk to western Szczecin and Toruń lies inland. Pomerania was fought over by Germanic and Slavic peoples for a millennium, before being incorporated almost fully within Poland after WWII.

Gdańsk

POP 460,000

Port cities are usually lively places with distinctive personalities, and Gdańsk is no exception. From its busy riverside waterfront to the Renaissance splendour of its charming narrow streets, there's plenty to like about this coastal city.

Few Polish cities occupy such a pivotal position in history as Gdańsk. Founded more than a millennium ago, it became the focus of territorial tensions when the Teutonic Knights seized it from Poland in 1308. The city joined the Hanseatic League in 1361 and became one of the richest ports in the Baltic through its membership of the trading organisation. Finally, the Thirteen Years' War ended in 1466 with the Knights' defeat and Gdańsk's return to Polish rule.

This to-and-fro between Germanic and Polish control didn't stop there, however – in 1793 Gdańsk was incorporated into Prussia and after the German loss in WWI it became the autonomous Free City of Danzig. The city's environs are where WWII began, when Nazi Germany bombarded Polish troops stationed at Westerplatte. Gdańsk suffered immense damage during the war, but upon its return to Poland in 1945 its historic centre was faithfully reconstructed.

In the 1980s, Gdańsk achieved international fame as the home of the Solidarity trade union, whose rise paralleled the fall of communism in Europe. Today it's a vibrant city and a great base for exploring the Baltic coast.

◉ Sights

MAIN TOWN

Royal Way HISTORIC ROUTE

The historic parade route of Polish kings runs from the western Upland Gate (Brama Wyżynna), which was built in the 1770s on the site of a 15th-century gate, onward through the Foregate (Przedbramie), which once housed a torture chamber, and 1614 Golden Gate (Złota Brama), and east to the 1568 Renaissance Green Gate (Zielona Brama). Along the way it passes through beautiful ul Długa (Long Street) and Długi Targ (Long Market).

Central Maritime Museum MUSEUM

(www.cmm.pl; ul Ołowianka 9; all sections 18/10zł; ⊙10am-4pm Tue-Sun) On the waterfront north of the 14th-century St Mary's Gate you'll find the 15th-century Gdańsk Crane (ul Szeroka 67/68; adult/concession 8/5zł; ⊙10am-4pm Tue-Sun), the largest of its kind in medieval Europe and capable of hoisting loads of up to 2000kg. It's part of this maritime history museum, which has a presence on both sides of the Motława River linked by its own regular ferry service.

On the west bank next to the crane is the spanking new Maritime Cultural Centre (ul Tokarska 21; adult/concession 12/8zł; ⊙10am-6pm Tue-Sun), with an exhibition of boats

from around the world and an interactive section popular with kids. The branch on the east bank offers a fascinating insight into Gdańsk's seafaring past, including the Sołdek Museum Ship (ul Ołowianka 9; adult/concession 8/5zł; ⊙10am-4pm Tue-Sun), built here just after WWII.

St Mary's Church CHURCH

(ul Podkramarska 5; tower adult/concession 5/3zł; ⊙8.30am-6pm, except during services) At the western end of picturesque ul Mariacka, with its gracious 17th-century burgher houses and amber shops, is this gigantic 14th-century place of worship. Watch little figures troop out at noon from its 14m-high astronomical clock, adorned with zodiacal signs. You can also climb the 405 steps of the tower for a giddy view over the town.

Amber Museum MUSEUM

(www.mhmg.gda.pl; Targ Węglowy; adult/concession 10/5zł, Mon free; ⊙11am-3pm Mon, 10am-7pm Tue-Sat, 11am-7pm Sun) Within the Foregate you can visit this museum, wherein you can marvel at the history of so-called 'Baltic gold'.

Historical Museum of Gdańsk MUSEUM

(www.mhmg.gda.pl; ul Długa 47; adult/concession 10/5zł, Mon free; ⊙11am-3pm Mon, 10am-7pm Tue-Sat, 11am-7pm Sun) Inside the towering Gothic Town Hall is this institution depicting photos of old Gdańsk and the damage caused to the city during WWII.

Neptune's Fountain FOUNTAIN

(Długi Targ) Near the Town Hall, legend says this decorative fountain (1633) once gushed forth *goldwasser*, the iconic Gdańsk liqueur.

Artus Court Museum MUSEUM

(www.mhmg.gda.pl; ul Długi Targ 43/44; adult/concession 10/5zł, free Mon; ⊙11am-3pm Mon, 10am-7pm Tue-Sat, 11am-7pm Sun) Merchants used to congregate in this building, which boasts lavish interior decoration. Also note the adjacent Golden House (Złota Kamienica; Długi Targ), built in 1618, which has a strikingly rich facade.

Dom Uphagena MUSEUM

(www.mhmg.gda.pl; ul Długa 12; adult/concession 10/5zł, Mon free; ⊙11am-3pm Mon, 10am-7pm Tue-Sat, 11am-7pm Sun) This historic 18th-century residence features ornate furniture.

Free City of Danzig Historical Zone MUSEUM

(ul Piwna 19/21; admission 5zł; ⊙11am-6pm) Small but intriguing display of items from

Gdańsk

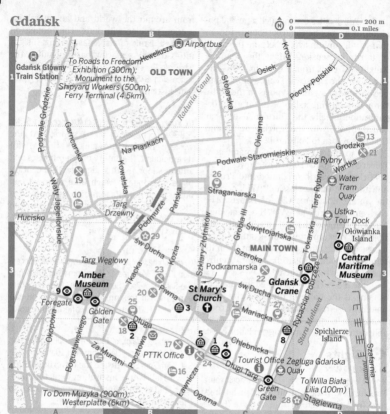

the interwar era when Gdańsk operated as a 'free city', independent of both Poland and Germany.

State Archaeological Museum
MUSEUM

(ul Mariacka 25/26; adult/concession 8/6zł; ☺10am-5pm Tue-Sun) Museum within St Mary's Gate, housing an overly generous number of formerly diseased ancient human skulls, displays of amber and river views from the adjacent **tower** (admission 5zł).

OLD TOWN

Almost totally destroyed in 1945, the Old Town has never been completely rebuilt, but contains some gems worth visiting.

TOP CHOICE Roads to Freedom Exhibition
MUSEUM

(ul Wały Piastowskie 24; adult/concession 6/4zł; ☺10am-6pm Tue-Sun) At the north end of the Old Town is this excellent museum. Its exhibits chart the decline and fall of Polish

communism and the rise of the Solidarity trade union. It's a place that anyone interested in Gdańsk's history should visit.

Monument to the Shipyard Workers
MONUMENT

(Plac Solidarności) A short walk further north, this soaring structure stands at the entrance to the Gdańsk Shipyards. It was erected in late 1980 in memory of 44 workers killed during the riots of December 1970 and was the first monument in a communist regime to commemorate the regime's victims.

OLIWA

Park Oliwski
GARDENS

(ul Cystersów; ☺8am-8pm) Some 9km northwest of the Main Town is the towering **Oliwa Cathedral** (ul Nowickiego 5; ☺9am-5pm), located within this lovely set of gardens. It was built in the 13th century with a Gothic facade and a long, narrow central nave. The famous baroque organ is used for recitals each hour

Gdańsk

between 10am and 3pm Monday to Saturday in July and August. There's an **Ethnographic Museum** (ul Cystersów 19; adult/concession 8/4zł, Fri free; ☺10am-5pm Tue-Sun) housed in the nearby Old Granary, and the **Modern Art Gallery** (ul Cystersów 18; adult/concession 10/6zł; ☺10am-5pm Tue-Sun) can be found in the former Abbots' Palace.

To reach the park, take the commuter train to the Gdańsk Oliwa station (3.60zł). From there, it's a 10-minute walk; head west up ul Poczty Gdańsk, turn right (north) along the highway and look for the signs to 'Ethnographic Museum' and 'Cathedral'.

WESTERPLATTE

Bus 106 (25 minutes) heads to Westerplatte every 15 minutes from a stop outside the Music Academy in Gdańsk. Alternatively, excursion boats sail from the Main Town to Westerplatte.

World War II Memorial   MEMORIAL
(ul Sucharskiego) WWII began at 4.45am on 1 September 1939, when the German battleship *Schleswig-Holstein* began shelling the Polish naval post at this location, 7km north of Gdańsk's Main Town. The 182-man Polish garrison held out against ferocious attacks for a week before surrendering.

The enormity of this event is marked by a hilltop **memorial**, a small **museum** (www.mhmg.gda.pl; ul Sucharskiego 1; adult/concession 3/2zł; ☺9am-7pm May-Sep) and **ruins** remaining from the Nazi German bombardment.

🎎 Festivals & Events

International Street & Open-Air Theatre Festival   THEATRE
(www.feta.pl; ☺Jul)

International Organ Music Festival   MUSIC
(☺Jul/Aug)

Sounds of the North Festival   MUSIC
(www.nck.org.pl; ☺Jul/Aug) Folkloric music festival.

St Dominic's Fair   SHOPPING
(www.mtgsa.pl; ☺Jul/Aug) Annual shopping and cultural fair.

International Shakespeare Festival   THEATRE
(www.shakespearefestival.pl; ☺Jul/Aug)

🛏 Sleeping

Accommodation can be tight in the warmer months. If you're having trouble finding a bed, check with the tourist office (p413). Also consider staying in nearby Sopot or Gdynia; the tourist offices there can help.

TOP CHOICE 3 City Hostel HOSTEL €

(📞58 354 5454; www.3city-hostel.pl; Targ Drzewny 12/14; dm from 50zł, r 180zł; 📶) Sparkling new hostel near the train station, with high ceilings, pleasant common areas, a kitchen and a lounge with a view. The cheapest beds are in Japanese-style capsules.

Kamienica Gotyk HOTEL €

(📞58 301 8567; www.gotykhouse.eu; ul Mariacka 1; s/d 280/310zł; 📶) This Gothic guesthouse claims to be Gdańsk's oldest residence. Inside, the rooms are compact but neat, with clean bathrooms. The location is impressive, with St Mary's Church and the cafes and shops of ul Mariacka just outside the door.

Dom Muzyka HOTEL €€

(📞58 326 0600; www.dommuzyka.pl; ul Łąkowa 1/2; s/d 252/344zł; 🅿📶) Gorgeous white rooms with arched ceilings and quality furniture, inside the Music Academy some 300m east of the city centre; trams 3, 8 and 9 will get you there from the train station. It's hard to spot from the street – head for the door on the city end of the courtyard within the big yellow-brick building.

Dom Zachariasza Zappio HOSTEL €

(📞58 322 0174; www.zappio.pl; ul Świętojańska 49; dm/s/d 50/99/158zł; 📶) This hostel is located in an atmospheric former convent next to St John's Church. Rooms are brightly furnished with contemporary furniture and there's a fantastic beer garden.

Happy Seven Hostel HOSTEL €

(📞58 320 8601; www.happyseven.com; ul Grodzka 16; dm from 45zł, d 230zł; 📶) Hostel in which each dorm has a light-hearted theme, including the 'Travel' dorm plastered with maps, and the 'Music', 'Sport' and 'Movie' dorms. The cool retro lounge contains a games console.

Kamienica Zacisze APARTMENTS €€

(📞69 627 4306; www.apartments.gdansk.pl; ul Ogarna 107; apt from 220zł; 📶) Set within a quiet courtyard off the street, this communist-era workers' dormitory building has been transformed into a set of light, airy apartments for up to nine people. Each apartment has high ceilings, a fully equipped kitchen and loads of space. Excellent value for the location and quality.

Apartments Poland APARTMENTS €€

(📞58 346 9864; www.apartmentpoland.com; apt €30-80) A company with renovated properties scattered through the Tri-City Area (Gdańsk–Sopot–Gdynia), including a number in central Gdańsk. Some are big enough for families or other groups.

Dom Harcerza HOTEL €

(📞58 301 3621; www.domharcerza.pl; ul Za Murami 2/10; dm 35zł, s/d from 60/120zł; 📶) The rooms are small but cosy at this place, which offers the best value and location for any budget-priced hotel. It's popular (so book ahead) and can get noisy when large groups are staying here. There's a charming old-fashioned restaurant on the ground floor.

Camping Nr 218 Stogi CAMPING GROUND €

(📞58 307 3915; www.kemping-gdansk.pl; ul Wydmy 9; site per person/tent 15/7zł, cabins 65-140zł; ⏰May-Sep) This camping ground is only 200m from the beach in the seaside holiday centre of Stogi, about 5.5km northeast of the Main Town. Tidy cabins sleep between two and five people and facilities include a volleyball court and children's playground. Take tram 8 or 13 from the main train station in Gdańsk.

Willa Biała Lilia HOTEL €

(📞58 301 7074; www.bialalilia.pl; ul Spichrzowa 16; s/d 260/340zł; 📶) The White Lily Villa is an attractive accommodation choice a short walk east of the Main Town on Spichlerze Island. Rooms are neat and clean; staff are helpful.

Hotel Hanza HOTEL €€€

(📞58 305 3427; www.hotelhanza.pl; ul Tokarska 6; s/d/ste from 450/530zł; 🅿📶) The Hanza is attractively perched along the waterfront near the Gdańsk Crane and offers elegant, tasteful rooms in a modern building. Some rooms have enviable views over the river.

Eating

For self-catering, visit **Kos Delikatesy** (ul Piwna 9/10; ⏰24hr) in the Main Town.

Restauracja Pod Łososiem POLISH €€€

(ul Szeroka 52/54; mains 60-85zł; ⏰noon-10pm) This is one of Gdańsk's oldest and most highly regarded restaurants. It is particularly famous for its salmon dishes and the gold-flecked liqueur *goldwasser*, which was invented here. Red-leather seats, brass chandeliers and a gathering of gas lamps fill out the posh interior.

Velevetka   KASHUBIAN €€€
(ul Długa 45; mains 20-69zł) This delightful eatery manages to evoke a rural theme without a single ancient agricultural knick-knack or trussed waitress in sight. Admire the heavy wooden furniture and soothing scenes of the Kashubian countryside, while munching through finely crafted regional dishes.

U Dzika   POLISH €€
(ul Piwna 59/61; mains 15-77zł; ⊘11am-10pm) Pleasant eatery with a nice outdoor terrace, specialising in *pierogi* (dumplings). If you're feeling adventurous, try the Fantasy Dumplings, comprising cottage cheese, cinnamon, raisins and peach.

Bar Mleczny Neptun   CAFETERIA €
(ul Długa 33/34; mains 2-16zł; ⊘7am-8pm Mon-Fri, 10am-6pm Sat & Sun; 🛜) This joint is a cut above your run-of-the-mill milk bar, with potted plants, lace curtains, decorative tiling and old lamps for decor.

Green Way   VEGETARIAN €
(ul Garncarska 4/6; mains 4-12zł; ⊘11am-8pm Mon-Fri, noon-7pm Sat & Sun; 🖉) Popular with local vegetarians, this eatery serves everything from soy cutlets to Mexican goulash in an unfussy green-and-orange space. There's another, more central, branch (ul Długa 11; mains 4-12zł; ⊘10am-8pm; 🖉) on the Royal Way.

Przystań Gdańska   POLISH €€
(ul Wartka 5; mains 17-43zł) An atmospheric place to enjoy outdoor dining, with a view along the river to the Gdańsk Crane. Serves Polish classics and a range of fish dishes.

🍷 Drinking

TOP CHOICE **Cafe Lamus**   BAR
(ul Lawendowa 8; ⊘noon-late; 🛜) Achingly cool retro-themed bar serving a range of beers from small Polish breweries, set up by a couple of locals after they returned from working in pubs in the UK. Enter from ul Straganiarska.

Cafe Ferber   CAFE-BAR
(ul Długa 77/78; ⊘9am-late; 🛜) It's startling to step from Gdańsk's historic main street into this modern cafe-bar, dominated by bright red panels, a suspended ceiling and boxy lighting. Partake of breakfast, well-made coffee, international wines and creative cocktails.

Kamienica   CAFE-BAR
(ul Mariacka 37/39) The best of the bunch on ul Mariacka is this excellent two-level cafe with a calm, sophisticated atmosphere and a charming patio. It's as popular for daytime coffee and cakes as it is for a sociable evening beverage.

☆ Entertainment

Miasto Aniołów   CLUB
(ul Chmielna 26) The City of Angels covers all the bases – late-night revellers can hit the spacious dance floor, crash in the chill-out area, or hang around the atmospheric deck overlooking the Motława River. Nightly DJs play disco and other dance-oriented sounds.

Parlament   CLUB
(www.parlament.com.pl; ul Św Ducha 2; ⊘8pm-late Thu-Sat) Hardly a talking shop, this long-lived club plays host to big dance events. There's retro music on Thursday, electronica on Friday and disco on Saturday.

State Baltic Opera Theatre   OPERA
(✆58 763 4906; www.operabaltycka.pl; Al Zwycięstwa 15) This venue is in the suburb of Wrzeszcz, not far from the train station at Gdańsk Politechnika.

ℹ Information

Jazz 'n' Java (ul Tkacka 17/18; per hr 6zł; ⊘10am-10pm) Internet access.
Main Post Office (ul Długa 22; ⊘24hr)
PTTK Office (✆58 301 9151; www.pttk-gdansk.pl; ul Długa 45; ⊘10am-6pm) Provides tourist information, along with internet access for 10zł per hour.
Tourist Office (✆58 305 7080; www.gdansk4u.pl; Długi Targ 28/29; ⊘9am-7pm Jun-Aug, to 5pm Sep-May)

ℹ Getting There & Away
Air
From **Lech Wałęsa Airport** (www.airport.gdansk.pl; ul Słowackiego 200), national carrier LOT has at least three daily flights to Warsaw and at least three daily to Frankfurt. Tickets can be bought at the **LOT office** (✆58 301 28 2223; ul Wały Jagiellońskie 2/4). Eurolot also flies twice daily to Wrocław and Kraków.

Gdańsk is also connected to a plethora of other European cities, including London via Ryanair and Wizz Air (three daily), and Dublin via Ryanair (four weekly).

The airport is accessible by bus 110 from the Gdańsk Wrzeszcz local commuter train station, or bus 210 or night bus N3 from outside the Gdańsk Główny train station. A private service, **Airportbus** (✆58 554 9393; www.airportbus.com.pl; ul Heweliusza 13; ticket 14.90zł), also runs from

TRAINS FROM GDAŃSK

Domestic Train

DESTINATION	PRICE (ZŁ)	DURATION	FREQUENCY
Białystok	63	7½hr	2 daily
Elbląg	16	1½hr	11 daily
Giżycko	56	5hr	2 daily
Kętrzyn	52	4¾hr	2 daily
Kraków	69	8-12hr	10 daily
Lublin	69	9hr	2 daily
Malbork	17	45min	at least hourly
Ostróda	24	3hr	2 daily
Olsztyn	40	3hr	6 daily
Poznań	58	5hr	8 daily
Szczecin	61	5½hr	3 daily
Toruń	46	3¾hr	9 daily
Warsaw	63	6¼hr	12 daily

International Train

DESTINATION	DURATION (HR)	FREQUENCY
Berlin (Germany)	6½	1 daily
Kaliningrad (Russia)	6	1 daily

the Mercure Hevelius hotel in the Old Town to the airport. Taxis cost 45zł to 55zł one way.

Boat

Polferries (☑22 830 0930; www.polferries.pl) offers daily services between Gdańsk and Nynäshamn (19 hours) in Sweden in summer (less frequently in the low season). The company uses the **Ferry Terminal** (ul Przemysłowa 1) in Nowy Port, about 5km north of the Main Town. The PTTK office in Gdańsk can provide information and sell tickets.

In the warmer months, **Żegluga Gdańska excursion boats** (www.zegluga.pl; ⊙10am-4pm Apr-Nov) leave regularly from the dock near the Green Gate in Gdańsk for Westerplatte (adult/concession return 45/22zł). From a quay further north along the dockside, **Ustka-Tour** (www.perlalew.pl; ⊙9am-7pm Apr-Oct) operates hourly cruises to Westerplatte (adult/concession return 40/22zł) aboard the *Czarna Perła* and *Galeon Lew*, replica 17th-century galleons. Just north of the galleon quay is the **Water Tram** (www.ztm.gda.pl; ⊙8.30am-7pm Jun-Aug), a ferry which heads to Hel (adult/concession 24/12zł, three daily) and Westerplatte (adult/concession 10/5zł, three daily). Bicycles cost an extra 5zł to transport.

Bus

The **bus station** (ul 3 Maja 12) is behind the main train station and connected to ul Podwale Grodzkie by an underground passageway. Useful PKS bus serves head to Frombork (18zł, 2¼ hours, three daily) and Warsaw (55zł, 5¾ hours, hourly). **Polski Bus** (www.polskibus.com) departs hourly to Ostróda (two hours) and Warsaw (5¾ hours); check fares and book online.

Train

The city's main train station, **Gdańsk Główny** (ul Podwale Grodzkie 1), is conveniently located on the western outskirts of the Old Town. Most long-distance trains actually start or finish at Gdynia, so make sure you get on/off quickly here.

❶ Getting Around

The local commuter train – the SKM – runs every 15 minutes from 6am to 7.30pm, and less frequently thereafter, between Gdańsk Główny and Gdynia Główna train stations, via Sopot and Gdańsk Oliwa train stations. Buy tickets at any station and validate them in the yellow boxes at the platform entrance, or purchase them prevalidated from vending machines on the platform.

Around Gdańsk

Gdańsk is part of the so-called Tri-City Area including Gdynia and Sopot, which are easy day trips from Gdańsk.

SOPOT
POP 38,700

Since the 19th century, Sopot, 12km north of Gdańsk, has been one of the Baltic coast's most fashionable seaside resorts. It has an easygoing atmosphere, good nightlife and long stretches of sandy beach.

From the train station, head left to busy ul Bohaterów Monte Cassino, one of Poland's most attractive pedestrian streets. Here you can find plenty of restaurants and bars, and the surreal Crooked House (Krzywy Domek; ul Bohaterów Monte Cassino 53) shopping centre. At the eastern end of the street off Plac Zdrojowy is Poland's longest pier (515m), the famous Molo (www.molo.sopot.pl; adult/concession 7/3.50zł; ⊘8am-11pm Jun-Aug, 8am-8pm May & Sep). Various attractions and cultural events can be found near and along the structure.

To the south, the Sopot Museum (www.muzeumsopotu.pl; ul Poniatowskiego 8; adult/concession 5/3zł, Thu free; ⊘10am-5pm Tue-Fri, noon-6pm Sat & Sun) has displays recalling the town's 19th-century incarnation as the German resort of Zoppot.

For tourist information, including accommodation, check with the tourist office (☑58 550 3783; www.sts.sopot.pl; Plac Zdrojowy 2; ⊘10am-8pm Jun-Sep, 10am-6pm Oct-May) in a modern building near the pier, which also houses a mineral water pump room and a lookout with a view of the Baltic.

From the Sopot train station, local SKM commuter trains run every 15 minutes to Gdańsk Główny (3.60zł, 15 minutes) and Gdynia Główna (3.60zł, 10 minutes) train stations. The Water Tram departs the pier in Sopot for Hel (adult/concession 22/11zł, three daily) from June to August.

GDYNIA
POP 249,000

As a young city with a busy port atmosphere, Gdynia, 9km north of Sopot, is less atmospheric than Gdańsk or Sopot. It was greatly expanded as a seaport after this coastal area (but not Gdańsk) became part of Poland following WWI.

From the southern end of Gdynia Główna train station, follow ul 10 Lutego east for about 1.5km to the Southern Pier. Here you'll find sights, shops and restaurants.

Moored on the pier's northern side are two interesting museum ships. First up is the curiously sky-blue destroyer Błyskawica (adult/concession 8/4zł; ⊘10am-5pm Tue-Sun Jun-Oct), which escaped capture in 1939 and went on to serve successfully with Allied naval forces throughout WWII. Beyond it is the beautiful three-masted frigate Dar Pomorza (www.cmm.pl; adult/concession 8/4zł; ⊘10am-4pm Feb-Nov), built in Hamburg in 1909 as a training ship for German sailors. There's information in English on the dockside.

For more information about Gdynia, including accommodation options, visit the tourist office (☑58 622 3766; www.gdyniaturystyczna.pl; ul 10 Lutego 24; ⊘9am-6pm Mon-Fri, 9am-4pm Sat & Sun) near the train station.

Local commuter trains link Gdynia Główna train station with Sopot (3.60zł, 10 minutes) and Gdańsk (5.40zł, 25 minutes, every 15 minutes). Trains also run to Hel (16zł, 1¾ hours, nine daily) and Lębork (17zł, one hour, half-hourly), where you can change for Łeba.

Stena Line (☑58 660 9200; www.stenaline.pl) uses the Terminal Promowy (ul Kwiatkowskiego 60), about 5km northwest of Gdynia. It offers twice-daily services between Gdynia and Karlskrona (between 10½ and 12½ hours) in Sweden.

MALBORK
POP 39,400

The magnificent Malbork Castle (☑55 647 0978; www.zamek.malbork.pl; ul Starościńska 1; adult/concession 40/30zł; ⊘9am-7pm 15 Apr-15 Sep, 10am-3pm 16 Sep-14 Apr) is the centrepiece of this town, 58km southeast of Gdańsk. It's the largest Gothic castle in Europe and was once known as Marienburg, headquarters of the Teutonic Knights. It was constructed by the order in 1276 and became the seat of their Grand Master in 1309. Damage sustained in WWII was repaired after the conflict's end and the castle was placed on the Unesco World Heritage List in 1997.

The entry fee includes a compulsory Polish-language tour, along with a free audio guide in English and other languages. Occasional English-language tours operate at a higher entry fee (adult/concession 48/38zł); otherwise, an English-speaking tour guide can be commissioned for 210zł. For one hour after the castle interiors have closed for the day, you can purchase a ticket to inspect the grounds for a bargain basement fee of adult/concession 7/4zł.

Malbork is an easy day trip from Gdańsk, but if you want to stay over, check with the

tourist office (☎55 647 4747; www.visitmalbork. pl; ul Kościuszki 54; ⏰8am-4pm Mon-Fri) for accommodation details. Places to eat can be found both at the castle and along the town's main street, ul Kościuszki.

The castle is 1km west of the train and bus stations. Leave the train station, turn right, cut across the highway, head down ul Kościuszki and follow the signs. Malbork is an easy day trip by train from Gdańsk (17zł, 45 minutes, at least hourly). Malbork is also connected to Olsztyn (36zł, two hours, six daily) and Toruń (22zł, 3¼ hours, seven daily including four operated by private company Arriva).

Toruń

POP 205,000

The first thing to strike you about Toruń, south of Gdańsk, is its collection of massive red-brick churches, looking more like fortresses than places of worship. The city is defined by its striking Gothic architecture, which gives its Old Town a distinctive appearance. Toruń is a pleasant place to spend a few days, offering a nice balance between a relaxing slow pace and engaging sights and entertainments.

Toruń is also famous as the birthplace of Nicolaus Copernicus, a figure you cannot escape as you walk the streets of his home town – you can even buy gingerbread men in his likeness. The renowned astronomer spent his youth here and the local university is named after him.

Historically, Toruń is intertwined with the Teutonic Knights, who established an outpost here in 1233. Following the Thirteen Years' War (1454–66), the Teutonic Order and Poland signed a peace treaty here, which returned to Poland a large area of land stretching from Toruń to Gdańsk.

Toruń was fortunate to escape major damage in WWII and as a result is the best-preserved Gothic town in Poland. The Old Town was added to Unesco's World Heritage List in 1997.

Toruń

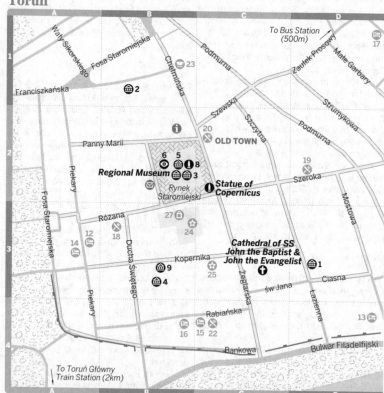

◉ Sights

Rynek Staromiejski
HISTORIC AREA

(Old Town Market Sq) The starting point for any exploration of Toruń is the Rynek Staromiejski. It's the focal point of the Old Town, lined by elegant facades and dominated by the massive 14th-century Old Town Hall (Ratusz Staromiejski).

In front of the Town Hall is an elegant statue of Copernicus. Look for other interesting items of statuary around the square, including a dog and umbrella from a famous Polish comic strip, a donkey that once served as a punishment device and a fabled violinist who saved Toruń from a plague of frogs.

Regional Museum
MUSEUM

(www.muzeum.torun.pl; Rynek Staromiejski 1; adult/concession 10/6zł; ⊙10am-6pm Tue-Sun May-Sep, to 4pm Tue-Sun Oct-Apr) Within the Town Hall, this institution features a fine collection of 19th- and 20th-century Polish art. Other displays recall the town's guilds and there's an exhibition of medieval stained glass and religious paintings. Climb the 40m-high tower (adult/concession 10/6zł; ⊙10am-4pm Tue-Sun Apr, to 8pm Tue-Sun May-Sep) for great views.

House of Copernicus
MUSEUM

(www.muzeum.torun.pl; ul Kopernika 15/17; adult/concession 10/7zł; ⊙10am-6pm Tue-Sun May-Sep, 10am-4pm Tue-Sun Oct-Apr) In 1473, Copernicus was allegedly born in the brick Gothic house that now contains this museum, presenting replicas of the great astronomer's instruments (though there's now some doubt he was really born here).

More engaging, if overpriced, is the museum's short audiovisual presentation (adult/concession 12/7zł) regarding Copernicus' life in Toruń, and the extravagantly titled World of Toruń's Gingerbread (adult/concession 10/6zł). In the latter, visitors are guided around the exhibition by a costumed medieval townswoman and given the chance to bake their own *pierniki* (gingerbread).

A combined ticket to all three attractions costs 20/15zł.

Cathedral of SS John the Baptist & John the Evangelist
CHURCH

(ul Żeglarska; adult/concession 3/2zł; ⊙9am-5.30pm Mon-Sat, 2-5.30pm Sun Apr-Oct) One block south of Rynek Staromiejski is this place of worship with its massive tower (adult/concession 6/4zł) and bell, founded in 1233 and completed more than 200 years later. A 3D movie about its history costs 2zł to view. No sightseeing is allowed during services.

Teutonic Knights' Castle Ruins
RUINS

(ul Przedzamcze; adult/concession 8/5zł, Mon free; ⊙10am-6pm) East of the remnants of the Old Town walls are the ruins of the Teutonic Castle, destroyed in 1454 by angry townsfolk protesting against the knights' oppressive regime. An occasional sound and light show (30zł) is staged here in summer.

Far Eastern Art Museum
MUSEUM

(www.muzeum.torun.pl; Rynek Staromiejski 35; adult/concession 7/4zł, Wed free; ⊙10am-6pm Tue-Sun May-Sep, to 4pm Tue-Sun Oct-Apr) The richly decorated, 15th-century House Under the Star, with its baroque facade and spiral wooden staircase, contains this collection of art from Asia.

POLAND TORUŃ

Explorers' Museum
MUSEUM

(www.muzeum.torun.pl; ul Franciszkańska 11) A street back from Rynek Staromiejski is this small but interesting display of artefacts from the collection of inveterate wanderer Antonio Halik and other travellers. At time of research it was closed pending renovation, but should have reopened by the time you read this – check with the tourist office for hours and entry fees.

Eskens' House
MUSEUM

(www.muzeum.torun.pl; ul Łazienna 16) This Gothic former residence houses city history displays, a collection of medieval weaponry and archaeological exhibits from the Iron and Bronze Ages, including a human skeleton buried in the distant past. At time of research it was closed for renovation, but should have now reopened.

Sleeping

Toruń is blessed with a generous number of hotels and hostels within converted historic buildings in its Old Town; but as they're fairly small, it pays to book ahead.

Hotel Karczma Spichrz
TOP CHOICE
HOTEL €€

(56 657 1140; www.spichrz.pl; ul Mostowa 1; s/d 250/310zł, apt from 290zł;) Situated within a historic granary on the waterfront, this

hotel's rooms are well supplied with personality, featuring massive exposed beams above elegant timber furniture. There's an excellent restaurant and bar within the establishment.

Green Hostel
HOSTEL €

(56 561 4000; www.greenhostel.eu; ul Małe Garbary 10; r from 100zł;) It may be labelled as a hostel, but there are no dorms. Instead, this budget accommodation boasts inexpensive rooms, a kitchen and a pleasant lounge. Note that most rooms share a bathroom and there's no breakfast.

Hotel Pod Czarną Różą
HOTEL €€

(56 621 9637; www.hotelczarnaroza.pl; ul Rabiańska 11; s/d 170/210zł;) 'Under the Black Rose' is spread between a historic inn and a newer wing facing the river, though its interiors present a uniformly clean, up-to-date look. Some doubles come with small but functional kitchens.

Orange Hostel
HOSTEL €

(56 652 0033; www.hostelorange.pl; ul Prosta 19; dm/s/d 30/50/90zł;) Orange is aimed at the international backpacker market. It's in a handy location, its decor is bright and cheerful, and its kitchen is an impressive place to practise the gentle art of self-catering.

Toruń

TRAINS FROM TORUŃ

DESTINATION	PRICE (ZŁ)	DURATION (HR)	FREQUENCY
Gdańsk & Gdynia	46	3¾	9 daily
Kraków	69	8½	3 daily
Łódź	34	3	10 daily
Malbork	22	3¼	7 daily
Olsztyn	34	2¼	8 daily
Poznań	24	2½	10 daily
Warsaw	48	2¾	11 daily
Wrocław	56	5	5 daily

Hotel Petite Fleur   HOTEL €€
(☎56 621 5100; www.petitefleur.pl; ul Piekary 25; s/d 210/270zł; 🖥) The Petite Fleur offers fresh, airy rooms in a renovated old town house, some with exposed original brickwork and rafters. It also has a French cellar restaurant.

Hotel Gotyk   HOTEL €€
(☎56 658 4000; www.hotel-gotyk.com.pl; ul Piekary 20; s/d 170/230zł; 🖥) Housed in a modernised 14th-century building just off Rynek Staromiejski. Rooms are very neat, with ornate furniture and high ceilings, and all come with sparkling bathrooms.

Hotel Retman   HOTEL €€
(☎56 657 4460; www.hotelretman.pl; ul Rabiańska 15; s/d 180/240zł; 🖥) Attractively decorated accommodation offering spacious, atmospheric rooms with red carpet and solid timber furniture. Downstairs is a good pub and restaurant.

Camping Nr 33 Tramp   CAMPING GROUND €
(☎56 654 7187; www.mosir.torun.pl; ul Kujawska 14; camping per person/tent 9/7zł, s/d from 50/76zł; ☾May-Sep) There's a choice of cabins or hotel-style rooms at this camping ground on the edge of the train line, along with an on-site snack bar. It's a five-minute walk west of the main train station.

Hotel 1231   HOTEL €€€
(☎56 619 0910; www.hotel1231.pl; ul Przedzamcze 6; s/d 340/400zł; ❄🖥) Elegant four-star accommodation in the shadow of the Old Town walls, with pleasantly appointed rooms and a cellar restaurant and bar.

✗ Eating & Drinking

Toruń is famous for its *pierniki*, which come in a variety of shapes and can be bought at **Sklep Kopernik** (Rynek Staromiejski 6). There's a handy **Biedronka supermarket** (ul Szeroka 22) in the Old Town.

Masala   INDIAN, POLISH €€
(Rynek Nowomiejski 8; mains 19-45zł; ☾10am-10pm; 🖉) Formerly known as Gospoda Pod Modrym Fartuchem, this 15th-century eatery on Rynek Nowomiejski (New Town Sq) has been visited by Polish kings and Napoleon. Polish dishes are joined by an array of Indian food, including a good vegetarian selection.

Bar Mleczny Pod Arkadami   CAFETERIA €
(ul Różana 1; mains 4-12zł; ☾9am-7pm Mon-Fri, 9am-4pm Sat & Sun) This classic milk bar is just off Rynek Staromiejski, with a range of low-cost dishes. It also has a takeaway window serving a range of tasty *zapiekanki* (toasted rolls with cheese, mushrooms and tomato sauce) and sweet waffles.

Oberża   POLISH €
(ul Rabiańska 9; mains 8-15zł; ☾11am-11pm Mon-Sat, to 9.30pm Sun; 🖥) This large self-service canteen stacks 'em high and sells 'em cheap for a hungry crowd of locals and tourists. Find your very own thatched mini-cottage among plentiful knick-knackery to enjoy *pierogi* (dumplings), soups, salads and other Polish mains.

Kuranty   POLISH, ITALIAN €€
(Rynek Staromiejski 29; mains 12-49zł; ☾11am-2am; 🖥) The menu is firmly based on the three Ps: pizza, pasta and *pierogi* (including a rather tasty baked version). Random photos and extraordinary art nouveau lightshades add to the atmosphere. Be warned: TVs stuck on the sports channel hang off the walls.

Kona Coast Cafe   CAFE
(ul Chełmińska 18; ☾9am-9pm Mon-Sat, 11am-6pm Sun; 🖥) Serves excellent freshly ground coffee,

along with homemade lemonade, chai and various cold drinks. There's also a light meal menu.

☆ Entertainment

Lizard King CLUB
(ul Kopernika 3; ☺7pm-late) Live-music venue with gigs ranging from local tribute bands to big rock acts from around Eastern and Central Europe.

Teatr Baj Pomorski PUPPETRY
(☑56 652 2029; www.bajpomorski.art.pl; ul Pienikarska 9) Puppet theatre shaped like a huge wooden cabinet, staging a variety of entertaining shows.

Dwór Artusa CLASSICAL MUSIC
(☑56 655 4929; Rynek Staromiejski 6) This place often presents classical music.

❶ Information

Ksero Uniwerek (ul Franciszkańska 5; per hr 4zł; ☺8am-7pm Mon-Fri, 9am-2pm Sat) Internet access.

Main Post Office (Rynek Staromiejski; ☺24hr)

Tourist Office (☑56 621 0930; www.torun.pl; Rynek Staromiejski 25; ☺9am-4pm Mon & Sat, to 6pm Tue-Fri, 11am-3pm Sun) Offers useful advice and hires out handheld MP3 players with English-language audio tours of the city (10zł per four hours).

❶ Getting There & Away

BUS The **bus station** (ul Dąbrowskiego) is a 10-minute walk north of the Old Town. From here, **Polski Bus** (www.polskibus.com) connects to Warsaw (3¾ hours, four daily) and Szczecin (6¼ hours, one daily); check fares and buy tickets online. However, most places can be reached more efficiently by train.

TRAIN The Toruń Główny train station is on the opposite side of the Vistula River and linked to the Old Town by bus 22 or 27 (get off at the first stop over the bridge). Some trains stop at the more convenient **Toruń Miasto train station** (Plac 18 Stycznia), about 500m east of the New Town.

Szczecin

POP 410,000 / TRANSPORT HUB

Szczecin (*shcheh*-cheen) is the major city and port of northwestern Poland. Though it's not the most beautiful of cities, it's a logical place to break a journey to or from Germany and has an international airport.

Decent midrange hotels handy for the train and bus stations include **Hotel Campanile** (☑91 481 7700; www.campanile.com; ul Wyszyńskiego 30; r from 219zł; ❋☏) and **Hotel Victoria** (☑91 434 3855; Plac Batorego 2; s/d 160/220zł; ☏). A budget option is **Hotelik Elka-Sen** (☑91 433 5604; www.elkasen.szczecin.pl; Al 3 Maja 1a; s/d 120/150zł; ☏), in the basement of an academic building.

WORTH A TRIP

BALTIC BEACHES

Between Gdańsk and the western city of Szczecin, there are numerous seaside towns with unpolluted waters and fine sandy beaches. Here are a few places for a sunbathing detour on your journey west along the Baltic coast towards the German border:

Hel Despite its name, this is an attractive place that's popular with windsurfers; it also houses a sanctuary for Baltic grey seals.

Łeba Pleasant holiday town with wide sandy beaches, the gateway to Słowiński National Park and its ever-shifting sand dunes.

Ustka Once the summer hang-out of German Chancellor Otto von Bismarck, this fishing port is full of atmosphere.

Darłowo A former medieval trading port with an impressive castle and two beaches linked by a pedestrian bridge over a river.

Kołobrzeg This coastal city offers historic attractions, spa treatments and Baltic cruises.

Międzyzdroje A popular seaside resort and the gateway to Wolin National Park.

Świnoujście On a Baltic island shared with Germany, this busy port town boasts a long sandy shore and pleasant parks.

For more details, check out Lonely Planet's *Poland* country guide, or www.poland.travel.

TRAINS FROM SZCZECIN

DESTINATION	PRICE (ZŁ)	DURATION (HR)	FREQUENCY
Berlin (Germany)	Varies	2	1 daily
Gdynia & Gdańsk	61	5½	3 daily
Poznań	46	2¾	at least hourly
Świnoujście	21	2	hourly
Warsaw	63	6½	7 daily
Wrocław	61	5	6 daily

You'll find plenty of restaurants and bars in the small but attractive Old Town northeast of the train station. There's a helpful tourist office (☑91 434 0440; www.szczecin. eu; Al Niepodległości 1; ☉9am-5pm Mon-Fri, 10am-2pm Sat) in the city's nearby commercial heart, and a similarly useful information centre (☑91 489 1630; www.zamek.szczecin.pl/ cikit; ul Korsarzy 34; ☉10am-6pm) in the imposing Castle of the Pomeranian Dukes next to the Old Town.

The airport (www.airport.com.pl) is in Goleniów, 45km northeast of the city. A shuttle bus (20zł) operated by Interglobus (☑91 485 0422; www.interglobus.pl) picks up from stops outside the LOT office and the train station before every flight, and meets all arrivals. Alternatively, a taxi should cost around 150zł to 200zł.

National carrier LOT flies between Szczecin and Warsaw three times a day. Book at the LOT office (☑91 488 3558; ul Wyzwolenia 17; ☉9am-5pm Mon-Fri), about 200m past the northern end of Al Niepodległości. There's also one or two flights daily to Kraków via Eurolot. International flights on Ryanair include London (four weekly) and Dublin (three weekly).

The bus station (Plac Grodnicki) and the nearby Szczecin Główny train station (ul Kolumba) are 600m southeast of the tourist office. Bus departures are of limited interest; however, from stand 3 in front of the train station Polski Bus heads once daily to Toruń (6¼ hours), continuing to Warsaw (10 hours).

Another way to reach Świnoujście is via the Bosman Express ferry (☑91 488 5564; http://www.wodolot.info.pl; ul Jana z Kolna 7; adult/ child 60/30zł; ☉Apr-Oct), which travels twice daily from a quay northeast of the Old Town across the waters of the Szczeciński Lagoon (1¼ hours).

WARMIA & MASURIA

The most impressive feature of Warmia and Masuria is its beautiful postglacial landscape dominated by thousands of lakes, linked to rivers and canals, which host aquatic activities, including yachting and canoeing. This picturesque lake district has little industry and remains unpolluted and attractive, especially in summer. Like much of northern Poland, the region has changed hands between Germanic and Polish rulers over the centuries.

Elbląg-Ostróda Canal

The longest navigable canal still used in Poland stretches 82km between Elbląg and Ostróda. Constructed between 1848 and 1876, this waterway linked several lakes in order to transport timber from inland forests to the Baltic. To overcome the 99.5m difference in water levels, the canal utilises an unusual system of five water-powered slipways so that boats are sometimes carried across dry land on rail-mounted trolleys.

Nowadays excursion boats run along the route, operated by Żegluga Ostródzka-Elbląska (☑Elbląg 55 232 4307, Ostróda 89 646 3871; www.zegluga.com.pl). Various tours of different lengths are available, but the most interesting is the 10-hour World of the Canal cruise (adult/concession 149/139zł; ☉May-Sep), which twice a week departs Elbląg at 8.30am, and in the other direction from Ostróda at 9am. The fare includes a bus transfer between boats in the middle of the trip, and a bus ride back to your starting point.

Along the way the canal boats pass beautiful green countryside replete with birdlife, navigating lakes and locks and the impressive 'inclined plane' slipways which raise or lower the vessels to the next section of canal.

POLAND ELBLĄG-OSTRÓDA CANAL

Boats each have a small cafe-bar that sells drinks and snacks.

Pensjonat Boss (✆55 239 3729; www.pensjonatboss.pl; ul Św Ducha 30; s/d 150/220zł) is a small hotel in Elbląg's Old Town, offering comfortable rooms above its own bar. **Camping Nr 61** (✆55 641 8666; www.camping61.com.pl; ul Panieńska 6; per person/tent 14/6zł, cabins 50-120zł; ☻May-Sep; 🛜), right at Elbląg's boat dock, is a pleasant budget option. In Ostróda, try **Hotel Promenada** (✆89 642 8100; www.hotelpromenada.pl; ul Mickiewicza 3; s/d from 160/200zł), 500m east of the bus and train stations.

Elbląg is accessible by frequent trains from Gdańsk (16zł, 1½ hours, 11 daily), Malbork (8zł, 30 minutes, hourly) and Olsztyn (19zł, 1¾ hours, 11 daily), and by bus from Frombork (7zł, 45 minutes, at least hourly).

Ostróda is reached by train from Olsztyn (10zł, 40 minutes, hourly), Toruń (28zł, two hours, eight daily) and Gdańsk (24zł, three hours, twice daily), and by hourly Polski Bus services directly from Warsaw (3¾ hours) and Gdańsk (two hours).

Buses also run regularly between Elbląg and Ostróda (21zł, 1½ hours, hourly).

Frombork

POP 2500

It may look like the most uneventful town in history, but Frombork was once home to the famous astronomer Nicolaus Copernicus. It's where he wrote his ground-breaking *On the Revolutions of the Celestial Spheres*, which established the theory that the earth travelled around the sun. Beyond the memory of its famous resident, it's a charming, sleepy settlement that was founded on the shore of the Vistula Lagoon in the 13th century. It was later the site of a fortified ecclesiastical township, erected on Cathedral Hill.

The hill is now occupied by the extensive **Nicolaus Copernicus Museum** (www.frombork.art.pl; ul Katedralna 8; ☻9am-5.30pm) with several sections requiring separate tickets. The 14th-century **cathedral** (adult/concession 6/3zł; ☻9.30am-4.30pm) contains the tomb of Copernicus himself. The main exhibition area is within the **Bishops' Palace** (adult/concession 6/3zł; ☻9am-4.30pm Tue-Sun), while the **belfry** (adult/concession 6/3zł; ☻9.30am-5pm) is home to an example of Foucault's pendulum. A short distance from the main museum, the **Hospital of the Holy Ghost** (adult/concession 6/3zł; ☻9.30am-5pm Tue-Sat) exhibits historical medical instruments and manuscripts.

Hotel Kopernik (✆55 243 7285; www.hotelkopernik.com.pl; ul Kościelna 2; s/d 150/220zł) is a comfortable modern hotel a short walk to the east of the museum bus stop. A budget option is **Camping Frombork** (✆506 803 151; www.campingfrombork.pl; ul Braniewska 14; per person/tent 10/5zł, d 50-140zł; ☻May-Sep), at the eastern end of town on the Braniewo road. It has basic cabins and a snack bar on the grounds.

The bus station is on the riverfront about 300m northwest of the museum. Frombork can be directly reached by bus from Elbląg (7zł, 45 minutes, at least hourly) and Gdańsk (18zł, 2¼ hours, three daily). The best place to get on and off is the bus stop directly below the museum on ul Kopernika.

Olsztyn

POP 175,000

Olsztyn (*ol-shtin*) is a pleasant, relaxed city whose rebuilt Old Town is home to cobblestone streets, art galleries, cafes, bars and restaurants. As a busy transport hub, it's also the logical base from which to explore the region, including the Great Masurian Lakes district.

It's also another city on the Copernicus trail, as the great astronomer once served as administrator of Warmia, commanding Olsztyn Castle from 1516 to 1520. From 1466 to 1772 the town belonged to the kingdom of Poland. With the first partition of the nation, Olsztyn became Prussian then German Allenstein, until it returned to Polish hands in 1945.

⊙ Sights

Old Town HISTORIC DISTRICT
Olsztyn's attractive historic centre was rebuilt after WWII destruction and centres on the **Rynek** (Market Sq). One of the Old Town's most striking features is the **High Gate** (ul Staromiejska, Old Town), a surviving fragment of the 14th-century city walls.

Museum of Warmia & Masuria MUSEUM
(ul Zamkowa 2; adult/concession 9/7zł; ☻10am-4pm Tue-Sun) West of the main square, the 14th-century **Castle of the Chapter of Warmia** contains this historical museum. Its exhibits feature Copernicus, who made some astronomical observations here in the early 16th century, along with collections of coins, art and armour.

Cathedral of St James the Elder CHURCH
(ul Długosza) This red-brick Gothic cathedral in the eastern Old Town dates from the

14th century and its 60m tower was added in 1596. The interior is an appealing blend of old and new decoration, including the bronze main doors that depict Pope John Paul II's visit in 1991.

🛏 Sleeping

TOP CHOICE **Hotel Dyplomat** HOTEL €€
(☎89 512 4141; www.hoteldyplomat.com; ul Dąbrowszczaków 28; s/d from 199/390zł; ❉❄🖰) Impressive new four-star hotel located midway between the train station and the Old Town. Its rooms are decked out with quality fittings and there's an excellent restaurant on the premises. Check the website for discounts.

Polsko-Niemieckie Centrum Młodzieży HOTEL €€
(☎89 534 0780; www.pncm.olsztyn.pl; ul Okopowa 25; s/d from 175/240zł; 🖰) This place devoted to Polish-German friendship is situated next to the castle. The rooms (some with views of the castle) are plain, but have gleaming bathrooms. There's a good sunlit restaurant off the foyer.

Hotel Wysoka Brama HOTEL €
(☎89 527 3675; www.hotelwysokabrama.olsztyn.pl; ul Staromiejska 1; s/d from 100/120zł; 🖰) Offers cheap but basic rooms in a very central location next to the Old Town's High Gate.

🍴 Eating & Drinking

TOP CHOICE **Chilli** INTERNATIONAL €€
(ul Kołłątaja 1; mains 18-54zł; ◷9am-late; 🖰) By day, this cool cafe-bar serves an international menu amid monochrome images of 20th-century America, to a background of chilled music. After dark it morphs into a smooth club with a lengthy cocktail menu.

Restauracja Staromiejska POLISH €€
(ul Stare Miasto 4/6; mains 20-39zł; ◷10am-10pm) In classy premises on the Rynek, this restaurant serves quality Polish standards at reasonable prices. There's a range of *pierogi* (dumplings) and *naleśniki* (crepes) on the menu.

Bar Dziupla POLISH €
(Rynek 9/10; mains 5-27zł; ◷8.30am-8.30pm) This small place is renowned among locals for its tasty Polish food, such as *pierogi*. It also does a good line in soups.

ℹ Information

The **tourist office** (☎89 535 3565; www.olsztyn.eu; ul Staromiejska 1; ◷8am-6pm Mon-Fri, 10am-3pm Sat & Sun May-Sep, 8am-4pm Mon-Fri Oct-Apr) is next to the High Gate in the Old Town and can help with finding accommodation. For snail mail, go to the **main post office** (ul Pieniężnego 21; ◷8am-8pm Mon-Fri, to 4pm Sat); for cybermail, visit the **library** (ul Stare

TRANSPORT FROM OLSZTYN

Bus

DESTINATIONT	PRICE (ZŁ)	DURATION (HR)	FREQUENCY
Białystok	46	5	6 daily
Lublin	61	8¾	1 daily
Warsaw	30	4	At least hourly

Train

DESTINATION	PRICE (ZŁ)	DURATION	FREQUENCY
Białystok	52	4½hr	2 daily
Elbląg	19	1¾hr	11 daily
Gdańsk & Gdynia	40	3hr	6 daily
Giżycko	21	2hr	5 daily
Kętrzyn	18	1½hr	5 daily
Malbork	36	2hr	6 daily
Ostróda	10	40min	hourly
Toruń	34	2¼hr	8 daily
Warsaw	48	4¾hr	3 daily

Miasto 33; internet free; ⊘9am-7pm Mon-Fri, to 2pm Sat) in the centre of the Rynek.

❶ Getting There & Away

BUS Useful buses travel to destinations around Poland from the **bus station** (ul Partyzantów), attached to the train station building.

TRAIN Trains depart from **Olsztyn Główny train station** (ul Partyzantów). Note that a smaller train station, **Olsztyn Zachodni** (ul Konopnickiej), is located nearer to the Old Town, about 300m west of the castle along ul Nowowiejskiego and ul Konopnickiej; but you're unlikely to find services such as taxis here.

Great Masurian Lakes

This region east of Olsztyn has more than 2000 lakes, which are remnants of long-vanished glaciers, surrounded by green hilly landscape. The largest lake is Lake Śniardwy (110 sq km). About 200km of canals connect these bodies of water, so the area is a prime destination for yachties and canoeists, as well as those who love to hike, fish and mountain bike. There are also regular excursion boats along the lakes from May to September.

Two towns that make good bases for exploring this lake country are Giżycko and Mikołajki. Both the Giżycko tourist office (☑87 428 5265; www.gizycko.turystyka.pl; ul Wyzwolenia 2; ⊘9am-5pm Mon-Fri & 10am-2pm Sat May-Sep, 9am-5pm Mon-Fri Oct-Apr) and the Mikołajki tourist office (☑87 421 6850; www.mikolajki.pl; Plac Wolności 3; ⊘10am-6pm Jun-Aug, 10am-6pm Mon-Sat May & Sep) supply useful maps for sailing and hiking, provide excursion boat schedules and assist with finding accommodation.

Nature aside, there are some interesting fragments of history in this region. The village of Święta Lipka boasts a superb 17th-century baroque church (www.swlipka.org.pl; admission free; ⊘8am-6pm except during Mass), noted for its lavishly decorated organ which features dancing angels. This mechanism is demonstrated several times daily.

A grimmer reminder of the past is the Wolf's Lair (Wilczy Szaniec; www.wolfsschanze.pl; adult/concession 15/10zł; ⊘8am-dusk) and its museum. Located at Gierłoż, 8km east of Kętrzyn, this ruined complex was Hitler's wartime headquarters for his invasion of the Soviet Union. In 1944 a group of high-ranking German officers led by Claus von Stauffenberg tried to assassinate the Nazi leader here via a bomb concealed in a briefcase. Though the explosion killed and wounded several people,

Hitler suffered only minor injuries. Von Stauffenberg and some 5000 people allegedly involved in the plot were subsequently executed. These dramatic events were reprised in the 2008 Tom Cruise movie *Valkyrie*.

On 24 January 1945, as the Red Army approached, the Germans blew up Wolfsschanze (as it was known in German) and most bunkers were at least partly destroyed. However, huge concrete slabs – some 8.5m thick – and twisted metal remain. It's a fascinating if eerie place to visit.

Święta Lipka and the Wolf's Lair are both most easily accessed from Kętrzyn; contact the tourist office (☑89 751 4765; www.it.ketrzyn.pl; Plac Piłsudskiego 10; ⊘9am-6pm Mon-Fri, 10am-3pm Sat & Sun) there for transport details, or consult Lonely Planet's *Poland* country guide.

From Olsztyn, there are trains to Kętrzyn (18zł, 1½ hours, five daily) that continue to Giżycko (21zł, two hours, five daily). You can also catch trains from Gdańsk directly to Kętrzyn (52zł, 4¾ hours, two daily) and Giżycko (56zł, five hours, five daily).

From Olsztyn, buses head to Kętrzyn (19zł, two hours, hourly), Giżycko (21zł, 2¼ hours, nine daily) and Mikołajki (22zł, two hours, two daily). Buses also run between Giżycko and Mikołajki (17zł, 50 minutes, four daily).

UNDERSTAND POLAND

History
Early History

Poland's history started with the Polanians (People of the Plains). During the early Middle Ages, these Western Slavs moved into the flatlands between the Vistula and Odra Rivers. Mieszko I, Duke of the Polanians, adopted Christianity in 966 and embarked on a campaign of conquest. A papal edict in 1025 led to Mieszko's son Bolesław Chrobry (Boleslaus the Brave) being crowned Poland's first king.

Poland's early success proved fragile and encroachment from Germanic peoples led to the relocation of the royal capital from Poznań to Kraków in 1038. More trouble loomed in 1226 when the Prince of Mazovia invited the Teutonic Knights to help convert the pagan tribes of the north. These Germanic crusaders used the opportunity to create their own state along the Baltic coast. The south had its own invaders to contend with and Kraków was attacked by Tatars twice in the mid-13th century.

The kingdom prospered under Kazimierz III 'the Great' (1333–70). During this period, many new towns sprang up, while Kraków blossomed into one of Europe's leading cultural centres.

When the daughter of Kazimierz's nephew, Jadwiga, married the Grand Duke of Lithuania, Jagiełło, in 1386, Poland and Lithuania were united as the largest state in Europe, eventually stretching from the Baltic to the Black Sea.

The Renaissance was introduced to Poland by the enlightened King Zygmunt during the 16th century, as he lavishly patronised the arts and sciences. By asserting that the earth travelled around the sun, Nicolaus Copernicus revolutionised the field of astronomy in 1543.

Invasion & Partition

The 17th and 18th centuries produced disaster and decline for Poland. First it was subject to Swedish and Russian invasions, and eventually it faced partition by surrounding empires. In 1773 Russia, Prussia and Austria seized Polish territory in the First Partition; by the time the Third Partition was completed in 1795, Poland had vanished from the map of Europe.

Although the country remained divided through the entire 19th century, Poles steadfastly maintained their culture. Finally, upon the end of WWI, the old imperial powers dissolved and a sovereign Polish state was restored.

Very soon, however, Poland was immersed in the Polish-Soviet War (1919–21). Under the command of Marshal Józef Piłsudski, Poland had to defend its newly gained eastern borders from long-time enemy Russia, now transformed into the Soviet Union and determined to spread its revolution westward. After two years of impressive fighting by the outnumbered Poles, an armistice was signed, retaining Vilnius and Lviv within Poland.

WWII & Communist Rule

Though Polish institutions and national identity flourished during the interwar period, disaster soon struck again. On 1 September 1939, a Nazi German blitzkrieg rained down from the west; soon after, the Soviets invaded Poland from the east, dividing the country with Germany. This agreement didn't last long, as Hitler soon transformed Poland into a staging ground for the Nazi invasion of the Soviet Union. Six million Polish inhabitants died during WWII (including the country's three million Jews), brutally annihilated in death camps.

At the war's end, Poland's borders were redrawn yet again. The Soviet Union kept the eastern territories and extended the country's western boundary at the expense of Germany. These border changes were accompanied by the forced resettlement of more than a million Poles, Germans and Ukrainians.

Peacetime brought more repression. After WWII, Poland endured four decades of Soviet-dominated communist rule, punctuated by waves of protests, most notably the paralysing strikes of 1980–81, led by the Solidarity trade union. Finally, in the open elections of 1989, the communists fell from power and in 1990 Solidarity leader Lech Wałęsa became Poland's first democratically elected president.

Looking West

The postcommunist transition brought radical changes, which induced new social hardships and political crises. But within a decade Poland had built the foundations for a market economy and reoriented its foreign relations towards the West. In March 1999, Poland was granted full NATO membership and it joined the EU in May 2004.

A period of Eurosceptic policies put forward by the Law and Justice party's government, eccentrically headed by the twin Kaczyński brothers as president (Lech) and prime minister (Jarosław), came to an end after parliamentary elections in 2007. The new centrist government of prime minister Donald Tusk's Civic Platform set a pro-business, pro-EU course.

Shockingly, President Kaczyński and numerous senior military and government officials were killed in an air crash in April 2010, during an attempted landing at Smolensk, Russia. They had been en route to a commemoration of the Soviet massacre of Polish officers in the nearby Katyń forest in 1940. In the resulting election, Tusk's party ally Bronisław Komorowski was elected as president.

The 2011 parliamentary elections were relatively uneventful, confirming Civic Platform's hold on power. However, one remarkable element was the emergence of a strongly pro-secular party, Palikot's Movement, which came from nowhere to gain 10% of the vote. Among its elected representatives were Poland's first transsexual member of parliament and its first openly gay MP. Two Poles of black African descent were also elected as Civic Platform MPs, a

POLAND HISTORY

reflection of the gradually changing nature of Polish society in the postcommunist era.

People

For centuries Poland was a multicultural country, home to Jewish, German and Ukrainian communities. Its Jewish population was particularly large and once numbered more than three million. However, after Nazi German genocide and the forced resettlements that followed WWII, the Jewish population declined to 10,000 and Poland became an ethnically homogeneous country, with some 98% of the population being ethnic Poles.

More than 60% of the citizens live in towns and cities. Warsaw is by far the largest urban settlement, followed by Kraków, Łódź, Wrocław, Poznań and Gdańsk. Upper Silesia (around Katowice) is the most densely inhabited area, while the northeastern border regions remain the least populated.

Between five and 10 million Poles live outside Poland. This émigré community, known as 'Polonia', is located mainly in the USA (particularly Chicago).

Poles are friendly and polite, but not overly formal. The way of life in large urban centres increasingly resembles Western styles and manners. However, Poles' sense of personal space may be a bit cosier than you are accustomed to – you may notice this trait when queuing for tickets or manoeuvring along city streets.

In the countryside, a more conservative culture dominates, evidenced by traditional gender roles and strong family ties. Both here and in urban settings, many Poles are devoutly religious. Roman Catholicism is the dominant Christian denomination, adhered to by more than 80% of Poles. The Orthodox church's followers constitute about 1% of the population, mostly living along a narrow strip on the eastern frontier.

The election of Karol Wojtyła, the archbishop of Kraków, as Pope John Paul II in 1978, and his triumphal visit to his homeland a year later, significantly enhanced the status of the church in Poland. The overthrow of communism was as much a victory for the Church as it was for democracy. The fine line between the Church and the state is often blurred in Poland and the Church is a powerful lobby on social issues.

Still, some Poles have grown wary of the Church's influence in society and politics, resulting in the success of outspokenly pro-secular candidates in recent parliamentary elections. However, Poland remains one of Europe's most religious countries and packed-out churches are not uncommon.

Arts

Literature

Poland has inherited a rich literary tradition dating from the 15th century, though its modern voice was shaped in the 19th century during the long period of foreign occupation. It was a time for nationalist writers such as the poet Adam Mickiewicz (1798–1855) and Henryk Sienkiewicz (1846–1916), who won a Nobel Prize in 1905 for *Quo Vadis?* This nationalist tradition was revived in the communist era when Czesław Miłosz was awarded a Nobel Prize in 1980 for *The Captive Mind.*

BOOKS

» *God's Playground: A History of Poland,* by Norman Davies. Offers an in-depth analysis of Polish history.

» *The Heart of Europe: A Short History of Poland* A condensed version of the above, also by Davies – has greater emphasis on the 20th century.

» *The Polish Way: A Thousand-Year History of the Poles and their Culture* by Adam Zamoyski. A superb cultural overview.

» *Rising '44* by Norman Davies. Vividly brings to life the wartime Warsaw Rising.

» *The Polish Revolution: Solidarity 1980–82* by Timothy Garton Ash. Entertaining and thorough.

» *Jews in Poland* by Iwo Cyprian Pogonowski. Provides a comprehensive record of half a millennium of Jewish life.

» Evocative works about rural life in interwar Poland include Bruno Schultz's *Street of Crocodiles* and Philip Marsden's *The Bronski House.*

At the turn of the 20th century, the avant-garde 'Young Poland' movement in art and literature developed in Kraków. The most notable representatives of this movement were writer Stanisław Wyspiański (1869–1907), also famous for his stained-glass work; playwright Stanisław Ignacy Witkiewicz (1885–1939), commonly known as Witkacy; and Nobel laureate Władysław Reymont (1867–1925). In 1996 Wisława Szymborska (b 1923) also received a Nobel Prize for her poetry.

Music

The most famous Polish musician was undoubtedly Frédéric Chopin (1810–49), whose music displays the melancholy and nostalgia that became hallmarks of the national style. Stanisław Moniuszko (1819–72) injected a Polish flavour into 19th-century Italian opera music by introducing folk songs and dances to the stage. His *Halka* (1858), about a peasant girl abandoned by a young noble, is a staple of the national opera houses.

Popular Polish musicians you might catch live in concert include the controversial Doda (pop singer); Andrzej Smolik (instrumentalist); Łzy (pop-rock band); Sofa (hip-hop/soul band); and Justyna Steczkowska (pop singer). Poland's equivalent of the Rolling Stones is Lady Pank, a rock band formed in 1982 and still going strong.

Visual Arts

Poland's most renowned painter was Jan Matejko (1838–93), whose monumental historical paintings hang in galleries throughout the country. Wojciech Kossak (1857–1942) is another artist who documented Polish history; he is best remembered for the colossal painting Panorama of Racławice (p399), on display in Wrocław.

A long-standing Polish craft is the fashioning of jewellery from amber. Amber is a fossil resin of vegetable origin that comes primarily from the Baltic region and appears in a variety of colours from pale yellow to reddish brown. The best places to buy it are Gdańsk, Kraków and Warsaw.

Polish poster art has received international recognition; the best selection of poster galleries is in Warsaw and Kraków.

Cinema

Poland has produced several world-famous film directors. The most notable is Andrzej Wajda, who received an Honorary Award at the 1999 Academy Awards. *Katyń*, his moving story of the Katyń massacre in WWII, was nominated for Best Foreign Language Film at the 2008 Oscars.

Western audiences are more familiar with the work of Roman Polański, who directed critically acclaimed films such as *Rosemary's Baby* and *Chinatown*. In 2002 Polański released the incredibly moving film *The Pianist*, which was filmed in Poland and set in the Warsaw Ghetto of WWII. The film went on to win three Oscars and the Cannes Palme d'Or.

The late Krzysztof Kieślowski is best known for the *Three Colours* trilogy. The centre of Poland's movie industry, and home to its prestigious National Film School, is Łódź.

Environment

Geography

Poland covers an area of 312,685 sq km – approximately as large as the UK and Ireland put together – and is bordered by seven nations and one sea.

The northern edge of Poland meets the Baltic Sea. This broad, 524km-long coastline is spotted with sand dunes and seaside lakes. Also concentrated in the northeast are many postglacial lakes – more than any country in Europe, except Finland.

The southern border is defined by the mountain ranges of the Sudetes and Carpathians. Poland's highest mountains are the rocky Tatras, a section of the Carpathian Range it shares with Slovakia. The highest peak of the Polish Tatras is Mt Rysy (2499m).

The area in between is a vast plain, sectioned by wide north-flowing rivers. Poland's longest river is the Vistula (Wisła), which winds 1047km from the Tatras to the Baltic. About a quarter of Poland is covered by forest. Some 60% of the forests are pine trees, but the share of deciduous species, such as oak, beech and birch, is increasing.

National Parks & Animals

Poland's fauna includes hare, red deer, wild boar and, less abundantly, elk, brown bear and wildcat. European bison, which once inhabited Europe in large numbers, were brought to the brink of extinction early in the 20th century and a few hundred now live in Białowieża National Park. The Great Masurian Lakes district attracts a vast array of bird life, such as storks and cormorants. The eagle, though rarely seen today, is Poland's national bird and appears on the Polish emblem.

POLAND ENVIRONMENT

Poland has 23 national parks, but they cover less than 1% of the country. No permit is necessary to visit these parks, but most have small admission fees. Camping in the parks is sometimes allowed, but only at specified sites. Poland also has a network of less strictly preserved areas called 'landscape parks', scattered throughout the country.

Food & Drink

Staples & Specialities

Various cultures have influenced Polish cuisine, including Jewish, Ukrainian, Russian, Hungarian and German. Polish food is hearty and filling, abundant in potatoes and dumplings, and rich in meat.

Poland's most famous dishes are *bigos* (sauerkraut with a variety of meats), *pierogi* (ravioli-like dumplings stuffed with cottage cheese, minced meat, or cabbage and wild mushrooms) and *barszcz* (red beetroot soup, better known by the Russian word *borsch*).

Hearty soups such as *żurek* (sour soup with sausage and hard-boiled eggs) are a highlight of Polish cuisine. Main dishes are made with pork, including *golonka* (boiled pig's knuckle served with horseradish) and *schab pieczony* (roast loin of pork seasoned with prunes and herbs). *Gołąbki* (cabbage leaves stuffed with mince and rice) is a tasty alternative. *Placki ziemniaczane* (potato pancakes) and *naleśniki* (crepes) are also popular dishes.

Poles claim the national drink, *wódka* (vodka), was invented in their country. It's usually drunk neat and comes in a number of flavours, including *myśliwska* (flavoured with juniper berries), *wiśniówka* (with cherries) and *jarzębiak* (with rowanberries). The most famous variety is *żubrówka* (bison vodka), flavoured with grass from the Białowieża Forest. Other notable spirits include *krupnik* (honey liqueur), *śliwowica* (plum brandy) and *goldwasser* (sweet liqueur containing flakes of gold leaf).

Poles also appreciate the taste of *zimne piwo* (cold beer); the top brands, found everywhere, include Żywiec, Tyskie, Lech and Okocim, while regional brands are available in every city.

Where to Eat & Drink

The cheapest place to eat Polish food is a *bar mleczny* (milk bar), a survivor from the communist era. These no-frills, self-service cafeterias are popular with budget-conscious locals and backpackers alike, though they have been disappearing at an alarming rate since government subsidies were withdrawn. Up the scale, the number and variety of *restauracja* (restaurants) has ballooned in recent years, especially in the big cities. Pizzerias have also become phenomenally popular with Poles. And though Polish cuisine features plenty of meat, there are vegetarian restaurants to be found in most cities.

Menus usually have several sections: *zupy* (soups), *dania drugie* (main courses) and *dodatki* (accompaniments). The price of the main course may not include a side dish – such as potatoes and salads – which you choose (and pay extra for) from the *dodatki* section. Also note that the price for some dishes (particularly fish and poultry) may be listed per 100g, so the price will depend on the total weight of the fish or meat.

Poles start their day with *śniadanie* (breakfast); the most important and substantial meal of the day, *obiad,* is normally eaten between 2pm and 5pm. The third meal is *kolacja* (supper). Most restaurants, cafes and cafe-bars are open from 11am to 11pm. It's rare for Polish restaurants to serve breakfast, though milk bars and snack bars are open from early morning.

After much delay, in late 2010 smoking was banned in shared areas of bars and restaurants, though these establishments are allowed to set up separate smoking areas. Don't be surprised, however, if the smoking section in some places is actually bigger than the so-called main bar!

SURVIVAL GUIDE

Directory A–Z

Accommodation

In Poland, budget accommodation spans camping grounds, dorms and doubles; at midrange and top-end, our price breakdown is based on a double room. Unless otherwise noted, rooms have private bathrooms and the rate includes breakfast.

€ less than 150zł/€35

€€ 150zł/€35 to 400zł/€95

€€€ more than 400zł/€95

CAMPING

Poland has hundreds of camping grounds and many offer good-value cabins and bungalows. Most open May to September, but some only open their gates between June and August. A handy campsite resource is the website of the **Polish Federation of Camping and Caravanning** (☏22 810 6050; www.pfcc.eu).

HOSTELS

Schroniska młodzieżowe (youth hostels) in Poland are operated by the **Polish Youth Hostel Association** (Polskie Towarzystwo Schronisk Młodzieżowych; ☏22 849 8128; www.ptsm.org. pl), a member of Hostelling International. Most open in July and August, and are often very busy with Polish students; the year-round hostels have more facilities. These youth hostels are open to all, with no age limit. Curfews are common and many hostels close between 10am and 5pm.

A large number of privately operated hostels operate in the main cities, geared towards international backpackers. They're open 24 hours and offer more modern facilities than the old youth hostels, though prices are higher. These hostels usually offer the use of washing machines (either free or paid), in response to the near-absence of laundromats in Poland.

A dorm bed can cost anything from 40zł to 80zł per person per night. Single and double rooms, if available, start at about 150zł a night.

HOTELS

Hotel prices often vary according to season, especially along the Baltic coast, and discounted weekend rates are common.

If possible, check the room before accepting. Don't be fooled by hotel reception areas, which may look great in contrast to the rest of the establishment. On the other hand, dreary scuffed corridors can sometimes open into clean, pleasant rooms.

Accommodation (sometimes with substantial discounts) can be reliably arranged via the internet through www.poland4u.com and www.hotelspoland.com.

MOUNTAIN REFUGES

PTTK (Polskie Towarzystwo Turystyczno-Krajoznawcze; ☏22 826 2251; www.pttk.pl) runs a chain of *schroniska górskie* (mountain refuges) for hikers. They're usually simple, with a welcoming atmosphere and serve cheap, hot meals. The more isolated refuges are obliged to accept everyone, so can be crowded in the high season. Refuges are normally open all year, but confirm with the nearest PTTK office before setting off.

PRIVATE ROOMS & APARTMENTS

Some destinations have agencies (usually called *biuro zakwaterowania* or *biuro kwater prywatnych*) that arrange accommodation in private homes. Rooms cost about 120/150zł per single/double. The most important factor to consider is location; if the home is in the suburbs, find out how far it is from reliable public transport.

During the high season, home owners also directly approach tourists. Also, private homes in smaller resorts and villages often have signs outside their gates or doors offering a *pokoje* (room) or *noclegi* (lodging).

In big cities such as Warsaw, Kraków, Wrocław and Gdańsk, some agencies offer self-contained apartments, which are an affordable alternative to hotels and allow for the washing of laundry.

Activities

CYCLING

As Poland is fairly flat, it's ideal for cyclists. Bicycle routes along the banks of the Vistula River are popular in Warsaw, Toruń and Kraków. Many of the national parks – including Tatra (near Zakopane) and Słowinski (near Łeba) – offer bicycle trails, as does the Great Masurian Lakes district. For more of a challenge, try cycling in the Bieszczady ranges around Sanok. Bikes can be rented at most resort towns and larger cities.

HIKING

Hikers can enjoy marked trails across the Tatra Mountains, where one of the most popular climbs is up the steep slopes of Mt Giewont (1894m). The Sudeten Mountains and the Great Masurian Lakes district also offer good walking opportunities. National parks worth hiking through include Białowieża National Park, Kampinos National Park just outside Warsaw, and Wielkopolska National Park outside Poznań. Trails are easy to follow and detailed maps are available at larger bookshops.

SKIING

Zakopane will delight skiers from December to March and facilities are cheaper than the ski resorts of Western Europe. Other sports on offer here include hang-gliding and paragliding. Another place to hit the snow is Szklarska Poręba in Silesia.

WATER SPORTS

Throngs of yachties, canoeists and kayakers enjoy the network of waterways in the Great

Masurian Lakes district every summer; boats are available for rent from lakeside towns and there are even diving excursions. Windsurfers can head to the beaches of the Hel peninsula.

Business Hours

Banks 8am to 5pm Monday to Friday, sometimes 8am to 2pm Saturday

Cafes & restaurants 11am to 11pm

Shops 10am to 6pm Monday to Friday, 10am to 2pm Saturday

Nightclubs 9pm to late

Embassies & Consulates

All diplomatic missions listed are located in Warsaw unless stated otherwise.

Australian Embassy (22 521 3444; www.australia.pl; ul Nowogrodzka 11)

Belarusian Embassy (22 742 0990; www.poland.mfa.gov.by; ul Wiertnicza 58)

Canadian Embassy (22 584 3100; www.canada.pl; ul Matejki 1/5)

French Embassy (22 529 3000; www.ambafrance-pl.org; ul Piękna 1)

French Consulate (12 424 5300; www.cracovie.org.pl; ul Stolarska 15, Kraków)

German Embassy (22 584 1700; www.warschau.diplo.de; ul Jazdów 12)

German Consulate (12 424 3000; www.krakau.diplo.de; ul Stolarska 7, Kraków)

Irish Embassy (22 849 6633; www.irlandia.pl; ul Mysia 5)

Netherlands Embassy (22 559 1200; www.nlembassy.pl; ul Kawalerii 10)

New Zealand Embassy (22 521 0500; www.nzembassy.com/poland; Al Ujazdowskie 51)

Russian Embassy (22 849 5111; http://warsaw.rusembassy.org; ul Belwederska 49)

South African Embassy (22 622 1031; warsaw.consular@dirco.gov.za; ul Koszykowa 54)

Ukrainian Embassy (22 622 4797; www.ukraine-emb.pl; Al Szucha 7)

UK Embassy (22 311 0000; www.ukinpoland.fco.gov.uk; ul Kawalerii 12)

UK Consulate (12 421 7030; ukconsul@sunley.pl; ul Św Anny 9, Kraków)

US Embassy (22 504 2000; http://poland.usembassy.gov; Al Ujazdowskie 29/31)

US Consulate (12 424 5100; http://krakow.usconsulate.gov; ul Stolarska 9, Kraków)

Food

Price ranges are based on the average cost of a main meal.

€ less than 20zł

€€ 20zł to 40zł

€€€ more than 40zł

Gay & Lesbian Travellers

Since the change of government in 2007, overt homophobia from state officials has declined; though with the Church remaining influential in social matters, gay acceptance in Poland is still a work in progress. The gay community is becoming more visible, however, and in 2010 Warsaw hosted **EuroPride** (www.europride.com), which was the first time this major event had been held in a former communist country. In late 2011 LGBT activist Robert Biedroń was elected as a member of the Polish parliament, its first openly gay representative.

In general though, the Polish gay and lesbian scene remains fairly discreet. Warsaw and Kraków are the best places to find gay-friendly bars, clubs and accommodation. The free tourist brochure, *The Visitor*, lists a few gay night spots, as do the **In Your Pocket** (www.inyourpocket.com) guides.

Another good source of information on gay Warsaw and Kraków is online at www.gayguide.net.

Internet Access

Internet access is near universal in Polish accommodation: either as wireless, via on-site computers, or both.

In the unlikely event that your lodgings are offline, you'll likely find an internet cafe nearby; expect to pay between 4zł and 5zł per hour. Also, some forward-thinking city councils have set up wireless access in their main market squares.

Media

The *Warsaw Business Journal* is aimed at the business community, while *Warsaw Insider* has more general-interest features, listings and reviews. *Warsaw Voice* is a weekly English-language news magazine with a business slant.

The free *Welcome to*... series of magazines covers Poznań, Kraków, Toruń, Zakopane and Warsaw monthly.

Recent newspapers and magazines from Western Europe and the USA are readily available at EMPiK bookshops and at newsstands in the foyers of upmarket hotels.

Poland has a mix of privately owned TV channels and state-owned nationwide channels. Foreign-language programs are painfully dubbed with one male voice covering all actors (that's men, women and children) and no lip-sync, so you can still hear the original language underneath. Most hotels offer English-language news channels.

Money

Poland is obliged by the terms of its accession to the EU to adopt the euro as its currency at some point in the future; but it's not likely to happen until at least 2016. In the meantime, the nation's currency is the złoty (*zwo*-ti), abbreviated to zł (international currency code PLN). It's divided into 100 groszy (gr). Denominations of notes are 10, 20, 50, 100 and 200 (rare) złoty; coins come in one, two, five, 10, 20 and 50 groszy and one, two and five złoty.

Bankomats (ATMs) accept most international credit cards and are easily found in the centre of all cities and most towns. Banks without an ATM may provide cash advances over the counter on credit cards.

Private *kantors* (foreign-exchange offices) are everywhere. They require no paperwork and charge no commission, though rates at *kantors* near tourist-friendly attractions or facilities can be poor.

Travellers cheques are more secure than cash, but *kantors* rarely change them and banks that do will charge a commission. A better option is a stored value cash card, which can be used in the same manner as a credit card; ask your bank about this before leaving home.

Post

Postal services are operated by Poczta Polska; the Poczta Główna (Main Post Office) in each city offers the widest range of services.

The cost of sending a normal-sized letter (up to 20g) or a postcard to other European countries is 2.40zł, rising to 3.20zł for North America and 4.50zł for Australia.

Public Holidays

New Year's Day 1 January

Epiphany 6 January

Easter Sunday March or April

Easter Monday March or April

State Holiday 1 May

Constitution Day 3 May

Pentecost Sunday Seventh Sunday after Easter

Corpus Christi Ninth Thursday after Easter

Assumption Day 15 August

All Saints' Day 1 November

Independence Day 11 November

Christmas 25 and 26 December

Safe Travel

Poland is a relatively safe country and crime has decreased significantly since the immediate postcommunism era. Be alert, however, for thieves and pickpockets around major train stations, such as Warszawa Centralna. Robberies have been a problem on night trains, especially on international routes. Try to share a compartment with other people if possible.

Theft from cars is a widespread problem, so keep your vehicle in a guarded car park whenever possible. Heavy drinking is common and drunks can be disturbing, though rarely dangerous.

As Poland is an ethnically homogeneous nation, travellers of a non-European appearance may attract curious glances from locals in outlying regions. Football (soccer) hooligans are not uncommon, so avoid travelling on public transport with them – especially if their team has lost!

Telephone

Polish telephone numbers have nine digits, with no area codes. To call Poland from abroad, dial the country code ☎48, then the Polish number. The international access code when dialling out of Poland is ☎00. For help, try the operators for local numbers (☎913), national numbers and codes (☎912), and international codes (☎908), but don't expect anyone to speak English.

The main mobile telephone providers are Plus, Orange, T-Mobile and Play, all of which offer prepaid SIM cards that come with call and data allowances. Such prepaid accounts are cheap by Western European standards and are easy to set up at local offices of these companies.

The cheapest way to make international calls from public telephones is via the prepaid international cards produced by various operators, which are available at post offices and kiosks. You can also buy magnetic phone cards from these places in order to make domestic calls.

Travellers with Disabilities

Poland is not set up well for people with disabilities, although there have been significant improvements in recent years. Wheelchair ramps are often only available at upmarket hotels and public transport will be a challenge for anyone with mobility problems. However, many hotels now have at least one room especially designed for disabled access – book ahead for these. There are also some low-floor trams running on bigger cities' public transport networks. Information on disability issues is available from Integracja (22 530 6570; www.integracja.org).

Visas

EU citizens do not need a visa to visit Poland and can stay indefinitely. Citizens of Australia, Canada, Israel, New Zealand, Switzerland and the USA can stay in Poland for up to 90 days without a visa.

However, since Poland's entry into the Schengen zone in December 2007, the 90-day visa-free entry period has been extended to all the Schengen countries; so if travelling from Poland through Germany and France, for example, you can't exceed 90 days in total. Once your 90 days is up, you must leave the Schengen zone for a minimum 90 days before you can once again enter it visa-free.

South African citizens do require a visa. Other nationals should check with Polish embassies or consulates in their countries for current visa requirements. Updates can be found at the website of the Ministry of Foreign Affairs (www.msz.gov.pl).

Websites

Commonwealth of Diverse Cultures (www.commonwealth.pl) Outlines Poland's cultural heritage.

Virtualtourist.com (www.virtualtourist. com) Poland section features postings by travellers.

Getting There & Away

Air

The majority of international flights to Poland arrive at Warsaw's Okęcie airport, while other important airports include Kraków, Gdańsk, Poznań and Wrocław. The national carrier LOT (801 703 703, 22 19572; www.lot. com) flies to all major European cities.

Other major airlines flying to/from Poland include the following:

Aeroflot (22 650 2511; www.aeroflot.com)

Air France (22 556 6400; www.airfrance. com)

Alitalia (22 556 6866; www.alitalia.it)

British Airways (00800 441 1592; www. ba.com)

EasyJet (703 103 988; www.easyjet.com)

Eurolot (22 574 0740; www.eurolot.com)

KLM (22 556 6444; www.klm.pl)

Lufthansa (22 338 1300; www.lufthansa.pl)

Ryanair (703 303 033; www.ryanair.com)

SAS (22 850 0500; www.flysas.com)

Wizz Air (703 603 993; www.wizzair.com)

Land

Since Poland is now within the Schengen zone, there are no border posts or border-crossing formalities between Poland and Germany, the Czech Republic, Slovakia and Lithuania. Below is a list of major road border crossings with Poland's non-Schengen neighbours that accept foreigners and are open 24 hours.

Belarus (South to north) Terespol, Kuźnica Białostocka

Russia (West to east) Gronowo, Bezledy

Ukraine (South to north) Medyka, Hrebenne, Dorohusk

If you're going to Russia or Lithuania and your train/bus passes through Belarus, you need a Belarusian transit visa and you must get it in advance.

BUS

International bus services are offered by dozens of Polish and international companies. One of the major operators is Eurolines Polska (22 621 3469; www.eurolinespolska.pl), which runs buses in all directions.

CAR & MOTORCYCLE

To drive a car into Poland, EU citizens need their driving licence from home, while other nationalities must obtain an International Drivers Permit in their home country. Also required are vehicle registration papers and liability insurance (Green Card).

TRAIN

Trains link Poland with every neighbouring country and beyond, but international train travel is not cheap. To save money on fares, investigate special train tickets and rail passes. Domestic trains in Poland are significantly cheaper, so you'll save money if you buy a ticket to a Polish border destination such as Szczecin or Prezmyśl, then take a local train.

You can search for international train connections and buy tickets from PKP Intercity (☑22 391 9757; www.intercity.pl). Another useful resource is the website of Polrail Service (www.polrail.com).

Do note that some international trains to/from Poland have been linked with theft. Keep an eye on your bags, particularly on the Prague–Warsaw and Prague–Kraków overnight trains.

Sea

Ferry services sail from Gdańsk (p414)and Gdynia (p415) to ports in Scandinavia. There are also car and passenger ferries from the Polish town of Świnoujście, operated by the following companies.

Polferries (www.polferries.pl) Offers daily services from Świnoujście to Ystad in Sweden (six hours), and to Copenhagen, Denmark (eight hours).

Unity Line (www.unityline.pl) Runs daily ferries between Świnoujście and the Swedish ports of Ystad (seven hours) and Trelleborg (eight hours).

Getting Around

Air

LOT (☑801 703 703, 22 19572; www.lot.com) flies several times a day from Warsaw to Gdańsk, Kraków, Poznań, Wrocław and Szczecin. A LOT subsidiary, Eurolot (☑22 574 0740; www.eurolot.com), serves the same airports.

Bicycle

Cycling is not great for getting around cities, but is often a good way to travel between villages. If you get tired, it's possible to place your bike in the luggage compartment at the front or rear of slow passenger trains (these are rarely found on faster services). You'll need a special ticket for your bike from the railway ticket office.

Bus

Buses can be useful on short routes and through the mountains in southern Poland; but usually trains are quicker and more comfortable, and private minibuses are quicker and more direct.

Most buses are operated by the state bus company, PKS. It provides two kinds of service from its bus terminals (*dworzec autobusowy PKS*): ordinary buses (marked in black on timetables); and fast buses (marked in red), which ignore minor stops.

Timetables are posted on boards and additional symbols next to departure times may indicate the bus runs only on certain days or in certain seasons. You can also check timetables online at www.e-podroznik.pl. Terminals usually have an information desk, but it's rarely staffed with English speakers. Tickets for PKS buses can sometimes be bought at the terminal, but more often from drivers. Note that all bus frequencies quoted in this chapter relate to the summer schedule.

The price of PKS bus tickets is determined by the length, in kilometres, of the trip; a bus fare will usually work out cheaper than a comparable train ticket. Minibuses charge set prices for journeys and these are normally posted in their windows or at the bus stop.

A useful alternative to PKS is the private company Polski Bus (www.polskibus.com), which operates modern double-decker buses (with free wi-fi on board) to destinations throughout Poland and beyond including Warsaw, Kraków, Gdańsk, Lublin, Wrocław, Vienna, Prague and Berlin. Fares vary dynamically in the manner of a budget airline and must be purchased in advance via the company's website.

Car & Motorcycle

FUEL & SPARE PARTS

Petrol stations sell several kinds of petrol, including 94-octane leaded, 95-octane unleaded, 98-octane unleaded and diesel. Most petrol stations are open from 6am to 10pm (from 7am to 3pm Sunday), though some operate around the clock. Garages are plentiful. Roadside assistance can be summoned by dialling ☑19637.

HIRE

Major international car-rental companies, such as Avis (☑22 650 4872; www.avis.pl), Hertz (☑22 500 1620; www.hertz.pl) and Europcar (☑22 650 2564; www.europcar.com.pl), are represented in larger cities and have smaller offices at airports. Rates are comparable to full-price rental in Western Europe.

Rental agencies will need to see your passport, your home driving licence (which must have been held for at least one year) and a credit card (for the deposit). You need to be at least 21 years of age to rent a car; sometimes 25 for a more expensive car.

ROAD RULES

The speed limit is 130km/h on motorways, 100km/h on two- or four-lane highways, 90km/h on other open roads and 50km/h in built-up areas. If the background of the sign bearing the town's name is white you must reduce speed to 50km/h; if the background is green there's no need to reduce speed (unless road signs indicate otherwise). Radar-equipped police are very active, especially in villages with white signs.

Unless signs state otherwise, cars may park on pavements as long as a minimum 1.5m-wide walkway is left for pedestrians. Parking in the opposite direction to traffic flow is allowed. The permitted blood alcohol level is a low 0.02%, so it's best not to drink if you're driving. Seat belts are compulsory, as are helmets for motorcyclists. Between October and February, all drivers must use headlights during the day (and night!).

Train

Trains will be your main means of transport. They're cheap, reliable and rarely overcrowded (except for July and August peak times). Polish State Railways (PKP; www.pkp.pl) operates trains to almost every tourist destination; its online timetable is very helpful, providing routes, fares and intermediate stations in English. A private company, Arriva (www.arriva.pl), also operates local services in the eastern part of Pomerania.

TRAIN TYPES

» **Express InterCity trains** only stop at major cities and are the fastest way to travel by rail. These trains require seat reservations.

» Down the pecking order are the older but cheaper **TLK trains** *(pociąg TLK)*. They're slower and more crowded, but are probably the type of train you'll most often catch. TLK trains also require seat reservations.

» **InterRegio trains** run between adjoining regions of Poland and often operate less frequently at weekends. No reservations are required.

» At the bottom of the hierarchy, slow **Regio trains**, also known as 'passenger trains' *(pociąg osobowy)* stop by every tree at the side of the track that could be imagined to be a station and are best used only for short trips. Seats can't be reserved.

CLASSES & FARES

Express InterCity and TLK trains carry two classes: *druga klasa* (2nd class) and *pierwsza klasa* (1st class), which is 50% more expensive.

Note that train fares quoted in this chapter are for a 2nd-class ticket on a TLK train, or the most likely alternative if the route is mainly served by a different type of train. Frequencies are as per the summer schedule.

In a couchette on an overnight train, compartments have four/six beds in 1st/2nd class. Sleepers have two/three people (1st/2nd class) in a compartment fitted with a washbasin, sheets and blankets. *Miejsca sypialne* (sleepers) and *kuszetki* (couchettes) can be booked at special counters in larger train stations; prebooking is recommended.

TIMETABLES

Train *odjazdy* (departures) are listed at train stations on a yellow board and *przyjazdy* (arrivals) on a white board. Ordinary trains are marked in black print, fast trains in red. The letter 'R' in a square indicates the train has compulsory seat reservation.

The timetables also show which *peron* (platform) it's using. The number applies to *both* sides of the platform. If in doubt, check the platform departure board or route cards on the side of carriages, or ask someone.

Full timetable and fare information in English can be found on the PKP website.

TICKETING

If a seat reservation is compulsory on your train, you will automatically be sold a *miejscówka* (reserved) seat ticket. If you do not make a seat reservation, you can travel on *any* train (of the type requested) to the destination indicated on your ticket on the date specified.

Your ticket will list the *klasa* (class); the *poc* (type) of train; where the train is travelling *od* (from) and *do* (to); the major town or junction the train is travelling *prez* (through); and the total *cena* (price). If more than one place is listed under the heading *prez* (via), ask the conductor *early* if you have to change trains at the junction listed or be in a specific carriage (the train may separate later).

If you get on a train without a ticket, you can buy one directly from the conductor for a small supplement (7zł) – but do it right away. If the conductor finds you first, you'll be fined for travelling without a ticket. You can always upgrade from 2nd to 1st class for a small extra fee (7zł), plus the additional fare.

Slovakia

Best Places to Eat

» Café Verne (p443)

» Cactus (p474)

» Reštaurácia Bašta (p449)

Best Places to Stay

» Ginger Monkey Hostel (p462)

» Grand Hotel Kempinski (p460)

» Skaritz (p442)

» Hotel Marrol's (p442)

Why Go?

No, it isn't a province of the Czech Republic. Going strong over two decades as an independent state after the breakup of Czechoslovakia, Slovakia out-trumps the Czechs for ancient castles, and boasts nature far wilder than its western neighbours. It savours wine over beer and, in its bashful heartland amid mountains and forests, cradles an entrancing folk culture most European nations have lost.

Slovakia's small size is possibly its biggest attraction. You can hike woodsy waterfall-filled gorges one day and yodel from peaks soaring more than 2500m the next. Dinky capital Bratislava is awash with quirky museums and backed by thick forests. With its rabbit-warren Old Town, it might just win world prize for most cafes per city resident.

Don't leave without heading east, to where fortresses tower over tradition-rich medieval towns such as Levoča or Bardejov and hiking trails lace the hills. Down a *slivovica* (firewaterlike plum brandy) and drink a toast for us – *nazdravie*!

When to Go
Bratislava

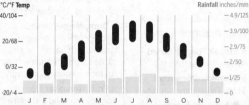

Sep Fewer crowds but clement weather. Wine season means it's time for alcohol-themed festivities.

Jun & Jul Festivals abound across the country. High Tatras hiking trails are all open.

Jan & Feb Peak ski season in the mountains, but many other sights are closed.

AT A GLANCE

» **Currency** Euro (€)

» **Language** Slovak

» **Money** ATMs widely available in cities

» **Visas** Not required for most visitors staying less than 90 days

Fast Facts

» **Area** 49,035 sq km

» **Capital** Bratislava

» **Country code** ☑02

» **Emergency** ☑112

Exchange Rates

Australia	A$1	€0.82
Canada	C$1	€0.77
Japan	¥100	€0.83
New Zealand	NZ$1	€0.65
UK	UK£1	€1.18
USA	US$1	€0.78

Set Your Budget

» **Budget hotel room** €30–60

» **Two-course meal** €15

» **Museum entrance** €3

» **Beer** €1.50

» **City transport ticket** €0.70

Resources

» **Slovak Tourist Board** (www.slovakia.travel)

» **Slovakia Document Store** (www.panorama.sk)

» **What's On Slovakia** (www.whatsonslovakia.com)

Connections

Though few airlines fly into Slovakia itself, Bratislava is just 60km from well-connected Vienna International Airport. By train from Bratislava, Budapest (three hours) and Prague (five hours) are easily reachable. Buses connect to Zakopane in Poland (two hours) from Poprad, and to Uzhhorod in Ukraine (2½ hours) via Košice.

ITINERARIES

Three Days

Two nights in Bratislava is enough to wander the Old Town streets and see some museums. The following day is best spent on a castle excursion, either to Devín or Trenčín. Or, better yet, spend all three days hiking in the rocky High Tatra mountains, staying central in the resort town of Starý Smokovec or in more off-beat Ždiar in the Belá Tatras.

One Week

After a day or two in Bratislava, venture east. Spend at least four nights around the Tatras so you have time to hike to a mountain hut as well as take day trips to the must-see Spiš Castle ruins, medieval Levoča, or to Slovenský Raj National Park for its highly rated Suchá Belá Gorge hike. For the last night or two, continue to Bardejov to marvel at its complete Renaissance town square, icon art and nearby wooden churches.

Essential Food & Drink

» **Sheep's cheese** *Bryndza* – sharp, soft and spreadable; *oštiepok* – solid and ball-shaped; *žinčina* – a traditional sheep's-whey drink (like sour milk).

» **Meaty moments** *Vývar* (chicken/beef broth served with *slížiky*, thin pasta strips, or liver dumplings); *kapustnica* (thick sauerkraut and meat soup, often with chorizo or mushrooms); baked duck/goose served in *lokše* (potato pancakes) and stewed cabbage.

» **Dumplings** Potato-based goodies in varieties such as *halušky* (mini-dumplings in cabbage or *bryndza* sauce topped with bacon) or *pirohy* (pocket-shaped dumplings stuffed with *bryndza* or smoked meat). For sweets, try *šulance* – walnut- or poppy-seed-topped dumplings.

» **Fruit firewater** Homemade or store-bought liquor, made from berries and pitted fruits, such as *borovička* (from juniper) and *slivovica* (from plums).

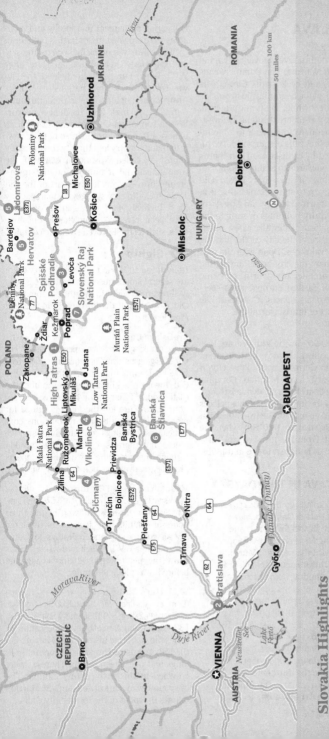

Slovakia Highlights

1 Hike between mountain huts in one of Europe's smallest alpine mountain ranges, the **High Tatras** (p456).

2 Linger over drinks at one of myriad sidewalk or riverfront cafes in Old Town **Bratislava** (p443).

3 Wander the ruins of **Spiš Castle** (p465), among the biggest in Europe.

4 Experience folk culture in traditional villages such as **Vlkolínec** (p450) and **Čičmany** (p450).

5 Seek out iconic, Unesco-listed wooden churches in isolated far-east Slovakia, such as **Hervatov** (p475) or **Ladomirová**.

6 Travel back in time at the spectacularly preserved ancient mining town of **Banská Štiavnica** (p454).

7 Climb creaking ladders past crashing waterfalls in the dramatic gorges of **Slovenský Raj National Park** (p468).

BRATISLAVA

🎵 02 / POP 432,800

Proximity to nature gives Slovakia's capital its strongest flavouring. The Danube wends through town and cycle paths through its verdant flood plain beginning just outside the centre. Meanwhile, a 30-minute walk from the train station are the densely forested Small Carpathians; the trailer to a mountainous extent that runs country-wide, virtually unimpeded by civilisation. Then there's ski runs and vineyards to amble among.

The charming – if tiny – Starý Mesto (Old Town) is the place to start appreciating Bratislava. Stroll narrow pedestrian streets of pastel 18th-century buildings or sample the nigh-on ubiquitous sidewalk cafes under the watchful gaze of the city castle, harking back to medieval times. Done with the old? In with the new: the city boasts intriguing Socialist-era architecture worth checking out and one of Eastern Europe's most spectacular modern art spaces. Contrasts like this are all part of Bratislava's allure.

History

Founded in AD 907, by the 12th century Bratislava (then called Poszony in Hungarian or Pressburg in German) was a large city in greater Hungary. King Matthias Corvinus founded a university here, Academia Istropolitana. Many of the imposing baroque palaces you see date to the reign of Austro-Hungarian empress Maria Theresa (1740–80), when the city flourished. From the 16th-century Turkish occupation of Budapest to the mid-1800s,

Hungarian parliament met locally and monarchs were crowned in St Martin's Cathedral.

'Bratislava' was officially born as the second city of a Czechoslovakian state after WWI. When Europe was redivided, the city was coveted by various nations – not least Austria (the population was predominantly German-speaking). US President Woodrow Wilson supported Czechoslovakian requests to have a Danube port included in their newly founded country and the city consequently almost got called Wilsonov. Post-WWII, the communists did a number on the town's architecture – razing a large part of the Old Town, including the synagogue, to make way for a highway. Bad architectural decisions have been reversed somewhat by positive ones, such as the Eurovea riverside complex.

⊙ Sights

In addition to those mentioned here, there are several small museums and increasingly well-regarded galleries scattered about the Old Town: ask at the info centre for the *Art Plan* leaflet.

Bratislava Castle   CASTLE
(www.snm.sk; grounds free, museum adult/child €4/2; ⊙grounds 9am-9pm, museum 10am-6pm Tue-Sun) Dominating the southwest of the Old Town on a hill above the Danube, the castle today is largely a 1950s reconstruction; an 1811 fire left the fortress ruined for more than a century and renovations continue. Most buildings contain administrative offices, but there is a museum of Slovakia through the ages, and lawns and ramparts provide great vantage points for city viewing.

Museum of Jewish Culture   MUSEUM
(www.snm.sk; Židovská 17; adult/child €7/2; ⊙11am-5pm Sun-Fri) The most moving of the three floors of exhibits here focuses on the large Jewish community and buildings lost during and after WWII. Black-and-white photos show the neighbourhood and synagogue before it was ploughed under.

St Martin's Cathedral   CHURCH
(Dóm sv Martina; cnr Kapitulská/Starometská; adult/child €2/free; ⊙9-11.30am & 1-5pm Mon-Sat, 1.30-4.30pm Sun) A relatively modest interior belies the elaborate history of St Martin's Cathedral: 11 Austro-Hungarian monarchs (10 kings and one queen, Maria Theresa) were crowned in this 14th-century church. The busy motorway almost touching St Martin's follows the moat of the former city walls.

BRATISLAVA IN TWO DAYS

Start the morning climbing the ramparts of **Bratislava Castle** for views of the barrel-tile Old Town roofs and concrete kingdom Petržalka. On your way down, visit the excellent **Museum of Jewish Culture** and magnificent **St Martin's Cathedral**, coronation place of Hungarian monarchs. Spend the afternoon strolling through the Old Town, winding up with an atmospheric meal at **Cafe Verne** or a Slovak-style party at **Nu Spirit Club**.

On the second day, take a trip out to **Devín Castle** to see poignant ruins from the 9th to the 18th centuries, or jump aboard a boat to **Danubiana Meulensteen Art Museum**.

BRATISLAVA: QUEEN OF QUIRK

Bratislava deserves a crown for queen of quirkiness when it comes to sightseeing. The most photographed sight? Not a church or a castle, but the bronze statue called the **Watcher** (cnr Panská & Rybárska) peeping from an imaginary manhole. He's not alone: look out around the Old Town for other questionable statuesque characters, including the **Photographer** and a timepiece-toting monk. Other unusual attractions include the following:

Museum of Clocks (www.muzeum.bratislava.sk; Židovská 1; adult/child €2.30/1.50; ⊙10am-5pm Tue-Fri, 11am-6pm Sat-Sun) Random old clocks, but they're contained in an interestingly narrow building.

Blue Church (Kostol Svätej Alžbety; Bezručova 2; ⊙Services 7/9.30/11am & 6.30pm) Every surface of the 1911 Church of St Elizabeth, more commonly known as the Blue Church, is an art nouveau fantasy dressed in cool sky-blue and deeper royal blue.

Michael's Gate & Tower (www.muzeum.bratislava.sk; Michalská 24; adult/child €4.30/2.50; ⊙10am-6pm Tue-Sun) Climb past the five small storeys of medieval weaponry in Bratislava's only remaining gate for superior Old Town views from the top.

Hviezdoslavovo Námestie   SQUARE

Embassies, restaurants and bars are the mainstay of the long, tree-lined plaza that anchors the pedestrian zone's southern extremity. At Hviezdoslavovo's east end, the ornate 1886 Slovak National Theatre (p444), one of the city's opera houses, steals the show. The theatre is not open for tours, but ticket prices are not prohibitive. The nearby neo-baroque 1914 **Reduta Palace** (Eugena Suchoň nám; ⊙1-7pm Mon, Tue, Thu & Fri, 8am-2pm Wed) houses the Slovak Philharmonic: refurbishment included adding the impressive €1.5 million organ.

Hlavné Námestie   SQUARE

Cafe tables outline pretty Hlavné nám (Main Sq), the site of numerous festival performances. **Roland's Fountain**, at the square's heart, is thought to have been built in 1572 as a fire hydrant of sorts. Flanking the northeast side of the square is the 1421 **Old Town Hall** (www.muzeum.bratislava.sk; adult/child €5/2; ⊙10am-5pm Tue-Fri, 11am-6pm Sat & Sun), home to the city museum. You'll often find a musician in traditional costume playing a *fujira* on the steps of the **Jesuit Church**, on the edge of adjoining Františkánske nám.

Slovak National Gallery   ART MUSEUM

(Slovenská Národná Galéria; www.sng.sk; Rázusovo nábr 2; adult/child €3.50/2; ⊙10am-5pm Tue-Sun) A socialist modernist building and an 18th-century palace make interesting co-hosts for the Slovak National Gallery. The nation's eclectic art collection contained here ranges from Gothic to graphic design.

Apponyi Palace   WINE MUSEUM

(www.muzeum.bratislava.sk; Radničná 1; adult/child €6/3; ⊙10am-5pm Tue-Fri, 11am-6pm Sat & Sun) Explore the area's winemaking heritage in the cellar exhibits of this restored 1761 palace. There's an excellent, interactive English-language audio.

Slovak National Museum   MUSEUM

(www.snm.sk; Vajanského nábr 2; adult/child €3.50/1.50; ⊙9am-5pm Tue-Sun) Changing exhibits on the lower floors, natural history on top.

Bratislava Forest Park   FOREST

(Bratislavský Lesný Park; 🚌203) Marked by the Kamzik TV mast (complete with viewing platform and vista-endowed restaurant) and visible north of the city is this vast, hilly forest park. There's a **cable car** (Skiareál Mariánky, Dusíkova; €3; ⊙every 15min 10am-5pm) but you're up here for the superb, scenic hiking and biking. It's a 20-minute walk uphill from the Koliba trolleybus terminal to the park entrance.

🏃 Activities

From April through September, **Slovak Shipping & Ports** (☎5293 2226; www.lod.sk; Fajnorovo nábr 2) runs 45-minute Bratislava return boat trips (adult/child €5/3.50) on the Danube. Its Devín sightseeing cruise (adult/child return €7/5) plies the waters to the castle, stops for one to two hours and returns to Bratislava in 30 minutes.

You can rent bikes from **Bratislava Sightseeing** (☎0907683112; www.bratislavasightseeing.com; Fajnorovo nábr; per hr/day €6/18; ⊙10am-6pm

Central Bratislava

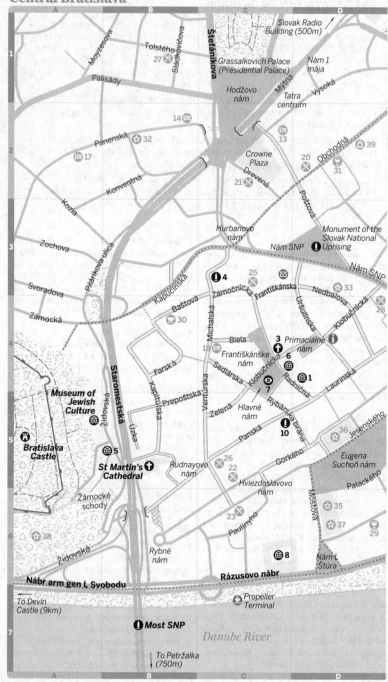

Slovak Radio Building (500m)

Grassalkovich Palace (Presidential Palace)

Nám 1 mája

Hodžovo nám

Tatra centrum

Crowne Plaza

Monument of the Slovak National Uprising

Nám SNP

Nám SNP

Hurbanovo nám

Museum of Jewish Culture

Bratislava Castle

St Martin's Cathedral

Primaciálne nám

Františkánske nám

Biela

Hlavné nám

Rudnayovo nám

Hviezdoslavovo nám

Rybné nám

Eugena Suchoň nám

Palackého

Nám L Štúra

Nábr arm gen L Svobodu

Rázusovo nábr

To Devín Castle (9km)

Propeller Terminal

Most SNP

Danube River

To Petržalka (750m)

Štefánikova

Tolstého

Sládkovičova

Moyzesova

Palisády

Panenská

Konventná

Kozia

Zochova

Svoradova

Zámocká

Pilárikova ulica

Kapucínska

Baštová

Michalská

Zámočnícka

Františkánska

Ursulínska

Klobučnícka

Nedbalova

Obchodná

Poštová

Mýtna

Vysoká

Drevená

Farská

Kapitulská

Prepoštská

Venturska

Zelena

Sedlárska

Klobučnícka

Radničná

Laurinská

Jesenského

Panská

Gorkého

Rybárska brána

Staromestská

Žiškova

Úzka

Žámocké schody

Židovská

Rudnayovo nám

Paulínyho

Mostová

Rybné nám

mid-May–mid-Sep), located in a children's playground along the waterfront.

👉 Tours

Authentic Slovakia   CULTURAL TOUR
(☏908308234; www.authenticslovakia.com; per 2/4hr tour €25/39) Want to know about the Slovakia the other tours don't tell you about? Sign up with these guys for forays to weird Socialist-era buildings and typical *krčmy* (Slovak pubs): authentic (uncensored) Slovakia.

FREE **Be Free Tours**   WALKING TOUR
(www.befreetours.com; ⊙11am & 4pm Tue-Sat, 4pm Sun & Mon) Lively, two-hour-plus English tour of the Old Town, leaving from the Hviezdoslav statue in Hviezdoslavovo nám. They also run pub crawls (Tuesdays, Thursdays and Saturdays).

🎎 Festivals & Events

Cultural Summer Festival   CULTURE
(http://visit.bratislava.sk; ⊙Jun-Sep) A smorgasbord of plays and performances comes to the streets and venues around town in summer.

Bratislava Jazz Days   MUSIC
(www.bjd.sk; ⊙Oct) World-class jazz takes centre stage for three days.

Christmas Market   SHOPPING
(⊙Nov & Dec) From 26 November, Hlavné nám fills with food and drink, crafts for sale and staged performances.

International Film Festival   FILM
(www.iffbratislava.sk; ⊙Nov) Showcases a great selection of offbeat worldwide cinema.

Fjúžn   CULTURE
(www.fjuzn.sk; ⊙Apr) Dunaj (p445), which is an important venue for world music year-round, hosts this annual celebration of Slovak minorities and their cultures.

🛏 Sleeping

For a full accommodation list, see www.bkis. sk. Getting a short-term rental flat in the old town (€65 to €120 per night) is a great way to stay super-central without paying hotel prices, plus you can self-cater. Family-run and friendly, the modern units of **Apartments Bratislava** (www.apartmentsbratislava. com) are our top choice. Many hostels also have kitchens.

Central Bratislava

TOP CHOICE **Skaritz** BOUTIQUE HOTEL €€
(☎5920 9770; www.skaritz.com; Michalská 4; r €75-100; P🐕🅿🛜) Few other spots in the Old Town so effortlessly combine century-old elegance and contemporary design touches. Nor could you ask for a more central location. Choose from 20 rooms and six apartments.

TOP CHOICE **Hotel Marrol's** BOUTIQUE HOTEL €€
(☎5778 4600; www.hotelmarrols.sk; Tobrucká 4; s/d €120/150, ste from €500; 🛜❄) The sort of place where you could imagine Kaiser Wilhelm puffing contentedly on a cigar: no member of aristocracy would feel out of place in these 54 sumptuous rooms and suites, or in the Jasmine spa. Considering it's a regular in world's best luxury hotel lists, prices are very proletariat-friendly.

Downtown Backpackers HOSTEL €
(☎5464 1191; www.backpackers.sk; Panenská 31; dm €17-18, d €52; 🐕@🛜) The first hostel in Bratislava, Backpackers is still a boozy (you

enter through a bar) bohemian classic. Red-brick walls and tapestries add character. Serves good food.

Penzión Virgo PENSION €€
(☎2092 1400; www.penzionvirgo.sk; Panenská 14; s/d/apt €61/74/85; 🐕@) Exterior-access rooms are arranged around a courtyard; light and airy despite dark-wood floors and baroque-accent wallpaper. Sip an espresso with the breakfast buffet (€5).

Penzión Zlatá Noha PENSION €
(☎5477 4922; ww.zlata-noha.sk; Bellova 2; s/d €39/49; 🛜; 🚌203) Up in leafy Koliba north of the Old Town, Zlatá Noha is a family-run enterprise offering some of the most decently priced rooms hereabouts. They're simply furnished but clean and the views down over vineyards across Bratislava will perk you up no end.

Hostel Blues HOSTEL €
(☎0905204020; www.hostelblues.sk; Špitálska 2; dm €15-20, d €52-63; 🐕@🛜) Choose from

five- to 10-bed single-sex or mixed dorms, or those with double bunk beds(!). Private rooms have their own bathrooms. Friendly staff also offer free sightseeing tours.

Tulip House Hotel BOUTIQUE HOTEL €€€
(☑3217 1819; www.tuliphouse.sk; Štúrova 10; ste incl breakfast €129-249; P❀❂@❂) Exquisite art nouveau property with a cafe-restaurant at street level.

Hotel-Penzión Arcus PENSION €€
(☑5557 2522; www.hotelarcus.sk; Moskovská 5; s/d incl breakfast €65/100; ❂❂) Family-run place with quite varied rooms (some with balcony, some with courtyard views). Pricey for what you get but sparkly clean. It's 500m north-east of Tesco, via Spitalska.

Austria Trend HOTEL €€
(☑5277 5800; www.austria-trend.sk; Vysoká 2a; r €90-150; P❀@) Newer business hotel on the edge of the Old Town.

✖ Eating

The pedestrian centre is chock-a-block with overpriced samey dining options. Scour between the cracks, however, and you'll find great cafes and a few decent restaurants, but many of the most authentic and atmospheric have been pushed further out. Decent Slovak food isn't easy to find. Reasonable eateries, both sit-down and takeaway, line Obchodná. That Slovak fave, the set lunch menu, can be a real steal. Many restaurants in Bratislava do not have English-language menus.

TOP CHOICE **Café Verne** INTERNATIONAL €€
(Hviezdoslavovo nám 18; mains €4-11; ❂9am-midnight; ❂) Lively, friendly, good-value dining in the old town: the Czech beers flow and everyone from expats to students wolfs down hearty no-nonsense grub, including Slovak staples and decent English breakfasts.

Bistro St Germain BISTRO €
(Obchodná 17; mains €4; ❂10am-10pm) Big surprise in a little courtyard off Obchodná: a wonderfully decorated, relaxed place to gossip over homemade lemonade, cupcakes or light lunches (creative salads, baguettes and the like).

TOP CHOICE **Bratislavský Meštiansky Pivovar** SLOVAKIAN €€€
(☑0944512265; Drevená 8; mains €3-19; ❂11am-midnight Mon-Thu & Sat, to 1am Fri, to 11pm Sun) This stylish microbrewery serves Bratisla-

va's freshest beer and offers creative Slovak cooking beneath vaulted ceilings and stylised Old Town artwork.

City Kebab TURKISH €
(Trnava Cesta & Tomašikova; kebabs & snacks €1-4; ❂7am-7pm Mon-Sat; ❂61) Bratislava's best Turkish food place. Behind it is the Fresh-market – stalls selling everything from *malokarpatské* (Small Carpathian) wine to myriad varieties of local mushrooms. It's 5km northeast of the city, towards the airport.

Lemon Tree THAI €€€
(☑5441 1244; www.lemontree.sk; Hviezdoslavovo nám 7; €5-15; ❂) Top-end Thai-Mediterranean restaurant with a 7th-floor upscale bar, Sky-bar, with great views. Reservations are a good idea.

Prašná Bašta SLOVAKIAN €€
(Zámočnicka 11; mains €6-15; ❂11am-11pm) This restaurant in the Old Town serves good Slovakian food in a charming round vaulted interior and one of the most private inner courtyards in the city.

Brasserie La Marine FRENCH €€€
(www.lamarine.sk; Pribinova; mains €11-21; ❂9am-11.30pm) A standout among the riverside eateries of the Eurovea mall, a 10-minute

---

SOCIALIST BRATISLAVA

The stint under socialism left its mark around town in bizarre and monumental ways.

Most SNP (New Bridge; www.u-f-o.sk; Viedenská cesta; observation deck adult/child €8/5; ❂10am-11pm) Colloquially called the UFO (pronounced 'ew-fo'), this Danube-spanning bridge is a modernist marvel from 1972 with a viewing platform and a restaurant with out-of-this-world prices.

Petržalka South of the Danube, this concrete jungle numbers among the largest Socialist housing developments in Eastern Europe.

Slavín War Memorial Huge memorial to the Soviets who fell in WWII, in a park of the same name yielding great city views.

Slovak Radio Building (Slovenský rozhlas; cnr Mýtna & Štefanovičova) A massive upside-down concrete pyramid; we'll leave the rest to your imagination.

walk east of the Old Town. It has one of the city's best wine lists and the food tastes just good enough to balance the high prices.

Traja Mušketieri PUB €€
(✆5443 0019; Sládkovičova 7; mains €6-12) This way-upmarket version of a medieval tavern comes with a poetic menu ('Treacherous Lady de Winter' is a skewered chicken stuffed with Parma ham). Courteous service; reservations recommended.

U Jakubu SLOVAKIAN €
(Nám SNP 24; mains €2-5; ⊙8am-6pm Mon-Fri) Self-service cafeteria with Slovakian classics.

Pesto & Co DELICATESSAN
(Špitálska 21; ⊙Mon-Sat) Everything Italian you've ever wanted from grappa to espresso, with regional recommendations from the charismatic owner.

Corny Café CAFE €
(Grösslingová 20; ⊙8am-10pm) As the cabinet inside showcases, this cosy, traditionally furnished joint offers coffee from almost anywhere you care to name (to buy and, on a rotational basis, to try). Then there's the delicious cakes, the tasty soups, the to-die-for quiches and a terrace by the Blue Church.

Shtoor CAFE €
(Panská 23; light lunches €3-5; 🛜✏️📱) Bursting onto the eating scene with tasty, cheap, healthy lunches, Shtoor has three locations in Bratislava but this, with two levels of seating, has the best (coffee- and cake-fuelled) atmosphere. Check the menus: written in old-fashioned Slovak as set down by Ľudovít Štúr, pioneer of Slovak literary language.

🍷 Drinking

From mid-April to October, sidewalk cafe tables sprout up in every corner of the pedestrian Old Town. Drinking without dining is normally fine. Hviezdoslavovo Nam has good options, as does Eurovea.

Prešporák CAFE
(Baštova 9; ⊙10am-11pm) Many are saying this does Bratislava's best coffee. Anyways, what with shelves of old books and more eccentric paraphernalia such as the huge model of a 16th-century sailing ship, it's a wonderful space to linger.

Slovak Pub SLOVAKIAN
(Obchodná 62; mains €5-10; ⊙10am-midnight Sun-Thu, 10am-2am Fri & Sat) It's touristy, but most

beers are available and it serves every traditional national dish you can think of, albeit far from top quality.

Nu Spirit Bar BAR
(Medená 16; ⊙10am-2am Mon-Fri, 5pm-4am Sat & Sun) Deservedly popular cellar bar with regular live music as underground as its location: jazz, electronica, soul.

☆ Entertainment

Check Slovak Spectator (www.spectator.sme.sk), the Bratislava Culture & Information Centre (www.bkis.sk) and Kam do Mesta (www.kamdomesta.sk) for the latest.

Nightclubs & Live Music

Cover charges for Bratislava's music bars and clubs are usually quite low (free to €5).

Apollon Club GAY & LESBIAN
(www.apollon-gay-club.sk; Panenská 24; ⊙6pm-3am Mon-Thu, 8pm-5am Fri & Sat, 8pm-1am Sun) The gay disco in town has two bars and three stages. Tuesday is karaoke night.

Nu Spirit Club NIGHTCLUB
(Šafárikovo nám 7; ⊙10pm-late, closed Sun & Mon) More of the same that Nu Spirit Bar offers, only in bigger, more danceable environs.

Hlava XXII CLUB
(Bazová 9; ⊙3pm-3am Tue-Sat) Jam sessions, blues and world beat – live. It's 1km northeast of centre, off Záhradnicka.

Subclub NIGHCLUB
(Nábrežie arm gen L Svobudu; ⊙10pm-4am Thu-Sat) An institution in the subterranean passageways under the castle. Techno, indie, hardcore dance etc pounds out to a younger, raucous crowd.

Sport

Bratislava's hallowed ice hockey team, HC Slovan, plays at the Ondrej Nepela Stadium (Odbojárov 9), which was revamped for the 2011 ice hockey world championship. Buy tickets at www.ticketportal.sk.

Performing Arts

Folk dance and music ensembles, like highly recommended Lúčnica (www.lucnica.sk), perform at venues around town; Dunaj caters to avant-garde tastes.

Slovak National Theatre THEATRE
(Slovenské Národné Divadlo (SND); www.snd.sk; Hviezdoslavovo nám) The national theatre company stages quality operas (Slavic and international), ballets and dramas in two

venues: the gilt decoration of the landmark Historic SND (Hviezdoslavovo nám, booking office cnr Jesenského & Komenského; ⊙8am-5.30pm Mon-Fri, 9am-1pm Sat) is a show in itself; the modern New SND (Pribinova 17; ⊙9am-5pm Mon-Fri) has a cafe.

Slovak Philharmonic　　　　　　THEATRE
(www.filharm.sk; Eugena Suchoň nám; tickets €5-20; ⊙9am-2pm Mon, 1-6pm Tue-Fri & before performances)

Dunaj　　　　　　　　　PERFORMING ARTS
(www.kcdunaj.sk; Nedbalova 3; ⊙4pm-late) Cultural centre hosting some of Slovakia's most interesting drama and music performances. Something's on almost nightly. Also has a bar with Old Town panoramas from the terrace.

 Shopping

There are several crystal, craft and jewellery stores, as well as souvenir booths, around Hlavné nám. Artisan galleries inhabit alleyways off Old Town streets.

Eurovea　　　　　　　　　　　　MALL
(Pribinova) A 10-minute walk east from the Old Town, this has all the western chain stores abutted by fancy riverside restaurants and the new Slovak National Theatre (New SND).

Úľuv　　　　　　　　　　　HANDICRAFTS
(www.uluv.sk; Obchodná 64) For serious folk-art shopping head to the main outlet of Úľuv, the national handicraft cooperative, where a courtyard is filled with artisans' studios. Look for *šupolienky*: expressive figures made from painted corn husks.

ℹ Information

Most cafes have wi-fi access; Hlavné nám and Hviezdoslavovo nám are free wi-fi zones. Bratislava has numerous banks and ATMs in the Old Town, with several branches on Poštova. There are also ATMs/exchange booths in the train and bus stations, and at the airport.

Bratislava Culture & Information Centre
(BKIS; ☑5443 3715, 16 186; www.bkis.sk; Klobučnícká 2; ⊙9am-6pm Mon-Fri, 9am-3pm Sat, 10am-3pm Sun) Amicable official tourist office. Brochures galore, including a small Bratislava guide.

Klar-i-net (Klariská 4; per hour €3.50; ⊙10am-10pm Mon-Fri, from 3pm Sat & Sun) Numerous well-equipped internet terminals.

Lonely Planet (www.lonelyplanet.com/slovakia/bratislava)

Main Police Station (☑158; Hrobákova 44) Main police station for foreigners, in Petržalka.

Main Post Office (Nám SNP 34-35) In a beautiful building.

Poliklinika Ruzinov (☑4827 9111; www.ruzinovskapoliklinika.sk, in Slovak; Ružinovská 10) Hospital with emergency services and 24-hour pharmacy.

Slovak Spectator (www.spectator.sme.sk) English-language weekly newspaper with current affairs and event listings.

Tatra Banka (Dunajská 4) English-speaking staff.

Visit Bratislava (http://visit.bratislava.sk) Comprehensive city tourist board site.

ℹ Getting There & Away

Bratislava is the main hub for trains, buses and the few planes that head in and out of the country.

Air

Keep in mind that Vienna's much busier international airport is only 60km west.

Airport Bratislava (BTS; www.airportbratislava.sk; Ivanská cesta) Nine kilometres northeast of the city centre. Flights connect to Italy, Spain, UK cities and more.

Danube Wings (www.danubewings.eu) The only airline with domestic services; has weekday flights (7am and 6pm) to Košice.

Boat

From April to October, plying the Danube is a cruisey way to get from Bratislava to Vienna.

Slovak Shipping & Ports (☑5293 2226; www.lod.sk; Fajnorova nábr 2, Hydrofoil Terminal) Several weekly hydrofoils to Vienna (€18 one way, 1¾ hours). Budapest services have been indefinitely cancelled.

Twin City Liner (☑0903 610 716; www.twincityliner.com; Rázusovo nábr, Propeller Terminal) Up to four boats daily to Vienna (€19 to €33 one way, 1½ hours).

Bus

Direct destinations include cities throughout Slovakia and Europe, but the train is usually comparably priced and more convenient. The **Main Bus Station** (Mlynské Nivy; 🚌Autobusová stanica, AS) is 1km east of the Old Town; locals call it 'Mlynské Nivy' (the street name). For schedules, see www.cp.atlas.sk.

Eurobus (www.eurobus.sk) Runs international routes.

Eurolines (📞5542 2734; www.slovaklines.sk) Contact for most international buses.

Slovenská Autobusová Doprava (SAD; www.sad.sk) National bus company.

Train

Rail is the main way to get around Slovakia and to neighbouring countries. Intercity and Eurocity (IC/EC) trains are quickest. *Ryclík* (R), or 'Fast' trains take slightly longer, but run more frequently and cost less. *Osobný* (Ob) trains are the milk runs. For schedules see www.cp.atlas.sk.

Main Train Station (Hlavná Stanica; www.slovakrail.sk; Predštanicné nám)

Getting Around

To/From the Airport

City bus no 61 links Bratislava airport with the main train station (20 minutes).

Standing taxis (over)charge about €20 to town; ask the price before you get in.

A regular bus (€7.70) connects Vienna, Vienna airport, Bratislava bus station and Bratislava Airport.

Car

Numerous international car-hire companies such as Hertz and Sixt have offices at the airport. Good smaller agencies include the following.

Buchbinder (📞4363 7821; www.buchbinder.sk) In-town pick-up possible for a fee.

Car Rental 24 (📞903 582 400; www.carrental24.sk) Has an office at the airport.

Public Transport

Bratislava has an extensive tram, bus and trolleybus network; though the Old Town is small, so you won't often need it. **Dopravný Podnik Bratislava** (DPB; www.dpb.sk; Hodžovo nám;

TRANSPORT FROM BRATISLAVA

International Bus

DESTINATION	PRICE (€)	DURATION (HR)	FREQUENCY (DAILY)
Budapest (Hungary)	6-14	2½-4	4
London (Britain)	76	23-24	1
Prague (Czech Republic)	14	4¼	5
Vienna (Austria)	8	1¼	12

Domestic Train

DESTINATION	PRICE (€)	DURATION (HR)	FREQUENCY (DAILY)
Košice	19	5½	12
Poprad	15	4	12
Trenčín	6.50	1½	12
Žilina	9.50	2½	12

International Train

DESTINATION	PRICE (€)	DURATION (HR)	FREQUENCY (DAILY)
Budapest (Hungary)	15	2¾	7
Moscow (Russia)	132	41	1
Prague (Czech Republic)	27	4¼	6
Vienna (Austria)	11	1	hourly
Warsaw (Poland)	63	10½	1

⊘6am-7pm Mon-Fri) is the public transport company; you'll find a route map online. The office is in the underground passage beneath Hodžovo nám. Check www.imhd.zoznam.sk for city-wide schedules.

Tickets cost €0.35/0.70/0.90 for 15/30/60 minutes. Buy at newsstands and validate on-board (or risk a legally enforceable €50 fine). Passes cost €4.50/8.30/10 for one/two/three days; buy at the DPB office, validate on board.

Important lines include the following:

Bus 93 Main Train Station to Hodžovo nám

Trolleybus 206 Main Bus Station to Hodžovo nám

Trolleybus 210 Main Bus Station to Main Train Station

Taxi

Standing cabs compulsively overcharge foreigners; an around-town trip should not cost above €10. To save, ask someone to help you order a taxi (not all operators speak English).

AA Euro Taxi (✆16 022)

Free Taxi (✆5596 9696) Cheap.

AROUND BRATISLAVA

Some of the best sights in Bratislava are actually way out of the centre. **Devín Castle** (www.muzeum.bratislava.sk; adult/child €3/1.50; ⊘10am-5pm Tue-Fri, to 7pm Sat & Sun May-Sep), 9km west, was once the military plaything of 9th-century warlord Prince Ratislav. The castle withstood the Turks but got blown up in 1809 by the French. Peer at older bits that have been unearthed and tour a reconstructed palace museum. Bus 29 links Devín with Bratislava's Nový Most (New Bridge) stop, under the bridge. Austria is just across the river from the castle.

Heading east out of the city you'll reach **Danubiana Meulensteen Art Museum** (www.danubiana.sk; Via Danubia, Čunovo; adult/child €6/3), Slovakia's most daring contemporary art museum, innovatively designed on a spit of sculpture-flanked land jutting into the Danube. Boat trips run from the city centre from June to October (€10/6 return, see website for details); otherwise take bus 91 from Nový Most to Čunovo and walk from the terminus (2.5km), or drive.

Hrad Červený Kameň (www.hradcervenykamen.sk; Slovak/foreign-language tour adult €6/7 child €3/3.50), aka the Red Stone Castle, is another member of Slovakia's fortified elite, exemplifying external Gothic resplendence along with interior baroque charm.

DON'T MISS

SMALL CARPATHIAN WINE ROUTE

Wine has been grown on Slovakian soil since at least the 6th century, when Celtic peoples exported their exotic-seeming drink to wine-deprived northern nations. Today there are six wine-growing regions. The Small Carpathians viticulture region extends northwest from Bratislava and is by far the most visitor-friendly, with many vineyards having open days. Twice a year (May and November) 80 wine cellars here open to visitors in the **Days of Open Wine Cellars**. For further information visit these websites:

Slovakwines.com (www.slovakwines.com) General information on Slovakia's wine-growing regions.

Small Carpathian Wine Route (www.mvc.sk) Focuses on this wine-growing region nearest Bratislava, with info on events (some in Slovak only).

The period-furnished rooms are interesting, but the vast cellar/dungeon complex is the highlight. The castle is not red at all, but white: the red refers to the stone it was built on. Two buses each hour connect Častá, the village below the castle, with Bratislava (€2, 1¼ hours).

WEST SLOVAKIA

Stupendous castles loom out of the crags of the Small Carpathians on the main trail northeast of Bratislava, with Trenčín's fortress one of the most magnificent along this heavily fortified stretch. The country's main spa, Piešťany, is en route, and vineyards cloak the fertile lower slopes.

Trenčín

✆032 / POP 56,400

High above the 18th- and 19th-century buildings of the Old Town, Trenčín's mighty castle has all the dark foreboding you'd want from a medieval fortress. Today's form dates from around the 15th century, but the city dates back much further. Roman legionnaires were stationed here (they called it Laugaricio) in the 2nd century AD: you can

PIEŠŤANY

Thermal waters bubble under much of the country, but it's Slovakia's premier spa site, **Piešťany** (www.spapiestany.sk), that attracts most visitors. Just across the river from Piešťany town, on **Kúpelne ostrov** (Spa Island) you can swim in thermal pools, breathe seasidelike air in a salt cave and be wrapped naked in hot mud. Many of the 19th-century buildings sport a new coat of Maria-Theresa-yellow paint; others are more modern. Reserve online for a stay, or head to the *kasa* (cashier) at **Napoleon 1** (☑033-775 7733; spa day package €36; ☺7.30am-7pm) to book day services. **Eva Pools** (adult/child €3/2; ☺11am-5pm) and **Balnea Esplanade Hotel** (per day adult/child €15/10, 3hr €10/7; ☺8am-10pm) have public swimming. Trains run from Bratislava (1¼ hours, €3.25, 12 daily, 87km) and you can continue on the same route to Trenčín (€2, 45 minutes) and the east.

read the inscription that's carved into a cliff in Trenčín to prove it! Afterwards, enjoy the sidewalk cafes and lively nightlife fuelled by the town's university population. The entire centre – including two large, interlocking pedestrian squares – is easily walkable.

◉ Sights & Activities

As well as the attractions listed here, there are other small museums around town that hold some interest, and historic buildings like the **Piarist Church** (Mierové nám) and the former 1913 **Synagogue** (Štúrovo nám) make for good exterior viewing.

Trenčín Castle
CASTLE

(www.muzeumtn.sk; adult/child €4.50/2.50; ☺9am-5.30pm) Spread-eagled domineeringly over a cliff above the Old Town, Trenčín's castle ranks as one of Slovakia's most impressive. Added to over virtually a millennium, much of what you see today is reconstruction – most recently from the 20th century – although there are remnants a-plenty dating to the earliest days. The lower echelons can be explored solo but to enter the keep and other furnished buildings you'll need a guide.

First noted in a Viennese chronicle of 1069, Trenčín Castle developed through the centuries until 1790 when it was damaged by fire.

From the town, climb stairs to reach the lowest level of fortifications and commanding views of the Váh River plain. Two levels higher, via a shop and eateries, you enter the towers and furnished palaces with one of the frequent tours (75 minutes, in Slovak only; call two days ahead to arrange English-speaking guides). The most evocative time to visit is during festivals or on

one of the castle's summer evening two-hour torchlight tours – complete with medieval sword fighting and staged frolics. Wonderful Brezina Forest Park – good for a stroll – lies alongside.

Roman Inscription
ANCIENT SITE

The town's unique claim to fame is a Roman inscription from AD 179; soldier's graffiti commemorating a battle against Germanic tribes. It's carved into the cliff behind the Hotel Elizabeth and can only be viewed through a window in the hotel's staircase; ask at reception.

Galéria Bazovského
MUSEUM

(www.gmab.sk; Palackého 27; adult/child €1.30/0.80; ☺9am-5pm Tue-Sun) Temporary exhibits represent leading 20th-century Slovakian and Czech art, while the permanent collection includes works by local painter Miloš Bazovský.

Town Gate Tower
LOOKOUT

(Mestská Veža; Sládkovičova; adult/child €1/0.50; ☺10am-8pm, closed Oct-May) An inconspicuous glass elevator and then six really steep flights of steps ascend to a 360-degree view of the Old Town.

Ostrov
BEACH

(off Mládežnícka) Floating in the middle of the Váh River, the Ostrov (island) is Trenčín's playground. A freely accessible, small, sandy beach, volleyball court and outdoor swimming pool are part of the attraction. It's just 200m north of the Old Town.

★ Festivals & Events

World music, jazz, rock, techno, hip hop and alternative music are all represented in July's **Bažant Pohoda Festival** (www.pohodafestival.sk), the largest music festival in Slovakia.

🛏 Sleeping

Penzión Svorad HOSTEL €
(☑7430 322; www.svorad-trencin.sk; Palackého 4; dm €18-32, d €28-40; ❄) Peeling linoleum, thin mattresses – but oh, what castle views at this dormitorylike pension (with private bathrooms).

Hotel Pod Hradom HOTEL €€
(☑7481 701; www.podhradom.sk; Matúšova 12; s €65-75, d €76-116; ❀) A well-kept 10-room lodging with its own restaurant on a wee, winding street en route to the castle.

Autocamping na Ostrove CAMPING GROUND €
(☑7434 013; www.slovanet.sk/camping; Ostrov; campsite from €6, bungalow d €17) Riverside bungalow camping ground on the island; has central space for tents.

Hotel Elizabeth HISTORIC HOTEL €€
(☑6506 111; www.hotelelizabeth.sk; Ul gen MR Štefánika 2; s/d €99/115; ❄❋) Newly refurbished, neo-baroque hotel with one of the country's better spas, offering 78 rooms (five are suites). The famous Roman inscription of AD 179 is on the cliff behind: ask at reception to see it.

🍴 Eating & Drinking

Numerous restaurants and cafes line Mierové nám and Štúrovo nám; choose any one for imbibing al fresco.

TOP CHOICE Reštaurácia Bašta SLOVAK €€
(Ostrov; mains €3-11; ❄24hr) Some of the freshest, cooked-to-order Slovak faves we've ever tasted – pork stuffed with spicy *klobasa*, *bryndza* (sheep's cheese) cream soup... Breakfasts are tasty too. Well worth the walk to the Ostrov (island).

TOP CHOICE La Piazzetta BAR
(Mierové nám 20; ❄10am-late) Slovakia's best Italian wine selection, in an amospheric, meticulously run cellar bar. There's great coffee and delectable edible accompaniments.

Cinema Movie Club Restaurant & Bar INTERNATIONAL €
(Palackého 33; mains €3-7; ❄8am-11pm Sun-Thu, 8am-late Fri & Sat; ❄) Student haunt with hearty weekday set lunch menus for under €4. Also shows films.

Restaurant Lánius CZECH €€
(☑744 1978; Mierové nám 20; mains €6-12; ❄11am-midnight) The rustic set-up – creaking beams, wood fireplace – matches the hearty Slovakian fare. The dining room up at the rear of the courtyard is most fun.

Steps Bar BAR
(Sládkovičova 4-6; ❄10am-1am Mon-Thu, 10am-4am Fri & Sat, 4pm-midnight Sun) A sidewalk cafe and upstairs bar that attracts a hip, college-age crowd.

ℹ Information

Culture & Information Centre (☑6504 711; www.visittrencin.sk; Mierové nám 9; ❄8am-6pm Mon-Fri, to 4pm Sat May-Sep, 8am-5pm Mon-Fri Oct-Apr) Relocated to the main square, this is a helpful, well-informed tourist office. Good free map available.

Library of Trenčín (Palackého; ❄8am-6pm Mon, Tue, Thu & Fri, 10am-7pm Wed, to noon-Sat) Internet upstairs (€1 per hour).

Main Post Office (Mierové nám 21)

VUB Bank (Mierové nám 37)

ℹ Getting There & Away

IC and EC trains run regularly to Trenčín from Bratislava (€6.50, 1½ hours), Žilina (€4.50, 1¼ hours) and Poprad (€10, 2¾ hours), among others.

CENTRAL SLOVAKIA

The rolling hills and lolling, forested mountains of central Slovakia are home to the shepherding tradition that defines Slovak culture. This is where the nation's own Robin Hood, Juraj Jánošík, once roamed. Limited train routes means a car is helpful for exploring here. Look roadside for farmers selling local sheep's cheese before you lose yourself in a picturesque valley. Some of the nation's most fabled castles also beckon and, further south, there's the ancient mining town of Banska Štiavnica.

Žilina

☑041 / POP 85,100

Žilina is agreeable enough, but its main draw is as a jumping-off point for forays into the Malá Fatra National Park, surrounding fortresses and folksy villages. The cultural and culinary scene is livening up, though – watch this space.

From the train station in the northeast, a walk along Národná takes you through Nám A Hlinku up to Mariánské nám, the main pedestrian square.

🛌 Sleeping & Eating

The tourist information office can recommend student dorms that take travellers in July and August. Interchangeable cafe-bars lie around Mariánske nám and Hlinka nám: look for names like Café Le Jour, on Hlinka.

Hotel Dubna Skala   HOTEL €€
(🖉5079 100; www.hoteldubnaskala.sk; Hurbanova 8; s/d €95/115; 🅿️❄️🛜) Modern boutique interiors fit surprisingly well within an ornately aged exterior. Within is a well-regarded wine-cellar restaurant and a cafe.

Penzion Central Park   GUESTHOUSE €€
(🖉5622 021; www.penzioncentralpark.sk; s/d €55/75; 🛜🎿) Impressive art nouveau facade meets with slick modern rooms. This pension caters primarily to business travellers but its location is perfect. A spa/swimming pool is attached.

TOP CHOICE **Voyage Voyage**   SLOVAK €€
(Mariánske nám 191; mains about €5) A modernised Slovakian menu in elegant, animated surrounds, with inventive dishes such as chicken fillet stuffed with peaches and cheese.

Trattoria   ITALIAN €€
(🖉5643 535; www.trattoria.sk; Jozefa Vuruma 5; pizzas €4-7) Cosy family-run Italian joint running the gamut of Italian foods and pleasing with most.

☆ Entertainment

TOP CHOICE **Stanica**   THEATRE
(www.stanica.sk; Závodská cesta 3) It's a theatre, arts centre, music venue and relaxed cafe-bar – but what's most incredible is how quickly this little oasis in the old train station has become Žilina's engine of bohemian creativity. May many follow its example.

ℹ️ Information

Main Post Office (Sládkovičova 1)
Tourist Information Office (TIK; 🖉7233 186; www.tikzilina.eu; Andrej Hlinka nám 9; ⏰9am-5pm Mon-Fri, plus 9am-2pm Sat & Sun May-Sep) Town and surrounding-area information available.
Volksbank (Národná 28) Bank and ATM near the train station.

ℹ️ Getting There & Away

Žilina is on the main Bratislava–Košice railway line. Four daily IC (and many more, slower, 'fast') trains head to Bratislava (€9.50, 2¾ hours), Trenčín (€4.50, 1¼ hours), Poprad (€7, 1¾ hours) and Košice (€11, three hours).

Around Žilina

Besides nearby Malá Fatra National Park, a few folk-culture sights within an hour of Žilina are well worth exploring. Martin, and Ružomberok to the east, are key transport hubs.

MARTIN

On the southern side of Malá Fatra National Park, Martin is primarily an industrial town but it sports several small museums and the country's largest *skanzen* (open-air village museum). Traditional buildings (*krčma* – or village pub – included) from all over the region have been moved to the **Museum of the Slovak Village** (Múzeum Slovenské Dediny; www.snm-em.sk; Malá Hora 2; adult/child €2/1; ⏰9am-4.30pm Tue-Sun). Contact the **Tourist Information Office** (🖉4238 776; www.tikmartin.sk; A Kmeťa 22; ⏰9am-5pm Mon-Fri) for more details.

From Žilina it's easiest to take the bus the 35km to Martin (€1.75, 45 minutes, half-hourly). The village museum is 4km southeast of the town. Take local bus 10 from the main station to the last stop and walk the remaining 1km up through the forest (or hail a taxi in town). Martin is also the beginning of Slovakia's best train journey, around Velká Fatra National Park south to Banska Bystrica (€3, 1¼ hours, seven daily).

ČIČMANY

If you've seen a brochure or postcard of Slovakia, you've probably seen a photograph of Čičmany (www.cicmany.viapvt.sk); dark log homes painted with white geometric patterns fill this traditional village. This is no *skanzen;* most houses are private residences, but **Radenov House** (Čičmany 42; adult/child €2/1.30; ⏰9am-4.30pm Tue-Sun Jun-Aug, 8am-3.30pm Tue-Sun Sep-May) is a museum. There's a gift shop, a small restaurant and a pension in the long, narrow settlement. Buses run the 50 minutes south of Žilina (€2) five times a day; return times allow hours to wander and photograph. One of Slovakia's best campsites, **Slnečné Skaly** (🖉904822692; http://camping-raj.sk; Rajecké Teplice; 2 adults & tent €7.50), awaits on the jaunt down near spa town Rajecké Teplice.

VLKOLÍNEC

The folksy mountain village of Vlkolínec, about 71km east and southeast of Žilina, is a Unesco-noted national treasure. The pastel paint and steep roofs on the 45 traditional plastered log cabins are remarkably well maintained. It's easy to imagine a *vlk* (wolf) wandering through this wooded mountainside settlement arranged along a small stream. You pay entry (adult/child €3/2, open 9am to 3pm) to walk around and one of the buildings has been turned into a small house museum, but this is still a living village – if just barely. Of the approximately 40 residents, almost half are schoolchildren. For more information, visit www.vlkolinec.sk.

Two weekday-only buses make the 25-minute (€0.50) journey to Vlkolínec from the Ružomberok train station; last return is at 3.15pm. Otherwise, driving or hiking the 6km uphill from Ružomberok is the only way to get to the village. Direct trains stop in Ružomberok en route to Bratislava (€11.50, 3½ hours, nine daily), Žilina (€3, 1¼ hours, hourly) and, in the other direction, to Poprad (€4.50, 1¼ hours, 17 daily).

Two kilometres west of Ružomberok, **Salaš Krajinka** (www.salaskrajinka.sk; E18; mains €3-9) is one of the country's best sheep dairy restaurants. Buy *bryndza* and other products on-site, or sit down for a full meal in the modern-rustic dining room with a glass wall looking into the barn.

ORAVSKÝ PODZÁMOK

Central Slovakia has numerous castles and ruins, but one of the most notorious is off the beaten track at the tiny community of Oravský Podzámok.

The classic 1922 vampire film *Nosferatu* featured the pointed towers of **Orava Castle** (Oravský hrad; www.oravamuzeum.sk; Oravský Podzámok; adult/child €5/3, with chapel €7/4; �8.30am-5pm, closed Apr), which rise from an impossibly narrow blade of rock above the village. This, one of Slovakia's most complete castles, dates from 1267. Later additions and reconstructions were made, most notably after a fire in 1800. The museum is chock full of weapons, folk art and period furniture. Legend has it the castle contains one mirror where the reflection will make you beautiful, and another that will make you ugly – make sure to ask the difference. Below the castle in the tiny village of Oravský Podzámok there's a pizza pub and a pension.

Buses run at least hourly between here and Ružomberok (€2, 45 minutes), where you can transfer to the Bratislava–Košice train line. Buses also run about every two hours to Žilina (€4, 1½ hours).

Malá Fatra National Park

🗐041

Sentinel-like formations stand watch at the rocky gorge entrance to valleys filled with pine-clad slopes and wave after wave of crescendoing peaks. *Vitajte* (welcome) to the Malá Fatra National Park (Národný Park Malá Fatra), incorporating a chocolate-box-pretty, 200-sq-km swathe of its namesake mountain range. The Vrátna Valley (Vrátna dolina), 25km east of Žilina, lies at the heart of the park. From here you can access the trailheads, ski lifts and a cable car to start your exploration. The straggling, one-street town of Terchová at the lower end of the valley has most services; Chata Vrátna is at the top. The village of Štefanová lies east of the main valley road, 1km uphill from Terchová.

⊙ Sights & Activities

Statue of Juraj Jánošík MONUMENT
Above Terchová sits an immense aluminium statue of Juraj Jánošík, Slovakia's Robin Hood. In early August, much festivity goes on beneath his likeness during the **Jánošík Days** folk festival.

Považké Museum MUSEUM
(www.pmza.sk; Sv Cyrila a Metoda 96; adult/child €2/1; ⊘9am-3.30pm Tue-Sun) Check out the exhibits (Slovak only) depicting the notorious highwayman Juraj Jánošík's exploits (and gruesome death) at this small museum in Terchová above the town info office.

Vrátna Valley PARK
(www.vratna.sk) The road to **Vrátna Valley** in Malá Fatra National Park runs south from Terchová through the crags of **Tiesňavy Gorge**, past picnic sites and scenic stops. The **cable car** (€8.50/10 one-way/return; ⊘8am-6pm mid-Dec–Apr & Jun-Sep, Sat & Sun only Oct–mid-Dec & May) at Vratna Výťah carries you from the top of the valley to **Snilovské saddle** (1524m) below two peaks, **Chleb** (1647m) and **Velký Kriváň** (1709m). Both are on the red ridge trail, one of the most popular in the park. A hike northeast from Chleb over **Hromové** (1636m), **Poludňový grúň** (1636m) and **Stoh** (1608m) to **Medziholie saddle** (1185m) takes about 5½ hours. From there you can descend on the green trail to Štefanová village where there's a bus stop, accommodation and restaurants. Further east, the precipitous gorge of **Horné Diery** is known as Jánošíkové Diery (Jánošík's Holes) for its rock formations

Malá Fatra National Park

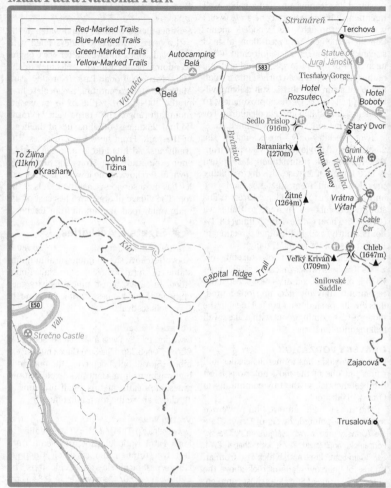

ravined by waterfalls. A challenging 2½-hour woodsy route, involving ascents by waterfall-splashed ladders, runs from Hotel Diery round to Hotel Boboty.

The main summer season is July and August; during other months businesses may close. For serious hiking, VKÚ's 1:50,000 Malá Fatra-Vrátna map (No 110) and Dajama's *Knapsacked Travel: Malá Fatra* are good. In summer, the **Organization for Sport Activities** (☑0903 546 600; www.splavovanie.sk; Starý Dvor; ⊙9am-5pm Jul & Aug) rents mountain bikes (€8) and organises rafting trips (€13 per person).

Vrátna Valley's 14 ski tows and lifts (8am to 4pm) are open December to April. Shacks with **ski rental** (per day from €12) keep the same hours and are located at Starý Dvor, where **ski passes** (main season pass per day adult/child €25/18) are also available.

🛏 Sleeping & Eating

Numerous private cottages are available for rent in the Terchová area, many listed on the information office website (http://www.ter-chova-info.sk/en/ubytovanie.php). No camping is allowed in the park. Eating options in the valley are limited to restaurants at the

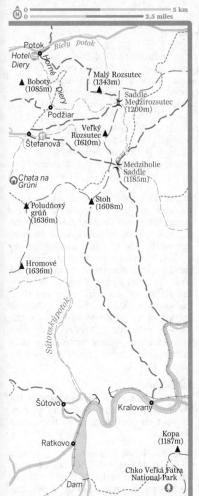

scene: attentive service and gleaming facilities (spa/sauna and appealing restaurant) give it the edge over some of the other old stalwarts. Rooms with gorgeous balcony views cost more. It lies 1km west of Starý Dvor.

Penzión Sagan
PENSION €

(📞0903 744 302; www.penzionsagan.sk; Štefanová 553; s/d incl breakfast €30/50; 🏊🛜) Impeccably kept, pine-clad rooms plus a little restaurant at this guesthouse (with games room) in Štefanová village.

Hotel Boboty
HOTEL €€

(📞5695 228; www.hotelboboty.sk; Nový Dvor; s/d €45/85; @🛜🏊) Services galore – sauna, massage, heated pool, billiards, free ski shuttle – are available at the valley's biggest lodging.

Chata na Grúni
MOUNTAIN HUT €

(📞5695 324; www.chatanagruni.sk; dm without/ with breakfast €12/19) Hikers' hut at the top of Gruni Ski Lift; four- to six-bed dorms and self-service restaurant.

Autocamping Belá
CAMPING GROUND €

(📞5695 135; http://camping.bela.sk; 2 adults with tent €8.50; ⏰May–mid-Oct; 🏊) Fine camping ground with 300 sites and a heated pool. There's a bus stop in front; 5km west of Terchová.

Vŕšky
SLOVAK €€

(📞5627 300; www.penzionvrsky.sk; Terchová; mains €6-14; 🏊🛜) Very popular restaurant with original takes on Slovak food and simple-but-spotless rooms in the pension (d €48). It's on the eastern edge of town on the road to Horné Diery.

Reštaurácia Starý Majer
SLOVAK €€

(📞5695 419; Starý Dvor; mains €5-10; ⏰10am-7pm Sep-May, to 8pm Jun-Aug) Dig into well-done traditional shepherds' dishes at rough-hewn outdoor tables, or inside among rustic farm implements.

main lodgings and a few food stands near the chairlifts and cable car.

TOP CHOICE Hotel Diery
HOTEL €

(📞5695 323; www.hotel-diery.com; Biely Potok; s/d €35/59) Substantial, minimalist rooms in a voluminous, affably run hotel that is also the proud owner of the best restaurant in Malá Fatra, the Koliba. Cuisine isn't Slovak here: it's Central European fusion – and tasty.

Hotel Rozsutec
HOTEL €€

(📞5008 034; www.hotelrozsutec.sk; s/d €45/80; 🛜🏊) A relatively new addition to the hotel

ℹ️ Information

Mountain Rescue Service (📞5695 232; www. hzs.sk) Also offers weather information.

Terchová Tourist Information Centre (📞5695 307; www.ztt.sk; Sv Cyrila a Metoda 96; ⏰8am-4pm Mon-Fri, 10am-1pm Sat & Sun) Maps for sale; ATM in building.

Turistcko-Informačna Chalupa (📞0907534354; www.uteczmesta.sk; Vrátňanská cesta, Terchová; ⏰8am-8pm) Private office that arranges lodgings and activities and provides information.

DON'T MISS

SLOVAKIA'S MOST-VISITED CASTLE

Bojnice Castle (www.bojnicecastle.sk; Bojnice zámok; adult/child €6.50/3; ⊙9am-5pm daily Jun-Sep, Tue-Sun May, 9am-3pm Tue-Sun Oct-Apr) is straight out of a fairy-tale dream, crowned with towers and turrets and crenulated mouldings. The original 12th-century fortification got an early-20th-century redo by the Pálffy family, who modelled it on French romantic castles. It's the country's most popular castle by visitor numbers. The time to visit is during the International Festival of Ghosts & Ghouls in May, when costumed guides put on shows. The palace also gets decked out for Christmas, Valentine's Day and various medieval events. The nearby city of Prievidza has bus connections to Žilina (€3.50, 1¼ hours, 10 daily) and Bratislava (€9.50, 3¼ hours, nine daily). From there take regular local buses 3 or 7 the 3km to Bojnice, a little town with lodging and restaurants.

❶ Getting There & Around

Hourly buses link Žilina with Terchová (€1.80, 40 minutes) and valley stops, terminating near Chata Vrátna at Vrátna Výťah (€2, one hour). Otherwise change in Terchová for local buses. Check schedules at www.cp.atlas.sk.

Banská Bystrica & Around

This area was a mining centre for greater Hungary from the 14th to the 18th centuries. The ancient mining town of Banská Štiavnica, as well as Bojnice Castle, are gems from its lavish past.

BANSKÁ BYSTRICA
📱 048 / POP 79,900

Slovakia's bustling, sixth-largest city, Banská Bystrica has attractions that combine handsome medieval architecture and a riveting insight into Slovakia's communist past. The excellent tourist office (📱415 5085; eng. ksibb.sk; Nám SNP 14; ⊙9am-6pm Mon-Fri, to 3pm Sat) is in the old town hall on the impressive main square. The key sight is arguably the country's best museum, the SNP Museum (www.muzeumsnp.sk; Kapitulská 23; adult/child €2/1; ⊙9am-6pm Tue-Sun May-Sep, to 4pm Tue-Sun Oct-Mar), documenting the Slovak national uprising and WWII Slovakia.

Direct trains serve Bratislava (€10, 3½ hours, every two hours) and, via a spectacular journey, Martin (€3.50, one hour, seven daily) near Malá Fatra National Park. Otherwise change at Zvolen or Vrútky. Destinations by bus include Liptovský Mikuláš (€4, 1¾ hours, hourly) near the High Tatras.

BANSKÁ ŠTIAVNICA
📱 045 / POP 10,500

A time-trapped medieval delight, Banská Štiavnica enjoyed a 16th-century heyday as an internationally renowned architectural showcase and grew to become the old Hungarian Kingdom's third-largest city. As the minerals ran out and mines closed, progress stopped, leaving buildings wonderfully untouched. Meandering among the steeply terraced hillsides now you'll see many of the same Old Town burghers' houses, churches and alleys that you would have seen then. Unesco recognised the town in 1972. At a fraction of its peak population today, the town is primarily a holiday destination with numerous mining-related attractions and two castles facing each other across the steep valley.

◉ Sights

Wandering the steep streets gazing at the buildings is the main attraction. In summer, the open-air pools high above town are a blessing.

Open-Air Mining Museum   MUSEUM
(JK Hella 12; adult/child €5/2.50; ⊙8am-4pm Tue-Sun by tour) Take a trip down into a former working mine, 2km west of the centre. One of numerous affiliates of the Slovak Mining Museum (www.muzeumbs.sk).

Old Castle   CASTLE
(Starozámocká 1; adult/child €4/2; ⊙9am-6pm daily May-Sep, 9am-4pm Tue-Sun Oct-Apr) Town history exhibits in a 16th-century stronghold.

New Castle   CASTLE
(Novozámocká 1; adult/child €2/1; ⊙9am-4pm May-Sep, 9am-4pm Tue-Sun Oct-Apr) A former lookout tower during the Hungarian-Turkish wars, the town's 'new' castle was constructed only five years after the old one; inside are exhibits on the historical struggle against Turkish invasion.

FREE Kalvária — CHURCH

(Calvary; www.kalvaria.sk; end of Pod Kalvlánou; ⊚9am-6pm daily May-Sep, 9am-4pm Tue-Sun Oct-Apr) A dramatic complex of 23 baroque religious buildings (19 chapels, three churches and a statue of the Virgin) cresting a hill 1km west of town.

🛏 Sleeping & Eating

Hostel 6 — HOSTEL €

(✆0905106705; www.hostel6.sk; Andreja Sládkoviča 6; dm/tr €13/39; ⊕@🖶) A hospitable little backpacker hostel with thoroughly modern amenities inside an old building. Choose from a private double, or five- or six-bed dorms. Great balcony views, full kitchen and laundry.

Penzión Príjemný Oddych — PENSION €

(✆6921 301; www.prijemnyoddych.sk; Starozámocká 3; r €43-49; 🖶) Distinctly *prijemný* (pleasing) hostelry below the Old Castle with a small on-site restaurant, playground and sauna.

Penzión Kachelman — SLOVAKIAN €

(✆6922 319; www.kachelman.sk; Kammerhofská 18; mains €5-10; 🕿) Rustic Renaissance-era inn/restaurant with a long and varied Slovak menu and pizzas (€3 to €4). It's close to the bus stop, below the Old Town centre. Budget-friendly doubles here are €37.

Art Cafe — CAFE €

(Academická 2; €2-7; ⊚8am-11pm) The best in town for wickedly strong coffee, fabulous cakes and lovingly prepared food, as well as beer and live music. Has an enticing terrace.

❶ Information

City Tourist Information Office (✆6949 653; www.banskastiavnica.sk; Nám sv Trojice 6; ⊚8am-6pm May-Sep, 8am-4pm Oct-Apr) Semiprecious stones for sale in addition to info; beside a branch of the mining museum. Two internet terminals (€1 per hour).

❶ Getting There & Away

Banská Štiavnica is not the easiest place to get to. Only one direct bus departs from Bratislava daily (€8.50, 3½ hours), at 4.40pm. Otherwise, all bus and train arrivals require a change in Zvolen or Banská Bystrica, which has three direct buses (€3, one hour). Check schedules at www.cp.atlas.sk.

From the train/bus stations it's a 2/1.5km climb uphill through the outskirts to Nám sv Trojice, the main Old Town square. Local buses and taxis are available to take you up into town.

TATRA MOUNTAINS

Alpine peaks in Slovakia? As you look upon the snow-strewn jagged mountains rising like an apparition east of Liptovský Mikuláš, you may think you're imagining things. But there they are indeed. The High Tatras are undoubtedly where the adventure-junkies head, along with those who can afford the luxury mountain resorts, mostly located here. Tucked into the eastern end of the peaks is the Belá Tatras: the loveliest and least-discovered region.

Poprad

♪052 / POP 54,300 / TRANSPORT HUB

Poprad will likely be your first experience of mountain country, being the nearest sizeable city to the High Tatras and a major transport hub for the region. Most visitors just experience the so-so city centre but the 16th-century neighbourhood of Spišská Sobota and a popular thermal water park might make you linger. From the adjacent train and bus stations the central pedestrian square, Nám sv Egídia, is a five-minute walk south on Alžbetina.

⊙ Sights & Activities

Spišská Sobota — NEIGHBOURHOOD

Sixteenth-century Spiš-style merchants' and artisans' houses line the Spišská Sobota town square. The suburb is 1.2km northeast of Poprad's train station.

Aqua City — SPA

(✆7851 111; www.aquacity.sk; Športová 1397; packages per day €16-29; ⊚8am-9pm) Sauna, swim, bubble and slide zones are all part of Poprad's thermal water park. The park employs admirably green initiatives; the heat and electricity derive from geothermal and solar sources.

Adventoura — ADVENTURE SPORTS

(✆903641549; www.adventoura.eu; Uherova 33) Dog sledding, hut-to-hut hikes, snowboarding...this company can organise the works. Day prices for trips around the Tatras start at about €90.

🛏 Sleeping & Eating

There's a large Billa grocery store off Jiřho Wolera just east of the bus station.

TOP CHOICE **Penzión Sabato** B&B €€
(☏7769 580; www.sabato.sk; Sobotské nám 6; r incl breakfast €90; 🛜) Exposed stone arches, a cobblestone courtyard and open-hearth restaurant reveal this inn's 17th-century age – as do romantically decorated rooms.

Penzión Plesnivec PENSION €
(☏911110410; www.penzion-plesnivec.sk; s/d €25/35; 🛜) The friendliest welcome in Poprad. Rooms are bright, clean and simple and in the tribally decorated traveller-friendly bar/common room, these folks can help with High Tatras planning. English and Spanish spoken. It's between Aqua City and Spišská Sobota.

Hotel Cafe Razy PENSION €
(☏7764 101; www.hotelcaferazy.sk; Nám Sv Egídia 58; s/d €29/39; 🛜) Sane and simple rooms upstairs; semi-crazy pub and pizza cafe down. Breakfast is €5. On the modern main square.

ℹ Information

City Information Centre (☏7721 700; www.poprad.sk; Dom Kultúry Štefániková 72; ⊙8am-5pm Mon-Fri, 9am-noon Sat) Town info only; lists private rooms.

ℹ Getting There & Away

AIR Poprad-Tatry International Airport (www.airport-poprad.sk; Na Letisko 100) is 5km west of the centre but doesn't receive any regular flights.

BUS Buses serve Levoča (€1.60, 45 minutes, hourly), Bardejov (€4.50, 2¼ hours, six daily) and Zakopane in Poland (€5, two hours, two daily April to October).

CAR Pick-up around town is available by pre-arrangement from **Car Rental Tatran** (☏0903 250 255; www.autopozicovnatatry.sk).

TRAIN Electric trains traverse the 14km or so to the High Tatras resorts. Mainline trains run directly to Bratislava (€16, four hours, hourly, four IC trains daily), Trenčín (€10, 2¾ hours, hourly, four IC trains daily) and Košice (€5, 1¼ hours, 24 daily).

High Tatras

☏052

The High Tatras (Vysoké Tatry), the tallest range in the Carpathian Mountains, tower over most of Eastern Europe. Some 25 peaks measure above 2500m. The massif is only 25km wide and 78km long, but photo opportunities are enough to get you fantasising about a National Geographic career – pristine snowfields, ultramarine mountain lakes, crashing waterfalls, undulating pine forests and shimmering alpine meadows. Most of this jagged range is part of the Tatra National Park (Tanap). Not that this fact has arrested development on the Slovakian ski slopes, much to the chagrin of watchdog groups like International Union for Conservation of Nature. The Tatra National Park complements a similar park across the peaks in Poland.

Midmountain, three main resort towns string west to east. Štrbské Pleso is the traditional ski centre and is most crowded, with construction galore. Eleven kilometres east, Smokovec is an amalgam of the Nový (New), Starý (Old), Dolný (lower) and Horný (upper) settlements. Here there's still a bit of a turn-of-the-20th-century heyday feel, plus numerous lodgings and the most services. Five kilometres further, Tatranská Lomnica is the quaintest, quietest village. All have mountain access by cable car, funicular or chairlift. Poprad is the closest city (with mainline train station and airport), 14km south of central Starý Smokovec.

When planning your trip, keep in mind that the highest trails are closed to snow from November to mid-June. June and July can be especially rainy; July and August are the warmest (and most crowded) months. Hotel prices and crowds are at their lowest from October to April.

◉ Sights & Activities

A 600km network of trails covers the alpine valleys and some peaks, with full-service mountain huts where hikers can stop for a meal or a rest along the way. Routes are colour coded and easy to follow. Pick up one of the numerous detailed maps and hiking guides available at bookstores and information offices. Park regulations require you to keep to trails and refrain from picking flowers. Be aware that many trails are rocky and uneven, watch for sudden thunderstorms on ridges where there's no protection, and know that the assistance of the Mountain Rescue Service is not free.

Distances for hikes in Slovakian national parks are officially given in hours rather than kilmetres. For hikes here we have therefore given hikes in hours, as per official trail estimates. Depending on the gradient and terrain, in the High Tatras a reasonably fit person can expect to hike between 2km and 5km per hour.

High Tatras

Legend:
- Red-Marked Trails
- Blue-Marked Trails
- Green-Marked Trails
- Yellow-Marked Trails

5 km
2.5 miles

To Ždiar (8km);
Poland (21km)

POLAND

EAST SLOVAKIA

CENTRAL SLOVAKIA

Belá Tatras (Belianske Tatry)

Vysoké Tatry

Tatranská Magistrála Trail

Studený Potok

Tatranská Matliare

Tatranská Lomnica

Hotel & Intercamp Tatranec

Lomnica
Eurocamp

Stará Lesná

Velká Lomnica

Velká Slavkov

Štart

Stará Lesna

Nová Lesná

Velká Slavkov

Skalnaté pleso

Gondola

Skalnaté Ski Lift

Cable Car

Lomnický štít (2634m)

Lomnické Sedlo (2190m)

Zamkovského Chata

Bilíkova chata

Hrebienok

Tatranská Lesná

Horný Smokovec

Dolný Smokovec

Velká Slavkov

To Poprad (6km)

Elektráka

Malá Studená Valley

Velká Studená Valley

Zbojnícka Chata

Slavkovský štít (2452m)

Východná Vysoká (2429m)

Funicular Railway

Magistrála Trail

Starý Smokovec

Nový Smokovec

Bielovodská Valley

Vysoká (2560m)

Gerlachovský štít (2654m)

Sliezsky dom

Koncistá (2538m)

Vysoké Tatry

Tatranská

Rysy (2499m)

Morskie Oko Lake

Velké Hincovo pleso

Malé Hincovo pleso

Czarny Staw

Vysoká (2499m)

Vysoké Tatry

Chata Popradské Pleso

Popradské pleso

Vyšné Hágy

Tatra National Park

Popradské Pleso

Furkotský štít (2405m)

Predné Solisko (2093m)

Chata pod Soliskom

Kriván (2494m)

Chairlift

Štrbské Pleso

Cog Railway

Elektráka

Tatranská Štrbá

Tatranská Lieskovec

537

534

539

E50

537

DON'T MISS

HIGH TATRAS HIKES

The 65km-long **Tatranská Magis-trála Trail** starts at the base of the Western (Zapadné) Tatras, but mostly runs beneath the peaks (between 1300m and 1800m) of the High Tatras. Because there's a relatively small elevation change, the trail is accessible by cable-assisted cars and lifts, and there are huts to stop and eat at; you need not be in peak mountaineering shape to experience it. Some of our favourite routes are Skalnaté pleso to Hrebienok (2½ hours), Štrbské Pleso to Popradské pleso (1¼ hours) and Skalnaté pleso to Chata pri Zelenom plese (2¼ hours).

SMOKOVEC RESORT TOWNS

From Starý Smokovec a **funicular railway** (www.vt.sk; adult/child return €7/5; ⏱7am-7pm Jul & Aug, 8am-5pm Sep-Jun) takes you up to **Hrebienok** (1280m). From here you have a great view of the **Velká Studená Valley** and a couple of hiking options. The red **Tatranská Magistrála Trail** transects the southern slopes of the High Tatras for 65km from start to finish. Bilíkova chata, a log-cabin lodge and restaurant, is only a 10-minute hike from Hrebienok. Following the Magistrála east on an easy trail section to **Studený Potok** waterfalls takes about 30 minutes. Heading west instead, you could follow the Magistrála to the lakeside **Sliezsky dom** hut (two hours), down a small green connector trail, to the yellow-marked trail back to Starý Smokovec (four hours total).

Mountain climbers scale to the top of **Slavkovský štít** (2452m) via the blue trail from Starý Smokovec (seven to eight hours return). To ascend the peaks without marked hiking trails (**Gerlachovský štít** included), you must hire a guide. Contact the **Mountain Guides Society Office** (☎4422 066; www.tatraguide.sk; Starý Smokovec 38; ⏱10am-6pm Mon-Fri, noon-6pm Sat & Sun, closed weekends Oct-May); guides cost from €150 and the society runs classes too.

At the top of the funicular, tow-assist snow sledging and summer tubing are to be had at **Funpark** (⏱10am-4pm Jul & Aug, from 9am Dec-Feb).

Rent mountain bikes at **Tatrasport** (www.tatry.net/tatrasport; Starý Smokovec 38; per day €12; ⏱8am-6pm), above the bus-station parking lot.

TATRANSKÁ LOMNICA & AROUND

While in the Tatras, you shouldn't miss the ride to the 2634m summit of **Lomnický štít** (bring a jacket!). From Lomnica, a **gondola** (www.vt.sk; adult/child return €15/10; ⏱8.30am-7pm Jul & Aug, to 4pm Sep-Jun) pauses midstation at **Štart** before it takes you to the winter-sports area, restaurant and lake at **Skalnaté pleso**. From there, a smaller **cable car** (www.vt.sk; adult/child return €24/17; ⏱8.30am-5.30pm Jul & Aug, to 3.30pm Sep-Jun) goes on to the summit. The second leg of the journey requires a time-reserved ticket. On sunny summer days time slots do sell out, so get in line early. You're given 50 minutes at the top to admire the views, walk the observation platforms and sip a beverage in the cafe before your return time.

One of the top Tatra day hikes starts from Skalnaté pleso, following the rocky Magistrála Trail west past amazingly open views back into the forest at **Zamkovského chata** (1¼ hours), an atmospheric mountain hut and restaurant. Continue downhill, along the even rockier, steeper path past the **Obrovský** and **Studený Potok** waterfalls on to Hrebienok (three hours total). From there the funicular takes you down to Starý Smokovec.

Get off the cable car at Štart and you're at **Funtools** (www.vt.sk; rides per hour €5; ⏱9am-6pm Jun-Sep), from where you can take a fast ride down the mountain on a two-wheeled scooter, a lugelike three-wheel cart or on a four-wheel modified skateboard.

Much winter-sport development has taken place on the slopes above Tatranská Lomnica; the area now counts about 30 skiable hectares. From Skalnaté pleso a high-speed winter **quadlift** (adult/child €8/5.50; ⏱9am-4pm) hoists riders to **Lomnické sedlo**, a 2190m saddle below the summit, and access to an advanced 6km-long ski run (1300m drop). A multimillion-euro renovation also added a high-speed **six-seat chairlift** (€10; ⏱9am-4pm) from the village up to Štart, snow-making capacity and a ski-in/ski-out car park. **Vysoké Tatry** (www.vt.sk; Tatranská Lomnica 7; day-lift ticket adult/child €24/17; ⏱9am-3.30pm Dec-Apr) sells passes from the base of the cable car, where ski rental (from €15 per day) and lockers are also available.

ŠTRBSKÉ PLESO & AROUND

Condo and hotel development continue unabated in the village but the namesake clear blue glacial lake (*pleso*) remains beautiful, surrounded by dark pine forest and rocky peaks. **Row boats** (per 45min €15-20; ⏱10am-6pm May-Sep) can be rented from the dock by Grand Hotel Kempinski: exorbitant, but you're on the water in front of Slovakia's most-photographed scenes.

In good weather the streets are overrun, as one of the most popular day hikes departs from here. Follow the red-marked **Magistrála Trail** uphill from the train station on a rocky forest trail for about 1¼ hours to **Popradské pleso**, an even more idyllic lake at 1494m. The busy mountain hut there has a large, self-service restaurant. You can return to the train line by following the paved road down to the Popradské pleso stop (45 minutes). Or the Magistrála zigzags dramatically up the mountainside from Popradské pleso and then traverses east towards Sliezsky dom and the Hrebienok funicular above Starý Smokovec (5¾ hours).

There is also a year-round **chairlift** (www.parksnow.sk; adult/child return €10/7; ⊗8am-3.30pm) up to **Chata pod Soliskom**, from where it's a one-hour walk north along a red trail to the 2093m summit of **Predné Solisko**.

Park Snow (www.parksnow.sk; day-lift ticket adult/child €19/13.50; ⊗8.30am-3.30pm), Štrbské Pleso's popular ski and snowboard resort, has two chairlifts, four tow lines, 12km of easy-to-moderate runs, one jump and a snow-tubing area.

🛏 Sleeping

For a full listing of Tatra lodgings, look online at www.tatryinfo.eu. Cheaper sleeps are available in small settlements like Nová Lesná down the hill or east over the ridge at Ždiar in the Belá Tatras. No wild/backcountry camping is permitted: there is a camping ground near Tatranská Lomnica. For the quintessential Slovak mountain experience, you can't beat hiking from one *chata* (a mountain hut; could be anything from a shack to a chalet) to the next, high up among the peaks. Food (optional meal service or restaurant) is always available. Beds fill up, so book ahead.

SMOKOVEC RESORT TOWNS

Look for reasonable, been-there-forever boarding houses with one-word names like 'Delta' just west of the Nový Smokovec electric train stop on the several no-name streets that run to the south.

TOP CHOICE Penzión Tatra PENSION €

(☑0903650802; www.tatraski.sk; Starý Smokovec 66; s/d incl breakfast €23/46; @🕿) Big and colourful modern rooms fill this classic 1900 alpinesque building above the train station. It's super-central. Billiard table and ski storage available.

Villa Siesta HOTEL €€

(☑4423 024; www.villasiesta.sk; Nový Smokovec 88; d €64, ste €83-113; 🕿) Light fills this airy, contemporary mountain villa furnished in natural hues. The full restaurant, sauna and jacuzzi are a bonus.

Grand Hotel HOTEL €€€

(☑4870 000; www.grandhotel.sk; Starý Smokovec 38; r €99-179; 🕿🖭) More than 100 years of history are tied up in Starý Smokovec's *grande dame*. Rooms could use an update.

Penzion Vesna PENSION €

(☑4422 774; www.penzionvesna.sk; Nový Smokovec 69; s/d €25/50) Rambling, good-value, family-run pension with some apartments available. Heading left over the electric railway tracks after the Palace Hotel, it's down a small road immediately to the left.

Bilíkova Chata MOUNTAIN HUT €

(☑4422 439; www.bilikovachata.sk; s/d without bathroom €28/56) Basic log-cabin hotel with full-service restaurant among the clouds; only a seven-minute walk from Hrebienok funicular station.

Zbojnícka Chata MOUNTAIN HUT €

(☑0903638000; www.zbojnickachata.sk; dm incl breakfast €20) Sixteen-bed dorm room, self-service eatery and small kitchen; at 1960m, a four-plus hours' hike up from Hrebienok.

TATRANSKÁ LOMNICA & AROUND

Look for private rooms (*privat* or *zimmer frei*), from €15 per person, on the back streets south and east of the train station. You can book ahead online at www.tatry.sk and www.tanap.sk/homes.html.

Grandhotel Praha HOTEL €€

(☑4467 941; www.grandhotelpraha.sk; Tatranská Lomnica; r incl breakfast €85-175; @🖭) Remember when travel was elegant and you dressed for dinner? Well, the 1899 Grandhotel's sweeping marble staircase and crystal chandeliers do. Rooms are appropriately classic and there's a snazzy spa here, high above the village.

Penzión Encian PENSION €

(☑4467 520; www.encian.eu; Tatranská Lomnica 32; s/d €30/47; @) Steep roofs, overflowing flowerboxes and a small restaurant hearth: Encian exudes mountain appeal. Breakfast buffet is €5.

MULTIRESORT SKI PASSES

Park Snow and Vysoký Tatry resorts, the ski concessions in Štrbské Pleso and Tatranská Lomnica have all joined forces to offer multiday, multiresort lift passes (three-day adult/child €93/65). The **Super Slovak Ski Pass** (www.vt.sk; 10-day adult €260) covers some of the main resorts as well as other smaller ski areas around Slovakia.

Penzion Daniela   PENSION €
(www.penziondaniela.sk; Tatranská Lomnica 40c; s/d €26/52) The five rooms are plainer than the rustic log chalet exterior suggests, but this is still Tatranská Lomnica's homeliest options.

Zamkovského Chata   MOUNTAIN HUT €
(☏4422 636; www.zamka.sk; per person €15-18) Atmospheric wood chalet with four-bed bunk rooms and restaurant; great hike stop midway between Skalnaté Pleso and Hrebienok.

Hotel & Intercamp Tatranec   CAMPING GROUND €
(☏4467 092; www.hoteltatranec.com; Tatranská Lomnica 202; campsite €7-10.50, d/cabin €85/96) Ageing six-person cabins, motel and restaurant – with an open tent field. North of the 'T Lomnica zast' stop on the train line to Studený Potok.

ŠTRBSKÉ PLESO & AROUND

Development and crowds make staying in this village our last choice, with one grand exception.

TOP CHOICE Grand Hotel Kempinski   LUXURY HOTEL €€€
(☏3262 554; www.kempinski.com/hightatras; Kupelna 6, Štrbské Pleso; r €400-450, ste €600-2800; ✳@≋) The swankiest Tatra accommodation is the classic, villalike Kempinski, enticing high-end travellers with evening turn-down service, heated marble bathroom floors and incredible lake views. See the mountains stretch before you through two-storey glass from the luxury spa.

Chata Pod Soliskom   MOUNTAIN HUT €
(☏0917 655 446; www.chatasolisko.sk; Štrbské Pleso; dm €16) Small log hostel (eight beds), nice terrace, no hiking required; next to the chairlift terminus at 1800m.

Chata Popradské Pleso   MOUNTAIN HUT €
(☏910948160; www.popradskepleso.sk; dm €14-18, s/d €23/46) Sizeable mountain hotel with restaurant and bar. It's a one-hour rugged hike up from the village or a paved hike up from Popradské pleso train stop.

Hotel Patria   HOTEL €€
(☏7848 999; s €81-121, d €110-164) This is where those Communist leaders holidayed back in the '70s...at least, that's the feel the gargantuan Hotel Patria gives. But somehow, we've got a soft spot for it. The rooms have views as good as the Kempinski and the restaurant's alright. It's on the other side of the lake from Štrbské Pleso, 1km from the village itself.

Eating & Drinking

The resort towns are close enough that it's easy to sleep in one and eat in another. There's at least one grocery store per town. Nightlife is limited here.

SMOKOVEC RESORT TOWNS

A couple of oft-changing discos are scattered around; ask for the latest when you arrive.

TOP CHOICE Reštaurácia Svišť   SLOVAKIAN €€
(Nový Smokovec 30; mains €6-13; ⊙6-11pm) From hearty dumplings to beef fillet with wine reduction, this stylish Slovakian restaurant does it all well – and it's surprisingly reasonably priced.

Pizzeria La Montanara   ITALIAN €
(Starý Smokovec 22; mains €3.50-6; ⊙11am-9pm) A local favourite, La Montanara serves good pies, pastas, soups and vegetables. It's above a grocery store on the eastern edge of town.

Koliba Smokovec   SLOVAK €
(Starý Smokovec 5; mains €7-15; ⊙3-10pm) A traditional rustic grill restaurant; some evening folk music. There's a **pension** (s/d €25/40) too.

Tatry Pub   PUB
(Tatra Komplex, Starý Smokovec; ⊙3pm-1am Sun-Thu, 3pm-3am Fri & Sat; 🖥) The official watering hole of the Mountain Guide Club is a lively place to drink, with a full schedule of dart tournaments, concerts etc.

Cafe Hoepfner   CAFE
(Starý Smokovec 22, Hotel Smokovec; cakes €1-3) Friendly, local cafe with cakes and coffees; live jazz on summer Saturday evenings.

TATRANSKÁ LOMNICA & AROUND

Hikers can carb-load at predictable Slovakian eateries by the train station. The restaurant at Grandhotel Praha has the best food; for the chairlift-bound there's decent pizza up at Štart cable-car station.

Reštaurácia U Medveda CZECH, SLOVAKIAN €€
(Tatranská Lomnica 88; mains €5-12) A good, off-the-beaten-track choice (south by the post office) for traditional cooking. Grilled specialities are a highlight.

Humno BAR
(Tatranská Lomnica; ⏱10am-midnight Sun-Thu, to 4am Fri & Sat) It's a club, it's cocktail bar, it's an après-ski... With capacity to hold 300, one of Lomnica's newest ventures can afford to be a little of everything. At the cable-car station base.

ŠTRBSKÉ PLESO & AROUND
Food stands line the road above the train station, on the way to the chair lift.

Reštaurácia Furkotka SLOVAKIAN €
(www.furkotka.sk; Štrbské Pleso; mains €3-6; ⏱11am-midnight) Easy...right outside the Štrbské Pleso electric railway station, here's your snug one-stop-shop for good food, beer, coffee, cake and alright **accommodation** (r per person €10-24).

Koliba Patria SLOVAKIAN €€
(southern lake shore, Štrbské Pleso; mains €6-15) Come here for the lovely lakeside terrace and complex meat dishes. It's certainly more refined than a typical *koliba* (rustic mountain restaurant serving Slovak sheep-herder specialities).

❶ Information
All three main resort towns have ATMs on the main street.

Emergency
Mountain Rescue Service (☏421-(0)52 7877 711, emergency 18 300; www.hzs.sk; Horný Smokovec 52) The main office of Slovakia.

Internet Access
U Michalka Café (Starý Smokovec 4; per hr €2; ⏱10am-10pm; 🖥) Pleasant cafe with four terminals, great tea and strudel.
Tatranská Lomnica Library (⏱9am-3.30pm Mon, Thu & Fri)

Tourist Information
Note that information offices do not book rooms; they hand out a brochure that lists some – not all – accommodation.
Tatra Information Office Starý Smokovec (TIK; ☏4423 440; Starý Smokovec 23; ⏱8am-8pm Mon-Fri, to 1pm Sat) Largest area info office, with the most brochures.
TIK Štrbské Pleso (☏4492 391; www.tatry-info.sk; Štrbské Pleso; ⏱8am-4pm) Provides good trail info especially; uphill north from the Hotel Toliar. Tiny museum (natural history mostly) to peruse.
TIK Tatranská Lomnica (☏4468 119; www.tatryinfo.sk; Cesta Slobody; ⏱10am-6pm Mon-Fri, 9am-1pm Sat) Has the most helpful staff; opposite Penzión Encian on the main street.

Travel Agencies
T-Ski Travel (☏0905 350 810; www.slovakiatravel.sk; Starý Smokovec 46; ⏱9am-4pm Mon-Thu, to 5pm Fri-Sun) Books lodgings, arranges

TRANSPORT FROM THE TATRAS

Bus

DESTINATION	DEPARTURE POINT	PRICE (€)	DURATION (MIN)	FREQUENCY
Starý Smokovec	Poprad	0.90	15	every 30 min
Štrbské Pleso	Poprad	1.60	60	every 45 min
Tatranská Lomnica	Poprad	1.20	35	hourly
Ždiar	Tatranská Lomnica	1	30	8 daily

Train

DESTINATION	DEPARTURE POINT	PRICE (€)	DURATION (MIN)
Starý Smokovec	Poprad	1.50	25
Starý Smokovec	Štrbské Pleso	1.50	40
Štrbské Pleso	Poprad	2	70
Tatranská Lomnica	Poprad	1.50	25-40
Tatranská Lomnica	Štrbské Pleso	2	60

ski and mountain-bike programs, offers rafting and other tours outside the Tatras. Located at the funicular station.

Websites

High Tatras Tourist Trade Association (www. tatryinfo.sk) Comprehensive overview of the area, including accommodation.

Tatra National Park (www.tanap.org) National park website.

Tatry.sk (www.tatry.sk) Official website of Tatra towns; look under 'Maps' for village layouts.

ℹ️ Getting There & Around

To reach the Tatras by public transport, switch in Poprad. From there a narrow-gauge electric train makes numerous stops in the resort towns along the main road; buses go to smaller, downhill villages as well. Either way, to get between Štrbské Pleso and Tatranská Lomnica, change in Starý Smokovec. Check schedules at www.cp.atlas.sk.

TRAIN From 6am until 10pm, electric trains (TEZ) run more or less hourly. Buy individual TEZ tickets at stations and block tickets (one to three) at tourist offices. Validate all on-board.

Belá Tatras

📞 052

Travel east over the High Tatra ridges and you start to hear Slovak spoken with a Polish accent. Goral folk culture is an intricate part of the experience in the small Belá Tatras (Belianské Tatry). Traditional wooden cottages, some with striking red-and-white graphic designs, are still being built today in the main village of Ždiar. A rustic, laid-back, more local-oriented atmosphere pervades here, from where it's an easy jaunt on to Poland (in peak season). Heck, it's almost close enough to walk.

ŽDIAR

Decorated timber cottages line Ždiar, the oldest Tatra settlement, inhabited since the 16th century. Goral traditions have been both bolstered and eroded by tourism. Several sections of the village are historical reservations, including the **Ždiar House Museum** (Ždiarsky Dom; €1; ⊙10am-4pm Tue-Fri, 10am-noon Sat & Sun), a tiny place with colourful local costumes and furnishings.

Cross over the main road from the museum and a green trail skirts the river through **Monkova Valley** (880m), a level hike with very little elevation change. After 45 minutes the trail climbs up over **Širkové saddle** (1826m) and gets you to **Kopské sad-**

dle (1750m) in about four hours total (seven hours return). Past this point you've crossed into the High Tatras; Chata pri Zelenom plese is an hour away and the cable car to Tatranská Lomnica is 2½ hours beyond that.

West of the main road are two ski areas; in summer one becomes **Bikepark Bachledova** (www.skibachledova.sk; ⊙9am-4pm mid-Jul–mid-Sep). Here you can rent mountain bikes (from €5 per hour), chairlift them up the hill (€5 per ride) and thunder down.

🛏️ Sleeping & Eating

Ždiar has multiple pensions and *privaty* (here private rooms are sizeable lodgings with shared-facility rooms for rent, from €11 per person). Odds are pretty good if you just show up, or check www.zdiar.sk under *ubytovanie*. If everywhere else is shut for food, Buffet Livia serves beer and goulash, goulash, goulash.

TOP CHOICE Ginger Monkey Hostel HOSTEL € (📞52 4498 084; www.gingermonkey.eu; Ždiar 294; dm/d €13/32; @🛜♨) Sublime mountain views from a comfy Goral-style house, round-the-clock tea, laundry, free breakfast and an unexpected sense of traveller camaraderie. Clearly the world-travelling owner/managers have picked up some tips... The place has a full kitchen, where a communal dinner may be cooking (by donation), or the whole group might go out eating (and drinking!) together. Don't just book one night; you'll end up extending. Cat, dog and chickens on site.

Penzión Kamzík PENSION € (📞4498 226; www.penzionkamzik.sk; Ždiar 513; s/d €11/22; 🛜) Cheerful staff, modern rooms, small restaurant, table tennis and sauna.

Goralska Karčma SLOVAKIAN € (Ždiar 460; mains €3-6) This *krčma* (traditional rural pub) serves all the regional specialities, like potato pancakes stuffed with a spicy sauté.

Rustika Pizzeria ITALIAN € (Ždiar 334; pizza €4-6; ⊙5-10pm) Wood-fired pizza in a rambling old log house midvillage.

Ždiarsky Dom SLOVAK € (Ždiar 55; mains €3-6) Rustic Slovakian cooking next door to the little museum.

ℹ️ Information

PLP Shop (📞0903 642 492; Ždiar 333; ⊙9am-noon & 3-6pm) Souvenir shop, info office and bicycle rental (from €12 per day) by Rustika Pizzeria.

ⓘ Getting There & Away

Bus is the only way to get to the Belá Tatras. Poland (open EU border) is 14km north of Ždiar. For Slovak schedules, check www.cp.atlas.sk; for Polish, see also http://strama.eu. Buses from Ždiar connect directly with Poprad (€2, one hour, nine daily), Starý Smokovec (€1.60, 40 minutes, 11 daily) and Tatranská Lomnica (€1, 30 minutes, hourly). Between April and October, buses from Poprad stop in Ždiar en route to Zakopane in Poland (€2.20, 50 minutes, two daily).

EAST SLOVAKIA

Life gets, well, more laid-back the further east you venture. Somehow picturesque towns such as Levoča and Bardejov have avoided modern bustle and unfortunate 20th-century architectural decisions, while the national parks beckon with untrammelled wildernesses that are free from those Tatras-bound tourists.

Kežmarok

⏀052 / POP 16,800

Snuggled beneath the broody High Tatras peaks, Kežmarok's pocket-sized Old Town square with distinctive churches and a small castle seems especially agreeable. The influence of original 13th-century Germanic settlers pervades the architecture even today. During July the European Folk Craft Market – one of the nation's largest – comes to town.

From the adjacent bus and train stations, 1km northwest of the pedestrian centre, follow Dr Alexandra street to the main square, Hlavné nám. The red-and-green, pseudo-Moorish New Evangelical Church (cnr Toporcerova & Hviezdoslavovo; admission €2; ⏀10am-noon & 2-4pm Tue-Sat, closed Nov-Apr), c 1894, dominates the south end of town. Admission covers entry to the more evocative Old Wooden Evangelical Church, built in 1717 without a single nail. It has an amazing interior of carved and painted wood, as well as an original organ.

At the other end of the square, the stumpy, mansionlike 15th-century Kežmarok Castle (www.kezmarok.com; Hradné nám 45; adult/child €3/1.50; ⏀9am-4pm by tour) is a museum with period furniture and archaeology exhibits.

You'll find cafes aplenty around pedestrianised Hlavné nám. If you're staying overnight, try the diminutive but elegant Hotel Hviezdoslav (Hlavne Nam; s/d €59/69) on this square, in the former house of the famed Slovak poet of the same name; it has a good restaurant. Bus connections also mean the town is a viable day trip from the High Tatras.

Kežmarok Information Agency (⏀4492 135; www.kezmarok.net; Hlavné nám 46; ⏀8.30am-4.15pm Mon-Fri, 8.30am-1pm Sat) has loads more information. Buses connect directly to Poprad (€1, 30 minutes, half-hourly), Tatranská Lomnica (€1, 30 minutes, hourly), Ždiar (€1.60, 40 minutes, four daily or change in Tatranská Lomnica) and Levoča (€1.30, one hour, four daily or change in Poprad).

Pieniny National Park

⏀052

People hit 21-sq-km Pieniny National Park (www.pieniny.sk) to raft the river beneath impressive 500m-tall cliffs. Along with a Polish park on the north bank, Pieniny protects the Dunajec Gorge, east of the Slovak village of Červený Kláštor.

At the mouth of the gorge, rooms in the fortified 14th-century Red Monastery (Červený Kláštor; www.muzeumcervenyklastor.sk; adult/child €3/1; ⏀8am-7pm Jul & Aug, 9am-5pm Apr-Jun, Sep & Oct, 10am-4pm Mon-Fri Nov-Mar) hold a diminutive museum, but the main reason why you're here is to float. There are two departure points for a river float trip (⏀4282 840; www.pltnictvo. sk; adult/child €10/5; ⏀9am-dusk May-Oct) on Rte 543: one opposite the monastery, another 1km upriver west of the village. Most visitors pile into one of the continually launching, traditional – and dry – *pltě* (shallow, flat-bottom wood rafts). But for €40 to €50 per person you can be outfitted for a wet, and slightly wilder, rubber-raft ride. Don't be expecting Class V thrills though. The Dunajec River is a fairly sedate 1½-hour experience terminating near the Slovak village of Lesnica.

To return to Červený Kláštor you can hike back the way you came, along an absorbing riverside trail through the 9km-long gorge, in two hours. Alternatively, 500m southeast of the river trip terminus is Chata Pieniny (⏀4285 031; www.chatapieniny.sk; mains €3-10) in Lesnica. Here, rent a bicycle for a one-way ride (€4) back through the gorge, or board a minibus that will transport you the 22km back by road (€3). In summer, folk musicians often play at the log *chata* and its buzzing restaurant: touristy, but fun.

Overnighters can pitch tents in the field outside Penzion Pltník (⏀4822 525; www. penzionpltnik.sk; Červený Kláštor 93; 2 adults & tent

€6.50, d €34) or check into one of the copious private rooms (usually signed *privaty*) on the road into Červený Kláštor.

Though Pieniny is only 42km north of Kežmarok, getting here is a challenge without your own vehicle. Travel agents in the High Tatras resorts can help arrange trips. Public buses run to Červený Kláštor from Poprad (€2.75, 1¾ hours), via Kežmarok (€2.25, 1¼ hour), once in the morning and twice in the afternoon. Several pedestrian bridges lead from here into Poland.

Levoča

☑ 053 / POP 14,900

So this is what Slovakia looked like in the 13th century... Unesco-listed Levoča is one of the few towns to still have its ancient defences largely intact. High medieval walls surround Old Town buildings and cobblestone alleyways. At the centre of it all stands the pride of the country's religious art and architecture collection, the Gothic Church of St Jacob. During the Middle Ages the king of Hungary invited Saxon Germans to colonise frontier lands. Levoča became central to the resulting Slavo-Germanic Spiš region, and became one of Slovakia's most important pilgrimage centres.

◉ Sights

Church of St Jacob   CHURCH
(Chrám Sv Jakuba; www.chramsvjakuba.sk; Nám Majstra Pavla; adult/child €2/1; ⊙by hourly tour 8.40am-4pm Tue-Sat, 1-4pm Sun) The spindles-and-spires Church of St Jacob, built in the 14th and 15th centuries, elevates your spirit with its soaring arches, precious art and rare furnishings, where the main attraction is Slovakia's tallest altar, an impressive 18m high.

The splendid Gothic altar (1517), created by Master Pavol of Levoča, is the main reason why people flock to this church on Levoča's main square. Little is known about the alter's sculptor, but his work is much revered. Cherubic representations of the Last Supper and the Madonna and Child are carved into the wood-and-paint masterpiece.

Buy tickets from the cashier inside the Municipal Weights House across the street from the north door. Entry is generally on the hour, but admissions are more frequent in summer and more sporadic off-season. The adjacent 16th-century cage of shame was built to punish naughty boys and girls.

Nám Majstra Pavla   SQUARE
Gothic and Renaissance eye candy abound on the main square, Nám Majstra Pavla. The private **Thurzov House** (1517), at No 7, has a characteristically frenetic Spiš Renaissance roofline. No 20 is the **Master Pavol Museum**, dedicated to the works of the city's most celebrated son. The 15th-century **Historic Town Hall** (Radnica) building, centre square, is really more interesting than the limited exhibits within. Temporary, town-related displays are on show at No 40, **Creative Culture in Spiš** (Výtarná Kultura na Spiši). One ticket gets you into all of the last three, as they are branches of the **Spiš Museum** (www.spisskemuzeum.com; adult/child €3/1.50; ⊙9.30am-3pm Tue-Fri).

Church of Mariánska Hora   CHURCH
From town you can see the Church of Mariánska Hora, 2km north, where the largest annual Catholic pilgrimage in Slovakia takes place in early July. You can walk or drive up for great views over Levoča: get directions in the tourist office.

🛏 Sleeping & Eating

Hotel U Leva   HOTEL €€
(☑4502 311; www.uleva.sk; Nám Majstra Pavla 24; s/d/apt €39/68/99; ❈🛜) Spread across two Old Town buildings, each of the 23 cleanly contemporary rooms is unique. All have muted jewel-tone walls enlivening them, and apartments come with kitchens. The fine restaurant (mains €7 to €13) combines atypical ingredients (brie, spinach) with time-honoured Slovak techniques.

Hotel Arkáda   HOTEL €
(☑4512 372; www.arkada.sk; Nám Majstra Pavla 26; s/d €36/52; @🛜) Furnishings in this Old Town building are mostly uninspired, but you can upgrade to a suite with antiques and arched ceilings for just €65. The cellar restaurant (mains €5 to €11) is much more atmospheric, with ancient brick vaults. Traditional and grilled dishes here attract quite a local following.

Oáza   PENSION €
(☑4514 511; www.ubytovanieoaza.sk; Nová 65; dm incl breakfast from €10) Simple two-bed rooms with shared bathroom, and four-bed rooms with bath and kitchen, are just what the budget doctor ordered.

U Janusa   SLOVAK
(Klaštorská 22; mains €4-11) Cosy traditional restaurant that doubles as a pension. Try the many kinds of *pirohy* (dumplings).

ℹ Information

Everything you'll likely need, banks and post office included, is on the main square.

Levonet Internet Café (Nám Majstra Pavla 38; per hr €2; ⊘10am-10pm)

Tourist Information Office (☑4513 763; http://eng.levoca.sk; Nám Majstra Pavla 58; ⊘9am-4pm Mon-Fri year-round, plus 9am-4pm Sat & Sun May-Sep)

ℹ Getting There & Away

Levoča is on the main E50 motorway between Poprad (28km) and Košice (94km). Bus travel is the most feasible option here.

The local bus stop at Nám Štefana Kluberta is much closer to town than the bus station, which is 1km southeast of centre. From the bus stop, follow Košicka west two blocks and you'll hit the main square.

Frequent coach services take you to the following destinations:

Košice (€4.50, two hours, seven daily)

Poprad (€1.60, 45 minutes, hourly) Most convenient onward mainline train connections.

Spišská Nová Ves (€1, 20 minutes, half-hourly) For Slovenský Raj National Park.

Spišské Podhradie (€1, 20 minutes, half-hourly) For Spiš Castle.

Spišské Podhradie

☑053 / POP 4000

Sprawling for 4 hectares above the village of Spišské Podhradie, ruined Spiš Castle is undoubtedly one of the largest in Europe. Even if you've never been, you may have seen pictures: the fortress is one of Slovakia's most-photographed sights. Two kilometres west, the medieval Spiš Chapter ecclesiastical settlement is also a Unesco World Heritage Site. In between, the village itself has basic services.

◉ Sights

Spiš Castle   CASTLE
(Spišský hrad; www.spisskemuzeum.com; adult/child €5/3; ⊘9am-7pm, closed Nov-Mar) Heralding from at least as early as the 13th century, Spiš Castle and its vast complex of ruins crown a ridge above Spišské Podhradie. Its claim to fame as one of Europe's largest castle complexes will certainly seem accurate as you explore. Highlights include the climb up the central tower for spectacular panoramic views across the Spiš region.

From the E50 motorway you catch glimpses of eerie outlines and stony ruins atop the hill on the eastern side of Spišské Podhradie

village. Can it really be that big? Indeed, Spiš Castle seemingly rambles on forever. If the reconstructed ruins are this impressive, imagine what the fortress was once like. Be sure to get the English audio tour that brings the past into focus through story and legend.

Chronicles first mention Spiš Castle in 1209 and the remaining central residential tower is thought to date from then. From there defenders allegedly repulsed the Tatars in 1241. Rulers and noble families kept adding fortifications and palaces during the 15th and 16th centuries, but by 1780 the site had already lost military significance and much was destroyed by fire. It wasn't until the 1970s that efforts were made to restore what remained. Few structures are whole, but there's a cistern, a Romanesque palace that contains the very small museum, and the chapel adjacent to it. Night tours and medieval festivals take place some summer weekends.

Be sure to climb the steep spiral staircase of the central tower for great views, and imagine yourself as a patrolling medieval guard as you traipse around this colossal fortress's outer walls.

Spiš Castle is 1km east of Spišské Podhradie, a healthy, uphill hike above the spur rail station. The easiest approach to the castle by car is off the E50 highway on the east (Prešov) side.

Spiš Chapter   MONASTERY
(Spišská Kapitula; adult/child €2/1) On the west side of Spišské Podhradie, you'll find still-active Spiš Chapter, a 13th-century Catholic complex encircled by a 16th-century wall. The pièce de résistance is St Martin's Cathedral (1273), towering above the community of quirky Gothic houses and containing some arresting 15th-century altars.

The Romanesque cathedral features twin towers and an ornate sanctuary; the altars are impressive trifold-painted sights. Spiš Chapter is part of the wider Spiš Castle & Levoča Unesco World Heritage Site. Buy tickets for the cathedral and pick up a guide from the (often-closed) information office at Spišská Kapitula 4. If you're travelling to Spiš Chapter by bus from Levoča, get off one stop (and 1km) before Spišské Podhradie, at Kapitula.

🛌 Sleeping & Eating

This is potentially a day trip from Levoča, the High Tatras or Košice, so there's little reason to stay over. The castle has food stands and the village has a grocery store.

Penzión Podzámok PENSION €

(☑4541 755; www.penzionpodzamok.sk; Podzámková 28; 2-4 bed r per person €13, without bathroom €8) Simple 42-bed guesthouse with a backyard view of the castle. It's in the village, north across the bridge. All meals are available: full board is an extra €13.50

TOP
CHOICE **Spišsky Salaš** MOUNTAIN HUT €

(☑4541 202; www.spisskysalas.sk; Levočská cesta 11; mains €3-5; ⓘ) Dig into lamb stew in the folksy dining room or on the covered deck, and watch the kids romp on rough-hewn play sets. The rustic log complex also has three simple rooms for rent (per person

€13). It's 3km west of Spiš Chapter, on the road toward Levoča. It's a great hike from here to Spiš Chapter and Spiš Castle.

ⓘ Getting There & Away

Spišské Podhradie is 15km east of Levoča and 78km northeast of Košice.

BUS Frequent buses connect with Levoča (€1, 20 minutes), Poprad (€2.15, 50 minutes) and Košice (€3.50, 1¾ hours).

TRAIN An inconvenient spur railway line heads to Spišské Podhradie from Spišské Vlachy (€0.75, 15 minutes, five daily), a station on the Bratislava–Košice main line. Check schedules at www.cp.atlas.sk.

Slovenský Raj & Around

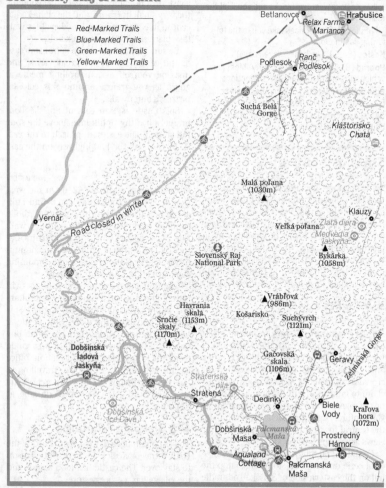

Slovenský Raj & Around

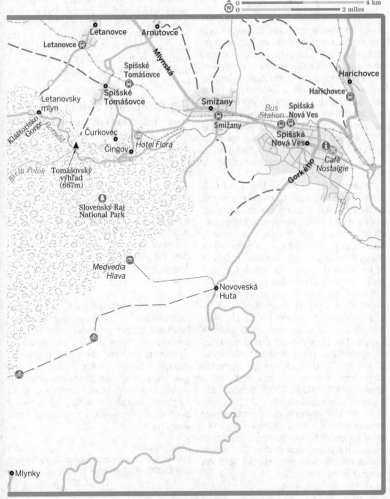

053

With rumbling waterfalls, sheer gorges and dense forests, Slovenský Raj lives up to the name of 'Slovak Paradise'. A few easier trails exist, but the one-way ladder-and-chain ascents make this a national park for the passionately outdoorsy. You cling to metal rungs headed up a precipice while an icy waterfall sprays you from a metre away: pure exhilaration.

The nearest major town is uninspiring Spišská Nová Ves, 23km southeast of Poprad. Of the three trailhead resort villages,

Podlesok, outside Hrabušice (16km southwest of Poprad), is our favourite – for its variety of hiking options and diverse lodging possibilities. Pretty Čingov, 5km west of Spišská Nová Ves, also has good lodgings. About 50km south, Dedinky is more a regular village with a pub and supermarket fronting a lake.

◉ Sights & Activities

Before you trek, pick up VKÚ's 1:25,000 *Slovenský Raj* hiking map (No 4) or Dajama's *Knapsacked Travel: The Slovak Paradise* hiking book, available at many tourist offices and bookshops countrywide. There

0 ____ 4 km
0 ____ 2 miles

Letanovce   Arnutovce
Letanovce
                Spišské
                Tomášovce   Mlynská   Harichovce
Letanovsky   Spišské   Harichovce
mlyn   Tomášovce   Smižany   Bus   Spišská
Kláštorisko Gorge Čurkovec   Station Nová Ves
                    Čingov Hotel Flora   Smižany
                                                   Spišská
Bielu Potok Tomášovský   Nová Ves
             vyhľad   Café
             (667m)   Nostalgie
        Slovenský Raj   Gorkého
        National Park

        Medvedia
        Hlava
                        Novoveská
                        Huta

Mlynky

BUSES FROM SPISŠKA NOVÁ VES

DESTINATION	PRICE(€)	DURATION (MIN)	FREQUENCY
Čingov	0.50	15	1 direct Mon-Fri or change in Spišské Tomášovce
Dedinky	2	70	2 direct Mon-Fri or change in Poprad
Levoča	0.85	20	10 Mon-Fri
Podlesok via Spišský Štvrtok	1.20	30	2 Mon-Fri
Poprad via Spišský Štvrtok	1.70	40	12 Mon-Fri

are several good biking trails crisscrossing the national park.

Slovenský Raj National Park　　　　PARK
(www.slovenskyraj.sk; Jul & Aug €1, Sep-Jun free) The national park has numerous trails that include one-way *roklina* (gorge) sections and take at least half a day. From Čingov a green trail leads up Hornád River Gorge an hour to **Tomašovský výhľad**, a rocky outcropping and overlook that is a good short-hike destination. Or continue to the green, one-way, technically aided **Kláštorisko Gorge** trail (at least eight hours). You can also reach the Kláštorisko Gorge ascent from Podlesok (six hours). There is accommodation available at **Kláštorisko Chata.**

Another excellent alternative from Podlesok is to hike on the six- to seven-hour circuit up the dramatic, ladder and technical-assist **Suchá Belá Gorge**, then east to Kláštorisko Chata, where you'll find a reconstructed 13th-century **monastery**, on a yellow then red trail. From there, take the blue trail down to the Hornád River, then follow the river gorge upstream to return to Podlesok.

One of the shortest, dramatic, technical-assist hikes starts at Biele Vody (15 minutes northeast of Dedinky via the red trail) and follows the green trail up **Zejmarská Gorge**. The physically fit can clamber up in 50 minutes; others huff and puff up in 90 minutes. To get back, you can follow the green trail down to Dedinky, or there's a **chairlift** (adult/child €1/0.50; ⏱9am-5pm Jun-Aug) that works sporadically.

The best viewpoint is at **Medvedia Hlava** in the east of the park. Slovenský Raj's forested gorges lie in one direction, the jagged teeth of the High Tatras in the other. Access it via a 4½ hour hike from Spišská Nová Ves tourist information centre.

Dobšinská Ice Cave　　　　CAVE
(www.ssj.sk; adult/child €7/3.50; ⏱9am-4pm Tue-Sun by hourly tour, closed Oct–mid-May) The fanciful frozen formations in this Unesco-noted ice cave are more dazzling in early June than September. A 15-minute hike leads up from the settlement of Dobšinská ľadová jaskyňa to where tours begin every hour or so.

🛌 Sleeping & Eating

Many lodgings have restaurants. Numerous food stands and eateries and a small grocery are available in Podlesok. The biggest supermarket is next to the bus station in Spišská Nová Ves.

TOP CHOICE Autocamp Podlesok　　　CAMPING GROUND €
(✆4299 165; www.podlesok.sk; campsite €4-8, cottages & huts per person €10; 🛜) The office at this lively camping ground provides substantial trail info and wi-fi. Pitch a tent (600 capacity) or choose from fairly up-to-date two-to-12-bed cabins and cottages with bathrooms.

🖊 Relax Farma Marianka　　　PENSION
(✆905714583; www.relaxfarmamarianka.sk; Betlanovce 83; per person €17; 🅿🛜👪) The hospitable owners of this big, well-kept eight-room pension can advise you about outdoor activities. Relax in the hot tub, meet the pigs or enjoy Janka's scrumptious organic cooking. From Hrabušice, head southeast towards the park: it's just passed the Podlesok turn-off where the road kinks sharp right.

Ranč Podlesok　　　PENSION €
(✆0918407077; www.rancpodlesok.sk; Podlesok 5; d/tr €30/45; 🛜👪) A blue park trail runs be-

hind this stone-and-log lodge and restaurant at the park's edge. There's sand volleyball too, if you fancy it. It's 1km past the Podlesok village area.

Penzión Lesnica   PENSION €

(☑449 1518; www.stefani.sk; Čingov 113; s/d incl breakfast €30/40) Nine simple, sunny-coloured rooms close to the trail fill up fast, so book ahead. The attached restaurant is one of the best local places for a Slovakian repast (mains €3 to €10).

Hotel Flora   HOTEL €

(☑449 1129; www.hotelfloraslovenskyraj.sk; Čingov 110; s/d incl breakfast €26/41; ☎) A certain mountain rusticity in the public areas but so-so rooms. The restaurant (mains €6 to €14) has a large, agreeable terrace.

Aqualand Cottage   HOSTEL €

(☑0948007735; www.aqualand.sk; dm €13, s/d without bathroom €25/32) A sprawling cottage-hostel with common room, toasty fireplace and two kitchens across the lake from Dedinky proper.

Koliba Zuzana   SLOVAKIAN €€

(☑0905278397; www.kolibazuzana.szm.sk; Dedinky 127; mains €3-10) Lakeside restaurant with terrace; two suites (€80) for rent upstairs.

Cafe Nostalgie   INTERNATIONAL €€

(Letná 49, Spisška Nová Ves; mains €5-10; ⊙10am-11pm) Next to the tourist information; probably the best thing in town. There's a quality international menu, including tasty Mexican options. If you've time to kill, kill it here.

❶ Information

Outside Spišská Nová Ves, lodgings are the best source of information; park info booths are open July through August. Get cash before you arrive

in the park; there is an ATM and exchange at Spišská Nová Ves train station. Helpful websites include www.slovenskyraj.sk.

Mountain Rescue Service (☑emergency 183 00; http://his.hzs.sk)

Tourist Information Booth (Čingov; ⊙9am-5pm, closed Sep-Jun)

Tourist Information Centre (☑4428 292; Letná 49, Spišská Nová Ves; ⊙8am-6pm Mon-Fri, 9am-1pm Sat, 2-6pm Sun) Helps with accommodation.

❶ Getting There & Around

Off season especially, you may consider hiring a car in Košice; connections to the park can be a chore. You'll have to transfer at least once, likely in Spišská Nová Ves.

BUS Buses run infrequently on weekends, more often in July and August. No buses run directly between trailhead villages. Carefully check schedules at www.cp.atlas.sk.

TRAIN Trains run from Spišska Nová Ves to Poprad (€1, 20 minutes, 12 daily) and Košice (€3.80, one hour, 15 daily). The train station is 1½ blocks east of the bus station.

Košice
☑055 / POP 234,000

The world may now finally realise what Košice residents have long known: that East Slovakia's industrial powerhouse has cosmopolitan clout and a buoyant cultural scene plonking it firmly on Europe's city break map, fiercely independent of Bratislava. The reason: as 2013's European Capital of Culture, Košice has accordingly initiated a new string of attractions including major arts installations in a combination of impressively revamped buildings, and eclectic events to enliven city streets.

ANDY WARHOL AND EAST SLOVAKIA

Andy Warhol wasn't born there, and took pains to disassociate himself from this area of Slovakia ('I come from nowhere', he once said) but Medzilaborce in far-eastern Slovakia is nevertheless where his parents grew up, before their move to the US. In 1991 the **Andy Warhol Museum** (☑421-57 7480 072; www.andywarhol.sk; Andyho Warhola 26, Medzilaborce; adult/child €3.50/1.75; ⊙10am-4.30pm Tue-Fri, midday-4.30pm Sat & Sun) opened in this unlikely location as a shrine to pop art (alongside numerous Warhol originals are works from Basquiat, Lichtenstein and the like). Trains run from Košice, normally changing at un-delightful Humenné (€6.75, three hours, six daily). South of the station, Mierová becomes Andyho Warhola and the museum is 600m along this street.

The folks at Košice's **Muza Hotel** (www.hotelmuza.sk; Pri prachárni 5) have collected (and display) many Andy Warhol originals. It's 3km south of the Old Town near the Carrefour Shopping Centre in Lunik VIII.

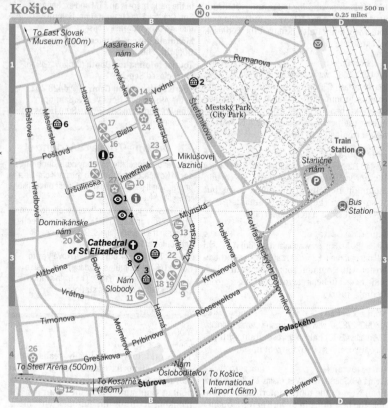

Košice

Košice was always a medieval gem awaiting discovery. New enhancements build on an arts scene already home to the paintings of Andy Warhol and one of Europe's loveliest theatres. Its vast oval-shaped *námestie* (central square) contains the largest collection of historical monuments in Slovakia and when the buzzing cafes and restaurants open up here of a mellow evening, it's hard not to love the city or, at least, want a spirited affair. Out of town, nature encroaches spectacularly with the delights of Central Europe's grandest cave network. It's the base of choice, too, for forays deeper into the tradition-seeped east.

Košice received its city coat of arms in 1369 before any other city in Central Europe and for centuries was eastern stronghold of the Hungarian kingdom. On 5 April 1945 the Košice Government Program – which made communist dictatorship in Czechoslovakia a virtual certainty – got announced here.

⊙ Sights

Hlavné Nám SQUARE

Almost all of the sights are in or around the town's long plazalike main square, Hlavná. Landscaped flowerbeds surround the central musical fountain, across from the 1899 State Theatre (p473). To the north stands a large baroque plague column from 1723. Look for the turn-of-the-20th-century, art nouveau Hotel Slávia (☑622 4395; www.hotel-slavia.sk; Hlavné Nám 63) at No 63. Shire Hall (1779), at No 27, is where the Košice Government Program was proclaimed in 1945; today there's a minor art gallery inside.

TOP CHOICE **Cathedral of St Elizabeth** CHURCH

(Dóm Sv Alžbety; Hlavné Nám; church free, attractions €1; ⊙1-5pm Mon, 9am-5pm Tue-Fri, 9am-1pm Sat) The dark and brooding 14th-century Cathedral of St Elizabeth wins the prize for the sight most likely to grace your Košice postcard home. You can't miss Europe's easternmost Gothic cathedral, which dominates the square. Below the church, the crypt contains the tomb of Duke Ferenc Rákóczi, who was exiled to Turkey after the failed 18th-century Hungarian revolt against Austria.

Don't forget to ascend the 160 narrow, circular stone steps up the church's tower for city views. Climbing the royal staircase as the monarchs once did provides an interior perspective: note the rare interlocking flights of steps. Just to the south, the 14th-century St Michael's Chapel (Kaplinka sv Michala) has sporadic entry hours.

Lower Gate Underground Museum MUSEUM

(Hlavné Nám; adult/child €1/0.50; ⊙10am-6pm Tue-Sun May-Sep) The underground remains of medieval Košice – lower gate, defence chambers, fortifications and waterways dating from the 13th to 15th centuries – were only uncovered during construction work in 1996. Get lost in the mazelike passages of the archaeological excavations at the south end of the square.

East Slovak Museum MUSEUM

(Východoslovenské múzeum; ☑622 0309; www.vsmuzeum.sk; Hviezdoslavovo 3; per exhibition €1; ⊙9am-5pm Tue-Sat, 9am-1pm Sun) Hidden treasure can be found at the East Slovak Museum. Workers found the secret stash of 2920 gold coins, dating from the 15th to 18th centuries, while renovating a house on Hlavná in 1935. There's a romp through various aspects of regional history, too, showcased through a former prison and a metal foundry. In the museum yard there's a relocated 1741 wooden church.

⌶ Sleeping

The City Information Centre has an annual town booklet that lists local accommodation, including university dorms open to the public in July and August.

TOP CHOICE **Hotel Bankov** HISTORIC HOTEL €€

(☑6324 522 ext 4; www.hotelbankov.sk; Dolný Bankov 2; s €85-135, d €95-145; P@🐾) Going strong since 1869, Slovakia's oldest hotel lies 4km northwest of central Košice in a verdant location overlooking woodland. Rooms are surprisingly good value, oozing old-world charm (beams, period furniture). There's an elegant restaurant and a wellness centre. There's complimentary taxi service for guests.

Chrysso Penzión BOUTIQUE HOTEL €€

(☑6230 450; www.penzionchrysso.sk; Zvonárska 3; s/d/apt €58/68/78; ✳🤚) Think design-driven details such as silk throws and sleek leather chairs in chocolate and cream. A wine-cellar-bar, terrace and restaurant downstairs are similarly stylish.

Ecohotel Dália BOUTIQUE HOTEL €€

(☑7994 321; www.hoteldalia.sk; Löfferova 1; s €59-89, d €74-109; P🤚) One of Slovakia's

NEW-LOOK KOŠICE

As 2013 European Capital of Culture, Košice has bolstered its appeal significantly. New/revamped attractions include the following:

Sándor Márai Memorial Room (☏625 8888; www.sandormarai.eu; Mäsiarska 35; ☺1-3pm) House museum about the life of one of Slovakia's most famous writers, Sándor Márai, who was born in Košice (although he wrote in Hungarian).

Kunsthalle (Hall of Art; Mestský Park, cnr Rumanova & Štefánikova) Grandiose former swimming pool dating from the 1930s, transformed into a major exhibition centre.

Kosarné (Culture Park; ☏6854 299; www.kulturpark.sk; Kukučínova 2) The old military barracks, now a nationally renowned cultural centre for performing arts and a music venue, with ateliers and a cafe-bar. Just south of the Old Town.

first ecohotels, the Dália has the whole shebang of green touches in its tucked-away location, including solar panelling, environmentally friendly toiletries and waste composting. Rooms have individual flourishes like hand-painted Chinese wallpaper. A wellness centre and a cafe-restaurant are on-site.

Hotel Zlatý Dukat
HOTEL €€

(☏7279 333; www.hotelzlatydukat.sk; Hlavná 16; s €75-79, d €85-89, ste €130-235; @☎) Luxury main-square hotel with touches such as flat-screen TVs, flowers and room service.

Penzión Slovakia
PENSION €

(☏7289 820; www.penzionslovakia.sk; Orliá 6; s/d/ste €45/55/65; ✿☎) Charming city guesthouse with grill restaurant downstairs.

K2
HOSTEL €

(☏6255 948; Štúrova 32; s/d without bathroom €16/27) These dowdy singles and doubles are the most centrally located budget option. No common room or kitchen; ask for a room away from the road.

✖ Eating

Med Malina
POLISH €€

(Hlavná 89; mains €7-11) The Polish owners cook up a variety of treats in this intimate little joint, like stuffed cabbage leaves or *zurek* (Polish potato soup).

TOP CHOICE Villa Regia
FINE DINING €€

(www.villaregia.sk; Dominikánske nám 3; mains €7-14; ☐) Steaks, seafood and vegetarian dishes get artistic treatment amid a rustic old-world atmosphere. The vaulted ceilings and stone walls extend to the upstairs pension rooms.

12 Apoštolov
SLOVAKIAN €€

(12 Apostles; Kováčska 51; mains €6-8) Košice's oldest restaurant has pulled its socks up to offer Slovakian-Hungarian cuisine as good as its surroundings are intense (stained-glass windows, church-pew seating).

Smelly Cat
CAFE €

(Zvonárska 6; ☺9am-10pm Mon-Thu, 10am-1am Fri & Sat, 2-10pm Sun) Books, big ancient sofas, wicked coffee, delectable cakes: a refined boho hang-out on an amicable pedestrian street.

Nech Sa Páči
CAFE €

(Hlavná 27; snacks €1-5; ☺10am-6pm Tue-Sun) Slickly designed cafe with a reputation for great breakfasts, coffees, desserts and cocktails. Has appealing outside seating; by the Cathedral of St Elizabeth.

Cafe Napoli
ITALIAN €€

(Hlavná 82; mains €4-11) Stylish young locals fill up this modern Italian restaurant, which does sublime pizza.

Cukráreň Aida
CAFE €

(Hlavná 81; cakes €1-3; ☺8am-9pm) The most popular ice-cream and cake shop in town; several branches on the main square.

♟ Drinking & Entertainment

For a city this small, options are plentiful. Any sidewalk cafe on the main square is great for a drink. Check free monthly publication *Kam do Mesta* (www.kamdomesta.sk) for entertainment listings.

Caffe Trieste
CAFE

(Uršulínska 2; ☺7.30am-7.30pm) Original of the mini-chain now found in Bratislava. Knock-out espresso, in slurp-it-and-go Italian fashion.

Krčma Nositel Radu Prce PUB
(Zvonárska 8) Return to the pre-1989 days:
Lenin posters and oh-so-communist ambience and prices. It's authentic, mind – not a theme bar. Cheapest beer around.

Villa Cassa BAR
(Vaznici 2; ⊗1pm-midnight Mon-Sat) Atmospheric wine bar offering more than 400 Slovak wines (plus others from across Europe).

Retro CLUB
(Kováčska 49; ⊗7.30pm-2am) The place to get wild hereabouts, among beautiful people aplenty.

Jazz Club CLUB
(http://jazzclub-ke.sk; Kováčska 39) DJs spin here most nights, but there are also occasional live concerts.

State Theatre THEATRE
(Štátne Divadlo Košice; ☎6221 234; www.sdke.sk; Hlavné Nám 58; ⊗box office 9am-5.30pm Mon-Fri, 10am-1pm Sat) Local opera and ballet companies stage performances in this 1899 neo-baroque theatre.

State Philharmonic Košice LIVE MUSIC
(Štátna Filharmónia Košice, House of the Arts; ☎6224 509; www.sfk.sk; Moyzesova 66) Concerts take place year-round but the spring musical festival is a good time to catch performances of the city's philharmonic.

Steel Aréna SPORTS
(www.steelarena.sk; Nerudova 12) The hometown's revered ice-hockey team, HC Košice, plays here. Buy tickets at www.ticketportal.sk.

ℹ Information

City Information Centre (☎6258 888; www.visitkosice.eu; Hlavná 59; ⊗9am-6pm Mon-Fri, 10am-4pm Sat & Sun) Ask for both the free annual town guide and the full-size colour brochure of historic sites. Good guided city tours can be arranged.

Internet Reading Room (Hlavná 48; per hr €1.60)

Ľudová Banka (Mlynská 29) Well-located ATM and exchange.

Police Station (☎159; Pribinova 6)

ℹ Getting There & Away

Check bus and train schedules at www.cp.atlas.sk.

AIR Košice International Airport (p479) is 6km southwest of the centre. **Danube Wings** (V5; www.danubewings.eu) has two daily flights to Bratislava (weekdays only). Vienna and Prague are also served.

BUS You can book ahead on some Ukraine-bound buses through **Eurobus** (www.eurobus.sk). Getting to Poland is easier from Poprad. Destinations include Bardejov (€4, 1¾ hours, nine daily), Levoča (€4.80, two hours, eight daily) and Uzhhorod (Ukraine; €7, two to three hours, two daily).

CAR Several international car-hire companies such as Avis and Eurocar have representatives at the airport. **Buchbinder** (☎6832 397; www.buchbinder.sk) is a smaller company with good rates and gratis pick-up in the city.

ℹ Getting Around

The Old Town is small, so you probably can walk everywhere. Transport tickets (€0.60 one zone) cover most buses and trams; buy them at newsstands and validate on board. Bus 23 between the airport and the train station requires a two-zone ticket (€1).

Around Košice

About 65km west of Košice lies Rožňava: the tourist office on the main square has information on how to visit the dramatic **Slovak Karst National Park** (Slovenský Kras; ☎58 7326 815; www.sopsr.sk/slovkras, in Slovak), undulating away outside town. Here more than 1000

TRAINS FROM KOŠICE

DESTINATION	PRICE (€)	DURATION (HR)	FREQUENCY (DAILY)
Bratislava	19	5-6	21
Lviv, Ukraine	60	13	1
Miskolc, Hungary	5	1¼	2
Poprad (High Tatras)	5	1¼	24
Spišská Nová Ves (Slovenský Raj)	4	1	23

caves, crevasses and abysses make up Central Europe's greatest karstic region. The subterranean highlight is Domica Cave (☑7882 010; tour with boat trip adult/child €7/3.50; ☺9am-4pm Jun-Aug, 9.30am-2pm Feb-May & Sep-Dec) near Dlhá Ves, where cave systems over 1000m long beg to be explored. There are boat trips, and 16 bat species.

South of Košice on the approach to Hungary is Slovakia's best-known wine region, Tokaj. Wine tastings and tours are available in several villages hereabouts; ask at Košice's City Information Centre (p473).

Bardejov

☑054 / POP 33,400

It's tough competition in the medieval wonderland of East Slovakia, but Bardejov wins the award for our favourite Old Town square, which would look barely a brick out of place 400 years ago. Bardejov received its royal charter in 1376 and grew rich on trade between Poland and Russia into the 16th century. The steep roofs and flat fronts of the Unesco-listed burghers' houses here each have their own unique plaster details or inscriptions.

A clutch of museums shed light on this region's Eastern-facing art and culture and the town makes a good springboard for further exploration. The area's wooden churches reflect a Carpatho-Rusyn heritage, shared with neighbouring parts of Ukraine and Poland. Just north in Bardejovské Kúpele you can cure some ills at a thermal spa or see examples of these churches in a rewarding open-air village museum.

◉ Sights

The main square, Radičné nám is a sight in itself, and you can walk along the old town walls and bastions along Na Hradbách.

Šariš Museum
MUSEUM

(www.muzeumbardejov.sk; ☺8am-noon & 12.30-4pm Tue-Sun) There are two local branches of the Šariš Museum worth seeing. Centre square, the Town Hall (Radničné nám 48; adult/child €1.50/1) contains altarpieces and a historical collection. Built in 1509, it was Slovakia's first Renaissance building. At the Icon Exposition (Radničné nám 27; adult/child €1.50/1), more than 130 dazzling icons and iconostases from the 16th to 19th centuries are displayed. This is an excellent opportunity to see the religious art that originally

decorated Greek Catholic and Orthodox wooden churches east of Bardejov.

Basilica of St Egídius
CHURCH

(Bazilika Sv Egídia; Radničné nám; adult/child €1.50/1; ☺9.30am-4pm Mon-Fri, 10am-3pm Sat, 11.30am-3pm Sun) The interior of this 15th-century basilica is packed with 11 Gothic altarpieces, built from 1460 to 1510. Each has thorough explanation in English.

🛏 Sleeping & Eating

Cafes can be found around Radničné nám.

el. Restaurant & Lodging
PENSION €

(☑4728 404; www.el-restaurant.sk; Stöcklova 43; s/d/apt incl breakfast €30/40/60; ☜) Three chirpy rooms up for grabs. It's very central and myriad chicken dishes are on the menu of the modern Slovakian restaurant downstairs.

Penzion Magura
PENSION €

(☑902374871; www.penzionmagura.sk; Andrasikova 31; s/d €27/39) There's oodles of space in these slickly finished rooms and a more traditional restaurant below.

Penzión Semafor
PENSION €

(☑0905830984; www.penzionsemafor.sk; Kellerova 13; s €26-33, d €39-43) Five bright doubles and an apartment in a family-run guesthouse. Nice and central.

TOP CHOICE Cactus
INTERNATIONAL €€

(www.cactus.sk; Štefánikova 61; mains €5-15; ☺7am-10pm) Crisp salads, juicy steaks, stuffed trout...the food is flamboyant and with a glut of influences from the Scandinavian to the French – as modern as Bardejov is ancient. It's a light, enticing space with a snug whisky-cigar bar next door.

La Bello
ITALIAN €€

(Radničné nám 50; mains €6.50) An atmospheric, Italianesque restaurant dishing up wood-fired pizzas. The local fave.

Stadión
SLOVAK €

(www.penzionstadion.sk; Družstevná 1; mains €5; ☺noon-8pm) No joke: this restaurant in the homonymous pension really is built into the football stadium – and it really does serve good food, in well-to-do sports-social-club-type environs. There are five rooms here (€28 to €48), including one apartment.

ℹ Information

ČSOB (Radničné nám 7) Exchange and ATM.
Main Post Office (Dlhý rad 14)

WOODEN CHURCHES

Travelling east from Bardejov, you come to a crossroads of Western and Eastern Christianity. From the 17th to the 19th centuries, nearly 300 dark-wood, onion-domed churches were erected hereabouts. Of the 40-odd remaining, eight have been recognised by Unesco. A handful celebrate Roman Catholic or Protestant faiths, but most belong to the Eastern rites of Greek Catholicism and Orthodoxy.

Typically they honour the Holy Trinity with three domes, three architectural sections and three doors on the icon screen. Richly painted icons and venerated representations of Christ and the saints decorate the iconostases and invariably every inch of the churches' interiors have also been hand-painted. These can be quite a sight, but it's not easy to get inside. These rural churches are remote, with limited or non-existant bus connections to them, and doors are kept locked. Sometimes there's a map posted showing where the key-keeper lives; sometimes he's next door and sometimes you're out of luck.

The time-pressed can guarantee seeing icons and an interior at the Icon Exhibition in Bardejov and the *skanzen* in Bardejovské Kúpele, 3km north. The medieval Roman Catholic church in **Hervatov** (www.saris.eu.sk/hervatov; Hervartov) is one of the closest to Bardejov, while **Ladomirová** north of Svidník has an impressive Greek Catholic church. If you're up for a further adventure, the following resources can help:

Drevené Chrámy (www.drevenechramy.sk) Great online resource with detailed information on 39 wooden churches.

Cultural Heritage of Slovakia: Wooden Churches Comprehensive, full-colour book by Miloš Dudas with photos and church descriptions; for sale at bookstores.

Bardejov Tourist Information Centre A highly recommended first port of call for logistics on visiting the churches.

Tourist Information Centre (☑4744 003; www.bardejov.sk; Radničné nám 21; ☉9am-5.30pm Mon-Fri, 11.30am-3.30pm Sat & Sun, closed Sat & Sun Oct-Apr) Info, maps, souvenirs etc.

❶ Getting There & Away

Bardejov is on a spur train line, so buses are most convenient although it's way off the international bus routes.

Buses go to and from Košice (€3.75, 1¾ hours, eight daily), Poprad (€4.50, 2¼ hours, six daily) and Bardejovské Kúpele (€0.55, 10 minutes, 12 daily).

Bardejovské Kúpele

Three short kilometres to the north of Bardejov you'll find the leafy, promenade-filled spa town of Bardejovské Kúpele where the hot, sulfurous water fizzes as it spouts out the taps. Overall, it's somewhat dilapidated, but to book a service like a massage or a mineral bath (from €10), go directly to the **Spa House** (Kúpelny dom; ☑4774 225; www.kupele-bj.sk; ☉8am-noon & 1-5pm Mon-Sat) at the top of the main pedestrian street. The town also has Slovakia's oldest *skanzen*, the **Museum of Folk Architecture** (Múzeum Ľudovej Architektúry; adult/child €1.30/0.70; ☉9.30am-5pm Tue-Sun, to 3pm Oct-Apr) where you can see painted interiors and iconostases of the area's nail-less wooden churches. An ancient (Unesco-listed) example from Zboj has been moved here. Still, hunting out the churches themselves in the surrounding countryside is more fun.

Frequent buses connect with Bardejov. If you have a car, park in the lot by the bus station at the base of the town and walk uphill; the whole place is pedestrian-only. At the base near the colonnade is the **Tourist Information Office** (☑4774 477; www.bardejovske-kupele.sk; Kino Žriedlo; ☉8am-4pm Mon-Fri, 10.30am-4pm Sat & Sun).

UNDERSTAND SLOVAKIA

History

Slavic tribes wandered west into what would become Slovakia some time around the 5th century; in the 9th century, the territory was part of the short-lived Great Moravian empire. It was about this time that the Magyars (Hungarians) set up shop next door and subsequently laid claim to the whole territory. When in the early 16th century the Turks moved into Budapest, Hungarian monarchs took up residence in Bratislava (known then as Pozsony in Hungarian). Being Hungarian frontierland, many fortresses were constructed here during the Middle Ages and can still be seen today.

It wasn't until the 19th century that Slovakia, thanks to national hero Ľudovít Štúr, successfully forged its own literary language. In the early 1900s Slovak intellectuals cultivated the ties with neighbouring Czechs that would take their nation into the united Czechoslovakia post-WWI. The day before Hitler's troops invaded Czechoslovakia in March 1939, Slovak leaders declared Slovakia a German protectorate and a brief period of sovereignty ensued. This was not a popular move and in August 1944 Slovak partisans instigated the ill-fated Slovak National Uprising (Slovenské Národné Povstanie, or SNP), a source of ongoing national pride (and innumerable street names).

After the reunification and communist takeover in 1948, power was centralised in Prague until 1989 when the Velvet Revolution brought down the iron curtain here. Elections in 1992 saw the left-leaning nationalist Movement for a Democratic Slovakia (HZDS) come to power. Scarcely a year later, without referendum, the Czechoslovak federation dissolved peacefully (albeit with far from universal support among Slovaks) on 1 January 1993, bringing Slovakia its first true independence.

Slovakia was accepted into NATO and the EU by 2004, became a Schengen member state in 2007 and adopted the euro as the national currency in January 2009. Respective renaissances as a major stag-party and ski-break destination in the early 2000s were catalysts for getting wider attention from international tourism.

People

A deeply religious and familial people, Slovaks have strong family ties and a deep sense of folk traditions. Today Roman Catholics form the majority (about 69%), but evangelicals are also numerous and East Slovakia has many Greek Catholic and Orthodox believers. The young are warm and open, but there can be residual communist reserve within older generations. Friendliness lurks just behind this stoicism. If you make friends with a family, the hospitality (and free-flowing liquor) may just knock you out. Thankfully, in the tourist industry, surly service is now the exception rather than the rule.

Government statistics estimate that Slovakia's population is 86% Slovak, 10% Hungarian and 1.7% Roma. This last figure is in dispute: some groups estimate the Roma population, most of which are based in Eastern Slovakia, to be much higher. The Roma are viewed by the general populace with an uncompromising suspicion – at best.

ICE-HOCKEY OBSESSION

Slovakia's national ice-hockey team is usually deemed one of the world's 10 strongest. (Not bad, considering the team was only created when Czechoslovakia dissolved in 1993.) Local club rivalries are quite heated, with the most popular teams being HC Slovan (p444) in Bratislava and HC Košice (p473) in Košice. These teams' two stadiums co-hosted the IIHF world championships in 2011. Bratislava's Ondrej Nepela Arena got a big-money overhaul for the event, so it doesn't seem like the ice-hockey fever will cool down anytime soon. Puck-pushing season is September to April, when games seem to be on TVs everywhere.

Arts

Traditional folk arts – from music to architecture – are still celebrated across the country. Indeed, attending one of the many village folk festivals in summer can be the highlight of a visit: colourful costumes, upbeat traditional music, hearty *klobasa* and beer are all part of the fun. The biggest is Východná Folk Festival (www.obec-vychodna.sk), in the small namesake village 32km west of Poprad.

Traditional Slovak folk instruments include the *fujara* (a 2m-long flute), the *konkovka* (a shepherd's flute), drums and cimbalom. Today you'll likely still see a folk troupe accompanied by fiddle, bass, clarinet and sometimes trumpet or accordion. National folk companies like Lučnica (www.lucnica.sk) and Sľuk (www.sluk.sk) perform country-wide. But each microregion has its own particular melodies and costumes.

Outside of festivals, the best place to experience folk culture is at a *skanzen* – an open-air museum where examples of traditional wooden cottages and churches have been gathered in village form. The houses are fully furnished in traditional style and frequent activities, especially around holidays, focus on folk culture. The largest *skanzen* (p450), in Martin, represents several regions while Bardejovské Kúpele's open-air village museum (p475) has good examples of the nailless wooden churches for which the area is known.

SLOVAKIA'S MUSICAL HERITAGE

Slovakia has a surprisingly rich classical music pedigree. The career of **Franz Liszt** began in the De Pauli Palace in Ventúska street in Old Town Bratislava, while **Ludwig van Beethoven** lived in Hlohovec, north of Bratislava, gave concerts in the capital and even dedicated a sonata (Piano Opus 78) to Therese Brunsvik, member of one of the most influential city families at that time. Hungarian composer **Béla Bartók** also lived for a time in Bratislava (then Pressburg).

Environment

A largely hilly, forested country, Slovakia sits at the heart of Europe (indeed Krahule, near Banska Bystricá, is one of several claimants to the title of 'geographical centre of Europe'). Straddling the northwestern end of the Carpathian Mountains, and with stupendous scenery, it's not surprising most Slovaks spend their weekends outdoors. National parks and protected areas comprise 20% of the territory and the entire country is laced with a network of trails.

Not to be missed is the High Tatras (Vysoké Tatry) National Park, protecting a 12km-long rocky mountain range that rises seemingly out of nowhere. The tallest peak, Gerlachovský štít, reaches an impressive 2654m. Then there are the lesser pine-clad ridges of Malá Fatra National Park, and Slovenský Raj National Park, where ladders and chain-assists make the challenging, narrow gorges accessible.

Unlike the mountainous north, south-western Slovakia is a fertile lowland hugging the Danube River, which forms the border with Hungary. Slovak rivers are prone to serious flooding: watch for warnings.

Food & Drink

Slovakia isn't known for its 'cuisine' as much as for home cooking. Soups like *cesnaková polievka* (garlic soup), clear with croutons and cheese, start most meals. The national dish is *bryndzové halušky*, gnocchilike dumplings topped with sheep's cheese and bacon fat. You'll also find *bryndza* sheep cheese on potato pancakes, in *pirohy* (dumplings) and served as a *natierka* (spread) with bread and raw onions. Don't pass up an opportunity to eat in a *salaš* or a *koliba* (rustic eateries named for traditional parts of a sheep-herder's camp), where such traditional specialities abound.

Much of what you'll see on regular menus is basic Central European fare: various fried meat schnitzels, hearty pork dishes and paprika-infused stews. It's all very meaty, but most towns have at least one (vegetarian-friendly) pizza place. For dessert, try sweet *pirohy* filled with plum jam and poppy seeds (the signature secret dessert ingredient hereabouts) or *ovocné knedličky* (fruit dumplings).

Spirits of Slovakia

Expect to be served a shot of *slivovica* (plum-based firewater), *borovička* (a potent berry-based clear liquor), Demänovka (a herbal liquor related to Czech Becherovka) or something similar.

Unlike the Czech Republic, Slovakia is not known for its *pivo* (beer). But the full-bodied Zlatý Bažant and dark, sweet Martiner are decent.

Wine is big, however. The Modra region squeezes out dry medium-bodied reds, like frankovka and kláštorné. Slovak reisling and müller-uhurgau varietals are fruity but on the dry side. One of the best-regarded is Tokaj, an amber-hued dessert wine from the east similar to the homonymous, and neighbouring, Hungarian wine region. If money is no object, there's also *l'adové víno*: wine concocted with frozen grapes foraged after the first snows and thus extremely sweet.

SURVIVAL GUIDE

Directory A–Z

Accommodation

Bratislava has more hostels and five-star hotels than midrange accommodation. Outside the capital, you'll find plenty of reasonable *penzióny* (guesthouses). Breakfast is usually available (sometimes included) at all lodgings and wi-fi is common and usually free. Many lodgings offer nonsmoking rooms. Parking is only a problem in Bratislava. A recommended booking resource in the capital city is Bratislava Hotels (www.bratislavahotels.com).

The below ranges are based on the price of a double room with private bathroom in tourist season.

€ less than €60

€€ €60 to €150

€€€ more than €150

Activities

Hiking The Mountain Rescue Service (☎421-(0)52 7877 711, emergency 18 300; www.hzs.sk; Horný Smokovec 52) provides hiking and weather information in addition to aid: the main office is in Horný Smokovec in the High Tatras.

Skiing Check out the snow conditions at www.skiinfo.sk.

Business Hours

Sight and attraction hours vary throughout the year; standard opening times for the tourist season (May through September) are listed below. Schedules vary from October to April; check ahead.

Banks 8am to 5pm Monday to Friday

Bars 11am to midnight Monday to Thursday, 11am to 2am Friday and Saturday, 4pm to midnight Sunday

Grocery stores 6.30am to 6pm Monday to Friday, 7am to noon Saturday

Post offices 8am to 5pm Monday to Friday, 8am to 11am Saturday

Nightclubs 4pm to 4am Wednesday to Sunday

Restaurants 10.30am to 10pm

Shops 9am to 6pm Monday to Friday, 9am to noon Saturday

Embassies & Consulates

Australia and New Zealand do not have embassies in Slovakia; the nearest are in Vienna and Berlin respectively. The following are in Bratislava:

Canadian Embassy (☎5920 4031; www.canadainternational.gc.ca/czech-tcheque/; Mostová 2, Carlton-Savoy Building)

French Embassy (☎5934 7111; www.ambafrance-sk.org; Hlavné nám 7)

German Embassy (☎5920 4400; www.pressburg.diplo.de; Hviezdoslavovo nám 10)

Netherlands Embassy (☎5262 5081; www.holandskoweb.com; Frana Kráľa 5)

UK Embassy (☎5998 2000; http://ukinslovakia.fco.gov.uk; Panská 16)

US Embassy (☎5443 0861; http://slovakia.usembassy.gov; Hviezdoslavovo nám 4)

Food

Restaurant review price indicators are based on the cost of a main course.

€ less than €6

€€ €6 to €12

€€€ more than €12

Gay & Lesbian Travellers

Homosexuality has been legal in Slovakia since the 1960s but this is a conservative, mostly Catholic, country. The GLBT scene is small in Bratislava and all but nonexistent elsewhere. Check out www.gay.sk.

Internet Access

Wi-fi is widely available at lodgings and cafes across the country; so much so that internet cafes are becoming scarce. For the laptopless, lodgings also often have computers you can use.

Money

» ATMs are quite common even in smaller towns, but shouldn't be relied upon in villages.

» Visa and MasterCard are accepted at most hotels and the top-end, popular restaurants in main tourist zones.

» Since January 2009, Slovakia's legal tender has been the euro. But you'll still hear reference to the former currency, the Slovak crown, or Slovenská koruna (Sk).

» Tipping 10% is fairly standard, though some locals tip less.

Post

Post office service is reliable, but be sure to hand your outgoing mail to a clerk; your postcard may languish in a box for quite some time.

Public Holidays

New Year's and Independence Day 1 January

Three Kings Day 6 January

Good Friday and Easter Monday March/April

Labour Day 1 May

Victory over Fascism Day 8 May

SS Cyril and Methodius Day 5 July

SNP Day 29 August

Constitution Day 1 September

Our Lady of Sorrows Day 15 September

All Saints' Day 1 November

Christmas 24 to 26 December

Telephone

Landline numbers can have either seven or eight digits. Mobile phone numbers (10 digits) are often used for businesses; they start with ⌾09. When dialling from abroad, you need to drop the zero from both city area codes and mobile phone numbers. Purchase local and international phone cards at newsagents. Dial ⌾00 to call out of Slovakia.

MOBILE PHONES
The country has GSM (900/1800MHz) and 3G UMTS networks operated by providers Orange, T-Mobile and O₂.

Tourist Information

Association of Information Centres of Slovakia (AICES; ⌾16 186; www.aices.sk) Runs an extensive network of city information centres.

Slovak Tourist Board (www.slovakia.travel) No Slovakia-wide information office exists; it's best to go online.

Travellers With Disabilities

Slovakia lags behind many EU states in accommodation for disabled travellers. **Slovak Union for the Disabled** (www.sztp.sk) works to change the status quo. Hotels and restaurants have few ramps or barrier-free rooms; pavements are far from universally smooth. There's some accessibility on public transport, including buses that lower, and special seating.

Visas

For a full list of visa requirements, see www.mzv.sk (under 'Ministry' and then 'Travel').
» No is visa required for EU citizens.
» Visitors from Australia, New Zealand, Canada, Japan and the US do not need a visa for up to 90 days.
» Visas are required for South African nationals, among others. For the full list see www.slovak-republic.org/visa-embassies.

Getting There & Away

Bratislava and Košice are the country's main entry/exit points. Flights, cars and tours can be booked online at lonelyplanet.com.

Entering Slovakia from the EU, indeed from most of Europe, is a breeze. Lengthy custom checks make arriving from the Ukraine more tedious.

Air

Bratislava's intra-European airport (BTS; www.airportbratislava.sk; Ivanská cesta), 9km northeast of the city centre, is small. Unless you're coming from the UK, which has several direct flights, your arrival will likely be by train. Vienna in Austria has the nearest international air hub.

AIRPORTS

Košice International Airport (KSC; www.airportkosice.sk)

Vienna International Airport (VIE; www.viennaairport.com) Austrian airport with regular buses that head the 60km east to Bratislava. Worldwide connections.

AIRLINES

The main airlines operating in Slovakia:

Austrian Airlines (www.aua.com) Connects Košice with Vienna.

Czech Airlines (www.czechairlines.com) Connects Košice with Prague.

Danube Wings (www.danubewings.eu) Connects Bratislava and Košice with Croatia.

Ryanair (www.ryanair.com) Connects Bratislava with numerous destinations across the UK and Italy, coastal Spain, Paris and Brussels.

Land

Border posts between Slovakia and fellow EU Schengen member states – Czech Republic, Hungary, Poland and Austria – are nonexistent. You can come and go at will. This makes checks at the Ukrainian border all the more strident, as you will be entering the EU. By bus expect one to two hours' wait; by car, much more.

BUS

Local buses connect Poprad and Ždiar with Poland. Eurobus (www.eurobus.sk)and Eurolines (www.slovaklines.sk) handle international routes across Europe from Bratislava and heading east to Ukraine from Košice.

CAR & MOTORCYCLE

Private vehicle requirements for driving in Slovakia are registration papers, a 'green card' (proof of third-party liability insurance), nationality sticker, first-aid kit and warning triangle.

TRAIN

See www.cp.atlas.sk for domestic and international train schedules. Direct trains connect Bratislava to Austria, the Czech Republic, Poland, Hungary and Russia; from Košice, trains connect to the Czech Republic, Poland, Ukraine and Russia. The fastest domestic trains are Intercity (IC) or Eurocity (EC). Rýclík (R), or 'fast' trains take slightly longer, but run more frequently and cost less. Osobný (Ob) trains are slowest (and cost least).

River

Danube riverboats offer an alternative way to get between Bratislava and Vienna.

Getting Around

Air

Danube Wings (V5; www.danubewings.eu) offers the only domestic air service: weekdays only, between Bratislava and Košice.

Bicycle

Roads are often narrow and potholed, and in towns cobblestones and tram tracks can prove dangerous for bike riders. Bike rental is uncommon outside mountain resorts. The cost of transporting a bike by rail is usually 10% of the train ticket.

Bus

Read timetables carefully; fewer buses operate on weekends and holidays. You can find up-to-date schedules online at www.cp.atlas. sk. The national bus company in Slovakia is Slovenská Autobusová Doprava (SAD; www.sad.sk).

Car & Motorcycle

» Foreign driving licences with photo ID are valid in Slovakia.
» *Nálepka* (toll stickers) are required on *all* green-signed motorways. Fines for not having them can be hefty. Buy at petrol stations (rental cars usually have them).
» City streetside parking restrictions are eagerly enforced. Always buy a ticket from a machine, attendant or newsagent in Old Town centres.
» Car hire is available in Bratislava and Košice primarily.

Local Transport

Towns all have good bus systems; villages have infrequent service. Bratislava also has trams and trolleybuses.
» Public transport generally operates from 4.30am to 11.30pm daily.
» City transport tickets are good for all local buses, trams and trolleybuses. Buy at newsstands and validate on board or risk serious fines (this is not a scam).

Train

Train is the way to travel in Slovakia; most tourist destinations are off the main Bratislava–Košice line. No online reservations; ticket machines are also rare. Reserve at train station offices. Visit www.cp.atlas.sk for up-to-date schedules. Slovak Republic Railways (ŽSR; ☑18 188; www.slovakrail. sk) has far-reaching, efficient national rail service.

Slovenia

Best Places to Eat

» Gostilna na Gradu (p490)
» Gostilna Ribič (p514)
» Gril Ranca (p513)
» Hiša Franko (p505)
» Gostilna Lectar (p497)

Best Places to Stay

» Antiq Palace Hotel & Spa (p489)
» Max Piran (p509)
» Hostel Pekarna (p513)
» Camping Bled (p497)
» Penzion Gasperin (p500)

Why Go?

It's a pint-sized place, with a surface area of just more than 20,000 sq km and two million people. But 'good things come in small packages', and never was that old chestnut more appropriate than in describing Slovenia. The country has everything from beaches, snowcapped mountains, hills awash in grape vines and wide plains blanketed in sunflowers to Gothic churches, baroque palaces and art nouveau buildings. Its incredible mixture of climates brings warm Mediterranean breezes up to the foothills of the Alps, where it can snow in summer.

The capital, Ljubljana, is a culturally rich city that values livability and sustainability over unfettered growth. This sensitivity towards the environment extends to rural and lesser-developed parts of the country as well. With more than half of its total area covered in forest, Slovenia really is one of the 'greenest' countries in the world.

When to Go
Ljubljana

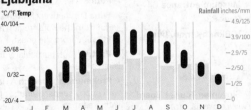

Apr–Jun Spring is a great time to be in the lowlands and the flower-carpeted valleys of the Julian Alps.

Sep This is the month made for everything – still warm enough to swim and tailor-made for hiking.

Dec–Mar Everyone (and their grandma) dons their skis in this winter-sport-mad country.

AT A GLANCE

» **Currency** Euro (€)

» **Language** Slovene

» **Money** ATMs are everywhere; banks open weekdays and Saturday morning

» **Visas** Not required for citizens of the EU, Australia, USA, Canada or New Zealand

Fast Facts

» **Area** 20,273 sq km

» **Capital** Ljubljana

» **Country code** ☑386

» **Emergency** Ambulance & fire ☑112, police ☑113

Exchange Rates

Australia	A$1	€0.82
Canada	C$1	€0.77
Japan	¥100	€0.83
New Zealand	NZ$1	€0.65
UK	UK£1	€1.18
USA	US$1	€0.78

Set Your Budget

» **Budget hotel room** €50

» **Two-course meal** €20

» **Museum entrance** €4

» **Beer** €3

» **100km by train/bus** €6/10

Resources

» **Slovenian Tourist Board** (www.slovenia.info)

» **E-uprava** (http://e-uprava.gov.si/e-unprava/en)

Connections

Border formalities with Slovenia's three European Union neighbours – Italy, Austria and Hungary – are nonexistent and all are accessible by train and bus. Venice can also be reached by boat from Piran. Expect a somewhat closer inspection of your documents when travelling to/from non-EU Croatia.

ITINERARIES

One Week

Spend a couple of days in Ljubljana, then head north to unwind in Bohinj or romantic Bled beside idyllic mountain lakes. Depending on the season, take a bus or drive over the hair-raising Vršič Pass into the valley of the vivid blue Soča River and take part in some adventure sports in Bovec or Kobarid before returning to Ljubljana.

Two Weeks

Another week will allow you to see just about everything: all of the above as well as the Karst caves at Škocjan and Postojna and the Venetian ports of Koper and Piran on the Adriatic. The country is small, so even the far eastern region, particularly the historically rich and picturesque city of Ptuj, is just a few hours away by car or train.

Essential Food & Drink

» **Pršut** Air-dried, thinly sliced ham from the Karst region not unlike Italian prosciutto.

» **Žlikrofi** Ravioli-like parcels filled with cheese, bacon and chives.

» **Žganci** The Slovenian stodge of choice – groats made from barley or corn but usually *ajda* (buckwheat).

» **Potica** A kind of nut roll eaten at teatime or as a dessert.

» **Wine** Distinctively Slovenian tipples include peppery red Teran from the Karst region and Malvazija, a straw-colour white wine from the coast.

» **Postrv** Trout, particularly the variety from the Soča River, is a real treat.

» **Prekmurska gibanica** A rich concoction of pastry filled with poppy seeds, walnuts, apples, and cheese and topped with cream.

» **Štruklji** Scrumptious dumplings made with curd cheese and served either savoury as a main course or sweet as a dessert.

» **Brinjevec** A very strong brandy made from fermented juniper berries (and a decidedly acquired taste).

LJUBLJANA

🎵 01 / POP 280,607

Slovenia's capital and largest city also happens to be one of Europe's greenest and most livable capitals. Car traffic is restricted in the centre, leaving the leafy banks of the emerald-green Ljubljanica River, which flows through the city's heart, free for pedestrians and cyclists. In summer, cafes set up terrace seating along the river, lending the feel of a perpetual street party. Slovenia's master of early-Modern, minimalist design, Jože Plečnik, graced Ljubljana with beautiful alabaster bridges and baubles, pylons and pyramids that are both elegant and playful. The museums, hotels and restaurants are among the best in the country.

History

Legacies of the Roman city of Emona – remnants of walls, dwellings, early churches, even a gilded statuette – can be seen everywhere. Ljubljana took its present form in the mid-12th century as Laibach under the Habsburgs, but it gained regional prominence in 1809,

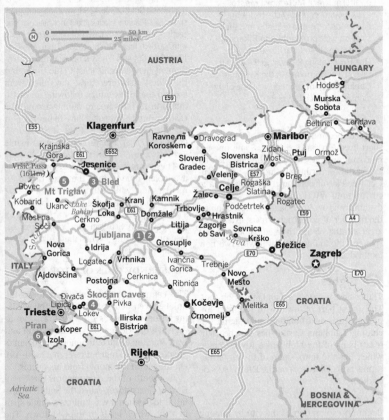

Slovenia Highlights

❶ Enjoy a flight up on the funicular to **Ljubljana Castle** (p484).

❷ Consider the genius of architect Jože Plečnik at Ljubljana's **National & University Library** (p485).

❸ Gaze at the natural perfection that is **Lake Bled** (p496).

❹ Gawk in awe at the 100m high walls of the incredible **Škocjan Caves** (p506).

❺ Climb to the top of the country's tallest mountain, **Mt Triglav** (p501).

❻ Get lost wandering the Venice-inspired, narrow alleyways of **Piran** (p508).

LJUBLJANA IN TWO DAYS

Take the funicular to **Ljubljana Castle**, then come down and explore the **Central Market** area. After a seafood lunch at **Ribca**, walk around the **Old Town** then cross the Ljubljanica River and walk north along Vegova ulica to **Kongresni Trg** and **Prešernov Trg**. Plan your evening over a fortifying libation at one of the many cafes along the Ljubljanica: low key at **Jazz Club Gajo** or alternative at **Metelkova Mesto**.

On your second day check out the city's museums and galleries, and then stroll or cycle on a **Ljubljana Bike**, stopping for an oh-so-local horse burger at **Hot Horse** along the way. In the evening, take in a performance at the **Križanke** or **Cankarjev Dom** and then visit one of the clubs you missed last night.

when it became the capital of Napoleon's short-lived 'Illyrian Provinces'. Some fine art nouveau buildings filled up the holes left by a devastating earthquake in 1895, and architect Jože Plečnik continued the remake of the city up until WWII. In recent years the city's dynamic mayor, Zoran Janković, has doubled the number of pedestrian streets, extended a great swathe of the river embankment and spanned the Ljubljanica River with two new footbridges.

⊙ Sights

The easiest way to see Ljubljana is on foot. The oldest part of town, with the most important historical buildings and sights (including Ljubljana Castle) lies on the right (east) bank of the Ljubljanica River. Center, which has the lion's share of the city's museums and galleries, is on the left (west) side of the river.

CASTLE AREA

Begin an exploration of the city by making the trek up to **Castle Hill** (Grajska Planota) to poke around grand Ljubljana Castle. The castle area offers a couple of worthwhile exhibitions, and the castle watchtower affords amazing views out over the city. The prospect of lunch at one of the city's best restaurants, Gostilna na Gradu (p490), provides an added inducement.

There are several ways to access the castle, with the easiest (and for kids, the most

fun) being a 70m-long **funicular** (vzpenjača; ☑reservations 306 42 00; www.ljubljanskigrad.si; Krekov trg 3-7; return adult/child €4/3; ⊙9am-11pm Apr-Sep, 10am-9pm Oct-Mar) that leaves from Old Town not far from the market (p491) on Vodnikov trg. If you'd like to get some exercise, you can hike the hill in about 20 minutes. There are three main walking routes: Študentovska ulica, which runs south from Ciril Metodov trg; steep Reber ulica from Stari trg; and Ulica na Grad from Gornji trg.

TOP CHOICE **Ljubljana Castle**　　　　CASTLE
(Ljubljanski Grad; ☑306 42 93; www.ljubljanskigrad. si; Grajska Planota 1; adult/child incl funicular and castle attractions €8/5, castle attractions only €6/3; with guided tour €10/8; ⊙9am-11pm May-Sep, 10am-9pm Oct-Apr) There's been a human settlement here since at least Celtic times, but the oldest structures these days date from around the 16th-century, following an earthquake in 1511. It's free to ramble around the castle grounds, but you'll have to pay to enter the **Watchtower**, the **Chapel of St George** (Kapela Sv Jurija) and to see the worthwhile **Exhibition on Slovenian History**.

There are several admission options available; some include the price of the funicular ride, while others include a **castle tour**. Consult the castle website for details. The **Ljubljana Castle Information Centre** (⊙9am-9pm Apr-Sep, 9am-6pm Oct-Mar) can advise on tours and events that might be on during your visit.

PREŠERNOV TRG & OLD TOWN

Prešernov Trg　　　　　　SQUARE, PLAZA
This central and beautiful square forms the link between Center and the Old Town. Taking pride of place is the **Prešeren monument** (1905), designed by Maks Fabiani and Ivan Zajc and erected in honour of Slovenia's greatest poet, France Prešeren (1800–49). On the plinth are motifs from his poems.

Just south of the monument is the **Triple Bridge** (Tromostovje), called the Špital (Hospital) Bridge when it was built as a single span in 1842, which leads to the Old Town. The prolific architect Jože Plečnik added the two sides in 1931.

To the east of the monument at No 5 is the Italianate Central Pharmacy (Centralna Lekarna), an erstwhile cafe frequented by intellectuals in the 19th century. To the north, on the corner of Trubarjeva cesta and Miklošičeva cesta, is the delightful Secessionist **Palača Urbanc** (Urbanc Palace) building from 1903.

Mestni Trg   SQUARE

The first of the Old Town's three 'squares' (the other two – Stari trg and Gornji trg – are more like narrow cobbled streets), Mestni trg (Town Square) is dominated by the town hall, in front of which stands the **Robba Fountain** (the original is now in the National Gallery).

Town Hall   TOWN HALL

(Mestna Hiša; ☑306 30 00; Mestni trg; ☉7.30am-4pm Mon-Fri) The seat of the city government and sometimes referred to as the *Magistrat* or *Rotovž*. It was erected in the late 15th century and rebuilt in 1718. The Gothic courtyard inside, arcaded on three levels, is where theatrical performances once took place and contains some lovely sgraffiti.

If you look above the south portal leading to a second courtyard you'll see a relief map of Ljubljana as it appeared in the second half of the 17th century.

Stari Trg   SQUARE

The 'Old Square' is the true heart of the Old Town. It is lined with 19th-century wooden shopfronts, quiet courtyards and cobblestone passageways. From behind the medieval houses on the eastern side, paths once led to Castle Hill, which was a source of water. The buildings fronting the river had large passageways built to allow drainage in case of flooding.

Gornji Trg   SQUARE

Upper Square is the eastern extension of Stari trg. The five **medieval houses** at Nos 7 to 15 have narrow side passages (some with doors) where rubbish was once deposited so that it could be washed down into the river.

FREE Botanical Garden   PUBLIC GARDEN

(Botanični Vrt; ☑427 12 80; www.botanicni-vrt.si; Ižanska cesta 15; ☉7am-8pm Jul & Aug, 7am-7pm Apr-Jun, Sep & Oct, 7am-5pm Nov-Mar) About 800m southeast of the Old Town along Karlovška cesta and over the Ljubljanica River, this 2.5-hectare botanical garden was founded in 1810 as a sanctuary of native flora. It contains 4500 species of plants and trees, about a third of which are indigenous,

CENTER

This large district on the left bank of the Ljubljanica is the nerve centre of modern Ljubljana. It is filled with shops, commercial offices, government departments and embassies. The region is divided into several distinct neighbourhoods centred on town squares.

Trg Francoske Revolucije   SQUARE

'French Revolution Sq' was for centuries the headquarters of the Teutonic Knights of the Cross (Križniki). They built a commandery here in the early 13th century, which was transformed into the **Križanke** (☑241 60 00; Trg Francoske Revolucije 1-2) monastery complex in the early 18th century. Today it serves as the headquarters of the Ljubljana Festival (p489).

TOP CHOICE National & University Library   HISTORIC BUILDING

(☑200 11 09; Turjaška ulica 1; ☉9am-6pm Mon-Fri, 9am-2pm Sat) This library is Plečnik's masterpiece, completed in 1941. To appreciate this great man's philosophy, enter through the main door (note the horse-head doorknobs) on Turjaška ulica – you'll find yourself in near darkness, entombed in black marble. As you ascend the steps, you'll emerge into a colonnade suffused with light – the light of knowledge, according to the architect's plans.

The **Main Reading Room** (Velika Čitalnica), now open to nonstudents only by group tour in summer, has huge glass walls and some stunning lamps, also designed by Plečnik.

City Museum   MUSEUM

(Mestni Muzej; ☑241 25 00; www.mestnimuzej.si; Gosposka ulica 15; adult/child €4/2.50; ☉10am-6pm Tue & Wed, Fri-Sun, 10am-9pm Thu) The excellent city museum focuses on Ljubljana's history, culture and politics via imaginative multimedia and interactive displays. The reconstructed Roman street that linked the eastern gates of Emona to the Ljubljanica and the collection of well-preserved classical finds in the basement are worth a visit in themselves.

The permanent 'Faces of Ljubljana' exhibit of celebrated and lesser-known *žabarji* ('froggers', as natives of the capital are known) is memorable. They host some very good special exhibitions too.

National Museum of Slovenia   MUSEUM

(Narodni Muzej Slovenije; ☑241 44 00; www.nms.si; Prešernova cesta 20; adult/child €3/2.50, 1st Sun of month free; ☉10am-6pm Fri-Wed, 10am-8pm Thu) Highlights include a highly embossed *Vače situla*, a Celtic pail from the late 6th century BC unearthed in a town east of Ljubljana, and a Stone Age bone flute discovered near Cerkno in western Slovenia in 1995. There are also examples of Roman glass and jewellery found in 6th-century Slavic graves, along with many other historical finds.

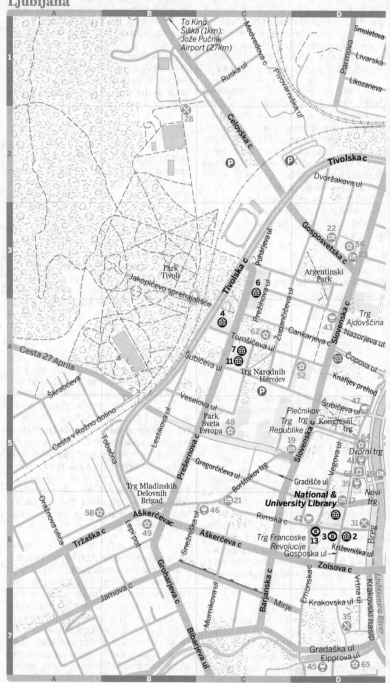

To Kino
Šiška (1km);
Jože Pučnik
Airport (27km)

Smoletova
Parmova
Livarska
Likozarieva

Ruska ul
Celovška c
Medvedova c
Pivovarniška ul

Tivolska c
Dvoržakova ul

Gosposvetska c

22
56
23

Argentinski
Park

Puharjeva ul
Tivolska c
Park
Tivoli
Jakopičevo sprehajališče

6
Prežihova ul
Župančičeva ul

Trg
Ajdovščina
43
Slovenska c
Nazorjeva ul

4
62
Tomšičeva ul
Cankarjeva ul

Čopova ul
7
11
Šubičeva ul
Trg Narodnih
Herojev
52
Knafljev prehod

Cesta 27 Aprila
Škrabčeva
Šubičeva ul
47

Veselova ul
Plečnikov
Trg
Republike
Kongresni
trg
64
48
Lestikova ul
Park
Sveta
Evropa
19
Slovenska c
Dvorni trg

Cesta v Rožno dolino
Tobačna
Gregorčičeva ul
Borštnikov trg
Vegova ul
Novi
trg
66
39

Trg Mladinskih
Delovnih
Brigad
Gradišče ul
National &
University Library
17

Prešernova c
21
46

58
Oražnova ulica
Aškerčevac
Snežniška ul
Aškerčeva c
Rimska c
42
Trg Francoske
Revolucije
Gosposka ul
13
3
2
31
Križevniška ul

49
Tržaška c
Lepi pot
Zoisova c

Grobarjeva c
Barjanska c
Emonska c
Vrtna ul
Krakovski nasip
Ljubljanica River

Jamova c
Murnikova ul
Mirje
Krakovska ul
35

Bibarjeva ul
Gradaška ul
Eipprova ul
45
65

28

P
P
P

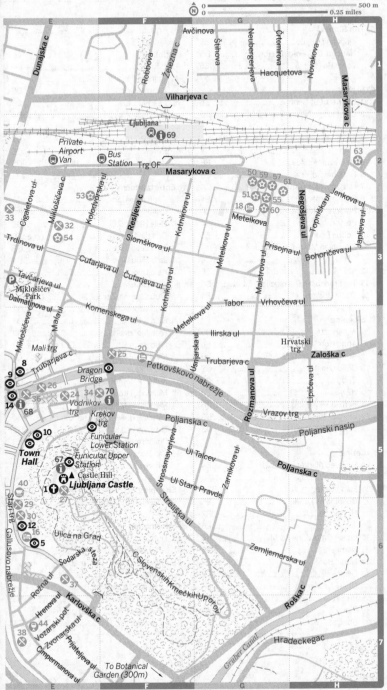

Avčinova

Štihova

Neubergerjeva

Čtomirova

Novakova

Hacquetova

Masarykova c

Vilharjeva c

Robbova

Železna c

Ljubljana

69

Private
Airport
Van

Bus
Station

Trg OF

63

Masarykova c

33

Cigaletova ul

Miklošičeva c

53

Kolodvorska ul

Resljeva c

50 59 57 61

51 55

18 60

Metelkova

32

54

Trdinova ul

Slomškova ul

Kotnikova ul

Metelkova ul

Negošjeva ul

Topniška ul

Jenkova ul

Maistrova ul

Masljeva ul

Cufarjeva ul

Čufarjeva ul

Prisojna ul

Bohoričeva ul

Tavčarjeva ul

Miklošičev
Park

Dalmatinova ul

Komenskega ul

Kotnikova ul

Tabor

Vrhovčeva ul

Hrvatski
trg

Zaloška c

Miklošičeva

Malju

Mali trg

Trubarjeva c

Metelkova ul

Ilirska ul

25

20

Usnjarska ul

Trubarjeva c

Rozmanova ul

Lipičeva ul

8

9

Petkovškovo nabrežje

Dragon
Bridge

26

24 34 70

36

Vodnikov
trg

68

14

Krekov
trg

Poljanska c

Vrazov trg

Poljanski nasip

Poljanska c

10

Strossmayerjeva

Ul Talcev

Zarnikova ul

**Town
Hall**

Funicular
Lower Station

67

Funicular Upper
Station

▲ Castle Hill

40

1

Ljubljana Castle

27

Ul Stare Pravde

29

30

12 16

5

Ulica na Grad

Sodarska steza

Streliška ul

Zemljemerska ul

Štari trg

Gallusovo nabrežje

37

C Slovenskih Kmečkih Uporol

Rožna ul

Karlovška c

Hrenova ul

Roška c

44

Vozarska ul

Zvonarska ul

Prijateljeva ul

38

Cimpermanova ul

**To Botanical
Garden (300m)**

Gruber Canal

Hradeckega c

Ljubljana

Check out the ceiling fresco in the foyer, which features an allegorical Carniola surrounded by important Slovenes from the past and the statues of the Muses and Fates relaxing on the stairway banisters.

Slovenian Museum of
Natural History   MUSEUM
(Prirodoslovni Muzej Slovenije; ☑241 09 40; www2. pms-lj.si; Prešernova cesta 20; adult/student €3/2.50, incl national museum €5/4; ☉10am-6pm Fri-Wed, 10am-8pm Thu; ℗) Housed in the same impressive building as the National Museum, the Natural History Museum contains the usual reassembled mammoth and whale skeletons, stuffed birds, reptiles and mammals. However, the mineral collections amassed by the philanthropic Baron Žiga Zois in the early 19th century and the display on Slovenia's unique salamander *Proteus anguinus* are worth a visit.

National Gallery   MUSEUM
(☑241 54 18; www.ng-slo.si; Prešernova cesta 24; adult/child €7/5, 1st Sun of month free; ☉10am-6pm Tue-Sun) Slovenia's foremost assembly of fine art is housed over two floors both in an old building dating to 1896 and an impressive modern wing.

Ljubljana Museum of Modern Art   MUSEUM
(☑241 68 00; www.mg-lj.si; Tomšičeva ulica 14; adult/student €5/2.50; ☉10am-6pm Tue-Sun) This museum houses the very best in Slovenian modern art. Keep an eye out for works by painters Tone Kralj *(Peasant Wedding)*, the expressionist France Mihelič *(The Quintet)* and the surrealist Štefan Planinc *(Primeval World series)* as well as sculptors such as Jakob Savinšek *(Protest)*.

The museum also owns works by the influential 1980s and 1990s multimedia group Neue Slowenische Kunst (NSK; *Suitcase for Spiritual Use: Baptism under Triglav)* and the artists' cooperative Irwin *(Kapital)*.

⚲ Tours

Two-hour walking tours (adult/child €10/5; ☉10am, 2pm & 5pm Apr-Oct), combined with a ride on the funicular or the tourist train up to the castle or a cruise on the Ljubljanica, are organised by the TIC. They depart daily from the town hall on Mestni trg.

✸ Festivals & Events

Druga Godba   WORLD MUSIC
(http://festival.drugagodba.si; ☉May-Jun) This festival of alternative and world music, takes place in the Križanke from late May to early June.

Ljubljana Festival   MUSIC & THEATRE
(www.ljubljanafestival.si; ☉Jul & Aug) The number-one event on Ljubljana's social calendar is the Ljubljana Festival, a celebration from early July to late August of music, opera, theatre and dance held at venues throughout the city, but principally in the open-air theatre at the Križanke.

International Ljubljana
Marathon   MARATHON
(www.ljubljanskimaraton.si; ☉Oct) Takes off on the last Saturday in October.

🛏 Sleeping

The TIC has comprehensive details of private rooms (from single/double €30/50) and apartments (from double/quad €55/80) though only a handful are central.

ᵀᴼᴾ/CHOICE **Antiq Palace**
Hotel & Spa   BOUTIQUE HOTEL €€€
(☑051 364 124; www.antiqpalace.com; Gosposka ulica 10 & Vegova ul 5a; s/d €180/210; ℗🖧❋@🛜) Easily the city's most luxurious sleeping option, the Antiq Palace occupies a 16th-century townhouse, about a block from the river. Accommodation is in 13 individually designed suites, each with several rooms and some stretching to 250 sq m in size. The list of amenities is a mile long. The target market is upscale honeymooners and businessmen on expenses.

Cubo   BOUTIQUE HOTEL €€€
(☑425 60 00; www.hotelcubo.com; Slovenska cesta 15; s/d €120/140) This sleek boutique hotel in the centre of town boasts high-end, minimalist design that could have stepped out of the pages of *Wallpaper* magazine. The owners have placed great emphasis on using the best construction materials and high-quality bedding to ensure a good night's sleep. The in-house restaurant is very good.

Celica Hostel   HOSTEL €€
(☑230 97 00; www.hostelcelica.com; Metelkova ulica 8; dm €19-25, s/d/tr cell €53/60/70; ℗@🛜) This stylishly revamped former prison (1882) in Metelkova has 20 'cells', designed by different artists and architects and complete with original bars. There are nine rooms and apartments with three to seven beds and a packed, popular 12-bed dorm. The ground floor is home to a cafe and restaurant (set lunch €5 to €7, open 7.30am to midnight)

and the hostel boasts its own gallery where everyone can show their work.

Slamič B&B
PENSION €€

(☑433 82 33; www.slamic.si; Kersnikova ulica 1; s €65-75, d €95-100, ste from €135; P❋@🛜) It's slightly away from the action but Slamič, a B&B above a famous cafe and teahouse, offers 11 bright rooms with antique(ish) furnishings and parquet floors. Choice rooms include the ones looking onto a back garden and the one just off an enormous terrace used by the cafe.

Penzion Pod Lipo
PENSION €€

(☑031 809 893; www.penzion-podlipo.com; Borštnikov trg 3; d/tr/q/ste €65/75/100/125; @) Sitting atop one of Ljubljana's oldest *gostilna* (inn-like restaurant) and a 400-year-old linden tree, this 10-room inn offers plain rooms, but excellent value in a part of the city that is filling up with bars and restaurants. We love the communal kitchen, the original hardwood floors and the east-facing terrace with deck chairs that catch the morning sun.

H2O
HOSTEL €

(☑041 662 266; www.h2ohostel.com; Petkovškovo nabrežje 47; dm €17-22, d €36-52, q €68-88; @🛜) One of our favourite hostels in Ljubljana, this six-room place wraps around a tiny courtyard bordering the Ljubljanica River and one room has views of the castle. Private doubles are available and guests have access to a common kitchen.

Antiq Hotel
BOUTIQUE HOTEL €€€

(☑421 35 60; www.antiqhotel.si; Gornji trg 3; s €75-120, d €85-150; ❋@🛜) This attractive boutique has been cobbled together from several townhouses in the Old Town. There are 16 spacious rooms and a multitiered back garden. The decor is kitsch with a smirk and there are fabulous touches everywhere. Among our favourite rooms are enormous No 8, with views of the Hercules Fountain, and No 13, with glimpses of Ljubljana Castle.

Zeppelin Hostel
HOSTEL €

(☑059 191 427; www.zeppelinhostel.com; 2 fl, Slovenska cesta 47; dm €18-24, d €49-60; @🛜) Located in the historic Evropa building on the corner of Gosposvetska cesta, this hostel offers clean and bright dorm rooms (four to eight beds) and doubles and is run by a young team of international travellers who keep their guests informed on parties and happenings around town.

Alibi Hostel
HOSTEL €

(☑251 12 44; www.alibi.si; Cankarjevo nabrežje 27; dm €15-18, d €40-50; ❋@) This very well-situated 106-bed hostel on the Ljubljanica has brightly painted, airy dorms with four to eight wooden bunks and a dozen doubles. There's a private suite at the top for six people.

🍴 Eating

TOP CHOICE Gostilna na Gradu
SLOVENIAN €€

(☑031 523 760; www.nagradu.si; Grajska planota 1; mains €8-14; ☉10am-midnight Mon-Sat, noon-6pm Sun) Be sure to plan a meal here at this marvelous traditional Slovenian restaurant during your visit to the castle. The chefs pride themselves on using only Slovenian-sourced breads, cheeses and meats, and age-old recipes to prepare a meal to remember. The castle setting is ideal. Book a table in advance to avoid disappointment.

Julija
MEDITERRANEAN €€

(☑425 64 63; http://julijarestaurant.com; Stari trg 9; €10.90-18.90; ☉noon-10pm) This is arguably the best of a trio of restaurants standing side by side on touristy Stari trg. We love the three-course set lunches served on the sidewalk terrace for €9. The cuisine here revolves around risottos and pastas, though the chicken breast special served in a spicy peanut sauce was one of the best meals on our trip.

Ribca
SEAFOOD €

(☑425 15 44; www.ribca.si; Adamič-Lundrovo nabrežje 1; dishes €5-8; ☉8am-4pm Mon-Fri, to 2pm Sat) One of the culinary joys of a visit to Ljubljana is the chance to sample inexpensive and well-prepared fish dishes. This basement seafood bar below the Plečnik Colonnade in Pogačarjev trg is one of the best for tasty fried squid, sardines and herrings. The setting is informal, though the cuisine is top notch. Set lunch on weekdays is €7.50.

Špajza
SLOVENIAN €€

(☑425 30 94; www.spajza-restaurant.si; Gornji trg 28; mains €15-25; ☉noon-11pm) This popular Old Town restaurant is the perfect spot for a splurge or romantic meal for two. The interior is decorated with rough-hewn tables and chairs, wooden floors, frescoed ceilings and nostalgic bits and pieces. The terrace in summer is a delight. The cooking is traditional Slovenian, with an emphasis on less-common mains like rabbit and veal.

Pri Škofu
SLOVENIAN €€

(📞426 45 08; Rečna ulica 8; mains €8-22; ⏰7am-11pm; 🔊) This wonderful little place in tranquil Krakovo, south of the centre, serves some of the best prepared local dishes and salads in Ljubljana, with an ever-changing menu. Weekday set lunches are good value at €8.

Lunch Café Marley & Me
INTERNATIONAL €€

(📞040 564 188; www.lunchcafe.si; Stari trg 9; mains from €7-20; ⏰11am-11pm; 🔊) The name couldn't be more misleading. It's more than a lunch cafe...and the 'Marley' bit? We just don't get it. Still, it's a very popular spot for lunch or dinner over salads, pastas and a variety of meats and seafood. There's sidewalk dining in nice weather.

Trta
ITALIAN €

(📞426 50 66; www.trta.si; Grudnovo nabrežje 21; pizza €8-10; ⏰11am-10pm Mon-Fri, noon-10.30pm Sat; 🔊) This award-winning pizzeria, with large pies cooked in a wood-fired oven, is slightly south of the centre, across the river opposite Trnovo.

Namasté
INDIAN €€

(📞425 01 59; www.restavracija-namaste.si; Breg 8; mains €10-20; ⏰11am-midnight Mon-Sat, to 10pm Sun; 🅿) Should you fancy a bit of Indian, head for this place on the left bank of the Ljubljanica. You won't get high-street-quality curry but the thalis and tandoori dishes are very good. The choice of vegetarian dishes is better than average and a set lunch costs between €6.50 €8.50. Eat along the river in nice weather.

Falafel
MIDDLE EASTERN €

(📞041 640 166; Trubarjeva cesta 40; sandwiches €4-6; ⏰11am-midnight Mon-Fri, noon-midnight Sat, 1-10pm Sun) Authentic Middle Eastern food, like falafel and hummus, served up to go or eat in at a few tables and chairs scattered about. Perfect choice for a quick meal on the run or the late-night munchies.

Hot Horse
BURGERS €

(📞521 14 27; www.hot-horse.si; Park Tivoli, Celovška cesta 25; snacks & burgers €3-6; ⏰9am-6pm Tue-Sun, 10am-6pm Mon) This little place in the city's biggest park supplies *Ljubljančani* (local people) with their favourite treat: horse burgers (€4). It's just down the hill from the Museum of Contemporary History.

Self-Catering
Self-caterers and those on a tight budget will want to head directly to Ljubljana's vast open-air market (Vodnikov trg; ⏰6am-6pm Mon-Fri, 6am-4pm Sat summer, 6am-4pm Mon-Sat winter) on Vodnikov trg, just across the Triple Bridge to the southeast of Prešernov trg. Here you'll find stalls selling everything from wild mushrooms and forest berries to honey and homemade cheeses. The covered market (Pogačarjev trg 1; ⏰7am-2pm Mon-Wed & Sat, 7am-4pm Thu & Fri) nearby sells meats and cheeses, and there's a fish market (Adamič-Lundrovo nabrežje 1; ⏰7am-4pm Mon-Fri, 7am-2pm Sat) too. You'll also find open-air fish stands selling plates of fried calamari for as low as €6. Another budget option is *burek*, pastry stuffed with cheese, meat or even apple. Reputedly the best places in town are Olimpije (Pražakova ulica 2; burek €2; ⏰24hr) southwest of the train and bus stations, and Nobel Burek (📞232 33 92; Miklošičeva cesta 30; burek €2, pizza slices €1.40; ⏰24hr).

🍷 Drinking

Few cities of this size have central Ljubljana's concentration of inviting cafes and bars, the vast majority with outdoor seating in the warmer months.

Bars & Pubs

TOP CHOICE Žmavc
BAR

(📞251 03 24; Rimska cesta 21; ⏰7.30am-1am Mon-Fri, from 10am Sat, from 6pm Sun; 🔊) A super-popular student hang-out west of Slovenska cesta, with *manga* comic-strip scenes and figures running halfway up the walls. There's a great garden terrace for summer-evening drinking, but try to arrive early to snag a table. Also excellent for morning coffee.

BiKoFe
BAR

(📞425 93 93; Židovska steza 2; ⏰7am-1am Mon-Fri, 10am-1pm Sat & Sun; 🔊) A favourite with the hipster crowd, this cupboard of a bar has mosaic tables, studenty art on the walls, soul and jazz on the stereo, and a giant water pipe on the menu for that long, lingering smoke outside. The shady outdoor patio is a great place to enjoy a recent purchase from the Behemot (📞251 13 92; www.behemot.si; Židovska steza 3; ⏰10am-8pm Mon-Fri, 10am-3pm Sat) bookshop across the street.

Dvorni Bar
WINE BAR

(📞251 12 57; www.dvornibar.net; Dvorni trg 2; ⏰8am-1am Mon-Sat, 9am-midnight Sun; 🔊) This wine bar is an excellent place to taste Slovenian vintages; it stocks more than 100 varieties and has wine tastings every month (usually the second Wednesday).

Šank Pub
PUB

(Eipprova ulica 19; ⊙7am-1am; 🖥) Down in studenty Trnovo, this raggedy little place with brick ceiling and wooden floor is a relaxed alternative to the nearby Sax. The Šank is one of a number of inviting bars and cafes along this stretch of Eipprova ulica.

Cafes & Teahouses

TOP CHOICE Nebotičnik
CAFE

(☎040 601 787; www.neboticnik.si; 12th fl, Štefanova ulica 1; ⊙9am-1am Sun-Wed, 9am-3am Thu-Sat; 🖥) After a decade-long hibernation this elegant cafe with its breathtaking terrace atop Ljubljana's famed art deco Skyscraper (1933) has reopened, and the 360-degree views are spectacular.

Le Petit Café
CAFE

(☎251 25 75; www.lepetit.si; Trg Francoske Revolucije 4; ⊙7.30am-1am; 🖥) Just opposite the Križanke, this pleasant, boho place offers great coffee and a wide range of breakfast goodies, lunches and light meals, plus a good restaurant on the 1st floor.

Čajna Hiša
TEAHOUSE

(☎421 24 40; Stari trg 3; ⊙9am-10.30pm Mon-Fri, 9am-3pm & 6-10pm Sat; 🖥) This elegant and centrally located teahouse takes its teas very seriously. They also serve light meals and there's a tea shop next door.

Open Cafe
GAY & LESBIAN

(☎041 391 371; www.open.si; Hrenova ulica 19; ⊙4pm-midnight; 🖥) This very stylish gay-owned-and-run cafe south of the Old Town has become the meeting point for Ljubljana's burgeoning queer culture. In June 2009 it was attacked by fascist homophobes who attempted to torch the place and some patrons fought back.

Zvezda
CAFE

(☎421 90 90; Wolfova ulica 14; ⊙7am-11pm Mon-Sat, 10am-8pm Sun; 🖥) The 'Star' has all the usual varieties of coffee and tea but is celebrated for its shop-made cakes, especially *skutina pečena* (€3), an eggy cheesecake.

☆ Entertainment

Ljubljana in Your Pocket (www.inyourpocket.com), which comes out every two months, is a good English source for what's on in the capital. Buy tickets for shows and events at the venue box office, online through **Eventim** (☎430 24 05; www.eventim.si), or at Ljubljana Tourist Information Centre (p494). Expect to pay around €10 to €20 for tickets to live acts, and less for club entry and DJ nights.

Nightclubs

Cirkus
CLUB

(Kinoklub Vič; ☎051 631 631; www.cirkusklub.si; Trg Mladinskih Delovnih Brigad 7; €5; ⊙8pm-5am Tue-Sat) This popular dance club, with DJs at the weekends, occupies the former Kinoklub Vič.

Klub K4
CLUB

(☎040 212 292; www.klubk4.org; Kersnikova ulica 4; ⊙10pm-2am Tue, 11pm-4am Wed & Thu, 11pm-6am Fri & Sat, 10pm-4am Sun) This evergreen venue in the basement of the Student Organisation of Ljubljana University (ŠOU) headquarters features rave-electronic music Friday and Saturday, with other styles of music on weeknights, and a popular gay and lesbian night on Sunday.

KMŠ
CLUB

(☎425 74 80; www.klubkms.si; Tržaška cesta 2; ⊙8am-10pm Mon-Fri, 9pm-5am Sat) Located in the deep recesses of a former tobacco factory complex, the Maribor Student Club stays comatose till Saturday when it turns into a raucous place with music and dancers all over the shop.

Live Music

Kino Šiška
INDIE & ROCK

(☎box office 030 310 110; www.kinosiska.si; Trg Prekomorskih brigad 3; ⊙5-8pm Mon-Fri, 10am-1pm Sat) This renovated old movie theatre has been reopened as an urban cultural centre, hosting mainly indie, rock and alternative bands from around Slovenia and the rest of Europe.

Orto Bar
ROCK

(☎232 16 74; www.orto-bar.com; Graboličeva ulica 1; ⊙9pm-4am Tue & Wed, to 5am Thu-Sat) A popular bar-club for late-night drinking and dancing with occasional live music, Orto is just five minutes' walk from Metelkova. Note the program takes a two-month hiatus in summer during July and August.

Jazz Club Gajo
JAZZ

(☎425 32 06; www.jazzclubgajo.com; Beethovnova ulica 8; ⊙7pm-2am Mon-Sat) Now in its 18th year, Gajo is the city's premier venue for live jazz and attracts both local and international talent. Jam sessions are at 8.30pm Monday.

Sax Pub
ROCK

(☎283 90 09; Eipprova ulica 7; ⊙noon-1am Mon, 10am-1am Tue-Sat, 4-10pm Sun) Two decades in

SOMETHING COMPLETELY DIFFERENT: METELKOVO MESTO

For a scruffy antidote to trendy clubs in Ljubljana, try **Metelkova Mesto** (Metelkova Town; www.metelkova.org; Masarykova cesta 24), an ex-army garrison taken over by squatters in the 1990s and converted into a free-living commune – a miniature version of Copenhagen's Christiania. In this two-courtyard block, a dozen idiosyncratic venues hide behind brightly tagged doorways, coming to life generally after midnight daily in summer and on Friday and Saturday the rest of the year. While it's certainly not for the genteel and the quality of the acts and performances varies with the night, there's usually a little of something for everyone on hand.

Entering the main 'city gate' from Masarykova cesta, the building to the right houses **Gala Hala** (☑431 70 63; www.galahala.com), with live bands and club nights, and **Klub Channel Zero** (www.ch0.org), with punk and hardcore. Above it on the 1st floor is **Galerija Mizzart** (www.mizzart.net) with a great exhibition space (the name is no comment on the quality of the creations – promise!).

Easy to miss in the first building to the left is the **Kulturni Center Q** (Q Cultural Centre) including **Tiffany** (www.kulturnicenterq.org/tiffany/klub) for gay men and **Klub Monokel** (www.klubmonokel.com) for lesbians. Due south is the ever-popular **Jalla Jalla Club** (www.metelkovamesto.org), a congenial pub with concerts. Beyond the first courtyard to the southwest, **Klub Gromka** (www.klubgromka.org) has folk concerts, theatre and lectures. Next door is **Menza pri Koritu** (☑434 03 45; www.menzaprikoritu.org), under the creepy ET-like figures, with performance and concerts. If you're staying at the Hostel Celica (p489), all of the action is just around the corner.

Trnovo and decorated with colourful murals and graffiti inside and out, the tiny Sax has live jazz at 9pm or 9.30pm on Thursday from late August to December and February to June. Canned stuff rules at other times.

Performing Arts

Cankarjev Dom OPERA, DANCE
(☑241 71 00, box office 241 72 99; www.cd-cc.si; Prešernova cesta 10; ☉box office 11am-1pm & 3-8pm Mon-Fri, 11am-1pm Sat, 1hr before performance) Ljubljana's premier cultural and conference centre has two large auditoriums (the Gallus Hall is said to have perfect acoustics) and a dozen smaller performance spaces offering a remarkable smorgasbord of performance arts. Buy tickets at the box office.

Opera & Ballet Ljubljana OPERA, DANCE
(☑box office 241 59 59; www.opera.si; Župančičeva ulica 1; ☉box office 10am-5pm Mon-Fri, 1hr before performance) Home to the Slovenian National Opera and Ballet companies, this historic neo-Renaissance theatre was fully renovated in 2011 and restored to its former luster.

Philharmonic Hall CLASSICAL
(Slovenska Filharmonija; ☑241 08 00; www.filharmonija.si; Kongresni trg 10; ☉7am-10pm) Home to the Slovenian Philharmonic Orchestra, this smaller but more atmospheric venue also stages concerts and hosts performances of the Slovenian Chamber Choir (Slovenski Komorni Zbor), which was founded in 1991.

Križanke CLASSICAL, THEATRE
(☑241 60 00, box office 241 60 26; www.ljubljanafestival.si; Trg Francoske Revolucije 1-2; ☉box office 10am-8pm Mon-Fri, 10am-1pm Sat Apr-Sep) The open-air theatre at this sprawling 18th-century monastery hosts the events of the Ljubljana Summer Festival. The smaller Knights Hall (Viteška Dvorana) is the venue for chamber concerts.

Cinema

Kinoteka CINEMA
(☑547 15 80; www.kinoteka.si; Miklošičeva cesta 28) Shows archival art and classic films in their original language (not always English).

Kino Dvor CINEMA
(Court Cinema; ☑239 22 13; www.kinodvor.org; Kolodvorska ulica 13) The sister cinema to Kinoteka nearby screens more contemporary films from around the world.

ℹ Information

Internet Access

Many cafes and restaurants offer free wi-fi for customers. Most hostels, and some hotels, maintain a public computer for guests to surf the internet. The Slovenia Tourist Information Centre has computers on-hand to check email (per 30 minutes €1).

Cyber Cafe Xplorer (☑430 19 91; Petkovškovo nabrežje 23; per 30min/1hr €2.50/4; ☺10am-10pm Mon-Fri, 2-10pm Sat & Sun; ☎) Ljubljana's best internet cafe; also has wi-fi and offers discount international calling.

Medical Services
Central Pharmacy (Centralna Lekarna; ☑230 61 00; Prešernov trg 5; ☺8am-7.30pm Mon-Fri, 8am-3pm Sat)

Health Centre Ljubljana (Zdravstveni Dom Ljubljana; ☑472 37 00; www.zd-lj.si; Metelkova ulica 9; ☺7.30am-7pm) For non-emergencies.

University Medical Centre Ljubljana (Univerzitetni Klinični Center Ljubljana; ☑522 50 50, emergencies 522 84 08; www4.kclj.si; Zaloška cesta 2; ☺24hr) University medical clinic with 24h accident and emergency service.

Money
There are ATMs at every turn, including a row of them outside the main Ljubljana Tourist Information Centre (TIC) office. At the train station you'll find a **bureau de change** (train station; ☺7am-8pm) changing cash for no commission but not travellers cheques.

Abanka (☑300 15 00; www.abanka.si; Slovenska cesta 50; ☺9am-1pm & 3pm-5pm Mon-Fri)

Nova Ljubljanska Banka (☑476 39 00; www.nlb.si; Trg Republike 2; ☺8am-6pm Mon-Fri)

Post
Main Post Office (Slovenska cesta 32; ☺8am-7pm Mon-Fri, to 1pm Sat) Holds poste restante for 30 days and changes money.

Tourist Information
Ljubljana Tourist Information Centre (TIC; ☑306 12 15; www.visitljubljana.si; Adamič-Lundrovo nabrežje 2; ☺8am-9pm Jun-Sep, 8am-7pm Oct-May) Knowledgeable and enthusiastic staff dispense information, maps and useful literature and help with accommodation. Maintains an excellent website. Has a helpful **branch** (☑433 94 75; www.visitljubljana.si; Trg OF 6; ☺8am-10pm Jun-Sep, 10am-7pm Mon-Fri, 8am-3pm Sat Oct-May) at the train station.

Slovenian Tourist Information Centre (STIC; ☑306 45 76; www.slovenia.info; Krekov trg 10; ☺8am-9pm Jun-Sep, 8am-7pm Oct-May) Good source of information for the rest of Slovenia, with internet and bicycle rental also available.

Travel Agency
STA Ljubljana (☑439 16 90, 041 612 711; www.sta-lj.com; 1st fl, Trg Ajdovščina 1; ☺10am-5pm Mon-Fri) Discount air fares for students and its cafe has internet access.

Trek Trek (☑425 13 92; www.trektrek.si; Bičevje ulica 5; ☺10am-5pm Mon-Fri) Specialising in adventure travel in Slovenia, with emphasis on trekking and cycling holidays.

Websites
In addition to the websites of the Slovenian Tourist Information Centre and Ljubljana Tourist Information Centre the following sites might be useful:

City of Ljubljana (www.ljubljana.si) Comprehensive information portal on every aspect of life and tourism direct from city hall.

In Your Pocket (www.inyourpocket.com) Insider info on the capital updated regularly.

Lonely Planet (www.lonelyplanet.com/slovenia/ljubljana)

🛈 Getting There & Away
Bus
Buses to destinations both within Slovenia and abroad leave from the **bus station** (Avtobusna Postaja Ljubljana; ☑234 46 00; www.ap-ljubljana.si; Trg Osvobodilne Fronte 4; ☺5.30am-10.30pm Sun-Fri, 5am-10pm Sat) just next to train station. Next to the ticket windows are multilingual information phones and a touchscreen computer. You do not usually have to buy a ticket in advance; just pay as you board the bus. But for long-distance trips on Friday, just before the school break and public holidays, book the day before to be safe. There's a **left luggage** (Trg OF 4; per day €2; ☺5.30am-10.30pm Sun-Fri, 5am-10pm Sat) area at window 3.

You can reach virtually anywhere in the country by bus.

Train
Domestic and international trains arrive at and depart from central Ljubljana's **train station** (Železniška Postaja; ☑291 33 32; www.slo-zeleznice.si; Trg Osvobodilne Fronte 6; ☺6am-10pm) where you'll find a separate Info Center next to the Ljubljana Tourist Information Centre branch. Buy domestic tickets from window nos 1 to 8 and international ones from either window no 9 or the Info Center. There are **coin lockers** (Trg OF 6; per day €2-3; ☺24hr) for left luggage on platform 1.

There's a surcharge of €1.55 on domestic InterCity (IC) and EuroCity (EC) train tickets.

🛈 Getting Around
To/From the Airport
The cheapest way to Ljubljana's **Jože Pučnik Airport** (LJU/Aerodrom Ljubljana; ☑04-206 19 81; www.lju-airport.si/eng; Zgornji Brnik 130a, Brnik) is by public bus (€4.10, 45 minutes, 27km) from stop No 28 at the bus station. These run at 5.20am and hourly from 6.10am to 8.10pm

TRANSPORT FROM LJUBLJANA

Bus

DESTINATION	PRICE (€)	DURATION (HR)	DISTANCE (KM)	FREQUENCY
Bled	6.20	1½	57	hourly
Bohinj	9	2	91	hourly
Koper	12	2½	122	5 daily with more in season
Maribor	14	3	141	2-4 four daily
Piran	14	3	140	up to 7 daily
Postojna	7	1	53	up to 24 daily

Train

DESTINATION	PRICE (€)	DURATION	DISTANCE (KM)	FREQUENCY
Bled	6.20	55min	51	up to 21 daily
Koper	9	2½hr	153	up to 4 daily with more in summer
Maribor	15	1¾hr	156	up to 25 daily
Murska Sobota	14	3¼hr	216	up to 5 daily

Monday to Friday; at the weekend there's a bus at 6.10am and then one every two hours from 9.10am to 7.10pm. Buy tickets from the driver.

A **private airport van** (☏051 321 414; www. airport-shuttle.si) also links Trg OF, near the bus station, with the airport (€9) up to 11 times daily between 5.20am and 10.30pm, and is a 30-minute trip. It goes from the airport to Ljubljana 10 times a day between 5.45am and 11pm.

A taxi from the airport to Ljubljana will cost from €40 to €45.

Bicycle

Ljubljana is a pleasure for cyclists, and there are bike lanes and special traffic lights everywhere.

Ljubljana Bike (☏306 45 76; www.visitljubljana. si; Krekov trg 10; per 2hr/day €2/8; ☺8am-7pm or 9pm Apr-Oct) rents two-wheelers in two-hour or full-day increments from April through October from the Slovenia Tourist Information Centre.

For short rides, you can hire bikes as needed from **Bicike(lj)** (www.bicikelj.si; subscription weekly/yearly €1/€3 plus hourly rate; ☺24hr) bike stands located around the city. To rent a bike requires pre-registration and subscription over the company website plus a valid credit or debit card. After registration simply submit your card or an Urbana public-transport card plus a PIN number. The first hour of the rental is free, the second hour costs €1, the third hour €2, and each additional hour €4. Bikes must be returned within 24 hours.

Public Transport

Ljubljana's city buses operate every five to 15 minutes from 5am (6am on Sunday) to around 10.30pm. A flat fare of €1.20 (good for 90 minutes of unlimited travel, including transfers) is paid with a stored-value magnetic **Urbana** (☏430 51 74; www.jh-lj.si/urbana) card, which can be purchased at newsstands, tourist offices and the **LPP Information Centre** (☏430 51 75; www.jhl.si; Slovenska cesta 56; ☺7am-7pm Mon-Fri) for €2; credit can then be added (from €1 to €50).

JULIAN ALPS

Slovenia's Julian Alps, part of the wider European Alpine range, is the epicentre for all things outdoors. If you're into adventure sports, head to this area. Much of the region, including the country's highest mountain, Mt Triglav, is protected as part of the Triglav National Park. The park has hiking and biking trails galore. The beautiful alpine lakes at Bled and Bohinj offer boating and swimming amid shimmering mountain backdrops. The region is not just about nature pursuits; you'll also find some of the country's most attractive and important historical towns, like Radovljica. These are unexpected treasure troves of Gothic, Renaissance and baroque architecture.

Lake Bled

📍04 / POP 10900

With its emerald-green lake, picture-postcard church on an islet, a medieval castle clinging to a rocky cliff and some of the highest peaks of the Julian Alps and the Karavanke as backdrops, Bled is Slovenia's most popular resort, drawing everyone from honeymooners lured by the over-the-top romantic setting to backpackers, who come for the hiking, biking, boating and canyoning possibilities. Bled can be overpriced and swarming with tourists in mid-summer. But as is the case with many popular destinations around the world, people come in droves – and will continue to do so – because the place is special.

◎ Sights

Lake Bled   LAKE
(Blejsko jezero) Bled's greatest attraction is its crystal blue-green lake, measuring just 2km by 1380m. The lake is lovely to behold from almost any vantage point, and makes a beautiful backdrop for the 6km walk along the shore. Mild thermal springs warm the water to a swimmable 26°C from June through August. You can rent boats, go diving or simply snap countless photos.

Bled Castle   CASTLE, MUSEUM
(Blejski Grad; www.blejski-grad.si; Grajska cesta 25; adult/child €8/3.50; ⊙8am-8pm Apr-Oct, 8am-6pm Nov-Mar) Perched atop a steep cliff more than 100m above the lake, Bled Castle is how most people imagine a medieval fortress to be, with towers, ramparts, moats and a terrace offering magnificent views. The castle houses a museum collection that traces the lake's history from earliest times to the development of Bled as a resort in the 19th century.

The castle, built on two levels, dates back to the early 11th century, although most of what stands here now is from the 16th century. For 800 years, it was the seat of the Bishops of Brixen. Among the museum holdings, there's a large collection of armour and weapons (swords, halberds and firearms from the 16th to 18th centuries).

Bled Island   ISLAND
(Blejski Otok; www.blejskiotok.si) Tiny, tear-shaped Bled Island beckons from the shore. There's a church and small museum, but the real thrill is the ride out by gondola (*pletna*). The boat sets you down on the south side at the monumental South Staircase (Južno Stopnišče), built in 1655.

Vintgar Gorge   NATURE PARK
(Soteska Vintgar; adult/child/student €4/2/3; ⊙8am-7pm late Apr-Oct) One of the easiest and most satisfying day trips from Bled is to Vintgar Gorge, some 4km to the northwest. The highlight is a 1600m wooden walkway, built in 1893 and continually rebuilt since. It criss-crosses the swirling Radovna River four times over rapids, waterfalls and pools before reaching 13m-high Šum Waterfall.

🏃 Activities

Several local outfits organise a wide range of outdoor activities in and around Bled, including trekking, mountaineering, rock climbing, ski touring, cross-country skiing, mountain biking, rafting, kayaking, canyoning, caving, horse riding and paragliding.

3glav Adventures   ADVENTURE SPORTS
(📞041 683 184; www.3glav-adventures.com; Ljubljanska cesta 1; ⊙9am-7pm Apr-Oct) The number-one adventure-sport specialists in Bled for warm-weather activities from 15 April to 15 October. The most popular trip is the Emerald River Adventure (€65), an 11-hour hiking and swimming foray into Triglav National Park. Also rents bikes (half-day/full day €8/15), conducts hot-air balloon flights (€150) and leads diving expeditions of Lake Bled (€70).

Gondola   BOATING
(Pletna; 📞041 427 155; per person return €12) Riding a piloted gondola out to Bled Island is the archetypal tourist experience. There is a convenient jetty just below the TIC and another in Mlino on the south shore. You get about half an hour to explore the island. In all, the trip to the island and back takes about 1¼ hours.

Horse-drawn Carriages   CARRIAGE
(Fijaker; 📞041 710 970; www.fijaker-bled.si) A romantic way to experience Bled is to take a horse-drawn carriage from the stand near the Festival Hall (Festivalna Dvorana; Cesta Svobode 11). A spin around the lake costs €40, and it's the same price to the castle; an extra 30 minutes inside costs €50. You can even get a carriage for four to Vintgar (adult/child €4/2; ⊙8am-7pm mid-May–Oct); the two-hour return trip costs €90.

🛌 Sleeping

Kompas has a list of private rooms and farmhouses, with singles/doubles starting at €24/38.

Hotel Triglav Bled HOTEL €€€
(☑575 26 10; www.hoteltriglavbled.si; Kolodvorska cesta 33; s €89-159, d €119-179, ste €139-209; P❋@🛜🏊) This 22-room boutique hotel in a painstakingly restored caravanserai that opened in 1906 raises the bar of accommodation standards in Bled. The rooms have hardwood floors and oriental carpets and are furnished with antiques. There's an enormous sloped garden that grows the vegetables served in the terrace restaurants. The location is opposite Bled Jezero train station.

TOP CHOICE Camping Bled CAMPGROUND €
(☑575 20 00; www.camping-bled.com; Kidričeva cesta 10c; adult €10.90-12.90, child €7.60-9, glamping huts €60-80; ☺Apr–mid-Oct; P@🛜) Bled's upscale campground is one of the nicest in the country and one of the few places around to try 'glamping' – aka glamorous camping – in this case, ecofriendly, all-natural A-frame huts, some equipped with hot-tubs. The campground setting is a well-tended rural valley at the western end of the lake, about 2.5km from the bus station.

Garni Hotel Berc HOTEL €€
(☑576 56 58; www.berc-sp.si; Pod Stražo 13; s €45-50, d €70-80; P@🛜) This purpose-built place, reminiscent of a Swiss chalet, has 15 rooms on two floors in a quiet location above the lake.

Penzion Mayer PENSION €€
(☑576 57 40; www.mayer-sp.si; Želeška cesta 7; s €57, d €77-82, apt €120-150; P@🛜) This flower-bedecked 12-room inn in a renovated 19th-century house is in a quiet location above the lake. The larger apartment is in a delightful wooden cabin and the in-house restaurant is excellent.

Traveller's Haven HOSTEL €
(☑041 396 545; www.travellers-haven.si; Riklijeva cesta 1; dm/d €19/48; P@🛜) This is arguably the nicest of several hostels clustered on a hillside on the eastern shore of the lake, about 500m north of the centre. The setting is a renovated villa, with six rooms (including one private double), a great kitchen and free laundry. Note the upstairs rooms get hot in mid-summer.

✖ Eating & Drinking

Vila Ajda SLOVENIAN €€
(☑576 83 20; www.vila-ajda.si; Cesta Svobode 27; mains €9-20; ☺11am-11pm; 🕿) Attractive destination restaurant with lovely views out over

---

WORTH A TRIP

RADOVLJICA

The town of Radovljica, an easy day trip from Bled, just 7km away, is filled with charming, historic buildings and blessed with stunning views of the Alps, including Mt Triglav. It was settled by the early Slavs and by the 14th century had grown into an important market town centred on a large rectangular square, today's **Linhartov trg**, and fortified with high stone walls. Much of the original architecture is still standing and looks remarkably unchanged from those early days.

Besides simply strolling historic Linhartov trg, don't miss the town's **Beekeeping Museum** (Čebelarski Muzej; www.muzeji-radovljica.si; Linhartov trg 1; adult/child €3/2; ☺10am-6pm Tue-Sun May-Oct, 8am-3pm Tue, Thu & Fri, 10am-noon & 3-5pm Wed, Sat & Sun Mar, Apr, Nov & Dec, 8am-3pm Tue-Fri Jan & Feb), which is more interesting than it sounds. The museum's collection of illustrated beehive panels from the 18th and 19th centuries, a folk art unique to Slovenia, is the largest in the country. Ask to see a short, instructive video in English.

Radovljica's other claim to fame is food, and the town is blessed with several excellent restaurants. Our favourite is the traditional **Gostilna Lectar** (☑537 48 00; www.lectar.com; Linhartov trg 2; mains €9-15; ☺noon-11pm; 🕿), an inviting guesthouse on the main square. Everything from relatively common dishes like veal goulash to harder to find items like 'beef tongue served with kohlrabi' are given a gourmet touch.

Across the street, **Gostilna Augustin** (☑531 41 63; Linhartov trg 15; mains €10-17; ☺10am-10pm) serves excellent Slovenian dishes to order. Don't miss the cellar dining room, which was once part of a prison (and may have seen an execution or two), and the wonderful back terrace with stunning views of Mt Triglav. Why not have lunch at one and dinner at the other?

Bled

500 m
0.25 miles

ŽELEČE

Cankarjeva c

Bled
Shopping Centre

Železka c

To Lesce-Bled
Train Station (4km);
Radovljica (8km)

Mladinska c

Seliška c

Ljubljanska c

Prešernova c

12

16

10

8

Spa
Park

C Svobode

1

5

6

Kidričeva c

14

7

15

PodStraža

C Svobode

Rečiška c

PRISTAVA

Bled
Castle

Grass
Beach

Gralska c

Straža Hill
(646m)

REČICA

Lake Bled

2

Minska c

13

4

Bled
Island

MLINO

Kidričeva c

Boardwalk

Kolodvorska c

Bled
Jezero

P

P

P

Mala Osojnica
(685m)

Bled

the lake and a menu that features traditional Slovenian cooking made from locally sourced ingredients. Eat outdoors in the garden in nice weather, or in the upscale dining room. Book in advance on warm evenings in summer.

Ostarija Peglez'n SEAFOOD €€
(☎574 42 18; http://ostarija-peglezn.mestna-izlozba.com; Cesta Svobode 19a; mains €8-18; ☺11am-11pm) One of the better restaurants in Bled, the Iron Inn is just opposite the landmark Grand Hotel Toplice. It has fascinating retro decor with lots of old household antiques and curios (including the eponymous iron) and serves some of the best fish dishes in town.

Penzion Mlino SLOVENIAN €€
(www.mlino.si; Cesta Svobode 45; mains €8-15; ☺noon-11pm; ☎) This is a wonderful choice for lunch along a quieter strip of the lake, about 3km outside the centre. The daily four-course set lunches (around €10) usually offer a fish choice, such as the unforgettable grilled trout we enjoyed on our stop.

Pizzeria Rustika PIZZA €
(☎576 89 00; www.pizzeria-rustika.com; Riklijeva cesta 13; pizza €6-10; ☺noon-11pm; ☎) Conveniently located on the same hill as many of Bled's hostels, so the best pizza in town is just a couple of minutes' walk away.

Pub Bled PUB
(Cesta Svobode 19a; ☺9am-2am Sun-Thu, 9am-3am Fri & Sat) This friendly pub above the Oštarija Peglez'n restaurant has great cocktails and, on some nights, a DJ.

Slaščičarna Šmon CAFE
(http://slascicarna-smon.mestna-izlozba.com; Grajska cesta 3; ☺7.30am-10pm; ☎) Bled's culinary speciality is *kremna rezina* (€2.40), a layer of vanilla custard topped with whipped cream and sandwiched between two layers of flaky pastry, and while Šmon may not be its place of birth, it remains the best place in which to try it.

❶ Information

A Propos Bar (☎574 40 44; Bled Shopping Centre, Ljubljanska cesta 4; per 15/30/60min €1.25/2.10/4.20; ☺8am-midnight Sun-Thu, to 1am Fri & Sat; ☎) In Bled Shopping Centre, wireless connection as well.

Gorenjska Banka (Cesta Svobode 15) Just north of the Park Hotel.

Kompas (☎572 75 01; www.kompas-bled.si; Bled Shopping Centre, Ljubljanska cesta 4; ☺8am-7pm Mon-Sat, 8am-noon & 4-7pm Sun) Full-service travel agency, organises excursions to Bohinj and Radovljica, airport transfers and transport, rents bikes and skis, sells fishing licenses and arranges accommodation in private homes and apartments.

Post Office (Ljubljanska cesta 10)

Tourist Information Centre Bled (☎574 11 22; www.bled.si; Cesta Svobode 10; ☺8am-7pm Mon-Sat, 11am-5pm Sun) Occupies a small office behind the Casino at Cesta Svobode 10; sells maps and souvenirs, rents bikes (half day/full day €8/11); has a computer for checking email.

❶ Getting There & Around

BUS Bled is well connected by bus. There are buses every 30 minutes to Radovljica (€1.80, 15 minutes, 7km) and around 20 buses daily run from Bled to Lake Bohinj (€3.60, 45 minutes) via Bohinjska Bistrica, with the first bus leaving around 5am and the last about 9pm. Buses depart at least hourly for Ljubljana (€6.50, 1¼ hours, 57km).

TRAIN Bled has two train stations, though neither is close to the centre. Mainline trains for Ljubljana (€6.50, 55 minutes, 51km, up to 21 daily), via Škofja Loka and Radovljica, use

Lesce-Bled station, 4km to the east of town. Trains to Bohinjska Bistrica (€1.60, 20 minutes, 18km, eight daily), from where you can catch a bus to Lake Bohinj, use the smaller Bled Jezero station, which is 2km west of central Bled.

Lake Bohinj

04 / POP 5275

Many visitors to Slovenia say they've never seen a more beautiful lake than Bled...that is, until they've seen Lake Bohinj, just 26km to the southwest. We'll refrain from weighing in on the Bled vs Bohinj debate other than to say we see their point. Admittedly, Bohinj lacks Bled's glamour, but it's less crowded and in many ways more authentic. It's an ideal summer holiday destination. People come primarily to chill out or go for a swim in the crystal-clear, blue-green water. There are lots of outdoor pursuits like kayaking, cycling, climbing and horse riding if you've got the energy.

⊙ Sights

Church of St John the Baptist   CHURCH
(Cerkev Sv Janeza Krstnika; Ribčev Laz; ⊙10am-noon & 4-7pm summer, by appointment other times) This church, on the northern side of the Sava Bohinjka river across the stone bridge, is what every medieval church should be: small, on a reflecting body of water and full of exquisite frescos. The nave is Romanesque, but the Gothic presbytery dates from about 1440.

Alpine Dairy Museum   MUSEUM
(Planšarski Muzej; www.bohinj.si; Stara Fužina 181; adult/child €3/2; ⊙11am-7pm Tue-Sun Jul & Aug, 10am-noon & 4-6pm Tue-Sun early Jan-Jun, Sep-late Oct) This museum in Stara Fužina, 1.5km north of Ribčev Laz, has a small collection related to Alpine dairy farming. The four rooms of the museum – once a cheese dairy itself – contain a mock-up of a mid-19th-century herder's cottage.

Savica Waterfall   WATERFALL
(Slap Savica; Ukanc; adult/child €2.50/1.25; ⊙9am-6pm Jul & Aug, 9am-5pm Apr-Jun, Sep & Oct; P) The magnificent Savica Waterfall, which cuts deep into a gorge 60m below, is 4km from the Hotel Zlatorog in Ukanc and can be reached by footpath from there.

🏃 Activities

While most people come to Bohinj to relax, there are more exhilarating pursuits available, including canyoning, caving, and para-

gliding from the top of Mt Vogel, among others. Two companies, Alpinsport and Perfect Adventure Choice (PAC) Sports, specialise in these activities.

Alpinsport   ADVENTURE SPORTS
(572 34 86; www.alpinsport.si; Ribčev Laz 53; ⊙9am-8pm Jul-Sep, 9am-7pm Oct-Jun) Rents sporting equipment, canoes, kayaks and bikes; also operates guided rafting, canyoning and caving trips. Located in a kiosk at the stone bridge over the Sava Bohinjka river in Ribčev Laz.

Bohinj Cable Car   HIKING, SKIING
(adult/child one way €9/7 return €13/9; ⊙every 30min 8am-6pm) The Bohinj cable car operates year-round, hauling skiiers in winter and hikers in summer. There are several day hikes and longer treks that set out from Mt Vogel (1922m).

Mrcina Ranč   HORSE RIDING
(041 790 297; www.ranc-mrcina.com; Studor; per hr €20) Mrcina Ranč in Studor, 5km from Ribčev Laz, offers a range of guided tours on horseback, lasting one hour to three days on sturdy Icelandic ponies.

PAC Sports   ADVENTURE SPORTS
(Perfect Adventure Choice; 572 34 61; www.pac-sports.com; Hostel Pod Voglom, Ribčev Laz; ⊙7am-11pm Jul & Aug, 10am-6pm Sep-Jun) Popular youth-oriented sports and adventure company, located in the Hostel pod Voglom, 3km west of Ribcev Laz on the road to Ukanc. Rents bikes, canoes and kayaks, and operates guided canyoning, rafting, paragliding and caving trips. In winter, they rent sleds and offer winter rafting near Vogel (per person €15).

Tourist Boat   BOATING
(Turistična Ladja; 574 75 90; one way adult/child €9/6.50, return €10.50/7.50; ⊙half-hourly 9.30am-5.30pm Jun–mid-Sep, 10am, 11.30am, 1pm, 2.30pm, 4pm & 5.30pm early Apr-May, 11.30am, 1pm, 2.30pm & 4pm mid-Sep–Oct) An easy family-friendly sail from Ribčev Laz to Ukanc and back.

🛏 Sleeping

The tourist office can help arrange accommodation in private rooms and apartments. Expect to pay anywhere from €38 to €50 for a two-person apartment.

TOP CHOICE **Penzion Gasperin**   PENSION €€
(041 540 805; www.bohinj.si/gasperin; Ribčev Laz 36a; r €48-60; P❀❄@⊙) This spotless

chalet-style guesthouse with 23 rooms is just 350m southeast of the TIC and run by a friendly British/Slovenian couple. Most rooms have balconies. The buffet breakfast is fresh and includes a sampling of local meats and cheeses.

Hotel Stare PENSION €€
(☑040 558 669; www.bohinj-hotel.com; Ukanc 128; per person €42-50; P@🐾) This beautifully appointed 10-room pension is situated on the Sava Bohinjka river in Ukanc and is surrounded by 3.5 hectares of lovely garden. If you really want to get away from it all without having to climb mountains, this is your place. Rates are half-board, including breakfast and dinner.

Hotel Jezero HOTEL €€€
(☑572 91 00; www.bohinj.si/alpinum/jezero; Ribčev Laz 51; s €65-75, d €120-140; P@🐾🏊) Further renovations have raised the standards at this 76-room place just across from the lake. It has a lovely indoor swimming pool, two saunas and a fitness centre.

Hostel Pod Voglom HOSTEL €
(☑572 34 61; www.hostel-podvoglom.com; Ribčev Laz 60; dm €18, r per person €23-26, without bathroom €20-22; P@) Bohinj's youth hostel, some 3km west of the centre of Ribčev Laz on the road to Ukanc, has 119 beds in 46 rooms in two buildings.

Autokamp Zlatorog CAMPGROUND €
(☑577 80 00; www.hoteli-bohinj.si; Ukanc 2; per person €6-9; ☉May-Sep) This pleasant, pine-shaded 2.5-hectare camping ground accommodating 500 guests is at the lake's western end, 4.5km from Ribčev Laz. Prices vary according to site location, with the most expensive – and desirable – sites right on the lake.

🍴 Eating

TOP CHOICE Gostilna Rupa SLOVENIAN €€
(☑572 34 01; www.apartmajikatrnjek.com/rupa; Srednja Vas 87; mains €8-16; ☉10am-midnight Jul & Aug, Tue-Sun Sep-Jun) If you're under your own steam, head for this country-style restaurant in the next village over from Studor and about 5km from Ribčev Laz. Among the excellent home-cooked dishes are *ajdova krapi*, crescent-shaped dumplings made from buckwheat and cheese, various types of local *klobasa* (sausage) and Bohinj trout.

Gostilna Mihovc SLOVENIAN €
(☑572 33 90; www.gostilna-mihovc.si; Stara Fužina 118; mains €7-10; ☉10am-midnight) This place in Stara Fužina is very popular – not least for its fiery homemade brandy. Try the *pasulj* (bean soup) with sausage (€6) or the beef *goláč* (goulash; €5.20). Live music on Friday and Saturday evenings. In

SLOVENIA LAKE BOHINJ

SUMMITING MT TRIGLAV

The 2864m limestone peak called Mt Triglav (Mt Three Heads) has been a source of inspiration and an object of devotion for Slovenes for more than a millennium. Under the Habsburgs in the 19th century, the 'pilgrimage' to Triglav became, in effect, a confirmation of one's ethnic identity, and this tradition continues to this day: a Slovene is expected to climb Triglav at least once in his or her life.

You can climb Slovenia's highest peak too, but Triglav is not for the unfit or faint-hearted. We strongly recommend hiring a guide for the ascent, even if you have some mountain-climbing experience under your belt. A local guide will know the trails and conditions, and can prove invaluable in helping to arrange sleeping space in mountain huts and providing transport. Guides can be hired through 3glav (p496) in Bled or Alpinsport in Bohinj, or book in advance through the **Alpine Association of Slovenia** (PZS; www.pzs.si/).

Triglav is inaccessible from middle to late October to late May. June and the first half of July are the rainiest times in the summer months, so late July, August and particularly September and early October are the best times to make the climb.

There are many ways to reach the top, with the most popular approaches coming from the south, either starting from **Pokljuka**, near Bled, or from the Savica Waterfall, near Lake Bohinj. You can also climb Triglav from the north and the east (Mojstrana and the Vrata Valley). All of the approaches offer varying degrees of difficulty and have their pluses and minuses. Note that treks normally require one or two overnight stays in the mountains.

summer book in advance to secure a garden table.

ⓘ Getting There & Away

Buses run regularly from Ljubljana (€9, two hours, 90km, hourly) to Bohinj Jezero and Ukanc – marked 'Bohinj Zlatorog' – via Bled and Bohinjska Bistrica. Around 20 buses daily run from Bled (€3.60, 45 minutes) to Bohinj Jezero (via Bohinjska Bistrica) and return, with the first bus leaving around 5am and the last about 9pm. From the end of June through August, **Alpetour** (☑532 04 45; www.alpetour.si) runs special tourist buses that leave from Ribčev Laz to Bohinjska Bistrica in one direction and to the Savica Waterfall (23 minutes) in the other.

Several trains daily make the run to Bohinjska Bistrica from Ljubljana (€6.70, two hours), though this route requires a change in Jesenice. There are also frequent trains between Bled's small Bled Jezero station (€1.60, 20 minutes, 18km, eight daily) and Bohinjska Bistrica.

Kranjska Gora

☑04 / POP 5510

Nestling in the Sava Dolinka Valley some 40km northwest of Bled, Kranjska Gora (Carniolan Mountain) is Slovenia's largest and best-equipped ski resort. It's at its most perfect under a blanket of snow, but its surroundings are wonderful to explore at other times as well. There are endless possibilities for hiking, cycling and mountaineering in Triglav National Park, which is right on the town's doorstep to the south, and few travellers will be unimpressed by a trip over Vršič Pass (1611m), the gateway to the Soča Valley.

◉ Sights & Activities

Most of the sights are situated along the main street, Borovška cesta, 400m south of where the buses stop. The endearing **Liznjek House** (Liznjekova Domačija; www.gornjesav-skimuzej.si; Borovška 63; adult/child €2.50/1.70; ☺10am-6pm Tue-Sat, 10am-5pm Sun), an 18th-century museum house, has a good collection of household objects and furnishings peculiar to the alpine region.

Kranjska Gora is best known as a winter resort, and chairlifts up to the **ski slopes** on Vitranc (1631m) are at the western end of town off Smerinje ulica. There are more ski slopes and a **ski-jumping facility** 6km to the west, near the villages of Rateče and Planica, which is home to the annual **Ski-Jumping World Cup Championships** (☑1 200 6241; www.planica.info; Planica; adult/child €20/3) in

mid-March. There are lots of places offering ski tuition and hiring out equipment, including **ASK Kranjska Gora Ski School** (☑588 53 02; www.ask-kg.com; Borovška c 99a; ☺9am-4pm Mon-Sat, 10am-6pm Sun mid-Dec–mid-Mar, 9am-3pm Mon-Fri mid-Mar–mid-Dec).

In summer, the town is quieter, but there are still plenty of things to do. Kranjska Gora makes an excellent base for **hiking** in the Triglav National Park, and Jasna Lake, the gateway to the park, is 2km to the south. The 1:30,000-scale *Kranjska Gora* hiking map is available at the **Tourist Information Centre** (TIC; ☑580 94 40; www.kranjska -gora.si; Tičarjeva cesta 2; ☺8am-7pm Mon-Sat, 9am-6pm Sun Jun-Sep & mid-Dec–mid-Mar, 8am-3pm Mon-Sat Apr, May & Oct–mid-Dec) for €9.

The hiking map also marks out 15 **cycling routes** of varying difficulty. Most ski-rental outfits hire out bikes in summer, including **Intersport** (www.intersport-bernik.com; Borovška cesta 88a; ☺8am-8pm mid-Dec–mid-Mar, 8am-8pm Mon-Sat, 8am-1pm Sun mid-Mar–mid-Dec). Expect to pay €10 for a full-day rental and helmet.

🛏 Sleeping & Eating

Accommodation costs peak from December to March and in mid-summer. Private rooms and apartments can be arranged through the Tourist Information Centre.

Hotel Kotnik HOTEL €€
(☑588 15 64; www.hotel-kotnik.si; Borovška cesta 75; s €50-60, d €72-80; P@☎) If you're not into big high-rise hotels with hundreds of rooms, choose this charming, bright-yellow, low-rise property. It has 15 cosy rooms, a great restaurant and pizzeria, and it couldn't be more central.

🏕 Natura Eco Camp Kranjska Gora CAMPGROUND €
(☑064 121 966; www.naturacamp-kranjskagora. com; Borovška cesta 62; adult €8-10, child €5-7, cabin & tree tent €25-30) This wonderful site, some 300m from the main road on an isolated horse ranch in a forest clearing, is as close to paradise as we've been for awhile. Pitch a tent or stay in one of the little wooden cabins or the unique tree tents – great pouches with air mattresses suspended from the branches.

Hotel Miklič HOTEL €€€
(☑588 16 35; www.hotelmiklic.com; Vitranška ulica 13; s €60-80, d €80-130; P@☎) This pristine 15-room small hotel south of the centre is

surrounded by luxurious lawns and flower beds and boasts an excellent restaurant and a small fitness room with sauna (€12 per hour). It's definitely a cut above most other accommodation in Kranjska Gora.

Hotel Kotnik
SLOVENIAN €€

(☑588 15 64; www.hotel-kotnik.si; Borovška c 75; mains €8-18; 🛜) One of Kranjska Gora's better eateries, the restaurant in this stylish inn, with bits of painted dowry chests on the walls, serves grilled meats – pepper steak is a speciality – that should keep you going for awhile. The adjoining pizzeria (pizza €6 to €9, open noon to 10.30pm) with the wood-burning stove is a great choice for something quicker.

Gostilna Pri Martinu
SLOVENIAN €

(☑582 03 00; Borovška c 61; mains €7-14; ⊙10am-11pm; 🛜) This atmospheric tavern-restaurant in an old house opposite the fire station is one of the best places in town to try local specialities, such as *ješprenj* (barley soup), *telečja obara* (veal stew) and *ričet* (barley stew with smoked pork ribs). One of the few places to offer a full three-course luncheon menu (€7).

ℹ Getting There & Away

Buses run hourly to Ljubljana (€8.70, two hours, 91km) via Jesenice (€3.10, 30 minutes, 24km), where you should change for Bled (€2.70, 20 minutes, 19km). There's just one direct departure to Bled (€4.80, one hour, 40km) on weekdays at 9.15am and at 9.50am on weekends.

Alpetour (☑201 31 30; www.alpetour.si) runs regular buses to Trenta (€4.70, 70 minutes, 30km) and Bovec (€6.70, two hours, 46km) from June through September via the Vršič Pass. Check the website for a timetable. There are normally about four departures daily (more at the weekend). Buy tickets from the driver.

Soča Valley

The Soča Valley region (Posočje) stretches from Triglav National Park to Nova Gorica, including the outdoor activity centres of Bovec and Kobarid. Threading through it is the magically aquamarine Soča River. Most people come here for the rafting, hiking and skiing, though there are plenty of historical sights and locations, particularly relating to WWI, when millions of troops fought on the mountainous battle front here.

BOVEC
☑05 / POP 1810

Soča Valley's de facto capital, Bovec, offers plenty in adventure-sports enthusiasts. With the Julian Alps above, the Soča River below and Triglav National Park all around, you could spend a week here hiking, kayaking, mountain biking and, in winter, skiing at Mt Kanin, Slovenia's highest ski station, without ever doing the same thing twice.

🏃 Activities

Rafting, kayaking and **canoeing** on the beautiful Soča River (10% to 40% gradient; Grades I to VI) are major draws. The season lasts from April to October.

Rafting trips of two to eight people over a distance of 8km to 10km (1½ hours) cost from €36 to €46 and for 21km (2½ hours) from €48 to €55, including neoprene long johns, windcheater, life jacket, helmet and paddle. Bring a swimsuit, T-shirt and towel. Canoes for two are €45 for the day; single kayaks €30. A number of beginners kayaking courses are also on offer (eg one-/two-days from €55/100). Longer guided kayak trips (up to 10km) are also available.

A 3km **canyoning** trip near the Soča, in which you descend through gorges and jump over falls attached to a rope, costs around €42.

Other popular activities include **cycling**, **hiking** and **fishing**. Visit the **Tourist Information Centre Bovec** (☑388 19 19; www.bovec.si; Trg Golobarskih Žrtev 8; ⊙8.30am-8.30pm summer, 9am-6pm winter) for specific information or check in with the following reputable agencies:

Soča Rafting
ADVENTURE SPORTS

(☑041-724 472, 389 62 00; www.socarafting.si; Trg Golobarskih Žrtev 14; ⊙9am-7pm year-round)

Top Extreme
ADVENTURE SPORTS

(☑041 620 636; www.top.si; Trg Golobarskih Žrtev 19; ⊙9am-7pm May-Sep)

Kanin Ski Centre
SKIING

(☑388 60 98; www.bovec.si; day pass adult/child/senior & student €22/16/18) The Kanin Ski Centre northwest of Bovec has skiing up to 2200m – the only real altitude alpine skiing in Slovenia. As a result, the season can be long, with good spring skiing in April and even May.

🛏 Sleeping & Eating

Private rooms are easy to come by in Bovec through the TIC.

TOP CHOICE Dobra Vila
BOUTIQUE HOTEL €€€

(☑389 64 00; www.dobra-vila-bovec.si; Mala Vas 112; d €120-145, tr €160-180; P❄🛜) This stunner of a 10-room boutique hotel is housed in an erstwhile telephone-exchange building dating to 1932. Peppered with interesting artefacts and objets d'art, it has its own library and wine cellar and a fabulous restaurant with a winter garden and outdoor terrace.

Martinov Hram
GUESTHOUSE €€

(☑388 62 14; www.martinov-hram.si; Trg Golobarskih Žrtev 27; s/d €33/54; P⚡) This lovely and very friendly guesthouse just 100m east of the centre has 14 beautifully furnished rooms and an excellent restaurant with an emphasis on specialities from the Bovec region.

Kamp Palovnik
CAMPGROUND €

(☑388 60 07; www.kamp-polovnik.com; Ledina 8; adult €6.50-7.50, child €5-5.75; ⊙Apr–mid-Oct; P) About 500m southeast of the Hotel Kanin, this is the closest camping ground to Bovec. It is small (just over a hectare with 70 sites) but located in an attractive setting.

Gostišče Stari Kovač
PIZZA €

(☑388 66 99; Rupa 3; starters €6.50-7, mains €8-11, pizza €5-7.50; ⊙noon-10pm Tue-Sun) The 'Old Blacksmith' is a good choice for pizza cooked in a wood-burning stove.

❶ Getting There & Away
Buses to Kobarid (€3.10, 30 minutes) depart up to six times a day. There are also buses to Ljubljana (€13.60, 3½ hours) via Kobarid and Idrija. From late June to August a service to Kranjska Gora (€6.70, two hours) via the Vršič Pass departs four times daily, continuing to Ljubljana.

KOBARID
☑05 / POP 1250

The charming town of Kobarid is quainter than nearby Bovec, and despite being surrounded by mountain peaks, Kobarid feels more Mediterranean than Alpine. On the surface not a whole lot has changed since Ernest Hemingway described Kobarid (then Caporetto) in *A Farewell to Arms* (1929) as 'a little white town with a campanile in a valley' with 'a fine fountain in the square'. Kobarid was a military settlement during Roman times, was hotly contested in the Middle Ages and was hit by a devastating earthquake in 1976, but the world will remember Kobarid as the site of the decisive battle of 1917 in which the combined forces of the Central Powers defeated the Italian army.

◎ Sights
Kobarid Museum
MUSEUM

(☑389 00 00; www.kobariski-muzej.si; Gregorčičeva ul 10; adult/child €5/2.50; ⊙9am-6pm Mon-Fri,

9am-7pm Sat & Sun summer, 10am-5pm Mon-Fri, 9am-6pm Sat & Sun winter) This museum is devoted almost entirely to the Soča Front and WWI. There are many photographs documenting the horrors of the front, military charts, diaries and maps, and two large relief displays showing the front lines and offensives through the Krn Mountains and the positions in the Upper Soča Valley. Don't miss the 20-minute multimedia presentation.

🏃 Activities
A free pamphlet and map titled *The Kobarid Historical Trail* outlines a 5km-long route that will take you past remnants of WWI troop emplacements to the impressive **Kozjak Stream Waterfalls** (Slapovi Potoka Kozjak) and **Napoleon Bridge** (Napoleonov Most) built in 1750. More ambitious is the hike outlined in the free *Pot Miru/Walk of Peace* brochure.

Kobarid gives Bovec a run for its money in adventure sports, and you'll find several outfits on or off the town's main square that can organise rafting (from €34), canyoning (from €45), kayaking (€40) and paragliding (€110) between April and October. Two recommended agencies are listed below:

X Point
ADVENTURE SPORTS

(☑041 692 290, 388 53 08; www.xpoint.si; Trg Svobode 6)

Positive Sport
ADVENTURE SPORTS

(☑040 654 475; www.positive-sport.com; Markova ulica 2)

🛏 Sleeping
TOP CHOICE Hiša Franko
GUESTHOUSE €€€

(☑389 41 20; www.hisafranko.com; Staro Selo 1; r €80-135; P⚡) This guesthouse in an old farmhouse 3km west of Kobarid in Staro Selo, halfway to the Italian border, has 10 themed rooms – we love the Moja Afrika (My Africa) and Soba Zelenega Čaja (Green Tea Room) ones – some of which have terraces and jacuzzis. Eat in their excellent restaurant.

Hotel Hvala
HOTEL €€€

(☑389 93 00; wwww.hotelhvala.si; Trg Svobode 1; s €72-76, d €104-112; P✳⚡) The delightful 'Hotel Thanks' (actually it's the family's name), has 31 rooms. A snazzy lift takes you on a vertical tour of Kobarid (don't miss both the Soča trout and Papa Hemingway at work); there's a bar, a Mediterranean-style cafe in the garden and a superb restaurant.

Kamp Koren CAMPGROUND €
(☎389 13 11; www.kamp-koren.si; Drežniške Ravne 33; per person pitch €11.50, chalets d/tr from €55/60; P 📶) The oldest camping ground in the valley, this 2-hectare site with 70 pitches is about 500m northeast of Kobarid on the left bank of the Soča River and just before the turn to Drežniške Ravne. In full view is the Napoleon Bridge.

Eating

In the centre of Kobarid you'll find two of Slovenia's best restaurants.

TOP CHOICE **Hiša Franko** SLOVENIAN €€
(☎389 41 20; www.hisafranko.com; Staro Selo 1; mains €22-24; ⊙noon-3pm & 6-11pm Tue-Sun) Foodies will love this superb gourmet restaurant in the guesthouse of the same name in Staro Selo, just west of town. Impeccable tasting menus, strong on locally sourced ingredients and which change according to the season, cost €50/75 for five/eight courses. It closes on Tuesday in winter.

Topli Val SEAFOOD €€
(Trg Svobode 1; starters €8-10, mains €9.50-25; ⊙noon-10pm) Seafood is the speciality here, and it's excellent – from the carpaccio of sea bass to the Soča trout and signature lobster with pasta. Expect to pay about €30 to €60 per person with a decent bottle of wine. There's a lovely front terrace and back garden open in warmer months.

Information

Tourist Information Centre Kobarid (☎380 04 90; www.dolina-soce.com; Trg Svobode 16; ⊙9am-1pm & 2-7pm Mon-Fri, 10am-1pm & 4-7pm Sat & Sun) Free internet.

Getting There & Around

There are half a dozen buses a day to Bovec (€3.10, 30 minutes). Other destinations include Ljubljana (€11.40 three hours) via Most na Soči train station (good for Bled and Bohinj). Daily in July and August, buses cross the spectacular Vršič Pass to Kranjska Gora (€6.70, three hours).

KARST & COAST

Slovenia's short coast (47km) is an area for both history and recreation. The southernmost resort town of Portorož has some decent beaches, but towns like Koper and Piran, famed for their Venetian Gothic architecture, are the main drawcards here. En route from Ljubljana or the Soča Valley, you'll cross the Karst, a huge limestone plateau and a land of olives, ruby-red Teran wine, *pršut* (air-dried ham), old stone churches and deep subterranean caves, including Postojna and Škocjan.

Postojna

☎05 / POP 8910

The karst cave at Postojna is one of the largest in the world and its stalagmite and stalactite formations are unequalled anywhere. It's a busy destination (visited by as many as a third of all tourists coming to Slovenia). The amazing thing is how the large crowds at the entrance seem to get swallowed whole by the size of the caves.

The small town of Postojna lies in the Pivka Valley at the foot of Sovič Hill (677m) with Titov trg at its centre. Postojna's bus station is at Titova cesta 36, about 250m southwest of Titov trg. The train station is on Kolodvorska cesta about 600m southeast of the square.

Sights

Postojna Cave CAVE
(☎700 01 00; www.postojnska-jama.si; Jamska c 30; adult/child/student €22.90/13.70/18.30; ⊙tours hourly 9am-6pm summer, 3 or 4 times from 10am daily winter) Slovenia's single most-popular tourist attraction, Postojna Cave is about 1.5km northwest of Postojna. The 5.7km-long cavern is visited on a 1½-hour tour – 4km of it by electric train and the rest on foot. Inside, impressive stalagmites and stalactites in familiar shapes stretch almost endlessly in all directions.

Proteus Vivarium MUSEUM
(www.turizem-kras.si; adult/child €8/4.80, with cave €27/16.20; ⊙9am-5.30pm May-Sep, 10.30am-3.30pm Oct-Apr) Just steps south of the Postojna Cave's entrance is Proteus Vivarium, a spelio-biological research station with a video introduction to underground zoology. A 45-minute tour then leads you into a small, darkened cave to peep at some of the endemic Proteus anguinus, a shy (and miniscule) salamander unique to Slovenia.

Sleeping & Eating

Hotel Kras HOTEL €€
(☎700 23 00; www.hotel-kras.si; Tržaška cesta 1; s €68-74, d €84-96, apt €100-120; P 📶) This rather flash, modern hotel has risen, phoenix-like, from the ashes of a decrepit old caravanserai in the heart of town, and now boasts 27 comfortable rooms with all the mod cons. If you've got the dosh, choose one

PREDJAMA CASTLE

The tiny village of Predjama (population 85), 10km northwest of Postojna, is home to remarkable **Predjama Castle** (☑700 01 03; www.postojnska-jama.eu; Predjama 1; adult/child/student €9/5.40/7.20; ⊙9am-7pm summer, 10am-4pm winter). The castle's lesson is clear: if you want to build an impregnable redoubt, put it in the gaping mouth of a cavern halfway up a 123m cliff. Its four storeys were built piece-meal over the years since 1202, but most of what you see today is 16th century. It looks simply unconquerable.

The castle holds great features for kids of any age – a drawbridge over a raging river, holes in the ceiling of the entrance tower for pouring boiling oil on intruders, a very dank dungeon, a 16th-century chest full of treasure (unearthed in the cellar in 1991), and a hiding place at the top called Erazem's Nook.

In mid-July, the castle hosts the **Erasmus Tournament**, a day of medieval duelling, jousting and archery.

The cave below Predjama Castle is a 6km network of galleries spread over four levels. Casual visitors can see about 900m of it; longer tours are available by prior arrangement only. **Gostilna Požar** (☑751 52 52; Predjama 2; meals from €11; ⊙10am-10pm Thu-Tue, daily Aug) is a simple restaurant next to the ticket kiosk and in heart-stopping view of the castle.

of the apartments on the top (5th) floor with enormous terraces.

Hotel Sport
HOTEL, HOSTEL €€
(☑720 22 44; www.sport-hotel.si; Kolodvorska c 1; dm €25, s/d from €55/70; P@🛜) A hotel of some sort or another since 1880, the Sport offers reasonable value for money, with 37 spick-and-span and comfortable rooms, including five with nine dorm beds each. There's a kitchen with a small eating area. It's 300m north of the centre.

Jamski Dvorec
INTERNATIONAL €€
(☑700 01 81; starters €6.50-10, mains €13.50-22; ⊙9am-6pm) Housed in a stunning 1920s-style building next to the entrance to the cave, the Cave Manor has fairly average international dishes but its set menus at €11 and €12 are a big attraction.

Čuk
PIZZA €
(☑720 13 00; Pot k Pivki 4; starters €5-7.50, pizza & pasta €6-9.50; ⊙10am-11pm Mon-Fri, 11am-midnight Sat, noon-11pm Sun) Excellent restaurant southwest of Titov trg, just off Tržaška cesta, Čuk takes its pizza seriously but offers a wide range of Slovenian mains too.

❶ Getting There & Away

BUS Services from Ljubljana to the coast as well as Ajdovščina stop in Postojna (€6, one hour, 53km, hourly). Other destinations include Koper (€6.90, 1¼ hours, 68km, four to seven daily) and Piran (€8.30, 1½ hours, 86km, three or four a day).

TRAIN Postojna is on the main train line linking Ljubljana (€4.90, one hour, 67km) with Sežana and Trieste via Divača (€2.90 to €4.45, 40 minutes, 37km), and is an easy day trip from the capital. You can also reach here from Koper (€5.90 to €10.30, 1½ hours, 86km) on one of up to seven trains a day.

Škocjan Caves
☑05

The immense system of the **Škocjan Caves** (☑708 21 10; www.park-skocjanske-jame.si; Škocjan 2; adult/child €15/7; ⊙10am-5pm), a Unesco World Heritage site, is more captivating than the larger one at Postojna, and for many travellers this will be the highlight of their trip to Slovenia.

Visitors walk in guided groups from the ticket office to the main entrance in the Globočak Valley. Through a tunnel built in 1933, you soon reach the head of the **Silent Cave**, a dry branch of the underground canyon that stretches for 500m. The first section, called **Paradise**, is filled with beautiful stalactites and stalagmites; the second part (called **Calvary**) was once the river bed. The Silent Cave ends at the **Great Hall**, a jungle of exotic dripstones and deposits; keep an eye out for the mighty stalagmites called the Giants and the Organ.

The sound of the Reka River heralds your entry into the **Murmuring Cave**, with walls 100m high. To get over the Reka and into Müller Hall, you must cross **Cerkevnik**

Bridge, some 45m high and surely the highlight of the trip.

Schmidl Hall, the final section, emerges into the Velika Dolina. From here you walk past Tominč Cave, where finds from a prehistoric settlement have been unearthed. A funicular takes you back to the entrance.

The temperature in the caves is constant at 12°C so bring along a light jacket or sweater. Good walking shoes, for the sometimes slippery paths, are recommended.

The nearest town with accommodation is Divača, 5km to the northwest. Gostilna Malovec (☑763 33 33; www.hotel-malovec.si; s/d €54/80; ☐@🖉) has a half-dozen basic but renovated rooms in a building beside its traditional restaurant.The nearby Orient Express (☑763 30 10; pizza €4.60-14; ☉11am-11pm Sun-Fri, 11am-2am Sat) is a popular pizzeria.

Buses from Ljubljana to Koper and the coast stop at Divača (€7.90, 1½ hours, half-hourly). Divača is also on the rail line to Ljubljana (€7.30, 1½ hours, hourly), with up to five trains a day to Koper (€4.05, 50 minutes) via Hrpelje-Kozina. The Škocjan Caves are about 5km by road southeast of the Divača train station – the route is signed. A courtesy van sometimes meets incoming Ljubljana trains.

Koper

☑05 / POP 24,725

Coastal Slovenia's largest town, Koper (Capodistria in Italian) at first glance appears to be a workaday city that scarcely gives tourism a second thought. Yet its central core is delightfully medieval and far less overrun than its ritzy cousin Piran, 18km down the coast. Known as Aegida to the ancient Greeks, Koper grew rich as a key port trading salt and was the capital of Istria under the Venetian republic during the 15th and 16th centuries. It remains Slovenia's most important port.

◉ Sights

The easiest way to see Koper's Old Town is to walk from the marina on Ukmarjev trg east along Kidričeva ulica to Titov trg and then south down Čevljarska ulica, taking various detours along the way.

Koper Regional Museum   MUSEUM
(☑663 35 70; www.pmk-kp.si; Kidričeva ul 19; adult/child €2/1.50; ☉9am-7pm Tue-Fri, to 1pm Sat & Sun) The Belgramoni-Tacco Palace houses this museum with displays of old maps and

photos of the port and coast, Italianate sculpture, and paintings dating from the 16th to 18th centuries. Note the wonderful bronze knocker on the door of Venus arising from a seashell.

Cathedral of the Assumption   CATHEDRAL
(Stolnica Marijinega Vnebovzetja; ☉7am-9pm) Opposite the Armoury in Titov trg is the Cathedral of the Assumption and its 36m-tall belfry, now called the City Tower. The cathedral, partly Romanesque and Gothic but mostly dating from the 18th century, has a white classical interior with a feeling of space and light that belies the sombre exterior.

FREE Beach   BEACH
(Kopališko nabrežje 1; ☉8am-7pm May-Sep) Koper's tiny beach, on the northwest edge of the Old Town, has a small bathhouse with toilets and showers, grassy areas for lying in the sun and a bar and cafe.

🛏 Sleeping

Hotel Koper   HOTEL €€€
(☑610 05 00; www.terme-catez.si; Pristaniška ul 3; s €76-92, d €120-150; ✳@🖋) This pleasant, 65-room property on the edge of the historic Old Town is the only really central hotel in town. Rates include entry to an aquapark. Choose a harbour-facing room.

Hotel Vodišek   HOTEL €€
(☑639 24 68; www.hotel-vodisek.com; Kolodvorska c 2; s €48-60, d €72-90; ☐✳@🖉) This small hotel with 35 reasonably priced rooms is in a shopping centre halfway between the Old Town and the train and bus stations. Guests get to use the hotel's bicycles for free.

Museum Hostel   APARTMENTS €
(☑041 504 466, 626 18 70; bozic.doris@siol.net; Muzejski trg 6; per person €20-25; 🖉) This place is more a series of apartments with kitchens and bathrooms than a hostel. Reception is at Museum Bife, a cafe-bar on Muzejski trg; the rooms are scattered nearby.

✕ Eating

Istrska Klet Slavček   ISTRIAN, SLOVENIAN €
(☑627 67 29; Župančičeva ul 39; dishes €3-12; ☉7am-10pm Mon-Fri) The Istrian Cellar, situated below the 18th-century Carli Palace, is one of the most colourful places for a meal in Koper's Old Town. Filling set lunches go for less than €8, and there's local Malvazija and Teran wine from the barrel.

LIPICA'S LIPIZZANER HORSES

The impact of Lipica has been far greater than its tiny size would suggest. It's here where the famed snow-white 'Lipizzaner' horses, made famous at Vienna's Spanish Riding School, were first bred in the late 16th century.

The breed got its start by pairing Andalusian horses from Spain with the local Karst breed the Romans once used to pull chariots. The white colour came two centuries later, when white Arabian horses got into the act.

The breed has subsequently become scattered – moved to Hungary and Austria after WWI, to the Sudetenland in Bohemia by the Germans during WWII, and then shipped off to Italy by the American army in 1945. Only 11 horses returned when operations resumed at Lipica in 1947.

Today, some 400 Lipizzaners remain at the **Lipica Stud Farm** (739 15 80; www.lipica.org; tour adult/child €11/5.50, training/classical performance €13/18; training & classical performance Tue, Fri & Sun Apr-Oct), while Lipizzaners are also bred in various locations around the world, including Piber in Austria, which breeds the horses for the Spanish Riding School. The stud farm offers equestrian fans a large variety of tours and riding presentations as well as lessons and carriage rides. Tour times are complicated; see the website for details.

Most people visit Lipica as a day trip from Sežana, 4km to the north, or Divača, 13km to the northeast, both of which are on the Ljubljana–Koper rail line. There is no public transport from either train station; a taxi will cost between €10 and €20.

For overnights, try the 59-room **Hotel Maestoso** (739 15 80; s/d €80/120;), managed by the stud farm. It has many upscale amenities, including a restaurant, swimming pool, sauna and tennis courts.

La Storia
ITALIAN €€

(626 20 18; www.lastoria.si; Pristaniška ul 3; mains €8.50-25) This Italian-style trattoria with sky-view ceiling frescos focuses on salads, pasta and fish dishes and has outside seating in the warmer months.

ℹ️ Information

Banka Koper (Kidričeva ul 14)

Pina Internet Cafe (627 80 72; Kidričeva ul 43; per hr adult/student €4.20/1.20; noon-10pm Mon-Fri, from 4pm Sat & Sun)

Post Office (Muzejski trg 3)

Tourist Information Centre Koper (664 64 03; www.koper.si; Praetorian Palace, Titov trg 3; 9am-8pm Jul & Aug, 9am-5pm Sep-Jun)

ℹ️ Getting There & Away

BUS Services run to Izola, Strunjan, Piran (€2.70, 30 minutes and Portorož every half-hour on weekdays. There's a handy bus stop at the corner of Piranška ulica. Some five daily buses make the run to Ljubljana (€11.10, 1¾ to 2½ hours). Buses to Trieste (€3, one hour) run along the coast via Ankaran and Muggia from Monday to Saturday. Destinations in Croatia include Rijeka (€11.20, two hours) and Rovinj (€12, three hours) via Poreč (€10, two hours).

TRAIN Half a dozen trains a day link Koper to Ljubljana (€10.70, 2½ hours, 153km) via Postojna and Divača.

Piran
05 / POP 4470

Picturesque Piran, sitting at the tip of a narrow peninsula, is everyone's favourite town on the coast. Its Old Town – one of the best preserved historical towns anywhere on the Adriatic – is a gem of Venetian architecture, but it can be a mob scene at the height of summer. In April or October, though, it's hard not to fall in love with the winding alleyways and tempting seafood restaurants.

👁 Sights

Tartinijev Trg
SQUARE

The **statue** of the nattily dressed gentleman in Tartinijev trg, an oval-shaped square that was the inner harbour until it was filled in 1894, is that of local boy-cum-composer Giuseppe Tartini (1692–1770). To the east is the **Church of St Peter** (Cerkev Sv Petra; Tartinijev trg), which contains the 14th-century **Piran Crucifix**. Across from the church is **Tartini House**, the composer's birthplace.

Sergej Mašera Maritime Museum
MUSEUM

(✆671 00 40; www.pommuz-pi.si; Cankarjevo nabrežje 3; adult/student & senior/child €3.50/2.50/2.10; ⊙9am-noon & 5-9pm Tue-Sun summer, 9am-5pm Tue-Sun winter) Located in the lovely 19th-century Gabrielli Palace on the waterfront, this museum focuses on the sea, sailing and salt-making. There are some old photographs showing salt workers going about their duties, as well as a wind-powered salt pump and little wooden weights in the form of circles and diamonds that were used to weigh salt during the Venetian republic.

Cathedral of St George
CATHEDRAL

(Stolna Cerkev Sv Jurija; Adamičeva ul 2) Piran's hilltop cathedral was founded in 1344 and rebuilt in baroque style in 1637. It's undergoing a massive renovation, and visitors are allowed only into the choir to view the magnificent marble altar and star-vaulted ceiling. If time allows, visit the attached **Parish Museum of St George** (✆673 34 40; admission €1; ⊙10am-1pm & 5-7pm Mon-Fri, 11am-7pm Sat & Sun), which contains paintings and a lapidary in the crypt.

Minorite Monastery
MONASTERY

(✆673 44 17; Bolniška ul 20) On your way up to Tartinijev trg are the Minorite Monastery with a wonderful cloister and the Church of St Francis Assisi, built originally in the early 14th century but enlarged and renovated over the centuries. Inside are ceiling frescos, a giant clam shell for donations and the Tartini family's burial plot.

🏃 Activities

The **Maona Tourist Agency** (✆673 45 20; www.maona.si; Cankarjevo nabrežje 7; ⊙9am-8pm Mon-Sat, 10am-1pm & 5-7pm Sun) and several other agencies in Piran and Portorož can book you on any number of cruises – from a loop that takes in the towns along the coast to day-long excursions to Brioni National Park and Rovinj in Croatia, or Venice and Trieste in Italy.

For swimming, Piran has several 'beaches' – rocky areas along Prešernovo nabrežje – where you might get your feet wet. They are a little better on the north side near Punta, but as long as you've come this far keep walking eastward on the paved path for just under 1km to Fiesa, which has a small but clean beach.

🛌 Sleeping

TOP CHOICE Max Piran
B&B €€

(✆041 692 928, 673 34 36; www.maxpiran.com; Ul IX Korpusa 26; d €60-70; ※@🛜) Piran's most romantic accommodation has just six rooms, each bearing a woman's name rather than number, in a delightful coral-coloured 18th-century townhouse.

Miracolo di Mare
B&B €€

(✆051 445 511, 921 76 60; www.miracolodimare.si; Tomšičeva ul 23; s €50-55, d €60-70; @🛜) A lovely B&B on the coast, the Wonder of the Sea has a dozen charming (though smallish) rooms, some of which (like No 3 and the breakfast room) look on to the most charming raised back garden in Piran. Floors and stairs are wooden (and original).

Val Hostel
HOSTEL €

(✆673 25 55; www.hostel-val.com; Gregorčičeva ul 38a; per person €22-27; @🛜) This excellent central hostel on the corner of Vegova ulica has 22 rooms (including a few singles), with shared shower, kitchen and washing machine. It's a deserved favourite with backpackers, and prices include breakfast.

Kamp Fiesa
CAMPGROUND €

(✆674 62 30; autocamp.fiesa@siol.net; adult/child €12/4; ⊙May-Sep; 🅿) The closest camping ground to Piran is at Fiesa, 4km by road but less than 1km if you follow the coastal path (obalna pešpot) east from the Cathedral of St George. It's tiny and gets crowded in summer, but it's in a quiet valley by two small ponds and right by the beach.

🍴 Eating

There's an outdoor **fruit and vegetable market** (Zelenjavni trg; ⊙7am-2pm Mon-Sat) in the small square behind the town hall.

TOP CHOICE Pri Mari
MEDITERRANEAN, SLOVENIAN €€

(✆041 616 488, 673 47 35; Dantejeva ul 17; mains €8.50-16; ⊙noon-11pm Tue-Sun summer, noon-10pm Tue-Sat, noon-6pm Sun winter) This stylish and welcoming restaurant run by an Italian-Slovenian couple serves inventive Mediterranean and Slovenian dishes. Be sure to book ahead.

Riva Piran
SEAFOOD €€

(✆673 22 25; Gregorčičeva ul 46; mains €8-28; ⊙11.30am-midnight) The best waterfront seafood restaurant, and worth patronising, is

Piran

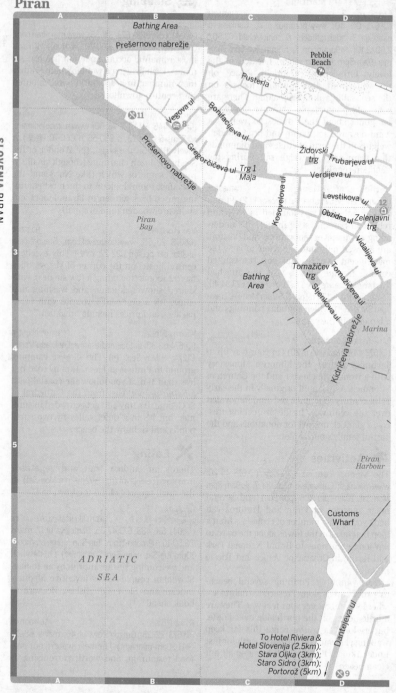

Bathing Area

Prešernovo nabrežje

Pusterla

Pebble Beach

Vegova ul

11

8

Bonifacijeva ul

Gregorčičeva ul

Prešernovo nabrežje

Trg 1 Maja

Piran Bay

Kosovelova ul

Židovski trg

Trubarjeva ul

Verdijeva ul

Levstikova ul

Obzidna ul

Zelenjavni trg

12

Vidalijeva ul

Tomažičev trg

Tomažičeva ul

Bathing Area

Stjenkova ul

Marina

Kidričeva nabrežje

Piran Harbour

Customs Wharf

ADRIATIC SEA

Dantejeva ul

To Hotel Riviera & Hotel Slovenija (2.5km); Stara Oljka (3km); Staro Sidro (3km); Portorož (5km)

9

Piran

◉ Sights

1	Cathedral of St George	E2
2	Church of St Peter	E3
3	Minorite Monastery	F3
	Parish Museum of St George	(see 1)
4	Sergej Mašera Maritime Museum	E4
5	Tartinijev Trg	E3

🛏 Sleeping

6	Max Piran	F2
7	Miracolo di Mare	E6
8	Val Hostel	B2

🍽 Eating

9	Pri Mari	D7
10	Restaurant Neptune	E5
11	Riva Piran	B2

🛍 Shopping

12	Fruit and Vegetable Market	D3

this classy place with attractive decor and sea views.

Restaurant Neptune SEAFOOD €
(☎673 41 11; Županičeva 7; mains €6-12; ⊙noon-4pm, 6pm-midnight) It's no bad thing to be more popular with locals than tourists, and this family-run place hits all the buttons – a friendly welcome, big seafood platters (as well as meat dishes and salads), and a good-value, daily two-course set lunch.

ℹ Information

Banka Koper (Tartinijev trg 12)
Caffe Neptun (☎041 724 237; www.caffeneptun.com; Dantejeva ul 4; per 20min €1; ⊙7am-1am; 🛜)
Post Office (Leninova ul 1)
Tourist Information Centre Piran (☎673 44 40, 673 02 20; www.portoroz.si; Tartinijev trg 2; ⊙9am-8pm summer, 9am-5pm winter)

ℹ Getting There & Away

BUS Services run every 20 to 30 minutes to Koper (€2.70, 30 minutes). Other destinations include Ljubljana (€12, three hours) via Divača and Postojna, and Nova Gorica (€10.30, 2¾ hours).

Some five buses go daily to Trieste (€10, 1¾ hours) in Italy, except Sundays. One bus a day heads south for Croatian Istria from June to September, stopping at the coastal towns of Umag, Poreč and Rovinj (€10.30, 2¾ hours).

CATAMARAN There are catamarans from the harbour to Trieste (adult/child €8.30/4.75, 30 minutes) in Italy daily except Wednesday, departing around 7pm.

MINIBUS From Tartinijev trg, minibuses (€1 on-board, €0.40 in advance from newsagencies, €6 for 20 rides) shuttle to Portorož every half-hour from 5.40am to 11pm continuously year-round.

Portorož

⚑05 / POP 2900

Every country with a coast has got to have a honky-tonk beach resort and Portorož (Portorose in Italian) is Slovenia's. But the 'Port of Roses' is making a big effort to scrub itself up. Portorož's sandy beaches are relatively clean, and there are pleasant spas and wellness centres where you can take the waters or cover yourself in curative mud.

🏃 Activities

The beaches (⊙8am-8pm Apr-Sep) at Portorož, including the main one, which accommodates 6000 fried and bronzed bodies, have water slides and outside showers, and beach chairs (€4.10) and umbrellas (€4.10) are available for rent. Beaches are off-limits between 11pm and 6am and camping is forbidden.

A couple of boats make the run between the main pier in Portorož and Izola in summer on trips lasting four hours. They include the Meja (☎041 664 132; adult/child €10/7; ⊙9.15am Tue & Fri) and the Svetko (☎041 623 191; adult/child €15/10.50; ⊙2.30pm daily). The Solinarka (☎031 653 682; www.solinarka.com; adult/child €12.50/6.25; ⊙varies) tour boat sails from Portorož to Piran and Strunjan and back.

Terme & Wellness Centre Portorož   SPA
(☎692 80 60; www.lifeclass.net; Obala 43; swimming pool 2/4hr pass Mon-Fri €8/12, Sat & Sun €10/15; ⊙8am-9pm Jun-Sep, 7am-7pm Oct-May, swimming pool 1-8pm Mon-Wed & Fri-Sun, 2-8pm Thu) This place is famous for treatments using sea water and by-products like mud, as well as a host of other therapies and beauty treatments. And there's a pool too.

🛏 Sleeping

Portorož counts upwards of two dozen hotels, and very few fit into the budget category. Many properties close for the winter in October and do not reopen until April or even May. The Maona Tourist Agency (☎674 03 63; Obala 14/b; ⊙9am-8pm Mon-Sat, 10am-1pm & 5-8pm Sun Jul & Aug, 9am-7pm Mon-Fri, 10am-7pm Sat, 10am-1pm Sun Sep-Jun) has

private rooms (s €18-21, d €26-40, tr €36-52) and apartments (apt for 2 €40-50), with prices varying depending on both the category and the season.

 Kaki Plac   CAMPGROUND €
(☎040 476 123; www.adrenaline-check/sea; Lucija; own tent €13, pitched tent €15, lean-to €20; ⊙Apr-Nov; P🐾) A small ecofriendly campsite tucked into the woods just outside Lucija on the outskirts of Portorož. Tents come with mattrasses and linen, some sit snugly under thatched Istrian lean-tos, so you can sleep like a traditional shepherd (sort of).

Hotel Riviera & Hotel Slovenija   HOTEL €€€
(☎692 00 00; www.lifeclass.net; Obala 33; s €142-185, d €184-250; P🌞@🏊) These four-star sister properties are joined at the hip and are good choices if you want to stay someplace central. The Riviera has 160 rooms, three fabulous swimming pools and an excellent wellness centre. The Slovenija is somewhat bigger with 183 rooms.

🍴 Eating

Staro Sidro   SEAFOOD €
(☎674 50 74; Obala 55; mains €8-19; ⊙noon-11pm Tue-Sun) A tried-and-true favourite, the Old Anchor is next to the lovely (and landmark) Vila San Marco. It specialises in seafood and has both a garden and a lovely terrace overlooking Obala and Portorož Bay.

Stara Oljka   BALKAN €€
(☎674 85 55; Obala 20; starters €5-9.60, mains €8.60-24; ⊙10am-midnight) The Old Olive Tree specialises in grills (Balkan, steaks etc), which you can watch being prepared in the open kitchen. There's a large and enticing sea-facing terrace.

ℹ Getting There & Away

BUS Buses leave Portorož for Koper (€2.30, 25 minutes) and Izola (€1.80, 15 minutes) about every 30 minutes throughout the year. Other destinations from Portorož and their daily frequencies are the same as those for Piran.

MINIBUS Minibuses make the loop from the Lucija camping grounds through central Portorož to Piran throughout the year.

EASTERN SLOVENIA

The rolling vine-covered hills of eastern Slovenia are attractive but less dramatic than the Julian Alps or, indeed, the coast. Two cities worth a detour include lively Maribor, Slovenia's second-largest city, and postcard-perfect Ptuj, less than 30km down the road.

Maribor

☑02 / POP 88,350

Despite being the nation's second-largest city, Maribor has only about a third the population of Ljubljana and often feels more like an overgrown provincial town. It has no unmissable sights but oozes charm thanks to its delightfully patchy Old Town along the Drava River. Pedestrianised central streets buzz with cafes and student life and the riverside Lent district hosts major cultural events – indeed, Maribor was European Capital of Culture in 2012.

◉ Sights

Grajksi Trg　　　　　　　　　SQUARE
The centre of the Old Town, this square is graced with the 17th-century **Column of St Florian**, dedicated to the patron saint of fire fighters.

Maribor Castle　　　　　　　　MUSEUM
(Grajski trg 2) On Grajski Trg, the centre of Maribor's Old Town, is Maribor's 15th-century castle. It contains a **Knights' Hall** (Viteška Dvorana) with a remarkable painted ceiling, the baroque **Loretska Chapel** and a magnificent **rococo staircase**.

Inside the castle, the **Maribor Regional Museum** (☑228 35 51; www.pmuzej-mb.si; Grajski trg; adult/child €3/2; ⊙9am-1pm & 4pm-7pm Mon-Fri, 9am-1pm Sat) has one of the richest collections in Slovenia. The building is undergoing renovation, so parts may be off-limits. On the ground floor there are archaeological, clothing and ethnographic exhibits, including florid, 19th-century beehive panels. Upstairs are rooms devoted to Maribor's history and guilds.

⌂ Sleeping

TOP CHOICE Hostel Pekarna　　　　HOSTEL €
(☑059 180 880; www.mkc-hostelpekarna.si; Ob železnici 16; dm/s/d €17/21/42; ☎♿) This bright and welcoming hostel south of the river is a converted army bakery. Facilities, from the dorms to the cafe, are up to the minute, and there are several apartments with kitchens.

Hotel Lent　　　　　　　　　HOTEL €€
(☑250 67 69; www.hotel-lent.si; Dravska ulica 9; s/d €69/89; ☀☎) Shiny riverside hotel in Lent, with a café out front. Rooms are stylishly decorated and comfortable, though the suites are tricked out in unexpected gangster bling.

✖ Eating

TOP CHOICE Gril Ranca　　　　　　BALKAN €
(☑252 55 50; Dravska ul 10; dishes €4.80-7.50; ⊙8am-11pm Mon-Sat, noon-9pm Sun) This place serves simple but scrumptious Balkan grills such as *pljeskavica* (spicy meat patties) and *čevapčiči* (spicy meatballs of beef or pork) in full view of the Drava. It's cool on a hot night.

Pri Florjanu　　　　　　MEDITERRANEAN €€
(☑059 084 850; Grajski trg 6; starters €5.50-7, mains €9-18; ⊙11am-10pm Mon-Thu, 11am-11pm Fri & Sat; ☑♿) A great spot in full view of the Column of St Florian, this stylish place has both an open front and an enclosed back terrace and a huge minimalist restaurant in between. It serves inspired Mediterranean food, with a good supply of vegetarian options.

❶ Information

Tourist Information Centre Maribor (☑234 66 11; www.maribor-pohorje.si; Partinzanska c 6a; ⊙9am-7pm Mon-Fri, 9am-6pm Sat & Sun) Very helpful TIC in kiosk opposite the Franciscan church.

❶ Getting There & Away

BUS Services are frequent to Celje (€6.7, 1½ hours), Murska Sobota (€6.30, 1¼ hours), Ptuj (€3.60, 45 minutes) and Ljubljana (€12.40, three hours).

TRAIN From Ljubljana there is the ICS express service (€15.20, 1¾ hours), or more frequent slower trains (€9, 2½ hours). Both stop at Celje.

Ptuj

☑02 / POP 19,010

Rising gently above a wide valley, Ptuj forms a symphony of red-tile roofs best viewed from across the Drava River. One of the oldest towns in Slovenia, Ptuj equals Ljubljana in terms of historical importance but the compact medieval core, with its castle, museums, monasteries and churches, can easily be seen in a day.

◉ Sights

Ptuj's Gothic centre, with its Renaissance and baroque additions, can be viewed on a 'walking tour' taking in Minoritski trg and Mestni trg, Slovenski trg, Prešernova ulica, Muzejski trg and Ptuj Castle.

Ptuj Castle
CASTLE

(Grad Ptuj; ☑787 92 45, 748 03 60; Na Gradu 1) Ptuj castle is an agglomeration of styles from the 14th to the 18th centuries. It houses the **Ptuj Regional Museum** (☑787 92 30; www.pok-muzej-ptuj.si; adult/child €4/2.50; ☉9am-6pm Mon-Fri, 9am-8pm Sat & Sun summer, 9am-5pm daily winter) but is worth the trip for views of Ptuj and the Drava. The shortest way to the castle is to follow narrow Grajska ulica, which leads to a covered wooden stairway and the castle's Renaissance **Peruzzi Portal** (1570).

✷ Festivals

Kurentovanje
CARNIVAL

(www.kurentovanje.net) Kurentovanje is a rite of spring celebrated for 10 days in February leading up to Shrove Tuesday; it's the most popular and best-known folklore event in Slovenia.

⛏ Sleeping

MuziKafe
HOTEL €€

TOP CHOICE

(☑787 88 60; www.muzikafe.si; Vrazov trg 1; ☏) This quirky cracker of a place is tucked away off Jadranska ulica. Everything is bright, with each room idiosyncratically decorated by the hotel's artist owners. There's a terrace café, plus a vaulted brick cellar for musical and artistic events.

Hotel Mitra
HOTEL €€€

(☑051 603 069, 787 74 55; www.hotel-mitra.si; Prešernova ul 6; s €62-88, d €106; 🅿❄@☏) This pleasant hotel has 25 generous-sized guest rooms and four humongous suites, each with its own name and story and specially commissioned paintings on the wall. There are lovely Oriental carpets on the original wooden floors and a wellness centre in an old courtyard cellar.

Hostel Eva
HOSTEL €

(☑040 226 522, 771 24 41; www.hostel-ptuj.si; Jadranska ul 22; per person €12-20) This welcoming, up-to-date hostel connected to a bike shop (per-day rental €10) has six rooms containing two to six beds and a large light-filled kitchen.

✗ Eating

Gostilna Ribič
GOSTILNA €€

TOP CHOICE

(☑749 06 35; Dravska ul 9; mains €9.50-20; ☉10am-11pm Sun-Thu, 10am-midnight Fri & Sat) Arguably the best restaurant in Ptuj, the Angler Inn faces the river, with an enormous terrace, and the speciality here is – not surprisingly – fish, especially herbed and baked pike perch. The seafood soup served in a bread loaf bowl is exceptional.

Amadeus
GOSTILNA €€

(☑771 70 51; Prešernova ul 36; mains €6.50-20; ☉noon-10pm Mon-Thu, noon-11pm Fri & Sat, noon-4pm Sun) This pleasant *gostilna* (inn-like restaurant) above a pub and near the foot of the road to the castle serves *štruklji* (dumplings with herbs and cheese), steak, pork and fish.

ℹ Information

Tourist Information Centre Ptuj (☑779 60 11; www.ptuj.info; Slovenski trg 5; ☉8am-8pm summer, 9am-6pm winter)

ℹ Getting There & Away

BUS Services to Maribor (€3.60, 45 minutes) go every couple of hours, less frequently at weekends.

TRAIN Connections are better for trains than buses, with plentiful departures to Ljubljana (€8 to €13.60) direct or via Pragersko. Up to a dozen trains go to Maribor (€2.90 to €5.90, 50 minutes).

UNDERSTAND SLOVENIA

History
Early Years

Slovenes can make a credible claim to having invented democracy. By the early 7th century, their Slavic ancestors had founded the Duchy of Carantania (Karantanija), based at Krn Castle (now Karnburg in Austria). Ruling dukes were elected by enobled commoners and invested before ordinary citizens.

This unique model was noted by the 16th-century French political philosopher Jean Bodin, whose work was a reference for Thomas Jefferson when he wrote the American Declaration of Independence in 1776.

Carantania (later Carinthia) was fought over by the Franks and Magyars from the 8th to 10th centuries, and later divided up among Austro-Germanic nobles and bishops.

The Habsburgs & Napoleon

Between the late 13th and early 16th centuries, almost all the lands inhabited by Slovenes, with the exception of the Venetian-controlled coastal towns, came under the domination of the Habsburgs, ruled from Vienna.

Austrian rule continued until 1918, apart from a brief interlude between 1809 and 1813 when Napoleon created six so-called Illyrian Provinces from Slovenian and Croatian regions and made Ljubljana the capital.

Napoleon proved a popular conqueror as his relatively liberal regime de-Germanised the education system. Slovene was taught in schools for the first time, leading to an awakening of national consciousness. In tribute, Ljubljana still has a French Revolution Sq (Trg Francoske Revolucije) with a column bearing a likeness of the French emperor.

World Wars I & II

Fighting during WWI was particularly savage along the Soča Valley – the Isonzo Front – which was occupied by Italy then retaken by German-led Austro-Hungarian forces. The war ended with the collapse of Austria-Hungary, which handed western Slovenia to Italy as part of postwar reparations.

Northern Carinthia, including the towns of Beljak and Celovec (now Villach and Klagenfurt), voted to stay with Austria in a 1920 plebiscite. What remained of Slovenia joined fellow Slavs (jug) in forming the Kingdom of Serbs, Croats and Slovenes, later Yugoslavia.

Nazi occupation in WWII was for the most part resisted by Slovenian partisans, though after Italy capitulated in 1943 the anti-partisan Slovenian Domobranci (Home Guards) were active in the west. To prevent their nemeses, the communists, from taking political control in liberated areas, the Domobranci threw their support behind the Germans.

The war ended with Slovenia regaining Italian-held areas from Piran to Bovec, but losing Trst (Trieste) and part of Gorica (Gorizia).

Tito's Yugoslavia

In Tito's Yugoslavia in the 1960s and '70s, Slovenia, with only 8% of the national population, was the economic powerhouse, creating up to 20% of the national GDP.

But by the 1980s the federation had become increasingly Serb-dominated, and Slovenes feared they would lose their political autonomy. In free elections, Slovenes voted overwhelmingly to break away from Yugoslavia and did so on 25 June 1991. A 10-day war that left 66 people dead followed; Yugoslavia swiftly signed a truce in order to concentrate on regaining control of coastal Croatia.

From Independence to Today

Shortly after the withdrawal of the federal army from Slovenian soil on 25 October 1991, Slovenia got a new constitution that provided for a bicameral parliamentary system of government.

The head of state, the president, is elected directly for a maximum of two five-year terms. Milan Kučan held that role from independence until 2002, when the late Janez Drnovšek (1950–2008), a former prime minister, was elected. Diplomat Danilo Türk has been president since 2007, having been re-elected in 2012.

Executive power is vested in the prime minister and his cabinet. The current premier is Janez Janša, who was returned to power in early 2012 after 3½ years in opposition.

Slovenia was admitted to the UN in 1992 as the 176th member-state. In May 2004, Slovenia entered the EU as a full member and less than three years later adopted the euro, replacing the tolar as the national currency.

People

The population of Slovenia is largely homogeneous. Just over 83% are ethnic Slovenes, with the remainder Serbs, Croats, Bosnians, Albanians and Roma; there are also small enclaves of Italians and Hungarians, who have special deputies looking after their interests in parliament.

Slovenes are ethnically Slavic, typically hardworking, multilingual and extrovert. Around 60% of Slovenes identify themselves as Catholics.

Arts

Slovenia's most cherished writer is the Romantic poet France Prešeren (1800–49). His patriotic yet humanistic verse was a driving force in raising Slovene national consciousness. Fittingly, a stanza of his poem 'Zdravljica' (A Toast) forms the lyrics of the national anthem.

Many of Ljubljana's most characteristic architectural features, including its recurring pyramid motif, were added by celebrated Slovenian architect Jože Plečnik (1872–1957), whose work fused classical building principles and folk-art traditions.

Postmodernist painting and sculpture were more or less dominated from the 1980s by the multimedia group NeueSlowenische Kunst (NSK) and the artists' cooperative Irwin. It also spawned the internationally known industrial-music group Laibach, whose leader, Tomaž Hostnik, died tragically in 1983 when he hanged himself from a *kozolec*, the traditional (and iconic) hayrack found only in Slovenia.

Slovenia's vibrant music scene embraces rave, techno, jazz, punk, thrash-metal and *chanson* (torch songs from the likes of Vita Mavrič); the most popular local rock group is Siddharta, formed in 1995 and still going strong. There's also been a folk-music revival: keep an ear out for the groups Katice and Katalena, who play traditional Slovenian music with a modern twist, and the vocalist Brina.

Films

Well-received Slovenian films in recent years include *Kruh in Mleko* (Bread & Milk, 2001), the tragic story by Jan Cvitkovič of a dysfunctional small-town family, and Damjan Kozole's *Rezerni Deli* (Spare Parts, 2003), about the trafficking of illegal immigrants through Slovenia from Croatia to Italy.

Much lighter fare is *Petelinji Zajtrk* (Rooster's Breakfast, 2007), a romance by Marko Naberšnik set on the Austrian border, and the bizarre US-made documentary *Big River Man* (John Maringouin, 2009) about an overweight marathon swimmer who takes on – wait for it – the Amazon and succeeds.

Environment

Slovenia is amazingly green; indeed, 58% of its total surface area is covered in forest and it's growing. Slovenia is home to almost 3200 plant species – some 70 of which are indigenous.

Triglav National Park is particularly rich in native flowering plants. Among the more peculiar endemic fauna in Slovenia is a blind salamander called *Proteus anguinus* that lives deep in Karst caves, can survive for years without eating and has been called a 'living fossil'.

Food & Drink

Slovenia boasts an incredibly diverse cuisine, but except for a few national favourites such as *žlikrofi* (pasta stuffed with cheese, bacon

and chives) and *jota* (hearty bean soup) and incredibly rich desserts like *gibanica* (a layer cake stuffed with nuts, cheese and apple), you're not likely to encounter many of these regional specialities on menus.

Dishes like *brodet* (fish soup) from the coast, *ajdovi žganci z ocvirki* (buckwheat 'porridge' with savoury pork crackling) and salad greens doused in *bučno olje* (pumpkin-seed oil) are generally eaten at home.

A *gostilna* or *gostišče* (inn) or *restavracija* (restaurant) more frequently serves *rižota* (risotto), *klobasa* (sausage), *zrezek* (cutlet/steak), *golaž* (goulash) and *paprikaš* (piquant chicken or beef 'stew'). *Riba* (fish) is excellent and usually priced by the *dag* (100g). Common in Slovenia are such Balkan favourites as *cevapčiči* (spicy meatballs of beef or pork) and *pljeskavica* (spicy meat patties), often served with *kajmak* (a type of clotted cream).

You can snack cheaply on takeaway pizza slices or pieces of *burek* (€2), flaky pastry stuffed with meat, cheese or apple. Alternatives include *štruklji* (cottage-cheese dumplings) and *palačinke* (thin sweet pancakes).

Wine, Beer & Brandy

Distinctively Slovenian wines include peppery red Teran (made from Refošk grapes in the Karst region), Cviček (a dry light red – almost rosé – wine from eastern Slovenia) and Malvazija (a straw-colour white from the coast that is light and dry). Slovenes are justly proud of their top vintages, but cheaper bar-standard *odprto vino* (open wine) sold by the decilitre (100mL) is just so-so.

Pivo (beer), whether *svetlo* (lager) or *temno* (porter), is best on *točeno* (draught) but always available in cans and bottles too.

There are dozens of kinds of *žganje* (fruit brandy) available, including *češnjevec* (made with cherries), *sadjevec* (mixed fruit), *brinjevec* (juniper), *hruška* (pears, also called *viljamovka*) and *slivovka* (plums).

SURVIVAL GUIDE

Directory A–Z

Accommodation

Accommodation runs the gamut from riverside camping grounds, hostels, mountain huts, cosy *gostišča* (inns) and farmhouses, to elegant castle hotels and five-star hotels in Ljubljana, so you'll usually have little trouble finding accommodation to fit your budget, except perhaps at the height of the season (July and August) on the coast, at Bled or Bohinj, or in Ljubljana.

The following price ranges refer to a double room, with en suite toilet and bath or shower and breakfast, unless otherwise indicated. Virtually every municipality in the land levies a tourist tax of between €0.50 and €1 per person per night.

€ less than €50

€€ €50 to €100

€€€ more than €100

FARMSTAYS

Hundreds of working farms in Slovenia offer accommodation to paying guests, either in private rooms in the farmhouse itself or in Alpine-style guesthouses. Many farms offer outdoor sport activities and allow you to help out with the farm chores if you feel so inclined.

Expect to pay about €15 per person in a room with shared bathroom and breakfast (from €20 for half-board) in the low season (September to mid-December and mid-January to June), rising in the high season (July and August) to a minimum €17 per person (from €25 for half-board).

For more information, contact the Association of Tourist Farms of Slovenia (Združenje Turističnih Kmetij Slovenije; ☑041 435 528, 03-425 55 11; www.farmtourism.si; Trnoveljska cesta 1) or check with the Slovenian Tourist Board.

Business Hours

The *delovni čas* (opening times) are usually posted on the door. *Odprto* is 'open', *zaprto* is 'closed'. The following hours are standard and reviews won't list business hours unless they differ from these.

Banks 9am to 5pm weekdays, and (rarely) from 8am until noon on Saturday.

Grocery stores 8am to 7pm weekdays and 8am until 1pm on Saturday.

Museums 10am to 6pm Tuesday to Sunday. Winter hours may be shorter.

Post offices 8am to 6pm or 7pm weekdays and until noon on Saturday.

Restaurant Hours vary but count on 11am to 10pm daily. Bars are usually open from 11am to midnight Sunday to Thursday and to 1am or 2am on Friday and Saturday.

Embassies & Consulates

All of the following are in Ljubljana:

Australian Consulate (☑01-234 86 75; Železna cesta 14; ⊗9am-1pm Mon-Fri)

Canadian Consulate (☑01-252 44 44; 49a Linhartova cesta; ⊗8am-noon Mon, Wed & Fri)

French Embassy (☑01-479 04 00; Barjanska cesta 1; ⊗8.30am-12.30pm Mon-Fri)

German Embassy (☑01-479 03 00; Prešernova cesta 27; ⊗9am-noon Mon-Thu, 9-11am Fri)

Irish Embassy (☑01-300 89 70; 1st fl, Palača Kapitelj, Poljanski nasip 6; ⊗9.30am-12.30pm & 2.30-4pm Mon-Fri)

Netherlands Embassy (☑01-420 14 61; 1st fl, Palača Kapitelj, Poljanski nasip 6; ⊗9am-noon Mon-Fri)

New Zealand Consulate (☑01-580 30 55; Verovškova ulica 57; ⊗8am-3pm Mon-Fri)

UK Embassy (☑01-200 39 10; 4th fl, Trg Republike 3; ⊗9am-noon Mon-Fri)

US Embassy (☑01-200 55 00; Prešernova cesta 31; ⊗9-11.30am & 1-3pm Mon-Fri)

Festivals & Events

The official website of the Slovenian Tourist Board (www.slovenia.info), maintains a comprehensive list of major cultural events.

Food

The following price ranges are a rough approximation for a two-course sit-down meal for one person, with a drink. Many restaurants offer an excellent-value set menu of two or even three courses at lunch. These typically run from €5 to €9.

€ less than €15

€€ €16 to €30

€€€ over €30

Gay & Lesbian Travellers

National laws ban discrimination in employment and other areas on the basis of sexual preference. In recent years a highly visible campaign against homophobia has been put in place across the country. Outside Ljubljana, however, there is little evidence of a gay presence, much less a lifestyle.

Roza Klub (Klub K4 ; www.klubk4.org; Kersnikova ulica 4; ⊗10pm-6am Sun Sep-Jun) in Ljubljana is made up of the gay and lesbian branches of KUC (www.skuc.org), which stands for Študentski Kulturni Center (Student Cultural

Centre) but is no longer student-orientated as such. It organises the gay and lesbian Ljubljana Pride (www.ljubljanapride.org) parade in late June and the Gay & Lesbian Film Festival (www.ljudmila.org/siqrd/fglf) in late November/early December. The gay male branch, Magnus (skucmagnus@hotmail.com), deals with AIDS prevention, networking and is behind the Kulturni Center Q (Q Cultural Centre) in Ljubljana's Metelkova Mesto, which includes Klub Tiffany for gay men and Klub Monokel for gay women.

A monthly publication called Narobe (Upside Down; www.narobe.si) is in Slovene only, though you might be able to at least glean some basic information from the listings.

Internet Access

Virtually every hotel and hostel now has internet access – a computer for guests' use (free or for a small fee), wi-fi – or both. Most of the country's tourist information centres offer free (or low-cost) access and many libraries in Slovenia have free terminals. Many cities and towns have at least one internet cafe (though they usually only have a handful of terminals), or even free wi-fi in town squares.

Money

The official currency is the euro. Exchanging cash is simple at banks, major post offices, travel agencies and *menjalnice* (bureaux de change), although many don't accept travellers cheques. Major credit and debit cards are accepted almost everywhere, and ATMs are ubiquitous.

Post

The Slovenian postal system (*Pošta Slovenije*), recognised by its bright yellow logo, offers a wide variety of services – from selling stamps and telephone cards to making photocopies and changing money. News stands also sell *znamke* (stamps). Post offices can sell you boxes.

Public Holidays

If a holiday falls on a Sunday, then the following Monday becomes the holiday.

New Year 1 and 2 January

Prešeren Day (Slovenian Culture Day) 8 February

Easter & Easter Monday March/April

Insurrection Day 27 April

Labour Day holidays 1 and 2 May

National Day 25 June

Assumption Day 15 August

Reformation Day 31 October

All Saints Day 1 November

Christmas Day 25 December

Independence Day 26 December

Telephone

Public telephones in Slovenia require a *telefonska kartica* or *telekartica* (telephone card) available at post offices and some newsstands. Phonecards cost €2.70/4/7.50/14.60 for 25/50/100/300 *impulzov* (impulses, or units).

To call Slovenia from abroad, dial the international access code, ☎386 (the country code for Slovenia), the area code (minus the initial zero) and the number. There are six area codes in Slovenia (☎01 to ☎05 and ☎07). To call abroad from Slovenia, dial ☎00 followed by the country and area codes and then the number. Numbers beginning with ☎80 in Slovenia are toll-free.

MOBILE PHONES

Network coverage amounts to more than 95% of the country. Mobile numbers carry the prefix ☎030 and ☎040 (SiMobil), ☎031, ☎041, ☎051 and ☎071 (Mobitel) and ☎070 (Tušmobil).

Slovenia uses GSM 900, which is compatible with the rest of Europe and Australia but not with the North American GSM 1900 or the totally different Japanese system. SIM cards with €5 credit are available for around €15 from SiMobil (www.simobil.si), Mobitel (www.mobitel.si) and Tušmobil (www.tusmobil.sil). Top-up scratch cards are available at post offices, news stands and petrol stations.

All three networks have outlets throughout Slovenia, including in Ljubljana.

Tourist Information

The Slovenian Tourist Board (Slovenska Turistična Organizacija, STO; ☎01-589 18 40; www.slovenia.info; Dunajska cesta 156), based in Ljubljana, is the umbrella organisation for tourist promotion in Slovenia, and produces a number of excellent brochures, pamphlets and booklets in English.

Walk-in visitors in Ljubljana can head to the Slovenian Tourist Information Centre (STIC, ☎306 45 76; www.slovenia.info; Krekov trg 10; ◷8am-9pm Jun-Sep, 8am-7pm Oct-May). In addition, the organisation oversees another five dozen or so local tourist offices and bureaus called 'tourist information centres' (TICs) across the country.

In the capital, the **Ljubljana Tourist Information Centre** (TIC; ☑306 12 15; www.visitljubljana.si; Adamič-Lundrovo nabrežje 2; ☺8am-9pm Jun-Sep, 8am-7pm Oct-May) knows just about everything there is to know about Ljubljana and almost as much about the rest of Slovenia. There's a branch at the train station.

Visas

Citizens of nearly all European countries, as well as Australia, Canada, Israel, Japan, New Zealand and the USA, do not require visas to visit Slovenia for stays of up to 90 days. Holders of EU and Swiss passports can enter using a national identity card.

Those who do require visas (including South Africans) can get them for up to 90 days at any Slovenian embassy or consulate – see the website of the **Ministry of Foreign Affairs** (www.mzz.gov.si) for a full listing. They cost €35 regardless of the type of visa or length of validity.

Getting There & Away

Border formalities with Slovenia's fellow European Union neighbours, Italy, Austria and Hungary, are virtually nonexistent. Croatia hopes to enter the EU in 2013 and plans to implement the Schengen border rules soon after. Until then expect a somewhat closer inspection of your documents – national ID (for EU citizens) or passport and, in some cases, visa when travelling to/from Croatia.

Air

Slovenia's only international airport is Ljubljana's **Jože Pučnik Airport** (LJU/Aerodrom Ljubljana; ☑04-206 19 81; www.lju-airport.si/eng; Zgornji Brnik 130a, Brnik) at Brnik, 27km north of Ljubljana. In the arrivals hall there's a **Slovenia Tourist Information Centre** (STIC; ☺11am-11pm Mon, Wed & Fri, 10am-10pm Tue & Thu, 10.30am-10.30pm Sat, 12.30pm-12.30am Sun) desk, a hotel-booking telephone and ATM. Car-rental agencies have outlets opposite the terminal.

From its base at Brnik, the Slovenian flag-carrier, **Adria Airways** (☑01-369 10 10, 080 13 00; www.adria-airways.com), serves some 20 European destinations on regularly scheduled flights.

Other airlines with regularly scheduled flights to and from Ljubljana include:

Air France (☑01-244 34 47; www.airfrance.com/si) Daily flights to Paris (CDG).

ČSA Czech Airlines (☑04-206 17 50; www.czechairlines.com) Flights to Prague.

EasyJet (☑04-206 16 77; www.easyjet.com) Low-cost daily flights to London Stansted.

JAT Airways (☑01-231 43 40; www.jat.com) Daily flights to Belgrade.

Lufthansa (☑01-434 72 46; www.lufthansa.com; Gosposvetska cesta 6) Code-shared flights with Adria.

Montenegro Airlines (☑04-259 42 52; www.montenegroairlines.com) Twice weekly flight to Podgorica.

Turkish Airlines (☑04-206 16 80; www.turkishairlines.com) Flights to Istanbul.

Land
BUS
International bus destinations from Ljubljana include Serbia, Germany, Croatia, Bosnia and Hercegovina, Macedonia, Italy and Scandinavia. You can also catch buses to Italy and Croatia from coastal towns, including Piran and Koper.

TRAIN
It is possible to travel to Italy, Austria, Germany, Croatia and Hungary by train; Ljubljana is the main hub, although you can, for example, hop on international trains in certain cities like Maribor and Ptuj). International train travel can be expensive. It is sometimes cheaper to travel as far as you can on domestic routes before crossing any borders.

Sea

Piran sends ferries to Trieste daily and catamarans to Venice at least once a week in season. There's also a catamaran between nearby Izola and Venice in summer months.

Getting Around
Bicycle
Cycling is a popular way of getting around. Bikes can be transported for €2.80 in the baggage compartments of some IC and regional trains. Larger buses can also carry bikes as luggage. Larger towns and cities have dedicated bicycle lanes and traffic lights.

ROAD RULES

» Drive on the right.

» Speed limits: 50km/h in town, 90km/h on secondary roads, 100km/h on highways; 130km/h on motorways.

» Seat belts are compulsory; motorcyclists must wear helmets.

» All motorists must illuminate their headlights throughout the day.

» Permitted blood-alcohol level for drivers is 0.05%.

Bus

Buy your ticket at the *avtobusna postaja* (bus station) or simply pay the driver as you board. In Ljubljana you should book your seat at least a day in advance if you're travelling on Friday, or to destinations in the mountains or on the coast on a public holiday. Bus services are restricted on Sunday and holidays.

A range of bus companies serve the country, but prices are uniform: €3.10/5.60/9.20/16.80 for 25/50/100/200km of travel.

Timetables in the bus station, or posted on a wall or column outside, list destinations and departure times. If you cannot find your bus listed or don't understand the schedule, get help from the *blagajna vozovnice* (information or ticket window), which are usually one and the same. *Odhodi* means 'departures' while *prihodi* is 'arrivals'.

Car & Motorcycle

Roads in Slovenia are generally good. There are two main motorway corridors – between Maribor and the coast (via the flyover at Črni Kal) and from the Karavanke Tunnel into Austria to Zagreb in Croatia – intersecting at the Ljubljana ring road, with a branch from Postojna to Nova Gorica. Motorways are numbered from A1 to A10 (for *avtocesta*).

Tolls are no longer paid separately on the motorways, instead all cars must display a *vinjeta* (road-toll sticker) on the windscreen. They cost €15/30/95 for a week/month/year for cars and €7.50/25/47.50 for motorbikes and are available at petrol stations, post offices and certain news stands and tourist information centres. These stickers will already be in place on a rental car; failure to display such a sticker risks a fine of up to €300.

Dial ☎1987 for roadside assistance.

HIRING A CAR

Renting a car in Slovenia allows access to cheaper out-of-centre hotels and farm or village homestays. Rentals from international firms such as Avis, Budget, Europcar and Hertz vary in price; expect to pay from €40/210 a day/week, including unlimited mileage, collision damage waiver (CDW), theft protection (TP), Personal Accident Insurance (PAI) and taxes. Some smaller agencies have somewhat more competitive rates; booking on the internet is always cheaper.

Train

Much of the country is accessible by rail, run by the national operator, Slovenian Railways (Slovenske Železnice, SŽ; ☎01-291 33 32; www.slo-zeleznice.si). The website has an easy-to-use timetable.

Figure on travelling at about 60km/h except on the fastest InterCity Slovenia (ICS) express trains that run between Ljubljana and Maribor (€13.60, 1¾ hours) at an average speed of 90km/h.

The provinces are served by *regionalni vlaki* (regional trains) and *primestni vlaki* (city trains), but the fastest are InterCity trains (IC).

An 'R' next to the train number on the timetable means seat reservations are available. If the 'R' is boxed, seat reservations are obligatory.

Purchase your ticket before travelling at the *železniška postaja* (train station); buying it from the conductor onboard costs an additional €2.50. Invalid tickets or fare dodging earn a €40 fine.

Switzerland

Includes »

Best Places to Eat

» Bottegone del Vino (p562)
» Wirtshaus Galliker (p544)
» Alpenrose (p554)
» Lötschberg AOC (p540)
» Whymper Stube (p538)

Best Places to Stay

» Hotel Bahnhof (p538)
» Hôtel Beau-Rivage Palace (p533)
» Hotel du Thèâtre (p553)
» Hotel Landhaus (p540)
» Palace Luzern (p544)

Why Go?

What giddy romance Zermatt, St Moritz and other glitterati-encrusted names evoke. This is *Sonderfall Schweiz* ('special case Switzerland'), a privileged neutral country, proudly idiosyncratic, insular and unique. Blessed with gargantuan cultural diversity, its four official languages alone say it all.

The Swiss don't do half-measures: Zürich, their most gregarious urban centre, has cutting-edge art, legendary nightlife and one of the world's highest living standards. The national passion for sweat, stamina and clingy Lycra takes 65 year olds across 2500m-high mountain passes for Sunday strolls, sees giggly three year olds skiing rings around grown-ups, prompts locals done with 'ordinary' marathons to sprint backwards up mountains – all in the name of good old-fashioned fun.

So don't depend just on your postcard images of Bern's chocolate-box architecture, the majestic Matterhorn or the thundering Rheinfall – Switzerland is a place that's so outrageously beautiful, it simply must be seen to be believed.

When to Go

Geneva

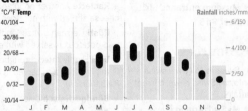

Dec–early Apr Carve through powder and drink gluhwein at an alpine resort.

May–Sep Hike in the shadow of the Matterhorn and be wowed by its mesmerising stance.

Aug Celebrate Swiss National Day on 1 August and witness Swiss national pride in full force.

AT A GLANCE

» **Currency** Swiss franc (Sfr)

» **Languages** French, German, Italian, Romansch

» **Money** ATMs readily available

» **Visas** Schengen rules apply

Fast Facts

» **Area** 41,285 sq km

» **Capital** Bern

» **Country code** ☑41

» **Emergency** police ☑117; fire☑118; ambulance ☑144

Exchange Rates

Australia	A$1	Sfr0.99
Canada	C$1	Sfr0.93
Euro	€1	Sfr1.22
Japan	¥100	Sfr1.01
New Zealand	NZ$1	Sfr0.79
UK	UK£1	Sfr1.44
USA	US$1	Sfr0.95

Set Your Budget

» **Budget hotel** Sfr80-100

» **Two-course meal** Sfr30

» **Museum entrance** Sfr15

» **Beer** Sfr5

Resources

» **Swiss Info** (www.swissinfo.ch) Swiss news, current affairs.

» **MySwitzerland** (www.myswitzerland.com) Swiss tourism.

Connections

Landlocked between France, Germany, Austria, Liechtenstein and Italy, Switzerland is well-linked. Geneva city buses run as far as the French border (a couple cross into France, continuing along the southern shore of Lake Geneva). Fast and frequent French TGV trains link Geneva and Lausanne with Paris. In the north, newly completed high-speed lines in France mean that Zürich is only four hours from Paris while Basel is but three. Basel also has fast ICE trains that serve major German cities, while Zürich is well linked to Stuttgart, Munich and Austria. Regular trains serve Milan from Zürich, Lucerne and Lugano.

ITINERARIES

One Week

Starting in vibrant Zürich, shop famous Bahnhofstrasse and find the medieval corners. Next, head to the Jungfrau region to explore some kick-ass alpine scenery (think James Bond racing an avalanche down a sheer snowy rock face). Take a pit stop in beautiful Lucerne before finishing up in country capital Bern.

Two Weeks

As above, then head west for French-immersion lessons in Geneva or lakeside Lausanne. Stop in Gruyères to dip into a cheesy fondue and overdose on meringues drowned in thick double cream. Zip to Zermatt or across to St Moritz to frolic in snow or green meadows, then loop east to taste the Italian side of Switzerland at lakeside Lugano.

Essential Food & Drink

» **Fondue** Switzerland's best-known dish, in which melted Emmental and Gruyère cheese are combined with white wine in a large pot and eaten with bread cubes.

» **Raclette** Another popular artery-hardener of melted cheese served with potatoes.

» **Rösti** German Switzerland's national dish of fried shredded potatoes is served with everything.

» **Veal** Highly rated throughout the country; in Zürich, veal is thinly sliced and served in a cream sauce (*Gschnetzeltes Kalbsfleisch*).

» **Bündnerfleisch** Dried beef, smoked and thinly sliced.

» **Chocolate** Good at any time of day and available in dozens of luscious flavours.

GENEVA

POP 192,400

Slick and cosmopolitan, Geneva (Genève in French, Genf in German) is a rare breed of city. It's one of Europe's priciest. Its people chatter in every language under the sun (184 nationalities comprise 45% of the city's population) and it's constantly thought of as the Swiss capital – which it isn't. This business-like city strung around the sparkling shores of Europe's largest alpine lake is, in fact, only Switzerland's second-largest city.

Yet the whole world is here: the UN, International Red Cross, International Labour Organization, World Health Organization – 200-odd governmental and nongovernmental international organisations fill the city's plush hotels with big-name guests, feast on an incredulous choice of cuisine and help prop up the overload of banks, jewellers and chocolate shops for which Geneva is known. Strolling manicured city parks, lake sailing and skiing next door in the Alps are weekend pursuits.

⊙ Sights

The city centre is so compact it's easy to see many of the main sights on foot.

Lake Geneva   LAKE

Begin your exploration of Europe's largest alpine lake by having a coffee on Île Rousseau, where a statue honours the celebrated freethinker. Cross to the southern side of the lake and walk west to the **Horloge Fleurie** (Flower Clock; Quai du Général-Guisan) in the Jardin Anglais. Geneva's most photographed clock, crafted from 6500 flowers, can be oddly disappointing after all the hype.

Far more rewarding is the iconic 140m-tall **Jet d'Eau** (Lake Geneva, Jetée des Eaux-Vives; admission free; ⊙9.30am-11.15pm Mar-Oct) on the lake's southern shore. When the fountain climaxes there are seven tonnes of water in the air, shooting up to create its sky-high plume, kissed by a rainbow on sunny days.

TOP CHOICE Old Town   HISTORIC AREA

The main street of the Vieille Ville (Old Town), Grand-Rue, shelters the **Espace Rousseau** (✆022 310 10 28; www.espace-rousseau.ch; Grand-Rue 40; adult/child Sfr5/3; ⊙11am-5.30pm Tue-Sun), where the 18th-century philosopher was born. It's Geneva's best area for walking; the Place du Bourg-de-Four is timeless and ringed by good cafes.

GENEVA IN TWO DAYS

Explore the left-bank parks, gardens and **Jet d'Eau**, then hit the **Old Town** for lunch and a stroll. Tummy full, take in a museum, followed by a dip in the water and an aperitif at **Bains des Pâquis**. On day two, plan a tour of **CERN** or **Palais des Nations**, followed by another stroll along the lake.

Nearby, the part-Romanesque, part-Gothic **Cathédrale de St-Pierre** (St Peter's Cathedral; Cour St-Pierre; admission free; ⊙9.30am-6.30pm Mon-Sat, noon-6.30pm Sun Jun-Sep, 10am-5.50pm Mon-Sat, noon-5.30pm Sun Oct-May) is where Protestant John Calvin preached from 1536 to 1564. Revel in the flamboyant **Chapel of the Maccabees**. Beneath the cathedral is the **site archéologique** (✆022 311 75 74; www.site-archeologique.ch; Cour St-Pierre 6; adult/child Sfr8/4; ⊙10am-5pm Tue-Sun), an interactive space safeguarding fine 4th-century mosaics and a 5th-century baptismal font.

You can trace Calvin's life in the neighbouring **Musée Internationale de la Réforme** (International Museum of the Reformation; ✆022 310 24 31; www.musee-reforme.ch; Rue du Cloître 4; adult/student/child Sfr8/3/2; ⊙10am-5pm Tue-Sun).

Palais des Nations   LANDMARK

(✆022 907 48 96; www.unog.ch; Av de la Paix 14; adult/child Sfr12/7; ⊙10am-noon & 2-4pm Mon-Fri Sep-Mar, 10am-noon & 2-4pm daily Apr-Jun, 10am-5pm daily Jul & Aug) The art deco Palais des Nations is the European arm of the UN and the home of 3000 international civil servants. You can see where decisions about world affairs are made on the hour-long tour. Afterwards check out the extensive gardens – don't miss the towering grey monument coated with heat-resistant titanium donated by the USSR to commemorate the conquest of space. An ID or passport is obligatory for admission. Tram 15 stops here.

International Red Cross
& Red Crescent Museum   MUSEUM

(Musée Internationale de la Croix Rouge et du Croissant-Rouge; ✆022 748 95 25; www.micr.org; Av de la Paix 17) Closed at the time of research, the museum was set to reopen in 2013 after a massive rethink. Visitors engage with displays along three themes: 'Defending

(Continued on page 528)

Switzerland Highlights

1 Discover the zest of **Zürich** (p550) with a daytime stroll along the city's sublime lake followed by a rollicking night out

2 Be wowed by the Eiger's monstrous north face on a ride

to the 'top of Europe', 3471m **Jungfraujoch** (p549)

3 Board a boat in **Geneva** (p523) for a serene lake cruise to Nyon or medieval Lausanne

4 Be surprised by Swiss capital **Bern** (p538): think medieval charm, folkloric fountains and a cafe and dining culture

5 Ride one of Switzerland's iconic scenic trains, such as one over the **Bernina Pass** (p563)

6 Gape at the iconic Matterhorn and wander around the car-free alpine village of **Zermatt** (p537)

7 Try out your Italian accent at **Lugano** (p561), which has a lovely, temperate lake setting

Geneva

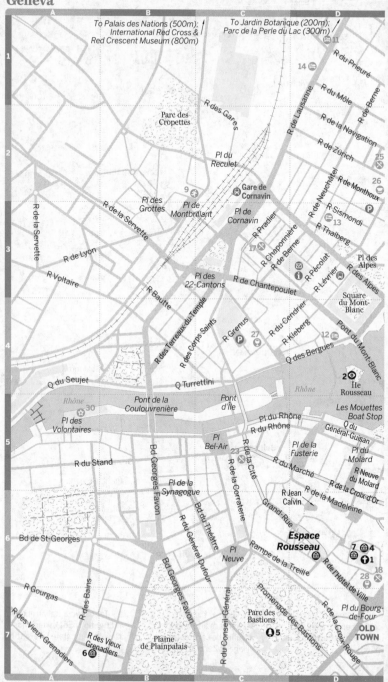

To Palais des Nations (500m);
International Red Cross &
Red Cross & Red Crescent Museum (800m)

To Jardin Botanique (200m);
Parc de la Perle du Lac (300m)

Parc des Cropettes

R des Gares

Pl du Reculet

Gare de Cornavin

Pl des Grottes

Pl de Montbrillant

Pl de Cornavin

R de la Servette

R de la Servette

R de Lyon

R Voltaire

R Baulte

Pl des 22-Cantons

R de Chantepoulet

R Pradier

R Chaponnière

R de Berne

Pl des Terreaux-du-Temple

R des Corps Saints

R Grenus

R du Cendrier

R Kleberg

Q des Bergues

R du Prieuré

R du Môle

R de la Navigation

R de Zürich

R de Neuchâtel

R de Monthoux

R Sismondi

R Thalberg

R Pécolat

R Lévrier

Pl des Alpes

Square du Mont-Blanc

Pont du Mont-Blanc

Q du Seujet

Q Turrettini

Pont de la Coulouvrenière

Pont d'Île

Rhône

Rhône

Île Rousseau

Les Mouettes Boat Stop

Q du Général-Guisan

Pl des Volontaires

Pl Bel-Air

Pl du Rhône

R du Rhône

Pl de la Fusterie

Pl du Molard

R du Stand

Bd Georges-Favon

Pl de la Synagogue

Bd du Théâtre

R de la Corraterie

R de la Cité

R du Marché

R Neuve du Molard

R de la Croix-d'Or

R Jean Calvin

R de la Madeleine

Grand-Rue

Bd de St-Georges

R du Général Dufour

Bd Georges-Favon

Pl Neuve

Rampe de la Treille

Espace Rousseau

R de l'Hôtel de Ville

R Gourgas

R des Bains

R des Vieux Grenadiers

R des Vieux Grenadiers

Plaine de Plainpalais

R du Conseil-Général

Parc des Bastions

Promenade des Bastions

R de la Croix-Rouge

Pl du Bourg-de-Four

OLD TOWN

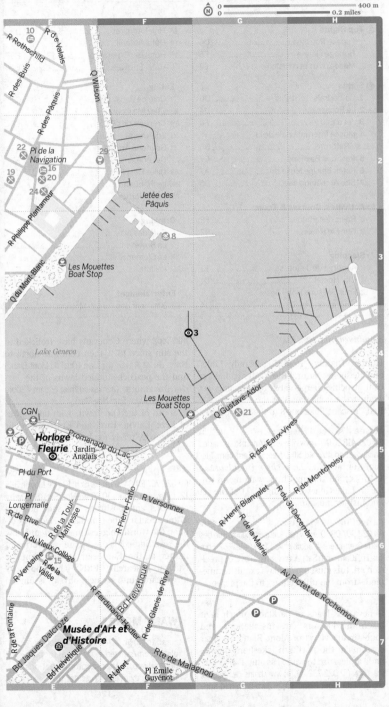

0 — 400 m
0 — 0.2 miles

R Rothschild
10
R de Valais
R des Buis
Q Wilson
R des Pâquis

22
Pl de la
Navigation
29
19
16
20
24
R Philippe Plantamour

Jetée des
Pâquis

8

Q du Mont-Blanc

Les Mouettes
Boat Stop

3

Lake Geneva

Les Mouettes
Boat Stop

Q Gustave-Ador
21

CGN

Promenade du Lac
R des Eaux-Vives

Horloge
Fleurie
Jardin
Anglais

Pl du Port

R de Montchoisy

Pl
Longemalle
R de Rive
R de la Tour-Maîtresse
R Pierre-Fatio
R Versonnex
R Henri Blanvalet
R de la Mairie
R du 31 Décembre

R du Vieux-Collège
R Verdaine
R de la
Vallée
15

Bd Helvétique
R Ferdinand-Hodler
R des Glacis de Rive

Av Pictet de Rochemont

R de la Fontaine
Bd Jacques Dalcroze
Musée d'Art et
d'Histoire

Bd Helvétique
R Lefort
Pl Émile
Guyénot
Rte de Malagnou

Geneva

(Continued from page 523)

Human Dignity', 'Restoring Family Links' and 'Reducing Natural Risks'. All highlight re cent atrocities perpetuated by humanity set against the noble goals of the Red Cross & Red Crescent. Take bus 8 to the Appia stop.

Musée d'Art et d'Histoire MUSEUM
(☑022 418 26 00; www.ville-ge.ch/mah; Rue Charles Galland 2; adult/child Sfr3/free; ⊙11am-6pm Tue-Sun) Konrad Witz' *La pêche miraculeuse* (c 1440–44), portraying Christ walking on water on Lake Geneva, is a highlight of the art and history museum.

Patek Phillipe Museum MUSEUM
(☑022 807 09 10; www.patekmuseum.com; Rue des Vieux Grenadiers 7; adult/child Sfr10/free; ⊙2-6pm Tue-Fri, 10am-6pm Sat) A treasure trove of precision art, this museum displays exquisite timepieces from the 16th century to the present.

Parks PARK
Geneva has loads of parkland, much of it lakefront. Flowers, art installations and soul-stirring views of Mont Blanc on clear days make the northern lakeshore promenade a pleasure to walk. Pass hip **Bains des Pâquis** (☑022 732 29 74; www.bains-des-paquis. ch; Quai du Mont-Blanc 30; ⊙9am-8pm mid-Apr–

mid-Sep), where Genevans have frolicked in the sun since 1872, then continue north to **Parc de la Perle du Lac** (Quai du Mont-Blanc) and the peacock-studded lawns of the **Jardin Botanique** (admission free; ⊙8am-7.30pm Apr-Oct, 9.30am-5pm Nov-Mar).

South of the Old Town, 4.5m-tall figures of Bèze, Calvin, Farel and Knox – in their nightgowns ready for bed – loom large in **Parc des Bastions**.

FREE **CERN** LABORATORY
(☑022 767 84 84; www.cern.ch; Rte de Meyrin 385 1217, Meyrin; ⊙tours 10.30am Mon-Sat) See why electrons and positrons are shot down a 27km circular tube (the Large Hadron Collider, the world's biggest machine) and how the resulting collisions create new forms of matter at the European Organisation for Nuclear Research (CERN). The laboratory for research into particle physics is funded

WANT MORE?

Head to **Lonely Planet** (www.lonely planet.com/switzerland/geneva) for planning advice, author recommendations, traveller reviews and insider tips.

FREE THRILLS

Bags of fabulous things to see and do in Geneva don't cost a cent. Our favourite freebies:

» Dashing like mad under the iconic Jet d'Eau (p523).

» Getting lost in the Old Town (p523).

» Hobnobbing with big-bang scientists at CERN (p528).

» Going green in the Jardin Botanique (p528).

» Flopping on the beach on the Bains des Pâquis (p528) jetty.

» Pedalling along the lake into France or towards Lausanne.

by 20 nations and can be visited on free tours (book at least one month in advance). Otherwise, enjoy **Microcosm** (☏022 767 84 84; admission free; ⊗8.30am-5.30pm Mon-Fri, 9am-5pm Sat), the on-site multimedia and interactive visitors centre. CERN is 8km west of Geneva; take tram 14.

✪ Festivals & Events

August's two-week **Fêtes de Genève** (www.fetes-de-geneve.ch) ushers in parades, open-air concerts, lakeside merry-go-rounds and fireworks. On 11 December, the **Escalade** celebrates the foiling of an invasion by the Duke of Savoy in 1602 with a costumed parade, the smashing and eating of chocolate cauldrons, and a day of running races around the Old Town.

🛏 Sleeping

When checking in, ask for your free public transport ticket covering unlimited bus travel for the duration of your hotel stay.

There are loads of cheap hotels southeast of the train station on and off the Rue des Alpes; although the neighbourhood can look gritty, the hotels are usually fine, albeit, at times, worn. Ask to see rooms.

Hôtel Bel'Esperance HOTEL €€
(☏022 818 37 37; www.hotel-bel-esperance.ch; Rue de la Vallée 1; s/d from Sfr105/160; @⊛) This two-star hotel is a two-second flit to the Old Town and offers extraordinary value for a pricey city like Geneva. Rooms are quiet and cared for, and those on the 1st floor share a kitchen. Ride the lift to the 5th floor to

flop in a chair on its wonderful flower-filled rooftop terrace.

Hotel Edelweiss HOTEL €€
(☏022 544 51 51; www.manotel.com; Place de la Navigation 2; r from Sfr160; ⊛@⊛) Plunge yourself into the heart of the Swiss Alps at this Heidi-style hideout, with its fireplace, wildflower-painted pine bedheads and big, cuddly St Bernard lolling over the banister.

Four Seasons Hôtel des Bergues LUXURY HOTEL €€€
(☏022 908 70 00; www.fourseasons.com/geneva; Quai des Bergues 33; r from Sfr625; ⊛@⊛) Geneva's oldest hotel continues to live up to its magnificent heritage. Chandelier-lit moulded ceilings, grandiose flower arrangements, original oil paintings in heavy gold frames and diamonds glittering behind glass is what this lakeside neoclassical gem from 1834 is all about.

La Cour des Augustins HOTEL €€
(☏022 322 21 00; www.lacourdesaugustins.com; Rue Jean-Violette 15; s/d from Sfr190/250; P⊛@⊛) 'Boutique gallery design hotel' is how this slick, contemporary space in Carouge markets itself. Disguised by a 19th-century facade, its crisp white interior screams cutting edge.

Hotel Admiral HOTEL €
(☏022 906 97 00; www.hoteladmiral.ch; Rue Pellegrino Rossi 8; s/d from Sfr90/100; ⊛@⊛) Excellent-value modest hotel between the train station and the lake. The street is slightly sleazy but the rooms are clean if small. There's an elevator, lavish complimentary buffet-breakfast and the staff are quite helpful.

Hôtel Auteuil HOTEL €€€
(☏022 544 22 22; www.manotel.com; Rue de Lausanne 33; r from Sfr320; P⊛@⊛) The star of this crisp, design-driven hotel near the station is its enviable collection of black-and-white photos of 1950s film stars in Geneva. Borrow the book from reception to find out precisely who's who and where.

Auberge de Jeunesse HOSTEL €
(☏022 732 62 60; www.yh-geneva.ch; Rue Rothschild 28-30; dm from Sfr29, d/q Sfr95/135; @⊛) At this well-equipped, HI-affiliated apartment block, rates include breakfast and bunk-bed dorms max out at 12 beds. Non HI-card holders pay Sfr6 more a night.

City Hostel HOSTEL €
(☏022 901 15 00; www.cityhostel.ch; Rue de Ferrier 2; dm from Sfr32, s/d from Sfr61/77; P@⊛)

Spanking clean is the trademark of this well-organised hostel, where two-bed dorms give travellers a chance to double up cheaply. Rates include sheets, towels and use of the kitchen. Reception is closed from noon to 1pm.

Eating

Geneva flaunts ethnic cuisines galore. If it's local and traditional you're after, dip into a cheese fondue or platter of pan-fried *filets de perche* (perch fillets). But beware: not all those cooked up are fresh from the lake. Many come frozen from Eastern Europe, so it's imperative to pick the right place to sample this simple Lake Geneva speciality.

Eateries crowd Place du Bourg-de-Four, Geneva's oldest square, in the lovely Old Town. Otherwise, head down the hill towards the river and Place du Molard, packed with tables and chairs for much of the year.

In Pâquis, there's a tasty line-up of more affordable restaurants on Place de la Navigation.

TOP CHOICE Les 5 Portes
BISTRO €

(☑022 731 84 38; Rue de Zürich 5; mains Sfr16-24; ⊙11am-11pm) The Five Doors is a fashionable Pâquis port of call that embraces every mood and moment. It has a rich, retro bistro feel yet works fine for just a glass of wine. The menu changes nightly and reflects what's fresh. Service is excellent and there is a long – and reasonable – wine list. Tables outside are good for a stylish pause.

Edelweiss
FONDUE €€

(☑022 544 51 51; Place de la Navigation 2; mains from Sfr35; ⊙6-10pm Mon-Sat) This chalet-style restaurant in the namesake hotel is a key address among Genevans for traditional cheese fondue. Choose from cheesy variations as well as other hearty old-time Swiss dishes.

Le Plantamour
DELI €

(www.leplantamour.ch; Rue Philippe Plantamour 37; mains Sfr8-15; ⊙7am-8pm Mon-Sat) No place cooks up a tastier, healthier lunch for an affordable Sfr15, than this modern delicatessen with a great terrace in a former baker's shop. Grab a pre-packaged salad or hot dish at the counter and take a seat outside.

Crêperie des Pâquis
FRENCH €

(www.creperie-paquis.com; Rue de Zürich 6; mains Sfr15-20; ⊙6pm-2am Mon, from 9am Tue-Fri, from 5pm Sat, from 11am Sun) Sweet and savoury, this laid-back address with seating both in and out to suit every taste cooks up fabulous crêpes with a mindboggling choice of fillings. Don't miss the daily specials chalked on the board.

Café de Paris
FRENCH €€

(www.cafe-de-paris.ch; Rue du Mont-Blanc 26; mains Sfr42; ⊙11am-11pm) A memorable dining experience since 1930. Everyone goes for the same thing here: green salad, beef steak with a killer herb-and-butter sauce, and as many *frites* (fries) as you can handle. A quick walk from the train station.

Chez Ma Cousine
CHICKEN €

(☑022 310 96 96; www.chezmacousine.ch; Place du Bourg-de-Four; mains Sfr15-17) *'On y mange du poulet'* (we eat chicken) is the tagline of this institution near the cathedral, which appeals for one good reason – generously handsome and homely portions of chicken, potatoes and salad at a price that can't possibly break the bank.

Gilles Desplanches
CAFE €

(☑022 810 30 28; www.gillesdesplanches.com; Rue de la Confédération 2; mains Sfr12-20; ⊙7am-7pm Mon-Wed & Fri, 7am-8pm Thu, 8am-7pm Sat, 10am-6pm Sun) One for serious chocolate fanatics. With its shocking-pink facade and exquisitely crafted cakes and chocolates alongside imaginative savoury tarts, this is one address that bursts at the seams at lunchtime. Good sandwiches, quiches, salads and more.

Drinking & Entertainment

Pâquis, the district in between the train station and lake, is particularly well endowed with bars. In summer the **paillote** (Quai du Mont-Blanc 30; ⊙to midnight), with wooden tables inches from the water, gets crammed.

For a dose of Bohemia, head to Carouge on tram 12. This shady quarter of 17th-century houses and narrow streets has galleries, hip bars and funky shops.

TOP CHOICE La Clémence
BAR

(☑022 312 24 98; www.laclemence.ch; Place du Bourg-de-Four 20; ⊙7am-1am Mon-Thu & Sun, to 2am Fri & Sat) Indulge in a glass of local wine or an artisanal beer at this venerable cafe-bar located on Geneva's loveliest square.

Café des Arts
CAFE

(☑022 321 58 85; Rue des Pâquis 15; ⊙11am-2am Mon-Fri, 8am-2am Sat & Sun) As much a place to drink as a daytime cafe, this Pâquis hangout lures a local crowd with its Parisian-style

TOP TWO GELATO SHOPS

Gelateria Arlecchino (☎022 736 70 60; Rue du 31 Décembre 1; per scoop Sfr3.50, milkshakes Sfr7) Left-bank choice a stone's throw from the Jet d'Eau. Chocolate and ginger, honey, peanut cream and mango are among the 40 flavours at this lip-licking parlour.

Gelatomania (☎022 741 41 44; Rue des Pâquis 25; per scoop Sfr3.50) Right-bank choice. A constant queue loiters outside this shop where ice-cream maniacs wrap their tongues around a plethora of exotic flavours and old faves.

terrace and artsy interior. Foodwise, think meal-sized salads, designer sandwiches and burgers (Sfr15 to Sfr20).

Le Cheval Blanc   BAR
(☎022 343 61 61; www.lechevalblanc.ch; Place de l'Octroi 15; ☺11.30am-1am or 2am Tue-Sat, 10.30am-1am Sun) The White Horse is a real Carouge favourite. Quaff cocktails and eat tapas – some of Geneva's best – at the pink neon-lit bar upstairs, then head downstairs to its club and concert space, Le Box.

La Bretelle   BAR
(☎022 732 75 96; Rue des Étuves 17; ☺6pm-2am) Little has changed since the 1970s, when this legendary bar opened. Live accordion accompanies French chansons most nights.

La Plage   BAR
(☎022 342 20 98; Rue Vautier 19; ☺11am-1am Mon-Thu, 10am-2am Fri & Sat, 5pm-1am Sun) With bare-wood tables, checked lino floor, green wooden shutters and tables outside, the Beach in Carouge is a timeless drinking hole.

Bar du Nord   BAR
(☎022 342 38 20; Rue Ancienne 66; ☺5pm-2am Thu-Fri, 9am-2am Sat) Bar du Nord, one of Carouge's oldest, is a stylish bar with Bauhaus-inspired furniture, the best whisky selection in town and a small courtyard terrace out back. The best nights are Thursday and Friday with good music (lots of electro) and DJs.

Le Chat Noir   LIVE MUSIC
(☎022 343 49 98; www.chatnoir.ch; Rue Vautier 13; ☺Tue-Sat) A hot address in Carouge packed most nights, the Black Cat is a lovely spot for

an after-work aperitif and, come dark, live music. There's also a small selection of tapas to nibble on.

Le Déclic   CLUB
(☎022 320 59 40; www.ledeclic.ch; Blvd du Pont d'Arve 28; ☺5pm-2am Mon-Fri, 9pm-2am Sat) A gay nightclub with numerous theme nights.

Bâtiment des Forces Motrices   PERFORMING ARTS
(☎022 322 12 20; www.bfm.ch; Place des Volontaires 4) Geneva's one-time riverside pumping station (1886) is now a striking space for classical music concerts, dance, ballet and other cultural events. Its Sunday morning Musique sur Rhône concerts are particularly delightful.

 Shopping

Designer shopping is wedged between Rue du Rhône and Rue de Rive; the latter has lots of chain stores. Grand-Rue in the Old Town and Carouge boast artsy boutiques.

ⓘ Information

Post Office (Rue du Mont-Blanc 18; ☺7.30am-6pm Mon-Fri, 9am-4pm Sat)

Tourist Office (☎022 909 70 00; www.geneve-tourisme.ch; Rue du Mont-Blanc 18; ☺9am-6pm Mon-Sat, 10am-4pm Sun) Offers good walking-tour information. The Geneva Pass (from Sfr25) offers free admissions and discounts.

ⓘ Getting There & Away

AIR Aéroport International de Genève (p574), 5km from town, has connections to major European cities and many others worldwide.

BOAT **CGN** (Compagnie Générale de Navigation; ☎084 881 18 48; www.cgn.ch) operates a web of scenic steamer-services from its Jardin Anglais jetty to other villages on Lake Geneva. Many only sail May to September, including those to/from Lausanne (Sfr43, 3½ hours). Eurail and Swiss Pass holders are valid on CGN boats or there is a one-day CGN boat pass (Sfr56).

BUS International buses depart from the **bus station** (☎022 732 02 30, 0900 320 320; www.coach-station.com; Place Dorcière).

TRAIN Trains run to major Swiss towns including at least every 30 minutes to/from Lausanne (Sfr22, 33 to 48 minutes), Bern (Sfr49, 1¾ hours) and Zürich (Sfr84, 2¾ hours).

International daily rail connections from Geneva include Paris by TGV (3¼ hours) and Milan (four hours).

ℹ Getting Around

TO/FROM THE AIRPORT Getting from the airport is easy with regular trains into Gare de Cornavin (Sfr3, eight minutes). Slower bus 10 (Sfr3) does the same 5km trip. A metered taxi costs from Sfr30 to Sfr50.

BICYCLE Pick up a bike at **Genève Roule** (☑022 740 13 43; www.geneveroule.ch; Place de Montbrillant 17; ⊙8am-6pm Mon-Sat) or its seasonal Jetée des Pâquis pick-up point for Sfr12/20 per day/weekend. May to October, borrow a bike (with advertisements on it) for free.

PUBLIC TRANSPORT Buses, trams, trains and boats service the city, and ticket dispensers are found at all stops. Most services are operated by **TPG** (www.tpg.ch; ⊙7am-7pm Mon-Fri, 7am-6pm Sat). Typical tickets cost Sfr3.50 (one hour); a day pass is Sfr8 when purchased after 9am. The same tickets are also valid on the yellow shuttle boats known as Les Mouettes (the seagulls) that criss-cross the lake every 10 minutes between 7.30am and 6pm.

LAKE GENEVA REGION

East of Geneva, Western Europe's biggest lake stretches like a giant liquid mirror between French-speaking Switzerland on its northern shore and France to the south. Known as Lake Geneva by many and Lac Léman to Francophones, the Swiss side of the lake cossets the elegant city of Lausanne, the pretty palm-tree-studded Riviera resort of Montreux, and the marvellous emerald spectacle of vines marching up steep hillsides in strict unison.

Nyon

POP 18,800

Of Roman origin but with a partly Celtic name (the 'on' comes from *dunon,* which means fortified enclosure), Nyon is a pretty lake town pierced at its hilltop-heart by the gleaming white turrets of a fairy-tale chateau and a tasty lunch address.

Nyon's castle was started in the 12th century, modified 400 years later and now houses the town's **Musée Historique et des Porcelaines** (www.chateaudenyon.ch; Place du Château; adult/child Sfr8/free; ⊙10am-5pm Tue-Sun).

Nyon is a perfect break on a boat trip between Geneva and Lausanne.

✕ Eating & Drinking

Good eating and drinking are a reward for a chateau visit, otherwise stick near the harbour for sensational gelato.

TOP CHOICE **L'Auberge du Château** ITALIAN €€
(☑022 361 00 32; www.aubergeduchateau.ch; Place du Château 8; mains Sfr30-50; ⊙8am-midnight, closed Sun Oct-Apr) No restaurant and cafe terrace has such a stunning view as this. Filling the pretty pedestrian square in front of Nyon's lovely chateau, tables look out on the Sleeping Beauty towers and lake beyond. The cuisine is Italian and creative – *taglierini* (pasta) with figs, simple homemade gnocchi and authentic pizza cooked in a wood-fired oven.

Caveau des Vignerons CAFE €
(Place du Château; samples from Sfr20; ⊙2-9pm Fri & Sat, 11am-8pm Sun) In the chateau's old stone cellars, the Caveau des Vignerons is where you can taste different Nyon wines by local producers. Pay Sfr20 to sample two reds and two whites with a plate of charcuterie.

TOP CHOICE **Gelateria Venezia** GELATO €
(Rue de Rive 44; ice cream Sfr3-7; ⊙11am-7pm) Slip your tongue into the extraordinary Italian-style ice cream here. From Nyon's CGN boat jetty on the lakefront, walk one block inland and look for the line outside the door.

ℹ Getting There & Away

Nyon is served by several trains per hour running between Geneva and Lausanne. There are year-round **CGN** (Compagnie Générale de Navigation; www.cgn.ch) boats to/from Geneva (Sfr22, 75 minutes); boats to Lausanne (Sfr33, two hours) run early April to mid-September.

Lausanne

POP 128,200

In a fabulous location overlooking Lake Geneva, Lausanne is an enchanting beauty with several distinct personalities: the former fishing village of Ouchy, with its summer beach-resort feel; Place St-François, with stylish, cobblestone shopping streets; and Flon, a warehouse district of bars, galleries and boutiques. It's also got a few good sights. One of the country's grandest Gothic cathedrals dominates its medieval centre.

◉ Sights & Activities

Downhill by the water in Ouchy, Lake Geneva is the source of many a sporting opportunity, including sailing, windsurfing, waterskiing and swimming; the tourist offices have details. Seasonal stands in front of Chateau d'Ouchy rent pedalos and kayaks, and cycling and rollerblading are big on the silky-smooth waterfront promenades. West of Ouchy, Vidy Beach, backed by thick woods and parklands, is one of Lake Geneva's few sandy beaches.

In the heart of the Vieille Ville (Old Town), the 9th-century medieval market square Place de la Palud – pretty as a picture – was originally bogland. For five centuries it has been home to the city government, now housed in the 17th-century Hôtel de Ville (town hall). A fountain pierces one end of the square, presided over by a brightly painted column topped by the allegorical figure of Justice, clutching scales and dressed in blue.

Cathédrale de Notre Dame   CHURCH
(⊙7am-7pm Mon-Fri, 8am-7pm Sat & Sun, to 5.30pm Sep-Mar) Lausanne's Gothic cathedral, Switzerland's finest, stands proudly at the heart of the Old Town. Raised in the 12th and 13th centuries on the site of earlier, humbler churches, it lacks the lightness of French Gothic buildings but is remarkable nonetheless.

Musée de l'Art Brut   MUSEUM
(☑021 315 25 70; www.artbrut.ch; Av des Bergières 11-13; adult/child Sfr10/free; ⊙11am-6pm Tue-Sun) This alluring museum showcases a fascinating amalgam of 15,000 works of art created by untrained artists – psychiatric patients, eccentrics and incarcerated criminals. The works offer a striking variety, at times a surprising technical capacity and in some cases an inspirational world view. The museum is about 600m northwest of Place St François; take bus 2 or 3 to the Beaulieu stop.

Musée Olympique   MUSEUM
(☑021 621 65 11; www.museum.olympic.org; Quai d'Ouchy 1) Lausanne is home to the International Olympic Committee and the Musée Olympique is easily the city's most lavish museum and a real must for sports buffs (and kids). Under renovation until late 2013, its usual home is a gorgeous building atop a tiered landscaped garden in the Parc Olympique.

🛏 Sleeping

Hotel guests get a Lausanne Transport Card covering unlimited use of public transport for the duration of their stay.

TOP CHOICE Hôtel Beau-Rivage Palace   HISTORIC HOTEL €€€
(☑021 613 33 33; www.beau-rivage-palace.ch; Place du Port 17-19; r from Sfr550; ❋@🛜≋) Easily the most stunningly located hotel in town and one of only two five-star options, this luxury lakeside address is suitably sumptuous. A beautifully maintained early-19th-century mansion set in immaculate grounds, it tempts with magnificent lake- and Alp-views and famous bars and restaurants.

Lausanne Guest House   GUESTHOUSE €
(☑021 601 80 00; www.lausanne-guesthouse.ch; Chemin des Épinettes 4; dm from Sfr39, r from Sfr100, without bathroom from Sfr90; P@🛜) An attractive mansion converted into quality backpacking accommodation near the train station. Many rooms have lake views and you can hang out in the garden or on the terrace.

Hôtel du Port   HOTEL €€
(☑021 612 04 44; www.hotel-du-port.ch; Place du Port 5; s/d from Sfr165/195; ⊜🛜) A perfect location in Ouchy, just back from the lake, makes this a good choice. The best doubles peep at the lake and suites slumber on the 3rd floor.

Hôtel du Marché   HOTEL €
(☑021 647 99 00; www.hoteldumarche-lausanne. ch; Rue Pré du Marché 42; s/d from Sfr115/145, without bathroom Sfr80/135) A five-minute walk from the Old Town, the no-frills rooms here are clean and spacious, and the kettle and complimentary tea and coffee in each room is a great touch.

🍴 Eating

TOP CHOICE Café St-Pierre   MODERN EUROPEAN €€
(☑021 326 36 36; www.cafesaintpierre.ch; Place Benjamin Constant 1; meals Sfr12-30; ⊙7.30am-midnight Tue & Wed, to 1am Thu, to 2am Fri, 11am-2am Sat, 11am-6pm Sun) The fact that every table is snapped up by noon while waiters buzz between tables and a constantly ringing telephone says it all – this hip cafe-bar rocks! Its interior is retro, trendy and relaxed, and the cuisine is contemporary European. Besides dinner there is tapas and weekend brunch. Reserve in advance.

Café Romand
SWISS €

(☎021 312 63 75; Place St François 2; mains Sfr20-30; ⏱11am-11pm Mon-Sat) Hidden in an unpromising-looking arcade, this Lausanne legend dating to 1951 is a welcome blast from the past. Everyone from bankers to punks pours into the broad, somewhat sombre dining area littered with timber tables to gorge on fondue, *pied de porc* (pork trotters) and other traditional dishes.

Café de Grancy
MODERN EUROPEAN €

(☎021 616 86 66; www.cafédegrancy.ch; Ave du Rond Point 1; mains Sfr20-35; ⏱8am-midnight; ☎) An old-time bar resurrected with colour and flair by young entrepreneurs, this spot is a hip hang-out with comfy lounges, weekend brunch and a tempting restaurant out back.

Café du Vieil Ouchy
SWISS €€

(☎021 616 21 94; Place du Port 3; mains Sfr20-40; ⏱9am-11pm Thu-Mon) A simple but charming location near the lake and metro for fondue, rösti and other classics. Follow up with a meringue smothered in thick double Gruyère cream.

🍸 Drinking & Entertainment

Lausanne is one of Switzerland's busier night-time cities. Look for the handy free listings booklet What's Up (www.whatsupmag.ch) in bars.

Bleu Lézard
BAR

(☎021 321 38 30; www.bleu-lezard.ch; Rue Enning 10; ⏱7am-late; ☎) This corner bar and bistro with royal-blue paintwork and wicker chairs to match is an old favourite that never loses its appeal – day or night (or at weekends for brunch). Lunch (mains from Sfr25), including some great veggie options, is served until 3pm and when your feet wanna jive to a live band, there's the basement music club, La Cave.

Great Escape
PUB

(☎021 312 31 94; www.the-great.ch; Rue de la Madeleine 18; ⏱11am-late) Beneath the whopping beams that hold up the roof of what could be a country house is a noisy pub with plenty of beers and ales on tap. Good burgers too.

Le Bourg
LIVE MUSIC

(☎021 625 07 07; www.lebourg.ch; Rue de Bourg 51; ⏱7pm-1am Wed-Thu, to 2am Fri-Sat) What was once an old cinema is now one of central Lausanne's happening drink dens and live music stages. Squeeze upstairs past the bar for a good view down to the stage area.

Le D! Club
CLUB

(☎021 351 51 40; www.dclub.ch; Place de Centrale 1; admission Sfr10-25; ⏱11pm-5am Wed-Sat) DJs spin funk to house at this heaving club. Take the stairs down from Rue du Grand Pont, turn right and descend to Place de Centrale.

❶ Information

The **tourist office** (☎021 613 73 21; www.lausanne-tourisme.ch; Place de la Navigation 4; ⏱9am-6pm Oct-Mar, to 7pm Apr-Sep) neighbours Ouchy metro station; there is also a branch at the train station (Place de la Gare 9; ⏱9am-7pm).

❶ Getting There & Around

Lausanne spans several steep hillsides, so prepare for some good walks.

BOAT The **CGN steamer service** (www.cgn.ch) runs early April to mid-September to/from Geneva (Sfr43, 3½ hours) via Nyon. Other services lace the lake.

PUBLIC TRANSPORT Buses and trolley buses service most destinations; the vital M2 metro line (single trip/day pass Sfr1.90/8.80) connects the lake (Ouchy) with the train station (Gare), cathedral area and Flon district.

TRAIN There are frequent trains to/from Geneva (Sfr22, 33 to 48 minutes) and Bern (Sfr32, 66 minutes).

Montreux
POP 24,600

In 1971 Frank Zappa was doing his thing in the Montreux casino when the building caught fire, casting a pall of smoke over Lake Geneva and inspiring the members of Deep Purple to pen their classic rock number 'Smoke on the Water'.

The showpiece of the Swiss Riviera has been a usually flame-free inspiration to writers, artists and musicians for centuries. Famous one-time residents include Lord Byron, Ernest Hemingway and the Shelleys. It's easy to see why: Montreux boasts stunning Alp views, tidy rows of pastel buildings and Switzerland's most extraordinary castle.

Crowds throng to the legendary (and not all-jazz) Montreux Jazz Festival (www.montreuxjazz.com) for a fortnight in early July. Free concerts take place every day, but big-name gigs cost Sfr75 to Sfr240.

GRYON & LEYSIN

Trek off the beaten track to lap up Swiss alpine charm in untouched **Gryon** (1130m), with great meadow hiking trails and **Chalet Martin** (024 498 33 21; www.gryon.com; dm from Sfr25, r Sfr70-90; P@), a Swiss-Australian–run hostel that travellers give rave reviews. The vibe is strictly laid-back and the place organises dozens of activities – paragliding, skiing and chocolate-tasting included. Take a train from Lausanne to Bex (Sfr19, 40 minutes, hourly), then the cogwheel train to Gryon (Sfr7, 30 minutes, hourly). The hostel is a five-minute signposted walk from the train stop.

Equally chilled is **Leysin**, a hub for skiers, boarders and hikers who throng to **Hiking Sheep** (024 494 35 35; www.hikingsheep.com; dm/r from Sfr30/80; P@). The tall, art deco house has a kitchen, great communal facilities, a pine-forested backyard and breathtaking views from its balconies. Find it a two-minute walk from Leysin-Grand Hôtel train station. Ride the cogwheel train from Aigle (Sfr12, 30 minutes, hourly), in turn linked by train with Lausanne (Sfr16, 30 minutes, hourly).

Sights

Château de Chillon CASTLE

(021 966 89 10; www.chillon.ch; Ave de Chillon 21; adult/child Sfr12/6; 9am-7pm Apr-Sep, 9.30am-6pm Mar & Oct, 10am-5pm Nov-Feb, last entry 1hr before close) Originally constructed on the shores of Lake Geneva in the 11th century, Château de Chillon was brought to the world's attention by Lord Byron and the world has been filing past ever since. Spend at least a couple of hours exploring its numerous courtyards, towers, dungeons and halls filled with arms, period furniture and artwork.

The castle is a lovely 45-minute lakefront walk from Montreux. Otherwise trolley bus 1 (Sfr2.50) passes every 10 minutes; better still, come on a CGN steamer from Montreux (Sfr10, 15 minutes).

Sleeping & Eating

Tralala Hôtel BOUTIQUE HOTEL €€

(021 963 49 73; www.tralalahotel.ch; Rue du Temple 2; r Sfr130-300;) A boutique hotel designed around Montreux' extraordinary musical heritage just had to open – and it has, perched up high from the lake in the old part of Montreux. Rooms come in three sizes – S ('Small & Sexy'), L or XL – and each one pays homage to a different artist.

Hôtel La Rouvenaz HOTEL €€

(021 963 27 36; www.rouvenaz.ch; Rue du Marché 1; r Sfr90-200; @) A stylish family-run spot with its own tasty Italian restaurant downstairs and wine bar next door. You cannot get any closer to the lake or the heart of the action. Its 15 rooms are lovely and mostly have views, plus there's a nice terrace.

Hôtel Masson HISTORIC HOTEL €€

(021 966 00 44; www.hotelmasson.ch; Rue Bonivard 5; r from Sfr200; P) In 1829, this vintner's mansion was converted into a hotel. Its old charm has remained intact and the hotel, set in magnificent grounds, is on the Swiss Heritage list of most beautiful hotels in the country. It lies back in the hills southeast of Montreux, best reached by taxi.

Café du Grütli SWISS €€

(021 963 42 65; Rue du Grand Chêne 8; mains Sfr18-30; Wed-Mon) This cheerful little eatery is hidden in the old part of town and provides good home cooking. Think rösti with ham, hearty meat dishes, salads and the inevitable fondue. It's a small hike uphill.

Getting There & Away

There are frequent trains to Lausanne (Sfr13, 25 minutes) and other lakeside points. Make the scenic journey to Interlaken via the **GoldenPass Line** (www.goldenpass.ch), with a change at Zweisimmen and a stop at the fabled ski resort of Gstaad (Sfr57, three hours, daily; rail passes valid).

Gruyères

POP 1800

Cheese and featherweight meringues drowned in thick cream are what this dreamy village is all about. Named after the emblematic *gru* (crane) brandished by the medieval Counts of Gruyères, it is a riot of 15th- to 17th-century houses tumbling down a hillock. Its heart is cobbled, a castle is its crowning glory and hard AOC Gruyère (the village is Gruyères but the 's' is dropped for the cheese) has been made for centuries in its surrounding Alpine pastures.

◎ Sights & Activities

Château de Gruyères
TOP CHOICE
CASTLE

(☎026 921 21 02; www.chateau-gruyeres.ch; adult/child Sfr10/3; ◎9am-6pm Apr-Oct, 10am-4.30pm Nov-Feb) This turreted castle is Gruyères' crowning glory. Inside, view period furniture, tapestries and modern 'fantasy art'. Don't miss the short footpath that weaves its way around the castle.

Musée HR Giger
MUSEUM

(☎026 921 22 00; adult/child Sfr12.50/4; ◎10am-6pm Apr-Oct, 1-5pm Tue-Fri, 10am-6pm Sat & Sun Nov-Mar) Fans of the *Alien* movies will relish this shrine to film designer HR Giger's expansive imagination. Just hope you don't feel any stomach cramps in the *Alien*-styled bar across the way...

Maison du Gruyère
TOP CHOICE
CHEESE FACTORY

(☎026 921 84 00; www.lamaisondugruyere.ch; adult/under 12yr Sfr7/6; ◎9am-7pm Apr-Sep, to 6pm Oct-Mar) The secrets behind Gruyères' famous cheese are revealed here at this slick visitors centre right across from the train station and at the base of the path up to the village. Cheese-making takes place several times daily and can be watched through windows. There's a cafe and a picnic-happy deli, which, besides cheese, sells myriad forms of Swiss chocolate.

Fromagerie d'Alpage de Moléson
CHEESE FACTORY

(☎026 921 10 44; www.fromagerie-alpage.ch; adult/child Sfr5/2; ◎9.30am-10pm May-Sep) At this 17th-century mountain chalet, 5km southwest of Gruyères in Moléson-sur-Gruyères, cheese is made a couple of times a day in summer using old-fashioned methods.

Sentier des Fromageries
WALKING

Cheese is still produced in a couple of traditional mountain chalets along the Sentier des Fromageries, a trail that takes walkers through green Gruyères pastures. Ask at the Maison du Gruyère for the brochure outlining the two-hour walk (7km to 8km).

Cailler
CHOCOLATE FACTORY

(www.cailler.ch; Rue Jules Bellet 7; adult/child Sfr10/free; ◎10am-6pm Apr-Oct, to 5pm Nov-Mar) Cailler has been making chocolate since 1825. Tours of its factory offer anecdotes, samples, demonstrations and a sort of sensory overload (no doubt exacerbated by the chance to buy factory seconds a mere 80m up the road). It gets packed on weekends and during holidays – and rightly so. Find the factory 2km north of Gruyères, in Broc, by following the signs to Nestlé.

✗ Eating

Browse a variety of cheese-themed restaurants that face onto the centre of Gruyères. There are several small inns here as well.

Chalet de Gruyères
SWISS €€

(☎026 921 21 54; www.chalet-gruyeres.ch; Rue du Château 53; fondues & raclettes from Sfr30; ◎lunch & dinner) A quintessential Gruyères address, this cosy wooden chalet strung with cow bells oozes Alpine charm – and fodder (fondue, raclette, grilled meats). There's a flower-bedecked terrace in the warmer months too.

ⓘ Information

There's a small **tourist office** (☎026 921 10 30; www.gruyeres.ch; Rue du Bourg 1; ◎10.30am-noon & 1.30-4.30pm Mon-Fri, plus 9am-5pm Sat & Sun Jul-Sep) near the entrance to town. It has an ATM and loads of regional info.

ⓘ Getting There & Away

Gruyères can be reached by train (Sfr17, 40 minutes, twice hourly) from Fribourg to Bulle, then another hourly train (Sfr5, 9 minutes). The village is a 10-minute walk uphill from the train station or you can take a free bus that meets trains.

Unusually for a Swiss train station, there are no lockers but you can leave your bags at the Maison du Gruyère across from the station.

VALAIS

This is Matterhorn country, an intoxicating land that seduces the toughest of critics with its endless panoramic vistas and breathtaking views. It's an earthy part of southern Switzerland where farmers were so poor a century ago they didn't have two francs to rub together, yet today it's a jet-set land where celebrities sip Sfr10,000 champagne cocktails from ice-carved goblets.

An area of extraordinary natural beauty, the outdoors here is so great it never goes out of fashion. Switzerland's 10 highest mountains – all over 4000m – rise to the sky here, while snow-fiends ski and board in one of Europe's top resorts, Zermatt. When snows melt and valleys turn lush green, hiking opportunities are boundless.

The main train line from Lake Geneva to Brig runs along the Rhône River at the base of the beautiful valley. Centuries-old vineyards climb the surrounding hillsides. At towns like Sion, you can stop for walks among the grapes, which take in wineries and hillside bistros. Tourist offices have maps of myriad routes.

Zermatt

POP 5850

Since the mid-19th century, Zermatt has starred among Switzerland's glitziest resorts. Today it attracts intrepid mountaineers and hikers, skiers who cruise at a snail's pace, spellbound by the scenery, and style-conscious darlings flashing designer togs in the lounge bars. But all are smitten with the **Matterhorn** (4478m), the Alps' most famous peak and an unfathomable monolith synonymous with Switzerland that you simply can't quite stop looking at.

◉ Sights

TOP
CHOICE **Matterhorn**
Glacier Paradise   CABLE CAR
(www.matterhornparadise.ch; adult/child from Sfr72/40; ⊙7am-4.20pm Jul & Aug, 8.30am-3.35pm mid-Oct–Dec, 8.30am-4.20pm rest of year) Views from Zermatt's cable cars and gondolas are all pretty remarkable, but the Matterhorn Glacier Paradise is the icing on the cake. Ride Europe's highest-altitude cable car up to 3883m and gawp at a top-of-the-beanstalk panorama of 14 glaciers and 38 mountain peaks over 4000m from the **Panoramic Platform**. Don't miss the **Glacier Palace**, an ice palace complete with glittering ice sculptures, a glacier crevasse to walk through and – one for the kids – an ice slide to swoosh down.

Gornergratbahn   RAILWAY
(www.gornergrat.ch; Bahnhofplatz 7; adult/child from Sfr40/20; ⊙2-3 departures hourly 7am-6pm May & mid-Oct–Nov, 7am-10pm Jun-Sep, every 20 min 7am-5.15pm Dec-Apr) This splendid cogwheel railway – Europe's highest – climbs through picture-postcard scenery to Gornergrat (3089m). Tickets allow you to get on and off en route; Matterhorn views abound.

Matterhorn Museum   MUSEUM
(☎027 967 41 00; www.matterhornmuseum.ch; Kirchplatz; adult/child Sfr10/5; ⊙11am-6pm Dec-Oct) This crystalline, state-of-the-art museum provides a fascinating insight into Valaisian village life, mountaineering, the dawn of tourism in Zermatt and the lives Matterhorn has claimed.

🏃 Activities

Zermatt is skiing heaven, with mostly long, scenic red runs, plus a smattering of blues for ski virgins and knuckle-whitening blacks for experts. The main skiing areas in winter are **Rothorn**, **Stockhorn** and **Klein Matterhorn**; 350km of ski runs in all with a link from Klein Matterhorn to the Italian resort of Cervinia and a freestyle park with half-pipe for snowboarders. A day pass covering all ski lifts in Zermatt (excluding Cervinia) costs Sfr67/57/34 per adult/student/child (Sfr75/64/38 including Cervinia).

Summer skiing (20km of runs, May to mid-October) and boarding (gravity park at Plateau Rosa on the Theodul glacier) are the most extensive in Europe.

Alpin Center   SKIING, HIKING
(☎027 966 24 60; www.alpincenter-zermatt.ch; Bahnhofstrasse 58; ⊙9am-noon & 3-7pm mid-Nov–Apr & Jul-Sep) This activities centre houses the ski school and mountain guides office. Climbs led by mountain guides can be arranged to major 4000ers, including Breithorn (Sfr165), Riffelhorn (Sfr257) and, for experts willing to acclimatise for a week, Matterhorn (Sfr998). The program also covers multiday hikes, glacier hikes to Gorner (Sfr120), snowshoeing (Sfr140) and ice-climbing (Sfr175).

Klein Matterhorn   SKIING
Klein Matterhorn is topped by Europe's highest cable-car station (3820m), providing access to Europe's highest skiing, Switzerland's most extensive summer skiing (25km of runs) and deep powder at the Italian resort of Cervinia. Broad and exhilarating, the No 7 run down from the border is a must-ski. Don't forget your passport.

If the weather is fine, take the lift up to the summit of Klein Matterhorn (3883m) for sweeping views over the Swiss Alps (from Mont Blanc to Aletschhorn) and deep into Italy.

🛏 Sleeping

Most places close May to mid-June and again from October to mid-November.

TOP CHOICE Hotel Bahnhof HOTEL €
(☏027 967 24 06; www.hotelbahnhof.com; Bahnhofstrasse; dm Sfr40-60, r Sfr80-220; ☞) Opposite the train station, these five-star budget digs have proper beds and spotless bathrooms that are a godsend after scaling or schussing down mountains all day. Rooms for four are fabulous for families. There's a kitchen for preparing your own breakfast.

Berggasthaus Trift GUESTHOUSE €
(☏079 408 70 20; www.zermatt.net/trift; dm/d with half-board from Sfr66/156; ☏Jul-Sep) Run by Hugo (a whizz on the alpenhorn) and Fabienne at the foot of the Triftgletscher. A stiff two-hour hike from Zermatt, it has simple rooms, mesmerising views of its glacial 4000m surrounds and a great terrace to kick back on over home-cured beef and oven-warm apple tart. Call in advance to ensure a bed.

Matterhorn Hostel HOSTEL €
(☏027 968 19 19; Schluhmattstrasse 32; dm Sfr36-56, r Sfr92-142; ☏reception 7.30-10am or 11am & 4-9pm or 10pm; ☞) Tucked in a 1960s wooden chalet, a two-minute walk from the lifts, this hostel is first-rate. Rooms are modern and its busy ground-floor bar cooks up a great vibe and great food.

🍴 Eating & Drinking

TOP CHOICE Whymper Stube SWISS €€
(☏027 967 22 96; www.whymper-stube.ch; Bahnhofstrasse 80; mains Sfr22-44) An advance reservation is essential at this legendary address, known for its excellent raclette and fondues, both cheese and meat. Service is relaxed and friendly, tables are packed tightly together, and the place has a real buzz.

Bayard Metzgerei SWISS €
(☏027 967 22 66; Bahnhofstrasse 9; sausages from Sfr6; ☏noon-6.30pm Jul-Sep, 4-6.30pm Dec-Mar) Join the line in the street for a sausage (pork, veal or beef) and chunk of bread to down with a beer on the hop – or at a bar stool with the sparrows in the alley by this butcher's shop.

Hennu Stall BAR
(☏027 966 35 10; Klein Matterhorn; ☏2-7pm) Last one down to this snow-bound 'chicken run' is a rotten egg. Hennu is the wildest après-ski shack on Klein Matterhorn. A metre-long 'ski' of shots will make you cluck all the way down to Zermatt.

Z'alt Hischi BAR
(☏027 967 42 62; www.hischibar.ch; Hinterdorfstrasse 44; ☏9pm-2am) Hidden on what must be Zermatt's most charming street, this busy watering hole comes packaged in an ancient, 'I've-seen-it-all' wooden chalet.

ℹ Information

The **tourist office** (☏027 966 81 00; www.zermatt.ch; Bahnhofplatz 5; ☏8.30am-6pm mid-Jun–Sep, 8.30am-noon & 1-6pm Mon-Fri, 8.30am-6pm Sat, 9.30am-noon & 4-6pm Sun rest of year) has all the bumph.

ℹ Getting There & Around

CAR Zermatt is car-free. Motorists have to park in Täsch (www.matterhornterminal.ch; per day Sfr14.50), load luggage onto a trolley (Sfr5) and ride the Zermatt Shuttle (adult/child Sfr8/4, 12 minutes, every 20 minutes from 6am to 9.40pm) train the last 5km to Zermatt.

TRAIN Trains depart regularly from Brig (Sfr37, 1½ hours) – a major rail hub – stopping at Visp en route. Zermatt is also the starting point of the popular *Glacier Express* to Graubünden.

BERN

POP 125,700

One of the planet's most underrated capitals, Bern is a fabulous find. With the genteel old soul of a Renaissance man and the heart of a high-flying 21st-century gal, the riverside city is both medieval and modern. The 15th-century Old Town is gorgeous enough to sweep you off your feet and make you forget the century (it's definitely worthy of its 1983 Unesco World Heritage site status). But the edgy vintage boutiques, artsy-intellectual bars and Renzo Piano's futuristic art museum crammed with Paul Klee pieces bring you firmly back into the present.

👁 Sights

TOP CHOICE Old Town HISTORIC AREA
Bern's flag-bedecked medieval centre is an attraction in its own right, with 6km of covered arcades and cellar shops/bars descending from the streets. After a devastating fire in 1405, the wooden city was rebuilt in today's sandstone. Unique to Bern are

GLACIER EXPRESS

Like a glacier faced with climate change, you'll have a hard time avoiding the hype for the **Glacier Express** (www.glacierexpress.ch), the train that links Zermatt with the eastern towns and resorts of Chur (1st-/2nd-class Sfr254/145, 5¾ hours), Davos (Sfr235/134, 7½ hours) and St Moritz (Sfr198/113, eight hours).

Although there is some stunning scenery of glacier-cleaved valleys and soaring peaks along the route, much of the run is down in valleys, so don't expect non-stop scenic thrills. Also eight hours on a train may test your endurance. You can shorten the duration by starting at the rail hub of Brig instead of Zermatt or just doing the leg between St Moritz and Chur (another rail hub).

Swiss Cards cover the entire route, while Eurail and InterRail are good for about 50% of the fare. See also the boxed text on p576.

the beautiful and deeply arcaded streets totalling some 6km in length and lined with shops, cafes and more.

Bern's **Zytglogge** (clock tower) is a focal point; crowds congregate around to watch its figures twirl rather somnolently at four minutes before the hour, after which the actual chimes begin.

Equally enchanting are the 11 decorative **fountains** (1545) depicting historical and folkloric characters. Most are along Marktgasse as it becomes Kramgasse and Gerechtigkeitsgasse, but the most famous lies in Kornhausplatz: the **Kindlifresserbrunnen** (Ogre Fountain) of a giant snacking on children.

Inside the 15th-century Gothic **Münster** (Cathedral; www.bernermuenster.ch; tower admission adult/child Sfr5/2; ⊙10am-5pm Tue-Sat, 11.30am-5pm Sun Easter-Nov, noon-4pm Tue-Fri, to 5pm Sat, 11.30am-4pm Sun rest of year, tower closes 30min earlier), a 344-step hike up the lofty spire – Switzerland's tallest – is worth the climb. Outside, pause on the **Münster Platform**, a gem of a park overlooking the Aare.

TOP CHOICE **Paul Klee Centre**   MUSEUM
(☑031 359 01 01; www.zpk.org; Monument im Fruchtland 3; adult/child Sfr20/7; ⊙10am-5pm Tue-Sun) The architecturally bold Paul Klee Centre is an eye-catching 150m-long building filled with modern art, with a huge emphasis on its namesake. Renzo Piano's curvaceous building swoops up and down like waves to create a trio of 'hills' that blend into the landscape east of town.

The middle hill houses the main exhibition space, showcasing 4000 rotating works from Klee's prodigious career. His works span mediums and are at times graphically precise, utterly playful and heart-tuggingly poignant. In the basement of another 'hill' is the fun-packed **Kindermuseum Creaviva**, an inspired children's art centre.

Take bus 12 from Bubenbergplatz to Zentrum Paul Klee (Sfr4.20, 15 minutes). By car the museum is right next to the Bern-Ostring exit off the A6.

Einstein Museum   MUSEUM
(☑031 312 00 91; www.einstein-bern.ch; Kramgasse 49; adult/student Sfr6/4.50; ⊙10am-5pm Feb-Dec) The world's most famous scientist developed his special theory of relativity in Bern in 1905. Find out more at the small museum inside the humble apartment where Einstein lived with his young family between 1903 and 1905 while working in the Bern patent office.

FREE Houses of Parliament   HISTORIC SITE
(Bundeshäuser; ☑031 332 85 22; www.parliament.ch; Bundesplatz; ⊙hourly tours 9am-4pm Mon-Sat) The 1902 home of the Swiss Federal Assembly is impressively ornate, with statues of the nation's founding fathers and a stained-glass dome adorned with cantonal emblems. Tours are offered when parliament is in recess; otherwise watch from the public gallery. Bring your passport to get in.

Bärengraben   BEAR PARK
(www.baerenpark-bern.ch; ⊙9.30am-5pm) After decades of living in a cramped concrete pit (and lots of protests from animal-rights advocates), Bern's iconic bears got a new spacious 6000-sq-metre open-air riverside park dotted with trees and terraces in 2009, in which a number of bears roam (although they still have access to the old pit). The bear park is at the eastern end of the Nydeggbrücke.

Kunstmuseum
MUSEUM

(☑031 328 09 44; www.kunstmuseumbern.ch; Hodlerstrasse 8-12; adult/child Sfr7/free; ☺10am-9pm Tue, to 5pm Wed-Sun) The permanent collection at the workmanlike Museum of Fine Arts includes works by Italian artists such as Fra Angelico and Swiss artists such as Ferdinand Hodler, alongside Picasso and Dalí pieces.

🛏 Sleeping

The tourist office books rooms and offers hotel deals.

TOP CHOICE Hotel Landhaus
HOTEL €

(☑031 331 41 66; www.albertfrida.ch; Altenbergstrasse 4; dm from Sfr33, r from Sfr160, without bathroom from Sfr120; P😐@🛜) Backed by the grassy slope of a city park and fronted by the river and Old Town spires, this historic hotel oozes character. Its soulful ground-floor restaurant, a tad Bohemian, draws a staunchly local crowd.

Hotel National
HOTEL €

(☑031 381 19 88; www.nationalbern.ch; Hirschengraben 24; s/d Sfr100/150, without bathroom from Sfr65/130; @🛜) A quaint, endearing hotel, the National charms with its wrought-iron lift and Persian rugs over wooden floors. All 58 rooms are unique. Breakfast at the in-house restaurant is included. It adheres to slow-food principles and is a local favourite.

Marthahaus Garni
HOTEL €

(☑031 332 41 35; www.marthahaus.ch; Wyttenbachstrasse 22a; s/d from Sfr115/145, without bathroom from Sfr70/105; 😐@🛜) Plum in a leafy residential location, this five-storey elevator building feels like a friendly boarding house. Clean, simple rooms are very white with a smattering of modern art, plus there's a kitchen.

Hotel City am Bahnhof
HOTEL €€

(☑031 311 53 77; www.fassbindhotels.com; Bubenbergplatz 7; r Sfr110-200; 🛜) Close to the train station, the 58 rooms here are business-standard and have decent desks. Ask for one of the rooms with a small terrace overlooking the action far below.

Hotel Belle Epoque
HOTEL €€

(☑031 311 43 36; www.belle-epoque.ch; Gerechtigkeitsgasse 18; s/d from Sfr170/240; 😐@🛜) A romantic Old Town hotel with opulent art-nouveau furnishings, the Belle Epoque's design ethos sees TVs tucked away into steamer-trunk-style cupboards so as not to spoil the look. It's a small operation, with a popular cafe.

SYHA Hostel
HOSTEL €

(☑031 326 11 11; www.youthhostel.ch/bern; Weihergasse 4; dm from Sfr36; ☺reception 7am-noon & 2pm-midnight; 😐@🛜) Prettily set along the river, this well-organised hostel sports spotless dorms and a leafy terrace, plus a good-value eatery. To get there, follow the paths downhill from the parliament building or ride the funicular.

Hotel Glocke Backpackers Bern
HOSTEL €

(☑031 311 37 71; www.bernbackpackers.com; Rathausgasse 75; dm incl breakfast Sfr35-47, d Sfr142, s/d without bathroom Sfr74/110 ; ☺reception 8-11am & 3-10pm; 😐@🛜) Its Old Town location makes this many backpacker's first choice, although street noise might irritate light sleepers.

🍴 Eating

Look for interesting cafes and bistros scattered amid the arcades on Old Town streets including Zeughausgasse, Rathausgasse, Marktgasse and Kramgasse.

TOP CHOICE Lötschberg AOC
SWISS €

(☑031 311 34 55; www.loetschberg-aoc.ch; Zeughausgasse 16; mains Sfr14-30; ☺9am-11pm) Take an all-Swiss wine and beer list, add cheese specialities from the Valais (including fondue and raclette, of course), toss in some salads, decorate the cheerful yellow walls with circular, wooden wine racks and you have one of the most dynamic Swiss restaurants in the country. This popular, casual spot serves exceptional Swiss fare without kitsch. Book for dinner.

Altes Tramdepot
SWISS €

(☑031 368 14 15; www.altestramdepot.ch; Am Bärengraben; mains Sfr16-20; ☺11am-12.30am) Even locals recommend this cavernous microbrewery by the bear pits. Swiss specialities snuggle up to wok-cooked stir-fries, pasta and international dishes on its bistro-styled menu. Sample some of the 20 seasonal beers brewed through the year.

Terrasse & Casa
ITALIAN €€

(☑031 350 50 01; www.schwellenmaetteli.ch; Damaziquai 11; mains Sfr25-45; ☺Terrasse 9am-midnight Mon-Sat, to 11pm Sun, Casa lunch & dinner Tue-Fri & Sun, dinner Sat) Dubbed 'Bern's Riviera', this twinset of classy hang-outs on the Aare is an experience. Terrasse is a glass shoebox with wooden decking over the

TOP QUICK EATS

Munch between meals on a *brezel* (pretzel; around Sfr3) smothered in salt crystals or sunflower, pumpkin or sesame seeds from kiosks, or a bag of piping-hot chestnuts crunched to the tune of the astronomical clock striking.

Sous le Pont Grab fries, falafel or a schnitzel from the graffiti-covered hole-in-the-wall next to the eponymous cafe-bar and dine at the graffiti-covered table in the graffiti-covered courtyard. Beer costs Sfr3.80/5.20 per 300/500mL glass.

Tibits (☑031 312 91 11; Bahnhofplatz 10; ⊗6.30am-11.30pm Mon-Wed, to midnight Thu-Sat, 8am-11pm Sun; ∅) This vegetarian buffet restaurant inside the train station is just the ticket for a quick healthy meal, any size, any time of day. Serve yourself, get it weighed and pay accordingly.

Markets (⊗8am-4pm Tue & Sat year-round, plus Thu Apr-Oct) Peruse choice produce and prepared goods at the markets held on Bundesplatz.

---

water and sun-loungers overlooking a weir, while Casa serves Italian food in a country-styled timber-framed house.

Kornhauskeller　　　MODERN EUROPEAN €€€
(☑031 327 72 72; Kornhausplatz 18; mains Sfr25-50; ⊗noon-11pm Mon-Sat, from 5pm Sun) Fine dining takes place beneath vaulted frescoed arches at Bern's surprisingly ornate former granary, now a stunning cellar restaurant serving Mediterranean cuisine. In its neighbouring cafe, punters lunch in the sun on the busy pavement terrace. The buzzy bar is open late.

Markthalle　　　INTERNATIONAL €
(Bubenbergplatz 9; meals Sfr12-35; ⊗6.30am-11.30pm Mon-Wed, to 12.30am Thu & Fri, 7.30am-12.30am Sat; ∅) Buzzing in atmosphere and quick-snack action, this covered market arcade near the train station is jam-packed with cheap eateries from around the world. You name it, it's here, to be eaten standing at bars or around plastic tables. More formal eateries offer table service.

🍷 Drinking & Entertainment

Bern has a healthy drinking scene. Several spaces, such as Kornhauskeller and Altes Tramdepot, are as much drinking as dining spots. A few bright and busy after-work aperitif-bars stud Gurtengasse near the Bundeshäuser and Rathäustrasse.

TOP
CHOICE **Café des Pyrénées**　　　BAR
(☑031 311 30 63; Kornhausplatz 17; ⊗Mon-Sat) With its mix of wine-quaffing trendies and beer-loving students, this Bohemian joint feels like a Parisian cafe-bar. It's dimly lit and not over-adorned.

Sous le Pont　　　BAR
(☑031 306 69 55; www.souslepont.ch; Neubrückstrasse 8; ⊗7pm-2am Tue-Sat) Delve into the grungy underground scene around the station in the bar of the semichaotic, alternative-arts centre, Reitschule. Find it in an old stone, graffiti-covered building – an old riding school built in 1897 – by the railway bridge.

Silo Bar　　　BAR
(☑031 311 54 12; www.silobar.ch; Mühlenplatz 11; ⊗10pm-3.30am Thu-Sat) By the water in the hip Matte quarter, Bern's monumental 19th-century corn house throbs with mainstream hits and a lively, predominantly student set.

Stadttheater Bern　　　PERFORMING ARTS
(☑031 329 51 51; www.stadttheaterbern.ch; Kornhausplatz 20) Opera, dance, classical music and plays (in German).

ℹ Information

Bern Tourismus (☑031 328 12 12; www.berninfo.com; Bahnhoftplatz; ⊗9am-8.30pm Jun-Sep, to 6.30pm Mon-Sat, 10am-5pm Sun Oct-May) Street-level floor of the train station. City tours, free hotel bookings, internet access (per hour Sfr12). There is a second office (☑031 328 12 12; Bärengraben; ⊗9am-6pm Jun-Sep,10am-4pm Mar-May & Oct, 11am-4pm Nov-Feb) in the Altes Tram depot by the bear pits.

Post Office (Schanzenstrasse 4; ⊗7.30am-9pm Mon-Fri, 8am-4pm Sat, 9am-4pm Sun)

ℹ Getting There & Around

AIR Bern-Belp airport (BRN; ☑031 960 21 21; www.alpar.ch), 9km southeast of the city centre, is a small airport with direct flights to/from Amsterdam, Barcelona, London, Munich and other cities. Most services are with the small regional carrier **SkyWork** (www.flyskywork.com). Bus 334 links with flights.

BICYCLE **Bern Rollt** (☑079 277 28 57; www.bernrollt.ch; 1st 4hr free, then per hr Sfr1; ⊙7.30am-9.30pm May-Oct) Pedal around with a bike, microscooter or skateboard, with kiosks inside the train station, at the western end of Zeughausgasse and just off Bubenbergplatz on Hirschengrasse.

PUBLIC TRANSPORT Buses and trams are operated by BernMobil (www.bernmobil.ch). Tickets are available from ticket machines and cost Sfr2.30 for up to six stops, or Sfr4.20 for a single journey within zones 1 & 2. Day passes cost Sfr12.

TRAINS Frequent trains connect to most Swiss towns, including Geneva (Sfr49, 1¾ hours), Basel (Sfr39, one hour) and Zürich (Sfr49, one hour).

Murten

POP 6100

Like something you'd build on the beach, this walled medieval village on the eastern shore of *Murten See* (Lac de Morat) isn't called Murten (Morat) – derived from the Celtic word *moriduno*, meaning 'fortress on the lake' – for nothing. In May 1476 the Burgundy duke Charles the Bold set off from Lausanne to besiege Murten, only to have 8000 of his men butchered or drowned in Murten Lake during the Battle of Murten (the Duke managed to run away). Even to-day, this German-speaking town marks the border with French-speaking Switzerland.

Murten is a cobblestone three-street town crammed with arcaded houses that make it feel like a mini-Bern. A string of hotel-res-taurants, culminating in a 13th-century **castle** (closed to visitors), line Rathausgasse; shops and eateries stud parallel Hauptgasse, capped by the medieval **Berntor city gate** at its eastern end.

The real highlights here are the nearly intact town **ramparts** (admission free; ⊙8am-9pm) – some of the best in Europe. Scale the wooden **Aufstieg auf die Ringmauer** (rampart stairs) behind the **Deutsche Kirche** (German Church) to reach the covered walk-way traversing part of the sturdy medieval walls. Alternate your views of the architec-turally harmonious old town with views out to where the battle ended French-speaking Charles' dreams of dominance.

The **Hotel Murtenhof & Krone** (☑026 672 90 30; www.murtenhof.ch; Rathausgasse 1-5; s/d from Sfr120/160, mains Sfr15-40; ⊙restaurant 11am-

10pm; ☎), in a 16th-century patrician's house, mixes old and new to create a spacious 58-room place to eat and sleep. Its terrace res-taurant cooks up first-class lake views and a traditional cuisine with a worldly hint of fu-sion. Book for terrace tables with views.

❶ Getting There & Away

The train station is 300m south of the city walls. Murten is a hub of hourly train services, includ-ing Bern (Sfr14, 35 minutes), Fribourg (Sfr12, 30 minutes) and Neuchâtel (Sfr13, 25 minutes).

Murten train station rents bicycles (per day Sfr33; ⊙9am to 4pm).

Navigation Lacs de Neuchâtel et Morat (☑032 729 96 00; www.navig.ch; adult/child Sfr25/12.50; ⊙Apr–mid-Oct) runs seasonal boats to/from Neuchâtel (1¾ hours).

Neuchâtel

POP 32,800

Its Old Town sandstone elegance, the airy Gallic nonchalance of its cafe life and the gay lakeside air that imbues the shoreline of its lake make Neuchâtel disarmingly charming.

The attractive Old Town streets are lined by fine, shuttered 18th-century man-sions and studded with fanciful gold-leaf fountains. The 15th-century **Chateau de Neuchâtel** (☑032 889 60 00; ⊙guided tours 10am-noon & 2-4pm Mon-Sat, 2-4pm Sun Apr-Sep) and the adjoining **Collegiate Church** are the centrepieces of the Old Town. The strik-ing cenotaph of 15 statues dates from 1372. Scale the nearby **prison tower** (☑032 717 71 02; Rue Jehanne de Hochberg 5; admission Sfr2; ⊙8am-6pm Apr-Sep) for broad views of town and lake.

Visit the **Musée d'Art et d'Histoire** (☑032 717 79 25; www.mahn.ch; Esplanade Léopold Robert 1; adult/under 16yr Sfr8/free, Wed free; ⊙11am-6pm Tue-Sun) to see beloved 18th-century clockwork figures.

Sample regional flavours such as *tripes à la Neuchâteloise* (Neuchâtel-style tripe) and roast pork and Neuchâtel blue-cheese sausage at **Le Jura Brasserie** (☑032 725 14 10; www.brasserielejura.ch; Rue de la Treille 7; meals Sfr20-50; ⊙cafe 9am-11pm Mon-Sat). The long menu changes daily.

The pedestrian zone and Place Pury (the local bus hub) are about 1km from the train station; walk down the hill along Ave de la Gare.

Trains serve Geneva (Sfr40, 65 minutes, hourly) and Bern (Sfr20, 35 minutes, hourly).

CENTRAL SWITZERLAND & BERNESE OBERLAND

The Bernese Oberland should come with a health warning – caution: may cause trembling in the north face of Eiger, uncontrollable bouts of euphoria at the foot of Jungfrau and 007 delusions at Schilthorn. Mark Twain wrote that no opiate compared to walking through this landscape – and he should know – and even when sober, the electric-green spruce forests, mountains so big they'll swallow you up, surreal china-blue skies, swirling glaciers and turquoise lakes seem hallucinatory. Up at Europe's highest train station, Jungfraujoch, husky-yapping mingles with a cacophony of 'oohs' and 'ahhs'. Just paces away, the serpentine Aletsch Glacier flicks out its tongue and you're surrounded by 4000m turrets and frosty stillness.

Lucerne

POP 76,200

Recipe for a gorgeous Swiss city: take a cobalt lake ringed by mountains of myth, add a medieval Old Town and sprinkle with covered bridges, sunny plazas, candy-coloured houses and waterfront promenades. Lucerne is bright, beautiful and has been Little Miss Popular since the likes of Goethe, Queen Victoria and Wagner savoured her views in the 19th century. Legend has it that an angel with a light showed the first settlers where to build a chapel in Lucerne, and today it still has amazing grace.

◉ Sights

Your first port of call should be the medieval Old Town, with its ancient rampart walls and towers. Wander the cobblestoned lanes and squares, pondering 15th-century buildings with painted facades and the two much-photographed covered bridges over the Reuss. **Kapellbrücke** (Chapel Bridge), dating from 1333, is Lucerne's best-known landmark. It's famous for its distinctive water tower and the spectacular 1993 fire that nearly destroyed it. Though it has been rebuilt, fire damage is still obvious on the 17th-century pictorial panels under the roof. In contrast are the spooky and dark *Dance of Death* panels under the roofline of **Spreuerbrücke** (Spreuer Bridge, 1408). Sinners repent!

Further explorations should include walks along – and boat rides across – the lake.

⊡ Museum

Sammlung Rosengart   MUSEUM
(☏041 220 16 60; www.rosengart.ch; Pilatusstrasse 10; adult/student Sfr18/16; ◉10am-6pm Apr-Oct, 11am-5pm Nov-Mar) Lucerne's blockbuster cultural attraction is the Rosengart Collection, occupying a graceful neoclassical pile. It showcases the outstanding stash of Angela Rosengart, a Swiss art dealer and close friend of Picasso. Alongside works by the great Spanish master are paintings and sketches by Cézanne, Kandinsky, Miró (including the stunning 1925 *Dancer II*), Matisse and Monet.

The basement has over 100 works of Paul Klee, which show the full range of his prodigious talents. The works are at times playful and introspective. Look for *Memory of a November Night's Adventure* (1922) among many great works.

Complementing the collection are some 200 photographs by David Douglas Duncan of the last 17 years of Picasso's life with his family in their home on the French Riviera. It's a portrait of the artist as an impish craftsman, lover and father.

Lion Monument   MONUMENT
(Löwendenkmal; Denkmalstrasse) Victorian attractions from the earliest days of mass tourism lure nostalgia buffs just north of the Old Town. By far the most touching is this 1820 10m-long monument carved on a limestone cliff face in a cute park. Lukas Ahorn's sculpture of a dying lion commemorates Swiss soldiers who died defending King Louis XVI during the French Revolution. Mark Twain once called it the 'saddest and most moving piece of rock in the world'.

Verkehrshaus   MUSEUM
(☏041 370 44 44; www.verkehrshaus.ch; Lidostrasse 5; adult/child Sfr30/15; ◉10am-6pm Apr-Oct, to 5pm Nov-Mar) Planes, trains and automobiles are the name of the game in the huge, family-oriented Transport Museum, east of the city centre, which is devoted to Switzerland's proud transport history. Switzerland's most popular museum, the sprawling complex has a fascinating railway hall that shows how the plucky Swiss scaled their mountains with iron. Take bus 6, 8 or 24 from Bahnhofplatz, or, better, enjoy the 2km walk along the lake.

🏃 Activities

Check out the cycling routes circumnavigating the lake; an easygoing and scenic option is the 16km pedal to Winkel via Kastanienbaum. You can rent bikes from Next Bike (📞041 508 08 00; www.nextbike.net; Lucerne Bahnhof; bikes per hour/day Sfr2/20) at the train station; register online or call and you're good to go.

Strandbad Lido
SWIMMING

(📞041 370 38 06; www.lido-luzern.ch; Lidostrasse 6a; adult/child Sfr7/free; ⏱9am-8pm mid-May–Sep) Perfect for a splash or sunbathe, this lakefront beach has a playground, volleyball court and heated outdoor pool. Or swim for free on the other bank of the lake by Seepark, off Alpenquai.

🎇 Festivals & Events

Lucerne's six-day Fasnacht celebrations are more boisterous and fun than Basel's carnival. The party kicks off on 'Dirty Thursday' with the emergence of the character 'Fritschi' from a window in the town hall, when bands of musicians and revellers take to the streets. The carnival moves through raucous celebrations climaxing on Mardi Gras (Fat Tuesday), and is over on Ash Wednesday.

June's Jodler Fest Luzern (www.jodlerfestluzern.ch) is a classic alpine shindig: think 12,000 Swiss yodellers, alphorn players and flag throwers.

🛏 Sleeping

TOP CHOICE Palace Luzern
HOTEL €€€

(📞041 416 16 16; www.palace-luzern.ch; Haldenstrasse 10; r from Sfr400; 🛜) This luxury belle époque hotel on the lakefront is a favourite with those looking for trad splendour. Inside it's all gleaming marble, chandeliers and turn-of-the-century grandeur. Go for a room with a view across the lake to the Alps beyond. Look for online deals for the smaller rooms in the eaves.

Backpackers Lucerne
HOSTEL €

(📞041 360 04 20; www.backpackerslucerne.ch; Alpenquai 42; dm/d from Sfr32/74; ⏱reception 7-10am & 4-11pm; @🛜) Right on the lake, this is a soulful place to crash with art-slung walls, bubbly staff, a well-equipped kitchen and immaculate dorms with balconies. It's a 15-minute walk southeast of the station.

Hotel De La Paix
HOTEL €

(📞041 418 80 00; www.ambassador.ch; Museggstrasse 2; r Sfr110-200; @🛜) Centrally located on the edge of the Old Town, this 31-room hotel is an excellent modest option. The lobby is minute but the rooms – especially corner ones – are very large and there are elevators. The included breakfast buffet is a good one.

Tourist Hotel
HOTEL €€

(📞041 410 24 74; www.touristhotel.ch; St-Karli-Quai 12; r Sfr90-170; P🚭🛜@) Don't be put off by the uninspired name and institutional-green facade of this central, riverfront cheapie. Rooms are cheerily modern – the cheaper ones have shared bathrooms – and there's a guest laundry.

Hotel Alpha
HOTEL €

(📞041 240 42 80; www.hotelalpha.ch; Zähringerstrasse 24; r Sfr75-140; @🛜) Easy on the eyes and wallet, this hotel is in a quiet residential area 10 minutes' walk from the Old Town. Rooms are simple, light and spotlessly clean; there are cheaper rooms with shared bathrooms.

The Hotel
HOTEL €€€

(📞041 226 86 86; www.the-hotel.ch; Sempacherstrasse 14; ste from Sfr430; ✳@🛜) This shamelessly hip hotel, bearing the imprint of architect Jean Nouvel, is all streamlined chic, with refined suites featuring stills from movie classics on the ceilings.

🍴 Eating & Drinking

Local specialities include fish from Lake Lucerne and chögalipaschtetli (vol-au-vents stuffed with meat and mushrooms).

There is an excellent market (⏱8am-3pm Sat) that runs along both sides of the Reuss.

TOP CHOICE Wirtshaus Galliker
SWISS €€

(📞041 240 10 01; Schützenstrasse 1; mains Sfr22-50; ⏱11.30am-2pm & 5-10pm Tue-Sat, closed Jul–mid-Aug) This old-style tavern has been passionately run by the Galliker family over four generations since 1856. Motherly waiters dish up Lucerne soul food (rösti, chögalipaschtetli and the like) that is batten-the-hatches filling. Book ahead for dinner.

Restaurant Schiff
SWISS €€

(📞041 418 52 52; Unter den Egg 8; mains Sfr20-45) Under the waterfront arcades and lit by tea lights at night, this restaurant has bags of charm. Try fish from Lake Lucerne and some of the city's most celebrated chögalipaschtetli.

Heini
CAFE €

(☑041 412 20 20; www.heini.ch; Falkenplatz; snacks from Sfr5) The original outlet for this lavish local chain of bakery-cafes is by the Lion Monument, but we prefer this modern version on a key square in the Old Town. Sandwiches and salads satisfy lunch needs but the real action here is in the display cases where the cakes, tortes and more will have you drooling. Find a table, then browse.

La Terraza
ITALIAN €€

(☑041 410 36 31; www.ristorante-laterrazza.ch; Metzgerrainle 9; mains Sfr18-45) Set in a 12th-century building that has housed fish sellers, dukes and scribes over the years, La Terraza oozes atmosphere. Think *bella* Italia with an urban edge. When the sun's out, sit on the riverfront terrace.

Rathaus Bräuerei
BREWERY €

(☑041 410 52 57; www.rathausbrauerei.ch; Unter den Egg 2; mains from Sfr15; ⊗8am-midnight) Sip house-brewed beer (try the bock) under the vaulted arches of this buzzy tavern, or nab a pavement table and watch the river flow. There are seasonal brews as well as excellent traditional German-Swiss fare. Nightly specials reflect the seasons.

La Madeleine
BAR

(www.lamadeleine.ch; Baselstrasse 15) This is a lovely little spot for a low-key gig, with two performance areas and a cosy-glam bar. Jazz, blues, pop, funk and more are played.

❶ Information

Lucerne Card (24/48/72hr Sfr19/27/33) Offers 50% discount on museum admissions, unlimited use of public transport and other reductions.

Luzern Tourism (☑041 227 17 17; www.luzern.com; Zentralstrasse 5; ⊗8.30am-7pm Mon-Sat, 9am-5pm Sun May-Oct, 8.30am-5.30pm Mon-Fri, 9am-5pm Sat & Sun Nov-Apr) Accessed from platform 3 of the train station.

❶ Getting There & Around

Frequent trains serve Bern (Sfr37, one hour), Geneva (Sfr76, 2¾ hours), Lugano (Sfr58, 2½ hours) and Zürich (Sfr24, one hour).

Trains also connect Lucerne and Interlaken East on the stunning GoldenPass Line via Meiringen (Sfr31, two hours).

SGV (www.lakelucerne.ch) operates boats (sometimes paddle-steamers) on Lake Lucerne daily. Services are extensive. Rail passes are good for free or discounted travel.

City buses leave from outside the Hauptbahnhof at Bahnhofplatz. Tickets cost Sfr2.40 for a journey around town; day passes are Sfr6.40.

Interlaken

POP 5300

Once Interlaken made the Victorians swoon with its dreamy mountain vistas, viewed from the chandelier-lit confines of its grand hotels. Today it makes daredevils scream with its adrenalin-loaded adventures. Straddling the glittering Lakes Thun and Brienz (thus the name), and dazzled by the pearly whites of Eiger, Mönch and Jungfrau, the scenery here is exceptional.

In fact you may want to stay closer to the amazing sights. Many tour groups use Interlaken as a base and the streets are lined with kitsch by day and rollicking bars by night. You may want to just stop off here as you head into the hills or avail yourself of the adventure operators here.

◉ Sights

Interlaken's central park, **Höhe-Matte**, has a few strategically placed cows munching on the grass. Their greatest interruption are the regular landings of paragliders.

Interlaken also has a small old town, **Unterseen**, across the Aare River.

🏃 Activities

Tempted to hurl yourself off a bridge, down a cliff or along a raging river? You're in the right place. Switzerland is the world's second-biggest adventure-sports centre and Interlaken is its busiest hub.

Almost every heart-stopping pursuit you can think of is offered here. You can white-water raft on the Lütschine, Simme and Saane Rivers, go canyoning in the Saxetet, Grimsel or Chli Schliere gorges, and canyon jump at the Gletscherschlucht near Grindelwald. If that doesn't grab you, there's paragliding, glacier bungee jumping, skydiving, ice climbing, hydrospeeding and, phew, much more.

Sample prices are around Sfr110 for rafting or canyoning, Sfr130 for bungee or canyon jumping, Sfr160 for tandem paragliding, Sfr180 for ice climbing, Sfr225 for hanggliding and Sfr430 for sky-diving. A half-day mountain-bike tour will set you back around Sfr25.

MOUNTAIN DAY TRIPS FROM LUCERNE

There are three classic day-trips to Alpine peaks from Lucerne, and all are marketed heavily. The summits offer a variety of walks and activities but the real appeal are the jaw-dropping views and the actual journeys themselves. Don't bother with these trips on cloudy days.

Mount Pilatus

Rearing above Lucerne from the southwest, Mt Pilatus (www.pilatus.com) is 2132m high. From May to October, you can reach Mt Pilatus on a classic 'golden round-trip'. Board the lake steamer from Lucerne to Alpnachstad, then rise with the world's steepest cog railway to Mt Pilatus. From the summit, cable cars bring you down to Kriens via Fräkmüntegg and Krienseregg, where bus 1 takes you back to Lucerne. The return trip costs Sfr91 (less with valid Swiss, Eurail or InterRail passes).

Mount Rigi

The Jungfrau peaks dominate the horizon from 1797m-high Rigi (www.rigi.ch). Two rival railways carry passengers to the top. One runs from Arth-Goldau (one-way/return Sfr40/64), the other from Vitznau (one-way/return Sfr45/72). Holders of Swiss, Eurail and InterRail passes receive a 50% discount on fares.

Mount Titlis

Central Switzerland's tallest mountain, Titlis (www.titlis.ch), has its only glacier and is reached on a breathtaking four-stage journey; the final link is on a revolving cable car. At Titlis station (3020m) the oohs and aahs come when you step out onto the terrace, where the panorama of glacier-capped peaks stretches to Eiger, Mönch and Jungfrau in the Bernese Oberland. The return trip to Titlis (45 minutes each way) costs Sfr90 from Engelberg. There are reductions of 50% for Swiss, Eurail and InterRail pass holders. Engelberg is at the end of a train line, about an hour from Lucerne (Sfr17). If on a day trip, check the Lucerne tourist office's Mt Titlis excursion tickets.

The major operators able to arrange most sports from May to September include the following. Advance bookings are essential.

Alpinraft (☎033 823 41 00; www.alpinraft.ch; Hauptstrasse 7)

Outdoor Interlaken (☎033 826 77 19; www.outdoor-interlaken.ch; Hauptstrasse 15)

Swissraft (☎033 821 66 55; www.swissraft-activity.ch; Obere Jungfraustrasse 72)

🛏 Sleeping

TOP CHOICE **Hotel Rugenpark** B&B €
(☎033 822 36 61; www.rugenpark.ch; Rugenparkstrasse 19; s/d from Sfr87/130, without bathroom from Sfr62/105; ⊗closed Nov–mid-Dec; P⊜@) Chris and Ursula have worked magic to transform this place into a sweet B&B. Rooms are humble, but the place is spotless and has been enlivened with colourful butterflies, beads and travel trinkets. Quiz your knowledgeable hosts for help and local tips.

Victoria-Jungfrau
Grand Hotel & Spa HOTEL €€€
(☎033 828 28 28; www.victoria-jungfrau.ch; Höheweg 41; s/d from Sfr560/680; P⊜@🛜🏊) The reverent hush and impeccable service evoke an era when only royalty and the seriously wealthy travelled. It's a perfect melding of well-preserved Victorian features and modern luxury.

Backpackers Villa Sonnenhof HOSTEL €
(☎033 826 71 71; www.villa.ch; Alpenstrasse 16; dm Sfr39-45, s Sfr69-79, d Sfr118-138; ⊗reception 7am-11pm; @🛜) Sonnenhof is a slick combination of ultramodern chalet and elegant art nouveau villa. Dorms are immaculate, and some have balconies with Jungfrau views. There's also a relaxed lounge, a well-equipped kitchen and a leafy garden for kicking back and enjoying the Jungfrau views.

Hôtel du Lac HOTEL €€
(☎033 822 29 22; www.dulac-interlaken.ch; Höheweg 225; s/d Sfr160/280) Smiley old-

fashioned service and a riverfront location near Interlaken Ost make this 19th-century hotel a solid choice. It has been in the same family for generations.

Walter's B&B
B&B €

(☑033 822 76 88; www.walters.ch; Oelestrasse 35; s/d without bathroom from Sfr50/66; 🛜) Walter is a real star with his quick smile, culinary skills and invaluable tips. Sure, the rooms are a blast from the 1970s (and have shared bathrooms), but they are super clean and you'd be hard pushed to find better value in Interlaken.

Balmer's Herberge
HOSTEL €

(☑033 822 19 61; www.balmers.ch; Hauptstrasse 23; dm from Sfr31, s/d from Sfr47/81; 🅿@🛜) Adrenalin junkies hail Balmer's for its fun frat-house vibe. These party-mad digs offer beer-garden happy hours, a pumping bar with DJs and chill-out hammocks for nursing your hangover.

✗ Eating & Drinking

Am Marktplatz is scattered with bakeries and bistros with alfresco seating. Höheweg, east of the park, is lined with ethnic eateries with reasonable prices.

The bars at Balmer's and Funny Farm are easily the liveliest drinking holes for revved-up party people.

Benacus
SWISS €€

(☑033 821 20 20; www.benacus.ch; Stadthausplatz; mains Sfr20-33; ⊙closed Sun) Supercool Benacus is a breath of urban air with its glass walls, slick wine-red sofas, lounge music and street-facing terrace. The German TV show *Funky Kitchen Club* is filmed here. The menu stars creative, seasonal flavours.

Sandwich Bar
SWISS €

(☑033 821 63 25; Rosenstrasse 5; snacks Sfr4-9; ⊙7.30am-7pm Mon-Fri, 8am-5pm Sat) This crimson-walled, zebra-striped cafe is a great snack spot. Choose your bread and get creative with fillings. Or try the soups, salads, toasties and locally made ice cream.

Schuh
CAFE €€

(☑033 822 94 41; www.schuh-interlaken.ch; Höheweg 56; meals from Sfr20; ⊙9am-11.30pm) A Viennese-style coffee house famous for its pastries, pralines and park-facing terrace. The menu covers all the bases, from rösti to Asian accents. The chocolate-making show (Sfr15) is touristy but fun; it runs at 5pm most days in the high season.

Goldener Anker
INTERNATIONAL €€

(☑033 822 16 72; www.anker.ch; Marktgasse 57; mains Sfr18-42; ⊙dinner; 🎵) This beamed restaurant covers a lot of bases with its menu, which runs from Switzerland to Asia with a brief stop in Mexico. Besides meaty mains, there are good salads and numerous veggie options. It has live music many nights with an equally polyglot line-up.

ⓘ Information

Tourist Office (☑033 826 53 00; www.interlakentourism.ch; Höheweg 37; ⊙8am-7pm Mon-Fri, to 5pm Sat, 10am-noon & 5-7pm Sun Jul & Aug, 8am-noon & 1.30-6pm Mon-Fri, 9am-noon Sat rest of year) Halfway between the stations. There's also a hotel booking board outside the office and at both train stations.

ⓘ Getting There & Away

The only way south for vehicles without a detour around the mountains is the car-carrying train from Kandersteg, south of Spiez.

There are two train stations. Interlaken West is slightly closer to the centre and is a stop for trains to Bern (Sfr27, one hour). Interlaken East is the rail hub for all lines, including the scenic ones up into the Jungfrau region and the lovely GoldenPass Line to Lucerne (Sfr31, two hours).

Jungfrau Region

If the Bernese Oberland is Switzerland's Alpine heart, the Jungfrau region is where yours will skip a beat. Presided over by glacier-encrusted monoliths Eiger, Mönch and Jungfrau (Ogre, Monk and Virgin), the scenery stirs the soul and strains the neck muscles. It's a magnet for skiers and snowboarders with its 214km of pistes, 44 lifts and much more; a one-day ski pass for Kleine Scheidegg–Männlichen, Grindelwald-First or Mürren-Schilthorn costs Sfr71.

Come summer, hundreds of kilometres of walking trails allow you to capture the landscape from many angles, but it never looks less than astonishing.

The Lauterbrunnen Valley branches out from Interlaken with sheer rock faces and towering mountains on either side, attracting an army of hikers and mountain bikers.

The main villages of Grindelwald, Wengen and Mürren, as well as the rail hub of Lauterbrunnen, all have ATMs. The first two are the only viable choices for staying during the off-season months of April and November.

JUNGFRAU ONLINE

The Jungfrau region's website, www. jungfrau.ch, is an excellent resource. It has 3D and downloadable maps of all the winter skiing areas and summer hiking trails, along with the complex thicket of train, cable car, bus and lift schedules.

It also has live cams from the peaks so you can do a final weather check before deciding to make the sizeable investment in time and money to ascend the summits.

🛈 Getting There & Around

Hourly trains (www.jungfrau.ch) depart for the Jungfrau region from Interlaken Ost station. Sit in the front half of the train for Lauterbrunnen (Sfr7.20) or the back half for Grindelwald (Sfr10.40).

From Grindelwald, trains ascend to Kleine Scheidegg (Sfr32), where you can transfer for Jungfraujoch. From Lauterbrunnen, trains ascend to Wengen (Sfr6.40) and continue to Kleine Scheidegg (Sfr24) for Jungfraujoch.

You can reach Mürren two ways from Lauterbrunnen: with a bus and cable car via Stechelberg (Sfr14.20) or with a cable car and train via Grütschalp (Sfr10.40). Do a circle trip for the full experience. Gimmelwald is reached by cable car from Stechelberg and Mürren. Many cable cars close for servicing in April and November.

Regional passes can save you money. The **Berner Oberland Regional Pass** (www.regiopass-berneroberland.ch; 7 days Sfr233) gives you three days' unlimited free travel and four days' discounted travel. The **Jungfraubahnen Pass** (www.jungfrau.ch; 6 days unlimited travel Sfr210, with Swiss Pass, Swiss Card or Half-Fare Card Sfr160) gives you six days unlimited travel though you still have to pay Sfr55 to Jungfraujoch.

GRINDELWALD

POP 3900

Grindelwald's charms were discovered by skiers and hikers in the late 19th century, making it one of Switzerland's oldest resorts and the Jungfrau's largest. It has lost none of its appeal over the decades, with archetypal alpine chalets and verdant pastures set against the chiselled features of the Eiger north face.

Grindelwald tourist office (☏033 854 12 12; www.grindelwald.ch; Dorfstrasse 110; ⏰8am-noon & 1.30-6pm Mon-Fri, 9am-noon & 1.30-5pm Sat & Sun) is at the Sportzentrum, 200m from the train station.

◎ Sights & Activities

The **Grindelwald-First** skiing area has runs stretching from Oberjoch at 2486m to the village at 1050m. In the summer it caters to hikers with 90km of trails at about 1200m, 48km of which are open year-round.

Gletscherschlucht   GLACIER
(Glacier Gorge; adult/child Sfr7/4; ⏰10am-5pm May-Oct, to 6pm Jul & Aug) Turbulent waters carve a path through the craggy Gletscherschlucht, a 30-minute walk south of the centre. A footpath weaves through tunnels hacked into cliffs – a popular spot for canyon- and bungee-jumping expeditions.

Grindelwald Sports   ADVENTURE SPORTS
(☏033 854 12 80; www.grindelwaldsports.ch; Dorfstrasse 110; ⏰8am-noon & 1.30-6pm, closed Sat & Sun in low season) In the tourist office, this outfit arranges mountain climbing, ski and snowboard instruction, canyon jumping and glacier bungee jumping at the Gletscherschlucht.

🛏 Sleeping & Eating

Gletschergarten TOP CHOICE   HOTEL €€
(☏033 853 17 21; www.hotel-gletschergarten.ch; Dorfstrasse; s Sfr120-150, d Sfr230-300; @) The sweet Breitenstein family make you feel at home in their rustic timber chalet, brimming with heirlooms from landscape paintings to family snapshots. Decked out in pine and flowery fabrics, the rooms have balconies facing Unterer Gletscher at the front and Wetterhorn (best for sunset) at the back.

Mountain Hostel   HOSTEL €
(☏033 854 38 38; www.mountainhostel.ch; dm Sfr37-44, r Sfr94-108; P@�) Near the Männlichen cable-car station, this is a good base for sports junkies. There's a beer garden, ski and bike room and TV lounge.

Hotel Tschuggen   HOTEL €€
(☏033 853 17 81; www.tschuggen-grindelwald.ch; Dorfstrasse 134; s Sfr70-95, d Sfr160-190; �) Monika and Robert extend a warm welcome at this dark-wood chalet in the centre of town. The light, simple rooms are spotlessly clean; opt for a south-facing double for terrific Eiger views.

Memory   SWISS €€
(☏033 854 31 31; Dorfstrasse; mains Sfr21-30; ⏰11.30am-10.30pm) Always packed, the Eiger Hotel's unpretentious restaurant rolls out tasty Swiss grub such as rösti and fon-

due. Try to bag a table on the street-facing terrace.

C & M
SWISS €€

(☏033 853 07 10; mains Sfr20-36; ⊗8.30am-11pm Wed-Mon) Just as appetising as the wide-ranging menu are the stupendous views to Unterer Gletscher from this gallery-style cafe's sunny terrace.

WENGEN
POP 1300

Photogenically poised on a mountain ledge, Wengen's celestial views include the silent majesty of the glacier-capped giant peaks as well as the shimmering ribbons of waterfalls spilling into the Lauterbrunnen Valley below.

The village is car-free and can only be reached by train. It's a fabulous hub for **hiking** for much of the year as well as **skiing** in winter. The **tourist office** (☏033 856 85 85; www.wengen.ch; ⊗9am-6pm Mon-Sat, 9am-noon & 1-6pm Sun, closed Sat & Sun Nov, Mar & Apr) has the usual bounty of maps and can help with the myriad rental chalets and rooms in addition to hotels.

Hotel Bären (☏033 855 14 19; www.baeren -wengen.ch; s Sfr90-150, d Sfr190-280; ☏) is close to the station. Loop back under the tracks and head down the hill to this snug log chalet with bright, if compact, rooms. The affable Brunner family serves a hearty breakfast.

For an excellent meal with ingredients sourced both organically and locally, try **Restaurant Eiger** (☏033 856 05 05; www. restaurant-eiger.ch; mains Sfr10-40; ⊗8am-11pm), which is right by the train station. It has casual meals during the day, including excellent fondue, which you can enjoy on the terrace. At night the seasonal menu is a creative treat. The **Coop Supermarket** by the train station is the best in the region.

JUNGFRAUJOCH

Sure, the world wants to see Jungfraujoch (3471m) and yes, tickets are expensive, but don't let that stop you. It's a once-in-a-lifetime trip and there's a reason why two million people a year visit Europe's highest train station. The icy wilderness of swirling glaciers and 4000m turrets that unfolds is truly enchanting.

Clear good weather is essential for the trip; check www.jungfrau.ch or call ☏033 828 79 31, and don't forget warm clothing, sunglasses and sunscreen. Up top, when you tire of the view (is this possible?), dash downhill on a snow disc (free) or on myriad other icy options.

From Interlaken Ost, the journey time is 2½ hours each way (return Sfr191; discounts with rail passes). The last train back is at 5.50pm in summer, and 4.40pm in winter. There are cheaper 'good morning' and 'good afternoon' tickets (Sfr140) with time restrictions.

SWITZERLAND JUNGFRAU REGION

JUNGFRAU REGION HIKING 101

There are hundreds of hikes along the hundreds of kilometres of trails in the Jungfrau Region. All include some of the world's most stunning scenery. Every skill and fortitude level is accommodated and options abound. Here are three to get you started.

Grütschalp to Mürren

Ride the cable car up from Lauterbrunnen and follow the trail along the railway tracks. The walk to Mürren takes about an hour and is mostly level. There are unbeatable views, Alpine woods and babbling glacier-fed streams.

Männlichen to Kleine Scheidegg

Reach the Männlichen lift station by cable cars from Wengen and Grindelwald. Now follow the well-marked, spectacular path down to Kleine Scheidegg. It takes about 90 minutes and you have nothing but Alps in front of you.

Kleine Scheidegg to Wengen

This downhill hike takes about three or more hours and gives you good views all the way. Parts are utterly silent while many stretches are quite steep. The odd mountain hut and cafe offer ample reasons to pause.

GIMMELWALD

POP 120

Decades ago some anonymous backpacker scribbled these words in the guestbook at the Mountain Hostel: 'If heaven isn't what it's cracked up to be, send me back to Gimmelwald.' Enough said. When the sun is out in Gimmelwald, this pipsqueak of a village will simply take your breath away. Sit outside and listen to the distant roar of avalanches on the sheer mountain faces arrayed before you.

The surrounding hiking trails include an easy one down from Mürren (30 to 40 minutes) and a steep one up from Stechelberg.

The rustic Mountain Hostel (☑033 855 17 04; www.mountainhostel.com; dm from Sfr28; ⊘reception 8.30am-noon & 6-11pm Apr–mid-Nov; @) is a backpacker's legend. A soak in its outdoor whirlpool with stunning views hits the spot every time. (And don't forget to sign the guestbook!) Esther's Guest House (☑033 855 54 88; www.esthersguesthouse.ch; s/d Sfr55/130, apt Sfr160-230; @⑦) is a sweet B&B with a tiny shop inside, where you can stock up on local goodies like Gimmelwald salami and Stechelberg honey.

MÜRREN

POP 500

Arrive on a clear evening when the sun hangs low on the horizon, and you'll think you've died and gone to heaven. Car-free Mürren *is* storybook Switzerland.

In summer, the Allmendhubel funicular (www.schilthorn.ch; return Sfr12.60; ⊘9am-5pm) takes you above Mürren to a panoramic restaurant. From here, you can set out on many walks, including the famous Northface Trail (1½ hours) via Schiltalp to the west, with spellbinding views of the Lauterbrunnen Valley and monstrous Eiger north face – bring binoculars to spy intrepid climbers.

The tourist office (☑033 856 86 86; www.mymuerren.ch; ⊘8.30am-7pm Mon-Sat, to 8pm Thu, to 6pm Sun, reduced hours in low season) is in the sports centre.

Sleeping options include Eiger Guesthouse (☑033 856 54 60; www.eigerguesthouse.

WANT MORE?

Head to Lonely Planet (www.lonelyplanet.com/switzerland/zurich) for planning advice, author recommendations, traveller reviews and insider tips.

com; r Sfr120-200; @⑦), by the train station, with the downstairs pub serving tasty food; and Hotel Jungfrau (☑033 856 64 64; www.hoteljungfrau.ch; s Sfr80-140, d Sfr160-280; @⑦), overlooking the nursery slopes from its perch above Mürren. It dates to 1894 and has a beamed lounge with open fire. Ten out of 10 much-lauded chalet Hotel Alpenruh (☑033 856 88 00; www.alpenruh-muerren.ch; s Sfr140-180, d Sfr200-280; ☻⑦), for service, food and unbeatable views to Jungfrau massif.

SCHILTHORN

There's a tremendous 360-degree panorama available from the 2970m Schilthorn (www.schilthorn.ch). On a clear day, you can see over 200 peaks, from Titlis to Mont Blanc and across to the German Black Forest. Note that this was the site of Blofeld's HQ in the under-appreciated 1969 James Bond film *On Her Majesty's Secret Service* (as the hype endlessly reminds you).

From Interlaken East a combined ticket to the summit costs Sfr125. From Mürren it's Sfr77 for the two long cable-car rides. There are discounts with rail passes.

ZÜRICH

POP 376,000

Zürich is an enigma. A savvy financial centre with possibly the densest public transport system in the world, it also has a gritty, post-industrial edge that always surprises. The nation's largest city has an evocative old town and lovely lakeside location. Its museums, shops and myriad restaurants can easily keep you busy for a couple of days, while its hip quarters will fill your nights.

⊙ Sights

Old Town   HISTORIC AREA

Explore the cobbled streets of the pedestrian Old Town lining both sides of the river.

The bank vaults beneath Bahnhofstrasse, the city's most elegant street, are said to be crammed with gold and silver. Indulge in affluent Züricher-watching and ogle at the luxury shops selling watches, clocks, chocolates, furs, porcelain and fashion labels galore.

Walk up to the Lindenhof, a large shady square that perches above the Old Town, for views down over the city and Limmat River.

As you walk, see how many of the city's 1221 fountains you can spot – each with a spout of drinkable glacier-fed water.

On Sundays all of Zürich strolls around its namesake lake. Take one short meander and you'll understand why: it's relaxing and simply sublime. On a clear day you'll glimpse the Alps in the distance.

Fraumünster CHURCH
(www.fraumuenster.ch; Münsterplatz; ⊙9am-6pm Apr-Oct, 10am-4pm Nov-Mar) The 13th-century cathedral is renowned for its stained-glass windows, designed by the Russian-Jewish master Marc Chagall (1887–1985).

Grossmünster CHURCH
(www.grossmuenster.ch; Grossmünsterplatz; ⊙10am-6pm Mar-Oct, to 5pm Nov-Feb) On the north bank of the river, the dual-towered Grossmünster was where, in the 16th century, the Protestant preacher Huldrych Zwingli first spread his message of 'pray and work' during the Reformation. The figure glowering from the south tower of the cathedral is Charlemagne, who ordered the original church built in the spot in the 10th century.

St Peterskirche CHURCH
(St Peter's Church; St Peterhofstatt; ⊙8am-6pm Mon-Fri, to 4pm Sat, 11am-5pm Sun) From any position in the city, it's impossible to overlook the 13th-century tower of St Peterskirche. Its prominent clock face, 8.7m in diameter, is Europe's largest.

Kunsthaus MUSEUM
(✆044 253 84 84; www.kunsthaus.ch; Heimplatz 1; adult/child Sfr15/free, Wed free; ⊙10am-8pm Wed-Fri, to 6pm Tue, Sat & Sun) Zürich's Fine Arts Museum boasts a rich collection of Alberto Giacometti stick-figure sculptures, Monets, Van Goghs, Rodin sculptures and other 19th- and 20th-century art. A large new addition is in the works for 2017; in the meantime the collection can feel chaotic.

Schweizerisches Landesmuseum MUSEUM
(Swiss National Museum; www.musee-suisse.ch; Museumstrasse 2; adult/child Sfr10/free; ⊙10am-5pm Tue-Sun, to 7pm Thu) Inside a purpose-built cross between a mansion and a castle sprawls an eclectic and imaginatively presented tour through Swiss history. Collections range from ancient arms to a series of rooms recreating the interiors of everything

TOASTING FROSTY

Sechseläuten (www.sechselaeuten.ch) is a spring festival on the third Monday of April that features guild members parading down the streets in historical costume. In one of Europe's more spectacular – and odd – traditions, a fireworks-filled 'snowman' (the *Böögg*) is ignited atop a huge pyre on Bellevueplatz to celebrate the end of winter. The entire country watches the spectacle on live TV and how long it takes for the snowman's head to explode is said to determine whether summer will be warm and sunny, or wet and dreary (six minutes is *very* good).

from a 15th-century convent to contemporary pads crammed with designer furniture. You can dart in from the train station between trains.

Activities
Zürich comes into its own in summer when its green lakeshore parks buzz with bathers, sun-seekers, in-line skaters, footballers, lovers, picnickers, party animals, preeners and police patrolling on rollerblades!

Swimming Areas SWIMMING
(admission Sfr6; ⊙9am-7pm May & Sep, to 8pm Jun-Aug) From mid-May to mid-September, outdoor swimming areas – think a rectangular wooden pier partly covered by a pavilion – open around the lake and up the Limmat River. Many offer massages, yoga and saunas, as well as snacks and rollicking bars. Our favourites include Seebad Enge (✆044 201 38 89; www.seebadenge.ch; Mythenquai 95; admission Sfr7), a trendy bar that opens until midnight in fine weather (it's about 700m southwest of Bürkliplatz); and Letten (✆044 362 92 00; Lettensteg 10; admission free), a hipster hangout where people swim, barbecue, play volleyball or just drink and loll on the grass and concrete.

Festivals & Events

Street Parade FESTIVAL
(www.street-parade.ch) This techno celebration in the middle of August is one of Europe's largest street parties.

Zürich

500 m
0.25 miles

G

Hadlaubstr
Toblerstr
Gladbachstr
Vogelsang
Hochstr
Rigistr
Gloriastr
Plattenstr
Zürichbergstr
Kantons-
schuit

F

Universitätsstr
Künstlergasse
Hirschengraben
Florhofgasse
Leonhardstr
Seilergraben
Neumarkt
Auf der Mauer
Zähringer-
str
Central
Niederdorfstr

E

Weinbergstr
Hochfarbstr
Walche
Brücke
Beatenplatz
Mühlesteg
Rudolf Brun
Brücke
Limmatquai
Beckenhofstr
Neumühlequai
Werdmühle-
platz
Lindenhof
Stampfenbachstr
Bahnhofplatz
Bahnhofstr
Rennweg
Fortunagasse
Münzplatz
Nordstr
Museumstr
Schützengasse
Uster-
str
Füsslistr
Löwenstr
Limmat
Beatengasse
Sihl
str

D

Wasserwerkstr
Kornhaus
Brücke
Ausstellungstr
Limmatstr
Langstr
Halterstr
Kaserenstr
Gessneralle
Steinmühle
platz
Talacker
23
Klingenstr
Zollstr
Hauptbahnhof
(Train Station)
Sihl str
Seinaust

C

Gasometerstr
Langstr
Mattengasse
4
Lagerstr
Zwingilstr
Teughaustr
Amkerstr
Müllerstr
Bäckerstr
Badenerstr
Werdstr
Neugasse
Staufacherquai
Kasernenstr
Gartenhofstr

B

Sihlhallenstr
7
22
Brauerstr
Müllerstr
Langstr
Badenerstr
Zweierstr
Schönbergstr
4
Stauffacherstr
Kanzleistr
9
Gartenhofstr

A

24
Hermann Greulich Str

1   **2**   **3**   **4**

Zürich

◎ Top Sights

◎ Sights

⊟ Sleeping

⊗ Eating

◉ Drinking

◉ Entertainment

SWITZERLAND ZÜRICH

🛏 Sleeping

Zürich accommodation prices are fittingly high for the main city of expensive Switzerland. You might consider options such as www.airbnb.com here.

TOP CHOICE **Hotel du Thèâtre** HOTEL €€
(☎044-2672670; www.hotel-du-theatre.ch; Seilergraben 69; s/d from Sfr155/205; ❋☎) Located in the lively Niederdorf and within walking distance to the train station, this boutique hotel is decorated with designer furniture and old film stills (an ode to the hotel's past – in the 1950s it was a combined theatre and hotel).

Pension für Dich
PENSION **€**

(☑044 317 91 60; www.fuerdich.ch; Stauffacher-strasse 141; s/d without bathroom from Sfr100/110; ☺🛜) These simple but fabulous apartments have been converted into comfy rooms – think retro furnishings meets Ikea. A number of rooms have balconies. There's a good cafe downstairs, plus you're smack in the centre of the Kreis 4 nightlife action.

Hotel Widder
HOTEL **€€€**

(☑044 224 25 26; www.widderhotel.ch; Rennweg 7; d from Sfr500; P❋@🛜) A stylish hotel in the equally grand Augustiner district, the Widder is a pleasing fusion of modernity and traditional charm. Rooms and public areas across the eight town houses here boast art and designer furniture.

Dakini
B&B **€**

(☑044 291 42 20; www.dakini.ch; Brauerstrasse 87; s/d from Sfr90/150; ☺@🛜) This relaxed B&B attracts a Bohemian crowd of artists and performers, academics and trendy tourists who don't bat an eyelid at its location near the red-light district. There's a communal kitchen. Take tram 8 to Bäckeranlange.

Hotel Rothaus
HOTEL **€**

(☑043 322 10 58; www.hotelrothaus.ch; Sihlhal-lenstrasse 1; s/d from Sfr100/140; ☺🛜) Smack in the middle of the Langstrasse action, this cheerful red-brick building is a real find. A variety of fresh, airy rooms are complemented by a busy little eatery-bar downstairs. Guests can rent bikes cheaply.

Hotel Otter
HOTEL **€€**

(☑044 251 22 07; Oberdorf-strasse 7; s/d/apt from Sfr125/155/200; 🛜) The Otter has 17 rooms with a variety of colour schemes ranging from white and blue stripes to olive green. You might get pink satin duvet covers. Studio apartment-style rooms with kitchens are another option. A popular bar, Wüste, is downstairs.

Hotel Seegarten
HOTEL **€€**

(☑0443883737; www.hotel-seegarten.ch; Seegar-tenstrasse 14; s/d from Sfr195/295; 🛜) Rattan furniture and vintage tourist posters give this place a rustic Mediterranean atmos-phere, which is reinforced by the proximity to the lake and the on-site Restaurant-Bar Latino. Take tram 2 or 4 to Kreuzstrasse.

SYHA Hostel
HOSTEL **€**

(☑043 399 78 00; www.youthhostel.ch; Mütschel-lenstrasse 114, Wollishofen; dm from Sfr42, s/d from Sfr118/138; @🛜) This bulbous, purple-red hostel features 290 beds, a swish 24-hour reception/dining hall and sparkling modern bathrooms. Dorms are small. Take tram 7 to Morgental, or S-Bahn to Wollishofen.

City Backpacker
HOSTEL **€**

(☑044 251 90 15; www.city-backpacker.ch; Nieder-dorfstrasse 5; dm Sfr37, s/d from Sfr77/118; ☺re-ception closed noon-3pm; @🛜) This youthful party hostel is friendly and well equipped, if a trifle cramped. Overcome the claustropho-bia in summer by hanging out on the roof terrace – the best spot in Zürich for sunset and cold beers.

🍴 Eating

Zürich has a thriving cafe culture and hundreds of restaurants – explore Nied-erdorfstrasse and its nearby backstreets. Langstrasse is another good area – on both sides of the tracks.

Alpenrose
SWISS **€€**

(☑044 271 39 19; Fabrikstrasse 12; mains Sfr24-42; ☺noon-11pm Wed-Sun) With its timber-clad walls, 'No Polka Dancing' warning and fine cuisine from regions all over the country, the Alpenrose makes for an inspired meal out. You could try risotto from Ticino or *Pizokel* (aka *Bizochel,* a kind of long and especially savoury noodle) from Graubünden or fresh perch fillets. Book.

Zeughauskeller
SWISS **€€**

(☑044 211 26 90; www.zeughauskeller.ch; Bahn-hofstrasse 28a; mains Sfr18-35; ☺11.30am-11pm; 🍴) The menu at this huge, atmospheric beer hall – set inside a former armoury – offers 20 different kinds of sausages as well as numerous other Swiss specialities of a car-nivorous and vegetarian variety. It's a local institution; expect queues during the week between noon and 2pm.

Café Schober
CAFE **€**

(www.conditorei-cafe-schober.ch; Napfgasse 4; snacks from Sfr10; ☺8am-7pm) Steady yourself for the best hot chocolate you've ever had at this grand cafe. On entry you'll see lavish displays of sweets, treats and other enticing edible baubles. Choose from several seating areas: red velvet, back garden, upstairs inti-mate etc. Holiday displays are stunning.

Les Halles
FRENCH **€€**

(☑044 273 11 25; www.les-halles.ch; Pfingst-weidstrasse 6; mains Sfr22-31; ☺11am-midnight Mon-Wed, to 1am Thu-Sat) This joyous scrum of timber tables in Kreis 5 is the best place in town to sit down to *Moules mit Frites* (mussels and fries). Hang at the bustling bar and shop at the market. It is one of several chirpy bar-restaurants in formerly derelict factory buildings in the area.

Schipfe 16   INTERNATIONAL €

(📞044 211 21 22; Schipfe 16; menus Sfr17-20; ⏱11am-2pm Mon-Fri) Overlooking the Limmat River from the historic Schipfe area, Schipfe 16 is a good-natured canteen-style spot in an unbeatable location on the river. Enjoy one of three daily menus (made with seasonal locally sourced ingredients) at outdoor tables.

Restaurant Brasserie Johanniter   SWISS €

(www.johanniter.com; Niederdorfstrasse 70; mains Sfr14-35; ⏱10am-midnight) In the very heart of the old town, this century-old traditional beer hall serves up Swiss standards (think lots of pork, veal and potatoes). There is a long list of daily specials and you can expect a hearty meal no matter what you order. Modestly sized, there is a suitably excellent selection of fresh beers available by the stein.

Kronenhalle   BRASSERIE €€€

(📞044 251 66 69; Rämistrasse 4; mains Sfr32-87; ⏱noon-11pm) A haunt of city movers-and-shakers in suits, the Crown Hall is a brasserie-style establishment with an old-world feel, white tablecloths and lots of dark wood. Impeccably mannered waiters move discreetly below Chagall, Miró, Matisse and Picasso originals.

Café Sprüngli   SWISS €

(📞044 224 47 31; www.spruengli.ch; Bahnhofstrasse 21; mains Sfr9-15; ⏱8am-5pm) Indulge in cakes, chocolate and coffee at this epicentre of sweet Switzerland, in business since 1836. You can have a light lunch too but, whatever you do, don't fail to check out the chocolate shop heaven around the corner on Paradeplatz.

Lily's   ASIAN €€

(📞044 440 18 85; www.lilys.ch; Langstrasse 197; ⏱11am-midnight) This trendy noodle-bar's convenient location and casual, upbeat atmosphere are fun, while the menu of Asian stir-fries and other classics is excellent. Dine at long tables and expect waits at prime times.

My Place   CAFE €

(www.myplacedesign.ch; Hottingerstrasse 4; meals from Sfr9; ⏱8am-10pm; 🔊) Ideally located close to the Kunsthaus, this sprightly cafe has excellent coffees and fresh fruit juices. It also has daily lunch specials that are healthy and seasonal.

Sternen Grill   SWISS €

(Theatrestrasse 22; snacks from Sfr7; ⏱11.30am-midnight) This is the city's most famous – and busiest – sausage stand; just follow the crowds streaming in. The classic *Kalbsbratwurst mit Gold Bürli* (veal sausage with bread roll) costs Sfr7. There are a few vegetarian options too.

🍷 Drinking & Entertainment

Options abound across town, but the bulk of the more animated drinking dens are in Züri-West, especially along Langstrasse in Kreis 4 and Hardstrasse in Kreis 5.

Züritipp (www.zueritipp.ch) comes out on Thursdays with the *TagesAnzeiger* newspaper, which is jammed with info about what's on.

Café Odeon   BAR

(📞044 251 16 50; www.odeon.ch; Am Bellevueplatz; ⏱9am-late) This one-time haunt of Lenin and the Dadaists is still a prime people-watching spot for gays and straights alike. Come for the art-nouveau interior, the OTT chandeliers and a whiff of another century. It serves food too.

Longstreet Bar   BAR

(📞044 241 21 72; www.longstreetbar.ch; Langstrasse 92; ⏱8pm-late Tue-Sat) The Longstreet is a music bar with a varied roll call of DJs coming in and out. Try to count the thousands of light bulbs in this purple-felt-lined one-time cabaret.

Café des Amis   CAFE

(www.desamis.ch; Nordstrasse 88; ⏱8am-late Tue-Fri, 9am-1am Sat, to 6pm Sun) A good weekend brunch stop (until 4pm), this is above all a popular new place to hang out and drink anything from coffee to cocktails. In summer, spread out in the generous, cobbled terrace area.

Barfussbar   BAR

(Barefoot Bar; 📞044 251 33 31; www.barfussbar.ch; Stadthausquai 12; ⏱11.30am-late Mon-Fri, 2pm-2am Sat, 3.30-11.30pm Sun) One of the first gay bars in the country and still going strong, Barfussbar now incorporates a sushi bar and has mellowed over the years – gays and straights feel equally at home.

Supermarket   CLUB

(📞044 440 20 05; www.supermarket.li; Geroldstrasse 17; ⏱11pm-late Thu-Sat) Looking like an

DON'T MISS

ZÜRI-WEST

The reborn part of the city, known as Züri-West and stretching west of the Hauptbahnhof, is primarily made up of two former working-class districts: Kreis 4 and Kreis 5. At night, it becomes a hedonists' playground.

Kreis 4, still a red-light district and centred on Langstrasse south of the tracks, is lined with eateries, bars and tawdry shops.

Langstrasse continues north over the railway lines into Kreis 5, where it quietens down a little but still offers plenty of options. The main focus of Kreis 5 action is along what promoters have dubbed the **Kulturmeile** (Culture Mile; www.kulturmeile.ch), Hardstrasse.

innocent little house, Supermarket boasts three cosy lounge bars around the dance floor, a covered back courtyard and an interesting roster of DJs playing house and techno. The crowd tends to be mid-20s. Take a train from Hauptbahnhof to Hardbrücke.

Kaufleuten   CLUB
(☎044 225 33 22; Pelikanplatz 18; ☺11pm-late Thu-Sat) An opulent art-deco theatre with a stage, mezzanine floor and bars arranged around the dance floor, Zürich's 'establishment' club plays house, hip hop and Latin rhythms to a slightly older crowd.

Moods   BLUES, JAZZ
(☎044 276 80 00; www.moods.ch; Schiffbaustrasse 6; ☺7.30pm-midnight Mon-Thu, to late Fri & Sat, 6-10pm Sun) One of the city's top jazz spots, although other musical genres such as Latin and world music grab the occasional spot on its calendar.

Tonhalle   CLASSICAL MUSIC
(☎044 206 34 34; www.tonhalle-orchester.ch; Claridenstrasse 7) An opulent venue used by Zürich's orchestra and chamber orchestra.

🛍 Shopping

For high fashion, head for Bahnhofstrasse and surrounding streets. Across the river, funkier boutiques are dotted about the lanes of Niederdorf. For grunge, preloved gear and some none-too-serious fun young stuff, have a stroll along Langstrasse in Kreis 4.

ℹ Information

Post Office (☺7am-9pm) Located inside the train station.

Zürich Tourism (☎044 215 40 00, hotel reservations 044 215 40 40; www.zuerich.com; ☺8am-8.30pm Mon-Sat, 8.30am-6.30pm Sun) Offers walking tours (Sfr25) most mornings at 11am. Located inside the train station.

ZürichCard (adult/child 24hr Sfr20/14, 72hr Sfr40/28) Excellent-value discount card available from the tourist office and airport train station. Provides free public transport, free museum admission and more.

ℹ Getting There & Away

AIR Zürich airport (ZRH; ☎043 816 22 11; www.zurich-airport.com), 10km north of the centre, is Switzerland's main airport.

TRAIN Zürich has services to all neighbouring countries. Destinations include Milan (4¼ hours), Munich (four hours), Paris (four hours) and Vienna (eight hours).

There are regular direct departures to most major Swiss towns, such as Basel (Sfr32, one hour), Bern (Sfr49, one hour), Geneva (Sfr84, 2¾ hours), Lucerne (Sfr24, one hour) and Lugano (Sfr62, 2¾ hours).

ℹ Getting Around

TO/FROM THE AIRPORT Up to nine trains an hour run each direction between the airport and the main train station (Sfr7, nine to 13 minutes). Most continue on to cities such as Lucerne and Geneva.

BICYCLE City bikes (www.zuerirollt.ch) can be picked up from the station at **Velogate** (☺8am-9.30pm) for free day use; if you keep it overnight it costs Sfr10.

BOAT Lake steamers (☎044 487 13 33; www.zsg.ch) run between April and October. They leave from Bürkliplatz. A small circular tour (Kleine Rundfahrt) takes 1½ hours (adult/child Sfr8.20/4.10) and departs every 30 minutes between 11am and 7.30pm. There are longer tours too.

PUBLIC TRANSPORT The comprehensive, unified bus, tram and S-Bahn **public transit system** (ZVV; www.zvv.ch) includes boats plying the Limmat River. Short trips under five stops are Sfr2.40; typical trips are Sfr4.20. A 24-hour pass for the city centre is Sfr8.40.

NORTHERN SWITZERLAND

This region is left off most people's Switzerland itineraries – which is precisely why you should visit! Sure, it is known for industry and commerce, but it also has some great attractions. Breathe in the sweet (OK slightly stinky) odours of black-and-white cows as you roll through the bucolic countryside. Take time to explore the tiny rural towns set among green rolling hills, and on Lake Constance (Bodensee) and the Rhine (Rhein) River on the German border.

Basel

POP 170,600

Basel is the closest Switzerland comes to having a seaport; the Rhine is navigable for decent-sized ships from this point until it reaches the North Sea in the Netherlands. Basel's year-round attractions, including the engaging Old Town, are mostly concentrated in Grossbasel (Greater Basel) on the south bank of the Rhine.

Sights & Activities

TOP CHOICE Old Town · HISTORIC AREA

The medieval Old Town in the heart of Basel is a delight. Start in **Marktplatz**, which is dominated by the astonishingly vivid red facade of the 16th century **Rathaus** (town hall). Just north, the Fischmarktplatz features the Gothic **Fischmarktbrunnen**, a splendid medieval fountain.

A walk about 400m west of Marktplatz through the former artisans' district along Spalenberg leads uphill to the 600-year-old **Spalentor** city gate, one of only three to survive the wall's demolition in 1866.

The narrow lanes that riddle the hillside between Marktplatz and the Spalentor form the most captivating part of old Basel. Lined by impeccably maintained, centuries-old houses, lanes like Spalenberg, Heuberg and Leonhardsberg are worth a gentle stroll.

TOP CHOICE Fondation Beyeler · GALLERY

(☑061 645 97 00; www.fondationbeyeler.ch; Baselstrasse 101, Riehen; adult/child Sfr25/6; ☺10am-6pm, to 8pm Wed) The art space to really knock your socks off is the Fondation Beyeler, housed in an open-plan building by Italian architect Renzo Piano. The quality of its 19th- and 20th-century paintings is matched only by the way Miró and Max Ernst sculptures are juxtaposed with similar tribal figures. Take tram 6 to Riehen.

Historisches Museum Basel · MUSEUM

(Basel History Museum; ☑061 205 86 00; www.hmb.ch; Barfüsserplatz; adult/child Sfr12/free;

☺10am-5pm Tue-Sun) Housed in the former Barfüsserkirche (the Barefooted Ones Church, after the barefoot Franciscan friars who founded it in the 14th century), the collections of the history museum include pre-Christian-era archaeological finds, a collection of religious objects from the cathedral and plenty of material documenting the city's development.

Kunstmuseum · GALLERY

(Museum of Fine Arts; ☑061 206 62 62; www.kunstmuseumbasel.ch; St Alban-Graben 16; adult/child Sfr15/free; ☺10am-5pm Tue-Sun) Art lovers can ogle at Switzerland's largest art collection, including works by Klee and Picasso.

Sleeping

Hotels are often full during Basel's trade fairs and conventions, so book ahead. Guests receive a pass for free travel on public transport.

TOP CHOICE Au Violon · HOTEL €

(☑061 269 87 11; www.au-violon.com; Im Lohnhof 4; s/d from Sfr125/150; ❋❸) The doors are one of the few hints that quaint, atmospheric Au Violon was a prison from 1835 to 1995. Most of the rooms are two cells rolled into one and either look onto a delightful cobblestone courtyard or have views of the Münster. Sitting on a leafy hilltop, it also has a well-respected restaurant.

Hotel Stadthof · HOTEL €

(☑061 261 87 11; www.stadthof.ch; Gerbergasse 84; s/d from Sfr80/130; ❸) Book ahead to snag one of nine rooms at this spartan but decent central hotel, located above a pizzeria on an Old Town square. The cheaper rooms share toilet and shower.

Der Teufelhof · BOUTIQUE HOTEL €€

(☑061 261 10 10; www.teufelhof.com; Leonhardsgraben 49; r from Sfr160) 'The Devil's Court' fuses two hotels into one. The Kunsthotel's nine rooms are each decorated by a different artist. The larger Galerie hotel annexe, a former convent, is more about stylish everyday design.

5 Signori · GUESTHOUSE €

(☑061 361 87 73; www.restaurantsignori.ch; Güterstrasse 183; r without bathroom from Sfr90; ❸) Just a 10-minute walk southeast of the train station, this simple but stylish guesthouse is located above an excellent restaurant, known for its freshly sourced ingredients. The rooms share bathrooms and there is a small, private terrace for guests to use.

THE JURA

The grandest towns in this clover-shaped canton are little more than enchanting villages. Deep, mysterious forests and impossible green clearings succeed one another across the low mountains of the Jura, and some 1200km of marked paths across the canton give hikers plenty of scope. This is the place for an escape.

The highlight is St Ursanne, a drop-dead-gorgeous medieval village with a 12th-century Gothic church, 16th-century town gate, clusters of ancient houses and a lovely stone bridge crossing the Doubs River right into the ramparts. Feast on thin crisp *tartes flambées* and apple cake to die for at **Hôtel-Restaurant de la Demi Lune** (032 461 35 31; www.demi-lune.ch; Rue Basse 2; r Sfr60-130).

The unexciting canton capital of Delémont (which is on the Basel–Geneva train line) has trains to St Ursanne (Sfr8, 15 minutes, hourly).

Hotel Krafft
HOTEL €

(061 690 91 30; www.hotelkrafft.ch; Rheingasse 12; s/d from Sfr75/125;) Design-savvy urbanites adore this place. Sculptural chandeliers dangle in the creaky-floored dining room (for fine food) overlooking the Rhine, and stainless-steel ornaments adorn each landing of the spiral staircase.

Basel Backpack
HOSTEL €

(061 333 00 37; www.baselbackpack.ch; Dornacherstrasse 192; dm Sfr32, s/d from Sfr80/100; @) Converted from a factory, this independent 81-bed hostel south of the main train station has cheerful, colour-coded eight-bed dorms and more sedate doubles and family rooms.

✗ Eating & Drinking

Head to the Marktplatz for a daily market and several stands selling excellent quick bites, such as local sausages and sandwiches.

St Alban Stübli
SWISS €€€

(061 272 54 15; www.st-alban-stuebli.ch; St Alban Vorstadt 74; mains Sfr40-60; 11.30am-2pm & 6-10pm Mon-Fri) Set in a lovely quiet street, this is your quintessential cosy local tavern with dim yellow lighting, plenty of timber and fine linen. Food fuses local with French.

Acqua
ITALIAN €€

(061 564 66 66; www.acquabasilea.ch; Binningerstrasse 14; mains Sfr17-42; lunch & dinner Tue-Fri, dinner Sat) For a special experience, head to these converted waterworks beside a quiet stream. The atmosphere is glam post-industrial; the food is Tuscan. Basel's beautiful people drink in the attached lounge-bar.

Zum Roten Engel
CAFE

(061 261 20 08; Andreasplatz 15; mains from Sfr15; 9am-midnight) This student-filled venue, spilling onto an irresistible, tiny cobblestone square, is great for a latte and snacks by day and a glass of wine or three in the evening. It's a temperate way to start the night. Sunday brunch is a treat.

Charon
FRENCH €€€

(061 261 99 80; www.restaurant-charon.ch; Schützengraben 62; mains Sfr40-50; 11.30am-2pm & 5-10pm Mon-Fri May-Sep, Tue-Sun Oct-Apr) In what looks like someone's home, this understated restaurant with art-nouveau decorative touches offers carefully prepared dishes leaning slightly to French tastes. Look for hearty country dishes sourced from the region.

Confiserie Schiesser
CAFE €

(www.confiserie-schiesser.ch; Marktplatz 19; snacks from Sfr5; 8am-6pm) Since 1870, this gemlike bakery and cafe has been creating sweet treats from bonbons to tortes to elaborate cakes. Browse the display cases and then head upstairs to the cafe for light meals and excellent coffee.

☆ Entertainment

Steinenvorstadt and Barfüsserplatz teem with teens and 20-somethings on the weekends. A faint whiff of grunge floats around Kleinbasel, the area around Rheingasse and Utengasse, with a few watering holes and something of a red-light zone to lend it edge.

Bird's Eye Jazz Club
JAZZ

(061 263 33 41; www.birdseye.ch; Kohlenberg 20; 8pm-midnight Tue-Sat Sep-May, Wed-Sat Jun-Aug) This is among Europe's top jazz dens, attracting local and headline foreign acts. Concerts start most evenings at 8.30pm.

Die Kuppel
CLUB

(061 270 99 39; www.kuppel.ch; Binningerstrasse 14; 9pm-late Tue, 10pm-late Thu-Sat) This is an

atmospheric wooden dome with a dance floor and cocktail bar located in a secluded park. Salsa, soul, house and '70s and '80s music are regularly on the bill. The closing time is late and flexible.

🛍 Shopping

The area around Marktplatz and Barfüsserplatz teems with shops, selling everything from fashion to fine foods. Long, pedestrian-only Freie Strasse, which runs southeast from Marktplatz, is lined with stores of all persuasions.

Spalenberg, a lovely climbing lane to explore in its own right, is home to a line-up of intriguing boutiques.

Läckerli Huus   FOOD
(www.laeckerli-huus.ch; Gerbergasse 57) Basel has a signature treat, *Leckerli*, which dates back to the Middle Ages. An oddly crunchy yet chewy biscuit, it combines honey, nuts and citrus flavours. You can buy it all over town but this is the original location of a company that makes the best example.

ℹ Information

Tourist Office (📞061 268 68 68; www.basel.com) The tourist office has branches at SBB Bahnhof (Bahnhof; ⊙8.30am-6pm Mon-Fri, 9am-5pm Sat, to 3pm Sun & holidays) and Stadtcasino (Steinenberg 14; ⊙9am-6.30pm Mon-Fri, to 5pm Sat, 10am-3pm Sun & holidays). The Stadtcasino branch organises two-hour English-language walking tours of the city centre (adult/child Sfr15/7.50), usually starting at 2.30pm Monday to Saturday, May through October, and on Saturdays the rest of the year.

ℹ Getting There & Away

AIR The **EuroAirport** (BSL or MLH; 📞061 325 31 11; www.euroairport.com), 5km northwest of town in France, is the main airport for Basel. It is a hub for easyJet and there are flights to major European cities.

TRAIN Basel is a major European rail hub. The main station, Basel SBB, has TGVs to France (Paris, three hours) and fast ICEs to major cities in Germany. There are frequent services to Freiburg (45 minutes), gateway to the Black Forest.

Services within Switzerland include frequent trains to Bern (Sfr39, one hour) and Zürich (Sfr32, one hour).

ℹ Getting Around

Bus 50 links the airport and Basel SBB (Sfr3.40, 20 minutes). Trams 8 and 11 link the station to Marktplatz (Sfr3.40, day pass Sfr9).

Schaffhausen & the Rhine

Schaffhausen is the kind of quaint medieval town one more readily associates with Germany (perhaps no coincidence given how close the border is). Ornate frescos and oriel windows adorn pastel-coloured houses in the pedestrian-only Altstadt (Old Town).

Prime views preen their feathers atop the 16th-century **Munot fortress** (admission free; ⊙8am-8pm May-Sep, 9am-5pm Oct-Apr), a 15-minute uphill walk through vineyards from town.

Westward along the river on foot (40 minutes) or aboard bus 1 or 6 to Neuhausen is **Rheinfall** (Rhine Falls; www.rhinefalls.ch; 🚌1, 6 or 9 to Neuhausen), waterfalls that, though only 23m tall, are deemed Europe's largest. The amount of water thundering down is extraordinary. Get off one stop after Migross in the centre, then follow signs leading to north bank of river.

The 45km **boat trip** (Untersee und Rhein; 📞052 634 08 88; www.urh.ch; Freier Platz; single Sfr47; ⊙Apr-Oct) from Schaffhausen to Constance (which is an excellent entry point

---

DON'T MISS

ST GALLEN'S TREASURE

St Gallen's 16th-century **Stiftsbibliothek** (abbey library; 📞071 227 34 16; www.stiftsbibliothek.ch; Klosterhof 6d; adult/child Sfr10/7; ⊙10am-5pm Mon-Sat, to 4pm Sun, closed late Nov) is one of the world's oldest and the finest example of rococo architecture. Along with the rest of the monastery complex surrounding it, the library forms a Unesco World Heritage site.

Filled with priceless books and manuscripts painstakingly handwritten by monks during the Middle Ages, it's a dimly lit confection of ceiling frescos, stucco, cherubs and parquetry. Only 30,000 of the total 150,000 volumes are in the library at any one time, and only a handful in display cases, arranged into special exhibitions. If there's a tour guide in the library at the time, you might see the monks' filing system, hidden in the wall panels.

There are regular trains from St Gallen to Bregenz in Austria (Sfr19, 35 minutes) and Zürich (Sfr29, 65 minutes via Winterthur).

into Germany; see p244) sails past one of the Rhine's more beautiful stretches. It passes meadows, castles and ancient villages, including Stein am Rhein, 20km to the east, where you could easily wear out your camera snapping pictures of the buildings in the picture-perfect Rathausplatz.

Direct hourly trains run to/from Schaffhausen and Zürich (Sfr27, 40 minutes to one hour).

Appenzellerland

Appenzellers are firmly rooted in tradition: the village Innerrhoden continues to hold a yearly open-air parliament and didn't permit women to vote until 1991.

Such devotion to rural tradition has an upside: locals go to great lengths to preserve their heritage. This area of impossibly green valleys, thick forests and mighty mountains is dotted with timeless villages and criss-crossed by endless hiking and cycling paths.

The pastel-hued village of Appenzell is a feast for the eyes and the stomach. Behind the gaily decorative coloured facades of its traditional buildings lie cafes, cake shops, cheese shops, delicatessens, butchers and restaurants all offering local specialities.

Hotel Appenzell (071 788 15 15; www.hotel-appenzell.ch; Landsgemeindeplatz; s/d from Sfr130/220; ⊙@) sits in a brightly decorated, typical Appenzeller building and is a solid choice to both sleep and sample seasonal cuisine, including vegetarian dishes and the local strong-smelling Appenzell cheese.

APPENZELL WALKS

Hiking trails abound around Appenzell. One more unusual one is the Barefoot Path from Gonten, 5km west of Appenzell, to Gontenbad (one hour), for which you really don't need shoes – think lush green moors and meadows. In Gontenbad, dip in mud-laden water from the moors at Natur-Moorbad (071 795 31 23; www.naturmoorbad.ch; Gontenbad; admission Sfr30; ⊙closed Tue), a moor bath dating to 1740, whose wholly natural products relieve stress or skin conditions (adding in nettles, ferns and other plants) or simply serve to luxuriate with sweet rose baths (Sfr86 for two).

The train station, 400m from the town centre, is also home to the tourist office (071 788 96 41; www.appenzell.ch; Hauptgasse 4; ⊙9am-noon & 1.30-6pm Mon-Fri, 10am-noon & 2-5pm Sat & Sun Apr-Oct, 9am-noon & 2-5pm Mon-Fri, 2-5pm Sat & Sun Nov-Mar). There is a train to St Gallen (Sfr7.20, 50 minutes, twice hourly).

TICINO

Switzerland meets Italy: the summer air is rich and hot, and the peacock-proud posers propel their scooters in and out of traffic. Italian weather, Italian style. And that's not to mention the Italian ice cream, Italian pizza, Italian architecture and Italian language.

South of the Alps, Ticino (Tessin in German and French) has a distinct look. The canton manages to perfectly fuse Swiss cool with Italian passion, as evidenced by a lusty love for Italian comfort food and full-bodied wines that's balanced by a healthy respect for rules and regulations.

❶ Getting There & Around

TRAIN Ticino is connected by a web of integrated trains (www.arcobaleno.ch; day pass Sfr20.40) that travel to Lugano, Locarno and Bellinzona, and reach into Italy. From Cadenazzo on the Locarno line there are trains to Milan's Malpensa airport (route S30; two hours, every two hours).

For an amazing scenic journey, take the Centovalli Express (www.centovalli.ch) from Locarno to Domodossola in Italy (two hours, hourly), where you can connect to Brig and points north in Switzerland. The views of gorges and rivers are incredible.

Locarno

POP 15,200

The rambling red enclave of Italianate town houses, piazzas and arcades ending at the northern end of Lake Maggiore, coupled with more hours of sunshine than anywhere else in Switzerland, give this laid-back town a summer resort atmosphere.

The lowest town in Switzerland, Locarno seemed like a soothing spot to host the 1925 peace conference that was intended to bring stability to Europe after WWI. It didn't work.

Locarno is on the northeast corner of Lago Maggiore, which mostly lies in Italy's Lombardy region. Navigazione Lago Maggiore (www.navigazionelaghi.it) operates boats across the entire lake.

BELLINZONA'S UNESCO CASTLES

Ticino's capital is a quiet stunner. Strategically placed at the conversion point of several valleys leading down from the Alps, Bellinzona is visually unique. Inhabited since Neolithic times, it is dominated by three grey-stone, fairy-tale medieval castles that have attracted everyone from Swiss invaders to painters such as JMW Turner. Turner may have liked the place, but Bellinzona has a surprisingly low tourist profile, in spite of its castles together forming a Unesco World Heritage site.

The main event is the medieval **Castelgrande** (www.bellinzonaunesco.ch; Mont San Michele; ⊘9am-6pm, later in summer), which is a 10-minute walk from the train station and is reached by an elevator. Skip the dull museum inside and focus on explorations of the ramparts where you can appreciate how these castles formed a strategic barrier to marauders heading up the pass north into Switzerland.

You can also roam the ramparts of the two larger castles; the **Castello di Montebello** (Salita ai Castelli; ☎091 825 13 42; castle admission free, museum adult/concession Sfr5/2; ⊘castle 8am-8pm mid-Mar–Oct, museum 10am-6pm mid-Mar–Oct) is a further 3.5km-hike on. Both castles are in great condition and offer panoramic views of the town and countryside.

The **tourist office** (☎091 825 21 31; www.bellinzonaturismo.ch; Piazza Nosetto; ⊘9am-6pm Mon-Fri, to noon Sat, reduced hours in winter) is in the restored Renaissance town hall in the centre of town.

Bellinzona is on the main train route connecting Zürich to Lugano (Sfr10.20, 22 to 30 minutes) and Italy. Trains also serve Locarno (Sfr8.20, 20 to 25 minutes).

⊙ Sights

Locarno's Italianate Old Town fans out from **Piazza Grande**, a photogenic ensemble of arcades and Lombard-style houses. A craft-and-produce market takes over the square every Thursday.

Santuario della
Madonna del Sasso
SANCTUARY

Don't miss the formidable Madonna del Sasso, located up on the hill, with panoramic views of the lake and town. The sanctuary was built after the Virgin Mary allegedly appeared in a vision in 1480. It features a church with 15th-century paintings, a small museum and several distinctive statues.

There is a funicular from the town centre, but the 20-minute climb is not demanding (take Via al Sasso off Via Cappuccini) and you pass some shrines on the way.

🛏 Sleeping & Eating

Lake Maggiore has a great variety of fresh and tasty fish, including *persico* (perch) and *corigone* (whitefish).

Vecchia Locarno
HOTEL €

(☎091 751 65 02; www.hotel-vecchia-locarno.ch; Via della Motta 10; s Sfr55-90, d Sfr100-140; 🐾) A sunny inner courtyard forms the centrepiece of this laid-back guesthouse. Rooms are bright and simple; the best have views over the Old Town and hills.

Osteria Chiara
ITALIAN €€

(☎091 743 32 96; www.osteriachiara.ch; Vicolo della Chiara 1; mains Sfr16-30; ⊘Tue-Sat; 🛆; 🚌Cannobio) Tucked away on a cobbled lane, this has the cosy feel of a grotto. Sit at granite tables beneath the pergola or at timber tables by the fireplace for homemade pasta. From the lake follow the signs up Vicolo dei Nessi.

ⓘ Getting There & Away

Locarno is well-linked to Ticino and the rest of Switzerland via Bellinzona. The scenic **Centovalli Express** (www.centovalli.ch) runs to Brig via Domodossola in Italy. The train station is five minutes away from Piazza Grande.

Lugano

POP 54,500

There is a distinct vibrant snappiness in the air in Lugano, Switzerland's southernmost tourist town, where visitors unravel the spaghetti maze of cobblestone streets while locals toil queitly in cash-stuffed banks – this is the country's third-most important banking centre.

A sophisticated slice of Italian life with colourful markets, upmarket shops, interlocking *piazze* and lakeside parks, lucky Lugano lounges on the northern shore of Lake Lugano, at the feet of Mts San Salvatore and Bré. It's a superb base for lake trips, water sports and hillside hikes.

◉ Sights & Activities

The **Centro Storico** (Old Town) is a 10-minute walk downhill from the train station; take the stairs or the fun funicular (Sfr1.10).

Wander through the mostly porticoed lanes woven around the busy main square, **Piazza della Riforma** – which is even more lively when the Tuesday- and Friday-morning markets are held. Via Nassa is the main shopping street and boasts a *Vogue*-worthy line-up of high-end stores.

Chiesa di Santa Maria degli Angioli CHURCH (St Mary of the Angel; Piazza Luini; ⊙7am-6pm) This simple Romanesque church contains two frescos by Bernardino Luini dating from 1529. Covering the entire wall that divides the church in two is a grand didactic illustration of the crucifixion of Christ. The closer you look, the more scenes of Christ's Passion are revealed. The power and vivacity of the colours are astounding.

Museo del Cioccolato Alprose MUSEUM (☎091 611 88 88; www.alprose.ch; Via Rompada 36, Caslano; adult/child Sfr3/1; ⊙9am-5.30pm Mon-Fri, to 4.30pm Sat & Sun) Chomp on a chocolate-coated history lesson: watch the sweet substance being made and taste it for free. Get there by the Ferrovia Ponte Tresa train (Sfr7).

Lago Lugano BOAT TOUR (www.lakelugano.ch; tours from Sfr25; ⊙Apr-Oct) Take a boat trip to one of the photogenic villages hugging the gorgeous shoreline – car-free **Gandria** is popular – and feast on traditional Ticinese dishes in your pick of quintessential Ticinese grottos.

🛌 Sleeping

Many hotels close for part of the winter.

TOP CHOICE **Hotel & Hostel Montarina** HOTEL, HOSTEL € (☎091 966 72 72; www.montarina.ch; Via Montarina 1; dm from Sfr27, s Sfr80-90, d Sfr110-130; P⚶🛜🏊) Occupying a bubblegum-pink villa dating to 1860, this hotel and hostel behind

the train station has lingering traces of old-world grandeur. Choose between the dorms in the vaulted basement, wood-floored antique rooms and contemporary rooms with private bathrooms. There's a shared kitchen-lounge, toys to amuse the kids, a swimming pool set in palm-dotted gardens and even a tiny vineyard.

Hotel International au Lac HOTEL €€ (☎091 922 75 41; www.hotel-international.ch; Via Nassa 88; s Sfr120-185, dSfr195-330; ⊙Apr-Oct; ✱🛜🏊) Choose a front room to gaze out across Lago Lugano at this century-old hotel on the lakefront. Rooms are comfortable, with a smattering of antique furniture, and the garden-fringed pool invites relaxation.

Acquarello HOTEL €€ (☎091 911 68 68; www.acquarello.ch; Piazza Cioccaro 9; r Sfr90-190; 🛜) You can't get more central than this modest yet rambling hotel right at the base of the funicular from the train station. Basic rooms may get some noise, but the better ones are bright and some ('superior') have sweeping lake views.

✕ Eating

For pizza or pasta, any of the places around Piazza della Riforma are pleasant and lively. For a salad bar and vegetarian joy, try **Manora** (Piazza Dante Alighieri; ⊙7.30am-9pm; 🍴) restaurant in the Manor department store.

TOP CHOICE **Bottegone del Vino** ITALIAN €€ (☎091 922 76 89; Via Magatti 3; mains Sfr20-45; ⊙11am-11pm Mon-Sat) This is a great place to taste fine local wines over an excellent meal. The menu changes daily and features fresh ingredients sourced locally. Knowledgeable waiters fuss around the tables, only too happy to suggest the perfect Ticino tipple (the basic house red is superb). Try the sublime acacia honey with cheese.

Grand Café Al Porto INTERNATIONAL €€€ (☎091 910 51 30; Via Pessina 3; mains Sfr31-48; ⊙8am-6.30pm Mon-Sat) This cafe, which began life way back in 1803, has several fine rooms for dining inside. Be sure to head upstairs to take a peek into the frescoed Cenacolo Fiorentino, once a monastery dining hall.

Gabbani CAFE, RESTAURANT € (☎091 921 34 70; www.gabbani.com; Piazza Cioccaro 1; meals from Sfr15; ⊙deli 8am-6pm, restaurant until late) This sprawling empire at the base of the funicular has been serving up the best in local food and drink since 1937. There's a bakery, deli (picnics!), food-to-go, cafe, bar and a fine restaurant. Have a morning coffee under the arches with a perfect little pastry. On the high floors there are stylish hotel rooms (from Sfr190).

L'Antica Osteria del Porto SWISS €€
(☑091 971 42 00; Via Foce 9; mains Sfr25-40; ☺9am-11pm Wed-Mon) Set back from Lugano's sailing club, this is the place for local fish and Ticinese dishes like polenta crostini with porcini. The terrace overlooking the Cassarate stream is pleasant, as are the lake views.

🍷 Drinking & Entertainment

Soho Café COCKTAIL BAR
(☑091 922 60 80; Corso Pestalozzi 3; ☺7am-1am Mon-Fri, 7pm-1am Sat) All those good-looking Lugano townies crowd in to this long, orange-lit bar for cocktails. Chilled DJ music creates a pleasant buzz.

New Orleans Club CLUB
(☑091 921 44 77; www.neworleansclublugano.com; Piazza Indipendenza 1; ☺5pm-1am Mon-Sat) A lively spot Thursday to Saturday nights with Latin, hip-hop and disco nights. A good cocktail bar other times.

ℹ Information

The **tourist office** (☑091 913 32 32; www.lugano-tourism.ch; Riva Giocondo Albertolli; ☺9am-7pm Mon-Fri, 10am-5pm Sat & Sun) also runs a seasonal booth at the train station.

ℹ Getting There & Away

Lugano is on the main line between Milan (60 to 90 minutes) and Zürich (Sfr62, 2¾ hours) and Lucerne (Sfr58, 2½ hours).

GRAUBÜNDEN

Don't be fooled by Graubünden's diminutive size on a map. This is topographic origami at its finest. Unfold the rippled landscape to find an outdoor adventurer's paradise riddled with more than 11,000km of walking trails, 600-plus lakes and 1500km of downhill ski slopes – including super swanky St Moritz and backpacker mecca Flims-Laax. You'll hear Italian, German and Romansch (the commonly used *crap* actually means peak).

WORTH A TRIP

BERNINA EXPRESS

The popular **Bernina Express** (www.berninaexpress.ch; ☺mid-May–early Dec) route runs from Lugano to St Moritz (Sfr72, six hours), Davos and the rail hub of Chur (Sfr101, 6½ hours). Fares include obligatory reservations. From Lugano to Tirano (in Italy) a bus is used for the scenic run along Italy's Lake Como.

The train route over the Bernina Pass between Tirano and St Moritz is one of Switzerland's most spectacular and is Unesco-recognised. Some trains feature open-top cars.

Flims-Laax

They say if the snow ain't falling anywhere else, you'll surely find some around Flims-Laax. These towns, along with tiny Falera, 20km west of Chur, form a single ski area known as the **Weisses Arena** (White Arena; www.alpenarena.ch), with 220km of slopes (most above 2000m) catering for all levels. Laax in particular is a mecca for snowboarders, who spice up the local nightlife too. The resort is barely two hours by train and bus from Zürich airport.

🏃 Activities

Ask clued-up snowboarders to rattle off their top Swiss resorts and Laax will invariably make the grade. The riders' mecca boasts both Europe's smallest and largest half-pipe, excellent free-style parks and many off-piste opportunities. Skiers are equally content to bash the pistes in the interlinked resorts. A day pass costs from Sfr70.

The **hiking** network spans 250km. The **Naturlehrpfad circuit** at the summit of Cassons is brilliant for spotting wild Alpine flowers and critters.

Try **river rafting** on a turbulent 17km stretch of the Vorderrhein between Ilanz and Reichenau with **Swissraft** (☑081 911 52 50; www.swissraft.ch; half-/full-day trips from Sfr110/160).

🛏 Sleeping & Eating

Riders Palace HOSTEL €
(☑081 927 97 00; www.riderspalace.ch; Laax Murschetg; dmSfr30-60,dSfr120-280; ☻) This design-focused boutique hostel draws a party-mad

LIECHTENSTEIN

If Liechtenstein (pop 36,400) didn't exist, someone would have invented it. A tiny German-speaking mountain principality (160 sq km) governed by an iron-willed monarch in the heart of 21st-century Europe, it certainly has novelty value. Only 25km long by 12km wide (at its broadest point) – just larger than Manhattan – Liechtenstein is mostly visited by people who want a glimpse of the castle and a spurious passport stamp. Stay a little longer and you can escape into its pint-sized Alpine wilderness.

History

Austrian prince Johann Adam Von Liechtenstein purchased the counties of Schellenberg (1699) and Vaduz (1712) from impoverished German nobles and gave them his name. Long a principality under the Holy Roman Empire, Liechtenstein gained independence in 1866. In 1923, it formed a customs union with Switzerland (today it uses the Swiss franc). Prince Hans Adam II ascended the throne in 1989. In 2003, he won sweeping powers to dismiss the elected government, appoint judges and reject proposed laws. The following year, he handed the day-to-day running of the country to his son Alois.

Vaduz

Vaduz is a postage-stamp-sized city with a postcard-perfect backdrop. Crouching at the foot of forested mountains, hugging the banks of the Rhine and crowned by a turreted castle, its location is visually stunning.

The centre itself is curiously modern and sterile, with its mix of tax-free luxury-goods stores and cube-shaped concrete buildings. Yet just a few minutes' walk brings you to traces of the quaint village that existed just 50 years ago and quiet vineyards where the Alps seem that bit closer.

Vaduz Castle is closed to the public, but is worth the climb for the vistas. Trails climb the hill from the end of Egertastrasse. To see how Vaduz once looked, amble northeast to Mitteldorf. This and the surrounding streets form a charming quarter of traditional houses and rose-strewn gardens.

---

crowd of young riders to its strikingly lit, bare concrete spaces. Choose between basic five-bed dorms, slick rooms with Philippe Starck tubs, and hi-tech suites complete with PlayStation and Dolby surround sound. It's 200m from the Laax lifts.

Posta Veglia HISTORIC HOTEL **€€**
(☑081 921 44 66; www.postaveglia.ch; Via Principala 54, Laax; s/d from Sfr150/250; ☎) Today this 19th-century post office delivers discreet service and rustic flavour. The seven country-cottage-style rooms and suites are filled with beams, antiques and mod cons like DVD players. The restaurant has creative takes on fusion cuisine.

ℹ Information

The main **tourist office** (☑081 920 92 00; www.alpenarena.ch; Via Nova; ⊗8am-6pm Mon-Fri, 8am-noon Sat mid-Jun–mid-Aug, 8am-5pm Mon-Sat mid-Dec–mid-Apr) is in Flims.

ℹ Getting There & Away

Postal buses run to Flims and the other villages in the White Arena area hourly from the rail hub of Chur (to Flims-Dorf Sfr13.20, 35 minutes). A free local shuttle bus connects the various villages.

St Moritz

POP 5200

Switzerland's original winter wonderland and the cradle of Alpine tourism, St Moritz (San Murezzan in Romansch) has been luring royals, celebrities and moneyed wannabes since 1864. With its shimmering aquamarine lake, emerald forests and aloof mountains, the town looks a million dollars.

Yet despite the string of big-name designer boutiques on Via Serlas and celebs bashing the pistes, this resort isn't all show. The real riches lie outdoors with superb carving on Corviglia, hairy black runs on Diavolezza and miles of hiking trails when the snow melts.

Historic and creakily elegant, the six-century-old **Gasthof Löwen** (☑238 11 41; www.hotel -loewen.li; Herrengasse 35; s/d from Sfr200/300; **P**🗋) has eight spacious rooms with antique furniture and modern bathrooms. There's a cosy bar, fine-dining restaurant and outdoor terrace overlooking grapevines.

Creaking wood floors and lilac walls create a rustic-chic backdrop for Swiss classics and Vaduz wines at the **Adler Vaduz** (☑232 21 31; www.adler.li; Herrengasse 2; mains Sfr18-50; ☺lunch & dinner Mon-Fri).

Around Vaduz

Outside Vaduz the air is crisp and clear with a pungent, sweet aroma of cow dung and flowers. The countryside is dotted with tranquil villages and enticing churches set to a craggy Alps backdrop.

Triesenberg, on a terrace above Vaduz, commands excellent views over the Rhine valley. It has a pretty, onion-domed church. Take bus 21 from Vaduz.

There are loads of well-marked **cycling** routes throughout Liechtenstein (look for signs with a cycle symbol; distances and directions will also be included), as well as 400km of **hiking trails**; see www.wanderwege-llv.li. The most famous is the **Fürstensteig trail**, a rite of passage for nearly every Liechtensteiner. Falling away to a sheer drop in parts, the four-hour hike begins at the Berggasthaus Gaflei (take bus 22 from Triesenberg).

Information

Liechtenstein's international phone prefix is ☑423. The **Liechtenstein Center** (☑239 63 00; www.tourismus.li; Städtle 37, Vaduz; ☺9am-5pm) offers brochures and souvenir passport stamps (Sfr3), as well as housing the **Philatelie Liechtenstein**, which will interest stamp collectors. The post office is nearby.

The nearest train stations are in the Swiss border towns of Buchs and Sargans. From each of these towns there are frequent buses to Vaduz (from Buchs/Sargans Sfr3.40/5.80; Swiss Pass valid). Buses run every 30 minutes from the Austrian border town of Feldkirch.

🏃 Activities

Skiers and snowboarders will revel in the 350km of runs in three key areas. Avid cross-country skiers can glide through snow-dusted woodlands and plains on 160km of groomed trails.

You can also hike or try your hand at golf (including on the frozen lake in winter), tennis, in-line skating, fishing, horse riding, sailing, windsurfing and river rafting, to mention just a few available activities.

See www.engadin.stmoritz.ch for year-round activities information.

Corviglia & Signal   SKIING
(day pass adult/child from Sfr73/24) For groomed slopes with big mountain vistas, head to Corviglia (2486m), accessible by funicular from Dorf. From Bad a cable car goes to Signal (shorter queues), giving access to the slopes of Piz Nair.

Diavolezza   SKIING
(day pass adult/child from Sfr62/20) Silhouetted by glaciated 4000ers, Diavolezza (2978m) is a must-ski for free-riders and fans of jaw-dropping descents.

🛏 Sleeping & Eating

Hotel Eden   HOTEL €€
(☑081 830 81 00; www.edenstmoritz.ch; Via Veglia 12; s Sfr160-190, d Sfr270-320; 🗋) Right in the heart of town, the Eden centres on an attractive central atrium and antique-strewn lounge where a fire crackles in winter. The old-style, pine-panelled rooms are cosy, and those on the top floor afford terrific lake- and mountain-views.

The Piz   HOTEL, B&B €€
(☑081 832 11 11; www.piz-stmoritz.ch; Via dal Bagn 6; s/d/apt Sfr120/210/500; 🗋) Splashes of crimson, hardwood floors and clean lines define this contemporary B&B in St Moritz Bad. Fitted with rain showers and mod gizmos, the rooms are sleek and comfy, though street noise may disturb light sleepers. The breakfast buffet is good.

WORTH A TRIP

SWISS NATIONAL PARK

The road west from Müstair stretches 34km over the Ofenpass (Pass dal Fuorn, 2149m), through the thick woods of Switzerland's only national park (☉Jun-Oct) and on to Zernez and the hands-on **Swiss National Park Centre** (☎081 851 41 41; www.national park.ch; adult/child Sfr7/3; ☉8.30am-6pm Jun-Oct, 9am-noon & 2-5pm Nov-May). Look for dolomite peaks, shimmering glaciers, larch woodlands, gentian-flecked pastures, clear waterfalls and high moors strung with topaz lakes.

Trains run regularly from Zernez to St Moritz (Sfr18.40, 45 minutes), stopping in scenic S-chanf, Zuoz and Celerina.

Jugendherberge St Moritz　　HOSTEL €
(☎081 836 61 11; www.youthhostel.ch/st.moritz; Stille Via Surpunt 60; dm/d Sfr60/150; @🛜) Budget beds are gold-dust rare in St Moritz, but you'll find one at this hostel edging the forest. The four-bed dorms and doubles are quiet and clean. There's a kiosk, games room and laundrette.

🍴**Hatecke**　　SWISS €€
(☎081 864 11 75; www.hatecke.ch; snacks & mains Sfr15-30; ☉9am-6.30pm Mon-Fri, to 6pm Sat) Organic, locally sourced *Bündnerfleisch* (smoked, air-dried beef) and melt-in-your-mouth venison ham are carved into wafer-thin slices on a century-old machine in this speciality shop. Take a seat on a sheepskin stool in the next-door cafe for a casual lunch.

Engiadina　　SWISS €€
(☎081 833 32 65; www.restaurant-engiadina.ch; Plazza da Scuola 2; fondue Sfr28-48; ☉11am-11pm Tue-Sun, closed May) A proper locals' place, Engiadina is famous for fondue, and that's the best thing to eat here. Champagne gives the melted cheese a kick. The pizza and polenta are also good.

🍷 Drinking

Around 20 bars and clubs pulsate in winter. While you shuffle to the beat, your wallet might also waltz itself wafer-thin: nights out with the glitterati in St Moritz can be expensive.

Bobby's Pub　　PUB
(☎081 834 42 83; Via dal Bagn 50a; ☉9.30am-1.30am) This laid-back and friendly English-style watering hole serves 30 different brews and attracts young snowboarders in season. It's among the few places open year-round.

ⓘ Information

Tourist Office (☎081 837 33 33; www.stmoritz. ch; Via Maistra 12; ☉9am-6.30pm Mon-Fri, 9am-12.30pm & 1.30-6.30pm Sat, 4-6pm Sun, shorter hours rest of year) Uphill from the train station.

ⓘ Getting There & Away

TRAIN Regular hourly trains (Sfr40, two hours) make the scenic run to/from the rail hub of Chur.

St Moritz is also an end point on the much-hyped *Glacier Express* (p539).

The *Bernina Express* (p563) provides seasonal links to Lugano, which include the stunning Unesco-recognised train line over the Bernina Pass to Tirano in Italy.

UNDERSTAND SWITZERLAND

History

The region's first inhabitants were a Celtic tribe, the Helvetii. The Romans arrived in 107 BC via the Great St Bernard Pass, but were gradually driven back by the Germanic Alemanni tribe, which settled in the region in the 5th century AD. Burgundians and Franks also came to the area, and Christianity was gradually introduced.

The territory was united under the Holy Roman Empire in 1032, but central control was never tight, and neighbouring nobles fought each other for local influence. Rudolph I spearheaded the Germanic Habsburg expansion and gradually brought the squabbling nobles to heel.

The Swiss Confederation

Upon Rudolph's death in 1291, local leaders saw a chance to gain independence. The forest communities of Uri, Schwyz and Nidwalden formed an alliance on 1 August 1291, which is seen as the origin of the Swiss Confederation (their struggles against the Habsburgs are idealised in the legend of William Tell). This union's success prompted other communities to join: Lucerne (1332), followed by Zürich (1351), Glarus and Zug (1352), and Bern (1353).

Encouraged by successes against the Habsburgs, the Swiss acquired a taste for territorial expansion and more land was seized. Fribourg, Solothurn, Basel, Schaffhausen and Appenzell joined the confederation, and the Swiss gained independence from the Holy Roman Emperor Maximilian I after their victory at Dornach in 1499.

Eventually, the Swiss over-extended themselves when they took on a superior force of French and Venetians at Marignano in 1515 and lost. Realising they could no longer compete against better-equipped larger powers, they declared their neutrality. Even so, Swiss mercenaries continued to serve in other armies for centuries, and earned an unrivalled reputation for skill and courage.

The Reformation during the 16th century caused upheaval throughout Europe. The Protestant teachings of Luther, Zwingli and Calvin spread quickly, although the inaugural cantons remained Catholic. This caused internal unrest that dragged on for centuries.

The French Republic invaded Switzerland in 1798 and established the Helvetic Republic. The Swiss vehemently resisted such centralised control, causing Napoleon to restore the former confederation of cantons in 1803. Yet France still retained overall jurisdiction.

Following Napoleon's defeat by the British and Prussians at Waterloo, Switzerland finally gained independence.

The Modern State

Throughout the gradual move towards one nation, each canton remained fiercely independent, to the extent of controlling coinage and postal services. The cantons lost these powers in 1848, when a new federal constitution was agreed upon, with Bern as the capital. The Federal Assembly was set up to take care of national issues, but the cantons retained legislative and executive powers to deal with local matters.

Having achieved political stability, Switzerland could concentrate on economic and social matters. Poor in mineral resources, it developed industries dependent on highly skilled labour. A network of railways and roads was built, opening up previously inaccessible regions of the Alps and helping the development of tourism.

The Swiss carefully guarded their neutrality in the 20th century. Their only involvement in WWI was organising units of the Red Cross (founded in Geneva in 1863 by Henri Dunant). Switzerland did join the League of Nations after peace was won, but only on the condition that its involvement was financial and economic rather than military. Apart from some accidental bombing, WWII left Switzerland largely unscathed.

SWITZERLAND HISTORY

IT ALL HAPPENED IN SWITZERLAND

» Albert Einstein came up with his theories of relativity and the famous formula $E=MC^2$ in Bern in 1905.

» Switzerland gave birth to the World Wide Web at the acclaimed CERN (European Organisation for Nuclear Research) institute outside Geneva.

» The first acid trip took place in Switzerland. In 1943 chemist Albert Hofmann was conducting tests for a migraine cure in Basel when he accidentally absorbed the lysergic acid diethylamide, or LSD compound through his fingertips.

» Of the 800 or so films produced by India's huge movie-making industry each year, more are shot in Switzerland than in any other foreign country. 'For the Indian public, Switzerland is the land of their dreams', film star Raj Mukherjee has said. Favourite destination shoots include the Bernese Oberland, Central Switzerland and Geneva.

» Switzerland's central Alpine region possesses one of Europe's richest traditions of myth and legend. Pontius Pilate is said to rise out of the lake on Mt Pilatus, near Lucerne, every Good Friday (the day he condemned Jesus Christ) to wash blood from his hands – and anybody who witnesses this event will allegedly die within the year. Tiny 'wild folk' with supernatural powers, called Chlyni Lüüt, were once reputed to inhabit Mt Rigi, also near Lucerne. Their children's spleens were removed at birth, giving them the ability to leap around mountain slopes.

Forever Neutral: A Nation Apart

Since the end of WWII, Switzerland has enjoyed an uninterrupted period of economic, social and political stability – thanks, in predictable Swiss fashion, to the neutrality that saw it forge ahead from an already powerful commercial, financial and industrial base while the rest of Europe was still picking up and rebuilding the broken pieces from the war. Zürich developed as an international banking and insurance centre, and the World Health Organization and a stash of other international bodies set up headquarters in Geneva. To preserve its much-vaunted neutrality, however, Switzerland opted to remain outside the UN (although Geneva has hosted its second-largest seat after the main New York headquarters from the outset) and, more recently, the European Union.

Then, in the late 1990s, a series of scandals forced Switzerland to begin reforming its famously secretive banking industry. In 1995, after pressure from Jewish groups, Swiss banks announced that they had discovered millions of dollars lying in dormant pre-1945 accounts, belonging to Holocaust victims and survivors. Three years later, amid allegations they'd been sitting on the money without seriously trying to trace its owners, the two largest banks, UBS and Credit Suisse, agreed to pay US$1.25 billion in compensation to Holocaust survivors and their families.

New Millennium

A hefty swing to the conservative right in the 2003 parliamentary elections served to further enhance Switzerland's standing as a nation staunchly apart. In 2006, the anti-EU, anti-immigration Swiss People's Party (SVP) called for the toughening up of immigration and political asylum laws; the policies were passed with an overwhelming majority at national referendum. Then there was the rumpus over its bid to ban building new minarets for Muslim calls to prayer – an idea that aroused much anger internationally, but was approved by the constitution after 57.7% of voters said 'yes' to the ban in a national referendum.

Isolationism aside, there have been concrete signs that Switzerland is opening up to the wider world. The country became the 190th member of the UN in 2002 (a referendum on the issue had last been defeated in 1986), and three years later it voted to join Europe's passport-free travel zone, Schengen (finally completing the process at the end of 2008). In another referendum the same year, the Swiss narrowly voted in favour of legalising civil unions for same-sex couples (but not marriage).

Yet few expect Switzerland to even consider joining either the EU or the euro single-currency zone any time soon (if ever). Traditionally, the western, French-speaking cantons have long desired both, while the German-speaking cantons (and Ticino) have generally been opposed.

Switzerland Today

Peaceful and prosperous, safe and sound, a magnet for the rich and a safe haven for wealth: this privileged land of quality living and global finance, of outdoor magnificence and Alpine aesthetic, found itself the victim of its own success in 2011 and 2012.

The Swiss franc, long recognised as one of the world's most stable currencies, had become so overvalued it was threatening the traditionally robust Swiss economy. So strong was the franc that Swiss exports were falling along with the number of incoming tourists as price-conscious visitors from abroad suddenly realised just how much a cup of coffee in Switzerland was going to cost them.

Even the Swiss were abandoning their local shops and hopping across the borders into cheaper France, Germany and Italy to do their weekly shop. So in 2011 the Swiss National Bank, in an unprecedented move, made the value of the Swiss franc tumble in an instant (by 9% in 15 minutes!) by pegging it at 1.20 to the euro. In the following year, the franc held at this new level, although visitors still reacted with shock at the price of a cup of coffee.

Meanwhile the normally staid world of Swiss banking was roiled by charges of vast scams involving international interest-rate rigging, a leaked list of accounts held by purported Greek tax dodgers and efforts by the German government to investigate similar actions by its citizens.

People

Switzerland's name may stand for everything from knives to watches, but don't expect this nation to take a stand for anyone other than itself. Militarily neutral for centuries, and armed to the teeth to make sure it stays that way, in Switzerland it's the Swiss Way or the highway.

With a population of almost 7.8 million, the country averages 176 people per sq km. Zürich is the largest city, followed by Geneva, Basel and Bern. Most people are of Germanic origin, as reflected in the breakdown of the four national languages. Around 20% of residents in Switzerland are not Swiss citizens.

The Swiss are polite, law-abiding people who usually see no good reason to break the rules. Living quietly with your neighbours is a national obsession. Good manners infuse the national psyche, and politeness is the cornerstone of all social intercourse. Always shake hands when being introduced to a Swiss, and kiss on both cheeks to greet and say goodbye to friends. Don't forget to greet shopkeepers when entering shops. When drinking with the Swiss, always wait until everyone has their drink and toast each of your companions, looking them in the eye and clinking glasses. Drinking before the toast is unforgivable, and will lead to seven years of bad sex...or so the superstition goes. Don't say you weren't warned.

In a few mountain regions such as Valais, people still wear traditional rural costumes, but dressing up is usually reserved for festivals. Yodelling, playing the alphorn and Swiss wrestling are also part of the alpine tradition.

Religion

The split between Roman Catholicism (42%) and Protestantism (35%) roughly follows cantonal lines. Strong Protestant areas include Zürich, Geneva, Vaud, Bern and Neuchâtel; Valais, Ticino, Fribourg, Lucerne and the Jura are predominantly Catholic.

Just over 4% of the population is Muslim.

Arts

Many foreign writers and artists, including Voltaire, Byron, Shelley and Turner, have visited and settled in Switzerland. Local and international artists pouring into Zürich during WWI spawned its Dadaist movement.

Paul Klee (1879–1940) is the best-known native painter. He created bold, hard-lined abstract works, which you can see in Bern and Lausanne. The writings of Genevan philosopher Jean-Jacques Rousseau (1712–78) played an important part in the development of democracy. Critically acclaimed postwar dramatists and novelists Max Frisch (1911–91) and Friedrich Dürrenmatt (1921–90) entertained readers with their dark satire, tragi-comedies and morality plays. On the musical front, Arthur Honegger (1892–1955) is Switzerland's most recognised composer.

The Swiss have made important contributions to graphic design and commercial art. Anyone who's ever used a computer will have interacted with their fonts, from Helvetica to Frutiger to Univers.

The father of modern architecture, Le Corbusier (1887–1965), who designed Notre Dame du Haut chapel at Ronchamps in France, Chandigarh in India and the UN headquarters in New York, was Swiss. One of the most acclaimed contemporary architectural teams on earth, Jacques Herzog and Pierre de Meuron, live and work in Basel. Winners of the prestigious Pritzker Prize in 2001, this pair created London's acclaimed Tate Modern museum building.

Gothic and Renaissance architecture are prevalent in urban areas, especially Bern. Rural Swiss houses vary according to region, but are generally characterised by ridged roofs with wide, overhanging eaves, and balconies and verandahs enlivened by colourful floral displays, especially geraniums.

Environment

Mountains make up 70% of Switzerland's 41,285 sq km. Farming is intensive and cows graze on the upper slopes as soon as the retreating snow line permits.

Europe's highest elevations smugly sit here. The Dufourspitze (4634m) of Monte Rosa in the Alps is Switzerland's highest point, but the Matterhorn (4478m), with its Toblerone-shaped cap is better known. Then of course there's Mont Blanc (4807m), a hulk of a mountain – Europe's highest – shared with France and Italy.

Switzerland's 1800 glaciers cover a 2000-sq-km area, but global warming means they're melting rapidly. The country's most famous mass of ice, rock and snow – the 23km-long Aletsch Glacier – shrunk 114.6m in 2006 alone and could shrink 80% by 2100 if things don't change, say experts. Six hundred people posed nude on the glacier in 2007 for a photo by New Yorker Spencer Tunick as part of a Greenpeace campaign calling for governments worldwide to act quickly.

The St Gotthard Mountains in Central Switzerland are the source of many lakes and rivers, including the Rhine and the Rhône. The Jura Mountains straddle the border with France, and peak at around 1700m. Between the two is the Mittelland, a region of hills also known as the Swiss Plateau, criss-crossed by rivers, ravines and winding valleys.

The ibex, with its huge, curved, ridged horns is the most distinctive alpine animal. In all, some 12,000 of this type of mountain goat roam Switzerland and prime ibex-spotting terrain is the country's only national park (169 sq km), unimaginatively called the Swiss National Park.

Switzerland is extremely environmentally friendly: its citizens produce less than 400kg of waste each per year (half the figure for the USA), are diligent recyclers and are actively encouraged to use public transport. Moreover, pioneering green travel-networks integrate the country's nonmotorised traffic routes: SwitzerlandMobility (www.switzerlandmobility.ch) maps out 169 routes for walkers (6300km), cyclists (8500km), mountain bikers (3300km), roller-bladers or -skaters (1000km) and canoeists (250km) countrywide, all perfectly signposted and easy to follow.

Food & Drink

There is far more to Swiss cuisine than chocolate, cheese and Swiss-German rösti. But the very best of Swiss dining in this essentially rural country is all about the nation's own foods. And you'd be nuts to miss it. While the chic city crowd feasts on international fare, the Swiss kitchen is extraordinarily rich thanks to French, German and Italian influences on the local dishes.

Cheese

First things first: not all Swiss cheese has holes. Emmental, the hard cheese from the Emme Valley east of Bern, does – as does the not dissimilar Tilsiter from the same valley. But, contrary to common perception, most of Switzerland's 450 different types of cheese (*käse* in German, *fromage* in French, *formaggio* in Italian) are hole-less.

Take the well-known hard cheese Gruyère made in the town of Gruyères near Fribourg, or the overwhelmingly stinky Appenzeller used in a rash of tasty, equally strong-smelling dishes in the same-name town in

SWISS CHOCOLATE

The Spanish conquistador Hernando Cortez brought the first load of cocoa to Europe in 1528. He could not have anticipated the subsequent demand for his cargo – especially among visitors! The Spaniards, and soon other Europeans, developed an insatiable thirst for the sweetened beverage produced from it. The solid stuff came later.

Swiss chocolate built its reputation in the 19th century, thanks to pioneering with familiar names such as François-Louis Cailler (1796–1852), Philippe Suchard (1797–1884), Henri Nestlé (1814–90), Jean Tobler (1830–1905), Daniel Peter (1836–1919) and Rodolphe Lindt (1855–1909).

Swiss supermarkets have shelves laden with myriad forms of chocolate at truly reasonable prices. Sample as many as you can.

northeastern Switzerland, or *Sbrinz*, Switzerland's oldest hard cheese and transalpine ancestor to Italian parmesan, ripened for 24 months to create its distinct taste.

Fondue & Raclette

It is hard to leave Switzerland without dipping into a fondue (from the French verb *fondre*, meaning 'to melt'). And you shouldn't! The main French contribution to the Swiss table, a pot of gooey melted cheese is placed in the centre of the table and kept on a slow burn while diners dip in cubes of crusty bread using slender two-pronged fondue forks. Just the sight of the creamy cheese languidly glistening on the bread is enough to make some diners swoon.

The classic fondue mix in Switzerland is equal amounts of Emmental and Gruyère cheese, grated and melted with white wine and a shot of kirsch (cherry-flavoured brandy); order a side platter of cold meats and tiny gherkins to accompany it.

Switzerland's other signature alpine cheese dish is raclette. Unlike fondue, raclette – both the name of the dish and the cheese at its gooey heart – is eaten year-round with boiled potatoes, cold meats and pickled onions or gherkins.

Other Dishes

Be sure not to miss rösti (fried, shredded potatoes). Baked to a perfect crisp, the shredded potato is mixed with seasonal mushrooms and bacon bits to create a perfect lunch, paired with nothing more than a simple green salad.

For a quintessential Swiss lunch, nothing beats an alfresco platter of air-dried beef, a truly sweet and exquisitely tender delicacy from Graubünden that is smoked, thinly sliced and served as *Bündnerfleisch.*

Veal is highly rated and is tasty when thinly sliced and smothered in a cream sauce such as *geschnetzeltes Kalbsfleisch* in Zürich.

Wine & Beer

Wine is considered an essential part of a meal and savouring local wine in Switzerland is an exquisite, gastronomic joy.

The bulk of Swiss wine production takes place in the French-speaking part of the country where vineyards line the shores of Lake Geneva, from where they stagger sharply up hillsides in tightly-packed terraces knitted together by ancient dry-stone walls.

Most of Lake Geneva's winemaking estates are found on either side of Lausanne in the canton of Vaud. Whites from the pea-green terraced vineyards of the Lavaux wine region between Lausanne and Montreux are so outstanding that the area has been designated a Unesco World Heritage site.

Drenched in an extra bonanza of sunshine and light from above the southern Alps, much of the land north of the Rhône River in western Valais is planted with vines – and this is where some of Switzerland's best wines are produced. Dryish white Fendant, the perfect accompaniment to fondue and raclette, and best served crisp cold, is the region's best-known wine. Dôle, made from Pinot noir and Gamay grapes, is the principal red blend and is as full bodied as an opera singer with its firm fruit flavour.

For beer, there are several bland lagers but there is a growing number of microbreweries. Ueli, Rappi, BFM, Felsenau and Trois Dames brew some excellent beers, many seasonal.

SURVIVAL GUIDE

Directory A–Z

Accommodation

From opulent palaces and castles to mountain refuges, nuclear bunkers, icy igloos or simple hay lofts, Switzerland sports traditional and creative accommodation in every price range.

The prices may seem steep – even the most inexpensive places are pricey compared with other parts of Europe. The upside is that standards are usually quite high.

In Switzerland, many budget hotels have cheaper rooms with shared toilet and shower facilities. From there the sky is truly the limit. Breakfast buffets can be extensive and tasty but are not always included in room rates.

When online looking for specials, besides the usual booking websites, take a gander at city and regional tourist authority websites where you can, at times, find excellent special deals.

Rates in cities and towns stay constant most of the year. In mountain resorts prices are seasonal (and can fall by 50% or more outside high season):

Low season mid-September to mid-December, mid-April to mid-June

Mid-season January to mid-February, mid-June to early July, September

High season July to August, Christmas, mid-February to Easter

PRICE RANGES

The following price ranges refer to a double room with a private bathroom, except in hostels or where otherwise specified. Quoted rates are for the high season and don't include breakfast unless otherwise noted.

€ less than Sfr150

€€ Sfr150 to Sfr350

€€€ more than Sfr350

HAY BARNS

If you're looking for a way to experience life on a Swiss farm, **Aventure sur la Paille/Schlaf im Stroh** (☏041 678 12 86; www.schlaf-im-stroh. ch) offers the ultimate adventure. When their cows are out to pasture in summer, or indeed even after they've been brought in for the winter come early October, farmers charge travellers Sfr20 to Sfr30 per adult and Sfr10 to Sfr20 per child to sleep on straw in their hay barns or lofts. Cotton undersheets and woolly blankets are provided, but guests need their own sleeping bags and pocket torch. Nightly rates include a farmhouse breakfast; showers and evening meals are extras.

HOSTELS

Switzerland has two types of hostels: Swiss Youth Hostels (SYHA; www.youthhostel.ch), affiliated with Hostelling International (HI), where nonmembers pay an additional 'guest fee' of Sfr6, and independent hostels which can be more charismatic. Prices listed for SYHA hostels may not include the guest fee. On average a dorm bed in either type costs Sfr31 to Sfr40, including sheets.

Backpacker hostels tend to be more flexible in their regulations, reception times and opening hours, and are usually free of school or youth groups. Membership is not required; over 30 such hostels are loosely affiliated under Swiss Backpackers (033 823 46 46; www.swissbackpackers.ch).

There are another 80 hostels in the shape of alpine chalets or rural farmhouses that offer hostel-style accommodation under the green umbrella group Naturfreundehaus (Friends of Nature; www.nfhouse.org).

Activities

There are dozens of ski resorts throughout the Alps, pre-Alps and Jura, and 200-odd different ski schools. Equipment hire is available at resorts, and ski passes allow unlimited use of mountain transport.

There is simply no better way to enjoy Switzerland's spectacular scenery than to walk through it. There are 50,000km of designated paths, often with a convenient inn or cafe located en route. Yellow signs marking the trail make it difficult to get lost, and each provides an average walking time to the next destination. Slightly more strenuous mountain paths have white-red-white markers. The Schweizer Alpen-Club (SAC; 031 370 18 18; www.sac-cas.ch; Monbijoustrasse 61, Bern) maintains huts for overnight stays at altitude and can also help with extra information.

Business Hours

The reviews in this chapter don't list hours unless they differ from the hours listed here.

Hours are given for the high season (April through October) and tend to decrease in the low season.

Banks 8.30am-4.30pm Mon-Fri, usually with late opening hours one day a week.

Offices 8am-noon & 2-5pm Mon-Fri.

Post Offices 7.30am-noon & 2-6.30pm Mon-Fri, to 11am Sat (typically; however, opening times vary).

Restaurants noon-2pm & 6-10pm.

Shops 9am-7pm Mon-Fri (sometimes with a one- to two-hour break for lunch at noon in small towns), 9am-6pm Sat. In cities, there's often shopping until 9pm on Thursday or Friday. Sunday sees some souvenir shops and supermarkets at some train stations open.

Discount Cards

Regular or long-term visitors to Switzerland may want to buy the **Swiss Museum Pass** (www.museumspass.ch; adult/family Sfr144/255), which covers entry to the permanent collection (only) of 450 museums.

In many resorts and cities there's a **visitors' card** (*Gästekarte*), which provides various benefits such as reduced prices for museums, swimming pools, public transport or cable cars. Cards are issued by your accommodation.

Electricity

The electricity current is 220V, 50Hz. Swiss sockets are recessed, three-holed, hexagonally shaped and incompatible with many plugs from abroad. They sometimes, however, take the standard European two-pronged plug.

Embassies & Consulates

For a list of embassies and consulates in Switzerland, go to www.eda.admin.ch. Embassies are in Bern but cities such as Zürich and Geneva have consulates.

Food

The following price ranges refer to a two-course meal.

€ less than Sfr25

€€ Sfr25 to Sfr45

€€€ more than Sfr45

THREE LANGUAGES

Located in the corner of Europe where Germany, France and Italy meet, Switzerland is a linguistic melting pot with three official federal languages: German (spoken by 64% of the population), French (19%) and Italian (8%). Swiss 'German' speakers write standard or 'high' German, but speak their own language: Schwyzertütsch has no official written form and is mostly unintelligible to outsiders.

A fourth language, Romansch, is spoken by less than 1% of the population, mainly in the canton of Graubünden. Derived from Latin, it's a linguistic relic that has survived in the isolation of mountain valleys. Romansch was recognised as a national language by referendum in 1938 and given federal protection in 1996.

English-speakers will have few problems being understood in the German-speaking parts. However, it is simple courtesy to greet people with the Swiss-German *grüezi* and to enquire *Sprechen Sie Englisch?* (Do you speak English?) before launching into English. In French Switzerland you shouldn't have too many problems either; in Italian-speaking Switzerland, people are more monolingual but you'll still encounter plenty of English-speakers.

Language Areas

Gay & Lesbian Travellers

Attitudes towards homosexuality are reasonably tolerant in Switzerland. Zürich and Geneva have particularly lively gay scenes.

Online resources:

Cruiser Magazine (www.cruiser.ch)

Pink Cross (www.pinkcross.ch)

Internet Access

Internet access in Switzerland – like most things – is expensive. Public wi-fi can easily cost Sfr5 for 30 minutes. Free hotspots are comparatively rare, even at cafes.

Maps

There's one great deal in Switzerland: maps. They are copious, beautifully detailed, lav-ishly rendered and given away for free at tourist offices.

Money

ATMs Automated teller machines (ATMs) – called Bancomats in banks and Postomats in post offices – are common.

Cash Swiss francs are divided into 100 centimes (*Rappen* in German-speaking Switzerland). There are notes for 10, 20, 50, 100, 200 and 1000 francs, and coins for 5, 10, 20 and 50 centimes, as well as for one, two and five francs. Euros are accepted by many tourism businesses.

Credit Cards The use of credit cards is slightly less widespread than in the UK or

USA and not all shops, hotels or restaurants accept them.

Moneychangers Exchange money at large train stations.

Tipping Not necessary, given that hotels, restaurants, bars and even some taxis are legally required to include a 15% service charge in bills. You can round up the bill after a meal for good service, as locals do.

Post

Postcards and letters sent to Europe cost Sfr1.30/1.20 priority/economy; to elsewhere they cost Sfr1.80/1.40.

Public Holidays

New Year's Day 1 January

Easter March/April (Good Friday, Easter Sunday and Monday)

Ascension Day 40th day after Easter

Whit Sunday & Monday Seventh week after Easter

National Day 1 August

Christmas Day 25 December

St Stephen's Day 26 December

Telephone

» The country code for Switzerland is ☎41. When calling Switzerland from abroad, drop the initial zero from the number; hence to call Bern, dial ☎41 31 (preceded by the overseas access code of the country you're dialling from).

» The international access code from Switzerland is ☎00. To call Britain (country code ☎44), start by dialling ☎00 44

» Telephone numbers with the code ☎0800 are toll-free; those with ☎0848 are charged at the local rate. Numbers beginning with 156 or 157 are charged at the premium rate.

» Mobile phone numbers start with the code ☎076, ☎078 or ☎079.

» SIM cards are widely available from train station ticket counters, exchange bureaus and mobile telephone shops. Several providers offer the same good deal: €20 for a SIM card that comes with €20 credit.

Tourist Information

Make the Swiss tourist board **Switzerland Tourism** (www.myswitzerland.com) your first port of call. Local tourist offices are extremely helpful and have reams of literature to give out, including maps (nearly always free).

Visas

For up-to-date details on visa requirements, go to the **Swiss Federal Office for Migration** (www.eda.admin.ch) and click 'Services'.

Visas are not required for passport holders from the UK, EU, Ireland, the USA, Canada, Australia, New Zealand, South Africa, Norway and Iceland.

Getting There & Away
Air

The main international airports:

Aéroport International de Genève (GVA; ☎0900 571 500; www.gva.ch) The country's second airport has decent international links.

EuroAirport (MLH or BSL; ☎+33 3 89 90 31 11; www.euroairport.com) France-based, serving Basel as well as Mulhouse in France and Freiburg, Germany. Has regional flights around Europe.

Zürich Airport (ZRH; ☎043 816 22 11; www.zurich-airport.com) Switzerland's main airport has flights to/from destinations worldwide. For flight information, SMS ZHR plus your flight number to ☎92 92.

Lake

Switzerland can be reached by ferry over several lakes.

Lake Constance (☎071 466 78 88; www.sbsag.ch) Austria (☎05574 42868; www.bodenseeschifffahrt.at; Austria); Germany (☎07531 3640 389; www.bsb-online.com; Germany)

Lake Geneva (☎0848 811 848; www.cgn.ch) From France.

Lago Maggiore (☎091 751 61 40; www.navigazionelaghi.it) From Italy.

Land
BUS

Eurolines (www.eurolines.com) has buses with connections across Western Europe.

CAR & MOTORCYCLE

There are fast, well-maintained highways to Switzerland through all bordering countries. The Alps present a natural barrier to entering Switzerland, so main roads gener-

PASSES & DISCOUNTS

Convenient discount passes make the Swiss transport system even more appealing. On extensive travel within Switzerland the following national travel passes generally offer better savings than Eurail or InterRail passes.

Swiss Pass The Swiss Pass entitles the holder to unlimited travel on almost every train, boat and bus service in the country, and on trams and buses in 41 towns, plus free entry to 400-odd museums. Reductions of 50% apply on funiculars, cable cars and private railways. Different passes are available, valid between four days (1st/2nd class US$460/288) and one month.

Swiss Flexi Pass This pass allows you to nominate a certain number of days (anywhere from three to six) during a month when you can enjoy unlimited travel.

Half-Fare Card Almost every Swiss owns one of these. As the name suggests, you pay only half the fare on trains with this card, plus you get some discounts on local-network buses, trams and cable cars. An adult one-year Half-Fare Card costs Sfr175 (photo necessary).

Swiss Card A variation on the Half-Fare Card that includes a round-trip ticket to/from a border area and is good for 30 days. It is sold abroad for US$300/200 1st/2nd class.

Junior Card The Sfr30 card gets free travel (on trains, buses and boats, even on some cable cars) for those aged six to 16 years when travelling with at least one of their parents. Children within that age bracket travelling with an adult who is not a relative get 50% off.

Regional Passes Network passes valid only within a particular region are available in several parts of the country. Such passes are available from train stations in the region.

ally head through tunnels. Smaller roads are more scenically interesting, but special care is needed when negotiating mountain passes.

TRAIN

Located in the heart of Europe, Switzerland is a hub of train connections to the rest of the continent. Zürich is the busiest international terminus, with service to all neighbouring countries. Destinations include Milan (4¼ hours), Munich (four hours) and Vienna (eight hours).

There are numerous TGV trains daily from Paris to several cities, including Geneva (three hours), Lausanne (3¾ hours), Basel (three hours) and Zürich (four hours). Basel is a hub for services to Germany: fast ICE trains serve most major German cities. An easy way into Germany from Zürich is via medieval Constance (Sfr31, 1¼ hours).

Getting Around

Swiss public transport is an efficient, fully integrated and comprehensive system, which incorporates trains, buses, boats and funiculars.

Marketed as the **Swiss Travel System** (www.swisstravelsystem.com), the network has a useful website and there are excellent free maps covering the country available at train stations and tourist offices.

Bicycle

You can hire bikes from most train stations for about Sfr10 per day. Local tourist offices often have good cycling information.

Boat

Ferries and steamers link towns and cities on many lakes, including Constance, Geneva, Lucerne, Lugano, Murten and Zürich.

Bus

Yellow postal buses are a supplement to the rail network, following postal routes and linking towns to the more inaccessible regions in the mountains. In all, routes cover some 8000km of terrain. Services are regular, and departures link to train schedules. Postbus stations are next to train stations and offer destination and timetable information.

SWITZERLAND'S SCENIC TRAINS

Swiss trains, buses and boats are more than a means of getting from A to B. Stunning views invariably make the journey itself the destination. Switzerland boasts the following routes among its classic sightseeing journeys.

Bear in mind that you can choose just one leg of the trip, and that scheduled services often ply the same routes for standard fares; these are cheaper than the named trains, which often have cars with extra-large windows and require reservations.

Bernina Express A spectacular bus and train journey between Lugano and St Mortiz/Davos/Chur. See p563.

Glacier Express A fabled journey between Zermatt and St Moritz, Chur or Davos. See p539.

Jungfrau Region You can spend days ogling stunning Alpine scenery from the trains, cable cars and more here. See p548.

GoldenPass Line (www.goldenpass.ch) Travels between Lucerne and Montreux in three sections; the Lucerne to Interlaken East leg is especially scenic.

Centovalli Express (www.centovalli.ch) An underappreciated gem of a line (two hours) that snakes along fantastic river gorges in Switzerland and Italy, travelling from Locarno to Domodossola. Trains run through the day and it is easy to connect to Brig and beyond from Domodossola in Italy.

Mont Blanc/St Bernard Expresses (www.tmrsa.ch) From Martigny to Chamonix, France, or over the St Bernard Pass.

Wilhelm Tell Express (www.williamtellexpress.ch; ⊙May-Oct) Begins with a placid 2½-hour cruise from Lucerne to Flüelen, where you get a train for the somewhat scenic run to Locarno and Lugano. This route is easily done with regular services.

Car

The **Swiss Touring Club** (Touring Club der Schweiz; ☑022 417 24 24; www.tcs.ch), Switzerland's largest motoring organisation, has reciprocal agreements with motoring organisations worldwide.

» You do not need an International Driving Permit to operate a vehicle in Switzerland. A licence from your home country is sufficient.

» Be prepared for winding roads, high passes and long tunnels.

» Normal speed limits are 50km/h in towns, 120km/h on motorways, 100km/h on semimotorways (designated by roadside rectangular pictograms showing a white car on a green background) and 80km/h on other roads.

» Mountain roads are well maintained. Some minor Alpine passes are closed from November to May – check with the local tourist offices before setting off.

Train

The Swiss rail network combines state-run and private operations. The **Swiss Federal Railway** (www.rail.ch) is abbreviated to SBB in German, CFF in French and FFS in Italian.

» All major train stations are connected to each other by hourly departures, at least between 6am and midnight, and most long-distance trains have a dining car.

» Second-class seats are perfectly acceptable, but cars are often close to full. First-class carriages are more comfortable, spacious and have fewer passengers.

» Powerpoints for laptops let you work aboard and some seats are in wi-fi hotspots – look for the insignia on the carriage.

» Ticket vending machines accept most major credit cards from around the world.

» Most stations have ticket counters.

» The SBB smartphone app is an excellent resource and can be used to store your tickets electronically.

» Check the SBB website for cheap Supersaver tickets on major routes.

» Most stations have 24-hour lockers (small/large locker Sfr6/9), usually accessible from 6am to midnight.

» Seat reservations (Sfr5) are advisable for longer journeys, particularly in the high season.

Survival Guide

Directory A–Z

Directory A-Z answers questions about Central Europe as a whole. For more detailed country-specific information, look in the Directory at the end of each destination chapter. Facilities vary based on whether you travel in the more westerly (Germany, Austria, Switzerland) or more easterly (Slovakia, Slovenia, Czech Republic, Poland, Hungary) countries of the region.

Accommodation

From splashy five-star hotels to homey pensions, Central Europe has a full range of accommodation. Hostels and student dormitories are more prevalent in cities, while hikers' huts are found only in the mountains. Top-end digs are rarely found outside cities or mountain resorts in the east but are more common in smaller towns of the west.

Accommodation can fill up at popular tourist destinations, especially during Christmas, New Year and Easter; it's advisable to book ahead in those cases. Tourist offices often have extensive accommodation lists and a few will help you book (sometimes for a small fee).

Agencies offering short-stay apartments can provide good value.

More and more accommodation is going smoke-free inside, but a few pensions to the east and south may not have any nonsmoking rooms.

Seasons

May to September Main tourist season.

July to August Peak travel time; expect crowds and book ahead.

October to April Off-season, rates drop dramatically (10% to 50%).

January to March Additional tourist/high season in the mountains.

Christmas, New Year and Easter Prices 20% to 30% higher than tourist season; reservations essential.

Camping

Camping provides the cheapest accommodation across the region, but, in cities, most camping grounds will be some distance from the centre, possibly with limited access by public transport.

» Expect a charge per tent or site, plus per person and per vehicle.

» In the west, well-maintained grounds exist for tents and some campsites offer bungalows, wooden cabins and caravan spaces. Campers are especially well catered for in Germany and Austria.

» In the east, minimal services are the norm; spartan cabins often ring a small open ground for pitching a tent.

» If you're on foot, the money you save by camping can quickly be eaten up by the cost of commuting to and from a town centre.

» It is illegal to camp anywhere but in designated areas in national parks or, with permission, on private property.

» Camping grounds may be open April to October, May to September, or June to August; a few private operations are open year-round.

Farmhouses

Villages or agrotourism (staying at a farmhouse)

PRICE RANGES

Individual price range breakdowns vary by country. In general:

€ Camping, hostel dorms with shared bathrooms; some provincial guesthouses and inns without catering.

€€ Pensions and guesthouses, some with bars or restaurants, and small hotels.

€€€ Upscale boutique properties, business hotels, international chain hotels, ski resorts and almost anything in Switzerland.

offer a distinctly local experience, often in picturesque rural areas. Some work may or may not be expected; in return, you might get fresh milk straight from the cow. In Switzerland, you can also stay in a hay barn. Reaching these remote outposts almost always requires having your own transport.

Guesthouses & Pensions

Small pensions and guesthouses are common in big cities and small villages across Central Europe.

» Priced lower than most hotels, they usually have loads more character. Think flower-fronted chalets or trendy apartment buildings.

» Typically, more personal service is available at a pension than a hotel.

» Most are small with less than a dozen rooms, but some are larger with saunas and other amenities.

» Small restaurants or bars are not uncommon.

» Some sort of breakfast is usually available.

» Wi-fi is widely available.

» More and more places have nonsmoking rooms.

Homestays & Rental Accommodation

Renting rooms in private homes is becoming less common regionwide. You'll find fewer opportunities in the west than in the east. Tourist offices and town websites have contacts of available options; travel agencies can sometimes book accommodation in local homes.

If you're approached at train and bus stations with offers of a room, ask lots of questions or visit the place before you agree.

In holiday villages around parks, lakes and mountains look for houses with 'Zimmer frei', 'sobe', 'privat' or 'szoba kiadó' (in German, Slovene, Slovak or Hungarian); just knock on the door and ask what's available.

Short-term apartment rental is a popular and affordable option. Corporate apartments are more upscale, with laundry facilities, parking, daily cleaning services and a concierge. In general, you can expect the following:

» An unoccupied apartment

» At least a kitchenette, if not a full kitchen

» Rates from €40 to €200 per day

» Room for two to five persons in prime locations

International private home and apartment resources include **Airbnb** (www.airbnb.com) and **Vacation Rental by Owner** (www.vrbo.com).

Hostels

Hostels offer the cheapest (secure) roof over your head in Central Europe and you do not have to be a youngster to take advantage of them. You can expect the following:

» Four to 10 bunks per room, ranging from €15 to €30, private rooms from €40 to €80

» Single and double rooms, where available, often cost as much as a pension

» Amenities often include internet access, a common room, kitchen, personal lockers and shared bathrooms

» Polskie Towarzystwo Schronisk Młodzieżowych (PTSM) hostels in Poland still have daytime lock-outs

» Big city hostels may offer organised tours

Local tourist offices list universities that open student dormitories as hostels in July and August. Other resources include the following:

» **Europe's Famous Hostels** (www.famoushostels.com)

» **Hostelling International** (www.hihostels.com)

» **Hostel World** (www.hostel-world.com)

» **Hostels.com** (www.hostels.com)

» **Hostelz** (www.hostelz.com)

Hotels

» In general, the more facilities (restaurant, swimming pool etc), the higher the rate.

» Wi-fi is widespread, air-conditioning less so (look for ⓦ or ❄ symbols in reviews).

» Hotel parking may be tight or nonexistent in cities.

» Breakfast is often available, if not included in all rates. Ask before you check in; the repast may cost extra but be mandatory.

» Discounts may be available for long stays or large groups.

» In larger places, inquire if there are less-expensive rooms with a washbasin in-room and toilet and shower down the hall.

» Off-season, in the eastern countries in particular, hotel owners may be open to a little bargaining.

Activities

While the cities of Central Europe offer nonstop entertainment, it's in the region's forests, on its lakes and rivers, and atop its mountains where you'll find some of the biggest thrills – and lungfuls of fresh air.

General tour companies include the following:

Backroads (www.backroads.com) Ecosensitive tour company offering a range of biking, hiking and multisport trips in the region.

Adventure Finder (www.adventurefinder.com) Single and multisport trips in Austria, Slovakia, Czech Republic and Germany.

Bird & Animal Watching

The countries of central Europe may not be the world's premier destinations for wildlife watching, but there are a few good sites – especially in Hungary.

TOURS

Ecotours (www.ecotours.hu) Birding, butterfly and wildlife tours in Hungary, Austria, Slovenia, Slovakia and Poland.

Probirder (www.probirder.com) Bird-watching tours in the Czech Republic, Hungary, Poland, Slovakia and Slovenia.

Wings (www.wingsbirds.com) Single-country birding tours in Germany, Austria and the Czech Republic.

RESOURCES

» *Birds of Europe* by Lars Svennson
» *Central and Eastern European Wildlife* by Gerard Gorman
» *Birding in Eastern Europe* by Gerard Gorman

Cycling

Cycling allows you to get up close to the scenery and the local people, keeping you fit in the process. Most airlines and long-distance bus companies transport bicycles. Note that bicycle theft can be an issue in cities. In the mountainous regions it can be heavy going, but this is offset by the dense concentration of things to see.

Hiking

Keen hikers can spend a lifetime exploring Central Europe's many trails. The mountains in Switzerland, Austria, Slovenia, Slovakia and Poland, especially, are criss-crossed with clearly marked paths and offer rewarding challenges for everyone from beginners to experts. Ramblers Holidays (www.ramblersholidays.co.uk) offers single-country hiking tours in Germany, Austria, Switzerland, Poland and Hungary.

» Public transport and cable cars will often get you to trailheads.

» Lodging and basic meals are often available at hikers' huts (may be a dorm-filled shack or hotel-like chalet).

» For high mountain hiking, July to early September; in lower ranges and forests, May through October.

DIFFICULTY INDICATORS

Red-white-red marker You need sturdy hiking boots and a pole.

Blue-white-blue marker Indicates the need for mountaineering equipment.

Skiing & Snowboarding

Central Europe is the continent's ski capital. Ski resorts in the Swiss Alps offer world-class facilities – and vistas that are incomparable in the region – but they are also the most expensive. Austria is generally slightly cheaper than Germany and Switzerland. A general rule of thumb is that the further east you travel, the less expensive the skiing.

» Ski season runs early December to late March; at higher altitudes it may extend an extra month either way.

» Snow conditions vary greatly from year to year and region to region, but January and February tend to be the best (and busiest).

Business Hours

Offices Closed Saturday and Sunday (including some tourist offices off-season).

Museums & Castles Closed Monday; may be closed additional days or completely from October through to April.

Banks & Post Offices Open 9am to 5pm Monday to Friday; may also be open on Saturday mornings.

Shops Open until 6pm or 7pm, some closed Sundays; megamarts never shut their doors.

Children

Central Europe is a great place to bring the young ones. There are well-established attractions geared towards children of all ages, especially in the more western countries. Lonely Planet's *Travel with Children* is an excellent general resource and includes topics ranging from children's health to games that will keep the kids amused.

» Highchairs, kids' menus and play areas are more common in restaurants in the western countries of the region.

» Cribs and cots are widely available in hotels and pensions.

» Most car-hire firms provide children's safety seats for a fee; they must be booked in advance.

» Selection of baby food, infant formulas, soy and cow's milk, disposable nappies (diapers) and the like is better in large cities than smaller ones.

Customs Regulations

Unless you cross the border into non-EU countries, you are generally unlikely to be subjected to a search. Duty-free goods are no longer sold to those travelling from one EU country to another.

For duty-free goods that are purchased at airports or on ferries outside the EU, the usual allowances apply:

Tobacco 200 cigarettes, 50 cigars or 250g of loose tobacco

Alcohol 1L of spirits or 2L of liquor with less than 22%

alcohol by volume; and 2L of wine

Perfume 50g of perfume and 250ml of eau de toilette

The following are the allowances for duty-*paid* items bought for personal use at normal shops and supermarkets:

Tobacco 800 cigarettes, 200 cigars or 1kg of loose tobacco

Alcohol 10L of spirits, 20L of fortified wine or aperitif, 90L of wine or 110L of beer

Perfume Unlimited quantities

Discount Cards

Note that seniors aged over 60 or 65 and students with ID may receive a discount at museums, sights and recreational facilities.

Camping Card International (CCI; www.campingcardinternational.com) Discount of 5% to 10% at affiliated camping grounds. Issued by camping federations, automobile associations and some campsites. May eliminate the need to leave your passport at reception.

Hostelling International Card (www.hihostels.com) Provides discounts at affiliated hostels, rarely mandatory, usually can be bought on-site.

International Student Identity Card (ISIC; www.isic.org) ID-style card with photograph. Provides discounts on various transport, sight admissions and inexpensive meals in some student cafeterias and restaurants. Teachers can get the International Teachers Identity Card (ITIC).

International Youth Travel Card (IYTC; www.myisic.com) Similar discounts and benefits as ISIC for non-students under age 26.

Euro26 Card (www.euro26.org) Discounts for non-students aged under 26.

Electricity

Check the voltage and cycle (usually 50Hz) used in your home country and your appliance. Modern battery chargers and electronic-device power supplies will *usually* adjust voltage automatically. Otherwise, don't mix 110/125V with 220/240V without a transformer.

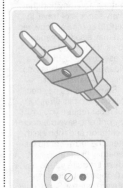

230V/50Hz

Embassies & Consulates

It's important to realise what your embassy can and cannot do for you while abroad. If you have all your money and documents stolen, it might assist with getting a new passport, but a loan for onward travel is almost always out of the question. Generally speaking, they won't be much help if you're in trouble that is remotely your own fault; you are bound by the laws of the country you are visiting.

Nations such as Australia, Canada, New Zealand and the US have embassies and consulates across Central Europe in capitals and major cities. You can find locations using these websites:

EMERGENCY NUMBERS

The EU-wide general emergency number is 112; Liechtenstein and Switzerland also use this number.

Australia (www.dfat.gov.au)
Canada (www.international.gc.ca)
New Zealand (www.mfat.govt.nz)
United Kingdom (www.fco.gov.uk)
United States (www.travel.state.gov)

Gay & Lesbian Travellers

Local attitudes towards public displays of same-sex affection vary widely among countries, and between large, urban centres and smaller, rural areas. Berlin, Munich and Vienna have vibrant and active gay scenes. It's a different story in the eastern countries of the region: most capital cities there have small gay scenes centred on one or two bars or clubs. Gay and lesbian venues are almost nonexistent outside urban centres.

Damron (www.damron.com) The USA's leading gay publisher offers guides to world cities.

International Gay & Lesbian Travel Association (www.iglta.org) Worldwide gay- and lesbian-friendly business listings (including accommodation and services); travel agent.

Spartacus International Gay Guide (www.spartacusworld.com) A male-only directory of gay entertainment venues.

Health

It is unlikely that you will encounter unusual health

problems in Central Europe, and if you do, standards of care are world-class. It's also important to have health insurance for your trip.

» Bring medications in their original, clearly labelled containers.

» Bring a list of your prescriptions (photocopies of the containers are good) including generic names, so you can get replacements if your bags go on holiday – carry this info separately.

» If you have health problems that may need treatment, bring a signed and dated letter from your physician describing your medical conditions and medications.

» If carrying syringes or needles, have a physician's letter documenting their medical necessity.

» If you need vision correction, carry a spare pair of contact lenses or glasses, and/or take your optical prescription with you.

Recommended Vaccinations

Though no vaccinations are specifically required for Central Europe, the World Health Organization (WHO) recommends that all travellers should be covered for diphtheria, tetanus, measles, mumps, rubella and polio. Be aware that most vaccines don't produce immunity until at least two weeks after they're given.

Availability & Cost of Health Care

Good, basic health care is readily available.

» In the east of the region, hospitals are most common in major cities.

» Pharmacies provide valuable advice on small issues, sell over-the-counter medicine and advise when more specialised help is required.

» The standard of dental care is usually good.

» Embassies, consulates, tourist offices and five-star hotels can usually recommend doctors or clinics with English-speaking staff.

Insurance

It's foolhardy to travel without insurance to cover theft, loss and medical problems. Start by seeing what your own insurance covers, be it medical, home owner's or renter's. You may find that many aspects of travel in Central Europe are covered. You may also find gaping holes. If you need to purchase coverage, there's a wide variety of policies, so check the small print.

Some policies pay doctors or hospitals directly, but most require you to pay upfront, save the documentation and then claim later. The former option is generally preferable, as it doesn't require you to pay out-of-pocket costs in a foreign country. Some policies also ask you to call back (reverse charges) to a centre in your home country, where an immediate assessment of your problem is made. Check that the policy covers ambulances or an emergency flight home.

If you're an EU citizen, the European Health Insurance Card (EHIC) covers you for most medical care. If you do need health insurance, strongly consider a policy that covers you for the worst possible scenario.

The policies handled by STA travel (www.statravel.com) and other student travel agencies are usually good value. In the UK, the website Money Supermarket (www.moneysupermarket.com) does an automated comparison of 450 partner policies and comes up with the best for your needs.

Worldwide travel insurance is available at www.lonelyplanet.com/travel_services. You can buy, extend and claim online anytime – even if you're already on the road.

Internet Access

Internet cafes are a thing of the past. Wi-fi is the main way people connect on the road. Make sure you have a web-based email account so that you can send and receive email on the road if you don't have a laptop or other web-enabled device with you.

» Some cities have free wi-fi zones, although you can usually find paid wi-fi in public areas such as train stations.

» Hostels are reliable places to find computer internet access.

» Free wi-fi (known as WLAN in Germany) is common at lodgings and in some restaurants and cafes. Always check for a signal or ask.

Legal Matters

You are required by law to prove your identity if asked by police, so always carry your passport, or an identity card if you're an EU citizen. Most regional authorities are friendly and helpful, especially if you have been a victim of a crime.

Maps

Buying a good regional map will make things easier if you are planning a trip across more than a couple of countries. When driving or cycling, an atlas can be invaluable.

» Freytag & Berndt's *Central Europe Road Atlas* is good for road trips; available worldwide.

» Hiking maps are recommended in the mountains; available locally.

Money

At the time of publication, the countries in Central Europe using the euro as their currency are Austria, Germany, Slovenia and Slovakia. The other countries use their own currencies, which are easily convertible, stable and reliable. Major international currencies such as the euro and the US dollar are easy to exchange. Hungary, Poland and the Czech Republic hope to convert to the euro in years to come. A useful internet site for calculating exchange rates is www. xe.com/ucc.

For security and flexibility, diversify your source of funds: carry an ATM card, a credit card and some cash.

ATMs

ATMs are widely available in cities and towns, including at transport arrival halls. Find a money machine before travelling to villages.

» Withdrawal fees are usually charged by both your domestic bank and the ATM operator.

» Check to see that there are no ancillary devices attached to the ATM and cover the key pad when entering your code to discourage theft.

» A few people report problems with their pin codes while abroad, so have a backup card or plan.

Credit Cards

Note that separate systems for processing the bill may be used for cash and charge, especially in the eastern countries. Announce that you intend to pay by card before requesting the cheque; once the bill arrives, it may be too late.

» Visa and MasterCard are commonly accepted at hotels, pensions, larger restaurants, train stations; occasionally accepted at smaller restaurants.

» American Express, Discover, Diners Club and others are accepted only rarely, at larger establishments.

Tipping

Adding 5% to 10% to a bill for service is common across Europe.

Travellers Cheques

International ATMs have eliminated the need for travellers cheques. Finding a place to cash these is difficult and commissions are generally high.

Travel Money Cards

In recent years prepaid cards – also called travel money cards, prepaid currency cards or cash passport cards – have become a popular way of carrying money.

These enable you to load a card with as much foreign currency as you want to spend. You then use it to withdraw cash at ATMs – the money comes off the card and not out of your account – or to make direct purchases in the same way you would with a Visa or MasterCard. You can reload it via telephone or online.

Advantages of a prepaid card include the following:

» You avoid foreign exchange fees as the money you put on your card is converted into foreign currency at the moment you load it.

» You can control your outlay by only loading as much as you want to spend.

» If the card is stolen your losses are limited to the balance on the card – it's not directly linked to your bank account.

» ATM withdrawal fees are lower.

» Americans and others who carry credit cards without embedded chips can use these cards (which have chips and PINs) for the many European purchases that require a card with a chip. Against this you'll need to weigh the costs. Fees are charged for buying the card and then every time you load it. ATM withdrawal fees also apply. You might also be charged a fee if you don't use the card for a certain period of time or to redeem any unused currency. Note also that if the card has an expiry date, you'll forfeit any money loaded onto the card after that date.

One source of travel money cards is Travelex (www. travelex.com).

Wire Transfers

Western Union (www.western union.com) enables you to wire money to thousands of offices across the region. The sender will be given a code that they then communicate to you and you take to the nearest office, along with your passport, to receive your cash.

GETTING YOUR TAX BACK

Sales tax applies to many goods and services in Europe; the amount – 10% to 20% – is already built into the price of the item. Luckily, when non-EU residents spend more than a certain amount (around €75) they can usually reclaim that tax when leaving the country. Note that none of this applies to EU residents. Even a US citizen living in London is not entitled to a rebate on items bought in Frankfurt. Conversely, an EU passport holder living in New York is.

Making a tax-back claim is straightforward:

» Check that the shop offers duty-free sales; often a sign will read 'Tax-Free Shopping'.

» When purchasing, ask the shop attendant for a tax-refund voucher, filled in with the correct amount and the date.

» Claim a refund directly at international airports (beware of very long lines), or have your claim documents stamped at ferry ports or border crossings and mailed back for a refund.

Photography

» Museums, castles and other Central European attractions may charge a fee for camera use (roughly equivalent to an additional ticket price).

» It is never a good idea, and may be illegal, to take photos of military installations or at airport immigration.

» Digital memory is easy to buy in Central Europe.

Post

Postal services are reliable throughout Central Europe.

Safe Travel

Central Europe is as safe – or unsafe – as any other part of the developed world. If you can handle yourself in the big cities of Western Europe, North America or Australia, you'll have little trouble dealing with the less pleasant sides of travel here. Here are a few tips:

» If possible, work out a list of places where you can be contacted.

» When hiking or skiing alone or in the back country, leave a note at your hotel or park headquarters stating your departure time, intended route and anticipated return.

Scams

Overall the region is quite safe, but there are a few scams to watch out for:

» Men, be wary of the attention of uber-gorgeous women who invite you to a club in eastern cities. The drinks may be absurdly priced (€100-plus) and enforcers may appear at the end of the night to walk you to the ATM. (Did you really think it was your charming good looks that attracted them?) Be careful and pay attention to your surroundings.

SCENE-SETTING MOVIES

Watching films based in Central Europe can provide background for an upcoming trip.

» *Goodbye Lenin* (2003) Comedy set in East Berlin; when a girl awakes from a coma postcommunism, her family pretends the Wall never fell.

» *The Sound of Music* (1965) Sure, you've seen it, but you need to practise your lines before prancing around Salzburg.

» *Schindler's List* (1993) The film to see about the Holocaust.

» *Kafka* (1991) Not much to do with the real Kafka, but Prague and its castle look beautiful in this black-and-white writer's mystery.

» *Latcho Drom* (1993) Haunting musical documentary following the historical migration of the Roma into modern-day Central Europe.

» *The Third Man* (1939) Trying to find some remnants of post-WWII Vienna will become an obsession after this great film noir by Carol Reed.

» There have been a few reports of unscrupulous people making quick, hi-tech duplicates of credit- or debit-card information. Be alert if your card leaves your possession for longer than necessary and check your charges from the road if possible.

Theft

Petty crime is as common here as elsewhere in Europe and your wariness should extend to other travellers.

» Make copies of all important documents, such as your passport and driving licence.

» Be aware of your belongings in tourist centres; pickpockets target anywhere you'll be distracted – from crowded transport to busy attractions.

» Be especially vigilant on overnight trains; keep your bags locked and avoid neck-hanging travel wallets that can be cut off easily.

» Avoid leaving luggage and other items in plain view in parked cars.

» In case of theft or loss, always report the incident to the police and ask for a statement; otherwise, your travel-insurance company won't pay.

Telephone

Treat your hotel phone and its often hidden and outrageous rates the same way you'd treat a thief. Using wi-fi in the room for Skype is the most common way to connect.

Mobile Phones

Travellers can easily purchase prepaid mobile phones (from €30) or SIM cards (from €10). GSM phones can be used throughout all countries in Central Europe. Mobile shops are everywhere. Shops in large train stations are especially adept at getting visitors set up.

You can bring your mobile phone from home and buy a local SIM card to enjoy cheap local calling rates if it is unlocked and compatible with European GSM networks. Check first.

If you bring your mobile phone from home, keep the following tips in mind:

» Check international roaming rates in advance; often they are very expensive.

» Check roaming fees for data usage for email and web connections; users of smart phones (eg iPhones) can get socked with huge fees. You may be able to buy a data package to limit your costs.

Time

» The time zone is GMT+1 hour.

» Central European countries employ daylight saving. Clocks usually push forward one hour on the last Sunday in March and set back one hour on the last Sunday in October.

» The 24-hour time system is usually used.

Tourist Information

Tourist information is widely available, with booths or tourist offices located in main city and town centres, and sometimes at airports and train stations. Services offered vary and smaller town offices may close on weekends off-season.

Austria (www.austria.info)

Czech Republic (www.czechtourism.com)

Germany (www.cometo germany.com)

Hungary (www.hungary.com)

Liechtenstein (www.tourismus.li)

Poland (www.poland.travel)

Slovakia (www.slovakia.travel)

Slovenia (www.slovenia.info)

Switzerland (www.my switzerland.com)

Visas

Although Switzerland and Liechtenstein are not members of the EU, all countries in Central Europe are part of the Schengen Agreement. Therefore all of Central Europe is considered one 'country' in terms of your 90-day or visa-length stay.

» Visitors from Australia, New Zealand, Canada, Japan and the US do not require a visa for up to 90 days; valid passport required.

» EU citizens do not require a visa; identity card required.

» Visas are sometimes required for South African nationals, among others.

» Many – but not all – of the border posts between the countries of the region have disappeared.

» Some countries require that your passport remain valid for at least three months beyond your expected departure; in practice, this is rarely checked.

» For those who do require visas, it's important to remember that these will have a 'use-by' date; you'll be refused entry after that period.

» Most countries do not issue visas on their borders, but you may be able to apply in a neighbouring country.

Weights & Measures

The metric system is used throughout Central Europe. In Germany, cheese and other food items are often sold per Pfund (500g).

Transport

GETTING THERE & AWAY

Central Europe is well connected to the wider world by air, and competition among low-cost carriers has made short air hops available from Europe and the UK. Taking the train (northwards from Turkey or Greece, for example, or eastwards from England, France or Spain) is a scenic and ecofriendly alternative.

The westernmost countries have the best connections, but from Europe you can get pretty much everywhere by rail with a change or two. Buses, bicycles and cars can also be used to enter the region. Flights, tours and rail tickets can be booked online at www.lonelyplanet.com/bookings.

Entering Central Europe

There is little hassle when entering the region through gateway airports or from EU border states. Crossings to take note of include the following:

From Belarus or Ukraine To Poland, Slovakia or Hungary; expect time delays and tight immigration and customs controls. Have necessary visas for Belarus and/or Ukraine, and no more than the permitted number of cigarettes.

From Romania, Serbia or Croatia To Hungary or Slovenia; involves no great problems as long as you have the necessary visas and documents.

Air

Frankfurt and Zürich are major international air hubs linked to points across the globe; Vienna is only slightly less connected. You can also reach major cities like Munich, Prague, Budapest and Warsaw from abroad. Airports in Ljubljana and Bratislava host intra-European flights only and tiny Liechtenstein has no airport.

Airlines

Large carriers take you to and from a host of world cities, and a web of low-cost airlines provide services across Europe.

Note that with cheap fares come many caveats. Some of the bare bones airlines are just that – expect non-reclining seats, nonexistent legroom and no window shades. At some far-flung airports, customer service may also be nonexistent – the same goes for convenience. Some airlines, such as Ryanair, are noted for their destination euphemisms, eg Frankfurt in Germany is called 'Frankfurt-Hahn', a small airport 120km west of Frankfurt (and its real airport) and two hours away by bus. Also beware of discount airline websites such as those of Air Berlin which show nonstop flights that are actually connections.

Land

Bicycle

Transporting a bicycle by plane is possible (taken apart or whole); check with the airline for regulations and fees.

Bus

Major urban centres are well connected by bus to European destinations. However, budget air and rail prices rival bus fares, so do your

WHAT'S THAT BAG WORTH TO YA?

Beware when booking low-cost carrier seats; extra costs add up super fast. Most charge fees for checked luggage and impose strict weight limits with oversize penalties. Flying with a set of Czech crystal could cost *waaaay* more than you bargained for. Other add-ons to take note of include phone-booking fees, assigned-seat fees, paper-ticket fees, priority-line fees, fresh-air fees... Oh, wait, they haven't started charging for oxygen – yet.

research before you decide to take what could be a slow, miserable journey.

Car & Motorcycle

No special requirements exist for driving into Central Europe. If you've hired a car elsewhere, make sure all the countries you plan to visit are insured by the rental agency.

Train

Regular train services connect Central Europe with practically every corner of the European continent. It's also possible to get here by rail from Central Asia, but it will require several days and/or transfers. In general all the Central European countries have good connections to large cities in neighbouring countries.

Sea

Though it's not the most common way of arriving, a few ferries do run to Central Europe. Compare prices and check routes at Ferry Savers (www.ferrysavers.com).

Germany To/from Scandinavia and the Baltic states

Poland To/from Denmark and Sweden

Slovenia To/from Italy

GETTING AROUND

Air

If you're travelling without checked luggage, booking at least two weeks ahead and willing to travel to alternative airports, European air flights can be quite affordable. Both major and low-cost carriers fly within the region; check the prices of both. Note that smaller nations, such as Hungary and Switzerland, have no useful internal flights.

Bicycle

Crossing Central Europe by bicycle is certainly doable.

Just remember that in addition to flat river plains, the region encompasses Europe's highest mountain peaks.

» Cycling is allowed on roads and highways, but not on limited-access motorways or autobahns.

» Numerous proper bike routes exist in western countries; further east you'll be relying on roadsides and rural routes.

» Helmets are not compulsory, but are advised.

» Rental outlets are more common in western than eastern countries; check with tourist offices.

» Most trains, and some buses, allow bicycle transport.

Boat

Seasonal boat travel on Central Europe's riverways is a cruisey, scenic – and very slow – way to get around. You won't save any money plying the waters, but you will gain a unique perspective on the region. Organised boat tours are also available.

Danube River (April to October) Ferries run from southern Germany to Austria, within Austria, and from Austria to Slovakia and into Hungary. The most popular route is Vienna–Bratislava–Budapest.

Moselle and Rhine Rivers Varying length routes within Germany.

Bus

Buses generally have a slight edge over trains and planes in terms of cost, but are slower and much less comfortable. They tend to be best for getting around mountainous areas and for reaching remote rural villages. International services link major cities only. Note that even if two towns in different countries appear close on the map, there's often no direct international service between them.

Europe's largest network of international buses is provided by a consortium of bus companies that operates under the name Eurolines (www.eurolines.com) There are many services and it's possible to travel very far for less than €100. Eurolines' various affiliates offer many national and regional bus passes.

Car & Motorcycle

Travelling by motor vehicle allows for greater flexibility compared to other forms of transport; you can get further off the beaten track and away from cities. But it does consume more carbon. Note that a car can be a major inconvenience in the region's urban centres, which have enthusiastically-enforced parking restrictions and many one-way streets.

CLIMATE CHANGE & TRAVEL

Every form of transport that relies on carbon-based fuel generates CO_2, the main cause of human-induced climate change. Modern travel is dependent on aeroplanes, which might use less fuel per kilometre per person than most cars but travel much greater distances. The altitude at which aircraft emit gases (including CO_2) and particles also contributes to their climate change impact. Many websites offer 'carbon calculators' that allow people to estimate the carbon emissions generated by their journey and, for those who wish to do so, to offset the impact of the greenhouse gases emitted with contributions to portfolios of climate-friendly initiatives throughout the world. Lonely Planet offsets the carbon footprint of all staff and author travel.

ViaMichelin (www.viamiche lin.com) is an excellent map source for route planning.

Automobile Associations

Ask your motoring organisation for details about free and reciprocal services offered by affiliated organisations around Europe. Some rental agreements include roadside assistance.

» For European residents, European Five Star Service is offered by AA; (www.theaa. com) and European Motoring Assistance is offered by RAC (www.rac.co.uk).

» For non-Europeans, it's often it's less expensive to arrange international coverage with your national motoring organisation before departure.

Driving Licence & Documentation

» Proof of insurance and of vehicle ownership or rental is required.

» EU, North American and Australian driving licences are generally acceptable.

» For any other type of licence, obtain an International Driving Permit (IDP) from your local motoring organisation.

» Every vehicle travelling across an international border should display a sticker that shows the country of registration.

Fuel

Fuel prices vary enormously from country to country, but

in general are similar to the UK and much higher than the US. Unleaded petrol and diesel are widely available. The Automobile Association (www.aaroadwatch.ie/ eupetrolprices) has a useful webpage tracking European fuel prices.

Hire

Hiring a vehicle is a relatively straightforward procedure across the region; you will find most rental options near airports and in capital cities. What to expect:

» The minimum rental age is between 21 and 25.

» A credit card is required.

» Manual transmission is standard; you'll pay much more for automatic.

» Price inclusions vary (Unlimited mileage? Collision waiver? Taxes?); be sure to ask ahead.

» Daily rates generally range from €25 to €75.

» Big international firms allow drop-off in a different town or country (for a fee).

» Local firms may charge less.

» Booking ahead will always save you money.

International consolidators include the following:

Autos Abroad (www.autos abroad.com)

Auto Europe (www.auto europe.com)

Kemwel (www.kemwel.com)

Insurance

» Third-party motor accident insurance is compulsory throughout the region.

» It is usually included with rental, covered by your private auto insurance or by some major credit cards.

» Europeans driving a private vehicle should get a Green Card, an internationally recognised proof of insurance, from their insurer.

» Check that the Green Card lists all the countries you intend to visit. If it doesn't, you will have to take out separate third-party cover in the country in question.

» You'll need this cover in the event of an accident outside the country where the vehicle is insured.

» Obtain a European Accident Statement from your insurance company.

» Never sign statements you can't read or understand – insist on a translation and sign it only if it's acceptable.

Road Conditions

Conditions and types of roads vary across the region, but it is possible to make some generalisations.

» Motorways (autobahns, autoroutes etc) provide the most direct routes and best-condition roads; they're usually four to six lanes, with 100km/h-plus speed limits and require a tariff (a motorway sticker or pass) for usage.

» Highways are good-condition roads and have more extensive coverage than motorways; speed limit may slow down through towns.

» Minor routes are normally more than adequate, with

many stops in towns and villages. Far-eastern Poland, Slovakia and Hungary have a few less-than-perfect rural roads.

» Horse-drawn conveyances, cyclists, pedestrians and domestic animals can be night-time hazards on narrow rural roads.

Road Rules

Contact an automobile association for the specific rules of each country. In many countries, driving infringements are subject to an on-the-spot fine; always ask for a receipt.

» Drive on the right-hand side of the road.

» Keep right except when overtaking, and use your indicators for any change of lane and when pulling away from the kerb.

» Speed limits are signposted. Generally: no speed limit on German autobahns unless marked, 110km/h or 120km/h on motorways, 100km/h on other highways, 80km/h on secondary and tertiary roads, and 50km/h or 60km/h in built-up areas.

» Use of seatbelts is mandatory; in most countries, children aged under 12 are not permitted in the front seat.

» Driving after drinking any alcohol is a very serious offence, with legal blood-alcohol limits between 0% (that's *zero*) and 0.08%.

» Turning right against a red light is prohibited, even after coming to a stop.

» In case of an accident, carrying and using a red reflector warning triangle is mandatory.

» Never pass a tram on the left or stop within 1m of tram tracks.

Hitching

Hitching is never entirely safe in any country and we don't recommend it. Travellers who decide to hitch should understand they are taking a small but potentially serious risk. Key points to remember including the following:

» Hitch in pairs for safety

» Solo women should never hitch.

» Don't hitch from city centres; take public transport to suburban exit routes.

» Hitching is usually illegal on motorways – stand on the slip roads or approach drivers at petrol stations and truck stops.

» Look presentable and cheerful, and make a cardboard sign in the local language indicating your intended destination.

» Never hitch where drivers can't stop in good time or without causing an obstruction. At dusk, give up and think about finding somewhere to stay.

» It is sometimes possible to arrange a lift in advance: scan student noticeboards in colleges or contact car-sharing agencies. Such agencies are particularly popular in Germany, where they're called Mitfahrzentrale.

Public Transport

Most Central European cities have excellent public transport systems, which comprise some combination of metros (subways), trains, trams and buses. Service is usually comprehensive. Major airports generally have fast-train or metro links to the city centre.

Tours

Central Europe is easy to explore independently – a package holiday may be worth considering if you have a specific interest or time is extremely limited.

Package tours, whether tailor-made or bog-standard, cater for all tastes, interests and ages. The internet is an excellent resource for finding unusual tours that might not receive media or trade attention. Many people have had memorable trips on tours organised by cultural institutions like the US Smithsonian institution (www.smithsonian .com) which run tours lead by experts in fields such as art. Try searching for your own interest (eg walking) with 'Europe tour' and see what you get.

River Tours

River cruiseships generally hold 100 to 300 passengers, meals are included and rooms can be posh – if small – with their own river views. Danube and Rhine River tours are popular.

Train

For our money, trains are the most atmospheric, comfortable and interesting way to make tracks in Central Europe. All of the major (and most of the minor) cities are on the rail network. It's perfectly feasible for train travel to be your only form of intercity transport. Overnight trains – where they still exist – have the added benefit of saving you a night's accommodation. Think before you schedule, however – a daytime train journey through the Alps is a trip highlight.

Deutsche Bahn (www.bahn. de) German national rail site, covers the schedules of all the nations of Central Europe (but only has prices for Germany). The schedule app for smartphones is excellent.

Man in Seat 61 (www. seat61.com) Invaluable train descriptions, rail passes and details of journeys to the far reaches of the continent.

Thomas Cook (www. thomascookpublishing.com) Publishes the *Thomas Cook European Timetable* book, which has long been the long-term travellers' bible. Comprehensive listing of train schedules and supplement and reservation requirements.

Classes & Tickets

» Most trains have a modern, aeroplane-like layout.

» Trains in Central Europe have 1st- and 2nd-class cars. 1st-class seats are larger, often with laptop outlets, and cost roughly 50% more than 2nd-class.

» Cabin compartments (four to eight seats facing each other) are found on some trains in the east.

» Longer routes have dining cars, but these are being replaced by snack bars and mobile carts.

» On busy routes, and during the peak summer season, reserve a seat in advance.

» In the east, it often pays to stick to the faster and generally newer IC (Intercity) or EC (Eurocity) trains in terms of cleanliness and comfort.

» Supplements apply on express (IC and EC) and highspeed (eg ICE and Railjet) trains. Reservations are often obligatory.

» Note that long-distance Central European trains sometimes split en route; make sure you're in the correct carriage.

» Most railways offer cheap tickets through their websites so it always worth checking online.

» Most railways offer free smartphone apps that are excellent for schedules and purchasing tickets.

Rail Passes

Think carefully about purchasing a rail pass. In particular, prices for the multitude of Eurail passes have become quite expensive. Spend a little time online checking the national railways' websites and determine what it would cost to do your trip by buying the tickets separately. More often than not, you'll find that you'll spend less than if you buy a Eurail pass.

Shop around as pass prices can vary between different outlets. Once purchased, take care of your pass as it cannot be replaced or refunded if lost or stolen. Passes get reductions on Eurostar through the Channel Tunnel and on certain ferry routes. In the USA, Rail Europe (www.raileurope.com) sells a variety of rail passes; note that its individual train tickets tend to be more expensive than what you'll pay buying from railway companies' own sites or in stations.

EURAIL

There are so many different Eurail (www.eurail.com)

RAIL PASS RATES

Eurail

AGE	CLASS	DURATION	PRICE (€)
12-25	2nd	1 month	586
12-25	2nd	15 days	369
over 26	1st	1 month	899
over 26	1st	15 days	567
12-25	2nd	10 days in 2 months	435
12-25	2nd	15 days in 2 months	571
over 26	1st	10 days in 2 months	668
over 26	1st	15 days in 2 months	876

InterRail

AGE	CLASS	DURATION	PRICE (€)
12-25	2nd	5 days in 10 days	181
12-25	2nd	10 days in 22 days	265
12-25	2nd	1 month	435
over 26	1st	5 days in 10 days	434
over 26	1st	10 days in 22 days	618
over 26	1st	1 month	1034
over 26	2nd	5 days in 10 days	276
over 26	2nd	10 days in 22 days	393
over 26	2nd	1 month	658

passes to choose from and such a wide variety of areas and time periods covered that you need to have a good idea of your itinerary before purchasing one. These passes can only be bought by residents of non-European countries and are supposed to be purchased before arriving in Europe. There are two types of pass: one for people between 12 and 25 years of age and one for people aged 26 and over.

Eurail passes are valid for unlimited travel on national railways and some private lines in Central Europe. Reductions are given on some ferry routes, on river/lake steamer services in various countries and on the Eurostar to/from the UK.

Pass types include the following:

Eurail Global All the European countries (despite the much grander-sounding name) for a set number of consecutive days or a set number of days within a period of time.

Eurail Saver Two to five people travelling together as a group for the entire trip can save about 15% on the various pass types above.

Eurail Selectpass Buyers choose which neighbouring countries it covers and for how long. Options are myriad and can offer significant savings over the other passes if, for example, you are only going to three or four countries. Use the Eurail website to calculate these.

Eurail likes to promote the hop-on/hop-off any train aspect of their passes. But when it comes to the most desirable high-speed trains this is not always the case. While German ICE trains may be used at will, French TGVs require a seat reservation and the catch is that these are not always available to pass holders on all trains. In addition, some of the high-speed services like Thalys trains require a fairly hefty surcharge from pass users.

EUROPEAN EAST PASS

Valid for travel in Austria, the Czech Republic, Hungary, Poland and Slovakia, this can be a handy pass. It is valid for five days of 1st- or 2nd-class travel within one month. It costs US$307 or US$214; with extra days available. No student discount. Available at Rail Europe (www.raileurope-world.com).

INTERRAIL

The InterRail (www.interrail net.com) pass is available to European residents of more than six months' standing (passport identification is required). Terms and conditions vary slightly from country to country, but in the country of origin there is a discount of around 50% on the normal fares. The pass covers up to 30 countries.

InterRail passes are generally cheaper than Eurail, but most high-speed trains require that you also buy a seat reservation and pay a supplement of €3 to €40 depending on the route.

InterRail passes are also available for individual countries. Compare these to passes offered by the national railways.

NATIONAL RAIL PASSES

If you're intending to travel extensively within one country, check what national rail passes are available as these can sometimes save you a lot of money. In a large country such as Germany where you might be covering long distances, a pass can make sense, whereas in a small country such as Slovenia it won't.

WANT MORE?

For in-depth language information and handy phrases, check out Lonely Planet's *Central Europe Phrasebook*. You'll find it at **shop.lonelyplanet.com**, or you can buy Lonely Planet's iPhone phrasebooks at the Apple App Store.

Language

This chapter offers basic vocabulary to help you get around Central Europe. If you read our coloured pronunciation guides as if they were English, you'll be understood. Note that the stressed syllables are indicated with italics.

Some of the phrases in this chapter have both polite and informal forms (indicated by the abbreviations 'pol' and 'inf' respectively). Use the polite form when addressing people you're meeting for the first time, who are older than you, officials and service staff. The abbreviations 'm' and 'f' indicate masculine and feminine gender respectively.

CZECH

An accent mark over a vowel in written Czech indicates it's pronounced as a long sound.

Note also that air is pronounced as in 'hair', aw as in 'law', oh as the 'o' in 'note', ow as in 'how', uh as the 'a' in 'ago', kh as the 'ch' in the Scottish *loch*, and zh as the 's' in 'pleasure'. Also, r is a rolled sound in Czech and the apostrophe (') indicates a slight y sound after a consonant.

Basics

Hello.	*Ahoj.*	uh·hoy
Goodbye.	*Na shledanou.*	nuh·skhle·duh·noh
Excuse me.	*Promiňte.*	pro·min'·te
Sorry.	*Promiňte.*	pro·min'·te
Please.	*Prosím.*	pro·seem
Thank you.	*Děkuji.*	dye·ku·yi
Yes./No.	*Ano./Ne.*	uh·no/ne

What's your name?		
Jak se jmenujete/ jmenuješ? (pol/inf)		yuhk se yme·nu·ye·te/ yme·nu·yesh
My name is ...		
Jmenuji se ...		yme·nu·yi se ...
Do you speak English?		
Mluvíte anglicky?		mlu·vee·te uhn·glits·ki
I don't understand.		
Nerozumím.		ne·ro·zu·meem

Accommodation

campsite	*tábořiště*	ta·bo·rzhish·tye
guesthouse	*penzion*	pen·zi·on
hotel	*hotel*	ho·tel
youth hostel	*mládežnická ubytovna*	mla·dezh·nyits·ka u·bi·tov·nuh
Do you have a ... room?	*Máte ... pokoj?*	ma·te ... po·koy
single	*jednolůžkový*	yed·no·loozh·ko·vee
double	*dvoulůžkový*	dvoh·loozh·ko·vee
How much is it per ...?	*Kolik to stojí ...?*	ko·lik to sto·yee ...
night	*na noc*	nuh nots
person	*za osobu*	zuh o·so·bu

Eating & Drinking

What would you recommend?
Co byste doporučil/ tso bis·te do·po·ru·chil/
doporučila? (m/f) do·po·ru·chi·luh

Do you have vegetarian food?
Máte vegetariánská ma·te ve·ge·tuh·ri·ans·ka
jídla? yeed·luh

I'll have ...	*Dám si ...*	dam si ...
Cheers!	*Na zdraví!*	nuh zdruh·vee
I'd like the ...,	*Chtěl/*	khtyel/
please.	*Chtěla bych*	khtye·luh bikh
	..., prosím. (m/f)	... pro·seem
bill	*účet*	oo·chet
menu	*jídelníček*	yee·del·nyee·chek
(bottle of) beer	*(láhev) piva*	(la·hef) pi·vuh
(cup of) coffee/tea	*(šálek) kávy/čaje*	(sha·lek) ka·vi/chuh·ye
water	*voda*	vo·duh
(glass of) wine	*(skleničku) vína*	(skle·nyich·ku) vee·nuh
breakfast	*snídaně*	snee·duh·nye
lunch	*oběd*	o·byed
dinner	*večeře*	ve·che·rzhe

Emergencies

Help!	*Pomoc!*	po·mots
Go away!	*Běžte pryč!*	byezh·te prich
Call ...!	*Zavolejte ...!*	zuh·vo·ley·te ...
a doctor	*lékaře*	lair·kuh·rzhe
the police	*policii*	po·li·tsi·yi

I'm lost.
Zabloudil/ zuh·bloh·dyil/
Zabloudila jsem. (m/f) zuh·bloh·dyi·luh ysem

Signs – Czech

Vchod	Entrance
Východ	Exit
Otevřeno	Open
Zavřeno	Closed
Zakázáno	Prohibited
Záchody/Toalety	Toilets

Numbers – Czech

1	jeden	ye·den
2	dva	dvuh
3	tři	trzhi
4	čtyři	chti·rzhi
5	pět	pyet
6	šest	shest
7	sedm	se·dm
8	osm	o·sm
9	devět	de·vyet
10	deset	de·set

I'm ill.
Jsem nemocný/ ysem ne·mots·nee/
nemocná. (m/f) ne·mots·na

Where are the toilets?
Kde jsou toalety? gde ysoh to·uh·le·ti

Shopping & Services

I'm looking for ...
Hledám ... hle·dam ...

How much is it?
Kolik to stojí? ko·lik to sto·yee

That's too expensive.
To je moc drahé. to ye mots druh·hair

bank	*banka*	buhn·kuh
post office	*pošta*	posh·tuh
tourist office	*turistická informační kancelář*	tu·ris·tits·ka in·for·muhch·nyee kuhn·tse·larzh

Transport & Directions

Where's the ...?
Kde je ...? gde ye ...

What's the address?
Jaká je adresa? yuh·ka ye uh·dre·suh

Can you show me (on the map)?
Můžete mi to moo·zhe·te mi to
ukázat (na mapě)? u·ka·zuht (nuh muh·pye)

One ... ticket to (Telč), please.	*... jízdenku do (Telče), prosim.*	... yeez·den·ku do (tel·che) pro·seem
one-way	*Jedno-směrnou*	yed·no-smyer·noh
return	*Zpáteční*	zpa·tech·nyee
bus	*autobus*	ow·to·bus
plane	*letadlo*	le·tuhd·lo
train	*vlak*	vluhk

GERMAN

In Central Europe, German is spoken in Germany, Austria, Liechtenstein and Switzerland and understood in many parts of the region.

Vowels in German can be short or long, which influences the meaning of words. Note that air is pronounced as in 'fair', aw as in 'saw', eu as the 'u' in 'nurse', ew as ee with rounded lips, ow as in 'now', kh as the 'ch' in the Scottish *loch* (pronounced at the back of the throat), r is also a throaty sound, and zh is pronounced as the 's' in 'pleasure'.

Basics

Hello.

(Austria)	Servus.	zer·vus
(Germany)	Guten Tag.	goo·ten taak
(Switzerland)	Grüezi.	grew·e·tsi
Goodbye.	Auf Wiedersehen.	owf vee·der·zey·en
Excuse me.	Entschuldigung.	ent·shul·di·gung
Sorry.	Entschuldigung.	ent·shul·di·gung
Please.	Bitte.	bi·te
Thank you.	Danke.	dang·ke
Yes.	Ja.	yaa
No.	Nein.	nain

What's your name?
Wie ist Ihr Name?   vee ist eer naa·me

My name is ...
Mein Name ist ...   main naa·me ist ...

Do you speak English?
Sprechen Sie Englisch?   shpre·khen zee eng·lish

I don't understand.
Ich verstehe nicht.   ikh fer·shtey·e nikht

Accommodation

campsite	Campingplatz	kem·ping·plats
guesthouse	Pension	paang·zyawn
hotel	Hotel	ho·tel
youth hostel	Jugend-herberge	yoo·gent·her·ber·ge

Signs – German

Eingang	Entrance
Ausgang	Exit
Offen	Open
Geschlossen	Closed
Verboten	Prohibited
Toiletten	Toilets

Do you have a ... room?	Haben Sie ein ...?	haa·ben zee ain ...
single	Einzelzimmer	ain·tsel·tsi·mer
double	Doppelzimmer mit einem Doppelbett	do·pel·tsi·mer mit ai·nem do·pel·bet

How much is it per ...?	Wie viel kostet es pro ...?	vee feel kos·tet es praw ...
night	Nacht	nakht
person	Person	per·zawn

Eating & Drinking

What would you recommend?
Was empfehlen Sie?   vas emp·fey·len zee

Do you have vegetarian food?
Haben Sie vegetarisches Essen?   haa·ben zee ve·ge·taa·ri·shes e·sen

I'll have ...
Ich hätte gern ...   ikh he·te gern ...

Cheers!
Prost!   prawst

I'd like the ..., please.	Bitte bringen Sie ...	bi·te bring·en zee ...
bill	die Rechnung	dee rekh·nung
menu	die Speise-karte	dee shpai·ze·kar·te

beer	Bier	beer
coffee	Kaffee	ka·fey
tea	Tee	tey
water	Wasser	va·ser
wine	Wein	vain

breakfast	Frühstück	frew·shtewk
lunch	Mittagessen	mi·taak·e·sen
dinner	Abendessen	aa·bent·e·sen

Emergencies

Help!
Hilfe!   hil·fe

Go away!
Gehen Sie weg!   gey·en zee vek

Call ...!	Rufen Sie ...!	roo·fen zee ...
a doctor	einen Arzt	ai·nen artst
the police	die Polizei	dee po·li·tsai

I'm lost.
Ich habe mich verirrt.   ikh haa·be mikh fer·irt

I'm ill.
Ich bin krank.   ikh bin krangk

Where are the toilets?
Wo ist die Toilette?   vo ist dee to·a·le·te

Numbers – German		
1	*eins*	ains
2	*zwei*	tsvai
3	*zdrei*	drai
4	*vier*	feer
5	*fünf*	fewnf
6	*sechs*	zeks
7	*sieben*	zee·ben
8	*acht*	akht
9	*neun*	noyn
10	*zehn*	tseyn

Shopping & Services

I'm looking for ...
Ich suche nach ... ikh *zoo*·khe nakh ...

How much is it?
Wie viel kostet das? vee feel *kos*·tet das

That's too expensive.
Das ist zu teuer. das ist tsoo *toy*·er

market	*Markt*	markt
post office	*Postamt*	*post*·amt
tourist office	*Fremden-verkehrs-büro*	*frem*·den·fer·kairs·bew·raw

Transport & Directions

Where's ...?
Wo ist ...? vaw ist ...

What's the address?
Wie ist die Adresse? vee ist dee a·*dre*·se

Can you show me (on the map)?
Können Sie es mir (auf der Karte) zeigen? *keu*·nen zee es meer (owf dair *kar*·te) *tsai*·gen

One ...ticket to (Berlin), please.	*Einen ... nach (Berlin), bitte.*	*ai*·nen ... naakh (ber·*leen*), *bi*·te
one-way	*einfache Fahrkarte*	*ain*·fa·khe *faar*·kar·te
return	*Rückfahr-karte*	*rewk*·faar·kar·te

boat	*Boot*	bawt
bus	*Bus*	bus
plane	*Flugzeug*	*flook*·tsoyk
train	*Zug*	tsook

HUNGARIAN

A symbol over a vowel in written Hungarian indicates it's pronounced as a long sound. Double consonants should be drawn out a little longer than in English.

Note that aw is pronounced as in 'law', eu as in 'nurse', ew as ee with rounded lips, and zh as the 's' in 'pleasure'. Also, r is rolled in Hungarian and the apostrophe (') indicates a slight y sound.

Basics

Hello.	*Szervusz.* (sg) *Szervusztok.* (pl)	*ser*·vus *ser*·vus·tawk
Goodbye.	*Viszlát.*	*vis*·lat
Excuse me.	*Elnézést kérek.*	el·*ney*·zeysht *key*·rek
Sorry.	*Sajnálom.*	*shoy*·na·lawm
Please.	*Kérem.* (pol) *Kérlek.* (inf)	*key*·rem *keyr*·lek
Thank you.	*Köszönöm.*	*keu*·seu·neum
Yes.	*Igen.*	*i*·gen
No.	*Nem.*	nem

What's your name?
Mi a neve/ neved? (pol/inf) mi o *ne*·ve/ *ne*·ved

My name is ...
A nevem ... o *ne*·vem ...

Do you speak English?
Beszél/Beszélsz angolul? (pol/inf) be·*seyl*/be·*seyls* on·*gaw*·lul

I don't understand.
Nem Értem. nem *eyr*·tem

Accommodation

campsite	*kemping*	*kem*·ping
guesthouse	*panzió*	*pon*·zi·aw
hotel	*szálloda*	*sal*·law·do
youth hostel	*ifjúsági szálló*	*if*·yū·sha·gi *sal*·lāw

Signs – Hungarian	
Bejárat	Entrance
Kijárat	Exit
Nyitva	Open
Zárva	Closed
Tilos	Prohibited
Toalett	Toilets

Numbers – Hungarian		
1	egy	ej
2	kettő	ket·tēū
3	három	ha·rawm
4	négy	neyj
5	öt	eut
6	hat	hot
7	hét	heyt
8	nyolc	nyawlts
9	kilenc	ki·lents
10	tíz	teez

Do you have a ... room?	Van Önnek kiadó egy ... szobája?	von eun·nek ki·o·dāw ed' ... saw·ba·yo
single	egyágyas	ej·a·dyosh
double	duplaágyas	dup·lo·a·dyosh

How much is it per ...?	Mennyibe kerül egy ...?	men'·nyi·be ke·rewl ej ...
night	éjszakára	ey·so·ka·ro
person	főre	fēū·re

Eating & Drinking

What would you recommend?
Mit ajánlana?   mit o·yan·lo·no

Do you have vegetarian food?
Vannak Önöknél   von·nok eu·neuk·neyl
vegetáriánus ételek?   ve·ge·ta·ri·a·nush ey·te·lek

I'll have ...
... kérek.   ... key·rek

Cheers! (to one person)
Egészségedre!   e·geys·shey·ged·re

Cheers! (to more than one person)
Egészségetekre!   e·geys·shey·ge·tek·re

I'd like the ...	... szeretném.	... se·ret·neym
bill	A számlát	o sam·lat
menu	Az étlapot	oz eyt·lo·pawt

(bottle of) beer	(üveg) sör	(ew·veg) sheur
(cup of) coffee/tea	(csésze) kávé/tea	(chey·se) ka·vey/te·o
water	víz	veez
(glass of) wine	(pohár) bor	(paw·har) bawr

breakfast	reggeli	reg·ge·li
lunch	ebéd	e·beyd
dinner	vacsora	vo·chaw·ro

Emergencies

Help!	Segítség!	she·geet·sheyg
Go away!	Menjen innen!	men·yen in·nen
Call a doctor!	Hívjon orvost!	heev·yawn awr·vawsht
Call the police!	Hívja a rendőrséget!	heev·yo o rend·ēūr·shey·get

I'm lost.
Eltévedtem.   el·tey·ved·tem

I'm ill.
Rosszul vagyok.   raws·sul vo·dyawk

Where are the toilets?
Hol a vécé?   hawl o vey·tsey

Shopping & Services

I'm looking for ...
Keresem a ...   ke·re·shem o ...

How much is it?
Mennyibe kerül?   men'·nyi·be ke·rewl

That's too expensive.
Ez túl drága.   ez tūl dra·go

market	piac	pi·ots
post office	postahivatal	pawsh·to·hi·vo·tol
tourist office	turistairoda	tu·rish·to·i·raw·do

Transport & Directions

Where's the ...?
Hol van a ...?   hawl von o ...

What's the address?
Mi a cím?   mi o tseem

Can you show me (on the map)?
Meg tudja mutatni   meg tud·yo mu·tot·ni
nekem (a térképen)?   ne·kem (o teyr·key·pen)

One ... ticket to (Eger), please.	Egy ... jegy (Eger)be.	ej ... yej (e·ger)·be
one-way	csak oda	chok aw·do
return	oda-vissza	aw·do·vis·so

bus	busz	bus
plane	repülőgép	re·pew·lēū·geyp
train	vonat	vaw·not

POLISH

Polish vowels are generally pronounced short. Nasal vowels are pronounced as though you're trying to force the air through your nose, and are indicated with n or m following the vowel.

Note that ow is pronounced as in 'how', kh as the 'ch' in the Scottish *loch*, and zh as the 's' in 'pleasure'. Also, r is rolled in Polish and the apostrophe (') indicates a slight y sound.

Basics

Hello.	*Cześć.*	cheshch
Goodbye.	*Do widzenia.*	do vee·*dze*·nya
Excuse me.	*Przepraszam.*	pshe·*pra*·sham
Sorry.	*Przepraszam.*	pshe·*pra*·sham
Please.	*Proszę.*	*pro*·she
Thank you.	*Dziękuję.*	jyen·*koo*·ye
Yes.	*Tak.*	tak
No.	*Nie.*	nye

What's your name?
Jak się pan/pani   yak shye pan/*pa*·nee
nazywa? (m/f pol)   na·*zi*·va
Jakie się nazywasz? (inf) yak shye na·*zi*·vash

My name is ...
Nazywam się ...   na·*zi*·vam shye ...

Do you speak English?
Czy pan/pani mówi   chi pan/*pa*·nee *moo*·vee
po angielsku? (m/f)   po an·*gyel*·skoo

I don't understand.
Nie rozumiem.   nye ro·*zoo*·myem

Accommodation

campsite	*kamping*	*kam*·peeng
guesthouse	*pokoje gościnne*	po·*ko*·ye gosh·*chee*·ne
hotel	*hotel*	*ho*·tel
youth hostel	*schronisko młodzieżowe*	skhro·*nees*·ko mwo·jye·*zho*·ve

Do you have a ... room?	*Czy jest pokój ...?*	chi yest *po*·kooy ...
single	*jedno-osobowy*	*yed*·no-o·so·*bo*·vi
double	*z podwójnym łóżkiem*	z pod·*vooy*·nim *woozh*·kyem

Signs – Polish

Wejście	Entrance
Wyjście	Exit
Otwarte	Open
Zamknięte	Closed
Wzbroniony	Prohibited
Toalety	Toilets

How much is it per ...?   *Ile kosztuje za ...?*   *ee*·le kosh·*too*·ye za ...

night	*noc*	nots
person	*osobę*	o·*so*·be

Eating & Drinking

What would you recommend?
Co by pan polecił? (m)   tso bi pan po·*le*·cheew
Co by pani poleciła? (f)   tso bi *pa*·nee po·le·*chee*·wa

Do you have vegetarian food?
Czy jest żywność   chi yest *zhiv*·noshch
wegetariańska?   ve·ge·tar·*yan*'·ska

I'll have ...	*Proszę ...*	*pro*·she ...
Cheers!	*Na zdrowie!*	na *zdro*·vye

I'd like the ..., please.	*Proszę o ...*	*pro*·she o ...
bill	*rachunek*	ra·*khoo*·nek
menu	*jadłospis*	ya·*dwo*·spees

(bottle of) beer	*(butelka) piwa*	(boo·*tel*·ka) *pee*·va
(cup of) coffee/tea	*(filiżanka) kawy/herbaty*	(fee·lee·*zhan*·ka) *ka*·vi/her·*ba*·ti
water	*woda*	*vo*·da
(glass of) wine	*(kieliszek) wina*	(kye·*lee*·shek) *vee*·na

breakfast	*śniadanie*	shnya·*da*·nye
lunch	*obiad*	*o*·byad
dinner	*kolacja*	ko·*la*·tsya

Emergencies

Help!	*Na pomoc!*	na *po*·mots
Go away!	*Odejdź!*	o·*deyj*

Call ...!	*Zadzwoń po ...!*	zad·*zvon*' po ...
a doctor	*lekarza*	le·*ka*·zha
the police	*policję*	po·*lee*·tsye

I'm lost.
Zgubiłem/   zgoo·*bee*·wem/
Zgubiłam się. (m/f)   zgoo·*bee*·wam shye

I'm ill.
Jestem chory/a. (m/f)   *yes*·tem *kho*·ri/a

Where are the toilets?
Gdzie są toalety?   gjye som to·a·*le*·ti

LANGUAGE SLOVAK

Numbers – Polish

1	jeden	ye·den
2	dwa	dva
3	trzy	tshi
4	cztery	chte·ri
5	pięć	pyench
6	sześć	sheshch
7	siedem	shye·dem
8	osiem	o·shyem
9	dziewięć	jye·vyench
10	dziesięć	jye·shench

Shopping & Services

I'm looking for ...
Szukam ... — shoo·kam

How much is it?
Ile to kosztuje? — ee·le to kosh·too·ye

That's too expensive.
To jest za drogie. — to yest za dro·gye

market	targ	tark
post office	urząd pocztowy	oo·zhond poch·to·vi
tourist office	biuro turystyczne	byoo·ro too·ris·tich·ne

Transport & Directions

Where's the ...?
Gdzie jest ...? — gjye yest ...

What's the address?
Jaki jest adres? — ya·kee yest ad·res

Can you show me (on the map)?
Czy może pan/pani mi pokazać (na mapie)? (m/f) — chi mo·zhe pan/pa·nee mee po·ka·zach (na ma·pye)

One ... ticket (to Katowice), please.	Proszę bilet ... (do Katowic).	pro·she bee·let ... (do ka·to·veets)
one-way	w jedną stronę	v yed·nom stro·ne
return	powrotny	po·vro·tni

boat	łódź	wooj
bus	autobus	ow·to·boos
plane	samolot	sa·mo·lot
train	pociąg	po·chonk

SLOVAK

An accent mark over a vowel in written Slovak indicates it's pronounced as a long sound.

Note that air is pronounced as in 'hair', aw as in 'law', oh as the 'o' in 'note', ow as in 'how', uh as the 'a' in 'ago', dz as the 'ds' in 'adds', kh as the 'ch' in the Scottish *loch*, and zh as the 's' in 'pleasure'. The apostrophe (') indicates a slight y sound.

Basics

Hello.	Dobrý deň.	do·bree dyen'
Goodbye.	Do videnia.	do vi·dye·ni·yuh
Excuse me.	Prepáčte.	pre·pach·tye
Sorry.	Prepáčte.	pre·pach·tye
Please.	Prosím.	pro·seem
Thank you.	Ďakujem	dyuh·ku·yem
Yes.	Áno.	a·no
No.	Nie.	ni·ye

What's your name?
Ako sa voláte? — uh·ko suh vo·la·tye

My name is ...
Volám sa ... — vo·lam suh ...

Do you speak English?
Hovoríte po anglicky? — ho·vo·ree·tye po uhng·lits·ki

I don't understand.
Nerozumiem. — nye·ro·zu·myem

Accommodation

campsite	táborisko	ta·bo·ris·ko
guesthouse	penzión	pen·zi·awn
hotel	hotel	ho·tel
youth hostel	nocľaháreň pre mládež	nots·lyuh·ha·ren' pre mla·dyezh

Do you have a single room?
Máte jednoposteľovú izbu? — ma·tye yed·no·pos·tye·lyo·voo iz·bu

Do you have a double room?
Máte izbu s manželskou posteľou? — ma·tye iz·bu s muhn·zhels·koh pos·tye·lyoh

Signs – Slovak

Vchod	Entrance
Východ	Exit
Otvorené	Open
Zatvorené	Closed
Zakázané	Prohibited
Záchody/Toalety	Toilets

How much is it per ...?	Koľko to stojí na ...?	koľ·ko to sto·yee nuh ...
night	noc	nots
person	osobu	o·so·bu

Eating & Drinking

What would you recommend?
Čo by ste mi odporučili?	cho bi stye mi od·po·ru·chi·li

Do you have vegetarian food?
Máte vegetariánske jedlá?	ma·tye ve·ge·tuh·ri·yan·ske yed·la

I'll have ...	Dám si ...	dam si ...
Cheers!	Nazdravie!	nuhz·druh·vi·ye

I'd like the ..., please.	Prosím si ...	pro·seem si ...
bill	účet	oo·chet
menu	jedálny lístok	ye·dal·ni lees·tok

(bottle of) beer	(fľaša) piva	(flyuh·shuh) pi·vuh
(cup of) coffee/tea	(šálka) kávy/čaju	(shal·kuh) ka·vi/chuh·yu
water	voda	vo·duh
(glass of) wine	(pohár) vína	(po·har) vee·nuh

breakfast	raňajky	ruh·nyai·ki
lunch	obed	o·bed
dinner	večera	ve·che·ruh

Emergencies

Help!	Pomoc!	po·mots
Go away!	Choďte preč!	khoď·tye prech

Call ...!	Zavolajte ...!	zuh·vo·lai·tye ...
a doctor	lekára	le·ka·ruh
the police	políciu	po·lee·tsi·yu

I'm lost.
Stratil/Stratila som sa. (m/f)	struh·tyil/struh·tyi·luh som suh

I'm ill.
Som chorý/chorá. (m/f)	som kho·ree/kho·ra

Where are the toilets?
Kde sú tu záchody?	kdye soo tu za·kho·di

Numbers – Slovak		
1	jeden	ye·den
2	dva	dvuh
3	tri	tri
4	štyri	shti·ri
5	päť	peť
6	šesť	shesť
7	sedem	se·dyem
8	osem	o·sem
9	deväť	dye·veť
10	desať	dye·suhť

Shopping & Services

I'm looking for ...
Hľadám ...	hlyuh·dam ...

How much is it?
Koľko to stojí?	koľ·ko to sto·yee

That's too expensive.
To je príliš drahé.	to ye pree·lish druh·hair

market	trh	trh
post office	pošta	posh·tuh
tourist office	turistická kancelária	tu·ris·tits·ka kuhn·tse·la·ri·yuh

Transport & Directions

Where's the ...?
Kde je ...?	kdye ye ...

What's the address?
Aká je adresa?	uh·ka ye uh·dre·suh

Can you show me (on the map)?
Môžete mi ukázať (na mape)?	mwo·zhe·tye mi u·ka·zuhť (nuh muh·pe)

One ... ticket (to Poprad), please.	Jeden ... lístok (do Popradu), prosím.	ye·den ... lees·tok (do pop·ruh·du) pro·seem
one-way	jedno-smerný	yed·no·smer·nee
return	spiatočný	spyuh·toch·nee

bus	autobus	ow·to·bus
plane	lietadlo	li·ye·tuhd·lo
train	vlak	vluhk

SLOVENE

We've used the symbols oh (as the 'o' in 'note') and ow (as in 'how') to help you pronounce vowels followed by the letters *l* and *v* in written

Slovene – at the end of a syllable these combinations produce a sound similar to the 'w' in English.

Note also that uh is pronounced as the 'a' in 'ago', zh as the 's' in 'pleasure', r is rolled, and the apostrophe (') indicates a slight y sound.

Basics

Hello.	Zdravo.	zdra·vo
Goodbye.	Na svidenje.	na svee·den·ye
Excuse me.	Dovolite.	do·vo·lee·te
Sorry.	Oprostite.	op·ros·tee·te
Please.	Prosim.	pro·seem
Thank you.	Hvala.	hva·la
Yes.	Da.	da
No.	Ne.	ne

What's your name?
Kako vam/ti
je ime? (pol/inf)   ka·ko vam/tee
ye ee·me

My name is ...
Ime mi je ...   ee·me mee ye ...

Do you speak English?
Ali govorite
angleško?   a·lee go·vo·ree·te
ang·lesh·ko

I don't understand.
Ne razumem.   ne ra·zoo·mem

Accommodation

campsite	kamp	kamp
guesthouse	gostišče	gos·teesh·che
hotel	hotel	ho·tel
youth hostel	mladinski hotel	mla·deen·skee ho·tel

Do you have a ... room?	Ali imate ... sobo?	a·lee ee·ma·te ... so·bo
single	enoposteljno	e·no·pos·tel'·no
double	dvoposteljno	dvo·pos·tel'·no

Signs – Slovene

Vhod	Entrance
Izhod	Exit
Odprto	Open
Zaprto	Closed
Prepovedano	Prohibited
Stranišče	Toilets

How much is it per ...?	Koliko stane na ...?	ko·lee·ko sta·ne na ...
night	noč	noch
person	osebo	o·se·bo

Eating & Drinking

What would you recommend?
Kaj priporočate?   kai pree·po·ro·cha·te

Do you have vegetarian food?
Ali imate
vegetarijansko
hrano?   a·lee ee·ma·te
ve·ge·ta·ree·yan·sko
hra·no

| I'll have ... | Jaz bom ... | yaz bom ... |
| Cheers! | Na zdravje! | na zdrav·ye |

I'd like the ..., please.	Želim ..., prosim.	zhe·leem ... pro·seem
bill	račun	ra·choon
menu	jedilni list	ye·deel·nee leest

(bottle of) beer	(steklenica) piva	(stek·le·nee·tsa) pee·va
(cup of) coffee/tea	(skodelica) kave/čaja	(sko·de·lee·tsa) ka·ve/cha·ya
water	voda	vo·da
(glass of) wine	(kozarec) vina	(ko·za·rets) vee·na

breakfast	zajtrk	zai·tuhrk
lunch	kosilo	ko·see·lo
dinner	večerja	ve·cher·ya

Emergencies

| Help! | Na pomoč! | na po·moch |
| Go away! | Pojdite stran! | poy·dee·te stran |

Call ...!	Pokličite ...!	pok·lee·chee·te ...
a doctor	zdravnika	zdrav·nee·ka
the police	policijo	po·lee·tsee·yo

I'm lost.
Izgubil/
Izgubila sem se. (m/f)   eez·goo·beew/
eez·goo·bee·la sem se

I'm ill.
Bolan/Bolna sem. (m/f)   bo·lan/boh·na sem

Where are the toilets?
Kje je stranišče?   kye ye stra·neesh·che

LANGUAGE SLOVENE

Shopping & Services

I'm looking for ...
Iščem ...   eesh·chem ...

How much is this?
Koliko stane?   ko·lee·ko sta·ne

That's too expensive.
To je predrago.   to ye pre·dra·go

market	tržnica	tuhrzh·nee·tsa
post office	pošta	posh·ta
tourist office	turistični urad	too·rees·teech·nee oo·rad

Transport & Directions

Where's the ...?
Kje je ...?   kye ye ...

What's the address?
Na katerem   na ka·te·rem
naslovu je?   nas·lo·voo ye

Can you show me (on the map)?
Mi lahko pokažete   mee lah·ko po·ka·zhe·te
(na zemljevidu)?   (na zem·lye·vee·doo)

Numbers – Slovene

1	en	en
2	dva	dva
3	trije	tree·ye
4	štirje	shtee·rye
5	pet	pet
6	šest	shest
7	sedem	se·dem
8	osem	o·sem
9	devet	de·vet
10	deset	de·set

One ... ticket to (Koper), please.	... vozovnico do (Kopra), prosim.	... vo·zov·nee·tso do (ko·pra) pro·seem
one-way	Enosmerno	e·no·smer·no
return	Povratno	pov·rat·no

boat	ladja	lad·ya
bus	avtobus	av·to·boos
plane	letalo	le·ta·lo
train	vlak	vlak

Behind the Scenes

SEND US YOUR FEEDBACK

We love to hear from travellers – your comments keep us on our toes and help make our books better. Our well-travelled team reads every word on what you loved or loathed about this book. Although we cannot reply individually to postal submissions, we always guarantee that your feedback goes straight to the appropriate authors, in time for the next edition. Each person who sends us information is thanked in the next edition – the most useful submissions are rewarded with a selection of digital PDF chapters.

Visit **lonelyplanet.com/contact** to submit your updates and suggestions or to ask for help. Our award-winning website also features inspirational travel stories, news and discussions.

Note: We may edit, reproduce and incorporate your comments in Lonely Planet products such as guidebooks, websites and digital products, so let us know if you don't want your comments reproduced or your name acknowledged. For a copy of our privacy policy visit lonelyplanet.com/privacy.

OUR READERS

Many thanks to the travellers who used the last edition and wrote to us with helpful hints, useful advice and interesting anecdotes:

Gail Barnea, Linda Dive, Bernard Donahue, Don Farrell, Bill Robinson, Rachel Van Ness

AUTHOR THANKS

Ryan Ver Berkmoes

Thanks to all the authors who worked so hard on this guidebook and to the ever-patient Elin Berglund. In Switzerland, thanks to Claudia Stehle for beers, Damien Simonis for being himself and Judy Slatyer and Peter for a splendid night. And big thanks to the eternally glistening Alexis Averbuck.

Mark Baker

I met many helpful people all along the way in researching the countries for this guide and their names would be too numerous to mention. I've lived in Prague for two decades now; a very special thanks to my good friends here. In Slovenia, the staff of the Slovenia Tourist Board deserve special mention.

Kerry Christiani

A big *Dankeschön* to all of the super-efficient tourism professionals who made the road to research a breeze, especially Cornelia Pirka in Vienna, Maria Altendorfer and team in Salzburg, and Colette Spiss-Verra in Innsbruck. Thanks to my Vienna friends Chiara and Karin for good times and invaluable tips. Thanks also go to Ryan Ver Berkmoes, my fellow authors and the entire Lonely Planet production team.

Steve Fallon

Thanks to Bea Szirti and Ildikó Nagy Moran for their helpful suggestions. Péter Lengyel showed me the correct wine roads to follow again and Gerard Gorman where the birds were. For hospitality on the road I am indebted to Regina Bruckner (Budapest), András Cseh (Eger), Zsuzsi Fábián (Kecskemét) and Shandor Madachy (Budapest). *Nagyon szépen köszönöm mindenkinek!* As always, I'd like to dedicate my share of this to partner Michael Rothschild, with love and gratitude.

Tim Richards

As always, I'm indebted to the staff of Poland's tourist offices, and the national train company PKP. *Dziękuję* to my Polish friends – Ewa, Magda and Andrzej – for their companionship and insights regarding their mother country.

I'm grateful to the members of the English Language Club in Kraków, who supplied both friendly conversation and advice on new places of interest. Thanks also to the generous inhabitants of Twitter for their random and useful assistance, particularly Magda Rakita for music tips.

Andrea Schulte-Peevers

Big heartfelt thanks to all these wonderful people who've plied me with tips, insights, information, ideas and encouragement (in no particular order): Henrik Tidefjärd, Miriam Bers, Petra Gümmer, Julia Schwarz, Frank Engster, Myriel Walter, Heinz 'Cookie' Gindullis, Heiner Schuster, Steffi Gretschel, Renate Freiling, Silke Neumann, Kirsten Schmidt, Michael Radder, Christoph Münch, Christoph Lehmann, Patrick Schwarzkopf, Danilo Hommel, Dr Jasper Freiherr von Richthofen, Julia Schröder, Jan Czyszke and, of course, David Peevers. Kudos to the entire Lonely Planet team responsible for producing such a kick-ass book.

Luke Waterson

To Josef for the Spišské Podhradie adventure; to the HRL girls; to Michaela in the High Tatras; to the entire Košice 2013 team; to Michal for the ride round the east; to Peter and Brano for the 'authentic' ride round Bratislava; to Giovanni and his great wine; to Majo for his hospitality in Slovenský Raj; and to the old women who opened up the wooden churches: d'akujem for the wonderful insight into your little-in-size, big-at-heart country.

ACKNOWLEDGMENTS

Climate map data adapted from Peel MC, Finlayson BL & McMahon TA (2007) 'Updated World Map of the Köppen-Geiger Climate Classification', Hydrology and Earth System Sciences, 11, 1633-44.

Cover photograph: Rothenburg ob der Tauber, Germany, Craig Pershouse/Getty Images.

THIS BOOK

This 10th edition of Lonely Planet's Central Europe guidebook is part of Lonely Planet's Europe series. Other titles in this series include *Western Europe, Eastern Europe, Mediterranean Europe, Southeastern Europe, Scandinavia* and *Europe on a Shoestring.* Lonely Planet also publishes phrasebooks for these regions.

This guidebook was commissioned in Lonely Planet's London office, and produced by the following:

Commissioning Editor Dora Whitaker

Coordinating Editors Elin Berglund, Samantha Forge

Coordinating Cartographer Valentina Kremenchutskaya

Coordinating Layout Designer Lauren Egan

Managing Editors Sasha Baskett, Annelies Mertens, Angela Tinson

Managing Cartographers Adrian Persoglia, Anthony Phelan, Amanda Sierp

Managing Layout Designer Chris Girdler

Assisting Editor Anne Mason

Assisting Layout Designers Adrian Blackburn, Frank Diem

Cover Research Kylie McLaughlin

Internal Image Research Aude Vauconsant

Language Content Branislava Vladisavljevic

Thanks to Joe Bindloss, Laura Crawford, Ryan Evans, Larissa Frost, Genesys India, Jouve India, Andi Jones, Lucy Monie, Darren O'Connell, Trent Paton, Dianne Schallmeiner, Kerrianne Southway, Helena Smith, Gerard Walker, Tracy Whitmey

index

000 Map pages
000 Photo pages

NOTES

how to use this book

These symbols will help you find the listings you want:

- ◉ Sights
- 🐬 Beaches
- 🏃 Activities
- 🎓 Courses
- 👉 Tours
- 🎆 Festivals & Events
- 🛏 Sleeping
- ✕ Eating
- 🍷 Drinking
- ☆ Entertainment
- 🛍 Shopping
- ℹ Information/ Transport

These symbols give you the vital information for each listing:

- 📞 Telephone Numbers
- 🕑 Opening Hours
- Ⓟ Parking
- Ⓝ Nonsmoking
- ❄ Air-Conditioning
- @ Internet Access
- 📶 Wi-Fi Access
- 🏊 Swimming Pool
- 🥗 Vegetarian Selection
- 📖 English-Language Menu
- 👪 Family-Friendly
- 🐾 Pet-Friendly
- 🚌 Bus
- ⛴ Ferry
- Ⓜ Metro
- Ⓢ Subway
- ⊖ London Tube
- 🚊 Tram
- 🚆 Train

Reviews are organised by author preference.

Look out for these icons:

TOP CHOICE — Our author's recommendation

FREE — No payment required

🌿 — A green or sustainable option

Our authors have nominated these places as demonstrating a strong commitment to sustainability – for example by supporting local communities and producers, operating in an environmentally friendly way, or supporting conservation projects.

Map Legend

Sights
- 🐬 Beach
- 🔺 Buddhist
- 🏰 Castle
- ✝ Christian
- 🕉 Hindu
- ☪ Islamic
- ✡ Jewish
- ❶ Monument
- 🏛 Museum/Gallery
- 🔲 Ruin
- 🍷 Winery/Vineyard
- 🐾 Zoo
- ◉ Other Sight

Activities, Courses & Tours
- 🤿 Diving/Snorkelling
- 🛶 Canoeing/Kayaking
- ⛷ Skiing
- 🏄 Surfing
- 🏊 Swimming/Pool
- 🚶 Walking
- 🏄 Windsurfing
- ◉ Other Activity/ Course/Tour

Sleeping
- 🛏 Sleeping
- 🏕 Camping

Eating
- ✕ Eating

Drinking
- 🍷 Drinking
- ☕ Cafe

Entertainment
- 🎭 Entertainment

Shopping
- 🛍 Shopping

Information
- 🏦 Bank
- 🏛 Embassy/ Consulate
- ➕ Hospital/Medical
- @ Internet
- 👮 Police
- ✉ Post Office
- ☎ Telephone
- 🚻 Toilet
- ℹ Tourist Information
- • Other Information

Transport
- ✈ Airport
- ⊗ Border Crossing
- 🚌 Bus
- ┼Ⓡ┼ Cable Car/ Funicular
- Cycling
- Ferry
- Monorail
- Ⓟ Parking
- 🏪 Petrol Station
- 🚕 Taxi
- Train/Railway
- Tram
- Ⓜ Underground Train Station
- • Other Transport

Routes
- Tollway
- Freeway
- Primary
- Secondary
- Tertiary
- Lane
- Unsealed Road
- Plaza/Mall
- Steps
-)═(Tunnel
- Pedestrian Overpass
- Walking Tour
- Walking Tour Detour
- Path

Geographic
- 🛖 Hut/Shelter
- 🗼 Lighthouse
- 👁 Lookout
- ▲ Mountain/Volcano
- 🌴 Oasis
- 🌳 Park
-)(Pass
- ⛺ Picnic Area
- 💧 Waterfall

Population
- ★ Capital (National)
- ◉ Capital (State/Province)
- ● City/Large Town
- • Town/Village

Boundaries
- — — — International
- — — — State/Province
- — — Disputed
- — — Regional/Suburb
- Marine Park
- Cliff
- Wall

Hydrography
- River, Creek
- Intermittent River
- Swamp/Mangrove
- Reef
- Canal
- Water
- Dry/Salt/ Intermittent Lake
- Glacier

Areas
- Beach/Desert
- + + + Cemetery (Christian)
- × × × Cemetery (Other)
- Park/Forest
- Sportsground
- Sight (Building)
- Top Sight (Building)

Tim Richards

Poland Tim taught English in Kraków in the 1990s, and was fascinated by Poland's post-communist transition. He's returned repeatedly for Lonely Planet, deepening his relationship with this beautiful, complex country. In 2011 Tim released a Kindle ebook collecting his media articles about Poland, *We Have Here the Homicide*. When he's not on the road for Lonely Planet, Tim is a freelance journalist in Melbourne, Australia, writing about travel and the arts. You can find his blog and social media contacts at www.iwriter.com.au.

Andrea Schulte-Peevers

Germany Born and raised in Germany and educated in London and at UCLA, Andrea has travelled the distance to the moon and back in her visits to some 65 countries. She's written about her native country for two decades and authored or contributed to some 60 Lonely Planet titles, including all editions of *Germany*, *Berlin* and *Pocket Berlin*. After years of living in LA, Andrea now makes her home in Berlin.

Luke Waterson

Slovakia Dividing his love affair with Slovakia between the castles, the mountains, *pirohy* (potato dumplings) and (more unexplainably) Soviet architecture, Luke has, besides contributions to 15 Lonely Planet titles, written for BBC Travel, the *Guardian*, Avalon Travel Publishing and a clutch of in-flight magazines (thus keeping you entertained even in mid-air). He lives on the very edge of Bratislava, conveniently located for slurping Small Carpathian wine, and his favourite weekend activity is hiking into the hills to a quirky *krčma* (rural pub).

Read more about Luke at:
lonelyplanet.com/members/lukewaterson

OUR STORY

A beat-up old car, a few dollars in the pocket and a sense of adventure. In 1972 that's all Tony and Maureen Wheeler needed for the trip of a lifetime – across Europe and Asia overland to Australia. It took several months, and at the end – broke but inspired – they sat at their kitchen table writing and stapling together their first travel guide, *Across Asia on the Cheap*. Within a week they'd sold 1500 copies. Lonely Planet was born.

Today, Lonely Planet has offices in Melbourne, London and Oakland, with more than 600 staff and writers. We share Tony's belief that 'a great guidebook should do three things: inform, educate and amuse'.

OUR WRITERS

Ryan Ver Berkmoes

Coordinating Author, Switzerland Ryan Ver Berkmoes first visited Switzerland in 1984 when he used it as his mail drop during a year-long backpacking trip. He next tried to visit Czechoslovakia but was denied access by a pudgy bureaucrat out of central casting. Since then he has delighted in numerous, hassle-free trips across Central Europe. These days he divides his time between Europe and the US. Follow him at ryanverberkmoes.com. He tweets at @ryanvb.

Mark Baker

Czech Republic, Slovenia Based permanently in Prague, Mark has lived and worked in Eastern Europe for more than 20 years, first as a journalist for The Economist Group and then for Bloomberg News and Radio Free Europe/Radio Liberty. He travels frequently throughout the region and counts Bulgaria, Slovenia and Romania among his favourite countries in Europe. In addition to this book, Mark is co-author of the Lonely Planet guides to Prague, Slovenia, and Romania and Bulgaria.

Kerry Christiani

Austria Ever since her first post-grad trip to Austria, Kerry has seized every available chance to travel to the country of Mozart, Maria and co. Picking the cream of Vienna's coffee houses, glimpsing September snow in the Alps above Innsbruck and finding out the truth about the von Trapps in Salzburg kept her busy for this edition. Kerry has worked on some 20 guidebooks, including Lonely Planet's *Austria*, *Germany* and *Switzerland*. She tweets @kerrychristiani and lists her latest work at www.kerrychristiani.com.

Steve Fallon

Hungary Steve, who has written every edition of Lonely Planet's *Hungary*, first visited Magyarország in the early 1980s by chance. It was a brief visit but he immediately fell in love with thermal baths, Tokaj wine and *bableves* (bean soup). Not able to survive on the occasional fleeting fix, he moved to Budapest in 1992, where he could enjoy all three in abundance. Now based in London, Steve returns to Hungary regularly for all these things and more: *pálinka* (fruit-flavoured brandy), art nouveau and the haunting voice of Marta Sebestyén.

OVER MORE
PAGE WRITERS

Published by Lonely Planet Publications Pty Ltd
ABN 36 005 607 983
10th edition – Oct 2013
ISBN 978 1 74220 421 5
© Lonely Planet 2013 Photographs © as indicated 2013
10 9 8 7 6 5 4 3 2 1
Printed in China